T0273829

Error Correction Coding

Error Correction Coding

Mathematical Methods and Algorithms

Second Edition

Todd K. Moon
Utah State University, Utah, USA

WILEY

This second edition first published 2021
© 2021 by John Wiley and Sons, Inc.

Edition History
John Wiley and Sons, Inc. (1e, 2005)

The right of Todd K. Moon to be identified as the author of this work has been asserted in accordance with law.

Registered Office
John Wiley & Sons, Inc., 111 River Street, Hoboken, NJ 07030, USA

Editorial Office
111 River Street, Hoboken, NJ 07030, USA

For details of our global editorial offices, customer services, and more information about Wiley products visit us at www.wiley.com.

Wiley also publishes its books in a variety of electronic formats and by print-on-demand. Some content that appears in standard print versions of this book may not be available in other formats.

Library of Congress Cataloging-in-Publication Data

Names: Moon, Todd K., author.
Title: Error correction coding : mathematical methods and algorithms / Todd K. Moon.
Description: Second edition. | Hoboken, NJ : Wiley, 2021. | Includes bibliographical references and index.
Identifiers: LCCN 2020027697 (print) | LCCN 2020027698 (ebook) | ISBN 9781119567479 (cloth) | ISBN 9781119567486 (adobe pdf) | ISBN 9781119567493 (epub)
Subjects: LCSH: Engineering mathematics. | Error-correcting codes (Information theory)
Classification: LCC TA331 .M66 2021 (print) | LCC TA331 (ebook) | DDC 621.3820285/572–dc23
LC record available at https://lccn.loc.gov/2020027697
LC ebook record available at https://lccn.loc.gov/2020027698

Cover Design: Wiley
Cover Image: © Putt Sakdhnagool/Getty Images

Set in 10/12pt NimbusRomNo9L by SPi Global, Chennai, India

Contents

Preface

The goals of this second edition are much the same as the first edition: to provide a comprehensive introduction to error correction coding suitable for the engineering practitioner and to provide a solid foundation leading to more advanced treatments or research. Since the first edition, the content has been modernized to include substantially more on LDPC code design and decoder algorithms, as well as substantial coverage of polar codes. The thorough introduction to finite fields and algebraic codes of the first edition has been retained, with some additions in finite geometries used for LDPC code design. As observed in the first edition, the sophistication of the mathematical tools used increases over time. While keeping with the sense that this is the first time most readers will have seen these tools, a somewhat higher degree of sophistication is needed in some places.

The presentation is intended to provide a background useful both to engineers, who need to understand algorithmic aspects for the deployment and implementation of error correction coding, and to researchers, who need sufficient background to prepare them to read, understand, and ultimately contribute to the research literature. The practical algorithmic aspects are built upon a firm foundation of mathematics, which are carefully motivated and developed.

Pedagogical Features

Since its inception, coding theory has drawn from richly interacting variety of mathematical areas, including detection theory, information theory, linear algebra, finite geometries, combinatorics, optimization, system theory, probability, algebraic geometry, graph theory, statistical designs, Boolean functions, number theory, and modern algebra. The level of sophistication has increased over time: algebra has progressed from vector spaces to modules; practice has moved from polynomial interpolation to rational interpolation; Viterbi makes way for SOVA and BCJR. This richness can be bewildering to students, particularly engineering students who may be unaccustomed to posing problems and thinking abstractly. It is important, therefore, to motivate the mathematics carefully.

Some of the major pedagogical features of the book are as follows.

- While most engineering-oriented error-correction-coding textbooks clump the major mathematical concepts into a single chapter, in this book the concepts are developed over several chapters so they can be put to more immediate use. I have attempted to present the mathematics "just in time," when they are needed and well-motivated. Groups and linear algebra suffice to describe linear block codes. Cyclic codes motivate polynomial rings. The design of cyclic codes motivates finite fields and associated number-theoretical tools. By interspersing the mathematical concepts with applications, a deeper and broader understanding is possible.

- For most engineering students, finite fields, the Berlekamp–Massey algorithm, the Viterbi algorithm, BCJR, and other aspects of coding theory are abstract and subtle. Software implementations of the algorithms bring these abstractions closer to a meaningful reality, bringing deeper understanding than is possible by simply working homework problems and taking tests. Even when students grasp the concepts well enough to do homework on paper, these programs provide a further emphasis, as well as tools to *help* with the homework. The understanding becomes *experiential*, more than merely conceptual.

  Understanding of any subject typically improves when the student him- or herself has the chance to teach the material to someone (or something) else. A student must develop an especially clear understanding of a concept in order to "teach" it to something as dim-witted and literal-minded as a computer. In this process the computer can provide feedback to the student through debugging and program testing that reinforces understanding.

  In the coding courses I teach, students implement a variety of encoders and decoders, including Reed–Solomon encoders and decoders, convolutional encoders, turbo code decoders, and LDPC decoders. As a result of these programming activities, students move beyond an on-paper understanding, gaining a perspective of what coding theory can do and how to put it to work. A colleague of mine observed that many students emerge from a first course in coding theory more

LabIntro.pdf

confused than informed. My experience with these programming exercises is that my students are, if anything, overconfident, and feel ready to take on a variety of challenges.

In this book, programming exercises are presented in a series of 13 Laboratory Exercises. These are supported with code providing most of the software "infrastructure," allowing students to focus on the particular algorithm they are implementing.

These labs also help with the coverage of the course material. In my course I am able to offload classroom instruction of some topics for students to read, with the assurance that the students will learn it solidly on their own as they implement it. (The Euclidean algorithm is one of these topics in my course.)

Research in error control coding can benefit from having a flexible library of tools for the computations, particularly since analytical results are frequently not available and simulations are required. The laboratory assignments presented here can form the foundation for a research library, with the added benefit that having written major components, the researcher can easily modify and extend them.

It is in light of these pedagogic features that this book bears the subtitle *Mathematical Methods and Algorithms*.

There is sufficient material in this book for a one- or two-semester course based on the book, even for instructors who prefer to focus less on implementational aspects and the laboratories.

Over 200 programs, functions and data files are associated with the text. The programs are written in MATLAB,[1] C, or C++. Some of these include complete executables which provide "tables" of primitive polynomials (over any prime field), cyclotomic cosets and minimal polynomials, and BCH codes (not just narrow sense), avoiding the need to tabulate this material. Other functions include those used to make plots and compute results in the book. These provide example of how the theory is put into practice. Other functions include those used for the laboratory exercises. The files are highlighted in the book by the icon

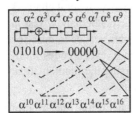

as in the marginal note above. The files are available at https://github.com/tkmoon/eccbook. Other aspects of the book include the following:

- Many recent advances in coding have resulted from returning to the perspective of coding as a detection problem. Accordingly, the book starts off with a digital communication framework with a discussion of **detection theory**.

- Recent codes such as polar codes or LDPC codes are capable of achieving capacity, or nearly so. It is important, therefore, to understand what capacity is and what it means to transmit at capacity. Chapter 1 also summarizes **information theory**, to put coding into its historical and modern context. Added in this second edition is an introduction to nonasymptotic information theory, which will be increasingly important in developing communication systems. The information theory informs EXIT chart analysis of turbo and LDPC codes.

---

[1] MATLAB is a registered trademark of The Mathworks, Inc.

- Pedagogically, Hamming codes are used to set the stage for the book by using them to demonstrate block codes, cyclic codes, trellises and Tanner graphs.

- Homework exercises are drawn from a variety of sources and are at a variety of levels. Some are numerical, testing basic understanding of concepts. Others provide the opportunity to prove or extend results from the text. Others extend concepts or provide new results. Because of the programming laboratories, exercises requiring decoding by hand of given bit sequences are few, since I am of the opinion that is better to know how to tell the computer than to do it by hand. I have drawn these exercises from a variety of sources, including problems that I faced as a student and those which I have given to students on homework and exams over the years.

- Number theoretic concepts such as divisibility, congruence, and the Chinese remainder theorem are developed at a point in the development where students can appreciate it.

- Occasionally connections between the coding theoretic concepts and related topics are pointed out, such as **public key cryptography** and **shift register sequences**. These add spice and motivate students with the understanding that the tools they are learning have broad applicability.

- There has been considerable recent progress made in decoding Reed–Solomon codes by re-examining their original definition. Accordingly, Reed–Solomon codes are defined both in this primordial way (as the image of a polynomial function) and also using a generator polynomial having roots that are consecutive powers of a primitive element. This sets the stage for several decoding algorithms for Reed–Solomon codes, including frequency-domain algorithms, **Welch–Berlekamp algorithm** and the **soft-input Guruswami–Sudan algorithm**.

- **Turbo codes**, including EXIT chart analysis, are presented, with both BCJR and SOVA decoding algorithms. Both probabilistic and likelihood decoding viewpoints are presented.

- **LDPC codes** are presented with an emphasis on the decoding algorithm. Density evolution analysis is also presented.

- **Polar Codes** are a family of codes developed since the first edition. They offer low complexity encode and decode with soft inputs and without iterative decoding. They also provably achieve channel capacity (as the code length goes to infinity). This book offers a deep introduction to polar codes, including careful description of encoding and decoding algorithms, with operational C++ code.

- Several **Applications** involving state-of-the-art systems illustrate how the concepts can be applied.

- **Space-time codes**, used for multi-antenna systems in fading channels, are presented.

Courses of Study

A variety of courses of study are possible. In the one-semester course I teach, I move quickly through principal topics of block, trellis, and iteratively–decoded codes. Here is an outline of one possible one-semester course:

Chapter 1: Major topics only.

Chapter 2: All.

Chapter 3: Major topics.

Chapter 4: Most. Leave CRC codes and LFSR to labs.

Chapter 5: Most. Touch on RSA.

Chapter 6: Most. Light on GFFT and variations.

Chapter 12: Most. Skip puncturing and stack-oriented algorithms.

Chapter 13: Most. Skip the V.34 material.

Chapter 14: Basic definition and the BCJR algorithm.

Chapter 15: Basic definition of LDPC codes and the sum-product decoder.

Chapter 17: Introduce the idea of

A guide in selecting material for this course is: follow the labs. To get through all 13 labs, selectivity is necessary.

An alternative two-semester course could be a semester devoted to block codes followed by a semester on trellis and iteratively decoded codes. A two semester sequence could move straight through the book, with possible supplements from the research literature on topics of particular interest to the instructor. A different two-semester approach would follow the outline above for one semester, followed by more advanced coverage of LDPC and polar codes.

Theorems, lemmas, corollaries, examples, and definitions are all numbered sequentially using the same counter in a chapter, which should make identifying these environments straightforward. Figures, tables, and equations each have their own counters. Definitions, examples, and proofs are terminated by the symbol □.

Use of Computers

comptut.pdf

The computer-based labs provide a means of working out some of the computational details that otherwise might require drudgery. These are primarily (with the exception of the first lab) to be done in C++, where the ability to overload operators and run at compiled speed make the language very well suited.

It may be helpful to have a "desk calculator" for homework and exploring ideas. Many tools exist now for this. The brief tutorial comptut.pdf provides an introduction to gap and magma, both of which can be helpful to students doing homework or research in this area. The sage package built on Python also provides considerable relevant capability.

Why This Book?

In my mind, the purposes of a textbook are these:

1. To provide a topographical map into the field of study, showing the peaks and the important roads to them. (However, in an area as rich as coding theory, it is impossible to be exhaustive.)

2. To provide specific details about important techniques.

3. To present challenging exercises that will strengthen students' understanding of the material and present new perspectives.

4. To have some reference value, so that practitioners can continue to use it.

5. To provide references to literature that will lead readers to make their own discoveries. With a rapidly-changing field, the references can only provide highlights; web-based searches have changed the nature of the game. Nevertheless, having a starting point in the literature is still important.

6. To present a breadth of ideas which will motivate students to innovate on their own.

A significant difficulty I have faced is selection. The terrain is so richly textured that it cannot be mapped out in a single book. Every communication or information theory conference and every issue of the *IEEE Transactions on Information Theory* yields new and significant results. Publishing restrictions and practicality limit this book from being encyclopedic. My role as author has been merely to select what parts of the map to include and to present them in a pedagogically useful way. In so doing, I have aimed to choose tools for the general practitioner and student (and of interest to me). Other than that selective role, no claim of creation is intended; I hope I have given credit as appropriate where it is due.

This book is a result of teaching a course in error correction coding at Utah State University for nearly three decades. Over that time, I have taught out of the books [45], [489], and [275], and my debt to these books is clear. Parts of some chapters grew out of lecture notes based on these books and the connections will be obvious. I have felt compelled to include many of the exercises from the first coding course I took out of [275]. These books have defined for me the *sine qua non* of error-correction coding texts. I am also indebted to [296] for its rich theoretical treatment, [401] for presentation of trellis coding material, [462] for discussion of bounds, [190] for exhaustive treatment of turbo coding methods, and to the many great researchers and outstanding expositors whose works have contributed to my understanding. More recently, the extensive coverage of LDPC codes in [391] has been extremely helpful, and motivated my own implementation of almost all of the decoding algorithms.

Acknowledgments

I am grateful for the supportive environment at Utah State University that has made it possible to undertake and to complete this task. Students in coding classes over the years have contributed to this material.

I have benefitted tremendously from feedback from careful readers and translators who have provided their own error correction from the first edition. Their negative acknowledgment protocols have improved the delivery of this packet of information. I thank you all!

To my six wonderful children — Leslie, Kyra, Kaylie, Jennie, Kiana, and Spencer — and presently twelve grandchildren, and my wife Barbara, who have seen me slip away too often and too long to write, I express my deep gratitude for their trust and patience. In the end, all I do is for them.

T.K.M
Logan, UT, October 2020

List of Program Files

List of Laboratory Exercises

List of Algorithms

List of Figures

List of Tables

List of Boxes

About the Companion Website

This book is accompanied by a companion website:

www.wiley.com/go/Moon/ErrorCorrectionCoding

The website includes:

- Solutions Manual
- Program Files

Part I

Introduction and Foundations

Chapter 1

A Context for Error Correction Coding

I will make weak things become strong unto them ...

—Ether 12:27

... he denies that any error in the machine is responsible for the so-called errors in the answers. He claims that the Machines are self correcting and that it would violate the fundamental laws of nature for an error to exist in the circuits of relays.

—Isaac Asimov
I, Robot

1.1 Purpose of This Book

Error control coding in the context of digital communication has a history dating back to the middle of the twentieth century. In recent years, the field has been revolutionized by codes which are capable of approaching the theoretical limits of performance, the *channel capacity*. This has been impelled by a trend away from purely combinatoric and discrete approaches to coding theory toward codes which are more closely tied to a physical channel and soft decoding techniques. The purpose of this book is to present error correction and detection coding covering both traditional concepts thoroughly as well as modern developments in soft-decision and iteratively decoded codes and recent decoding algorithms for algebraic codes. An attempt has been made to maintain some degree of balance between the mathematics and their engineering implications by presenting both the mathematical methods used in understanding the codes as well as the algorithms which are used to efficiently encode and decode.

1.2 Introduction: Where Are Codes?

Error correction coding is the means whereby errors which may be introduced into digital data as a result of transmission through a communication channel can be corrected based upon received data. Error detection coding is the means whereby errors can be detected based upon received information. Collectively, error correction and error detection coding are *error control coding*. Error control coding can provide the difference between an operational communications system and a dysfunctional system. It has been a significant enabler in the telecommunications revolution, portable computers, the Internet, digital media, and space exploration. Error control coding is nearly ubiquitous in modern, information-based society. Every compact disc, CD-ROM, or DVD employs codes to protect the data embedded in the plastic disk. Every flash drive (thumb drive) and hard disk drive employs correction coding. Every phone call made over a digital cellular phone employs it. Every frame of digital television is protected by error correction coding. Every packet transmitted over the Internet has a protective coding "wrapper" used to determine if the packet has been received correctly. Even everyday commerce takes advantage of error detection coding, as the following examples illustrate.

Example 1.1   The ISBN (international standard book number) is used to uniquely identify books. An ISBN such as 0-201-36186-8 can be parsed as

$$\underbrace{0}_{\text{country}} - \underbrace{20}_{\text{publisher}} - \underbrace{1 - 36186 -}_{\text{book no.}} \underbrace{8}_{\text{check}} .$$

Hyphens do not matter. The first digit indicates a country/language, with 0 for the United States. The next two digits are a publisher code. The next six digits are a publisher-assigned book number. The last digit is a check digit, used to validate if the code is correct using what is known as a weighted code. An ISBN is checked as follows: the cumulative sum of the digits is computed, then the cumulative sum of the cumulative sum is computed. For a valid ISBN, the sum-of-the-sum must be equal to 0, modulo 11. The character X is used for the check digit 10. For this ISBN, we have

Digit	Cumulative Sum	Cumulative Sum
0	0	0
2	2	2
0	2	4
1	3	7
3	6	13
6	12	25
1	13	38
8	21	59
6	27	86
8	35	121

The final sum-of-the-sum is 121, which is equal to 0 modulo 11 (i.e., the remainder after dividing by 11 is 0). □

Example 1.2   The Universal Product Codes (UPC) employed on the bar codes of most merchandise employ a simple error detection system to help ensure reliability in scanning. In this case, the error detection system consists of a simple parity check. A UPC consists of a 12-digit sequence, which can be parsed as

$$\underbrace{0 \;\; 16000}_{\substack{\text{manufacturer} \\ \text{identification} \\ \text{number}}} \;\; \underbrace{66610}_{\substack{\text{item} \\ \text{number}}} \;\; \underbrace{8}_{\substack{\text{parity} \\ \text{check}}} .$$

Denoting the digits as $u_1, u_2, \ldots, u_{12}$, the parity digit u_{12} is determined such that

$$3(u_1 + u_3 + u_5 + u_7 + u_9 + u_{11}) + (u_2 + u_4 + u_6 + u_8 + u_{10} + u_{12})$$

is a multiple of 10. In this case,

$$3(0 + 6 + 0 + 6 + 6 + 0) + (1 + 0 + 0 + 6 + 1 + 8) = 70.$$

If, when a product is scanned, the parity condition does not work, the operator is flagged so that the object may be re-scanned. □

1.3   The Communications System

Appreciation of the contributions of coding and understanding its limitations require some awareness of information theory and how its major theorems delimit the performance of a digital communication system. Information theory is increasingly relevant to coding theory, because with recent advances in theory it is now possible to achieve the performance bounds of information theory. By contrast, in the past, the bounds were more of a backdrop to the action on the stage of coding research and practice. Part of this success has come by placing the coding problem more fully in its communications context, marrying the coding problem more closely to the signal detection problem instead of treating the coding problem mostly as one of discrete combinatorics.

Information theory treats *information* almost as a physical quantity which can be measured, transformed, stored, and moved from place to place. A fundamental concept of information theory is that information is conveyed by the resolution of uncertainty. Information can be measured by the amount of uncertainty resolved. For example, if a digital source always emits the same value, say 1, then no information is gained by observing that the source has produced, yet again, the output 1, since there was no uncertainty about the outcome to begin with. Probabilities are used to mathematically describe the uncertainty. For a discrete random variable X (i.e., one which produces discrete outputs, such as $X = 0$ or $X = 1$), the information conveyed by observing an outcome x is defined as $-\log_2 P(X = x)$ bits. (If the logarithm is base 2, the units of information are in **bits**. If the natural logarithm is employed, the units of information are in **nats**.) For example, if $P(X = 1) = 1$ (the outcome 1 is certain), then observing $X = 1$ yields $-\log_2(1) = 0$ bits of information. On the other hand, observing $X = 0$ in this case yields $-\log_2(0) = \infty$: total surprise at observing an impossible outcome. The *entropy* is the *average information*. For a binary source X having two outcomes occurring with probabilities p and $1 - p$, the binary entropy function, denoted as either $H_2(X)$ (indicating that it is the entropy of the source) or $H_2(p)$ (indicating that it is a function of the outcome probabilities) is

$$H_2(X) = H_2(p) = E[-\log_2 P(X)] = -p \log_2(p) - (1 - p) \log_2(1 - p) \text{ bits.}$$

A plot of the binary entropy function as a function of p is shown in Figure 1.1. The peak information of 1 bit occurs when $p = \frac{1}{2}$.

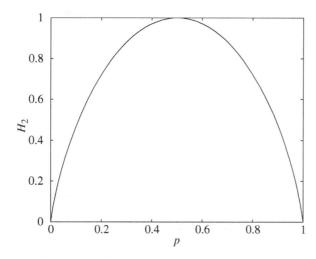

Figure 1.1: The binary entropy function $H_2(p)$.

Example 1.3 A fair coin is tossed once per second, with the outcomes being "head" and "tail" with equal probability. Each toss of the coin generates an event that can be described with $H_2(0.5) = 1$ bit of information. The sequence of tosses produces information at a rate of 1 bit/second. An unfair coin, with $P(\text{head}) = 0.01$ is tossed. The average information generated by each throw in this case is $H_2(0.01) = 0.0808$ bits. Another unfair coin, with $P(\text{head}) = 1$ is tossed. The information generated by each throw in this case is $H_2(1) = 0$ bits. □

For a source X having M outcomes $x_1, x_2, \ldots, x_M$, with probabilities $P(X = x_i) = p_i, i = 1, 2, \ldots, M$, the entropy is

$$H(X) = E[-\log_2 P(X)] = -\sum_{i=1}^{M} p_i \log_2 p_i \text{ bits.} \tag{1.1}$$

Note: The "bit" as a measure of entropy (or information content) is different from the "bit" as a measure of storage. For the unfair coin having P(head) $= 1$, the actual information content determined by a toss of the coin is 0: there is no information gained by observing that the outcome is again 1. For this process with this unfair coin, the entropy rate — that is, the amount of actual information it generates — is 0. However, if the coin outcomes were for some reason to be stored directly, without the benefit of some kind of coding, each outcome would require 1 bit of storage (even though they don't represent any new information).

With the prevalence of computers in our society, we are accustomed to thinking in terms of "bits" — e.g., a file is so many bits long, the register of a computer is so many bits wide. But these are "bits" as a measure of storage size, not "bits" as a measure of actual information content. Because of the confusion between "bit" as a unit of information content and "bit" as an amount of storage, the unit of information content is sometimes — albeit rarely — called a *Shannon*, in homage to the founder of information theory, Claude Shannon.[1]

A digital communication system embodies functionality to perform physical actions on information. Figure 1.2 illustrates a fairly general framework for a single digital communication link. In this link, digital data from a *source* are encoded and modulated (and possibly encrypted) for communication over a *channel*. At the other end of the channel, the data are demodulated, decoded (and possibly decrypted), and sent to a sink. The elements in this link all have mathematical descriptions and theorems from information theory which govern their performance. The diagram indicates the realm of applicability of three major theorems of information theory.

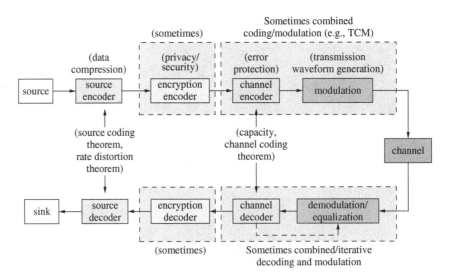

Figure 1.2: A general framework for digital communications.

There are actually many kinds of codes employed in a communication system. In the description below, we point out where some of these codes arise. Throughout the book we make some connections between these codes and our major focus of study, error correction codes.

The source is the data to be communicated, such as a computer file, a video sequence, or a telephone conversation. For our purposes, it is represented in digital form, perhaps as a result of an

---

[1] This mismatch of object and value is analogous to the physical horse, which may or may not be capable of producing one "horsepower" of power, 550 ft-lbs/second. Thermodynamicists can dodge the issue by using the SI unit of Watts for power, information theorists might sidestep confusion by using the Shannon. Both of these units honor founders of their respective disciplines.

analog-to-digital conversion step. Information-theoretically, sources are viewed as streams of random numbers governed by some probability distribution.

Every source of data has a measure of the information that it represents, which (in principle) can be exactly quantified in terms of entropy.

The source encoder performs data compression by removing redundancy.

As illustrated in Example 1.3, the number of bits used to store the information from a source may exceed the number of bits of actual information content. That is, the number of bits to represent the data may exceed the number of mathematical bits — Shannons — of actual information content.

The amount a particular source of data can be compressed without any loss of information (*lossless* compression) is governed theoretically by the *source coding theorem* of information theory, which states that a source of information can be represented without any loss of information in such a way that the amount of storage required (in bits) is equal to the amount of information content — the entropy — in bits or Shannons. To achieve this lower bound, it may be necessary for long blocks of the data to be jointly encoded.

Example 1.4 For the unfair coin with $P(\text{head}) = 0.01$, the entropy is $H(0.01) = 0.0808$. Therefore, 10,000 such (independent) tosses convey 808 bits (Shannons) of information, so theoretically the information of 10,000 tosses of the coin can be represented exactly using only 808 (physical) bits of information. $\square$

Thus a bit (in a computer register) in principle *can* represents an actual (mathematical) bit of information content, if the source of information is represented correctly.

In compressing a data stream, a source encoder removes redundancy present in the data. For compressed binary data, 0 and 1 occur with equal probability in the compressed data (otherwise, there would be some redundancy which could be exploited to further compress the data). Thus, it is frequently assumed at the channel coder that 0 and 1 occur with equal probability.

The source encoder employs special types of codes to do the data compression, called collectively source codes or data compression codes. Such coding techniques include Huffman coding, run-length coding, arithmetic coding, Lempel–Ziv coding, and combinations of these, all of which fall beyond the scope of this book.

If the data need to be compressed below the entropy rate of the source, then some kind of distortion must occur. This is called lossy data compression. In this case, another theorem governs the representation of the data. It is possible to do lossy compression in a way that minimizes the amount of distortion for a given rate of transmission. The theoretical limits of lossy data compression are established by the *rate–distortion theorem* of information theory. One interesting result of rate–distortion theory says that for a binary source having equiprobable outcomes, the minimal rate to which the data can be compressed with the average distortion per bit equal to p is

$$r = 1 - H_2(p) \quad p \le \frac{1}{2}. \tag{1.2}$$

Lossy data compression uses its own kinds of codes as well.

Example 1.5 In the previous example, suppose that a channel is available that only provides 800 bits of information to convey 10,000 tosses of the biased coin. Since this number of bits is less than allowed by the source coding theorem, there must be some distortion introduced. From above, the source rate is 0.0808 bits of information per toss. The rate we are sending over this restricted channel is $800/10\,000 = 0.08$ bits/toss. The rate at which tosses are coded is

$$r = \frac{800}{808} = 0.9901.$$

The distortion is

$$p = H_2^{-1}(1 - r) = H_2^{-1}(1 - 0.9901) = H_2^{-1}(0.0099) = 0.00085.$$

That is, out of 10,000 coin tosses, transmission at this rate would introduce distortion in (0.00085) $(10,000) = 8.5$ bits.

$\square$

The encrypter hides or scrambles information so that unintended listeners are unable to discern the information content. The codes used for encryption are generally different from the codes used for error correction.

Encryption is often what the layperson frequently thinks of when they think of "codes," as in secret codes, but as we are seeing, there are many other different kinds of codes.

As we will see, however, the mathematical tools used in error correction coding can be applied to some encryption codes. In particular, we will meet RSA public key encryption as an outgrowth of number theoretic tools to be developed, and McEliece public key encryption as a direct application of a particular family of error correction codes.

The channel coder is the first step in the error correction or error detection process.

The channel coder adds redundant information to the stream of input symbols in a way that allows errors which are introduced into the channel to be corrected. **This book is primarily dedicated to the study of the channel coder and its corresponding channel decoder.**

It may seem peculiar to remove redundancy with the source encoder, then turn right around and add redundancy back in with the channel encoder. However, the redundancy in the source typically depends on the source in an unstructured way and may not provide uniform protection to all the information in the stream, nor provide any indication of how errors occurred or how to correct them. The redundancy provided by the channel coder, on the other hand, is introduced in a structured way, precisely to provide error control capability.

Treating the problems of data compression and error correction separately, rather than seeking a jointly optimal source/channel coding solution, is asymptotically optimal (as the block sizes get large). This fact is called the *source–channel separation theorem* of information theory. (There has been work on combined source/channel coding for finite — practical — block lengths, in which the asymptotic theorems are not invoked. This work falls outside the scope of this book.)

Because of the redundancy introduced by the channel coder, there must be more symbols at the output of the coder than at the input. Frequently, a channel coder operates by accepting a block of k input symbols and producing at its output a block of n symbols, with $n > k$. The **rate** of such a channel coder is

$$R = k/n,$$

so that $R < 1$.

The input to the channel coder is referred to as the *message symbols* (or, in the case of binary codes, the *message bits*). The input may also be referred to as the *information symbols* (or bits).

The modulator converts symbol sequences from the channel encoders into signals appropriate for transmission over the channel. Many channels require that the signals be sent as a continuous-time voltage, or an electromagnetic waveform in a specified frequency band. The modulator provides the appropriate channel-conforming representation.

Included within the modulator block one may find codes as well. Some channels (such as magnetic recording channels) have constraints on the maximum permissible length of runs of 1s. Or they might have a restriction that the sequence must be DC-free. Enforcing such constraints employs special codes. Treatment of such runlength-limited codes appears in [275]; see also [209].

Some modulators employ mechanisms to ensure that the signal occupies a broad bandwidth. This *spread-spectrum* modulation can serve to provide multiple-user access, greater resilience to jamming, low probability of detection, and other advantages. (See, e.g., [509].) Spread-spectrum systems frequently make use of pseudorandom sequences, some of which are produced using linear feedback shift registers as discussed in Appendix 4.A.

The channel is the medium over which the information is conveyed. Examples of channels are telephone lines, internet cables, fiber-optic lines, microwave radio channels, high-frequency channels, cell phone channels, etc. These are channels in which information is conveyed between two distinct places. Information may also be conveyed between two distinct times, for example, by writing information onto a computer disk, then retrieving it at a later time. Hard drives, CD-ROMs, DVDs, and solid-state memory are other examples of channels.

As signals travel through a channel, they are corrupted. For example, a signal may have noise added to it; it may experience time delay or timing jitter, or suffer from attenuation due to propagation distance and/or carrier offset; it may be reflected by multiple objects in its path, resulting in constructive and/or destructive interference patterns; it may experience inadvertent interference from other channels, or be deliberately jammed. It may be filtered by the channel response, resulting in interference among symbols. These sources of corruption in many cases can all occur simultaneously.

For purposes of analysis, channels are frequently characterized by mathematical models, which (it is hoped) are sufficiently accurate to be representative of the attributes of the actual channel, yet are also sufficiently abstracted to yield tractable mathematics. Most of our work in this book will assume one of two idealized channel models, the binary symmetric channel (BSC) and the additive white Gaussian noise channel (AWGNC), which are described in Section 1.5. While these idealized models do not represent all of the possible problems a signal may experience, they form a starting point for many, if not most, of the more comprehensive channel models. The experience gained by studying these simpler channel models forms a foundation for more accurate and complicated channel models. (As exceptions to the AWGN or BSC rule, in Section 14.7, we comment briefly on convolutive channels and turbo equalization, while in Chapter 19, coding for quasi-static Rayleigh flat fading channels are discussed.)

As suggested by Figure 1.2, the channel encoding and modulation may be combined in what is known as *coded modulation*.

Channels have different information-carrying capabilities. For example, a dedicated fiber-optic line is capable of carrying more information than a plain-old-telephone-service (POTS) pair of copper wires. Associated with each channel is a quantity known as the **capacity**, C, which indicates how much information it can carry **reliably**.

The information a channel can reliably carry is intimately related to the use of error correction coding. The governing theorem from information theory is Shannon's **channel coding theorem**, which states essentially this: Provided that the rate R of transmission is less than the capacity C, *there exists* a code such that the probability of error can be made arbitrarily small.

The demodulator/equalizer receives the signal from the channel and converts it into a sequence of symbols. This typically involves many functions, such as filtering, demodulation, carrier synchronization, symbol timing estimation, frame synchronization, and matched filtering, followed by a detection step in which decisions about the transmitted symbols are made. We will not concern ourselves in this book with these very important details (many of which are treated in textbooks on digital communication, such as [367]), but will focus on issues related to channel encoding and decoding.

The channel decoder exploits the redundancy introduced by the channel encoder to correct any errors that may have been introduced. As suggested by the figure, demodulation, equalization, and decoding may be combined. Particularly in recent work, turbo equalizers (introduced in Chapter 14) are used in a powerful combination.

The decrypter removes any encryption.

The source decoder provides an uncompressed representation of the data.

The sink is the ultimate destination of the data.

As this summary description has indicated, there are many different kinds of codes employed in communications. This book treats only error correction (or detection) codes. There is a certain duality between some channel coding methods and some source coding methods. So, studying error correction does provide a foundation for other aspects of the communication system.

1.4   Basic Digital Communications

The study of modulation/channel/demodulation/detection falls in the realm of "digital communications," and many of its issues (e.g., filtering, synchronization, carrier tracking) lie beyond the scope of this book. Nevertheless, some understanding of digital communications is necessary here because modern coding theory has achieved some of its successes by careful application of detection theory, in particular in maximum *a posteriori* (MAP) and maximum likelihood (ML) receivers. Furthermore, performance of codes is often plotted in terms of signal-to-noise ratio (SNR), which is understood in the context of the modulation of a physical waveform. Coded modulation relies on signal constellations beyond simple binary modulation, so an understanding of them is important.

The material in this section is standard for a digital communications course. However, it is germane to our treatment here because these concepts are employed in the development of soft-decision decoding algorithms.

1.4.1   Binary Phase-Shift Keying

In digital communication, a stream of bits (i.e., a sequence of 1s and 0s) is mapped to a waveform for transmission over the channel. Binary phase-shift keying (BPSK) is a form of amplitude modulation in which a bit is represented by the sign of the transmitted waveform. (It is called "phase-shift" keying [PSK] because the sign change represents a $180°$ phase shift.) Let $\{ \ldots, b_{-2}, b_{-1}, b_0, b_1, b_2, \ldots \}$ represent a sequence of bits, $b_i \in \{0, 1\}$ which arrive at a rate of 1 bit every T seconds. The bits are assumed to be randomly generated with probabilities $P_1 = P(b_i = 1)$ and $P_0 = P(b_i = 0)$. While typically 0 and 1 are equally likely, we will initially retain a measure of generality and assume that $P_1 \neq P_0$ necessarily. It will frequently be of interest to map the set $\{0, 1\}$ to the set $\{-1, 1\}$. We will denote $\tilde{b}_i$ as the ± 1-valued bit corresponding to the $\{0, 1\}$-valued bit b_i. Either of the mappings

$$\tilde{b}_i = (2b_i - 1) \quad \text{or} \quad \tilde{b}_i = -(2b_i - 1)$$

may be used in practice, so some care is needed to make sure the proper mapping is understood.

Here, let $a_i = \sqrt{E_b}(2b_i - 1) = -\sqrt{E_b}(-1)^{b_i} = \sqrt{E_b}\tilde{b}_i$ be a mapping of bit b_i (or $\tilde{b}_i$) into a transmitted signal amplitude. This signal amplitude multiplies a waveform $\varphi_1(t)$, where $\varphi_1(t)$ is a unit-energy signal,

$$\int_{-\infty}^{\infty} \varphi_1(t)^2 \, dt = 1,$$

which has support[2] over $[0, T]$. Thus, a bit b_i arriving at time iT can be represented by the signal $a_i \varphi_1(t - iT)$. The energy required to transmit a single bit b_i is

$$\int_{-\infty}^{\infty} (a_i \varphi_1(t))^2 \, dt = E_b.$$

Thus, E_b is the energy expended per bit.

It is helpful to think of the transmitted signals $\sqrt{E_b} \varphi_1(t)$ and $-\sqrt{E_b} \varphi_1(t)$ as points $\sqrt{E_b}$ and $-\sqrt{E_b}$ in a one-dimensional **signal space**, where the coordinate axis is the "$\varphi_1(t)$" axis. The two points in the signal space are plotted with their corresponding bit assignment in Figure 1.3. The points in the signal space employed by the modulator are called the **signal constellation**, so Figure 1.3 is a signal constellation with two points (or signals).

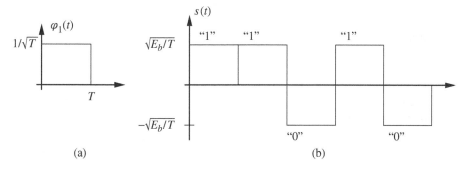

Figure 1.3 Signal constellation for BPSK.

A sequence of bits to be transmitted can be represented by a juxtaposition of $\varphi_1(t)$ waveforms, where the waveform representing bit b_i starts at time iT. Then the sequence of bits is represented by the signal

$$s(t) = \sum_i a_i \varphi_1(t - iT). \tag{1.3}$$

Example 1.6 With $\varphi_1(t)$ as shown in Figure 1.4(a) and the bit sequence $\{1, 1, 0, 1, 0\}$, the signal $s(t)$ is as shown in Figure 1.4(b).

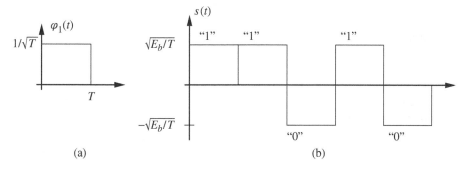

(a)   (b)

Figure 1.4: Juxtaposition of signal waveforms.

□

1.4.2 More General Digital Modulation

The concept of signal spaces generalizes immediately to higher dimensions and to larger signal constellations; we restrict our attention here to no more than two dimensions. Let $\varphi_2(t)$ be a unit-energy

---

[2] Strictly speaking, functions not having this limited support can be used, but assuming support over $[0, T]$ makes the discussion significantly simpler. Also, the signal $\varphi_i(t)$ can in general be complex, but we restrict attention here to real signals.

function which is orthogonal to $\varphi_1(t)$. That is,

$$\int_{-\infty}^{\infty} \varphi_2(t)^2 \, dt = 1 \quad \text{and} \quad \int_{-\infty}^{\infty} \varphi_1(t)\varphi_2(t) \, dt = 0.$$

In this case, we are defining "orthogonality" with respect to the inner product

$$\langle \varphi_1(t), \varphi_2(t) \rangle = \int_{-\infty}^{\infty} \varphi_1(t)\varphi_2(t) \, dt.$$

We say that $\{\varphi_1(t), \varphi_2(t)\}$ form an *orthonormal set* if they both have unit energy and are orthogonal:

$$\langle \varphi_1(t), \varphi_1(t) \rangle = 1 \quad \langle \varphi_2(t), \varphi_2(t) \rangle = 1 \quad \langle \varphi_1(t), \varphi_2(t) \rangle = 0.$$

The orthonormal functions $\varphi_1(t)$ and $\varphi_2(t)$ define the coordinate axes of a two-dimensional signal space, as suggested by Figure 1.5. Corresponding to every point (x_1, y_1) of this two-dimensional signal space is a signal (i.e., a function of time) $s(t)$ obtained as a linear combination of the coordinate functions:

$$s(t) = x_1 \varphi_1(t) + y_1 \varphi_2(t).$$

That is, there is a one-to-one correspondence between "points" in space and their represented signals. We can represent this as

$$s(t) \leftrightarrow (x_1, y_1).$$

The geometric concepts of distance and angle can be expressed in terms of the signal space points. For example, let

$$\begin{aligned}
s_1(t) &= x_1 \varphi_1(t) + y_1 \varphi_2(t) \quad (\text{i.e., } s_1(t) \leftrightarrow (x_1, y_1)) \\
s_2(t) &= x_2 \varphi_1(t) + y_2 \varphi_2(t) \quad (\text{i.e., } s_2(t) \leftrightarrow (x_2, y_2))
\end{aligned} \tag{1.4}$$

We define the squared distance between $s_1(t)$ and $s_2(t)$ as

$$d^2(s_1(t), s_2(t)) = \int_{-\infty}^{\infty} (s_1(t) - s_2(t))^2 \, dt, \tag{1.5}$$

and the inner product between $s_1(t)$ and $s_2(t)$ as

$$\langle s_1(t), s_2(t) \rangle = \int_{-\infty}^{\infty} s_1(t) s_2(t) \, dt. \tag{1.6}$$

Rather than computing distance using the integral (1.5), we can equivalently and more easily compute using the coordinates in signal space (see Figure 1.5):

$$d^2(s_1(t), s_2(t)) = (x_1 - x_2)^2 + (y_1 - y_2)^2. \tag{1.7}$$

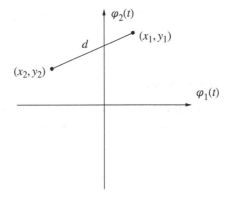

Figure 1.5: Two-dimensional signal space.

This is the familiar squared **Euclidean distance** between the points (x_1, y_1) and (x_2, y_2). Also, rather than computing the inner product using the integral (1.6), we equivalently compute using the coordinates in signal space:

$$\langle s_1(t), s_2(t) \rangle = x_1 x_2 + y_1 y_2. \tag{1.8}$$

This is the familiar inner product (or dot product) between the points (x_1, y_1) and (x_2, y_2):

$$\langle (x_1, y_1), (x_2, y_2) \rangle = x_1 x_2 + y_1 y_2.$$

The significance is that we can use the signal space geometry to gain insight into the nature of the signals, using familiar concepts of distance and angle.

We can use this two-dimensional signal space for digital information transmission as follows. Let $M = 2^m$, for some integer m, be the number of points in the signal constellation. M-ary transmission is obtained by placing M points $(a_{1k}, a_{2k}), k = 0, 1, \ldots, M - 1$, in this signal space and assigning a unique pattern of m bits to each of these points. These points are the signal constellation. Let

$$S = \{(a_{1k}, a_{2k}), k = 0, 1, \ldots, M - 1\}$$

denote the set of points in the signal constellation.

Example 1.7 Figure 1.6 shows eight points arranged in two-dimensional space in a constellation known as 8-PSK. Each point has a 3-bit designation. The signal corresponding to the point (a_{1k}, a_{2k}) is selected by three input bits and transmitted. Thus, the signal

$$s_k(t) = a_{1k} \varphi_1(t) + a_{2k} \varphi_2(t), \quad (a_{1k}, a_{2k}) \in S$$

carries 3 bits of information.

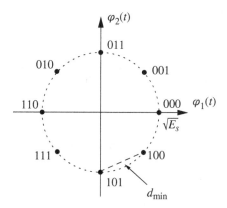

Figure 1.6: 8-PSK signal constellation.

Note that the assignments of bits to constellation points in Figure 1.6 is such that adjacent points differ by only 1 bit. Such an assignment is called Gray code order. Since it is most probable that errors will move from a point to an adjacent point, this reduces the probability of bit error. □

Associated with each signal $s_k(t) = a_{1k} \varphi_1(t) + a_{2k} \varphi_2(t)$ and signal constellation point $(a_{1k}, a_{2k}) \in S$ is a signal energy,

$$E_k = \int_{-\infty}^{\infty} (s_k(t))^2 \, dt = a_{1k}^2 + a_{2k}^2.$$

The *average signal energy* E_s is obtained by averaging all the signal energies, usually by assuming that each signal point is used with equal probability:

$$E_s = \frac{1}{M} \sum_{k=0}^{M-1} \int_{-\infty}^{\infty} s_k(t)^2 \, dt = \frac{1}{M} \sum_{k=0}^{M-1} (a_{1k}^2 + a_{2k}^2).$$

The average energy per signal E_s can be related to the average energy per bit E_b by

$$E_b = \frac{\text{energy per signal}}{\text{number of bits/signal}} = \frac{E_s}{m}.$$

To send a sequence of bits using M-ary modulation, the bits are partitioned into blocks of m successive bits, where the data rate is such that m bits arrive every T_s seconds. The ith m-bit set is then used to index a point $(a_{1i}, a_{2i}) \in S$. This point corresponds to the signal which is transmitted over the signal interval for the m bits. These signals are juxtaposed to form the transmitted signal:

$$s(t) = \sum_i a_{1i}\varphi_1(t - iT_s) + a_{2i}\varphi_2(t - iT_s), \quad (a_{1i}, a_{2i}) \in S. \tag{1.9}$$

The point (a_{1i}, a_{2i}) is thus the point set at time i. Equation (1.9) can be expressed in its signal space vector equivalent, by simply letting $\mathbf{s}_i = [a_{1i}, a_{2i}]^T$ denote the vector transmitted at time i.

In what follows, we will express the operations in terms of the two-dimensional signal space. Restricting to a one-dimensional signal space (as for BPSK transmission), or extending to higher-dimensional signal spaces is straightforward.

In most channels, the signal $s(t)$ is mixed with some carrier frequency before transmission. However, for simplicity, we will restrict attention to the baseband transmission case.

1.5 Signal Detection

1.5.1 The Gaussian Channel

The signal $s(t)$ is transmitted over the channel. Of all the possible disturbances that might be introduced by the channel, we will deal primarily with additive white Gaussian noise (AWGN), resulting in the received signal

$$r(t) = s(t) + n(t). \tag{1.10}$$

In an AWGN channel, the signal $n(t)$ is a white Gaussian noise process, having the properties that

$$E[n(t)] = 0 \quad \forall t,$$

$$R_n(\tau) = E[n(t)n(t - \tau)] = \frac{N_0}{2}\delta(\tau),$$

and all sets of samples are jointly Gaussian distributed. The quantity $N_0/2$ is the (two-sided) noise power spectral density.

Due to the added noise, the signal $r(t)$ is typically not a point in the signal constellation, nor, in fact, is $r(t)$ probably even *in* the signal space — it cannot be expressed as a linear combination of the basis functions $\varphi_1(t)$ and $\varphi_2(t)$. The detection process to be described below corresponds to the geometric operations of (1) projecting $r(t)$ onto the signal space; and (2) finding the closest point in the signal space to this projected function.

At the receiver, optimal detection requires first passing the received signal through a filter "matched" to the transmitted waveform. This is the projection operation, projecting $r(t)$ onto the signal space. To detect the ith signal starting at iT_s, the received signal is correlated with the waveforms

$\varphi_1(t - iT_s)$ and $\varphi_2(t - iT_s)$ to produce the point (R_{1i}, R_{2i}) in signal space[3]:

$$R_{1i} = \langle r(t), \varphi_1(t - iT_s) \rangle = \int_{-\infty}^{\infty} r(t)\varphi_1(t - iT_s) \, dt,$$

$$R_{2i} = \langle r(t), \varphi_2(t - iT_s) \rangle = \int_{-\infty}^{\infty} r(t)\varphi_2(t - iT_s) \, dt. \tag{1.11}$$

The integral is over the support of $\varphi_1(t)$ and $\varphi_2(t)$. For example, if $\varphi_1(t)$ has support over $[0, T_s]$, then the limits of integration in (1.11) are $\int_{iT_s}^{(i+1)T_s}$. The processing in (1.11) is illustrated in Figure 1.7. Using (1.9) and (1.10), it is straightforward to show that

$$R_{1i} = a_{1i} + N_{1i} \quad \text{and} \quad R_{2i} = a_{2i} + N_{2i}, \tag{1.12}$$

where (a_{1i}, a_{2i}) is the transmitted point in the signal constellation for the ith symbol. The point (a_{1i}, a_{2i}) is not known at the receiver — it is, in fact, what the receiver needs to decide — so at the receiver a_{1i} and a_{2i} are random variables.

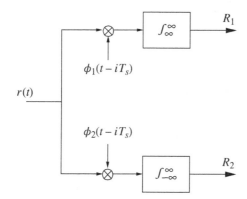

Figure 1.7: Correlation processing (equivalent to matched filtering).

The noise random variables N_{1i} and N_{2i} defined by

$$N_{1i} = \int_{iT_s}^{(i+1)T_s} \varphi_1(t - iT_s)n(t) \, dt \quad \text{and} \quad N_{2i} = \int_{iT_s}^{(i+1)T_s} \varphi_2(t - iT_s)n(t) \, dt$$

have the following properties: N_{1i} and N_{2i} are Gaussian random variables, with

$$E[N_{1i}] = 0 \quad \text{and} \quad E[N_{2i}] = 0 \tag{1.13}$$

and[4]

$$\text{var}[N_{1i}] \triangleq \sigma^2 = \frac{N_0}{2} \quad \text{and} \quad \text{var}[N_{2i}] \triangleq \sigma^2 = \frac{N_0}{2} \tag{1.14}$$

and

$$E[N_{1i}N_{2i}] = 0; \tag{1.15}$$

---

[3] The operation in (1.11) can equivalently be performed by passing $r(t)$ through filters with impulse response $\varphi_1(-t)$ and $\varphi_2(-t)$ and sampling the output at time $t = iT_s$. This is referred to as a *matched filter*. The matched filter implementation and the correlator implementation provide identical outputs.

[4] The symbol $\triangleq$ means "is defined to be equal to."

that is, N_{1i} and N_{2i} are uncorrelated and hence, being Gaussian, are independent. The probability density function (pdf) for N_{1i} or N_{2i} is

$$p_N(n_i) = \frac{1}{\sqrt{2\pi}\sigma} e^{-\frac{1}{2\sigma^2} n_i^2}.$$

It will be convenient to express (1.12) in vector form. Let $\mathbf{R}_i = [R_{1i}, R_{2i}]^T$ (received vector), $\mathbf{S}_i = [a_{1i}, a_{2i}]^T$ (sent vector), and $\mathbf{N}_i = [N_{1i}, N_{2i}]^T$ (noise vector). Then

$$\mathbf{R}_i = \mathbf{S}_i + \mathbf{N}_i.$$

Then $\mathbf{N}_i$ is jointly Gaussian distributed, with 0 mean and covariance matrix

$$E[\mathbf{N}_i \mathbf{N}_i^T] = \sigma^2 \begin{bmatrix} 1 & 0 \\ 0 & 1 \end{bmatrix} = \sigma^2 I = R_N.$$

Explicitly, the pdf of the vector $\mathbf{N}_i$ is

$$p_{\mathbf{N}}(\mathbf{n}) = \frac{1}{2\pi\sqrt{\det(R_N)}} \exp\left[-\frac{1}{2}\mathbf{n}^T R_N^{-1}\mathbf{n}\right] = \frac{1}{2\pi\sigma^2}\exp\left[-\frac{1}{2\sigma^2}(n_1^2 + n_2^2)\right].$$

1.5.2 MAP and ML Detection

Let $\mathbf{S}$ denote the transmitted value, where $\mathbf{S} \in \mathcal{S}$ is chosen with prior probability $P(\mathbf{S} = \mathbf{s})$, or, more briefly, $P(\mathbf{s})$. The receiver uses the received point $\mathbf{R} = \mathbf{r}$ to make a decision about what the transmitted signal $\mathbf{S}$ is. Let $P(\mathbf{s}|\mathbf{r})$ be used to denote $P(\mathbf{S} = \mathbf{s}|\mathbf{R} = \mathbf{r}) = P_{\mathbf{S}|\mathbf{R}}(\mathbf{S} = \mathbf{s}|\mathbf{R} = \mathbf{r})$ for an observed value of the random variable $\mathbf{R} = \mathbf{r}$. Conditioned on knowing that the transmitted signal is $\mathbf{S} = \mathbf{s}$, $\mathbf{R}$ is a Gaussian random variable with conditional density

$$
\begin{aligned}
p_{R|S}(\mathbf{r}|\mathbf{s}) = p_N(\mathbf{r} - \mathbf{s}) &= \frac{1}{2\pi\sqrt{\det(R_N)}}\exp\left[-\frac{1}{2}(\mathbf{r}-\mathbf{s})^T R_N^{-1}(\mathbf{r}-\mathbf{s})\right] \\
&= C\exp\left[-\frac{1}{2\sigma^2}\|\mathbf{r}-\mathbf{s}\|^2\right],
\end{aligned}
\tag{1.16}
$$

where $\|\mathbf{r} - \mathbf{s}\|^2$ is the squared Euclidean distance between $\mathbf{r}$ and $\mathbf{s}$ and C is a quantity that does not depend on either $\mathbf{R}$ or $\mathbf{S}$. The quantity $p_{R|S}(\mathbf{r}|\mathbf{s})$ is called the *likelihood function*. The likelihood function $p_{R|S}(\mathbf{r}|\mathbf{s})$ is typically viewed as a function of the *conditioning* argument, with the observed values $\mathbf{r}$ as fixed parameters.

The signal point $\mathbf{s} \in \mathcal{S}$ depends uniquely upon the transmitted bits mapped to the signal constellation point. Conditioning upon knowing the transmitted signal is thus equivalent to conditioning on knowing the transmitted bits. Thus, the notation $p(\mathbf{r}|\mathbf{s})$ is used interchangeably with $p(\mathbf{r}|\mathbf{b})$, when $\mathbf{s}$ is the signal used to represent the bits $\mathbf{b}$. For example, for BPSK modulation, we could write either $p(r|s = \sqrt{E_b})$ or $p(r|b = 1)$ or even $p(r|\tilde{b} = 1)$, since by the modulation described above the amplitude $\sqrt{E_b}$ is transmitted when the input bit is $b = 1$ (or $\tilde{b} = 1$).

Let us denote the estimated decision as $\hat{\mathbf{s}} = [\hat{a}_1, \hat{a}_2]^T \in \mathcal{S}$. We will use the notation $P(\mathbf{s}|\mathbf{r})$ as a shorthand for $P(\mathbf{S} = \mathbf{s}|\mathbf{r})$.

Theorem 1.8 *The decision rule which minimizes the probability of error is to choose $\hat{\mathbf{s}}$ to be that value of $\mathbf{s}$ which maximizes $P(\mathbf{S} = \mathbf{s}|\mathbf{r})$, where the possible values of $\mathbf{s}$ are those in the signal constellation $\mathcal{S}$. That is,*

$$\hat{\mathbf{s}} = \arg\max_{\mathbf{s}\in\mathcal{S}} P(\mathbf{s}|\mathbf{r}).
\tag{1.17}$$

Proof Let us denote the constellation as $S = \{\mathbf{s}_i, i = 1, 2, \ldots, M\}$. Let $p(\mathbf{r}|\mathbf{s}_i)$ denote the pdf of the received signal when $\mathbf{S} = \mathbf{s}_i$ is the transmitted signal. Let Ω denote the space of possible received values; in the current case $\Omega = \mathbb{R}^2$. Let us partition the space Ω into regions Ω_i, where the decision rule is expressed as: set $\hat{\mathbf{s}} = \mathbf{s}_i$ if $\mathbf{r} \in \Omega_i$. That is,

$$\Omega_i = \{\mathbf{r} \in \Omega \ : \ \text{decide } \hat{\mathbf{s}} = \mathbf{s}_i\}.$$

The problem, then, is to determine the partitions Ω_i. By the definition of the partition, the conditional probability of a correct answer when $\mathbf{S} = \mathbf{s}_i$ is sent is

$$P(\hat{\mathbf{s}} = \mathbf{s}_i|\mathbf{S} = \mathbf{s}_i) = \int_{\Omega_i} p(\mathbf{r}|\mathbf{s}_i)\, d\mathbf{r}.$$

Denote the conditional probability of error when signal $\mathbf{S} = \mathbf{s}_i$ is sent as $P_i(\mathcal{E})$:

$$P_i(\mathcal{E}) = P(\hat{\mathbf{s}} \neq \mathbf{s}_i|\mathbf{S} = \mathbf{s}_i).$$

Then we have

$$P_i(\mathcal{E}) = 1 - P(\hat{\mathbf{s}} = \mathbf{s}_i|\mathbf{S} = \mathbf{s}_i) = 1 - \int_{\Omega_i} p(\mathbf{r}|\mathbf{s}_i)\, d\mathbf{r}.$$

The average probability of error is

$$P(\mathcal{E}) = \sum_{i=1}^{M} P_i(\mathcal{E})P(\mathbf{S} = \mathbf{s}_i) = \sum_{i=1}^{M} P(\mathbf{S} = \mathbf{s}_i)\left[1 - \int_{\Omega_i} p(\mathbf{r}|\mathbf{s}_i)\, d\mathbf{r}\right] d\mathbf{r}$$

$$= 1 - \sum_{i=1}^{M} \int_{\Omega_i} p(\mathbf{r}|\mathbf{s}_i)P(\mathbf{S} = \mathbf{s}_i)\, d\mathbf{r}.$$

The probability of a correct answer is

$$P(C) = 1 - P(\mathcal{E}) = \sum_{i=1}^{M} \int_{\Omega_i} p(\mathbf{r}|\mathbf{s}_i)P(\mathbf{S} = \mathbf{s}_i)\, d\mathbf{r} = \sum_{i=1}^{M} \int_{\Omega_i} P(\mathbf{S} = \mathbf{s}_i|\mathbf{r})p(\mathbf{r})\, d\mathbf{r}.$$

Since $p(\mathbf{r}) \geq 0$, to maximize $P(C)$, the region of integration Ω_i should be chosen precisely so that it covers the region where $P(\mathbf{S} = \mathbf{s}_i|\mathbf{r})$ is the largest possible. That is,

$$\Omega_i = \{\mathbf{r} \ : \ P(\mathbf{S} = \mathbf{s}_i|\mathbf{r}) > P(\mathbf{S} = \mathbf{s}_j|\mathbf{r}), i \neq j\}.$$

This is equivalent to (1.17). $\qquad\square$

Using Bayes' rule we can write (1.17) as

$$\hat{\mathbf{s}} = \arg\max_{\mathbf{s} \in S} P(\mathbf{s}|\mathbf{r}) = \arg\max_{\mathbf{s} \in S} \frac{p_{R|S}(\mathbf{r}|\mathbf{s})P(\mathbf{s})}{p_R(\mathbf{r})}.$$

Since the denominator of the last expression does not depend on $\mathbf{s}$, we can further write

$$\boxed{\hat{\mathbf{s}} = \arg\max_{\mathbf{s} \in S} p_{R|S}(\mathbf{r}|\mathbf{s})P(\mathbf{s}).} \tag{1.18}$$

This is called the MAP decision rule. In the case that all the prior probabilities are equal (or are assumed to be equal), this rule can be simplified to

$$\boxed{\hat{\mathbf{s}} = \arg\max_{\mathbf{s} \in S} p_{R|S}(\mathbf{r}|\mathbf{s}).}$$

This is called the ML decision rule.

Note: We will frequently suppress the subscript on a pdf or distribution function, letting the arguments themselves indicate the intended random variables. We could thus write $p(\mathbf{r}|\mathbf{s})$ in place of $p_{R|S}(\mathbf{r}|\mathbf{s})$.

Once the decision $\hat{\mathbf{s}}$ is made, the corresponding bits are determined by the bit-to-constellation mapping. The output of the receiver is thus an estimate of the bits.

By the form of (1.16), we see that the ML decision rule for the Gaussian noise channel selects that point $\hat{\mathbf{s}} \in S$ which is closest to $\mathbf{r}$ in squared **Euclidean distance**, $\|\mathbf{r} - \hat{\mathbf{s}}\|^2$.

1.5.3 Special Case: Binary Detection

For the case of binary transmission in a one-dimensional signal space, the signal constellation consists of the points $S = \{\sqrt{E_b}, -\sqrt{E_b}\}$, corresponding, respectively, to the bit $b = 1$ or $b = 0$ (respectively, using the current mapping). The corresponding likelihood functions are

$$p(r|s = \sqrt{E_b}) = \frac{1}{\sqrt{2\pi}}e^{-\frac{1}{2\sigma^2}(r-\sqrt{E_b})^2} \quad p(r|s = -\sqrt{E_b}) = \frac{1}{\sqrt{2\pi}}e^{-\frac{1}{2\sigma^2}(r+\sqrt{E_b})^2}.$$

These densities are plotted in Figure 1.8(a). We see $r|s = \sqrt{E_b}$ is a Gaussian with mean $\sqrt{E_b}$. The MAP decision rule compares the weighted densities $p(r|s = \sqrt{E_b})P(s = \sqrt{E_b})$ and $p(r|s = -\sqrt{E_b})P(s = -\sqrt{E_b})$. Figure 1.8(b) shows these densities in the case that $P(s = -\sqrt{E_b}) > P(s = \sqrt{E_b})$. Clearly, there is a threshold point τ at which

$$p(r|s = \sqrt{E_b})P(s = \sqrt{E_b}) = p(r|s = -\sqrt{E_b})P(s = -\sqrt{E_b}).$$

In this case, the decision rule (1.18) simplifies to

$$\hat{s} = \begin{cases} \sqrt{E_b}(\text{i.e., } b_i = 1) & \text{if } r > \tau \\ -\sqrt{E_b}(\text{i.e., } b_i = 0) & \text{if } r < \tau. \end{cases} \tag{1.19}$$

The threshold value can be computed explicitly as

$$\tau = \frac{\sigma^2}{2\sqrt{E_b}} \ln \frac{P(s = -\sqrt{E_b})}{P(s = \sqrt{E_b})}. \tag{1.20}$$

In the case that $P(s = \sqrt{E_b}) = P(s = -\sqrt{E_b})$, the decision threshold is at $\tau = 0$, as would be expected.

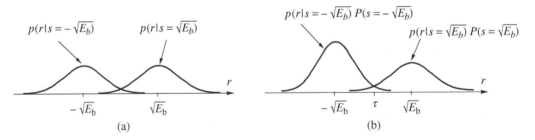

Figure 1.8: Conditional densities in BPSK modulation. (a) Conditional densities; (b) weighted conditional densities.

Binary detection problems are also frequently expressed in terms of *likelihood ratios*. For binary detection, the problem is one of determining, say, if $b = 1$ or if $b = 0$. The detection rule (1.18) becomes a test between

$$p(r|b = 1)P(b = 1) \quad \text{and} \quad P(r|b = 0)P(b = 0).$$

This can be expressed as a *ratio*,

$$\frac{p(r|b=1)P(b=1)}{p(r|b=0)P(b=0)}.$$

In the case of equal priors, we obtain the likelihood ratio

$$L(r) = \frac{p(r|b=1)}{p(r|b=0)}.$$

For many channels, it is more convenient to use the *log likelihood ratio*

$$\Lambda(r) = \log \frac{p(r|b=1)}{p(r|b=0)},$$

where the natural logarithm is usually used. The decision is made that $\hat{b} = 1$ if $\Lambda(r) > 0$ and $\hat{b} = 0$ if $\Lambda(r) < 0$.

For the Gaussian channel with BPSK modulation, we have

$$\Lambda(r) = \log \frac{p(r|a=\sqrt{E_b})}{p(r|a=-\sqrt{E_b})} = \log \frac{\exp(-\frac{1}{2\sigma^2}(r-\sqrt{E_b})^2)}{\exp(-\frac{1}{2\sigma^2}(r+\sqrt{E_b})^2)} = \frac{2\sqrt{E_b}}{\sigma^2}r = L_c r, \qquad (1.21)$$

where $L_c = \frac{2\sqrt{E_b}}{\sigma^2}$ is called the **channel reliability**.[5]

The quantity $\Lambda(r) = L_c r$ can be used as *soft information* in a decoding system. The quantity $\text{sign}(\Lambda(r))$ is referred to as *hard information* in a decoding system. Most early error correction decoding algorithms employed hard information — actual estimated bit values — while there has been a trend toward increasing use of soft information decoders, which generally provide better performance.

Note: Beginning in Section 1.7, error correction coding is used, and the transmitted BPSK amplitudes are $\pm\sqrt{E_c}$, where $E_c = RE_b$. Using these amplitudes,

$$\Lambda(r) = \log \frac{p(r|a=\sqrt{E_c})}{p(r|a=-\sqrt{E_c})} = \frac{2\sqrt{E_c}}{\sigma^2}r$$

so that the channel reliability is $L_c = 2\sqrt{E_c}/\sigma^2$.

1.5.4 Probability of Error for Binary Detection

Even with optimum decisions at the demodulator, errors can still be made with some probability (otherwise, error correction coding would not ever be needed). For binary detection problems in Gaussian noise, the probabilities can be expressed using the $Q(x)$ function, which is the probability that a unit Gaussian $N \sim \mathcal{N}(0,1)$ exceeds x:

$$Q(x) = P(N > x) = \frac{1}{\sqrt{2\pi}} \int_x^\infty e^{-n^2/2}\, dn.$$

The Q function has the properties that

$$Q(x) = 1 - Q(-x) \quad Q(0) = \frac{1}{2} \quad Q(-\infty) = 1 \quad Q(\infty) = 0.$$

---

[5] In some sources (e.g., [178]) the channel reliability L_c is expressed alternatively as equivalent to $2E_b/\sigma^2$. This is in some ways preferable, since it is unitless.

For a Gaussian random variable Z with mean μ and variance σ^2, $Z \sim \mathcal{N}(\mu, \sigma^2)$, it is straightforward to show that

$$P(Z > x) = \frac{1}{\sqrt{2\pi}\sigma} \int_x^{\infty} e^{-(z-\mu)^2/2\sigma^2} \, dz = Q\left(\frac{x - \mu}{\sigma}\right).$$

Suppose there are two points a and b along an axis, and that

$$R = s + N,$$

where s is one of the two points, and $N \sim \mathcal{N}(0, \sigma^2)$. The distributions $P(R|s = a)P(s = a)$ and $P(R|s = b)P(s = b)$ are plotted in Figure 1.9. A decision threshold τ is also shown. When a is sent, an error is made when $R > \tau$. Denoting $\mathcal{E}$ as the error event, this occurs with probability

$$P(\mathcal{E}|s = a) = P(R > \tau) = \frac{1}{\sqrt{2\pi}\sigma} \int_\tau^{\infty} e^{-\frac{1}{2\sigma^2}(r-a)^2} \, dr = Q\left(\frac{\tau - a}{\sigma}\right).$$

When b is sent, an error is made when $R < \tau$, which occurs with probability

$$P(\mathcal{E}|s = b) = P(R < \tau) = 1 - P(R > \tau) = 1 - Q\left(\frac{\tau - b}{\sigma}\right) = Q\left(\frac{b - \tau}{\sigma}\right).$$

The overall probability of error is

$$\begin{aligned} P(\mathcal{E}) &= P(\mathcal{E}|s = a)P(s = a) + P(\mathcal{E}|s = b)P(s = b) \\ &= Q\left(\frac{\tau - a}{\sigma}\right)P(s = a) + Q\left(\frac{b - \tau}{\sigma}\right)P(s = b). \end{aligned} \tag{1.22}$$

An important special case is when $P(s = a) = P(s = b) = \frac{1}{2}$. Then the decision threshold is at the midpoint $\tau = (a + b)/2$. Let $d = |b - a|$ be the distance between the two signals. Then (1.22) can be written

$$\boxed{P(\mathcal{E}) = Q\left(\frac{d}{2\sigma}\right).} \tag{1.23}$$

Even in the case that the signals are transmitted in multidimensional space, provided that the covariance of the noise is of the form $\sigma^2 I$, the probability of error is still of the form (1.23). That is, if

$$\mathbf{R} = \mathbf{s} + \mathbf{N}$$

are n-dimensional vectors, with $\mathbf{N} \sim \mathcal{N}(\mathbf{0}, \sigma^2 I)$, and $\mathbf{S} \in \{\mathbf{a}, \mathbf{b}\}$ are two equiprobable transmitted vectors, then the probability of decision error is $P(\mathcal{E}) = Q\left(\frac{d}{2\sigma}\right)$, where $d = \| \mathbf{a} - \mathbf{b} \|$ is the Euclidean distance between vectors. This formula is frequently used in characterizing the performance of codes.

For the particular case of BPSK signaling, we have $a = -\sqrt{E_b}$, $b = \sqrt{E_b}$, and $d = 2\sqrt{E_b}$. The probability $P(\mathcal{E})$ is denoted as P_b, the "probability of a bit error." Thus,

$$P_b = Q\left(\frac{\tau + \sqrt{E_b}}{\sigma}\right)P(-\sqrt{E_b}) + Q\left(\frac{\sqrt{E_b} - \tau}{\sigma}\right)P(\sqrt{E_b}). \tag{1.24}$$

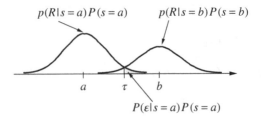

Figure 1.9: Distributions when two signals are sent in Gaussian noise.

When $P(\sqrt{E_b}) = P(-\sqrt{E_b})$, then $\tau = 0$. Recalling that the variance for the channel is expressed as $\sigma^2 = \frac{N_0}{2}$, we have for BPSK transmission

$$\boxed{P_b = Q(\sqrt{E_b}/\sigma) = Q\left(\sqrt{\frac{2E_b}{N_0}}\right).} \tag{1.25}$$

bpskprobplot.m
bpskprob.m

The quantity E_b/N_0 is frequently called the (bit) SNR.

Figure 1.10 shows the probability of bit error for a BPSK as a function of the SNR in dB (decibel), where

$$E_b/N_0 \text{ dB} = 10\log_{10} E_b/N_0,$$

for the case $P(\sqrt{E_b}) = P(-\sqrt{E_b})$.

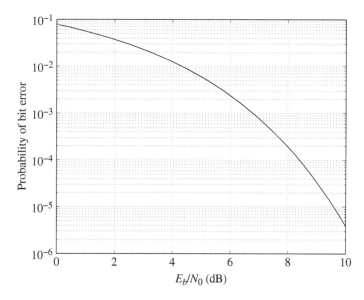

Figure 1.10: Probability of error for BPSK signaling.

1.5.5 Bounds on Performance: The Union Bound

For some signal constellations, exact expressions for the probability of error are difficult to obtain. In many cases it is more convenient to obtain a *bound* on the probability of error using the union bound. (See Box 1.1.) Consider, for example, the 8-PSK constellation in Figure 1.11. If the point labeled $\mathbf{s}_0$ is transmitted, then an error occurs if the received signal falls in either shaded area. Let A be the event that the received signal falls on the incorrect side of threshold line L_1 and let B be the event that the received signal falls on the incorrect side of the line L_2. Then

$$\Pr(\text{symbol decoding error}|\mathbf{s}_0 \text{ sent}) = P(A \cup B).$$

The events A and B are not disjoint, as is apparent from Figure 1.11. The exact probability computation is made more difficult by the overlapping region. Using the union bound, however, the probability of error can be bounded as

$$\Pr(\text{symbol decoding error}|\mathbf{s}_0 \text{ sent}) \le P(A) + P(B).$$

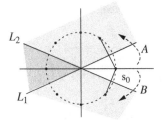

Figure 1.11: Probability of error bound for 8-PSK modulation.

Box 1.1: The Union Bound

For sets A and B, we have $P(A \cup B) = P(A) + P(B) - P(A \cap B)$.

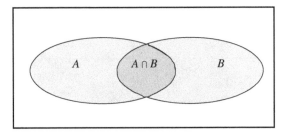

Then, since $P(A \cap B) \geq 0$, clearly $P(A \cup B) \leq P(A) + P(B)$.

The event A occurs with the probability that the transmitted signal falls on the wrong side of the line L_1; similarly for B. Assuming that the noise is independent Gaussian with variance σ^2 in each coordinate direction, this probability is

$$P(A) = Q\left(\frac{d_{\min}}{2\sigma}\right),$$

where $d_{\min}$ is the minimum distance between signal points. Denote the probability of a symbol error by P_s. Assuming that all symbols are sent with equal probability, we have $P_s =$ Pr(symbol decoding error$|\mathbf{s}_0$ sent), where the probability is bounded by

$$P_s \leq 2Q\left(\frac{d_{\min}}{2\sigma}\right). \tag{1.26}$$

The factor 2 multiplying the Q function is the number of nearest neighbors around each constellation point. The probability of error is dominated by the minimum distance between points: better performance is obtained with larger distance. As E_s/N_0 (the symbol SNR) increases, the probability of falling in the intersection region decreases and the bound (1.26) becomes increasingly tight. More generally, the probability of detection error for a symbol s which has K neighbors in signal space at a distance $d_{\min}$ from it can be bounded by

$$P_s \leq KQ\left(\frac{d_{\min}}{2\sigma}\right), \tag{1.27}$$

and the bound becomes increasingly tight as the SNR increases.

For signal constellations larger than BPSK, it is common to plot the probability of a *symbol* error *vs.* the SNR in E_s/N_0, where E_s is the average signal energy. However, when the bits are assigned in

Gray code order, then a symbol error is likely to be an adjacent symbol. One symbol thus results in 1 bit error, out of the $\log_2 M$ bits the symbol represents, so

$$P_b \approx \frac{1}{\log_2 M} P_s \quad \text{for sufficiently large SNR.} \tag{1.28}$$

1.5.6   The Binary Symmetric Channel

The BSC is a simplified channel model which contemplates only the transmission of bits over the channel; it does not treat details such as signal spaces, modulation, or matched filtering. The BSC accepts 1 bit per unit of time and transmits that bit with a probability of error p. A representation of the BSC is shown in Figure 1.12. An incoming bit of 0 or 1 is transmitted through the channel unchanged with probability $1 - p$, or flipped with probability p. The sequence of output bits in a BSC can be modeled as

$$R_i = S_i \oplus N_i, \tag{1.29}$$

where $R_i \in \{0, 1\}$ are the output bits, $S_i \in \{0, 1\}$ are the input bits, $N_i \in \{0, 1\}$ represents the possible bit errors, where N_i is 1 if an error occurs on bit i. The addition in (1.29) is **modulo 2 addition** (without carry), according to the addition table

$$0 \oplus 0 = 0 \quad 0 \oplus 1 = 1 \quad 1 \oplus 1 = 0,$$

so that if $N_i = 1$, then R_i is the bit complement of S_i. The BSC is an instance of a *memoryless channel*. This means each of the errors N_i is statistically independent of all the other N_i. The probability that bit i has an error is $P(N_i = 1) = p$, where p is called the BSC crossover probability. The sequence $\{N_i, i \in \mathbb{Z}\}$ can be viewed as an independent and identically distributed (i.i.d.) Bernoulli(p) random process.

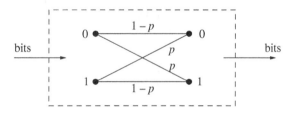

Figure 1.12: A binary symmetric channel.

Suppose that S is sent over the channel and R is received. The likelihood function $P(R|S)$ is

$$P(R|S) = \begin{cases} 1 - p & \text{if } R = S \\ p & \text{if } R \neq S. \end{cases} \tag{1.30}$$

Now suppose that the sequence $\mathbf{s} = [s_1, s_2, \ldots, s_n]$ is transmitted over a BSC and that the received sequence is $\mathbf{R} = [r_1, r_2, \ldots, r_n]$. Because of independent noise samples, the likelihood function factors,

$$P(\mathbf{R}|\mathbf{S}) = \prod_{i=1}^{n} P(R_i|S_i). \tag{1.31}$$

Each factor in the product is of the form (1.30). Thus, there is a factor $(1 - p)$ every time R_i agrees with S_i, and a factor p every time R_i differs from S_i. To represent this, we introduce the *Hamming distance*.

Definition 1.9 The **Hamming distance** between a sequence $\mathbf{x} = [x_1, x_2, \ldots, x_n]$ and a sequence $\mathbf{y} = [y_1, y_2, \ldots, y_n]$ is the number of positions that the corresponding elements differ:

$$\boxed{d_H(\mathbf{x}, \mathbf{y}) = \sum_{i=1}^{n} [x_i \neq y_i].}$$

(1.32)

Here we have used the notation (Iverson's convention [166])

$$[x_i \neq y_i] = \begin{cases} 1 & \text{if } x_i \neq y_i \\ 0 & \text{if } x_i = y_i. \end{cases}$$

□

Using the notation of Hamming distance, we can write the likelihood function (1.31) as

$$P(\mathbf{R}|\mathbf{S}) = \underbrace{(1-p)^{n-d_H(\mathbf{R},\mathbf{S})}}_{\substack{\text{number of places} \\ \text{they are the same}}} \underbrace{p^{d_H(\mathbf{R},\mathbf{S})}}_{\substack{\text{number of places} \\ \text{they differ}}}.$$

The likelihood function can also be written as

$$P(\mathbf{R}|\mathbf{S}) = \left(\frac{p}{1-p}\right)^{d_H(\mathbf{R},\mathbf{S})} (1-p)^n.$$

Consider now the detection problem of deciding if the sequence $\mathbf{S}_1$ or the sequence $\mathbf{S}_2$ was sent, where each occur with equal probability. The ML decision rule says to choose that value of $\mathbf{S}$ for which $\frac{p}{1-p}^{d_H(\mathbf{R},\mathbf{S})} (1-p)^n$ is the largest. Assuming that $p < \frac{1}{2}$, this corresponds to choosing that value of $\mathbf{S}$ for which $d_H(\mathbf{R}, \mathbf{S})$ is the smallest, that is, the vector $\mathbf{S}$ nearest to $\mathbf{R}$ in Hamming distance.

We see that for detection in a Gaussian channel, the *Euclidean* distance is the appropriate distance for detection. For the BSC, the *Hamming* distance is the appropriate distance for detection.

1.5.7 The BSC and the Gaussian Channel Model

At a sufficiently coarse level of detail, the modulator/demodulator system with the AWGN channel can be viewed as a BSC. The modulation, channel, and detector collectively constitute a "channel" which accepts bits at the input and emits bits at the output. The end-to-end system viewed at this level, as suggested by the dashed box in Figure 1.13(b), forms a BSC. The crossover probability p can be computed based on the system parameters,

$$p = P(\text{bit out} = 0|\text{bit in} = 1) = P(\text{bit out} = 1|\text{bit in} = 0) = P_b = Q(\sqrt{2E_b/N_0}).$$

In many cases the probability of error is computed using a BSC with an "internal" AWGN channel, so that the probability of error is produced as a function of E_b/N_0.

1.6 Memoryless Channels

A memoryless channel is one in which the output r_n at the nth symbol time depends only on the input at time n. Thus, given the input at time n, the output at time n is statistically independent of the outputs at other times. That is, for a sequence of received signals

$$\mathbf{R} = (R_1, R_2, \ldots, R_m)$$

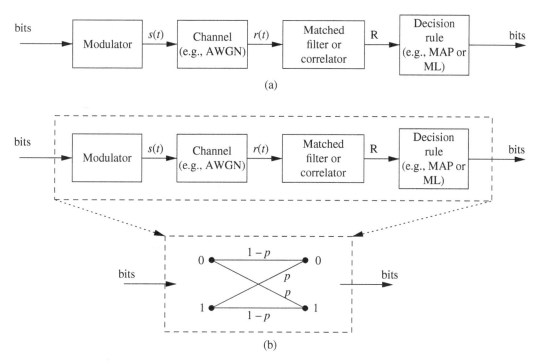

Figure 1.13: (a) System diagram showing modulation, channel, and demodulation; (b) BSC equivalent.

depending on transmitted signals $S_1, S_2, \ldots, S_m$, the likelihood function

$$p(R_1, R_2, \ldots, R_m | S_1, S_2, \ldots, S_m)$$

can be factored as

$$p(R_1, R_2, \ldots, R_m | S_1, S_2, \ldots, S_m) = \prod_{i=1}^{m} p(R_i | S_i).$$

Both the additive Gaussian channel and the BSC that have been introduced are memoryless channels. We will almost universally assume that the channels are memoryless channels. The bursty channels discussed in Chapter 10 and the convolutive channel introduced in Chapter 14 are exceptions to this.

1.7 Simulation and Energy Considerations for Coded Signals

In channel coding with rate $R = k/n$, k input bits yield n coded bits at the output of the encoder, where $n > k$. A transmission budget which allocates E_b Joules/bit for the uncoded data must spread that energy over more coded bits. Let

$$E_c = RE_b$$

denote the "energy per coded bit." We thus have $E_c < E_b$. Consider the framework shown in Figure 1.14. From point "a" to point "b," there is conventional (uncoded) BPSK modulation passing through an AWGN channel, except that the energy per bit is E_c, so that the amplitudes in the BPSK modulator are $\pm\sqrt{E_c}$, instead of $\pm\sqrt{E_b}$, as they would be in the uncoded case.

Thus, at point "b" the probability of error of the coded bits appearing at point "a" can be computed as

$$P_{b,\text{coded}} = Q\left(\sqrt{\frac{2E_c}{N_0}}\right).$$

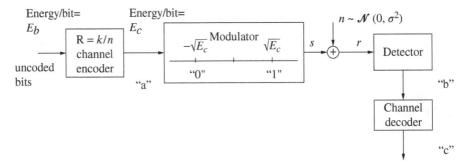

Figure 1.14: Energy for a coded signal.

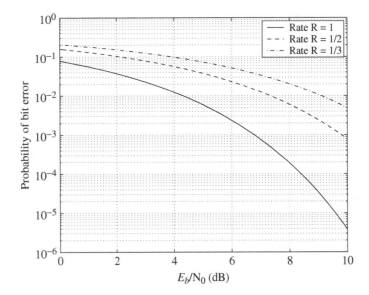

Figure 1.15: Probability of error for coded bits, before correction.

Since $E_c < E_b$, this is *worse* performance than uncoded BPSK would have had. Figure 1.15 shows the probability of error of coded bits for $R = 1/2$ and $R = 1/3$ error correction codes at point "b" in Figure 1.14. At the receiver, the detected coded bits are passed to the channel decoder, the error correction stage, which attempts to correct errors. Clearly, in order to be of any value, the code must be strong enough so that the bits emerging at point "c" of Figure 1.14 can compensate for the lower energy per bit in the channel, plus correct other errors. Fortunately, we will see that this is in fact the case.

Now consider how this system might be simulated in software. It is common to simulate the modulator at point "a" of Figure 1.14 as having fixed amplitudes and to adjust the variance σ^2 of the noise n in the channel. One of the primary considerations, therefore, is how to set σ^2.

Frequently it is desired to simulate performance at a particular SNR, expressed in dB, denoted as $(E_b/N_0)_{dB}$). Let $\gamma = E_b/N_0$ denote the desired SNR at which to simulate. The SNR in dB is converted to γ by

$$\gamma = 10^{(SNR)_{dB}/10}$$

Recalling that $\sigma^2 = N_0/2$, and knowing γ, we have

$$\gamma = \frac{E_b}{2\sigma^2},$$

so

$$\sigma^2 = \frac{E_b}{2\gamma}.$$

Since $E_b = E_c/R$, we have

$$\sigma^2 = \frac{E_c}{2R\gamma}.$$

It is also common in simulation to normalize so that the simulated signal amplitude is $E_c = 1$.

1.8 Some Important Definitions and a Trivial Code: Repetition Coding

In this section, we introduce the important coding concepts of code rate, Hamming distance, minimum distance, Hamming spheres, and the generator matrix. These concepts are introduced by means of a simple, even trivial, example of an error correction code, the repetition code.

Let $\mathbb{F}_2$ denote the set (field) with two elements in it, 0 and 1. In this field, arithmetic operations are defined as:

$$0 + 0 = 0 \quad 0 + 1 = 1 \quad 1 + 0 = 1 \quad 1 + 1 = 0$$

$$0 \cdot 0 = 0 \quad 0 \cdot 1 = 0 \quad 1 \cdot 0 = 0 \quad 1 \cdot 1 = 1.$$

Let $\mathbb{F}_2^n$ denote the (vector) space of n-tuples of elements of $\mathbb{F}_2$.

Suppressing for the moment a few details, here is a useful definition: an (n, k) binary code is a set of 2^k distinct points in $\mathbb{F}_2^n$. Another way of putting this: an (n, k) binary code is a code that accepts k bits as input and produces n bits as output. (We will be interested in linear codes, as the details unfold.)

Definition 1.10 The **rate** of an (n, k) code is

$$R = \frac{k}{n}.$$

□

The $(n, 1)$ **repetition code**, where n is odd, is the code obtained by repeating the 1-bit input n times in the output codeword. That is, the codeword representing the input 0 is a block of n 0s and the codeword representing the input 1 is a block of n 1s. The *code C* consists of the set of two codewords

$$C = \{[0, 0, \ldots, 0], [1, 1, \ldots, 1]\} \subset \mathbb{F}_2^n.$$

Letting m denote the message, the corresponding codeword is

$$\mathbf{c} = \underbrace{[m, m, m, \ldots, m]}_{n \text{ copies}}.$$

This is a rate $R = 1/n$ code.

Encoding can be represented as a matrix operation. Let G be the $1 \times n$ **generator matrix** given by

$$G = \begin{bmatrix} 1 & 1 & \cdots & 1 \end{bmatrix}.$$

Then the encoding operation is

$$\mathbf{c} = mG.$$

1.8.1 Detection of Repetition Codes Over a BSC

Let us first consider decoding of this code when transmitted through a BSC with crossover probability $p < 1/2$. Denote the output of the BSC by

$$\mathbf{r} = \mathbf{c} \oplus \mathbf{n},$$

where the addition is modulo 2 and $\mathbf{n}$ is a binary vector of length n, with 1 in the positions where the channel errors occur. Assuming that the codewords are selected with equal probability, ML decoding is appropriate. As observed in Section 1.5.6, the ML decoding rule selects the codeword in C which is closest to the received vector $\mathbf{r}$ in Hamming distance. For the repetition code, this decoding rule can be expressed as a majority decoding rule: if the majority of received bits are 0, decode a 0; otherwise, decode a 1. For example, take the $(7, 1)$ repetition code and let $m = 1$. Then the codeword is $\mathbf{c} = [1, 1, 1, 1, 1, 1, 1]$. Suppose that the received vector is

$$\mathbf{r} = [1, 0, 1, 1, 0, 1, 1].$$

Since 5 out of the 7 bits are 1, the decoded value is

$$\hat{m} = 1.$$

An error *detector* can also be established. If the received vector $\mathbf{r}$ is not one of the codewords, we *detect* that the channel has introduced one or more errors into the transmitted codeword.

The codewords in a code C can be viewed as points in n-dimensional space. For example, Figure 1.16(a) illustrates the codewords as points $(0, 0, 0)$ and $(1, 1, 1)$ in three-dimensional space. (Beyond three dimensions, of course, the geometric viewpoint cannot be plotted, but it is still valuable conceptually.) In this geometric setting, we use the **Hamming distance** to measure distances between points.

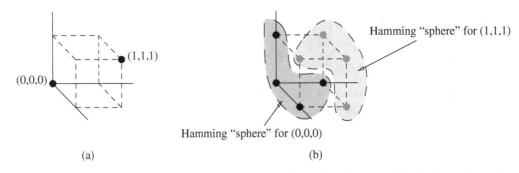

Figure 1.16: A $(3, 1)$ binary repetition code. (a) The code as points in space; (b) the Hamming spheres around the points.

Definition 1.11 The **minimum distance** $d_{\min}$ of a code C is the smallest Hamming distance between any two codewords in the code:

$$d_{\min} = \min_{\mathbf{c}_i, \mathbf{c}_j \in C, \mathbf{c}_i \neq \mathbf{c}_j} d_H(\mathbf{c}_i, \mathbf{c}_j).$$

□

The two codewords in the $(n, 1)$ repetition code are clearly (Hamming) distance n apart.

In this geometric setting, the ML decoding algorithm may be expressed as: Choose the codeword $\hat{\mathbf{c}}$ which is closest to the received vector $\mathbf{r}$. That is,

$$\hat{\mathbf{c}} = \arg \min_{\mathbf{c} \in C} d_H(\mathbf{r}, \mathbf{c}).$$

Definition 1.12 The **Hamming sphere** of radius t around a codeword $\mathbf{c}$ consists of all vectors which are at a Hamming distance $\leq t$ from $\mathbf{c}$.

□

For example, for the $(3, 1)$ repetition code, the codewords and the points in their Hamming spheres are

Codeword	Points in its sphere
(0,0,0)	(0,0,0),(0,0,1),(0,1,0),(1,0,0)
(1,1,1)	(1,1,1),(1,1,0),(1,0,1),(0,1,1),

as illustrated in Figure 1.16(b).

When the Hamming spheres around each codeword are all taken to have the same radius, the largest such radius producing nonoverlapping spheres is determined by the separation between the *nearest* two codewords in the code, d_{min}. The radius of the spheres in this case is $t = \lfloor (d_{min} - 1)/2 \rfloor$, where the notation $\lfloor x \rfloor$ means to take the greatest integer $\leq x$. Figure 1.17 shows the idea of these Hamming spheres. The black squares represent codewords in n-dimensional space and black dots represent other vectors in n-dimensional space. The dashed lines indicate the boundaries of the Hamming spheres around the codewords. If a vector $\mathbf{r}$ falls inside the sphere around a codeword, then it is closer to that codeword than to any other codeword. By the ML criterion, $\mathbf{r}$ should decode to that codeword inside the sphere. When all the spheres have radius $t = \lfloor (d_{min} - 1)/2 \rfloor$, this decoding rule is referred to as bounded distance decoding.

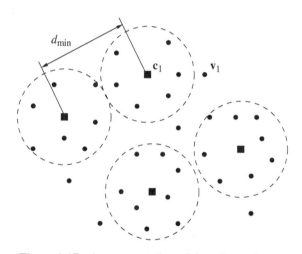

Figure 1.17: A representation of decoding spheres.

The decoder will make a decoding error if the channel noise moves the received vector $\mathbf{r}$ into a sphere other than the sphere the true codeword is in. Since the centers of the spheres lie a distance at least d_{min} apart, the decoder is guaranteed to *decode* correctly provided that no more than t errors occur in the received vector $\mathbf{r}$. The number t is called the **random error correction capability** of the code. If d_{min} is even and two codewords lie exactly d_{min} apart and the channel introduces $d_{min}/2$ errors, then the received vector lies right on the boundary of two spheres. In this case, given no other information, the decoder must choose one of the two codewords arbitrarily; half the time it will make an error.

Note from Figure 1.17 that in a bounded distance decoder there may be vectors that fall outside the Hamming spheres around the codewords, such as the vector labeled $\mathbf{v}_1$. If the received vector $\mathbf{r} = \mathbf{v}_1$, then the nearest codeword is $\mathbf{c}_1$. A bounded distance decoder, however, would not be able to decode if $\mathbf{r} = \mathbf{v}_1$, since it can only decode those vectors that fall in spheres of radius t. The decoder might have to declare a decoding failure in this case.

A true ML decoder, which chooses the nearest codeword to the received vector, would be able to decode. Unfortunately, ML decoding is computationally very difficult for large codes. Most of the algebraic decoding algorithms in this book are only bounded distance decoders. An interesting exception are the decoders presented in Chapters 7 and 11, which actually produce *lists* of codeword candidates. These decoders are called *list decoders*.

If the channel introduces fewer than $d_{\min}$ errors, then these can be *detected*, since **r** cannot be another codeword in this case. In summary, for a code with minimum distance $d_{\min}$:

$$\begin{aligned}
\text{Guaranteed error correction capability:} \quad & t = \lfloor (d_{\min} - 1)/2 \rfloor \\
\text{Guaranteed error detection capability:} \quad & d_{\min} - 1
\end{aligned}$$

Having defined the repetition code, let us now characterize its probability of error performance as a function of the BSC crossover probability p. For the $(n, 1)$ repetition code, $d_{\min} = n$, and $t = (n - 1)/2$ (remember n is odd). Suppose in particular that $n = 3$, so that $t = 1$. Then the decoder will make an error if the channel causes either 2 or 3 bits to be in error. Using P_e^n to denote the probability of decoding error for a code of length n, we have

$$P_e^3 = \text{Prob(2 channel errors)} + \text{Prob(3 channel errors)}$$

$$= 3p^2(1 - p) + p^3 = 3p^2 - 2p^3.$$

If $p < \frac{1}{2}$, then $P_e^3 < p$, that is, the decoder will have fewer errors than using the channel without coding.

Let us now examine the probability of decoding error for a code of length n. Note that it doesn't matter what the transmitted codeword was; the probability of error depends only on the error introduced by the channel. Clearly, the decoder will make an error if more than half of the received bits are in error. More precisely, if more than t bits are in error, the decoder will make an error. The probability of error can be expressed as

$$P_e^n = \sum_{i=t+1}^{n} \text{Prob}(i \text{ channel errors occur out of } n \text{ transmitted bits}).$$

The probability of exactly i bits in error out of n bits, where each bit is drawn at random with probability p is[6]

$$\binom{n}{i} p^i (1 - p)^{n-i},$$

so that

$$P_e^n = \sum_{i=t+1}^{n} \binom{n}{i} p^i (1 - p)^{n-i}$$

$$= \binom{n}{t+1} (1 - p)^n \left(\frac{p}{1 - p} \right)^{t+1} + \text{terms of higher degree in } p.$$

It would appear that as the code length increases, and thus t increases, the probability of decoder error decreases. (This is substantiated in Exercise 1.16b.) Thus, it is possible to obtain *arbitrarily small* probability of error, but at the cost of a very low rate: $R = 1/n \to 0$ as $P_e^N \to 0$.

Let us now consider using this repetition code for communication over the AWGN channel. Let us suppose that the transmitter has $P = 1$ Watt (W) of power available and that we want to send information at 1 bit/second. There is thus $E_b = 1$ Joule (J) of energy available for each bit of information. Now the information is coded using an $(n, 1)$ repetition code. To maintain the information rate of 1 bit/second, we must send n coded bits/second. With n times as many bits to send, there is still only 1 W of power available, which must be shared among all the coded bits. The energy available for each coded bit, which we denote as E_c, is $E_c = E_b/n$. Thus, because of coding, there is less energy available for each bit to convey information! The probability of error for the AWGN channel (i.e., the

---

[6] The binomial coefficient is $\binom{n}{i} = \frac{n!}{i!(n-i)!}$.

binary crossover probability for the effective BSC) is

$$p = Q(\sqrt{2E_c/N_0}) = Q(\sqrt{2E_b/nN_0}).$$

The crossover probability p is higher as a result of using a code! However, the hope is that the error decoding capability of the overall system is better. Nevertheless, for the repetition code, this hope is in vain.

Figure 1.18 shows the probability of error for repetition codes (here, consider only the hard-decision decoding). The coded performance is worse than the uncoded performance, and the performance gets worse with increasing n.

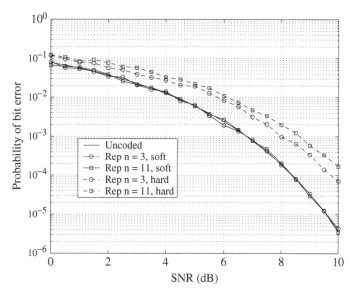

Figure 1.18: Performance of the $(3, 1)$ and $(11, 1)$ repetition code over BSC using both hard- and soft-decision decoding.

1.8.2 Soft-Decision Decoding of Repetition Codes Over the AWGN

Let us now consider decoding over the AWGN using a *soft-decision* decoder. Since the repetition code has a particularly simple codeword structure, it is straightforward to describe the soft-decision decoder and characterize its probability of error.

The likelihood function is

$$p(\mathbf{r}|\mathbf{c}) = \prod_{i=1}^{n} p(r_i|c_i),$$

so that the log likelihood ratio

$$\Lambda(\mathbf{r}) = \log \frac{p(\mathbf{r}|m = 1)}{p(\mathbf{r}|m = 0)}$$

can be computed using (1.21) as

$$\Lambda(\mathbf{r}) = L_c \sum_{i=1}^{n} r_i.$$

Then the decoder decides $\hat{m} = 1$ if $\Lambda(\mathbf{r}) > 0$, or $\hat{m} = 0$ if $\Lambda(\mathbf{r}) < 0$. Since the threshold is 0 and L_c is a positive constant, the decoder decides

$$\hat{m} = \begin{cases} 1 & \text{if } \sum_{i=1}^{n} r_i > 0 \\ 0 & \text{if } \sum_{i=1}^{n} r_i < 0. \end{cases}$$

The soft-decision decoder performs superior to the hard-decision decoder. Suppose the vector $(-\sqrt{E_c}, -\sqrt{E_c}, \ldots, -\sqrt{E_c})$ is sent (corresponding to the all-zero codeword). If one of the r_i happens to be greater than 0, but other of the r_i are correspondingly less than 0, the erroneous positive quantities might be canceled out by the other symbols. In fact, it is straightforward to show (see Exercise 1.18) that the probability of error for the $(n, 1)$ repetition code with soft-decision decoding is

$$P_b = Q(\sqrt{2E_b/N_0}). \tag{1.33}$$

That is, it is the same as for uncoded transmission — still not effective as a code, but better than hard-decision decoding.

While these simple-minded repetition codes do not, by themselves, make good error correction codes, repetition codes will be shown in Chapter 15 to be a component of very powerful codes, the repeat accumulate codes.

1.8.3 Simulation of Results

While it is possible for these simple codes to compute explicit performance curves, it is worthwhile to consider how the performance might also be simulated, since other codes that we will examine may be more difficult to analyze. The program here illustrates a framework for simulating the performance of codes. The probability of error is estimated by running codewords through a simulated Gaussian channel until a specified number of errors has occurred. Then the estimated probability of error is the number of errors counted divided by the number of bits generated.

Figure 1.18 shows the probability of error for uncoded transmission and both hard- and soft-decision decoding of $(3, 1)$ and $(11, 1)$ codes.

1.8.4 Summary

This lengthy example on a nearly useless code has introduced several concepts that will be useful for other codes:

- The concept of minimum distance of a code.
- The probability of decoder error.
- The idea of a generator matrix.
- The fact that not every code is good!
- Recognition that soft-decision decoding is superior to hard-input decoding in terms of probability of error.

Prior to the proof of Shannon's channel coding theorem and the research it engendered, communication engineers were in a quandary. It was believed that to obtain totally reliable communication, it would be necessary to transmit using very slow rates, essentially employing repetition codes to catch any errors and using slow symbol rate to increase the energy per bit. However, Shannon's theorem dramatically changed this perspective, indicating that it is not necessary to slow the rate of communication to zero. It is only necessary to use better codes. It is hardly an overstatement that information-theoretic understanding has driven the information age!

1.9 Hamming Codes

As a second example we now introduce are Hamming codes. These are codes which are much better than repetition codes and were the first important codes discovered. Hamming codes lie at the intersection of many different kinds of codes, so we will also use them to briefly introduce several important themes which will be developed throughout the course of this book. These themes include: generator matrices; parity check matrices; syndromes; generator polynomials; parity check polynomials; trellises; and Tanner graphs. These themes, touched on here, will be fully developed in later chapters.

A $(7, 4)$ Hamming code produces $n = 7$ bits of output for every $k = 4$ bits of input. Hamming codes are *linear block codes*, which means that the encoding operation can be described in terms of a 4×7 generator matrix, such as

$$G = \begin{bmatrix} 1 & 1 & 0 & 1 & 0 & 0 & 0 \\ 0 & 1 & 1 & 0 & 1 & 0 & 0 \\ 0 & 0 & 1 & 1 & 0 & 1 & 0 \\ 0 & 0 & 0 & 1 & 1 & 0 & 1 \end{bmatrix}. \tag{1.34}$$

The codewords are obtained as linear combination of the *rows* of G, where all the operations are computed modulo 2 in each vector element, that is, in the field $\mathbb{F}_2$. The code is the *row space* of G. For a message vector $\mathbf{m} = [m_1, m_2, m_3, m_4]$ the codeword is

$$\mathbf{c} = \mathbf{m}G.$$

For example, if $\mathbf{m} = [1, 1, 0, 0]$, then

$$\mathbf{c} = \mathbf{m}G = [1, 1, 0, 1, 0, 0, 0] \oplus [0, 1, 1, 0, 1, 0, 0] = [1, 0, 1, 1, 1, 0, 0].$$

It can be verified that the minimum distance of the Hamming code is $d_{\min} = 3$, so the code is capable of correcting 1 error in every block of n bits.

The codewords for this code are

$$\begin{aligned} &[0,0,0,0,0,0,0], [1,1,0,1,0,0,0], [0,1,1,0,1,0,0], [1,0,1,1,1,0,0] \\ &[0,0,1,1,0,1,0], [1,1,1,0,0,1,0], [0,1,0,1,1,1,0], [1,0,0,0,1,1,0] \\ &[0,0,0,1,1,0,1], [1,1,0,0,1,0,1], [0,1,1,1,0,0,1], [1,0,1,0,0,0,1] \\ &[0,0,1,0,1,1,1], [1,1,1,1,1,1,1], [0,1,0,0,0,1,1], [1,0,0,1,0,1,1]. \end{aligned} \tag{1.35}$$

The Hamming decoding algorithm presented here is slightly more complicated than for the repetition code. (There are other decoding algorithms.)

Every (n, k) linear block code has associated with it a $(n - k) \times n$ matrix H called the *parity check matrix*, which has the property that $GH^T = \mathbf{0}$ (all the operations are performed modulo 2). This means that a vector $\mathbf{v} \in \mathbb{F}_2^n$ (a vector of binary elements)

$$\mathbf{v}H^T = \mathbf{0} \text{ if and only if the vector } \mathbf{v} \text{ is a codeword.} \tag{1.36}$$

The parity check matrix is not unique. For the generator G of (1.34), the parity check matrix can be written as

$$H = \begin{bmatrix} 1 & 0 & 1 & 1 & 1 & 0 & 0 \\ 0 & 1 & 0 & 1 & 1 & 1 & 0 \\ 0 & 0 & 1 & 0 & 1 & 1 & 1 \end{bmatrix}. \tag{1.37}$$

The matrix H can be expressed in terms of its columns as

$$H = \begin{bmatrix} \mathbf{h}_1 & \mathbf{h}_2 & \mathbf{h}_3 & \mathbf{h}_4 & \mathbf{h}_5 & \mathbf{h}_6 & \mathbf{h}_7 \end{bmatrix}.$$

It may be observed that (for the Hamming code) the columns of H consist of the binary representations of the numbers 1 through $7 = n$, though not in numerical order. On the basis of this observation, we can generalize to other Hamming codes. Hamming codes of length $n = 2^m - 1$ and dimension $k = 2^m - m - 1$ exist for every $m \geq 2$, having parity check matrices whose columns are binary representations of the numbers from 1 through n.

1.9.1 Hard-Input Decoding Hamming Codes

Suppose that a codeword $\mathbf{c}$ is sent and the vector through a BSC is

$$\mathbf{r} = \mathbf{c} \oplus \mathbf{n} \text{ (addition modulo 2)}.$$

The first decoding step is to compute the *syndrome*

$$\mathbf{s} = \mathbf{r}H^T = (\mathbf{c} \oplus \mathbf{n})H^T = \mathbf{n}H^T$$

(all operations in $\mathbb{F}_2$). Because of Property (1.36), the syndrome depends only on the error $\mathbf{n}$ and not on the transmitted codeword. The codeword information is "projected away."

Since a Hamming code is capable of correcting only a single error, suppose that $\mathbf{n}$ is all zeros except at a single position,

$$\mathbf{n} = [n_1, n_2, n_3, \ldots, n_7] = [0, \ldots, 0, 1, 0, \ldots, 0],$$

where the 1 is equal to n_i. (That is, the error is in the ith position.)

Let us write H^T in terms of its rows:

$$H^T = \begin{bmatrix} \mathbf{h}_1^T \\ \mathbf{h}_2^T \\ \vdots \\ \mathbf{h}_n^T \end{bmatrix}.$$

Then the syndrome is

$$\mathbf{s} = \mathbf{r}H^T = \mathbf{n}H^T = \begin{bmatrix} n_1 & n_2 & \cdots & n_n \end{bmatrix} \begin{bmatrix} \mathbf{h}_1^T \\ \mathbf{h}_2^T \\ \vdots \\ \mathbf{h}_n^T \end{bmatrix} = \mathbf{h}_i^T.$$

The error position i is the column i of H that is equal to the (transpose of) the syndrome $\mathbf{s}^T$.

Algorithm 1.1 Hamming Code Decoding

---

1. For the received binary vector $\mathbf{r}$, compute the syndrome $\mathbf{s} = \mathbf{r}H^T$. If $\mathbf{s} = \mathbf{0}$, then the decoded codeword is $\hat{\mathbf{c}} = \mathbf{r}$.

2. If $\mathbf{s} \neq \mathbf{0}$, then let i denote the column of H which is equal to $\mathbf{s}^T$. There is an error in position i of $\mathbf{r}$. The decoded codeword is $\hat{\mathbf{c}} = \mathbf{r} + \mathbf{n}_i$, where $\mathbf{n}_i$ is a vector which is all zeros except for a 1 in the ith position.

This decoding procedure fails if more than one error occurs.

Example 1.13 Suppose that the message

$$\mathbf{m} = [m_1, m_2, m_3, m_4] = [0, 1, 1, 0]$$

is encoded, resulting in the codeword

$$\mathbf{c} = [0, 1, 1, 0, 1, 0, 0] + [0, 0, 1, 1, 0, 1, 0] = [0, 1, 0, 1, 1, 1, 0].$$

When $\mathbf{c}$ is transmitted over a BSC, the vector

$$\mathbf{r} = [0, 1, 1, 1, 1, 1, 0]$$

is received. The decoding algorithm proceeds as follows:

1. The syndrome $\mathbf{s} = [0, 1, 1, 1, 1, 1, 0]H^T = [1, 0, 1]$ is computed.

2. This syndrome corresponds to column 3 of H. The decoded value is therefore

$$\hat{\mathbf{c}} = \mathbf{r} + [0, 0, 1, 0, 0, 0, 0] = [0, 1, 0, 1, 1, 1, 0],$$

which is the transmitted codeword.

□   hamcode74pe.m
       nchoosektest.m

The expression for the probability of bit error is significantly more complicated for Hamming codes than for repetition codes. We defer on the details of these computations to the appropriate location (Section 3.7) and simply plot the results here. The available energy per encoded bit is

$$E_c = E_b(k/n) = 4E_b/7,$$

so, as for the repetition code, there is less energy available per bit. This represents a loss of $10\log_{10}(4/7) = -2.4$ dB of energy per transmitted bit compared to the uncoded system. The decrease in energy per bit is not as great as for the repetition code, since the rate is higher. Figure 1.19 shows the probability of bit error for uncoded channels (the solid line), and for the coded bits — that is, the bits coded with energy E_c per bit — (the dashed line). The figure also shows the probability of bit error for the bits *after* they have been through the decoder (the dash-dot line). In this case, the decoded bits *do* have a lower probability of error than the uncoded bits. For the uncoded system, to achieve a probability of error of $P_b = 10^{-6}$ requires an SNR of 10.5 dB, while for the coded system, the same probability of error is achieved with 10.05 dB. The code was able to overcome the 2.4 dB of loss due to rate, and add another 0.45 dB of improvement. We say that the *coding gain* of the system (operated near 10 dB) is 0.45 dB: we can achieve the same performance as a system expending 10.5 dB SNR per bit, but with only 10.05 dB of expended transmitter energy per bit.

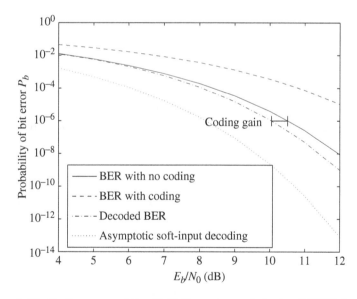

Figure 1.19: Performance of the $(7, 4)$ Hamming code in the AWGN channel.

Also shown in Figure 1.19 is the asymptotic (most accurate for large SNR) performance of soft-decision decoding. This is somewhat optimistic, having better performance than might be achieved in practice. But it does show the potential that soft-decision decoding has: it is significantly better than the hard-input decoding.

1.9.2   Other Representations of the Hamming Code

In the brief introduction to the Hamming code, we showed that the encoding and decoding operations have matrix representations. This is because Hamming codes are **linear block codes**, which will be explored in Chapter 3. There are other representations for Hamming and other codes. We briefly introduce these here as bait and lead-in to further chapters. As these representations show, descriptions of codes involve algebra, polynomials, graph theory, and algorithms on graphs, in addition to the linear algebra we have already seen.

1.9.2.1   An Algebraic Representation

The columns of the parity check matrix H can be represented using a symbol for each column. For example, we could write

$$H = \begin{bmatrix} 1 & 0 & 1 & 1 & 1 & 0 & 0 \\ 0 & 1 & 0 & 1 & 1 & 1 & 0 \\ 0 & 0 & 1 & 0 & 1 & 1 & 1 \end{bmatrix}$$

as

$$H = \begin{bmatrix} \beta_1 & \beta_2 & \beta_3 & \beta_4 & \beta_5 & \beta_6 & \beta_7 \end{bmatrix},$$

where each β_i represents a 3-tuple. Then the syndrome $\mathbf{s} = \mathbf{r}H^T$ can be represented as

$$\mathbf{s} = \sum_{i=1}^{7} r_i \beta_i.$$

Then $\mathbf{s} = \beta_j$ for some j, which indicates the column where the error occurred. This turns the decoding problem into a straightforward algebra problem.

A question we shall take up later is how to generalize this operation. That is, can codes be defined which are capable of correcting more than a single error, for which finding the errors can be computed using algebra? In order to explore this question, we will need to carefully define how to perform algebra on discrete objects (such as the columns of H) so that addition, subtraction, multiplication, and division are defined in a meaningful way. Such algebraic operations are defined in Chapters 2 and 5.

1.9.2.2   A Polynomial Representation

Examination of the codewords in (1.35) reveals an interesting fact: if $\mathbf{c}$ is a codeword, then so is every cyclic shift of $\mathbf{c}$. For example, the codeword $[1, 1, 0, 1, 0, 0, 0]$ has the cyclic shifts

$$[0, 1, 1, 0, 1, 0, 0], [0, 0, 1, 1, 0, 1, 0], [0, 0, 0, 1, 1, 0, 1], [1, 0, 0, 0, 1, 1, 0],$$

$$[0, 1, 0, 0, 0, 1, 1], [1, 0, 1, 0, 0, 0, 1],$$

which are also codewords. Codes for which all cyclic shifts of every codeword are also codewords are called **cyclic** codes. As we will find in Chapter 4, Hamming codes, like most block codes of modern interest, are cyclic codes. In addition to the representation using a generator matrix, cyclic codes can also be represented using polynomials. For the $(7, 4)$ Hamming code, there is a *generator polynomial* $g(x) = x^3 + x + 1$ and a corresponding *parity-check polynomial* $h(x) = x^4 + x^2 + x + 1$, which is a polynomial such that $h(x)g(x) = x^7 + 1$. In general, for a cyclic code of length n, a generator polynomial $g(x)$ must divide $x^n + 1$ (without remainder, operations in $\mathbb{F}_2$), and the quotient is the parity check polynomial,

$$h(x) = \frac{x^n + 1}{g(x)},$$

where the operations are done in $\mathbb{F}_2$. The encoding operation can be represented using polynomial multiplication (with coefficient operations modulo 2). For this reason, the study of polynomial operations and the study of algebraic objects built out of polynomials is of great interest. The parity check polynomial can be used to check if a polynomial is a code polynomial: A polynomial $r(x)$ is a code polynomial if and only if $r(x)h(x)$ is a multiple of $x^n + 1$, so that

$$\frac{r(x)h(x)}{x^n + 1}$$

divides with remainder 0. This provides a parity check condition: for this Hamming code $(n = 7)$ compute $r(x)h(x)$ modulo $x^7 + 1$. If this is not equal to 0, then $r(x)$ is not a code polynomial.

Example 1.14   The message $\mathbf{m} = [m_0, m_1, m_2, m_3] = [0, 1, 1, 0]$ can be represented as a polynomial as

$$m(x) = m_0 + m_1 x + m_2 x^2 + m_3 x^3 = 0 \cdot 1 + 1 \cdot x + 1 \cdot x^2 + 0 \cdot x^3 = x + x^2.$$

The code polynomial is obtained by $c(x) = m(x)g(x)$, or

$$c(x) = (x + x^2)(1 + x + x^3) = (x + x^2 + x^4) + (x^2 + x^3 + x^5)$$
$$= x + 2x^2 + x^3 + x^4 + x^5 = x + x^3 + x^4 + x^5,$$

(where $2x^2 = 0$ modulo 2), which corresponds to the code vector $\mathbf{c} = [0, 1, 0, 1, 1, 1, 0]$.   □

1.9.2.3   A Trellis Representation

As we will see in Chapter 12, there is a graph associated with a block code. This graph is called the *Wolf trellis* for the code. We shall see that paths through the graph correspond to vectors $\mathbf{v}$ that satisfy the parity check condition $\mathbf{v}H^T = \mathbf{0}$. For example, Figure 1.20 shows the trellis corresponding to the parity check matrix (1.37). The trellis states at the kth stage are obtained by taking all possible binary linear combinations of the first k columns of H. In Chapter 12, we will develop a decoding algorithm which essentially finds the best path through the graph. One such decoding algorithm is called the *Viterbi algorithm*. Such decoding algorithms will allow us to create soft-decision decoding algorithms for block codes.

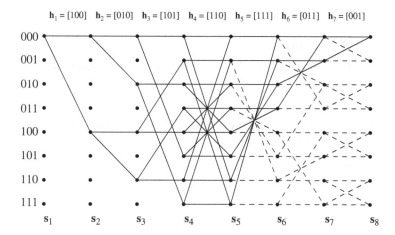

Figure 1.20: The trellis of a $(7, 4)$ Hamming code.

The Viterbi algorithm is also used for decoding codes which are defined using graphs similar to that of Figure 1.20. Such codes are called *convolutional codes*.

1.9.2.4 The Tanner Graph Representation

Every linear block code also has another graph which represents it called the *Tanner graph*. For a parity check matrix, the Tanner graph has one node to represent each column of H (the "bit nodes," denoted by c_i in the figure) and one node to represent each row of H (the "check nodes," denoted by z_i in the figure). Edges occur only between bit nodes and check nodes. There is an edge between a bit node and a check node if there is a 1 in the parity check matrix at the corresponding location. For example, for the parity check matrix of (1.37), the Tanner graph representation is shown in Figure 1.21. Algorithms to be presented in Chapter 15 describe how to propagate information through the graph in order to perform decoding. These algorithms are usually associated with codes which are iteratively decoded, such as turbo codes and low-density parity-check codes. These modern families of codes have very good behavior, sometimes nearly approaching capacity.

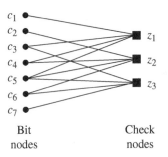

Figure 1.21: The Tanner graph for a $(7, 4)$ Hamming code.

1.10 The Basic Questions

The two simple codes we have examined so far bring out issues relevant for the codes we will investigate:

1. How is the code described and represented?

2. How is encoding accomplished?

3. How is decoding accomplished? (This frequently takes some cleverness!)

4. How are codewords to be represented, encoded, and decoded, in a computationally tractable way?

5. What is the performance of the code? What are the properties of the code? (e.g., How many codewords? What are the weights of the codewords?)

6. Are there other families of codes which can provide better coding gains?

7. How can these codes be found and described?

8. Are there constraints on allowable values of n, k, and $d_{\min}$?

9. Is there some limit to the amount of coding gain possible?

10. For a given available SNR, is there a lower limit on the probability of error that can be achieved?

Questions of this nature shall be addressed throughout the remainder of this book, presenting the best answers available at this time.

1.11 Historical Milestones of Coding Theory

We present in Table 1.1 a brief summary of major accomplishments in coding theory and some of the significant contributors to that theory, or expositors who contributed by bringing together the significant contributions to date. Some dates and contributions may not be exactly as portrayed here; it is difficult to sift through the sands of recent history. Also, significant contributions to coding are made *every month*, so this cannot be a complete list.

1.12 A Bit of Information Theory

This section serves as an appendix to this introductory chapter, providing background on the basic definitions and concepts of information theory. As information-theoretic concepts are invoked throughout this book, readers may want to refer to this section for this background material.

1.12.1 Information- Theoretic Definitions for Discrete Random Variables

1.12.1.1 Entropy and Conditional Entropy

Definition 1.15 Let X be a discrete random variable taking values in a set $\mathcal{X} = \{x_1, x_2, \ldots, x_m\}$ with probabilities $P(X = x_i)$, $x_i \in \mathcal{X}$. Different notations for these probabilities are $p_X(x_i)$, $p(x_i)$, or p_i. The **entropy** of X is

$$H(X) = E[-\log_2 P(X)] = -\sum_{x \in \mathcal{X}} P(X = x) \log_2 P(X = x) = -\sum_{i=1}^{m} p_i \log_2 p_i$$

$$= -\sum_{x \in \mathcal{X}} p_X(x) \log_2 p_X(x).$$

When logarithm base is 2, the units of entropy are in *bits*. When the logarithm base is e (natural log), the units of entropy are in *nats* . □

The entropy represents the uncertainty there is about X prior to its measurement; equivalently, it is the amount of information gained when X is measured. The entropy of X depends on the *probabilities* with which X takes on its values, not the particular *values* that X takes on, so it is a function of p_X, not $\mathcal{X}$.

When the base of logarithms is 2 (as above), then the entropy is in units of *bits*. When the base of logarithms is e, the entropy is in units of *nats*. Writing the base of the entropy as $H_b(X)$, it is straightforward to show that

$$H_b(X) = (\log_b a)H_a(X).$$

For example,

$$H_e(X) = (\log_e 2)H_2(X).$$

Thus, to convert from bits to nats, multiply by $\log_e 2$.

It is straightforward to show that for any distribution, $H(X) \geq 0$.

Example 1.16 Let

$$X = \begin{cases} 1 & \text{with probability } p \\ 0 & \text{with probability } 1 - p. \end{cases}$$

Then

$$H(X) = -p \log p - (1 - p) \log(1 - p).$$

This is also denoted as $H(p)$ (since it depends only on p).

For example, when $p = 0.1$, then $H(X) = 0.469$ bits (using $\log_2$) and $H(X) = 0.3251$ nats (using $\log_e$). □

Table 1.1: Historical Milestones

Year	Milestone	Year	Milestone
1948	Shannon publishes "A Mathematical Theory of Communication" [404]	1973	Forney elucidates the Viterbi algorithm [128]
1950	Hamming describes Hamming codes [181]	1975	Sugiyama et al. propose the use of the Euclidean algorithm for decoding [424]
1954	Reed [362] and Muller [321] both present Reed–Muller codes and their decoders	1977	MacWilliams and Sloane produce the encyclopedic *The Theory of Error Correcting Codes* [292]
1955	Elias introduces convolutional codes [109]		*Voyager* deep space mission uses a concatenated RS/convolutional code (see [305])
1957	Prange introduces cyclic codes [348]		
1959	A. Hocquenghem [201] and ...	1978	Wolf introduces a trellis description of block codes [488]
1960	Bose and Ray-Chaudhuri [48] describe BCH codes	1980	14,400 BPS modem commercially available (64-QAM) (see [138])
	Reed and Solomon produce eponymous codes [364]		Sony and Phillips standardize the compact disc, including a shortened Reed–Solomon code
	Peterson provides a solution to BCH decoding [336]	1981	Goppa introduces algebraic-geometry codes [163, 164]
1961	Peterson produces his book [337], later extended and revised by Peterson and Weldon [338]	1982	Ungerboeck describes trellis-coded modulation [452]
1962	Gallager introduces LDPC codes [148]	1983	Lin and Costello produce their engineering textbook [271]
	2400 BPS modem commercially available (4-PSK) (see [138])		Blahut publishes his textbook [45]
1963	The Fano algorithm for decoding convolutional codes introduced [113]	1984	14,400 BPS TCM modem commercially available (128-TCM) (see [138])
	Massey unifies the study of majority logic decoding [297]	1985	19,200 BPS TCM modem commercially available (160-TCM) (see [138])
1966	Forney produces an in-depth study of concatenated codes [126] introduces generalized minimum distance decoding [127]	1993	Berrou, Glavieux, and Thitimajshima announce turbo codes [39]
1967	Berlekamp introduces a fast algorithm for BCH/Reed–Solomon decoding [36]	1994	The $\mathbb{Z}_4$ linearity of families of nonlinear codes is announced [182]
	Rudolph initiates the study of finite geometries for coding [385]	1995	MacKay resuscitates LDPC codes [290]
	4800 BPS modem commercially available (8-PSK) (see [138])		Wicker publishes his textbook [483]
1968	Berlekamp produces *Algebraic Coding Theory* [33]	1996	33,600 BPS modem (V.34) modem is commercially available (see [136])
	Gallager produces *Information theory and reliable communication* [147]	1998	Alamouti describes a space-time code [8]
1969	Jelinek describes the stack algorithm for decoding convolutional codes [219]	1999	Guruswami and Sudan present a list decoder for RS and AG codes [172]
	Massey introduces his algorithm for BCH decoding [295]	2000	Aji and McEliece [6] (and others [255]) synthesize several decoding algorithms using message passing ideas
	Reed–Muller code flies on *Mariner* deep space probes using Green machine decoder	2002	Hanzo, Liew, and Yeap characterize turbo algorithms in [187]
1971	Viterbi introduces the algorithm for ML decoding of convolutional codes [468]	2003	Koetter and Vardy extend the GS algorithm for soft-decision decoding of RS codes [251]
	9600 BPS modem commercially available (16-QAM) (see [138])	2004	Lin and Costello second edition [272]
1972	The BCJR algorithm is described in the open literature [21]	2009	Arıkan invents polar codes [16]
		2020	Moon produces what is hoped to be a valuable 2nd Edition!

Now suppose that $Y = f(X)$ for some probabilistic function $f(X)$. (For example, Y might be the output of a noisy channel that has X as the input, such that $Y = X + N$ for a discrete random variable N.) Let $\mathcal{Y}$ denote the set of possible Y outcomes. Let $P_Y(y) = P(Y = y)$. X and Y are jointly distributed with joint probability $P_{XY}(x, y)$. The conditional probability of X, given that $Y = y$ is

$$P(X|Y = y) = \frac{P_{XY}(X, y)}{P_Y(y)}.$$

$H(X|y)$ is the uncertainty remaining about X when Y is measured as $Y = y$:

$$H(X|y) = E[-\log_2 P_{X|Y}(X|y)] = -\sum_{x \in \mathcal{X}} P_{X|Y}(x|y) \log_2 P_{X|Y}(x|y) \text{ (bits)}.$$

Then the average uncertainty in X averaged over the outcomes Y is called the *conditional entropy*, $H(X|Y)$, computed as

$$H(X|Y) = \sum_{y \in \mathcal{Y}} H(X|y) P_Y(y) = -\sum_{y \in \mathcal{Y}} \sum_{x \in \mathcal{X}} P_{X|Y}(x|y) P_Y(y) \log_2 P_{X|Y}(x|y)$$

$$= -\sum_{y \in \mathcal{Y}} \sum_{x \in \mathcal{X}} P_{XY}(x, y) \log_2 P_{X|Y}(x|y) \text{ (bits)}.$$

The **joint entropy** is defined by

$$H(X, Y) = -\sum_{x \in \mathcal{X}} \sum_{y \in \mathcal{Y}} P_{XY}(x, y) \log_2 P_{XY}(x, y).$$

It is straightforward to show that

$$H(X, Y) = H(X) + H(Y|X).$$

This is referred to as the *chain rule* for entropy. This has the interpretation: The uncertainty in the joint variables (X, Y) is the uncertainty in X plus the uncertainty remaining in Y when X is given. By symmetry,

$$H(X, Y) = H(Y) + H(X|Y).$$

This rule also holds if all arguments are conditioned on the same event:

$$H(X, Y|Z) = H(X|Z) + H(Y|X, Z).$$

The chain rule for conditional entropy can be extended to multiple variables:

$$H(X_1, X_2, \ldots, X_n) = \sum_{i=1}^{n} H(X_i|X_{i-1}, \ldots, X_1)$$

$$= H(X_1) + H(X_2|X_1) + H(X_3|X_2, X_1) + \cdots + H(X_n|X_{n-1}, \ldots, X_1).$$

1.12.1.2 Relative Entropy, Mutual Information, and Channel Capacity

Definition 1.17 Let $P(x)$ and $Q(x)$ be two probability mass functions on the outcomes in $\mathcal{X}$. The **Kullback–Leibler distance** $D(P||Q)$ between two probability mass functions, also known as the **relative entropy** or the **cross entropy** is

$$D(P||Q) = E_P\left[\log \frac{P(x)}{Q(x)}\right] = \sum_{x \in \mathcal{X}} P(x) \log \frac{P(x)}{Q(x)}.$$

□

Lemma 1.18 $D(P||Q) \geq 0$, with equality if and only if $p = q$; that is, if the two distributions are the same.

Proof We use the inequality $\log x \leq x - 1$, with equality only at $x = 1$ (where the log is $\log_e$). This inequality appears so frequently in information theory it has been termed the information theory inequality. Then

$$
D(P||Q) = \sum_{x \in \mathcal{X}} P(x) \log \frac{P(x)}{Q(x)} = -\sum_{x \in \mathcal{X}} P(x) \log \frac{Q(x)}{P(x)}
$$

$$
\geq \sum_{x \in \mathcal{X}} P(x) \left[1 - \frac{Q(x)}{P(x)} \right] \quad \text{(information theory inequality)}
$$

$$
= \sum_{x \in S} P(x) - Q(x) = 0.
$$

$\square$

Definition 1.19 Let X be a random variable taking values in the set $\mathcal{X}$ and let Y be a random variable taking values in the set $\mathcal{Y}$, and let X and Y be jointly and marginally distributed as $P_{XY}(x, y)$, $P_X(x)$, and $P_Y(y)$, respectively. The **mutual information** between X and Y is the Kullback–Leibler distance between the joint distribution $P_{XY}(x, y)$ and the product of the marginals $P_X(x)P_Y(y)$:

$$
I(X; Y) = D(P_{XY}||P_X P_Y) = \sum_{x \in \mathcal{X}} \sum_{y \in \mathcal{Y}} P_{XY}(x, y) \log \frac{P_{XY}(x, y)}{P_X(x)P_Y(y)}. \tag{1.38}
$$

$\square$

If X and Y are independent, so that $P_{XY}(x, y) = P_X(x)P_Y(y)$, then $I(X; Y) = 0$. That is, Y tells no information at all about X. From the definition,

$$
I(X; Y) = I(Y; X) \quad \text{and} \quad I(X; X) = H(X).
$$

Using the definitions, mutual information can also be written as

$$
I(X; Y) = H(X) - H(X|Y).
$$

This is shown as follows:

$$
I(X; Y) = \sum_{x,y} P_{XY}(x, y) \log \frac{P_{XY}(x, y)}{P_X(x)P_Y(y)}
$$

$$
= \sum_{x,y} P_{XY}(x, y) \log \frac{P_{X|Y}(x|y)}{P_X(x)}
$$

$$
= -\sum_{x,y} P_{XY}(x, y) \log P_X(x) + \sum_{x,y} P_{XY}(x, y) \log P_{X|Y}(x|y)
$$

$$
= -\sum_{x} P_X(x) \log P_X(x) - \left(-\sum_{x,y} P_{XY}(x, y) \log P_{X|Y}(x|y) \right)
$$

$$
= H(X) - H(X|Y).
$$

The mutual information is the difference between the average uncertainty in X and the uncertainty in X there still is after measuring Y. Thus, it quantifies how much information Y tells about X. Since the Definition (1.38) is symmetric, also

$$
I(X; Y) = H(Y) - H(Y|X).
$$

We can also write

$$I(X;Y) = H(X) + H(Y) - H(X,Y).$$

In light of Lemma 1.18, we see that mutual information $I(X;Y)$ can never be negative.

Definition 1.20 The *conditional mutual information* of random variables X and Y given Z is

$$I(X;Y|Z) = H(X|Z) - H(X|Y,Z). \tag{1.39}$$

$\square$

Similar to entropy, mutual information has a chain rule:

$$\begin{aligned}
I(X_1, X_2, \ldots, X_n; Y) &= \sum_{i=1}^{n} I(X_i; Y|X_{i-1}, X_{i-2}, \ldots, X_1) \\
&= I(X_1; Y) + I(X_2; Y|X_1) + I(X_3; Y|X_2, X_1) \\
&\quad + \cdots + I(X_n; Y|X_{n-1}, X_{n-2}, \ldots, X_1).
\end{aligned} \tag{1.40}$$

1.12.2 Data Processing Inequality

Let X, Y, and Z be random variables described by mass functions (or pdfs, in the case of continuous random variables). By the properties of conditional probability, for any three such random variables, the joint density factors as

$$p(x, y, z) = p(x)p(y|x)p(z|x, y).$$

(Here, the argument is used to also denote the random variables involved). In the particular case the X, Y, and Z form a Markov chain (in that order), the joint probability mass function (or pdf) can be factored as

$$p(x, y, z) = p(x)p(y|x)p(z|y),$$

that is, $p(z|x, y) = p(z|y)$, so that Z is conditionally independent of X given Y. Variables X, Y, and Z forming a Markov chain are conditionally independent, given Y, since

$$p(x, z|y) = \frac{p(x, y, z)}{p(y)} = \frac{p(x)p(y|x)p(z|y)}{p(y)} = \frac{p(x, y)p(z|y)}{p(y)} = p(x|y)p(z|y).$$

The following theorem is known as the data processing inequality.

Theorem 1.21 *If X, Y and Z form a Markov chain (in that order), then*

$$I(X;Y) \geq I(X;Z).$$

Proof Expand the mutual information using the chain rule in two different ways:

$$\begin{aligned}
I(X;Y,Z) &= I(X;Z) + I(X;Y|Z) \\
&= I(X;Y) + I(X;Z|Y).
\end{aligned}$$

Since, as observed above, X and Z are conditionally independent given Y, $I(X;Z|Y) = 0$, so

$$I(X;Y) = I(X;Z) + I(X;Y|Z).$$

Since $I(X;Y|Z) \geq 0$, it follows that

$$I(X;Y) \geq I(X;Z).$$

$\square$

An interpretation of this can be given in light of Figure 1.22. X is an input to a channel (or system) which produces an output Y. There is some information that Y provides about X, as determined by $I(X; Y)$. The Y data is processed by some processing block (which is not limited in any way) to produce an output Z. What the data processing inequality teaches is that Z cannot provide more information about X than was already available from Y. (It might provide a more useful representation, but it cannot create information that is not there originally.)

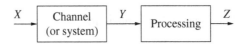

Figure 1.22: Illustration of data processing inequality.

1.12.3 Channels

From an information theoretic view, a channel is a model of the medium by which an input is conveyed to an output, often in a setting of communication. Since communication in the presence of noise involves random perturbations to the input, a channel is described by a transition probability, as follows.

Definition 1.22 A **discrete channel** is a system with an input alphabet $\mathcal{X}$ and an output alphabet $\mathcal{Y}$, with a transition probability $P_{Y|X}(y|x)$ (or, more briefly, $p(y|x)$), which is the probability of observing the output symbol $y \in \mathcal{Y}$ when the input symbol is $x \in \mathcal{X}$.   □

A channel is said to be **memoryless** if the probability distribution of the output depends only on the input at the corresponding time, and is conditionally independent of channel inputs or outputs at other times. Let $\mathbf{x} = x_1, x_2, \ldots, x_n$ be a sequence of inputs and $\mathbf{y} = y_1, y_2, \ldots, y_n$ be the corresponding sequence of outputs. Then for a memoryless channel, the joint conditional probability factors:

$$p(\mathbf{y}|\mathbf{x}) = \prod_{i=1}^{n} p(y_i|x_i).$$

1.12.3.1 Binary Symmetric Channel

An important example of a channel is the **BSC**. This models a situation in which bits, having alphabet $\mathcal{X} = \{0, 1\}$, may be flipped as they traverse the channel. A transmitted 0 is received (correctly) as a 0 with probability $1 - p$, and as a 1 (incorrectly) with probability p, and correspondingly for a transmitted 1. Thus, p is the probability that a bit is corrupted as it passed through the channel. p is referred to as the crossover probability. A model for the BSC is shown in Figure 1.23(a).

For the BSC, the mutual information between the input and the output is

$$I(X; Y) = H(Y) - H(Y|X)$$

$$= H(Y) - \sum_{x \in \{0,1\}} p(x) H(Y|X = x)$$

$$= H(Y) - \sum_{x} p(x) H(P) = H(Y) - H(p)$$

$$\leq 1 - H(p).$$

The last inequality is because Y is a binary random variable (maximum entropy = 1). When the probability distribution on the input is $P_X(0) = P_X(1) = \frac{1}{2}$, then by symmetry $P_Y(0) = P_Y(1) = \frac{1}{2}$, and the mutual information is maximized.

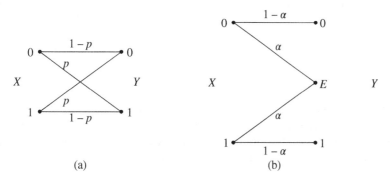

Figure 1.23: BSC and BEC models. (a) Binary symmetric channel with crossover; (b) binary erasure channel with erasure probability.

A useful representation of the channel transition probabilities $p(y|x)$ is as a **transition matrix** whose xth row and yth column represents $p(y|x)$. For the BSC, the transmission matrix is

$$p(y|x) = \begin{bmatrix} 1-p & p \\ p & 1-p \end{bmatrix}.$$

1.12.3.2 Binary Erasure Channel

Another important channel is the **binary erasure channel** (BEC). In the BEC, bits are not corrupted but some bits are lost. This might model, for example, an internet connection in which when packets are received, the bits in the channel are (essentially) reliably received, but some packets may be lost, resulting in lost bits.

A model for the BEC is shown in Figure 1.23(b). The input alphabet is binary, $\mathcal{X} = \{0, 1\}$, and the output alphabet has three symbols, 0, 1, and a symbol denoting an erasure, $\mathcal{Y} = \{0, 1, \mathsf{E}\}$. The probability that a symbol is erased is α:

$$P(Y = E|X = 0) = P(Y = E|X = 1) = \alpha.$$

The transition matrix is

$$p(y|x) = \begin{bmatrix} 1-\alpha & \alpha & 0 \\ 0 & \alpha & 1-\alpha \end{bmatrix}.$$

The mutual information between the input and the output is

$$I(X; Y) = H(Y) - H(Y|X) = H(Y) - H(\alpha)$$

where $H(Y|X) = H(\alpha)$ (the entropy for a binary channel with crossover probability p). It can be shown that $H(Y)$ is maximized when $P(X = 1) = P(X = 0) = \frac{1}{2}$, and in that case,

$$I(X; Y) = 1 - \alpha.$$

1.12.3.3 Noisy Typewriter

Less practical, but helpful to think about the nature of channels, is the noisy typewriter channel. In this case, the input set and output sets are $\mathcal{X} = \mathcal{Y} = \{A, B, C, \ldots, Z\}$. The channel input is either received unchanged, or the next letter in the alphabet is received, with probability $\frac{1}{2}$. The mutual information is

$$I(X;Y) = H(Y) - H(Y|X).$$

For every given X, there are two possible outcomes Y, so $H(Y|X) = 1$ bit. When all input symbols are equally likely, then all output symbols are equally likely and $H(Y) = \log_2 26$ bits. For the uniform input probabilities, then,

$$I(X;Y) = \log_2 26 - 1 = \log_2 13.$$

1.12.3.4 Symmetric Channels

Definition 1.23 [82, p. 190] A channel is said to be **symmetric** if the rows of the channel transition matrix are permutations of each other and the columns are permutations of each other.

A channel is said to be **weakly symmetric** if every row of the transition matrix is a permutation of every other row, and all the column sums $\sum_x p(y|x)$ are equal. □

The BSC introduced above is an example of a symmetric channel, but the BEC is not a symmetric channel. However, the BEC is weakly symmetric.

1.12.4 Channel Capacity

Definition 1.24 The **channel capacity** C of a channel with input X and output Y is defined as the maximum mutual information between X and Y, where the maximum is taken over all possible input distributions.

$$C = \max_{P_X(x)} I(X;Y).$$

□

For a (weakly) symmetric channel, let $\mathbf{r}$ denote the probabilities of one of the rows and let $H(\mathbf{r})$ be the entropy computed using these probabilities. The mutual information is

$$I(X;Y) = H(Y) - H(Y|X) = H(Y) - H(\mathbf{r}).$$

The entropy of Y is bounded by $\log |\mathcal{Y}|$, so

$$I(X;Y) = \log |\mathcal{Y}| - H(\mathbf{r}).$$

For a symmetric channel, when the input distribution is uniform, $P_X(x) = 1/|\mathcal{X}|$, then the output distribution is also uniform, so $H(Y) = \log |\mathcal{Y}|$. Thus

$$C = \max_{p(x)} I(X;Y) = \log |\mathcal{Y}| - H(\mathbf{r}). \tag{1.41}$$

For the BSC with crossover probability p, the capacity is

$$\boxed{C = 1 - H_2(p),}$$

which is achieved when the input symbols are chosen with $P(X = 0) = P(X = 1) = \frac{1}{2}$. For the BEC with erasure probability α, the capacity is

$$\boxed{C = 1 - \alpha,}$$

which is achieved when the input symbols are chosen with $P(X = 0) = P(X = 1) = \frac{1}{2}$.

1.12.5 Information Theoretic Definitions for Continuous Random Variables

Let Y be a continuous random variable taking on values in an (uncountable) set $\mathcal{Y}$, with pdf $p_Y(y)$. The differential entropy is defined as

$$H(Y) = -E[\log_2 p_Y(y)] = -\int_{\mathcal{Y}} p_Y(y) \log_2 p_Y(y) \, dy.$$

Whereas entropy for discrete random variables is always nonnegative, differential entropy (for a continuous random variable) can be positive or negative.

Example 1.25 Let $Y \sim \mathcal{N}(0, \sigma^2)$. Then

$$H(Y) = -E\left[\log_2 \frac{1}{\sqrt{2\pi}\sigma} e^{-Y^2/2\sigma^2}\right] = -E\left[\log_2 \frac{1}{\sqrt{2\pi}\sigma} + \log_2(e)\left(-\frac{1}{2\sigma^2}\right)(Y^2)\right]$$

$$= \log_2(e)\frac{1}{2\sigma^2}E[Y^2] + \frac{1}{2}\log_2 2\pi\sigma^2$$

$$= \frac{1}{2}\log_2(e) + \frac{1}{2}\log_2 2\pi\sigma^2 = \frac{1}{2}\log_2 2\pi e\sigma^2 \text{(bits)}.$$

□

It can be shown that, of all continuous random variables having mean 0 and variance σ^2, the Gaussian $\mathcal{N}(0, \sigma^2)$ has the largest differential entropy.

Let X be a discrete-valued random variable taking on values in the alphabet $\mathcal{X}$ with probability $\Pr(X = x) = P_X(x), x \in \mathcal{X}$ and let X be passed through a channel which produces a continuous-valued output Y for $Y \in \mathcal{Y}$. A typical example of this is the AWGNC, where

$$Y = X + N,$$

and $N \sim \mathcal{N}(0, \sigma^2)$. Let

$$p_{XY}(x, y) = p_{Y|X}(y|x)P_X(x)$$

denote the joint distribution of X and Y and let

$$p_Y(y) = \sum_{x \in \mathcal{X}} p_{XY}(x, y) = \sum_{x \in \mathcal{X}} p_{Y|X}(y|x)P_X(x)$$

denote the pdf of Y. Then the mutual information $I(X; Y)$ is computed as

$$I(X; Y) = D(p_{XY}(X, Y) || P_X(X)p_Y(Y)) = \int_{\mathcal{Y}} \sum_{\mathcal{X}} p_{XY}(x, y) \log_2 \frac{p_{XY}(x, y)}{p_Y(y)P_X(x)} \, dy$$

$$= \sum_{x \in \mathcal{X}} \int_{y \in \mathcal{Y}} p_{Y|X}(y|x)P_X(x) \log_2 \frac{p_{Y|X}(y|x)}{\sum_{x' \in \mathcal{X}} p_{Y|X}(y|x')P_X(x')} \, dy.$$

Example 1.26 Suppose $\mathcal{X} = \{a, -a\}$ (e.g., BPSK modulation with amplitude a) with probabilities $P(X = a) = P(X = -a) = \frac{1}{2}$. Let $N \sim \mathcal{N}(0, \sigma^2)$ and let

$$Y = X + N.$$

Because the channel has only binary inputs, this is referred to as the *binary* additive white Gaussian noise channel (BAWGNC). Then

$$
\begin{aligned}
I(X;Y) &= \frac{1}{2}\left[\int_{-\infty}^{\infty} p(y|a)\log_2\frac{p(y|a)}{\frac{1}{2}(p(y|a)+p(y|-a))}\right.\\
&\qquad\left.+\,p(y|-a)\log_2\frac{p(y|-a)}{\frac{1}{2}(p(y|a)+p(y|-a))}\ dy\right]\\
&= \frac{1}{2}\int_{-\infty}^{\infty} p(y|a)\log_2 p(y|a)+p(y|-a)\log_2 p(y|-a) \qquad (1.42)\\
&\quad -\,(p(y|a)+p(y|-a))\log_2\left[\frac{1}{2}(p(y|a)+p(y|-a))\right]\ dy\\
&= \frac{1}{2}\Big[-H(Y)-H(Y)\\
&\qquad -\int_{-\infty}^{\infty}(p(y|a)+p(y|-a))\log_2\left[\frac{1}{2}(p(y|a)+p(y|-a))\right]\ dy\Big]\\
&= \boxed{-\int_{-\infty}^{\infty}\phi(y,a,\sigma^2)\log_2\phi(y,a,\sigma^2)\ dy-\frac{1}{2}\log_2 2\pi e\sigma^2 \ \text{(bits)},} \qquad (1.43)
\end{aligned}
$$

where we define the function

$$
\phi(y,a,\sigma^2)=\frac{1}{\sqrt{8\pi\sigma^2}}[e^{-(y-a)^2/2\sigma^2}+e^{-(y+a)^2/2\sigma^2}].
$$

$\square$

When both the channel input X and the output Y are continuous random variables, then the mutual information is

$$
I(X;Y)=D(p_{XY}(X,Y)||P_X(x)p_Y(Y))=\int_{\mathcal{X}}\int_{\mathcal{Y}}p_{XY}(x,y)\log_2\frac{p_{XY}(x,y)}{p_Y(y)P_X(x)}\ dy\ dx.
$$

Example 1.27   Let $X\sim\mathcal{N}(0,\sigma_x^2)$ and $N\sim\mathcal{N}(0,\sigma_n^2)$, independent of X. Let $Y=X+N$. Then $Y\sim\mathcal{N}(0,\sigma_x^2+\sigma_n^2)$.

$$
\begin{aligned}
I(X;Y) &= H(Y)-H(Y|X)=H(Y)-H(X+N|X)=H(Y)-H(N|X)\\
&= H(Y)-H(N)=\frac{1}{2}\log_2 2\pi e\sigma_y^2-\frac{1}{2}\log_2 2\pi e\sigma_n^2\\
&= \boxed{\frac{1}{2}\log_2\left(1+\frac{\sigma_x^2}{\sigma_n^2}\right)\ \text{(bits).}} \qquad (1.44)
\end{aligned}
$$

The quantity σ_x^2 represents the average power in the transmitted signal X and σ_n^2 represents the average power in the noise signal N. This channel is called the AWGNC. $\square$

As for the discrete channel, the channel capacity C of a channel with input X and output Y is the maximum mutual information between X and Y, where the maximum is over all input distributions. In Example 1.26, the maximizing distribution is, in fact, the uniform distribution, $P(X=a)=P(X=-a)=\frac{1}{2}$, so (1.43) is the capacity for the BAWGNC. In Example 1.27, the maximizing distribution is, in fact, the Gaussian distribution (since this maximizes the entropy of the output), so (1.44) is the capacity for the AWGNC.

1.12.6   The Channel Coding Theorem

The channel capacity has been *defined* as the maximum mutual information between the input and the output. But Shannon's channel coding theorem, tells us what the capacity *means*. Recall that an error correction code has a rate $R = k/n$, where k is the number of input symbols and n is the number of output symbols, the length of the code. The channel coding theorem says this:

> Provided that the coded rate of transmission R is less than the channel capacity, for any given probability of error ϵ specified, there is an error correction code of length n_0 such that there exist codes of length n exceeding n_0 for which the decoded probability of error is less than ϵ.

That is, provided that we transmit at a rate less than capacity, arbitrarily low probabilities of error can be obtained, if a sufficiently long error correction code is employed. The capacity is the amount of information that can be transmitted *reliably* through the channel *per channel use*.

A converse to the channel coding theorem states that for a channel with capacity C, if $R > C$, then the probability of error is bounded away from zero: reliable transmission is not possible.

The channel coding theorem is an *existence* theorem; it tells us that codes exist that can be used for reliable transmission, but not how to find practical codes. Shannon's remarkable proof used random codes. But as the code gets long, the decoding complexity of a truly random (unstructured) code goes up exponentially with the length of the code. Since Shannon's proof, engineers and mathematicians have been looking for ways of constructing codes that are both good (meaning they can correct a lot of errors) and practical, meaning that they have some kind of structure that makes decoding of sufficiently low complexity that decoders can be practically constructed.

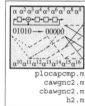

```
plocapcmp.m
cawgnc2.m
cbawgnc2.m
h2.m
```

Figure 1.24 shows a comparison of the capacity of the AWGNC and the BAWGNC channels as a function of E_c/σ^2 (an SNR measure). In this figure, we observe that the capacity of the AWGNC increases with SNR beyond 1 bit per channel use, while the BAWGNC asymptotes to a maximum of 1 bit per channel use — if only binary data is put into the channel, only 1 bit of useful information can be obtained. It is always the case that

$$C_{\text{AWGNC}} > C_{\text{BAWGNC}}.$$

Over all possible input distributions, the Gaussian distribution is information maximizing, so C_{AWGNC} is an upper bound on capacity for any modulation or coding that might be employed. However, at very low SNRs, C_{AWGNC} and C_{BAWGNC} are very nearly equal.

Figure 1.24 also shows the capacity of the equivalent BSC, with crossover probability $p = Q(\sqrt{E_c/\sigma^2})$ and capacity $C_{\text{BSC}} = 1 - H_2(p)$. This corresponds to hard-input decoding. Clearly, there is some loss of potential rate due to hard-input decoding, although the loss diminishes as the SNR increases.

1.12.7 "Proof" of the Channel Coding Theorem

In this section, we present a "proof" of the channel coding theorem. While mathematically accurate, it is not complete. The arguments can be considerably tightened, but are sufficient to show the main ideas of coding. Also, the proof is only presented for the discrete input/discrete channel case. The intuition, however, generally carries over to the Gaussian channel.

An important preliminary concept is the "asymptotic equipartition property" (AEP). Let X be a random variable taking values in a set $\mathcal{X}$. Let $\mathbf{X} = (X_1, X_2, \ldots, X_n)$ be an i.i.d. (independent, identically distributed) random vector and let $\mathbf{x}$ denote an outcome of $\mathbf{X}$.

Theorem 1.28 *(AEP) Let $X = (X_1, X_2, \ldots, X_n)$, where X_i are i.i.d., and let $x = (x_1, x_2, \ldots, x_n)$ be a particular draw. As $n \to \infty$*

$$P(X = x) \approx 2^{-nH(X)}, \quad x \in \mathcal{T}, \tag{1.45}$$

The interpretation of this theorem is as follows. Note that the probability $2^{-nH(X)}$ is a function of the distribution of X, not the particular outcome $\mathbf{x}$. By the AEP, most of the probability of a draw of $\mathbf{X}$ is "concentrated" in a set that occurs with probability $2^{-nH(X)}$. the typical set. That is, a "typical" outcome

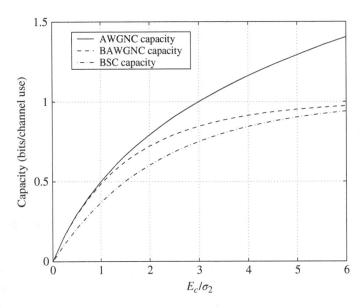

Figure 1.24: Capacities of AWGNC, BAWGNC, and BSC.

is likely to occur, while an outcome which is not "typical" is not likely to occur. Since the "typical" outcomes all have approximately the same probability, given by (1.45), there must be approximately $2^{nH(X)}$ outcomes in the typical set $\mathcal{T}$.

Proof We sketch the main idea of the proof. Let the outcome space for a random variable Y be $\mathcal{Y} = \{b_1, b_2, \ldots, b_K\}$, occurring with probabilities $P_i = P(Y = b_i)$. Out of n samples of the i.i.d. variable Y, let n_i be the number of outcomes that are equal to b_i. By the law of large numbers,[7] when n is large,

$$\frac{n_i}{n} \approx P_i. \tag{1.46}$$

The product of n observations can be written as

$$
\begin{aligned}
y_1 y_2 \cdots y_n &= b_1^{n_1} b_2^{n_2} \cdots b_K^{n_K} = [b_1^{(n_1/n)} b_2^{(n_2/n)} \cdots b_K^{(n_K/n)}]^n \\
&= \left[2^{\frac{n_1}{n}\log_2 b_1} 2^{\frac{n_2}{n}\log_2 b_2} \cdots 2^{\frac{n_K}{n}\log_2 b_K} \right]^n = \left[2^{\sum_{i=1}^{K} \frac{n_i}{n}\log_2 b_i} \right]^n \\
&\approx \left[2^{\sum_{i=1}^{K} P_i \log_2 b_i} \right]^n \quad \text{(by (1.46))} \\
&= [2^{E[\log_2 Y]}]^n. \tag{1.47}
\end{aligned}
$$

Now suppose that Y is, in fact, a function of a random variable X, $Y = f(X)$, where, specifically, this function is the probability mass function of X: $f(x) = P_X(x) = P(X = x)$. Then

$$y_1 y_2 \cdots y_n = f(x_1) f(x_2) \cdots f(x_n) = \prod_{i=1}^{n} P_X(x_i) = P(\mathbf{X} = \mathbf{x}).$$

Also, by (1.47),

$$y_1 y_2 \cdots y_n = f(x_1) f(x_2) \cdots f(x_n) = \prod_{i=1}^{n} p_X(x_i) \approx [2^{E[\log_2 p_X(X)]}]^n = 2^{-nH(X)}.$$

This establishes (1.45).   □

---

[7] Thorough proof of the AEP merely requires putting all of the discussion in the formal language of the weak law of large numbers.

Let X be a binary source with entropy $H(X)$ and let each X be transmitted through a memoryless channel to produce the output Y. Consider transmitting the sequence of i.i.d. outcomes $x_1, x_2, \ldots, x_n$. While the number of possible sequences is $M = 2^n$, the typical set has only about $2^{nH(X)}$ sequences in it. Let the total possible number of output sequences $\mathbf{y} = y_1, y_2, \ldots, y_n$ be N. There are about $2^{nH(Y)} \leq N$ typical output sequences. For each typical output sequence $\mathbf{y}$ there are approximately $2^{nH(X|Y)}$ input sequences that could have caused it. Furthermore, each input sequence $\mathbf{x}$ typically could produce $2^{nH(Y|X)}$ output sequences. This is summarized in Figure 1.25(a).

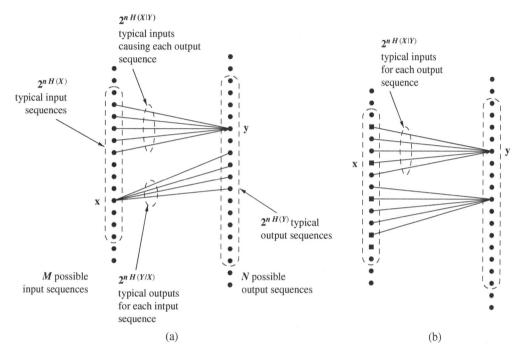

Figure 1.25: Relationship between input and output entropies for a channel. Each • or ■ represents a sequence. (a) Basic input output relationship; (b) ■ represents codewords.

Now let X be coded by a rate-R code to produce a coded sequence which selects, out of the 2^n possible input sequences, only 2^{nR} of these. In Figure 1.25(b), these coded sequences are denoted with filled squares, ■. The mapping which selects the 2^{nR} points is the *code*. Rather than select any particular code, we contemplate using all possible codes *at random* (using, however, only the typical sequences). Under the random code, a sequence selected at random is a codeword with probability

$$\frac{2^{nR}}{2^{nH(X)}} = 2^{n(R-H(X))}.$$

Now consider the problem of correct decoding. A sequence $\mathbf{y}$ is observed. It can be decoded correctly if there is only one code vector $\mathbf{x}$ that could have caused it. From Figure 1.25(b), the probability that none of the points in the "fan" leading to $\mathbf{y}$ other than the original code point is a codeword is

$$P = (\text{probability a point } \mathbf{x} \text{ is not a codeword})^{(\text{typical number of inputs for this } \mathbf{y})}$$

$$= (1 - 2^{n(R-H(X))})^{2^{nH(X|Y)}}.$$

If we now choose $R < \max_{P_X(x)} H(X) - H(X|Y)$, that is, choose $R <$ the capacity C, then

$$R - H(X) + H(X|Y) < 0$$

for any input distribution $P_X(x)$. In this case,

$$R - H(X) = -H(X|Y) - \eta$$

for some $\eta > 0$. Then

$$P = (1 - 2^{n(-H(X|Y)-\eta)})^{2^{nH(X|Y)}}.$$

Expanding out using the binomial expansion,

$$P = 1 - \binom{2^{nH(X|Y)}}{1} 2^{n(-H(X|Y)-\eta)} + \text{higher order terms},$$

so as $n \to \infty$,

$$P \to 1 - 2^{-n\eta} \to 1.$$

Thus, the probability that none of the points except the original code point leading to **y** is a codeword approaches 1, so that the probability of decoding error — due to multiple codewords mapping to a single received vector — approaches 0.

We observe that if the *average* of an ensemble approaches zero, then there are elements in the ensemble that must approach 0. Thus, among all the possible codes in the ensemble, there are codes for which the probability of error approaches zero as $n \to \infty$.

There are two other ways of viewing the coding rate requirement. The $2^{nH(Y|X)}$ typical sequences resulting from transmitting a vector **x** must partition the $2^{nH(Y)}$ typical output sequences, so that each observed output sequence can be attributed to a unique input sequence. The number of subsets in this partition is

$$\frac{2^{nH(Y)}}{2^{nH(Y|X)}} = 2^{n(H(Y)-H(Y|X))},$$

so the condition $R < H(Y) - H(Y|X)$ must be enforced. Alternatively, the $2^{nH(X)}$ typical input sequences must be partitioned so that the $2^{nH(X|Y)}$ typical input sequences associated with an observation **y** are disjoint. There must be $2^{n(H(X)-H(X|Y))}$ distinct subsets, so again the condition $R < H(X) - H(X|Y)$ must be enforced.

Let us summarize what we learn from the proof of the channel coding theorem:

- As long as $R < C$, arbitrarily reliable transmission is possible.

- The code lengths, however, may have to be long to achieve the desired reliability. The closer R is to C, the larger we would expect n to need to be in order to obtain some specified level of performance.

- Since the theorem was based on ensembles of random codes, it does not specify what the best code should be. We don't know how to "design" the best codes, we only know that they exist.

- However, random codes have a high probability of being good. So we are likely to get a good code simply by picking one at random!

So what, then, is the issue? Why the need for decades of research in coding theory, if a code can simply be selected at random? The answer has to do with the complexity of representing and decoding the code. To represent a random code of length n, there must be memory to store all the codewords, which requires $n2^{Rn}$ bits. Furthermore, to decode a received word **y**, ML decoding for a random code requires that a received vector **y** must be compared with all 2^{Rn} possible codewords. For a $R = 1/2$ code with $n = 1000$ (a relatively modest code length and a low-rate code), 2^{500} comparisons must be made for each received vector. This is prohibitively expensive, beyond practical feasibility for even massively parallel computing systems, let alone a portable communication device.

Ideally, we would like to explore the space of codes parameterized by rate, probability of decoding error, block length (which governs latency), and encoding and decoding complexity, identifying thereby all achievable tuples of $(R, P, n, \chi_E, \chi_D)$, where P is the probability of error and χ_E and χ_D are the encoding and decoding complexities. This is an overwhelmingly complex task. The essence of coding research has taken the pragmatic stance of identifying families of codes which have some kind of algebraic or graphical *structure* that will enable representation and decoding with manageable complexity. In some cases what is sought are codes in which the encoding and decoding can be accomplished readily using algebraic methods — essentially so that decoding can be accomplished by solving sets of equations. In other cases, codes employ constraints on certain graphs to reduce the encoding and decoding complexity. Most recently, families of codes have been found for which very long block lengths can be effectively obtained with low complexity using very sparse representations, which keep the decoding complexity in check. Describing these codes and their decoding algorithms is the purpose of this book.

The end result of the decades of research in coding is that the designer has a rich palette of code options, with varying degrees of rate and encode and decode complexity. This book presents many of the major themes that have emerged from this research.

1.12.8 Capacity for the Continuous-Time AWGN Channel

Let X_i be a zero-mean random variable with $E[X_i^2] = \sigma_x^2$ which is input to a discrete AWGN channel, so that

$$R_i = X_i + N_i,$$

where the N_i are i.i.d. $N_i \sim \mathcal{N}(0, \sigma_n^2)$. The capacity of this channel is

$$C = \frac{1}{2}\log_2\left(1 + \frac{\sigma_x^2}{\sigma_n^2}\right) \text{ bits/channel use.}$$

Now consider sending a continuous-time signal $x(t)$ according to

$$x(t) = \sum_{i=1}^{n} X_i \varphi_i(t),$$

where the $\varphi_i(t)$ functions are orthonormal over $[0, T]$. Let us suppose that the transmitter power available is P watts, so that the energy dissipated in T seconds is $E = PT$. This energy is also expressed as

$$E = \int_0^T x^2(t)\, dt = \sum_{i=1}^{n} X_i^2.$$

We must therefore have

$$\sum_{i=1}^{n} X_i^2 = PT$$

or $nE[X_i^2] = PT$, so that $\sigma_x^2 = PT/n$.

Now consider transmitting a signal $x(t)$ through a continuous-time channel with bandwidth W. By the sampling theorem (frequently attributed to Nyquist, but in this context it is frequently called *Shannon's* sampling theorem), a signal of bandwidth W can be exactly characterized by $2W$ samples/second — any more samples than this cannot convey any more information about this bandlimited signal. So we can get $2W$ independent channel uses per second over this bandlimited channel. There are $n = 2WT$ symbols transmitted over T seconds.

If the received signal is

$$R(t) = x(t) + N(t),$$

where $N(t)$ is a white Gaussian noise random process with two-sided power spectral density $N_0/2$, then in the discrete-time sample

$$R_i = x_i + N_i,$$

where $R_i = \int_0^T R(t)\varphi_i(t)\,dt$, the variance of N_i is $\sigma^2 = N_0/2$. The capacity for this bandlimited channel is

$$C = \left(\frac{1}{2}\log_2\left(1 + \frac{PT/n}{N_0/2}\right) \text{ bits/channel use}\right)(2W \text{ channel uses/second})$$

$$= W\log_2\left(1 + \frac{2PT}{nN_0}\right) \text{ bits/second}.$$

Now, using $n = 2WT$, we obtain

$$C = W\log_2(1 + P/N_0W) \text{ bits/second}. \tag{1.48}$$

Since P is the average transmitted power, in terms of its units, we have

$$P = \frac{\text{energy}}{\text{second}} = (\text{energy/bit})(\text{bits/second}).$$

Since E_b is the energy/bit and the capacity is the rate of transmission in bits per second, we have $P = E_b R_b = E_b C$ (when transmitting at capacity), giving

$$C = W\log_2\left(1 + \frac{C}{W}\frac{E_b}{N_0}\right). \tag{1.49}$$

Let $\eta = C/W$ be the spectral efficiency in bits/second/Hz; this is the data rate available for each Hertz of channel bandwidth. From (1.49),

$$\eta = \log_2\left(1 + \eta\frac{E_b}{N_0}\right)$$

or

$$E_b/N_0 = \frac{2^\eta - 1}{\eta}. \tag{1.50}$$

For BPSK the spectral efficiency is $\eta = 1$ bit/second/Hz, so (1.50) indicates that it is theoretically possible to transmit arbitrarily reliably at $E_b/N_0 = 1$, which is 0 dB. In principle, then, it should be possible to devise a coding scheme which could transmit BPSK-modulated signals arbitrarily reliably at an SNR of 0 dB. By contrast, for uncoded transmission when $E_b/N_0 = 9.6$ dB, the BPSK performance shown in Figure 1.10 has $P_b = 10^{-5}$. There is at least 9.6 dB of coding gain possible. The approximately 0.44 dB of gain provided by the (7,4) Hamming code of Section 1.9 falls over 9 dB short of what is theoretically possible!

plotcbawgn2.m
cbawgnc.m
cawgnc.m
philog.m
phifun.m

1.12.9   Transmission at Capacity with Errors

By the channel coding theorem, zero probability of error is (asymptotically) attainable provided that the transmission rate is less than the capacity. What if we allow a nonvanishing probability of error. What is the maximum rate of transmission? Or, equivalently, for a given rate, which is the minimum SNR that will allow transmission at that rate, with a specified probability of error?

The theoretical tools we need to address these questions are the separation theorem and rate–distortion theory. The separation theorem says that we can separately consider and optimally (at least, asymptotically) data compression and error correction. Suppose that the source has a rate of r bits/second. First, compress the information so that the bits of the compressed signal match the bits of the source signal with probability p. From rate-distortion theory, this produces a source at rate $1 - H_2(p)$ per source bit (see (1.2)). These compressed bits, at a rate $r(1 - H_2(p))$ are then transmitted over the channel with vanishingly small probability of error. We must therefore have $r(1 - H_2(p)) < C$. The maximum rate achievable with average distortion (i.e., probability of bit error) p, which we denote

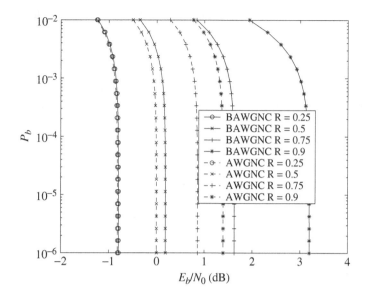

Figure 1.26: Capacity lower bounds on P_b as a function of SNR.

as $C^{(p)}$, is therefore

$$C^{(p)} = \frac{C}{1 - H_2(p)}.$$

Figure 1.26 shows the required SNR E_b/N_0 for transmission at various rates for both the BAWGNC and the AWGNC. For any given line in the plot, the region to the right of the plot is achievable — it should theoretically be possible to transmit at that probability of error at that SNR. Curves such as these therefore represent a goal to be achieved by a particular code: we say that we are transmitting at capacity if the performance falls on the curve.

We note the following from the plot:

- At very low SNR, the binary channel and the AWGN channel have very similar performance. This was also observed in conjunction with Figure 1.24.

- The higher the rate, the higher the required SNR.

- The vertical asymptote (as $P_b \to 0$) is the capacity C for that channel.

1.12.10 The Implication of the Channel Coding Theorem

The implication of the channel coding theorem, fundamentally, is that for a block code of length n and rate $R = k/n$, the probability of a block decoding error can be bounded as

$$P(E) \leq 2^{-nE_b(R)}, \tag{1.51}$$

where $E_b(R)$ is a positive function of R for $R < C$. Work on a class of codes known as convolutional codes — to be introduced in Chapter 12 has shown (see, e.g., [471]) that

$$P(E) \leq 2^{-(m+1)nE_c(R)}, \tag{1.52}$$

where m is the memory of the code and $E_c(R)$ is positive for $R < C$. The problem, as we shall see (and what makes coding such a fascinating topic) is that, in the absence of some kind of structure, as either

n or m grow, the complexity can grow exponentially. How should this structure be introduced, to make the encoders and decoders tractable, while producing good error correction capability?

1.12.11 Non-Asymptotic Information Theory

The channel coding theorem described above is an *asymptotic* theory, asserting the existence of codes producing low probability of error, *as the code length n goes to infinity*. This asymptotic theory serves best when the code lengths are long. Recent technological developments, however, are pushing toward short codes. For example, in a cybercontrol system, near real-time response cannot wait around for a long codeword to be formed, so short codewords protecting brief data packets are needed to move data around in a responsive way. Thus, it becomes increasingly of interest to consider what the information-theoretic performance limits are for short codes. These issues are addressed by finite-block length, non-asymptotic information theory, briefly developed in this section.

A code (not necessarily linear) may be described by the parameters (n, M, ϵ), where:

- n is the length of the code;
- M is the number of codewords in the code;
- ϵ is the probability of error that the code achieves.

Since M messages can be indexed by $\log_2 M$ bits, the rate of the code (the number of bits to select a codeword divided by the codeword length) is

$$R = \frac{\log_2 M}{n}.$$

Expressed in this language, Shannon's channel coding theorem can be expressed as: there exists sequences of codes described by (n, M_n, ϵ_n) such that

$$R = \lim_{n \to \infty} \frac{\log_2 M_n}{n} > 0.$$

that is, there is a positive asymptotic rate, and

$$\epsilon_n \to 0.$$

Here, M_n is the maximum number of codewords associated with a code of length n, and ϵ_n is the probability of error associated with the code of length n.

Let

$$M^*(n, \epsilon) = \max\{M : \exists (n, M, \epsilon) - \text{code}\}$$

be the maximum number of codewords of length n such that it is possible to recover the original message with probability at least $1 - \epsilon$. $M^*(n, \epsilon)$ is basic to non-asymptotic information theory.

Shannon's asymptotic result can be expressed as

$$\lim_{\epsilon \to 0} \lim_{n \to \infty} \frac{1}{n} M^*(n, \epsilon) = C,$$

where C is the capacity. For any $0 < \epsilon < 1$, it is also true that

$$\lim_{n \to \infty} \frac{1}{n} M^*(n, \epsilon) \leq C.$$

Thus,

$$\log_2 M^*(n, \epsilon) = nC + o(n).$$

We define the *information density* as

$$i_{X;Y}(x;y) = \log \frac{P_{XY}(x,y)}{P_X(x)P_Y(y)}$$

The expectation of the information density is the mutual information,

$$E[i_{X;Y}(x;y)] = I(X;Y).$$

Under asymptotic information theory,

$$\lim_{n\to\infty} \frac{1}{n}\log_2 M^*(n,\epsilon) = E[i_{X;Y}(x,y)] = C.$$

Asymptotic information theory is thus seen to be a first-order theory, accounting for only the mean value of the information density.

1.12.11.1 Discrete Channels

Under non-asymptotic information theory, it can be shown [343, Section 3.2.2] that for a discrete channel (such as a BSC with crossover probability δ) the *Gaussian approximation* holds:

$$\frac{1}{n}\log_2 M^*(n,\epsilon) = C - \sqrt{\frac{V}{n}}Q^{-1}(\epsilon) + \frac{1}{2n}\log_2 n + \frac{1}{n}O(1). \tag{1.53}$$

Here, Q^{-1} is the inverse of the Q function defined by

$$Q(x) = \int_x^\infty \frac{1}{\sqrt{2\pi}}e^{-y^2/2}\,dy.$$

Also, V is called the *channel dispersion*, and is computed as the *variance* of the information density:

$$V = \text{var}[i_{X;Y}(x,y)].$$

For the BSC, it can be shown by computation that

$$V = \delta(1-\delta)\left(\log\frac{1-\delta}{\delta}\right)^2,$$

so that

$$\frac{1}{n}\log_2 M^*(n,\epsilon) \approx C - \sqrt{\frac{\delta(1-\delta)}{n}}Q^{-1}(\epsilon)\log_2\frac{1-\delta}{\delta} + \frac{1}{2n}\log_2 n. \tag{1.54}$$

There are two other bounds that are interesting to compare with the Gaussian approximation. An upper bound is expressed as follows.

Theorem 1.29 *[343, Theorem 40, p. 51] For a BSC with crossover probability δ, the size M of an (n, M, ϵ) code is bounded by*

$$M \leq \frac{1}{\beta_{1-\epsilon}^n}, \tag{1.55}$$

where $\beta_{1-\epsilon}^n$ is computed as follows.

- *Let $\alpha = 1 - \epsilon$.*

- *Determine the integer L and the number $\lambda \in [0,1)$ such that*

$$\alpha = (1-\lambda)\alpha_L + \lambda\alpha_{L+1},$$

where

$$\alpha_\ell = \sum_{k=0}^{\ell-1} \binom{n}{k} (1-\delta)^{n-k} \delta^k.$$

(Since α_ℓ is an increasing function of ℓ, select L as the smallest value such that $\alpha_\ell > \alpha$, then λ will be within its bounds.)

- *Compute*

$$\beta_{1-\epsilon}^n = (1-\lambda)\beta_L + \lambda\beta_{L+1},$$

where

$$\beta_t = 2^{-n} \sum_{k=0}^{t} \binom{n}{k}.$$

The proof is provided in [343]. This theorem describes a non-asymptotic converse to the channel coding theorem: in order to achieve a given probability of error ϵ, the number of codewords in the code cannot exceed $1/\beta_{1-\epsilon}^n$. This provides an upper bound on the rate of the code.

Another bound is provided by the following.

Theorem 1.30 *[343, Corollary 39, p. 49] For the BSC with crossover probability δ, there exists an (n, M, ϵ) code (where ϵ represents the average probability of error) such that*

$$\epsilon \leq \sum_{t=0}^{n} \binom{n}{t} \delta^t (1-\delta)^{n-t} \min\left(1, (M-1)2^{-n} \sum_{s=0}^{t} \binom{n}{s}\right). \tag{1.56}$$

This is an existence theorem. For a given probability of error, codes with a small number of codewords M (low rate) could be used. But this theorem promises that there *exist* codes bounding the probability of error ϵ. This provides a lower bound on what values of M are possible.

To employ this as a bound, a value of M which achieves the bound (1.56) is found. In the plot below, this was done by a binary search on the value $\log_2 M/n$, starting with a bracketing solution of $M = 2$ and a value of M large enough that the right-hand side of (1.56) exceeds ϵ.

Figure 1.27 shows these bounds for a BSC with crossover probability $\delta = 0.11$ (giving a capacity $C = 1 - H(\delta) = 0.5$) and maximal block error $\epsilon = 10^{-3}$, compared with the capacity $C = 1 - H(\delta) = 0.5$. While (1.55) and (1.56) are actual bounds and not approximations, the plot shows that the Gaussian approximation (1.54) closely tracks these bounds, and has the benefit of being much easier to compute than the bounds. As the figure shows, there is a substantial gap between the asymptotic rate (Capacity $C = 0.5$) and the non-asymptotic rate — at lengths of $n = 2000$ bits, the rate achieving $\epsilon = 10^{-3}$ is only about 0.43, so only 88% of the asymptotic capacity is achievable even at $n = 2000$.

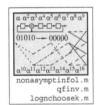
nonasymptinfo1.m
qfinv.m
lognchoosek.m

For the BEC channel, the Gaussian approximation is [343, Section 3.3.2]

$$\frac{1}{n} \log M^*(n, \epsilon) = (1-\delta) \log 2 - \sqrt{\frac{\delta(1-\delta)}{n}} Q^{-1}(\epsilon) \log 2 + \frac{1}{n} O(1). \tag{1.57}$$

1.12.11.2 The AWGN Channel

For the Gaussian channel (a continuous channel), with codewords $(c_1, c_2, \ldots, c_n)$ satisfying the power constraint

$$\sum_{i=1}^{n} c_i^2 = nP$$

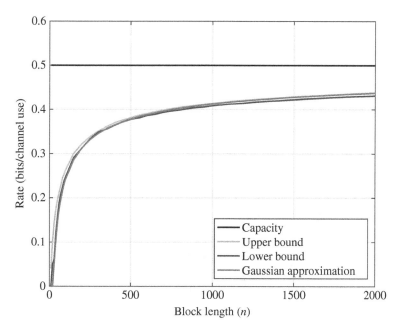

Figure 1.27: Rate-block length tradeoff for the BSC with $\delta = 0.11$ and maximal block error rate $\epsilon = 10^{-3}$.

having unit-covariance noise, let $M^*(n, \epsilon, P)$ denote the number of codewords in a code of length satisfying the power constraint. Shannon's (asymptotic) capacity is

$$\lim_{\epsilon \to 0} \lim_{n \to \infty} \frac{1}{n} \log M^*(n, \epsilon, P) = \frac{1}{2} \log(1 + P) \triangleq C(P).$$

For the non-asymptotic theory,

$$\frac{1}{n} M^*(n, \epsilon, P) \leq C(P) - \sqrt{\frac{V(P)}{n}} Q^{-1}(\epsilon) + \frac{1}{n} O(1).$$

Here, $V(P)$ is the channel dispersion

$$V(P) = \frac{P}{2} \frac{P + 2}{(P + 1)^2} (\log e)^2.$$

It can be shown [343] that this approximation closely tracks other bounds.

Figure 1.28 shows the asymptotic rate (capacity) compared with the Gaussian approximation. Again, the finite length effect is clear. Even with a codelength of $n = 2000$, only 88% of the channel capacity is achievable.

1.12.11.3 Comparison of Codes

Polyanskiy [343] suggests the use of M^* as a means of comparing different codes. For a code with M codewords, he defines (for the AWGN channel) the ratio

$$R_{\text{norm}}(\epsilon) = \frac{\log M}{\log M^*(n, \epsilon, \gamma_{\min}(\epsilon))},$$

where $\gamma_{\min}(\epsilon)$ is the smallest SNR at which the code will admit decoding with probability of error less than ϵ. Practically, $M^*(n, \epsilon, \gamma_{\min}(\epsilon))$ is approximated using (1.57) with negligible loss in accuracy.

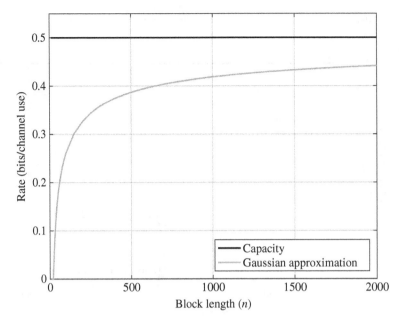

Figure 1.28: Rate-block length tradeoff for the Gaussian channel with $P = 1$ and maximal block error rate $\epsilon = 10^{-3}$.

"Better" codes should have $R_{\text{norm}}(\epsilon)$ which is near 1. A comparison of the sorts of codes discussed in this book is provided in [343].

Programming Laboratory 1:

Simulating a Communications Channel

Objective

In this lab, you will simulate a BPSK communication system and a coded system with a Hamming code employing hard-input decoding rules.

Background

Reading: Sections 1.5, 1.7, 1.9.

In the case of BPSK, an exact expression for the probability of error is available, (1.25). However, in many more interesting communication systems, a closed-form expression for the probability of error is not available or is difficult to compute. Results must be therefore obtained by simulation of the system.

One of the great strengths of the signal-space viewpoint is that probability of error simulations can be made based only on points in the signal space. In other words, it suffices to simulate random variables as in the matched filter output (1.12), rather than creating the continuous-time functions as in (1.10). (However, for other kinds of questions, a simulation of the continuous-time function might be necessary. For example, if you are simulating the effect of synchronization, timing jitter, delay, or fading, simulating the time signal is probably necessary.)

A framework for simulating a communication system from the signal space point of view for the purpose of computing the probability of error is as follows:

Algorithm 1.2 Outline for Simulating Digital Communications

---

1 Initialization: Store the points in the signal constellation. Fix E_b (typically $E_b = 1$).
2 FOR each signal-to-noise ratio $\gamma = E_b/N_0$:
3   Compute $N_0 = E_b/\gamma$ and $\sigma^2 = N_0/2$.
4   DO:
5   Generate some random bit(s) (the "transmitted" bits). according to the bit probabilities
6   Map the bit(s) into the signal constellation (e.g., BPSK or 8-PSK) to create signal **s**.
7   Generate a Gaussian random vector **n** (noise) with variance $\sigma^2 = N_0/2$ in each signal direction.

8 Add the noise to the signal to create the matched filter output signal $\mathbf{r} = \mathbf{s} + \mathbf{n}$.

9 Perform a detection on the symbol.
   (e.g., find closest point in signal constellation to $\mathbf{r}$).

10 From the detected symbol, determine the detected bits.

11 Compare detected bits with the transmitted bits.

12 Accumulate the number of bits in error.

13 UNTIL at least N bit errors have been counted.

14 The estimated probability of error at this SNR is
$$P_e \approx \frac{\text{number of errors counted}}{\text{number of bits generated}}$$

15 End FOR

As a general rule, the more errors N you count, the smaller will be the variance of your estimate of the probability of error. However, the bigger N is, the longer the simulation will take to run. For example, if the probability of error is near 10^{-6} at some particular value of SNR, around 1 million bits must be generated before you can expect an error. If you choose $N = 100$, then 100 million bits must be generated to estimate the probability of error, for just that *one* point on the plot!

Use of Coding in Conjunction with the BSC

For an (n, k) code having rate $R = k/n$ transmitted with energy per bit equal to E_b, the energy per coded bit is $E_c = E_b R$. It is convenient to fix the coded energy per bit in the simulation. To simulate the BSC channel with coding, the following outline can be used.

Algorithm 1.3 Outline for Simulating (n, k)-coded Digital Communications

---

1 Initialization: Store the points in the signal constellation.
   Fix E_c (typically $E_c = 1$). Compute R.

2 FOR each signal-to-noise ratio $\gamma = E_b/N_0$:

3   Compute $N_0 = E_c/(R\gamma)$ and $\sigma^2 = N_0/2$.

4   Compute the BSC crossover probability $p = Q(\sqrt{2E_c/N_0})$.

5   DO:

6   Generate a block of k "transmitted" input bits
       and accumulate the number of bits generated

7   Encode the input bits to n codeword bits

8   Pass the n bits through the BSC
       (flip each bit with probability p)

9   Run the n bits through the decoder to produce k output bits

10   Compare the decoded output bits with the input bits

11   Accumulate the number of bits in error

12   UNTIL at least N bit errors have been counted.

13   The estimated probability of error is
$$P_e \approx \frac{\text{number of errors counted}}{\text{number of bits generated}}$$

14 End FOR

The encoding and decoding operations depend on the kind of code used. In this lab, you will use codes which are among the simplest possible, the Hamming codes.

Since for linear codes the codeword is irrelevant, the simulation can be somewhat simplified by assuming that the input bits are all zero so that the codeword is also all zero. For the Hamming code, the simulation can be arranged as follows:

Algorithm 1.4 Outline for Simulating (n, k) Hamming-coded Digital Communications

---

1 Fix E_c (typically $E_c = 1$). Compute R.

2 FOR each signal-to-noise ratio $\gamma = E_b/N_0$:

3   Compute $N_0 = E_c/(R\gamma)$ and $\sigma^2 = N_0/2$.

4   Compute the BSC crossover probability $p = Q(\sqrt{2E_c/N_0})$.

5   DO:

6   Generate $\mathbf{r}$ as a vector of n random bits which are 1
       with probability p

7   Increment the number of bits generated by k.

8   Compute the syndrome $\mathbf{s} = \mathbf{r}H^T$.

9   If $\mathbf{s} \neq 0$, determine the error location based on the column
       of H which is equal to $\mathbf{s}$ and complement that bit of $\mathbf{r}$

10   Count the number of decoded bits (out of k) in $\mathbf{r}$ which
       match the all-zero message bits

11   Accumulate the number of bits in error.

12   UNTIL at least N bit errors have been counted.

13   Compute the probability of error.

14 End FOR

The **coding gain** for a coded system is the difference in the SNR required between uncoded and coded systems achieving the same probability of error. Usually the coding gain is expressed in dB.

Assignment

Preliminary Exercises

Show that if X is a random variable with mean 0 and variance 1 then
$$Y = aX + b$$
is a random variable with mean b and variance a^2.

Programming Part

BPSK Simulation

1. Write a program that will simulate a BPSK communication system with unequal prior bit probabilities. Using your program, create data from which to plot the probability of bit error obtained from your simulation for SNRs in the range from 0 to 10 dB, for the three cases that $P_0 = 0.5$ (in which case your

plot should look much like Figure 1.10), $P_0 = 0.25$, and $P_0 = 0.1$. Decide on an appropriate value of N.

2. Prepare data from which to plot the theoretical probability of error (1.24) for the same three values of P_0. (You may want to combine these first two programs into a single program.)

3. Plot the simulated probability of error on the same axes as the theoretical probability of error. The plots should have E_b/N_0 in dB as the horizontal axis and the probability as the vertical axis, plotted on a logarithmic scale (e.g., semilogy in MATLAB).

4. Compare the theoretical and simulated results. Comment on the accuracy of the simulation and the amount of time it took to run the simulation. Comment on the importance of theoretical models (where it is possible to obtain them).

5. Plot the probability of error for $P_0 = 0.1$, $P_0 = 0.25$ and $P_0 = 0.5$ on the same axes. Compare them and comment.

8-PSK Simulation

1. Write a program that will simulate an 8-PSK communication system with equal prior bit probabilities. Use a signal constellation in which the points are numbered in Gray code order. Make your program so that you can estimate both the symbol error probability and the bit error probability. Decide on an appropriate value of N.

2. Prepare data from which to plot the bound on the probability of symbol error P_s using (1.26) and probability of bit error P_b using (1.28).

3. Plot the simulated probability of symbol error and bit error on the same axes as the bounds on the probabilities of error.

4. Compare the theoretical and simulated results. Comment on the accuracy of the bound compared to the simulation and the amount of time it took to run the simulation.

Coded BPSK Simulation

1. Write a program that will simulate performance of the $(7, 4)$ Hamming code over a BSC channel with channel crossover probability $p = Q(\sqrt{2E_b/N_0})$ and plot the probability of error as a function of E_b/N_0 in dB. On the same plot, plot the theoretical probability of error for uncoded BPSK transmission. Identify what the coding gain is for a probability of error $P_b = 10^{-5}$.

2. Repeat this for a $(15, 11)$ Hamming code. (See page 112 and Equations (3.6) and (3.4).)

Resources and Implementation Suggestions

- A unit Gaussian random variable has mean 0 and variance 1. Given a unit Gaussian random variable, using the preliminary exercise, it is straightforward to generate a Gaussian random variable with any desired variance.

  The function gran provides a unit Gaussian random variable, generated using the Box–Muller transformation of two uniform random variables. The function gran2 returns two unit Gaussian random variables. This is useful for simulations in two-dimensional signal constellations.

- There is nothing in this lab that makes the use of C++ imperative, as opposed to C. However, you may find it useful to use C++ in the following ways:

  (a) Create an AWGN class to represent a 1-D or 2-D channel.

  (b) Create a BSC class.

  (c) Create a Hamming code class to take care of encoding and decoding (as you learn more about coding algorithms, you may want to change how this is done).

  (d) In the literature, points in two-dimensional signal constellations are frequently represented as points in the complex plane. You may find it convenient to do similarly, using the complex number capabilities that are present in C++.

- Since the horizontal axis of the probability of error plot is expressed as a ratio E_b/N_0, there is some flexibility in how to proceed. Given a value of E_b/N_0, you can either fix N_0 and determine E_b, or you can fix E_b and determine N_0. An example of how this can be done is in testrepcode.cc.

- The function uran generates a uniform random number between 0 and 1. This can be used to generate a bit which is 1 with probability p.

- The Q function, used to compute the theoretical probability of error, is implemented in the function qf.

- There are two basic approaches to generating the sequence of bits in the simulation. One way is to generate and store a large array of bits (or their resulting signals) then processing them all together. This is effective in a language such as MATLAB, where vectorized operations are faster than using for loops. The other way, and the way recommended here, is to generate each signal separately and to process it separately. This is recommended because it is not necessarily known in advance how many bits should be generated. The number of bits to be generated could be extremely large — in the millions or even billions when the probability of error is small enough.

- For the Hamming encoding and decoding operation, vector/matrix multiply operations over GF(2) are required, such as $\mathbf{c} = \mathbf{m}G$. (GF(2) is addition/subtraction/multiplication/division modulo 2.) These could be done in the conventional way using nested for loops. However, for short binary codes, a computational simplification is possible. Write G in terms of its columns as

$$G = \begin{bmatrix} \mathbf{g}_1 & \mathbf{g}_2 & \cdots & \mathbf{g}_n \end{bmatrix}.$$

Then the encoding process can be written as a series of vector/vector products (inner products)

$$\mathbf{c} = [c_1, c_2, \dots, c_n]$$
$$= \begin{bmatrix} \mathbf{m}\mathbf{g}_1 & \mathbf{m}\mathbf{g}_2 & \cdots & \mathbf{m}\mathbf{g}_n \end{bmatrix}.$$

Let us consider the inner product operation: it consists of element-by-element multiplication, followed by a sum.

Let m be an integer variable, whose bits represent the elements of the message vector $\mathbf{m}$. Also, let $g[i]$ be an integer variable in C whose bits represent the elements of the column $\mathbf{g}_i$. Then the element-by-element multiplication involved in the product $\mathbf{m}\mathbf{g}_i$ can be written simply using the bitwise-and operator & in C. How, then, to sum up the elements of the resulting vector? One way, of course, is to use a for loop, such as:

```
// Compute c=m*G, where m is a
// bit-vector, and G is represented by
// g[i]
c = 0;    // set vector of bits to 0
for(i = 0; i < n; i++) {
   mg = m & g[i];
   // mod-2 multiplication
   // of all elements
   bitsum=0;
   for(j = 0, mask=1; j < n; j++) {
   // mask selects a single bit
      if(mg & mask) {
```

```
         bitsum++;
         // accumulate if the bit != 0
      }
      mask «= 1;
      // shift mask over by 1 bit
   }
   bitsum = bitsum % 2; // mod-2 sum
   c = c | bitsum*(1«i);
   // assign to vector of bits ...
}
```

However, for sufficiently small codes (such as in this assignment) the inner for loop can be eliminated by *precomputing* the sums. Consider the table below. For a given number m, the last column provides the sum of all the bits in m, modulo 2.

m	m (binary)	$\sum m$	$s[m] = \sum m \pmod 2$
0	0000	0	0
1	0001	1	1
2	0010	1	1
3	0011	2	0
4	0100	1	1
5	0101	2	0
6	0110	2	0
7	0111	3	1
8	1000	1	1
9	1001	2	0
10	1010	2	0
11	1011	3	1
12	1100	2	0
13	1101	3	1
14	1110	3	1
15	1111	4	0

To use this in a program, precompute the table of bit sums, then use this to look up the result. An outline follows:

```
// Compute the table s, having all
// the bit sums modulo 2
// ...

// Compute c=m*G, where
// m is a bit-vector, and
// G is represented by g[i]
c = 0;
for(i = 0; i < n; i++) {
    c = c | s[m & g[i]]*(1«i);
    // assign to vector of bits
}
```

1.13   Exercises

1.1   Weighted codes. Let $s_1, s_2, \ldots, s_n$ be a sequence of digits, each in the range $0 \le s_i < p$, where p is a prime number. The weighted sum is

$$W = ns_1 + (n-1)s_2 + (n-2)s_3 + \cdots + 2s_{n-1} + s_n.$$

The final digit s_n is selected so that W modulo p is equal to 0. That is, $W \equiv 0 \pmod p$. W is called the checksum.

(a) Show that the weighted sum W can be computed by computing the cumulative sum sequence $t_1, t_2, \ldots, t_n$ by

$$t_1 = s_1, t_2 = s_1 + s_2, \ldots, t_n = s_1 + s_2 + \cdots + s_n$$

then computing the cumulative sum sequence

$$w_1 = t_1, w_2 = t_1 + t_2, \ldots, w_n = t_1 + t_2 + \cdots + t_n,$$

with $W = w_n$.

(b) Suppose that the digits s_k and s_{k+1} are interchanged, with $s_k \ne s_{k+1}$, and then a new checksum W' is computed. Show that if the original sequence satisfies $W \equiv 0 \pmod p$, then the modified sequence cannot satisfy $W' \equiv 0 \pmod p$. Thus, interchanged digits can be detected.

(c) For a sequence of digits of length $< p$, suppose that digit s_k is altered to some $s_k' \ne s_k$, and a new checksum W' is computed. Show that if the original sequence satisfies $W \equiv 0 \pmod p$, then the modified sequence cannot satisfy $W' \equiv 0 \pmod p$. Thus, a single modified digit can be detected. Why do we need the added restriction on the length of the sequence?

(d) See if the ISBN 0-13-139072-4 is valid.

(e) See if the ISBN 0-13-193072-4 is valid.

1.2   See if the UPCs 0 59280 00020 0 and 0 41700 00037 9 are valid.

1.3   A coin having $P(\text{head}) = 0.001$ is tossed 10,000 times, each toss independent. What is the lower limit on the number of bits it would take to accurately describe the outcomes? Suppose it were possible to send only 100 bits of information to describe all 10,000 outcomes. What is the minimum average distortion per bit that must be accrued sending the information in this case?

1.4   Show that the entropy of a source X with M outcomes described by (1.1) is maximized when all the outcomes are equally probable: $p_1 = p_2 = \cdots = p_M$.

1.5   Show that (1.7) follows from (1.5) using (1.4).

1.6   Show that (1.12) is true and that the mean and variance of N_{1i} and N_{2i} are as in (1.13) and (1.14).

1.7   Show that the decision rule and threshold in (1.19) and (1.20) are correct.

1.8   Show that (1.24) is correct.

1.9   Show that if X is a random variable with mean 0 and variance 1 then $Y = aX + b$ is a random variable with mean b and variance a^2.

1.10   Show that the detection rule for 8-PSK

$$\hat{\mathbf{s}} = \arg \max_{\mathbf{s} \in S} \mathbf{r}^T \mathbf{s}$$

follows from (1.18) when all points are equally likely.

1.11   Consider a series of M BSCs, each with transition probability p, where the outputs of each BSC is connected to the inputs of the next in the series. Show that the resulting overall channel is a BSC and determine the crossover probability as a function of M. What happens as $M \to \infty$? *Hint*: To simplify, consider the difference of $(x+y)^n$ and $(x-y)^n$.

1.12 [319] **Bounds and approximations to the Q function**. For many analyses it is useful to have analytical bounds and approximations to the Q function. This exercise introduces some of the most important of these.

(a) Show that

$$\sqrt{2\pi}Q(x) = \frac{1}{x}e^{-x^2/2} - \int_x^\infty \frac{1}{y^2}e^{-y^2/2}dy \quad x > 0.$$

Hint: integrate by parts.

(b) Show that

$$0 < \int_x^\infty \frac{1}{y^2}e^{-y^2/2}\,dy < \frac{1}{x^3}e^{-x^2/2}.$$

(c) Hence conclude that

$$\frac{1}{\sqrt{2\pi}x}e^{-x^2/2}(1 - 1/x^2) < Q(x) < \frac{1}{\sqrt{2\pi}x}e^{-x^2/2} \quad x > 0.$$

(d) Plot these lower and upper bounds on a plot with $Q(x)$ (use a log scale).

(e) Another useful bound is $Q(x) \le \frac{1}{2}e^{-x^2/2}$. Derive this bound. *Hint*: Identify $[Q(\alpha)]^2$ as the probability that the zero-mean unit-Gaussian random variables lie in the shaded region shown on the left in Figure 1.29, (the region $[\alpha, \infty) \times [\alpha, \infty)$). This probability is exceeded by the probability that (x, y) lies in the shaded region shown on the right (extended out to ∞). Evaluate this probability.

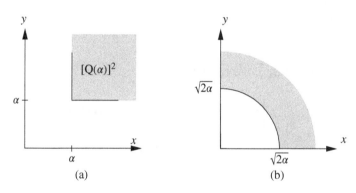

(a)   (b)

Figure 1.29: Regions for bounding the Q function.

1.13 Let $V_2(n, t)$ be the number of points in a Hamming sphere of "radius" t around a binary codeword of length n. That is, it is the number of points within a Hamming distance t of a binary vector. Determine a formula for $V_2(n, t)$.

1.14 Show that the Hamming distance satisfies the triangle inequality. That is, for three binary vectors $\mathbf{x}$, $\mathbf{y}$, and $\mathbf{z}$ of length n, show that

$$d_H(\mathbf{x}, \mathbf{z}) \le d_H(\mathbf{x}, \mathbf{y}) + d_H(\mathbf{y}, \mathbf{z}).$$

1.15 Show that for BPSK modulation with amplitudes $\pm\sqrt{E_c}$, the Hamming distance d_H and the Euclidean distance d_E between a pair of codewords are related by $d_E = 2\sqrt{E_c d_H}$.

1.16 In this problem, we will demonstrate that the probability of error for a repetition code decreases exponentially with the code length. Several other useful facts will also be introduced by this problem.

(a) Show that

$$2^{-nH_2(p)} = (1-p)^n \left(\frac{p}{1-p} \right)^{np}.$$

(b) For the fact

$$\text{If } 0 \le p \le \frac{1}{2} \text{ then } \sum_{0 \le i \le pn} \binom{n}{i} \le 2^{nH_2(p)},$$

justify the following steps of its proof

$$1 = (p + (1-p))^n \ge \sum_{0 \le i \le pn} \binom{n}{i} p^i (1-p)^{n-i}$$

$$\ge \sum_{0 \le i \le pn} \binom{n}{i} (1-p)^n \left(\frac{p}{1-p} \right)^{pn}$$

$$= 2^{-nH_2(p)} \sum_{0 \le i \le pn} \binom{n}{i}.$$

(c) Show that the probability of error for a repetition code can be written as

$$P_e^n = \sum_{j=0}^{n-(t+1)} \binom{n}{j} (1-p)^j p^{(n-j)},$$

where $t = \lfloor (n-1)/2 \rfloor$.

(d) Show that

$$P_e^n \le [2\sqrt{p(1-p)}]^n$$

1.17 [292, p. 14] Identities on $\binom{n}{k}$. We can define

$$\binom{x}{m} = \begin{cases} \frac{x(x-1)(x-2)\cdots(x-m+1)}{m!} & \text{if } m \text{ is a positive integer} \\ 1 & \text{if } m = 0 \\ 0 & \text{otherwise.} \end{cases}$$

Show that

(a) $\binom{n}{k} = \frac{n!}{k!(n-k)!}$ if k is a nonnegative integer.

(b) $\binom{n}{k} = 0$ if n is an integer and $k > n$ is a nonzero integer.

(c) $\binom{n}{k} + \binom{n}{k-1} = \binom{n+1}{k}$.

(d) $(-1)^k \binom{-n}{k} = \binom{n+k-1}{k}$.

(e) $\sum_{k=0}^{n} \binom{n}{k} = 2^n$.

(f) $\sum_{k \text{ even}} \binom{n}{k} = \sum_{k \text{ odd}} \binom{n}{k} = 2^{n-1}$ if $n \ge 1$.

(g) $\sum_{k=0}^{n} (-1)^k \binom{n}{k} = 0$ if $n \ge 1$.

1.18 Show that for soft-decision decoding on the $(n, 1)$ repetition code, (1.33) is correct.

1.19 For the $(n, 1)$ code used over a BSC with crossover probability p, what is the probability that an error event occurs which is not detected?

1.20 Hamming code decoding.

(a) For G in (1.34) and H in (1.37), verify that $GH^T = \mathbf{0}$. (Recall that operations are computed modulo 2.)

(b) Let $\mathbf{m} = [1, 1, 0, 0]$. Determine the transmitted Hamming codeword when the generator of (1.34) is used.

(c) Let $\mathbf{r} = [1, 1, 1, 1, 1, 0, 0]$. Using Algorithm 1.1, determine the transmitted codeword $\mathbf{c}$. Also determine the transmitted message $\mathbf{m}$.

(d) The message $\mathbf{m} = [1, 0, 0, 1]$ is encoded to form the codeword $\mathbf{c} = [1, 1, 0, 0, 1, 0, 1]$. The vector $\mathbf{r} = [1, 0, 1, 0, 1, 0, 0]$ is received. Decode $\mathbf{r}$ to obtain $\hat{\mathbf{c}}$. Is the codeword $\hat{\mathbf{c}}$ found the same as the original $\mathbf{c}$? Why or why not?

1.21 For the $(7, 4)$ Hamming code generator polynomial $g(x) = 1 + x + x^3$, generate all possible code polynomials $c(x)$. Verify that they correspond to the codewords in (1.35). Take a nonzero codeword $c(x)$ and compute $c(x)h(x)$ modulo $x^7 + 1$. Do this also for two other nonzero codewords. What is the check condition for this code?

1.22 Is it possible that the polynomial $g(x) = x^4 + x^3 + x^2 + 1$ is a generator polynomial for a cyclic code of length $n = 7$?

1.23 For the parity check matrix

$$H = \begin{bmatrix} 1 & 0 & 1 & 0 & 0 \\ 0 & 1 & 0 & 1 & 0 \\ 0 & 1 & 1 & 0 & 1 \end{bmatrix}$$

draw the Wolf trellis and the Tanner graph.

1.24 Let X be a random variable taking on the values $\mathcal{A}_x = \{a, b, c, d\}$ with probabilities

$$P(X = a) = \frac{1}{2} \quad P(X = b) = \frac{1}{4} \quad P(X = c) = \frac{1}{8} \quad P(X = d) = \frac{1}{8}.$$

Determine $H(X)$. Suppose that 100 measurements of independent draws of X are made per second. Determine what the entropy rate of this source is. Determine how to encode the X data to achieve this rate.

1.25 Show that the information inequality $\log x \leq x - 1$ is true.

1.26 Show that for a discrete random variable X, $H(X) \geq 0$.

1.27 Show that $I(X; Y) \geq 0$ and that $I(X; Y) = 0$ only if X and Y are independent. *Hint*: Use the information inequality.

1.28 Show that the formulas $I(X; Y) = H(X) - H(X|Y)$ and $I(X; Y) = H(Y) - H(Y|X)$ follow from the Definition (1.38).

1.29 Show that $H(X) \geq H(X|Y)$. *Hint*: Use the previous two problems.

1.30 Show that the mutual information $I(X; Y)$ can be written as

$$I(X; Y) = \sum_{x \in \mathcal{A}_x} P_X(x) \sum_{y \in \mathcal{A}_y} P_{Y|X}(y|x) \log_2 \frac{P_{Y|X}(y|x)}{\sum_{x' \in \mathcal{A}_x} P_X(x') P_{Y|X}(y|x')}$$

1.31 For a BSC with crossover probability p having input X and output Y, let the probability of the inputs be $P(X = 0) = q$ and $P(X = 1) = 1 - q$.

(a) Show that the mutual information is

$$I(X; Y) = H(Y) + p \log_2 p + (1 - p) \log_2 (1 - p).$$

(b) By maximizing over q show that the channel capacity per channel use is

$$C = 1 - H_2(p) \text{ (bits)}.$$

1.32 Consider the channel model shown here, which accepts three different symbols.

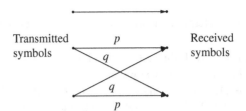

The first symbol is not affected by noise, while the second and third symbols have a probability p of not being corrupted, and a probability q of being changed into the other of the pair. Let $\alpha = -p \log p - q \log q$, and let P be the probability that the first symbol is chosen and let Q be the probability that either of the other two is chosen, so that $P + 2Q = 1$.

   (a) Show that $H(X) = -P \log P - 2Q \log Q$.

   (b) Show that $H(X|Y) = 2Q\alpha$.

   (c) Choose the input distribution (i.e., choose P and Q) in such a way to maximize $I(X;Y) = H(X) - H(X|Y)$) subject to $P + 2Q = 1$. What is the capacity for this channel?

1.33 Let $X \sim \mathcal{U}(-a, a)$ (that is, X is uniformly distributed on $[-a, a]$). Compute $H(X)$. Compare $H(X)$ with the entropy of a Gaussian distribution having the same variance.

1.34 Let $g(x)$ denote the pdf of a random variable X with variance σ^2. Show that

$$H(X) \leq \frac{1}{2} \log_2 2\pi e \sigma^2.$$

with equality if and only if X is Gaussian. *Hint*: Let $p(x)$ denote the pdf of a Gaussian r.v. with variance σ^2 and consider $D(g||p)$. Also, note that $\log p(x)$ is quadratic in x.

1.35 Show that $H(X + N|X) = H(N)$.

1.14 References

The information age was heralded with Shannon's work [404]. Thorough coverage of information theory appears in [82], [147] and [498]. The books [300] and [471] place coding theory in its information theoretic context. Our discussion of the AEP follows [26], while our "proof" of the channel coding theorem closely follows Shannon's original [404]. More analytical proofs appear in the textbooks cited above. See also [458]. Discussion about tradeoffs with complexity are in [376], as is the discussion in Section 1.12.9. Non-asymptotic information theory is developed in the masterful dissertation [343].

The detection theory and signal space background is available in most books on digital communication. See, for example, [26, 319, 344, 354].

Hamming codes were presented in [181]. The trellis representation was presented first in [488]; a thorough treatment of the concept appears in [273]. The Tanner graph representation appears in [432]; see also [148]. Exercise 1.16b comes from [458, p. 21].

The discussion relating to simulating communication systems points out that such simulations can be very slow. Faster results can in some cases be obtained using *importance sampling*. Some references on importance sampling are [123, 279, 403].

Part II

Block Codes

Chapter 2

Groups and Vector Spaces

2.1 Introduction

Linear block codes form a group and a vector space. Hence, the study of the properties of this class of codes benefits from a formal introduction to these concepts. The codes, in turn, reinforce the concepts of groups and subgroups that are valuable in the remainder of our study.

Our study of groups leads us to cyclic groups, subgroups, cosets, and factor groups. These concepts, important in their own right, also build insight in understanding the construction of extension fields which are essential for some coding algorithms to be developed.

2.2 Groups

A **group** formalizes some of the basic rules of arithmetic necessary for cancellation and solution of some simple algebraic equations.

Definition 2.1 A **binary operation** $*$ on a set is a rule that assigns to each ordered pair of elements of the set (a, b) some element of the set. (Since the operation returns an element in the set, this is actually defined as *closed* binary operation. We assume that all binary operations are closed.) □

Example 2.2 On the set of positive integers, we can define a binary operation $*$ by $a * b = \min(a, b)$. □

Example 2.3 On the set of real numbers, we can define a binary operation $*$ by $a * b = a$ (i.e., the first argument). □

Example 2.4 On the set of real numbers, we can define a binary operation $*$ by $a * b = a + b$. That is, the binary operation is regular addition. □

Definition 2.5 A **group** $\langle G, * \rangle$ is a set G together with a binary operation $*$ on G such that:

G1 The operator is **associative**: for any $a, b, c \in G$, $(a * b) * c = a * (b * c)$.

G2 There is an element $e \in G$ called the **identity element** such that $a * e = e * a = a$ for all $a \in G$.

G3 For every $a \in G$, there is an element $b \in G$ known as the **inverse** of a such that $a * b = b * a = e$. The inverse of a is sometimes denoted as a^{-1} (when the operator $*$ is multiplication-like) or as $-a$ (when the operator $*$ is addition-like).

Where the operation is clear from context, the group $\langle G, * \rangle$ may be denoted simply as G. □

It should be noted that the notation $*$ and a^{-1} are generic labels to indicate the concept. The particular notation used is modified to fit the context. Where the group operation is addition, the operator $+$ is used and the inverse of an element a is more commonly represented as $-a$. When the group operation is multiplication, either $\cdot$ or juxtaposition is used to indicate the operation and the inverse is denoted as a^{-1}.

Error Correction Coding: Mathematical Methods and Algorithms, Second Edition. Todd K. Moon
© 2021 John Wiley & Sons, Inc. Published 2021 by John Wiley & Sons, Inc.
Companion website: www.wiley.com/go/Moon/ErrorCorrectionCoding

Definition 2.6 If G has a finite number of elements, it is said to be a finite group. The **order** of a finite group G, denoted $|G|$, is the number of elements in G. □

This definition of order (of a group) is to be distinguished from the order of an element, given below.

Definition 2.7 A group $\langle G, * \rangle$ is **commutative** if $a * b = b * a$ for every $a, b \in G$. □

Example 2.8 The set $\langle \mathbb{Z}, + \rangle$, which is the set of integers under addition, forms a group. The identity element is 0, since $0 + a = a + 0 = a$ for any $a \in \mathbb{Z}$. The inverse of any $a \in \mathbb{Z}$ is $-a$.
   This is a commutative group. □

As a matter of convention, a group that is commutative with an additive-like operator is said to be an **Abelian** group (after the mathematician N.H. Abel).

Example 2.9 The set $\langle \mathbb{Z}, \cdot \rangle$, the set of integers under multiplication, does *not* form a group. There is a multiplicative identity, 1, but there is not a multiplicative inverse for every element in $\mathbb{Z}$. □

Example 2.10 The set $\langle \mathbb{Q} \backslash \{0\}, \cdot \rangle$, the set of rational numbers excluding 0, is a group with identity element 1. The inverse of an element a is $a^{-1} = 1/a$. □

The requirements on a group are strong enough to introduce the idea of cancellation. In a group G, if $a * b = a * c$, then $b = c$ (this is left cancellation). To see this, let a^{-1} be the inverse of a in G. Then

$$a^{-1} * (a * b) = a^{-1} * (a * c) = (a^{-1} * a) * c = e * c = c$$

and $a^{-1} * (a * b) = (a^{-1} * a) * b = e * b = b$, by the properties of associativity and identity.

Under group requirements, we can also verify that solutions to linear equations of the form $a * x = b$ are unique. Using the group properties we get immediately that $x = a^{-1}b$. If x_1 and x_2 are two solutions, such that $a * x_1 = b = a * x_2$, then by cancellation we get immediately that $x_1 = x_2$.

Example 2.11 Let $\langle \mathbb{Z}_5, + \rangle$ denote addition on the numbers $\{0, 1, 2, 3, 4\}$ modulo 5. The operation is demonstrated in tabular form in the table below:

+	0	1	2	3	4
0	0	1	2	3	4
1	1	2	3	4	0
2	2	3	4	0	1
3	3	4	0	1	2
4	4	0	1	2	3

Clearly 0 is the identity element. Since 0 appears in each row and column, every element has an inverse. By the uniqueness of solution, we must have every element appearing in every row and column, as it does. By the symmetry of the table it is clear that the operation is Abelian (commutative). Thus, we verify that $\langle \mathbb{Z}_5, + \rangle$ is an Abelian group.

   (Typically, when using a table to represent a group operation $a * b$, the first operand a is the row and the second operand b is the column in the table.) □

In general, we denote the set of numbers $0, 1, \ldots, n - 1$ with addition modulo n by $\langle \mathbb{Z}_n, + \rangle$ or, more briefly, $\mathbb{Z}_n$.

Example 2.12 Consider the set of numbers $\{1, 2, 3, 4, 5\}$ using the operation of multiplication modulo 6. The operation is shown in the following table:

$\cdot$	1	2	3	4	5
1	1	2	3	4	5
2	2	4	0	2	4
3	3	0	3	0	3
4	4	2	0	4	2
5	5	4	3	2	1

The number 1 acts as an identity, but this does not form a group, since not every element has a multiplicative inverse. In fact, the only elements that have a multiplicative inverse are those that are relatively prime to 6, that is, those numbers that don't share a divisor with 6 other than 1. We will see this example later in the context of rings. □

One way to construct groups is to take the Cartesian, or direct, product of groups. Given groups $\langle G_1, * \rangle, \langle G_2, * \rangle, \ldots, \langle G_r, * \rangle$, the direct product group $G_1 \times G_2 \times \cdots \times G_r$ has elements $(a_1, a_2, \ldots, a_r)$, where each $a_i \in G_i$. The operation in G is defined element-by-element. That is, if

$$(a_1, a_2, \ldots, a_r) \in G \quad \text{and} \quad (b_1, b_2, \ldots, b_r) \in G,$$

then

$$(a_1, a_2, \ldots, a_r) * (b_1, b_2, \ldots, b_r) = (a_1 * b_1, a_2 * b_2, \ldots, a_r * b_r).$$

Example 2.13 The group $\langle \mathbb{Z}_2 \times \mathbb{Z}_2, + \rangle$ consists of 2-tuples with addition defined element-by-element modulo 2. An addition for the group table is shown here:

$+$	(0,0)	(0,1)	(1,0)	(1,1)
(0,0)	(0,0)	(0,1)	(1,0)	(1,1)
(0,1)	(0,1)	(0,0)	(1,1)	(1,0)
(1,0)	(1,0)	(1,1)	(0,0)	(0,1)
(1,1)	(1,1)	(1,0)	(0,1)	(0,0)

This group is called the Klein 4-group. □

Example 2.14 This example introduces the idea of *permutations* as elements in a group. It is interesting because it introduces a group operation that is function composition, as opposed to the mostly arithmetic group operations presented to this point.

A permutation of a set A is a one-to-one, onto function (a bijection) of a set A onto itself. It is convenient for purposes of illustration to let A be a set of n integers. For example,

$$A = \{1, 2, 3, 4\}.$$

A permutation p can be written in the notation

$$p = \begin{pmatrix} 1 & 2 & 3 & 4 \\ 3 & 4 & 1 & 2 \end{pmatrix},$$

which means that

$$1 \to 3 \quad 2 \to 4 \quad 3 \to 1 \quad 4 \to 2.$$

There are $n!$ different permutations on n distinct elements.

We can think of p as an operator expressed in prefix notation. For example,

$$p \circ 1 = 3 \quad \text{or} \quad p \circ 4 = 2.$$

Let $p_1 = p$ and

$$p_2 = \begin{pmatrix} 1 & 2 & 3 & 4 \\ 4 & 3 & 1 & 2 \end{pmatrix}$$

The *composition* permutation $p_2 \circ p_1$ first applies p_1, then p_2, so that

$$p_2 \circ p_1 = \begin{pmatrix} 1 & 2 & 3 & 4 \\ 4 & 3 & 1 & 2 \end{pmatrix} \circ \begin{pmatrix} 1 & 2 & 3 & 4 \\ 3 & 4 & 1 & 2 \end{pmatrix} = \begin{pmatrix} 1 & 2 & 3 & 4 \\ 1 & 2 & 4 & 3 \end{pmatrix}.$$

This is again another permutation, so the operation of composition of permutations is closed under the set of permutations. The identity permutation is

$$e = \begin{pmatrix} 1 & 2 & 3 & 4 \\ 1 & 2 & 3 & 4 \end{pmatrix}.$$

There is an inverse permutation under composition. For example,

$$p_1^{-1} = \begin{pmatrix} 1 & 2 & 3 & 4 \\ 3 & 4 & 1 & 2 \end{pmatrix}.$$

It can be shown that composition of permutations is associative: for three permutations p_1, p_2, and p_3, then $(p_1 \circ p_2) \circ p_3 = p_1 \circ (p_2 \circ p_3)$.

Thus, the set of all $n!$ permutations on n elements forms a group, where the group operation is function composition. This group is referred to as the **symmetric group** on n letters. The group is commonly denoted by S_n.

It is also interesting to note that the composition is *not* commutative. This is clear from this example since

$$p_2 \circ p_1 \neq p_1 \circ p_2.$$

So S_4 is an example of a noncommutative group. □

2.2.1 Subgroups

Definition 2.15 A subgroup $\langle H, * \rangle$ of a group $\langle G, * \rangle$ is a group formed from a subset of elements in a group G with the same operation $*$. Notationally, we may write $H < G$ to indicate that H is a subgroup of G. (There should be no confusion using $<$ with comparisons between numbers because the operands are different in each case.) □

If the elements of H are a strict subset of the elements of G (i.e., $H \subset G$ but not $H = G$), then the subgroup is said to be a **proper** subgroup. If $H = G$, then H is an improper subgroup of G. The subgroups $H = \{e\} \subset G$ (e is the identity) and $H = G$ are said to be trivial subgroups.

Example 2.16 Let $G = \langle \mathbb{Z}_6, + \rangle$, the set of numbers $\{0, 1, 2, 3, 4, 5\}$ using addition modulo 6. Let $H = \langle \{0, 2, 4\}, + \rangle$, with addition taken modulo 6. As a set, $H \subset G$. It can be shown that H forms a group.

Let $K = \langle \{0, 3\}, + \rangle$, with addition taken modulo 6. Then K is a subgroup of G. □

Example 2.17 A variety of familiar groups can be arranged as subgroups. For example,

$$\langle \mathbb{Z}, + \rangle < \langle \mathbb{Q}, + \rangle < \langle \mathbb{R}, + \rangle < \langle \mathbb{C}, + \rangle.$$

□

Example 2.18 The group of permutations on four letters, S_4, has a subgroup formed by the permutations

$$p_0 = \begin{pmatrix} 1 & 2 & 3 & 4 \\ 1 & 2 & 3 & 4 \end{pmatrix} \qquad p_1 = \begin{pmatrix} 1 & 2 & 3 & 4 \\ 2 & 3 & 4 & 1 \end{pmatrix}$$

$$p_2 = \begin{pmatrix} 1 & 2 & 3 & 4 \\ 3 & 4 & 1 & 2 \end{pmatrix} \qquad p_3 = \begin{pmatrix} 1 & 2 & 3 & 4 \\ 4 & 1 & 2 & 3 \end{pmatrix}$$

$$p_4 = \begin{pmatrix} 1 & 2 & 3 & 4 \\ 2 & 1 & 4 & 3 \end{pmatrix} \qquad p_5 = \begin{pmatrix} 1 & 2 & 3 & 4 \\ 4 & 3 & 2 & 1 \end{pmatrix}$$

$$p_6 = \begin{pmatrix} 1 & 2 & 3 & 4 \\ 3 & 2 & 1 & 4 \end{pmatrix} \qquad p_7 = \begin{pmatrix} 1 & 2 & 3 & 4 \\ 1 & 4 & 3 & 2 \end{pmatrix} \qquad\qquad (2.1)$$

Compositions of these permutations are closed. These permutations correspond to the ways that the corners of a square can be moved to other corners by rotation about the center and reflection across edges or across diagonals (without bending the square). The geometric depiction of these permutations and the group operation table are shown here:

	p_0	p_1	p_2	p_3	p_4	p_5	p_6	p_7
p_0	p_0	p_1	p_2	p_3	p_4	p_5	p_6	p_7
p_1	p_1	p_2	p_3	p_0	p_7	p_6	p_4	p_5
p_2	p_2	p_3	p_0	p_1	p_5	p_4	p_7	p_6
p_3	p_3	p_0	p_1	p_2	p_6	p_7	p_5	p_4
p_4	p_4	p_6	p_5	p_7	p_0	p_2	p_1	p_3
p_5	p_5	p_7	p_4	p_6	p_2	p_0	p_3	p_1
p_6	p_6	p_5	p_7	p_4	p_3	p_1	p_0	p_2
p_7	p_7	p_4	p_6	p_5	p_1	p_3	p_2	p_0

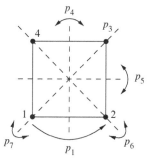

This group is known as D_4. D_4 has a variety of subgroups of its own. (Can you find them?)   □

2.2.2 Cyclic Groups and the Order of an Element

In a group G with operation $*$ or multiplication operation, we use the notation a^n to indicate $a * a * a * \cdots * a$, with the operand a appearing n times. Thus, $a^1 = a$, $a^2 = a * a$, etc. We take a^0 to be the identity element in the group G. We use a^{-2} to indicate $(a^{-1})(a^{-1})$, and a^{-n} to indicate $(a^{-1})^n$.

For a group with an additive operator $+$, the notation na is often used, which means $a + a + a + \cdots + a$, with the operand appearing n times. Throughout this section we use the a^n notation; making the switch to the additive operator notation is straightforward.

Let G be a group and let $a \in G$. Any subgroup containing a must also contain a^2, a^3, and so forth. The subgroup must contain $e = aa^{-1}$, and hence a^{-2}, a^{-3}, and so forth, are also in the subgroup.

Definition 2.19 For any $a \in G$, the set $\{a^n | n \in \mathbb{Z}\}$ generates a subgroup of G called the **cyclic subgroup**. The element a is said to be the **generator** of the subgroup. The cyclic subgroup generated by a is denoted as $\langle a \rangle$.   □

Definition 2.20 If every element of a group can be generated by a single element, the group is said to be **cyclic**.   □

Example 2.21   The group $\langle \mathbb{Z}_5, + \rangle$ is cyclic, since every element in the set can be generated by $a = 2$ (under the appropriate addition law):

$$2, \quad 2+2 = 4, \quad 2+2+2 = 1, \quad 2+2+2+2 = 3, \quad 2+2+2+2+2 = 0.$$

In this case we could write $\mathbb{Z}_5 = \langle 2 \rangle$. Observe that there are several generators for $\mathbb{Z}_5$.   □

The permutation group S_3 is not cyclic: there is no element which generates the whole group.

Definition 2.22   In a group G, with $a \in G$, the smallest positive n such that a^n is equal to the identity in G is said to be the **order** of a. If no such n exists, a is of **infinite order**.   □

The order of an element should not be confused with the order of a group, which is the number of elements in the group.

In $\mathbb{Z}_5$, the computations above show that the element 2 is of order 5. In fact, the order of every nonzero element in $\mathbb{Z}_5$ is 5.

Example 2.23   Let $G = \langle \mathbb{Z}_6, + \rangle$. Then

$$\langle 2 \rangle = \{0, 2, 4\} \quad \langle 3 \rangle = \{0, 3\} \quad \langle 5 \rangle = \{0, 1, 2, 3, 4, 5\} = \mathbb{Z}_6.$$

It is easy to verify that an element $a \in \mathbb{Z}_6$ is a generator for the whole group if and only if a and 6 are relatively prime.   □

2.2.3   Cosets

Definition 2.24   Let H be a subgroup of $\langle G, * \rangle$ (where G is not necessarily commutative) and let $a \in G$. The **left coset** of H, $a * H$, is the set $\{a * h | h \in H\}$. The **right coset** of H is similarly defined, $H * a = \{h * a | h \in H\}$.   □

Of course, in a commutative group, the left and right cosets are the same.

Figure 2.1 illustrates the idea of cosets. If G is the group $\langle \mathbb{R}^3, + \rangle$ and H is the white plane shown, then the cosets of H in G are the *translations* of H.

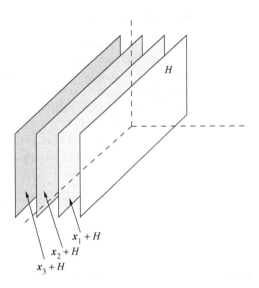

Figure 2.1: An illustration of cosets.

Let G be a group and let H be a subgroup of G. Let $a * H$ be a (left) coset of H in G. Then clearly $b \in a * H$ if and only if $b = a * h$ for some $h \in H$. This means (by cancellation) that we must have

$$a^{-1} * b \in H.$$

Thus, to determine if a and b are in the same (left) coset of H, we determine if $a^{-1} * b \in H$.

Example 2.25 Let $G = \langle \mathbb{Z}, + \rangle$ and let

$$S_0 = 3\mathbb{Z} = \{ \dots, -6, -3, 0, 3, 6, \dots \}.$$

Then S_0 is a subgroup of G. Now let us form the cosets

$$S_1 = S_0 + 1 = \{ \dots, -5, -2, 1, 4, 7, \dots \}$$

and

$$S_2 = S_0 + 2 = \{ \dots, -4, -1, 2, 5, 8, \dots \}.$$

Note that neither S_1 nor S_2 are groups (they do not contain the identity). The sets $S_0, S_1,$ and S_2 collectively cover the original group,

$$G = S_0 \cup S_1 \cup S_2.$$

Let us check whether $a = 4$ and $b = 6$ are in the same coset of S_0 by checking whether $(-a) + b \in S_0$. Since $-a + b = 2 \notin S_0$, a and b are not in the same coset. □

2.2.4 Lagrange's Theorem

Lagrange's theorem prescribes the size of a subgroup compared to the size of its group. This little result is used in a variety of ways in the developments to follow.

Lemma 2.26 *Every coset of H in a group G has the same number of elements.*

Proof We will show that every coset has the same number of elements as H. Let $a * h_1 \in a * H$ and let $a * h_2 \in a * H$ be two elements in the coset $a * H$. If $a * h_1 = a * h_2$, then by cancellation we must have $h_1 = h_2$. Thus, the elements of a coset are uniquely identified by the elements in H. □

We summarize some important properties about cosets:

Reflexive An element a is in the same coset as itself.

Symmetric If a and b are in the same coset, then b and a are in the same coset.

Transitive If a and b are in the same coset, and b and c are in the same coset, then a and c are in the same coset.

Reflexivity, symmetricity, and transitivity are properties of the relation "in the same coset."

Definition 2.27 A relation which has the properties of being **reflexive**, **symmetric**, and **transitive** is said to be an **equivalence relation**. □

An important fact about equivalence relations is that every equivalence relation *partitions* its elements into disjoint sets. Let us consider here the particular case of cosets.

Lemma 2.28 *The distinct cosets of H in a group G are disjoint.*

Proof Suppose A and B are distinct cosets of H; that is, $A \neq B$. Assume that A and B are not disjoint, then there is some element c which is common to both. We will show that this implies that $A \subset B$. Let $b \in B$. For any $a \in A$, a and c are in the same coset (since c is in A). And c and b are in the same coset (since c is in B). By transitivity, a and b must be in the same coset. Thus, every element of A is in B, so $A \subset B$. Turning the argument around, we find that $B \subset A$. Thus, $A = B$.

This contradiction shows that distinct A and B must also be disjoint. $\qquad\square$

Theorem 2.29 (*Lagrange's theorem*) *Let G be a group of finite order and let H be a subgroup of G. Then the order of H divides[1] the order of G. That is, $|H|$ divides $|G|$.*

Proof The set of cosets partition G into disjoint sets, each of which has the same number of elements, $|H|$. These disjoint sets completely cover G, since every element $g \in G$ is in some coset, $g * H$. So the number of elements of G must be equal to a multiple of $|H|$. $\qquad\square$

Lagrange's theorem can be stated more succinctly using a notation which we now introduce:

Definition 2.30 The vertical bar $\mid$ means **divides**. We write $a \mid b$ if a divides b (without remainder). $\qquad\square$

Then Lagrange's theorem can be written: If $|G| < \infty$ and $H < G$, then $|H| \big| |G|$.
One implication of Lagrange's theorem is the following.

Lemma 2.31 *Every group of prime order is cyclic.*

Proof Let G be of prime order, let $a \in G$, and denote the identity in G by e. Let $H = \langle a \rangle$, the cyclic subgroup generated by a. Then $a \in H$ and $e \in H$. But by Theorem 2.29, the order of H must divide the order of G. Since G is of prime order, then we must have $|H| = |G|$; hence a generates G, so G is cyclic. $\qquad\square$

2.2.5 Induced Operations; Isomorphism

Example 2.32 Let us return to the three cosets S_0, S_1, and S_2 defined in Example 2.25. We thus have a set of three objects, $S = \{S_0, S_1, S_2\}$. Let us define an addition operation on S as follows: for A, B and $C \in S$,

$$A + B = C \quad \text{if and only if } a + b = c \text{ for any } a \in A, b \in B \text{ and some } c \in C.$$

That is, addition of the sets is defined by **representatives** in the sets. The operation is said to be the induced operation on the cosets. For example,

$$S_1 + S_2 = S_0,$$

taking as representatives, for example, $1 \in S_1$, $2 \in S_2$ and noting that $1 + 2 = 3 \in S_0$. Similarly,

$$S_1 + S_1 = S_2,$$

taking as representatives $1 \in S_1$ and noting that $1 + 1 = 2 \in S_2$. Based on this induced operation, an addition table can be built for the set S:

$+$	S_0	S_1	S_2
S_0	S_0	S_1	S_2
S_1	S_1	S_2	S_0
S_2	S_2	S_0	S_1

---

[1] That is, divides without remainder.

It is clear that this addition table defines a group, which we can call $\langle S, + \rangle$. Now compare this addition table with the addition table for $\mathbb{Z}_3$:

+	0	1	2
0	0	1	2
1	1	2	0
2	2	0	1

Structurally, the two addition tables are identical: entries in the second table are obtained merely by replacing S_k with k, for $k = 0, 1, 2$. We say that the group $\langle S, + \rangle$ and the group $\langle \mathbb{Z}_3, + \rangle$ are **isomorphic**.   □

Definition 2.33 Two groups $\langle G, * \rangle$ and $\langle \mathcal{G}, \diamond \rangle$ are said to be (group) **isomorphic** if there exists a one-to-one, onto function $\phi : G \to \mathcal{G}$ called the **isomorphism** such that for every $a, b \in G$ (Box 2.1),

$$\phi(\underbrace{a * b}_{\substack{\text{operation} \\ \text{in } G}}) = \underbrace{\phi(a) \diamond \phi(b)}_{\substack{\text{operation} \\ \text{in } \mathcal{G}}}. \tag{2.2}$$

The fact that groups G and $\mathcal{G}$ are isomorphic are denoted by $G \cong \mathcal{G}$.   □

We can thus write $S \cong \mathbb{Z}_3$ (where the operations are unstated but understood from context).

Whenever two groups are isomorphic they are, for all practical purposes, the same thing. Different objects in the groups may have different names, but they represent the same sorts of relationships among themselves.

Box 2.1: One-to-One and Onto Functions.

A function $\phi : G \to \mathcal{G}$ is said to be **one-to-one** if $\phi(a) = \phi(b)$ implies $a = b$ for every a and b in G. That is, two distinct values $a, b \in G$ with $a \neq b$ do not map to the same value of ϕ. A one-to-one function is also called an **injective** function.
A contrasting example is $\phi(x) = x^2$, where $\phi : \mathbb{R} \to \mathbb{R}$, which is *not* one-to-one since $4 = \phi(2)$ and $4 = \phi(-2)$.

Definition 2.34 A function $\phi : G \to \mathcal{G}$ is said to be **onto** if for every $g \in \mathcal{G}$, there is an element $a \in G$ such that $\phi(a) = g$. An onto function is also called an **surjective** function. □

That is, the function goes onto everything in $\mathcal{G}$. A contrasting example is $\phi(x) = x^2$, where $\phi : \mathbb{R} \to \mathbb{R}$, since the point $g = -3$ is not mapped onto by ϕ from any point in $\mathbb{R}$.

Definition 2.35 A function which is one-to-one and onto (i.e., surjective and injective) is called **bijective**.   □

Bijective functions are always invertible. If $\phi : G \to \mathcal{G}$ is bijective, then $|G| = |\mathcal{G}|$ (the two sets have the same cardinality).

Definition 2.36 Let $\langle G, * \rangle$ be a group, H a subgroup and let $S = \{H_0 = H, H_1, H_2, \ldots, H_M\}$ be the set of cosets of H in G. Then the **induced operation** between cosets A and B in S is defined by

$$A * B = C \text{ if and only if } a * b = c$$

for any $a \in A$, $b \in B$ and some $c \in C$, provided that this operation is well defined. The operation is **well defined** if for every $a \in A$ and $b \in B$, $a * b \in C$; there is thus no ambiguity in the induced operation.   □

For commutative groups, the induced operation is always well defined. However, the reader should be cautioned that for noncommutative groups, the operation is well defined only for normal subgroups.[2]

Example 2.37   Consider the group $G = \langle \mathbb{Z}_6, + \rangle$ and let $H = \{0, 3\}$. The cosets of H are

$$H_0 = \{0, 3\} \quad H_1 = 1 + H = \{1, 4\} \quad H_2 = 2 + H = \{2, 5\}.$$

Then, under the induced operation, for example, $H_2 + H_2 = H_1$ since $2 + 2 = 4$ and $4 \in H_1$. We could also choose different representatives from the cosets. We get

$$5 + 5 = 4$$

in G. Since $5 \in H_2$ and $4 \in H_1$, we again have $H_2 + H_2 = H_1$. If by choosing different elements from the addend cosets, we were to end up with a different sum coset, the operation would not be well defined. Let us write the addition table for $\mathbb{Z}_6$ reordered and separated out by the cosets. The induced operation is clear. We observe that H_0, H_1 and H_2 themselves constitute a group, with addition table also shown.

	+	0	3	1	4	2	5
H_0	0	0	3	1	4	2	5
	3	3	0	4	1	5	2
H_1	1	1	4	2	5	3	0
	4	4	1	5	2	0	3
H_2	2	2	5	3	0	4	1
	5	5	2	0	3	1	4

+	H_0	H_1	H_2
H_0	H_0	H_1	H_2
H_1	H_1	H_2	H_0
H_2	H_2	H_0	H_1

The group of cosets is clearly isomorphic to $\langle \mathbb{Z}_3, + \rangle$: $\{H_0, H_1, H_2\} \cong \mathbb{Z}_3$.   □

From this example, we see that the cosets themselves form a group.

Theorem 2.38   *If H is a subgroup of a commutative group $\langle G, * \rangle$, the induced operation $*$ on the set of cosets of H satisfies*

$$(a * b) * H = (a * H) * (b * H).$$

Furthermore, the operation is well defined.

The proof is explored in Exercise 2.13. This defines an operation. Clearly, H itself acts as an identity for the operation defined on the set of cosets. Also, by Theorem 2.38, $(a * H) * (a^{-1} * H) = (a * a^{-1}) * H = H$, so every coset has an inverse coset. Thus, the set of cosets of H form a group.

Definition 2.39   The group formed by the cosets of H in a commutative[3] group G with the induced operation is said to be the **factor group** of G modulo H, denoted by G/H. The cosets are said to be the **residue classes** of G modulo H.   □

In the last example, we could write $\mathbb{Z}_3 \cong \mathbb{Z}_6/H$. From Example 2.32, the group of cosets was also isomorphic to $\mathbb{Z}_3$, so we can write

$$\mathbb{Z}/3\mathbb{Z} \cong \mathbb{Z}_3.$$

In general, it can be shown that

$$\mathbb{Z}/n\mathbb{Z} \cong \mathbb{Z}_n.$$

---

[2] A subgroup H of a group G is **normal** if $g^{-1} H g = H$ for all $g \in G$. Clearly all Abelian groups are normal.

[3] Or of a normal subgroup in a noncommutative group.

Example 2.40 A **lattice** is formed by taking all possible integer linear combinations of a set of basis vectors. That is, let $\mathbf{v}_1, \mathbf{v}_2, \ldots, \mathbf{v}_n$ be a set of linearly independent vectors, let $V = \left[\mathbf{v}_1, \mathbf{v}_2, \ldots, \mathbf{v}_n\right]$. Then a lattice is formed from these basis vectors by

$$\Lambda = \{V\mathbf{z} : \mathbf{z} \in \mathbb{Z}^n\}.$$

For example, the lattice formed by $V = \begin{bmatrix} 1 & 0 \\ 0 & 1 \end{bmatrix}$ is the set of points with integer coordinates in the plane, denoted as $\mathbb{Z}^2$.

For the lattice $\Lambda = \mathbb{Z}^2$, let $\Lambda' = 2\mathbb{Z}^2$ be a subgroup. Then the cosets

$$S_0 = \Lambda' \text{(denoted by } \bullet\text{)} \qquad S_1 = (1,0) + \Lambda' \text{(denoted by } \circ\text{)}$$
$$S_2 = (0,1) + \Lambda' \text{(denoted by } \square\text{)} \qquad S_3 = (1,1) + \Lambda' \text{(denoted by } \Diamond\text{)}$$

are indicated in Figure 2.2. It is straightforward to verify that

$$\Lambda/\Lambda' \cong \mathbb{Z}_2 \times \mathbb{Z}_2.$$

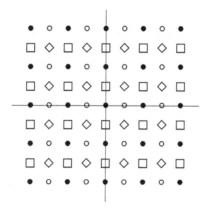

Figure 2.2: A lattice partitioned into cosets.

Such decompositions of lattices into subsets find application in trellis coded modulation, as we shall see in Chapter 13. □

2.2.6 Homomorphism

For *isomorphism*, two sets G and $\mathcal{G}$ are structurally the same, as defined by (2.2), and they have the same number of elements (since there is a bijective function $\phi : G \to \mathcal{G}$). From an algebraic point of view, G and $\mathcal{G}$ are identical, even though they may have different names for their elements.

Homomorphism is a somewhat weaker condition: the sets must have the same algebraic structure, but they might have different numbers of elements.

Definition 2.41 The groups $\langle G, * \rangle$ and $\langle \mathcal{G}, \diamond \rangle$ are said to be (group) **homomorphic** if there exists a function (that is not necessarily one-to-one) $\phi : G \to \mathcal{G}$ called the **homomorphism** such that

$$\phi(\underbrace{a * b}_{\substack{\text{operation} \\ \text{in } G}}) = \underbrace{\phi(a) \diamond \phi(b)}_{\substack{\text{operation} \\ \text{in } \mathcal{G}}}. \qquad (2.3)$$

□

Example 2.42   Let $G = \langle \mathbb{Z}, + \rangle$ and let $\mathcal{G} = \langle \mathbb{Z}_n, + \rangle$. Let $\phi : G \to \mathcal{G}$ be defined by $\phi(a) = a \bmod n$, the remainder when a is divided by n. Let $a, b \in \mathbb{Z}$. We have (see Exercise 2.32)

$$\phi(a + b) = \phi(a) + \phi(b).$$

Thus, $\langle \mathbb{Z}, + \rangle$ and $\langle \mathbb{Z}_n, + \rangle$ are homomorphic, although they clearly do not have the same number of elements.   □

Theorem 2.43   *Let* $\langle G, * \rangle$ *be a commutative group and let H be a subgroup, so that G/H is the factor group. Let $\phi : G \to G/H$ be defined by $\phi(a) = a * H$. Then ϕ is a homomorphism. The homomorphism ϕ is said to be the* natural *or* canonical homomorphism.

Proof   Let $a, b \in G$. Then by Theorem 2.38,

$$\phi(\ \underbrace{a * b}_{\substack{\text{operation} \\ \text{in } G}}\ ) = \underbrace{\phi(a) * \phi(b)}_{\substack{\text{operation} \\ \text{in } G/H}}.$$

□

Definition 2.44   The **kernel of a homomorphism** ϕ of a group G into a group $\mathcal{G}$ is the set of all elements of G which are mapped onto the identity element of $\mathcal{G}$ by ϕ.   □

Example 2.45   For the canonical map $\mathbb{Z} \to \mathbb{Z}_n$ of Example 2.42, the kernel is $n\mathbb{Z}$, the set of multiples of n.   □

2.3   Fields: A Prelude

We shall have considerably more to say about fields in Chapter 5, but we introduce the concept here since fields are used in defining vector spaces and simple linear block codes.

Definition 2.46   A **field** $\langle \mathbb{F}, +, \cdot \rangle$ is a set of objects $\mathbb{F}$ on which the operations of addition and multiplication, subtraction (or additive inverse), and division (or multiplicative inverse) apply in a manner analogous to the way these operations work for real numbers.

In particular, the addition operation $+$ and the multiplication operation $\cdot$ (or juxtaposition) satisfy the following:

F1 Closure under addition: For every a and b in $\mathbb{F}$, $a + b$ is also in $\mathbb{F}$.

F2 Additive identity: There is an element in $\mathbb{F}$, which we denote as 0, such that $a + 0 = 0 + a = a$ for every $a \in \mathbb{F}$.

F3 Additive inverse (subtraction): For every $a \in \mathbb{F}$, there exists an element b in $\mathbb{F}$ such that $a + b = b + a = 0$. The element b is frequently called the additive inverse of a and is denoted as $-a$.

F4 Associativity: $(a + b) + c = a + (b + c)$ for every $a, b, c \in \mathbb{F}$.

F5 Commutativity: $a + b = b + a$ for every $a, b \in \mathbb{F}$.

The first four requirements mean that the elements of $\mathbb{F}$ form a **group** under addition; with the fifth requirement, a **commutative group** is obtained.

. . . .

F6 Closure under multiplication: For every a and b in $\mathbb{F}$, $a \cdot b$ is also in $\mathbb{F}$.

F7 Multiplicative identity: There is an element in $\mathbb{F}$, which we denote as 1, such that $a \cdot 1 = 1 \cdot a = a$
for every $a \in \mathbb{F}$ with $a \neq 0$.

F8 Multiplicative inverse: For every $a \in \mathbb{F}$ with $a \neq 0$, there is an element $b \in \mathbb{F}$ such that $a \cdot b =$
$b \cdot a = 1$. The element b is called the multiplicative inverse, or reciprocal, of a and is denoted as
a^{-1}.

F9 Associativity: $(a \cdot b) \cdot c = a \cdot (b \cdot c)$ for every $a, b, c \in \mathbb{F}$.

F10 Commutativity: $a \cdot b = b \cdot a$ for every $a, b \in \mathbb{F}$.

Thus, the nonzero elements of $\mathbb{F}$ form a commutative group under multiplication.

....

F11 Multiplication distributes over addition: $a \cdot (b + c) = a \cdot b + a \cdot c$.

The field $\langle \mathbb{F}, +, \cdot \rangle$ is frequently referred to simply as $\mathbb{F}$. A field with q elements in it may be denoted
as $\mathbb{F}_q$. □

Example 2.47 The field with two elements in it, $\mathbb{F}_2 = \mathbb{Z}_2 = GF(2)$ has the following addition and multiplication
tables

+	0	1
0	0	1
1	1	0

$\cdot$	0	1
0	0	0
1	0	1

"exclusive or"   "and"

The field $GF(2)$ is very important to our work, since it is the field where the operations involved in *binary* codes
work. However, we shall have occasion to use many other fields as well. □

Example 2.48 The field $\mathbb{F}_5 = \mathbb{Z}_5 = GF(5)$ has the following addition and multiplication tables:

+	0	1	2	3	4
0	0	1	2	3	4
1	1	2	3	4	0
2	2	3	4	0	1
3	3	4	0	1	2
4	4	0	1	2	3

$\cdot$	0	1	2	3	4
0	0	0	0	0	0
1	0	1	2	3	4
2	0	2	4	1	3
3	0	3	1	4	2
4	0	4	3	2	1

□

There are similarly constructed fields for every prime p, denoted by either $GF(p)$ or $\mathbb{F}_p$.

Example 2.49 A field with four elements can be constructed with the following operation tables:

+	0	1	2	3
0	0	1	2	3
1	1	0	3	2
2	2	3	0	1
3	3	2	1	0

$\cdot$	0	1	2	3
0	0	0	0	0
1	0	1	2	3
2	0	2	3	1
3	0	3	1	2

(2.4)

This field is called $GF(4)$. Note that it is definitely *not* the same as $\langle \mathbb{Z}_4, +, \cdot \rangle$! (Why not?) We learn in Chapter 5
how to construct such a field. □

Just as for groups, we can define the concepts of isomorphism and homomorphism. Two fields $\langle F, +, \cdot \rangle$ and $\langle \mathcal{F}, +, \cdot \rangle$ are (field) isomorphic if there exists a bijective function $\phi : F \to \mathcal{F}$ such that for every $a, b \in F$,

$$\phi(\underbrace{a+b}_{\substack{\text{operation} \\ \text{in } F}}) = \underbrace{\phi(a) + \phi(b)}_{\substack{\text{operation} \\ \text{in } \mathcal{F}}} \qquad \phi(\underbrace{ab}_{\substack{\text{operation} \\ \text{in } F}}) = \underbrace{\phi(a)\phi(b)}_{\substack{\text{operation} \\ \text{in } \mathcal{F}}}.$$

For example, the field $\mathcal{F}$ defined on the elements $\{-1, 1\}$ with operation tables

+	-1	1
-1	-1	1
1	1	-1

$\cdot$	-1	1
-1	-1	-1
1	-1	1

is isomorphic to the field $GF(2)$ defined above, with ϕ mapping $0 \to -1$ and $1 \to 1$. Fields F and $\mathcal{F}$ are homomorphic if such a structure-preserving map ϕ exists which is not necessarily bijective.

2.4 Review of Linear Algebra

Linear block codes are based on concepts from linear algebra. In this section, we review concepts from linear algebra which are immediately pertinent to our study of linear block codes.

Up to this point, our examples have dealt primarily with binary alphabets having the symbols $\{0, 1\}$. As your algebraic and coding-theoretic skills are deepened, you will learn that larger alphabets are feasible and often desirable for good codes. However, rather than presenting the algebra first and the codes second, it seems pedagogically worthwhile to present the basic block coding concepts first using binary alphabets and introduce the algebra for larger alphabets later. For the sake of generality, we present definitions in terms of larger alphabets, but for the sake of concrete exposition we present examples in this chapter using binary alphabets. For now, understand that we will eventually need to deal with alphabets with more than two symbols. We denote the number of symbols in the alphabet by q, where $q = 2$ usually in this chapter. Furthermore, the alphabets we use usually form a finite **field**, denoted here as $\mathbb{F}_q$, which is briefly introduced in Section 2.3 and thoroughly developed in Chapter 5.

Definition 2.50 Let V be a set of elements called **vectors** and let $\mathbb{F}$ be a field of elements called **scalars**. An addition operation $+$ is defined between vectors. A scalar multiplication operation $\cdot$ (or juxtaposition) is defined such that for a scalar $a \in \mathbb{F}$ and a vector $\mathbf{v} \in V$, $a \cdot \mathbf{v} \in V$. Then V is a **vector space** over $\mathbb{F}$ if $+$ and $\cdot$ satisfy the following:

V1 V forms a commutative group under $+$.

V2 For any element $a \in \mathbb{F}$ and $\mathbf{v} \in V$, $a \cdot \mathbf{v} \in V$.

Combining V1 and V2, we must have $a \cdot \mathbf{v} + b \cdot \mathbf{w} \in V$ for every $\mathbf{v}, \mathbf{w} \in V$ and $a, b \in \mathbb{F}$.

V3 The operations $+$ and $\cdot$ distribute:

$$(a+b) \cdot \mathbf{v} = a \cdot \mathbf{v} + b \cdot \mathbf{v} \quad \text{and} \quad a \cdot (\mathbf{u} + \mathbf{v}) = a \cdot \mathbf{u} + a \cdot \mathbf{v}$$

for all scalars $a, b \in \mathbb{F}$ and vectors $\mathbf{v}, \mathbf{u} \in V$.

V4 The operation $\cdot$ is associative: $(a \cdot b) \cdot \mathbf{v} = a \cdot (b \cdot \mathbf{v})$ for all $a, b \in \mathbb{F}$ and $\mathbf{v} \in V$.

$\mathbb{F}$ is called the scalar field of the vector space V. $\square$

Example 2.51

1. The set of n-tuples $(v_0, v_1, \ldots, v_{n-1})$, with elements $v_i \in \mathbb{R}$ forms a vector space which we denote as $\mathbb{R}^n$, with addition defined element-by-element,

$$(v_0, v_1, \ldots, v_{n-1}) + (u_0, u_1, \ldots, u_{n-1}) = (v_0 + u_0, v_1 + u_1, \ldots, v_{n-1} + u_{n-1}),$$

and scalar multiplication defined by

$$a \cdot (v_0, v_1, \ldots, v_{n-1}) = (av_0, av_1, \ldots, av_{n-1}). \tag{2.5}$$

2. The set of n-tuples of $(v_0, v_1, \ldots, v_{n-1})$ with elements $v_i \in \mathbb{F}_2$ forms a vector space which we denote as $\mathbb{F}_2^n$. There are 2^n elements in the vector space $\mathbb{F}_2^n$. For $n = 3$, the elements of the vector space are

$$\begin{array}{cccc} (0,0,0) & (0,0,1) & (0,1,0) & (0,1,1) \\ (1,0,0) & (1,0,1) & (1,1,0) & (1,1,1) \end{array}$$

3. In general, the set $V = \mathbb{F}_q^n$ of n-tuples of elements of the field $\mathbb{F}_q$ with element-by-element addition and scalar multiplication as in (2.5) constitutes a vector space. We call an n-tuple of elements of $\mathbb{F}_q$ simply an n-vector.

$\square$

Definition 2.52 Let $\mathbf{v}_1, \mathbf{v}_2, \ldots, \mathbf{v}_k$ be vectors in a vector space V and let $a_1, a_2, \ldots, a_k$ be scalars in $\mathbb{F}$. The operation

$$a_1\mathbf{v}_1 + a_2\mathbf{v}_2 + \cdots a_k\mathbf{v}_k$$

is said to be a **linear combination** of the vectors.

$\square$

Notationally, observe that the linear combination

$$a_1\mathbf{v}_1 + a_2\mathbf{v}_2 + \cdots + a_k\mathbf{v}_k$$

can be obtained by forming a matrix G by stacking the vectors as columns,

$$G = \begin{bmatrix} \mathbf{v}_1 & \mathbf{v}_2 & \cdots & \mathbf{v}_k \end{bmatrix}$$

then forming the product with the column vector of coefficients:

$$a_1\mathbf{v}_1 + a_2\mathbf{v}_2 + \cdots a_k\mathbf{v}_k = \begin{bmatrix} \mathbf{v}_1 & \mathbf{v}_2 & \cdots & \mathbf{v}_k \end{bmatrix} \begin{bmatrix} a_1 \\ a_2 \\ \vdots \\ a_k \end{bmatrix}. \tag{2.6}$$

Alternatively, the vectors $\mathbf{v}_i$ can be envisioned as *row* vectors and stacked as rows. The linear combination can be obtained by the product with a row vector of coefficients:

$$a_1\mathbf{v}_1 + a_2\mathbf{v}_2 + \cdots a_k\mathbf{v}_k = \begin{bmatrix} a_1 & a_2 & \cdots & a_k \end{bmatrix} \begin{bmatrix} \mathbf{v}_1 \\ \mathbf{v}_2 \\ \vdots \\ \mathbf{v}_k \end{bmatrix}.$$

Definition 2.53 Let V be a vector space. A set of vectors $G = \{\mathbf{v}_1, \mathbf{v}_2, \ldots, \mathbf{v}_k\}$, each in V, is said to be a **spanning set** for V if every vector $\mathbf{v} \in V$ can be written as a linear combination of the vectors in G. That is, for every $\mathbf{v} \in V$, there exists a set of scalars $a_1, a_2, \ldots, a_k$ such that $\mathbf{v} = a_1\mathbf{v}_1 + a_2\mathbf{v}_2 + \cdots + a_k\mathbf{v}_k$.

For a set of vectors G, the set of vectors obtained from every possible linear combination of vectors in G is called the **span** of G, span(G).

$\square$

It may be verified that the span of a set of vectors is itself a vector space. In light of the notation in (2.6), it is helpful to think of G as a *matrix* whose columns are the vectors $\mathbf{v}_i$, and not simply as a set of vectors. If G is interpreted as a matrix, we take span(G) as the set of linear combinations of the columns of G. The space obtained by the linear combination of the columns of a matrix G is called the **column space** of G. The space obtained by the linear combination of the rows of a matrix G is called the **row space** of G.

It may be that there is redundancy in the vectors of a spanning set, in the sense that not all of them are needed to span the space because some of them can be expressed in terms of other vectors in the spanning set. In such a case, the vectors in the spanning set are not linearly independent:

Definition 2.54 A set of vectors $\mathbf{v}_1, \mathbf{v}_2, \ldots, \mathbf{v}_k$ is said to be **linearly dependent** if a set of scalars $\{a_1, a_2, \ldots, a_k\}$ exists, with not all $a_i = 0$ such that

$$a_1\mathbf{v}_1 + a_2\mathbf{v}_2 + \cdots + a_k\mathbf{v}_k = 0.$$

A set of vectors which is not linearly dependent is **linearly independent**.   □

From the definition, if a set of vectors $\{\mathbf{v}_1, \ldots, \mathbf{v}_k\}$ is linearly independent and there exists a set of coefficients $\{a_1, \ldots, a_k\}$ such that

$$a_1\mathbf{v}_1 + a_2\mathbf{v}_2 + \cdots + a_k\mathbf{v}_k = \mathbf{0},$$

then it must be the case that $a_1 = a_2 = \cdots = a_k = 0$.

Definition 2.55 A spanning set for a vector space V that has the smallest possible number of vectors in it is called a **basis** for V.

The number of vectors in a basis for V is the **dimension** of V.   □

Clearly the vectors in a basis must be linearly independent (or it would be possible to form a smaller set of vectors).

Example 2.56 Let $V = \mathbb{F}_2^4$, the set of binary 4-tuples and let

$$G = \left[\begin{bmatrix} 1 \\ 0 \\ 1 \\ 0 \end{bmatrix}, \begin{bmatrix} 0 \\ 1 \\ 1 \\ 0 \end{bmatrix}, \begin{bmatrix} 1 \\ 1 \\ 0 \\ 0 \end{bmatrix} \right]$$

be a set of vectors.

Let $W = \text{span}(G)$;

$$W = \left\{ \begin{bmatrix} 0 \\ 0 \\ 0 \\ 0 \end{bmatrix}, \begin{bmatrix} 1 \\ 0 \\ 1 \\ 0 \end{bmatrix}, \begin{bmatrix} 0 \\ 1 \\ 1 \\ 0 \end{bmatrix}, \begin{bmatrix} 1 \\ 1 \\ 0 \\ 0 \end{bmatrix} \right\}.$$

It can be verified that W is a vector space.

The set G is a spanning set for W, but it is not a spanning set for V. However, G is not a basis for W; the set G has some redundancy in it, since the third vector is a linear combination of the first two:

$$\begin{bmatrix} 1 \\ 1 \\ 0 \\ 0 \end{bmatrix} = \begin{bmatrix} 1 \\ 0 \\ 1 \\ 0 \end{bmatrix} + \begin{bmatrix} 0 \\ 1 \\ 1 \\ 0 \end{bmatrix}.$$

The vectors in G are not linearly independent. The third vector in G can be removed, resulting in the set

$$G' = \left\{ \begin{bmatrix} 1 \\ 0 \\ 1 \\ 0 \end{bmatrix}, \begin{bmatrix} 0 \\ 1 \\ 1 \\ 0 \end{bmatrix} \right\},$$

which has $\text{span}(G') = W$.

No spanning set for W has fewer vectors in it than does G', so $\dim(W) = 2$.   □

Theorem 2.57 *Let V be a k-dimensional vector space defined over a scalar field with a finite number of elements q in it. Then the number of elements in V is $|V| = q^k$.*

Proof Every vector $\mathbf{v}$ in V can be written as

$$\mathbf{v} = a_1\mathbf{v}_1 + a_2\mathbf{v}_2 + \cdots + a_k\mathbf{v}_k.$$

Thus, the number of elements in V is the number of distinct k-tuples $(a_1, a_2, \ldots, a_k)$ that can be formed, which is q^k.   □

Definition 2.58 Let V be a vector space over a scalar field $\mathbb{F}$ and let $W \subset V$ be a vector space. That is, for any $\mathbf{w}_1$ and $\mathbf{w}_2 \in W$, $a\mathbf{w}_1 + b\mathbf{w}_2 \in W$ for any $a, b \in \mathbb{F}$. Then W is called a **vector subspace** (or simply a subspace) of F.   □

Example 2.59 The set W in Example 2.56 is a vector space, and is a subset of V. So W is a vector subspace of V. Note, as specified by Theorem 2.57, that W has $4 = 2^2$ elements in it.   □

We now augment the vector space with a new operator called the **inner product**, creating an inner product space.

Definition 2.60 Let $\mathbf{u} = (u_0, u_1, \ldots, u_{n-1})$ and $\mathbf{v} = (v_0, v_1, \ldots, v_{n-1})$ be vectors in a vector space V, where $u_i, v_i \in \mathbb{F}$. The **inner product** is a function that accepts two vectors and returns a scalar. It may be written as $\langle \mathbf{u}, \mathbf{v} \rangle$ or as $\mathbf{u} \cdot \mathbf{v}$. It is defined as

$$\langle \mathbf{u}, \mathbf{v} \rangle = \mathbf{u} \cdot \mathbf{v} = \sum_{i=0}^{n-1} u_i \cdot v_i.$$

□

It is straightforward to verify the following properties:

1. Commutativity: $\mathbf{u} \cdot \mathbf{v} = \mathbf{v} \cdot \mathbf{u}$
2. Associativity: $a \cdot (\mathbf{u} \cdot \mathbf{v}) = (a \cdot \mathbf{u}) \cdot \mathbf{v}$
3. Distributivity: $\mathbf{u} \cdot (\mathbf{v} + \mathbf{w}) = \mathbf{u} \cdot \mathbf{v} + \mathbf{u} \cdot \mathbf{w}$.

In physics and elementary calculus, the inner product is often called the dot product and is used to describe the physical concept of orthogonality. We similarly define orthogonality for the vector spaces of interest to us, even though there may not be a physical interpretation.

Definition 2.61 Two vectors $\mathbf{u}$ and $\mathbf{v}$ are said to be **orthogonal** if $\mathbf{u} \cdot \mathbf{v} = 0$. When $\mathbf{u}$ and $\mathbf{v}$ are orthogonal, this is sometimes denoted as $\mathbf{u} \perp \mathbf{v}$.   □

Combining the idea of vector subspaces with orthogonality, we get the concept of a dual space:

Definition 2.62 Let W be a k-dimensional subspace of a vector space V. The set of all vectors $\mathbf{u} \in V$ which are orthogonal to all the vectors of W is called the **dual space** of W (sometimes called the **orthogonal complement** of W or **dual space**), denoted $W^\perp$. (The symbol $W^\perp$ is sometimes pronounced "W perp," for "perpendicular.") That is,

$$W^\perp = \{\mathbf{u} \in V : \mathbf{u} \cdot \mathbf{w} = 0 \text{ for all } \mathbf{w} \in W\}.$$

$\square$

Geometric intuition regarding dual spaces frequently may be gained by thinking in three-dimensional space $\mathbb{R}^3$ and letting W be a plane through the origin and $W^\perp$ a line through the origin orthogonal to the plane.

Example 2.63 Let $V = \mathbb{F}_2^4$ and let W be as in Example 2.56. Then it can be verified that

$$W^\perp = \left\{ \begin{bmatrix} 0 \\ 0 \\ 0 \\ 0 \end{bmatrix}, \begin{bmatrix} 0 \\ 0 \\ 0 \\ 1 \end{bmatrix}, \begin{bmatrix} 1 \\ 1 \\ 1 \\ 0 \end{bmatrix}, \begin{bmatrix} 1 \\ 1 \\ 1 \\ 1 \end{bmatrix} \right\}.$$

Note that

$$W^\perp = \text{span}\left(\left\{ \begin{bmatrix} 0 \\ 0 \\ 0 \\ 1 \end{bmatrix}, \begin{bmatrix} 1 \\ 1 \\ 1 \\ 0 \end{bmatrix} \right\} \right)$$

and that $\dim(W^\perp) = 2$.

$\square$

This example demonstrates the important principle stated in the following theorem.

Theorem 2.64 *Let V be a finite-dimensional vector space of n-tuples, $\mathbb{F}^n$, with a subspace W of dimension k. Let $U = W^\perp$ be the dual space of W. Then*

$$\dim(W^\perp) = \dim(V) - \dim(W) = n - k.$$

Proof Let $\mathbf{g}_1, \mathbf{g}_2, \ldots, \mathbf{g}_k$ be a basis for W and let

$$G = \begin{bmatrix} \mathbf{g}_1 & \mathbf{g}_2 & \cdots & \mathbf{g}_k \end{bmatrix}.$$

This is a rank k matrix, meaning that the dimension of its column space is k and the dimension of its row space is k. Any vector $\mathbf{w} \in W$ is of the form $\mathbf{w} = G\mathbf{x}$ for some vector $\mathbf{x} \in \mathbb{F}^k$. Any vector $\mathbf{u} \in U$ must satisfy $\mathbf{u}^T G\mathbf{x} = 0$ for all $\mathbf{x} \in \mathbb{F}^k$. This implies that $\mathbf{u}^T G = 0$. (That is, $\mathbf{u}$ is orthogonal to every basis vector for W.)

Let $\{\mathbf{h}_1, \mathbf{h}_2, \ldots, \mathbf{h}_r\}$ be a basis for $W^\perp$, then extend this to a basis for the whole n-dimensional space, $\{\mathbf{h}_1, \mathbf{h}_2, \ldots, \mathbf{h}_r, \mathbf{f}_1, \mathbf{f}_2, \ldots, \mathbf{f}_{n-r}\}$. Every vector $\mathbf{v}$ in the row space of G is expressible (not necessarily uniquely) as $\mathbf{v} = \mathbf{b}^T G$ for some vector $\mathbf{b} \in V$. But since $\{\mathbf{h}_1, \mathbf{h}_2, \ldots, \mathbf{h}_r, \mathbf{f}_1, \mathbf{f}_2, \ldots, \mathbf{f}_{n-r}\}$ spans V, $\mathbf{b}$ must be a linear combination of these vectors:

$$\mathbf{b} = a_1 \mathbf{h}_1 + a_2 \mathbf{h}_2 + \cdots + a_r \mathbf{h}_r + a_{r+1} \mathbf{f}_1 + \cdots + a_n \mathbf{f}_{n-r}.$$

So a vector $\mathbf{v}$ in the row space of G can be written as

$$\mathbf{v} = a_1 \mathbf{h}_1^T G + a_2 \mathbf{h}_2^T G + \cdots + a_n \mathbf{f}_{n-r}^T G,$$

from which we observe that the row space of G is spanned by the vectors

$$\{\mathbf{h}_1^T G, \mathbf{h}_2^T G, \ldots, \mathbf{h}_r^T G, \mathbf{f}_1^T G, \ldots, \mathbf{f}_{n-r}^T G\}.$$

The vectors $\{\mathbf{h}_1, \mathbf{h}_2, \ldots, \mathbf{h}_r\}$ are in $W^\perp$, so that $\mathbf{h}_i^T G = \mathbf{0}$ for $i = 1, 2, \ldots, r$. The remaining vectors $\{\mathbf{f}_1^T G, \ldots, \mathbf{f}_{n-r}^T G\}$ remain to span the k-dimensional row space of G. Hence, we must have $n - r \geq k$. Furthermore, these vectors are linearly independent, because if there is a set of coefficients $\{a_i\}$ such that

$$a_1(\mathbf{f}_1^T G) + \cdots + a_{n-r}(\mathbf{f}_{n-r}^T G) = \mathbf{0},$$

then

$$(a_1 \mathbf{f}_1^T + \cdots + a_{n-r} \mathbf{f}_{n-r}^T) G = \mathbf{0}.$$

But the vectors $\mathbf{f}_i$ are not in $W^\perp$, so we must have

$$a_1 \mathbf{f}_1^T + \cdots + a_{n-r} \mathbf{f}_{n-r}^T = 0.$$

Since the vectors $\{\mathbf{f}_i\}$ are linearly independent, we must have $a_1 = a_2 = \cdots = a_{n-r} = 0$. Therefore, we must have dim span$(\{\mathbf{f}_1^T G, \ldots, \mathbf{f}_{n-r}^T G\}) = k$, so $n - r = k$. $\square$

2.5 Exercises

2.1 A group can be constructed by using the rotations and reflections of a regular pentagon into itself. The group operator is "followed by" (e.g., a reflection ρ "followed by" a rotation r). This is a permutation group, as in Example 2.14.

   (a) How many elements are in this group?

   (b) Construct the group (i.e., show the "multiplication table" for the group).

   (c) Is it an Abelian group?

   (d) Find a subgroup with five elements and a subgroup with two elements.

   (e) Are there any subgroups with four elements? Why?

2.2 Show that only one group exists with three elements "up to isomorphism." That is, there is only one way of filling out a binary operation table that satisfies all the requirements of a group.

2.3 Show that there are two groups with four elements, up to isomorphism. One of these groups is isomorphic to $\mathbb{Z}_4$. The other is called the Klein 4-group.

2.4 Prove that in a group G, the identity element is unique.

2.5 Prove that in a group G, the inverse a^{-1} of an element a is unique.

2.6 Let $G = \langle \mathbb{Z}_{16}, + \rangle$, the group of integers modulo 16. Let $H = \langle 4 \rangle$, the cyclic group generated by the element $4 \in G$.

   (a) List the elements of H.

   (b) Determine the cosets of G/H.

   (c) Draw the "addition" table for G/H.

   (d) To what group is G/H isomorphic?

2.7 Show that if G is an Abelian group and $\mathcal{G}$ is isomorphic to G, then $\mathcal{G}$ is also Abelian.

2.8 Let G be a cyclic group and let $\mathcal{G}$ be isomorphic to G. Show that $\mathcal{G}$ is also a cyclic group.

2.9 Let G be a cyclic group with generator a and let $\mathcal{G}$ be a group isomorphic to G. If $\phi : G \to \mathcal{G}$ is an isomorphism, show that for every $x \in G$, x may be written as a^j (for some j, using multiplicative notation) and that $\phi(x)$ is determined by $\phi(a)$.

2.10 An automorphism of a group G is an isomorphism of the group with itself, $\phi : G \to G$. Using Exercise 2.9, how many automorphisms are there of $\mathbb{Z}_2$? of $\mathbb{Z}_6$? of $\mathbb{Z}_8$? of $\mathbb{Z}_{17}$?

2.11 [144] Let G be a finite Abelian group of order n, and let r be a positive integer relatively prime to n (i.e., they have no factors in common except 1). Show that the map $\phi_r : G \to G$ defined by $\phi_r(a) = a^r$ is an isomorphism of G onto itself (an automorphism). Deduce that the equation $x^r = a$ always has a unique solution in a finite Abelian group G if r is relatively prime to the order of G.

2.12 Show that the induced operation defined in Definition 2.36 is well defined if G is commutative.

2.13 Prove Theorem 2.38.

2.14 Show for the lattice with coset decomposition in Figure 2.2 that $\Lambda/\Lambda' \cong \mathbb{Z}_2 \times \mathbb{Z}_2$.

2.15 Let G be a cyclic group with generator a and let $\phi : G \to G'$ be a homomorphism onto a group G'. Show that the value of ϕ on every element of G is determined by the value of the homomorphism $\phi(a)$.

2.16 Let G be a group and let $a \in G$. Let $\phi : \mathbb{Z} \to G$ be defined by $\phi(n) = a^n$. Show that ϕ is a homomorphism. Describe the image of ϕ in G.

2.17 Show that if G, G', and G'' are groups and $\phi : G \to G'$ and $\psi : G' \to G''$ are homomorphisms, then the composite function $\psi \circ \phi : G \to G''$ is a homomorphism.

2.18 Consider the set $S = \{0, 1, 2, 3\}$ with the operations

+	0	1	2	3
0	0	1	2	3
1	1	2	3	0
2	2	3	0	1
3	3	0	1	2

$\cdot$	0	1	2	3
0	0	0	0	0
1	0	1	2	3
2	0	2	3	1
3	0	3	1	2

Is this a field? If not, why not?

2.19 Construct the addition and multiplication tables for $\langle \mathbb{Z}_4, +, \cdot \rangle$ and compare to the tables in equation (2.4). Does $\langle \mathbb{Z}_4, +, \cdot \rangle$ form a field?

2.20 Use the representation of $GF(4)$ in (2.4) to solve the following pair of equations:

$$2x + y = 3$$

$$x + 2y = 3.$$

2.21 Show that the vectors in a basis must be linearly independent.

2.22 Let $G = \{\mathbf{v}_1, \mathbf{v}_2, \ldots, \mathbf{v}_k\}$ be a basis for a vector space V. Show that for every vector $\mathbf{v} \in V$, there is a *unique* representation for $\mathbf{v}$ as a linear combination of the vectors in G.

2.23 Show that if $\mathbf{u}$ is orthogonal to every basis vector for W, then $\mathbf{u} \perp W$.

2.24 Let V be a vector space, and let $W \subset V$ be a subspace. The dual space $W^\perp$ of W is the set of vectors in V which are orthogonal to every vector in W. Show that the dual space $W^\perp$ is a subspace of V.

2.25 Show that the set of binary polynomials (i.e., polynomials with binary coefficients, with operations in $GF(2)$) with degree less than r forms a vector space over $GF(2)$ with dimension r.

2.26 What is the dimension of the vector space spanned by the vectors

$$\{(1, 1, 0, 1, 0, 1), (0, 1, 0, 1, 1, 1), (1, 1, 0, 0, 1, 1), (0, 1, 1, 1, 0, 1), (1, 0, 0, 0, 0, 0)\}$$

over $GF(2)$?

2.27 Find a basis for the dual space to the vector space spanned by

$$\{(1, 1, 1, 0, 0), (0, 1, 1, 1, 0), (0, 0, 1, 1, 1)\}.$$

2.28 Let $S = \{\mathbf{v}_1, \mathbf{v}_2, \ldots, \mathbf{v}_n\}$ be an arbitrary basis for the vector space V. Let $\mathbf{v}$ be an arbitrary vector in V; it may be expressed as the linear combination

$$\mathbf{v} = a_1 \mathbf{v}_1 + a_2 \mathbf{v}_2 + \cdots + a_n \mathbf{v}_n.$$

Develop an expression for computing the coefficients $\{a_i\}$ in this representation.

2.29 Is it true that if $\mathbf{x}, \mathbf{y}$ and $\mathbf{z}$ are linearly independent vectors over $GF(q)$ then so also are $\mathbf{x} + \mathbf{y}$, $\mathbf{y} + \mathbf{z}$ and $\mathbf{z} + \mathbf{x}$?

2.30 Let V be a vector space and let $\mathbf{v}_1, \mathbf{v}_2, \ldots, \mathbf{v}_k \in V$. Show that span($\{\mathbf{v}_1, \mathbf{v}_2, \ldots, \mathbf{v}_k\}$) is a vector space.

2.31 Let U and V be linear subspaces of a vector space S. Show that the intersection $U \cap V$ is also a subspace of S.

2.32 Let $G = \langle \mathbb{Z}, + \rangle$ and let $\mathcal{G} = \langle \mathbb{Z}_n, + \rangle$. Let $\phi : G \to \mathcal{G}$ be defined by $\phi(a) = a \bmod n$. Show that $\phi(a + b) = \phi(a) + \phi(b)$.

2.33 In this exercise, let $\mathbf{x} \cdot \mathbf{y}$ denote the inner product *over the real numbers*. Let $\mathbf{x}$ and $\mathbf{y}$ be vectors of length n with elements from the set $\{-1, 1\}$. Show that $d_H(\mathbf{x}, \mathbf{y}) = \frac{n - \mathbf{x} \cdot \mathbf{y}}{2}$.

2.6 References

Group theory is presented in a variety of books; see, for example, [42] or [144]. Our summary of linear algebra was drawn from [45, 483] and [319]. Some of the exercises were drawn from [483] and [144].

Chapter 3

Linear Block Codes

3.1 Basic Definitions

Consider a source that produces symbols from an alphabet $\mathcal{A}$ having q symbols, where $\mathcal{A}$ forms a field. We refer to a tuple $(c_0, c_1, \ldots, c_{n-1}) \in \mathcal{A}^n$ with n elements as an n-vector or an n-tuple.

Definition 3.1 An (n, k) **block code** C over an alphabet of q symbols is a set of q^k n-vectors called **codewords** or **code vectors**. Associated with the code is an **encoder** which maps a **message**, a k-tuple $\mathbf{m} \in \mathcal{A}^k$, to its associated codeword. $\qquad\square$

For a block code to be useful for error correction purposes, there should be a one-to-one correspondence between a message $\mathbf{m}$ and its codeword $\mathbf{c}$. However, for a given code C, there may be more than one possible way of mapping messages to codewords.

A block code can be represented as an exhaustive list, but for large k this would be prohibitively complex to store and decode. The complexity can be reduced by imposing some sort of mathematical structure on the code. The most common requirement is linearity.

Definition 3.2 A block code C over a field $\mathbb{F}_q$ of q symbols of length n and q^k codewords is a q-ary **linear** (n, k) code if and only if its q^k codewords form a k-dimensional vector subspace of the vector space of all the n-tuples $\mathbb{F}_q^n$. The number n is said to be the **length** of the code and the number k is the **dimension** of the code. The **rate** of the code is $R = k/n$. $\qquad\square$

In some literature, an (n, k) linear code is denoted using square brackets, $[n, k]$. A linear code may also be designated as $(n, k, d_{\min})$, where $d_{\min}$ is the minimum distance of the code (as discussed below).

For a linear code, the sum of any two codewords is also a codeword. More generally, any linear combination of codewords is a codeword.

Definition 3.3 The **Hamming weight** wt$(\mathbf{c})$ of a codeword $\mathbf{c}$ is the number of nonzero components of the codeword. The minimum weight $w_{\min}$ of a code C is the smallest Hamming weight of any nonzero codeword: $w_{\min} = \min_{\mathbf{c} \in C, \mathbf{c} \neq 0} \text{wt}(\mathbf{c})$. $\qquad\square$

Recall from Definition 1.11 that the minimum distance is the smallest Hamming distance between any two codewords of the code.

Theorem 3.4 *For a linear code C, the minimum distance $d_{\min}$ satisfies $d_{\min} = w_{\min}$. That is, the minimum distance of a linear block code is equal to the minimum weight of its nonzero codewords.*

Proof The result relies on the fact that linear combinations of codewords are codewords. If $\mathbf{c}_i$ and $\mathbf{c}_j$ are codewords, then so is $\mathbf{c}_i - \mathbf{c}_j$. The distance calculation can then be "translated to the origin":

$$d_{\min} = \min_{\mathbf{c}_i, \mathbf{c}_j \in C, \mathbf{c}_i \neq \mathbf{c}_j} d_H(\mathbf{c}_i, \mathbf{c}_j) = \min_{\mathbf{c}_i, \mathbf{c}_j \in C, \mathbf{c}_i \neq \mathbf{c}_j} d_H(\mathbf{c}_i - \mathbf{c}_j, \mathbf{c}_j - \mathbf{c}_j) = \min_{\mathbf{c} \in C, \mathbf{c} \neq 0} w(\mathbf{c}).$$
$\qquad\square$

An (n, k) code with minimum distance $d_{\min}$ is sometimes denoted as an $(n, k, d_{\min})$ code.

As described in Section 1.8.1, the random error correcting capability of a code with minimum distance $d_{\min}$ is $t = \lfloor (d_{\min} - 1)/2 \rfloor$.

Error Correction Coding: Mathematical Methods and Algorithms, Second Edition. Todd K. Moon
© 2021 John Wiley & Sons, Inc. Published 2021 by John Wiley & Sons, Inc.
Companion website: www.wiley.com/go/Moon/ErrorCorrectionCoding

3.2   The Generator Matrix Description of Linear Block Codes

Since a linear block code C is a k-dimensional vector space, there exist k linearly independent vectors which we designate as $\mathbf{g}_0, \mathbf{g}_1, \ldots, \mathbf{g}_{k-1}$ such that every codeword $\mathbf{c}$ in C can be represented as a linear combination of these vectors,

$$\mathbf{c} = m_0\mathbf{g}_0 + m_1\mathbf{g}_1 + \cdots + m_{k-1}\mathbf{g}_{k-1}, \tag{3.1}$$

where $m_i \in \mathbb{F}_q$. (For binary codes, all arithmetic in (3.1) is done modulo 2; for codes of $\mathbb{F}_q$, the arithmetic is done in $\mathbb{F}_q$.) Thinking of the $\mathbf{g}_i$ as row vectors[1] and stacking up, we form the $k \times n$ matrix G,

$$G = \begin{bmatrix} \mathbf{g}_0 \\ \mathbf{g}_1 \\ \vdots \\ \mathbf{g}_{k-1} \end{bmatrix}.$$

Let

$$\mathbf{m} = \begin{bmatrix} m_0 & m_1 & \cdots & m_{k-1} \end{bmatrix}.$$

Then (3.1) can be written as

$$\mathbf{c} = \mathbf{m}G, \tag{3.2}$$

and every codeword $\mathbf{c} \in C$ has such a representation for some vector $\mathbf{m}$. Since the rows of G generate (or span) the (n, k) linear code C, G is called a **generator matrix** for C. Equation (3.2) can be thought of as an encoding operation for the code C. Representing the code thus requires storing only k vectors of length n (rather than the q^k vectors that would be required to store all codewords of a nonlinear code).

Note that the representation of the code provided by G is not unique. From a given generator G, another generator G' can be obtained by performing row operations (nonzero linear combinations of the rows). Then an encoding operation defined by $\mathbf{c} = \mathbf{m}G'$ maps the message $\mathbf{m}$ to a codeword in C, but it is not necessarily the same codeword that would be obtained using the generator G.

Example 3.5   The $(7, 4)$ Hamming code of Section 1.9 has the generator matrix

$$G = \begin{bmatrix} 1 & 1 & 0 & 1 & 0 & 0 & 0 \\ 0 & 1 & 1 & 0 & 1 & 0 & 0 \\ 0 & 0 & 1 & 1 & 0 & 1 & 0 \\ 0 & 0 & 0 & 1 & 1 & 0 & 1 \end{bmatrix}. \tag{3.3}$$

To encode the message $\mathbf{m} = \begin{bmatrix} 1 & 0 & 0 & 1 \end{bmatrix}$, add the first and fourth rows of G (modulo 2) to obtain

$$\mathbf{c} = \begin{bmatrix} 1 & 1 & 0 & 0 & 1 & 0 & 1 \end{bmatrix}.$$

Another generator is obtained by replacing the first row of G with the sum of the first two rows of G:

$$G' = \begin{bmatrix} 1 & 0 & 1 & 1 & 1 & 0 & 0 \\ 0 & 1 & 1 & 0 & 1 & 0 & 0 \\ 0 & 0 & 1 & 1 & 0 & 1 & 0 \\ 0 & 0 & 0 & 1 & 1 & 0 & 1 \end{bmatrix}.$$

For $\mathbf{m}$ the corresponding codeword is

$$\mathbf{c}' = \mathbf{m}G' = \begin{bmatrix} 1 & 0 & 1 & 0 & 0 & 0 & 1 \end{bmatrix}.$$

This is a different codeword than $\mathbf{c}$, but is still a codeword in C.   □

---

[1] Most signal processing and communication work employs column vectors by convention. However, a venerable tradition in coding theory has employed row vectors and we adhere to that through most of the book.

Definition 3.6 Let C be an (n, k) block code (not necessarily linear). An encoder is **systematic** if the message symbols $m_0, m_1, \ldots, m_{k-1}$ may be found explicitly and unchanged in the codeword. That is, there are coordinates $i_0, i_1, \ldots, i_{k-1}$ (which are most frequently sequential, $i_0, i_0 + 1, \ldots, i_0 + k - 1$) such that $c_{i_0} = m_0, c_{i_1} = m_1, \ldots, c_{i_{k-1}} = m_{k-1}$.

For a linear code, the generator for a systematic encoder is called a *systematic generator*. $\quad\square$

It should be emphasized that being systematic is a property of the encoder and not a property of the code. For a linear block code, the encoding operation represented by G is systematic if an identity matrix can be identified among the rows of G. Neither the generator G nor G' of Example 3.5 are systematic.

Frequently, a systematic generator is written in the form

$$
G = \begin{bmatrix} P & I_k \end{bmatrix} = \begin{bmatrix}
p_{0,0} & p_{0,1} & \cdots & p_{0,n-k-1} & 1 & 0 & 0 & \cdots & 0 \\
p_{1,0} & p_{1,1} & \cdots & p_{1,n-k-1} & 0 & 1 & 0 & \cdots & 0 \\
p_{2,0} & p_{2,1} & \cdots & p_{2,n-k-1} & 0 & 0 & 1 & \cdots & 0 \\
\vdots & \vdots & & \vdots & & & & & \vdots \\
p_{k-1,0} & p_{k-1,1} & \cdots & p_{k-1,n-k-1} & 0 & 0 & 0 & \cdots & 1
\end{bmatrix}, \tag{3.4}
$$

where I_k is the $k \times k$ identity matrix and P is a $k \times (n - k)$ matrix which generates *parity* symbols. The encoding operation is

$$
\mathbf{c} = \mathbf{m} \begin{bmatrix} P & I_k \end{bmatrix} = \begin{bmatrix} \mathbf{m}P & \mathbf{m} \end{bmatrix} .n.
$$

The codeword is divided into two parts: the part $\mathbf{m}$ consists of the message symbols, and the part $\mathbf{m}P$ consists of the **parity check symbols**.

Performing elementary row operations (replacing a row with linear combinations of some rows) does not change the row span, so that the same code is produced. If two columns of a generator are interchanged, then the corresponding positions of the code are changed, but the distance structure of the code is preserved.

Definition 3.7 Two linear codes which are the same except for a permutation of the components of the code are said to be **equivalent** codes. $\quad\square$

Let G and G' be generator matrices of equivalent codes. Then G and G' are related by the following operations:

1. Column permutations,
2. Elementary row operations.

Given an arbitrary generator G, it is possible to put it into the form (3.4) by performing Gaussian elimination with pivoting.

Example 3.8 For G of (3.3), an equivalent generator in systematic form is

$$
G'' = \begin{bmatrix}
1 & 1 & 0 & 1 & 0 & 0 & 0 \\
0 & 1 & 1 & 0 & 1 & 0 & 0 \\
1 & 1 & 1 & 0 & 0 & 1 & 0 \\
1 & 0 & 1 & 0 & 0 & 0 & 1
\end{bmatrix}. \tag{3.5}
$$

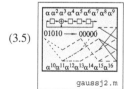
gaussj2.m

For the Hamming code with this generator, let the message be $\mathbf{m} = [m_0, m_1, m_2, m_3]$ and let the corresponding codeword be $\mathbf{c} = [c_0, c_1, \ldots, c_6]$. Then the parity bits are obtained by

$$c_0 = m_0 + m_2 + m_3$$

$$c_1 = m_0 + m_1 + m_2$$

$$c_2 = m_1 + m_2 + m_3$$

and the systematically encoded bits are $c_3 = m_0$, $c_4 = m_1$, $c_5 = m_2$ and $c_6 = m_3$.   □

3.2.1 Rudimentary Implementation

Implementing encoding operations for binary codes is straightforward, since the multiplication operation corresponds to the `and` operation and the addition operation corresponds to the `exclusive-or` operation. For software implementations, encoding is accomplished by straightforward matrix/vector multiplication. This can be greatly accelerated for binary codes by packing several bits into a single word (e.g., 32 bits in an `unsigned int` of 4 bytes). The multiplication is then accomplished using the bit `exclusive-or` operation of the language (e.g., the `^` operator of C). Addition must be accomplished by looping through the bits, or by precomputing bit sums and storing them in a table, where they can be immediately looked up.

3.3 The Parity Check Matrix and Dual Codes

Since a linear code C is a k-dimensional vector subspace of $\mathbb{F}_q^n$, by Theorem 2.64 there must be a dual space to C of dimension $n - k$.

Definition 3.9 The dual space to an (n, k) code C of dimension k is the $(n, n - k)$ **dual code** of C, denoted by $C^{\perp}$. A code C such that $C = C^{\perp}$ is called a **self-dual code**.   □

As a vector space, $C^{\perp}$ has a basis which we denote by $\{\mathbf{h}_0, \mathbf{h}_1, \ldots, \mathbf{h}_{n-k-1}\}$. We form a matrix H using these basis vectors as rows:

$$H = \begin{bmatrix} \mathbf{h}_0 \\ \mathbf{h}_1 \\ \vdots \\ \mathbf{h}_{n-k-1} \end{bmatrix}.$$

This matrix is known as the **parity check matrix** for the code C. The generator matrix and the parity check matrix for a code satisfy

$$\boxed{GH^T = \mathbf{0}.}$$

The parity check matrix has the following important property:

Theorem 3.10 *Let C be an (n, k) linear code over $\mathbb{F}_q$ and let H be a parity check matrix for C. A vector $\mathbf{v} \in \mathbb{F}_q^n$ is a codeword if and only if*

$$\mathbf{v}H^T = \mathbf{0}.$$

That is, the codewords in C lie in the (left) nullspace of H.

(Sometimes additional linearly dependent rows are included in H, but the same result still holds.)

Proof Let $\mathbf{c} \in C$. By the definition of the dual code, $\mathbf{h} \cdot \mathbf{c} = \mathbf{0}$ for all $\mathbf{h} \in C^{\perp}$. Any row vector $\mathbf{h} \in C^{\perp}$ can be written as $\mathbf{h} = \mathbf{x}H$ for some vector $\mathbf{x}$. Since $\mathbf{x}$ is arbitrary, and in fact can select individual rows of H, we must have $\mathbf{ch}_i^T = 0$ for $i = 0, 1, \ldots, n - k - 1$. Hence $\mathbf{c}H^T = \mathbf{0}$.

Conversely, suppose that $\mathbf{v}H^T = 0$. Then $\mathbf{v}\mathbf{h}_i^T = 0$ for $i = 0, 1, \ldots, n-k-1$, so that $\mathbf{v}$ is orthogonal to the basis of the dual code, and hence orthogonal to the dual code itself. Hence, $\mathbf{v}$ must be in the code C. □

When G is in systematic form (3.4), a parity check matrix is readily determined:

$$H = \begin{bmatrix} I_{n-k} & -P^T \end{bmatrix}. \tag{3.6}$$

(For the field $\mathbb{F}_2$, $-1 = 1$, since 1 is its own additive inverse.) Frequently, a parity check matrix for a code is obtained by finding a generator matrix in systematic form and employing (3.6).

Example 3.11 For the systematic generator G'' of (3.5), a parity check matrix is

$$H = \begin{bmatrix} 1 & 0 & 0 & 1 & 0 & 1 & 1 \\ 0 & 1 & 0 & 1 & 1 & 1 & 0 \\ 0 & 0 & 1 & 0 & 1 & 1 & 1 \end{bmatrix}. \tag{3.7}$$

It can be verified that $G''H^T = \mathbf{0}$. Furthermore, even though G is not in systematic form, it still generates the same code so that $GH^T = \mathbf{0}$. H is a generator for a $(7,3)$ code, the dual code to the $(7,4)$ Hamming code. □

The condition $\mathbf{c}H^T = \mathbf{0}$ imposes linear constraints among the bits of $\mathbf{c}$ called the **parity check equations**.

Example 3.12 The parity check matrix of (3.7) gives rise to the equations

$$c_0 + c_3 + c_5 + c_6 = 0$$
$$c_1 + c_3 + c_4 + c_5 = 0$$
$$c_2 + c_4 + c_5 + c_6 = 0$$

or, equivalently, some equations for the parity symbols are

$$c_0 = c_3 + c_5 + c_6$$
$$c_1 = c_3 + c_4 + c_5$$
$$c_2 = c_4 + c_5 + c_6.$$

□

A parity check matrix for a code (whether systematic or not) provides information about the minimum distance of the code.

Theorem 3.13 *Let a linear block code C have a parity check matrix H. The minimum distance $d_{\min}$ of C is equal to the smallest positive number of columns of H which are linearly dependent. That is, all combinations of $d_{\min} - 1$ or fewer columns are linearly independent, so there is some set of $d_{\min}$ columns which are linearly dependent.*

Proof Let the columns of H be designated as $\mathbf{h}_0, \mathbf{h}_1, \ldots, \mathbf{h}_{n-1}$. Then since $\mathbf{c}H^T = \mathbf{0}$ for any codeword $\mathbf{c}$, we have

$$\mathbf{0} = c_0\mathbf{h}_0 + c_1\mathbf{h}_1 + \cdots + c_{n-1}\mathbf{h}_{n-1},$$

that is, a linear combination of columns of H. Let $\mathbf{c}$ be the codeword of smallest weight, $w = \text{wt}(\mathbf{c}) = d_{\min}$, with nonzero positions only at indices $i_1, i_2, \ldots, i_w$. Then

$$c_{i_1}\mathbf{h}_{i_1} + c_{i_2}\mathbf{h}_{i_2} + \cdots + c_{i_w}\mathbf{h}_{i_w} = 0.$$

Clearly, the columns of H corresponding to the elements of $\mathbf{c}$ are linearly dependent.

On the other hand, if there were a linearly dependent set of $u < w$ columns of H, then there would be a codeword of weight u. □

Example 3.14   For the parity check matrix H of (3.7), the parity check condition is

$$\mathbf{c}H^T = \begin{bmatrix} c_0, c_1, c_2, c_3, c_4, c_5, c_6 \end{bmatrix} \begin{bmatrix} 1 & 0 & 0 \\ 0 & 1 & 0 \\ 0 & 0 & 1 \\ 1 & 1 & 0 \\ 0 & 1 & 1 \\ 1 & 1 & 1 \\ 1 & 0 & 1 \end{bmatrix}$$

$$= c_0[1,0,0] + c_1[0,1,0] + c_2[0,0,1] + c_3[1,1,0] + c_4[0,1,1] + c_5[1,1,1] + c_6[1,0,1].$$

The first, second, and fourth rows of H^T are linearly dependent, and no fewer rows of H^T are linearly dependent. □

3.3.1   Some Simple Bounds on Block Codes

Theorem 3.13 leads to a relationship between $d_{\min}$, n, and k:

Theorem 3.15 *The **Singleton bound**. The minimum distance for an (n,k) linear code is bounded by*

$$d_{\min} \leq n - k + 1. \tag{3.8}$$

Note: Although this bound is proved here for linear codes, it is also true for nonlinear codes. (See [292].)

Proof   An (n,k) linear code has a parity check matrix with $n-k$ linearly independent rows. Since the row rank of a matrix is equal to its column rank, $rank(H) = n-k$. Any collection of $n-k+1$ columns must therefore be linearly dependent. Thus, by Theorem 3.13, the minimum distance cannot be larger than $n-k+1$. □

A code for which $d_{\min} = n - k + 1$ is called a **maximum distance separable** (MDS) code.

Thinking geometrically, around each code point is a cloud of points corresponding to non-codewords. (See Figure 1.17.) For a q-ary code, there are $(q-1)n$ vectors at a Hamming distance 1 away from a codeword, $(q-1)^2 \binom{n}{2}$ vectors at a Hamming distance 2 away from a codeword and, in general, $(q-1)^l \binom{n}{l}$ vectors at a Hamming distance l from a codeword.

Example 3.16   Let C be a code of length $n = 4$ over $GF(3)$, so $q = 3$. Then the vectors at a Hamming distance of 1 from the $[0,0,0,0]$ codeword are

$$[1,0,0,0], [0,1,0,0], [0,0,1,0], [0,0,0,1]$$

$$[2,0,0,0], [0,2,0,0], [0,0,2,0], [0,0,0,2].$$
□

The vectors at Hamming distances $\leq t$ away from a codeword form a "sphere" called the **Hamming sphere** of radius t. The number of vectors in a Hamming sphere up to radius t for a code of length n over an alphabet of q symbols is denoted $V_q(n,t)$, where

$$V_q(n,t) = \sum_{j=0}^{t} \binom{n}{j} (q-1)^j. \tag{3.9}$$

The bounded distance decoding sphere of a codeword is the Hamming sphere of radius $t = \lfloor (d_{\min} - 1)/2 \rfloor$ around the codeword. Equivalently, a code whose random error correction capability is t must have a minimum distance between codewords satisfying $d_{\min} \geq 2t + 1$.

The **redundancy** of a code is essentially the number of parity symbols in a codeword. More precisely we have

$$r = n - \log_q M,$$

where M is the number of codewords. For a linear code we have $M = q^k$, so $r = n - k$.

Theorem 3.17 (The Hamming Bound) *A t-random error correcting q-ary code C must have redundancy r satisfying*

$$r \geq \log_q V_q(n, t).$$

Proof Each of M spheres in C has radius t. The spheres do not overlap, or else it would not be possible to decode t errors. The total number of points enclosed by the spheres must be $\leq q^n$. We must have

$$M V_q(n, t) \leq q^n$$

so

$$q^n / M \geq V_q(n, t),$$

from which the result follows by taking $\log_q$ of both sides. $\square$

A code satisfying the Hamming bound with equality is said to be a **perfect code.** Actually, being perfect codes does not mean the codes are the best possible codes; it is simply a designation regarding how points fall in the Hamming spheres. The set of perfect codes is actually quite limited. It has been proved (see [292]) that the entire set of perfect codes is:

1. The set of all n-tuples, with minimum distance $= 1$ and $t = 0$.

2. Odd-length binary repetition codes.

3. Binary and nonbinary Hamming codes (linear) or other nonlinear codes with equivalent parameters.

4. The binary $(23, 12, 7)$ Golay code G_{23}.

5. The ternary (i.e., over $GF(3)$) $(11, 6, 5)$ code G_{11} and the $(23, 11, 5)$ code G_{23}. These codes are discussed in Chapter 8.

3.4 Error Detection and Correction Over Hard-Output Channels

Definition 3.18 Let $\mathbf{r}$ be an n-vector over $\mathbb{F}_q$ and let H be a parity check matrix for a code C. The vector

$$\boxed{\mathbf{s} = \mathbf{r}H^T} \tag{3.10}$$

is called the **syndrome** of $\mathbf{r}$. $\square$

By Theorem 3.10, $\mathbf{s} = \mathbf{0}$ if and only if $\mathbf{r}$ is a codeword of C. In medical terminology, a syndrome is a pattern of symptoms that aids in diagnosis; here $\mathbf{s}$ aids in diagnosing if $\mathbf{r}$ is a codeword or has been corrupted by noise. As we will see, it also aids in determining what the error is.

3.4.1 Error Detection

The syndrome can be used as an *error detection* scheme. Suppose that a codeword $\mathbf{c}$ in a binary linear block code C over $\mathbb{F}_q$ is transmitted through a hard channel (e.g., a binary code over a BSC) and that the n-vector $\mathbf{r}$ is received. We can write

$$\mathbf{r} = \mathbf{c} + \mathbf{e},$$

where the arithmetic is done in $\mathbb{F}_q$, and where $\mathbf{e}$ is the *error vector*, being 0 in precisely the locations where the channel does not introduce errors. The received vector $\mathbf{r}$ could be any of the vectors in $\mathbb{F}_q^n$, since any error pattern is possible. Let H be a parity check matrix for C. Then the syndrome

$$\mathbf{s} = \mathbf{r}H^T = (\mathbf{c} + \mathbf{e})H^T = \mathbf{e}H^T.$$

From Theorem 3.10, $\mathbf{s} = \mathbf{0}$ if $\mathbf{r}$ is a codeword. However, if $\mathbf{s} \neq \mathbf{0}$, then an error condition has been *detected*: we do not know what the error is, but we do know that an error has occurred. (Some additional perspective to this problem is provided in Box 3.1.)

Box 3.1: Error Correction and Least Squares

The hard-input decoding problem is: Given $\mathbf{r} = \mathbf{m}G + \mathbf{e}$, compute $\mathbf{m}$. Readers familiar with least-squares problems (see, e.g., [319]) will immediately recognize the structural similarity of the decoding problem to least squares. If a least-squares solution were possible, the decoded value could be written as

$$\hat{\mathbf{m}} = \mathbf{r}G^T(GG^T)^{-1},$$

reducing the decoding problem to numerical linear algebra. Why cannot least-squares techniques be employed here? In the first place, it must be recalled that in least squares, the distance function d is induced from an inner product, $d(x, y) = \langle x - y, x - y \rangle^{1/2}$, while in our case the distance function is the Hamming distance — which measures the likelihood — which is not induced from an inner product. The Hamming distance is a function $\mathbb{F}_q^n \times \mathbb{F}_q^n \to \mathbb{N}$, while the inner product is a function $\mathbb{F}_q^n \times \mathbb{F}_q^n \to \mathbb{F}_q$: the codomains of the Hamming distance and the inner product are different.

3.4.2 Error Correction: The Standard Array

Let us now consider one method of decoding linear block codes transmitted through a hard channel using maximum likelihood (ML) decoding. As discussed in Section 1.8.1, ML decoding of a vector $\mathbf{r}$ consists of choosing the codeword $\mathbf{c} \in C$ that is closest to $\mathbf{r}$ in Hamming distance. That is,

$$\hat{\mathbf{c}} = \arg\min_{\mathbf{c} \in C} d_H(\mathbf{c}, \mathbf{r}).$$

Let the set of codewords in the code be $\{\mathbf{c}_0, \mathbf{c}_1, \ldots, \mathbf{c}_{M-1}\}$, where $M = q^k$. Let us take $\mathbf{c}_0 = \mathbf{0}$, the all-zero codeword. Let V_i denote the set of n-vectors which are closer to the codeword $\mathbf{c}_i$ than to any other codeword. (Vectors which are equidistant to more than one codeword are assigned into a set V_i at random.) The sets $\{V_i, i = 0, 1, \ldots, M - 1\}$ partition the space of n-vectors into M disjoint subsets. If $\mathbf{r}$ falls in the set V_i, then, being closer to $\mathbf{c}_i$ than to any other codeword, $\mathbf{r}$ is decoded as $\mathbf{c}_i$. So, decoding can be accomplished if the V_i sets can be found.

The *standard array* is a representation of the partition $\{V_i\}$. It is a two-dimensional array in which the columns of the array represent the V_i. The standard array is built as follows. First, every codeword $\mathbf{c}_i$ belongs in its own set V_i. Writing down the set of codewords thus gives the first row of the array. From the remaining vectors in $\mathbb{F}_q^n$, find the vector $\mathbf{e}_1$ of smallest weight. This must lie in the set V_0, since it is closest to the codeword $\mathbf{c}_0 = \mathbf{0}$. But

$$d_H(\mathbf{e}_1 + \mathbf{c}_i, \mathbf{c}_i) = d_H(\mathbf{e}_1, \mathbf{0}),$$

for each i, so the vector $\mathbf{e}_1 + \mathbf{c}_i$ must also lie in V_i for each i. So $\mathbf{e}_1 + \mathbf{c}_i$ is placed into each V_i. The vectors $\mathbf{e}_1 + \mathbf{c}_i$ are included in their respective columns of the standard array to form the second row of the standard array. The procedure continues, selecting an unused vector of minimal weight and adding it to each codeword to form the next row of the standard array, until all q^n possible vectors have been used in the standard array. In summary:

1. Write down all the codewords of the code C.

2. Select from the remaining unused vectors of $\mathbb{F}_q^n$ one of minimal weight, $\mathbf{e}$. Write $\mathbf{e}$ in the column under the all-zero codeword, then add $\mathbf{e}$ to each codeword in turn, writing the sum in the column under the corresponding codeword.

3. Repeat step 2 until all q^n vectors in $\mathbb{F}_q^n$ have been placed in the standard array.

Example 3.19 For a $(7, 3)$ code, a generator matrix is

$$G = \begin{bmatrix} 0 & 1 & 1 & 1 & 1 & 0 & 0 \\ 1 & 0 & 1 & 1 & 0 & 1 & 0 \\ 1 & 1 & 0 & 1 & 0 & 0 & 1 \end{bmatrix}.$$

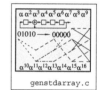

genstdarray.c

The codewords for this code are

| row 1 | 0000000 | 0111100 | 1011010 | 1100110 | 1101001 | 1010101 | 0110011 | 0001111 |

From the remaining 7-tuples, one of minimal weight is selected; take (1000000). The second row is obtained by adding this to each codeword:

row 1	0000000	0111100	1011010	1100110	1101001	1010101	0110011	0001111
row 2	1000000	1111100	0011010	0100110	0101001	0010101	1110011	1001111

Now, proceed until all 2^n vectors are used, selecting an unused vector of minimum weight and adding it to all the codewords. The result is shown in Table 3.1. □

Table 3.1: The Standard Array for a Code

Row 1	0000000	0111100	1011010	1100110	1101001	1010101	**0110011**	0001111
Row 2	1000000	1111100	0011010	0100110	0101001	0010101	1110011	1001111
Row 3	0100000	0011100	1111010	1000110	1001001	1110101	0010011	0101111
Row 4	0010000	0101100	1001010	1110110	1111001	1000101	0100011	0011111
Row 5	0001000	0110100	1010010	1101110	1100001	1011101	0111011	0000111
Row 6	0000100	0111000	1011110	1100010	1101101	1010001	0110111	0001011
Row 7	0000010	0111110	1011000	1100100	1101011	1010111	0110001	0001101
Row 8	0000001	0111101	1011011	1100111	1101000	1010100	0110010	0001110
Row 9	1100000	1011100	0111010	0000110	0001001	0110101	1010011	1101111
Row 10	1010000	1101100	0001010	0110110	0111001	0000101	1100011	1011111
Row 11	0110000	0001100	1101010	1010110	1011001	1100101	0000011	0111111
Row 12	1001000	1110100	0010010	0101110	0100001	0011101	1111011	1000111
Row 13	**0101000**	0010100	1110010	1001110	1000001	1111101	**0011011**	0100111
Row 14	0011000	0100100	1000010	1111110	1110001	1001101	0101011	0010111
Row 15	1000100	1111000	0011110	0100010	0101101	0010001	1110111	1001011
Row 16	1110000	1001100	0101010	0010110	0011001	0100101	1000011	1111111

The horizontal lines in the standard array separate the error patterns of different weights.

We make the following observations:

1. There are q^k codewords (columns) and q^n possible vectors, so there are q^{n-k} rows in the standard array. We observe, therefore, that: an (n,k) code is capable of correcting q^{n-k} different error patterns.

2. The difference (or sum, over $GF(2)$) of any two vectors in the same row of the standard array is a code vector. In a row, the vectors are $\mathbf{c}_i + \mathbf{e}$ and $\mathbf{c}_j + \mathbf{e}$. Then

$$(\mathbf{c}_i + \mathbf{e}) - (\mathbf{c}_j + \mathbf{e}) = \mathbf{c}_i - \mathbf{c}_j,$$

which is a codeword, since linear codes form a vector subspace.

3. No two vectors in the same row of a standard array are identical. Because otherwise we have

$$\mathbf{e} + \mathbf{c}_i = \mathbf{e} + \mathbf{c}_j, \text{ with } i \neq j,$$

which means $\mathbf{c}_i = \mathbf{c}_j$, which is impossible.

4. Every vector appears exactly once in the standard array. We know every vector must appear at least once, by the construction. If a vector appears in both the lth row and the mth row, we must have

$$\mathbf{e}_l + \mathbf{c}_i = \mathbf{e}_m + \mathbf{c}_j$$

for some i and j. Let us take $l < m$. We have

$$\mathbf{e}_m = \mathbf{e}_l + \mathbf{c}_i - \mathbf{c}_j = \mathbf{e}_l + \mathbf{c}_k$$

for some k. This means that $\mathbf{e}_m$ is on the lth row of the array, which is a contradiction.

The rows of the standard array are called **cosets**. Each row is of the form

$$\mathbf{e} + C = \{\mathbf{e} + \mathbf{c} : \mathbf{c} \in C\}.$$

That is, the rows of the standard array are translations of C. These are the same cosets we met in Section 2.2.3 in conjunction with groups.

The vectors in the first column of the standard array are called the **coset leaders**. They represent the error patterns that can be corrected by the code under this decoding strategy. The decoder of Example 3.19 is capable of correcting all errors of weight 1, seven different error patterns of weight 2, and one error pattern of weight 3.

To decode with the standard array, we first locate the received vector $\mathbf{r}$ in the standard array. Then identify

$$\mathbf{r} = \mathbf{e} + \mathbf{c}$$

for a vector $\mathbf{e}$ which is a coset leader (in the left column) and a codeword $\mathbf{c}$ (on the top row). Since we designed the standard array with the smallest error patterns as coset leaders, the error codeword so identified in the standard array is the ML decision. The coset leaders are called the *correctable error patterns*.

Example 3.20   For the code of Example 3.19, let

$$\mathbf{r} = [0,0,1,1,0,1,1]$$

(shown in bold in the standard array) then its coset leader is $\mathbf{e} = [0,1,0,1,0,0,0]$ and the codeword is $\mathbf{c} = [0,1,1,0,\ 0,1,1]$, which corresponds to the message $\mathbf{m} = [0,1,1]$, since the generator is systematic. $\square$

Example 3.21   It is interesting to note that for the standard array of Example 3.19, not all $\binom{7}{2} = 21$ patterns of two errors are correctable. Only seven patterns of two errors are correctable. However, there is one pattern of three errors which is correctable.

The minimum distance for this code is clearly 4, since the minimum weight of the nonzero codewords is 4. Thus, the code is guaranteed to correct only $\lfloor (4-1)/2 \rfloor = 1$ error and, in fact it does correct all patterns of single errors. □

As this decoding example shows, the standard array decoder may have coset leaders with weight higher than the random-error-correcting capability of the code $t = \lfloor (d_{min} - 1)/2 \rfloor$.

This observation motivates the following definition.

Definition 3.22 A **complete error correcting decoder** is a decoder that given the received word $\mathbf{r}$, selects the codeword $\mathbf{c}$ which minimizes $d_H(\mathbf{r}, \mathbf{c})$. That is, it is the ML decoder for the BSC channel. □

If a standard array is used as the decoding mechanism, then complete decoding is achieved. On the other hand, if the rows of the standard array are filled out so that *all* instances of up to t errors appear in the table, and all other rows are left out, then a bounded distance decoder is obtained.

Definition 3.23 A t-error correcting **bounded distance decoder** selects the codeword $\mathbf{c}$ given the received vector $\mathbf{r}$ if $d_H(\mathbf{r}, \mathbf{c}) \leq t$. If no such $\mathbf{c}$ exists, then a **decoder failure** is declared. □

Example 3.24 In Table 3.1, only up to row 8 of the table would be used in a bounded distance decoder, which is capable of correcting up to $t = \lfloor (d_{min} - 1)/2 \rfloor = \lfloor (4-1)/2 \rfloor = 1$ error. A received vector $\mathbf{r}$ appearing in rows 9 through 16 of the standard array would result in a decoding failure. □

A perfect code can be understood in terms of the standard array: it is one for which there are no "leftover" rows: for binary codes all $\binom{n}{t}$ error patterns of weight t and all lighter error patterns appear as coset leaders in the table, with no "leftovers." (For q-ary codes, the number of error patterns is $(q-1)^t \binom{n}{t}$.)

What makes it "perfect" then, is that the bounded distance decoder is also the ML decoder.

The standard array can, in principle, be used to decode any linear block code, but suffers from a major problem: the memory required to represent the standard array quickly become excessive, and decoding requires searching the entire table to find a match for a received vector $\mathbf{r}$. For example, a (256,200) binary code — not a particularly long code by modern standards — would require $2^{256} \approx 1.2 \times 10^{77}$ vectors of length 256 bits to be stored in it and every decoding operation would require on average searching through half of the table.

A first step in reducing the storage and search complexity (which doesn't go far enough) is to use **syndrome decoding**. Let $\mathbf{e} + \mathbf{c}$ be a vector in the standard array. The syndrome for this vector is $\mathbf{s} = (\mathbf{e} + \mathbf{c})H^T = \mathbf{e}H^T$. Furthermore, every vector in the coset has the same syndrome: $(\mathbf{e} + \mathbf{c})H^T = \mathbf{e}H^T$. We therefore only need to store syndromes and their associated error patterns. This table is called the syndrome decoding table. It has q^{n-k} rows but only two columns, so it is smaller than the entire standard array. But is still impractically large in many cases.

With the syndrome decoding table, decoding is done as follows:

1. Compute the syndrome, $\mathbf{s} = \mathbf{r}H^T$.

2. In the syndrome decoding table look up the error pattern $\mathbf{e}$ corresponding to $\mathbf{s}$.

3. Then $\mathbf{c} = \mathbf{r} + \mathbf{e}$.

Example 3.25 For the code of Example 3.19, a parity check matrix is

$$H = \begin{bmatrix} 1 & 0 & 0 & 0 & 0 & 1 & 1 \\ 0 & 1 & 0 & 0 & 1 & 0 & 1 \\ 0 & 0 & 1 & 0 & 1 & 1 & 0 \\ 0 & 0 & 0 & 1 & 1 & 1 & 1 \end{bmatrix}.$$

The syndrome decoding table is

Error	Syndrome
0000000	0000
1000000	1000
0100000	0100
0010000	0010
0001000	0001
0000100	0111
0000010	1011
0000001	1101
1100000	1100
1010000	1010
0110000	0110
1001000	1001
0101000	**0101**
0011000	0011
1000100	1111
1110000	1110

Suppose that $\mathbf{r} = [0, 0, 1, 1, 0, 1, 1]$, as before. The syndrome is

$$\mathbf{s} = \mathbf{r}H^T = \begin{bmatrix} 0 & 1 & 0 & 1 \end{bmatrix},$$

(in bold in the table) which corresponds to the coset leader $\mathbf{e} = \begin{bmatrix} 0 & 1 & 0 & 1 & 0 & 0 & 0 \end{bmatrix}$. The decoded codeword is then

$$\hat{\mathbf{c}} = [0, 0, 1, 1, 0, 1, 1] + [0, 1, 0, 1, 0, 0, 0] = [0, 1, 1, 0, 0, 1, 1],$$

as before.   □

Despite the significant reduction compared to the standard array, the memory requirements for the syndrome decoding table are still very high. It is still infeasible to use this technique for very long codes. Additional algebraic structure must be imposed on the code to enable decoding long codes.

3.5   Weight Distributions of Codes and Their Duals

The weight distribution of a code plays a significant role in calculating probabilities of error.

Definition 3.26 Let C be an (n, k) code. Let A_i denote the number of codewords of weight i in C. Then the set of coefficients $\{A_0, A_1, \ldots, A_n\}$ is called the **weight distribution** for the code.

It is convenient to represent the weight distribution as a polynomial,

$$A(z) = A_0 + A_1 z + A_2 z^2 + \cdots + A_n z^n. \tag{3.11}$$

This polynomial is called the **weight enumerator**.   □

The weight enumerator is (essentially) the z-transform of the weight distribution sequence.

Example 3.27   For the code of Example 3.19, there is one codeword of weight 0. The rest of the codewords all have weight 4. So $A_0 = 1$, $A_4 = 7$. Thus,

$$A(z) = 1 + 7z^4.$$

□

There is a relationship, known as the *MacWilliams identities*, between the weight enumerator of a linear code and its dual. This relationship is of interest because for many codes it is possible to directly characterize the weight distribution of the dual code, from which the weight distribution of the code of interest is obtained by the MacWilliams identity.

Theorem 3.28 (The MacWilliams Identities). *Let C be an (n, k) linear block code over $\mathbb{F}_q$ with weight enumerator $A(z)$ and let $B(z)$ be the weight enumerator of $C^\perp$. Then*

$$B(z) = q^{-k}(1 + (q-1)z)^n A\left(\frac{1-z}{1+(q-1)z}\right), \tag{3.12}$$

or, turning this around algebraically,

$$A(z) = q^{-(n-k)}(1 + (q-1)z)^n B\left(\frac{1-z}{1+(q-1)z}\right). \tag{3.13}$$

For binary codes with $q = 2$, the MacWilliams identities are

$$B(z) = \frac{1}{2^k}(1+z)^n A\left(\frac{1-z}{1+z}\right) \qquad A(z) = \frac{1}{2^{n-k}}(1+z)^n B\left(\frac{1-z}{1+z}\right).$$

The proof of this theorem reveals some techniques that are very useful in coding. We give the proof for codes over $\mathbb{F}_2$, but it is straightforward to extend to larger fields (once you are familiar with them). The proof relies on the **Hadamard transform**. For a function f defined on $\mathbb{F}_2^n$, the Hadamard transform $\hat{f}$ of f is

$$\hat{f}(\mathbf{u}) = \sum_{\mathbf{v} \in \mathbb{F}_2^n} (-1)^{\langle \mathbf{u}, \mathbf{v} \rangle} f(\mathbf{v}) = \sum_{\mathbf{v} \in \mathbb{F}_2^n} (-1)^{\sum_{i=0}^{n-1} u_i v_i} f(\mathbf{v}), \quad \mathbf{u} \in \mathbb{F}_2^n,$$

where the sum is taken over all 2^n n-tuples $\mathbf{v} = (v_0, v_1, \ldots, v_{n-1})$, where each $v_i \in \mathbb{F}_2$. The inverse Hadamard transform is

$$f(\mathbf{u}) = \frac{1}{2^n} \sum_{\mathbf{v} \in \mathbb{F}_2^n} (-1)^{\langle \mathbf{u}, \mathbf{v} \rangle} \hat{f}(\mathbf{v}).$$

Lemma 3.29 *If C is an (n, k) binary linear code and f is a function defined on $\mathbb{F}_2^n$,*

$$\sum_{\mathbf{u} \in C^\perp} f(\mathbf{u}) = \frac{1}{|C|} \sum_{\mathbf{u} \in C} \hat{f}(\mathbf{u}) \quad or \quad \sum_{\mathbf{u} \in C} f(\mathbf{u}) = \frac{1}{|C^\perp|} \sum_{\mathbf{u} \in C^\perp} \hat{f}(\mathbf{u}).$$

Here $|C|$ denotes the number of elements in the code C.

Proof *of lemma.*

$$\sum_{\mathbf{u} \in C} \hat{f}(\mathbf{u}) = \sum_{\mathbf{u} \in C} \sum_{\mathbf{v} \in \mathbb{F}_2^n} (-1)^{\langle \mathbf{u}, \mathbf{v} \rangle} f(\mathbf{v}) = \sum_{\mathbf{v} \in \mathbb{F}_2^n} f(\mathbf{v}) \sum_{\mathbf{u} \in C} (-1)^{\langle \mathbf{u}, \mathbf{v} \rangle}$$

$$= \sum_{\mathbf{v} \in C^\perp} f(\mathbf{v}) \sum_{\mathbf{u} \in C} (-1)^{\langle \mathbf{u}, \mathbf{v} \rangle} + \sum_{\mathbf{v} \in C \setminus \{\mathbf{0}\}} f(\mathbf{v}) \sum_{\mathbf{u} \in C} (-1)^{\langle \mathbf{u}, \mathbf{v} \rangle},$$

where $\mathbb{F}_2^n$ has been partitioned into two disjoint sets, the dual code $C^\perp$ and the nonzero elements of the code, $C \setminus \{\mathbf{0}\}$. In the first sum, $\langle \mathbf{u}, \mathbf{v} \rangle = 0$, so the inner sum is $|C|$. In the second sum, for every $\mathbf{v}$ in the outer sum, $\langle \mathbf{u}, \mathbf{v} \rangle$ takes on the values 0 and 1 equally often as $\mathbf{u}$ varies over C in the inner sum, so the inner sum is 0. Therefore,

$$\sum_{\mathbf{u} \in C} \hat{f}(\mathbf{u}) = \sum_{\mathbf{v} \in C^\perp} f(\mathbf{v}) \sum_{\mathbf{u} \in C} (1) = |C| \sum_{\mathbf{v} \in C^\perp} f(\mathbf{v}).$$

$\square$

Proof of Theorem 3.28. The weight enumerators of the code and its dual can be written as

$$A(z) = \sum_{\mathbf{u} \in C} z^{\text{wt}(\mathbf{u})} \quad B(z) = \sum_{\mathbf{u} \in C^\perp} z^{\text{wt}(\mathbf{u})}.$$

Let $f(\mathbf{u}) = z^{\text{wt}(\mathbf{u})}$. Its Hadamard transform is

$$\hat{f}(\mathbf{u}) = \sum_{\mathbf{v} \in \mathbb{F}_2^n} (-1)^{\langle \mathbf{u}, \mathbf{v} \rangle} z^{\text{wt}(\mathbf{v})}.$$

Writing out the inner product and the weight function explicitly on the vectors $\mathbf{u} = (u_0, u_1, \ldots, u_{n-1})$ and $\mathbf{v} = (v_0, v_1, \ldots, v_{n-1})$, we have

$$\hat{f}(\mathbf{u}) = \sum_{\mathbf{v} \in \mathbb{F}_2^n} (-1)^{\sum_{i=0}^{n-1} u_i v_i} \prod_{i=0}^{n-1} z^{v_i} = \sum_{\mathbf{v} \in \mathbb{F}_2^n} \prod_{i=0}^{n-1} (-1)^{u_i v_i} z^{v_i}.$$

The sum over the 2^n values of $\mathbf{v} \in \mathbb{F}_2^n$ can be expressed as n nested summations over the binary values of the elements of $\mathbf{v}$:

$$\hat{f}(\mathbf{u}) = \sum_{v_0=0}^{1} \sum_{v_1=0}^{1} \cdots \sum_{v_{n-1}=0}^{1} \prod_{i=0}^{n-1} (-1)^{u_i v_i} z^{v_i}.$$

Now the distributive law can be used to pull the product out of the summations,

$$\hat{f}(\mathbf{u}) = \prod_{i=0}^{n-1} \sum_{v_i=0}^{1} (-1)^{u_i v_i} z^{v_i}.$$

If $u_i = 0$, then the inner sum is $1 + z$. If $u_i = 1$, then the inner sum is $1 - z$. Thus,

$$\hat{f}(\mathbf{u}) = (1+z)^{n - \text{wt}(\mathbf{u})} (1-z)^{\text{wt}(\mathbf{u})} = \left(\frac{1-z}{1+z} \right)^{\text{wt}(\mathbf{u})} (1+z)^n. \tag{3.14}$$

The weight enumerator for the dual code is

$$B(z) = \sum_{\mathbf{u} \in C^\perp} z^{\text{wt}(\mathbf{u})} = \sum_{\mathbf{u} \in C^\perp} f(\mathbf{u}) = \frac{1}{|C|} \sum_{\mathbf{u} \in C} \hat{f}(\mathbf{u}) \quad \text{(by Lemma 3.29)}$$

$$= \frac{1}{|C|} \sum_{\mathbf{u} \in C} \left(\frac{1-z}{1+z} \right)^{\text{wt}(\mathbf{u})} (1+z)^n \quad \text{(by (3.14))}$$

$$= \frac{1}{|C|} (1+z)^n \sum_{\mathbf{u} \in C} \left(\frac{1-z}{1+z} \right)^{\text{wt}(\mathbf{u})} = \frac{1}{|C|} (1+z)^n A(z) \Big|_{z=(1-z)/(1+z)}.$$

$\square$

3.6 Binary Hamming Codes and Their Duals

We now formally introduce a family of binary linear block codes, the Hamming codes, and their duals.

Definition 3.30 For any integer $m \geq 2$, a $(2^m - 1, 2^m - m - 1, 3)$ binary code (where the 3 in the designation refers to the minimum distance of the code) may be defined by its $m \times n$ parity check matrix H, which is obtained by writing all possible binary m-tuples, except the all-zero tuple, as the columns of H. For example, simply write out the m-bit binary representation for the numbers from 1 to n in order. Codes equivalent to this construction are called **Hamming codes**. $\square$

For example, when $m = 4$, we get

$$H = \begin{bmatrix} 1 & 0 & 1 & 0 & 1 & 0 & 1 & 0 & 1 & 0 & 1 & 0 & 1 & 0 & 1 \\ 0 & 1 & 1 & 0 & 0 & 1 & 1 & 0 & 0 & 1 & 1 & 0 & 0 & 1 & 1 \\ 0 & 0 & 0 & 1 & 1 & 1 & 1 & 0 & 0 & 0 & 0 & 1 & 1 & 1 & 1 \\ 01 & 02 & 03 & 04 & 05 & 06 & 07 & 18 & 19 & 110 & 111 & 112 & 113 & 114 & 115 \end{bmatrix}$$

as the parity check matrix for a $(15, 11)$ Hamming code. However, it is usually convenient to reorder the columns — resulting in an equivalent code — so that the identity matrix which is interspersed throughout the columns of H appears in the first m columns. We therefore write

$$H = \begin{bmatrix} 1 & 0 & 0 & 0 & 1 & 1 & 0 & 1 & 1 & 0 & 1 & 0 & 1 & 0 & 1 \\ 0 & 1 & 0 & 0 & 1 & 0 & 1 & 1 & 0 & 1 & 1 & 0 & 0 & 1 & 1 \\ 0 & 0 & 1 & 0 & 0 & 1 & 1 & 1 & 0 & 0 & 0 & 1 & 1 & 1 & 1 \\ 01 & 02 & 04 & 18 & 03 & 05 & 06 & 07 & 19 & 110 & 111 & 112 & 113 & 114 & 115 \end{bmatrix}.$$

It is clear from the form of the parity check matrix that for any m there exist three columns which add to zero; for example,

$$\begin{bmatrix} 1 \\ 0 \\ 0 \\ 0 \end{bmatrix}, \quad \begin{bmatrix} 0 \\ 1 \\ 0 \\ 0 \end{bmatrix}, \quad \text{and} \quad \begin{bmatrix} 1 \\ 1 \\ 0 \\ 0 \end{bmatrix},$$

so by Theorem 3.13 the minimum distance is 3; Hamming codes are capable of correcting 1 bit error in the block, or detecting up to 2 bit errors.

An algebraic decoding procedure for Hamming codes was described in Section 1.9.1.

The dual to a $(2^m - 1, 2^m - m - 1)$ Hamming code is a $(2^m - 1, m)$ code called a **simplex code** or a **maximal-length feedback shift register code**.

Example 3.31   The parity check matrix of the $(7, 4)$ Hamming code of (3.7) can be used as a generator of the $(7, 3)$ simplex code with codewords

$$\begin{array}{ll} 0000000 & 1001011 \\ 0101110 & 0010111 \\ 1100101 & 1011100 \\ 0111001 & 1110010 \end{array}$$

Observe that except for the zero codeword, all codewords have weight 4.   □

In general, all of the nonzero codewords of the $(2^m - 1, m)$ simplex code have weight 2^{m-1} (see Exercise 3.12) and every pair of codewords is at a distance 2^{m-1} apart (which is why it is called a simplex). For example, for the $m = 2$ case, the codewords $\{(000), (101), (011), (110)\}$ form a tetrahedron. Thus, the weight enumerator of the dual code is

$$B(z) = 1 + (2^m - 1)z^{2^{m-1}}. \tag{3.15}$$

From the weight enumerator of the dual, we find using (3.13) that the weight distribution of the Hamming code is

$$A(z) = \frac{1}{n + 1}[(1 + z)^n + n(1 - z)(1 - z^2)^{(n-1)/2}]. \tag{3.16}$$

Example 3.32   For the $(7, 4)$ Hamming code, the weight enumerator is

$$A(z) = \frac{1}{8}[(1 + z)^7 + 7(1 - z)(1 - z^2)^3] = 1 + 7z^3 + 7z^4 + z^7. \tag{3.17}$$

□

Example 3.33   For the $(15, 11)$ Hamming code, the weight enumerator is

$$A(z) = \frac{1}{16}((1 + z)^{15} + 15(1 - z)(1 - z^2)^7)$$

$$= 1 + 35z^3 + 105z^4 + 168z^5 + 280z^6 + 435z^7 + 435z^8 + 280z^9 + 168z^{10} \qquad (3.18)$$

$$+ 105z^{11} + 35z^{12} + z^{15}.$$

□

3.7   Performance of Linear Codes

There are several different ways that we can characterize the error detecting and correcting capabilities of codes at the output of the channel decoder [483].

$P(E)$ is the **probability of decoder error**, also known as the **word error rate**. This is the probability that the codeword at the output of the decoder is not the same as the codeword at the input of the encoder.

$P_b(E)$ or P_b is the **probability of bit error**, also known as the **bit error rate.** This is the probability that the decoded message bits (extracted from a decoded codeword of a binary code) are not the same as the encoded message bits. Note that when a decoder error occurs, there may be anywhere from 1 to k message bits in error, depending on what codeword is sent, what codeword was decoded, and the mapping from message bits to codewords.

$P_u(E)$ is the **probability of undetected codeword error**, the probability that errors occurring in a codeword are not detected.

$P_d(E)$ is the **probability of detected codeword error**, the probability that one or more errors occurring in a codeword are detected.

P_{u_b} is the **undetected bit error rate**, the probability that a decoded message bit is in error and is contained within a codeword corrupted by an undetected error.

P_{d_b} is the **detected bit error rate**, the probability that a received message bit is in error and is contained within a codeword corrupted by a detected error.

$P(F)$ is the **probability of decoder failure**, which is the probability that the decoder is unable to decode the received vector (e.g., for a bounded distance decoder) and is able to determine that it cannot decode.

In what follows, bounds and exact expressions for these probabilities will be developed.

3.7.1   Error Detection Performance

All errors with weight up to $d_{\min} - 1$ can be detected, so in computing the probability of detection, only error patterns with weight $d_{\min}$ or higher need be considered. If a codeword $\mathbf{c}$ of a linear code is transmitted and the error pattern $\mathbf{e}$ happens to be a codeword, $\mathbf{e} = \mathbf{c}'$, then the received vector

$$\mathbf{r} = \mathbf{c} + \mathbf{c}'$$

is also a codeword. Hence, the error pattern would be undetectable. Thus, the probability that an error pattern is undetectable is precisely the probability that it is a codeword.

We consider only errors in transmission of binary codes over the BSC with crossover probability p. (Extension to codes with larger alphabets is discussed in [483].) The probability of any particular pattern of j errors in a codeword is $p^j(1 - p)^{n-j}$. Recalling that A_j is the number of codewords in C of weight j, the probability that j errors form a codeword is $A_j p^j(1 - p)^{n-j}$. The probability of undetectable error in a codeword is then

$$P_u(E) = \sum_{j=d_{\min}}^{n} A_j p^j (1-p)^{n-j}. \tag{3.19}$$

The probability of a detected codeword error is the probability that one or more errors occur minus the probability that the error is undetected:

$$P_d(E) = \sum_{j=1}^{n} \binom{n}{j} p^j (1-p)^{n-j} - P_u(E) = 1 - (1-p)^n - P_u(E).$$

Computing these probabilities requires knowing the weight distribution of the code, which is not always available. It is common, therefore, to provide *bounds* on the performance. A bound on $P_u(E)$ can be obtained by observing that the probability of undetected error is bounded above by the probability of occurrence of *any* error patterns of weight greater than or equal to $d_{\min}$. Since there are $\binom{n}{j}$ different ways that j positions out of n can be changed,

$$P_u(E) \leq \sum_{j=d_{\min}}^{n} \binom{n}{j} p^j (1-p)^{n-j}. \tag{3.20}$$

A bound on $P_d(E)$ is simply

$$P_d(E) \leq 1 - (1-p)^n.$$

Example 3.34 For the Hamming $(7,4)$ code with $A(z) = 1 + 7z^3 + 7z^4 + z^7$,

$$P_u(E) = 7p^3(1-p)^4 + 7p^4(1-p)^3 + p^7.$$

If $p = 0.01$ then $P_u(E) \approx 6.79 \times 10^{-6}$. The bound (3.20) gives $P_u(E) < 3.39 \times 10^{-5}$. □

The corresponding bit error rates can be bounded as follows. The undetected bit error rate P_{u_b} can be lower-bounded by assuming the undetected codeword error corresponds to only a single message bit error. P_{u_b} can be upper-bounded by assuming that the undetected codeword error corresponds to all k message bits being in error. Thus,

$$\frac{1}{k} P_u(E) \leq P_{u_b} \leq P_u(E).$$

Similarly for P_{d_b}:

$$\frac{1}{k} P_d(E) \leq P_{d_b} \leq P_d(E).$$

Example 3.35 Figure 3.1 illustrates the detection probabilities for a BSC derived from a BPSK system, with $p = Q(\sqrt{2RE_b/N_0})$, for a Hamming $(15,11)$ code. The weight enumerator is in (3.18). For comparison, the probability of an undetected error for the uncoded system is shown, in which *any* error is undetected, so $P_{u,\text{uncoded}} = 1 - (1 - p_{\text{uncoded}})^k$, where $p_{\text{uncoded}} = Q(\sqrt{2E_b/N_0})$. Note that the upper bound on P_u is not very tight, but the upper bound on P_d is tight — they are indistinguishable on the plot, since they differ by $P_u(E)$, which is orders of magnitude smaller than $P_d(E)$. The uncoded probability of undetected error is much greater than the coded P_u.

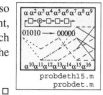

probdeth15.m
probdet.m

□

3.7.2 Error Correction Performance

An error pattern is correctable if and only if it is a coset leader in the standard array for the code, so the probability of correcting an error is the probability that the error is a coset leader. Let α_i denote

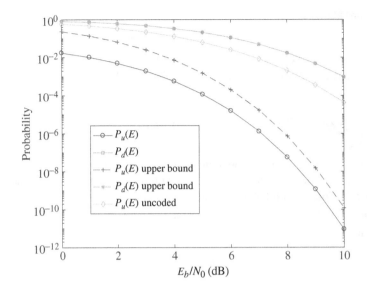

Figure 3.1: Error detection performance for a $(15, 11)$ Hamming code.

the number of coset leaders of weight i. The numbers $\alpha_0, \alpha_1, \ldots, \alpha_n$ are called the **coset leader weight distribution**. Over a BSC with crossover probability p, the probability of j errors forming one of the coset leaders is $\alpha_j p^j (1 - p)^{n-j}$. The probability of a decoding error is thus the probability that the error is *not* one of the coset leaders

$$P(E) = 1 - \sum_{j=0}^{n} \alpha_j p^j (1 - p)^{n-j}.$$

This result applies to any linear code with a *complete decoder*.

Example 3.36   For the standard array in Table 3.1, the coset leader weight distribution is

$$\alpha_0 = 1 \quad \alpha_1 = 7 \quad \alpha_2 = 7 \quad \alpha_3 = 1.$$

If $p = 0.01$, then $P(E) = 0.0014$.   □

Most hard-decision decoders are bounded-distance decoders, selecting the codeword $\mathbf{c}$ which lies within a Hamming distance of $\lfloor (d_{\min} - 1)/2 \rfloor$ of the received vector $\mathbf{r}$. An exact expression for the probability of error for a bounded-distance decoder can be developed as follows. Let P_l^j be the probability that a received word $\mathbf{r}$ is exactly Hamming distance l from a codeword of weight j.

Lemma 3.37   *[[483], p. 249]*

$$P_l^j = \sum_{r=0}^{l} \binom{j}{l-r} \binom{n-j}{r} p^{j-l+2r}(1 - p)^{n-j+l-2r}.$$

Proof   Assume (without loss of generality) that the all-zero codeword was sent. Let $\mathbf{c}$ be a codeword of weight j, where $j \neq 0$. Let the coordinates of $\mathbf{c}$ which are 1 be called the 1-coordinates and let the coordinates of $\mathbf{c}$ which are 0 be called the 0-coordinates. There are thus j 1-coordinates and $n - j$ 0-coordinates of $\mathbf{c}$. Consider now the ways in which the received vector $\mathbf{r}$ can be a Hamming distance l away from $\mathbf{c}$. To differ in l bits, it must differ in an integer r number of 0-coordinates and $l - r$

1-coordinates, where $0 \leq r \leq l$. The number of ways that $\mathbf{r}$ can differ from $\mathbf{c}$ in r of the 0-coordinates is $\binom{n-j}{r}$. The total probability of $\mathbf{r}$ differing from $\mathbf{c}$ in exactly r 0-coordinates is

$$\binom{n-j}{r} p^r (1-p)^{n-j-r}.$$

The number of ways that $\mathbf{r}$ can differ from $\mathbf{c}$ in $l-r$ of the 1-coordinates is $\binom{j}{j-(l-r))} = \binom{j}{l-r}$. Since the all-zero codeword was transmitted, the $l-r$ coordinates of $\mathbf{r}$ must be 0 (there was no crossover in the channel) and the remaining $j-(l-r)$ bits must be 1. The total probability of $\mathbf{r}$ differing from $\mathbf{c}$ in exactly $l-r$ 1-coordinates is

$$\binom{j}{l-r} p^{j-l+r}(1-p)^{l-r}.$$

The probability P_l^j is obtained by multiplying the probabilities on the 0-coordinates and the 1-coordinates (they are independent events since the channel is memoryless) and summing over r:

$$P_l^j = \sum_{r=0}^{l} \binom{n-j}{r} p^r (1-p)^{n-j-r} \binom{j}{l-r} p^{j-l+r}(1-p)^{l-r}$$

$$= \sum_{r=0}^{l} \binom{j}{l-r} \binom{n-j}{r} p^{j-l+2r}(1-p)^{n+l-j-2r}.$$

$\square$

The probability of error is now obtained as follows.

Theorem 3.38 *For a binary (n,k) code with weight distribution $\{A_i\}$, the probability of decoding error for a bounded distance decoder is*

$$P(E) = \sum_{j=d_{\min}}^{n} A_j \sum_{l=0}^{\lfloor (d_{\min}-1)/2 \rfloor} P_l^j. \tag{3.21}$$

Proof Assume that the all-zero codeword was sent. For a particular codeword of weight $j \neq 0$, the probability that the received vector $\mathbf{r}$ falls in the decoding sphere of that codeword is

$$\sum_{l=0}^{\lfloor (d_{\min}-1)/2 \rfloor} P_l^j.$$

Then the result follows by adding up over all possible weights, scaled by the number of codewords of weight j, A_j.

$\square$

The probability of decoder failure for the bounded distance decoder is the probability that the received codeword does not fall into any of the decoding spheres,

$$P(F) = 1 - \underbrace{\sum_{j=0}^{\lfloor (d_{\min}-1)/2 \rfloor} \binom{n}{j} p^j (1-p)^{n-j}}_{\substack{\text{probability of} \\ \text{falling in correct} \\ \text{decoding sphere}}} - \underbrace{P(E)}_{\substack{\text{probability of} \\ \text{falling in the incorrect} \\ \text{decoding sphere}}}.$$

Exact expressions to compute $P_b(E)$ require information relating the weight of the message bits and the weight of the corresponding codewords. This information is summarized in the number β_j, which is the total weight of the message blocks associated with codewords of weight j.

Example 3.39 For the $(7,4)$ Hamming code, $\beta_3 = 12, \beta_4 = 16$, and $\beta_7 = 4$. That is, the total weight of the messages producing codewords of weight 3 is 12; the total weight of messages producing codewords of weight 4 is 16.   □

Modifying (3.21), we obtain

$$P_b(E) = \frac{1}{k} \sum_{j=d_{min}}^{n} \beta_j \sum_{l=0}^{\lfloor (d_{min}-1)/2 \rfloor} P_l^j.$$

(See `hamcode74pe.m`.) Unfortunately, while obtaining values for β_j for small codes is straightforward computationally, appreciably large codes require theoretical expressions which are usually unavailable.

The probability of decoder error can be easily bounded by the probability of *any* error patterns of weight greater than $\lfloor (d_{min} - 1)/2 \rfloor$:

$$P(E) \leq \sum_{j=\lfloor (d_{min}+1)/2 \rfloor}^{n} \binom{n}{j} p^j (1-p)^{n-j}.$$

An easy bound on probability of failure is the same as the bound on this probability of error.

Bounds on the probability of bit error can be obtained as follows. A lower bound is obtained by assuming that a decoder error causes a single bit error out of the k message bits. An upper bound is obtained by assuming that all k message bits are incorrect when the block is incorrectly decoded. This leads to the bounds

$$\frac{1}{k}P(E) \leq P_b(E) \leq P(E).$$

3.7.3 Performance for Soft-Decision Decoding

While all of the decoding in this chapter has been for hard-input decoders, it is interesting to examine the potential performance for soft-decision decoding. Suppose the codewords of an (n, k, d_{min}) code C are modulated to a vector $\mathbf{s}$ using BPSK having energy $E_c = RE_b$ per coded bit and transmitted through an AWGN with variance $\sigma^2 = N_0/2$. The transmitted vector $\mathbf{s}$ is a point in n-dimensional space. In Exercise 1.15, it is shown that the Euclidean distance between two BPSK modulated codewords is related to the Hamming distance between the codewords by

$$d_E = 2\sqrt{E_c d_H}.$$

Suppose that there are K codewords (on average) at a distance d_{min} from a codeword. By the union bound (1.27), the probability of a block decoding error is given by

$$P(E) \approx KQ\left(\frac{d_{E,min}}{2\sigma}\right) = KQ\left(\sqrt{\frac{2Rd_{min}E_b}{N_0}}\right).$$

Neglecting the multiplicity constant K, we see that we achieve essentially comparable performance compared to uncoded transmission when

$$\frac{E_b}{N_0} \text{ for uncoded} = \frac{Rd_{min}E_b}{N_0} \text{ for coded}.$$

The asymptotic coding gain is the factor by which the coded E_b/N_0 can be decreased to obtain equivalent performance. (It is called asymptotic because it applies only as the SNR becomes large enough that the union bound can be regarded as a reasonable approximation.) In this case the asymptotic coding gain is

$$Rd_{min}.$$

Recall that Figure 1.19 illustrated the advantage of soft-input decoding compared with hard-input decoding.

3.8   Erasure Decoding

An erasure is an error in which the error location is *known*, but the value of the error is not. Erasures can arise in several ways. In some receivers the received signal can be examined to see if it falls outside acceptable bounds. If it falls outside the bounds, it is declared as an erasure. (For example, for BPSK signaling, if the received signal is too close to the origin, an erasure might be declared.)

Example 3.40   Another way that an erasure can occur in packet-based transmission is as follows. Suppose that a sequence of codewords $\mathbf{c}_1, \mathbf{c}_2, \ldots, \mathbf{c}_N$ are written into the *rows* of a matrix

c_{10}	c_{11}	c_{12}	$\cdots$	c_{1n-1}
c_{20}	c_{21}	c_{22}	$\cdots$	c_{2n-1}
$\vdots$	$\vdots$	$\vdots$	$\vdots$	$\vdots$
c_{N0}	c_{N1}	c_{N2}	$\cdots$	c_{Nn-1}

then the *columns* are read out, giving the data sequence

$$[c_{10}, c_{20}, \ldots, c_{N0}], [c_{11}, c_{21}, \ldots, c_{N1}], [c_{12}, c_{22}, \ldots, c_{N2}], \ldots, [c_{1n-1}, c_{2n-1}, \ldots, c_{Nn-1}].$$

Suppose that these are now sent as a sequence of n data packets, each of length N, over a channel which is susceptible to packet loss, but where the loss of a packet is known at the receiver (such as the Internet using a protocol that does not guarantee delivery, such as UDP). At the receiver, the packets are written into a matrix in column order — leaving an empty column corresponding to lost packets — then read out in row order. Suppose in this scheme that one of the packets, say the third, is lost in transmission. Then the data in the receiver interleaver matrix would look like

c_{10}	c_{11}	c_{12}	$\cdots$	c_{1n-1}
c_{20}	c_{21}	c_{22}	$\cdots$	c_{2n-1}
$\vdots$	$\vdots$	$\vdots$	$\vdots$	$\vdots$
c_{N0}	c_{N1}	c_{N2}	$\cdots$	c_{Nn-1}

where the gray boxes indicate lost data. While a lost packet results in an entire column of lost data, it represents only one erased symbol from the de-interleaved codewords, a symbol whose location is known.   □

Erasures can also sometimes be dealt with using concatenated coding techniques, where an inner code declares erasures at some symbol positions, which an outer code can then correct.

BOX 3.2: The UDP Protocol [SD1]

UDP — user datagram protocol — is one of the protocols in the TCP/IP protocol suite. The most common protocol, TCP, ensures packet delivery by acknowledging each packet successfully received, retransmitting packets which are garbled or lost in transmission. UDP, on the other hand, is an open-ended protocol which does not guarantee packet delivery. For a variety of reasons, it incurs lower delivery latency and as a result, it is of interest in near real-time communication applications. The application designer must deal with dropped packets using, for example, error correction techniques.

Consider the erasure capability for a code of distance d_{min}. A single erased symbol removed from a code (with no additional errors) leaves a code with a minimum distance at least $d_{min} - 1$. Thus, f erased symbols can be "filled" provided that $f < d_{min}$. For example, a Hamming code with $d_{min} = 3$ can correct up to 2 erasures.

Now suppose that there are both errors and erasures. For a code with $d_{\min}$ experiencing a single erasure, there are still $n-1$ unerased coordinates and the codewords are separated by a distance of at least $d_{\min}-1$. More generally, if there are f erased symbols, then the distance among the remaining digits is at least $d_{\min}-f$. Letting t_f denote the random error decoding distance in the presence of f erasures, we can correct up to

$$t_f = \lfloor (d_{\min} - f - 1)/2 \rfloor$$

errors. If there are f erasures and e errors, they can be corrected provided that

$$2e + f < d_{\min}. \tag{3.22}$$

Since correcting an error requires determination of both the error position and the error value, while filling an erasure requires determination only of the error value, essentially twice the number of erasures can be filled as errors corrected.

3.8.1 Binary Erasure Decoding

We consider now how to simultaneously fill f erasures and correct e errors in a binary code with a given decoding algorithm [[483], p. 229]. In this case, all that is necessary is to determine for each erasure whether the missing value should be a one or a zero. An erasure decoding algorithm for this case can be described as follows:

1. Place zeros in all erased coordinates and decode using the usual decoder for the code. Call the resulting codeword c_0.

2. Place ones in all erased coordinates and decode using the usual decoder for the code. Call the resulting codeword c_1.

3. Find which of c_0 and c_1 is closest to r. This is the output code.

Let us examine why this decoder works. Suppose we have $(2e + f) < d_{\min}$ (so that correct decoding is possible). In assigning 0 to the f erased coordinates, we thereby generated e_0 errors, $e_0 \leq f$, so that the total number of errors to be corrected is $(e_0 + e)$. In assigning 1 to the f erased coordinates, we make e_1 errors, $e_1 \leq f$, so that the total number of errors to be corrected is $(e_1 + e)$. Note that $e_0 + e_1 = f$, so that either e_0 or e_1 is less than or equal to $f/2$. Thus, either

$$2(e + e_0) \leq 2(e + f/2) \quad \text{or} \quad 2(e + e_1) \leq 2(e + f/2),$$

and $2(e + f/2) < d_{\min}$, so that one of the two decodings must be correct.

Erasure decoding for nonbinary codes depends on the particular code structure. For example, decoding of Reed–Solomon codes is discussed in Section 6.7.

3.9 Modifications to Linear Codes

We introduce some minor modifications to linear codes. These are illustrated for some particular examples in Figure 3.2.

Definition 3.41 An (n, k, d) code is **extended** by adding an additional parity coordinate, producing an $(n+1, k, d+1)$ code.   □

Example 3.42 We demonstrate the operations by modifying a $(7, 4, 3)$ Hamming code. A parity check matrix for the $(7, 4, 3)$ Hamming code is

$$H = \begin{bmatrix} 1 & 0 & 0 & 1 & 0 & 1 & 1 \\ 0 & 1 & 0 & 1 & 1 & 1 & 0 \\ 0 & 0 & 1 & 0 & 1 & 1 & 1 \end{bmatrix}.$$

The parity check matrix for an extended Hamming code, with an extra check bit that checks the parity of all the bits, can be written as

$$H = \begin{bmatrix} 1 & 0 & 0 & 1 & 0 & 1 & 1 & 0 \\ 0 & 1 & 0 & 1 & 1 & 1 & 0 & 0 \\ 0 & 0 & 1 & 0 & 1 & 1 & 1 & 0 \\ 1 & 1 & 1 & 1 & 1 & 1 & 1 & 1 \end{bmatrix}.$$

The last row is the overall check bit row. By linear operations, this can be put in equivalent systematic form

$$H = \begin{bmatrix} 1 & 0 & 0 & 0 & 1 & 1 & 0 & 1 \\ 0 & 1 & 0 & 0 & 0 & 1 & 1 & 1 \\ 0 & 0 & 1 & 0 & 1 & 1 & 1 & 0 \\ 0 & 0 & 0 & 1 & 1 & 0 & 1 & 1 \end{bmatrix}$$

with the corresponding generator

$$G = \begin{bmatrix} 1 & 0 & 1 & 1 & 1 & 0 & 0 & 0 \\ 1 & 1 & 1 & 0 & 0 & 1 & 0 & 0 \\ 0 & 1 & 1 & 1 & 0 & 0 & 1 & 0 \\ 1 & 1 & 0 & 1 & 0 & 0 & 0 & 1 \end{bmatrix}.$$

See Figure 3.2. □

Definition 3.43 A code is **punctured** by deleting one of its parity symbols. An (n, k) code becomes an $(n-1, k)$ code. □

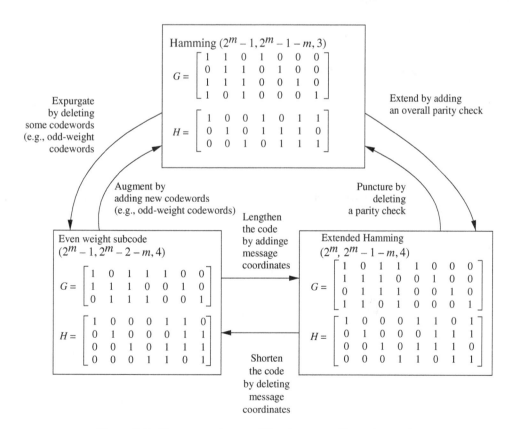

Figure 3.2: Demonstrating modifications on a Hamming code.

Puncturing an extended code can return it to the original code (if the extended symbols are the ones punctured). Puncturing can reduce the weight of each codeword by its weight in the punctured positions. The minimum distance of a code is reduced by puncturing if the minimum weight codeword is punctured in a nonzero position. Puncturing an (n, k, d) code p times can result in a code with minimum distance as small as $d - p$.

Definition 3.44 A code is **expurgated** by deleting some of its codewords. It is possible to expurgate a linear code in such a way that it remains a linear code. The minimum distance of the code may increase.   □

Example 3.45 If all the odd-weight codewords are deleted from the $(7, 4)$ Hamming code, an even-weight subcode is obtained.   □

Definition 3.46 A code is **augmented** by adding new codewords. It may be that the new code is not linear. The minimum distance of the code may decrease.   □

Definition 3.47 A code is **shortened** by deleting a message symbol. This means that a row is removed from the generator matrix (corresponding to that message symbol) and a column is removed from the generator matrix (corresponding to the encoded message symbol). An (n, k) code becomes an $(n - 1, k - 1)$ code.

Shortened cyclic codes are discussed in more detail in Section 4.12.   □

Definition 3.48 A code is **lengthened** by adding a message symbol. This means that a row is added to the generator matrix (for the message symbol) and a column is added to represent the coded message symbol. An (n, k) code becomes an $(n + 1, k + 1)$ code.   □

3.10 Best-Known Linear Block Codes

Tables of the best-known linear block codes are available. An early version appears in [292]. More recent tables can be found at [50].

3.11 Exercises

3.1   Find, by trial and error, a set of four binary codewords of length three such that each word is at least a distance of 2 from every other word.

3.2   Find a set of 16 binary words of length 7 such that each word is at least a distance of 3 from every other word. *Hint*: Hamming code.

3.3   Perhaps the simplest of all codes is the binary parity check code, a $(n, n - 1)$ code, where $k = n - 1$. Given a message vector $\mathbf{m} = (m_0, m_1, \ldots, m_{k-1})$, the codeword is $\mathbf{c} = (m_0, m_1, \ldots, m_{k-1}, b)$, where $b = \sum_{j=0}^{k-1} m_j$ (arithmetic in $GF(2)$) is the *parity bit*. Such a code is called an even parity code, since all codewords have even parity — an even number of 1 bits.

(a)   Determine the minimum distance for this code.

(b)   How many errors can this code correct? How many errors can this code detect?

(c)   Determine a generator matrix for this code.

(d)   Determine a parity check matrix for this code.

   (e) Suppose that bit errors occur independently with probability p_c. The probability that a parity check is satisfied is the probability that an even number of bit errors occur in the received codeword. Verify the following expression for this probability:

$$\sum_{i=0,i\,even}^{n} \binom{n}{i} p_c^i (1-p_c)^{n-i} = \frac{1+(1-2p_c)^n}{2}.$$

3.4   For the $(n, 1)$ repetition code, determine a parity check matrix.

3.5   [483] Let $p = 0.1$ be the probability that any bit in a received vector is incorrect. Compute the probability that the received vector contains undetected errors given the following encoding schemes:

   (a) No code, word length $n = 8$.

   (b) Even parity (see Exercise 3.3), word length $n = 4$.

   (c) Odd parity, word length $n = 9$. (Is this a linear code?)

   (d) Even parity, word length $= n$.

3.6   [272] Let C_1 be an (n_1, k, d_1) binary linear systematic code with generator $G_1 = \begin{bmatrix} P_1 & I_k \end{bmatrix}$. Let C_2 be an (n_2, k, d_2) binary linear systematic code with generator $G_2 = \begin{bmatrix} P_2 & I_k \end{bmatrix}$. Form the parity check matrix for an $(n_1 + n_2, k)$ code as

$$H = \begin{bmatrix} & P_1^T \\ I_{n_1+n_2-k} & I_k \\ & P_2^T \end{bmatrix}.$$

   Show that this code has minimum distance at least $d_1 + d_2$.

3.7   The generator matrix for a code over $GF(2)$ is given by

$$G = \begin{bmatrix} 1 & 1 & 1 & 0 & 1 & 0 \\ 1 & 0 & 0 & 1 & 1 & 1 \\ 0 & 0 & 1 & 0 & 1 & 1 \end{bmatrix}.$$

   Find a generator matrix and parity check matrix for an equivalent systematic code.

3.8   The generator and parity check matrix for a binary code C are given by

$$G = \begin{bmatrix} 1 & 0 & 1 & 0 & 1 & 1 \\ 0 & 1 & 1 & 1 & 0 & 1 \\ 0 & 1 & 1 & 0 & 1 & 0 \end{bmatrix} \quad H = \begin{bmatrix} 1 & 1 & 0 & 1 & 1 & 0 \\ 1 & 0 & 1 & 0 & 1 & 1 \\ 0 & 1 & 0 & 0 & 1 & 1 \end{bmatrix}. \tag{3.23}$$

   This code is small enough that it can be used to demonstrate several concepts from throughout the chapter.

   (a) Verify that H is a parity check matrix for this generator.

   (b) Draw a logic diagram schematic for an implementation of an encoder for the nonsystematic generator G using "and" and "xor" gates.

   (c) Draw a logic diagram schematic for an implementation of a circuit that computes the syndrome.

   (d) List the vectors in the orthogonal complement of the code (that is, the vectors in the dual code $C^\perp$).

   (e) Form the standard array for code C.

(f) Form the syndrome decoding table for C.

(g) How many codewords are there of weight $0, 1, \ldots, 6$ in C? Determine the weight enumerator $A(z)$.

(h) Using the generator matrix in (3.23), find the codeword with $\mathbf{m} = [1, 1, 0]$ as message bits.

(i) Decode the received word $\mathbf{r} = [1, 1, 1, 0, 0, 1]$ using the generator of (3.23).

(j) Determine the weight enumerator for the dual code.

(k) Write down an explicit expression for $P_u(E)$ for this code. Evaluate this when $p = 0.01$.

(l) Write down an explicit expression for $P_d(E)$ for this code. Evaluate this when $p = 0.01$.

(m) Write down an explicit expression for $P(E)$ for this code. Evaluate this when $p = 0.01$.

(n) Write down an explicit expression for $P(E)$ for this code, assuming a bounded distance decoder is used. Evaluate this when $p = 0.01$.

(o) Write down an explicit expression for $P(F)$ for this code. Evaluate this when $p = 0.01$.

(p) Determine the generator G for an extended code, in systematic form.

(q) Determine the generator for a code which has expurgated all codewords of odd weight. Then express it in systematic form.

3.9   [271] Let a binary systematic $(8, 4)$ code have parity check equations

$$c_0 = m_1 + m_2 + m_3$$

$$c_1 = m_0 + m_1 + m_2$$

$$c_2 = m_0 + m_1 + m_3$$

$$c_3 = m_0 + m_2 + m_3.$$

(a) Determine the generator matrix G for this code in systematic form. Also determine the parity check matrix H.

(b) Using Theorem 3.13, show that the minimum distance of this code is 4.

(c) Determine $A(z)$ for this code. Determine $B(z)$.

(d) Show that this is a self-dual code.

3.10 Show that a self-dual code has a generator matrix G which satisfies $GG^T = 0$.

3.11 Given a code with a parity check matrix H, show that the coset with syndrome $\mathbf{s}$ contains a vector of weight w if and only if some linear combination of w columns of H equals $\mathbf{s}$.

3.12 Show that all of the nonzero codewords of the $(2^m - 1, m)$ simplex code have weight 2^{m-1}. *Hint*: Start with $m = 2$ and work by induction.

3.13 Show that (3.13) follows from (3.12).

3.14 Show that (3.16) follows from (3.15) using the MacWilliams identity.

3.15 Let $f(u_1, u_2) = u_1 u_2$, for $u_i \in \mathbb{F}_2$. Determine the Hadamard transform $\hat{f}$ of f.

3.16 The weight enumerator $A(z)$ of (3.11) for a code C is sometimes written as

$$W_A(x, y) = \sum_{i=0}^{n} A_i x^{n-i} y^i.$$

In this problem, consider binary codes, $q = 2$.

(a) Show that $A(z) = W_A(x, y)|_{x=1, y=z}$.

(b) Let $W_B(x, y) = \sum_{i=0}^{n} B_i x^{n-i} y^i$ be the weight enumerator for the code dual to C. Show that the MacWilliams identity can be written as

$$W_B(x, y) = \frac{1}{q^k} W_A(x + y, x - y)$$

or

$$W_A(x, y) = \frac{1}{q^{n-k}} W_B(x + y, x - y). \tag{3.24}$$

(c) In the following subproblems, assume a binary code. Let $x = 1$ in (3.24). We can write

$$\sum_{i=0}^{n} A_i y^i = \frac{1}{2^{n-k}} \sum_{i=0}^{n} B_i (1 + y)^{n-i} (1 - y)^i. \tag{3.25}$$

Set $y = 1$ in this and show that $\sum_{i=0}^{n} \frac{A_i}{2^k} = 1$. Justify this result.

(d) Now differentiate (3.25) with respect to y and set $y = 1$ to show that

$$\sum_{i=1}^{n} \frac{i A_i}{2^k} = \frac{1}{2}(n - B_1).$$

If $B_1 = 0$, this gives the average weight.

(e) Differentiate (3.25) v times with respect to y and set $y = 1$ to show that

$$\sum_{i=v}^{n} \binom{i}{v} \frac{A_i}{2^k} = \frac{1}{2^v} \sum_{i=0}^{v} (-1)^i \binom{n-i}{v-i} B_i.$$

Hint: Define $(x)_+^n = \begin{cases} 0 & n < 0 \\ x^n & n \geq 0 \end{cases}$. We have the following generalization of the product rule for differentiation:

$$\frac{d^v}{dy^v}(y + a)^p (y + b)^q = \sum_{j=0}^{v} \binom{v}{j} \frac{p!}{(p-j)!}(y + a)_+^{p-j} \frac{q!}{(q-(v-j))!}(y + b)_+^{q-(v-j)}.$$

(f) Now set $y = 1$ in (3.24) and write

$$\sum_{i=0}^{n} A_i x^{n-i} = \frac{1}{2^{n-k}} \sum_{i=0}^{n} B_i (x + 1)^{n-i} (x - 1)^i.$$

Differentiate v times with respect to x and set $x = 1$ to show that

$$\sum_{i=0}^{n-v} \binom{n-i}{v} A_i = 2^{k-v} \sum_{i=0}^{v} \binom{n-i}{n-v} B_i, \quad v = 0, 1, \ldots, n. \tag{3.26}$$

3.17 Let C be a binary (n, k) code with weight enumerator $A(z)$ and let $\overline{C}$ be the extended code of length $n + 1$,

$$\overline{C} = \left\{ (c_0, c_1, \ldots, c_n) : (c_0, \ldots, c_{n-1}) \in C, \sum_{i=0}^{n} c_i = 0 \right\}.$$

Determine the weight enumerator for $\overline{C}$.

3.18 [272] Let C be a binary linear code with both even- and odd-weight codewords. Show that the number of even-weight codewords is equal to the number of odd-weight codewords.

3.19 Show that for a binary code, $P_u(E)$ can be written as:

(a) $P_u(E) = (1 - p)^n \left[A\left(\frac{p}{1-p}\right) - 1 \right]$

(b) and $P_u(E) = 2^{k-n} B(1 - 2p) - (1 - p)^n$.

3.20 [483] Find the lower bound on required redundancy for the following codes.

(a) A single-error correcting binary code of length 7.

(b) A single-error correcting binary code of length 15.

(c) A triple-error correcting binary code of length 23.

(d) A triple-error correcting 4-ary code (i.e., $q = 4$) of length 23.

3.21 Show that all odd-length binary repetition codes are perfect.

3.22 Show that Hamming codes achieve the Hamming bound.

3.23 Determine the weight distribution for a binary Hamming code of length 31. Determine the weight distribution of its dual code.

3.24 The parity check matrix for a nonbinary Hamming code of length $n = (q^m - 1)/(q - 1)$ and dimension $k = (q^m - 1)/(q - 1) - m$ with minimum distance 3 can be constructed as follows. For each q-ary m-tuple of the base-q representation of the numbers from 1 to $q^m - 1$, select those for which the first nonzero element is equal to 1. The list of all such m-tuples as columns gives the generator H.

(a) Explain why this gives the specified length n.

(b) Write down a parity check matrix in systematic form for the $(5, 3)$ Hamming code over the field of four elements.

(c) Write down the corresponding generator matrix. *Note*: in this field, every element is its own additive inverse: $1 + 1 = 0$, $2 + 2 = 0$, $3 + 3 = 0$.

3.25 [272] Let G be the generator matrix of an (n, k) binary code C and let no column of G be all zeros. Arrange all the codewords of C as rows of a $2^k \times n$ array.

(a) Show that no column of the array contains only zeros.

(b) Show that each column of the array consists of 2^{k-1} zeros and 2^{k-1} ones.

(c) Show that the set of all codewords with zeros in particular component positions forms a subspace of C. What is the dimension of this subspace?

(d) Show that the minimum distance $d_{\min}$ of this code must satisfy the following inequality, known as the **Plotkin bound**:

$$d_{\min} \le \frac{n2^{k-1}}{2^k - 1}.$$

3.26 [272] Let Γ be the ensemble of *all* the binary systematic linear (n, k) codes.

(a) Prove that a nonzero binary vector $\mathbf{v}$ is contained in exactly $2^{(k-1)(n-k)}$ of the codes in Γ or it is in none of the codes in Γ.

(b) Using the fact that the nonzero n-tuples of weight $d - 1$ or less can be in at most

$$2^{(k-1)(n-k)} \sum_{i=1}^{d-1} \binom{n}{i}$$

(n, k) systematic binary linear codes, show that there exists an (n, k) linear code with minimum distance of at least d if the following bound is satisfied:

$$\sum_{i=1}^{d-1} \binom{n}{i} < 2^{n-k}.$$

(c) Show that there exists an (n, k) binary linear code with minimum distance at least d that satisfies the following inequality:

$$2^{n-k} \le \sum_{i=0}^{d} \binom{n}{i}.$$

This provides a lower bound on the minimum distance attainable with an (n, k) linear code known as the **Gilbert–Varshamov bound**.

3.27 Define a linear $(5, 3)$ code over $GF(4)$ by the generator matrix

$$G = \begin{bmatrix} 1 & 0 & 0 & 1 & 1 \\ 0 & 1 & 0 & 1 & 2 \\ 0 & 0 & 1 & 1 & 3 \end{bmatrix}.$$

    (a) Find the parity check matrix.

    (b) Prove that this is a single-error-correcting code.

    (c) Prove that it is a double-erasure-correcting code.

    (d) Prove that it is a perfect code.

3.28 [271] Let H be the parity check matrix for an (n, k) linear code C. Let C' be the extended code whose parity check matrix H' is formed by

$$H' = \begin{bmatrix} 0 & & & & \\ 0 & & & H & \\ \vdots & & & & \\ 0 & & & & \\ \hline 1 & 1 & 1 & \cdots & 1 \end{bmatrix}.$$

    (a) Show that every codeword of C' has even weight.

    (b) Show that C' can be obtained from C by adding an extra parity bit called the overall parity bit to each codeword.

3.29 The $[\mathbf{u}|\mathbf{u} + \mathbf{v}]$ construction: Let C_i, $i = 1, 2$ be linear binary (n, k_i) block codes with generator matrix G_i and minimum distance d_i. Define the code C by

$$C = |C_1|C_1 + C_2| = \{[\mathbf{u}|\mathbf{u} + \mathbf{v}] : \mathbf{u} \in C_1, \mathbf{v} \in C_2\}.$$

    (a) Show that C has the generator

$$G = \begin{bmatrix} G_1 & G_1 \\ 0 & G_2 \end{bmatrix}.$$

    (b) Show that the minimum distance of C is

$$d_{\min} = \min(2d_1, d_2).$$

3.12 References

The definitions of generator, parity check matrix, distance, and standard arrays are standard; see, for example, [271, 483]. The MacWilliams identity appeared in [291]. Extensions to nonlinear codes appear in [292]. The discussion of probability of error in Section 3.7 is drawn closely from [483]. Our discussion on modifications follows [483], which, in turn, draws from [33]. Our analysis of soft-input decoding was drawn from [26]. Classes of perfect codes are in [444].

Chapter 4

Cyclic Codes, Rings, and Polynomials

4.1 Introduction

We have seen that linear block codes can be corrected using the standard array, but that for long codes the storage and computation time can be prohibitive. Furthermore, we have not yet seen any mechanism by which the generator or parity check matrix can be *designed* to achieve a specified minimum distance or other criteria. In this chapter, we introduce *cyclic codes*, which have additional algebraic structure to make encoding and decoding more efficient. Following the introduction in this chapter, additional algebraic tools and concepts are presented in Chapter 5, which will provide for design specifications and lead to efficient algebraic decoding algorithms.

Cyclic codes are based on polynomial operations. A natural algebraic setting for the operations on polynomials is the algebraic structure of a *ring*.

4.2 Basic Definitions

Given a vector $\mathbf{c} = (c_0, c_1, \ldots, c_{n-2}, c_{n-1}) \in GF(q)^n$, the vector

$$\mathbf{c}' = (c_{n-1}, c_0, c_1, \ldots, c_{n-2})$$

is said to be a *cyclic shift* of $\mathbf{c}$ to the right. A shift by r places to the right produces the vector $(c_{n-r}, c_{n-r+1}, \ldots, c_{n-1}, c_0, c_1, \ldots, c_{n-r-1})$.

Definition 4.1 An (n, k) block code C is said to be **cyclic** if it is linear and if for every codeword $\mathbf{c} = (c_0, c_1, \ldots, c_{n-1})$ in C, its right cyclic shift $\mathbf{c}' = (c_{n-1}, c_0, \ldots, c_{n-2})$ is also in C.[1]   □

Example 4.2 We observed in Section 1.9.2.2 that the Hamming $(7, 4)$ code is cyclic; see the codeword list in (1.35).   □

The operations of shifting and cyclic shifting can be conveniently represented using polynomials. The vector

$$\mathbf{c} = (c_0, c_1, \ldots, c_{n-1})$$

is represented by the polynomial

$$c(x) = c_0 + c_1 x + \cdots + c_{n-1} x^{n-1},$$

using the obvious one-to-one correspondence. We write this correspondence as

$$(c_0, c_1, \ldots, c_{n-1}) \leftrightarrow c_0 + c_1 x + \cdots + c_{n-1} x^{n-1}.$$

A (noncyclic) shift is represented by polynomial multiplication:

$$xc(x) = c_0 x + c_1 x^2 + \cdots + c_{n-1} x^n$$

---

[1] A generalization of cyclic codes is quasi-cyclic codes. These are discussed in Section 16.4.

Error Correction Coding: Mathematical Methods and Algorithms, Second Edition. Todd K. Moon.
© 2021 John Wiley & Sons, Inc. Published 2021 by John Wiley & Sons, Inc.
Companion website: www.wiley.com/go/Moon/ErrorCorrectionCoding

so

$$(0, c_0, c_1, \ldots, c_{n-1}) \leftrightarrow c_0 x + c_1 x^2 + \cdots + c_{n-1} x^n.$$

To represent the *cyclic* shift, we move the coefficient of x^n to the constant coefficient position by taking this product modulo $x^n - 1$. Dividing $xc(x)$ by $x^n - 1$ using the usual polynomial division with remainder (i.e., the "division algorithm"; see Box 4.1), we obtain

$$xc(x) = \underbrace{c_{n-1}}_{\text{quotient}} (x^n - 1) + \underbrace{(c_0 x + c_1 x^2 + \cdots + c_{n-2} x^{n-1} + c_{n-1})}_{\text{remainder}}$$

so that the remainder upon dividing by $x^n - 1$ is

$$xc(x) \ (\text{mod}) x^n - 1 = c_{n-1} + c_0 x + \cdots + c_{n-2} x^{n-1}.$$

Box 4.1: The Division Algorithm

Let $p(x)$ be a polynomial of degree n and let $d(x)$ be a polynomial of degree m. That is, $\deg(p(x)) = n$ and $\deg(d(x)) = m$. Then the "division algorithm" for polynomials asserts that there exist polynomials $q(x)$ (the quotient) and $r(x)$ (the remainder), where $0 \le \deg(r(x)) < m$ and

$$p(x) = q(x)d(x) + r(x).$$

The actual "algorithm" is polynomial long division with remainder. We say that $p(x)$ is equivalent to $r(x)$ modulo $d(x)$ and write this as

$$p(x) \equiv r(x) \ \mod d(x)$$

or

$$p(x) \ (\text{mod}) d(x) = r(x).$$

If $r(x) = 0$, then $d(x)$ divides $p(x)$, which we write as $d(x) \mid p(x)$. If $d(x)$ does not divide $p(x)$, this is denoted as $d(x) \nmid p(x)$.

4.3 Rings

We now introduce an algebraic structure, the **ring**, which is helpful in our study of cyclic codes. We have met the concept of a group in Chapter 2. Despite their usefulness in a variety of areas, groups are still limited because they have only one operation associated with them. Rings, on the other hand, have two operations associated with them.

Definition 4.3 A **ring** $\langle R, +, \cdot \rangle$ is a set R with two binary operations $+$ (addition) and $\cdot$ (multiplication) defined on R such that:

R1 $\langle R, + \rangle$ is an Abelian (commutative) group. We typically denote the additive identity as 0.

R2 The multiplication operation $\cdot$ is associative: $(a \cdot b) \cdot c = a \cdot (b \cdot c)$ for all $a, b, c \in R$.

R3 The left and right distributive laws hold:

$$a(b + c) = ab + ac,$$

$$(a + b)c = (ac) + (bc).$$

A ring is said to be a **commutative ring** if $a \cdot b = b \cdot a$ for every $a, b \in R$.

The ring $\langle R, +, \cdot \rangle$ is frequently referred to simply as R.

A ring is said to be a **ring with identity** if $\cdot$ has an identity element. This is typically denoted as 1. □

Notice that we do not require that the multiplication operation form a group: there may not be multiplicative inverses in a ring (even if it has an identity). Nor is the multiplication operation necessarily commutative. All of the rings that we deal with in this book are rings with identity.

Some of the elements of a ring *may* have a multiplicative inverse. An element a in a ring having a multiplicative inverse is said to be a **unit**.

Example 4.4 The set of 2×2 matrices under usual definitions of addition and multiplication form a ring. (This ring is not commutative, nor does every element have an inverse.) □

Example 4.5 $\langle \mathbb{Z}_6, +, \cdot \rangle$ forms a ring.

+	0	1	2	3	4	5		$\cdot$	0	1	2	3	4	5
0	0	1	2	3	4	5		0	0	0	0	0	0	0
1	1	2	3	4	5	0		1	0	1	2	3	4	5
2	2	3	4	5	0	1		2	0	2	4	0	2	4
3	3	4	5	0	1	2		3	0	3	0	3	0	3
4	4	5	0	1	2	3		4	0	4	2	0	4	2
5	5	0	1	2	3	4		5	0	5	4	3	2	1

It is clear that multiplication under $\mathbb{Z}_6$ does *not* form a group. But $\mathbb{Z}_6$ still satisfies the requirements to be a ring. □

Let R be a ring and let $a \in R$. For an integer n, let na denote $a + a + \cdots + a$ with n arguments. If $n < 0$, $-na$ denotes $(-a) + (-a) + \cdots + (-a)$, with $|n|$ arguments.

Definition 4.6 If a positive integer n exists such that $na = 0$ for all $a \in R$, then the *smallest* such positive integer n is the **characteristic of the ring** R. If no such positive integer exists, the R is said to be a ring of characteristic 0. □

Example 4.7 In the ring $\mathbb{Z}_6$, the characteristic is 6. In the ring $\langle \mathbb{Z}_n, +, \cdot \rangle$, the characteristic is n. In the ring $\mathbb{Q}$, the characteristic is 0. □

4.3.1 Rings of Polynomials

Let R be a ring. A polynomial $f(x)$ of degree n with coefficients in R is

$$f(x) = \sum_{i=0}^{n} a_i x^i,$$

where $a_n \neq 0$. The symbol x is said to be an indeterminate.

Definition 4.8 The set of all polynomials with an indeterminate x with coefficients in a ring R, using the usual operations for polynomial addition and multiplication, forms a ring called the **polynomial ring**. It is denoted as $R[x]$. □

Example 4.9   Let $R = \langle \mathbb{Z}_6, +, \cdot \rangle$ and let $S = R[x] = \mathbb{Z}_6[x]$. Then some elements in S are: $0, 1, x, 1 + x, 4 + 2x$, $5 + 4x$, etc. Example operations are

$$(4 + 2x) + (5 + 4x) = 3$$

$$(4 + 2x)(5 + 4x) = 2 + 2x + 2x^2.$$

□

Example 4.10 $\mathbb{Z}_2[x]$ is the ring of polynomials with coefficients that are either 0 or 1 with operations modulo 2. As an example of arithmetic in this ring,

$$(1 + x)(1 + x) = 1 + x + x + x^2 = 1 + x^2,$$

since $x + x = 0$ in $\mathbb{Z}_2$.

□

polyadd.m
polysub.m
polymult.m
polydiv.m
polyaddm.m
polysubm.m
polymultm.m

It is clear that polynomial multiplication does not, in general, have an inverse. For example, in the ring of polynomials with real coefficients $\mathbb{R}[x]$, there is no polynomial solution $f(x)$ to

$$f(x)(x^2 + 3x + 1) = x^3 + 2x + 1.$$

Polynomials can represent a sequence of numbers in a single collective object. One reason polynomials are of interest is that polynomial multiplication is equivalent to convolution. The convolution of the sequence

$$\mathbf{a} = \{a_0, a_1, a_2, \ldots, a_n\}$$

with the sequence

$$\mathbf{b} = \{b_0, b_1, b_2, \ldots, b_m\}$$

can be accomplished by forming the polynomials

$$a(x) = a_0 + a_1 x + a_2 x^2 + \cdots + a_n x^n$$

$$b(x) = b_0 + b_1 x + b_2 x^2 + \cdots + b_m x^m$$

and multiplying them

$$c(x) = a(x)b(x).$$

Then the coefficients of

$$c(x) = c_0 + c_1 x + c_2 x^2 + \cdots + c_{n+m} x^{n+m}$$

are equal to the values obtained by convolving $\mathbf{a} * \mathbf{b}$.

4.4   Quotient Rings

Recall the idea of factor groups introduced in Section 2.2.5: Given a group and a subgroup, a set of cosets was formed by "translating" the subgroup. We now do a similar construction over a ring of polynomials. We assume that the underlying ring is commutative (to avoid certain technical issues). We begin with a particular example, then generalize.

Consider the ring of polynomials $GF(2)[x]$ (polynomials with binary coefficients) and a polynomial $x^3 - 1$.[2] Let us divide the polynomials up into equivalence classes depending on their remainder modulo $x^3 + 1$. For example, the polynomials in

$$S_0 = \{0, x^3 + 1, x^4 + x, x^5 + x^2, x^6 + x^3, \ldots\}$$

---

[2] In a ring of characteristic 2, $x^n - 1 = x^n + 1$. However, in other rings, the polynomial should be of the form $x^n - 1$.

all have remainder 0 when divided by $x^3 + 1$. We write $S_0 = \langle x^3 + 1 \rangle$, the set generated by $x^3 + 1$. The polynomials in

$$S_1 = \{1, x^3, x^4 + x + 1, x^5 + x^2 + 1, x^6 + x^3 + 1, \dots\}$$

all have remainder 1 when divided by $x^3 + 1$. We can write

$$S_1 = 1 + S_0 = 1 + \langle x^3 + 1 \rangle.$$

Similarly, the other equivalence classes are

$$S_2 = \{x, x^3 + x + 1, x^4, x^5 + x^2 + x, x^6 + x^3 + x, \dots\}$$
$$= x + S_0$$
$$S_3 = \{x + 1, x^3 + x, x^4 + 1, x^5 + x^2 + x + 1, x^6 + x^3 + x + 1, \dots\}$$
$$= x + 1 + S_0$$
$$S_4 = \{x^2, x^3 + x^2 + 1, x^4 + x^2 + x, x^5, x^6 + x^3 + x^2, \dots\}$$
$$= x^2 + S_0$$
$$S_5 = \{x^2 + 1, x^3 + x^2, x^4 + x^2 + x + 1, x^5 + 1, x^6 + x^3 + x^2 + 1, \dots\}$$
$$= x^2 + 1 + S_0$$
$$S_6 = \{x^2 + x, x^3 + x^2 + x + 1, x^4 + x^2, x^5 + x, x^6 + x^3 + x^2 + x, \dots\}$$
$$= x^2 + x + S_0$$
$$S_7 = \{x^2 + x + 1, x^3 + x^2 + x, x^4 + x^2 + 1, x^5 + x + 1, x^6 + x^3 + x^2 + x + 1, \dots\}$$
$$= x^2 + x + 1 + S_0.$$

Thus, $S_0, S_1, \dots, S_7$ form the cosets of $\langle GF(2)[x], + \rangle$ modulo the subgroup $\langle x^3 + 1 \rangle$. These equivalence classes exhaust all possible remainders after dividing by $x^3 + 1$. It is clear that every polynomial in $GF(2)[x]$ falls into one of these eight sets.

Just as we defined an induced group operation for the cosets of Section 2.2.5 to create the factor group, so we can define induced ring operations for both $+$ and $\cdot$ for the equivalence classes of polynomials modulo $x^3 + 1$ by operation on representative elements. This gives us the addition and multiplication tables shown in Figure 4.1.

Let $R = \{S_0, S_1, \dots, S_7\}$. From the addition table, $\langle R, + \rangle$ clearly forms an Abelian group, with S_0 as the identity. For the multiplicative operation, S_1 clearly acts as an identity. However, not every element has a multiplicative inverse, so $\langle R \backslash S_0, \cdot \rangle$ does not form a group. However, $\langle R, +, \cdot \rangle$ does define a **ring**. The ring is denoted as $GF(2)[x]/\langle x^3 + 1 \rangle$ or sometimes by $GF(2)[x]/(x^3 + 1)$, the *ring*

+	S_0	S_1	S_2	S_3	S_4	S_5	S_6	S_7
S_0	S_0	S_1	S_2	S_3	S_4	S_5	S_6	S_7
S_1	S_1	S_0	S_3	S_2	S_5	S_4	S_7	S_6
S_2	S_2	S_3	S_0	S_1	S_6	S_7	S_4	S_5
S_3	S_3	S_2	S_1	S_0	S_7	S_6	S_5	S_4
S_4	S_4	S_5	S_6	S_7	S_0	S_1	S_2	S_3
S_5	S_5	S_4	S_7	S_6	S_1	S_0	S_3	S_2
S_6	S_6	S_7	S_4	S_5	S_2	S_3	S_0	S_1
S_7	S_7	S_6	S_5	S_4	S_3	S_2	S_1	S_0

$\cdot$	S_0	S_1	S_2	S_3	S_4	S_5	S_6	S_7
S_0	S_0	S_0	S_0	S_0	S_0	S_0	S_0	S_0
S_1	S_0	S_1	S_2	S_3	S_4	S_5	S_6	S_7
S_2	S_0	S_2	S_4	S_6	S_1	S_3	S_5	S_7
S_3	S_0	S_3	S_6	S_5	S_5	S_6	S_3	S_0
S_4	S_0	S_4	S_1	S_5	S_2	S_6	S_3	S_7
S_5	S_0	S_5	S_3	S_6	S_6	S_3	S_5	S_0
S_6	S_0	S_6	S_5	S_3	S_3	S_5	S_6	S_0
S_7	S_0	S_7	S_7	S_0	S_7	S_0	S_0	S_7

Figure 4.1: Addition and multiplication tables for $GF(2)[x]/\langle x^3 + 1 \rangle$.

of polynomials in $GF(2)[x]$ *modulo* $x^3 + 1$. We denote the ring $GF(2)[x]/\langle x^n - 1\rangle$ by R_n. We denote the ring $\mathbb{F}_q[x]/\langle x^n - 1\rangle$ as $R_{n,q}$.

Each equivalence class can be identified uniquely by its element of lowest degree.

$$S_0 \leftrightarrow 0 \quad S_1 \leftrightarrow 1$$
$$S_2 \leftrightarrow x \quad S_3 \leftrightarrow x + 1$$
$$S_4 \leftrightarrow x^2 \quad S_5 \leftrightarrow x^2 + 1$$
$$S_6 \leftrightarrow x^2 + x \quad S_7 \leftrightarrow x^2 + x + 1$$

Let $\mathcal{R} = \{0, 1, x, x+1, x^2, x^2+1, x^2+x, x^2+x+1\}$. Define the addition operation in $\mathcal{R}$ as conventional polynomial addition, and the multiplication operation as polynomial multiplication, followed by computing the remainder modulo $x^3 + 1$. Then $\langle \mathcal{R}, +, \cdot\rangle$ forms a ring.

Definition 4.11 Two rings $\langle R, +, \cdot\rangle$ and $\langle \mathcal{R}, +, \cdot\rangle$ are said to be (ring) **isomorphic** if there exists a bijective function $\phi : R \to \mathcal{R}$ called the **isomorphism** such that for every $a, b \in R$,

$$\underbrace{\phi\ (a+b)}_{\substack{\text{operation}\\ \text{in } R}} = \underbrace{\phi(a) + \phi(b)}_{\substack{\text{operation}\\ \text{in } \mathcal{R}}} \quad \underbrace{\phi\ (a \cdot b)}_{\substack{\text{operation}\\ \text{in } R}} = \underbrace{\phi(a) \cdot \phi(b)}_{\substack{\text{operation}\\ \text{in } \mathcal{R}}} \tag{4.1}$$

Ring homomorphism is similarly defined: the function ϕ no longer needs to be bijective, but (4.1) still applies. $\square$

Clearly the rings R (where operation is by representative elements, defined in the tables above) and $\mathcal{R}$ (defined by polynomial operations modulo $x^3 + 1$) are isomorphic.

Note that we can factor $x^3 + 1 = (x+1)(x^2+x+1)$. Also note from the table that in R, $S_3 S_7 = S_0$. Equivalently, in $\mathcal{R}$,

$$(x+1)(x^2+x+1) = 0.$$

This is clearly true, since to multiply, we compute the conventional product $(x+1)(x^2+x+1) = x^3 + 1$, then compute the remainder modulo $x^3 + 1$, which is 0. We shall make use of analogous operations in computing syndromes.

More generally, for a field $\mathbb{F}$, the ring of polynomials $\mathbb{F}[x]$ can be partitioned by a polynomial $f(x)$ of degree m into a ring consisting of q^m different equivalence classes, with one equivalence class for each remainder modulo $f(x)$, where $q = |\mathbb{F}|$. This ring is denoted as $\mathbb{F}[x]/\langle f(x)\rangle$ or $\mathbb{F}[x]/f(x)$. A question that arises is under what conditions this ring is, in fact, a field? As we will develop much more fully in Chapter 5, the ring $\mathbb{F}[x]/f(x)$ is a field if and only if $f(x)$ cannot be factored over $\mathbb{F}[x]$. In the example above we have

$$x^3 + 1 = (x+1)(x^2+x+1),$$

so $x^3 + 1$ is reducible and we do not get a field.

4.5   Ideals in Rings

Definition 4.12 Let R be a ring. A nonempty subset $I \subseteq R$ is an **ideal** if it satisfies the following conditions:

I1 I forms a group under the addition operation in R.

I2 For any $a \in I$ and any $r \in R$, $ar \in I$. $\square$

Example 4.13

1. For any ring R, 0 and R are (trivial) ideals in R.

2. The set $I = \{0, x^5 + x^4 + x^3 + x^2 + x + 1\}$ forms an ideal in R_6. For example, let $1 + x + x^2 \in R_6$. Then

$$(1 + x + x^2)(x^5 + x^4 + x^3 + x^2 + x + 1)$$
$$= x^7 + x^5 + x^4 + x^3 + x^2 + 1 \pmod{x^6 + 1}$$
$$= x^5 + x^4 + x^3 + x^2 + x + 1 \in I.$$

$\square$

Example 4.14 Let R be a ring and let $R[x_1, x_2, \ldots, x_n]$ be the ring of polynomials in the n indeterminates $x_1, x_2, \ldots, x_n$.

Ideals in the polynomial ring $R[x_1, \ldots, x_n]$ may be generated by a finite number of polynomials. Let $f_1, f_2, \ldots, f_s$ be polynomials in $R[x_1, \ldots, x_n]$. Let $\langle f_1, f_2, \ldots, f_s \rangle$ be the set

$$\langle f_1, f_2, \ldots, f_s \rangle = \left\{ \sum_{i=1}^{s} h_i f_i : h_1, \ldots, h_s \in R[x_1, \ldots, x_n] \right\}.$$

That is, it is the set of all polynomials which are linear combinations of the $\{f_i\}$. The set $\langle f_1, \ldots, f_s \rangle$ is an ideal.

Thus, an ideal is similar to a subspace, generated by a set of basis vectors, except that to create a subspace, the coefficients are scalars, whereas for an ideal, the coefficients are polynomials. $\square$

The direction toward which we are working is the following:

> Cyclic codes form ideals in a ring of polynomials.

In fact, for cyclic codes the ideals are principal, as defined by the following.

Definition 4.15 An ideal I in a ring R is said to be **principal** if there exists some $g \in I$ such that every element $a \in I$ can be expressed as a product $a = mg$ for some $m \in R$. For a principal ideal, such an element g is called the **generator element.** The ideal generated by g is denoted as $\langle g \rangle$:

$$\langle g \rangle = \{hg : h \in R\}.$$

$\square$

Theorem 4.16 *Let I be an ideal in $\mathbb{F}_q[x]/(x^n - 1)$. Then*

1. *There is a unique monic polynomial $g(x) \in I$ of minimal degree.*[3]

2. *I is principal with generator $g(x)$.*

3. *$g(x)$ divides $(x^n - 1)$ in $\mathbb{F}_q[x]$.*

Proof There is at least one ideal (so the result is not vacuous, since the entire ring is an ideal). There is a lower bound on the degrees of polynomials in the ideal. Hence there must be at least one polynomial in the ideal of minimal degree, which may be normalized to be monic. Now to show uniqueness, let $g(x)$ and $f(x)$ be monic polynomials in I of minimal degree with $f \neq g$. Then $h(x) = g(x) - f(x)$ must be in I since I forms a group under addition, and $h(x)$ must be of lower degree, contradicting the minimality of the degree of g and f.

---

[3] A polynomial is monic if the coefficient of the *leading term* — the term of highest degree — is equal to 1.

To show that I is principal, we assume (to the contrary) that there is an $f(x) \in I$ that is not a multiple of $g(x)$. Then by the division algorithm

$$f(x) = m(x)g(x) + r(x)$$

with $\deg(r) < \deg(g)$. But $m(x)g(x) \in I$ (definition of an ideal) and $r = f - mg \in I$ (definition of ideal), contradicting the minimality of the degree of g, unless $r = 0$.

To show that $g(x)$ divides $(x^n - 1)$, we assume to the contrary that $g(x)$ does not divide $(x^n - 1)$. By the division algorithm

$$x^n - 1 = h(x)g(x) + r(x)$$

with $0 \le \deg(r) < \deg(g)$. But $h(x)g(x) \in I$ and $r(x) = (x^n - 1) - h(x)g(x)$ is the additive inverse of $h(x)g(x) \in I$, and so is in I, contradicting the minimality of the degree of g.   □

If a monic polynomial $g(x)$ divides $(x^n - 1)$, then it can be used to generate an ideal: $I = \langle g(x) \rangle$.

In the ring $\mathbb{F}_q[x]/(x^n - 1)$, different ideals can be obtained by selecting different divisors $g(x)$ of $x^n - 1$.

Example 4.17   By multiplication, it can be shown that in $GF(2)[x]$,

$$x^7 + 1 = (x + 1)(x^3 + x + 1)(x^3 + x^2 + 1).$$

In the ring $GF(2)[x]/(x^7 + 1)$, there are ideals corresponding to the different factorizations of $x^7 + 1$, so there are the following nontrivial ideals:

$$\langle x + 1 \rangle \quad \langle x^3 + x + 1 \rangle \quad \langle x^3 + x^2 + 1 \rangle$$

$$\langle (x + 1)(x^3 + x + 1) \rangle \quad \langle (x + 1)(x^3 + x^2 + 1) \rangle \quad \langle (x^3 + x + 1)(x^3 + x^2 + 1) \rangle.$$

□

4.6   Algebraic Description of Cyclic Codes

Let us return now to cyclic codes. As mentioned in Section 4.1, cyclic shifting of a polynomial $c(x)$ can be represented by $xc(x)$ modulo $x^n - 1$. Now think of $c(x)$ as an element of $GF(q)[x]/(x^n - 1)$. Then *in that ring*, $xc(x)$ is a cyclic shift, since operations in the ring are defined modulo $x^n - 1$. Any power of x times a codeword yields a codeword so that, for example,

$$(c_{n-1}, c_0, c_1, \ldots, c_{n-2}) \leftrightarrow xc(x)$$

$$(c_{n-2}, c_{n-1}, c_0, \ldots, c_{n-3}) \leftrightarrow x^2 c(x)$$

$$\vdots$$

$$(c_1, c_2, \ldots, c_{n-1}, c_0) \leftrightarrow x^{n-1} c(x),$$

where the arithmetic on the right is done in the ring $GF(q)[x]/(x^n - 1)$. Furthermore, multiples of these codewords are also codewords, so that $a_1 xc(x)$ is a codeword for $a_1 \in GF(q)$, $a_2 x^2 c(x)$ is a codeword for $a_2 \in GF(q)$, etc. Furthermore, any linear combination of such codewords must be a codeword (since the code is linear). Let C be a cyclic code over $GF(q)$ and let $c(x) \in GF(q)[x]/(x^n - 1)$ be a polynomial representing a codeword in C. If we take a polynomial $a(x) \in GF(q)[x]/(x^n - 1)$ of the form

$$a(x) = a_0 + a_1 x + \cdots + a_{n-1} x^{n-1}$$

then

$$c(x)a(x)$$

is simply a linear combination of cyclic shifts of $c(x)$, which is to say, a linear combination of codewords in C. Thus, $c(x)a(x)$ is also a codeword. Since linear codes form a group under addition we see that **a cyclic code is an ideal in** $GF(q)[x]/(x^n - 1)$. From Theorem 4.16, we can immediately make some observations about cyclic codes:

- An (n, k) cyclic code has a unique minimal-degree, monic polynomial $g(x)$ of degree $n - k$, which is the generator of the ideal. This is called the **generator polynomial** for the code

$$g(x) = g_0 + g_1 x + g_2 x^2 + \cdots + g_{n-k} x^{n-k},$$

  and let $r = n - k$ (the redundancy of the code).

- Every code polynomial in the code can be expressed as a multiple of the generator

$$c(x) = m(x)g(x),$$

  where $m(x)$ is a *message polynomial*. The degree of $m(x)$ is (strictly) less than k,

$$m(x) = m_0 + m_1 x + \cdots + m_{k-1} x^{k-1}.$$

  There are k independently selectable coefficients in $m(x)$, so the dimension of the code is k. Then $c(x) = m(x)g(x)$ has degree $\leq n - 1$, so that n coded symbols can be represented:

$$c(x) = c_0 + c_1 x + c_2 x^2 + \cdots + c_{n-1} x^{n-1}$$
$$= (g_0 + g_1 x + \cdots + g_{n-k} x^{n-k})(m_0 + m_1 x + m_2 x^2 + \cdots + m_{k-1} x^{k-1}).$$

- The generator is a factor of $x^n - 1$ in $GF(q)[x]$.

Example 4.18 We consider cyclic codes of length 15 with binary coefficients. By multiplication it can be verified that

$$x^{15} - 1 = (1 + x)(1 + x + x^2)(1 + x + x^4)(1 + x + x^2 + x^3 + x^4)(1 + x^3 + x^4).$$

So there are polynomials of degrees 1, 2, 4, 4, and 4 which can be used to construct generators. The product of any combination of these can be used to construct a generator polynomial. If we want a generator of, say, degree 10, we could take

$$g(x) = (1 + x + x^2)(1 + x + x^4)(1 + x + x^2 + x^3 + x^4).$$

If we want a generator of degree 5 we could take

$$g(x) = (1 + x)(1 + x + x^4)$$

or

$$g(x) = (1 + x)(1 + x + x^2 + x^3 + x^4).$$

In fact, in this case, we can get generator polynomials of any degree from 1 to 15. So we can construct the (n, k) codes

$$(15, 1), (15, 2), \ldots, (15, 15).$$

$\square$

4.7 Nonsystematic Encoding and Parity Check

A message vector $\mathbf{m} = \begin{bmatrix} m_0 & m_1 & \ldots & m_{k-1} \end{bmatrix}$ corresponds to a message polynomial

$$m(x) = m_0 + \cdots + m_{k-1} x^{k-1}.$$

Then the code polynomial corresponding to $m(x)$ is obtained by the **encoding operation** of polynomial multiplication:

$$c(x) = m(x)g(x)$$
$$= (m_0 g(x) + m_1 x g(x) + \cdots + m_{k-1} x^{k-1} g(x)).$$

This is not a systematic encoding operation; systematic encoding is discussed below. The encoding operation can be written as

$$c(x) = \begin{bmatrix} m_0 & m_1 & m_2 & \cdots & m_{k-1} \end{bmatrix} \begin{bmatrix} g(x) \\ xg(x) \\ x^2 g(x) \\ \vdots \\ x^{k-1} g(x) \end{bmatrix}.$$

This can also be expressed as

$$\mathbf{c} = \begin{bmatrix} m_0, m_1, \ldots, m_{k-1} \end{bmatrix} \begin{bmatrix} g_0 & g_1 & \cdots & g_r & & & & \\ & g_0 & g_1 & \cdots & g_r & & & \\ & & g_0 & g_1 & \cdots & g_r & & \\ & & & \ddots & \ddots & & \ddots & \\ & & & & g_0 & g_1 & \cdots & g_r & \\ & & & & & g_0 & g_1 & \cdots & g_r \end{bmatrix},$$

(where empty locations are equal to 0) or

$$\mathbf{c} = \mathbf{m}G,$$

where G is a $k \times n$ matrix. A matrix such as this which is constant along the diagonals is said to be a **Toeplitz** matrix.

Example 4.19 Let $n = 7$ and let

$$g(x) = (x^3 + x + 1)(x + 1) = 1 + x^2 + x^3 + x^4,$$

so that the code is a $(7, 3)$ code. Then a generator matrix for the code can be expressed as

$$G = \begin{bmatrix} 1 & 0 & 1 & 1 & 1 & 0 & 0 \\ 0 & 1 & 0 & 1 & 1 & 1 & 0 \\ 0 & 0 & 1 & 0 & 1 & 1 & 1 \end{bmatrix}.$$

The codewords in the code are as shown in Table 4.1.

Table 4.1: Codewords in the Code Generated by $g(x) = 1 + x^2 + x^3 + x^4$

m	$m(x)g(x)$	Code Polynomial	Codeword
(0,0,0)	$0g(x)$	0	0000000
(1,0,0)	$1g(x)$	$1 + x^2 + x^3 + x^4$	1011100
(0,1,0)	$xg(x)$	$x + x^3 + x^4 + x^5$	0101110
(1,1,0)	$(x + 1)g(x)$	$1 + x + x^2 + x^5$	1110010
(0,0,1)	$x^2 g(x)$	$x^2 + x^4 + x^5 + x^6$	0010111
(1,0,1)	$(x^2 + 1)g(x)$	$1 + x^3 + x^5 + x^6$	1001011
(0,1,1)	$(x^2 + x)g(x)$	$x + x^2 + x^3 + x^6$	0111001
(1,1,1)	$(x^2 + x + 1)g(x)$	$1 + x + x^4 + x^6$	1100101

□

For a cyclic code of length n with generator $g(x)$, there is a corresponding polynomial $h(x)$ of degree k satisfying $h(x)g(x) = x^n - 1$. This polynomial is called the **parity check polynomial**. Since codewords are exactly the multiples of $g(x)$, then for a codeword,

$$c(x)h(x) = m(x)g(x)h(x) = m(x)(x^n - 1) \equiv 0 \quad (\text{in } GF(q)[x]/(x^n - 1)).$$

Thus, a polynomial $r(x)$ can be examined to see if it is a codeword: $r(x)$ is a codeword if and only if $r(x)h(x) \pmod{x^n - 1}$ is equal to 0.

As for linear block codes, we can define a *syndrome*. This can be accomplished by several ways. One way is to define the **syndrome polynomial** corresponding to the received data $r(x)$ as

$$s(x) = r(x)h(x) \pmod{x^n - 1}. \tag{4.2}$$

$s(x)$ is identically zero if and only if $r(x)$ is a codeword.

Let us construct a parity check matrix corresponding to the parity check polynomial $h(x)$. Let $c(x)$ represent a code polynomial in C, so $c(x) = m(x)g(x)$ for some message $m(x) = m_0 + m_1 x + \cdots + m_{k-1}x^{k-1}$. Then

$$c(x)h(x) = m(x)g(x)h(x) = m(x)(x^n - 1) = m(x)x^n - m(x).$$

Since $m(x)$ has degree less than k, then powers $x^k, x^{k+1}, \ldots, x^{n-1}$ do not appear[4] in $m(x)x^n - m(x)$. Thus, the coefficients of $x^k, x^{k+1}, \ldots, x^{n-1}$ in the product $c(x)h(x)$ must be 0,

$$\sum_{i=0}^{k} h_i c_{l-i} = 0 \quad \text{for } l = k, k+1, \ldots, n-1. \tag{4.3}$$

This can be expressed as

$$\begin{bmatrix} h_k & h_{k-1} & h_{k-2} & \cdots & h_0 & & & \\ & h_k & h_{k-1} & h_{k-2} & \cdots & h_0 & & \\ & & h_k & h_{k-1} & h_{k-2} & \cdots & h_0 & \\ & & & \ddots & & & & \ddots \\ & & & & h_k & h_{k-1} & h_{k-2} & \cdots & h_0 \end{bmatrix} \begin{bmatrix} c_0 \\ c_1 \\ c_2 \\ \vdots \\ c_{n-1} \end{bmatrix} = \mathbf{0}. \tag{4.4}$$

Thus, the parity check matrix H can be expressed as the $(n-k) \times n$ Toeplitz matrix

$$H = \begin{bmatrix} h_k & h_{k-1} & h_{k-2} & \cdots & h_0 & & & \\ & h_k & h_{k-1} & h_{k-2} & \cdots & h_0 & & \\ & & h_k & h_{k-1} & h_{k-2} & \cdots & h_0 & \\ & & & \ddots & & & & \ddots \\ & & & & h_k & h_{k-1} & h_{k-2} & \cdots & h_0 \end{bmatrix}.$$

Example 4.20 For the $(7, 3)$ cyclic code of Example 4.19 generated by $g(x) = x^4 + x^3 + x^2 + 1$, the parity check polynomial is

$$h(x) = \frac{x^7 + 1}{x^4 + x^3 + x^2 + 1} = x^3 + x^2 + 1.$$

The parity check matrix is

$$H = \begin{bmatrix} 1 & 1 & 0 & 1 & & & \\ & 1 & 1 & 0 & 1 & & \\ & & 1 & 1 & 0 & 1 & \\ & & & 1 & 1 & 0 & 1 \end{bmatrix}.$$

It can be verified that $GH^T = \mathbf{0}$ (in $GF(2)$). $\qquad\square$

---

[4] This "trick" of observing which powers are absent is a very useful one, and we shall see it again.

4.8 Systematic Encoding

With only a little more effort, cyclic codes can be encoded in systematic form. We take the message vector and form a message polynomial from it,

$$\mathbf{m} = (m_0, m_1, \ldots, m_{k-1}) \leftrightarrow m(x) = m_0 + m_1 x + \cdots + m_{k-1} x^{k-1}.$$

Now take the message polynomial and shift it to the right $n - k$ positions:

$$x^{n-k} m(x) = m_0 x^{n-k} + m_1 x^{n-k+1} + \cdots + m_{k-1} x^{n-1}.$$

Observe that the vector corresponding to this is

$$\underbrace{(0, 0, \ldots, 0}_{n-k}, m_0, m_1, \ldots, m_{k-1}) \leftrightarrow x^{n-k} m(x).$$

Now divide $x^{n-k} m(x)$ by the generator $g(x)$ to obtain a quotient and remainder

$$x^{n-k} m(x) = q(x) g(x) + d(x),$$

where $q(x)$ is the quotient and $d(x)$ is the remainder, having degree less than $n - k$. We use the notation $R_{g(x)}[\cdot]$ to denote the operation of computing the remainder of the argument when dividing by $g(x)$. Thus, we have

$$d(x) = R_{g(x)}[x^{n-k} m(x)].$$

By the degree of $d(x)$, it corresponds to the code sequence

$$(d_0, d_1, \ldots, d_{n-k-1}, 0, 0, \ldots, 0) \leftrightarrow d(x).$$

Now form

$$\boxed{x^{n-k} m(x) - d(x) = q(x) g(x).} \tag{4.5}$$

Since the left-hand side is a multiple of $g(x)$, it must be a codeword. It has the vector representation

$$(\underbrace{-d_0, -d_1, \ldots, -d_{n-k-1}}_{\text{parity}}, \underbrace{m_0, m_1, \ldots, m_{k-1}}_{\text{message}}) \leftrightarrow x^{n-k} m(x) - d(x).$$

The message symbols appear explicitly in the last k positions of the vector. Parity symbols appear in the first $n - k$ positions. This gives us a systematic encoding.

Example 4.21   We demonstrate systematic coding in the $(7, 3)$ code from Example 4.19. Let $\mathbf{m} = (1, 0, 1) \leftrightarrow m(x) = 1 + x^2$.

1. Compute $x^{n-k} m(x) = x^4 m(x) = x^4 + x^6$.

2. Employ the division algorithm:

$$x^4 + x^6 = (1 + x + x^2)(1 + x^2 + x^3 + x^4) + (1 + x).$$

   The remainder is $(1 + x)$.

3. The code polynomial is

$$c(x) = x^{n-k} m(x) - d(x) = (1 + x) + (x^4 + x^6) \leftrightarrow (\underbrace{1, 1, 0, 0}_{1+x}, \underbrace{1, 0, 1}_{\mathbf{m}}).$$

□

A systematic representation of the generator matrix is also readily obtained. Dividing x^{n-k+i} by $g(x)$ using the division algorithm we obtain

$$x^{n-k+i} = q_i(x)g(x) + b_i(x), \quad i = 0, 1, \ldots, k-1,$$

where $b_i(x) = b_{i,0} + b_{i,1}x + \cdots + b_{i,n-k-1}x^{n-k-1}$ is the remainder. Equivalently,

$$x^{n-k+i} - b_i(x) = q_i(x)g(x),$$

so $x^{n-k+i} - b_i(x)$ is a multiple of $g(x)$ and must be a codeword. Using these codewords for $i = 0, 1, \ldots, k-1$ to form the rows of the generator matrix, we obtain

$$G = \begin{bmatrix} -b_{0,0} & -b_{0,1} & \cdots & -b_{0,n-k-1} & 1 & 0 & 0 & \cdots & 0 \\ -b_{1,0} & -b_{1,1} & \cdots & -b_{1,n-k-1} & 0 & 1 & 0 & \cdots & 0 \\ -b_{2,0} & -b_{2,1} & \cdots & -b_{2,n-k-1} & 0 & 0 & 1 & \cdots & 0 \\ \vdots & & & & & & & & \\ -b_{k-1,0} & -b_{k-1,1} & \cdots & -b_{k-1,n-k-1} & 0 & 0 & 0 & \cdots & 1 \end{bmatrix}.$$

The corresponding parity check matrix is

$$H = \begin{bmatrix} 1 & 0 & 0 & \cdots & 0 & b_{0,0} & b_{1,0} & b_{2,0} & \cdots & b_{k-1,0} \\ 0 & 1 & 0 & \cdots & 0 & b_{0,1} & b_{1,1} & b_{2,1} & \cdots & b_{k-1,1} \\ 0 & 0 & 1 & \cdots & 0 & b_{0,2} & b_{1,2} & b_{2,2} & \cdots & b_{k-1,2} \\ \vdots & & & & & & & & \\ 0 & 0 & 0 & \cdots & 1 & b_{0,n-k-1} & b_{1,n-k-1} & b_{2,n-k-1} & \cdots & b_{k-1,n-k-1} \end{bmatrix}.$$

Example 4.22 Let $g(x) = 1 + x + x^3$. The $b_i(x)$ polynomials are obtained as follows:

$$\begin{array}{llll} i = 0: & x^3 & = g(x) + (1+x) & b_0(x) = 1 + x \\ i = 1: & x^4 & = xg(x) + (x + x^2) & b_1(x) = x + x^2 \\ i = 2: & x^5 = (x^2 + 1)g(x) + (1 + x + x^2) & b_2(x) = 1 + x + x^2 \\ i = 3: & x^6 = (x^3 + x + 1)g(x) + (1 + x^2) & b_3(x) = 1 + x^2 \end{array}$$

The generator and parity matrices are

$$G = \begin{bmatrix} 1 & 1 & 0 & 1 & 0 & 0 & 0 \\ 0 & 1 & 1 & 0 & 1 & 0 & 0 \\ 1 & 1 & 1 & 0 & 0 & 1 & 0 \\ 1 & 0 & 1 & 0 & 0 & 0 & 1 \end{bmatrix} \quad H = \begin{bmatrix} 1 & 0 & 0 & 1 & 0 & 1 & 1 \\ 0 & 1 & 0 & 1 & 1 & 1 & 0 \\ 0 & 0 & 1 & 0 & 1 & 1 & 1 \end{bmatrix}.$$ $\square$

For systematic encoding, error detection can be readily accomplished. Consider the systematically encoded codeword

$$\mathbf{c} = (-d_0, -d_1, \ldots, -d_{n-k-1}, m_0, m_1, \ldots, m_{k-1}) = (-\mathbf{d}, \mathbf{m}).$$

We can perform error *detection* as follows:

1. Estimate a message based on the systematic message part of $\mathbf{r}$. Call this $\mathbf{m}'$.

2. Encode $\mathbf{m}'$. Compare the parity bits from this to the received parity bits. If they don't match, then an error is detected.

Example 4.23 We repeat the encoding for the $(7, 3)$ code of Example 4.19 using systematic encoding. The codewords in the code are as shown in Table 4.2. $\square$

Table 4.2: Systematic Codewords in the Code Generated by $g(x) = 1 + x^2 + x^3 + x^4$

m	$m(x)$	$x^4 m(x)$	$d(x) = R_{g(x)}[x^4 m(x)]$	Code Polynomial	Codeword
(0,0,0)	0	0	0	0	0000 000
(1,0,0)	1	x^4	$1 + x^2 + x^3$	$1 + x^2 + x^3 + x^4$	1011 100
(0,1,0)	x	x^5	$1 + x + x^2$	$1 + x + x^2 + x^5$	1110 010
(1,1,0)	$1 + x$	$x^4 + x^5$	$x + x^3$	$x + x^3 + x^4 + x^5$	0101 110
(0,0,1)	x^2	x^6	$x + x^2 + x^3$	$x + x^2 + x^3 + x^6$	0111 001
(1,0,1)	$1 + x^2$	$x^4 + x^6$	$1 + x$	$1 + x + x^4 + x^6$	1100 101
(0,1,1)	$x + x^2$	$x^5 + x^6$	$1 + x^3$	$1 + x^3 + x^5 + x^6$	1001 011
(1,1,1)	$1 + x + x^2$	$x^4 + x^5 + x^6$	x^2	$x^2 + x^4 + x^5 + x^6$	0010 111

4.9 Some Hardware Background

One of the justifications for using cyclic codes, and using the polynomial representation in general, is that there are efficient hardware configurations for performing the encoding operation. In this section, we present circuits for computing polynomial multiplication and division. In Section 4.10, we put this to work for encoding operations. Some of these architectures are also used in conjunction with the convolutional codes, to be introduced in Chapter 12.

4.9.1 Computational Building Blocks

The building blocks employed here consist of three basic elements. We express the operations over an arbitrary field $\mathbb{F}$.

One-bit memory storage The symbol $\boxed{D}$ is a storage element which holds one symbol in the field $\mathbb{F}$. (Most typically, in the field $GF(2)$, it is 1 bit of storage, like a D flip-flop.) The $\boxed{D}$ holds its symbol of information (either a 0 or a 1) until a clock signal (not portrayed in the diagrams) is applied. Then the signal appearing at the input is "clocked" through to the output and also stored internally. In all configurations employed here, all of the $\boxed{D}$ elements are clocked simultaneously. As an example, consider the following system of five $\boxed{D}$ elements:

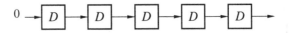

This cascaded configuration is called a *shift register*. In this example, the connection on the left end is permanently attached to a "0.". If the storage elements are initially loaded with the contents $(1, 0, 1, 0, 0)$, then as the memory elements are clocked, the contents of the shift register change as shown here:

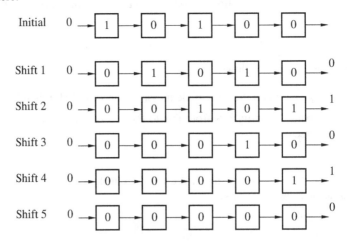

This is frequently represented in tabular form:

Initial:	1	0	1	0	0
Shift 1:	0	1	0	1	0
Shift 2:	0	0	1	0	1
Shift 3:	0	0	0	1	0
Shift 4:	0	0	0	0	1
Shift 5:	0	0	0	0	0

Further clockings of the system result in no further changes: the state (the contents of the memory elements) of the system remains in the all-zero state.

Adder The symbol $\oplus$ has two inputs and one output, which is computed as the sum of the inputs (in the field $\mathbb{F}$).

Multiplication The symbol $\otimes_{g_i}$ has one input and one output, which is computed as the product of the input and the number g_i (in the field $\mathbb{F}$). For the binary field the coefficients are either 0 or 1, represented by either no connection or a connection, respectively.

4.9.2 Sequences and Power Series

In the context of these implementations, we represent a sequence of numbers $\{a_0, a_1, a_2, \ldots, a_n\}$ by a polynomial $y(x) = a_0 + a_1 x + \cdots + a_n x^n = \sum_{i=0}^{n} a_i x^i$. Multiplication by x yields

$$xy(x) = a_0 x + a_1 x^2 + \cdots + a_n x^{n+1},$$

which is a representation of the sequence $\{0, a_0, a_1, \ldots, a_n\}$ — a right-shift or delay of the sequence. The x may thus be thought of as a "delay" operator (just as z^{-1} in the context of Z-transforms). Such representations are sometimes expressed using the variable D (for "delay") as $y(D) = a_0 + a_1 D + \cdots + a_n D^n$. This polynomial representation is sometimes referred to as the D-transform. Multiplication by D ($= x$) represents a delay operation. There are two different kinds of circuit representations presented for polynomial operations. In some operations, it is natural to deal with the *last* element of a sequence first. That is, for a sequence $\{a_0, a_1, \ldots, a_k\}$, represented by $a(x) = a_0 + a_1 x + \cdots + a_k x^k$, first a_k enters the processing, then a_{k-1}, and so forth. This seems to run counter to the idea of x as a "delay," where temporally a_0 would seem to come first. But when dealing with a block of data, it is not a problem to deal with any element in the block and it is frequently more convenient to use this representation.

On the other hand, when dealing with a stream of data, it may be more convenient to deal with the elements "in order," first a_0, then a_1, and so forth.

The confusion introduced by these two different orders of processing is exacerbated by the fact that two different kinds of realizations are frequently employed, each of which presents its coefficients in opposite order from the other. For (it is hoped) clarity, representations for both last-element-first and first-element-first realizations are presented here for many of the operations of interest.

4.9.3 Polynomial Multiplication

4.9.3.1 Last-Element-First Processing

Let $a(x) = a_0 + a_1 x + \cdots + a_k x^k$ and let $h(x) = h_0 + h_1 x + \cdots + h_r x^r$. The product

$$b(x) = a(x)h(x)$$

$$= a_0 h_0 + (a_0 h_1 + a_1 h_0)x + \cdots + (a_k h_{r-1} + a_{k-1} h_r)x^{r+k-1} + a_k h_r x^{r+k}$$

$$= b_0 + b_1 x + \cdots + b_{r+k} x^{r+k}$$

can be computed using a circuit as shown in Figure 4.2. (This circuit should be familiar to readers acquainted with signal processing, since it is simply an implementation of a finite impulse response filter.) The operation is as follows: The registers are first cleared. The last symbol a_k is input

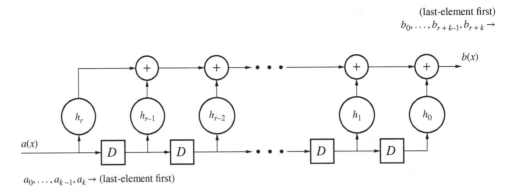

Figure 4.2: A circuit for multiplying two polynomials, last-element first.

first. The first output is $a_k h_r$, which is the last symbol of the product $a(x)h(x)$. At the next step, a_{k-1} arrives and the output is $a_{k-1}h_r + a_k h_{r-1}$. At the next step, a_{k-2} arrives and the output is $(a_{k-2}h_r + a_{k-1}h_{r-1} + a_k h_{r-2})$, and so forth. After a_0 is clocked in, the system is clocked r times more to produce a total of $k + r + 1$ outputs. A second circuit for multiplying polynomials is shown in Figure 4.3. This circuit has the advantage for hardware implementation that the addition is not cascaded through a series of addition operators. Hence this configuration is suitable for higher-speed operation.

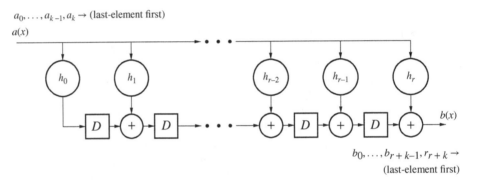

Figure 4.3: A circuit for multiplying two polynomials, last-element first, with high-speed operation.

4.9.3.2 First-Element-First Processing

The circuits in this section are used for filtering streams of data, such as for the convolutional codes described in Chapter 12.

Figure 4.4 shows a circuit for multiplying two polynomials, first-element first. Note that the coefficients are reversed relative to Figure 4.2. In this case, a_0 is fed in first, resulting in the output $a_0 h_0$ at the first step. At the next step, a_1 is fed in, resulting in the output $a_0 h_1 + a_1 h_0$, and so forth.

Figure 4.5 shows another high-speed circuit for multiplying two polynomials, first-element first.

It may be observed that these filters are FIR (finite impulse response) filters.

4.9.4 Polynomial Division

4.9.4.1 Last-Element-First Processing

Computing quotients of polynomials, and more importantly, the remainder after division, plays a significant role in encoding cyclic codes. The circuits of this section will be applied to that end.

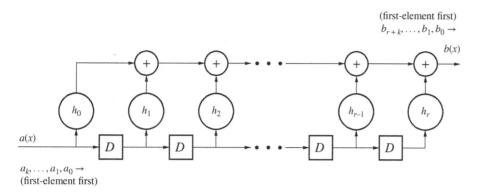

Figure 4.4: A circuit for multiplying two polynomials, first-element first.

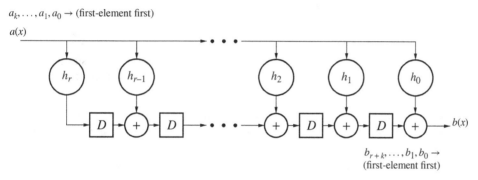

Figure 4.5: A circuit for multiplying two polynomials, first-element first, with high-speed operation.

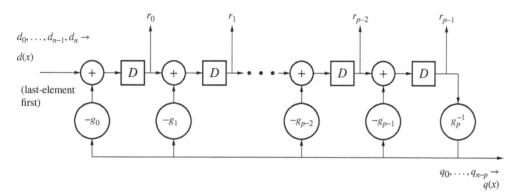

Figure 4.6: A circuit to perform polynomial division.

Figure 4.6 illustrates a device for computing the quotient and remainder of the polynomial division

$$\frac{d(x)}{g(x)},$$

where the dividend $d(x)$ represents a sequence of numbers

$$d(x) = d_0 + d_1 x + d_2 x^2 + \cdots + d_n x^n,$$

and the divisor $g(x)$ represents a sequence of numbers

$$g(x) = g_0 + g_1 x + g_2 x^2 + \cdots + g_p x^p.$$

The coefficient g_p is nonzero; for binary polynomials the coefficient $-g_p^{-1}$ has the value of 1. The polynomial $g(x)$ is sometimes called the **connection polynomial**. The remainder $r(x)$ must be of degree $\leq p - 1$, since the divisor has degree p:

$$r(x) = r_0 + r_1 x + \cdots + r_{p-1} x^{p-1},$$

and the quotient $q(x)$ can be written

$$q(x) = q_0 + q_1 x + \cdots + q_{n-p} x^{n-p}.$$

Readers familiar with signal processing will recognize the device of Figure 4.6 as an implementation of an all-pole filter.

The division device of Figure 4.6 operates as follows:

1. All the memory elements are initially cleared to 0.

2. The coefficients of $d(x)$ are clocked into the left register for p steps, starting with d_n, the coefficient of x^n in $d(x)$. This initializes the registers and has no direct counterpart in long division as computed by hand.

3. The coefficients of $d(x)$ continue to be clocked in on the left. The bits which are shifted out on the right represent the coefficients of the quotient $d(x)/g(x)$, starting from the highest-order coefficient.

4. After all the coefficients of $d(x)$ have been shifted in, the contents of the memory elements represent the remainder of the division, with the highest-order coefficient r_{p-1} on the right.

Example 4.24 Consider the division of the polynomial $d(x) = x^8 + x^7 + x^5 + x + 1$ by $g(x) = x^5 + x + 1$. The polynomial long division is

$$
\begin{array}{r}
x^3 + x^2 + 1 \\
x^5 + x + 1\,\overline{\big)\,x^8 + x^7 + x^5_{\;A} + x + 1} \\
x^8 + x^4 + x^3 \\
\hline
x^7 + x^5 + x^4 + x^3_{\;B} + x + 1 \\
x^7 + x^3 + x^2 \\
\hline
x^5 + x^4 + x^2_{\;C} + x + 1 \\
x^5 + x + 1 \\
\hline
x^4 + x^2_{\;D} \\
\end{array}
\tag{4.6}
$$

The circuit for performing this division is shown in Figure 4.7. The operation of the circuit is detailed in Table 4.3. The shaded components of the table correspond to the shaded functions in the long division in 4.6. The Input column of the table shows the coefficient of the dividend polynomial $d(x)$, along with the monomial term x^i that is represented, starting with the coefficient of x^8. The Register column shows the shift register contents, along with the polynomial represented. As the algorithm progresses, the degree of the polynomial represented by the shift register decreases down to a maximum degree of $p - 1$.

Initially, the shift register is zeroed out. After five shifts, the shift registers hold the top coefficients of $d(x)$, indicated by A in the table, and also shown highlighted in the long division. The shift register holds the coefficient of the highest power on the right, while the long division has the highest power on the left. With the next shift,

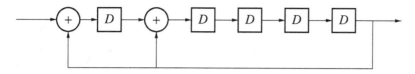

Figure 4.7: A circuit to divide by $g(x) = x^5 + x + 1$.

Table 4.3: Computation Steps for Long Division Using a Shift Register Circuit

	Input Symbol on j th Shift		Shift Register Contents After j Shifts							Output Symbol on j th Shift	
j	Bit	Polynomial Term			Bits					Polynomial Representation	Bit	Polynomial Term
0	–	–	0	0	0	0	0					
1	1	(x^8)	1	0	0	0	0					
2	1	(x^7)	1	1	0	0	0					
3	0	(x^6)	0	1	1	0	0					
4	1	(x^5)	1	0	1	1	0					
5	0	(x^4)	0	1	0	1	1	A:	$x^5 + x^7 + x^8$	1	x^3
6	0	(x^3)	1	1	1	0	1	B:	$x^3 + x^4 + x^5 + x^7$	1	x^2
7	0	(x^2)	1	0	1	1	0	C:	$x^2 + x^4 + x^5$	0	x^1
8	1	(x^1)	1	1	0	1	1		$x + x^2 + x^4 + x^5$	1	x^0
9	1	1	0	0	1	0	1	D:	$x^2 + x^4$		

the divisor polynomial $g(x)$ is subtracted (or added) from the dividend. The shift registers then hold the results B. The operations continue until the last coefficient of $d(x)$ is clocked in. After completion, the shift registers contain the remainder, $r(x)$, shown as D. Starting from step 5, the right register output represents the coefficients of the quotient. □

4.9.5 Simultaneous Polynomial Division and Multiplication

4.9.5.1 First-Element-First Processing

Figure 4.8 shows a circuit that computes the output

$$b(x) = a(x)\frac{h(x)}{g(x)},$$

where

$$\frac{h(x)}{g(x)} = \frac{h_0 + h_1 x + \cdots + h_r x^r}{g_0 + g_1 x + \cdots + g_r x^r}$$

with $g_0 = 1$. (If $g_0 = 0$, then a noncausal filter results. If $g_0 \neq 0$ and $g_0 \neq 1$, then a constant can be factored out of the denominator.) This form is referred to as the *controller canonical form* or the *first companion form* in the controls literature [145, 239]. Figure 4.9 also computes the output

$$b(x) = a(x)\frac{h(x)}{g(x)}.$$

This form is referred to as the *alternative first companion form* or the *observability form* in the controls literature.

Example 4.25 Figure 4.10 shows the controller form for a circuit implementing the transfer function

$$H(x) = \frac{1 + x}{1 + x^3 + x^4}.$$

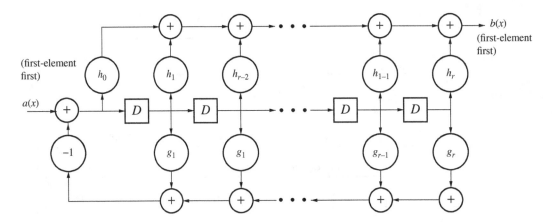

Figure 4.8: Realizing $h(x)/g(x)$ (first-element first), controller canonical form.

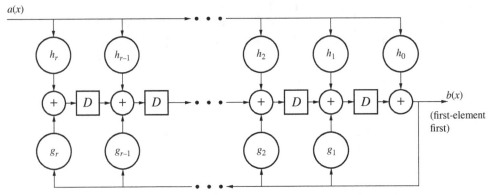

Figure 4.9: Realizing $h(x)/g(x)$ (first-element first), observability form.

For the input sequence $a(x) = 1 + x + x^2$ the output can be computed as

$$b(x) = a(x)\frac{1+x}{1+x^3+x^4} = \frac{(1+x+x^2)(1+x)}{1+x^3+x^4} = \frac{1+x^3}{1+x^3+x^4}$$
$$= 1 + x^4 + x^7 + x^8 + x^{10} + \cdots,$$

as can be verified using the long division $1 + x^3 + x^4 \overline{)1 + x^3}$. The operation of the circuit with this input is detailed in the following table. The column labeled "b" shows the signal at the point "b" in Figure 4.10.

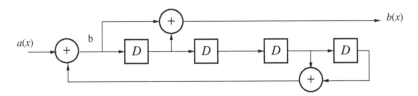

Figure 4.10: Circuit realization of $H(x) = (1+x)/(1+x^3+x^4)$, controller form.

k	a_k	b	Output	Next State	k	a_k	b	Output	Next State
				0000	5	0	0	$0\,(x^5)$	0011
0	1	1	1	1000	6	0	0	$0\,(x^6)$	0001
1	1	1	$0\,(x)$	1100	7	0	1	$1\,(x^7)$	1000
2	1	1	$0\,(x^2)$	1110	8	0	0	$1\,(x^8)$	0100
3	0	1	$0\,(x^3)$	1111	9	0	0	$0\,(x^9)$	0010
4	0	0	$1\,(x^4)$	0111	10	0	1	$1\,(x^{10})$	1001

Figure 4.11 shows a circuit in the observability form. The following table details its operation for the same input sequence $a(x) = 1 + x + x^2$.

k	a_k	Output	Next State	k	a_k	Output	Next State
			0000	5	0	$0\,(x^5)$	0110
0	1	1	1101	6	0	$0\,(x^6)$	0011
1	1	$0\,(x)$	0111	7	0	$1\,(x^7)$	1101
2	1	$0\,(x^2)$	0010	8	0	$1\,(x^8)$	1010
3	0	$0\,(x^3)$	0001	9	0	$0\,(x^9)$	0101
4	0	$1\,(x^4)$	1100	10	0	$1\,(x^{10})$	1110

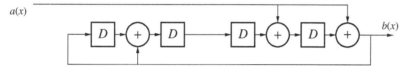

Figure 4.11: Circuit realization of $H(x) = (1 + x)/(1 + x^3 + x^4)$, observability form.

□

Circuits for simultaneous multiplication and division last-element first can be obtained by combining the circuit of Figure 4.2 with the circuit of Figure 4.6. An example is given in Section 4.12.

4.10 Cyclic Encoding

Let $g(x) = 1 + g_1 x + \cdots + g_{n-k-1} x^{n-k-1} + x^{n-k}$ be the generator for a cyclic code. Nonsystematic encoding of the message polynomial $m(x) = m_0 + m_1 x + \cdots + m_{k-1} x^{k-1}$ can be accomplished by shifting $m(x)$ (starting from the high-order symbol m_{k-1}) into either of the circuits shown in Figure 4.2 or 4.3, redrawn with the coefficients of $g(x)$ in Figure 4.12.

To compute a systematic encoding, the steps are accomplished using the circuitry shown in Figure 4.13.

1. Compute $x^{n-k} m(x)$. The shift by x^{n-k} is accomplished in the circuitry by feeding the message $m(x)$ on the *right* side of the circuit, $n - k$ delay units to the right of the left end. The message is clocked in the order $m_{k-1}, m_{k-2}, \ldots, m_0$.

2. Divide by $g(x)$ and compute the remainder, $d(x)$. The "gate" in the feedback path is open, so the signal $x^{n-k} m(x)$ passes through the feedback path, which performs the division. The switch on the right is in position A, so that $x^{n-k} m(x)$ also shifts to the output to form the systematic part of the codeword.

    After clocking $x^{n-k} m(x)$ into the system, the registers contain the remainder $d(x) = R_{g(x)}[x^{n-k} m(x)]$.

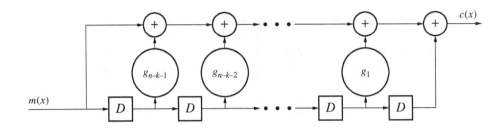

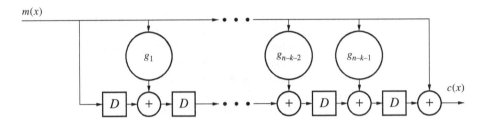

Figure 4.12: Nonsystematic encoding of cyclic codes.

3. Compute $x^{n-k}m(x) - d(x)$. The "gate" on the top is opened so no further feedback occurs, the switch on the right is moved to position B, and the register is clocked $n - k$ times to clock the register contents out to the codeword output, changing the sign (only for nonbinary codes).

Example 4.26 For the $(7,4)$ binary Hamming code with generator $g(x) = 1 + x + x^3$, the systematic encoder circuit is shown in Figure 4.14. For the message $\mathbf{m} = (0,1,1,1)$ with polynomial $m(x) = x + x^2 + x^3$, the contents of the registers are shown here.

Input		Register Contents		
	0	0	0	(Initial state)
1	1	1	0	
1	1	0	1	
1	0	1	0	
0	0	0	1	(Parity bits, $d(x) = x^2$)

The sequence of output bits is

$$\mathbf{c} = (0,0,1,\ 0,1,1,1).$$

$\square$

Systematic encoding can also be accomplished using the parity check polynomial $h(x) = h_0 + h_1 x + \cdots + h_k x^k$. Since $h_k = 1$, we can write the condition (4.3) as

$$c_{l-k} = -\sum_{i=0}^{k-1} h_i c_{l-i} \quad l = k, k+1, \ldots, n-1. \tag{4.7}$$

Given the systematic part of the message $c_{n-k} = m_0, c_{n-k+1} = m_1, \ldots, c_{n-1} = m_{k-1}$, the parity check bits $c_0, c_1, \ldots, c_{n-k-1}$ can be found from (4.7). A circuit for doing the computations is shown in Figure 4.15. The operation is as follows.

1. With gate 1 open (passing message symbols) and gate 2 closed and with the syndrome register cleared to 0, the message $m(x) = m_0 + m_1 x + \cdots + m_{k-1} x^{k-1}$ is shifted into simultaneously the

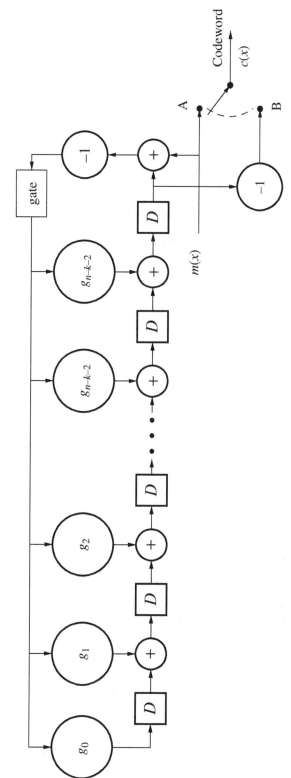

Figure 4.13: Circuit for systematic encoding using $g(x)$.

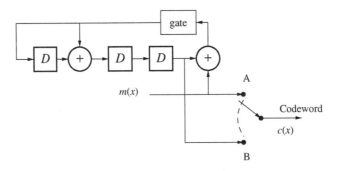

Figure 4.14: Systematic encoder for the $(7, 4)$ code with generator $g(x) = 1 + x + x^3$.

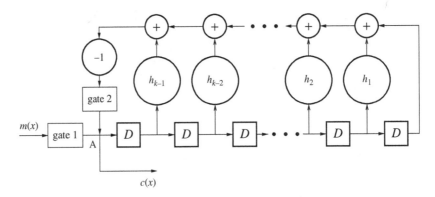

Figure 4.15: A systematic encoder using the parity check polynomial.

registers and into the channel, starting with the symbol m_{k-1}. At the end of k shifts, the registers contain the symbols $m_0, m_1, \ldots, m_{k-1}$, reading from left to right.

2. Then gate 1 is closed and gate 2 is opened. The first parity check digit

$$c_{n-k-1} = -(h_0 c_{n-1} + h_1 c_{n-2} + \cdots + h_{k-1} c_{n-k})$$
$$= -(m_{k-1} + h_1 m_{k-2} + \cdots + h_{k-1} m_0)$$

is produced and appears at the point labeled A. c_{n-k-1} is simultaneously clocked into the channel and into the buffer register (through gate 2).

3. The computation continues until all $n - k$ parity check symbols have been produced.

Example 4.27   For the $(7, 4)$ code generator $g(x) = x^3 + x + 1$, the parity check polynomial is

$$h(x) = \frac{x^7 - 1}{x^3 + x + 1} = x^4 + x^2 + x + 1.$$

Figure 4.16 shows the systematic encoder circuit. (The -1 coefficient is removed because of the binary field.) Suppose $m(x) = x + x^2 + x^3$. The bits $(0, 1, 1, 1)$ are shifted in (with the 1bit shifted first). Then the contents of the registers are shown here.

	Registers			Output
0	1	1	1	(Initial)
1	0	1	1	1
0	1	0	1	0
0	0	1	0	0

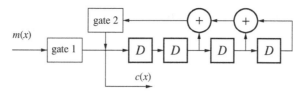

Figure 4.16: A systematic encoder for the Hamming code using $h(x)$.

The sequence of output bits is

$$\mathbf{c} = (0, 0, 1, \ 0, 1, 1, 1),$$

which is the same as produced by the encoding in Example 4.26. □

4.11 Syndrome Decoding

We now examine the question of decoding binary cyclic codes. Recall that for any linear code, we can form a standard array, or we can use the reduced standard array using syndromes. For cyclic codes it is possible to exploit the cyclic structure of the codes to further decrease the memory requirements.

Recall that the syndrome was initially defined as $s(x) = r(x)h(x) \pmod{x^n - 1}$. However, we can define the syndrome an alternative way. Since a codeword must be a multiple of $g(x)$, when we divide $r(x)$ by $g(x)$, the remainder is zero exactly when $r(x)$ is a codeword. Thus, we can employ the division algorithm to obtain a syndrome. We write

$$r(x) = q(x)g(x) + s(x),$$

where $q(x)$ is the quotient (which is usually not used for decoding) and $s(x)$ is the remainder polynomial having degree less than the degree of $g(x)$:

$$s(x) = s_0 + s_1 x + \cdots + s_{n-k-1} x^{n-k-1}.$$

Thus, to compute the syndrome we can use polynomial division. A circuit such as that in Figure 4.6 can be used to compute the remainder.

We have the following useful result about cyclic codes and syndromes.

Theorem 4.28 *Let $s(x)$ be the syndrome corresponding to $r(x)$, so $r(x) = q(x)g(x) + s(x)$. Let $r^{(1)}(x)$ be the polynomial obtained by cyclically right-shifting $r(x)$ and let $s^{(1)}(x)$ denote its syndrome. Then $s^{(1)}(x)$ is the remainder obtained when dividing $xs(x)$ by $g(x)$. In other words, syndromes of shifts of $r(x) \pmod{x^n - 1}$ are shifts of $s(x) \pmod{g(x)}$.*

Proof With $r(x) = r_0 + r_1 x + \cdots + r_{n-1} x^{n-1}$ the cyclic shift $r^{(1)}(x)$ is

$$r^{(1)}(x) = r_{n-1} + r_0 x + \cdots + r_{n-2} x^{n-1},$$

which can be written as

$$r^{(1)}(x) = xr(x) - r_{n-1}(x^n - 1).$$

Using the division algorithm and the fact that $x^n - 1 = g(x)h(x)$,

$$q^{(1)}(x)g(x) + s^{(1)}(x) = x[q(x)g(x) + s(x)] - r_{n-1}g(x)h(x),$$

where $s^{(1)}(x)$ is the remainder from dividing $r^{(1)}(x)$ by $g(x)$. Rearranging, we have

$$xs(x) = [q^{(1)}(x) + r_{n-1}h(x) - xq(x)]g(x) + s^{(1)}(x).$$

Thus, $s^{(1)}(x)$ is the remainder from dividing $xs(x)$ by $g(x)$, as claimed. □

By induction, the syndrome $s^{(i)}(x)$ that corresponds to cyclically shifting $r(x)$ i times to produce $r^{(i)}(x)$ is obtained from the remainder of $x^i s(x)$ when divided by $g(x)$. This can be accomplished in hardware simply by clocking the circuitry that computes the remainder $s(x)$ i times: the shift register motion corresponds to multiplication by x, while the feedback corresponds to computing the remainder upon division by $g(x)$.

Example 4.29 For the $(7,4)$ code with generator $g(x) = x^3 + x + 1$, let $r(x) = x + x^2 + x^4 + x^5 + x^6$ be the received vector. That is, $\mathbf{r} = (0,1,1,0,1,1,1)$. Then the cyclic shifts of $r(x)$ and their corresponding syndromes are shown here.

Polynomial	Syndrome
$r(x) = x + x^2 + x^4 + x^5 + x^6$	$s(x) = x$
$r^{(1)}(x) = 1 + x^2 + x^3 + x^5 + x^6$	$s^{(1)}(x) = x^2$
$r^{(2)}(x) = 1 + x + x^3 + x^4 + x^6$	$s^{(2)}(x) = 1 + x$
$r^{(3)}(x) = 1 + x + x^2 + x^4 + x^5$	$s^{(3)}(x) = x + x^2$
$r^{(4)}(x) = x + x^2 + x^3 + x^5 + x^6$	$s^{(4)}(x) = 1 + x + x^2$
$r^{(5)}(x) = 1 + x^2 + x^3 + x^4 + x^6$	$s^{(5)}(x) = 1 + x^2$
$r^{(6)}(x) = 1 + x + x^3 + x^4 + x^5$	$s^{(6)}(x) = 1$

Figure 4.17 shows the circuit which divides by $g(x)$, producing the remainder $s(x) = s_0 + s_1 x + s_2 x^2$ in its registers. Suppose the gate is initially open and $r(x)$ is clocked in, producing the syndrome $s(x)$. Now the gate is closed and the system is clocked six more times. The registers contain successively the syndromes $s^{(i)}(x)$ corresponding to the cyclically shifted polynomials $r^{(i)}(x)$, as shown in Table 4.4.

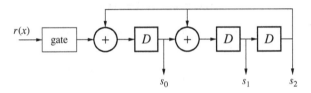

Figure 4.17: A syndrome computation circuit for a cyclic code example.

Table 4.4: Computing the Syndrome and Its Cyclic Shifts

Clock	Input	Registers			Syndrome
Initial:		0	0	0	
1	1	1	0	0	
2	1	1	1	0	
3	1	1	1	1	
4	0	1	0	1	
5	1	0	0	0	
6	1	1	0	0	
7	0	0	1	0	$s(x) = x$
. . . . (turn off gate)					
8		0	0	1	$s^{(1)}(x) = x^2$
9		1	1	0	$s^{(2)}(x) = 1 + x$
10		0	1	1	$s^{(3)}(x) = x + x^2$
11		1	1	1	$s^{(4)}(x) = 1 + x + x^2$
12		1	0	1	$s^{(5)}(x) = 1 + x^2$
13		0	0	0	$s^{(6)}(x) = 0$ (syndrome adjustment)

We only need to compute one syndrome **s** for an error **e** and all cyclic shifts of **e**, so the size of the syndrome table can be reduced by n. Furthermore, we can compute the shifts necessary using the same circuit that computes the syndrome in the first place.

This observation also indicates a means of producing error correcting hardware. Consider the decoder shown in Figure 4.18. This decoder structure is called a **Meggitt decoder**.

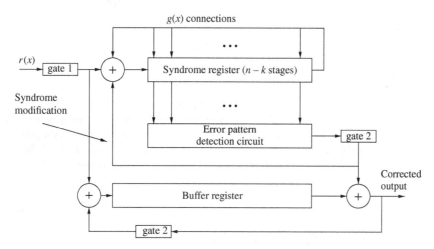

Figure 4.18: Cyclic decoder when $r(x)$ is shifted in the left end of the syndrome register.

The operation of the circuit is as follows. The error pattern detection circuit is a combinatorial logic circuit that examines the syndrome bits and outputs a 1 if the syndrome corresponds to an error in the *highest* bit position, $e_{n-1} = 1$.

- With gate 1 open and gate 2 closed and with the syndrome register cleared to 0, the received vector is shifted into the buffer register and the syndrome register for n clocks. At the end of this, the syndrome register contains the syndrome for $r(x)$.

- Now gate 1 is closed and gate 2 is opened. The error pattern detection circuit outputs $e_{n-1} = 1$ if it has determined that the (current) highest bit position is in error, so that $e(x) = x^{n-1}$. The modified polynomial, denoted by $r_1(x)$, is $r_1(x) = r_0 + r_1 x + \cdots + r_{n-2}x^{n-2} + (r_{n-1} + e_{n-1})x^{n-1}$. Now cyclically shift $r_1(x)$ to produce $r_1^{(1)}(x) = (r_{n-1} + e_{n-1}) + r_0 x + \cdots + r_{n-2}x^{n-1}$. The corresponding syndrome $s_1^{(1)}(x)$ is the remainder of $r_1^{(1)}(x)$ divided by $g(x)$. Since the remainder of $xr(x)$ is $s^{(1)}(x)$ and the remainder of xx^{n-1} is 1, the new syndrome is

$$s_1^{(1)}(x) = s^{(1)}(x) + 1.$$

Therefore, the syndrome register can be adjusted so that it reflects the modification made to $r(x)$ by adding a 1 to the left end of the register. (If only single error correction is possible, then this update is unnecessary.)

The modified value is output and is also fed back around through gate 2.

- Decoding now proceeds similarly on the other bits of $r(x)$. As each error is detected, the corresponding bit is complemented and the syndrome register is updated to reflect the modification. Operation continues until all the bits of the buffer register have been output.

At the end of the decoding process, the buffer register contains the corrected bits.

The key to decoding is designing the error pattern detection circuit.

Example 4.30 Consider again the decoder for the code with generator $g(x) = x^3 + x + 1$. The following table shows the error vectors and their corresponding syndrome vectors and polynomials.

Error	Error Polynomial	Syndrome	Syndrome Polynomial
0000000	$e(x) = 0$	000	$s(x) = 0$
1000000	$e(x) = 1$	100	$s(x) = 1$
0100000	$e(x) = x$	010	$s(x) = x$
0010000	$e(x) = x^2$	001	$s(x) = x^2$
0001000	$e(x) = x^3$	110	$s(x) = 1 + x$
0000100	$e(x) = x^4$	011	$s(x) = x + x^2$
0000010	$e(x) = x^5$	111	$s(x) = 1 + x + x^2$
0000001	$e(x) = x^6$	101	$s(x) = 1 + x^2$

(From this table, we recognize that the received polynomial $r(x)$ in Example 4.29 has an error in the second bit, since $s(x) = x$ is the computed syndrome.) However, what is of immediate interest is the error in the *last* position, $\mathbf{e} = (0000001)$ or $e(x) = x^6$, with its syndrome $s(x) = 1 + x^2$. In the decoder of Figure 4.19, the pattern is detected with a single three-input and gate with the middle input inverted. When this pattern is detected, the outgoing right bit of the register is complemented and the input bit of the syndrome register is complemented. The decoding circuit is thus as shown in Figure 4.19.

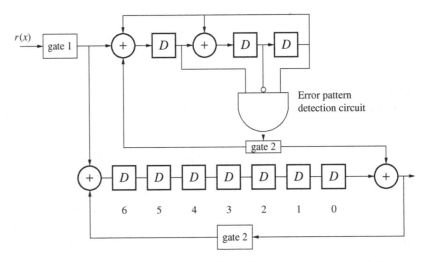

Figure 4.19: Decoder for a $(7, 4)$ Hamming code, input on the left.

Suppose now that $r(x) = x + x^2 + x^4 + x^5 + x^6$, as in Example 4.29. As this is shifted in, the syndrome $s(x) = x$ is computed. Now the register contents are clocked out, producing in succession the syndromes shown in Table 4.4. At clock tick 12 (which is 5 ticks after the initial the pattern was shifted in), $s^{(5)}(x) = 1 + x^2$ appears in the syndrome register, signaling an error in the right bit of the register. The bit of the buffer register is complemented on its way to output, which corresponds to the second bit of the received codeword. The next syndrome becomes 0, corresponding to a vector with no errors. The corrected codeword is thus

$$c(x) = x^2 + x^4 + x^5 + x^6,$$

corresponding to a message polynomial $m(x) = x + x^2 + x^3$.

The overall operation of the Meggitt decoder of Figure 4.19 is shown in Table 4.5. The input is shifted into the syndrome register and the buffer register. (The erroneous bit is indicated underlined.) After being shifted in, the syndrome register is clocked (with no further input) while the buffer register is cyclically shifted. At step 12, the syndrome pattern is detected as corresponding to an error in the right position. This is corrected. The syndrome is simultaneously adjusted, so that no further changes are made in the last two steps.   □

Table 4.5: Operation of the Meggitt Decoder, Input from the Left

Step	Input	Syndrome Register	Buffer Register
1	1	100	1000000
2	1	110	1100000
3	1	111	1110000
4	0	101	0111000
5	1	000	1011100
6	1	100	1101110
7	0	010	0110111
8		001	1011011
9		110	1101101
10		011	1110110
11		111	0111011
12		101	1011101 (error corrected)
13		000	0101110
14		000	0010111

In some cases, the Meggitt decoder is implemented with the received polynomial shifted in to the *right* of the syndrome register, as shown in Figure 4.20. Since shifting $r(x)$ into the right end of the syndrome register is equivalent to multiplying by x^{n-k}, the syndrome after $r(x)$ has been shifted in is $s^{(n-k)}(x)$, the syndrome corresponding to $r^{(n-k)}(x)$. Now decoding operates as before: if $s^{(n-k)}(x)$ corresponds to an error pattern with $e(x)$ with $e_{n-1} = 1$, then bit r_{n-1} is corrected. The effect of the error must also be removed from the syndrome. The updated syndrome, denoted $s_1^{(n-k)}(x)$ is the sum of $s^{(n-k)}(x)$ and the remainder resulting from dividing x^{n-k-1} by $g(x)$. Since x^{n-k-1} has degree less than the degree of $g(x)$, this remainder is, in fact, equal to x^{n-k-1}. The updated syndrome is thus

$$s_1^{(n-k)}(x) = s^{(n-k)}(x) + x^{(n-k-1)}.$$

This corresponds to simply updating the right coefficient of the syndrome register.

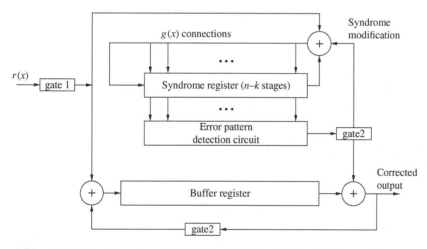

Figure 4.20: Cyclic decoder when $r(x)$ is shifted into the right end of the syndrome register.

Example 4.31 When the error pattern $e(x) = x^6$ is fed into the right-hand side of the syndrome register of a $(7, 4)$ Hamming code, it appears as $x^3 x^6 = x^9$. The remainder upon dividing x^9 by $g(x)$ is $s^{(3)}(x) = R_{g(x)}[x^9] = x^2$. Thus, the syndrome to look for in the error pattern detection circuit is x^2. Figure 4.21 shows the corresponding decoder circuit. □

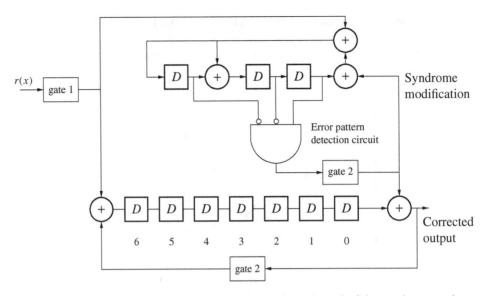

Figure 4.21: Hamming decoder with input fed into the right end of the syndrome register.

Table 4.6: Operation of the Meggitt Decoder, Input from the Right

Step	Input	Syndrome Register	Buffer Register
1	1	110	1000000
2	1	101	1100000
3	1	010	1110000
4	0	001	0111000
5	1	000	1011100
6	1	110	1101110
7	0	011	0110111
8		111	1011011
9		101	1101101
10		100	1110110
11		010	0111011
12		001	1011101 (error corrected)
13		000	0101110
14		000	0010111

If this decoder is used with the received polynomial $r(x) = x + x^2 + x^4 + x^5 + x^6$ (as before), then the syndrome register and buffer register contents are as shown in Table 4.6. Initially the received polynomial is shifted in. As before, the erroneous bit is shown underlined. After step $n = 7$, the syndrome register is clocked with no further input. At step 12, the syndrome pattern detects the error in the right position. This is corrected in the buffer register adjusted in the syndrome register.

Example 4.32   We present decoders for the $(31, 26)$ Hamming code generated by $g(x) = 1 + x^2 + x^5$.

Figure 4.22(a) shows the decoder when the received polynomial is shifted in on the left. The error pattern $e(x) = x^{30}$ results in the syndrome $s(x) = R_{g(x)}[x^{30}] = x^4 + x$.

Figure 4.22(b) shows the decoder when the received polynomial is shifted in on the right. The error pattern $e(x) = x^{30}$ results in the shifted syndrome

$$s(x) = R_{g(x)}[x^{30}x^5] = R_{g(x)}[x^{35}] = x^4.$$

□

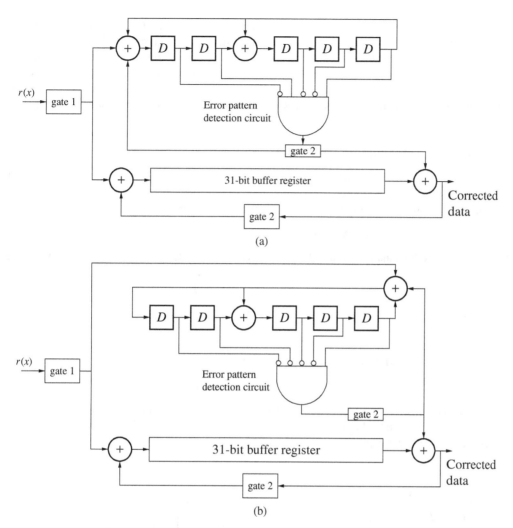

Figure 4.22: Meggitt decoders for the $(31, 26)$ Hamming code. (a) Input from the left end; (b) Input from the right end.

4.12 Shortened Cyclic Codes

Shortened block codes were introduced in Section 3.9. In this section, we deal in particular about shortened cyclic codes [272]. Let C be an (n, k) cyclic code and let $C' \subset C$ be the set of codewords for which the l high-order message symbols are equal to 0. That is, the symbols $m_{k-l}, m_{k-l+1}, \ldots, m_{k-2}, m_{k-1}$ are all set to 0, so all messages are of the form

$$m(x) = m_0 + m_1 x + \cdots + m_{k-l-1} x^{k-l-1}.$$

There are 2^{k-l} codewords in C', forming a linear $(n - l, k - l)$ subcode of C. The minimum distance of C' is at least as large as that of C. C' is called a shortened cyclic code.

The shortened cyclic code C' is not, in general, cyclic. However, since C is cyclic, the encoding and decoding of C' can be accomplished using the same cyclic-oriented hardware as for C, since the deleted message symbols do not affect the parity check or syndrome computations. However, care must be taken that the proper number of cyclic shifts is used.

Let $r(x) = r_0 + r_1 x + \cdots + r_{n-l-1} x^{n-l-1}$ be the received polynomial. Consider a decoder in which $r(x)$ is clocked into the right end of the syndrome register, as in Figure 4.20. Feeding $r(x)$ into the right-end register corresponds to multiplying $r(x)$ by x^{n-k}. However, since the code is of length $n - l$, what is desired is multiplication by $x^{n-(k-l)} = x^{n-k+l}$. Thus, the syndrome register must be cyclically clocked another l times after $r(x)$ has been shifted into the register. While this is feasible, it introduces an additional decoder latency of l clock steps. We now show two different methods to eliminate this latency.

4.12.1   Method 1: Simulating the Extra Clock Shifts

In this method, $r(x)$ is fed into the syndrome computation register in such a way in $n - k$ shifts the effect of $n - k + l$ shifts is obtained.

Using the division algorithm to divide $x^{n-k+l} r(x)$ by $g(x)$, we obtain

$$x^{n-k+l} r(x) = q_1(x)g(x) + s^{(n-k+l)}(x), \tag{4.8}$$

where $s^{(n-k+l)}(x)$ is the remainder and is the desired syndrome for decoding the digit r_{n-l-1}. Now divide x^{n-k+l} by $g(x)$,

$$x^{n-k+l} = q_2(x)g(x) + \rho(x),$$

where $\rho(x) = \rho_0 + \rho_1 x + \cdots + \rho_{n-k-1} x^{n-k-1}$ is the remainder. This can also be expressed as

$$\rho(x) = x^{n-k+l} + q_2(x)g(x) \tag{4.9}$$

(for binary operations). Multiply (4.9) by $r(x)$ and use (4.8) to write

$$\rho(x)r(x) = [q_1(x) + q_2(x)r(x)]g(x) + s^{(n-k+l)}(x).$$

From this equation, it is seen that the desired syndrome $s^{(n-k+l)}(x)$ can be obtained by multiplying $r(x)$ by $\rho(x)$ then computing the remainder modulo $g(x)$. Combining the first-element-first circuits of Figures 4.2 and 4.6, we obtain the circuit shown in Figure 4.23.

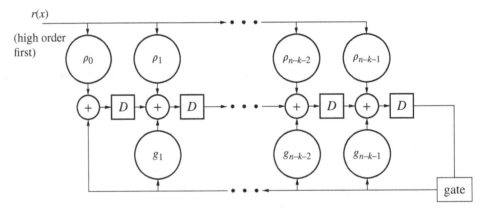

Figure 4.23: Multiply $r(x)$ by $\rho(x)$ and compute the remainder modulo $g(x)$.

The error pattern detection circuit for this implementation is the same as for the unshortened code.

Example 4.33   Consider the Hamming $(7,4)$ code generated by $g() = 1 + x + x^3$ whose decoder is shown in Figure 4.21. Shortening this code by $l = 2$, a $(5,2)$ code is obtained. To find $\rho(x)$, we have

$$\rho(x) = R_{g(x)}[x^{n-k+l}] = R_{g(x)}[x^5] = x^2 + x + 1.$$

Figure 4.24 shows the decoder for this code.   □

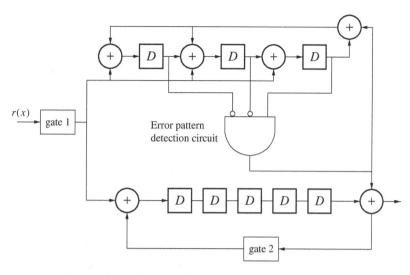

Figure 4.24: Decoder for a shortened Hamming code.

4.12.2 Method 2: Changing the Error Pattern Detection Circuit

Another way to modify the decoder is to change the error pattern detection circuit so that it looks for patterns corresponding to the shifted input, but still retains the usual syndrome computation circuit. The error pattern detection circuit is designed to produce a 1 when the syndrome register corresponds to a correctable error pattern $e(x)$ with an error at the right position, that is, at position x^{n-l-1}. When this happens, the received digit r_{n-l-1} is corrected and the effect of the error digit e_{n-l-1} is removed from the syndrome register via syndrome modification.

Let $e(x) = x^{n-l-1}$. Since this is input on the right end, this is equivalent to $x^{n-l-1}x^{n-k} = x^{2n-l-k-1}$. The syndrome pattern to watch for is obtained by $\sigma(x) = R_{g(x)}[x^{2n-l-k-1}]$.

Example 4.34 Consider again the $(7,4)$ Hamming code shortened to a $(5,2)$ code. The error pattern at position $x^{n-l-1} = x^4$ appearing on the right-hand side as $x^{2n-l-k-1} = x^7$. The syndrome to watch for is

$$\sigma(x) = R_{g(x)}[x^7] = 1.$$

□

4.13 Binary CRC Codes

The term Cyclic Redundancy Check (CRC) code has come to be jargon applied to cyclic codes used as error *detection* codes: they indicate when error patterns have occurred over a sequence of bits, but not where the errors are nor how to correct them. They are commonly used in networking in conjunction with protocols which call for retransmission of erroneous data packets. Typically, CRCs are *binary* codes, with operations taking place in $GF(2)$. A CRC is a cyclic code, that is, the code polynomials are multiples of a generator polynomial $g(x) \in GF(2)[x]$.

CRCs are simply cyclic codes, so the same encoding and decoding concepts as any other cyclic code applies. In this section, however, we will introduce an efficient byte-oriented algorithm for computing syndromes.

We use the notation $R_{g(x)}[\cdot]$ to denote the operation of computing the remainder of the argument when dividing by $g(x)$. The entire cyclic encoding operation can thus be written, as described in Section 4.8, as

$$c(x) = x^r m(x) + R_{g(x)}[x^r m(x)].$$

Example 4.35 Let $g(x) = x^{16} + x^{15} + x^2 + 1$ and $m(x) = x^{14} + x^{13} + x^{11} + x^{10} + x^8 + x^5 + x^2 + x + 1$ corresponding to the message bits

$$\mathbf{m} = [\underbrace{0, 1, 1, 0, 1, 1, 0, 1}_{d_0}, \underbrace{0, 0, 1, 0, 0, 1, 1, 1}_{d_1}]$$

$$= [m_{15}, m_{14}, \ldots, m_1, m_0].$$
$$m(x) = x^{14} + x^{13} + x^{11} + x^{10} + x^8 + x^5 + x^2 + x + 1.$$

The vector $\mathbf{m}$ is written here with m_0 on the right. Since $\deg(g(x)) = n - k = 16$, to encode we first multiply $m(x)$ by x^{16}:

$$x^{16}m(x) = x^{30} + x^{29} + x^{27} + x^{26} + x^{24} + x^{21} + x^{18} + x^{17} + x^{16}, \qquad (4.10)$$

then divide by $g(x)$ to obtain the remainder

$$d(x) = x^{14} + x^{13} + x^{11} + x^{10} + x^9 + x^7 + x^6 + x^4 + x^2. \qquad (4.11)$$

The code polynomial is

$$\begin{aligned} c(x) &= x^{16}m(x) + d(x) \\ &= x^{30} + x^{29} + x^{27} + x^{26} + x^{24} + x^{21} + x^{18} + x^{17} + x^{16} \\ &\quad + x^{14} + x^{13} + x^{11} + x^{10} + x^9 + x^7 + x^6 + x^4 + x^2. \end{aligned}$$

The operation can also be represented using bit vectors instead of polynomials. From (4.10),

$$x^{16}m(x) \leftrightarrow [0, 1, 1, 0, 1, 1, 0, 1, 0, 0, 1, 0, 0, 1, 1, 1 | 0, 0, 0, 0, 0, 0, 0, 0, 0, 0, 0, 0, 0, 0, 0, 0]$$

(with the highest power of x corresponding to the bit on the left of this vector) and from (4.11),

$$d(x) \leftrightarrow [0, 0, 0, 0, 0, 0, 0, 0, 0, 0, 0, 0, 0, 0, 0, 0 | 0, 1, 1, 0, 1, 1, 1, 0, 1, 1, 0, 1, 0, 1, 0, 0].$$

Adding these two vectors, we find

$$\mathbf{c} = [0, 1, 1, 0, 1, 1, 0, 1, 0, 0, 1, 0, 0, 1, 1, 1 | 0, 1, 1, 0, 1, 1, 1, 0, 1, 1, 0, 1, 0, 1, 0, 0].$$

The message vector $\mathbf{m}$ is clearly visible in the codeword $\mathbf{c}$.   □

Suppose now that the effect of the channel is represented by

$$r(x) = c(x) + e(x).$$

To see if any errors occurred in transmission over the channel, $r(x)$ is divided by $g(x)$ to find $s(x) = R_{g(x)}[r(x)]$. The polynomial $s(x)$ is the syndrome polynomial. Note that

$$s(x) = R_{g(x)}[r(x)] = R_{g(x)}[c(x) + e(x)] = R_{g(x)}[c(x)] + R_{g(x)}[e(x)] = R_{g(x)}[e(x)],$$

since $R_{g(x)}[c(x)] = 0$ for any code polynomial $c(x)$.

If $s(x) \neq 0$, then $e(x) \neq 0$, that is, one or more errors have occurred and they have been detected. If $s(x) = 0$, then it is concluded $r(x)$ has not been corrupted by errors, so that the original message $m(x)$ may be immediately extracted from $r(x)$.

Note, however, that if an error pattern occurs which is exactly one of the code polynomials, say $e(x) = c_1(x)$ for some code polynomial $c_1(x)$, then

$$s(x) = R_{g(x)}[c(x) + c_1(x)] = R_{g(x)}[c(x)] + R_{g(x)}[c_1(x)] = 0.$$

In other words, there are error patterns that can occur which are not detected by the code: an error pattern is undetectable if and only if $e(x)$ is a code polynomial.

Let us consider how many such undetected error patterns there are.

- Suppose there is a single bit in error, $e(x) = x^i$ for $0 \leq i \leq n - 1$. If the polynomial $g(x)$ has more than one nonzero term, it cannot divide x^i evenly, so there is a nonzero remainder. Thus, all single-bit errors can be detected.

- Suppose that $g(x)$ has $(1 + x)$ as a factor. Then it can be shown that all codewords have even parity, so that *any* odd number of bit errors can be detected.

- A *burst error* of length B is any error pattern for which the number of bits between the first and last errors (inclusive) is B. For example, the bit sequence $\ldots,0,0,1,1,0,1,1,0,1,0,\ldots$ has a burst error of length 7.

  Let $e(x)$ be an error burst of length $r = n - k$ or less. Then

$$e(x) = x^i(1 + e_1 x + \cdots + e_{n-k-1}x^{n-k-1})$$

  for some i, $0 \leq i \leq k$. Since $g(x)$ is of degree $n - k$ and has a nonzero constant term, that is

$$g(x) = 1 + g_1 x + \cdots + g_{n-k-1}x^{n-k-1} + x^{n-k},$$

  then $R_{g(x)}[e(x)]$ cannot be zero, so the burst can be detected.

- Consider now a burst of errors of length $n - k + 1$, with error polynomial $e(x) = x^i(1 + e_1 x + \cdots + e_{n-k-1}x^{n-k-1} + x^{n-k})$. There are 2^{n-k-1} possible error patterns of this form for each value of i. Of these, all but error bursts of the form $e(x) = x^i g(x)$ are detectable. The fraction of undetectable bursts of length $n - k + 1$ is therefore $2^{-(n-k-1)}$.

- For bursts of length $l > n - k + 1$ starting at position i, all 2^{l-2} of the bursts are detectable except those of the form

$$e(x) = x^i a(x) g(x)$$

  for some $a(x) = a_0 + a_1 x + \cdots + a_{l-n+k-1}x^{l-n+k-1}$ with $a_0 = a_{l-n+k-1} = 1$. The number of undetectable bursts is $2^{l-n+k-2}$, so the fraction of undetectable bursts is 2^{-n+k}.

Example 4.36 Let $g(x) = x^{16} + x^{15} + x^2 + 1$. This can be factored as $g(x) = (1 + x)(1 + x + x^{15})$, so the CRC is capable of detecting any odd number of bit errors. It can be shown that the smallest integer m such that $g(x)$ divides $1 + x^m$ is $m = 32767$, so by Exercise 4.37, the CRC is able to detect any pattern of two errors — a double-error pattern — provided that the code block length $n \leq 32767$. All burst errors of length 16 or less are detectable. Bursts of length 17 are detectable with probability 0.99997. Bursts of length ≥ 18 are detectable with probability 0.99998. □

Table 4.7 [489, p. 123, 364], lists commonly used generator polynomials for CRC codes of various lengths.

4.13.1 Byte-Oriented Encoding and Decoding Algorithms

The syndrome computation algorithms described above are well-adapted to bit-oriented hardware implementations. However, CRCs are frequently used to check the integrity of files or data packets on computer systems which are intrinsically byte-oriented. An algorithm is presented here which produces the same result as a bit-oriented algorithm, but which operates on a byte at a time. The algorithm is faster because it deals with larger pieces of data and also because it makes use of parity information which is computed in advance and stored. It thus has higher storage requirements than the bitwise encoding algorithm but lower operational complexity; for a degree 16 polynomial, 256 2-byte integers must be stored.

Consider a block of N bytes of data, as in a file or a data packet. We think of the first byte of data as corresponding to higher powers of x in its polynomial representation, since polynomial division

Table 4.7: CRC Generators

CRC Code	Generator Polynomial
CRC-4	$g(x) = x^4 + x^3 + x^2 + x + 1$
CRC-7	$g(x) = x^7 + x^6 + x^4 + 1$
CRC-8	$g(x) = x^8 + x^7 + x^6 + x^4 + x^2 + 1$
CRC-12	$g(x) = x^{12} + x^{11} + x^3 + x^2 + x + 1$
CRC-ANSI	$g(x) = x^{16} + x^{15} + x^2 + 1$
CRC-CCITT	$g(x) = x^{16} + x^{12} + x^5 + 1$
CRC-SDLC	$g(x) = x^{16} + x^{15} + x^{13} + x^7 + x^4 + x^2 + x + 1$
CRC-24	$g(x) = x^{24} + x^{23} + x^{14} + x^{12} + x^8 + 1$
CRC-32a	$g(x) = x^{32} + x^{30} + x^{22} + x^{15} + x^{12} + x^{11} + x^7 + x^6 + x^5 + x$
CRC-32b	$g(x) = x^{32} + x^{26} + x^{23} + x^{22} + x^{16} + x^{12} + x^{11} + x^{10} + x^8$ $+ x^7 + x^5 + x^4 + x^2 + x + 1$

requires dealing first with highest powers of x. This convention allows the file to be processed in storage order. The data are stored in bytes, as in

$$d_0, d_1, \ldots, d_{N-1},$$

where d_i represents an 8-bit quantity. For a byte of data d_i, let $d_{i,7}, d_{i,6}, \ldots, d_{i,0}$ denote the bits, where $d_{i,0}$ is the least-significant bit (LSB) and $d_{i,7}$ is the most significant bit (MSB). The byte d_i, the "next byte" to be processed, has a corresponding polynomial representation

$$b_{i+1}(x) = d_{i,7}x^7 + d_{i,6}x^6 + \cdots + d_{i,1}x + d_{i,0}.$$

The algorithm described below reads in a byte of data and computes the CRC parity check information for all of the data up to that byte. It is described in terms of a CRC polynomial $g(x)$ of degree 16, but generalization to other degrees is straightforward. For explicitness of examples, the generator polynomial $g(x) = x^{16} + x^{15} + x^2 + 1$ (CRC-ANSI) is used throughout. Let $m^{[i]}(x)$ denote the message polynomial formed from the $8i$ bits of the first i data bytes $\{d_0, d_1, \ldots, d_{i-1}\}$,

$$m^{[i]}(x) = d_{0,7}x^{8i-1} + d_{0,6}x^{8i-2} + \cdots + d_{i-1,1}x + d_{i-1,0},$$

and let $p^{[i]}(x)$ denote the corresponding parity polynomial of degree ≤ 15,

$$p^{[i]}(x) = \underbrace{p^{[i]}_{15}x^{15} + p^{[i]}_{14}x^{14} + \cdots + p^{[i]}_8 x^8}_{\text{upper byte. crc1}} + \underbrace{p^{[i]}_7 x^7 + \cdots + p^{[i]}_1 x + p^{[i]}_0}_{\text{lower byte. crc0}}.$$

(For the future, note that this is divided into 2 bytes, an upper most significant byte and a lower least significant byte.) By the operation of cyclic encoding,

$$p^{[i]}(x) = R_{g(x)}[x^{16}m^{[i]}(x)],$$

that is,

$$x^{16}m^{[i]}(x) = q(x)g(x) + p^{[i]}(x) \tag{4.12}$$

for some quotient polynomial $q(x)$.

Let us now augment the message by one more byte. This is done by shifting the current message polynomial eight positions (bits) and inserting the new byte in the empty bit positions. We can write

$$m^{[i+1]}(x) = \underbrace{x^8 m^{[i]}(x)}_{\text{Shift 8 positions}} + \underbrace{b_{i+1}(x)}_{\text{add new byte}},$$

where $b_{i+1}(x)$ represents the new data. The new parity polynomial is computed by

$$p^{[i+1]}(x) = R_{g(x)}[x^{16}m^{[i+1]}(x)] = R_{g(x)}[x^{16}(x^8 m^{[i]}(x) + b_{i+1}(x))]. \tag{4.13}$$

Using (4.12), we can write (4.13) as

$$p^{[i+1]}(x) = R_{g(x)}[x^8 g(x)q(x) + x^8 p^{[i]}(x) + x^{16}b_{i+1}(x)].$$

This can be expanded as

$$p^{[i+1]}(x) = R_{g(x)}[x^8 g(x)q(x)] + R_{g(x)}[x^8 p^{[i]}(x) + x^{16}b_{i+1}(x)],$$

or

$$p^{[i+1]}(x) = R_{g(x)}[x^8 p^{[i]}(x) + x^{16}b_{i+1}(x)]$$

since $g(x)$ evenly divides $x^8 g(x)q(x)$. The argument can be expressed in expanded form as

$$
\begin{aligned}
x^8 p^{[i]}(x) + x^{16}b_{i+1}(x) &= p_{15}^{[i]}x^{23} + p_{14}^{[i]}x^{22} + \cdots + p_1^{[i]}x^9 + p_0^{[i]}x^8 \\
&\quad + d_{i,7}x^{23} + d_{i,6}x^{22} + \cdots + d_{i,1}x^{17} + d_{i,0}x^{16} \\
&= (d_{i,7} + p_{15}^{[i]})x^{23} + (d_{i,6} + p_{14}^{[i]})x^{22} + \cdots + (d_{i,0} + p_8^{[i]})x^{16} \\
&\quad + p_7^{[i]}x^{15} + p_6^{[i]}x^{14} + \cdots + p_0^{[i]}x^8.
\end{aligned}
$$

Let $t_j = d_{i,j} + p_{j+8}^{[i]}$ for $j = 0, 1, \ldots, 7$. The 8 bits of t are the 8 bits in the new byte plus the eight MSBs of $p^{[i]}(x)$. Then

$$x^8 p^{[i]}(x) + x^{16}b_{i+1}(x) = t_7 x^{23} + t_6 x^{22} + \cdots + t_0 x^{16} + p_7^{[i]}x^{15} + p_6^{[i]}x^{14} + \cdots + p_0^{[i]}x^8.$$

The updated parity is thus

$$
\begin{aligned}
p^{[i+1]}(x) &= R_{g(x)}[t_7 x^{23} + t_6 x^{22} + \cdots + t_0 x^{16} + p_7^{[i]}x^{15} + p_6^{[i]}x^{14} + \cdots + p_0^{[i]}x^8] \\
&= R_{g(x)}[t_7 x^{23} + t_6 x^{22} + \cdots + t_0 x^{16}] + R_{g(x)}[p_7^{[i]}x^{15} + p_6^{[i]}x^{14} + \cdots + p_0^{[i]}x^8] \\
&= R_{g(x)}[t_7 x^{23} + t_6 x^{22} + \cdots + t_0 x^{16}] + p_7^{[i]}x^{15} + p_6^{[i]}x^{14} + \cdots + p_0^{[i]}x^8,
\end{aligned}
$$

where the last equality follows since the degree of the argument of the second $R_{g(x)}$ is less than the degree of $g(x)$.

There are $2^8 = 256$ possible remainders of the form

$$R_{g(x)}[t_7 x^{23} + t_6 x^{22} + \cdots + t_0 x^{16}]. \tag{4.14}$$

For each 8-bit combination $t = (t_7, t_6, \ldots, t_0)$, the remainder in (4.14) can be computed and stored in advance. For example, when $t = 1$ (i.e., $t_0 = 1$ and other t_i are 0) we find

$$R_{g(x)}[x^{16}] = x^{15} + x^2 + 1,$$

which has the representation in bits [1,0,0,0, 0,0,0,0, 0,0,0,0, 0,1,0,1], or in hex, 8005. Table 4.8 shows the remainder values for all 256 possible values of t, where the hex number $R(t)$ represents the bits of the syndrome. Let $\tilde{t}(x) = t_7 x^{23} + t_6 x^{22} + \cdots + t_0 x^{16}$ and let $R(t) = R_{g(x)}[\tilde{t}(x)]$ (i.e., the polynomial represented by the data in Table 4.8). The encoding update rule is summarized as

$$p^{[i+1]}(x) = \underbrace{p_7^{[i]}x^{15} + p_6^{[i]}x^{14} + \cdots + p_0^{[i]}x^8}_{\text{upper byte. New crc1}} + \underbrace{R(t)}_{\text{lower byte. New crc0}}.$$

Table 4.8: Lookup Table for CRC-ANSI

t	$R(t)$	t	$R(t)$	t	$R(t)$	t	$R(t)$	t	$R(t)$	t	$R(t)$	t	$R(t)$	t	$R(t)$
0	0000	1	8005	2	800f	3	000a	4	801b	5	001e	6	0014	7	8011
8	8033	9	0036	a	003c	b	8039	c	0028	d	802d	e	8027	f	0022
10	8063	11	0066	12	006c	13	8069	14	0078	15	807d	16	8077	17	0072
18	0050	19	8055	1a	805f	1b	005a	1c	804b	1d	004e	1e	0044	1f	8041
20	80c3	21	00c6	22	00cc	23	80c9	24	00d8	25	80dd	26	80d7	27	00d2
28	00f0	29	80f5	2a	80ff	2b	00fa	2c	80eb	2d	00ee	2e	00e4	2f	80e1
30	00a0	31	80a5	32	80af	33	00aa	34	80bb	35	00be	36	00b4	37	80b1
38	8093	39	0096	3a	009c	3b	8099	3c	0088	3d	808d	3e	8087	3f	0082
40	8183	41	0186	42	018c	43	8189	44	0198	45	819d	46	8197	47	0192
48	01b0	49	81b5	4a	81bf	4b	01ba	4c	81ab	4d	01ae	4e	01a4	4f	81a1
50	01e0	51	81e5	52	81ef	53	01ea	54	81fb	55	01fe	56	01f4	57	81f1
58	81d3	59	01d6	5a	01dc	5b	81d9	5c	01c8	5d	81cd	5e	81c7	5f	01c2
60	0140	61	8145	62	814f	63	014a	64	815b	65	015e	66	0154	67	8151
68	8173	69	0176	6a	017c	6b	8179	6c	0168	6d	816d	6e	8167	6f	0162
70	8123	71	0126	72	012c	73	8129	74	0138	75	813d	76	8137	77	0132
78	0110	79	8115	7a	811f	7b	011a	7c	810b	7d	010e	7e	0104	7f	8101
80	8303	81	0306	82	030c	83	8309	84	0318	85	831d	86	8317	87	0312
88	8330	89	8335	8a	833f	8b	033a	8c	832b	8d	032e	8e	0324	8f	8321
90	0360	91	8365	92	836f	93	036a	94	837b	95	037e	96	0374	97	8371
98	8353	99	0356	9a	035c	9b	8359	9c	0348	9d	834d	9e	8347	9f	0342
a0	03c0	a1	83c5	a2	83cf	a3	03ca	a4	83db	a5	03de	a6	03d4	a7	83d1
a8	83f3	a9	03f6	aa	03fc	ab	83f9	ac	03e8	ad	83ed	ae	83e7	af	03e2
b0	83a3	b1	03a6	b2	03ac	b3	83a9	b4	03b8	b5	83bd	b6	83b7	b7	03b2
b8	0390	b9	8395	ba	839f	bb	039a	bc	838b	bd	038e	be	0384	bf	8381
c0	0280	c1	8285	c2	828f	c3	028a	c4	829b	c5	029e	c6	0294	c7	8291
c8	82b3	c9	02b6	ca	02bc	cb	82b9	cc	02a8	cd	82ad	ce	82a7	cf	02a2
d0	82e3	d1	02e6	d2	02ec	d3	82e9	d4	02f8	d5	82fd	d6	82f7	d7	02f2
d8	02d0	d9	82d5	da	82df	db	02da	dc	82cb	dd	02ce	de	02c4	df	82c1
e0	8243	e1	0246	e2	024c	e3	8249	e4	0258	e5	825d	e6	8257	e7	0252
e8	0270	e9	8275	ea	827f	eb	027a	ec	826b	ed	026e	ee	0264	ef	8261
f0	0220	f1	8225	f2	822f	f3	022a	f4	823b	f5	023e	f6	0234	f7	8231
f8	8213	f9	0216	fa	021c	fb	8219	fc	0208	fd	820d	fe	8207	ff	0202

Values for t and $R(t)$ are expressed in hex.

In words: The lower (least significant) byte of the updated parity is from $R(t)$, looked up in the table. The upper (most significant byte) of the updated parity is obtained from the lower byte of the previous parity, shifted over 8 bits.

The algorithm described above in terms of polynomials can be efficiently implemented in terms of byte-oriented arithmetic on a computer. The parity check information is represented in 2 bytes, `crc1` and `crc0`, with `crc1` representing the high-order parity byte. Together, [`crc1`, `crc0`] forms the 2-byte (16 bit) parity. Also, let $R(t)$ denote the 16-bit parity corresponding to the t, as in Table 4.8. The operation $\oplus$ indicates bitwise modulo-2 addition (i.e., exclusive or). The fast CRC algorithm is summarized in Algorithm 4.1.

Example 4.37 A file consists of 2 bytes of data, $d_0 = 109$ and $d_1 = 39$, or in hexadecimal notation, $d_0 = 6D_{16}$ and $d_1 = 27_{16}$. This corresponds to the bits

$$0110\ 1101\ 0010\ 0111,$$

$$\underbrace{\qquad\qquad}_{d_0}\ \underbrace{\qquad\qquad}_{d_1}$$

Algorithm 4.1 Fast CRC encoding for a stream of bytes

Input: A sequence of bytes $d_0, d_1, \ldots, d_N - 1$.

1   Initialization: Clear the parity information: Set $[\texttt{crc1}, \texttt{crc0}] = [0,0]$.

2   For $i = 0$ to $N - 1$:

3   Compute $t = d_i \oplus \texttt{crc1}$

4       $[\texttt{crc1}, \texttt{crc0}] = [\texttt{crc0}, 0] \oplus R(t)$

5   End

6   Output: Return the 16-bit parity $[\texttt{crc1}, \texttt{crc0}]$.

---

with the LSB on the right, or, equivalently, the polynomial

$$x^{14} + x^{13} + x^{11} + x^{10} + x^8 + x^5 + x^2 + x + 1.$$

(It is the same data as in Example 4.35.) The steps of the algorithm are as follows:

1   $\texttt{crc1}, \texttt{crc0} = [0,0]$

2   $i = 0$:

3       $t = d_0 \oplus \texttt{crc1} = 6D_{16} + 0 = 6D_{16}$

4       $[\texttt{crc1}, \texttt{crc0}] = [\texttt{crc0}, 0] \oplus R(t) = [0, 0] \oplus 816D_{16}$

2   $i = 1$:

3       $t = d_1 \oplus \texttt{crc1} = 27_{16} \oplus 81_{16} = A6_{16}$

4       $[\texttt{crc1}, \texttt{crc0}] = [\texttt{crc0}, 0] \oplus R(t) = [6D_{16}, 0] \oplus 03D4_{16} = 6ED4_{16}$

6 Return $6ED4_{16}$.

The return value corresponds to the bits

$$0110 \quad 1110 \quad 1101 \quad 0100$$

which has polynomial representation

$$p(x) = x^{14} + x^{13} + x^{11} + x^{10} + x^9 + x^7 + x^6 + x^4 + x^2.$$

This is the same parity as obtained in Example 4.35.   □

4.13.2   CRC Protecting Data Files or Data Packets

When protecting data files or data packets using CRC codes, the CRC codeword length is selected in bytes. As suggested in Example 4.36, for the CRC-16 code the number of bits in the codeword should be less than 32767, so the number of bytes in the codeword should be less than 4095. That is, the number of message bytes should be less than 4093. Let K denote the number of message bytes and let N denote the number of code bytes, for example, $N = K + 2$.

The encoded file is, naturally, longer than the unencoded file, since parity bytes is included. In encoding a file, the file is divided into blocks of length K. Each block of data is written to an encoded file, followed by the parity bytes. At the end of the file, if the number of bytes available is less than K, a shorter block is written out, followed by its parity bytes.

In decoding (or checking) a file, blocks of N bytes are read in and the parity for the block is computed. If the parity is not zero, one or more error has been detected in that block. At the end of the file, if the block size is shorter, the appropriate block length read in is used.

Appendix 4.A   Linear Feedback Shift Registers

Closely related to polynomial division is the linear feedback shift register (LFSR). This is simply a divider with no input — the output is computed based on the initial condition of its storage elements.

With proper feedback connections, the LFSR can be used to produce a sequence with many properties of random noise sequences (for example, the correlation function approximates a δ function). These pseudonoise sequences are widely used in spread spectrum communication and as synchronization sequences in common modem protocols. The LFSR can also be used to provide an important part of the representation of Galois fields, which are fundamental to many error correction codes (see Chapter 5). The LFSR also reappears in the context of decoding algorithms for BCH and Reed–Solomon codes, where an important problem is to determine a shortest LFSR and its initial condition which could produce a given output sequence (see Chapter 6).

Appendix 4.A.1 Basic Concepts

A binary LFSR circuit is built using a polynomial division circuit with no input. Eliminating the input to the division circuit of Figure 4.6, we obtain the LFSR shown in Figure 4.25. Since there is no input, the output generated is due to the initial state of the registers. Since there are only a finite number of possible states for this digital device, the circuit must eventually return to a previous state. The number of steps before a state reappears is called the **period** of the sequence generated by the circuit. A binary LFSR with p storage elements has 2^p possible states. Since the all-zero state never changes, it is removed from consideration, so the longest possible period is $2^p - 1$.

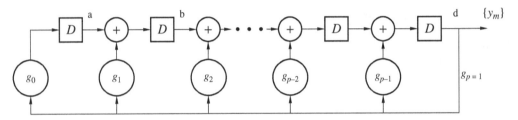

Figure 4.25: Linear feedback shift register.

Example 4.38   Figure 4.26 illustrates the LFSR with connection polynomial $g(x) = 1 + x + x^2 + x^4$. Table 4.9 shows the sequence of states and the output of the LFSR when it is loaded with the initial condition $(1, 0, 0, 0)$. The sequence of states repeats after seven steps, so the output sequence is periodic with period 7. Table 4.10 shows the sequence of states for the same connection polynomial when the LFSR is loaded with the initial condition $(1, 1, 0, 0)$, which again repeats after seven steps. Of the 15 possible nonzero states of the LFSR, these two sequences exhaust all but one of the possible states. The sequence for the last remaining state, corresponding to an initial condition $(1, 0, 1, 1)$, is shown in Table 4.11; this repeats after only one step.

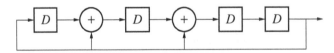

Figure 4.26: Linear feedback shift register with $g(x) = 1 + x + x^2 + x^4$.

□

Example 4.39   Figure 4.27 illustrates the LFSR with connection polynomial $g(x) = 1 + x + x^4$. Table 4.12 shows the sequence of states and the output of the LFSR when it is loaded with the initial condition $(1, 0, 0, 0)$. In this case, the shift register sequences through 15 states before it repeats.   □

Definition 4.40   A sequence generated by a connection polynomial $g(x)$ of degree n is said to be a **maximal length** sequence if the period of the sequence is $2^n - 1$.   □

Table 4.9: LFSR Example with $g(x) = 1 + x + x^2 + x^4$
and Initial State 1

Count	State				Output
0	1	0	0	0	0
1	0	1	0	0	0
2	0	0	1	0	0
3	0	0	0	1	1
4	1	1	1	0	0
5	0	1	1	1	1
6	1	1	0	1	1
7	1	0	0	0	0

Table 4.10: LFSR Example with $g(x) = 1 + x + x^2 + x^4$] and
Initial State $1 + x$

Count	State				Output
0	1	1	0	0	0
1	0	1	1	0	0
2	0	0	1	1	1
3	1	1	1	1	1
4	1	0	0	1	1
5	1	0	1	0	0
6	0	1	0	1	1
7	1	1	0	0	0

Table 4.11: LFSR Example with $g(x) = 1 + x + x^2 + x^4$] and Initial
State $1 + x^2 + x^3$

Count	State				Output
0	1	0	1	1	1
1	1	0	1	1	1

Thus, the output sequence of Example 4.39 is a maximal-length sequence, while the output sequences of Example 4.38 are not. A connection polynomial which produces a maximal-length sequence is a **primitive polynomial**. A program to exhaustively search for primitive polynomials modulo p for arbitrary (small) p is primfind.

primitive.txt

primfind.c

The sequence of outputs of the LFSR satisfies the equation

$$y_m = \sum_{j=0}^{p-1} g_j y_{m-p+j}.$$ (4.15)

This may be seen as follows. Denote the output sequence of the LFSR in Figure 4.25 by $\{y_m\}$. For immediate convenience, assume that the sequence is infinite $\{\ldots, y_{-2}, y_{-1}, y_0, y_1, y_2, \ldots\}$ and represent this sequence as a formal power series

$$y(x) = \sum_{i=-\infty}^{\infty} y_i x^i.$$

Consider the output at point "a" in Figure 4.25. Because of the delay x, at point "a" the signal is

$$g_0 x y(x),$$

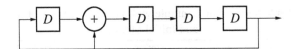

Figure 4.27: Linear feedback shift register with $g(x) = 1 + x + x^4$.

Table 4.12: LFSR example with $g(x) = 1 + x + x^4]$ and Initial State 1

Count	State				Output
0	1	0	0	0	0
1	0	1	0	0	0
2	0	0	1	0	0
3	0	0	0	1	1
4	1	1	0	0	0
5	0	1	1	0	0
6	0	0	1	1	1
7	1	1	0	1	1
8	1	0	1	0	0
9	0	1	0	1	1
10	1	1	1	0	0
11	0	1	1	1	1
12	1	1	1	1	1
13	1	0	1	1	1
14	1	0	0	1	1
15	1	0	0	0	0

where the factor x represents the delay through the memory element. At point "b," the signal is

$$g_0 x^2 y(x) + g_1 x y(x).$$

Continuing likewise through the system, at the output point "d" the signal is

$$(g_0 x^p + g_1 x^{p-1} + \cdots + g_{p-1} x)y(x),$$

which is the same as the output signal:

$$(g_0 x^p + g_1 x^{p-1} + \cdots + g_{p-1} x)y(x) = y(x). \qquad (4.16)$$

Equation (4.16) can be true only if coefficients of corresponding powers of x match. This produces the relationship

$$y_i = \sum_{j=0}^{p-1} g_j y_{i-p+j}. \qquad (4.17)$$

Letting $g_j^* = g_{p-j}$, (4.17) can be written in the somewhat more familiar form as a convolution,

$$y_i = \sum_{j=1}^{p} g_j^* y_{i-j}. \qquad (4.18)$$

Equation (4.18) can also be rewritten as

$$\sum_{j=0}^{p} g_j^* y_{i-j} = 0 \qquad (4.19)$$

with the stipulation that $g_0^* = 1$.

The polynomial $g^*(x)$ with coefficients $g_j^* = g_{p-j}$ is sometimes referred to as the **reciprocal polynomial**. That is, $g^*(x)$ has its coefficients in the reverse order from $g(x)$. (The term "reciprocal" does not mean that $h(x)$ is a multiplicative inverse of $g(x)$; it is just a conventional name.) The reciprocal polynomial of $g(x)$ is denoted as $g^*(x)$. If $g(x)$ is a polynomial of degree p with nonzero constant term (i.e., $g_0 = 1$ and $g_p = 1$), then the reciprocal polynomial can be obtained by

$$g^*(x) = x^p g(1/x).$$

It is clear in this case that the reciprocal of the reciprocal is the same as the original polynomial. However, if $g_0 = 0$, then the degree of $x^p g(1/x)$ is less than the degree of $g(x)$ and this latter statement is not true.

With the understanding that the output sequence is periodic with period $2^p - 1$, so that $y_{-1} = y_{2^p-2}$, (4.19) is true for all $i \in \mathbb{Z}$. Because the sum in (4.19) is equal to 0 for all i, the polynomial $g^*(x)$ is said to be an *annihilator* of $y(x)$.

Example 4.41 For the coefficient polynomial $g(x) = 1 + x + x^2 + x^4$, the reciprocal polynomial is $g^*(x) = 1 + x^2 + x^3 + x^4$ and the LFSR relationship is

$$y_i = y_{i-2} + y_{i-3} + y_{i-4} \quad \text{for all } i \in \mathbb{Z}. \tag{4.20}$$

For the output sequence of Table 4.9 $\{0, 0, 0, 1, 0, 1, 1, 0, \dots\}$, it may be readily verified that (4.20) is satisfied. □

The LFSR circuit diagram is sometimes expressed in terms of the reciprocal polynomials, as shown in Figure 4.28. It is important to be careful of the conventions used.

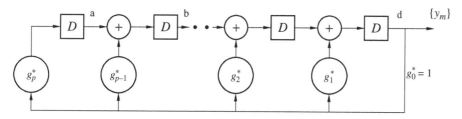

Figure 4.28: Linear feedback shift register, reciprocal polynomial convention.

Appendix 4.A.2   Connection With Polynomial Division

The output sequence produced by an LFSR has a connection with polynomial long division. To illustrate this, let us take $g(x) = 1 + x + x^2 + x^4$, as in Example 4.38. The reciprocal polynomial is $g^*(x) = 1 + x^2 + x^3 + x^4$. Let the dividend polynomial be $d(x) = x^3$. (The relationship between the sequence and the dividend are explored in Exercise 4.43.) The power series obtained by dividing $d(x)$ by $g^*(x)$, with $g^*(x)$ written in order of increasing degree, is obtained by formal long division:

$$
\begin{array}{r}
x^3 + x^5 + x^6 \ \cdots \\[2pt]
\hline
1 + x^2 + x^3 + x^4 \,\big|\, x^3 \\
x^3 + x^5 + x^6 + x^7 \\
\hline
x^5 + x^6 + x^7 \\
x^5 + \quad x^7 + x^8 + x^9 \\
\hline
x^6 + \quad x^8 + x^9 \\
x^6 + \quad x^8 + x^9 + x^{10} \\
\hline
x^{10}
\end{array}
$$

The quotient polynomial corresponds to the sequence $\{0, 0, 0, 1, 0, 1, 1, \ldots\}$, the same as the output sequence shown in Table 4.9.

Let $y_0, y_1, \ldots$ be an infinite sequence produced by an LFSR, which we represent with $y(x) = y_0 + y_1 x + y_2 x^2 + \cdots = \sum_{n=0}^{\infty} y_n x^n$. Furthermore, represent the initial state of the shift register as $y_{-1}, y_{-2}, \ldots, y_{-p}$. Using the recurrence relation (4.18) we have

$$y(x) = \sum_{n=0}^{\infty} \sum_{j=1}^{p} g_j^* y_{n-j} x^n = \sum_{j=1}^{p} g_j^* x^j \sum_{n=0}^{\infty} y_{n-j} x^{n-j}$$

$$= \sum_{j=1}^{p} g_j^* x^j \left[(y_{-j} x^{-j} + \cdots + y_{-1} x^{-1}) + \sum_{n=0}^{\infty} y_n x^n \right]$$

$$= \sum_{j=1}^{p} g_j^* x^j [(y_{-j} x^{-j} + \cdots + y_{-1} x^{-1}) + y(x)]$$

so that

$$y(x) = \frac{\sum_{j=1}^{p} g_j^* x^j (y_{-j} x^{-j} + \cdots + y_{-1} x^{-1})}{1 - \sum_{j=1}^{p} g_j^* x^j} \tag{4.21}$$

$$= \frac{\sum_{j=1}^{p} g_j^* (y_{-j} + y_{-j+1} x + \cdots + y_{-1} x^{j-1})}{g^*(x)}.$$

Example 4.42 Returning to Example 4.38, with the periodic sequence $y_{-1} = 1$, $y_{-2} = 1$, $y_{-3} = 0$, and $y_{-4} = 1$. From (4.21), we find

$$y(x) = \frac{x^3}{g^*(x)} = \frac{x^3}{1 + x^2 + x^3 + x^4},$$

as before.   □

Theorem 4.43 *Let $y(x)$ be produced by a LFSR with connection polynomial $g(x)$ of degree p. If $y(x)$ is periodic with period N, then $g^*(x) \mid (x^N - 1)d(x)$, where $d(x)$ is a polynomial of degree $< p$.*

Proof By the results above, $y(x) = \frac{d(x)}{g^*(x)}$ for a polynomial $d(x)$ with $\deg(d(x)) < p$. If $y(x)$ is periodic, then

$$y(x) = (y_0 + y_1 x + \cdots + y_{N-1} x^{N-1}) + x^N (y_0 + y_1 x + \cdots + y_{N-1} x^{N-1})$$

$$+ x^{2N} (y_0 + y_1 x + \cdots + y_{N-1} x^{N-1}) + \cdots$$

$$= (y_0 + y_1 x + \cdots + y_{N_1} x^{N-1})(1 + x^N + x^{2N} + \cdots)$$

$$= -\frac{(y_0 + y_1 x + \cdots + y_{N-1} x^{N-1})}{x^N - 1}.$$

So

$$\frac{d(x)}{g^*(x)} = -\frac{(y_0 + y_1 x + \cdots + y_{N-1} x^{N-1})}{x^N - 1}$$

or $g^*(x)(y_0 + y_1 x + \cdots + y_{N-1} x^{N-1}) = -d(x)(x^N - 1)$, establishing the result.   □

For a given $d(x)$, the period is the smallest N such that $g^*(x) \mid (x^N - 1)d(x)$.

Example 4.44 The polynomial $g^*(x) = 1 + x^2 + x^3 + x^4$ can be factored as

$$g^*(x) = (1 + x)(1 + x + x^3).$$

Taking $N = 1$ and $d(x) = 1 + x + x^3$, we see that $y(x)$ has period 1. This is the sequence shown in Table 4.11. We note that $g^*(x) \mid x^7 - 1$, so that any $d(x)$ of appropriate degree will serve. □

As a sort of converse to the previous theorem, we have the following.

Theorem 4.45 *If $g^*(x) \mid x^N - 1$, then $y(x) = \frac{1}{g^*(x)}$ is periodic with period N or some divisor of N.*

Proof Let $q(x) = \frac{x^N - 1}{g^*(x)} = y_0 + y_1 x + \cdots + y_{N-1} x^{N-1}$. Then

$$\frac{1}{g^*(x)} = \frac{y_0 + y_1 + \cdots + y_{N-1} x^{N-1}}{1 - x^N} = (y_0 + y_1 x + \cdots + y_{N-1} x^{N-1})(1 + x^N + x^{2N} + \cdots)$$

$$= (y_0 + y_1 x + \cdots + y_{N-1} x^{N-1}) + x^N (y_0 + y_1 x + \cdots + y_{N-1} x^{N-1}) + \cdots,$$

which represents a periodic sequence. □

Theorem 4.46 *If the sequence $y(x)$ produced by the connection polynomial $g(x)$ of degree p has period $2^p - 1$ — that is, $y(x)$ a maximal-length sequence — then $g^*(x)$ is irreducible.*

Proof Since the shift register moves through $2^p - 1$ states before repeating, the shift register must progress through all possible nonzero conditions. Therefore, there is some "initial condition" corresponding to $d(x) = 1$. Without loss of generality we can take $y(x) = 1/g^*(x)$.

Suppose that $g^*(x)$ factors as $a^*(x)b^*(x)$, where $\deg(a^*(x)) = p_1$ and $\deg(b^*(x)) = p_2$, with $p_1 + p_2 = p$. Then

$$y(x) = \frac{1}{g^*(x)} = \frac{1}{a^*(x)b^*(x)} = \frac{c(x)}{a^*(x)} + \frac{d(x)}{b^*(x)}$$

by partial fraction expansion. $c(x)/a^*(x)$ represents a series with period at most $2^{r_1} - 1$ and $d(x)/b^*(x)$ represents a series with period at most $2^{r_2} - 1$. The period of the sum $\frac{c(x)}{a^*(x)} + \frac{d(x)}{b^*(x)}$ is at most the least common multiple of these periods, which must be less than the product of the periods:

$$(2^{p_1} - 1)(2^{p_2} - 1) = 2^p - 3.$$

But this is less than the period $2^p - 1$, so $g^*(x)$ must not have such factors. □

As mentioned above, irreducibility does not imply maximal-length. The polynomial $g^*(x) = 1 + x + x^2 + x^3 + x^4$ divides $x^5 + 1$. But by Theorem 4.45, $y(x) = 1/g^*(x)$ has period 5, instead of the period 15 that a maximal-length sequence would have. What is needed for the polynomial to be primitive.

Appendix 4.A.3   Some Algebraic Properties of Shift Sequences

Let $y(x)$ be a sequence with period N. Then $y(x)$ can be considered an element of $R_N = GF(2)[x]/(x^N - 1)$. Let $g(x)$ be a connection polynomial and $g^*(x)$ be its reciprocal. Let $w(x) = g^*(x)y(x)$, where computation occurs in the ring R_N, and let $w(x) = w_0 + w_1 x + \cdots + w_{N-1} x^{N-1}$. The coefficient w_i of this polynomial is computed by

$$w_i = \sum_{j=0}^{p} g_p^* y_{i-j}.$$

However, by (4.19), this is equal to 0. That is, $g^*(x)y(x) = 0$ in the ring R_N. In this case, we say that $g^*(x)$ *annihilates* the sequence $y(x)$. Let $V(g^*)$ be the set of sequences annihilated by $g^*(x)$. We observe that $V(g^*)$ is an ideal in the ring R_n and has a generator $h^*(x)$ which must divide $x^N - 1$. The generator

$h^*(x)$ is the polynomial factor of $(x^N - 1)/g^*(x)$ of smallest positive degree. If $(X^N - 1)/g^*(x)$ is irreducible, then $h^*(x) = (X^N - 1)/g^*(x)$.

Example 4.47 Let $g(x) = 1 + x + x^2 + x^4$, as in Example 4.38. Then $g^*(x) = 1 + x^2 + x^3 + x^4$. This polynomial divides $x^7 + 1$:

$$h^*(x) = \frac{x^7 + 1}{g^*(x)} = 1 + x^2 + x^3.$$

The polynomial $y(x) = h^*(x)$ corresponds to the output sequence $1, 0, 1, 1, 0, 0, 0$ and its cyclic shifts, which appears in Table 4.9.

The polynomial $y(x) = (1 + x)h^*(x) = 1 + x + x^2 + x^4$ corresponds to the sequence $1, 1, 1, 0, 1$ and its cyclic shifts, which appears in Table 4.10.

The polynomial $y(x) = (1 + x + x^3) * h^*(x) = 1 + x + x^2 + x^3x^4 + x^5 + x^6$ corresponds to the sequence $1, 1, 1, 1, 1, 1$ and its cyclic shifts. This sequence appears in Table 4.11. This sequence also happens to have period 2. □

Example 4.48 For the generator polynomial $g(x) = 1 + x + x^4$ and its reciprocal $g^*(x) = 1 + x^3 + x^4$. This polynomial divides $x^{15} + 1$:

$$h^*(x) = \frac{x^{15} + 1}{g^*(x)} = 1 + x^3 + x^4 + x^6 + x^8 + x^9 + x^{10} + x^{11}.$$

The polynomial $y(x) = h^*(x)$ corresponds to the sequence $1, 0, 0, 1, 1, 0, 1, 0, 1, 1, 1, 1$, which appears in Table 4.12.   □

Programming Laboratory 2: Polynomial Division and Linear Feedback Shift Registers

Objective

Computing quotients and remainders in polynomial division is an important computational step for encoding and decoding cyclic codes. In this lab, you are to create a C++ class which performs these operations for binary polynomials. You will also create an LFSR class, **which will be used in the construction of a Galois field class.**

Preliminary Exercises

Reading: Sections 4.9 and Appendix 4.A.1.

1) Let $g(x) = x^4 + x^3 + x + 1$ and $d(x) = x^8 + x^7 + x^5 + x^4 + x^3 + x + 1$.

   (a) Perform polynomial long division of $d(x)$ and $g(x)$, computing the quotient and remainder, as in Example 4.24.

   (b) Draw the circuit configuration for dividing by $g(x)$.

   (c) Trace the operation of the circuit for the $g(x)$ and $d(x)$ given, identifying the polynomials represented by the shift register contents at each step of the algorithm, as in Table 4.3. Also, identify the quotient and the remainder produced by the circuit.

2) For the connection polynomial $g(x) = x^4 + x^3 + x + 1$, trace the LFSR when the initial register contents are $(1, 0, 0, 0)$, as in Example 4.38. Also, if this does not exhaust all possible 15 states of the LFSR, determine other initial states and the sequences they generate.

Programming Part: `BinLFSR`

Create a C++ class `BinLFSR` which implements an LFSR for a connection polynomial of degree ≤ 32 (or the number of bits stored in an unsigned int). Store the state of the LFSR in an `unsigned int` variable. Create a constructor with arguments

```
BinLFSR(unsigned int g, int n, unsigned int
    // initstate=1);
```

The first argument `g` is a representation of the connection polynomial. For example, `g = 0x17` represents the bits 10111, which represents the polynomial

$g(x) = x^4 + x^2 + x + 1$. The second argument n is the degree of the connection polynomial. The third argument has a default value, corresponding to the initial state $(1, 0, 0, \ldots, 0)$. Use a single unsigned int internally to hold the state of the shift register. The class should have member functions as follows:

```
BinLFSR(void) { g=n=state=mask=mask1=0;}
    // default constructor
BinLFSR(unsigned int g, int n, unsigned int
    // initstate=1);
    // constructor
~BinLFSR() {};
    // destructor
void setstate(unsigned int state);
    // Set the initial state of the LFSR
unsigned char step(void);
    // Step the LFSR one step,
    // and return 1-bit output
unsigned char step(unsigned int &state);
    // Step the LFSR one step,
    // return 1-bit output
    // and the new state
void steps(int nstep, unsigned char *outputs);
    // Step the LFSR nstep times,
    // returning the array of 1-bit outputs
```

Test the class as follows:

1. Use the LFSR class to generate the three sequences of Example 4.38.

2. Use the LFSR class to generate the output sequence and the sequence of states shown in Table 4.12.

Resources and Implementation Suggestions

The storage of the polynomial divider and LFSR could be implemented with a character array, as in

```
unsigned char *storage = new unsigned char[n];
```

Shifting the registers would require a for loop. However, since the degree of the coefficient polynomial is of degree ≤ 32, all the memory can be contained in a single 4-byte unsigned integer, and the register shift can be accomplished with a single-bit shift operation.

- The operator $\ll$ shifts bits left, shifting 0 into the LSBs. Thus, if a=3, then a$\ll$2 is equal to 12. The number 1$\ll$m is equal to 2^m for $m \geq 0$.

- The operator $\gg$ shifts bits right, shifting in 0 to the MSB. Thus, if a=13, then a$\gg$2 is equal to 3.

- Hexadecimal constants can be written using 0xnnnn, as in 0xFF (the number 255), or 0x101

(the number 257). Octal constants can be written using 0nnn, as in 0123, which has the bit pattern 001 010 011.

- The bitwise and operator & can be used to mask bits off. For example, if a = 0x123, then in b = a & 0xFF;, b is equal to 0x23. To retain the lowest m bits of a number, mask it with ((1$\ll$m)-1).

- The algorithms can be implemented either by shifting right using $\gg$ or by shifting left using $\ll$. For a few reasons, it makes sense to shift left, so that the input comes into the LSB and the output comes out of the most significant bit. This may be initially slightly confusing, since the pictures portray shifts to the right.

- **As a tutorial, the code for the LFSR is provided.**

Algorithm 4.2 BinLFSR
File: BinLFSR.h
        BinLFSR.cc
        testBinLFSR.cc
        MakeLFSR

The class declarations are given in BinLFSR.h. The class definitions are given in BinLFSR.cc. In this case, the definitions are short enough that it would make sense to merge the .cc file into the .h file, but they are separated for pedagogical reasons.[5] A simple test program is test-BinLFSR.cc. A very simple makefile (if you choose to use make) is in MakeLFSR.

Programming Part: BinPolyDiv

Create a C++ class BinPolyDiv which implements a polynomial divisor/remainder circuit, where the degree of $g(x)$ is < 32. The constructor has arguments representing the divisor polynomial and its degree:

```
BinPolyDiv(unsigned char *g, int p);
```

The class should have member functions div and remainder which compute, respectively, the quotient and the remainder, with arguments as follows:

```
unsigned int div(unsigned char *d,    // dividend
            int ddegree,
            unsigned char *q,
            unsigned int &quotientdegree,
            unsigned int &remainderdegree);

unsigned int remainder(unsigned char *d,
```

```
    int n,
    int &remainderdegree);
```

The dividend d is passed in as an unsigned char array, 1 bit per character, so that arbitrarily long dividend polynomials can be accommodated. The remainder is returned as a single integer whose bits represent the storage register, with the least-significant bit representing the coefficient of smallest degree of the remainder. Internally, the remainder should be stored in a single unsigned int.

Test your function on the polynomials $g(x) = x^4 + x^3 + x + 1$ and $d(x) = x^8 + x^7 + x^5 + x^4 + x^3 + x + 1$ from the Preliminary Exercises. Also test your function on the polynomials from Example 4.24.

Algorithm 4.3 BinPolyDiv
File: BinPolyDiv.h
       BinPolyDiv.cc
       testBinPolyDiv.cc

Follow-On Ideas and Problems

A binary $\{0, 1\}$ sequence $\{y_n\}$ can be converted to a binary ± 1 sequence z_n by $z_n = (-1)^{y_n}$. For a binary ± 1 sequence $\{z_0, z_1, \ldots, z_{N-1}\}$ with period N, define the cyclic autocorrelation by

$$r_z(\tau) = \frac{1}{N} \sum_{i=0}^{N-1} z_i z_{((i+\tau))},$$

where $((i + \tau))$ denotes $i + \tau$ modulo N.

Using your LFSR class, generate the sequence with connection polynomial $g(x) = 1 + x + x^4$ and compute and plot $r_z(\tau)$ for $\tau = 0, 1, \ldots, 15$. (You may want to make the plots by saving the computed data to a file, then plotting using some convenient plotting tool such as MATLAB.) You should observe that there is a single point with correlation 1 (at $\tau = 0$) and that the correlation at all other lags is $-1/N$.

The shape of the correlation function is one reason that maximal length sequences are called pseudonoise sequences: the correlation function approximates a δ function (with the approximation improving for longer N).

As a comparison, generate a sequence with period 7 using $g(x) = 1 + x + x^2 + x^4$ and plot $r_z(\tau)$ for this sequence.

Programming Laboratory 3: CRC Encoding and Decoding

Objective

In this lab, you become familiar with cyclic encoding and decoding, both in bit-oriented and byte-oriented algorithms.

Preliminary

Reading: Section 4.13.

Verify that the remainder $d(x)$ in (4.11) is correct by dividing $x^{16}m(x)$ by $g(x)$. (You may want to do this both by hand and using a test program invoking BinPolyDiv, as a further test on your program.)

Programming Part

1. Write a C++ class CRC16 which computes the 16-bit parity bits for a stream of data, where $g(x)$ is a generator polynomial of degree 16. The algorithm should use the polynomial division idea (that is, a bit-oriented algorithm. You may probably want to make use of a BinPolyDiv object from Lab 2 in

your class). Here is a class declaration you might find useful:

```
class CRC16 {
protected:
    BinPolyDiv div;     // the divider object
public:
    CRC16(unsigned int crcpoly); // constructor
    int CRC(unsigned char *data, int len);
    // Compute the CRC for the data
    // data=data to be encoded
    // len = number of bytes to be encoded
    // Return value: the 16 bits of
    // parity
    // (data[0] is associated with the
    // highest power of x^n)
};
```

Test your program first using Example 4.35.

2. Write a standalone program crcenc which encodes a file, making use of your CRC16 class. Use $g(x) = x^{16} + x^{15} + x^2 + 1$. The program should accept three command line arguments:

   crcenc K filein fileout

   where K is the message block length (in bytes), filein is the input file, and fileout is the encoded file.

3. Write a standalone program `crcdec` which decodes a file, making use of your CRC class. The program should accept three arguments:

```
crcdec K filein fileout
```

where `K` is the message block length (in bytes), `filein` is an encoded file, and `fileout` is a decoded file.

4. Test `crcenc` and `crcdec` by first encoding then decoding a file, then comparing the decoded file with the original. (A simple compare program is `cmpsimple`.) The decoded file should be the same as the original file. Use a message block length of 1024 bytes. Use a file of 1,000,000 random bytes created using the `makerand` program for the test.

5. Test your programs further by passing the encoded data through a binary symmetric channel using the `bsc` program. Try channel crossover probabilities of 0.00001, 0.001, 0.01, and 0.1. Are there any blocks of data that have errors that are not detected?

6. Write a class `FastCRC16` which uses the byte-oriented algorithm to compute the parity bits for a generator $g(x)$ of degree 16. A sample class definition follows:

```
class FastCRC16 {
protected:
    static int *crctable;
    unsigned char crc0, crc1;
    // the two bytes of parity
public:
    FastCRC16(unsigned int crcpoly);  // constructor
    int CRC(unsigned char *data, int len);
    // Compute the CRC for the data
    // data[0] corresponds to the
    // highest powers of x
};
```

The table of parity values (as in Table 4.8) should be stored in a static class member variable (see the discussion below about static variables). The constructor for the class should allocate space for the table and fill the table, if it has not already been built.

7. Test your program using the data in Example 4.37.

8. Write a standalone program `fastcrcenc` which encodes a file using `FastCRC16`. Use $g(x) = x^{16} + x^{15} + x^2 + 1$. The program should have the same arguments as the program `crcenc`. Test your program by encoding some data and verify that the encoded file is the same as for a file encoded using `crcenc`.

9. Write a decoder program `fastcrcdec` which decodes using `FastCRC16`. Verify that it decodes correctly.

10. How much faster is the byte-oriented algorithm?

Resources and Implementation Suggestions

Static Member Variables A static member variable of a class is a variable that is associated with the class. However, all instances of the class share that same data, so the data are not really part of any particular object. To see why these might be used, suppose that you want to build a system that has two `FastCRC16` objects in it:

```
FastCRC16 CRC1(g);   // instantiate two objects
FastCRC16 CRC2(g);
```

The `FastCRC16` algorithm needs the data from Table 4.8. This data could be represented using member data as in

```
class FastCRC16 {
protected:
    int *crctable;
    unsigned char crc0, crc1;
    // the two bytes of parity
public:
    FastCRC16(int crcpoly);  // constructor
    int CRC(unsigned char *data, int len);
};
```

However, there are two problems with this:

1. Each object would have its own table. This wastes storage space.

2. Each object would have to construct its table, as part of the constructor routine. This wastes time.

As an alternative, the lookup table could be stored in a static member variable. Then it would only need to be constructed once (saving computation time) and only stored once (saving memory). The tradeoff is that it is not possible by this arrangement to have two or more different lookup tables in the same system of software at the same time. (There are ways to work around this problem, however. You should try to think of a solution on your own.)

The declaration `static int *crctable;` which appears in the `.h` file does not define the variable. There must be a definition somewhere, in a C++ source file that is only compiled once. Also, since it is a static object, in a sense external to the class, its definition must be fully scoped. Here is how it is defined:

```
// File: FastCRC.cc

// ...
#include "FastCRC.h"
```

```
int *FastCRC16::crctable=0;
```

This defines the pointer and initializes it to 0. Allocation of space for the table and computation of its contents is accomplished by the constructor:

```
// Constructor for FastCRC16 object
FastCRC16::FastCRC16(int crcpoly) {
    if(FastCRC16::crctable==0) {
        // the table has not been allocated yet
        FastCRC16::crctable = new int[256];
        // Now build the tables
        // ...
    }
    // ...
}
```

Static member variables do not necessarily disappear when an object goes out of scope. We shall use static member variables again in the Galois field arithmetic implementation.

Command Line Arguments For operating systems which provide a command-line interface, reading the command line arguments into a program is very straightforward. The arguments are passed in to the `main` routine using the variables `argc` and `argv`. These may then be parsed and used. `argc` is the total number of arguments on the command line, including the program name. If there is only the program name (with no other arguments), then `argc==1`. `argv` is an array of pointers to the string commands. `argv[0]` is the name of the program being run.

As an example, to read the arguments for `crcenc K filein fileout`, you could use the following code:

```
// Program crcenc

// ...
```

```
main(int argc, char *argv[]) {
    int K;
    char *infname, *outfname;

    // ...
    if(argc!=4) {
    // check number of arguments is as expected
        cout « "Usage: " « argv[0] «
            "K infile outfile" « endl;
        exit(-1);
    }
    K = atoi(argv[1]);
    // read blocksize as an integer
    infname = argv[2];
    // pointer to input file name
    outfname = argv[3];
    // pointer to output file name
    // ...
}
```

Picking Out All the Bits in a File To write the bit-oriented decoder algorithm, you need to pick out all the bits in an array of data. Here is some sample code:

```
// d is an array of unsigned characters
// with 'len' elements
unsigned char bits[8];
// an array that hold the bits of one byte of d

for(int i = 0; i > len; i++) {
    // work through all the bytes of data
    for(int j = 7; j >= 0; j-) {
        // work through the bits in each byte
        bits[j] = (data[i]&(1«j)) != 0;
    }
    // bits now has the bits of d[i] in it
    // ...
}
```

4.14 Exercise

4.1 List the codewords for the $(7,4)$ Hamming code. Verify that the code is cyclic.

4.2 In a ring with identity (that is, multiplicative identity), denote this identity as 1. Prove:

(a) The multiplicative identity is unique.

(b) If an element a has both a right inverse b (i.e., an element b such that $ab = 1$) and a left inverse c (i.e., an element c such that $ca = 1$), then $b = c$. In this case, the element a is said to have an inverse (denoted by a^{-1}). Show that the inverse of an element a, when it exists, is unique.

(c) If a has a multiplicative inverse a^{-1}, then $(a^{-1})^{-1} = a$.

(d) The set of units of a ring forms a group under multiplication. (Recall that a unit of a ring is an element that has a multiplicative inverse.)

(e) If $c = ab$ and c is a unit, then a has a right inverse and b has a left inverse.

(f) In a ring, a nonzero element a such that $ax = 0$ for $x \neq 0$ is said to be a zero divisor. Show that if a has an inverse, then a is not a zero divisor.

4.3 Construct the ring $R_4 = GF(2)[x]/(x^4 + 1)$. That is, construct the addition and multiplication tables for the ring. Is R_4 a field?

4.4 Let R be a commutative ring and let $a \in R$. Let $I = \{b \in R : ab = 0\}$. Show that I is an ideal of R.

4.5 An element a of a ring R is nilpotent if $a^n = 0$ for some positive integer n. Show that the set of all nilpotent elements in a commutative ring R is an ideal.

4.6 Let A and B be ideals in a ring R. The sum $A + B$ is defined as $A + B = \{a + b : a \in A, b \in B\}$. Show that $A + B$ is an ideal in R. Show that $A \subset A + B$.

4.7 Show that in the ring $\mathbb{Z}_{15}$ the polynomial $p(x) = x^2 - 1$ has more than two zeros. In a field there would be only two zeros. What may be lacking in a ring that leads to "too many" zeros?

4.8 In the ring $R_4 = GF(2)[x]/(x^4 + 1)$, multiply $a(x) = 1 + x^2 + x^3$ and $b(x) = x + x^2$. Also, cyclically convolve the sequences $\{1, 0, 1, 1\}$ and $\{0, 1, 1\}$. What is the relationship between these two results?

4.9 For the $(15, 11)$ binary Hamming code with generator $g(x) = x^4 + x + 1$:

(a) Determine the parity check polynomial $h(x)$.

(b) Determine the generator matrix G and the parity check matrix H for this code in nonsystematic form.

(c) Determine the generator matrix G and the parity check matrix H for this code in systematic form.

(d) Let $m(x) = x + x^2 + x^3$. Determine the code polynomial $c(x) = g(x)m(x)$.

(e) Let $m(x) = x + x^2 + x^3$. Determine the systematic code polynomial $c(x) = x^{n-k}m(x) + R_{g(x)}[x^{n-k}m(x)]$, where $R_{g(x)}[\ ]$ computes the remainder after division by $g(x)$.

(f) For the codeword $c(x) = 1 + x + x^3 + x^4 + x^5 + x^9 + x^{10} + x^{11} + x^{13}$, determine the message if nonsystematic encoding is employed.

(g) For the codeword $c(x) = 1 + x + x^3 + x^4 + x^5 + x^9 + x^{10} + x^{11} + x^{13}$, determine the message if systematic encoding is employed.

(h) Let $r(x) = x^{14} + x^{10} + x^5 + x^3$. Determine the syndrome for $r(x)$.

(i) Draw the systematic encoder circuit for this code using the $g(x)$ feedback polynomial.

(j) Draw the decoder circuit for this circuit with $r(x)$ input on the left of the syndrome register. Determine in particular the error pattern detection circuit.

(k) Draw the decoder circuit for this circuit with $r(x)$ input on the right of the syndrome register. Determine in particular the error pattern detection circuit.

(l) Let $r(x) = x^{13} + x^{10} + x^9 + x^5 + x^2 + 1$. Trace the execution of the Meggitt decoder with the input on the left, analogous to Table 4.5.

(m) Let $r(x) = x^{13} + x^{10} + x^9 + x^5 + x^2 + 1$. Trace the execution of the Meggitt decoder with the input on the right, analogous to Table 4.6.

4.10 Let $f(x)$ be a polynomial of degree m in $\mathbb{F}[x]$, where $\mathbb{F}$ is a field. Show that if a is a root of $f(x)$ (so that $f(a) = 0$), then $(x - a)\ f(x)$. *Hint*: Use the division algorithm. Inductively, show that $f(x)$ has at most m roots in $\mathbb{F}$.

4.11 The following are code polynomials from binary cyclic codes. Determine the highest-degree generator $g(x)$ for each code.

(a) $c(x) = 1 + x^4 + x^5$

(b) $c(x) = 1 + x + x^2 + x^3 + x^4 + x^5 + x^6 + x^7 + x^8 + x^9 + x^{10} + x^{11} + x^{12} + x^{13} + x^{14}$

(c) $c(x) = x^{13} + x^{12} + x^9 + x^5 + x^4 + x^3 + x^2 + 1$

(d) $c(x) = x^8 + 1$

(e) $c(x) = x^{10} + x^7 + x^5 + x^4 + x^3 + x^2 + x + 1$

4.12 Let $g(x) = g_0 + g_1 x + \cdots + g_{n-k} x^{n-k}$ be the generator for a cyclic code. Show that $g_0 \neq 0$.

4.13 Show that $g(x) = 1 + x + x^4 + x^5 + x^7 + x^8 + x^9$ generates a binary (21,12) cyclic code. Devise a syndrome computation circuit for this code. Let $r(x) = 1 + x^4 + x^{16}$ be a received polynomial. Compute the syndrome of $r(x)$. Also, show the contents of the syndrome computation circuit as each digit of $r(x)$ is shifted in.

4.14 [272] Let $g(x)$ be the generator for a binary (n,k) cyclic code C. The reciprocal of $g(x)$ is defined as

$$g^*(x) = x^{n-k} g(1/x).$$

(In this context, "reciprocal" does *not* mean multiplicative inverse.)

(a) As a particular example, let $g(x) = 1 + x^2 + x^4 + x^6 + x^7 + x^{10}$. Determine $g^*(x)$. The following subproblems deal with arbitrary cyclic code generator polynomials $g(x)$.

(b) Show that $g^*(x)$ also generates an (n,k) cyclic code.

(c) Let C^* be the code generated by $g^*(x)$. Show that C and C^* have the same weight distribution.

(d) Suppose C has the property that whenever $c(x) = c_0 + c_1 x + c_{n-1} x^{n-1}$ is a codeword, so is its reciprocal $c^*(x) = c_{n-1} + c_{n-2} x + \cdots + c_0 x^{n-1}$. Show that $g(x) = g^*(x)$. Such a code is said to be a *reversible* cyclic code.

4.15 [272] Let $g(x)$ be the generator polynomial of a binary cyclic code of length n.

(a) Show that if $g(x)$ has $x + 1$ as a factor, then the code contains no codevectors of odd weight.

(b) Show that if $x + 1$ is *not* a factor of $g(x)$, then the code contains the all-one codeword.
    Hint: The following is true for any ring $\mathbb{F}[x]$:

$$1 - x^n = (1 - x)(1 + x + x^2 + \cdots + x^{n-1}).$$

(c) Show that the code has minimum weight at least 3 if n is the smallest integer such that $g(x)$ divides $x^n - 1$.

4.16 Let $A(z)$ be the weight enumerator for a binary cyclic code C with generator $g(x)$. Suppose furthermore that $x + 1$ is not a factor of $g(x)$. Show that the code generated by $\tilde{g}(x) = (x + 1)g(x)$ has weight enumerator $\tilde{A}(z) = \frac{1}{2}[A(z) + A(-z)]$.

4.17 Let $g(x)$ be the generator polynomial of an (n,k) cyclic code C. Show that $g(x^\lambda)$ generates an $(\lambda n, \lambda k)$ cyclic code that has the same minimum weight as the code generated by $g(x)$.

4.18 Let C be a $(2^m - 1, 2^m - m - 1)$ Hamming code. Show that if a Meggitt decoder with input on the right-hand side is used, as in Figure 4.20, then the syndrome to look for to correct the digit r_{n-1} is $s(x) = x^{m-1}$. *Hint*: $g(x)$ divides $x^{2^m - 1} + 1$. Draw the Meggitt decoder for this Hamming code decoder.

4.19 [45] The code of length 15 generated by $g(x) = 1 + x^4 + x^6 + x^7 + x^8$ is capable of correcting 2 errors. (It is a (15,7) BCH code.) Show that there are 15 correctable error patterns in which the highest-order bit is equal to 1. Devise a Meggitt decoder for this code with the input applied to the right of the syndrome register. Show that the number of syndrome patterns to check can be reduced to 8.

4.20 Let $g(x)$ be the generator of a $(2^m - 1, 2^m - m - 1)$ Hamming code and let $\tilde{g}(x) = (1 + x)g(x)$. Show that the code generated by $\tilde{g}(x)$ has minimum distance exactly 4.

(a) Show that there exist distinct integers i and j such that $x^i + x^j$ is not a codeword generated by $g(x)$. Write $x^i + x^j = q_1(x)g(x) + r_1(x)$.

(b) Choose an integer k such that the remainder upon dividing x^k by $g(x)$ is not equal to $r_1(x)$. Write $x^i + x^j + x^k = q_2(x)g(x) + r_2(x)$.

(c) Choose an integer l such that when x^l is divided by $g(x)$ the remainder is $r_2(x)$. Show that l is not equal to i, j, or k.

(d) Show that $x^i + x^j + x^k + x^l = [q_2(x) + q_3(x)]g(x)$ and that $x^i + x^j + x^k + x^l$ is a multiple of $(x + 1)g(x)$.

4.21 [272] An error pattern of the form $e(x) = x^i + x^{i+1}$ is called a double-adjacent-error pattern. Let C be the $(2^m - 1, 2^m - m - 2)$ cyclic code generated by $g(x) = (x + 1)p(x)$, where $p(x)$ is a primitive polynomial of degree m.

Show that no two double-adjacent-error patterns can be in the same coset of a standard array for C. Also show that no double-adjacent-error pattern and single-error pattern can be in the same coset of the standard array. Conclude that the code is capable of correcting all the single-error patterns and all the double-adjacent-error patterns.

4.22 [272] Let $c(x)$ be a code polynomial in a cyclic code of length n and let $c^{(i)}(x)$ be its ith cyclic shift. Let l be the smallest positive integer such that $c^{(l)}(x) = c(x)$. Show that l is a factor of n.

4.23 Verify that the circuit shown in Figure 4.2 computes the product $a(x)h(x)$.

4.24 Verify that the circuit shown in Figure 4.3 computes the product $a(x)h(x)$.

4.25 Verify that the circuit shown in Figure 4.4 computes the product $a(x)h(x)$.

4.26 Verify that the circuit shown in Figure 4.5 computes the product $a(x)h(x)$.

4.27 Let $h(x) = 1 + x^2 + x^3 + x^4$. Draw the multiplier circuit diagrams as in Figures 4.4, and 4.5.

4.28 Let $r(x) = 1 + x^3 + x^4 + x^5$ be the input to the decoder in Figure 4.21. Trace the execution of the decoder by following the contents of the registers. If the encoding is systematic, what was the transmitted message?

4.29 Cyclic code dual.

(a) Let C be a cyclic code. Show that the dual code $C^\perp$ is also a cyclic code.

(b) Given a cyclic code C with generator polynomial $g(x)$, describe how to obtain the generator polynomial for the dual code $C^\perp$.

4.30 As described in Section 3.6, the dual to a Hamming code is a $(2^m - 1, m)$ maximal-length code. Determine the generator matrix for a maximal-length code of length $2^m - 1$.

4.31 Let C be an (n, k) binary cyclic code with minimum distance d_{min} and let $C' \subset C$ be the shortened code for which the l high-order message bits are equal to 0. Show that C' has 2^{k-l} codewords and is a linear code. Show that the minimum distance d'_{min} of C' is at least as large as d_{min}.

4.32 For the binary $(31, 26)$ Hamming code generated using $g(x) = 1 + x^2 + x^5$ shortened to a $(28,23)$ Hamming code.

(a) Draw the decoding circuit for the $(28, 23)$ shortened code using the method of simulating extra clock shifts.

(b) Draw the decoding circuit for the $(28, 23)$ shortened code using the method of changing the error pattern detection circuit.

4.33 Explain why CRC codes can be thought of as shortened cyclic codes.

4.34 Let $g(x) = 1 + x^2 + x^4 + x^5$. Determine the fraction of all burst errors of the following lengths that can be detected by a cyclic code using this generator: (a) burst length = 4; (b) burst length = 5; (c) burst length = 6; (d) burst length = 7; (e) burst length = 8.

4.35 Let $g(x) = x^8 + x^7 + x^6 + x^4 + x^2 + 1$ be the generator polynomial for a CRC code.

(a) Let $m(x) = 1 + x + x^3 + x^6 + x^7 + x^{12} + x^{16} + x^{21}$. Determine the CRC-encoded message $c(x)$.

   (b) The CRC-encoded polynomial $r(x) = x^2 + x^3 + x^5 + x^6 + x^7 + x^8 + x^{10} + x^{11} + x^{14} + x^{17} + x^{20} + x^{23} + x^{26} + x^{28}$ is received. Has an error been made in transmission?

4.36 Verify the entry for $t = 3$ in Table 4.8. Also verify the entry for $t =$ dc.

4.37 A double-error pattern is one of the form $e(x) = x^i + x^j$ for $0 \le i < j \le n - 1$. If $g(x)$ does not have x as a factor and does not evenly divide $1 + x^{j-i}$, show that any double-error pattern is detectable.

4.38 A file containing the 2 bytes $d_0 = 56 = 38_{16}$ and $d_1 = 125 = 7\mathrm{D}_{16}$ is to be CRC encoded using the CRC-ANSI generator polynomial $g(x) = x^{16} + x^{15} + x^2 + 1$.

   (a) Convert these data to a polynomial $m(x)$.

   (b) Determine the CRC-encoded data $c(x) = x^r m(x) + R_{g(x)}[x^r m(x)]$ and represent the encoded data as a stream of bits.

   (c) Using the fast CRC encoding of Algorithm 4.1, encode the data. Verify that it corresponds to the encoding obtained previously.

4.39 The output sequence of an LFSR with connection polynomial $g(x)$ can be obtained by formal division of some dividend $d(x)$ by $g^*(x)$. Let $g(x) = 1 + x + x^4$. Show by computational examples that when the connection polynomial is reversed (i.e., reciprocated), the sequence generated by it is reversed (with possibly a different starting point in the sequence). Verify this result analytically.

4.40 Show that (4.17) follows from (4.16). Show that (4.18) follows from (4.17).

4.41 Show that the circuit in Figure 4.29 produces the same sequence as that of Figure 4.25. (Of the two implementations, the one in Figure 4.25 is generally preferred, since the cascaded summers of Figure 4.29 result in propagation delays which inhibit high-speed operations.)

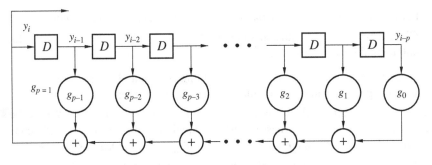

Figure 4.29: Another LFSR circuit.

4.42 Figure 4.30 shows an LFSR circuit with the outputs of the memory elements labeled as state variables x_1 through x_p. Let

$$\mathbf{x}[k] = \begin{bmatrix} x_1[k] \\ x_2[k] \\ \vdots \\ x_p[k] \end{bmatrix}.$$

   (a) Show that for the state labels as in Figure 4.30 that the state update equation is

$$\mathbf{x}[k+1] = M\mathbf{x}[k],$$

where M is the companion matrix

$$M = \begin{bmatrix} 0 & 0 & 0 & 0 & \cdots & 0 & -g_0 \\ 1 & 0 & 0 & 0 & \cdots & 0 & -g_1 \\ 0 & 1 & 0 & 0 & \cdots & 0 & -g_2 \\ 0 & 0 & 1 & 0 & \cdots & 0 & -g_3 \\ \vdots & & & & & & \\ 0 & 0 & 0 & 0 & \cdots & 1 & -g_{p-1} \end{bmatrix}.$$

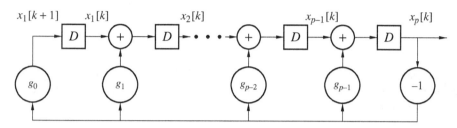

Figure 4.30: An LFSR with state labels.

(b) The characteristic polynomial of a matrix is $p(x) = \det(xI - M)$. Show that

$$p(x) = g_0 + g_1 x + g_2 x^2 + \cdots + g_{p-1} x^{p-1} = g(x).$$

(c) It is a fact that every matrix satisfies its own characteristic polynomial. That is, $p(M) = 0$. (This is the Cayley–Hamilton theorem.) Use this to show that if $g(x) \mid (1 - x^k)$ then $M^k = I$.

(d) The period k of an LFSR with initial vector $\mathbf{x}[0]$ is the smallest k such that $M^k = I$. Interpret this in light of the Cayley–Hamilton theorem, if $p(x)$ is irreducible.

(e) A particular output sequence $\{x_p[0], x_p[1], \ldots, \}$ is to be produced from this LFSR. Determine what the initial vector $\mathbf{x}[0]$ should be to obtain this sequence. (That is, what is the initial value of the LFSR register?)

4.43 Given a sequence $y(x)$ produced by dividing by the reciprocal polynomial of $g(x)$,

$$y(x) = \frac{d(x)}{g^*(x)},$$

determine what $d(x)$ should be to obtain the given $y(x)$.
The sequence $\{0, 1, 0, 0, 1, 1, 0, 1, 0, 1, 1, 1, 1, \ldots\}$ is generated by the polynomial $g^*(x) = 1 + x^3 + x^4$. Determine the numerator polynomial $d(x)$.

4.44 Show that the set of sequences annihilated by a polynomial $g^*(x)$ is an ideal.

4.45 [266] A Barker code is a binary-valued sequence $\{b_n\}$ of length n whose autocorrelation function has values of 0, 1, and n. Only nine such sequences are known, shown in Table 4.13.

(a) Compute the autocorrelation value for the Barker sequence $\{b_5\}$.

(b) Contrast the autocorrelation function for a Barker code with that of a maximal-length LFSR sequence.

4.46 [193] A nonbinary LFSR: It is known that $x^3 + x + \beta$ is irreducible for some values of $\beta \in GF(2^7)$. Find a $\beta \in GF(128)$ such that $x^3 + x + \beta$ is not only irreducible, but also *primitive*. Form the extension field $GF(128)$ using the primitive polynomial $g(\alpha) = \alpha^7 + \alpha^3 + 1$. (This could be used, for example, as a 7-bit scrambler.)
Answer: The value of β can be found by checking each nonzero element of $GF(128)$ in succession, building (in software) an LFSR and clocking to see if the LFSR generates all

Table 4.13: Barker Codes

n	$\{b_n\}$
2	$[1, 1]$
2	$[-1, 1]$
3	$[1, 1, -1]$
4	$[1, 1, -1, 1]$
4	$[1, 1, 1, -1]$
5	$[1, 1, 1, -1, 1]$
7	$[1, 1, 1, -1, -1, 1, -1]$
11	$[1, 1, 1, -1, -1, -1, 1, -1, -1, 1, -1]$
13	$[1, 1, 1, 1, 1, -1, -1, 1, 1, -1, 1, -1, 1]$

possible nonzero values. Each register in the LFSR holds 7 bits, so the three registers can take $2^{3\cdot7} - 1 = 2^{21} - 1 = 2,097,151$ distinct states. By this exhaustive search, it is found that $\beta = \alpha^3$ generates a primitive sequence.

4.15   References

Cyclic codes were explored by Prange [350, 352, 353]. Our presentation owes much to Wicker [483], who promotes the idea of cyclic codes as ideals in a ring of polynomials. The Meggitt decoder is described in [306]. Our discussion of the Meggitt decoder closely follows [271]; many of the exercises were also drawn from that source.

The tutorial paper [360] provides an overview of CRC codes, comparing five different implementations and also providing references to more primary literature.

Much of the material on polynomial operations was drawn from [338]. The table of primitive polynomials is from [509], which in turn was drawn from [338]. An early but still important and thorough work on LFSRs is [160]. See also [158, 159]. The circuit implementations presented here can take other canonical forms. For other realizations, consult a book on digital signal processing, such as [328], or controls [145, 239]. The paper [510] has some of the fundamental algebraic results in it. An example of maximal length sequences to generate modem synchronization sequences is provided in [212]. The paper [394] has descriptions of correlations of maximal length sequences under decimation.

Chapter 5

Rudiments of Number Theory and Algebra

5.1 Motivation

We have seen that the cyclic structure of a code provides a convenient way to encode and reduces the complexity of decoders for some simple codes compared to linear block codes. However, there are several remaining questions to be addressed in approaching practical long code designs and effective decoding algorithms.

1. The cyclic structure means that the error pattern detection circuitry must only look for errors in the last digit. This reduces the amount of storage compared to the syndrome decoding table. However, for long codes, the complexity of the error pattern detection circuitry may still be considerable. It is therefore of interest to have codes with additional *algebraic* structure, in addition to the cyclic structure, that can be exploited to develop efficient decoding algorithms.

2. The decoders presented in Chapter 4 are for *binary* codes: knowing the location of errors is sufficient to decode. However, there are many important nonbinary codes, for which both the error locations and values must be determined. We have presented no theory yet for how to do this.

3. We have seen that generator polynomials $g(x)$ must divide $x^n - 1$. Some additional algebraic tools are necessary to describe how to find such factorizations over arbitrary finite fields.

4. Finally, we have not presented yet a *design* methodology, by which codes having a specified minimum distance might be designed.

This chapter develops mathematical tools to address these issues. In reality, the amount of algebra presented in this chapter is both more and less than is needed. It is more than is needed, in that concepts are presented which are not directly called for in later chapters (even though their presence helps put other algebraic notions more clearly in perspective). It is less than is needed, in that the broad literature of coding theory uses all of the algebraic concepts presented here, and much more. An attempt has been made to strike a balance in presentation.

Example 5.1   We present another example motivating the use of the algebra over finite fields [33]. This example will preview many of the concepts to be developed in this chapter, including modulo operations, equivalence, the Euclidean algorithm, irreducibility, and operations over a finite field.

We have seen in Section 1.9.2 that the decoding algorithm for the Hamming code can be expressed purely in an algebraic way: finding the (single) error can be expressed as finding the solution to a single algebraic equation. It is possible to extend this to a two-error-correcting code whose solution is found by solving two polynomial equations in two unknowns. We demonstrate this by a particular example, starting from a Hamming $(31, 26)$ code having a parity check matrix

$$H = \begin{bmatrix} 0 & 0 & 0 & \cdots & 1 & 1 \\ 0 & 0 & 0 & \cdots & 1 & 1 \\ 0 & 0 & 0 & \cdots & 1 & 1 \\ 0 & 1 & 1 & \cdots & 1 & 1 \\ 1 & 0 & 1 & \cdots & 0 & 1 \end{bmatrix}.$$

Error Correction Coding: Mathematical Methods and Algorithms, Second Edition. Todd K. Moon.
© 2021 John Wiley & Sons, Inc. Published 2021 by John Wiley & Sons, Inc.
Companion website: www.wiley.com/go/Moon/ErrorCorrectionCoding

The 5-tuple in the ith column is obtained from the binary representation of the integer i. As in Section 1.9.2, we represent the 5-tuple in the ith column as a single "number," denoted by γ_i, so we write

$$H = \begin{bmatrix} \gamma_1 & \gamma_2 & \gamma_3 & \cdots & \gamma_{30} & \gamma_{31} \end{bmatrix}.$$

Let us now attempt to move beyond a single error correction code by appending five additional rows to H. We will further assume that the five new elements in each column are some function of column number. That is, we assume that we can write H as

$$H = \begin{bmatrix} 0 & 0 & 0 & \cdots & 1 & 1 \\ 0 & 0 & 0 & \cdots & 1 & 1 \\ 0 & 0 & 0 & \cdots & 1 & 1 \\ 0 & 1 & 1 & \cdots & 1 & 1 \\ 1 & 0 & 1 & \cdots & 0 & 1 \\ f_1(1) & f_1(2) & f_1(3) & \cdots & f_1(30) & f_1(31) \\ f_2(1) & f_2(2) & f_2(3) & \cdots & f_2(30) & f_2(31) \\ f_3(1) & f_3(2) & f_3(3) & \cdots & f_3(30) & f_3(31) \\ f_4(1) & f_4(2) & f_4(3) & \cdots & f_4(30) & f_4(31) \\ f_5(1) & f_5(2) & f_5(3) & \cdots & f_5(30) & f_5(31) \end{bmatrix}. \tag{5.1}$$

The function $\mathbf{f}(i) = [f_1(i), f_2(i), f_3(i), f_4(i), f_5(i)]^T$ has binary components, so $f_i(i) \in \{0, 1\}$. This function tells what binary pattern should be associated with each column. Another way to express this is to note that $\mathbf{f}$ maps binary 5-tuples to binary 5-tuples. We can also use our shorthand notation. Let $f(\gamma)$ be the symbol represented by the 5-tuple $(f_1(i), f_2(i), f_3(i), f_4(i), f_5(i))$, where i is the integer corresponding to $\gamma_i = \gamma$. Using our shorthand notation, we could write (5.1) as

$$H = \begin{bmatrix} \gamma_1 & \gamma_2 & \gamma_3 & \cdots & \gamma_{30} & \gamma_{31} \\ f(\gamma_1) & f(\gamma_2) & f(\gamma_3) & \cdots & f(\gamma_{30}) & f(\gamma_{31}) \end{bmatrix}.$$

The problem now is to select a function $\mathbf{f}$ so that H represents a code capable of correcting two errors, and does so in such a way that an algebraic solution is possible. To express the functions $\mathbf{f}$, we need some way of dealing with these γ_i 5-tuples as algebraic objects in their own right, with arithmetic defined to add, subtract, multiply, and divide. That is, the γ_i need to form a *field*, as defined in Section 2.3, or (since there are only finitely many of them) a *finite field*. Addition in the field is straightforward: we could define addition element-by-element. But how do we multiply in a meaningful, nontrivial way? How do we divide?

The key is to think of each 5-tuple as corresponding to a polynomial of degree ≤ 4. For example:

$$(0, 0, 0, 0, 0) \leftrightarrow 0$$

$$(0, 0, 0, 0, 1) \leftrightarrow 1$$

$$(0, 0, 0, 1, 0) \leftrightarrow x$$

$$(0, 0, 1, 0, 0) \leftrightarrow x^2$$

$$(1, 0, 1, 0, 1) \leftrightarrow x^4 + x^2 + 1.$$

Note that each coefficient of the polynomials is binary; we assume that addition is modulo 2 (i.e., over GF(2)). Clearly, addition of polynomials accomplishes exactly the same thing as addition of the vectors. (They are **isomorphic**.)

How can we multiply? We want our polynomials representing the 5-tuples to have degree ≤ 4, and yet when we multiply the degree may exceed that. For example,

$$(x^3 + x + 1)(x^4 + x^3 + x + 1) = x^7 + x^6 + x^5 + x^4 + x^2 + 1.$$

To reduce the degree, we choose some polynomial $M(x)$ of degree 5, and **reduce the product modulo** $M(x)$. That is, we divide by $M(x)$ and take the remainder. Let us take $M(x) = x^5 + x^2 + 1$. When we divide $x^7 + x^6 + x^5 + x^4 + x^2 + 1$ by $M(x)$, we get a quotient of $x^2 + x + 1$, and a remainder of $x^3 + x^2 + x$. We use the remainder:

$$(x^3 + x + 1)(x^4 + x^3 + x + 1) = x^7 + x^6 + x^5 + x^4 + x^2 + 1$$

$$\equiv x^3 + x^2 + x \pmod{x^5 + x^2 + 1}.$$

Our modulo operations allow us now to add, subtract, and multiply these 5-tuples, considered as polynomials modulo some $M(x)$. Can we divide? More fundamentally, given a polynomial $a(x)$, is there some other polynomial $s(x)$ — we may consider it a multiplicative inverse or a reciprocal — such that

$$a(x)s(x) \equiv 1 \mod M(x).$$

The answer lies in the oldest algorithm in the world, the Euclidean algorithm. (More details later!) For now, just be aware that if $M(x)$ is **irreducible** — it cannot be factored — then we can define division so that all of the 5-tuples γ_i have a multiplicative inverse except $(0, 0, 0, 0, 0)$.

Let us return now to the problem of creating a two-error-correcting code. Suppose that there are two errors, occurring at positions i_i and i_2. Since the code is linear, it is sufficient to consider

$$\mathbf{r} = (0, 0, \dots, \underbrace{1}_{i_1}, \dots, \underbrace{1}_{i_2}, 0, \dots, 0).$$

We find

$$\mathbf{r}H^T = (s_1, s_2)$$

with

$$\begin{aligned} \gamma_{i_1} + \gamma_{i_2} &= s_1 \\ f(\gamma_{i_1}) + f(\gamma_{i_2}) &= s_2. \end{aligned} \tag{5.2}$$

If the two equations in (5.2) are functionally independent, then we have two equations in two unknowns, which we could solve for γ_{i_1} and γ_{i_2} which, in turn, will determine the error locations i_1 and i_2.

Let us consider some possible simple functions. One might be a simple multiplication: $f(\gamma) = a\gamma$. But this would lead to the two equations

$$\gamma_{i_1} + \gamma_{i_2} = s_1 \quad a\gamma_{i_1} + a\gamma_{i_2} = s_2,$$

representing the dependency $s_2 = as_1$; the new parity check equations would tell us nothing new.

We could try $f(\gamma) = \gamma + a$; this would not help, since we would always have $s_2 = s_1$.

Let us try some powers. Say $f(\gamma) = \gamma^2$. We would then obtain

$$\gamma_{i_1} + \gamma_{i_2} = s_1 \quad \gamma_{i_1}^2 + \gamma_{i_2}^2 = s_2.$$

These looks like independent equations, but we have to remember that we are dealing with operations modulo 2. Notice that

$$s_1^2 = (\gamma_{i_1} + \gamma_{i_2})^2 = \gamma_{i_1}^2 + \gamma_{i_2}^2 + 2\gamma_{i_1}\gamma_{i_2} = \gamma_{i_1}^2 + \gamma_{i_2}^2 = s_2.$$

We have only the redundant $s_1^2 = s_2$: the second equation is the square of the first and still conveys no new information.

Try $f(\gamma) = \gamma^3$. Now the decoder equations are

$$\gamma_{i_1} + \gamma_{i_2} = s_1 \quad \gamma_{i_1}^3 + \gamma_{i_2}^3 = s_2.$$

These are independent!

Now let's see what we can do to solve these equations algebraically. In a finite field, we can do conventional algebraic manipulation, keeping in the back of our mind how we do multiplication and division.

We can write

$$s_2 = \gamma_{i_1}^3 + \gamma_{i_2}^3 = (\gamma_{i_1} + \gamma_{i_2})(\gamma_{i_1}^2 - \gamma_{i_1}\gamma_{i_2} + \gamma_{i_2}^2) = s_1(\gamma_{i_1}^2 + \gamma_{i_1}\gamma_{i_2} + \gamma_{i_2}^2) = s_1(\gamma_{i_1}\gamma_{i_2} - s_1^2)$$

(where the signs have changed with impunity because these values are based on $GF(2)$). Hence we have the two equations

$$\gamma_{i_1} + \gamma_{i_2} = s_1 \quad \gamma_{i_1}\gamma_{i_2} = s_1^2 + \frac{s_2}{s_1}$$

if $s_1 \neq 0$. We can combine these two equations into a quadratic:

$$\gamma_{i_1}(s_1 + \gamma_{i_1}) = s_1^2 + \frac{s_2}{s_1},$$

or

$$\gamma_{i_1}^2 + s_1\gamma_{i_1} + \left(s_1^2 + \frac{s_2}{s_1}\right) = 0,$$

or

$$1 + s_1\gamma_{i_1}^{-1} + \left(s_1^2 + \frac{s_2}{s_1}\right)\gamma_{i_1}^{-2} = 0.$$

For reasons to be made clear later, it is more useful to deal with the reciprocals of the roots. Let $z = \gamma_{i_1}^{-1}$. We then have the equation

$$q(z) = 1 + s_1 z + \left(s_1^2 + \frac{s_2}{s_1}\right)z^2 = 0.$$

The polynomial $q(z)$ is said to be an *error locator polynomial*: the reciprocals of its roots tell the γ_{i_1} and γ_{i_2}, which, in turn, tell the locations of the errors.

If there is only one error, then $\gamma_{i_1} = s_1$ and $\gamma_{i_1}^3 = s_2$ and we end up with the equation $1 + s_1\gamma^{-1} = 0$. If there are no errors, then $s_1 = s_2 = 0$.

Let us summarize the steps we have taken. First, we have devised a way of operating on 5-tuples as single algebraic objects, defining addition, subtraction, multiplication, and division. This required finding some irreducible polynomial $M(x)$ which works behind the scenes. Once we have got this, the steps are as follows:

1. We compute the syndrome $\mathbf{r}H^T$.

2. From the syndrome, we set up the error locator polynomial. We note that there must be some relationship between the sums of the powers of roots and the coefficients.

3. We then find the roots of the polynomial, which determine the error locations.

For binary codes, knowing where the error is suffices to correct the error. For nonbinary codes, there is another step: knowing the error location, we must also determine the error value at that location. This involves setting up another polynomial, the error evaluation polynomial, whose roots determine the error values.

The above steps establish the outline for this and the next chapters. Not only will we develop more fully the arithmetic, but we will be able to generalize to whole families of codes, capable of correcting many errors. However, the concepts are all quite similar to those demonstrated here.

(It is historically interesting that it took roughly 10 years of research to bridge the gap between Hamming and the code presented above. Once this was accomplished, other generalizations followed quickly.) □

5.2 Number Theoretic Preliminaries

We begin with some notation and concepts from elementary number and polynomial theory.

5.2.1 Divisibility

Definition 5.2 An integer b is **divisible** by a nonzero integer a if there is an integer c such that $b = ac$. This is indicated notationally as $a|b$ (read "a divides b"). If b is not divisible by a, we write $a \nmid b$. Let $a(x)$ and $b(x)$ be polynomials in $F[x]$ (that is, the ring of polynomials with coefficients in F) where F is a field and assume that $a(x)$ is not identically 0. Then $b(x)$ is divisible by a polynomial $a(x)$ if there is some polynomial $c(x) \in F[x]$ such that $b(x) = a(x)c(x)$; this is indicated by $a(x)|b(x)$. □

Example 5.3 For $a(x)$ and $b(x)$ in $\mathbb{R}[x]$, with

$$b(x) = 112 + 96x + 174x^2 + 61x^3 + 42x^4 \quad \text{and} \quad a(x) = \frac{3}{4}x^2 + \frac{5}{7}x + 2$$

we have $a(x)|b(x)$ since $b(x) = 28(2 + x + 2x^2)a(x)$. □

The following properties of divisibility of integers are straightforward to show.

Lemma 5.4 *[325] For integers,*

1. $a|b$ implies $a|bc$ for any integer c.

2. *$a|b$ and $b|c$ imply $a|c$.*

3. *$a|b$ and $a|c$ imply $a|(bs + ct)$ for any integers s and t.*

4. *$a|b$ and $b|a$ imply $a = \pm b$.*

5. *$a|b$, $a > 0$ and $b > 0$ imply $a \leq b$.*

6. *if $m \neq 0$, then $a|b$ if and only if $ma|mb$.*

7. *if $a|b$ and $c|d$ then $ac|bd$.*

These properties apply with a few modifications to polynomials with coefficients from a finite field. Property (4) is different for polynomials: if $a(x)|b(x)$ and $b(x)|a(x)$, then $a(x) = cb(x)$, where c is a nonzero element of the field of coefficients. Property (5) is also different for polynomials: $a(x)|b(x)$ implies $\deg(a(x)) \leq \deg(b(x))$.

An important fact regarding division is expressed in the following theorem.

Theorem 5.5 (Division algorithm) *For any integers a and b with $a > 0$, there exist* unique *integers q and r such that*

$$b = qa + r,$$

where $0 \leq r < a$. The number q is the quotient and r is the remainder.

For polynomials, for $a(x)$ and $b(x)$ in $F[x]$, F a field, there is a unique representation

$$b(x) = q(x)a(x) + r(x),$$

where $\deg(r(x)) < \deg(a(x))$.

Proof [325, p. 5] We provide a partial proof for integers. Form the arithmetic progression

$$\ldots, b - 3a, b - 2a, b - a, b, b + a, b + 2a, b + 3a, \ldots$$

extending indefinitely in both directions. In this sequence select the smallest non-negative element and denote it by r; this satisfies the inequality $0 \leq r < a$ and implicitly defines q by $r = b - qa$. □

Example 5.6 With $b = 23$ and $a = 7$ we have

$$23 = 3 \cdot 7 + 2.$$

The quotient is 3 and the remainder is 2. □

Example 5.7 With $b(x) = 2x^3 + 3x + 2$ and $a(x) = x^2 + 7$ in $\mathbb{R}[x]$,

$$b(x) = (2x)(x^2 + 7) + (-11x + 2).$$

□

Definition 5.8 If $d|a$ and $d|b$, then d is said to be a **common divisor** of a and b.

A common divisor $g > 0$ such that every common divisor of a and b divides g is called the **greatest common divisor** (GCD) and is denoted by (a, b).

Integers a and b with a GCD equal to 1 are said to be **relatively prime**. The integers $a_1, a_2, \ldots, a_k$ are **pairwise** relatively prime if $(a_i, a_j) = 1$ for $i \neq j$.

If $d(x)|a(x)$ and $d(x)|b(x)$ then $d(x)$ is said to be a **common divisor** of $a(x)$ and $b(x)$. If either $a(x)$ or $b(x)$ is not zero, the common divisor $g(x)$ such that every common divisor of $a(x)$ and $b(x)$ divides $g(x)$ is referred to as the **GCD** of $a(x)$ and $b(x)$ and is denoted by $(a(x), b(x))$.

The GCD of polynomials $(a(x), b(x))$ is, by convention, normalized so that it is a *monic* polynomial.

If the GCD of $a(x)$ and $b(x)$ is a constant (which can be normalized to 1), then $a(x)$ and $b(x)$ are said to be **relatively prime**. □

Example 5.9 If $a = 24$ and $b = 18$ then, clearly, $(a, b) = (24, 18) = 6$. □

Example 5.10 By some trial and error (to be reduced to an effective algorithm), we can determine that $(851, 966) = 23$. □

Example 5.11 With $a(x) = 4x^3 + 10x^2 + 8x + 2$ and $b(x) = 8x^3 + 14x^2 + 7x + 1$ in $\mathbb{R}[x]$, it can be shown that

$$(a(x), b(x)) = x^2 + \frac{3}{2}x + \frac{1}{2}.$$
□

Useful properties of the GCD:

Theorem 5.12

1. *For any positive integer m, $(ma, mb) = m(a, b)$.*
2. *As a consequence of the previous result, if $d|a$ and $d|b$ and $d > 0$, then*

$$\left(\frac{a}{d}, \frac{b}{d}\right) = \frac{1}{d}(a, b).$$

3. *If $(a, b) = g$, then $(a/g, b/g) = 1$.*
4. *If $(a, c) = (b, c) = 1$, then $(ab, c) = 1$.*
5. *If $c|ab$ and $(b, c) = 1$ then $c|a$.*
6. *Every divisor d of a and b divides (a, b). This follows immediately from (3) in Lemma 5.4 (or from the definition).*
7. *$(a, b) = |a|$ if and only if $a|b$.*
8. *$(a, (b, c)) = ((a, b), c)$ (associativity).*
9. *$(ac, bc) = |c|(a, b)$ (distributivity).*

5.2.2 The Euclidean Algorithm and Euclidean Domains

The Euclidean algorithm is perhaps the oldest algorithm in the world, being attributed to Euclid over 2000 years ago and appearing in his *Elements*. It was formulated originally to find the greatest common divisor of two integers. It has since been generalized to apply to elements in an algebraic structure known as a *Euclidean domain*. The powerful algebraic consequences include a method for solving a key step in the decoding of Reed–Solomon and BCH codes.

To understand the Euclidean algorithm, it is perhaps most helpful to first see the Euclidean algorithm in action, without worrying formally yet about how it works. The Euclidean algorithm works by simple repeated division: Starting with two numbers, a and b, divide a by b to obtain a remainder. Then divide b by the remainder, to obtain a new remainder. Proceed in this manner, dividing the last divisor by the most recent remainder, until the remainder is 0. Then the last nonzero remainder is the GCD (a, b).

Example 5.13 Find $(966, 851)$. Let $a = 966$ and $b = 851$. Divide a by b and express in terms of quotient and remainder. The results are expressed in equation and "long division" form:

$$966 = 851 \cdot 1 + 115$$

$$
\begin{array}{r}
1 \\
851 \overline{\smash{)}966} \\
\underline{851} \\
115
\end{array}
$$

Now take the divisor (851) and divide it by the remainder (115):

$$851 = 115 \cdot 7 + 46$$

$$
\begin{array}{rr}
7 & 1 \\
115 \overline{\smash{)}851} & 851 \overline{\smash{)}966} \\
\underline{805} & \underline{851} \\
46 & 115
\end{array}
$$

Now take the divisor (115) and divide it by the remainder (46):

$$115 = 46 \cdot 2 + 23$$

$$
\begin{array}{rrr}
2 & 7 & 1 \\
46 \overline{\smash{)}115} & 115 \overline{\smash{)}851} & 851 \overline{\smash{)}966} \\
\underline{92} & \underline{805} & \underline{851} \\
23 & 46 & 115
\end{array}
$$

Now take the divisor (46) and divide it by the remainder (23):

$$46 = 23 \cdot 2 + 0$$

$$
\begin{array}{rrrr}
2 & 2 & 7 & 1 \\
23 \overline{\smash{)}46} & 46 \overline{\smash{)}115} & 115 \overline{\smash{)}851} & 851 \overline{\smash{)}966} \\
\underline{23} & \underline{92} & \underline{805} & \underline{851} \\
0 & 23 & 46 & 115
\end{array}
$$

The remainder is now 0; the last nonzero remainder 23 is the GCD:

$$(966, 851) = 23.$$

$\square$

Example 5.14 In this example, we perform computations over $\mathbb{Z}_5[x]$, that is, operations modulo 5. Determine $(a(x), b(x)) = (x^7 + 3x^6 + 4x^4 + 2x^3 + x^2 + 4, x^6 + 3x^3 + 2x + 4)$, where $a(x), b(x) \in \mathbb{Z}_5[x]$.

$$(x^7 + 3x^6 + 4x^4 + 2x^3 + x^2 + 4) = (x + 3)(x^6 + 3x^3 + 2x + 4) + (x^4 + 3x^3 + 4x^2 + 2)$$
$$(x^6 + 3x^3 + 2x + 4) = (x^2 + 2x)(x^4 + 3x^3 + 4x^2 + 2) + (3x^2 + 3x + 4) \qquad (5.3)$$
$$(x^4 + 3x^3 + 4x^2 + 2) = (2x^2 + 4x + 3)(3x^2 + 3x + 4) + 0.$$

With the degree of the last remainder equal to zero, we take the last nonzero remainder, $3x^2 + 3x + 4$ and normalize it to obtain the GCD:

$$g(x) = 3^{-1}(3x^2 + 3x + 4) = 2(3x^2 + 3x + 4) = x^2 + x + 3.$$

For future reference, the polynomials $s(t)$ and $t(x)$ for this GCD are

$$s(x) = 3x^2 + x \quad t(x) = 2x^3 + 2x + 2.$$

$\square$

The Euclidean algorithm is established with the help of the following theorems and lemmas.

Theorem 5.15 *If $g = (a, b)$, then there exist integers s and t such that*

$$g = (a, b) = as + bt.$$

For polynomials, if $g(x) = (a(x), b(x))$, then there are polynomials $s(x)$ and $t(x)$ such that

$$g(x) = a(x)s(x) + b(x)t(x). \tag{5.4}$$

Proof [325] We provide the proof for the integer case; modification for the polynomial case is straightforward.

Consider the linear combinations $as + bt$ where s and t range over all integers. The set of integers $E = \{as + bt, s \in \mathbb{Z}, t \in \mathbb{Z}\}$ contains positive and negative values and 0. Choose s_0 and t_0 so that $as_0 + bt_0$ is the smallest positive integer in the set: $l = as_0 + bt_0 > 0$. We now establish that $l|a$; showing that $l|b$ is analogous. By the division algorithm, $a = lq + r$ with $0 \leq r < l$. Hence $r = a - ql = a - q(as_0 + bt_0) = a(1 - qs_0) + b(-qt_0)$, so r itself is in the set E. However, since l is the smallest positive integer in R, r must be 0, so $a = lq$, or $l|a$.

Since g is the GCD of a and b, we may write $a = gm$ and $b = gn$ for some integers m and n. Then $l = as_0 + bt_0 = g(ms_0 + nt_0)$, so $g|l$. Since it cannot be that $g < l$, since g is the *greatest* common divisor, it must be that $g = l$. $\qquad\square$

From the proof of this theorem, we make the following important observation: the GCD $g = (a, b)$ is the smallest positive integer value of $as + bt$ as s and t range over all integers.

Lemma 5.16 *For any integer n, $(a, b) = (a, b + an)$.*

For any polynomial $n(x) \in F[x]$, $(a(x), b(x)) = (a(x), b(x) + a(x)n(x))$.

Proof Let $d = (a, b)$ and $g = (a, b + an)$. By Theorem 5.15 there exist s_0 and t_0 such that $d = as_0 + bt_0$. Write this as

$$d = a(s_0 - nt_0) + (b + an)t_0 = as_1 + (b + an)t_0.$$

It follows (from Lemma 5.4 part (3)) that $g|d$. We now show that $d|g$. Since $d|a$ and $d|b$, we have that $d|(an + b)$. Since g is the GCD of a and $an + b$ and any divisor of a and $an + b$ must divide the GCD, it follows that $d|g$. Since $d|g$ and $g|d$, we must have $g = d$.

(For polynomials, the proof is almost exactly the same, except that it is possible that $g(x) = d(x)$ only if both are monic.) $\qquad\square$

We demonstrate the use of this theorem and lemma by an example.

Example 5.17 Determine $g = (966, 851)$; this is the same as in Example 5.13, but now we keep track of a few more details. By the division algorithm,

$$966 = 1 \cdot 851 + 115. \tag{5.5}$$

By Lemma 5.16,

$$g = (851, 966) = (851, 966 - 1 \cdot 851) = (851, 115) = (115, 851).$$

Thus, the problem has been reduced using the lemma to one having smaller numbers than the original, but with the same GCD. Applying the division algorithm again,

$$851 = 7 \cdot 115 + 46 \tag{5.6}$$

hence, again applying Lemma 5.16,

$$(115, 851) = (115, 851 - 7 \cdot 115) = (115, 46) = (46, 115).$$

Again, the GCD problem is reduced to one with smaller numbers. Proceeding by application of the division algorithm and the property, we obtain successively

$$115 = 2 \cdot 46 + 23 \tag{5.7}$$

$$(46, 115) = (46, 115 - 2 \cdot 46) = (46, 23) = (23, 46)$$

$$46 = 2 \cdot 23 + 0$$

$$(23, 46) = 23.$$

Chaining together the equalities, we obtain

$$(966, 851) = 23.$$

We can find the s and t in the representation suggested by Theorem 5.15,

$$(966, 851) = 966s + 851t,$$

by working the equations backward, substituting in for the remainders from each division in reverse order

$$23 = 115 - 2 \cdot 46 \qquad\qquad \text{"23" from (5.7)}$$
$$= 115 - 2 \cdot (851 - 7 \cdot 115) = -2 \cdot 851 + 15 \cdot 115 \qquad\qquad \text{"46" from (5.6)}$$
$$= -2 \cdot 851 + 15(966 - 1 \cdot 851) = 15 \cdot 966 - 17 \cdot 851 \qquad\qquad \text{"115" from (5.5)}$$

so $s = 15$ and $t = -17$. $\qquad\qquad\qquad\qquad\qquad\qquad\qquad\qquad\qquad\qquad\qquad\qquad\qquad\quad\square$

Example 5.18 It can be shown that for the polynomials in Example 5.14,

$$s(x) = 3x^2 + x \quad t(x) = 2x^3 + 2x + 2.$$

$\qquad\qquad\qquad\qquad\qquad\qquad\qquad\qquad\qquad\qquad\qquad\qquad\qquad\qquad\qquad\qquad\qquad\qquad\qquad\quad\square$

Having seen the examples and the basic theory, we can now be a little more precise. In fullest generality, the Euclidean algorithm applies to algebraic structures known as Euclidean domains.

Definition 5.19 [144, p. 301] A **Euclidean domain** is a set D with operations $+$ and $\cdot$ satisfying:

1. D forms a commutative ring with identity. That is, D has an operation $+$ such that $\langle D, + \rangle$ is a commutative group. Also, there is a commutative operation "multiplication," denoted using $\cdot$ (or merely juxtaposition), such that for any a and b in D, $a \cdot b$ is also in D. The distributive property also applies: $a \cdot (b + c) = a \cdot b + a \cdot c$ for any $a, b, c \in D$. Also, there is an element 1, the multiplicative identity, in D such that $a \cdot 1 = 1 \cdot a = a$.

2. Multiplicative cancellation holds: if $ab = cb$ and $b \neq 0$, then $a = c$.

3. Every $a \in D$ has a **valuation** $v(a) : D \to \mathbb{N} \cup \{-\infty\}$ such that:

    (a) $v(a) \geq 0$ for all $a \in D$ (except when $a = 0$).
    (b) $v(a) \leq v(ab)$ for all $a, b \in D$, $b \neq 0$.
    (c) For all $a, b \in D$ with $v(a) > v(b)$ there is a $q \in D$ (quotient) and $r \in D$ (remainder) such that

    $$a = qb + r$$

    with $v(r) < v(b)$ or $r = 0$. $v(b)$ is never $-\infty$ except possibly when $b = 0$. The valuation v is also called a Euclidean function.

$\qquad\qquad\qquad\qquad\qquad\qquad\qquad\qquad\qquad\qquad\qquad\qquad\qquad\qquad\qquad\qquad\qquad\qquad\qquad\quad\square$

We have seen two examples of Euclidean domains:

1. The ring of integers under integer addition and multiplication, where the valuation is $v(a) = |a|$ (the absolute value). Then the statement

    $$a = qb + r$$

    is obtained simply by integer division with remainder (the division algorithm).

2. Let F be a field. Then $F[x]$ is a Euclidean domain with valuation function $v(a(x)) = \deg(a(x))$ (the degree of the polynomial $a(x) \in F[x]$). It is conventional for this domain to take $v(0) = -\infty$. Then the statement

    $$a(x) = q(x)b(x) + r(x)$$

    follows from polynomial division.

The Euclidean algorithm can be stated in two versions. The first simply computes the GCD.

Theorem 5.20 (The Euclidean Algorithm)   *Let a and b be nonzero elements in a Euclidean domain. Then by repeated application of the division algorithm in the Euclidean domain, we obtain a series of equations:*

$$a = bq_1 + r_1 \qquad r_1 \neq 0 \ \text{ and } \ v(r_1) < v(b)$$

$$b = r_1 q_2 + r_2 \qquad r_2 \neq 0 \ \text{ and } \ v(r_2) < v(r_1)$$

$$r_1 = r_2 q_3 + r_3 \qquad r_3 \neq 0 \ \text{ and } \ v(r_3) < v(r_2)$$

$$\vdots$$

$$r_{j-2} = r_{j-1} q_j + r_j \quad r_j \neq 0 \ \text{ and } \ v(r_j) < v(r_{j-1})$$

$$r_{j-1} = r_j q_{j+1} + 0 \qquad\qquad (r_{j+1} = 0).$$

Then $(a, b) = r_j$, the last nonzero remainder of the division process.

gcd.c

That the theorem stops after a finite number of steps follows since every remainder must be smaller (in valuation) than the preceding remainder and the (valuation of the) remainder must be nonnegative. That the final nonzero remainder is the GCD follows from property Lemma 5.16.

This form of the Euclidean algorithm is very simple to code. Let $\lfloor a/b \rfloor$ denote the "quotient" without remainder of a/b, that is, $a = \lfloor a/b \rfloor b + r$. Then recursion in the Euclidean algorithm may be expressed   as

$$q_i = \lfloor r_{i-2}/r_{i-1} \rfloor$$
$$r_i = r_{i-2} - r_{i-1} q_i \tag{5.8}$$

for $i = 1, 2, \ldots$ (until   termination)   with $r_{-1} = a$ and $r_0 = b$.

The second version of the Euclidean algorithm, sometimes called the **extended Euclidean algorithm**, computes $g = (a, b)$ and also the coefficients s and t of Theorem 5.15 such that

$$as + bt = g.$$

The values for s and t are computed by finding intermediate quantities s_i and t_i satisfying

$$as_i + bt_i = r_i \tag{5.9}$$

at every step of the algorithm. The formula to update s_i and t_i is (see Exercise 5.18)

$$s_i = s_{i-2} - q_i s_{i-1}$$
$$t_i = t_{i-2} - q_i t_{i-1}, \tag{5.10}$$

for $i = 1, 2, \ldots$ (until termination), with

$$s_{-1} = 1 \quad s_0 = 0$$
$$t_{-1} = 0 \quad t_0 = 1. \tag{5.11}$$

The Extended Euclidean Algorithm is as shown in Algorithm 5.1.

The following are some facts about the GCD which are proved using the Euclidean algorithm. Analogous results hold for polynomials. (It is helpful to verify these properties using small integer examples.)

Lemma 5.21

1. *For integers, (a, b) is the smallest positive value of $as + bt$, where s and t range over all integers.*

2. *If $as + bt = 1$ for some integers s and t, then $(a, b) = 1$; that is, a and b are relatively prime. Thus, a and b are relatively prime if and only if there exist s and t such that $as + bt = 1$.*

Algorithm 5.1 Extended Euclidean Algorithm

1   Initialization: Set s and t as in (5.11).
2   Let $r_{-1} = a, r_0 = b, s_{-1} = 1, s_0 = 0, t_{-1} = 0, t_0 = 1, i = 0$
3   while($r_i \neq 0$){   Repeat until remainder is 0
4       $i = i + 1$
5       $q_i = \lfloor r_{i-2}/r_{i-1} \rfloor$ Compute quotient
6       $r_i = r_{i-2} - q_i r_{i-1}$ Compute remainder
7       $s_i = s_{i-2} - q_i s_{i-1}$ Compute s and t values
8       $t_i = t_{i-2} - q_i t_{i-1}$
9   }
10   Return: $s = s_{i-1}, t = t_{i-1}, g = r_{i-1}$

5.2.3   An Application of the Euclidean Algorithm: The Sugiyama Algorithm

The Euclidean algorithm, besides computing the GCD, has a variety of other applications. Here, the Euclidean algorithm is put to use as a means of solving the problem of finding the shortest LFSR which produces a given output. This problem, as we shall see, is important in decoding BCH and Reed–Solomon codes. (The Berlekamp–Massey algorithm is another way of arriving at this solution.)

We introduce the problem as a prediction problem. Given a set of $2p$ data points $\{b_k\} = \{b_k, k = 0, 1, \ldots, 2p - 1\}$ satisfying the LFSR equation[1]

$$b_k = -\sum_{j=1}^{v} t_j b_{k-j}, \quad k = v, v + 1, \ldots, 2p - 1 \qquad (5.12)$$

we want to find the coefficients $\{t_j\}$ so that (5.12) is satisfied. That is, we want to find coefficients to predict b_k using prior values. Furthermore, we want the number of nonzero coefficients v to be as small as possible. Equation (5.12) can also be written as

$$\sum_{j=0}^{v} t_j b_{k-j} = 0, \quad k = v, v + 1, \ldots, 2p - 1, \qquad (5.13)$$

with $t_0 = 1$. One way to find the coefficients $\{t_j\}$, given a set $\{b_j\}$, is to explicitly set up and solve the Toeplitz matrix equation

$$\begin{bmatrix} b_{v-1} & b_{v-2} & b_{v-3} & \cdots & b_0 \\ b_v & b_{v-1} & b_{v-2} & \cdots & b_1 \\ b_{v+1} & b_v & b_{v-1} & \cdots & b_2 \\ \vdots & & & & \vdots \\ b_{2p-2} & b_{2p-3} & b_{2p-4} & \cdots & b_{p-1} \end{bmatrix} \begin{bmatrix} t_1 \\ t_2 \\ t_3 \\ \vdots \\ t_v \end{bmatrix} = \begin{bmatrix} -b_v \\ -b_{v+1} \\ -b_{v+2} \\ \vdots \\ -b_{2p-1} \end{bmatrix}.$$

That is, v rows of this matrix can be selected to obtain a square matrix. The value of v is not known however, so different values of v would need to be tried to select the smallest v which could work.

The Sugiyama algorithm is an efficient way of solving this problem which guarantees that $t(x)$ has minimal degree. The Sugiyama algorithm thus provides a means of synthesizing LFSR coefficients of smallest degree that produces the sequence $\{b_k\}$.

---

[1] Comparison with (4.18) shows that this equation has a $-$ where (4.18) does not. This is because (4.18) is expressed over $GF(2)$.

Since the LFSR recursion (5.13) is a convolution, this suggests considering relationships related to polynomial multiplication. Let us represent the sequence and the LFSR in terms of polynomials by

$$b(x) = \sum_{i=0}^{2p-1} b_i x^i \quad \text{and} \quad t(x) = 1 + \sum_{i=1}^{v} t_i x^i$$

and consider the product $\theta(x) = b(x)t(x)$. Expanding the product out term by term, we find

$$\theta(x) = b(x)t(x) = (b_0 + b_1 x + b_2 x + \cdots + b_{2p-1}x^{2p-1})(t_0 + t_1 x + t_2 x^2 + \cdots + t_v x^v)$$

$$= \underbrace{\theta_0 + \theta_1 x + \theta_2 x^2 + \cdots + \theta_{v-1}x^{v-1}}_{\text{incomplete sums 1}} + \underbrace{\theta_v x^\mu + \cdots \theta_{2p-1}x^{2p-1}n}_{\text{complete sums}}$$

$$+ \underbrace{\theta_{2p}x^{2p} + \cdots + \theta_{v+2p-1}x^{v+2p-1}}_{\text{incomplete sums 2}}$$

$$= \underbrace{b_0 t_0 + (b_1 t_0 + b_0 t_1)x + (b_2 t_0 + b_1 t_1 + b_0 t_2)x^2}_{\text{incomplete sums 1}} \tag{5.14}$$

$$+ \cdots + \underbrace{(b_{v-1}t_0 + b_{v-2}t_1 + \cdots b_0 t_{v-1})x^{v-1}}_{\text{incomplete sums 1 (cont'd)}} \tag{5.15}$$

$$+ \underbrace{(b_v t_0 + b_{v-1}t_1 + \cdots + b_0 t_v)x^v + (b_{v+1}t_0 + b_v t_1 + \cdots + b_1 t_v)x^{v+1}}_{\text{complete sums}} \tag{5.16}$$

$$+ \cdots + \underbrace{(b_{2p-1}t_0 + \cdots + b_{2p-1-v}t_v)x^{2p-1}}_{\text{complete sums (cont'd)}} \tag{5.17}$$

$$+ \underbrace{(b_{2p-1}t_1 + b_{2p-2}t_2 + \cdots + b_{2p-1-v}t_v)x^{2p} + \cdots + b_{2p-1}t_v x^{v+2p-1}}_{\text{incomplete sums 2}}. \tag{5.18}$$

In this product, the coefficients in the sum terms "complete sums" in (5.16) and (5.17) involve $v + 1$ terms and are each 0 by (5.13). The terms in the "incomplete sums 1" (5.14) and (5.15) are not necessarily zero because they do not have all $v + 1$ terms in the sum (5.13). These terms collectively form a polynomial of degree $\leq v - 1$. The terms in the "incomplete sums 2" (5.18) are not necessarily zero and these terms collectively form a polynomial whose lowest term may have degree $2p$. (Thinking in terms of convolution, the "incomplete sums" terms involve where the sequences $\{b_i\}$ and $\{t_i\}$ are sliding into and out of full overlap, and the "complete sums" terms involve where the sequences being convolved are fully overlapping.) Because the "complete sums" terms are 0, the product may be written as

$$b(x)t(x) = r(x) - x^{2p}s(x), \tag{5.19}$$

where here

$$r(x) = b_0 t_0 + (b_1 t_0 + b_0 t_1)x + (b_2 t_0 + b_1 t_1 + b_0 t_2)x^2 + \cdots + (b_{v-1}t_0 + b_{v-2}t_1 + \cdots + b_0 t_{v-1})x^{v-1}$$

with $\deg(r(x)) < v$ and

$$s(x) = -((b_{2p-1}t_1 + b_{2p-2}t_2 + \cdots + b_{2p-1-v}t_v) + \cdots + b_{2p-1}t_v x^{v-1}).$$

Example 5.22 In this example, computations are done in $\mathbb{Z}_5$. The sequence $\{2, 3, 4, 2, 2, 3\}$, corresponding to the polynomial $b(x) = 2 + 3x + 4x^2 + 2x^3 + 2x^4 + 3x^5$, can be generated (as can be found using techniques described below or the Berlekamp–Massey algorithm) using the coefficients $t_1 = 3, t_2 = 4, t_3 = 2$, so that $t(x) = 1 + 3x + 4x^2 + 2x^3$. We have $p = 3$ and $v = 3$. Then in $\mathbb{Z}_5[x]$,

$$b(x)t(x) = 2 + 4x + x^2 + x^6 + x^7 + x^8 = \underbrace{(2 + 4x + x^2)}_{r(x)} + \underbrace{x^6(1 + x + x^2)}_{-x^{2p}s(x)}. \tag{5.20}$$

The terms x^3, x^4, and x^5 are missing, corresponding to terms with "complete sums." We identify

$$r(x) = 2 + 4x + x^2 \quad s(x) = -(1 + x + x^2).$$

□

The linear relationship (5.13) implies and is implied by the structure of (5.19). Equation (5.19) can also be expressed as

$$\frac{r(x) - b(x)t(x)}{x^{2p}} = s(x),$$

that is, $x^{2p}|(r(x) - b(x)t(x))$. As is described below, this means that we can also write

$$b(x)t(x) \equiv r(x) \ (\mathrm{mod} \ x^{2p}).$$

There are two ways of interpreting this relationship. The first is, as observed, that $x^{2p}|(r(x) - b(x)t(x))$. The second is to work with remainders modulo x^{2p}, which results in discarding all terms of degree x^{2p} or higher. For example, if $b(x)$ and $t(x)$ are multiplied together, then taking the result and discarding terms of degree $2p$ or higher, the result is $r(x)$.

Equation (5.19) can also be expressed as

$$x^{2p}s(x) + b(x)t(x) = r(x). \tag{5.21}$$

Equation (5.21) has the form of the equation related to the GCD in the extended Euclidean algorithm in (5.4), where in the Euclidean algorithm we set $a(x) = x^{2p}$ and $b(x)$ is formed from the sequence $\{b_k\}$. Rather than iterating the extended Euclidean algorithm until a remainder $r_i(x) = 0$, iteration continues until $\deg(r_i(x)) < p$. Then the polynomial $t_i(x)$ returned by the extended Euclidean algorithm (normalized so that the constant coefficient is equal to 1) is the desired connection polynomial.

Example 5.23 Given the sequence $\{2, 3, 4, 2, 2, 3\}$, where the coefficients are in $\mathbb{Z}_5$, calling the gcd function with $a(x) = x^6$ and $b(x) = 2 + 3x + 4x^2 + 2x^3 + 2x^4 + 3x^5$ results after three iterations in

$$r_i(x) = 3 + x + 4x^2 \quad s_i(x) = 1 + x + x^2 \quad t_i(x) = 4 + 2x + x^2 + 3x^3.$$

Normalizing $t_i(x)$ and the other polynomials by scaling by $4^{-1} = 4$, we find

$$t(x) = 4(4 + 2x + x^2 + 3x^3) = 1 + 3x + 4x^2 + 2x^3$$
$$r(x) = 4(3 + x + 4x^2) = 2 + 4x + x^2$$
$$s(x) = 4(1 + x + x^2) = 4 + 4x + 4x^2 = -(1 + x + x^2).$$

These correspond to the polynomials in (5.20).

□

One of the useful attributes of the Sugiyama algorithm is that it determines the coefficients $\{t_1, \ldots, t_p\}$ satisfying (5.13) with the *smallest* value of v. Put another way, it determines the $t(x)$ of smallest degree satisfying (5.19).

Example 5.24 To see this, consider the sequence $\{2, 3, 2, 3, 2, 3\}$. This can be generated by the polynomial $t_1(x) = 1 + 3x + 4x^2 + 2x^3$, since

$$b(x)t_1(x) = 2 + 4x + 4x^2 + 3x^6 + x^7 + x^8 = (2 + 4x + 4x^2) + x^6(3 + x + x^2).$$

However, as a result of calling the Sugiyama algorithm, we obtain the polynomial

$$t(x) = 1 + x,$$

so

$$b(x)t(x) = 2 + 3x^6.$$

It may be observed (in retrospect) that the sequence of coefficients in b happen to satisfy $b_k = -b_{k-1}$, consistent with the $t(x)$ obtained.   □

5.2.4 Congruence

Operations modulo an integer are fairly familiar. We frequently deal with operations on a clock modulo 24, "If it is 10:00 now, then in 25 hours it will be 11:00," or on a week modulo 7, "If it is Tuesday, then in eight days it will be Wednesday." The concept of congruence provides a notation to capture the idea of modulo operations.

Definition 5.25 If an integer $m \neq 0$ divides $a - b$, then we say that a is **congruent** to b modulo m and write $a \equiv b \pmod{m}$. If a polynomial $m(x) \neq 0$ divides $a(x) - b(x)$, then we say that $a(x)$ is congruent to $b(x)$ modulo $m(x)$ and write $a(x) \equiv b(x) \pmod{m(x)}$.

In summary:

$$\boxed{a \equiv b \pmod{m} \text{ if and only if } m|(a-b).}$$ (5.22)
                                                                                                            □

Example 5.26

1. $7 \equiv 20 \pmod{13}$.

2. $7 \equiv -6 \pmod{13}$.   □

Congruences have the following basic properties.

Theorem 5.27 *[325, Theorem 2.1,Theorem 2.3, Theorem 2.4] For integers a, b, c, d, x, y, m:*

1. $a \equiv b \pmod{m} \Leftrightarrow b \equiv a \pmod{m} \Leftrightarrow b - a \equiv 0 \pmod{m}$.

2. *If $a \equiv b \pmod{m}$ and $b \equiv c \pmod{m}$ then $a \equiv c \pmod{m}$.*

3. *If $a \equiv b \pmod{m}$ and $c \equiv d \pmod{m}$ then $ax + cy \equiv bx + dy \pmod{m}$.*

4. *If $a \equiv b \pmod{m}$ and $c \equiv d \pmod{m}$ then $ac \equiv bd \pmod{m}$. From this it follows that if $a \equiv b \pmod{m}$ then $a^n \equiv b^n \pmod{m}$.*

5. *If $a \equiv b \pmod{m}$ and $d|m$ and $d > 0$ then $a \equiv b \pmod{d}$.*

6. *If $a \equiv b \pmod{m}$ then for $c > 0$, $ac \equiv bc \pmod{mc}$.*

7. *$ax \equiv ay \pmod{m}$ if and only if $x \equiv y \pmod{m/(a,m)}$.*

8. *If $ax \equiv ay \pmod{m}$ and $(a,m) = 1$ then $x \equiv y \pmod{m}$.*

9. *If $a \equiv b \pmod{m}$ then $(a,m) = (b,m)$.*

From the definition, we note that if $n|a$, then $a \equiv 0 \pmod{n}$.

5.2.5 The ϕ Function

Definition 5.28 The **Euler totient function** $\phi(n)$ is the number of positive integers less than n that are relatively prime to n. This is also called the **Euler** ϕ function, or sometimes just the ϕ function. □

Example 5.29

1. $\phi(5) = 4$ (the numbers 1, 2, 3, 4 are relatively prime to 5).
2. $\phi(4) = 2$ (the numbers 1 and 3 are relatively prime to 4).
3. $\phi(6) = 2$ (the numbers 1 and 5 are relatively prime to 6).

□

It can be shown that the ϕ function can be written as

$$\phi(n) = n \prod_{p|n} \left(1 - \frac{1}{p}\right) = n \prod_{p|n} \frac{p-1}{p},$$

where the product is taken over all primes p dividing n.

Example 5.30
$$\phi(189) = \phi(3 \cdot 3 \cdot 3 \cdot 7) = 189(1 - 1/3)(1 - 1/7) = 108.$$

$$\phi(64) = \phi(2^6) = 64(1 - 1/2) = 32.$$

□

We observe that:

1. $\phi(p) = p - 1$ if p is prime.
2. For distinct primes p_1 and p_2,

$$\phi(p_1 p_2) = (p_1 - 1)(p_2 - 1). \tag{5.23}$$

3. $\phi(p^m) = p^{m-1}(p - 1)$ for p prime.
4. $\phi(p^m q^n) = p^{m-1} q^{n-1}(p - 1)(q - 1)$ for distinct primes p and q.
5. For positive integers m and n with $(m, n) = 1$,

$$\phi(mn) = \phi(m)\phi(n). \tag{5.24}$$

5.2.6 Some Cryptographic Payoff

With all the effort so far introducing number theory, it is interesting to put it to work on a problem of practical interest: public key cryptography using the RSA algorithm. This is really a topic distinct from error correction coding, but the application is important in modern communication and serves to motivate some of these theoretical ideas.

In a symmetric public key encryption system, a user B has a private "key" which is only known to B and a public "key" which may be known to any interested party, C. A message encrypted by one key (either the public or private) can be decrypted by the other.

For example, if C wants to send a sealed letter so that only B can read it, C encrypts using B's public key. Upon reception, B can read it by deciphering using his private key. Or, if B wants to send a letter that is known to come from only him, B encrypts with his private key. Upon receipt, C can successfully decrypt only using B's public key.

Public key encryption relies upon a "trapdoor": an operation which is exceedingly difficult to compute unless some secret information is available. For the RSA encryption algorithm, the secret information is number theoretic: it relies upon the difficulty of factoring very large integers.

5.2.6.1 Fermat's Little Theorem

Theorem 5.31

1. *(Fermat's little theorem)[2] If p is a prime and if a is an integer such that $(a, p) = 1$ (i.e., p does not divide a), then p divides $a^{p-1} - 1$. Stated another way, if $a \not\equiv 0 \pmod{p}$,*

$$a^{p-1} \equiv 1 \pmod{p}.$$

2. *(Euler's generalization of Fermat's little theorem) If n and a are integers such that $(a, n) = 1$, then*

$$a^{\phi(n)} \equiv 1 \pmod{n},$$

where ϕ is the Euler ϕ function. For any prime p, $\phi(p) = p - 1$ and we get Fermat's little theorem.

Example 5.32

1. Let $p = 7$ and $a = 2$. Then $a^{p-1} - 1 = 2^6 - 1 = 63$ and $p | 2^6 - 1$.

2. Compute the remainder of 8^{103} when divided by 13. Note that

$$103 = 8 \cdot 12 + 7.$$

Then with all computations modulo 13,

$$8^{103} = (8^{12})^8 (8^7) \equiv (1^8)(8^7) \equiv (-5)^7 \equiv (-5)^6 (-5) \equiv (25)^3 (-5) \equiv (-1)^3 (-5) \equiv 5.$$

In the first step 8^{12} can be found as follows. With $n = 13$, $\phi(n) = 12$, and $(8, 13) = 1$. By Euler's generalization, $8^{\phi(n)} \equiv 1$ modulo 13.

□

Proof of Theorem 5.31.

1. The nonzero elements in the group $\mathbb{Z}_p$, $\{1, 2, \ldots, p-1\}$ form a group of order $p - 1$ under multiplication. By Lagrange's theorem (Theorem 2.29), the order of any element in a group divides the order of the group, so for $a \in \mathbb{Z}_p$ with $a \neq 0$, $a^{p-1} = 1$ in $\mathbb{Z}_p$. If $a \in \mathbb{Z}$ and $a \notin \mathbb{Z}_p$, write $a = (\tilde{a} + kp)$ for some $k \in \mathbb{Z}$ and for $0 \leq \tilde{a} < p$, then reduce modulo p.

2. Let G_n be the set of elements in $\mathbb{Z}_n$ that are relatively prime to n. Then (it can be shown that) G_n forms a group under multiplication. Note that the group G_n has $\phi(n)$ elements in it. Now let $a \in \mathbb{Z}_n$ be relatively prime to n. Then a is in the group G_n. Since the order of an element divides the order of the group, we have $a^{\phi(n)} \equiv 1 \pmod{n}$. If $a \notin \mathbb{Z}_n$, write $a = (\tilde{a} + kn)$ where $\tilde{a} \in \mathbb{Z}_n$. Then reduce modulo n.

□

---

[2] Fermat's little theorem should not be confused with "Fermat's last theorem," proved by A. Wiles, which states that $x^n + y^n = z^n$ has no solution over the integers if $n > 2$.

5.2.6.2 RSA Encryption

Named after its inventors, Ron Rivest, Adi Shamir, and Leonard Adleman [378], the RSA encryption algorithm gets its security from the difficulty of factoring *large* numbers. The steps in setting up the system are:

- Choose two distinct random prime numbers p and q (of roughly equal length for best security) and compute $n = pq$. Note that $\phi(n) = (p-1)(q-1)$.

- Randomly choose an encryption key e, an integer e such that the GCD $(e, (p-1)(q-1)) = 1$. By the extended Euclidean algorithm, there are numbers d and f such that $de - f(p-1)(q-1) = 1$, or

$$de = 1 + (p-1)(q-1)f.$$

  That is, $d \equiv e^{-1} \pmod{(p-1)(q-1)}$. (If the value of d returned by the Euclidean algorithm is negative, then, since the computations are done modulo $(p-1)(q-1)$, a positive value can be obtained by adding multiples of $(p-1)(q-1)$ to d until a positive integer is obtained.)

- Publish the pair of numbers $\{e, n\}$ as the public key. Retain the pair of numbers $\{d, n\}$ as the private key. The factors p and q of n are never disclosed.

To **encrypt** (say, using the public key), break the message m (as a sequence of numbers) into blocks m_i of length less than the length of n. Furthermore, assume that $(m_i, n) = 1$ (which is highly probable, since n has only two factors). For each block m_i, compute the encrypted block c_i by

$$c_i = m_i^e \pmod{n}.$$

(If $e < 0$, then find the inverse modulo n.) To **decrypt** (using the corresponding private key) compute

$$c_i^d \pmod{n} = m_i^{de} \pmod{n} = m_i^{f(p-1)(q-1)+1} \pmod{n} = m_i m_i^{f(p-1)(q-1)} \pmod{n}.$$

Since $(m_i, n) = 1$,

$$m_i^{f(p-1)(q-1)} = (m_i^f)^{(p-1)(q-1)} = (m_i^f)^{\phi(n)} \equiv 1 \pmod{n},$$

so that

$$c_i^d \pmod{n} = m_i,$$

as desired.

To crack this, a person knowing n and e would have to factor n to find d. While multiplication (and computing powers) is easy and straightforward, factoring very large integers is very difficult.

Example 5.33 Let $p = 47$ and $q = 71$ and $n = 3337$. (This is clearly too short to be of cryptographic value.) Then

$$(p-1)(q-1) = 3220.$$

The encryption key e must be relatively prime to 3220; take $e = 79$. Then we find by the Euclidean algorithm that $d = 1019$. The public key is $(79, 3337)$. The private key is $(1019, 3337)$.

To encode the message block $m_1 = 688$, we compute

$$c_1 = (688)^{79} \pmod{3337} = 1570.$$

To decrypt this, exponentiate

$$c_1^d = (1570)^{1019} \pmod{3337} = 688.$$

□

In practical applications, primes p and q are usually chosen to be at least several hundred digits long. This makes factoring $n = pq$ exceedingly difficult!

5.3   The Chinese Remainder Theorem

The material from this section is not used until Section 7.4.2.

Example 5.34   The integer $x = 1028$ has the property that

$$x \equiv 0 \;(\text{mod } 4) \quad x \equiv 2 \;(\text{mod } 27) \quad x \equiv 3 \;(\text{mod } 25). \tag{5.25}$$

In this forward direction, computation is very straightforward. But suppose you are given only the equivalences in (5.25), and it is desired to determine the integer x. The method of solution is found using the Chinese Remainder Theorem (CRT).   □

In its simplest interpretation, the CRT is a method for finding the *simultaneous* solution to the set of congruences

$$x \equiv a_1 \;(\text{mod } m_1) \quad x \equiv a_2 \;(\text{mod } m_2) \quad \ldots \quad x \equiv a_r \;(\text{mod } m_r). \tag{5.26}$$

However, the CRT applies not only to integers, but to other Euclidean domains, including rings of polynomials. The CRT provides an interesting isomorphism between rings which is useful in some decoding algorithms.

One approach to the solution of (5.26) would be to find the solution *set* to each congruence separately, then determine if there is a point in the intersection of these sets. The following theorem provides a more constructive solution.

Theorem 5.35   *If $m_1, m_2, \ldots, m_r$ are pairwise relatively prime elements with positive valuation in a Euclidean domain R, and $a_1, a_2, \ldots, a_r$ are any elements in the Euclidean domain, then the set of congruences in (5.26) have common solutions. Let $m = m_1 m_2 \cdots m_r$. If x_0 is a solution, then so is $x = x_0 + km$ for any $k \in R$.*

Proof   Let $m = \prod_{j=1}^{r} m_j$. Observe that $(m/m_j, m_j) = 1$ since the m_is are relatively prime. By Theorem 5.15, there are unique elements s and t such that

$$(m/m_j)s + m_j t = 1,$$

which is to say that

$$(m/m_j)s \equiv 1 \;(\text{mod } m_j).$$

Let $b_j = s$ in this expression, so that we can write

$$(m/m_j)b_j \equiv 1 \;(\text{mod } m_j). \tag{5.27}$$

Also $(m/m_j)b_j \equiv 0 \;(\text{mod } m_i)$ if $i \neq j$ since $m_i | m$. Form a solution x_0 by

$$x_0 = \sum_{j=1}^{r} (m/m_j)b_j a_j. \tag{5.28}$$

Then

$$x_0 \equiv (m/m_i)b_i a_i \equiv a_i \;(\text{mod } m_i).$$

Uniqueness is straightforward to verify, as is the fact that $x = x_0 + km$ is another solution.   □

It is convenient to introduce the notation $M_i = m/m_i$. The solution (5.28) can be written as $x_0 = \sum_{j=1}^{r} \gamma_j a_j$, where

$$\gamma_j = \frac{m}{m_j} b_j = M_j b_j \tag{5.29}$$

with b_j determined by the solution to (5.27). Observe that γ_j depends only upon the set of moduli $\{m_i\}$ and not upon x. If the γ_js are precomputed, then the synthesis of x from the $\{a_i\}$ is a simple inner product.

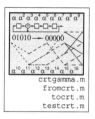

crtgamma.m
fromcrt.m
tocrt.m
testcrt.m

Example 5.36 Find a solution x to the set of congruences

$$x \equiv 0 \ (\text{mod } 4) \quad x \equiv 2 \ (\text{mod } 27) \quad x \equiv 3 \ (\text{mod } 25).$$

Since the moduli m_i are powers of distinct primes, they are pairwise relative prime. Then $m = m_1 m_2 m_3 = 2700$. Using the Euclidean algorithm it is straightforward to show that $(m/4)b_1 \equiv 1 \ (\text{mod } 4)$ has solution $b_1 = -1$. Similarly

$$b_2 = 10 \quad b_3 = -3.$$

The solution to the congruences is given by

$$x = (m/4)(-1)(0) + (m/27)(10)(2) + (m/25)(-3)(3) = 1028.$$

$\square$

The CRT provides a means of representing integers in the range $0 \le x < m$, where $m = m_1 m_2 \cdots m_r$ and the m_i are pairwise relatively prime. Let $R/\langle m \rangle$ denote the ring of integers modulo m and let $R/\langle m_i \rangle$ denote the ring of integers modulo m_i. Given a number $x \in R/\langle m \rangle$, it can be decomposed into an r-tuple $[x_1, x_2, \ldots, x_r]$ by

$$x \equiv x_i \ (\text{mod } m_i), \quad i = 1, 2, \ldots, r,$$

where $x_i \in R/\langle m_i \rangle$. Going the other way, an r-tuple of numbers $[x_1, x_2, \ldots, x_r]$ with $0 \le x_i < m_i$ can be converted into the number x they represent using (5.28). If we let $\underline{x} = [x_1, x_2, \ldots, x_r]$, then the correspondence between a number x and its representation using the CRT can be represented as

$$x \leftrightarrow \underline{x}.$$

We also denote this as

$$\underline{x} = \text{CRT}(x) \quad x = \text{CRT}^{-1}(\underline{x}).$$

Ring operations can be equivalently computed in the original ring $R/\langle m \rangle$, or in each of the rings $R/\langle m_i \rangle$ separately.

Example 5.37 Let $m_1 = 4, m_2 = 27, m_3 = 25$. Let $x = 25$; then $\underline{x} = [1, 25, 0]$. Let $y = 37$; then $\underline{y} = [1, 10, 12]$. The sum $z = x + y = 62$ has $\underline{z} = [2, 8, 12]$, which represents $\underline{x} + \underline{y}$, added element by element, with the first component modulo 4, the second component modulo 27, and the third component modulo 25.

The product $z = x \cdot y = 925$ has $\underline{z} = [1, 7, 0]$, corresponding to the element-by-element product (modulo 4, 27, and 25, respectively).

$\square$

More generally, we have a ring isomorphism by the CRT. Let $\pi_i : R/\langle m \rangle \to R/\langle m_i \rangle, i = 1, 2, \ldots, r$ denote the ring homomorphism defined by $\pi_i(a) = a \ (\text{mod } m_i)$. We define the homomorphism $\chi : R/\langle m \rangle \to R/\langle m_1 \rangle \times R/\langle m_2 \rangle \times \cdots \times R/\langle m_r \rangle$ by $\chi = \pi_1 \times \pi_2 \times \cdots \times \pi_r$, that is,

$$\chi(a) = (a \bmod m_1, a \bmod m_2, \ldots, a \bmod m_r). \tag{5.30}$$

testcrtp.m
tocrtpoly.m
fromcrtpoly.m
crtgammapoly.m

Then χ defines a ring isomorphism: both the additive and multiplicative structure of the ring are preserved, and the mapping is bijective.

Example 5.38 The CRT can be applied to any Euclidean domain, not just integers.

Suppose the Euclidean domain is $\mathbb{R}[x]$ (polynomials with real coefficients) and the polynomials are

$$m_1(x) = (x-1) \quad m_2(x) = (x-2)^2 \quad m_3(x) = (x-3)^3.$$

These are clearly pairwise relatively prime, as can be verified with the Euclidean algorithm.

Let

$$f(x) = x^5 + 4x^4 + 5x^3 + 2x^2 + 3x + 2,$$

then

$$f(x) \ (\mathrm{mod}\ m_1(x)) \equiv a_1(x) = 17$$

$$f(x) \ (\mathrm{mod}\ m_2(x)) \equiv a_2(x) = 279x - 406$$

$$f(x) \ (\mathrm{mod}\ m_3(3)) \equiv a_3(x) = 533x^2 - 2211x + 2567.$$

We find that

$$m(x) = m_1(x)m_2(x)m_3(x) = x^6 - 14x^5 + 80x^4 - 238x^3 + 387x^2 - 324x + 108.$$

The polynomial $f(x)$ can be represented as the 3-tuple of moduli polynomials:

$$f(x) \leftrightarrow (17, \ 279x - 406, \ 533x^2 - 2211 + 2567) = \underline{f}_1(x). \qquad \Box$$

5.3.1   The CRT and Interpolation

5.3.1.1   The Evaluation Homomorphism

Let $\mathbb{F}$ be a field and let $R = \mathbb{F}[x]$. Let $f(x) \in R$ and let $m_1(x) = x - u_1$. Then computing the remainder of $f(x)$ modulo $x - u_1$ gives exactly $f(u_1)$.

Example 5.39   Let $f(x) = x^4 + 3x^3 + 2x^2 + 4 \in \mathbb{R}[x]$ and let $m_1(x) = x - 3$. Then computing $f(x)/m_1(x)$ by long division, we obtain the quotient and remainder

$$f(x) = (x-3)(x^3 + 6x^2 + 20x + 60) + 184.$$

But we also find that

$$f(3) = 184.$$

So $f(x) \bmod (x-3) = 184 = f(3)$. $\qquad \Box$

Thus, we can write

$$f(x) \bmod (x-u) = f(u).$$

The mapping $\pi_i : \mathbb{F}[x] \to \mathbb{F}$ defined by

$$\pi_i(f(x)) = f(u_i) = f(x) \ (\mathrm{mod}\ (x-u_i))$$

is called the **evaluation homomorphism**. It can be shown that it is, in fact, a homomorphism: for two polynomials $f(x), g(x) \in \mathbb{F}[x]$,

$$\pi_i(f(x) + g(x)) = \pi_i(f(x)) + \pi_i(g(x)) \quad \pi_i(f(x)g(x)) = \pi_i(f(x))\pi_i(g(x)).$$

5.3.1.2   The Interpolation Problem

Suppose we are given the following problem: Given a set of points (u_i, a_i), $i = 1, 2, \ldots, r$, determine an **interpolating** polynomial $f(x) \in \mathbb{F}[x]$ of degree $< r$ such that

$$f(u_1) = a_1, f(u_2) = a_2, \ldots, f(u_r) = a_r. \qquad (5.31)$$

Now let $f(x) = f_0 + f_1 x + \cdots + f_{r-1} x^{r-1}$. Since $\deg(f(x)) < r$, we can think of $f(x)$ as being in $\mathbb{F}[x]/(x^r - 1)$. Also let $m_i(x) = x - u_i \in \mathbb{F}[x]$ for $i = 1, 2, \ldots, r$ where the $u_1, u_2, \ldots, u_r \in F$ are pairwise *distinct*. Then the $m_i(x)$ are pairwise relatively prime.

By the evaluation homomorphism, the set of constraints (5.31) can be expressed as

$$f(x) \equiv a_1 \pmod{m_1(x)} \quad f(x) \equiv a_2 \pmod{m_2(x)} \quad f(x) \equiv a_r \pmod{m_r(x)}.$$

So solving the interpolation problem simply becomes an instance of solving a CRT.

The interpolating polynomial is found using the CRT. Let $m(x) = \prod_{i=1}^{r}(x - u_i)$. By the proof of Theorem 5.35, we need functions $b_j(x)$ such that

$$(m(x)/m_j(x))b_j(x) \equiv 1 \pmod{m_j}$$

and

$$(m(x)/m_j(x))b_j(x) \equiv 0 \pmod{m_k}.$$

That is,

$$\left[\prod_{i=1, i \neq j}^{r} (x - u_i) \right] b_j(x) \equiv 1 \pmod{m_j},$$

and

$$\left[\prod_{i=1, i \neq j}^{r} (x - u_i) \right] b_j(x) \equiv 0 \pmod{m_k}$$

for $k \neq j$. Let

$$b_j(x) = \prod_{i=1, i \neq j}^{r} \frac{1}{(u_j - u_i)}$$

and let

$$l_j(x) = (m(x)/m_j(x))b_j(x) = \prod_{i=1, i \neq j}^{r} \frac{(x - u_i)}{(u_j - u_i)}. \tag{5.32}$$

Since

$$l_j(u_j) = 1 \quad \text{and} \quad l_j(u_k) = 0, \quad j \neq k,$$

we see that $b_j(x)$ satisfies the necessary requirements. By (5.28), the interpolating polynomial is then simply

$$f(x) = \sum_{j=1}^{r} (m(x)/m_j(x))b_j(x)a_j = \sum_{j=1}^{r} a_j l_j(x). \tag{5.33}$$

This form of an interpolating polynomial is called a *Lagrange interpolator*. The basis functions $l_i(x)$ are called *Lagrange interpolants*. By the CRT, this interpolating polynomial is unique modulo $m(x)$.

The Lagrange interpolator can be expressed in another convenient form. Let

$$m(x) = \prod_{i=1}^{r}(x - u_i).$$

Then the derivative[3] is

$$m'(x) = \sum_{k=1}^{r} \prod_{i \neq k}(x - u_i)$$

---

[3] Or formal derivative, if the field of operations is not real or complex.

so that

$$m'(u_j) = \prod_{i \neq j} (u_j - u_i).$$

(See also Definition 6.35.) The interpolation formula (5.33) can now be written as

$$f(x) = \sum_{i=1}^{r} a_i \frac{m(x)}{(x - u_i)} \frac{1}{m'(u_i)}. \tag{5.34}$$

Example 5.40   An important instance of interpolation is the discrete Fourier transform (DFT). Let $f(x) = f_0 + f_1 x + \cdots + f_{N-1} x^{N-1}$, with $x = z^{-1}$, be the Z-transform of a complex cyclic sequence. Then $f(x) \in \mathbb{C}[x]/\langle x^N - 1 \rangle$, since it is a polynomial of degree $\leq N - 1$. Let $m(x) = x^N - 1$. The N roots of $m(x)$ are the complex numbers $e^{-ij2\pi/N}$, $i = 0, 1, \ldots, N - 1$. Let $\omega = e^{-j2\pi/N}$; this is a primitive Nth root of unity. Then the factorization of $m(x)$ can be written as

$$m(x) = x^N - 1 = \prod_{i=0}^{N-1} (x - \omega^i),$$

where the factors are pairwise relative prime. Define the evaluations

$$F_k = \pi_k(f(x)) = f(\omega^k) = \sum_{i=0}^{N-1} f_i \omega^{ik}, \quad k = 0, 1, \ldots, N - 1.$$

Expressed another way, $F_k = f(x) \pmod{x - \omega^k}$. The coefficients $\{f_k\}$ may be thought of as existing in a "time domain," while the coefficients $\{F_k\}$ may be thought of as existing in a "frequency domain."

By the ring isomorphism, for functions in the "time domain," multiplication is polynomial multiplication (modulo $x^N - 1$). That is, for polynomials $f(x)$ and $g(x)$, multiplication is $f(x)g(x) \pmod{x^N - 1}$, which amounts to cyclic convolution.

For functions in the "transform domain," multiplication is element by element. That is, for sequences $(F_0, F_1, \ldots, F_{N-1})$ and $(G_0, G_1, \ldots, G_{N-1})$, multiplication is element by element as complex numbers:

$$(F_0 G_0, F_1 G_1, \ldots, F_{N-1} G_{N-1}).$$

Thus, the ring isomorphism validates the statement: (cyclic) convolution in the time domain is equivalent to multiplication in the frequency domain.   □

5.4   Fields

Fields were introduced in Section 2.3. We review the basic requirements here, in comparison with a ring. In a ring, not every element has a multiplicative inverse. In a field, the familiar arithmetic operations that take place in the usual real numbers are all available: $\langle F, + \rangle$ is an Abelian group. (Denote the additive identity element by 0.) The set $F \backslash \{0\}$ (the set F with the additive identity removed) forms a **commutative** group under multiplication. Denote the multiplicative identity element by 1. Finally, as in a ring the operations $+$ and $\cdot$ distribute: $a \cdot (b + c) = a \cdot b + a \cdot c$ for all $a, b, c \in F$.

In a field, all the elements except the additive identity form a group, whereas in a ring, there may not even be a multiplicative identity, let alone an inverse for every element. Every field is a ring, but not every ring is a field.

Example 5.41 $\langle \mathbb{Z}_5, +, \cdot \rangle$ forms a field; every nonzero element has a multiplicative inverse. So this set forms not only a ring but also a group. Since this field has only a finite number of elements in it, it is said to be a **finite field**.

However, $\langle \mathbb{Z}_6, +, \cdot \rangle$ does not form a field, since not every element has a multiplicative inverse.   □

One way to obtain finite fields is described in the following.

Theorem 5.42 *The ring $\langle \mathbb{Z}_p, +, \cdot \rangle$ is a field if and only if p is a prime.*

Before proving this, we need the following definition and lemma.

Definition 5.43 In a ring R, if $a, b \in R$ with both a and b not equal to zero but $ab = 0$, then a and b are said to be **zero divisors**. □

Lemma 5.44 *In a ring $\mathbb{Z}_n$, the zero divisors are precisely those elements that are not relatively prime to n.*

Proof Let $a \in \mathbb{Z}_n$ be not equal to 0 and be not relatively prime to n. Let d be the GCD of n and a. Then $a(n/d) = (a/d)n$, which, being a multiple of n, is equal to 0 in $\mathbb{Z}_n$. We have thus found a number $b = n/d$ such that $ab = 0$ in $\mathbb{Z}_n$, so a is a zero divisor in $\mathbb{Z}_n$.

Conversely, suppose that there is an $a \in \mathbb{Z}_n$ relatively prime to n such that $ab = 0$. Then it must be the case that

$$ab = kn$$

for some integer k. Since n has no factors in common with a, then it must divide b, which means that $b = 0$ in $\mathbb{Z}_n$. □

Observe from this lemma that if p is a prime, there are *no* divisors of 0 in $\mathbb{Z}_p$. We now turn to the proof of Theorem 5.42.

Proof of Theorem 5.42.

We have already shown that if p is not prime, then there are zero divisors and hence $\langle \mathbb{Z}_p, +, \cdot \rangle$ cannot form a field. Let us now show that if p is prime, $\langle \mathbb{Z}_p, +, \cdot \rangle$ is a field.

We have already established that $\langle \mathbb{Z}_p, + \rangle$ is a group. The key remaining requirement is to establish that $\langle \mathbb{Z}_p \backslash \{0\}, \cdot \rangle$ forms a group. The multiplicative identity is 1 and multiplication is commutative. The key remaining requirement is to establish that every nonzero element in $\mathbb{Z}_p$ has a multiplicative inverse.

Let $\{1, 2, \ldots, p-1\}$ be a list of the nonzero elements in $\mathbb{Z}_p$, and let $a \in \mathbb{Z}_p$ be nonzero. Form the list

$$\{1a, 2a, \ldots, (p-1)a\}. \tag{5.35}$$

Every element in this list is distinct, since if any two were identical, say $ma = na$ with $m \neq n$, then $a(m - n) = 0$, which is impossible since there are no zero divisors in $\mathbb{Z}_p$. Thus, the list (5.35) contains all nonzero elements in $\mathbb{Z}_p$ and is a permutation of the original list. Since 1 is in the original list, it must appear in the list in (5.35). □

5.4.1 An Examination of $\mathbb{R}$ and $\mathbb{C}$

Besides the finite fields $\langle \mathbb{Z}_p, +, \cdot \rangle$ with p prime, there are other finite fields. These fields are *extension fields* of $\mathbb{Z}_p$. However, before introducing them, it is instructive to take a look at how the field of complex numbers $\mathbb{C}$ can be constructed as a field extension from the field of real numbers $\mathbb{R}$.

Recall that there are several representations for complex numbers. Sometimes it is convenient to use a "vector" notation, in which a complex number is represented as (a, b). Sometimes it is convenient to use a "polynomial" notation $a + bi$, where i is taken to be a root of the polynomial $x^2 + 1$. However, since there is some preconception about the meaning of the symbol i, we replace it with the symbol α, which doesn't carry the same connotations (yet). In particular, α is not (yet) the symbol for $\sqrt{-1}$. You may think of $a + b\alpha$ as being a polynomial of degree ≤ 1 in the "indeterminate" α. There is also a polar notation for complex numbers, in which the complex number is written as $a + ib = re^{i\theta}$ for the appropriate r and θ. Despite the differences in notation, it should be borne in mind that they all represent the same number.

Given two complex numbers we *define* the addition component-by-component in the vector notation (a, b) and (c, d), where $a, b, c,$ and d are all in $\mathbb{R}$, based on the addition operation of the underlying field $\mathbb{R}$. The set of complex number thus forms a two-dimensional *vector space* of real numbers. We define

$$(a, b) + (c, d) = (a + c, b + d). \tag{5.36}$$

It is straightforward to show that this addition operation satisfies the group properties for addition, based on the group properties it inherits from $\mathbb{R}$.

Now consider the "polynomial notation." Using the conventional rules for adding polynomials, we obtain

$$a + b\alpha + c + d\alpha = (a + c) + (b + d)\alpha,$$

which is equivalent to (5.36).

How, then, to define multiplication in such a way that all the field requirements are satisfied? If we simply multiply using the conventional rules for polynomial multiplication,

$$(a + b\alpha)(c + d\alpha) = ac + (ad + bc)\alpha + bd\alpha^2, \tag{5.37}$$

we obtain a quadratic polynomial, whereas complex numbers are represented as polynomials having degree ≤ 1 in the variable α.

To reduce the degree as needed, polynomial multiplication must be followed by another step, computing the *remainder* modulo some other polynomial. Let us pick the polynomial

$$g(\alpha) = 1 + \alpha^2$$

to divide by. Dividing the product in (5.37) by $g(\alpha)$

$$
\begin{array}{r}
bd \\
\alpha^2 + 1 \overline{\smash{\big)}\, bd\alpha^2 + (ad + bc)\alpha + ac} \\
\underline{bd\alpha^2 + bd} \\
(ad + bc)\alpha + ac - bd
\end{array}
$$

we obtain the remainder $(ac - bd) + (ad + bc)\alpha$. Summarizing this, we now *define* the product of $(a + b\alpha)$ by $(c + d\alpha)$ by the following two steps:

1. Multiply $(a + b\alpha)$ by $(c + d\alpha)$ as polynomials.
2. Compute the remainder of this product when divided by $g(\alpha) = \alpha^2 + 1$.

That is, the multiplication is defined in the ring $\mathbb{R}[\alpha]/g(\alpha)$, as described in Section 4.4.

Of course, having established the pattern, it is not necessary to carry out the actual polynomial arithmetic: by this two-step procedure we have obtained the familiar formula

$$(a + b\alpha) \cdot (c + d\alpha) = (ac - bd) + (ad + bc)\alpha$$

or, in vector form,

$$(a, b) \cdot (c, d) = (ac - bd, ad + bc).$$

As an important example, suppose we want to multiply the complex numbers (in vector form) $(0, 1)$ times $(0, 1)$, or (in polynomial form) α times α. Going through the steps of computing the product and the remainder we find

$$\alpha \cdot \alpha = -1. \tag{5.38}$$

In other words, in the arithmetic that we have defined, the element α satisfies the equation

$$\alpha^2 + 1 = 0. \tag{5.39}$$

In other words, the indeterminate α *acts like the number* $\sqrt{-1}$. This is a result of the fact that multiplication is computed modulo of the polynomial $g(\alpha) = \alpha^2 + 1$: the symbol α is (now by construction) a root of the polynomial $g(x)$. To put it another way, the remainder of a polynomial $\alpha^2 + 1$ divided by $\alpha^2 + 1$ is exactly 0. So, by this procedure, any time $\alpha^2 + 1$ appears in any computation, it may be replaced with 0.

Let us take another look at the polynomial multiplication in (5.37):

$$(a + b\alpha)(c + d\alpha) = ac + (ad + bc)\alpha + bd\alpha^2. \tag{5.40}$$

Using (5.38), we can replace α^2 in (5.40) wherever it appears with expressions involving lower powers of α. We thus obtain

$$(a + b\alpha)(c + d\alpha) = ac + (ad + bc)\alpha + bd(-1) = (ac - bd) + (ad + bc)\alpha,$$

as expected. If we had an expression involving α^3 it could be similarly simplified and expressed in terms of lower powers of α:

$$\alpha^3 = \alpha \cdot \alpha^2 = \alpha \cdot (-1) = -\alpha.$$

Using the addition and multiplication as defined, it is (more or less) straightforward to show that we have created a field which is, in fact, the field of complex numbers $\mathbb{C}$.

As is explored in the exercises, it is important that the polynomial $g(\alpha)$ used to define the multiplication operation *not* have roots in the base field $\mathbb{R}$. If $g(\alpha)$ were a polynomial so that $g(b) = 0$ for some $b \in \mathbb{R}$, then the multiplication operation defined would not satisfy the field requirements, as there would be zero divisors. A polynomial $g(x)$ that cannot be factored into polynomials of lower degree is said to be irreducible. By the procedure above, we have taken a polynomial equation $g(\alpha)$ which has no real roots (it is irreducible) and *created* a new element α which is the root of $g(\alpha)$, defining along the way an arithmetic system that is mathematically useful (it is a field). The new field $\mathbb{C}$, with the new element α in it, is said to be an **extension field** of the base field $\mathbb{R}$.

At this point, it might be a tempting intellectual exercise to try to extend $\mathbb{C}$ to a bigger field. However, we won't attempt this because:

1. The extension created is sufficient to demonstrate the operations necessary to extend a finite field to a larger finite field; and (more significantly)

2. It turns out that $\mathbb{C}$ does not have any further extensions: it already contains the roots of all polynomials in $\mathbb{C}[x]$, so there are no other polynomials by which it could be extended. This fact is called the **fundamental theorem of algebra**.

There are a couple more observations that may be made about operations in $\mathbb{C}$. First, we point out again that addition in the extension field is easy, being simply element-by-element addition of the vector representation. Multiplication has its own special rules, determined by the polynomial $g(\alpha)$. However, if we represent complex numbers in polar form,

$$a + b\alpha = r_1 e^{j\theta_1} \quad c + d\alpha = r_2 e^{j\theta_2},$$

then multiplication is also easy: simply multiply the magnitudes and add the angles:

$$r_1 e^{j\theta_1} \cdot r_2 e^{j\theta_2} = r_1 r_2 e^{j(\theta_1 + \theta_2)}.$$

Analogously, we will find that addition in the Galois fields we construct is achieved by straightforward vector addition, while multiplication is achieved either by some operation which depends on a polynomial g, or by using a representation loosely analogous to the polar form for complex numbers, in which the multiplication is more easily computed.

5.4.2 Galois Field Construction: An Example

A subfield of a field is a subset of the field that is also a field. For example, $\mathbb{Q}$ is a subfield of $\mathbb{R}$. A more potent concept is that of an extension field. Viewed one way, it simply turns the idea of a subfield around: an extension field E of a field F is a field in which F is a subfield. The field F in this case is said to be the **base field**. But more importantly is the way that the extension field is constructed. Extension fields are constructed to create roots of irreducible polynomials that do not have roots in the base field.

Definition 5.45 A nonconstant polynomial $f(x) \in R[x]$ is **irreducible over** R if $f(x)$ cannot be expressed as a product $g(x)h(x)$ where both $g(x)$ and $h(x)$ are polynomials of degree less than the degree of $f(x)$ and $g(x) \in R[x]$ and $h(x) \in R[x]$. □

In this definition, the ring (or field) in which the polynomial is irreducible makes a difference. For example, the polynomial $f(x) = x^2 - 2$ is irreducible over $\mathbb{Q}$, but over the real numbers we can write

$$f(x) = (x + \sqrt{2})(x - \sqrt{2}),$$

so $f(x)$ is reducible over $\mathbb{R}$.

We have already observed that $\langle \mathbb{Z}_p, +, \cdot \rangle$ forms a field when p is prime. It turns out that *all* finite fields have order equal to some power of a prime number, p^m. For $m > 1$, the finite fields are obtained as extension fields to $\mathbb{Z}_p$ using an irreducible polynomial in $\mathbb{Z}_p[x]$ of degree m. These finite fields are usually denoted by $GF(p^m)$ or $GF(q)$ where $q = p^m$, where GF stands for "Galois field," named after the French mathematician Èveriste Galois (See Box 5.1).

Box 5.1: Èveriste Galois (1811–1832)

The life of Galois is a study in brilliance and tragedy. At an early age, Galois studied the works in algebra and analysis of Abel and Lagrange, convincing himself (justifiably) that he was a mathematical genius. His mundane schoolwork, however, remained mediocre. He attempted to enter the Ècole Polytechnique, but his poor academic performance resulted in rejection, the first of many disappointments. At the age of seventeen, he wrote his discoveries in algebra in a paper which he submitted to Cauchy, who lost it. Meanwhile, his father, an outspoken local politician who instilled in Galois a hate for tyranny, committed suicide after some persecution. Sometime later, Galois submitted another paper to Fourier. Fourier took the paper home and died shortly thereafter, thereby resulting in another lost paper. As a result of some outspoken criticism against its director, Galois was expelled from the normal school he was attending. Yet another paper presenting his works in finite fields was a failure, being rejected by the reviewer (Poisson) as being too incomprehensible.

Disillusioned, Galois joined the National Guard, where his outspoken nature led to some time in jail for a purported insult against Louis Philippe. Later he was challenged to a duel — probably a setup — to defend the honor of a woman. The night before the duel, Galois wrote a lengthy letter describing his discoveries. The letter was eventually published in *Revue Encyclopèdique*. Alas, Galois was not there to read it: he was shot in the stomach in the duel and died the following day of peritonitis at the tender age of 20.

We demonstrate the extension process by constructing the operations for the field $GF(2^4)$, analogous to the way the complex field was constructed from the real field. Any number in $GF(2^4)$ can be represented as a 4-tuple (a, b, c, d), where $a, b, c, d \in GF(2)$. Addition of these numbers is defined to be element-by-element, modulo 2: For $(a_1, a_2, a_3, a_4) \in GF(2^4)$ and $(b_1, b_2, b_3, b_3) \in GF(2^4)$, where $a_i \in GF(2)$ and $b_i \in GF(2)$,

$$(a_1, a_2, a_3, a_4) + (b_1, b_2, b_3, b_4) = (a_1 + b_1, a_2 + b_2, a_3 + b_3, a_4 + b_4).$$

Example 5.46 Add the numbers $(1, 0, 1, 1) + (0, 1, 0, 1)$. Recall that in $GF(2)$, $1 + 1 = 0$, so that we obtain

$$(1, 0, 1, 1) + (0, 1, 0, 1) = (1, 1, 1, 0).$$

□

To define the multiplicative structure, we need an irreducible polynomial of degree 4. The polynomial $g(x) = 1 + x + x^4$ is irreducible over $GF(2)$. (This can be verified since $g(0) = 1$ and $g(1) = 1$, which eliminates linear factors and it can be verified by exhaustion that the polynomial cannot be factored into quadratic factors.) In the extension field $GF(2^4)$, define α to be a root of g:

$$\alpha^4 + \alpha + 1 = 0,$$

or

$$\alpha^4 = 1 + \alpha. \tag{5.41}$$

A 4-tuple (a, b, c, d) representing a number in $GF(2^4)$ has a representation in polynomial form

$$a + b\alpha + c\alpha^2 + d\alpha^3.$$

Now take successive powers of α beyond α^4:

$$\begin{aligned}
\alpha^4 &= 1 + \alpha, \\
\alpha^5 &= \alpha(\alpha^4) = \alpha + \alpha^2, \\
\alpha^6 &= \alpha^2(\alpha^4) = \alpha^2 + \alpha^3, \\
\alpha^7 &= \alpha^3(\alpha^4) = \alpha^3(1 + \alpha) = \alpha^3 + 1 + \alpha,
\end{aligned} \tag{5.42}$$

and so forth. In fact, because of the particular irreducible polynomial $g(x)$ which we selected, powers of α up to α^{14} are all distinct and $\alpha^{15} = 1$. Thus, all 15 of the nonzero elements of the field can be represented as powers of α. This gives us something analogous to a "polar" form; we call it the "power" representation. The relationship between the vector representation, the polynomial representation, and the "power" representation for $GF(2^4)$ is shown in Table 5.1. The fact that a 4-tuple has a corresponding representation as a power of α is denoted using $\leftrightarrow$. For example,

$$(0, 1, 0, 0) \leftrightarrow \alpha \quad (0, 1, 1, 0) \leftrightarrow \alpha^5.$$

The Vector Representation (integer) column of the table is obtained from the Vector Representation column by binary-to-decimal conversion, with the least-significant bit on the left.

Example 5.47 In $GF(2^4)$ multiply the Galois field numbers $1 + \alpha + \alpha^3$ and $\alpha + \alpha^2$. Step 1 is to multiply these "as polynomials" (where the arithmetic of the coefficients takes place in $GF(2)$):

$$(1 + \alpha + \alpha^3) \cdot (\alpha + \alpha^2) = \alpha + \alpha^3 + \alpha^4 + \alpha^5.$$

Step 2 is to reduce using Table 5.1 or, equivalently, to compute the remainder modulo $\alpha^4 + \alpha + 1$:

$$\alpha + \alpha^3 + \alpha^4 + \alpha^5 = \alpha + \alpha^3 + (1 + \alpha) + (\alpha + \alpha^2) = 1 + \alpha + \alpha^2 + \alpha^3.$$

So in $GF(2^4)$,

$$(1 + \alpha + \alpha^3) \cdot (\alpha + \alpha^2) = 1 + \alpha + \alpha^2 + \alpha^3.$$

Table 5.1: Power, Vector, and Polynomial Representations of $GF(2^4)$ as an Extension Using $g(\alpha) = 1 + \alpha + \alpha^4$

Polynomial Representation				Vector Representation	Vector Representation (integer)	Power Representation α^n	Logarithm n	Zech Logarithm $z(n)$
0				0 0 0 0	0	–	–	–
1				1 0 0 0	1	$1 = \alpha^0$	0	–
	α			0 1 0 0	2	α	1	4
		α^2		0 0 1 0	4	α^2	2	8
			α^3	0 0 0 1	8	α^3	3	14
1 +	α			1 1 0 0	3	α^4	4	1
	α +	α^2		0 1 1 0	6	α^5	5	10
		α^2 +	α^3	0 0 1 1	12	α^6	6	13
1 +	α	+	α^3	1 1 0 1	11	α^7	7	9
1		+ α^2		1 0 1 0	5	α^8	8	2
	α	+	α^3	0 1 0 1	10	α^9	9	7
1 +	α +	α^2		1 1 1 0	7	α^{10}	10	5
	α +	α^2 +	α^3	0 1 1 1	14	α^{11}	11	12
1 +	α +	α^2 +	α^3	1 1 1 1	15	α^{12}	12	11
1		+ α^2 +	α^3	1 0 1 1	13	α^{13}	13	6
1		+	α^3	1 0 0 1	9	α^{14}	14	3

Note that $\alpha^{15} = 1$. (The Zech logarithm is explained in Section 5.6.)

In vector notation, we could also write

$$(1, 1, 0, 1) \cdot (0, 1, 1, 0) = (1, 1, 1, 1).$$

This product can also be computed using the power representation. Since $(1, 1, 0, 1) \leftrightarrow \alpha^7$ and $(0, 1, 1, 0) \leftrightarrow \alpha^5$, we have

$$(1, 1, 0, 1) \cdot (0, 1, 1, 0) \leftrightarrow \alpha^7 \alpha^5 = \alpha^{12} \leftrightarrow (1, 1, 1, 1).$$

The product is computed simply using the laws of exponents (adding the exponents). □

Example 5.48 In $GF(2^4)$, compute $\alpha^{12} \cdot \alpha^5$. In this case, we would get

$$\alpha^{12} \cdot \alpha^5 = \alpha^{17}.$$

However since $\alpha^{15} = 1$,

$$\alpha^{12} \cdot \alpha^5 = \alpha^{17} = \alpha^{15} \alpha^2 = \alpha^2.$$

  □

We compute $\alpha^a \alpha^b = \alpha^c$ by finding $c = (a + b) \pmod{p^m - 1}$.

Since the exponents are important, a nonzero number is frequently represented by the exponent. The exponent is referred to as the logarithm of the number.

It should be pointed that this power (or logarithm) representation of the Galois field exists because of the particular polynomial $g(\alpha)$ which was chosen. The polynomial is not only irreducible, it is also *primitive* which means that successive powers of α up to $2^m - 1$ are all unique, just as we have seen.

While different irreducible polynomials can be used to construct the field there is, in fact, only one field with q elements in it, up to isomorphism.

Tables which provide both addition and multiplication operations for $GF(2^3)$ and $GF(2^4)$ are provided inside the back cover of this book.

5.4.3 Connection with Linear Feedback Shift Registers

The generation of a Galois field can be represented using an LFSR with $g(x)$ as the connection polynomial by labeling the registers as $1, \alpha, \alpha^2$, and α^3, as shown in Figure 5.1. As the LFSR is clocked, successive powers of α are represented by the state of the LFSR. The sequence of register contents as the LFSR is clocked n steps is shown in the table below.

n	1	α	α^2	α^3
0	1	0	0	0
1	0	1	0	0
2	0	0	1	0
3	0	0	0	1
4	1	1	0	0
5	0	1	1	0
6	0	0	1	1
7	1	1	0	1
8	1	0	1	0
9	0	1	0	1
10	1	1	1	0
11	0	1	1	1
12	1	1	1	1
13	1	0	1	1
14	1	0	0	1
15	1	0	0	1

The register contents correspond exactly with the nonzero vectors of the Vector Representation column of Table 5.1. The state contents provide the vector representation, while the count provides the exponent in the power representation.

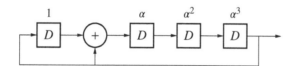

Figure 5.1: LFSR labeled with powers of α to illustrate Galois field elements.

5.5 Galois Fields: Mathematical Facts

Having presented an example of constructing a Galois field, we now lay out some aspects of the theory.

We first examine the additive structure of finite fields, which tells us what size any finite field can be. Recalling Definition 4.6, that the characteristic is the smallest positive integer m such that $m(1) = 1 + 1 + \cdots + 1 = 0$, we have the following.

Lemma 5.49 *The characteristic of a field must be either 0 or a prime number.*

Proof If the field has characteristic 0, the field must be infinite. Otherwise, suppose that the characteristic is a finite number k. Assume k is a composite number. Then $k(1) = 0$ and there are integers $m \neq 1$ and $n \neq 1$ such that $k = mn$. Then

$$0 = k(1) = (mn)(1) = m(1)n(1) = 0.$$

But a field has no zero divisors, so either m or n is the characteristic, violating the minimality of the characteristic. $\square$

It can be shown that any field of characteristic 0 contains the field $\mathbb{Q}$.

On the basis of this lemma, we can observe that in a finite field $GF(q)$, there are p elements (p a prime number) $\{0, 1, 2 = 2(1), \ldots, (p-1) = (p-1)(1)\}$ which behave as a field (i.e., we can define addition and multiplication on them as a field). Thus, $\mathbb{Z}_p$ (or something isomorphic to it, which is the same thing) is a subfield of every Galois field $GF(q)$. In fact, a stronger assertion can be made:

Theorem 5.50 *The order q of every finite field $GF(q)$ must be a power of a prime.*

Proof By Lemma 5.49, every finite field $GF(q)$ has a subfield of prime order p. We will show that $GF(q)$ acts like a vector space over its subfield $GF(p)$.

Let $\beta_1 \in GF(q)$, with $\beta_1 \neq 0$. Form the elements $a_1\beta_1$ as a_1 varies over the elements $\{0, 1, \ldots, p-1\}$ in $GF(p)$. The product $a_1\beta_1$ takes on p distinct values. (For if $x\beta_1 = y\beta_1$ we must have $x = y$, since there are no zero divisors in a field.) If by these p products we have "covered" all the elements in the field, we are done: they form a vector space over $GF(p)$.

If not, let β_2 be an element which has not been covered yet. Then form $a_1\beta_1 + a_2\beta_2$ as a_1 and a_2 vary independently. This must lead to p^2 distinct values in $GF(q)$. If still not done, then continue, forming the linear combinations

$$a_1\beta_1 + a_2\beta_2 + \cdots + a_m\beta_m$$

until all elements of $GF(q)$ are covered. Each combination of coefficients $\{a_1, a_2, \ldots, a_m\}$ corresponds to a distinct element of $GF(q)$. Therefore, there must be p^m elements in $GF(q)$. $\square$

This theorem shows that all finite fields have the structure of a vector space of dimension m over a finite field $\mathbb{Z}_p$. For the field $GF(p^m)$, the subfield $GF(p)$ is called the **ground field.**

This proof raises an important point about the representation of a field. In the construction of $GF(2^4)$ in Section 5.4.2, we formed the field as a vector space over the basis vectors 1, α, α^2, and α^3. (Or, more generally, to form $GF(p^m)$, we would use the elements $\{1, \alpha, \alpha^2, \ldots, \alpha^{m-1}\}$ as the basis vectors.) However, another set of basis vectors could be used. Any set of m linearly independent nonzero elements of $GF(p^m)$ can be used as a basis set. For example, for $GF(2^4)$ we could construct the field as all linear combinations of $\{1 + \alpha, \alpha + \alpha^2, 1 + \alpha^3, \alpha + \alpha^2 + \alpha^3\}$. The multiplicative relationship prescribed by the irreducible polynomial still applies. While this is not as convenient a construction for most purposes, it is sometimes helpful to think of representations of a field in terms of different bases.

Theorem 5.51 *If x and y are elements in a field of characteristic p,*

$$(x + y)^p = x^p + y^p.$$

This rule is sometimes called "freshman exponentiation," since it is erroneously employed by some students of elementary algebra.

Proof By the binomial theorem,

$$(x + y)^p = \sum_{i=0}^{p} \binom{p}{i} x^i y^{p-i}.$$

For a prime p and for any integer $i \neq 0$ and $i \neq p$, $p | \binom{p}{i}$ so that $\binom{p}{i} \equiv 0 \pmod{p}$. Thus, all the terms in the sum except the first and the last are p times some quantity, which are equal to 0 since the characteristic of the field is p. $\square$

This theorem extends by induction in two ways: both to the number of summands and to the exponent: If $x_1, x_2, \ldots, x_k$ are in a field of characteristic p, then

$$\left(\sum_{i=1}^{k} x_i\right)^{p^r} = \sum_{i=1}^{k} x_i^{p^r} \tag{5.43}$$

for all $r \geq 0$.

We now consider some multiplicative questions related to finite fields.

Definition 5.52 Let $\beta \in GF(q)$. The **order**[4] of β, written $\mathrm{ord}(\beta)$ is the smallest positive integer n such that $\beta^n = 1$. □

Definition 5.53 An element with order $q - 1$ in $GF(q)$ (i.e., it generates all the nonzero elements of the field) is called a **primitive element**. □

In other words, a primitive element has the highest possible order.

We saw in the construction of $GF(2^4)$ that the element we called α has order 15, making it a primitive element in the field. We also saw that the primitive element enables the "power representation" of the field, which makes multiplication particularly easy. The questions addressed by the following lemmas are: Does a Galois field always have a primitive element? How many primitive elements does a field have?

Lemma 5.54 If $\beta \in GF(q)$ and $\beta \neq 0$ then $\mathrm{ord}(\beta)|(q - 1)$.

Proof Let $t = \mathrm{ord}(\beta)$. The set $\{\beta, \beta^2, \ldots, \beta^t = 1\}$ forms a subgroup of the nonzero elements in $GF(q)$ under multiplication. Since the order of a subgroup must divide the order of the group (Lagrange's theorem, Theorem 2.29), the result follows. □

Example 5.55 In the field $GF(2^4)$, the element α^3 has order 5, since

$$(\alpha^3)^5 = \alpha^{15} = 1,$$

and $5|15$. In fact, we have the sequence

$$\alpha^3, \quad (\alpha^3)^2 = \alpha^6, \quad (\alpha^3)^3 = \alpha^9, \quad (\alpha^3)^4 = \alpha^{12}, \quad (\alpha^3)^5 = \alpha^{15} = 1.$$

□

Lemma 5.56 Let $\beta \in GF(q)$. $\beta^s = 1$ if and only if $\mathrm{ord}(\beta)|s$.

Proof Let $t = \mathrm{ord}(\beta)$. Let s be such that $\beta^s = 1$. Using the division algorithm, write $s = at + r$ where $0 \leq r < t$. Then $1 = \beta^s = \beta^{at}\beta^r = \beta^r$. By the minimality of the order (it must be the *smallest* positive integer), we must have $r = 0$.

Conversely, if $\mathrm{ord}(\beta)|s$, then $\beta^s = \beta^{qt} = (\beta^t)^q = 1$, where $t = \mathrm{ord}(\beta)$ and $q = s/t$. □

Lemma 5.57 If α has order s and β has order t and $(s, t) = 1$, then $\alpha\beta$ has order st.

Example 5.58 Before embarking on the proof, an example of this lemma. In $GF(2^4)$, α^3 and α^5 have orders that are relatively prime, being 5 and 3, respectively. It may be verified that $\alpha^3\alpha^5 = \alpha^8$ has order 15 (it is primitive). □

---

[4] The nomenclature is unfortunate, since we already have defined the order of a group and the order of an element within a group.

Proof First,

$$(\alpha\beta)^{st} = (\alpha^s)^t(\beta^t)^s = 1.$$

Might there be a smaller value for the order than st?

Let k be the order of $\alpha\beta$. Since $(\alpha\beta)^k = 1$, $\alpha^k = \beta^{-k}$. Since $\alpha^s = 1$, $\alpha^{sk} = 1$, and hence $\beta^{-sk} = 1$. Furthermore, $\alpha^{tk} = \beta^{-tk} = 1$. By Lemma 5.56, $s|tk$. Since $(s,t) = 1$, k must be a multiple of s.

Similarly, $\beta^{-sk} = 1$ and so $t|sk$. Since $(s,t) = 1$, k must be a multiple of t.

Combining these, we see that k must be a multiple of st. In light of the first observation, we have $k = st$. □

Lemma 5.59 *In a finite field, if* $ord(\alpha) = t$ *and* $\beta = \alpha^i$, *then*

$$\operatorname{ord}(\beta) = \frac{t}{(i,t)}.$$

Proof If $ord(\alpha) = t$, then $\alpha^s = 1$ if and only if $t|s$ (Lemma 5.56).

Let $ord(\beta) = u$. Note that $i/(i,t)$ is an integer. Then

$$\beta^{t/(i,t)} = (\alpha^i)^{t/(i,t)} = (\alpha^t)^{i/(i,t)} = 1.$$

Thus, $u|t/(i,t)$. We also have

$$(\alpha^i)^u = 1$$

so $t|iu$. This means that $t/(i,t)|u$. Combining the results, we have $u = t/(i,t)$. □

Theorem 5.60 *For a Galois field* $GF(q)$, *if* $t|q-1$ *then there are* $\phi(t)$ *elements of order t in* $GF(q)$, *where* $\phi(t)$ *is the Euler totient function.*

Proof Observe from Lemma 5.54 that if $t \nmid q-1$, then there are no elements of order t in $GF(q)$. So assume that $t|q-1$; we now determine how many elements of order t there are.

Let α be an element with order t. Then by Lemma 5.59, if $\beta = \alpha^i$ for some i such that $(i,t) = 1$, then β also has order t. The number of such is is $\phi(t)$.

Could there be other elements not of the form α^i having order t? Any element having order t is a root of the polynomial $x^t - 1$. Each element in the set $\{\alpha, \alpha^2, \alpha^3, \ldots, \alpha^t\}$ is a solution to the equation $x^t - 1 = 0$. Since a polynomial of degree t over a field has no more than t roots (see Theorem 5.69 below), there are no elements of order t not in the set. □

The following theorem is a corollary of this result:

Theorem 5.61 *There are* $\phi(q-1)$ *primitive elements in* $GF(q)$.

Example 5.62 In $GF(7)$, the numbers 5 and 3 are primitive:

$$5^1 = 5, \quad 5^2 = 4, \quad 5^3 = 6, \quad 5^4 = 2, \quad 5^5 = 3, \quad 5^6 = 1.$$
$$3^1 = 3, \quad 3^2 = 4, \quad 3^3 = 6, \quad 3^4 = 4, \quad 3^5 = 5, \quad 3^6 = 1.$$

We also have $\phi(q-1) = \phi(6) = 2$, so these are the only primitive elements. □

Because primitive elements exist, the nonzero elements of the field $GF(q)$ can always be written as powers of a primitive element. If $\alpha \in GF(q)$ is primitive, then

$$\{\alpha, \alpha^2, \alpha^3, \ldots, \alpha^{q-2}, \alpha^{q-1} = 1\}$$

is the set of all nonzero elements of $GF(q)$. If we let $GF(q)^*$ denote the set of nonzero elements of $GF(q)$, we can write

$$GF(q)^* = \langle \alpha \rangle.$$

If $\beta = \alpha^i$ is also primitive (i.e., $(i, q-1) = 1$), then the nonzero elements of the field are also generated by

$$\{\beta, \beta^2, \beta^3, \ldots, \beta^{q-2}, \beta^{q-1} = 1\},$$

that is, $GF(q)^* = \langle \beta \rangle$. Despite the fact that these are different generators, these are not different fields, only different representations, so $\langle \alpha \rangle$ is isomorphic to $\langle \beta \rangle$. We thus talk of *the* Galois field with q elements, since there is only one.

Theorem 5.63 *Every element of the field $GF(q)$ satisfies the equation $x^q - x = 0$. Furthermore, they constitute the entire set of roots of this equation.*

Proof Clearly, the equation can be written as $x(x^{q-1} - 1) = 0$. Thus, $x = 0$ is clearly a root. The nonzero elements of the field are all generated as powers of a primitive element α. For an element $\beta = \alpha^i \in GF(q)$, $\beta^{q-1} = (\alpha^i)^{q-1} = (\alpha^{q-1})^i = 1$. Since there are q elements in $GF(q)$, and at most q roots of the equation, the elements of $GF(q)$ are all the roots. $\quad\square$

An extension field E of a field $\mathbb{F}$ is a **splitting field** of a nonconstant polynomial $f(x) \in \mathbb{F}[x]$ if $f(x)$ can be factored into linear factors over E, but not in any proper subfield of E. Theorem 5.63 thus says that $GF(q)$ is the splitting field for the polynomial $x^q - x$.

As an extension of Theorem 5.63, we have

Theorem 5.64 *Every element in a field $GF(q)$ satisfies the equation*

$$x^{q^n} - x = 0$$

for every $n \geq 0$.

Proof When $n = 0$, the result is trivial; when $n = 1$, we have Theorem 5.63, giving $x^q = x$. The proof is by induction: Assume that $x^{q^{n-1}} = x$. Then $(x^{q^{n-1}})^q = x^q = x$, or $x^{q^n} = x$. $\quad\square$

A field $GF(p)$ can be extended to a field $GF(p^m)$ for any $m > 1$. Let $q = p^m$. The field $GF(q)$ can be further extended to a field $GF(q^r)$ for any r, by extending by an irreducible polynomial of degree r in $GF(q)[x]$. This gives the field $GF(p^{mr})$.

5.6 Implementing Galois Field Arithmetic

Lab 5 describes one way of implementing Galois field arithmetic in a computer using two tables. In this section, we present a way of computing operations using one table of *Zech logarithms*, as well as some concepts for hardware implementation.

5.6.1 Zech Logarithms

In a Galois field $GF(2^m)$, the Zech logarithm $z(n)$ is defined by

$$\alpha^{z(n)} = 1 + \alpha^n, \quad n = 1, 2, \ldots, 2^m - 2.$$

Table 5.1 shows the Zech logarithm for the field $GF(2^4)$. For example, when $n = 2$, we have

$$1 + \alpha^2 = \alpha^8$$

so that $z(2) = 8$.

In the Zech logarithm approach to Galois field computations, numbers are represented using the exponent. Multiplication is thus natural. To see how to add, consider the following example:

$$\alpha^3 + \alpha^5.$$

The first step is to factor out the term with the smallest exponent,

$$\alpha^3(1 + \alpha^2).$$

Now the Zech logarithm is used: $1 + \alpha^2 = \alpha^{z(2)} = \alpha^8$. So

$$\alpha^3 + \alpha^5 = \alpha^3(1 + \alpha^2) = \alpha^3\alpha^8 = \alpha^{11}.$$

The addition requires one table lookup and one multiply operation. It has been found that in many implementations, the use of Zech logarithms can significantly improve execution time.

5.6.2 Hardware Implementations

We present examples for the field $GF(2^4)$ generated by $g(x) = 1 + x + x^4$. Addition is easily accomplished by simple mod-2 addition for numbers in vector representation.

Multiplication of the element $\beta = b_0 + b_1\alpha + b_2\alpha^2 + b_3\alpha^3$ by the primitive element α is computed using $\alpha^4 = 1 + \alpha$ as

$$\alpha\beta = b_0\alpha + b_1\alpha^2 + b_2\alpha^3 + b_3\alpha^4 = b_3 + (b_0 + b_3)\alpha + b_1\alpha^2 + b_2\alpha^3.$$

These computations can be obtained using an LFSR as shown in Figure 5.2. Clocking the registers once fills them with the representation of $\alpha\beta$.

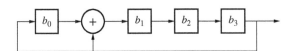

Figure 5.2: Multiplication of β by α.

Multiplication by specific powers of α can be accomplished with dedicated circuits. For example, to multiply $\beta = b_0 + b_1\alpha + b_2\alpha^2 + b_3\alpha^3$ by $\alpha^4 = 1 + \alpha$, we have

$$\beta\alpha^4 = \beta + \alpha\beta = (b_0 + b_3) + (b_0 + b_1 + b_3)\alpha + (b_1 + b_2)\alpha^2 + (b_2 + b_3)\alpha^3,$$

which can be represented as shown in Figure 5.3.

Finally, we present a circuit which multiplies two arbitrary Galois field elements. Let $\beta = b_0 + b_1\alpha + b_2\alpha^2 + b_3\alpha^3$ and let $\gamma = c_0 + c_1\alpha + c_2\alpha^2 + c_3\alpha^3$. Then $\beta\gamma$ can be written in a Horner-like notation as

$$\beta\gamma = (((c_3\beta)\alpha + c_2\beta)\alpha + c_1\beta)\alpha + c_0\beta.$$

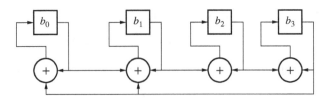

Figure 5.3: Multiplication of an arbitrary β by α^4.

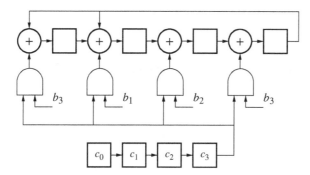

Figure 5.4: Multiplication of β by an arbitrary field element.

Figure 5.4 shows a circuit for this expression. Initially, the upper register is cleared. Then at the first clock the register contains $c_3\beta$. At the second clock the register contains $c_3\beta\alpha + c_2\beta$, where the multiplication by α comes by virtue of the feedback structure. At the next clock the register contains $(c_3\beta\alpha + c_2\beta)\alpha + c_1\beta$. At the final clock the register contains the entire product.

5.7 Subfields of Galois Fields

Elements in a base field $GF(q)$ are also elements of its extension field $GF(q^m)$. Given an element $\beta \in GF(q^m)$ in the extension field, it is of interest to know if it is an element in the base field $GF(q)$. The following theorem provides the answer.

Theorem 5.65 *An element* $\beta \in GF(q^m)$ *lies in* $GF(q)$ *if and only if* $\beta^q = \beta$.

Proof If $\beta \in GF(q)$, then by Lemma 5.54, $\text{ord}(\beta)|(q-1)$, so that $\beta^q = \beta$.

Conversely, assume $\beta^q = \beta$. Then β is a root of $x^q - x = 0$. Now observe that all q elements of $GF(q)$ satisfy this polynomial and it can only have q roots. Hence $\beta \in GF(q)$. $\square$

By induction, it follows that an element $\beta \in GF(q^n)$ lies in the subfield $GF(q)$ if $\beta^{q^n} = \beta$ for any $n \geq 0$.

Example 5.66 The field $GF(4)$ is a subfield of $GF(256)$. Let α be primitive in $GF(256)$. We desire to find an element in $GF(4) \subset GF(256)$. Let $\beta = \alpha^{85}$. Then, invoking Theorem 5.65

$$\beta^4 = \alpha^{85\cdot4} = \alpha^{255}\alpha^{85} = \beta.$$

So $\beta \in GF(4)$ and $GF(4)$ has the elements $\{0, 1, \beta, \beta^2\} = \{0, 1, \alpha^{85}, \alpha^{170}\}$. $\square$

Theorem 5.67 $GF(q^k)$ *is a subfield of* $GF(q^j)$ *if and only if* $k|j$.

The proof relies on the following lemma.

Lemma 5.68 *If* n, r, *and* s *are positive integers and* $n \geq 2$, *then* $n^s - 1|n^r - 1$ *if and only if* $s|r$.

Proof of Theorem 5.67. If $k|j$, say $j = mk$, then $GF(q^k)$ can be extended using an irreducible polynomial of degree m over $GF(q^k)$ to obtain the field with $(q^k)^m = q^j$ elements.

Conversely, let $GF(q^k)$ be a subfield of $GF(q^j)$ and let β be a primitive element in $GF(q^k)$. Then $\beta^{q^k-1} = 1$. As an element of the field $GF(q^j)$, it must also be true (see, e.g., Theorem 5.63) that

$\beta^{q^j-1} = 1$. From Lemma 5.56, it must be the case that $q^k - 1 | q^j - 1$ and hence, from Lemma 5.68, it follows that $k|j$.   □

As an example of this, Figure 5.5 illustrates the subfields of $GF(2^{24})$.

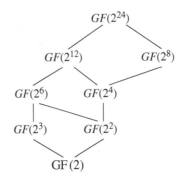

Figure 5.5: Subfield structure of $GF(2^{24})$.

5.8   Irreducible and Primitive Polynomials

We first present a result familiar from polynomials over complex numbers.

Theorem 5.69 *A polynomial of degree d over a field $\mathbb{F}$ has at most d roots in any field containing $\mathbb{F}$.*

This theorem seems obvious, but in fact over a *ring* it is not necessarily true! The quadratic polynomial $x^2 - 1$ has four roots in $\mathbb{Z}_{15}$, namely 1, 4, 11, and 14 [33].

Proof Every polynomial of degree 1 (i.e., a linear polynomial) is irreducible. Since the degree of a product of several polynomials is the sum of their degrees, a polynomial of degree d cannot have more than d linear factors. By the division algorithm, $(x - \beta)$ is a factor of a polynomial $f(x)$ if and only if $f(\beta) = 0$ (see Exercise 5.47). Hence $f(x)$ can have at most d roots.   □

While any irreducible polynomial can be used to construct the extension field, computation in the field is easier if a primitive polynomial is used. We make the following observation:

Theorem 5.70 *Let p be prime. An irreducible mth-degree polynomial $f(x) \in GF(p)[x]$ divides $x^{p^m-1} - 1$.*

Example 5.71 $(x^3 + x + 1)|(x^7 + 1)$ in $GF(2)$ (this can be shown by long division).   □

It is important to understand the implication of the theorem: an irreducible polynomial divides $x^{p^m-1} - 1$, but just because a polynomial divides $x^{p^m-1} - 1$ does not mean that it is irreducible. (Showing irreducibility is much harder than that!)

Proof Let $GF(q) = GF(p^m)$ be constructed using the irreducible polynomial $f(x)$, where α denotes the root of $f(x)$ in the field: $f(\alpha) = 0$. By Theorem 5.63, α is a root of $x^{p^m-1} - 1$ in $GF(q)$. Using the division algorithm write

$$x^{p^m-1} - 1 = g(x)f(x) + r(x), \tag{5.44}$$

where $\deg(r(x)) < m$. Evaluating (5.44) at $x = \alpha$ in $GF(q)$, we obtain

$$0 = 0 + r(\alpha).$$

But the elements of the field $GF(q)$ are represented as polynomials in α of degree $< m$, so since $r(\alpha) = 0$ it must be that $r(x)$ is the zero polynomial, $r(x) = 0$. $\qquad \square$

A slight generalization, proved similarly using Theorem 5.64, is the following:

Theorem 5.72 *If $f[x] \in GF(q)[x]$ is an irreducible polynomial of degree m, then*

$$f(x)|(x^{q^k} - x)$$

for any k such that $m|k$.

Definition 5.73 An irreducible polynomial $p(x) \in GF(p^r)[x]$ of degree m is said to be **primitive** if the smallest positive integer n for which $p(x)$ divides $x^n - 1$ is $n = p^{rm} - 1$. $\qquad \square$

Example 5.74 Taking $f(x) = x^3 + x + 1$, it can be shown by exhaustive checking that $f(x) \nmid x^4 + 1, f(x) \nmid x^5 + 1$, and $f(x) \nmid x^6 + 1$, but $f(x)|x^7 + 1$. In fact,

$$x^7 - 1 = (x^3 + x + 1)(x^4 + x^2 + x + 1).$$

Thus, $f(x)$ is primitive. $\qquad \square$

The following theorem provides the motivation for using primitive polynomials.

Theorem 5.75 *The roots of an mth degree primitive polynomial $p(x) \in GF(p)[x]$ are primitive elements in $GF(p^m)$.*

That is, any of the roots can be used to generate the nonzero elements of the field $GF(p^m)$.

Proof Let α be a root of an mth-degree primitive polynomial $p(x)$. We have

$$x^{p^m - 1} - 1 = p(x)q(x)$$

for some $q(x)$. Observe that

$$\alpha^{p^m - 1} - 1 = p(\alpha)q(\alpha) = 0q(\alpha) = 0,$$

from which we note that

$$\alpha^{p^m - 1} = 1.$$

Now the question is, might there be a smaller power t of α such that $\alpha^t = 1$? If this were the case, then we would have

$$\alpha^t - 1 = 0.$$

There would therefore be some polynomial $x^t - 1$ that would have α as a root. However, any root of $x^t - 1$ must also be a root of $x^{p^m - 1} - 1$, because $\text{ord}(\alpha)|p^m - 1$. To see this, suppose (to the contrary) that $\text{ord}(\alpha) \nmid p^m - 1$. Then

$$p^m - 1 = k\,\text{ord}(\alpha) + r$$

for some r with $0 < r < \text{ord}(\alpha)$. Therefore, we have

$$1 = \alpha^{p^m - 1} = \alpha^{k\,\text{ord}(\alpha) + r} = \alpha^r,$$

which contradicts the minimality of the order.

Thus, all the roots of $x^t - 1$ are the roots of $x^{p^m-1} - 1$, so

$$x^t - 1 \mid x^{p^m-1} - 1.$$

We show below that all the roots of an irreducible polynomial are of the same order. This means that $p(x) \mid x^t - 1$. But by the definition of a primitive polynomial, we must have $t = p^m - 1$. □

All the nonzero elements of the field can be **generated as powers of the roots of the primitive polynomial.**

Example 5.76 The polynomial $p(x) = x^2 + x + 2$ is primitive in $GF(5)$. Let α represent a root of $p(x)$, so that $\alpha^2 + \alpha + 2 = 0$, or $\alpha^2 = 4\alpha + 3$. The elements in $GF(25)$ can be represented as powers of α as shown in the following table.

0	$\alpha^0 = 1$	$\alpha^1 = \alpha$	$\alpha^2 = 4\alpha + 3$	$\alpha^3 = 4\alpha + 2$
$\alpha^4 = 3\alpha + 2$	$\alpha^5 = 4\alpha + 4$	$\alpha^6 = 2$	$\alpha^7 = 2\alpha$	$\alpha^8 = 3\alpha + 1$
$\alpha^9 = 3\alpha + 4$	$\alpha^{10} = \alpha + 4$	$\alpha^{11} = 3\alpha + 3$	$\alpha^{12} = 4$	$\alpha^{13} = 4\alpha$
$\alpha^{14} = \alpha + 2$	$\alpha^{15} = \alpha + 3$	$\alpha^{16} = 2\alpha + 3$	$\alpha^{17} = \alpha + 1$	$\alpha^{18} = 3$
$\alpha^{19} = 3\alpha$	$\alpha^{20} = 2\alpha + 4$	$\alpha^{21} = 2\alpha + 1$	$\alpha^{22} = 4\alpha + 1$	$\alpha^{23} = 2\alpha + 2$

As an example of some arithmetic in this field,

$$(3\alpha + 4) + (4\alpha + 1) = 2\alpha$$

$$(3\alpha + 4)(4\alpha + 1) = \alpha^9 \alpha^{22} = \alpha^{31} = (\alpha^{24})(\alpha^7) = 2\alpha.$$

□

primfind.c

The program `primfind` finds primitive polynomials in $GF(p)[x]$, where the prime p can be specified. It does this by recursively producing *all* polynomials (or all of those of a weight you might specify) and evaluating whether they are primitive by using them as feedback polynomials in an LFSR. Those which generate maximal length sequences are primitive.

5.9 Conjugate Elements and Minimal Polynomials

From Chapter 4, we have seen that cyclic codes have a generator polynomial $g(x)$ dividing $x^n - 1$. Designing cyclic codes with a specified code length n thus requires the facility to factor $x^n - 1$ into factors with certain properties. In this section, we explore aspects of this factorization question.

It frequently happens that the structure of a code is defined over a field $GF(q^m)$, but it is desired to employ a generator polynomial $g(x)$ over the base field $GF(q)$. For example, we might want a binary generator polynomial — for ease of implementation — but need to work over a field $GF(2^m)$ for some m. How to obtain polynomials having coefficients in the base field but roots in the larger field is our first concern. The concepts of conjugates and minimal polynomials provide a language to describe the polynomials we need.

We begin with a reminder and analogy from polynomials with real coefficients. Suppose we are given a complex number $x_1 = (2 + 3i)$. Over the (extension) field $\mathbb{C}$, there is a polynomial $x - (2 + 3i) \in \mathbb{C}[x]$ which has x_1 as a root. But suppose we are asked to find the polynomial with *real* coefficients that has x_1 as a root. We are well acquainted with the fact that the roots of real polynomials come in complex conjugate pairs, so we conclude immediately that a real polynomial with root x_1 must also have a root $x_2 = (2 - 3i)$. We say that x_2 is a *conjugate* root to x_1. A polynomial having these roots is

$$(x - (2 + 3i))(x - (2 - 3i)) = x^2 - 4x + 13.$$

Note in particular that the coefficients of the resulting polynomials are in $\mathbb{R}$, which was the base field for the extension to $\mathbb{C}$.

This concept of conjugacy has analogy to finite fields. Suppose that $f(x) \in GF(q)[x]$ has $\alpha \in GF(q^m)$ as a root. (That is, the polynomial has coefficients in the *base field*, while the root comes from an extension field.) What are the other roots of $f(x)$ in this field?

Theorem 5.77 *Let* $GF(q) = GF(p^r)$ *for some* $r \geq 1$. *Let* $f(x) = \sum_{j=0}^{d} f_j x^j \in GF(q)[x]$. *That is,* $f_i \in GF(q)$. *Then*

$$f(x^{q^n}) = [f(x)]^{q^n}$$

for any $n \geq 0$.

Proof

$$[f(x)]^{q^n} = \left[\sum_{j=0}^{d} f_j x^j\right]^{q^n} = \sum_{j=0}^{d} f_j^{q^n} (x^j)^{q^n} \qquad \text{(by (5.43))}$$

$$= \sum_{j=0}^{d} f_j (x^{q^n})^j \qquad \text{(by Theorem 5.65)}$$

$$= f(x^{q^n}).$$

$\square$

Thus, if $\beta \in GF(q^m)$ is a root of $f(x) \in GF(q)[x]$, then β^{q^n} is also a root of $f(x)$. This motivates the following definition.

Definition 5.78 Let $\beta \in GF(q^m)$. The **conjugates** of β with respect to a subfield $GF(q)$ are $\beta, \beta^q, \beta^{q^2}, \beta^{q^3}, \ldots$. (This list must, of course, repeat at some point since the field is finite.)

The conjugates of β with respect to $GF(q)$ form a set called the **conjugacy class** of β with respect to $GF(q)$.

$\square$

Example 5.79

1. Let $\alpha \in GF(2^3)$ be primitive. The conjugates of α with respect to $GF(2)$ are

$$\alpha, \alpha^2, (\alpha^{2^2}) = \alpha^4, (\alpha^{2^3}) = \alpha.$$

So the conjugacy class of α is $\{\alpha, \alpha^2, \alpha^4\}$.

Let $\beta = \alpha^3$, an element not in the conjugacy class of α. The conjugates of β with respect to $GF(2)$ are

$$\beta = \alpha^3, \quad (\alpha^3)^2 = \alpha^6, \quad (\alpha^3)^{2^2} = \alpha^{12} = \alpha^7 \alpha^5 = \alpha^5, \quad (\alpha^3)^{2^3} = \alpha^{24} = \alpha^{21} \alpha^3 = \alpha^3.$$

So the conjugacy class of β is $\{\alpha^3, \alpha^6, \alpha^5\}$.

The only other elements of $GF(2^3)$ are 1, which always forms its own conjugacy class, and 0, which always forms its own conjugacy class.

We observe that the conjugacy classes of the elements of $GF(2^3)$ form a partition of $GF(2^3)$.

2. Let $\beta \in GF(16)$ be an element such that $\text{ord}(\beta) = 3$. (Check for consistency: since $3|15$, there are $\phi(3) = 2$ elements of order 3 in $GF(16)$.) The conjugacy class of β with respect to $GF(2)$ is

$$\beta, \beta^2, \beta^{2^2} = \beta^4 = \beta.$$

So there are two elements in this conjugacy class, $\{\beta, \beta^2\}$.

3. Find all the conjugacy classes in $GF(2^4)$ with respect to $GF(2)$.

Let $\alpha \in GF(2^4)$ be primitive. Pick α and list its conjugates with respect to $GF(2)$:

$$\alpha, \alpha^2, \alpha^4, \alpha^8, \alpha^{16} = \alpha,$$

so the first conjugacy class is $\{\alpha, \alpha^2, \alpha^4, \alpha^8\}$. Now pick an element unused so far. Take α^3 and write its conjugates:

$$\alpha^3, (\alpha^3)^2 = \alpha^6, (\alpha^3)^4 = \alpha^{12}, (\alpha^3)^8 = \alpha^9, (\alpha^3)^{16} = \alpha^3,$$

so the next conjugacy class is $\{\alpha^3, \alpha^6, \alpha^9, \alpha^{12}\}$. Take another unused element, α^5:

$$\alpha^5, (\alpha^5)^2 = \alpha^{10}, (\alpha^5)^4 = \alpha^5,$$

so the next conjugacy class is $\{\alpha^5, \alpha^{10}\}$. Take another unused element, α^7:

$$\alpha^7, (\alpha^7)^2 = \alpha^{14}, (\alpha^7)^4 = \alpha^{13}, (\alpha^7)^8 = \alpha^{11}, (\alpha^7)^{16} = \alpha^7,$$

so the next conjugacy class is $\{\alpha^7, \alpha^{14}, \alpha^{13}, \alpha^{11}\}$. The only unused elements now are 0, with conjugacy class $\{0\}$, and 1, with conjugacy class $\{1\}$.

4. Find all the conjugacy classes in $GF(2^4)$ with respect to $GF(4)$.

   Let α be primitive in $GF(2^4)$. The conjugacy classes with respect to $GF(4)$ are:

$$\{\alpha, \alpha^4\} \quad \{\alpha^2, \alpha^8\} \quad \{\alpha^3, \alpha^{12}\} \quad \{\alpha^5\}$$

$$\{\alpha^6, \alpha^9\} \quad \{\alpha^7, \alpha^{13}\} \quad \{\alpha^{10}\} \quad \{\alpha^{11}, \alpha^{14}\}.$$

$\square$

Definition 5.80 [5] The smallest positive integer d such that $n | q^d - 1$ is called the **multiplicative order of q modulo n**. $\square$

Lemma 5.81 *Let $\beta \in GF(q^m)$ have $ord(\beta) = n$ and let d be the multiplicative order of q modulo n. Then $\beta^{q^d} = \beta$. The d elements $\beta, \beta^q, \beta^{q^2}, \ldots, \beta^{q^{d-1}}$ are all distinct.*

Proof Since $ord(\beta) = n$ and $n | q^d - 1$, $\beta^{q^d-1} = 1$, so $\beta^{q^d} = \beta$.

To check distinctness, suppose that $\beta^{q^k} = \beta^{q^i}$ for $0 \le i < k < d$. Then $\beta^{q^k - q^i} = 1$, which by Lemma 5.56 implies that $n | q^k - q^i$, that is, $q^k \equiv q^i \pmod{n}$. By Theorem 5.27, item 5.27, it follows that $q^{k-i} \equiv 1 \pmod{n/(n, q^i)}$, that is, $q^{k-i} \equiv 1 \pmod{n}$ (since q is a power of a prime, and $n | q^d - 1$). By definition of d, this means that $d | k - i$, which is not possible since $i < k < d$. $\square$

5.9.1 Minimal Polynomials

In this section, we examine the polynomial in $GF(q)[x]$ which has an element $\beta \in GF(q^m)$ and all of its conjugates as roots.

Definition 5.82 Let $\beta \in GF(q^m)$. The **minimal polynomial** of β with respect to $GF(q)$ is the smallest-degree, nonzero, monic polynomial $p(x) \in GF(q)[x]$ such that $p(\beta) = 0$. $\square$

Returning to the analogy with complex numbers, we saw that the polynomial with $f(x) = x^2 - 4x + 13$ with *real* coefficients has the *complex* number $x_1 = 2 + 3i$ as a root. Furthermore, it is clear that there is no real polynomial of smaller degree which has x_1 as a root. We would say that $x^2 - 4x + 13$ is the minimal polynomial of $2 + 3i$ with respect to the real numbers.

Some properties for minimal polynomials:

Theorem 5.83 *[483, Theorem 3.2] For each $\beta \in GF(q^m)$ there exists a unique monic polynomial $p(x)$ of minimal degree in $GF(q)[x]$ such that:*

---

[5] This is yet another usage of the word "order."

1. $p(\beta) = 0$.

2. *The degree of* $p(x) \leq m$.

3. *If there is a polynomial* $f(x) \in GF(q)[x]$ *such that* $f(\beta) = 0$ *then* $p(x) | f(x)$.

4. $p(x)$ *is irreducible in* $GF(q)[x]$.

Proof Existence: Given an element $\beta \in GF(q^m)$, write down the $(m+1)$ elements $1, \beta, \beta^2, \ldots, \beta^m$ which are elements of $GF(q^m)$. Since $GF(q^m)$ is a vector space of dimension m over $GF(q)$, these $m+1$ elements must be linearly dependent. Hence there exist coefficients $a_i \in GF(q)$ such that $a_0 + a_1\beta + \cdots + a_m\beta^m = 0$; these are the coefficients of a polynomial $p(x) = \sum_{i=0}^{m} a_i x^i$ which has β as the root. (It is straightforward to make this polynomial monic.) This also shows that the degree of $p(x) \leq m$.

Uniqueness: Suppose that there are two minimal polynomials of β, which are normalized to be monic; call them $f(x)$ and $g(x)$. These must both have the same degree. Then there is a polynomial $r(x)$ having $\deg(r(x)) < \deg(f(x))$ such that

$$f(x) = g(x) + r(x).$$

Since β is a root of f and g, we have

$$0 = f(\beta) = g(\beta) + r(\beta).$$

so that $r(\beta) = 0$. Since a minimal polynomial $f(x)$ has the smallest nonzero degree polynomial such that $f(\beta) = 0$, it must be the case that $r(x) = 0$ (i.e., it is the zero polynomial), so $f(x) = g(x)$.

Divisibility: Let $p(x)$ be a minimal polynomial. If there is a polynomial $f(x)$ such that $f(\beta) = 0$, we write using the division algorithm

$$f(x) = p(x)q(x) + r(x),$$

where $\deg(r) < \deg(p)$. But then $f(\beta) = p(\beta)q(\beta) + r(\beta) = 0$, so $r(\beta) = 0$. By the minimality of the degree of $p(x)$, $r(x) = 0$, so $p(x) | f(x)$.

Irreducibility: If $p(x)$ factors, so $p(x) = f(x)g(x)$, then either $f(\beta) = 0$ or $g(\beta) = 0$, again a contradiction to the minimality of the degree of $p(x)$. $\qquad\square$

We observe that primitive polynomials are the minimal polynomials for primitive elements in a finite field.

Let $p(x) \in GF(q)[x]$ be a minimal polynomial for β. Then $\beta^q, \beta^{q^2}, \ldots, \beta^{q^{d-1}}$ are also roots of $p(x)$. Could there be other roots of $p(x)$? The following theorem shows that the conjugacy class for β contains all the roots for the minimal polynomial of β.

Theorem 5.84 *[33, Theorem 4.410] Let* $\beta \in GF(q^m)$ *have order n and let d be the multiplicative order of q mod n. Then the coefficients of the polynomial* $p(x) = \prod_{i=0}^{d-1}(x - \beta^{q^i})$ *are in $GF(q)$. Furthermore, $p(x)$ is irreducible. That is, $p(x)$ is the minimal polynomial for β.*

Proof From Theorem 5.77 we see that $p(\beta) = 0$ implies that $p(\beta^q) = 0$ for $p(x) \in GF(q)[x]$. It only remains to show that the polynomial having the conjugates of β as its roots has its coefficients in $GF(q)$. Write

$$[p(x)]^q = \prod_{i=0}^{d-1}(x - \beta^{q^i})^q = \prod_{i=0}^{d-1}(x^q - \beta^{q^{i+1}}) \qquad \text{(by Theorem 5.51)}$$

$$= \prod_{i=1}^{d-1}(x^q - \beta^{q^i}) = \prod_{i=0}^{d-1}(x^q - \beta^{q^i}) \qquad \text{(since } \beta^{q^d} = \beta = \beta^{q^0}\text{)}.$$

Thus, $[p(x)]^q = p(x^q)$. Now writing $p(x) = \sum_{i=0}^{d} p_i x^i$, we have

$$[p(x)]^q = \left(\sum_{i=0}^{d} p_i x^i \right)^q = \sum_{i=0}^{d} p_i^q x^{iq} \qquad (5.45)$$

and

$$p(x^q) = \sum_{i=0}^{d} p_i x^{iq}. \qquad (5.46)$$

The two polynomials in (5.45) and (5.46) are identical, so it must be that $p_i^q = p_i$, so $p_i \in GF(q)$.

If $p(x) = g(x)h(x)$, where $g(x) \in GF(q)[x]$ and $h(x) \in GF(q)[x]$ are monic, then $p(\beta) = 0$ implies that $g(\beta) = 0$ or $h(\beta) = 0$. If $g(\beta) = 0$, then $g(\beta^q) = g(\beta^{q^2}) = \cdots = g(\beta^{q^{d-1}}) = 0$. g thus has d roots, so $g(x) = p(x)$. Similarly, if $h(\beta) = 0$, then it follows that $h(x) = p(x)$. $\square$

As a corollary, we have the following.

Corollary 5.85 *[483, p. 58] Let $f(x) \in GF(q)[x]$ be irreducible. Then all of the roots of $f(x)$ have the same order.*

Proof Let $GF(q^m)$ be the smallest field containing all the roots of the polynomial $f(x)$ and let $\beta \in GF(q^m)$ be a root of $f(x)$. Then $\mathrm{ord}(\beta) | q^m - 1$ (Lemma 5.54). By the theorem, the roots of $f(x)$ are the conjugates of β and so are of the form $\{\beta, \beta^q, \beta^{q^2}, \ldots\}$. Since $q = p^r$ for some r, it follows that $(q, q^m - 1) = 1$. Also, if $t | q^m - 1$, then $(q, t) = 1$. By Lemma 5.59 we have

$$\mathrm{ord}(\beta^{q^k}) = \frac{\mathrm{ord}(\beta)}{(q^k, \ \mathrm{ord}(\beta))} = \mathrm{ord}(\beta).$$

Since this is true for any k, each root has the same order. $\square$

Example 5.86 According to Theorem 5.84, we can obtain the minimal polynomial for an element β by multiplying the factors $(x - \beta^{q^i})$. In what follows, you may refer to the conjugacy classes determined in Example 5.79.

1. Determine the minimal polynomial for each conjugacy class in $GF(8)$ with respect to $GF(2)$. To do the multiplication, a representation of the field is necessary; we use the representation using primitive polynomial $g(x) = x^3 + x + 1$. Using the conjugacy classes we found before in $GF(8)$, we obtain the minimal polynomials shown in Table 5.2.

2. Determine the minimal polynomial for each conjugacy class in $GF(2^4)$ with respect to $GF(2)$. Use Table 5.1 as a representation. The minimal polynomials are shown in Table 5.3.

3. Determine the minimal polynomial for each conjugacy class in $GF(2^5)$ with respect to $GF(2)$. Using the primitive polynomial $x^5 + x^2 + 1$, it can be shown that the minimal polynomials are as shown in Table 5.4.

4. Determine the minimal polynomials in $GF(4^2)$ with respect to $GF(4)$. Use the representation obtained from the subfield $GF(4) = \{0, 1, \alpha^5, \alpha^{10}\} \subset GF(16)$ from Table 5.1. The result is shown in Table 5.5.
                                                                                                      $\square$

Table 5.2: Conjugacy Classes over $GF(2^3)$ with Respect to $GF(2)$

Conjugacy Class	Minimal Polynomial
$\{0\}$	$M_-(x) = x$
$\{1\}$	$M_0(x) = x + 1$
$\{\alpha, \alpha^2, \alpha^4\}$	$M_1(x) = (x - \alpha)(x - \alpha^2)(x - \alpha^4) = x^3 + x + 1$
$\{\alpha^3, \alpha^6, \alpha^5\}$	$M_3(x) = (x - \alpha^3)(x - \alpha^5)(x - \alpha^6) = x^3 + x^2 + 1$

Table 5.3: Conjugacy Classes over $GF(2^4)$ with Respect to $GF(2)$

Conjugacy Class	Minimal Polynomial
$\{0\}$	$M_-(x) = x$
$\{1\}$	$M_0(x) = x + 1$
$\{\alpha, \alpha^2, \alpha^4, \alpha^8\}$	$M_1(x) = (x - \alpha)(x - \alpha^2)(x - \alpha^4)(x - \alpha^8)$ $= x^4 + x + 1$
$\{\alpha^3, \alpha^6, \alpha^9, \alpha^{12}\}$	$M_3(x) = (x - \alpha^3)(x - \alpha^6)(x - \alpha^9)(x - \alpha^{12})$ $= x^4 + x^3 + x^2 + x + 1$
$\{\alpha^5, \alpha^{10}\}$	$M_5(x) = (x - \alpha^5)(x - \alpha^{10}) = x^2 + x + 1$
$\{\alpha^7, \alpha^{11}, \alpha^{13}, \alpha^{14}\}$	$M_7(x) = (x - \alpha^7)(x - \alpha^{11})(x - \alpha^{13})(x - \alpha^{14})$ $= x^4 + x^3 + 1$

Table 5.4: Conjugacy Classes over $GF(2^5)$ with Respect to $GF(2)$

Conjugacy Class	Minimal Polynomial
$\{0\}$	$M_-(x) = x$
$\{1\}$	$M_0(x) = x + 1$
$\{\alpha, \alpha^2, \alpha^4, \alpha^8, \alpha^{16}\}$	$M_1(x) = (x - \alpha)(x - \alpha^2)(x - \alpha^4)(x - \alpha^8)(x - \alpha^{16})$ $= x^5 + x^2 + 1$
$\{\alpha^3, \alpha^6, \alpha^{12}, \alpha^{17}, \alpha^{24}\}$	$M_3(x) = (x - \alpha^3)(x - \alpha^6)(x - \alpha^{12})(x - \alpha^{17})(x - \alpha^{24})$ $= x^5 + x^4 + x^3 + x^2 + 1$
$\{\alpha^5, \alpha^9, \alpha^{10}, \alpha^{18}, \alpha^{20}\}$	$M_5(x) = (x - \alpha^5)(x - \alpha^9)(x - \alpha^{10})(x - \alpha^{18})(x - \alpha^{20})$ $= x^5 + x^4 + x^2 + x + 1$
$\{\alpha^7, \alpha^{14}, \alpha^{19}, \alpha^{25}, \alpha^{28}\}$	$M_7(x) = (x - \alpha^7)(x - \alpha^{14})(x - \alpha^{19})(x - \alpha^{25})(x - \alpha^{28})$ $= x^5 + x^3 + x^2 + x + 1$
$\{\alpha^{11}, \alpha^{13}, \alpha^{21}, \alpha^{22}, \alpha^{26}\}$	$M_{11}(x) = (x - \alpha^{11})(x - \alpha^{13})(x - \alpha^{21})(x - \alpha^{22})(x - \alpha^{26})$ $= x^5 + x^4 + x^3 + x + 1$
$\{\alpha^{15}, \alpha^{23}, \alpha^{27}, \alpha^{29}, \alpha^{30}\}$	$M_{15}(x) = (x - \alpha^{15})(x - \alpha^{23})(x - \alpha^{27})(x - \alpha^{29})(x - \alpha^{30})$ $= x^5 + x^3 + 1$

Table 5.5: Conjugacy Classes over $GF(4^2)$ with Respect to $GF(4)$

Conjugacy Class	Minimal Polynomial
$\{0\}$	$M_-(x) = x$
$\{1\}$	$M_0(x) = x + 1$
$\{\alpha, \alpha^4\}$	$M_1(x) = (x + \alpha)(x + \alpha^4) = x^2 + x + \alpha^5$
$\{\alpha^2, \alpha^8\}$	$M_2(x) = (x + \alpha^2)(x + \alpha^8) = x^2 + x + \alpha^{10}$
$\{\alpha^3, \alpha^{12}\}$	$M_3(x) = (x + \alpha^3)(x + \alpha^{12}) = x^2 + \alpha^{10}x + 1$
$\{\alpha^5\}$	$M_5(x) = x + \alpha^5$
$\{\alpha^6, \alpha^9\}$	$M_6(x) = (x + \alpha^6)(x + \alpha^9) = x^2 + \alpha^5 x + 1$
$\{\alpha^7, \alpha^{13}\}$	$M_7(x) = (x + \alpha^7)(x + \alpha^{13}) = x^2 + \alpha^5 x + \alpha^5$
$\{\alpha^{10}\}$	$M_{10}(x) = x + \alpha^{10}$
$\{\alpha^{11}, \alpha^{14}\}$	$M_{11}(x) = (x + \alpha^{11})(x + \alpha^{14}) = x^2 + \alpha^{10}x + \alpha^{10}$

As this example suggests, the notation $M_i(x)$ is used to denote the minimal polynomial of the conjugacy class that α^i is in, where i is the smallest exponent in the conjugacy class.

It can be shown that (see [268, p. 96]) for the minimal polynomial $m(x)$ of degree d in a field of $GF(q^m)$ that $d|m$.

5.10   Factoring $x^n - 1$

We now have the theoretical tools necessary to describe how to factor $x^n - 1$ over arbitrary finite fields for various values of n. When $n = q^m - 1$, from Theorem 5.63, every nonzero element of $GF(q^m)$ is a root of $x^{q^m-1} - 1$, so

$$x^{q^m-1} - 1 = \prod_{i=0}^{q^m-2} (x - \alpha^i) \tag{5.47}$$

for a primitive element $\alpha \in GF(q^m)$. To provide a factorization of $x^{q^m-1} - 1$ over the field $GF(q)$, the factors in $(x - \alpha^i)$ (5.47) can be grouped together according to conjugacy classes, which then multiply together to form minimal polynomials. Thus, $x^{q^m-1} - 1$ can be expressed as a product of the minimal polynomials of the nonzero elements.

Example 5.87

1. The polynomial $x^7 - 1 = x^{2^3-1} - 1$ can be factored over $GF(2)$ as a product of the minimal polynomials shown in Table 5.2.
   $$x^7 - 1 = (x + 1)(x^3 + x + 1)(x^3 + x^2 + 1).$$

2. The polynomial $x^{15} - 1 = x^{2^4-1} - 1$ can be factored over $GF(2)$ as a product of the minimal polynomials shown in Table 5.3.
   $$x^{15} - 1 = (x + 1)(x^4 + x + 1)(x^4 + x^3 + x^2 + x + 1)(x^2 + x + 1)(x^4 + x^3 + 1).$$
   $\square$

We now pursue the slightly more general problem of factoring $x^n - 1$ when $n \neq q^m - 1$. An element $\beta \neq 1$ such that $\beta^n = 1$ and not for lower powers of n is called a primitive nth root of unity. The first step is to determine a field $GF(q^m)$ (that is, to determine m) in which nth roots of unity can exist. Once the field is found, factorization is accomplished using minimal polynomials in the field.

Theorem 5.60 tells us that if

$$n | q^m - 1, \tag{5.48}$$

then there are $\phi(n)$ elements of order n in $GF(q^m)$. Finding a field $GF(q^m)$ with nth roots of unity thus requires finding an m such that $n | q^m - 1$, which is usually done by trial and error.

Example 5.88   Determine an extension field $GF(3^m)$ in which 13th roots of unity exist. We see that $13 | 3^3 - 1$, so that 13th roots exist in the field $GF(3^3)$. $\square$

Once the field is found, we let β be an element of order n in the field $GF(q^m)$. Then β is a root of $x^n - 1$ in that field, and so are the elements $\beta^2, \beta^3, \ldots, \beta^{n-1}$. That is,

$$x^n - 1 = \prod_{i=0}^{n-1} (x - \beta^i).$$

The roots are divided into conjugacy classes to form the factorization over $GF(q)$.

Example 5.89   Determine an extension field $GF(2^m)$ in which 5th roots of unity exist and express the factorization in terms of polynomials in $GF(2)[x]$. Using (5.48) we check:

$$5 \nmid (2 - 1) \quad 5 \mid (2^2 - 1) \quad 5 \mid (2^3 - 1) \quad 5 | (2^4 - 1).$$

So in $GF(16)$ there are primitive fifth roots of unity. For example, if we let $\beta = \alpha^3$, α primitive, then $\beta^5 = \alpha^{15} = 1$. The roots of $x^5 - 1 = x^5 + 1$ in $GF(16)$ are

$$1, \beta, \beta^2, \beta^3, \beta^4,$$

which can be expressed in terms of the primitive element α as

$$1, \alpha^3, \alpha^6, \alpha^9, \alpha^{12}.$$

Using the minimal polynomials shown in Table 5.3 we have

$$x^5 + 1 = (x+1)M_3(x) = (x+1)(x^4 + x^3 + x^2 + x + 1).$$

$\square$

Example 5.90 We want to find a field $GF(2^m)$ which has 25th roots of unity. We need

$$25|(2^m - 1).$$

By trial and error we find that when $m = 20$, $25|2^m - 1$. Now let us divide the roots of $2^{20} - 1$ into conjugacy classes. Let β be a primitive 25th root of unity. The other roots of unity are the powers of β: $\beta^0, \beta^1, \beta^2, \ldots, \beta^{24}$. Let us divide these powers into conjugacy classes:

$$\{1\}$$

$$\{\beta, \beta^2, \beta^4, \beta^8, \beta^{16}, \beta^7, \beta^{14}, \beta^3, \beta^6, \beta^{12}, \beta^{24}, \beta^{23}, \beta^{21}, \beta^{17}, \beta^9, \beta^{18}, \beta^{11}, \beta^{22}, \beta^{19}, \beta^{13}\}$$

$$\{\beta^5, \beta^{10}, \beta^{20}, \beta^{15}\}$$

Letting $M_i(x) \in GF(2)[x]$ denote the minimal polynomial having β^i for the smallest i as a root, we have the factorization $x^{25} + 1 = M_0(x)M_1(x)M_5(x)$.

$\square$

Example 5.91 Let us find a field $GF(7^m)$ in which $x^{15} - 1$ has roots; this requires an m such that

$$15|7^m - 1.$$

$m = 4$ works. Let γ be a primitive 15th root of unity in $GF(7^4)$. Then $\gamma^0, \gamma^1, \ldots, \gamma^{14}$ are roots of unity. Let us divide these up into conjugacy classes with respect to $GF(7)$:

$$\{1\}, \{\gamma, \gamma^7, \gamma^{49} = \gamma^4, \gamma^{7^3} = \gamma^{13}\}, \{\gamma^2, \gamma^{14}, \gamma^8, \gamma^{11}\}, \{\gamma^3, \gamma^6, \gamma^{12}, \gamma^9\}, \{\gamma^5\}, \{\gamma^{10}\}$$

Thus, $x^{15} - 1$ factors into six irreducible polynomials in $GF(7)$.

$\square$

5.11 Cyclotomic Cosets

Definition 5.92 The cyclotomic cosets modulo n with respect to $GF(q)$ contain the *exponents* of the n distinct powers of a primitive nth root of unity with respect to $GF(q)$, each coset corresponding to a conjugacy class. These cosets provide a shorthand representation for the conjugacy class.

cyclomin.cc

Example 5.93 For Example 5.91, $n = 15$ and $q = 7$. The cyclotomic cosets and the corresponding conjugacy classes are shown in Table 5.6.

$\square$

"Tables" of cyclotomic cosets and minimal polynomials for $GF(2^m)$ are available using the program `cyclomin`.

Table 5.6: Cyclotomic Cosets Modulo 15 with Respect to $GF(7)$

Conjugacy Class		Cyclotomic Cosets
$\{1\}$	$\leftrightarrow$	$\{0\}$
$\{\gamma, \gamma^7, \gamma^4, \gamma^{13}\}$	$\leftrightarrow$	$\{1, 7, 4, 13\}$
$\{\gamma^2, \gamma^{14}, \gamma^8, \gamma^{11}\}$	$\leftrightarrow$	$\{2, 14, 8, 11\}$
$\{\gamma^3, \gamma^6, \gamma^{12}, \gamma^9\}$	$\leftrightarrow$	$\{3, 6, 12, 9\}$
$\{\gamma^5\}$	$\leftrightarrow$	$\{5\}$
$\{\gamma^{10}\}$	$\leftrightarrow$	$\{10\}$

Appendix 5.A   How Many Irreducible Polynomials Are There?

The material in this appendix is not needed later in the book. However, it introduces several valuable analytical techniques and some useful facts.

A finite field $GF(q^m)$ can be constructed as an extension of $GF(q)$ if an irreducible polynomial of degree m over $GF(q)$ exists. The question of the existence of finite fields of order any prime power, then, revolves on the question of the existence of irreducible polynomials of arbitrary degree. Other interesting problems are related to *how many* such irreducible polynomials there are.

To get some insight into the problem, let us first do some exhaustive enumeration of irreducible polynomials with coefficients over $GF(2)$. Let I_n denote the number of irreducible polynomials of degree n. The polynomials of degree 1, x and $x + 1$, are both irreducible, so $I_1 = 2$. The polynomials of degree 2 are

$$x^2 \text{ (reducible)} \qquad\qquad x^2 + 1 = (x + 1)^2 \text{ (reducible)}$$

$$x^2 + x = x(x + 1) \text{ (reducible)} \quad x^2 + x + 1 \text{ (irreducible)}.$$

So $I_2 = 1$.

In general, there are 2^n polynomials of degree n. Each of these can either be factored into products of powers of irreducible polynomials of lower degree, or are irreducible themselves. Let us count how many different ways the set of binary cubics might factor. It can factor into a product of an irreducible polynomial of degree 2 and a polynomial of degree 1 in $I_2 I_1 = 2$ ways:

$$x(x^2 + x + 1) \quad (x + 1)(x^2 + x + 1).$$

It can factor into a product of three irreducible polynomials of degree 1 in four ways:

$$x^3 \quad x^2(x + 1) \quad x(x + 1)^2 \quad (x + 1)^3$$

The remaining cubic binary polynomials,

$$x^3 + x + 1 \quad \text{and} \quad x^3 + x^2 + 1$$

must be irreducible, so $I_3 = 2$.

This sort of counting can continue, but becomes cumbersome without some sort of mechanism to keep track of the various combinations of factors. This is accomplished using a *generating function* approach.

Definition 5.94 A **generating function** of a sequence $A_0, A_1, A_2, \ldots$ is the formal power series

$$A(z) = \sum_{k=0}^{\infty} A_k z^k.$$

$\square$

The generating function is analogous to the z-transform of discrete-time signal processing, allowing us to formally manipulate sequences of numbers by polynomial operations. Generating functions $A(z)$ and $B(z)$ can be added (term by term), multiplied (using polynomial multiplication)

$$A(z)B(z) = \sum_{i=0}^{\infty} \left(\sum_{k=0}^{i} B_k A_{i-k} \right) z^i = \sum_{i=0}^{\infty} \left(\sum_{k=0}^{i} A_k B_{i-k} \right) z^i$$

and (formal) derivatives computed,

$$\text{if } A(z) = \sum_{k=0}^{\infty} A_k z^k \text{then } A'(z) = \sum_{k=1}^{\infty} k A_k z^{k-1},$$

with operations taking place in some appropriate field.

The key theorem for counting the number of irreducible polynomials is the following.

Theorem 5.95 *Let $f(x)$ and $g(x)$ be relatively prime, monic irreducible polynomials over $GF(q)$ of degrees m and n, respectively. Let C_k be the number of monic polynomials of degree k whose only irreducible factors are $f(x)$ and $g(x)$. Then the moment generating function for C_k is*

$$C(z) = \frac{1}{1 - z^m} \frac{1}{1 - z^n}.$$

That is, $C_k = \sum_i B_i A_{k-i}$, where A_i is the i th coefficient in the generating function $A(z) = 1/(1 - z^m)$ and B_i is the i th coefficient in the generating function $B(z) = 1/(1 - z^n)$.

Example 5.96   Let $f(x) = x$ and $g(x) = x + 1$ in $GF(2)[x]$. The set of polynomials whose factors are $f(x)$ and $g(x)$ are those with linear factors, for example,

$$p(x) = (f(x))^a (g(x))^b, \quad a, b \geq 0.$$

According to the theorem, the weight enumerator for the number of such polynomials is

$$\frac{1}{(1 - z)^2}.$$

This can be shown to be equal to

$$\frac{1}{(1 - z)^2} = \sum_{k=0}^{\infty} (k + 1) z^k = 1 + 2z + 3z^2 + \cdots. \tag{5.49}$$

That is, there are two polynomials of degree 1 ($f(x)$ and $g(x)$), three polynomials of degree 2 ($f(x)g(x), f(x)^2$ and $g(x)^2$), four polynomials of degree 3, and so on.   □

Proof Let A_k be the number of monic polynomials in $GF(q)[x]$ of degree k which are powers of $f(x)$. The kth power of $f(x)$ has degree km, so

$$A_k = \begin{cases} 1 & \text{if } m|k \\ 0 & \text{otherwise.} \end{cases}$$

We will take $A_0 = 1$ (corresponding to $f(x)^0 = 1$). The generating function for the A_k is

$$A(z) = 1 + z^m + z^{2m} + \cdots = \frac{1}{1 - z^m}.$$

$A(z)$ is called the *enumerator by degree* of the powers of $f(z)$.

Similarly, let B_k be the number of monic polynomials in $GF(q)[x]$ of degree k which are powers of $g(x)$; arguing as before we have $B(z) = 1/(1 - z^n)$.

With C_k the number of monic polynomials of degree k whose only factors are $f(x)$ and $g(x)$, we observe that if $\deg(g(x)^b) = nb = i$, then $\deg(f(x)^a) = ma = k - i$ for every $0 \leq i \leq k$. Thus,

$$C_k = \sum_{i=0}^{k} B_i A_{k-i}$$

or, equivalently,

$$C(z) = A(z)B(z).$$

□

The theorem can be extended by induction to multiple sets of polynomials, as in the following corollary.

Corollary 5.97 *Let $S_1, S_2, \ldots, S_N$ be sets of polynomials such that any two polynomials in different sets are relatively prime. The set of polynomials which are products of a polynomial from each set has an enumerator by degree $\prod_{i=1}^{N} A_i(z)$, where $A_i(z)$ is the enumerator by degree of the set S_i.*

Example 5.98 For the set of polynomials formed by products of $x, x+1$ and $x^2+x+1 \in GF(2)[x]$, the enumerator by degree is

$$\left(\frac{1}{1-z}\right)^2 \frac{1}{1-z^2} = 1 + 2z + 4z^2 + 6z^3 + 9z^4 + \cdots$$

That is, there are six different ways to form polynomials of degree 3, and nine different ways to form polynomials of degree 4. (Find them!) □

Let I_m be the number of monic irreducible polynomials of degree m. Applying the corollary, the set which includes I_1 irreducible polynomials of degree 1, I_2 irreducible polynomials of degree 2, and so forth, has the enumerator by the degree

$$\prod_{m=1}^{\infty} \left(\frac{1}{1-z^m}\right)^{I_m}.$$

Let us now extend this to a base field $GF(q)$. We observe that the set of all monic polynomials in $GF(q)[x]$ of degree k contains q^k polynomials in it. So the enumerator by degree of the set of polynomials of degree k is

$$\sum_{k=0}^{\infty} q^k z^k = \frac{1}{1-qz}.$$

Furthermore, the set of all products of powers of irreducible polynomials is precisely the set of all monic polynomials. Hence, we have the following.

Theorem 5.99 *[33, Theorem 3.32]*

$$\frac{1}{1-qz} = \prod_{m=1}^{\infty} \left(\frac{1}{1-z^m}\right)^{I_m}. \tag{5.50}$$

Equation (5.50) does not provide a very explicit formula for computing I_m. However, it can be manipulated into more useful forms. Reciprocating both sides, we obtain

$$(1-qz) = \prod_{m=1}^{\infty} (1-z^m)^{I_m}. \tag{5.51}$$

Taking the formal derivative of both sides and rearranging, we obtain

$$\frac{q}{1-qz} = \sum_{m=1}^{\infty} \frac{mI_m z^{m-1}}{1-z^m}. \tag{5.52}$$

Multiplying both sides by z and expanding both sides of (5.52) in formal series, we obtain

$$\sum_{k=1}^{\infty} (qz)^k = \sum_{m=1}^{\infty} mI_m \sum_{k=1}^{\infty} (z^m)^k = \sum_{m=1}^{\infty} mI_m \sum_{\substack{k:k\neq 0 \\ m|k}} z^k = \sum_{k=1}^{\infty} \sum_{m:m|k} mI_m z^k.$$

Equating the kth terms of the sums on the left and right sides of this equation, we obtain the following theorem.

Theorem 5.100

$$q^k = \sum_{m|k} m I_m, \tag{5.53}$$

where the sum is taken of all m which divide k, including 1 and k.

This theorem has the following interpretation. By Theorem 5.72, in a field of order q, the product of all distinct monic polynomials whose degrees divide k divides $x^{q^k} - x$. The degree of $x^{q^k} - x$ is q^k, the left-hand side of (5.53). The degree of the product of all distinct monic polynomials whose degrees divide k is the sum of the degrees of those polynomials. Since there are I_m distinct monic irreducible polynomials, the contribution to the degree of the product of those polynomials is $m I_m$. Adding all of these up, we obtain the right-hand side of (5.53). This implies the following:

Theorem 5.101 *[33, Theorem 4.415] In a field of order q, $x^{q^k} - x$ factors into the product of all monic irreducible polynomials whose degrees divide k.*

Example 5.102 Let us take $q = 2$ and $k = 3$. The polynomials whose degrees divide $k = 3$ have degree 1 or 3. The product of the binary irreducible polynomials of degree 1 and 3 is

$$x(x+1)(x^3 + x + 1)(x^3 + x^2 + 1) = x^8 + x.$$

$\square$

Theorem 5.100 allows a sequence of equations to be built up for determining I_m for any m. Take for example $q = 2$:

$$
\begin{aligned}
k = 1: \quad & 2 = (1)I_1 & \longrightarrow I_1 = 2 \\
k = 2: \quad & 4 = (1)I_1 + 2I_2 & \longrightarrow I_2 = 1 \\
k = 3: \quad & 8 = (1)I_1 + 3I_3 & \longrightarrow I_3 = 2. \\
& \quad \vdots
\end{aligned}
$$

Appendix 5.A.1 Solving for I_m Explicitly: The Moebius Function

However, Equation (5.53) only implicitly determines I_m. An explicit formula can also be found. Equation (5.53) is a special case of a summation of the form

$$f(k) = \sum_{m|k} g(m) \tag{5.54}$$

in which $f(k) = q^k$ and $g(m) = m I_m$. Solving such equations for $g(m)$ can be accomplished using the number-theoretic function known as the Moebius (or Möbius) function μ.

Definition 5.103 The function $\mu(n) : \mathbb{Z}^+ \to \mathbb{Z}^+$ is the **Moebius function**, defined by

$$
\mu(n) = \begin{cases}
1 & \text{if } n = 1 \\
(-1)^r & \text{if } n \text{ is the product of } r \text{ distinct primes} \\
0 & \text{if } n \text{ contains any repeated prime factors.}
\end{cases}
$$

$\square$

Theorem 5.104 *The Moebius function satisfies the following formula:*

$$
\sum_{d|n} \mu(d) = \begin{cases}
1 & \text{if } n = 1 \\
0 & \text{if } n > 1.
\end{cases} \tag{5.55}
$$

The proof is developed in Exercise 5.81. This curious "delta-function-like" behavior allows us to compute an inverse of some number-theoretic sums, as the following theorem indicates.

Theorem 5.105 (Moebius inversion formula) *If* $f(n) = \sum_{d|n} g(d)$ *then*

$$g(n) = \sum_{d|n} \mu(d) f(n/d).$$

Proof Let $d|n$. Then from the definition of $f(n)$, we have

$$f(n/d) = \sum_{k|(n/d)} g(k).$$

Multiplying both sides of this by $\mu(d)$ and summing over divisors d of n, we obtain

$$\sum_{d|n} \mu(d) f(n/d) = \sum_{d|n} \sum_{k|(n/d)} \mu(d) g(k).$$

The order of summation can be interchanged as

$$\sum_{d|n} \mu(d) f(n/d) = \sum_{k|n} \sum_{d|(n/k)} \mu(d) g(k) = \sum_{k|n} g(k) \sum_{d|(n/k)} \mu(d).$$

By (5.55), $\sum_{d|(n/k)} \mu(d) = 1$ if $n/k = 1$, that is, if $n = k$, and is zero otherwise. So the double summation collapses down to a $g(n)$.   □

Returning now to the problem of irreducible polynomials, (5.53) can be solved for I_m using the Moebius inversion formula of Theorem 5.105,

$$m I_m = \sum_{d|m} \mu(d) q^{(m/d)} \quad \text{or} \quad I_m = \frac{1}{m} \sum_{d|m} \mu(d) q^{(m/d)}. \tag{5.56}$$

Programming Laboratory 4: Programming the Euclidean Algorithm

Objective

The Euclidean algorithm is important both for modular arithmetic in general and also for specific decoding algorithms for BCH/Reed–Solomon codes. In this lab, you are to implement the Euclidean algorithm over both integers and polynomials.

Preliminary Exercises

Reading: Sections 5.2.2 and 5.2.3.
1) In $\mathbb{Z}_5[x]$, determine $g(x) = (2x^5 + 3x^4 + 4x^3 + 3x^2 + 2x + 1, x^4 + 2x^3 + 3x^2 + 4x + 3)$ and also $s(x)$ and $t(x)$ such that
$$a(x)s(x) + b(x)t(x) = (a(x), b(x)).$$

2) Compute $(x^3 + 2x^2 + x + 4, x^2 + 3x + 4)$, operations in $\mathbb{R}[x]$, and also find polynomials $s(x)$ and $t(x)$ such that
$$a(x)s(x) + b(x)t(x) = (a(x), b(x)).$$

Background

Code is provided which implements modulo arithmetic in the class `ModAr`, implemented in the files indicated in Algorithm 5.2.

Algorithm 5.2 Modulo Arithmetic
File: `ModAr.h`
         `ModArnew.h`
         `testmodarnew1.cc`

Code is also provided which implements polynomial arithmetic in the class `polynomialT`, using the files indicated in Algorithm 5.3. This class is templatized, so that the coefficients can come from a variety of fields or rings. For example, if you want a polynomial with `double` coefficients or `int` coefficients or `ModAr` coefficients, the objects are declared as

```
polynomialT<double> p1;
polynomialT<nt> p2;
polynomialT<ModAr> p3;
```

Algorithm 5.3 Templatized Polynomials
File: `polynomialT.h`
     `polynomialT.cc`
     `testpoly1.cc`

Programming Part

1) Write a C or C++ function that performs the Euclidean algorithm on integers a and b, returning g, s, and t such that $g = as + bt$. The function should have declaration

```
void gcd(int a, int b, int &g, int &s, int &t);
```

Test your algorithm on $(24, 18)$, $(851, 966)$, and other pairs of integers. Verify in each case that $as + bt = g$.

2) Write a function that computes the Euclidean algorithm on `polynomialT<TYPE>`. The function should have declaration

```
template <class T> void
gcd(const polynomialT<T> &a,
   const polynomialT<T> &b, polynomialT<T> &g,
   polynomialT<T> &s, polynomialT<T> &t);
```

Also, write a program to test your function. Algorithm 5.4 shows a test program and the framework for the program,

showing how to instantiate the function with `ModAr` and double polynomial arguments.

Algorithm 5.4 Polynomial GCD
File: `testgcdpoly.cc`
     `gcdpoly.cc`

Test your algorithm as follows:

(a) Compute $(3x^7 + 4x^6 + 3x^4 + x^3 + 1, 4x^4 + x^3 + x)$ and $t(x)$ and $s(x)$ for polynomials in $\mathbb{Z}_5[x]$. Verify that $a(x)s(x) + b(x)t(x) = g(x)$.

(b) Compute $(2x^5 + 3x^4 + 4x^3 + 3x^2 + 2x + 1, x^4 + 2x^3 + 3x^2 + 4x + 3)$ and $s(x)$ and $t(x)$ for polynomials in $\mathbb{Z}_5[x]$. Verify that $a(x)s(x) + b(x)t(x) = g(x)$.

(c) Compute $(2 + 8x + 10x^2 + 4x^3, 1 + 7x + 14x^2 + 8x^3)$ and $s(x)$ and $t(x)$ for polynomials in $\mathbb{R}[x]$. For polynomials with real coefficients, extra care must be taken to handle roundoff. Verify that $a(x)s(x) + b(x)t(x) = g(x)$.

3) Write a function which applies the Sugiyama algorithm to a sequence of data or its polynomial representation.

4) Test your algorithm over $\mathbb{Z}_5[x]$ by finding the shortest polynomial generating the sequence $\{3, 2, 3, 1, 4, 0, 4, 3\}$. Having found $t(x)$, compute $b(x)t(x)$ and identify $r(x)$ and $s(x)$ and verify that they are consistent with the result found by the Sugiyama algorithm.

5) In $\mathbb{Z}_5[x]$, verify that the sequence $\{3, 2, 1, 0, 4, 3, 2, 1\}$ can be generated using the polynomial $t_1(x) = 1 + 2x + 4x^2 + 2x^3 + x^4$. Then use the Sugiyama algorithm to find the shortest polynomial $t(x)$ generating the sequence and verify that it works.

Programming Laboratory 5: Programming Galois Field Arithmetic

Objective

Galois fields are fundamental to algebraic block codes. This lab provides a tool to be used for BCH and Reed–Solomon codes. It builds upon the LFSR code produced in Lab 2.

Preliminary Exercises

Reading: Section 5.4.

Write down the vector, polynomial, and power representations of the field $GF(2^3)$ generated with the polynomial $g(x) = 1 + x + x^3$. Based on this, write down the tables `v2p` and `p2v` for this field. (See the implementation suggestions for the definition of these tables.)

Programming Part

Create a C++ class GFNUM2m with overloaded operators to implement arithmetic over the field $GF(2^m)$ for an arbitrary $m < 32$. This is similar in structure to class ModAr, except that the details of the arithmetic are different.

Test all operations of your class: +, -, *, /, ^+, +=, -=, *=, /=, +^=+, ==, != for the field generated by $g(x) = 1 + x + x^4$ by comparing the results the computer provides with results you calculate by hand. Then test for $GF(2^3)$ generated by $g(x) = 1 + x + x^3$.

The class GFNUM2m of Algorithm 5.5 provides the declarations and definitions for the class. In this representation, the field elements are represented intrinsically in the *vector* form, with the vector elements stored as the bits in a single int variable. This makes addition fast (bit operations). Multiplication of Galois field elements is easier when they are in exponential form and addition is easier when they are in vector form. Multiplication here is accomplished by converting to the power representation, adding the exponents, then converting back to the vector form. In the GFNUM2m provided, all of the basic field operations are present except for completing the construction operator initgf which builds the tables v2p and p2v. The main programming task, therefore, is to build these tables. This builds upon the LFSR functions already written.

Algorithm 5.5 $GF(2^m)$

File: GFNUM2m.h
       GF2.h
       GFNUM2m.cc
       testgfnum.cc

To make the conversion between the vector and power representations, two arrays are employed. The array v2p converts from vector to power representation and the array p2v converts from power to vector representation.

Example 5.106 In the field $GF(2^4)$ represented in Table 5.1, the field element $(1, 0, 1, 1)$ has the power representation α^7. The vector $(1, 0, 1, 1)$ can be expressed as an integer using binary-to-decimal conversion (LSB on the right) as 11. We thus think of 11 as the vector representation. The number v2p[11] converts from the vector representation, 11, to the exponent of the power representation, 7.

Turned around the other way, the number α^7 has the vector representation (as an integer) of 11. The number p2v[7] converts from the exponent of the power representation to the number 11. The conversion tables for the field are

i	v2p[i]	p2v[i]	i	v2p[i]	p2v[i]
0	–	1	8	3	5
1	0	2	9	14	10
2	1	4	10	9	7
3	4	8	11	7	14
4	2	3	12	6	15
5	8	6	13	13	13
6	5	12	14	11	9
7	10	11	15	12	–

To get the whole thing working, the arrays p2v and v2p need to be set up. To this end, a *static* member function initgf(int m, int g) is created. Given the degree of the extension m and the coefficients of $g(x)$ in the bits of the integer g, initgf sets up the conversion arrays. This can take advantage of the LFSR programmed in Lab 2. Starting with an initial LFSR state of 1, the v2p and p2v arrays can be obtained by repeatedly clocking the LFSR: the state of the LFSR represents the vector representation of the Galois field numbers, while the number of times the LFSR has been clocked represents the power representation.

There are some features of this class which bear remarking on:

- The output format (when printing) can be specified in either vector or power form. In power form, something like A^+3 is printed; in vector form, an integer like 8 is printed. The format can be specified by invoking the static member function setouttype, as in

```
GFNUM2m::setouttype(vector);
    // set vector output format
GFNUM2m::setouttype(power);
    // set power output format
```

- The v2p and p2v arrays are stored as static arrays. This means that (for this implementation) all field elements must come from the same size field. It is not possible, for example, to have some elements to be $GF(2^4)$ and other elements to be $GF(2^8)$. (You may want to give some thought to how to provide for such flexibility in a memory efficient manner.)

- A few numbers are stored as static data in the class. The variable gfm represents the number m in $GF(2^m)$. The variable gfN represents the number $2^m - 1$. These should be set up as part of the initgf function. These numbers are used in various operators (such as multiplication, division, and> exponentiation).

- Near the top of the header are the lines

```
extern GFNUM2m ALPHA;
    // set up a global alpha
extern GFNUM2m& A;
    // and a reference to alpha
    // for shorthand
```

These declare the variables `ALPHA` and `A`, the latter of which is a reference to the former. These variables can be used to represent the variable α in your programs, as in

```
GFNUM2m a;
a = (A^4) + (A^8);//
```

```
// a is alpha^4 + alpha^8
```

The *definitions* of these variables should be provided in the `GFNUM2m.cc` file.

Write your code, then extensively test the arithmetic using $GF(2^4)$ (as shown above) and $GF(2^8)$. For the field $GF(2^8)$, use the primitive polynomial $p(x) = 1 + x^2 + x^3 + x^4 + x^8$:

```
GFNUM2m::initgf(8,0x11D);
    //   1 0001 1101
    //   x^8 + x^4 + x^3 + x^2 + 1
```

5.12 Exercise

5.1 Referring to the computations outlined in Example 5.1:

(a) Write down the polynomial equivalents for $\gamma_1, \gamma_2, \ldots, \gamma_{31}$. (That is, find the binary representation for γ_i and express it as a polynomial.)

(b) Write down the polynomial representation for γ_i^3, using operations modulo $M(x) = 1 + x^2 + x^5$.

(c) Explicitly write down the 10×31 binary parity check matrix H in (5.1).

5.2 Prove the statements in Lemma 5.4 that apply to integers.

5.3 [325] Let s and $g > 0$ be integers. Show that integers x and y exist satisfying $x + y = s$ and $(x, y) = g$ if and only if $g|s$.

5.4 [325] Show that if $m > n$, then $(a^{2^n} + 1)|(a^{2^m} - 1)$.

5.5 Wilson's theorem: Show that if p is a prime, then $(p - 1)! \equiv -1 \pmod{p}$.

5.6 Let $f(x) = x^{10} + x^9 + x^5 + x^4$ and $g(x) = x^2 + x + 1$ be polynomials in $GF(2)[x]$. Write $f(x) = g(x)q(x) + r(x)$, where $\deg(r(x)) < \deg(g(x))$.

5.7 Uniqueness of division algorithm: Suppose that for integers $a > 0$ and b there are two representations

$$b = q_1 a + r_1 \quad b = q_2 a + r_2,$$

with $0 \leq r_1 < a$ and $0 \leq r_2 < a$. Show that $r_1 = r_2$.

5.8 Let $R_a[b]$ be the remainder of b when divided by a, where a and b are integers. That is, by the division algorithm, $b = qa + R_a[b]$. Prove the following by relating both sides to the division algorithm.

(a) $R_a[b + c] = R_a[R_a[b] + R_a[c]]$.

(b) $R_a[bc] = R_a[R_a[b]R_a[c]]$.

(c) Do these results extend to polynomials?

5.9 Find the GCD g of 6409 and 42823. Also, find s and t such that $6409s + 42823t = g$.

5.10   Use the extended Euclidean algorithm over $\mathbb{Z}_p[x]$ to find $g(x) = (a(x), b(x))$ and the polynomials $s(x)$ and $t(x)$ such that $a(x)s(t) + b(x)t(x) = g(x)$ for

    (a) $a(x) = x^3 + x + 1$, $b(x) = x^2 + x + 1$ for $p = 2$ and $p = 3$.

    (b) $a(x) = x^6 + x^5 + x + 1$, $b(x) = x^4 + x^3$, $p = 2$ and $p = 3$.

5.11   Let $a \in \mathbb{Z}_n$. Describe how to use the Euclidean algorithm to find an integer $b \in \mathbb{Z}_n$ such that $ab = 1$ in $\mathbb{Z}_n$, if such a b exists and determine conditions when such a b exists.

5.12   Show that all Euclidean domains with a finite number of elements are fields.

5.13   Prove the GCD properties in Theorem 5.12.

5.14   Let a and b be integers. The **least common multiple** (LCM) m of a and b is the smallest positive integer such that $a|m$ and $b|m$. The LCM of a and b is frequently denoted $[a, b]$ (For polynomials $a(x)$ and $b(x)$, the LCM is the polynomial $m(x)$ of smallest degree such that $a(x)|m(x)$ and $b(x)|m(x)$.)

    (a)   If s is any common multiple of a and b (that is, $a|r$ and $b|r$) and $m = [a, b]$ is the least common multiple of a and b, then $m|s$. *Hint*: division algorithm.

    (b)   Show that for $m > 0$, $[ma, mb] = m[a, b]$.

    (c)   Show that $[a, b](a, b) = |ab|$

5.15   Let C_1 and C_2 be cyclic codes of length n generated by $g_1(x)$ and $g_2(x)$, respectively, with $g_1(x) \neq g_2(x)$. Let $C_3 = C_1 \cap C_2$. Show that C_3 is also a cyclic code and determine its generator polynomial $g_3(x)$. If d_1 and d_2 are the minimum distances of C_1 and C_2, respectively, what can you say about the minimum distance of C_3?

5.16   Show that $\sum_{i=1}^{p-1} i^{-2} \equiv 0 \pmod{p}$, where p is a prime. *Hint*: The sum of the squares of the first n natural numbers is $n(n + 1)(2n + 1)/6$.

5.17   [472] Show that $\{as + bt : s, t \in \mathbb{Z}\} = \{k(a, b) : k \in \mathbb{Z}\}$ for all $a, b \in \mathbb{Z}$.

5.18   Show that the update equations for the extended Euclidean algorithm in (5.10) are correct. That is, show that the recursion (5.10) produces s_i and t_i satisfying the equation $as_i + bt_i = r_i$ for all i. *Hint*: Show for the initial conditions given in (5.11) that (5.9) is satisfied for $i = -1$ and $i = 0$. Then do a proof by induction.

5.19   [45] **A matrix formulation of the Euclidean algorithm**. For polynomials $a(x)$ and $b(x)$, use the notation $a(x) = \left\lfloor \frac{a(x)}{b(x)} \right\rfloor b(x) + r(x)$ to denote the division algorithm, where $q(x) = \left\lfloor \frac{a(x)}{b(x)} \right\rfloor$ is the quotient. Let $\deg(a(x)) > \deg(b(x))$. Let $a^{(0)}(x) = a(x)$ and $b^{(0)}(x) = b(x)$ and $A^{(0)}(x) = \begin{bmatrix} 1 & 0 \\ 0 & 1 \end{bmatrix}$. Let

$$q^{(k)}(x) = \left\lfloor \frac{a^{(k)}(x)}{b^{(k)}(x)} \right\rfloor$$

$$A^{(k+1)}(x) = \begin{bmatrix} 0 & 1 \\ 1 & -q^{(k)}(x) \end{bmatrix} A^{(k)}(x)$$

$$\begin{bmatrix} a^{(k+1)}(x) \\ b^{(k+1)}(x) \end{bmatrix} = \begin{bmatrix} 0 & 1 \\ 1 & -q^{(k)}(x) \end{bmatrix} \begin{bmatrix} a^{(k)}(x) \\ b^{(k)}(x) \end{bmatrix}.$$

    (a)   Show that $\begin{bmatrix} a^{(k+1)}(x) \\ b^{(k+1)}(x) \end{bmatrix} = A^{(k+1)} \begin{bmatrix} a(x) \\ b(x) \end{bmatrix}$.

    (b)   Show that $b^{(K)}(x) = 0$ for some integer K.

    (c)   Show that $\begin{bmatrix} a^{(K)}(x) \\ 0 \end{bmatrix} = A^{(K)}(x) \begin{bmatrix} a(x) \\ b(x) \end{bmatrix}$. Conclude that any divisor of both $a(x)$ and $b(x)$ also divides $a^{(K)}(x)$. Therefore, $(a(x), b(x))|a^{(K)}(x)$.

(d) Show that

$$\begin{bmatrix} a(x) \\ b(x) \end{bmatrix} = \left[\prod_{k=1}^{K} \begin{bmatrix} q^{(k)}(x) & 1 \\ 1 & 0 \end{bmatrix} \right] \begin{bmatrix} a^{(K)}(x) \\ 0 \end{bmatrix}.$$

Hence conclude that $a^{(K)}(x)|a(x)$ and $a^{(K)}(x)|b(x)$, and therefore that $a^{(K)}(x)|(a(x), b(x))$.

(e) Conclude that $a^{(K)}(x) = \gamma(a(x), b(x))$ for some scalar γ. Furthermore, show that $a^{(K)}(x) = A_{11}^{(K)}(x)a(x) + A_{12}^{(K)}(x)b(x)$.

5.20 [472] **More on the matrix formulation of the Euclidean algorithm.** Let

$$R^0 = \begin{bmatrix} s_{-1} & t_{-1} \\ s_0 & t_0 \end{bmatrix} = \begin{bmatrix} 1 & 0 \\ 0 & 1 \end{bmatrix} \quad \text{and} \quad Q^{(i)} = \begin{bmatrix} 0 & 1 \\ 1 & -q^{(i)}(x), \end{bmatrix}$$

where $q^{(i)}(x) = \lfloor r_{i-2}/r_{i-1} \rfloor$ and let $R^{(i+1)} = Q^{(i+1)}R^{(i)}$. Show that:

(a) $\begin{bmatrix} r_{i-1}(x) \\ r_i(x) \end{bmatrix} = R^{(i)} \begin{bmatrix} a(x) \\ b(x) \end{bmatrix}$, $0 \le i \le K$, where K is the last index such that $r_K(x) \ne 0$.

(b) $R^{(i)} = \begin{bmatrix} s_{i-1} & t_{i-1} \\ s_i & t_i \end{bmatrix}$, $0 \le i \le K$.

(c) Show that any common divisor of r_i and r_{i+1} is a divisor of r_K and that $r_K|r_i$ and $r_K|r_{i+1}$ for $-1 \le i < K$.

(d) $s_i t_{i+1} - s_{i+1} t_i = (-1)^{i+1}$, so that $(s_i, t_i) = 1$. *Hint:* determinant of $R^{(i+1)}$.

(e) $s_i a + t_i b = r_i$, $-1 \le i \le K$.

(f) $(r_i, t_i) = (a, t_i)$.

5.21 [304] Properties of the extended Euclidean algorithm. Let q_i, r_i, s_i, and t_i be defined as in Algorithm 5.1. Let n be the value of i such that $r_n = 0$ (the last iteration). Using proofs by induction, show that the following relationships exist among these quantities:

$$t_i r_{i-1} - t_{i-1} r_i = (-1)^i a \qquad 0 \le i \le n$$

$$s_i r_{i-1} - s_{i-1} r_i = (-1)^{i+1} b \qquad 0 \le i \le n$$

$$s_i t_{i-1} - s_{i-1} t_i = (-1)^{i+1} \qquad 0 \le i \le n$$

$$s_i a + t_i b = r_i \qquad -1 \le i \le n$$

$$\deg(s_i) + \deg(r_{i-1}) = \deg(b) \qquad 1 \le i \le n$$

$$\deg(t_i) + \deg(r_{i-1}) = \deg(a) \qquad 0 \le i \le n.$$

5.22 Continued fractions and the Euclidean algorithm. Let u_0 and u_1 be in a field $\mathbb{F}$ or ring of polynomials over a field $\mathbb{F}[x]$. A continued fraction representation of the ratio u_0/u_1 is a fraction of the form

$$\frac{u_0}{u_1} = a_0 + \cfrac{1}{a_1 + \cfrac{1}{a_2 + \cdots \cfrac{1}{a_{j-1} + \cfrac{1}{a_j}}}}. \qquad (5.57)$$

For example,

$$\frac{51}{22} = 2 + \cfrac{1}{3 + \cfrac{1}{7}}.$$

The continued fraction (5.57) can be denoted as $\langle a_0, a_1, \ldots, a_j \rangle$.

(a) Given u_0 and u_1, show how to use the Euclidean algorithm to find the $a_0, a_1, \ldots, a_j$ in the continued fraction representation of u_0/u_1. *Hint*: by the division algorithm, $u_0 = u_1 a_0 + u_2$. This is equivalent to $u_0/u_1 = a_0 + 1/(u_1/u_2)$.

(b) Determine the continued fraction expansion for $u_0 = 966$, $u_1 = 815$. Verify that it works.

(c) Let $u_0(x), u_1(x) \in \mathbb{Z}_5[x]$, where $u_0(x) = 1 + 2x + 3x^2 + 4x^3 + 3x^5$ and $u_1(x) = 1 + 3x^2 + 2x^3$. Determine the continued fraction expansion for $u_0(x)/u_1(x)$.

5.23 [304] Padé Approximation and the Euclidean Algorithm. Let $A(x) = a_0 + a_1 x + a_2 x^2 + \cdots$ be a power series with coefficients in a field $\mathbb{F}$. A (μ, ν) Padé approximant to $A(x)$ is a rational function $p(x)/q(x)$ such that $q(x)A(x) \equiv p(x) \pmod{x^{N+1}}$, where $\mu + \nu = N$ and where $\deg(p(x) \le \mu$ and $\deg(q(x)) \le \nu$. That is, $A(x)$ agrees with the expansion $p(x)/q(x)$ for terms up to x^N. The Padé condition can be written as $q(x)A_N(x) \equiv p(x) \pmod{x^{N+1}}$, where $A_N(x)$ is the Nth truncation of $A(x)$,

$$A_N(x) = a_0 + a_1 x + \cdots + a_N x^N.$$

(a) Describe how to use the Euclidean algorithm to obtain a sequence of polynomials $r_j(x)$ and $t_j(x)$ such that $t_j(x)A_N(x) \equiv r_j(x) \pmod{x^{N+1}}$.

(b) Let $\mu + \nu = \deg(a(x)) - 1$, with $\mu \ge \deg((a(x), b(x))$. Show that there exists a unique index j such that $\deg(r_j) \le \mu$ and $\deg(t_j) \le \nu$. *Hint*: See the last property in Exercise 5.21

(c) Let $A(x) = 1 + 2x + x^3 + 3x^7 + x^9 + \cdots$ be a power series. Determine a Padé approximation with $\mu = 5$ and $\nu = 3$; that is, an approximation to the truncated series $A_8(x) = 1 + 2x + x^3 + 3x^7$.

5.24 Let I_1 and I_2 be ideals in $\mathbb{F}[x]$ generated by $g_1(x)$ and $g_2(x)$, respectively.

(a) The LCM of $g_1(x)$ and $g_2(x)$ is the polynomial $g(x)$ of smallest degree such that $g_1(x)|g(x)$ and $g_2(x)|g(x)$. Show that $I_1 \cap I_2$ is generated by the LCM of $g_1(x)$ and $g_2(x)$.

(b) Let $I_1 + I_2$ mean the smallest ideal which contains I_1 and I_2. Show that $I_1 + I_2$ is generated by the greatest common divisor of $g_1(x)$ and $g_2(x)$.

5.25 Using the extended Euclidean algorithm, determine the shortest linear feedback shift register that could have produced the sequence $[1, 4, 2, 2, 4, 1]$ with elements in $\mathbb{Z}_5$.

5.26 Prove statements (1)–(9) of Theorem 5.27.

5.27 If x is an even number, then $x \equiv 0 \pmod 2$. What congruence does an odd integer satisfy? What congruence does an integer of the form $x = 7k + 1$ satisfy?

5.28 [325] Write a single congruence equivalent to the pair of congruences $x \equiv 1 \pmod 4$ and $x \equiv 2 \pmod 3$.

5.29 Compute: $\phi(190)$, $\phi(191)$, $\phi(192)$.

5.30 [325] Prove the following divisibility facts:

(a) $n^6 - 1$ is divisible by 7 if $(n, 7) = 1$.

(b) $n^7 - n$ is divisible by 42 for any integer n.

(c) $n^{12} - 1$ is divisible by 7 if $(n, 7) = 1$.

(d) $n^{6k} - 1$ is divisible by 7 if $(n, 7) = 1$, k a positive integer.

(e) $n^{13} - n$ is divisible by 2, 3, 5, 7, and 13 for any positive integer n.

5.31 Prove that

$$\phi(n) = n \prod_{p|n} \left(1 - \frac{1}{p}\right),$$

where the product is taken over all primes p dividing n. Hint: write $n = p_1^{e_1} p_2^{e_2} \cdots p_r^{e_r}$.

5.32 In this exercise, you will prove an important property of the Euler ϕ function:

$$\sum_{d|n} \phi(d) = n, \tag{5.58}$$

where the sum is over all the numbers d that divide n.

(a) Suppose $n = p^e$, where p is prime. Show that (5.58) is true.

(b) Now proceed by induction. Suppose that (5.58) is true for integers with k or fewer distinct prime factors. Consider any integer N with $k + 1$ distinct prime factors. Let p denote one of the prime factors of N and let p^e be the highest power of p that divides N. Then $N = p^e n$, where n has k distinct prime factors. As d ranges over the divisors of n, the set $d, pd, p^2 d, \ldots, p^e d$ ranges over the divisors of N. Now complete the proof.

5.33 Let G_n be the elements in $\mathbb{Z}_n$ that are relatively prime to n. Show that G_n forms a group under multiplication.

5.34 RSA Encryption: Let $p = 97$ and $q = 149$. Encrypt the message $m = 1234$ using the public key $\{e, n\} = \{35, 14453\}$. Determine the private key $\{d, n\}$. Then decrypt.

5.35 A message is encrypted using the public key $\{e, n\} = \{23, 64777\}$. The encrypted message is $c = 1216$. Determine the original message m. (That is, crack the code.) Check your answer by re-encoding it using e.

5.36 Find all integers that simultaneously satisfy the congruences $x \equiv 2 \pmod 4$, $x \equiv 1 \pmod 9$, and $x \equiv 2 \pmod 5$.

5.37 Find a polynomial $f(x) \in \mathbb{Z}_5[x]$ simultaneously satisfying the three congruences

$$f(x) \equiv 2 \pmod{x - 1} \quad f(x) \equiv 3 + 2x \pmod{(x - 2)^2}$$

$$f(x) \equiv x^2 + 3x + 2 \pmod{(x - 3)^3}.$$

5.38 Evaluation homomorphism: Show that $f(x) \pmod{x - u} = f(u)$. Show that $\pi : \mathbb{F}[x] \to \mathbb{F}$ defined by $\pi_u(f(x)) = f(u)$ is a ring homomorphism.

5.39 Determine a Lagrange interpolating polynomial $f(x) \in \mathbb{R}[x]$ such that

$$f(1) = 3 \quad f(2) = 6 \quad f(3) = 1.$$

5.40 Let $(x_1, y_1), (x_2, y_2), \ldots, (x_N, y_N)$ be points.

(a) Write down the Lagrange interpolants $l_i(x)$ for these points.

(b) Write down a polynomial $f(x)$ that interpolates through these points.

5.41 An interesting identity. In this exercise you will prove that for $p_1, p_2, \ldots, p_N$ all distinct, the following identity holds:

$$\sum_{i=1}^{N} \prod_{n=1, n \neq i}^{N} \frac{p_i}{p_i - p_n} = 1$$

in any field.

(a) Verify the identity when $N = 2$ and $N = 3$.

(b) Let $f(x) = x^{N-1}$. Find a Lagrange interpolating polynomial $g(x)$ for the points $(p_1, p_1^{N-1}), (p_2, p_2^{N-1}), \ldots, (p_N, p_N^{N-1})$.

(c) Determine the $(N - 1)$st derivative of $g(x)$, $g^{(N-1)}(x)$.

(d) Determine the $(N - 1)$st derivative of $f(x)$, $f^{(N-1)}(x)$.

(e) Show that the identity is true.

(f) Based on this identity, prove the following facts:

    i. $\sum_{i=1}^{N} \prod_{n=1, n \neq i}^{N} \frac{i}{i-n} = 1$. Based on this, show that

$$\frac{1}{N!} \sum_{i=1}^{N} (-1)^{N-i} \binom{N}{i} i^N = 1.$$

    ii. $\sum_{i=1}^{N} \prod_{n=1, n \neq i}^{N} \frac{n}{n-i} = 1$. Based on this, show that

$$\sum_{i=1}^{N} (-1)^{i-1} \binom{N}{i} = 1.$$

    iii. $\sum_{i=1}^{N} \prod_{n=1, n \neq i}^{N} \frac{1}{1-x^{n-i}} = 1, x \neq 1$.

    iv. $\sum_{i=1}^{N} \prod_{n=1, n \neq i}^{N} \frac{1}{1-(n/i)^x} = 1$ for all $x \neq 0$.

5.42 Let $l_j(x)$ be a Lagrange interpolant, as in (5.32). Show that $\sum_{j=1}^{r} l_j(x) = 1$.

5.43 Show that $x^5 + x^3 + 1$ is irreducible over $GF(2)$.

5.44 Determine whether each of the following polynomials in $GF(2)[x]$ is irreducible. If irreducible, determine if it is also primitive.

    (a) $x^2 + 1$ (d) $x^4 + x^2 + 1$ (g) $x^5 + x^3 + x^2 + x + 1$

    (b) $x^2 + x + 1$ (e) $x^4 + x^2 + x^2 + x + 1$.   (h) $x^5 + x^2 + 1$

    (c) $x^3 + x + 1$ (f) $x^4 + x^3 + x + 1$ (i) $x^6 + x^5 + x^4 + x + 1$

5.45 Let $p(x) \in GF(2)[x]$ be $p(x) = x^4 + x^3 + x^2 + x + 1$. This polynomial is irreducible. Let this polynomial be used to create a representation of $GF(2^4)$. Using this representation of $GF(2^4)$, do the following:

    (a) Let α be a root of $p(x)$. Show that α is not a primitive element.

    (b) Show that $\beta = \alpha + 1$ is primitive.

    (c) Find the minimal polynomial of $\beta = \alpha + 1$.

5.46 Solve the following set of equations over $GF(2^4)$, using the representation in Table 5.1.

$$\alpha x + \alpha^5 y + z = \alpha$$

$$\alpha^2 x + \alpha^3 y + \alpha^8 z = \alpha^4$$

$$\alpha^2 x + y + \alpha^9 z = \alpha^{10}.$$

5.47 Show that $(x - \beta)$ is a factor of a polynomial $f(x)$ if and only if $f(\beta) = 0$.

5.48 Create a table such as Table 5.1 for the field $GF(2^3)$ generated by the primitive polynomial $x^3 + x + 1$, including the Zech logarithms.

5.49 Construct the field $GF(8)$ using the primitive polynomial $p(x) = 1 + x^2 + x^3$, producing a table similar to Table 5.1. Use β to represent the root of $p(x)$: $\beta^3 + \beta^2 + 1 = 0$.

5.50 Extension of $GF(3)$:

    (a) Prove that $p(x) = x^2 + x + 2$ is irreducible in $GF(3)$.

    (b) Construct the field $GF(3^2)$ using the primitive polynomial $x^2 + x + 2$.

5.51 Let $g(x) = (x^2 - 3x + 2) \in \mathbb{R}[x]$. Show that in $\mathbb{R}[x]/\langle g(x) \rangle$ there are zero divisors, so that this does not produce a field.

5.52 Let $f(x)$ be a polynomial of degree n over $GF(2)$. The reciprocal of $f(X)$ is defined as

$$f^*(x) = x^n f(1/x).$$

(a) Find the reciprocal of the polynomial

$$f(x) = 1 + x + x^5.$$

(b) Let $f(x)$ be a polynomial with nonzero constant term. Prove that $f(x)$ is irreducible over $GF(2)$ if and only if $f^*(x)$ is irreducible over $GF(2)$.

(c) Let $f(x)$ be a polynomial with nonzero constant term. Prove that $f(x)$ is primitive if and only if $f^*(x)$ is primitive.

5.53 Extending Theorem 5.51. Show that

$$\left(\sum_{i=1}^{k} x_i\right)^p = \sum_{i=1}^{k} x_i^p.$$

Show that

$$(x + y)^{p^r} = x^{p^r} + y^{p^r}.$$

5.54 Prove Lemma 5.68.

5.55 Show that, over any field, $x^s - 1 \mid x^r - 1$ if and only if $s \mid r$.

5.56 [33, p. 29] Let $d = (m, n)$. Show that $(x^m - 1, x^n - 1) = x^d - 1$. *Hint*: Let r_k denote the remainders for the Euclidean algorithm over integers computing (m, n), with $r_{k-2} = q_k r_{k-1} + r_k$, and let $r^{(k)}$ be the remainder for the Euclidean algorithm over polynomials computing $(x^m - 1, x^n - 1)$. Show that

$$x^{r_k}\left[\sum_{i=0}^{q_k-1} (x^{r_{k-1}})^i\right] (x^{r_{k-1}} - 1) = x^{q_k r_{k-1} + r_k} - x^{r_k},$$

so that

$$x^{r_{k-1}} - 1 = x^{r_k}\left[\sum_{i=0}^{q_k-1} (x^{r_{k-1}})^i\right] (x^{r_{k-1}} - 1) + x^{r_k} - 1.$$

5.57 The set of Gaussian integers $\mathbb{Z}[i]$ is made by adjoining $i = \sqrt{-1}$ to $\mathbb{Z}$:

$$\mathbb{Z}[i] = \{a + bi : a, b \in \mathbb{Z}\}.$$

(This is analogous to adjoining $i = \sqrt{-1}$ to $\mathbb{R}$ to form $\mathbb{C}$.) For $a \in \mathbb{Z}[i]$, define the valuation function $v(a) = aa^*$, where $*$ denotes complex conjugation. $v(a)$ is also called the **norm**. $\mathbb{Z}[i]$ with this valuation forms a Euclidean domain.

(a) Show that $v(a)$ is a Euclidean function. *Hint*: Let $a = a_1 + a_2 i$ and $b = b_1 + b_2 i$, $a/b = Q + iS$ with $Q, S \in \mathbb{Q}$ and $q = q_1 + iq_2, q_1, q_2 \in \mathbb{Z}$ be the nearest integer point to (a/b) and let $r = a - bq$. Show that $v(r) < v(b)$ by showing that $v(r)/v(b) < 1$.

(b) Show that the units in $\mathbb{Z}[i]$ are the elements with norm 1.

(c) Compute the GCDs of 6 and $3 + i$ in $\mathbb{Z}[i]$. Express them as linear combinations of 6 and $3 + i$.

5.58 The **trace** is defined as follows: For $\beta \in GF(p^r)$, $Tr(\beta) = \beta + \beta^p + \beta^{p^2} + \cdots + \beta^{p^{r-1}}$. Show that the trace has the following properties:

(a) For every $\beta \in GF(p^r)$, $Tr(\beta) \in GF(p)$.

(b) There is at least one element $\beta \in GF(p^r)$ such that $Tr(\beta) \neq 0$.

(c) The trace is a $GF(p)$-linear function. That is, for $\beta, \gamma \in GF(p)$ and $\delta_1, \delta_2 \in GF(p^r)$,

$$Tr[\beta\delta_1 + \gamma\delta_2] = \beta Tr[\delta_1] + \gamma Tr[\delta_2].$$

5.59 Square roots in finite fields: Show that every element in $GF(2^m)$ has a square root. That is, for every $\beta \in GF(2^m)$, there is an element $\gamma \in GF(2^m)$ such that $\gamma^2 = \beta$.

5.60 [472, p. 238] Let $q = p^m$ and let t be a divisor of $q - 1$, with prime factorization $t = p_1^{e_1} p_2^{e_2} \cdots p_r^{e_r}$. Prove the following:

    (a) For $\alpha \in GF(q)$ with $\alpha \neq 0$, $\mathrm{ord}(\alpha) = t$ if and only if $\alpha^t = 1$ and $\alpha^{t/p_i} \neq 1$ for $i = 1, 2, \ldots, r$.

    (b) $GF(q)$ contains an element β_i of order $p_i^{e_i}$ for $i = 1, 2, \ldots, r$.

    (c) If $\alpha \in GF(q)$ and $\beta \in GF(q)$ have $(\mathrm{ord}(\alpha), \mathrm{ord}(\beta)) = 1$, then $\mathrm{ord}(\alpha\beta) = \mathrm{ord}(\alpha)\,\mathrm{ord}(\beta)$.

    (d) $GF(q)$ has an element of order t.

    (e) $GF(q)$ has a primitive element.

5.61 Let $f(x) = (x - a_1)^{r_1} \cdots (x - a_l)^{r_l}$. Let $f'(x)$ be the formal derivative of $f(x)$. Show that $(f(x), f'(x)) = (x - a_1)^{r_1-1} \cdots (x - a_l)^{r_l-1}$.

5.62 The polynomial $f(x) = x^2 - 2$ is irreducible over $\mathbb{Q}[x]$ because $\sqrt{2}$ is irrational. Prove that $\sqrt{2}$ is irrational.

5.63 Express the following as products of binary irreducible polynomials over $GF(2)[x]$. (a) $x^7 + 1$. (b) $x^{15} + 1$.

5.64 Construct all binary cyclic codes of length 7. (That is, write down the generator polynomials for all binary cyclic codes of length 7.)

5.65 Refer to Theorem 4.16. List all of the distinct ideals in the ring $GF(2)[x]/(x^{15} - 1)$ by their generators.

5.66 [483] List by dimension all of the binary cyclic codes of length 31.

5.67 [483] List by dimension all of the 8-ary cyclic codes of length 33. *Hint*:

$$x^{33} - 1 = (x + 1)(x^2 + x + 1)(x^{10} + x^7 + x^5 + x^3 + 1)(x^{10} + x^9 + x^5 + x + 1)$$

$$(x^{10} + x^9 + x^8 + x^7 + x^6 + x^5 + x^4 + x^3 + x^2 + x + 1).$$

5.68 List the dimensions of all the binary cyclic codes of length 19. *Hint*:

$$x^{19} + 1 = (x + 1) \sum_{i=0}^{18} x^i.$$

5.69 Let β be an element of $GF(2^m)$, with $\beta \neq 0$ and $\beta \neq 1$. Let $q(x)$ be the minimal polynomial of β. What is the shortest cyclic code with $q(x)$ as the generator polynomial?

5.70 Let $\beta \in GF(q)$ have minimal polynomial $m(x)$ of degree d. Show that the reciprocal $x^d m(1/x)$ is the minimal polynomial of β^{-1}.

5.71 Let $\alpha \in GF(2^{10})$ be primitive. Find the conjugates of α with respect to $GF(2)$, $GF(4)$, and $GF(32)$.

5.72 In the field $GF(9)$ constructed with the primitive polynomial $x^2 + x + 2$ (see Exercise 5.50), determine the minimal polynomials of all the elements with respect to $GF(3)$ and determine the cyclotomic cosets.

5.73 [483] Determine the degree of the minimal polynomial of β with respect to $GF(2)$ for a field element β with the following orders: (a) $\mathrm{ord}(\beta) = 3$. Example: $\{\beta, \beta^2, \beta^4 = \beta\}$, so there are two conjugates. Minimal polynomial has degree 2. (b) $\mathrm{ord}(\beta) = 5$. (c) $\mathrm{ord}(\beta) = 7$. (d) $\mathrm{ord}(\beta) = 9$.

5.74 For each of the following polynomials, determine a field $GF(2^m)$ where the polynomials can be factored into polynomials in $GF(2)[x]$. Determine the cyclotomic cosets in each case and the number of binary irreducible polynomials in the factorization.

    (a) $x^9 + 1$ (c) $x^{13} + 1$ (e) $x^{19} + 1$

    (b) $x^{11} + 1$ (d) $x^{17} + 1$ (f) $x^{29} + 1$

5.75 Let $g(x)$ be the generator of a cyclic code over $GF(q)$ of length n and let q and n be relatively prime. Show that the vector of all 1s is a codeword if and only if $g(1) \neq 0$.

5.76 Let $g(x) = x^9 + \beta^2 x^8 + x^6 + x^5 + \beta^2 x^2 + \beta^2$ be the generator for a cyclic code of length 15 over $GF(4)$, where $\beta = \beta^2 + 1$ is primitive over $GF(4)$.

   (a) Determine $h(x)$.

   (b) Determine the dimension of the code.

   (c) Determine the generator matrix G and the parity check matrix H for this code.

   (d) Let $r(x) = \beta x^3 + \beta^2 x^4$. Determine the syndrome for $r(x)$.

   (e) Draw a circuit for a systematic encoder for this code.

   (f) Draw a circuit which computes the syndrome for this code.

5.77 [483] Let $\langle f(x), h(x) \rangle$ be the ideal $I \subset GF(2)[x]/(x^n - 1)$ formed by all linear combinations of the form $a(x)f(x) + b(x)g(x)$, where $a(x), b(x) \in GF(2)[x]/(x^n - 1)$. By Theorem 4.16, I is principal. Determine the generator for I.

5.78 Let $A(z) = \sum_{n=0}^{\infty} A_n z^n$ and $B(z) = \sum_{n=0}^{\infty} B_n z^n$ be generating functions and let $C(z) = A(z)B(z)$. Using the property of a formal derivative that $A'(z) = \sum_{n=0}^{\infty} n A_n z^{n-1}$, show that $C'(z) = A'(z)B(z) + A(z)B'(z)$. By extension, show that if $C(z) = \prod_{i=1}^{k} A_i(z)$, show that

$$\frac{\left[\prod_{i=1}^{k} A_i(z) \right]'}{\prod_{i=1}^{k} A_i(z)} = \sum_{i=1}^{k} \frac{[A_i(z)]'}{A_i(z)}.$$

5.79 Show how to make the transition from (5.51) to (5.52).

5.80 Show that:

   (a) For an LFSR with an irreducible generator $g(x)$ of degree p, the period of the sequence is a factor of $2^p - 1$.

   (b) If $2^p - 1$ is prime, then every irreducible polynomial of degree p produces a maximal-length shift register.

       Incidentally, if $2^n - 1$ is a prime number, it is called a **Mersenne prime**. A few values of n which yield Mersenne primes are: $n = 2, 3, 5, 7, 13, 17, 19, 31, 61, 89$.

5.81 Prove Theorem 5.104.

5.82 Using Exercise 5.32 and Theorem 5.105, show that

$$\phi(n) = \sum_{d|n} \mu(d)(n/d).$$

5.83 Let $q = 2$. Use (5.56) to determine I_1, I_2, I_3, I_4, and I_5.

5.13 References

The discussion of number theory was drawn from [325] and [472]. Discussions of the computational complexity of the Euclidean algorithm are in [247] and [472]. The Sugiyama algorithm is discussed in [424] and [304]. Fast Euclidean algorithm implementations are discussed in [44]. Continued fractions are discussed in [325]; Padé approximation appears in [304, 309, 472]. A delightful introduction to applications of number theory appears in [399]. Modern algebra can be found in [33, 42, 144, 472, 483]. More advanced treatments can be found in [206, 215], while a thorough treatment of finite fields is in [268, 269]. Zech logarithms and some of their interesting properties are presented in [399]. Our discussion of hardware implementations is drawn from [271], while the format of the add/multiply tables inside the back cover is due to [351]. Discussion of irreducible polynomials was drawn closely from [33]. The RSA algorithm was presented first in [378]; for introductory discussions, see also [472] and [399]. The algebraic approach using the CRT for fast transforms in multiple dimensions is explored in [356].

Chapter 6

BCH and Reed–Solomon Codes: Designer Cyclic Codes

The most commonly used cyclic error-correcting codes may be the BCH and Reed–Solomon (RS) codes. The BCH code is named after Bose, Ray–Chaudhuri, and Hocquenghem (see the references at the end of the chapter), who published work in 1959 and 1960 which revealed a means of designing codes over $GF(2)$ with a specified design distance. Decoding algorithms were then developed by Peterson and others.

The RS codes are also named after their inventors, who published them in 1960. It was later realized that RS codes and BCH codes are related and that their decoding algorithms are quite similar.

This chapter describes the construction of BCH and RS codes and several decoding algorithms. Decoding of these codes is an extremely rich area. Chapter 7 describes other "modern" decoding algorithms.

6.1 BCH Codes

6.1.1 Designing BCH Codes

BCH codes are cyclic codes and hence may be specified by a generator polynomial. A BCH code over $GF(q)$ of length n capable of correcting at least t errors is specified as follows:

1. Determine the smallest m such that $GF(q^m)$ has a primitive nth root of unity β.

2. Select a nonnegative integer b. Frequently, $b = 1$.

3. Write down a list of $2t$ *consecutive* powers of β:

$$\beta^b, \beta^{b+1}, \ldots, \beta^{b+2t-1}.$$

   Determine the minimal polynomial with respect to $GF(q)$ of each of these powers of β. (Because of conjugacy, frequently these minimal polynomials are not distinct.)

4. The generator polynomial $g(x)$ is the least common multiple (LCM) of these minimal polynomials. The code is a $(n, n - \deg(g(x)))$ cyclic code.

Because the generator is constructed using minimal polynomials with respect to $GF(q)$, the generator $g(x)$ has coefficients in $GF(q)$, and the code is over $GF(q)$.

Definition 6.1 If $b = 1$ in the construction procedure, the BCH code is said to be **narrow sense**. If $n = q^m - 1$, then the BCH code is said to be **primitive**. □

Because not all codes are primitive, in this chapter we distinguish between the β used to form the roots of the generator polynomial, and a primitive element α in $GF(q^m)$. (See, for example, Example 6.5.)

Two fields are involved in the construction of the BCH codes. The "small field" $GF(q)$ is where the generator polynomial has its coefficients and is the field where the elements of the codewords are. The "big field" $GF(q^m)$ is the field where the generator polynomial has its roots. For encoding purposes, it is sufficient to work only with the small field. However, as we shall see, decoding requires operations

Error Correction Coding: Mathematical Methods and Algorithms, Second Edition. Todd K. Moon
© 2021 John Wiley & Sons, Inc. Published 2021 by John Wiley & Sons, Inc.
Companion website: www.wiley.com/go/Moon/ErrorCorrectionCoding

in the big field. (It will be seen that for RS codes both the encode and decode operations take place in the "big" field.)

Example 6.2 Let $n = 31 = 2^5 - 1$ for a primitive code with $m = 5$ and let β be a root of the primitive polynomial $x^5 + x^2 + 1$ in $GF(2^5)$. (That is, β is an element with order n.)

Let us take $b = 1$ (narrow-sense code) and construct a single-error- correcting binary BCH code. That is, we have $t = 1$. The $2t$ consecutive powers of β are β, β^2. The minimal polynomials of β and β^2 with respect to $GF(2)$ are the same (they are conjugates). Let us denote this minimal polynomial by $M_1(x)$. Since β is primitive, $M_1(x) = x^5 + x^2 + 1$ (see Table 5.4). Then

$$g(x) = M_1(x) = x^5 + x^2 + 1.$$

Since $\deg(g) = 5$, we have a $(31, 26)$ code. (This is, in fact, a Hamming code.)

As a variation on this, consider now a non-narrow-sense code with $b = 2$. The $2t$ consecutive powers of β are

$$\beta^2, \beta^3.$$

The root β^3 is in a different conjugacy class than the root β^2, so another minimal polynomial must be included. The minimal polynomial for β^2 is $M_1(x)$ (from above) and the minimal polynomial for β^3 is $M_3(x) = x^5 + x^4 + x^3 + x^2 + 1$. The generator polynomial is

$$g(x) = M_1(x)M_3(x) = (x^5 + x^2 + 1)(x^5 + x^4 + x^3 + x^2 + 1) = x^{10} + x^9 + x^8 + x^6 + x^5 + x^3 + 1.$$

The code is a $(31, 21)$ code. In this case, the non-narrow-sense choice of $b = 2$ has led to a lower rate code. However, the following example indicates that the story is not yet complete. $\square$

Example 6.3 As before, let $n = 31$, but now construct a $t = 2$-error-correcting code, with $b = 1$, and let β be a primitive element. We form $2t = 4$ consecutive powers of β: $\beta, \beta^2, \beta^3, \beta^4$. Dividing these into conjugacy classes with respect to $GF(2)$, we have $\{\beta, \beta^2, \beta^4\}, \{\beta^3\}$. Using Table 5.4 we find the minimal polynomials

$$M_1(x) = x^5 + x^2 + 1 \quad M_3(x) = x^5 + x^4 + x^3 + x^2 + 1$$

so that

$$g(x) = \text{LCM}[M_1(x), M_3(x)] = (x^5 + x^2 + 1)(x^5 + x^4 + x^3 + x^2 + 1)$$
$$= x^{10} + x^9 + x^8 + x^6 + x^5 + x^3 + 1.$$

This gives a $(31, 31 - 10) = (31, 21)$ binary cyclic code.

Comparing with the previous example, we see that in the previous case, with $b = 2$, additional roots were "accidentally" included in the conjugacy class by the minimal polynomial so that the code which was designed in that example is actually a two-error-correcting code.

As these examples show, it can happen that the actual correction capability of a BCH code exceeds the design-correction capability.

Let us now repeat the design for a $t = 2$-error-correcting code, but with a non-narrow-sense $b = 2$. The roots are

$$\beta^2, \beta^3, \beta^4, \beta^5,$$

which have minimal polynomials:

$$\beta^2, \beta^4 : M_2(x)$$
$$\beta^3 : M_3(x)$$
$$\beta^5 : M_5(x).$$

The conjugacy classes for these three polynomials are (see Table 5.4)

$$\{\alpha, \alpha^2, \alpha^4, \alpha^8, \alpha^{16}\}, \quad \{\alpha^3, \alpha^6, \alpha^{12}, \alpha^{17}, \alpha^{24}\}, \quad \{\alpha^5, \alpha^9, \alpha^{10}, \alpha^{18}, \alpha^{20}\}.$$

The exponents of the pooled roots are

$$1, 2, 3, 4, 5, 6, \quad 8, 9, 10, 12, 16, 17, 18, 20, 24.$$

Since there is a run of six consecutive roots, this code actually is capable of correcting three errors. The generator is

$$g(x) = M_1(x)M_3(x)M_5(x) = x^{15} + x^{11} + x^{10} + x^9 + x^8 + x^7 + x^5 + x^3 + x^2 + x + 1.$$

$\square$

Example 6.4 As before, let $n = 31$, but now construct a $t = 3$-error-correcting code, with $b = 1$. We form $2t = 6$ consecutive powers of β:

$$\beta, \beta^2, \beta^3, \beta^4, \beta^5, \beta^6.$$

Divided into conjugacy classes with respect to $GF(2)$, we have

$$\{\beta, \beta^2, \beta^4\}, \quad \{\beta^3, \beta^6\}, \quad \{\beta^5\}.$$

Denote the minimal polynomials for these sets as $M_1(x)$, $M_3(x)$, and $M_5(x)$, respectively. Using Table 5.4 we find that the minimal polynomials for elements in these classes are

$$M_1(x) = x^5 + x^2 + 1 \quad M_3(x) = x^5 + x^4 + x^3 + x^2 + 1$$

$$M_5(x) = x^5 + x^4 + x^2 + x + 1$$

so the generator is

$$g(x) = \text{LCM}[M_1(x), M_3(x), M_5(x)] = M_1(x)M_3(x)M_5(x)$$
$$= x^{15} + x^{11} + x^{10} + x^9 + x^8 + x^7 + x^5 + x^3 + x^2 + x + 1.$$

This gives a $(31, 31 - 15) = (31, 16)$ binary cyclic code. $\square$

Example 6.5 Construct a generator for a quaternary, narrow-sense BCH 2-error- correcting code of length $n = 51$. For a quaternary code, we have $q = 4$. The smallest m such that $51|q^m - 1$ is $m = 4$, so the arithmetic takes place in the field $GF(4^4) = GF(256)$. Let α be primitive in the field $GF(256)$. The element $\beta = \alpha^5$ is a 51st root of unity. The subfield $GF(4)$ in $GF(256)$ can be represented (see Example 5.66) using the elements $\{0, 1, \alpha^{85}, \alpha^{170}\}$. The $2t$ consecutive powers of β are $\beta, \beta^2, \beta^3, \beta^4$. Partitioned into conjugacy classes with respect to $GF(4)$, these powers of β are $\{\beta, \beta^4\}, \{\beta^2\}, \{\beta^3\}$. The conjugacy classes for these powers of β are

$$\{\beta, \beta^4, \beta^{16}, \beta^{64}\} \quad \{\beta^2, \beta^8, \beta^{32}, \beta^{128}\} \quad \{\beta^3, \beta^{12}, \beta^{48}, \beta^{192}\}$$

with corresponding minimal polynomials

$$p_1(x) = x^4 + \alpha^{170}x^3 + x^2 + x + \alpha^{170}$$
$$p_2(x) = x^4 + \alpha^{85}x^3 + x^2 + \alpha^{85}$$
$$p_3(x) = x^4 + \alpha^{170}x^3 + x^2 + \alpha^{170}x + 1.$$

These are in $GF(4)[x]$, as expected. The generator polynomial is

$$g(x) = p_1(x)p_2(x)p_3(x)$$
$$= x^{12} + \alpha^{85}x^{11} + \alpha^{170}x^{10} + x^8 + \alpha^{170}x^6 + \alpha^{170}x^5 + \alpha^{170}x^4 + \alpha^{85}x^3$$
$$+ \alpha^{85}x^2 + \alpha^{85}x + 1.$$

$\square$

6.1.2 The BCH Bound

The BCH bound is the proof that the constructive procedure described above produces codes with at least the specified minimum distance.

We begin by constructing a parity check matrix for the code. Let $c(x) = m(x)g(x)$ be a code polynomial. Then, for $j = b, b+1, \ldots, b+2t-1$,

$$c(\beta^j) = m(\beta^j)g(\beta^j) = m(\beta^j)0 = 0,$$

since these powers of β are, by design, the roots of $g(x)$. Writing $c(x) = c_0 + c_1 x + \cdots + c_{n-1}x^{n-1}$, we have

$$c_0 + c_1 \beta^j + c_2 (\beta^j)^2 + \cdots + c_{n-1}(\beta^j)^{n-1} = 0 \quad j = b, b+1, \ldots, b+2t-1.$$

The parity check conditions can be expressed in the form

$$\begin{bmatrix} 1 & \beta^j & \beta^{2j} & \cdots & \beta^{(n-1)j} \end{bmatrix} \begin{bmatrix} c_0 \\ c_1 \\ c_2 \\ \vdots \\ c_{n-1} \end{bmatrix} = 0 \quad j = b, b+1, \ldots, b+2t-1.$$

Let $\delta = 2t + 1$; δ is called the **design distance** of the code. Stacking the row vectors for different values of j, we obtain a parity check matrix H,

$$H = \begin{bmatrix} 1 & \beta^b & \beta^{2b} & \cdots & \beta^{(n-1)b} \\ 1 & \beta^{b+1} & \beta^{2(b+1)} & \cdots & \beta^{(n-1)(b+1)} \\ \vdots \\ 1 & \beta^{b+\delta-3} & \beta^{2(b+\delta-3)} & \cdots & \beta^{(n-1)(b+\delta-3)} \\ 1 & \beta^{b+\delta-2} & \beta^{2(b+\delta-2)} & \cdots & \beta^{(n-1)(b+\delta-2)} \end{bmatrix}. \tag{6.1}$$

With this in place, there is one more important result needed from linear algebra to prove the BCH bound.

A **Vandermonde matrix** is a square matrix of the form

$$V = V(x_0, x_1, \ldots, x_{n-1}) = \begin{bmatrix} 1 & x_0 & x_0^2 & \cdots & x_0^{n-1} \\ 1 & x_1 & x_1^2 & \cdots & x_1^{n-1} \\ 1 & x_2 & x_2^2 & \cdots & x_2^{n-1} \\ \vdots \\ 1 & x_{n-1} & x_{n-1}^2 & \cdots & x_{n-1}^{n-1} \end{bmatrix} \tag{6.2}$$

or the transpose of such a matrix.

Lemma 6.6 *Let V be a $n \times n$ matrix as in (6.2). Then*

$$\det(V) = \prod_{0 \le j < k \le n-1} (x_k - x_j).$$

Thus, as long as the x_i are all distinct, the Vandermonde matrix is invertible.

Proof The determinant is a polynomial function of the elements of the matrix of total degree

$$1 + 2 + \cdots + n - 1 = n(n-1)/2.$$

We note that if any $x_i = x_0$, $i \neq 0$, then the determinant is equal to 0, since the determinant of a matrix with two identical columns is equal to 0. This suggests that we can think of the determinant as a polynomial of degree $n - 1$ in the variable x_0. Thus, we can write

$$\det(V) = (x_0 - x_1)(x_0 - x_2) \cdots (x_0 - x_{n-1}) p_0(x_1, x_2, \ldots, x_{n-1}),$$

where p_0 is some polynomial function of its arguments. Similarly, we can think of $\det(V)$ as a polynomial in x_1 of degree $n - 1$, having roots at locations $x_0, x_2, \ldots, x_{n-1}$:

$$\det(V) = (x_1 - x_0)(x_1 - x_2) \cdots (x_1 - x_{n-1}) p_1(x_0, x_2, \ldots, x_{n-1}).$$

This applies to all the elements, so

$$\det(V) = \prod_{0 \leq j < k \leq n-1} (x_k - x_j) p(x_0, x_1, \ldots, x_{n-1})$$

for some function p which is polynomial in its arguments. The product

$$\prod_{0 \leq j < k \leq n-1} (x_k - x_j)$$

has total degree

$$(n - 1) + n - 2 + \cdots + 1 = n(n - 1)/2.$$

Comparing the degrees of both sides, we see that $p = 1$. $\qquad\square$

Theorem 6.7 (**The BCH Bound**) *Let C be a q-ary (n, k) cyclic code with generator polynomial $g(x)$. Let $GF(q^m)$ be the smallest extension field of $GF(q)$ that contains a primitive nth root of unity and let β be a primitive nth root of unity in that field. If $g(x)$ is the minimal-degree polynomial in $GF(q)[x]$ having 2t consecutive roots of the form $g(\beta^b) = g(\beta^{b+1}) = g(\beta^{b+2}) = \cdots = g(\beta^{b+2t-1})$, then the minimum distance of the code satisfies $d_{\min} \geq \delta = 2t + 1$; that is, the code is capable of correcting at least t errors.*

In designing BCH codes we may, in fact, exceed the design distance, since extra roots as consecutive powers of β are often included with the minimal polynomials. For RS codes, on the other hand, the minimum distance for the code is exactly the design distance.

Proof Let $\mathbf{c} \in C$, with corresponding polynomial representation $c(x)$. As we have seen in (6.1), a parity check matrix for the code can be written as

$$H = \begin{bmatrix} 1 & \beta^b & \beta^{2b} & \cdots & \beta^{(n-1)b} \\ 1 & \beta^{b+1} & \beta^{2(b+1)} & \cdots & \beta^{(n-1)(b+1)} \\ \vdots & & & & \\ 1 & \beta^{b+\delta-3} & \beta^{2(b+\delta-3)} & \cdots & \beta^{(n-1)(b+\delta-3)} \\ 1 & \beta^{b+\delta-2} & \beta^{2(b+\delta-2)} & \cdots & \beta^{(n-1)(b+\delta-2)} \end{bmatrix}.$$

By Theorem 3.13, the minimum distance of a linear code C is equal to the minimum positive number of columns of H which are linearly dependent. Also, the minimum distance of a code is the smallest nonzero weight of the codewords.

We do a proof by contradiction. Suppose there is a codeword $\mathbf{c}$ of weight $w < \delta$. We write the nonzero components of $\mathbf{c}$ as $[c_{i_1}, c_{i_2}, \ldots, c_{i_w}]^T = \mathbf{d}^T$. Then since $H\mathbf{c} = 0$, we have

$$\begin{bmatrix} \beta^{i_1 b} & \beta^{i_2 b} & \beta^{i_3 b} & \cdots & \beta^{i_w b} \\ \beta^{i_1(b+1)} & \beta^{i_2(b+1)} & \beta^{i_3(b+1)} & \cdots & \beta^{i_w(b+1)} \\ \vdots & & & & \\ \beta^{i_1(b+\delta-3)} & \beta^{i_2(b+\delta-3)} & \beta^{i_3(b+\delta-3)} & \cdots & \beta^{i_w(b+\delta-3)} \\ \beta^{i_1(b+\delta-2)} & \beta^{i_2(b+\delta-2)} & \beta^{i_3(b+\delta-2)} & \cdots & \beta^{i_w(b+\delta-2)} \end{bmatrix} \begin{bmatrix} c_{i_1} \\ c_{i_2} \\ \vdots \\ c_{i_{w-1}} \\ c_{i_w} \end{bmatrix} = \mathbf{0}.$$

Table 6.1: Weight Distribution of the Dual of a
Double-Error-Correcting Primitive Binary BCH Code of Length
$n = 2^m - 1, m \geq 3, m$ Odd

Codeword Weight i	Number of Codewords of Weight i, B_i
0	1
$2^{m-1} - 2^{(m-1)/2}$	$(2^{m-2} + 2^{(m-3)/2})(2^m - 1)$
2^{m-1}	$(2^{m-1} + 1)(2^m - 1)$
$2^{m-1} + 2^{(m-1)/2}$	$(2^{m-2} - 2^{(m-3)/2})(2^m - 1)$

From the first w rows, we obtain

$$
\begin{bmatrix}
\beta^{i_1 b} & \beta^{i_2 b} & \beta^{i_3 b} & \cdots & \beta^{i_w b} \\
\beta^{i_1(b+1)} & \beta^{i_2(b+1)} & \beta^{i_3(b+1)} & \cdots & \beta^{i_w(b+1)} \\
\vdots & & & & \\
\beta^{i_1(b+w-2)} & \beta^{i_2(b+w-2)} & \beta^{i_3(b+w-2)} & \cdots & \beta^{i_w(b+w-2)} \\
\beta^{i_1(b+w-1)} & \beta^{i_2(b+w-1)} & \beta^{i_3(b+w-1)} & \cdots & \beta^{i_w(b+w-1)}
\end{bmatrix}
\begin{bmatrix}
c_{i_1} \\ c_{i_2} \\ \vdots \\ c_{i_{w-1}} \\ c_{i_w}
\end{bmatrix} = \mathbf{0}.
$$

Let H' be the square $w \times w$ matrix on the LHS of this equation. Since $\mathbf{d} \neq 0$, we must have that H' is singular, so that $\det(H') = 0$. Note that

$$
\det(H') = \beta^{i_1 b + i_2 b + \cdots + i_w b} \det
\begin{bmatrix}
1 & 1 & \cdots & 1 \\
\beta^{i_1} & \beta^{i_2} & \cdots & \beta^{i_w} \\
\vdots & & & \\
\beta^{i_1(w-2)} & \beta^{i_2(w-2)} & \cdots & \beta^{i_w(w-2)} \\
\beta^{i_1(w-1)} & \beta^{i_2(w-1)} & \cdots & \beta^{i_w(w-1)}
\end{bmatrix}.
$$

But the latter matrix is a Vandermonde matrix: its determinant is zero if and only if $\beta^{i_j} = \beta^{i_k}$ for some j and k, $j \neq k$. Since $0 \leq i_k < n$ and β is of order n, the β^{i_k} elements along the second row are all distinct. There is thus a contradiction. We conclude that a codeword with weight $w < \delta$ cannot exist. □

It should be mentioned that there are extensions to the BCH bound. In the BCH bound, only a single consecutive block of roots of the generator is considered. The Hartman–Tzeng bound and the Roos bound, by contrast, provide bounds on the error-correction capability of BCH codes based on multiple sets of consecutive roots. For these, see [190, 191, 381].

6.1.3 Weight Distributions for Some Binary BCH Codes

While the weight distributions of most BCH codes are not generally known, weight distributions for the *duals* of all double- and triple-error-correcting binary primitive BCH codes have been found [248, 296, p. 451, 669], [275, pp. 177–178]. From the dual weight distributions, the weight distributions of these BCH codes can be obtained using the MacWilliams identity; see Tables 6.1–6.4.

Example 6.8 In Example 6.3, we found the generator for a double-error- correcting code of length $n = 31 = 2^5 - 1$ to be

$$g(x) = x^{10} + x^9 + x^8 + x^6 + x^5 + x^3 + 1.$$

Table 6.2: Weight Distribution of the Dual of a Double-Error-Correcting Primitive Binary Narrow-Sense BCH Code, $n = 2^m - 1$, $m \geq 4$, m Even

Codeword Weight i	Number of Codewords of Weight i, B_i
0	1
$2^{m-1} - 2^{m/2}$	$\frac{1}{3}2^{(m/2)-2}(2^{(m-2)/2} + 1)(2^m - 1)$
$2^{m-1} - 2^{(m/2)-1}$	$\frac{1}{3}2^{m/2}(2^{m/2} + 1)(2^m - 1)$
2^{m-1}	$(2^{m-2} + 1)(2^m - 1)$
$2^{m-1} + 2^{(m/2)-1}$	$\frac{1}{3}2^{m/2}(2^{m/2} - 1)(2^m - 1)$
$2^{m-1} + 2^{m/2}$	$\frac{1}{3}2^{(m/2)-2}(2^{(m-2)/2} - 1)(2^m - 1)$

Table 6.3: Weight Distribution of the Dual of a Triple-Error-Correcting Primitive Binary Narrow-Sense BCH Code, $n = 2^m - 1$, $m \geq 5$, m Odd

Codeword Weight i	Number of Codewords of Weight i, B_i
0	1
$2^{m-1} - 2^{(m+1)/2}$	$\frac{1}{3}2^{(m-5)/2}(2^{(m-3)/2} + 1)(2^{m-1} - 1)(2^m - 1)$
$2^{m-1} - 2^{(m-1)/2}$	$\frac{1}{3}2^{(m-3)/2}(2^{(m-1)/2} + 1)(5 \cdot 2^{m-1} + 4)(2^m - 1)$
2^{m-1}	$(9 \cdot 2^{2m-4} + 3 \cdot 2^{m-3} + 1)(2^m - 1)$
$2^{m-1} + 2^{(m-1)/2}$	$\frac{1}{3}2^{(m-3)/2}(2^{(m-1)/2} - 1)(5 \cdot 2^{m-1} + 4)(2^m - 1)$
$2^{m-1} + 2^{(m+1)/2}$	$\frac{1}{3}2^{(m-5)/2}(2^{(m-3)/2} - 1)(2^{m-1} - 1)(2^m - 1)$

From Table 6.1, we obtain

Codeword Weight i	Number of Codewords of Weight i, B_i
0	1
12	310
16	527
20	186

The corresponding weight enumerator for the dual code is

$$B(x) = 1 + 310x^{12} + 527x^{16} + 186x^{20}.$$

Using the MacWilliams identity (3.13) we have

bchweight.m

Table 6.4: Weight Distribution of the Dual of a Triple-Error-Correcting Primitive Binary Narrow-Sense BCH Code, $n = 2^m - 1$, $m \geq 6$, m Even

Codeword Weight i	Number of Codewords of Weight i, B_i
0	1
$2^{m-1} - 2^{(m/2)+1}$	$\frac{1}{960}(2^{m-1} + 2^{(m/2)+1})(2^m - 4)(2^m - 1)$
$2^{m-1} - 2^{m/2}$	$\frac{7}{48}2^m(2^{m-1} + 2^{m/2})(2^m - 1)$
$2^{m-1} - 2^{(m/2)-1}$	$\frac{2}{15}(2^{m-1} + 2^{(m/2)-1})(3 \cdot 2^m + 8)(2^m - 1)$
2^{m-1}	$\frac{1}{64}(29 \cdot 2^{2m} - 4 \cdot 2^m + 64)(2^m - 1)$
$2^{m-1} + 2^{(m/2)-1}$	$\frac{2}{15}(2^{m-1} - 2^{(m/2)-1})(3 \cdot 2^m + 8)(2^m - 1)$
$2^{m-1} + 2^{m/2}$	$\frac{7}{48}2^m(2^{m-1} - 2^{m/2})(2^m - 1)$
$2^{m-1} + 2^{(m/2)+1}$	$\frac{1}{960}(2^{m-1} - 2^{(m/2)+1})(2^m - 4)(2^m - 1)$

$$
\begin{aligned}
A(x) &= 2^{-(n-k)}(1+x)^n B\left(\frac{1-x}{1+x}\right) \\
&= 2^{-10}(1+x)^{31}\left[1 + 310\left[\frac{1-x}{1+x}\right]^{12} + 527\left[\frac{1-x}{1+x}\right]^{16} + 186\left[\frac{1-x}{1+x}\right]^{20}\right] \\
&= 1 + 186x^5 + 806x^6 + 2635x^7 + 7905x^8 + 18{,}910x^9 + 41{,}602x^{10} + 85{,}560x^{11} \\
&\quad + 142{,}600x^{12} + 195{,}300x^{13} + 251{,}100x^{14} + 301{,}971x^{15} + 301{,}971x^{16} \\
&\quad + 251{,}100x^{17} + 195{,}300x^{18} + 142{,}600x^{19} + 85{,}560x^{20} + 41{,}602x^{21} + 18{,}910x^{22} \\
&\quad + 7905x^{23} + 2635x^{24} + 806x^{25} + 186x^{26} + x^{31}.
\end{aligned}
$$

□

6.1.4 Asymptotic Results for BCH Codes

The Varshamov–Gilbert bound (see Exercise 3.26) indicates that if the rate R of a block code is fixed, then there exist binary (n, k) codes with distance $d_{\min}$ satisfying $k/n \geq R$ and $d_{\min}/n \geq H_2^{-1}(1 - R)$. It is interesting to examine whether a sequence of BCH codes can be constructed which meets this bound.

Definition 6.9 [[292], p. 269] A family of codes over $GF(q)$ for a fixed q is said to be **good** if it contains an infinite sequence of codes $C_1, C_2, \ldots$, where C_i is an (n_i, k_i, d_i) code such that both the rate $R_i = k_i/n_i$ and the relative distance d_i/n_i approach a nonzero limit as $i \to \infty$. □

bchdesigner

The basic result about BCH codes (which we do not prove here; see [[292], p. 269]) is this:

Theorem 6.10 *There does not exist a sequence of primitive BCH codes over $GF(q)$ with both k/n and d/n bounded away from zero.*

That is, as codes of a given rate become longer, the fraction of errors that can be corrected diminishes to 0.

Nevertheless, for codes of moderate length (up to n of a few thousand), the BCH codes are widely used as components in many coding systems (often used as components in concatenated coding systems.

The program `bchdesigner` can be used to design a binary BCH code for a given code length n, design-correction capability t, and starting exponent b.

6.2 Reed–Solomon Codes

There are actually two distinct constructions for RS codes. While these initially appear to describe different codes, it is shown in Section 6.8.1 using Galois Field Fourier transform (GFFT)techniques that the families of codes described are in fact equivalent. Most of the encoders and decoders in this chapter are concerned with the second code construction. However, there are important theoretical reasons to be familiar with the first code construction as well.

6.2.1 Reed–Solomon Construction 1

Definition 6.11 Let β be a primitive element in $GF(q^m)$ (e.g., $\beta = \alpha$) and let $n = q^m - 1$. Let $\mathbf{m} = (m_0, m_1, \ldots, m_{k-1}) \in GF(q^m)^k$ be a message vector and let $m(x) = m_0 + m_1 x + \cdots + m_{k-1}x^{k-1} \in GF(q^m)[x]$ be its associated polynomial. Then the encoding is defined by the mapping $\rho : m(x) \mapsto \mathbf{c}$ by

$$(c_0, c_1, \ldots, c_{n-1}) \overset{\triangle}{=} \rho(m(x)) = (m(1), m(\beta), m(\beta^2), \ldots, m(\beta^{n-1})).$$

That is, $\rho(m(x))$ evaluates $m(x)$ at all the nonzero elements of $GF(q^m)$.

The RS code of length $n = q^m - 1$ and dimension k over $GF(q^m)$ is the image under ρ of all polynomials in $GF(q^m)[x]$ of degree less than or equal to $k - 1$.

More generally, a RS code can be defined by taking $n \leq q^m - 1$, choosing n distinct elements out of $GF(q^m)$, $\beta_1, \beta_2, \ldots, \beta_n$ known as the **support set**, and defining the encoding operation as

$$\rho(m(x)) = (m(\beta_1), m(\gamma_2), \ldots, m(\beta_n)).$$

The code is the image of the support set under ρ of all polynomials in $GF(q^m)[x]$ of degree less than k. □

Example 6.12 Let $GF(q^m) = GF(2^3) = GF(8)$. A $(7, 3)$ RS code can be obtained by writing down all polynomials of degree 2, $m(x) = m_0 + m_1 x + x_2 x^2$, with coefficients $m_i \in GF(8)$, then evaluating them at the nonzero elements in the field. Such polynomials are, for example, $m(x) = \alpha + \alpha^3 x^2$ or $m(x) = \alpha^5 + \alpha^2 x + \alpha^4 x^2$ ($8^3 = 512$ polynomials in all). We will see that $d_{min} = 5$, so this is a two-error-correcting code. □

Some properties of the RS codes are immediate from the definition.

Lemma 6.13 *The RS code is a linear code.*

The proof is immediate.

Lemma 6.14 *The minimum distance of an (n, k) RS code is $d_{min} = n - k + 1$.*

Proof Since $m(x)$ is of degree $k - 1$ it has at most $k - 1$ zeros in it in the field $GF(q^m)$, there are at most $k - 1$ zero positions in each nonzero codeword. Thus, $d_{min} \geq n - (k - 1)$. However, by the Singleton bound (see Section 3.3.1), we must have $d_{min} \leq n - k + 1$. So $d_{min} = n - k + 1$. □

RS codes achieve the Singleton bound and are thus maximum distance separable codes.

This construction of RS codes came first historically [364] and leads to important generalizations, some of which are introduced in Section 6.9.2. Recently a powerful decoding algorithm has been developed based on this viewpoint (see Section 7.6). However, the following construction has been important because of its relation with BCH codes and their associated decoding algorithms.

6.2.2   Reed–Solomon Construction 2

In constructing BCH codes, we looked for generator polynomials over $GF(q)$ (the small field) so we dealt with minimal polynomials. Since the minimal polynomial for an element β must have all the conjugates of β as roots, the product of the minimal polynomials usually exceeds the number $2t$ of roots specified.

The situation is somewhat different with RS codes. With RS codes, we can operate in the bigger field:

Definition 6.15 A RS code is a q^m-ary BCH code of length $n = q^m - 1$.   □

In $GF(q^m)$, the minimal polynomial for any element β is simply $(x - \beta)$. Selecting the $2t$ roots of the generator polynomial as

$$\beta^b, \beta^{b+1}, \ldots, \beta^{b+2t-1},$$

where β is a primitive element in $GF(q^m)$, the generator for a RS code is

$$g(x) = (x - \beta^b)(x - \beta^{b+1}) \cdots (x - \beta^{b+2t-1}).$$

There are no "extra" roots of $g(x)$ included due to conjugates in the minimal polynomials, so the degree of g is exactly equal to $2t$. Thus, $n - k = 2t$ for a RS code. The design distance is $\delta = n - k + 1$.

Example 6.16 Let $n = 7$. We want to design a narrow-sense ($b = 1$) double-error-correcting ($t = 2$) RS code. Let $\beta = \alpha$ be a root of the primitive polynomial $x^3 + x + 1$. The $2t = 4$ consecutive powers of β are β, β^2, β^3, and β^4. The generator polynomial is

$$g(x) = (x - \beta)(x - \beta^2)(x - \beta^3)(x - \beta^4) = x^4 + \beta^3 x^3 + x^2 + \beta x + \beta^3.$$

Note that the coefficients of $g(x)$ are in $GF(8)$, the extension ("big") field. We have designed a $(7, 3)$ code with 8^3 codewords.   □

Example 6.17 Let $n = 2^4 - 1 = 15$ and consider a primitive, narrow-sense, three-error-correcting code over $GF(2^4)$, where the field is constructed modulo of the primitive polynomial $x^4 + x + 1$. Let $\beta = \alpha$ be a primitive element in the field. The code generator has

$$\beta, \beta^2, \beta^3, \beta^4, \beta^5, \beta^6$$

as roots. The generator of the $(15, 9)$ code is

$$g(x) = (x - \beta)(x - \beta^2)(x - \beta^3)(x - \beta^4)(x - \beta^5)(x - \beta^6)$$
$$= \beta^6 + \beta^9 x + \beta^6 x^2 + \beta^4 x^3 + \beta^{14} x^4 + \beta^{10} x^5 + x^6.$$

A $(15, 9)$ code is obtained.   □

Example 6.18 Let $n = 2^8 - 1 = 255$ and consider a primitive, narrow-sense, three-error-correcting code over $GF(2^8)$, where the field is represented using the primitive polynomial $p(x) = 1 + x^2 + x^3 + x^4 + x^8$. Let $\beta = \alpha$ be a primitive element in the field. The generator is

$$g(x) = (x - \beta)(x - \beta^2)(x - \beta^3)(x - \beta^4)(x - \beta\alpha^5)(x - \beta^6)$$
$$= \beta^{21} + \beta^{181} x + \beta^9 x^2 + \beta^{137} x^3 + \beta^2 x^4 + \beta^{167} x^5 + x^6.$$

This gives a $(255, 249)$ code.   □

Codes defined over $GF(256)$, such as this, are frequently of interest in many computer-oriented applications, because every field symbol requires 8 bits — 1 byte — of data.

The remainder of this chapter deals with RS codes obtained via this second construction.

6.2.3 Encoding Reed–Solomon Codes

RS codes may be encoded just as any other cyclic code (provided that the arithmetic is done in the right field). Given a message vector $\mathbf{m} = (m_0, m_1, \ldots, m_{k-1})$ and its corresponding message polynomial $m(x) = m_0 + m_1 x + \cdots + m_{k-1}x^{k-1}$, where each $m_i \in GF(q)$, the systematic encoding process is

$$c(x) = m(x)x^{n-k} - R_{g(x)}[m(x)x^{n-k}]$$

where, as before, $R_{g(x)}[\cdot]$ denotes the operation of taking the remainder after division by $g(x)$.

Typically, the code is over $GF(2^m)$ for some m. The message symbols m_i can then be formed by grabbing m bits of data, then interpreting these as the *vector* representation of the $GF(2^m)$ elements.

Example 6.19 For the code from Example 6.17, the 4-bit data

$$5, 2, 1, 6, 8, 3, 10, 15, 4$$

are to be encoded. The corresponding message polynomial is

$$m(x) = 5 + 2x + x^2 + 6x^3 + 8x^4 + 3x^5 + 10x^6 + 15x^7 + 4x^8.$$

Using the vector to power conversion

$$5 = 0101_2 \leftrightarrow \alpha^8 \quad 2 = 0010_2 \leftrightarrow \alpha \quad 1 = 0001_2 \leftrightarrow 1$$

and so forth, the message polynomial (expressed in power form) is

$$m(x) = \alpha^8 + \alpha x + x^2 + \alpha^5 x^3 + \alpha^3 x^4 + \alpha^4 x^5 + \alpha^9 x^6 + \alpha^{12} x^7 + \alpha^2 x^8.$$

The systematically encoded code polynomial is

$$c(x) = \alpha^8 + \alpha^2 x + \alpha^{14}x^2 + \alpha^3 x^3 + \alpha^5 x^4 + \alpha x^5 + \alpha^8 x^6 + \alpha x^7 + x^8 + \alpha^5 x^9 + \alpha^3 x^{10} + \alpha^4 x^{11}$$
$$+ \alpha^9 x^{12} + \alpha^{12} x^{13} + \alpha^2 x^{14},$$

where the message is explicitly evident.

The following code fragment shows how to reproduce this example using the classes GFNUM2m and polynomialT:

```
int k=9;
int n=15;
GFNUM2m::initgf(4,0x13);   // 1 0011 = d^4+d+1
POLYC(GFNUM2m, m,{5,2,1,6,8,3,10,15,4});   // the message data
polynomialT<GFNUM2m> c;           // code polynomial
//
// ... build the generator g

c = (m<<(n-k)) + (m<<(n-k))% g;          // encode operation: pretty easy!

cout << "message=" << m << endl;
cout << "code=" << c << endl;
```
□

Using groups of m bits as the vector representation of the Galois field element is particularly useful when $m = 8$, since 8 bits of data correspond to 1 byte. Thus, a computer data file can be encoded by simply grabbing k bytes of data, then using those bytes as the coefficients of $m(x)$: no conversion of any sort is necessary (unless you want to display the answer in power form).

6.2.4 MDS Codes and Weight Distributions for RS Codes

We observed in Lemma 6.14 that RS codes are maximum distance separable (MDS), that is, $d_{\min} = n - k + 1$. Being MDS gives sufficient theoretical leverage that the weight distribution for RS codes can be explicitly described. We develop that result through a series of lemmas [[292], p. 318].

Lemma 6.20 *A code C is MDS if and only if every set of $n - k$ columns of its parity check matrix H are linearly independent.*

Proof By Theorem 3.13, a code C contains a code of weight w if and only if w columns of H are linearly dependent. Therefore, C has $d_{\min} = n - k + 1$ if and only if no $n - k$ or fewer columns of H are linearly dependent. □

Lemma 6.21 *If an (n, k) code C is MDS, then so is the $(n, n - k)$ dual code $C^\perp$. That is, $C^\perp$ has $d_{\min} = k + 1$.*

Proof Let $H = \begin{bmatrix} \mathbf{h}_1 & \dots & \mathbf{h}_n \end{bmatrix}$ be an $(n - k) \times n$ parity check matrix for C. Then H is a generator matrix for $C^\perp$. Suppose that for some message vector $\mathbf{m}$ there is a codeword $\mathbf{c} = \mathbf{m}H \in C^\perp$ with weight $\leq k$. Then $\mathbf{c}$ has zero elements in $\geq n - k$ positions. Let the zero elements of $\mathbf{c}$ have indices $\{i_1, i_2, \dots, i_{n-k}\}$. Write

$$H = \begin{bmatrix} \mathbf{h}_1 & \mathbf{h}_2 & \cdots & \mathbf{h}_n \end{bmatrix}.$$

Then the zero elements of $\mathbf{c}$ are obtained from

$$\mathbf{0} = \mathbf{m} \begin{bmatrix} h_{i_1} & h_{i_2} & \cdots & h_{i_{n-k}} \end{bmatrix} \stackrel{\triangle}{=} \mathbf{m}\tilde{H}.$$

We thus have a $(n - k) \times (n - k)$ submatrix $\tilde{H}$ of H which is singular. Since the row-rank of a matrix is equal to the column-rank, there must therefore be $n - k$ columns of H which are linearly dependent. This contradicts the fact that C has minimum distance $n - k + 1$, so the minimal weight codeword of $C^\perp$ must be $d_{\min} > k$. By the Singleton bound, we must have $d_{\min} = k + 1$. □

Lemma 6.22 *Every k columns of a generator matrix G of an MDS are linearly independent. (This means that any k symbols of the codeword may be taken as systematically encoded message symbols.)*

Proof Let G be the $k \times n$ generator matrix of an MDS code C. Then G is the parity check matrix for $C^\perp$. Since $C^\perp$ has minimum distance $k + 1$, any combination of k rows of G must be linearly independent. Thus, any $k \times k$ submatrix of G must be nonsingular. So by row reduction on G, any $k \times k$ submatrix can be reduced to the $k \times k$ identity, so that the corresponding k message symbols can appear explicitly. □

Lemma 6.23 *The number of codewords in a q-ary (n, k) MDS code C of weight $d_{\min} = n - k + 1$ is $A_{n-k+1} = (q - 1)\binom{n}{n-k+1}$.*

Proof By Lemma 6.22, select an arbitrary set of k coordinates as message positions for a message $\mathbf{m}$ of weight 1. The systematic encoding for these coordinates thus has $k - 1$ zeros in it. Since the minimum distance of the code is $n - k + 1$, all the $n - k$ parity symbols therefore must be nonzero. Since there are $\binom{n}{n-k+1} = \binom{n}{k-1}$ different ways of selecting the zero coordinates and $q - 1$ ways of selecting the nonzero message symbol,

$$A_{n-k+1} = (q - 1)\binom{n}{k-1}.$$
□

Lemma 6.24 *(Weight distribution for MDS codes) The number of codewords of weight j in a q-ary (n, k) MDS code is*

$$A_j = \binom{n}{j} (q-1) \sum_{i=0}^{j-d_{\min}} (-1)^i \binom{j-1}{i} q^{j-d_{\min}-i}. \qquad (6.3)$$

reedsolwt.m

Proof Using (3.26) from Exercise 3.16, generalized to q-ary codes we have

$$\sum_{i=0}^{n-j} \binom{n-i}{j} A_i = q^{k-j} \sum_{i=0}^{j} \binom{n-i}{j-i} B_i, \quad j = 0, 1, \ldots, n.$$

Since $A_i = 0$ for $i = 1, \ldots, n-k$ and $B_i = 0$ for $i = 1, \ldots, k$, this becomes

$$\binom{n}{j} + \sum_{i=n-k+1}^{n-j} \binom{n-i}{j} A_i = q^{k-j} \binom{n}{j}, \quad j = 0, 1, \ldots, k-1.$$

Setting $j = k - 1$, we obtain

$$A_{n-k+1} = (q-1) \binom{n}{k-1},$$

as in Lemma 6.23. Setting $j = k - 2$, we obtain

$$\binom{k-1}{k-2} A_{n-k+1} + A_{n-k+2} = \binom{n}{k-2} (q^2 - 1),$$

from which

$$A_{n-k+2} = \binom{n}{k-2} [(q^2 - 1) - (n-k+2)(q-1)].$$

Proceeding similarly, it may be verified that

$$A_{n-k+r} = \binom{n}{k-r} \sum_{j=0}^{r-1} (-1)^j \binom{n-k+r}{j} (q^{r-j} - 1).$$

Letting $j = n - k + r$, it is straightforward from here to verify (6.3). □

Complete weight enumerators for RS codes are described in [47].

6.3 Decoding BCH and RS Codes: The General Outline

There are many algorithms which have been developed for decoding BCH or RS codes. In this chapter, we introduce a general approach. In Chapter 7, we present other approaches which follow a different outline.

The algebraic decoding BCH or RS codes has the following general steps:

1. Computation of the *syndrome*.

2. Determination of an *error locator polynomial*, whose roots provide an indication of where the errors are. There are many different ways of finding the locator polynomial. These methods include Peterson's algorithm for BCH codes, the Berlekamp–Massey algorithm for BCH codes; the Peterson–Gorenstein–Zierler algorithm for RS codes, the Berlekamp–Massey algorithm for RS codes, and the Euclidean algorithm. In addition, there are techniques based upon Galois-field Fourier transforms, and many other methods not described in this book.

3. Finding the roots of the error locator polynomial. This is usually done using the *Chien search*, which is an exhaustive search over all the elements in the field.

4. For RS codes or nonbinary BCH codes, the error *values* must also be determined. This is typically accomplished using Forney's algorithm.

6.3.1 Computation of the Syndrome

Let $g(x)$ be the generator polynomial for a BCH or RS code, with roots $\beta^b, \beta^{b+1}, \ldots, \beta^{b+2t-1}$, where β is an element of order n. Since

$$g(\beta^b) = g(\beta^{b+1}) = \cdots = g(\beta^{b+2t-1}) = 0$$

it follows that a codeword $\mathbf{c} = (c_0, \ldots, c_{n-1})$ with polynomial $c(x) = c_0 + \cdots + c_{n-1}x^{n-1}$ has

$$c(\beta^b) = \cdots = c(\beta^{b+2t-1}) = 0.$$

For a received polynomial $r(x) = c(x) + e(x)$, we compute

$$S_j = r(\beta^j) = c(\beta^j) + e(\beta^j) = e(\beta^j), \quad j = b, b+1, \ldots, b+2t-1.$$

The values $S_b, S_{b+1}, \ldots, S_{b+2t-1}$ are called the *syndromes* of the received data.

Suppose that $\mathbf{r}$ has v errors in it which are at locations $i_1, i_2, \ldots, i_v$, with corresponding error values in these locations $e_{i_j} \neq 0$. The errors can be represented by the error polynomial

$$e(x) = \sum_{k=0}^{n-1} e_k x^k = \sum_{\ell=1}^{v} e_{i_\ell} x^{i_\ell}.$$

Then

$$S_j = e(\beta^j) = \sum_{\ell=1}^{v} e_{i_\ell} (\beta^j)^{i_\ell} = \sum_{\ell=1}^{v} e_{i_\ell} (\beta^{i_\ell})^j, \quad j = b, b+1, \ldots, b+2t-1.$$

Let

$$X_\ell = \beta^{i_\ell}.$$

Then we can write

$$S_j = \sum_{\ell=1}^{v} e_{i_\ell} X_\ell^j \quad j = b, b+1, \ldots, b+2t-1. \tag{6.4}$$

If we know the X_ℓ, then we know the location of the errors. For example, suppose we know that $X_1 = \beta^4$. Then it is known that $i_1 = 4$, that is, the error is in the received digit r_4. We thus call the X_ℓ the **error locators**. In practice, the number of errors v is not known in advance, so this is another unknown in the decoding problem.

In a field of characteristic q and for a BCH code where $e_{i_\ell} \in GF(q)$,

$$(S_j)^q = \sum_{\ell=1}^{v} (e_{i_\ell}(X_\ell^j))^q = \sum_{\ell=1}^{v} e_{i_\ell}^q X_\ell^{jq} = \sum_{\ell=1}^{v} e_{i_\ell} X_\ell^{jq} = S_{jq}. \tag{6.5}$$

For *binary codes* we have $e_{i_\ell} = 1$ (that is, if there is an error, it must be 1), so

$$S_j = \sum_{\ell=1}^{v} X_\ell^j \quad j = b, b+1, \ldots, b+2t-1. \tag{6.6}$$

For binary codes (i.e., binary BCH codes), this means that once the error locations are known, no further computations are necessary to determine the error values. However, looking ahead to RS decoding, we'll set the problem up first including the error values. For binary BCH codes, (6.5) becomes $S_j = S_{2j}$.

6.3.2 The Error Locator Polynomial

The next stage in the decoding problem is to determine the error locators X_ℓ given the syndromes S_j. The problem is stated as follows: Given $S_j, j = b, b + 1, \ldots, b + 2t - 1$, determine the number of errors v and the error locators $X_\ell, \ell = 1, 2, \ldots, v$.

The problem can be set up as an algebra problem using (6.4) as

$$S_b = e_{i_1} X_1^b + e_{i_2} X_2^b + \cdots + e_{i_v} X_v^b$$
$$S_{b+1} = e_{i_1} X_1^{b+1} + e_{i_2} X_2^{b+1} + \cdots + e_{i_v} X_v^{b+1}$$
$$\vdots$$
$$S_{b+2t-1} = e_{i_1} X_1^{b+2t-1} + e_{i_2} X_2^{b+2t-1} + \cdots + e_{i_v} X_v^{b+2t-1}.$$

Rather than attacking this system of nonlinear algebraic equations directly, a new polynomial is introduced, the *error locator polynomial*, which casts the problem in a different, more tractable, setting. The error locator polynomial is defined as

$$\Lambda(x) = \prod_{\ell=1}^{v} (1 - X_\ell x) = \Lambda_v x^v + \Lambda_{v-1} x^{v-1} + \cdots + \Lambda_1 x + \Lambda_0$$
$$= \sum_{i=0}^{v} \Lambda_i x^i, \tag{6.7}$$

where $\Lambda_0 = 1$. By this definition, if x is the reciprocal of any of the error locators, that is, $x = X_\ell^{-1}$, then $\Lambda(x) = 0$. The roots of the error locator polynomial are at the *reciprocals* (in the field arithmetic) of the error locators.

Example 6.25 Suppose in $GF(16)$ (with β primitive) we find that $x = \beta^4$ is a root of an error locator polynomial $\Lambda(x)$. Then the error locator is $(\beta^4)^{-1} = \beta^{11}$, indicating that there is an error in r_{11}. □

Once the error locator polynomial is determined, then the error locations can be found by finding its roots.

6.3.3 Chien Search

Algorithms for solving for the error locator polynomial given the syndromes are discussed in sections below. Assume for the moment that we actually have the error locator polynomial. The next step is to find the roots of the error locator polynomial. The field of interest is $GF(q^m)$. Being a finite field, we can examine every element of the field to determine if it is a root. (Other root-finding methods over continuous fields, such as Newton's method, cannot work in the usual way in a finite field.) There exist other ways of factoring polynomials over finite fields (see, e.g., [33, 472]), but for the fields usually used for error-correction codes and the number of roots involved, the Chien search may be the most efficient. The Chien search is essentially a way of organizing an exhaustive search over every nonzero element of a finite field. In digital hardware, it can evaluate at a finite field value every tick of the clock.

Suppose, for example, that $v = 3$ and the error locator polynomial is

$$\Lambda(x) = 1 + \Lambda_1 x + \Lambda_2 x^2 + \Lambda_3 x^3.$$

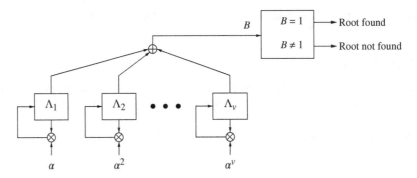

Figure 6.1: Chien search algorithm.

Let α be primitive in $GF(q^m)$. We evaluate $\Lambda(x)$ at each nonzero elements $x = \alpha^0 = 1, x = \alpha, \ldots,$ $x = \alpha^{q^m-1}$ in succession. This gives us the following:

$$\Lambda(1) = 1 + \Lambda_1(1) + \Lambda_2(1)^2 + \Lambda_3(1)^3$$

$$\Lambda(\beta) = 1 + \Lambda_1 \alpha + \Lambda_2 \alpha^2 + \Lambda_3 \alpha^3$$

$$\Lambda(\alpha^2) = 1 + \Lambda_1 \alpha^2 + \Lambda_2(\alpha^2)^2 + \Lambda_3(\alpha^2)^3$$

$$\vdots$$

$$\Lambda(\alpha^{q^m-1}) = 1 + \Lambda_1 \alpha^{q^m-1} + \Lambda_2(\alpha^{q^m-1})^2 + \Lambda_3(\alpha^{q^m-1})^3.$$

The computations in this sequence can be efficiently embodied in the hardware depicted in Figure 6.1. A set of v registers are loaded initially with the coefficients of the error locator polynomial, $\Lambda_1, \Lambda_2, \ldots, \Lambda_v$. The initial output is the sum

$$B = \sum_{j=1}^{v} \Lambda_j = \Lambda(x) - 1|_{x=1}.$$

If $B = 1$, then an error has been located (since then $\Lambda(x) = 0$). At the next stage, each register is multiplied by $\alpha^j, j = 1, 2, \ldots, v$, so the register contents are $\Lambda_1 \alpha, \Lambda_2 \alpha^2, \ldots, \Lambda_v \alpha^v$. The output is the sum

$$B = \sum_{j=1}^{v} \Lambda_j \alpha^j = \Lambda(x) - 1|_{x=\beta}.$$

The registers are multiplied again by successive powers of α, resulting in evaluation at β^2. This procedure continues until $\Lambda(x)$ has been evaluated at $q^m - 1$ powers of β.

If v roots are found, then these roots determine the error locations. If the roots are not distinct or there are not v roots found by the Chien search (i.e., they would lie in some extension field), then the received word is not within distance t of any codeword. The corresponding error pattern is said to be an uncorrectable error pattern. The decoder algorithm can check for this condition and declare a **decoder failure** if v roots are not found.

6.4 Finding the Error Locator Polynomial

Let us return to the question of finding the error locator polynomial using the syndromes. Take the definition of the error locator polynomial (6.7) and multiply the equation by $e_{i_\ell} X_\ell^j$:

$$\Lambda(x) e_{i_\ell} X_\ell^j = \sum_{i=0}^{v} \Lambda_i x^i e_{i_\ell} X_\ell^j,$$

then evaluate at $x = X_\ell^{-1}$ (resulting in 0 on the left) and sum over $\ell = 1, 2, \ldots, v$. This results in the equation

$$0 = \sum_{\ell=1}^{v} \sum_{i=0}^{v} \Lambda_i e_{i_\ell} X_\ell^{j-i} = \sum_{i=0}^{v} \Lambda_i \sum_{\ell=1}^{v} e_{i_\ell} X_\ell^{j-i}.$$

From (6.4), the inner sum is S_{j-i}, resulting in

$$\sum_{i=0}^{v} \Lambda_i S_{j-i} = 0, \quad \Lambda_0 = 1. \tag{6.8}$$

This equation is valid for j such that $j - i$ falls in the range $b, b+1, \ldots, b + 2t - 1$. Recalling that $\Lambda_0 = 1$, we can write

$$S_j = -\sum_{i=1}^{v} \Lambda_i S_{j-i}, \quad j = b + v, b + v + 1, \ldots, b + 2t - 1. \tag{6.9}$$

This has produced a *linear* relationship between the syndromes and the coefficients of the error locator polynomial.

Equation (6.9) can be stacked up in matrix form as

$$\begin{bmatrix} S_{b+v-1} & \cdots & S_{b+1} & S_b \\ S_{b+v} & \cdots & S_{b+2} & S_{b+1} \\ S_{b+v+1} & \cdots & S_{b+3} & S_{b+2} \\ \vdots & & & \\ S_{b+2t-2} & \cdots & S_{b+2t-v-1} & S_{b+2t-v} \end{bmatrix} \begin{bmatrix} \Lambda_1 \\ \vdots \\ \Lambda_{v-1} \\ \Lambda_v \end{bmatrix} = - \begin{bmatrix} S_{b+v} \\ S_{b+v+1} \\ S_{b+v+2} \\ \vdots \\ S_{b+2t-1} \end{bmatrix} \tag{6.10}$$

The matrix is a $(2t - v) \times v$ matrix. If $t \geq v$ (that is, the error-correction design is greater than or equal to the number of errors), then there are enough equations to solve uniquely for $\Lambda_1, \ldots, \Lambda_v$. The matrix is a Toeplitz matrix (constant on the diagonals). Let Mv be the $v \times v$ Toeplitz submatrix of the form in (6.10).

At this point it is convenient to **relabel the indices of the syndromes**. In this indexing, the first syndrome, obtained by evaluating at $S_b = r(\beta^b)$, is *called S_1*. The second syndrome $S_{b+1} = r(\beta^{b+1})$ is *called S_2*, and so forth. This is merely a relabeling and does not change the functional relationship between the syndromes. The syndromes

$$S_b, S_{b+1}, \ldots, S_{b+2t-1}$$

are thus written in relabeled form as

$$S_1, S_2, \ldots, S_{2t},$$

(that is, as if $b = 1$). This indicates that the same linear relationship (6.9) applies regardless of whether a code is narrow sense or not. Under this relabeling, (6.9) becomes

$$S_j = -\sum_{i=1}^{v} \Lambda_i S_{j-i} \quad j = v + 1, \ldots, 2t \quad \text{(reindexed)}.$$

(This labeling is closer to how the data would be represented in a computer representation.) Similarly, under the relabeling, (6.10) becomes

$$\begin{bmatrix} S_v & \cdots & S_2 & S_1 \\ S_{1+v} & \cdots & S_3 & S_2 \\ S_{2+v} & \cdots & S_4 & S_3 \\ \vdots & & & \\ S_{2t-1} & \cdots & S_{2t-v+1} & S_{2t-v} \end{bmatrix} \begin{bmatrix} \Lambda_1 \\ \vdots \\ \Lambda_{v-1} \\ \Lambda_v \end{bmatrix} = - \begin{bmatrix} S_{1+v} \\ S_{2+v} \\ \vdots \\ S_{2t} \end{bmatrix} \quad \text{(reindexed)}.$$

The number of unknowns v is not known in advance and so must be determined as part of the of the solution process. One way to accomplish this is the Peterson–Gorenstein–Zierler decoder, which operates as follows:

1. Set $v = t$.

2. Form M_v and compute the determinant $\det(M_v)$ to determine if M_v is invertible. If it is not invertible, set $v \leftarrow v - 1$ and repeat this step.

3. If M_v is invertible, solve for the coefficients $\Lambda_1, \Lambda_2, \ldots, \Lambda_v$.

6.4.1 Simplifications for Narrow-Sense Binary Codes; Peterson's Algorithm

We consider here the case narrow-sense BCH codes. The syndrome equation (6.6) becomes

$$
\begin{aligned}
S_1 &= X_1 + X_2 + \cdots + X_v \\
S_2 &= X_1^2 + X_2^2 + \cdots + X_v^2 \\
&\;\vdots \\
S_{2t} &= X_1^{2t} + X_2^{2t} + \cdots + X_v^{2t}.
\end{aligned}
\tag{6.11}
$$

The equations are said to be *power-sum symmetric functions*. This gives us $2t$ equations in the v unknown error locators.

There are other relationships between the syndromes and the coefficients of the error-location polynomial. To develop some insight, we consider various cases:

- $v = 1$: $\Lambda(x) = (1 - X_1 x) = 1 + \Lambda_1 x$ so $\Lambda_1 = -X_1$.

- $v = 2$: $\Lambda(x) = (1 - X_1 x)(1 - X_2 x) = 1 + x(-X_1 - X_2) + X_1 X_2 x^2 = 1 + \Lambda_1 x + \Lambda_2 x^2$ so

$$
\Lambda_1 = -(X_1 + X_2) \quad \Lambda_2 = X_1 X_2.
$$

- $v = 3$: $\Lambda(x) = (1 - X_1 x)(1 - X_2 x)(1 - X_3 x) = 1 + x(-X_1 - X_2 - X_3) + x^2(X_1 X_2 + X_1 X_3 + X_2 X_3) + x^3(-X_1 X_2 X_3)$ so

$$
\Lambda_1 = -(X_1 + X_2 + X_3) \quad \Lambda_2 = X_1 X_2 + X_1 X_3 + X_2 X_3 \quad \Lambda_3 = -X_1 X_2 X_3.
$$

In general, for an error locator polynomial of degree v,

$$
\begin{aligned}
\Lambda_0 &= 1 \\
\Lambda_1 &= -\sum_{i=1}^{v} X_i = X_1 + X_2 + \cdots + X_v \\
\Lambda_2 &= \sum_{i<j} X_i X_j = X_1 X_2 + X_1 X_3 + \cdots + X_1 X_v + \cdots + X_{v-1} X_v \\
\Lambda_3 &= -\sum_{i<j<k} X_i X_j X_k = X_1 X_2 X_3 + X_1 X_2 X_4 + \cdots + X_{v-2} X_{v-1} X_v \\
&\;\vdots \\
\Lambda_v &= (-1)^v X_1 X_2 \cdots X_v.
\end{aligned}
\tag{6.12}
$$

Equations of the form (6.12) are referred to as the elementary symmetric functions of the error locators (so called because if the error locators $\{X_i\}$ are permuted, the same values are computed).

The following theorem provides additional relationships between the syndromes and the coefficients of the error-locating polynomial.

Theorem 6.26 *The syndromes (6.11) and the coefficients of the error locator polynomial are related by*

$$
\begin{aligned}
S_k + \Lambda_1 S_{k-1} + \cdots + \Lambda_{k-1} S_1 + k\Lambda_k &= 0 \quad 1 \leq k \leq v \\
S_k + \Lambda_1 S_{k-1} + \cdots + \Lambda_{v-1} S_{k-v+1} + \Lambda_v S_{k-v} &= 0 \quad k > v.
\end{aligned}
\tag{6.13}
$$

(The second equation is the same as (6.9).) That is,

$$
\begin{aligned}
k = 1 &: \ S_1 + \Lambda_1 = 0 \\
k = 2 &: \ S_2 + \Lambda_1 S_1 + 2\Lambda_2 = 0 \\
&\ \vdots \\
k = v &: \ S_v + \Lambda_1 S_{v-1} + \Lambda_2 S_{v-2} + \cdots + \Lambda_{v-1} S_1 + v\Lambda_v = 0 \\
k = v+1 &: \ S_{v+1} + \Lambda_1 S_v + \Lambda_2 S_{v-1} + \cdots + \Lambda_v S_1 = 0 \\
k = v+2 &: \ S_{v+2} + \Lambda_1 S_{v+1} + \Lambda_2 S_v + \cdots + \Lambda_v S_2 = 0 \\
&\ \vdots \\
k = 2t &: \ S_{2t} + \Lambda_1 S_{2t-1} + \Lambda_2 S_{2t-2} + \cdots + \Lambda_v S_{2t-v} = 0.
\end{aligned}
\tag{6.14}
$$

The theorem is proved in Appendix 6.A.

Because of (6.5) with $q = 2$, the even-numbered equations in (6.14) do not convey new information. For binary codes, Newton's identities are subject to further simplifications. $kS_j = 0$ if k is even and $kS_j = S_j$ if k is odd. The odd-numbered equations can be written as

$$
S_1 + \Lambda_1 = 0
$$

$$
S_3 + \Lambda_1 S_2 + \Lambda_2 S_1 + \Lambda_3 = 0
$$

$$
\vdots
$$

$$
S_{2t-1} + \Lambda_1 S_{2t-2} + \cdots + \Lambda_t S_{t-1} = 0,
$$

which can be expressed in the matrix equation

$$
\begin{bmatrix}
1 & 0 & 0 & 0 & \cdots & 0 & 0 \\
S_2 & S_1 & 1 & 0 & \cdots & 0 & 0 \\
S_4 & S_3 & S_2 & S_1 & \cdots & 0 & 0 \\
\vdots & & & & & & \\
S_{2t-4} & S_{2t-5} & S_{2t-6} & S_{2t-7} & \cdots & S_{t-2} & S_{t-3} \\
S_{2t-2} & S_{2t-3} & S_{2t-4} & S_{2t-5} & \cdots & S_t & S_{t-1}
\end{bmatrix}
\begin{bmatrix}
\Lambda_1 \\ \Lambda_2 \\ \vdots \\ \Lambda_t
\end{bmatrix}
=
\begin{bmatrix}
-S_1 \\ -S_3 \\ \vdots \\ -S_{2t-1}
\end{bmatrix},
\tag{6.15}
$$

or $A\Lambda = -\mathbf{S}$. If there are in fact t errors, the matrix is invertible, as we can determine by computing the determinant of the matrix. If it is not invertible, remove two rows and columns, then try again. Once Λ is found, we find its roots. This matrix-based approach to solving for the error locator polynomial is called *Peterson's algorithm* for decoding binary BCH codes.

For small numbers of errors, we can provide explicit formulas for the coefficients of $\Lambda(x)$, which may be more efficient than the more generalized solutions suggested below [307].

1-error correction

$\Lambda_1 = S_1$.

2-error correction

$\Lambda_1 = S_1, \Lambda_2 = (S_3 + S_1^3)/(S_1)$.

3-error correction

$\Lambda_1 = S_1, \Lambda_2 = (S_1^2 S_3 + S_5)/(S_1^3 + S_3), \Lambda_3 = (S_1^3 + S_3) + S_1 \Lambda_2$.

4 error correction

$$
\Lambda_1 = S_1, \quad \Lambda_2 = \frac{S_1(S_7 + S_1^7) + S_3(S_1^5 + S_5)}{S_3(S_1^3 + S_3) + S_1(S_1^5 + S_5)},
$$

$$\Lambda_3 = S_1^3 + S_3 + S_1\Lambda_2, \quad \Lambda_4 = \frac{(S_5 + S_1^2 S_3) + (S_1^3 + S_3)\Lambda_2}{S_1}.$$

5-error correction

$\Lambda_1 = S_1,$

$$\Lambda_2 = \frac{(S_1^3 + S_3)[(S_1^9 + S_9) + S_1^4(S_5 + S_1^2 S_3) + S_3^2(S_1^3 + S_3)] + (S_1^5 + S_5)(S_7 + S_1^7) + S_1(S_3^2 + S_1 S_5)}{(S_1^3 + S_3)[(S_7 + S_1^7) + S_1 S_3(S_1^3 + S_3)] + (S_5 + S_1^2 S_3)(S_1^5 + S_5)}$$

$$\Lambda_3 = (S_1^3 + S_3) + S_1\Lambda_2$$

$$\Lambda_4 = \frac{(S_1^9 + S_9) + S_3^2(S_1^3 + S_3) + S_1^4(S_5 + S_1^2 S_3) + \Lambda_2[(s_7 + S_1^7) + S_1 S_3(S_1^3 + S_3)]}{S_1^5 + S_5}$$

$$\Lambda_5 = S_5 + S_1^2 S_3 + S_1 S_4 + \Lambda_2(S_1^3 + S_3).$$

For large numbers of errors, Peterson's algorithm is quite complex. Computing the sequence of determinants to find the number of errors is costly. So is solving the system of equations once the number of errors is determined. We therefore look for more efficient techniques.

Example 6.27   Consider the $(31, 21)$ two-error-correcting code introduced in Example 6.3, with generator $g(x) = x^{10} + x^9 + x^8 + x^6 + x^5 + x^3 + 1$ having roots at $\alpha, \alpha^2, \alpha^3,$ and α^4. Suppose the codeword

$$c(x) = 1 + x^3 + x^4 + x^5 + x^6 + x^8 + x^{10} + x^{14} + x^{16} + x^{17} + x^{18} + x^{20} + x^{21} + x^{23} + x^{24} + x^{25}$$

is transmitted and

$$r(x) = 1 + x^3 + x^5 + x^6 + x^8 + x^{10} + x^{14} + x^{16} + x^{17} + x^{20} + x^{21} + x^{23} + x^{24} + x^{25}$$

is received. The syndromes are

$$S_1 = r(\alpha) = \alpha^{17} \quad S_2 = r(\alpha^2) = \alpha^3 \quad S_3 = r(\alpha^3) = 1 \quad S_4 = r(\alpha^4) = \alpha^6.$$

Using the results above, we find

$$\Lambda_1 = S_1 = \alpha^{17} \quad \Lambda_2 = \frac{S_3 + S_1^3}{S_1} = \alpha^{22},$$

so that $\Lambda(x) = 1 + \alpha^{17}x + \alpha^{22}x^2$. The roots of this polynomial (found, e.g., using the Chien search) are at $x = \alpha^{13}$ and $x = \alpha^{27}$. Specifically, we could write

$$\Lambda(x) = \alpha^{22}(x + \alpha^{13})(x + \alpha^{27}).$$

The *reciprocals* of the roots are at α^{18} and α^4, so that the errors in transmission occurred at locations 4 and 18,

$$e(x) = x^4 + x^{18}.$$

It can be seen that $r(x) + e(x)$ is in fact equal to the transmitted codeword.   □

6.4.2 Berlekamp–Massey Algorithm

While Peterson's method involves straightforward linear algebra, it is computationally complex in general. Starting with the matrix A in (6.15), it is examined to see if it is singular. This involves either attempting to solve the equations (e.g., by Gaussian elimination or equivalent), or computing the determinant to see if the solution can be found. If A is singular, then the last two rows and columns are dropped to form a new A matrix. Then the attempted solution must be *recomputed* starting over with the new A matrix.

The Berlekamp–Massey algorithm takes a different approach. Starting with a *small* problem, it works up to increasingly longer problems until it obtains an overall solution. However, at each stage it is able to reuse information it has already learned. Whereas as the computational complexity of the Peterson method is $O(v^3)$, the computational complexity of the Berlekamp–Massey algorithm is $O(v^2)$.

We observed in (6.9) that

$$S_j = -\sum_{i=1}^{v} \Lambda_i S_{j-i}, \quad j = v+1, v+2, \ldots, 2t. \tag{6.16}$$

(The syndromes are reindexed so the indices are in the range $1, 2, \ldots, 2t$ if the code is not narrow sense.) This formula describes the output of a linear feedback shift register (LFSR) with coefficients $\Lambda_1, \Lambda_2, \ldots, \Lambda_v$ and an initial fill of $S_1, S_2, \ldots, S_v$. In order for this formula to work, we must find the Λ_j coefficients in such a way that the LFSR generates the known sequence of syndromes $S_1, S_2, \ldots, S_{2t}$. Furthermore, by the maximum likelihood principle, the number of errors v determined must be the smallest that is consistent with the observed syndromes. We therefore want to determine the *shortest* such LFSR that produces the syndrome sequence $S_1, S_2, \ldots, S_{2t}$.

In the Berlekamp–Massey algorithm, we build the LFSR that produces the entire sequence $\{S_1, S_2, \ldots, S_{2t}\}$ by successively modifying an existing LFSR, if necessary, to produce increasingly longer sequences. We start with an LFSR that could produce S_1. We determine if that LFSR could also produce the sequence $\{S_1, S_2\}$; if it can, then no modifications are necessary. If the sequence cannot be produced using the current LFSR configuration, we determine a new LFSR that can produce the longer sequence. Proceeding inductively in this way, we start from an LFSR capable of producing the sequence $\{S_1, S_2, \ldots, S_{k-1}\}$ and modify it, if necessary, so that it can also produce the sequence $\{S_1, S_2, \ldots, S_k\}$. At each stage, the modifications to the LFSR are accomplished so that the LFSR is the shortest possible. By this means, after completion of the algorithm the shortest LFSR has been found that is able to produce $\{S_1, S_2, \ldots, S_{2t}\}$; its coefficients correspond to the error locator polynomial $\Lambda(x)$ of *smallest* degree.

Since we build up the LFSR using information from prior computations, we need a notation to represent the $\Lambda(x)$ used at different stages of the algorithm. Let L_k denote the length of the LFSR produced at stage k of the algorithm. Let

$$\Lambda^{[k]}(x) = 1 + \Lambda_1^{[k]} x + \cdots + \Lambda_{L_k}^{[k]} x^{L_k}$$

be the *connection polynomial* at stage k, indicating the connections for the LFSR capable of producing the output sequence $\{S_1, S_2, \ldots, S_k\}$. That is,

$$S_j = -\sum_{i=1}^{L_k} \Lambda_i^{[k]} S_{j-i} \quad j = L_k + 1, \ldots, k. \tag{6.17}$$

Note: It is important to realize that some of the coefficients in $\Lambda^{[k]}(x)$ may be zero, so that L_k may be different from the degree of $\Lambda^{[k]}(x)$. In realizations which use polynomial arithmetic, it is important to keep in mind what the length is as well as the degree.

At some intermediate step, suppose we have a connection polynomial $\Lambda^{[k-1]}(x)$ of length L_{k-1} that produces $\{S_1, S_2, \ldots, S_{k-1}\}$ for some $k - 1 < 2t$. We check if this connection polynomial also produces

S_k by computing the output

$$\hat{S}_k = -\sum_{i=1}^{L_{k-1}} \Lambda_i^{[k-1]} S_{k-i}.$$

If $\hat{S}_k$ is equal to S_k, then there is no need to update the LFSR, so $\Lambda^{[k]}(x) = \Lambda^{[k-1]}(x)$ and $L_k = L_{k-1}$. Otherwise, there is some nonzero *discrepancy* associated with $\Lambda^{[k-1]}(x)$,

$$d_k = S_k - \hat{S}_k = S_k + \sum_{i=1}^{L_{k-1}} \Lambda_i^{[k-1]} S_{k-i} = \sum_{i=0}^{L_{k-1}} \Lambda_i^{[k-1]} S_{k-i}. \tag{6.18}$$

In this case, we update the connection polynomial using the formula

$$\boxed{\Lambda^{[k]}(x) = \Lambda^{[k-1]}(x) + Ax^\ell \Lambda^{[m-1]}(x),} \tag{6.19}$$

where A is some element in the field, ℓ is an integer, and $\Lambda^{[m-1]}(x)$ is one of the prior connection polynomials produced by our process associated with nonzero discrepancy d_m. (Initialization of this inductive process is discussed in the proof of Theorem 6.29.) Using this new connection polynomial, we compute the new discrepancy, denoted by d_k', as

$$
\begin{aligned}
d_k' &= \sum_{i=0}^{L_k} \Lambda_i^{[k]} S_{k-i} \\
&= \sum_{i=0}^{L_{k-1}} \Lambda_i^{[k-1]} S_{k-i} + A \sum_{i=0}^{L_{m-1}} \Lambda_i^{[m-1]} S_{k-i-\ell}.
\end{aligned} \tag{6.20}
$$

Now, let $\ell = k - m$. Then, by comparison with the definition of the discrepancy in (6.18), the second summation gives

$$A \sum_{i=0}^{L_{m-1}} \Lambda_i^{[m-1]} S_{m-i} = A d_m.$$

Thus, if we choose $A = -d_m^{-1} d_k$, then the summation in (6.20) gives

$$d_k' = d_k - d_m^{-1} d_k d_m = 0.$$

So the new connection polynomial produces the sequence $\{S_1, S_2, \ldots, S_k\}$ with no discrepancy.

6.4.3 Characterization of LFSR Length in Massey's Algorithm

The update in (6.19) is, in fact, the heart of Massey's algorithm. If all we need is an algorithm to find a connection polynomial, no further analysis is necessary. However, the problem was to find the *shortest* LFSR producing a given sequence. We have produced a means of finding an LFSR, but have no indication yet that it is the shortest. Establishing this requires some additional effort in the form of two theorems.

Theorem 6.28 *Suppose that an LFSR with connection polynomial $\Lambda^{[k-1]}(x)$ of length L_{k-1} produces the sequence $\{S_1, S_2, \ldots, S_{k-1}\}$, but not the sequence $\{S_1, S_2, \ldots, S_k\}$. Then any connection polynomial that produces the latter sequence must have a length L_k satisfying*

$$L_k \geq k - L_{k-1}.$$

Proof The theorem is only of practical interest if $L_{k-1} < k - 1$; otherwise, it is trivial to produce the sequence. Let us take, then, $L_{k-1} < k - 1$. Let

$$\Lambda^{[k-1]}(x) = 1 + \Lambda_1^{[k-1]}x + \cdots + \Lambda_{L_{k-1}}^{[k-1]}x^{L_{k-1}}$$

represent the connection polynomial which produces $\{S_1, \ldots, S_{k-1}\}$ and let

$$\Lambda^{[k]}(x) = 1 + \Lambda_1^{[k]}x + \cdots + \Lambda_{L_k}^{[k]}x^{L_k}$$

denote the connection polynomial which produces $\{S_1, S_2, \ldots, S_k\}$. Now we do a proof by contradiction. Assume (contrary to the theorem) that

$$L_k \leq k - 1 - L_{k-1}. \tag{6.21}$$

From the definitions of the connection polynomials, we observe that

$$-\sum_{i=1}^{L_{k-1}} \Lambda_i^{[k-1]} S_{j-i} \begin{cases} = S_j & j = L_{k-1} + 1, \ L_{k-1} + 2, \ldots, k - 1 \\ \neq S_k & j = k \end{cases} \tag{6.22}$$

and

$$-\sum_{i=1}^{L_k} \Lambda_i^{[k]} S_{j-i} = S_j \quad j = L_k + 1, \ L_k + 2, \ldots, k. \tag{6.23}$$

In particular, from (6.23), we have

$$S_k = -\sum_{i=1}^{L_k} \Lambda_i^{[k]} S_{k-i}. \tag{6.24}$$

The values of S_i involved in this summation range from S_{k-1} to S_{k-L_k}. The indices of these values form a set $\{k - L_k, k - L_k + 1, \ldots, k - 1\}$. By the (contrary) assumption made in (6.21), we have $k - L_k \geq L_{k-1} + 1$, so that the set of indices $\{k - L_k, k - L_k + 1, \ldots, k - 1\}$ are a subset of the set of indices $\{L_{k-1} + 1, L_{k-1} + 2, \ldots, k - 1\}$ appearing in (6.22). Thus, each S_{k-i} appearing on the right-hand side of (6.24) can be replaced by the summation expression from (6.22) and we can write

$$S_k = -\sum_{i=1}^{L_k} \Lambda_i^{[k]} S_{k-i} = \sum_{i=1}^{L_k} \Lambda_i^{[k]} \sum_{j=1}^{L_{k-1}} \Lambda_j^{[k-1]} S_{k-i-j}.$$

Interchanging the order of summation, we have

$$S_k = \sum_{j=1}^{L_{k-1}} \Lambda_j^{[k-1]} \sum_{i=1}^{L_k} \Lambda_i^{[k]} S_{k-i-j}. \tag{6.25}$$

Now setting $j = k$ in (6.22), we obtain

$$S_k \neq -\sum_{i=1}^{L_{k-1}} \Lambda_i^{[k-1]} S_{k-i}. \tag{6.26}$$

In this summation the indices of S form the set $\{k - L_{k-1}, \ldots, k - 1\}$. By the (contrary) assumption (6.21), $L_k + 1 \leq k - L_{k-1}$, so the sequence of indices $\{k - L_{k-1}, \ldots, k - 1\}$ is a subset of the range $L_k + 1, \ldots, k$ of (6.23). Thus, we can replace each S_{k-i} in the summation of (6.26) with the expression from (6.23) to obtain

$$S_k \neq \sum_{i=1}^{L_{k-1}} \Lambda_i^{[k-1]} \sum_{j=1}^{L_k} \Lambda_j^{[k]} S_{k-i-j}. \tag{6.27}$$

Comparing (6.25) with (6.27), the double summations are the same, but the equality in the first case and the inequality in the second case indicate a contradiction. Hence, the assumption on the length of the LFSRs must have been incorrect. By this contradiction, we must have

$$L_k \geq k - L_{k-1}.$$

If we take this to be the case, the index ranges which gave rise to the substitutions leading to the contradiction do not occur. □

Since the shortest LFSR that produces the sequence $\{S_1, S_2, \ldots, S_k\}$ must also produce the first part of that sequence, we must have $L_k \geq L_{k-1}$. Combining this with the result of the theorem, we obtain

$$L_k \geq \max(L_{k-1}, k - L_{k-1}). \tag{6.28}$$

We observe that the shift register cannot become shorter as more outputs are produced.

We have seen how to update the LFSR to produce a longer sequence using (6.19) and have also seen that there is a lower bound on the length of the LFSR. We now show that this lower bound can be achieved with equality, thus providing the *shortest* LFSR which produces the desired sequence.

Theorem 6.29 *In the update procedure, if $\Lambda^{[k]}(x) \neq \Lambda^{[k-1]}(x)$, then a new LFSR can be found whose length satisfies*

$$L_k = \max(L_{k-1}, k - L_{k-1}). \tag{6.29}$$

Proof We do a proof by induction. To check when $k = 1$ (which also indicates how to get the algorithm started), take $L_0 = 0$ and $\Lambda^{[0]}(x) = 1$. We find that

$$d_1 = S_1.$$

If $S_1 = 0$, then no update is necessary. If $S_1 \neq 0$, then we take $\Lambda^{[m]}(x) = \Lambda^{[0]}(x) = 1$, so that $l = 1 - 0 = 1$. Also, take $d_m = 1$. The updated polynomial is

$$\Lambda^{[1]}(x) = 1 + S_1 x,$$

which has degree L_1 satisfying

$$L_1 = \max(L_0, 1 - L_0) = 1.$$

In this case, (6.17) is vacuously true for the sequence consisting of the single point $\{S_1\}$.

Now let $\Lambda^{[m-1]}(x)$, $m < k - 1$, denote the *last* connection polynomial before $\Lambda^{[k-1]}(x)$ with $L_{m-1} < L_{k-1}$ that can produce the sequence $\{S_1, S_2, \ldots, S_{m-1}\}$ but not the sequence $\{S_1, S_2, \ldots, S_m\}$. Then

$$L_m = L_{k-1};$$

hence, in light of the inductive hypothesis (6.29),

$$L_m = m - L_{m-1} = L_{k-1}, \quad \text{or} \quad L_{m-1} - m = -L_{k-1}. \tag{6.30}$$

By the update formula (6.19) with $l = k - m$, we note that

$$L_k = \max(L_{k-1}, k - m + L_{m-1}).$$

Using $L_{m-1} - m$ from (6.30), we find that

$$L_k = \max(L_{k-1}, k - L_{k-1}).$$

□

In the update step, we observe that the new length is the same as the old length if $L_{k-1} \geq k - L_{k-1}$, that is, if

$$2L_{k-1} \geq k.$$

In this case, the connection polynomial is updated, but there is no change in length.

The shift-register synthesis algorithm, known as Massey's algorithm, is presented first in pseudocode as Algorithm 6.1, where we use the notations

$$c(x) = \Lambda^{[k]}(x)$$

to indicate the "current" connection polynomial and

$$p(x) = \Lambda^{[m-1]}(x)$$

to indicate a "previous" connection polynomial. Also, N is the number of input symbols ($N = 2t$ for many decoding problems).

Algorithm 6.1 Massey's Algorithm

Input: $S_1, S_2, \ldots, S_N$ (a sequence putatively produced by an LFSR of unknown length)
Output: Connection polynomial $c(x)$
Initialize:
$L = 0$ (the length of the current LFSR)
$c(x) = 1$ (the current connection polynomial)
$p(x) = 1$ (the connection polynomial before last length change)
$\ell = 1$ (ℓ is $k - m$, the amount of shift in update)
$d_m = 1$ (previous discrepancy)
for $k = 1$ to N
  $d = S_k + \sum_{i=1}^{L} c_i S_{k-i}$ (compute discrepancy)
  if ($d = 0$) (no change in polynomial)
    $\ell = \ell + 1$
  else
    if ($2L \geq k$) then (no-length change in update)
      $c(x) = c(x) - d d_m^{-1} x^\ell p(x)$
      $\ell = \ell + 1$
    else (update c with length change)
      $t(x) = c(x)$ (temporary storage)
      $c(x) = c(x) - d d_m^{-1} x^\ell p(x)$
      $L = k - L$
      $p(x) = t(x)$
      $d_m = d$
      $\ell = 1$
    end
  end
end
return the polynomial $c(x)$

---

masseymodM.m

Example 6.30 For the sequence $S = \{1, 1, 1, 0, 1, 0, 0\}$ the feedback connection polynomial obtained by a call to `massey` is $\{1, 1, 0, 1\}$, which corresponds to the polynomial

$$c(x) = 1 + x + x^3.$$

Thus, the elements of S are related by

$$S_j = S_{j-1} + S_{j-3},$$

for $j \geq 3$. Details of the operation of the algorithm are presented in Table 6.5.   □

Table 6.5: Evolution of the Berlekamp–Massey Algorithm for the Input Sequence $\{1,1,1,0,1,0,0\}$

k	S_k	d_k	$c(x)$	L	$p(x)$	ℓ	d_m
1	1	1	$1+x$	1	1	1	1
2	1	0	$1+x$	1	1	2	1
3	1	0	$1+x$	1	1	3	1
4	0	1	$1+x+x^3$	3	$1+x$	1	1
5	1	0	$1+x+x^3$	3	$1+x$	2	1
6	0	0	$1+x+x^3$	3	$1+x$	3	1
7	0	0	$1+x+x^3$	3	$1+x$	4	1

Table 6.6: Berlekamp–Massey Algorithm for a Double-Error-Correcting Code

k	S_k	d_k	$c(x)$	L	$p(x)$	ℓ	d_m
1	α^{17}	α^{17}	$1+\alpha^{17}x$	1	1	1	α^{17}
2	α^3	0	$1+\alpha^{17}x$	1	1	2	α^{17}
3	1	α^8	$1+\alpha^{17}x+\alpha^{22}x^2$	2	$1+\alpha^{17}x$	1	α^8
4	α^6	0	$1+\alpha^{17}x+\alpha^{22}x^2$	2	$1+\alpha^{17}x$	2	α^8

Example 6.31   For the $(31,21)$ binary double-error- correcting code with decoding in Example 6.27, let us employ the Berlekamp–Massey algorithm to find the error-locating polynomial. Recall from that example that the syndromes are $S_1=\alpha^{17}$, $S_2=\alpha^3$, $S_3=1$, and $S_4=\alpha^6$. Running the Berlekamp–Massey algorithm over $GF(32)$ results in the computations shown in Table 6.6. The final connection polynomial $c(x)=1+\alpha^{17}x+\alpha^{22}x^2$ is the error- location polynomial previously found using Peterson's algorithm. (In the current case, there are more computations using the Berlekamp–Massey algorithm, but for longer codes with more errors, the latter would be more efficient.)   □

6.4.4   Simplifications for Binary Codes

Consider again the Berlekamp–Massey algorithm computations for decoding a BCH code, as presented in Table 6.6. Note that d_k is 0 for every even k. This result holds in all cases for BCH Codes.

Lemma 6.32 *When the sequence of input symbols to the Berlekamp–Massey algorithm are syndromes from a binary BCH code, then the discrepancy d_k is equal to 0 for all even k (when 1-based indexing is used).*

As a result, there is never an update for these steps of the algorithm, so they can be merged into the next step. This cuts the complexity of the algorithm approximately in half. A restatement of the algorithm for BCH decoding is presented below.

Algorithm 6.2 Massey's Algorithm for Binary BCH Decoding

Input: $S_1, S_2, \ldots, S_N$, where $N=2t$
Initialize:
$L=0$ (the current length of the LFSR)
$c(x)=1$ (the current connection polynomial)
$p(x)=1$ (the connection polynomial before last length change)
$\ell=1$ (ℓ is $k-m$, the amount of shift in update)
$d_m=1$ (previous discrepancy)
for $k=1$ to N in steps of 2

$d = S_k + \sum_{i=1}^{L} c_i S_{k-i}$ (compute discrepancy)
if ($d = 0$) (no change in polynomial)
    $\ell = \ell + 1$
else
    if ($2L \geq k$) then (no-length change in update)
        $c(x) = c(x) - d d_m^{-1} x^\ell p(x)$
        $\ell = \ell + 1$
    else (update c with length change)
        $t(x) = c(x)$ (temporary storage)
        $c(x) = c(x) - d d_m^{-1} x^\ell p(x)$
        $L = k - L$
        $p(x) = t(x)$
        $d_m = d$
        $\ell = 1$
    end
  end
  $l = l + 1$; (accounts for the values of k skipped)
end

Example 6.33 Returning to the $(31, 21)$ code from the previous example, if we call the BCH-modified Berlekamp–Massey algorithm with the syndrome sequence $S_1 = \alpha^{17}$, $S_2 = \alpha^3$, $S_3 = 1$, and $S_4 = \alpha^6$, we obtain the results in Table 6.7. Only two steps of the algorithm are necessary and the same error locator polynomial is obtained as before. □

The odd-indexed discrepancies are zero due to the fact that for binary codes, the syndromes S_j have the property that

$$(S_j)^2 = S_{2j}. \tag{6.31}$$

We call this condition the syndrome conjugacy condition. Equation (6.31) follows from (6.6) and freshman exponentiation.

For the example we have been following,

$$S_1^2 = (\alpha^{17})^2 = \alpha^3 = S_2 \quad S_2^2 = (\alpha^3)^2 = \alpha^6 = S_4.$$

Example 6.34 We now present an entire decoding process for the three-error-correcting $(15, 5)$ binary code generated by

$$g(x) = 1 + x + x^2 + x^4 + x^5 + x^8 + x^{10}.$$

Suppose the all-zero vector is transmitted and the received vector is

$$\mathbf{r} = (0, 1, 0, 1, 0, 0, 0, 0, 1, 0, 0, 0, 0, 0, 0).$$

Then $r(x) = x + x^3 + x^8$.

Table 6.7: Berlekamp-Massey Algorithm for a Double-Error-Correcting Code: Simplifications for the Binary Code

k	S_k	d_k	$c(x)$	L	$p(x)$	ℓ	d_m
0	α^{17}	α^{17}	$1 + \alpha^{17}x$	1	1	2	α^{17}
2	1	α^8	$1 + \alpha^{17}x + \alpha^{22}x^2$	2	$1 + \alpha^{17}x$	2	α^8

Step 1 Compute the syndromes. Evaluating $r(x)$ at $x = \alpha, \alpha^2, \ldots, \alpha^6$, we find the syndromes

$$S_1 = \alpha^{12} \quad S_2 = \alpha^9 \quad S_3 = \alpha^3 \quad S_4 = \alpha^3 \quad S_5 = 0 \quad S_6 = \alpha^6.$$

Step 2 Compute the error locator polynomial.

A call to the binary Berlekamp–Massey algorithm yields the following computations.

k	S_k	d_k	$c(x)$	L	$p(x)$	l	d_m
1	α^{12}	α^{12}	$1 + \alpha^{12}x$	1	1	2	α^{12}
3	α^3	α^2	$1 + \alpha^{12}x + \alpha^5 x^2$	2	$1 + \alpha^{12}x$	2	α^2
5	0	α^2	$1 + \alpha^{12}x + \alpha^{10}x^2 + \alpha^{12}x^3$	3	$1 + \alpha^{12}x + \alpha^5 x^2$	2	α^2

The error locator polynomial is thus

$$\Lambda(x) = 1 + \alpha^{12}x + \alpha^{10}x^2 + \alpha^{12}x^3.$$

Step 3 Find the roots of the error locator polynomial. Using the Chien search function, we find roots at α^7, α^{12}, and α^{14}. Inverting these, the error locators are

$$X_1 = \alpha^8 \quad X_2 = \alpha^3 \quad X_3 = \alpha,$$

indicating that errors at positions 8, 3, and 1.

Step 4 Determine the error values: for a binary BCH code, any errors have value 1.

Step 5 Correct the errors: Add the error values (1) at the error locations, to obtain the decoded vector of all zeros.

6.5   Nonbinary BCH and RS Decoding

For nonbinary BCH or RS decoding, some additional work is necessary. Since the recursion (6.4) applies to nonbinary codes, finding the error-locating polynomial using the Berlekamp–Massey algorithm is unchanged. After the errors are located, however, the error values must also be computed. In light of (6.4), the latter equation can be written as

$$\Lambda_v S_{j-v} + \Lambda_{v-1} S_{j-v+1} + \cdots + \Lambda_1 S_{j-1} + \Lambda_0 S_j = 0.$$

Because (6.9) holds, the Berlekamp–Massey algorithm (in its nonbinary formulation) can be used to find the coefficients of the error locator polynomial, just as for binary codes.

6.5.1   Forney's Algorithm

Having found the error-locator polynomial and its roots, there is still one more step for the nonbinary BCH or RS codes: we have to find the error values. Let us return to the syndrome,

$$S_j = \sum_{\ell=1}^{v} e_{i_\ell} X_\ell^j, \quad j = b, b+1, \ldots, b+2t-1.$$

Knowing the error locators (obtained from the roots of the error locator polynomial) it is straightforward to set up and solve a set of linear equations:

$$\begin{bmatrix} X_1^b & X_2^b & X_3^b & \cdots & X_v^b \\ X_1^{b+1} & X_2^{b+1} & X_3^{b+1} & \cdots & X_v^{b+1} \\ \vdots & & & & \\ X_1^{b+2t-1} & X_2^{b+2t-1} & X_3^{b+2t-1} & \cdots & X_v^{b+2t-1} \end{bmatrix} \begin{bmatrix} e_{i_1} \\ e_{i_2} \\ \vdots \\ e_{i_v} \end{bmatrix} = \begin{bmatrix} S_b \\ S_{b+1} \\ \vdots \\ S_{b+2t-1} \end{bmatrix}. \tag{6.32}$$

However, there is a method which is computationally easier and in addition provides us a key insight for another way of doing the decoding. It may be observed that the matrix in (6.32) is essentially a Vandermonde matrix. There exist fast algorithms for solving Vandermonde systems (see, e.g., [161]). One of these which applies specifically to this problem is known as *Forney's algorithm*.

Before presenting the formula, a few necessary definitions must be established. A *syndrome polynomial* is defined as

$$S(x) = S_b + S_{b+1}x + S_{b+2}x^2 + \cdots + S_{b+2t-1}x^{2t-1} = \sum_{j=0}^{2t-1} S_{b+j}x^j. \tag{6.33}$$

Since the syndromes satisfy a linear recursion as in (6.8), a polynomial relationship of the form described in Section 5.2.3 must exist, so that there exists a polynomial $\Omega(x)$ of degree $< t$ such that

$$\boxed{\Omega(x) = S(x)\Lambda(x) \pmod{x^{2t}}.} \tag{6.34}$$

The polynomial $\Omega(x)$ is called the *error-evaluator polynomial*.[1] Equation (6.34) is called the **key equation**. Note that the effect of computing modulo x^{2t} can be interpreted as discarding all terms of degree $2t$ or higher. As we will see, the key equation provides not only a tool for computing error values, but also a method for finding the error locator polynomial $\Lambda(x)$ using the Euclidean algorithm.

Definition 6.35 Let $f(x) = f_0 + f_1 x + f_2 x^2 + \cdots + f_t x^t$ be a polynomial with coefficients in some field $\mathbb{F}$. The **formal derivative** $f'(x)$ of $f(x)$ is computed using the conventional rules of polynomial differentiation:

$$f'(x) = f_1 + 2f_2 x + 3f_3 x^2 + \cdots + tf_t x^{t-1}, \tag{6.35}$$

where, as usual, mf_i for $m \in \mathbb{Z}$ and $f_i \in \mathbb{F}$ denotes repeated addition:

$$mf_i = \underbrace{f_i + f_i + \cdots + f_i}_{m \text{ summands}}.$$

□

There is no implication of any kind of limiting process in formal differentiation: it simply corresponds to formal manipulation of symbols. Based on this definition, it can be shown that many of the conventional rules of differentiation apply. For example, the product rule holds:

$$[f(x)g(x)]' = f'(x)g(x) + f(x)g'(x).$$

If $f(x) \in \mathbb{F}[x]$, where $\mathbb{F}$ is a field of characteristic 2, then $f'(x)$ has no odd-powered terms. In a field of characteristic 2,

$$f'(x) = \begin{cases} f_1 + f_3 x^2 + \cdots + f_t x^{t-1} & \text{if } t \text{ is odd} \\ f_1 + f_3 x^2 + \cdots + f_{t-1}x^{t-2} & \text{if } t \text{ is even.} \end{cases}$$

Theorem 6.36 (Forney's algorithm) *The error values for a RS code based on the roots of the generator polynomial $g(x) = (x - \beta^b)(x - \beta^{b+1})\cdots(x - \beta^{b+2t-1})$ are computed by*

$$e_{i_k} = -\frac{\Omega(X_k^{-1})}{X_k^{b-1}\Lambda'(X_k^{-1})}, \tag{6.36}$$

---

[1] Some authors define $S(x) = S_b x + S_{b+1}x^2 + \cdots + S_{b+2t-1}x^{b+2t-1}$, in which case they define $\Omega(x) = (1 + S(x))\Lambda(x) \pmod{x^{2t+1}}$ and obtain $e_{i_k} = -X_k\Omega(X_k^{-1})/\Lambda'(X_k^{-1})$.

where $\Lambda'(x)$ is the formal derivative of $\Lambda(x)$. Thus, when $b = 1$ (narrow-sense code),

$$e_{i_k} = -\frac{\Omega(X_k^{-1})}{\Lambda'(X_k^{-1})}.$$

Proof First note that over any ring,

$$(1 - x^{2t}) = (1 - x)(1 + x + x^2 + \cdots + x^{2t-1}) = (1 - x)\sum_{j=0}^{2t-1} x^j. \tag{6.37}$$

With the syndrome values $S_j = \sum_{\ell=1}^{v} e_{i_\ell}(\beta^j)^{i_\ell}$ for $j = b, \ldots, b + 2t - 1$, the syndrome polynomial is

$$S(x) = \sum_{j=b}^{b+2t-1} \sum_{\ell=1}^{v} e_{i_\ell} X_\ell^j x^{j-b}$$

$$= \sum_{j=0}^{2t-1} \sum_{\ell=1}^{v} e_{i_\ell} X_\ell^{j+b} x^j \quad (\text{replace } j - b \text{ by } j).$$

Observe that

$$\Omega(x) = S(x)\Lambda(x) \pmod{x^{2t}}$$

$$= \left(\sum_{j=0}^{2t-1} \sum_{\ell=1}^{v} e_{i_\ell} X_\ell^{j+b} x^j\right)\left(\prod_{i=1}^{v}(1 - X_i x)\right) \pmod{x^{2t}}$$

$$= \sum_{\ell=1}^{v} e_{i_\ell} X_\ell^b \sum_{j=0}^{2t-1} (X_\ell x)^j \prod_{i=1}^{v}(1 - X_i x) \pmod{x^{2t}}$$

$$= \sum_{\ell=1}^{v} e_{i_\ell} X_\ell^b \left[(1 - X_\ell x)\sum_{j=0}^{2t-1}(X_\ell x)^j\right] \prod_{i\neq\ell}(1 - X_i x) \pmod{x^{2t}}.$$

From (6.37),

$$(1 - X_\ell x)\sum_{j=0}^{2t-1}(X_\ell x)^j = 1 - (X_\ell x)^{2t}.$$

Since $(X_\ell x)^{2t} \pmod{x^{2t}} = 0$, we have

$$S(x)\Lambda(x) \pmod{x^{2t}} = \sum_{\ell=1}^{v} e_{i_\ell} X_\ell^b \prod_{i\neq\ell}(1 - X_i x) = \Omega(x).$$

The trick now is to isolate a particular e_{i_k} on the right-hand side of this expression. To this end, evaluate $\Omega(x)$ at $x = X_k^{-1}$:

$$\Omega(X_k^{-1}) = \sum_{\ell=1}^{v} e_{i_\ell} X_\ell^b \prod_{i\neq\ell}(1 - X_i X_k^{-1}).$$

Every in the sum results in a product that has a zero in it, except the term when $\ell = k$, since that factor is skipped. We thus obtain

$$\Omega(X_k^{-1}) = e_{i_k} X_k^b \prod_{i\neq k}(1 - X_i X_k^{-1}).$$

We can thus write

$$e_{i_k} = \frac{\Omega(X_k^{-1})}{X_k^b \prod_{i \neq k}(1 - X_i X_k^{-1})}. \tag{6.38}$$

Once $\Omega(x)$ is known, the error values can thus be computed. However, there are some computational simplifications.

The formal derivative of $\Lambda(x)$ is

$$\Lambda'(x) = \frac{d}{dx}\prod_{i=1}^{v}(1 - X_i x) = -\sum_{l=1}^{v} X_l \prod_{i \neq l}(1 - X_i x).$$

Then

$$\Lambda'(X_k^{-1}) = -X_k \prod_{i \neq k}(1 - X_i X_k^{-1}).$$

Substitution of this result into (6.38) yields (6.36). $\qquad\qquad\square$

Example 6.37 Working over $GF(8)$ constructed with the primitive polynomial $1 + x + x^3$, in a code where $t = 2$, suppose $S(x) = \alpha^6 + \alpha^3 x + \alpha^4 x^2 + \alpha^3 x^3$. We find (say using the B–M algorithm and the Chien search) that the error locator polynomial is

$$\Lambda(x) = 1 + \alpha^2 x + \alpha x^2 = (1 + \alpha^3 x)(1 + \alpha^5 x).$$

That is, the error locators (reciprocals of the roots of $\Lambda(x)$) are $X_1 = \alpha^3$ and $X_2 = \alpha^5$. We have

$$\Omega(x) = (\alpha^6 + \alpha^3 x + \alpha^4 x^2 + \alpha^3 x^3)(1 + \alpha^2 x + \alpha x^2) \ (\text{mod } x^4) = (\alpha^6 + x + \alpha^4 x^5) \ (\text{mod } x^4) = \alpha^6 + x$$

and

$$\Lambda'(x) = \alpha^2 + 2\alpha x = \alpha^2.$$

So

$$e_{i_k} = -\left.\frac{\alpha^6 + x}{\alpha^2}\right|_{x=X_k^{-1}} = \alpha^4 + \alpha^5 X_k^{-1}.$$

Using the error locator $X_1 = \alpha^3$, we find

$$e_3 = \alpha^4 + \alpha^5(\alpha^3)^{-1} = \alpha$$

and for the error locator $X_2 = \alpha^5$,

$$e_5 = \alpha^4 + \alpha^5(\alpha^5)^{-1} = \alpha^5.$$

The error polynomial is $e(x) = \alpha x^3 + \alpha^5 x^5$. $\qquad\qquad\square$

Example 6.38 We consider the entire decoding process for $(15, 9)$ code of Example 6.17, using the message and code polynomials in Example 6.19. Suppose the received polynomial is

$$r(x) = \alpha^8 + \alpha^2 x + \underline{\alpha^{13} x^2} + \alpha^3 x^3 + \alpha^5 x^4 + \alpha x^5 + \alpha^8 x^6 + \alpha x^7 + \underline{\alpha x^8} + \alpha^5 x^9 + \alpha^3 x^{10}$$
$$+ \alpha^4 x^{11} + \alpha^9 x^{12} + \alpha^{12} x^{13} + \underline{\alpha^5 x^{14}}.$$

(Errors are in the underlined positions.)

The syndromes are

$$S_1 = r(\alpha) = \alpha^{13} \quad S_2 = r(\alpha^2) = \alpha^4 \quad S_3 = r(\alpha^3) = \alpha^8$$
$$S_4 = r(\alpha^4) = \alpha^2 \quad S_5 = r(\alpha^5) = \alpha^3 \quad S_6 = r(\alpha^6) = \alpha^8$$

so

$$S(x) = \alpha^{13} + \alpha^4 x + \alpha^8 x^2 + \alpha^2 x^3 + \alpha^3 x^4 + \alpha^8 x^5$$

Table 6.8: Berlekamp–Massey Algorithm for a Triple-Error-Correcting Code

k	S_k	d_k	$c(x)$	L	$p(x)$	ℓ	d_m
1	α^{13}	α^{13}	$1 + \alpha^{13}x$	1	1	1	α^{13}
2	α^4	α^{13}	$1 + \alpha^6 x$	1	1	2	α^{13}
3	α^8	α	$1 + \alpha^6 x + \alpha^3 x^2$	2	$1 + \alpha^6 x$	1	α
4	α^2	α^5	$1 + \alpha^{12}x + \alpha^{12}x^2$	2	$1 + \alpha^6 x$	2	α
5	α^3	α^{10}	$1 + \alpha^{12}x + \alpha^8 x^2 + x^3$	3	$1 + \alpha^{12}x + \alpha^{12}x^2$	1	α^{10}
6	α^8	α^5	$1 + \alpha^3 x + \alpha^{11}x^2 + \alpha^9 x^3$	3	$1 + \alpha^{12}x + \alpha^{12}x^2$	2	α^{10}

and the error locator polynomial determined by the Berlekamp–Massey algorithm is

$$\Lambda(x) = 1 + \alpha^3 x + \alpha^{11}x^2 + \alpha^9 x^3.$$

The details of the Berlekamp–Massey computations are shown in Table 6.8.

The roots of $\Lambda(x)$ are at α, α^7, and α^{13}, so the error locators (the reciprocal of the roots) are

$$X_1 = \alpha^{14} \quad X_2 = \alpha^8 \quad X_3 = \alpha^2,$$

corresponding to errors at positions 14, 8, and 2. The error evaluator polynomial is

$$\Omega(x) = \alpha^{13} + x + \alpha^2 x^2.$$

Then the computations to find the error values are:

$$X_1 = \alpha^{14} : \quad \Omega(X_1^{-1}) = \alpha^6 \quad \Lambda'(X_1^{-1}) = \alpha^5 \quad e_{14} = \alpha$$
$$X_2 = \alpha^8 : \quad \Omega(X_2^{-1}) = \alpha^2 \quad \Lambda'(X_2^{-1}) = \alpha^{13} \quad e_8 = \alpha^4$$
$$X_3 = \alpha^2 : \quad \Omega(X_3^{-1}) = \alpha^{13} \quad \Lambda'(X_3^{-1}) = \alpha^{11} \quad e_2 = \alpha^2$$

The error polynomial is thus

$$e(x) = \alpha^2 x^2 + \alpha^4 x^8 + \alpha x^{14}$$

and the decoded polynomial is

$$\alpha^8 + \alpha^2 x + \alpha^{14}x^2 + \alpha^3 x^3 + \alpha^5 x^4 + \alpha x^5 + \alpha^8 x^6 + \alpha x^7 + x^8 + \alpha^5 x^9 + \alpha^3 x^{10}$$
$$+ \alpha^4 x^{11} + \alpha^9 x^{12} + \alpha^{12} x^{13} + \alpha^2 x^{14},$$

which is the same as the original codeword $c(x)$.   □

6.6 Euclidean Algorithm for the Error Locator Polynomial

We have seen that the Berlekamp–Massey algorithm can be used to construct the error locator polynomial. In this section, we show that the Euclidean algorithm can also be used to construct error locator polynomials. This approach to decoding is often called the Sugiyama algorithm [424].

We return to the key Equation (6.34):

$$\Omega(x) = S(x)\Lambda(x) \;(\mathrm{mod}\; x^{2t}). \tag{6.39}$$

Given only $S(x)$ and t, we desire to determine the error locator polynomial $\Lambda(x)$ and the error evaluator polynomial $\Omega(x)$. As stated, this problem seems hopelessly underconstrained. However, recall that (6.39) means that $x^{2t}|(\Omega(x) - S(x)\Lambda(x))$, so

$$\Theta(x)x^{2t} + \Lambda(x)S(x) = \Omega(x)$$

for some polynomial $\Theta(x)$. (See (5.22).) Also recall that the extended Euclidean algorithm returns, for a pair of elements (a, b) from a Euclidean domain, a pair of elements (s, t) such that

$$as + bt = c,$$

where c is the GCD of a and b. In our case, we run the extended Euclidean algorithm to obtain a sequence of polynomials $\Theta^{[k]}(x)$, $\Lambda^{[k]}(x)$, and $\Omega^{[k]}(x)$ satisfying

$$\Theta^{[k]}(x)x^{2t} + \Lambda^{[k]}(x)S(x) = \Omega^{[k]}(x).$$

This is exactly the circumstance described in Section 5.2.3. Recall that the stopping criterion there is based on the observation that the polynomial we are here calling $\Omega(x)$ must have degree $< t$.

The steps to decode using the Euclidean algorithm are summarized as follows:

1. Compute the syndromes and the syndrome polynomial $S(x) = S_b + S_{b+1}x + \cdots + S_{b+2t-1}x^{2t-1}$.
2. Run the Euclidean algorithm with $a(x) = x^{2t}$ and $b(x) = S(x)$, until $\deg(r_i(x)) < t$. Then $\Omega(x) = r_i(x)$ and $\Lambda(x) = t_i(x)$.
3. Find the roots of $\Lambda(x)$ and the error locators X_i.
4. Solve for the error values using (6.36).

Actually, since $\Lambda(x)$ has $\Lambda_0 = 1$, it may be necessary to normalize, $\Lambda(x) = t_i(x)/t_i(0)$.

Example 6.39   For the syndrome polynomial

$$S(x) = \alpha^{13} + \alpha^4 x + \alpha^8 x^2 + \alpha^2 x^3 + \alpha^3 x^4 + \alpha^8 x^5$$

of the triple-error-correcting polynomial of Example 6.38, let

$$a(x) = x^6 \quad b(x) = S(x).$$

Then calling the Euclidean algorithm to stop when the degree of $r_i(x)$ is less than 3 yields

$$s_i(x) = \alpha^{14} + \alpha^6 x + \alpha^2 x^2$$
$$t_i(x) = 1 + \alpha^3 x + \alpha^{11} x^2 + \alpha^9 x^3$$
$$r_i(x) = \alpha^{13} + x + \alpha^2 x^2.$$

The error locator polynomial is

$$\Lambda(x) = t_i(x) = 1 + \alpha^3 x + \alpha^{11} x^2 + \alpha^9 x^3,$$

as before.   □

In terms of computational efficiency, it appears that the Berlekamp–Massey algorithm procedure may be slightly better than the Euclidean algorithm for binary codes, since the Berlekamp–Massey deals with polynomials no longer than the error locator polynomial, while the Euclidean algorithm may have intermediate polynomials of higher degree. However, the computational complexity is probably quite similar. Also, the error evaluator polynomial $\Omega(x)$ is automatically obtained as a useful byproduct of the Euclidean algorithm method.

6.7 Erasure Decoding for Nonbinary BCH or RS Codes

Erasures and binary erasure decoding were introduced in Section 3.8. Here we describe erasure decoding for nonbinary BCH or RS codes.

Let the received word $\mathbf{r}$ have v errors and f erasures, with the errors at $i_1, i_2, \ldots, i_v$ and the erasures at $j_1, j_2, \ldots, j_f$, and with $v + f/2 \leq t$. We employ error locators as before, $X_1, X_2, \ldots, X_v$, with $X_k = \alpha^{i_k}$. Now introduce erasure locators

$$Y_1 = \alpha^{j_1} \quad Y_2 = \alpha^{j_2} \quad \cdots \quad Y_f = \alpha^{j_f}.$$

The decoder must find the number of errors v, the errors locators X_k, the error values e_{i_k} at the error locations, and values at the erasures f_{j_k}.

Define the *erasure locator polynomial* as

$$\Gamma(x) = \prod_{l=1}^{f}(1 - Y_l x),$$

which is known, since the erasure locations are known.

Since received symbol values are necessary to compute the syndromes, it is convenient to (temporarily) fill in the erased symbol locations with zeros. Let $\tilde{r}(x)$ denote the received polynomial setting the erasures to 0. Then

$$S_j = \tilde{r}(\alpha^j) = \sum_{k=1}^{v} e_{i_k} X_k^j + \sum_{k=1}^{f} f_{i_k} Y_k^j, \quad j = b, b+1, \ldots, b+2t-1.$$

As before, we create a syndrome polynomial,

$$S(x) = \sum_{\ell=0}^{2t-1} S_{b+\ell} x^\ell.$$

The product of the locator polynomials $\Lambda(x)\Gamma(x)$ locates all the errors and erasures. Multiplying this by the syndrome polynomial results in a situation analogous to that described in Section 5.2.3, resulting in the key equation

$$\Lambda(x)\Gamma(x)S(x) = \Omega(x) \ (\mathrm{mod}\ x^{2t})$$

for a polynomial $\Omega(x)$ with $\deg(\Omega(x)) < 2t$.

The Euclidean algorithm can be used to solve for $\Lambda(x)$ and $\Omega(x)$. Let

$$\Xi(x) = \Gamma(x)S(x) \ (\mathrm{mod}\ x^{2t})$$

be used to represent the data that are known once the syndromes are computed, we can write the key equation as

$$\Lambda(x)\Xi(x) = \Omega(x) \ (\mathrm{mod}\ x^{2t}).$$

This can be used in the Euclidean algorithm, using $\Xi(x)$ in place of $S(x)$, setting $a(x) = x^{2t}$ and $b(x) = \Xi(x)$ and stoping when

$$\deg(r_i(x)) \leq \begin{cases} t + \dfrac{f}{2} & \text{if } f \text{ is even} \\ t + \dfrac{f-1}{2} & \text{if } f \text{ is odd.} \end{cases}$$

Once $\Lambda(x)$ is known, its roots are found (as usual).

The error and erasure values can then be found using a modification of Forney's algorithm. The polynomial

$$\Phi(x) = \Lambda(x)\Gamma(x),$$

called the *combined error/erasure locator polynomial* is computed. Then

$$e_{i_k} = -\frac{\Omega(X_k^{-1})}{\Phi'(X_k^{-1})} \quad \text{and} \quad f_{j_k} = -\frac{\Omega(Y_k^{-1})}{\Phi'(Y_k^{-1})}.$$

testRSerasure.cc

Example 6.40 Let $GF(16)$ be represented using the primitive polynomial $1 + x + x^4$. A narrow-sense $(15, 9)$ RS code with $t = 3$ has generator polynomial (expressed in vector notation) as $g(x) = 12 + 10x + 12x^2 + 3x^3 + 9x^4 + 7x^5 + x^6$. The message

$$\mathbf{m} = \begin{bmatrix} 5, 2, 1, 6, 8, 3, 10, 15, 4 \end{bmatrix}$$

is encoded to produce the codeword

$$\mathbf{c} = \begin{bmatrix} 5, 4, \underline{9}, 8, 6, \underline{2}, 5, 2, 1, 6, 8, 3, 10, 15, 4 \end{bmatrix}.$$

The received data is

$$\mathbf{r} = \begin{bmatrix} 5, 4, E, 8, 6, E, 5, 2, \underline{2}, 6, 8, 3, 10, 15, \underline{6} \end{bmatrix}.$$

The erasure locations are at 2 and 5, and the error locations are at 8 and 14. The error polynomial is $e(x) = 3x^8 + 2x^{14}$.
Forming $\tilde{r}(x)$ by setting the erasures to 0, we have

$$\tilde{r}(x) = 5 + 4x + 8x^3 + 6x^4 + 5x^6 + 2x^7 + 2x^8 + 6x^9 + 8x^{10} + 3x^{11} + 10x^{12} + 15x^{13} + 6x^{14}.$$

The syndromes are

$$S_j = \tilde{r}(\alpha^j), \quad j = 1, 2, \ldots, 6$$

$$= \{0, 9, 4, 4, 3, 0\}.$$

The erasure locator polynomial is $\Gamma(x) = (1 - \alpha^x x)(1 - \alpha^5 x) = 1 + 2x + 11x^2$, and

$$\Xi(x) = \Gamma(x)S(x) \pmod{x^{2t}} = 9x + 5x^2 + x^4 + 12x^5.$$

Calling the Euclidean algorithm with $a(x) = x^6$ and $b(x) = \Xi(x)$, we obtain the following:

i	$r_i(x)$	$q_i(x)$	$s_i(x)$	$t_i(x)$
-1	x^6		1	0
0	$\Xi(x)$		0	1
1	$4x + 11x^2 + 4x^3 + 8x^4$	$8 + 10x$	1	$8 + 10x$
2	$3x + 10x^2 + 13x^3$	$11 + 8x$	$11 + 8x$	$6 + 14x + 15x^2$

At this point, $\deg(r_i(x)) < t$, so the Euclidean algorithm is stopped.
    The polynomials $\Lambda(x)$ and $\Omega(x)$ are obtained by normalizing $t_2(x)$ and $r_2(x)$, respectively. With $t(x) = t_2(x) = 6 + 14x + 15x^2$, normalize by $6^{-1} = (\alpha^5)^{-1} = \alpha^{10} = 7$ to obtain

$$\Lambda(x) = 7(6 + 14x + 15x^2) = 1 + 12x + 11x^2$$

and

$$\Omega(x) = 7(r_2(x)) = 7(3x + 10x^2 + 13x^3) = 9x + 3x^2 + 5x^3.$$

The Chien search finds the roots of the error locator polynomial at $\{\alpha, \alpha^7\}$, so the error locators are at $\{\alpha^8, \alpha^{14}\}$. The combined erasure/error locator polynomial is

$$\Phi(x) = \Lambda(x)\Gamma(x) = 1 + 14x + 11x^2 + 8x^3 + 9x^4$$

with derivative

$$\Phi'(x) = 14 + 8x^2.$$

The error and erasure values are

$$e_{14} = \frac{\Omega(\alpha^{n-14})}{\Phi'(\alpha^{n-14})} = 2 \quad e_8 = \frac{\Omega(\alpha^{n-8})}{\Phi'(\alpha^{n-8})} = 3 \quad f_2 = \frac{\Omega(\alpha^{n-2})}{\Phi'(\alpha^{n-2})} = 9 \quad f_5 = \frac{\Omega(\alpha^{n-5})}{\Phi'(\alpha^{n-5})} = 2.$$

Adding these values into their respective symbol locations gives a correctly decoded codeword. ☐

Example 6.41   For a triple-error-correcting $(t = 3)$ RS code over $GF(16)$ constructed using the primitive polynomial $1 + x + x^4$, suppose that

$$r(x) = \alpha^5 x^{11} + \alpha^6 x^9 + E x^7 + E x^6 + \alpha^{11} x^5 + x^4 + \alpha^{11} x^3 + \alpha^6 x^2 + \alpha^{12},$$

where E denotes that the position is erased. The erasure locations are thus at $j_1 = 7$ and $j_2 = 6$, the erasure locators are $Y_1 = \alpha^7$ and $Y_2 = \alpha^6$. The erasure locator polynomial is

$$\Gamma(x) = (1 - \alpha^6 x)(1 - \alpha^7 x) = 1 + \alpha^{10} x + \alpha^{13} x^2.$$

Let

$$\tilde{r}(x) = r(x)|_{\text{erasures removed}}$$
$$= \alpha^5 x^{11} + \alpha^6 x^9 + \alpha^{11} x^5 + x^4 + \alpha^{11} x^3 + \alpha^6 x^2 + \alpha^{12}.$$

The syndromes are

$$S_1 = \tilde{r}(\alpha) = 1 \quad S_2 = \tilde{r}(\alpha^2) = 0 \quad S_3 = \tilde{r}(\alpha^3) = \alpha^9$$
$$S_4 = \tilde{r}(\alpha^4) = \alpha^{12} \quad S_5 = \tilde{r}(\alpha^5) = \alpha^2 \quad S_6 = \tilde{r}(\alpha^6) = \alpha^8,$$

so $S(x) = 1 + \alpha^9 x^2 + \alpha^{12} x^3 + \alpha^2 x^4 + \alpha^8 x^5$. Let

$$\Xi(x) = \Gamma(x)S(x) \bmod x^{2t} = \alpha^{13} x^5 + \alpha^2 x^4 + \alpha^6 x^3 + \alpha^{10} x^2 + \alpha^{10} x + 1.$$

By Euclid, we find that

$$\Lambda(x) = 1 + \alpha^{11} x,$$

which has a root at $x = \alpha^4$, so there is an error at $i_1 = 11$ and $X_1 = \alpha^{11}$. We find

$$\Omega(x) = \Lambda(x)\Xi(x) \bmod x^{2t} = \alpha^7 x^2 + \alpha^{14} x + 1$$

and

$$\Phi(x) = \Lambda(x)\Gamma(x) = \alpha^9 x^3 + x^2 + \alpha^{14} x + 1.$$

The error value is

$$e_1 = \frac{\Omega(X_1^{-1})}{\Phi'(X_1^{-1})} = \alpha^5$$

and the erasure values are

$$f_1 = \frac{\Omega(Y_1^{-1})}{\Phi'(Y_1^{-1})} = \alpha$$
$$f_2 = \frac{\Omega(Y_2^{-1})}{\Phi'(Y_2^{-1})} = \alpha^{14}.$$

The decoded polynomial is

$$\hat{c}(x) = \alpha^6 x^9 + \alpha x^7 + \alpha^{14} x^6 + \alpha^{11} x^5 + x^4 + \alpha^{11} x^3 + \alpha^6 x^2 + \alpha^{12}.$$

☐

6.8   Galois Field Fourier Transform Methods

Just as a discrete Fourier transform (DFT) can be defined over real or complex numbers, so it is possible to define a Fourier transform over a sequence of Galois field numbers. This transform yields valuable insight into the structure of the code and new decoding algorithms.

Recall (see, e.g., [328]) that the DFT of a real (or complex) vector $\mathbf{x} = (x_0, x_1, \ldots, x_{n-1})$ is the vector $\mathbf{X} = (X_0, X_1, \ldots, X_{n-1})$ with components

$$X_k = \sum_{j=0}^{n-1} x_j e^{-2\pi i j k / n},$$

(where $i = \sqrt{-1}$) and that the inverse DFT computes the elements of $\mathbf{x}$ from $\mathbf{X}$ by

$$x_j = \frac{1}{n} \sum_{k=0}^{n-1} X_k e^{2\pi i j k / n}.$$

The quantity $e^{-2\pi i/n}$ is a primitive nth root of unity in the complex numbers, that is, a complex number with order n. In a similar way, we can define a DFT of length n over a finite field having an element of order n. These concepts are now extended to finite fields.

Definition 6.42 Let $\mathbf{v} = (v_0, v_1, \ldots, v_{n-1})$ be a vector over $GF(q)$ (or $GF(q^m)$) of length n such that $n | q^m - 1$ for some positive integer m. Let $\alpha \in GF(q^m)$ have order n. The **Galois Field Fourier Transform** (GFFT) of $\mathbf{v}$ is the vector $\mathbf{V} = (V_0, V_1, \ldots, V_{n-1})$ with components $V_j \in GF(q^m)$

$$V_j = \sum_{i=0}^{n-1} \alpha^{ij} v_i \quad j = 0, 1, \ldots, n-1. \tag{6.40}$$

We write $\mathbf{V} = \mathcal{F}[\mathbf{v}]$ and $\mathbf{v} \leftrightarrow \mathbf{V}$ to denote the Fourier transform relationship between $\mathbf{v}$ and $\mathbf{V}$, where the type of Fourier transform (a GFFT) is obtained from the context.   □

Theorem 6.43 *In a field $GF(q)$ with characteristic p, the inverse GFFT of the vector $\mathbf{V} = (V_0, V_1, \ldots, V_{n-1})$ is the vector $\mathbf{v}$ with components*

$$v_i = n^{-1} \sum_{j=0}^{n-1} \alpha^{-ij} V_j, \tag{6.41}$$

where n^{-1} is the multiplicative inverse of n modulo p.

Proof   [[483], p. 194] Note that α is a root of $x^n - 1$. We can write

$$x^n - 1 = (x - 1)(x^{n-1} + x^{n-2} + \cdots + x + 1).$$

Evaluating $x^n - 1$ at $x = \alpha^r$ for some integer r, we have

$$(\alpha^r)^n - 1 = (\alpha^n)^r - 1 = 0.$$

If $r \not\equiv 0 \pmod{n}$, then α^r must be a zero of $(x^{n-1} + x^{n-2} + \cdots + x + 1)$. We therefore have

$$\sum_{j=0}^{n-1} \alpha^{rj} = 0 \quad r \not\equiv 0 \pmod{n}.$$

When $r \equiv 0 \pmod{n}$, we get

$$\sum_{j=0}^{n-1} \alpha^{rj} = \sum_{j=0}^{n-1} 1 \equiv n \pmod{p}.$$

Substituting (6.40) into (6.41),

$$\sum_{j=0}^{n-1} \alpha^{-ij} V_j = \sum_{j=0}^{n-1} \alpha^{-ij} \sum_{k=0}^{n-1} \alpha^{kj} v_k$$

$$= \sum_{k=0}^{n-1} v_k \sum_{j=0}^{n-1} \alpha^{(k-i)j}$$

$$= v_i n \pmod{p}.$$

Multiplying both sides by $n^{-1} \pmod{p}$, we obtain the desired result. $\square$

Cyclic convolution of the sequences $\mathbf{a} = (a_0, a_1, \ldots, a_{n-1})$ and $\mathbf{b} = (b_0, b_1, \ldots, b_{n-1})$ is denoted by

$$\mathbf{c} = \mathbf{a} \circledast \mathbf{b},$$

where $\circledast$ denotes cyclic convolution. The elements of $\mathbf{c}$ in the convolution are given by

$$c_i = \sum_{k=0}^{n-1} a_k b_{((i-k))},$$

where $((i - k))$ is used as a shorthand for $(i - k) \pmod{n}$. That is, the indices in $i - k$ "wrap around" in a cyclic manner modulo n. One of the most important results from digital signal processing is the convolution theorem; as applied to the DFT it says that the DFT of sequence obtained by cyclic convolution of $\mathbf{a}$ and $\mathbf{b}$ is the element-by-element product of the DFTs of $\mathbf{a}$ and $\mathbf{b}$. An identical result holds for the GFFT.

Theorem 6.44 *If*

$$a \leftrightarrow A$$

$$b \leftrightarrow \mathbf{B}$$

$$c \leftrightarrow \mathbf{C}$$

are all sequences of length n in a finite field GF(q) such that $n | q^m - 1$ for some m, then

$$C_j = A_j B_j \quad j = 0, 1, \ldots, n-1$$

if and only if

$$c = a \circledast b$$

(cyclic convolution) — that is,

$$c_i = \sum_{k=0}^{n-1} a_k b_{((i-k))}.$$

Furthermore,

$$c_j = a_j b_j \quad j = 0, 1, \ldots, n-1$$

if and only if

$$C = n^{-1} A \circledast B;$$

that is,

$$C_i = n^{-1} \sum_{k=0}^{n-1} A_k B_{((i-k))}.$$

Proof [[483], p. 195] We prove the first part of the theorem. We compute the inverse GFFT of **C**:

$$c_i = n^{-1} \sum_{j=0}^{n-1} \alpha^{-ij} C_j = n^{-1} \sum_{j=0}^{n-1} \alpha^{-ij} A_j B_j$$

$$= n^{-1} \sum_{j=0}^{n-1} \alpha^{-ij} \left(\sum_{k=0}^{n-1} \alpha^{kj} a_k \right) B_j = n^{-1} \sum_{k=0}^{n-1} a_k \sum_{j=0}^{n-1} \alpha^{-(i-k)j} B_j$$

$$= \sum_{k=0}^{n-1} a_k b_{((i-k))}.$$

□

Let us now turn our attention from vectors to polynomials.

Definition 6.45 The **spectrum** of the polynomial (codevector) $v(x) = v_0 + v_1 x + \cdots + v_{n-1} x^{n-1}$ is the GFFT of $\mathbf{v} = (v_0, v_1, \ldots, v_{n-1})$. □

We refer to the original vector $\mathbf{v} = (v_0, v_1, \ldots, v_{n-1})$ as a vector in the "time domain" (even though time has nothing to do with it) and its corresponding transform **V** as being in the "frequency domain." V_j is said to be the *j*th frequency component of **v**.

Given a polynomial $v(x)$, note that

$$v(\alpha^j) = v_0 + v_1 \alpha^j + v_2 \alpha^{2j} + \cdots + v_{n-1} \alpha^{(n-1)j} = \sum_{i=0}^{n-1} v_i \alpha^{ij} = V_j. \tag{6.42}$$

Thus, the *j*th component of the GFFT of **v** is obtained by evaluating $v(x)$ at $x = \alpha^j$. Let us also define a polynomial based on $\mathbf{V} = (V_0, V_1, \ldots, V_{n-1})$ by

$$V(x) = V_0 + V_1 x + V_2 x^2 + \cdots + V_{n-1} x^{n-1}.$$

Then

$$V(\alpha^{-i}) = V_0 + V_1 \alpha^{-i} + V_2 \alpha^{-2i} + \cdots + V_{n-1} \alpha^{-(n-1)i} = \sum_{j=0}^{n-1} V_j \alpha^{-ij} = n v_i. \tag{6.43}$$

Based on (6.42) and (6.43), we can immediately prove the following theorem.

Theorem 6.46 α^j *is a zero of* $v(x)$ *if and only if the jth frequency component of the spectrum of* $v(x)$, V_j, *equals zero.*

α^{-i} *is a zero of* $V(x)$ *if and only if the ith time component* v_i *of the inverse transform* **v** *of* **V** *equals zero.*

Recall the basic idea of a minimal polynomial: a polynomial $p(x)$ has its coefficients in the base field $GF(q)$ if and only if its roots are conjugates of each other. We have a similar result for the GFFT:

Theorem 6.47 [[483], p. 196] *Let* **V** *be a vector of length n over* $GF(q^m)$, *where* $n | q^m - 1$ *and* $GF(q^m)$ *has characteristic p. The inverse transform* **v** *of* **V** *contains elements exclusively from the subfield* $GF(q)$ *if and only if*

$$V_j^q \pmod{p} \equiv V_{qj \pmod{n}}, \quad j = 0, 1, \ldots, n-1.$$

Proof Recall that in $GF(p^t)$,

$$(a + b)^{p^r} = a^{p^r} + b^{p^r}.$$

Also recall that an element $\beta \in GF(q^m)$ is in the subfield $GF(q)$ if and only if $\beta^q = \beta$.

Let $v_i \in GF(q)$. Then

$$V_j^q = \left(\sum_{i=0}^{n-1} \alpha^{ij} v_i \right)^q = \sum_{i=0}^{n-1} \alpha^{qij} v_i^q = \sum_{i=0}^{n-1} \alpha^{i(qj)} v_i = V_{qj(\bmod\ n)}.$$

Conversely, assume $V_j^q = V_{qj\ (\bmod\ n)}$. From the definition of the GFFT,

$$V_j^q = \left(\sum_{i=0}^{n-1} \alpha^{ij} v_i \right)^q = \sum_{i=0}^{n-1} \alpha^{iqj} v_i^q$$

and

$$V_{qj\ (\bmod\ n)} = \sum_{i=0}^{n-1} \alpha^{iqj} v_i,$$

hence

$$\sum_{i=0}^{n-1} \alpha^{iqj} v_i^q = \sum_{i=0}^{n-1} \alpha^{iqj} v_i.$$

Let $k = qj$ (mod n). Since $n = q^m - 1$, q and n must be relatively prime, so that as j ranges from 0 to $n - 1$, k takes on all values in the same range, so we conclude the $v_i = v_i^q$.   □

Example 6.48   Let us illustrate the idea of the spectrum of a polynomial by considering the spectra of the minimal polynomials in $GF(8)$. The conjugacy classes and their minimal polynomials are shown here:

Conjugacy Class	Minimal Polynomial
$\{0\}$	$M_-(x) = x$
$\{\alpha^0\}$	$M_0(x) = x + 1$
$\{\alpha, \alpha^2, \alpha^4\}$	$M_1(x) = (x - \alpha)(x - \alpha^2)(x - \alpha^4) = x^3 + x + 1$
$\{\alpha^3, \alpha^5, \alpha^6\}$	$M_3(x) = (x - \alpha^3)(x - \alpha^6)(x - \alpha^5) = x^3 + x^2 + 1$

Now let us find the GFFT of the sequences obtained from the coefficients of the polynomials:

$$M_-(x): \quad \mathcal{F}(0100000) = (\alpha^j)_{j=0}^6 = (1, \alpha, \alpha^2, \alpha^3, \alpha^4, \alpha^5, \alpha^6)$$

$$M_0(x): \quad \mathcal{F}(1100000) = (1 + 1\alpha^j)_{j=0}^6 = (0, \alpha^3, \alpha^6, \alpha, \alpha^5, \alpha^4, \alpha^2)$$

$$M_1(x): \quad \mathcal{F}(1101000) = (1 + \alpha^j + \alpha^{3j})_{j=0}^6 = (1, 0, 0, \alpha^4, 0, \alpha^2, \alpha)$$

$$M_3(x): \quad \mathcal{F}(1011000) = (1 + \alpha^{2j} + \alpha^{3j})_{j=0}^6 = (1, \alpha^4, \alpha, 0, \alpha^2, 0, 0).$$

Note that the positions of the zeros in the spectra correspond to the roots of the minimal polynomials.   □

We can now state the BCH bound in terms of spectra:

Theorem 6.49 *[[483], p. 197] Let $n | q^m - 1$ for some m. A q-ary n-tuple with weight $\leq \delta - 1$ that also has $\delta - 1$ consecutive zeros in its spectrum must be the all-zero vector. That is, the minimum weight of the code is $\geq \delta$.*

Proof Let $\mathbf{c}$ have weight v, having exactly nonzero coordinates at $i_1, i_2, \ldots, i_v$. Define the locator polynomial $\Lambda(x)$ whose zeros correspond to the nonzero coordinates of $\mathbf{c}$:

$$\Lambda(x) = (1 - x\alpha^{-i_1})(1 - x\alpha^{-i_2}) \cdots (1 - x\alpha^{-i_v}) = \Lambda_0 + \Lambda_1 x + \cdots + \Lambda_v x^v.$$

We regard this polynomial as a polynomial in the frequency domain. The *inverse* transform of $\Lambda(x)$ (i.e., its coefficient sequence) is a time domain vector λ that has zero coordinates in the exact positions where $\mathbf{c}$ has nonzero coordinates. Also, at the positions where $c_i = 0$, the λ_i are not zero. Thus, $c_i \lambda_i = 0$ for all i. By the convolution theorem, we must therefore have $\mathbf{C} \circledast \Lambda = 0$.

Assume $\mathbf{c}$ has weight $\leq \delta - 1$, while $\mathbf{C}$ has $\delta - 1$ consecutive zeros (possibly consecutive by "wrapping around" the end of the vector $\mathbf{C}$ in a cyclic manner). From the definition, $\Lambda_0 = 1$. Cyclic convolution in the frequency domain gives us

$$\sum_{k=0}^{n-1} \Lambda_k C_{((i-k))} = 0$$

so

$$C_i = -\sum_{k=1}^{\delta-1} \Lambda_k C_{((i-k))}.$$

Substituting the sequence of $\delta - 1$ zeros into C_i gives $C_i = 0$; proceeding forward from that index shows that all the C_is are 0, so that $\mathbf{C} = \mathbf{0}$. □

Based on our transform interpretation, we have the following definition (construction) for a RS code: A RS code can be obtained by selecting as codewords all vectors whose transforms have $\delta - 1 = 2t$ consecutive zeros. That is, a vector $\mathbf{c}$ is a codeword in a code with minimum distance $2t + 1$ if its transform $\mathbf{C} = \mathcal{F}[\mathbf{c}]$ has a consecutive sequence of $2t$ zeros (where the sequence of zeros starts from some fixed index in the transform vector).

This definition of the code can be used to establish another encoding mechanism for RS codes. Given a message sequence $\mathbf{m} = (m_0, m_1, \ldots, m_{k-1})$, form the vector

$$\mathbf{C} = \begin{bmatrix} \mathbf{0}_{2t} & \mathbf{m} \end{bmatrix}.$$

Then the corresponding codeword is

$$\mathbf{c} = \mathcal{F}^{-1}[\mathbf{C}].$$

However, this encoding is not systematic.

6.8.1 Equivalence of the Two Reed–Solomon Code Constructions

In Section 6.2, two seemingly inequivalent constructions were presented for RS codes. Based on Theorem 6.49, a RS codeword has a consecutive sequence of $2t = d_{\min} - 1$ zeros in its GFFT. We furthermore know that the minimum distance of a RS code is $d_{\min} = n - k + 1$. We now show that the codewords constructed according to Construction 1 (Section 6.2.1) have a consecutive sequence of $n - k$ zeros in their spectrum, as required.

Let $m(x) = m_0 + m_1 x + \cdots + m_{k-1} x^{k-1}$ and let the codeword constructed according to Construction 1 be

$$\mathbf{c} = (m(1), m(\alpha), \ldots, m(\alpha^{n-1})),$$

so that

$$c_i = m(\alpha^i) = \sum_{\ell=0}^{k-1} m_\ell \alpha^{il}, \quad i = 0, 1, \ldots, n-1. \tag{6.44}$$

Now compute the GFFT of **c** as

$$C_{-j} = \sum_{i=0}^{n-1} c_i \alpha^{-ij},$$

where the index $-j$ is to be interpreted cyclically (which is legitimate, since $\alpha^n = 1$). Substituting from (6.44) into the transform,

$$C_{-j} = \sum_{i=0}^{n-1} \sum_{\ell=0}^{k-1} m_\ell \alpha^{-ij} \alpha^{i\ell} = \sum_{\ell=0}^{k-1} m_\ell \left[\sum_{i=0}^{n-1} \alpha^{i(\ell-j)} \right].$$

The inner summation is 0 if $\ell \neq j \pmod{n}$. This is the case for $-j = k, k+1, \ldots, n-1$, which is $n-k$ consecutive values of j. Thus, there are $n-k$ consecutive zeros in the GFFT of every codeword.

6.8.2 Frequency-Domain Decoding

We present in this section one way of using the GFFT to decode a BCH or RS code. Let $\mathbf{r} = \mathbf{c} + \mathbf{e}$ be a received vector and let **R**, **C**, and **E** denote the corresponding transformed vectors. By the linearity of the transform, we have

$$\mathbf{R} = \mathbf{C} + \mathbf{E},$$

where

$$E_j = \sum_{i=0}^{n-1} \alpha^{ij} e_i.$$

Assume the code is a narrow-sense code. Then the first $2t$ coordinates of **C** are equal to zero, so that $\mathbf{R}_j = \mathbf{E}_j$ for $j = 0, 1, \ldots, 2t-1$. (These are the syndromes for the decoder.) Completion of the decoding requires finding the the remaining $n - 2t$ coordinates of **E**, after which we can find **e** by inverse GFFT.

Let $\Lambda(x) = \prod_{i=1}^{\nu}(1 - X_i x)$, treating the coefficients as a spectrum Λ. The inverse transform $\lambda = \mathcal{F}^{-1}[\Lambda]$ yields a vector which has zeros at the coordinates corresponding to the zeros of $\Lambda(x)$, so λ has a zero wherever **e** is nonzero. Thus,

$$\lambda_i e_i = 0, \quad i = 0, 1, \ldots, n-1.$$

Translating the product back to the frequency domain, we have by the convolution formula $\Lambda \circledast \mathbf{E} = \mathbf{0}$, or

$$\sum_{k=0}^{n-1} \Lambda_k E_{((j-k))} = 0, \quad j = 0, 1, \ldots, n-1.$$

Now assume that ν errors have occurred, so that the degree of $\Lambda(x)$ is ν. Then $\Lambda_k = 0$ for $k > \nu$. We obtain the familiar LFSR relationship

$$\sum_{k=0}^{\nu} \Lambda_k E_{((j-k))} = 0, \quad j = 0, 1, \ldots, n-1$$

or, since $\Lambda_0 = 1$,

$$E_j = -\sum_{k=1}^{\nu} \Lambda_k E_{j-k}. \tag{6.45}$$

This expresses an LFSR relationship between the transformed errors E_j and the coefficients of the error locator polynomial. Given the $2t$ known values of the transformed errors $\{E_0, E_1, \ldots, E_{2t-1}\}$, the error locator polynomial can be found using any of the methods described previously (such as the Berlekamp–Massey algorithm or the Euclidean algorithm). Knowing the Λ_i coefficients, the remainder of the E_j values can be found using (6.45). Then knowing **E**, the error vector in the "time" domain can be found by an inverse Fourier transform: $\mathbf{e} = \mathcal{F}^{-1}[\mathbf{E}]$. Note that unless a fast inverse Fourier transform is available, this is essentially the same as a Chien search.

6.9 Variations and Extensions of Reed–Solomon Codes

In this section, we briefly describe several variations on RS and BCH codes. More detail can be found in [292].

6.9.1 Simple Modifications

Several simple modifications are possible, of the sort described in Section 3.9.

An (n, k) RS code can be *punctured* by deleting any of its symbols, resulting in a $(n - 1, k)$ code.

An (n, k) RS code C can be *extended* by adding additional parity check symbols. A code is *singly* extended by adding a single parity symbol. Interestingly enough, a single-extended RS code is still MDS. To see this, let $\mathbf{c} = (c_0, c_1, \ldots, c_{q-2})$ be a codeword from a $(q - 1, k)$ q-ary narrow-sense t-error-correcting code and let

$$c_{q-1} = -\sum_{j=0}^{q-2} c_j$$

be an overall parity check digit. Then an extended codeword is $(c_0, c_1, \ldots, c_{q-1})$. To see that this extended code is still MDS, we must show that the distance has, in fact, increased. To this end, suppose that $\mathbf{c}$ has, in fact, minimum weight $d_{\min}$ in C. Let $c(x)$ be the corresponding code polynomial. The generator for the code is

$$g(x) = (x - \alpha)(x - \alpha^2) \cdots (x - \alpha^{2t}).$$

Now

$$c(1) = \sum_{i=0}^{q-2} c_i.$$

If $c(1) \neq 0$, then $c_{q-1} \neq 0$, so the new codeword in the extended code has minimum distance $d_{\min} + 1$. If $c(1) = 0$, then $c(x)$ must be of the form $c(x) = u(x)(x - 1)g(x)$ for some polynomial $u(x)$. That is, $c(x)$ is a code polynomial in the code having generator

$$g'(x) = (x - 1)(x - \alpha)(x - \alpha^2) \cdots (x - \alpha^{2t}).$$

By the BCH bound, this code must have minimum distance $d_{\min} + 1$. Since the new code is $(n + 1, k)$ with minimum distance $d_{\min} + 1$, it is MDS.

It is also possible to form a double-extended RS code which is MDS [292]. However, these extended codes are not, in general, cyclic.

6.9.2 Generalized Reed–Solomon Codes and Alternant Codes

Recall that according to Construction 1 of RS codes, codewords are obtained by

$$\mathbf{c} = (m(1), m(\alpha), \ldots, m(\alpha^{n-1})). \tag{6.46}$$

Now choose a vector $\mathbf{v} = (v_1, v_2, \ldots, v_n)$ whose elements are all nonzero. Then a generalization of (6.46) is

$$\mathbf{c} = (v_1 m(1), v_2 m(\alpha), \ldots, v_n m(\alpha^{n-1})).$$

Somewhat more generally, we have the following.

Definition 6.50 Let $\boldsymbol{\alpha} = (\alpha_1, \alpha_2, \ldots, \alpha_n)$ be n distinct elements of $GF(q^m)$ and let $\mathbf{v} = (v_1, v_2, \ldots, v_n)$ have nonzero (but not necessarily distinct) elements from $GF(q^m)$. Then the **generalized RS code**, denoted by $GRS_k(\boldsymbol{\alpha}, \mathbf{v})$, consists of all vectors

$$(v_1 m(\alpha_1), v_2 m(\alpha_2), \ldots, v_n m(\alpha_n))$$

as $m(x)$ ranges over all polynomials of degree $< k$. □

The $GRS_k(\boldsymbol{\alpha}, \mathbf{v})$ code is an (n, k) code and can be shown (using the same argument as for Construction 1) to be MDS.

The parity check matrix for the $GRS_k(\boldsymbol{\alpha}, \mathbf{v})$ code can be written as

$$H = \begin{bmatrix} y_1 & y_2 & \cdots & y_n \\ \alpha_1 y_1 & \alpha_2 y_2 & \cdots & \alpha_n y_n \\ \vdots & & & \\ \alpha_1^{r-1} y_1 & \alpha_2^{r-1} y_2 & \cdots & \alpha_n^{r-1} y_n \end{bmatrix}$$

$$= \begin{bmatrix} 1 & 1 & \cdots & 1 \\ \alpha_1 & \alpha_2 & \cdots & \alpha_n \\ \alpha_1^2 & \alpha_2^2 & \cdots & \alpha_n^2 \\ \vdots & & & \\ \alpha_1^{r-1} & \alpha_2^{r-1} & \cdots & \alpha_n^{r-1} \end{bmatrix} \begin{bmatrix} y_1 & & & \\ & y_2 & & \\ & & \ddots & \\ & & & y_n \end{bmatrix} \triangleq XY. \tag{6.47}$$

Here, $\mathbf{y} = (y_1, y_2, \ldots, y_n)$ with $y_i \in GF(q^m)$ and $y_i \neq 0$, is such that $GRS_k(\boldsymbol{\alpha}, \mathbf{v})^\perp = GRS_{n-k}(\boldsymbol{\alpha}, \mathbf{y})$.

If $H = XY$ is a parity check matrix, then for an invertible matrix C, $\tilde{H} = CXY$ is an equivalent parity check matrix.

While the elements of codewords of a $GRS_k(\boldsymbol{\alpha}, \mathbf{v})$ code are in general in $GF(q^m)$, it is possible to form a code from codewords whose elements lie in the base field $GF(q)$.

Definition 6.51 An **alternant** code $\mathcal{A}(\boldsymbol{\alpha}, \mathbf{y})$ consists of all codewords of $GRS_k(\boldsymbol{\alpha}, \mathbf{v})$ whose components all lie in $GF(q)$. (We say that $\mathcal{A}(\boldsymbol{\alpha}, \mathbf{y})$ is the **restriction** of $GRS_k(\boldsymbol{\alpha}, \mathbf{v})$ to $GF(q)$.) That is, $\mathcal{A}(\boldsymbol{\alpha}, \mathbf{y})$ is the set of all vectors $\mathbf{c} \in GF(q)^n$ such that $H\mathbf{c} = \mathbf{0}$, for H in (6.47). Another way of saying this is that $\mathcal{A}$ is the **subfield subcode** of $GRS_k(\boldsymbol{\alpha}, \mathbf{v})$. □

Since we have an expression for a parity check matrix for the GRS code, it is of interest to find a parity check matrix for the alternant code. That is, we want to find a parity check matrix $\tilde{H}$ over $GF(q)$ corresponding to the parity check matrix H over $GF(q^m)$. This can be done as follows. Pick a basis $\alpha_1, \alpha_2, \ldots, \alpha_m$ for $GF(q^m)$ over $GF(q)$. (Recall that $GF(q^m)$ can be written as a vector space of elements of $GF(q)$.) A convenient basis set is $\{1, \alpha, \alpha^2, \ldots, \alpha^{m-1}\}$, but any linearly independent set can do. Then, for each element H_{ij} of H, write

$$H_{ij} = \sum_{l=1}^{m} h_{ijl} \alpha_l,$$

where each $h_{ijl} \in GF(q)$. Now define $\tilde{H}$ to be the $(n-k)m \times n$ matrix obtained from H by replacing each entry H_{ij} by the column vector of components in $(h_{ij1}, h_{ij2}, \ldots, h_{ijm})$, so that

$$\tilde{H} = \begin{bmatrix} h_{111} & h_{121} & & h_{1n1} \\ h_{112} & h_{122} & \cdots & h_{1n2} \\ \vdots & \vdots & & \vdots \\ h_{11m} & h_{12m} & & h_{1nm} \\ \vdots & & & \\ h_{r11} & h_{r21} & & h_{rn1} \\ h_{r12} & h_{r22} & \cdots & h_{rn2} \\ \vdots & \vdots & & \vdots \\ h_{r1m} & h_{r2m} & & h_{rnm} \end{bmatrix}.$$

It can be argued that the dimension of the code must satisfy $k \geq n - mr$.

One of the important properties about alternant codes is the following:

Theorem 6.52 *[[292], p. 334] $\mathcal{A}(\boldsymbol{\alpha}, \mathbf{y})$ has minimum distance $d_{\min} \geq n - k + 1$.*

Proof Suppose $\mathbf{c}$ is a codeword having weight $\leq r = n - k$. Then $H\mathbf{c} = XY\mathbf{c} = \mathbf{0}$. Let $\mathbf{b} = Y\mathbf{c}$. Since Y is diagonal and invertible, $\text{wt}(\mathbf{b}) = \text{wt}(\mathbf{c})$. Then $X\mathbf{b} = \mathbf{0}$. However, X is a full-rank Vandermonde matrix, so this is impossible. $\qquad\square$

In summary, we have a code of length n, dimension $k \geq n - mr$ and minimum distance $d_{\min} \geq n - r$.

The family of alternant codes encompasses a variety of interesting codes, depending on how the field and subfield are chosen. BCH and RS codes are alternant codes. So are Goppa codes, which are described next.

6.9.3 Goppa Codes

Goppa codes start off with a seemingly different definition but are, in fact, instances of alternant codes.

Definition 6.53 Let $L = \{\alpha_1, \alpha_2, \ldots, \alpha_n\}$ where each $\alpha_i \in GF(q^m)$. Let $G(x) \in GF(q^m)[x]$ be the **Goppa polynomial**, where each $\alpha_i \in L$ is *not* a root of G. That is, $G(\alpha_i) \neq 0$ for all $\alpha_i \in L$. For any vector $\mathbf{a} = (a_1, a_2, \ldots, a_n)$ with elements in $GF(q)$, associate the rational function

$$R_{\mathbf{a}}(x) = \sum_{i=1}^{n} \frac{a_i}{x - \alpha_i}.$$

Then the **Goppa code** $\Gamma(L, G)$ consists of all vectors $\mathbf{a} \in GF(q)^n$ such that

$$R_{\mathbf{a}}(x) \equiv 0 \pmod{G(x)}. \tag{6.48}$$

If $G(x)$ is irreducible, then $\Gamma(L, G)$ is an irreducible Goppa code. $\qquad\square$

As we will see, Goppa codes have good distance properties: $d_{\min} \geq \deg(G) + 1$.

Goppa codes are linear codes. The parity check matrix can be found using (6.48), which can be re-expressed as: $R_{\mathbf{a}}(x) = 0$ in the ring $GF(q^m)[x]/G(x)$. Note that in this ring, $x - \alpha_i$ does have an inverse, since it does not divide $G(x)$. The inverse is

$$(x - \alpha_i)^{-1} = -\frac{G(x) - G(\alpha_i)}{x - \alpha_i} G(\alpha_i)^{-1}, \tag{6.49}$$

as can be shown by observing that

$$-(x - \alpha_i)\frac{G(x) - G(\alpha_i)}{x - \alpha_i} G(\alpha_i)^{-1} \equiv 1 \pmod{G(x)}$$

by applying the definition of $\equiv$. Let $G(x) = \sum_{i=0}^{r} g_i x^i$ with $g_r \neq 0$. It can be verified by long division and collection of terms that

$$
\begin{aligned}
\frac{G(x) - G(\alpha_i)}{x - \alpha_i} &= g_r(x^{r-1} + x^{r-2}\alpha_i + \cdots + \alpha_i^{r-1}) + g_{r-1}(x^{r-2} + \cdots + \alpha_i^{r-2}) \\
&\quad + \cdots + g_2(x + \alpha_i) + g_1.
\end{aligned}
\tag{6.50}
$$

Substituting (6.49) into (6.48), we have that $\mathbf{a}$ is in $\Gamma(L, G)$ if and only if

$$\sum_{i=1}^{n} a_i \frac{G(x) - G(\alpha_i)}{x - \alpha_i} G(\alpha_i)^{-1} = 0 \tag{6.51}$$

as a polynomial (and not just modulo $G(x)$). Since the polynomial must be 0, the coefficients of each x^i must each be zero individually. Substituting (6.50) into (6.51) and equating each of the coefficients of $x^{r-1}, x^{r-2}, \ldots, 1$ to 0, we see that $\mathbf{a}$ is in $\Gamma(l, G)$ if and only if $H\mathbf{a} = \mathbf{0}$, where

$$
H = \begin{bmatrix}
g_r G(\alpha_1)^{-1} & \cdots & g_1 G(\alpha_n)^{-1} \\
(g_{r-1} + \alpha_1 g_r) G(\alpha_1)^{-1} & \cdots & (g_{r-1} + \alpha_n g_r) G(\alpha_n)^{-1} \\
\vdots & & \\
(g_1 + \alpha_1 g_2 + \cdots + \alpha_1^{r-1} g_r) G(\alpha_1)^{-1} & \cdots & (g_1 + \alpha_n g_2 + \cdots + \alpha_n^{r-1} g_r) G(\alpha_n)^{-1}
\end{bmatrix}.
$$

Note that the matrix H can be written as

$$
H = \begin{bmatrix}
g_r & 0 & 0 & \cdots & 0 \\
g_{r-1} & g_r & 0 & \cdots & 0 \\
g_{r-2} & g_{r-1} & g_r & \cdots & 0 \\
\vdots & & & & \\
g_1 & g_2 & g_3 & \cdots & g_r
\end{bmatrix}
\begin{bmatrix}
1 & 1 & \cdots & 1 \\
\alpha_1 & \alpha_2 & \cdots & \alpha_n \\
\alpha_1^2 & \alpha_2^2 & \cdots & \alpha_n^2 \\
\vdots & & & \\
\alpha_1^{r-1} & \alpha_2^{r-1} & \cdots & \alpha_n^{r-1}
\end{bmatrix}
$$

$$
\times \begin{bmatrix}
G(\alpha_1)^{-1} & & & \\
& G(\alpha_2)^{-1} & & \\
& & \ddots & \\
& & & G(\alpha_n)^{-1}
\end{bmatrix}
$$

or $H = CXY$. Since C is lower triangular with a nonzero along the diagonal, C is invertible. It follows that an equivalent parity check matrix is

$$
\tilde{H} = XY = \begin{bmatrix}
G(\alpha_1)^{-1} & \cdots & G(\alpha_n)^{-1} \\
\alpha_1 G(\alpha_1)^{-1} & \cdots & \alpha_n G(\alpha_n)^{-1} \\
\vdots & & \\
\alpha_1^{r-1} G(\alpha_1)^{-1} & \cdots & \alpha_n^{r-1} G(\alpha_n)^{-1}
\end{bmatrix}.
$$

We observe from the structure of the parity check matrix (compare with (6.47)) that the Goppa code is an alternant code, with $\mathbf{y} = (G(\alpha_1)^{-1}, \ldots, G(\alpha_n)^{-1})$. In fact, it can be shown that the $\Gamma(L, G)$ code can be obtained as the restriction to $GF(q)$ of the $GRS_{n-r}(\boldsymbol{\alpha}, \mathbf{v})$ code, where

$$
v_i = \frac{G(\alpha_i)}{\prod_{j \neq i}(\alpha_i - \alpha_j)}.
$$

6.9.4 Decoding Alternant Codes

Efficient algorithms exist for decoding alternant codes [[292], Section 12.9]. These exactly parallel the steps used for decoding RS codes: (1) A syndrome is computed (the details are somewhat different than for RS codes); (2) An error locator polynomial is found, say, using the Berlekamp–Massey or the Euclidean algorithm; (3) The roots are found; and (4) Error values are computed if necessary. A decoding algorithm for Goppa codes also appears in [334].

6.9.5 Cryptographic Connections: The McEliece Public Key Cryptosystem

In this section, we present another connection between error-correction coding and cryptography. In this case, we show how an error-correction code can be used to make a public key encryption system. The original system was based on Goppa codes (hence its inclusion in this context), but other codes might also be used.

The person A wishing to communicate picks an irreducible polynomial $G(x)$ of degree t over $GF(2^m)$ "at random" and constructs the generator matrix G for the (n, k) Goppa code using $G(x)$. This code is capable of correcting any pattern of up to t errors. Note that there are efficient decoding algorithms for this code.

Now A scrambles the generator G by selecting a random dense invertible $k \times k$ matrix S and a random $n \times n$ permutation matrix P. He computes $\tilde{G} = SGP$. A message $\mathbf{m}$ would be encoded using this generator as

$$\tilde{\mathbf{c}} = (\mathbf{m}S)GP = (\tilde{\mathbf{m}}G)P.$$

Since P simply reorders the elements of the codeword corresponding to the message $\tilde{\mathbf{m}}$, the code with generator $\tilde{G}$ has the same minimum distance as the code with generator G. The **public key** for this system is the scrambled generator $\tilde{G}$. The **private key** is the set (S, G, P).

Encryption of a message $\mathbf{m}$ is accomplished using the public key by computing

$$\mathbf{e} = \mathbf{m}\tilde{G} + \mathbf{z},$$

where $\mathbf{z}$ is a random "noise" vector of length n and weight t. $\mathbf{e}$ is transmitted as the encrypted information.

Because the encoding is not systematic and there is noise added, the message is not explicitly evident in $\mathbf{e}$. The encrypted message $\mathbf{m}$ could be discovered if $\mathbf{e}$ could be decoded (in the error-correction coding sense). However, the scrambled matrix $\tilde{G}$ no longer has the algebraic structure that provides an efficient decoding algorithm. Optimal decoding without some structure to exploit can have NP-complete complexity [35]. Hence, a recipient of $\mathbf{e}$ can recover $\mathbf{m}$ only with extreme effort.

Decryption of $\mathbf{e}$ knowing (S, G, P), however, is straightforward. Knowing P, first compute $\tilde{\mathbf{e}} = \mathbf{e}P^{-1}$. Note that while the noise is permuted, no additional noise terms are added. Now decode using a fast Goppa decoder, effectively getting rid of the noise $\mathbf{z}$, to obtain the scrambled message $\tilde{\mathbf{m}} = \mathbf{m}S$. Finally, invert to obtain $\mathbf{m} = \tilde{\mathbf{m}}S^{-1}$.

Programming Laboratory 6: Programming the Berlekamp–Massey Algorithm

Background

Reading: Sections 6.4.2, 6.4.3 and 6.4.4.

The Berlekamp–Massey algorithm provides one of the key steps in the decoding of BCH or RS codes. Specifically, it provides a means to determine the error-locating polynomial given the syndromes.

We have encountered LFSRs in previous labs: in binary form in Lab 2 and in the context of the Sugiyama algorithm in Lab 4. The problem addressed by the Berlekamp–Massey algorithm is to find the coefficients $\{c_1, c_2, \ldots, c_v\}$ satisfying (6.16) with the *smallest* v. (The Sugiyama algorithm introduced in Lab 4 provides another solution to this same problem.) The LFSR coefficients are represented in a polynomial, the *connection polynomial*

$$c(x) = 1 + c_1 x + c_2 x^2 + \cdots + c_v x^v.$$

The Berlekamp–Massey algorithm is described in Algorithm 6.1 on page 25. Simplifications for binary BCH codes are presented in Algorithm 6.2 on page 26.

Assignment

Preliminary Exercises

1) For operations in $\mathbb{Z}_5$, work through the Berlekamp–Massey algorithm for the sequence $\{2, 3, 4, 2, 2, 3\}$. Verify that the sequence of connection polynomials is

Initial:	$c = 1$	$L = 0$
$k = 1$	$c = 1 + 3x$	$L = 1$
$k = 2$	$c = 1 + x$	$L = 1$
$k = 3$	$c = 1 + x + 4x^2$	$L = 2$
$k = 4$	$c = 1 + 2x$	$L = 2$
$k = 5$	$c = 1 + 2x + 2x^2 + 2x^3$	$L = 3$
$k = 6$	$c = 1 + 3x + 4x^2 + 2x^3$	$L = 3$

2) For operations in $GF(2)$, work through the Berlekamp–Massey algorithm for the sequence $\{1, 1, 1, 0, 1, 0, 0\}$. Verify that the sequence of connection polynomials is

Initial:	$c = 1$	$L = 0$
$k = 1$	$c = 1 + x$	$L = 1$
$k = 2$	$c = 1 + x$	$L = 1$
$k = 3$	$c = 1 + x$	$L = 1$
$k = 4$	$c = 1 + x + x^3$	$L = 3$
$k = 5$	$c = 1 + x + x^3$	$L = 3$
$k = 6$	$c = 1 + x + x^3$	$L = 3$
$k = 7$	$c = 1 + x + x^3$	$L = 3$

3) For operations in $GF(2^4)$, work through the Berlekamp–Massey algorithm for the sequence $\{0, \alpha^3, \alpha^4, \alpha^7\}$. Verify that the sequence of connection polynomials is

Initial:	$c = 1$	$L = 0$
$k = 1$	$c = 1$	$L = 0$
$k = 2$	$c = 1 + \alpha^3 x^2$	$L = 2$
$k = 3$	$c = 1 + \alpha x + \alpha^3 x^2$	$L = 2$
$k = 4$	$c = 1 + \alpha x + \alpha^{10} x^2$	$L = 2$

Programming Part

1. Write a function berlmass which: **Either**
   - Accepts a sequence of numbers of arbitrary type and returns a connection polynomial for an LFSR generating that sequence. The function should have the following declaration:

   ```
   template <class T> polynomialT<T> berlmass
   (const T* s, int n);
   // Accept a sequence s of type T and length n
   // (s[0] ... s[n-1])
   // and return a connection polynomial c of
   // shortest length generating that sequence.
   ```

   - **Or,** accepts an array of numbers of arbitrary type and an argument into which the coefficients of the connection polynomial are written. The function should have the following declaration:

   ```
   template <class T> void berlmass2
   (const T* s, int n, T* c, int & L)
   // s = input coefficients s[0],s[1],...
     s[n-1]
   // c = connection polynomial coefficients.
   // (Must be allocated prior to calling)
   // L = degree of connection polynomial
   ```

   You may want to create a class BCH which encapsulates one of these functions. (See the discussion below.) The difference between these is that the first form deals explicitly with the polynomial, while the second deals only with the coefficients. Tradeoffs between these are discussed below.

2. Test your function using the examples from the preliminary exercises.

Algorithm 6.3 Test BM Algorithm
File: testBM.cc
        berlmass.cc
        berlmass2.cc

3. Over $GF(16)$ verify that the sequence $\{\alpha^8, \alpha, \alpha^{13}, \alpha^2, \alpha^5, \alpha^{11}\}$ is generated by the LFSR with connection polynomial $1 + \alpha^8 x + \alpha^2 x^2$.

4. Over $GF(16)$ verify that the sequence $\{0, 0, \alpha^5, 0, 1, \alpha^{10}\}$ is produced by $1 + \alpha^{10} x^2 + \alpha^5 x^3$.

5. Write a function berlmassBCH which accepts data satisfying the syndrome conjugacy condition (6.31) and computes the connection polynomial using the reduced complexity algorithm. Test your algorithm by verifying that:
   (a) For the sequence $\{1, 1, \alpha^{10}, 1, \alpha^{10}, \alpha^5\}$ the connection polynomial is $1 + x + \alpha^5 x^3$, with computations over $GF(2^4)$.
   (b) For the sequence $\{\alpha^{14}, \alpha^{13}, 1, \alpha^{11}, \alpha^5, 1\}$ the connection polynomial is $1 + \alpha^{14} x + \alpha^{11} x^2 + \alpha^{14} x^3$, with computations over $GF(2^4)$.

Resources and Implementation Suggestions

Two implementations are sugaggested for the algorithms, one which employs polynomials and the other which employs arrays. The polynomial implementation is somewhat easier to write than the array implementation, since the single statement

```
c = c - (p << shift)*(d/dm);
```

suffices to provide the update in (6.19). The algorithm outlined in Algorithm 6.1 can thus be almost literally translated into C++.

There are a couple of precautions, however. First, in the update, there may be cancellations in the higher order terms of the polynomial, so the actual degree of the polynomial $c(x)$ is less than the expected degree L. However, L should not be modified. The impact of this is that when the discrepancy is computed, the actual degree of $c(x)$ should be used, not L. The discrepancy can be computed as in the following piece of code:

```
// compute the discrepancy
// in the polynomial implementation
d = s[k]; for(j=1; j <= c.getdegree(); j++) {  // sum
  d += c[j]*s[k-j];
}
```

The other thing to be aware of is that there is internal memory allocation and deallocation that take place whenever a polynomialT is assigned to a polynomialT of different degree. This introduces an operational overhead to the algorithm.

Which brings up the array form: By implementing the operations explicitly using arrays, the overhead of memory management can be (almost) eliminated and only a little more work is necessary. For example, the update formula (6.19) can be represented using a simple loop:

```
// update the polynomial
for(j = shift; j <= L; j++) {
  // Compute: c = c - (p<< shift)*(d/dm);
  c[j] -= p[j-shift]*ddm;
}
```

The function must have passed to it an array of sufficient size to hold the polynomial. Also, it must allocate arrays of sufficient size to represent the largest possible `t` and `p` polynomials, then de-allocate them on exit. However, there is a caution associated with this implementation: if the function is called repeatedly, the prior data in `c` does mess up the computations. Additional care is necessary to ensure that terms that should be 0 actually are — the simple loop above does not suffice for this purpose.

This brings up the final implementation suggestion: the function would be most cleanly represented using a class with internal storage allocation. Then the necessary internal space could be allocated once upon instantiation of an object then used repeatedly. You may therefore want to write it this way (and use arrays internally).

Programming Laboratory 7: Programming the BCH Decoder

Objective

In this lab you implement a BCH decoder and thoroughly test it.

Preliminary Exercises

Reading: Sections 6.3 and 6.4.

1. For the field $GF(2^4)$ generated by $1 + x + x^4$, show that the minimal polynomials of α, α^3, and α^5 are

$$M_1(x) = 1 + x + x^4$$
$$M_3(x) = 1 + x + x^2 + x^3 + x^4$$
$$M_5(x) = 1 + x + x^2.$$

2. Show that the generator for a $(15, 5)$ three-error-correcting binary BCH code is

$$g(x) = 1 + x + x^2 + x^4 + x^5 + x^8 + x^{10}.$$

3. Determine the actual minimum weight of this code.

Programming Part

1. Write a class `ChienSearch` which implements the Chien search algorithm over $GF(2^m)$. In the interest of speed, the class constructor should allocate space necessary for the registers as well as space for the computed roots. A member function should accept an error locator polynomial (or an array of its coefficients) and compute all the roots of the polynomial.

Algorithm 6.4 Chien Search
File: `ChienSearch.h`
`ChienSearch.cc`
`testChien.cc`

Test your algorithm by verifying that over $GF(2^4)$ the roots of the error locator polynomial

$$\Lambda(x) = 1 + x + \alpha^5 x^3$$

are at α^3, α^{10}, and α^{12}.

2. Build a BCH decoder class which decodes a vector of n binary elements.

3. Thoroughly test your decoder on the $(15, 5)$ BCH code with generator

$$g(x) = 1 + x + x^2 + x^4 + x^5 + x^8 + x^{10}$$

over the field $GF(2^4)$. You should correct all patterns of up to three errors. The test program in Algorithm 6.5 provides an exhaustive test of *all* patterns of three errors (with some duplication).

Your finished decoder should finish without any uncorrected errors. It is important to make sure that you are able to successfully decode all error patterns. This test is likely to shake out several minor problems with the functions you have written. After all errors are corrected, you can be quite confident in the functions you have written.

Algorithm 6.5 BCH Decoder
File: `BCHdec.h`
`BCHdec.cc`
`testBCH.cc`

4. Modify the BCH decoder to use the reduced-complexity Berlekamp–Massey algorithm

for BCH syndromes (the one described in Section 6.4.4) to find the error locator polynomial from the syndromes. Ensure that your decoder is still able to decode all patterns of up to three errors.

5. Modify the BCH decoder to use the Sugiyama algorithm from lab 4 to find the error locator polynomial from the syndromes. Ensure that your decoder is still able to decode all patterns of up to three errors.

Resources and Implementation Suggestions

1. The syndromes are numbered $s_1, s_2, \ldots, s_{2t}$, whereas the discussion surrounding the Berlekamp–Massey algorithm used zero-based indexing, $y_0, y_1, \ldots, y_{2t-1}$. There is no difficulty here: simply interpret $y_j = s_{j+1}$ and call the Berlekamp–Massey algorithm with an array such that the first element contains the first syndrome.

2. If you represent the received vector as a polynomial polynomialT<GFNUM2m>, then evaluating it to compute the syndromes is very straightforward using the ( ) operator in class polynomialT.

   If you choose to represent it as an array (to avoid memory management overhead), for efficiency the polynomial evaluation should be done using *Horner's rule*. As an example, to evaluate a cubic polynomial, you would not want to use

```
p = c[0] + c[1]*x + c[2]*x*x + c[3]*x*x*x;
```

since multiplications are wasted in repeatedly computing products of x. Instead, it is better to write in nested form as

```
p = ((c[3]*x+c[2])*x+c[1])*x+c[0];
```

This nesting can be efficiently coded as

```
p = c[j=n];
while(j>0)
    p = p*x + c[-j];
```

3. If you use an array implementation of the Berlekamp–Massey algorithm (in contrast to a polynomialT implementation) you may need to take special care that the coefficients of the connection polynomial are zeroed out properly.

Follow-On Ideas and Problems

The BCH codes described in this lab are narrow sense, in that the roots of the polynomial $g(x)$ contain the list $\beta, \beta^2, \ldots, \beta^{2t}$ for a primitive element β. A non-narrow-sense BCH code uses the roots

$$\beta^b, \beta^{b+1}, \ldots, \beta^{b+2t-1}$$

for an arbitrary b. Describe how the decoding algorithm is modified for non-narrow-sense BCH codes.

Programming Laboratory 8: Reed–Solomon Encoding and Decoding

Objective

In this lab you are to extend the binary BCH decoder implemented in Lab 7 to nonbinary RS codes. In addition, instead of simply decoding random errors, you will create a systematic encoder.

Background

Reading: Sections 6.3–6.5 and 6.6.

Programming Part

1. Create a class RSenc which implements a Reed–Solomon encoder for primitive, narrow-sense codes. Verify that the function works by encoding

the data as in Example 6.19. Your class declaration might be as in RSenc.h.

Algorithm 6.6 Reed-Solomon Encoder Declaration
File: RSenc.h
       RSenc.cc

2. Create a class RSdec which implements a Reed–Solomon decoder for primitive, narrow-sense codes. Use the Berlekamp–Massey algorithm to find $\Lambda(x)$, followed by the Chien search to find the error locators and the Forney algorithm to find the error values. You should be able to use much of the code that you have written previously (the Berlekamp–Massey algorithm, the Chien search from the BCH lab) as well as create new code

for the Forney algorithm. A declaration for the class might be as in RSdec.h.

Algorithm 6.7 Reed-Solomon Decoder Declaration
File: RSdec.h
        RSdec.cc

After creating an RSdec object, a call to the decode member function converts the array r to the decoded array dec.

3. Test your decoder by decoding 10,000 patterns of up to 3 errors for the $(255, 249)$ code over the field $GF(2^8)$ using $p(x) = x^8 + x^4 + x^3 + x^2 + 1$. A program which does this testing is testRS.cc.

Algorithm 6.8 Reed-Solomon Decoder Testing
File: testRS.cc

4. After you have tested and debugged your decoder, replace the Berlekamp–Massey algorithm with the Euclidean algorithm to determine $\Lambda(x)$ and $\Omega(x)$. Test the resulting algorithm as before, ensuring that many random patterns of up to three errors are decoded.

5. After you have tested and debugged your encoder and decoder objects, you are ready to use them to protect data files on the computer. rsencode is a program to encode data using a $(255, 255 - 2t)$ RS code, where t defaults to 3, but can be set using a command-line argument. The corresponding decoder program is rsdecode.

Algorithm 6.9 Reed-Solomon File Encoder and Decoder
File: rsencode.cc
        rsdecode.cc

In the program, special care is taken to handle the last block of data, writing out the length of the block if it is less than 255.

Starting with this source code, use your encoder and decoder objects to build complete encoder and decoder programs, rsencode and rsdecode. Test your encoders and decoders on short files (<249 bytes) and longer files. Test the program when the encoded data is corrupted (say, using the bsc program).

Algorithm 6.10 Binary Symmetric Channel Simulator
File: bsc.c

Appendix 6.A   Proof of Newton's Identities

Newton's identities relate the coefficients of a polynomial to the power sum identities obtained from the roots of the polynomial. We derive them here in the general case, then make application to the error locator polynomial.

Let

$$f(x) = (x - x_1)(x - x_2) \cdots (x - x_n)$$
$$= x^n - \sigma_1 x^{n-1} + \sigma_2 x^{n-2} + \cdots + (-1)^{n-1}\sigma_{n-1}x + (-1)^n \sigma_n.$$

The power sums are $s_k = x_1^k + x_2^k + \cdots + x_n^k$, $k = 1, 2, \ldots, n$, and the elementary symmetric functions are

$$\sigma_1 = x_1 + \cdots + x_n$$
$$\sigma_2 = x_1 x_2 + x_1 x_3 + \cdots + x_1 x_n + \cdots x_{n-1} x_n$$
$$\vdots$$
$$\sigma_n = x_1 x_2 \cdots x_n.$$

Theorem 6.54 *(Newton's Identities) The elementary symmetric functions σ_k and the power sum symmetric functions s_k are related by*

$$s_k - \sigma_1 s_{k-1} + \cdots + (-1)^{k-1}\sigma_{k-1}s_1 + (-1)^k k\sigma_k = 0 \quad 1 \le k \le n \tag{6.52}$$
$$s_k - \sigma_1 s_{k-1} + \cdots + (-1)^{n-1}\sigma_{n-1}s_{k-n+1} + (-1)^n s_{k-n}\sigma_n = 0 \quad k > n.$$

Proof Let σ_i^n be the ith elementary symmetric function in n variables and let s_i^n be the symmetric power sum function in n variables. Also, let $\sigma_0^n = 1$ and $\sigma_i^n = 0$ if $i < 0$ or $i > n$. Then the two Newton's identities (6.13) are subsumed into the single relationship

$$s_k^n - \sigma_1^n s_{k-1}^n + \cdots + (-1)^{k-1}\sigma_{k-1}^n s_1^n + (-1)^k k\sigma_k^n = 0 \quad \text{for all } k \ge 1, \tag{6.53}$$

or, more concisely,

$$\sum_{j=0}^{k-1}[(-1)^j s_{k-j}^n \sigma_j^n] + (-1)^k k\sigma_k^n = 0 \quad \text{for all } k \ge 1. \tag{6.54}$$

The proof of (6.53) relies on the observations that

$$s_k^m = s_k^{m-1} + x_m^k, \quad m = 1, 2, \ldots, n \tag{6.55}$$

and

$$\sigma_i^m = \sigma_i^{m-1} + x_m \sigma_{i-1}^{m-1}, \quad i = 1, \ldots, n; \quad m = 0, \ldots, n. \tag{6.56}$$

The former equation is by definition and the latter is by the multiplication operation. We do induction on the number of variables. When $m = n = 1$, (6.54) implies $s_1^1 = \sigma_1^1$, which is true by direct computation. Assume (6.54) is true for $n - 1$; we obtain the inductive hypothesis

$$\sum_{j=0}^{k-1}[(-1)^j s_{k-j}^{n-1} \sigma_j^{n-1}] + (-1)^k k\sigma_k^{n-1} = 0. \tag{6.57}$$

Then for n, using (6.55) and (6.56),

$$\sum_{j=0}^{k-1}[(-1)^j s_{k-j}^n \sigma_j^n] + (-1)^k k\sigma_k^n$$

$$= \sum_{j=0}^{k-1}(-1)^j (\underbrace{s_{k-j}^{n-1}}_{a} + \underbrace{x_n^{k-j}}_{b})(\underbrace{\sigma_j^{n-1}}_{c} + \underbrace{x_n\sigma_{j-1}^{n-1}}_{d}) + (-1)^k k(\underbrace{\sigma_k^{n-1}}_{e} + \underbrace{x_n\sigma_{k-1}^{n-1}}_{f})$$

$$= \underbrace{\sum_{j=0}^{k-1}(-1)^j s_{k-j}^{n-1}\sigma_j^{n-1} + (-1)^k k\sigma_k^{n-1}}_{a\times c + e = A} + \underbrace{x^n\left[\sum_{j=0}^{k-1}(-1)^j s_{k-j}^{n-1}\sigma_{j-1}^{n-1} + (-1)^k k\sigma_{k-1}^{n-1}\right]}_{a\times d + f = B}$$

$$+ \underbrace{\sum_{j=0}^{k-1}(-1)^j x_n^{k-j}\sigma_j^{n-1}}_{b\times c} + \underbrace{\sum_{j=0}^{k-1}(-1)^j x_n^{k-j+1}\sigma_{j-1}^{n-1}}_{b\times d}.$$
$$\underbrace{\phantom{\sum_{j=0}^{k-1}(-1)^j x_n^{k-j}\sigma_j^{n-1} + \sum_{j=0}^{k-1}(-1)^j x_n^{k-j+1}\sigma_{j-1}^{n-1}}}_{C}$$

The terms in A are equal to zero by (6.57). The terms in B are

$$B = x^n \left[\left(-\sum_{l=0}^{k-2} (-1)^l s_{(k-1)-l}^{n-1} \sigma_l^{n-1} - (-1)^{k-1}(k-1)\sigma_{k-1}^{n-1} \right) - (-1)^{k-1}\sigma_{k-1}^{n-1} \right]$$

$$= -x^n (-1)^{k-1} \sigma_{k-1}^{n-1}$$

using (6.57) again. The terms in C cancel each other except for one term, so that

$$C = (-1)^{k-1} x_n \sigma_{k-1}^{n-1}.$$

Thus, $B + C = 0$ and $\sum_{j=0}^{k-1} s_{k-j}^n \sigma_j^n + (-1)^k k \sigma_k^n = 0$. $\qquad\square$

Since $f(x)$ is of the form $f(x) = \prod_{i=1}^{n}(x - X_i)$ and $\Lambda(x)$ is of the form $\Lambda(x) = \prod_{i=1}^{n}(1 - X_i x)$, it follows that $\Lambda(x) = x^n f(1/x)$, so that $\Lambda_i = (-1)^i \sigma_i$. This gives the form of the Newton identities shown in (6.13).

6.11 Exercise

6.1 For a binary, narrow-sense, triple-error-correcting BCH code of length 15, constructed using the polynomial $x^4 + x + 1$:

    (a) Compute a generator polynomial for this code.

    (b) Determine the rate of the code.

    (c) Construct the parity check matrix and generator matrix for this code.

6.2 Find the generator $g(x)$ for a narrow-sense, binary double-error-correcting code of blocklength $n = 63$.

6.3 Find a generator polynomial for a narrow-sense, double-error- correcting binary BCH code of length 21.

6.4 Find a generator for a narrow-sense, double-error-correcting quaternary BCH code of length 21.

6.5 Compute the weight distribution of a double-error-correcting binary BCH code of length $n = 15$.

6.6 Construct a narrow-sense RS code of length 15 and design distance 3. Find the generator polynomial and the parity-check and generator matrices. How does the rate of this code compare with the rate of the code found in Exercise 1.1?

6.7 Compute the weight distribution of an $(8, 3)$ 8-ary MDS code.

6.8 Show that when a MDS code is punctured, it is still MDS. *Hint*: Puncture, then use the Singleton bound.

6.9 Show that when a MDS code is shortened, it is still MDS. *Hint*: Let C be MDS and let C_i be the subset of codewords in C which are 0 in the ith position. Shorten on coordinate i, and use the Singleton bound.

6.10 [272] Show for a binary BCH t-error-correcting code of length n that, if $2t + 1 | n$, then the minimum distance of the code is exactly $2t + 1$. *Hint*: Write $n = q(2t + 1)$ and show that $(x^n + 1)/(x^q + 1)$ is a code polynomial of weight exactly $2t + 1$. See Exercise 5.55.

6.11 Find $g(x)$ for a narrow-sense, double-error-correcting RS code using $\alpha \in GF(2^4)$ as the primitive element. For this code, suppose the received data produces the syndromes $S_1 = \alpha^4$, $S_2 = 0$, $S_3 = \alpha^8$, and $S_4 = \alpha^2$. Find the error locator polynomial and the error locations using the Peterson–Gorenstein–Zierler decoder.

6.12 For a triple-error-correcting, primitive, narrow-sense, binary BCH code of length 15, suppose that

$$r(x) = x^{12} + x^{11} + x^9 + x^8 + x^7 + x^6 + x^3 + x^2 + 1.$$

(a) Determine the syndromes S_1, S_2, S_3, S_4, S_5, and S_6.
(b) Check that $S_2 = S_1^2$, $S_4 = S_2^2$, and $S_6 = S_3^2$.
(c) Using the Peterson–Gorenstein–Zierler algorithm, determine the error locator polynomial and the decoded codeword.
(d) Find the error locator polynomial using the (nonbinary) Berlekamp–Massey algorithm. Provide the table illustrating the operation of the Berlekamp–Massey algorithm.
(e) Find the error locator polynomial using the binary Berlekamp–Massey algorithm. Provide the table illustrating the operation of the Berlekamp–Massey algorithm.
(f) Find the error locator polynomial using the Euclidean algorithm (the Sugiyama algorithm). Show the steps in the operations of the algorithm.

6.13 For a triple-error-correcting, primitive, narrow-sense, binary BCH code of length 15, suppose that

$$r(x) = x^{13} + x^9 + x^4 + x^3 + 1.$$

(a) Determine the syndromes S_1, S_2, S_3, S_4, S_5, and S_6.
(b) Check that $S_2 = S_1^2$, $S_4 = S_2^2$, and $S_6 = S_3^2$.
(c) Find the error locator polynomial $\Lambda(x)$ using the (nonbinary) Berlekamp–Massey algorithm. Provide the table illustrating the operation of the Berlekamp–Massey algorithm. Also, find the factorization of $\Lambda(x)$, and determine the error locations and the decoded codeword.
(d) Find the error locator polynomial using the binary Berlekamp–Massey algorithm. Provide the table illustrating the operation of the Berlekamp–Massey algorithm. Compare the error locator polynomial with that found using the Berlekamp–Massey algorithm.
(e) Find the error locator polynomial using the Euclidean algorithm (the Sugiyama algorithm). Show the steps in the operations of the algorithm. Compare with the error locator polynomial found using the Berlekamp–Massey algorithm.

6.14 For a triple-error-correcting, narrow-sense, RS code of length 15, suppose that

$$r(x) = \alpha^4 x^{12} + \alpha^7 x^9 + \alpha^2 x^7 + x^6 + \alpha^{10} x^5 + \alpha x^4 + \alpha^{12} x^3 + \alpha^4 x^2 + \alpha^{13}.$$

(a) Determine the syndromes S_1, S_2, S_3, S_4, S_5, and S_6.
(b) Find the error locator polynomial $\Lambda(x)$ using the Berlekamp–Massey algorithm. Provide the table illustrating the operation of the Berlekamp–Massey algorithm. Also, find the factorization of $\Lambda(x)$ and determine the error locations.
(c) Determine the error values using Forney's algorithm and determine the decoded codeword.
(d) Find the error locator polynomial using the Euclidean algorithm (the Sugiyama algorithm). Show the steps in the operations of the algorithm. Compare with the error locator polynomial found using the Berlekamp–Massey algorithm.

6.15 For a triple-error-correcting, narrow-sense, RS code of length 15, suppose that

$$r(x) = \alpha^{11} x^9 + \alpha^3 x^7 + \alpha x^6 + \alpha^7 x^5 + \mathsf{E} x^4 + \mathsf{E} x^3 + \alpha^4 x^2 + \alpha^9 x + \alpha^9,$$

where E denotes that the position is erased.

(a) Determine the erasure locator polynomial $\Gamma(x)$.
(b) Determine $\tilde{r}(x)$ and the syndromes S_1, S_2, S_3, S_4, S_5, and S_6.

(c) Find $\Xi(x)$.

(d) Using the Berlekamp–Massey or Euclidean algorithm determine $\Lambda(x)$ and find the error locations.

(e) Determine the error and erasure values using Forney's algorithm, and determine the decoded codeword.

6.16 As a review, carefully describe the decoding steps for a non-narrow-sense code.

6.17 The Berlekamp–Massey algorithm (Algorithm 6.1) requires division in the field, that is, finding a multiplicative inverse. This can be more complex than multiplication or addition. Is it possible to modify the algorithm so that it still produces an error locator polynomial, but does not require any divisions?

6.18 Let C be the $(2^m - 1, k)$ RS code with minimum distance d. Show that C contains the primitive $(2^m - 1, k)$ binary BCH code C' of length $2^m - 1$ with design distance d. This is an example of a subfield subcode.

6.19 [272] Is there a binary t-error-correcting BCH code of length $n = 2^m + 1$ for $m \geq 3$ and $t < 2^{m-1}$. If so, determine its generator polynomial.

6.20 [272] Let $b = -t$. Let C be a BCH code with design distance $d = 2t + 2$ whose generator polynomial has $\beta^{-t}, \ldots, \beta^{-1}, 1, \beta, \ldots, \beta^t$ and their conjugates as roots. Show that this is a reversible cyclic code. (See Exercise 4.14a.) Also, show that if t is odd, then the minimum distance of this code is at least $2t + 4$.

6.21 [272] A t-error-correcting RS code of length $n = 2^m - 1$ over $GF(2^m)$ has the following parity check matrix:

$$H = \begin{bmatrix} 1 & \alpha & \alpha^2 & \cdots & \alpha^{n-1} \\ 1 & \alpha^2 & \alpha^4 & \cdots & \alpha^{2(n-1)} \\ \vdots & & & & \\ 1 & \alpha^{2t} & \alpha^{4t} & \cdots & \alpha^{2t(n-1)} \end{bmatrix},$$

where α is primitive in $GF(2^m)$. Now form the parity check matrix

$$H' = \begin{bmatrix} 0 & 1 & \\ 0 & 0 & \\ \vdots & \vdots & H \\ 0 & 0 & \\ 1 & 0 & \end{bmatrix}.$$

Show that the code with parity check matrix H' also has minimum distance $2t + 1$. *Hint*: Consider $2t \times 2t$ submatrices. For submatrices including the first columns, think of the cofactor expansion.

6.22 Let $m(x) = m_0 + m_1 x + \cdots + m_{k-1} x^{k-1} \in GF(2^m)[x]$. Form the polynomial

$$c(x) = m(1) + m(\alpha)x + m(\alpha^2)x^2 + \cdots + m(\alpha^{2^m-2})x^{2^m-2}.$$

Show that $c(x)$ has $\alpha, \alpha^2, \ldots, \alpha^{2^m-k-1}$ as roots. What can you conclude about the set of all $\{c(x)\}$ as $m(x)$ varies?

6.23 Let $\mathbf{v} = [v_0, v_1, \ldots, v_{n-1}], v_i \in GF(q)$ be a sequence and let $v(x) = v_0 + v_1 x + \cdots + v_{n-1}x^{n-1}$. Let $V_j = v(\alpha^j) = \sum_{i=0}^{n-1} v_i \alpha^{ij}, j = 0, 1, \ldots, n-1$, where α is a primitive nth root of unity. The **Mattson–Solomon polynomial** (see [[292], p. 239]) is defined as

$$A(z) = \sum_{j=0}^{n-1} A_{n-j} z^j = \sum_{j=1}^{n} A_j z^{n-j}.$$

(a) Show that $A_0 = A_n$.

(b) Show that the a_i can be recovered from $A(z)$ by $a_i = n^{-1}A(\alpha^i)$.

(c) Show that if the a_i are binary valued and operations take place in a field $GF(2^m)$, then $R_{z^n+1}[A(z)^2] = A(z)$.

(d) Show that if $c(x) = R_{x^n+1}[a(x)b(x)]$ (that is, the product modulo $x^n + 1$), then $C(z) = A(z) \odot B(z)$, where $\odot$ denotes the element-by-element product, $A(z) \odot B(z) = \prod_{i=0}^{n-1} A_i B_i z^i$, and conversely.

6.24 Using the definition of the formal derivative in (6.35) for operations over the commutative ring with identity $R[x]$, where R is a ring:

(a) Show that $[f(x)g(x)]' = f'(x)g(x) + f(x)g'(x)$.

(b) Show that if $f^2(x)|g(x)$ then $f(x)|g'(x)$.

(c) Show that $(f_1 f_2)^{(n)} = \sum_{i=0}^{n} \binom{n}{i} f_1^{(i)} f_2^{(n-i)}$, where $()^{(n)}$ denotes the nth formal derivative.

(d) Show that $(f_1 f_2 \cdots f_r)' = \sum_{i=1}^{r} f_i' \prod_{j \neq i} f_j$.

(e) From the latter conclude that with $f = f_1 f_2 \cdots f_r$,

$$\frac{f'}{f} = \frac{f_1'}{f_1} + \cdots + \frac{f_r'}{f_r}.$$

This is a partial fraction decomposition of f'/f.

(f) Let u be a simple root of $f(x)$ and let $g(x) = f(x)/(x - u)$. Show that $f'(u) = g(u)$.

(g) Show that if f has a repeated root at u, then $(x - u)$ is a factor of (f, f').

6.25 Prove Lemma 6.32. *Hint*: Use the fact that $S_{2v} = S_v^2$ for binary codes. Start with an LFSR

$$S_j = \sum_{i=1}^{L} c_i S_{j-i}$$

capable of producing the outputs $\{S_1, S_2, \ldots, S_{2v-1}\}$ (that is, S_{2v-1} is an odd-numbered output).

6.26 Express Massey's algorithm in a form appropriate for using 0-based indexing; that is, when the syndromes are numbered $S_0, S_1, \ldots, S_{N-1}$, where $N = 2t$.

6.27 Compute the GFFT in $GF(8)$ of the vector represented by the polynomial $v(x) = 1 + \alpha^2 x + \alpha^3 x^4 + \alpha^6 x^5$. Also, compute the inverse GFFT of $V(x)$ and ensure that $v(x)$ is obtained.

6.28 Let $\{a_i\}$ be a sequence of length n, $\{a_i\} = \{a_0, a_1, \ldots, a_{n-1}\}$. Let $\{a_{((i-1))}\}$ denote the cyclic shift of the sequence $\{a_i\}$. Let $\{a_i\} \leftrightarrow \{A_j\}$ denote that there is a GFFT relationship between the sequences. Prove the following properties of the GFFT.

Cyclic shift property: $\{a_{((i-1))}\} \leftrightarrow \{\alpha^j A_j\}$

Modulation property: $\{\alpha^i a_i\} \leftrightarrow \{A_{((j+1))}\}$

6.29 Determine the GFFT of the vector $v_i = \alpha^{ri}$. Determine the GFFT of the vector $v_i = \beta \delta_{i-l}$; that is, it has value $v_i = \beta$ when $i = l$ and value $v_i = 0$ when $i \neq l$. Assume $0 \leq l < n$.

6.30 List the minimal polynomials over $GF(16)$. Compute the GFFT of the corresponding vectors and note the positions of the zeros of the spectra compared to the roots of the minimal polynomials.

6.31 Computing the GFFT. Let $v_i \in GF(2^m)$, $i = 0, 1, \ldots, n-1$. Let

$$V_j = \beta^{j^2} \sum_{i=0}^{n-1} \beta^{-(j-i)^2} (\beta^{i^2} v_i). \tag{6.58}$$

Show when β is a square root of α that V_j of (6.58) is equal to V_j of (6.40). That is, (6.58) can be used to compute the GFFT. This is called the Bluestein chirp algorithm. The chirp transform can be computed as a pointwise product of v_i by β^{i^2} followed by a cyclic convolution with β^{-i^2}.

6.32 Describe how to obtain a (mn, mk) binary code from a (n, k) code over $GF(2^m)$. Let d be the minimum distance of the (n, k) code and let d_m be the minimum distance of the (mn, mk) code. How does $d_m/(mn)$ compare with d/n in general?

6.33 Let $M_i(x)$ be the minimal polynomial of α^i, where α^i is a primitive element in $GF(2^n)$. Let

$$h^*(x) = \frac{x^{2^n-1} + 1}{\text{LCM}(M_1(x), M_2(x), \ldots, M_{2k}(x))}$$

and let $V(h^*)$ be the set of sequences of length $2^n - 1$ which are annihilated by $h^*(x)$. Show that for any two sequences $a, b \in V(g^*)$, $\text{wt}(a + b) > 2k$.

6.34 (Justeson codes) Let C be an (n, k) RS code over $GF(q^m)$. Let $\mathbf{c} = (c_0, c_1, \ldots, c_{n-1})$ be a codeword in C. Form the $2 \times n$ matrix by

$$M = \begin{bmatrix} c_0 & c_1 & c_2 & \cdots & c_{n-1} \\ \alpha^0 c_0 & \alpha^1 c_1 & \alpha^2 c_2 & \cdots & \alpha^{n-1} c_{n-1} \end{bmatrix}.$$

Replace each $GF(q^m)$ element of this matrix by a $GF(q)$ m-tuple, resulting in a $2m \times N$ matrix. The set of such matrices produces the *Justeson codes*, a q-ary code whose codewords have length $2mN$ obtained by stacking up the elements of the matrix into a vector.

(a) Show that the Justeson code is linear.

(b) Explain why at least $n - k + 1$ of the columns of a matrix M are nonzero.

(c) Explain why no two nonzero columns can be the same.

(d) Let I be an integer satisfying

$$\sum_{i=1}^{I} (q-1)^i \binom{2m}{i} \leq n - k + 1.$$

Show that the minimum distance of the Justeson code is lower-bounded by

$$d_{\min} \geq \sum_{i=1}^{I} i(q-1)^i \binom{2m}{i}.$$

Hint: In a $2m$-tuple there are $\binom{2m}{i}$ ways of picking i nonzero places and $q - 1$ different nonzero values. The minimum distance is greater than or equal to the sum of the weights of the columns.

It can be shown that [45] asymptotically $d_{\min}/n \geq 0.11(1 - 2R)$, where $R = k/2n$ is the rate of the code. Thus, Justeson codes have a fractional distance bounded away from 0 if $R < 1/2$.

6.12 References

RS codes were presented first in [364]; these are, of course, structurally similar to the BCH codes announced in [201] and [48]. The first decoding algorithms were based on solving Toeplitz systems; this is the essence of the Peterson decoding algorithm [336]. The generalization to nonbinary codes appears in [165]. The Berlekamp–Massey algorithm was presented in [33] and [295]. The Forney algorithm appears in [125] and the Chien search appears in [70]. More information about weight distributions of BCH codes appears in [245]. The theoretical aspects of these codes are considerably richer than this chapter can contain and could cover several chapters. Interested readers are referred to [292].

There are many other decoding algorithms to explore for these codes. It is possible to scale the Berlekamp–Massey algorithm so that no divisions are required to produce an error-locator polynomial

[52]; this may be of interest in hardware implementations. See also [122, 448]. However, computing the error value still requires divisions. Decoding algorithms based on finite-field Fourier transforms have been developed; for a thorough survey see [45]. See also [484] for a systolic decoding algorithm and [363] for an algorithm based on Fermat transforms. A work which shows the underlying similarity of the Euclidean algorithm-based methods and the Berlekamp–Massey based methods is [74]. Other RS decoding algorithms are described in [69, 116–118, 153, 278, 413] and the book [485], which provides some discussion of hardware considerations.

Blahut [45] has made many of the contributions to GFFT methods for coding theory; the presentation here closely follows [483]. Berlekamp–Massey algorithm is presented in [295]; our presentation closely follows that of [319]. A very theoretical description of BCH and RS codes appears in [292], with considerable material devoted to MDS codes. A fascinating discussion of RS and BCH codes from a finite-field perspective, leading to many generalizations of RS codes is [46].

The discussion of Newton's identities is suggested by an exercise in [83]. The discussion of alternant and Goppa codes is summarized from [292]. A decoding algorithm for Goppa codes appears in [334]. McEliece public key cryptosystem was presented in [301].

Chapter 7

Alternate Decoding Algorithms for Reed–Solomon Codes

7.1 Introduction: Workload for Reed–Solomon Decoding

In this chapter, we present two alternatives to the decoding algorithms presented in Chapter 6. The first is based upon a new key equation and is called **remainder decoding**. The second method is a list decoder capable of decoding beyond the design distance of the code.

A primary motivation behind the remainder decoder is that implementations of it may have lower decode complexity. The decode complexity for a conventional decoding algorithm for an (n, k) code having redundancy $\rho = n - k$ is summarized by the following steps:

1. Compute the syndromes. ρ syndromes must be computed, each with a computational cost of $O(n)$, for a total cost of $O(\rho n)$. Furthermore, all syndromes must be computed, regardless of the number of errors.

2. Find the error-locator polynomial and the error evaluator. This has a computation cost $O(\rho^2)$ (depending on the approach).

3. Find the roots of the error-locator polynomial. This has a computation cost of $O(\rho n)$ using the Chien search.

4. Compute the error values, with a cost of $O(\rho^2)$.

Thus, if $\rho < n/2$, the most expensive steps are computing the syndromes and finding the roots. In remainder decoding, decoding takes place by computing remainders instead of syndromes; the remaining steps retain similar complexity. This results in potentially faster decoding. Furthermore, as we demonstrate, it is possible to find the error-locator polynomial using a highly parallelizable algorithm. The general outline for the new decoding algorithm is as follows:

1. Compute the remainder polynomial $r(x) = R(x) \bmod g(x)$, with complexity $O(n)$ (using very simple hardware).

2. Compute an error-locator polynomial $W(x)$ and an associated polynomial $N(x)$. The complexity is $O(\rho^2)$. Architectures exist for parallel computation.

3. Find the roots of the error-locator polynomial, complexity $O(\rho n)$.

4. Compute the error values, complexity $O(\rho^2)$.

7.2 Derivations of Welch–Berlekamp Key Equation

We present in this section two derivations of a new key equation called the Welch–Berlekamp (WB) key equation. The first derivation uses the definition of the remainder polynomial. The second derivation shows that the WB key equation can be obtained from the conventional Reed–Solomon key equation.

Error Correction Coding: Mathematical Methods and Algorithms, Second Edition. Todd K. Moon
© 2021 John Wiley & Sons, Inc. Published 2021 by John Wiley & Sons, Inc.
Companion website: www.wiley.com/go/Moon/ErrorCorrectionCoding

7.2.1　The Welch–Berlekamp Derivation of the WB Key Equation

The generator polynomial for an (n, k) RS code can be written as

$$g(x) = \prod_{i=b}^{b+d-2} (x - \alpha^i),$$

which is a polynomial of degree $d - 1$, where $d = d_{\min} = 2t + 1 = n - k + 1$. We denote the received polynomial as $R(x) = c(x) + E(x)$. We designate the first $d - 1$ symbols of $R(x)$ as *check symbols*, and the remaining k symbols as *message symbols*. This designation applies naturally to systematic encoding of codewords, but we use it even in the case that systematic encoding is not employed. Let $L_c = \{0, 1, \ldots, d - 2\}$ be the index set of the check locations, with corresponding check locators $L_{\alpha^c} = \{\alpha^k, 0 \le k \le d - 2\}$. Also, let $L_m = \{d - 1, d, \ldots, n - 1\}$ denote the index set of the message locations, with corresponding message locators $L_{\alpha^m} = \{\alpha^k, d - 1 \le k \le n - 1\}$.

We define the *remainder polynomial* as

$$r(x) = R(x) \bmod g(x)$$

and write $r(x)$ in terms of its coefficients as

$$r(x) = \sum_{i=0}^{d-2} r_i x^i.$$

The degree of $r(x)$ is $\le d - 2$. This remainder can be computed using conventional LFSR hardware that might be used for the encoding operation, with computational complexity $O(n)$.

Lemma 7.1 $r(x) \equiv E(x) \bmod g(x)$ *and* $r(\alpha^k) = E(\alpha^k)$ *for* $k \in \{b, b + 1, \ldots, b + d - 2\}$.

Proof Since $R(x) = m(x)g(x) + E(x)$ for some message polynomial $m(x)$, the remainder polynomial does not depend upon the transmitted codeword. Thus,

$$r(x) \equiv E(x) \bmod g(x).$$

We can write $E(x) = q(x)g(x) + e(x)$ for some divisor polynomial $q(x)$. Thus, $E(x) \equiv e(x) \bmod g(x)$. Then $E(\alpha^k) = q(\alpha^k)g(\alpha^k) + e(\alpha^k) = e(\alpha^k) = r(\alpha^k)$ for $k \in \{b, b + 1, \ldots, b + d - 2\}$. $\qquad\square$

Notation: At some points in the development, it is convenient to use the notation $r_k = r[\alpha^k]$ to indicate the remainder at index k (with locator α^k). Similarly, we will use $Y[\alpha^k]$ to indicate an error value at index k.

7.2.1.1　Single error in a message location

To derive the WB key equation, we assume initially that a single error occurs. We need to make a distinction between whether the error location e is a message location or a check location. Initially we assume that $e \in L_m$ with error value Y. We thus take $E(x) = Yx^e$, or the (error position, error value) = $(\alpha^e, Y) = (X, Y)$. The notation $Y = Y[X]$ is also used to indicate the error value at the error locator X.

When $e \in L_m$, then the modulo operation $Yx^e \bmod g(x)$ "folds" the polynomial back into the lower order terms, as pictured in Figure 7.1. Evaluating $r(x)$ at generator root locations, we have by Lemma 7.1,

$$r(\alpha^k) = E(\alpha^k) = Y(\alpha^k)^e = YX^k, \quad k \in \{b, b + 1, \ldots, b + d - 2\}, \tag{7.1}$$

where $X = \alpha^e$ is the error locator. It follows that

$$r(\alpha^k) - Xr(\alpha^{k-1}) = YX^k - XYX^{k-1} = 0, \quad k \in \{b + 1, b + 2, \ldots, b + d - 2\}.$$

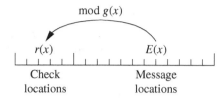

Figure 7.1: Remainder computation when errors are in message locations.

Define the polynomial $u(x) = r(x) - Xr(\alpha^{-1}x)$, which has degree less than $d - 1$. Then $u(x)$ has roots at $\alpha^{b+1}, \alpha^{b+2}, \ldots, \alpha^{b+d-2}$, so that $u(x)$ is divisible by the polynomial

$$p(x) = \prod_{i=b+1}^{b+d-2} (x - \alpha^k) = \sum_{i=0}^{d-2} p_i x^i,$$

which has degree $d - 2$. Thus, $u(x)$ must be a *scalar* multiple of $p(x)$,

$$u(x) = ap(x) \tag{7.2}$$

for some $a \in GF(q)$. Equating coefficients between $u(x)$ and $p(x)$, we obtain

$$r_i(1 - X\alpha^{-i}) = ap_i, \quad i = 0, 1, \ldots, d - 2.$$

That is,

$$r_i(\alpha^i - X) = a\alpha^i p_i, \quad i = 0, 1, \ldots, d - 2. \tag{7.3}$$

We define the error-locator polynomial as $W_m(x) = x - X = x - \alpha^e$. (This definition is different from the error locator we defined for the conventional decoding algorithm, since the roots of $W_m(x)$ are the message locators, not the reciprocals of message locators.) Using $W_m(x)$, we see from (7.3) that

$$r_i W_m(\alpha^i) = a\alpha^i p_i, \quad i = 0, 1, \ldots, d - 2. \tag{7.4}$$

Since the error is in a message location, $e \in L_m$, $W_m(\alpha^i)$ is not zero for $i = 0, 1, \ldots, d - 2$. We can solve for r_i as

$$r_i = a\alpha^i p_i / W_m(\alpha^i). \tag{7.5}$$

We now eliminate the coefficient a from (7.5). The error value Y can be computed using (7.1), choosing $k = b$:

$$Y = Y[X] = X^{-b} r(\alpha^b) = X^{-b} \sum_{i=0}^{d-2} r_i \alpha^{ib} = X^{-b} \sum_{i=0}^{d-2} \frac{a\alpha^i p_i}{W_m(\alpha^i)} \alpha^{ib} = aX^{-b} \sum_{i=0}^{d-2} \frac{\alpha^{i(b+1)} p_i}{(\alpha^i - X)}.$$

Define

$$f(x) = x^{-b} \sum_{i=0}^{d-2} \frac{\alpha^{i(b+1)} p_i}{(\alpha^i - x)}, \quad x \in L_{\alpha^m},$$

which can be precomputed for all values of $x \in L_{\alpha^m}$. Then

$$Y = af(X)$$

or $a = Y/f(X)$. We thus write (7.4) as

$$r_i = \frac{Y\alpha^i p_i}{f(X)W_m(\alpha^i)}. \tag{7.6}$$

7.2.1.2 Multiple errors in message locations

Now assume that there are $v \geq 1$ errors, with error locators $X_i \in L_{\alpha^m}$ and corresponding error values $Y_i = Y[X_i]$ for $i = 1, 2, \ldots, v$. Corresponding to each error there is a "mode" yielding a relationship $r(\alpha^k) = Y_i X_i^k$, each of which has a solution of the form (7.6). Thus, by linearity, we can write

$$r_k = r[\alpha^k] = p_k \alpha^k \sum_{i=1}^{v} \frac{Y_i}{f(X_i)(\alpha^k - X_i)}, \quad k = 0, 1, \ldots, d-2. \tag{7.7}$$

Now define the function

$$F(x) = \sum_{i=1}^{v} \frac{Y_i}{f(X_i)(x - X_i)} \tag{7.8}$$

having poles at the error locations. This function can be written as

$$F(x) = \sum_{i=1}^{v} \frac{Y_i}{f(X_i)(x - X_i)} = \frac{N_m(x)}{W_m(x)},$$

where

$$W_m(x) = \prod_{i=1}^{v}(x - X_i)$$

is the error-locator polynomial for the errors among the symbol locations and where $N_m(x)$ is the numerator obtained by adding together the terms in $F(x)$. It is clear that $\deg(N_m(x)) < \deg(W_m(x))$. Note that the representation in (7.8) corresponds to a partial fraction expansion of $N_m(x)/W_m(x)$. Using this notation, (7.7) can be written

$$r_k = p_k \alpha^k F(\alpha^k) = p_k \alpha^k N_m(\alpha^k)/W_m(\alpha^k)$$

or

$$N_m(\alpha^k) = \frac{r_k}{p_k \alpha^k} W_m(\alpha^k), \quad k \in L_c = \{0, 1, \ldots, d-2\}. \tag{7.9}$$

$N_m(x)$ and $W_m(x)$ have the degree constraints $\deg(N_m(x)) < \deg(W_m(x))$ and $\deg(W_m(x)) \leq \lfloor (d-1)/2 \rfloor = t$, since no more than t errors can be corrected. Equation (7.9) has the form of the **key equation** we seek.

7.2.1.3 Errors in check locations

For a single error occurring in a check location $e \in L_c$, then $r(x) = E(x)$ — there is no "folding" by the modulo operation. Then $u(x) = r(x) - Xr(\alpha^{-1}x)$ must be identically 0, so the coefficient a in (7.2) is equal to 0. We can write

$$r_k = \begin{cases} Y & k = e \\ 0 & \text{otherwise.} \end{cases}$$

If there are errors in both check locations and message locations, let $E_m = \{i_1, i_2, \ldots, i_{v_1}\} \subset L_m$ denote the error locations among the message locations and let $E_c = \{i_{v_1+1}, \ldots, i_v\} \subset L_c$ denote the error locations among the check locations. Let $E_{\alpha^m} = \{\alpha^{i_1}, \alpha^{i_2}, \ldots, \alpha^{i_{v_1}}\}$ and $E_{\alpha^c} = \{\alpha^{i_{v_1+1}}, \ldots, \alpha^{i_v}\}$ denote the corresponding error locators. The (error location, error value) pairs for the errors in message locations are (X_i, Y_i), $i = 1, 2, \ldots, v_1$. The pairs for errors in check locations are (X_i, Y_i), $i = v_1 + 1, \ldots, v$. Then by linearity,

$$r_k = p_k \alpha^k \sum_{i=1}^{v_1} \frac{Y_i}{f(X_i)(\alpha^k - X_i)} + \begin{cases} Y_j & \text{if error locator } X_j = \alpha^k \text{ is in a check location} \\ 0 & \text{otherwise.} \end{cases} \tag{7.10}$$

Because of the extra terms added on in (7.10), Equation (7.9) does not apply when $k \in E_c$, so we have

$$N_m(\alpha^k) = \frac{r_k}{p_k \alpha^k} W_m(\alpha^k), \quad k \in L_c \backslash E_c. \tag{7.11}$$

To account for the errors among the check symbols, let $W_c(x) = \prod_{i \in E_c}(x - \alpha^i)$ be the error-locator polynomial for errors in check locations. Let

$$N(x) = N_m(x)W_c(x) \quad \text{and} \quad W(x) = W_m(x)W_c(x).$$

Since $N(\alpha^k) = W(\alpha^k) = 0$ for $k \in E_c$, we can write

$$\boxed{N(\alpha^k) = \frac{r_k}{p_k \alpha^k} W(\alpha^k), \quad k \in L_c = \{0, 1, \ldots, d-2\}.} \tag{7.12}$$

That is, the equation is now satisfied for *all* values of k in L_c. Equation (7.12) is the WB **key equation**, to be solved subject to the conditions

$$\deg(N(x)) < \deg(W(x)) \quad \deg(W(x)) \le (d-1)/2.$$

The polynomial $W(x)$ is the error-locator polynomial, having roots at *all* the error locators. We write (7.12) as

$$\boxed{N(x_i) = W(x_i)y_i \quad i = 1, 2, \ldots, m = 2t = d - 1} \tag{7.13}$$

for "points" $(x_i, y_i) = (\alpha^{i-1}, r_{i-1}/(p_{i-1}\alpha^{i-1})), i = 1, 2, \ldots, m = 2t$.

Example 7.2   Consider a $(15, 9)$ triple-error-correcting RS code over $GF(16)$ generated by $1 + x + x^4$ with $b = 2$. The generator for the code is

$$g(x) = \alpha^{12} + \alpha^{14}x + \alpha^{10}x^2 + \alpha^7 x^3 + \alpha x^4 + \alpha^{11}x^5 + x^6.$$

The function $p(x)$ is

$$p(x) = \alpha^{10} + \alpha^9 x + \alpha^{11}x^2 + \alpha^6 x^3 + \alpha^9 x^4 + x^5.$$

The function $f(x)$ evaluated at message locators is tabulated as

$$
\begin{array}{cccccccccc}
x: & \alpha^6 & \alpha^7 & \alpha^8 & \alpha^9 & \alpha^{10} & \alpha^{11} & \alpha^{12} & \alpha^{13} & \alpha^{14} \\
f(x): & 1 & \alpha^8 & \alpha^{12} & \alpha^2 & \alpha^{11} & \alpha^7 & \alpha^7 & \alpha^8 & \alpha^5
\end{array}
$$

Suppose the received data is $R(x) = \alpha^5 x^4 + \alpha^7 x^9 + \alpha^8 x^{12}$ (three errors). Then

$$r(x) = R(x) \ (\text{mod } g(x)) = \alpha^2 + \alpha x + \alpha^6 x^3 + \alpha^3 x^5.$$

The (x_i, y_i) data appearing in the key equation are

$$
\begin{array}{ccccccc}
i & 1 & 2 & 3 & 4 & 5 & 6 \\
x_i & 1 & \alpha & \alpha^2 & \alpha^3 & \alpha^4 & \alpha^5 \\
y_i & \alpha^7 & \alpha^6 & 0 & \alpha^{12} & 0 & \alpha^{13}
\end{array}
$$

$\square$

Hereafter we will refer to the $N(x)$ and $W(x)$ as $N_1(x)$ and $W_1(x)$, referring to the first (WB) derivation.

7.2.2 Derivation from the Conventional Key Equation

A WB-type key equation may also be obtained starting from the conventional key equation and syndromes. Let us denote the syndromes as

$$S_i = R(\alpha^{b+i}) = r(\alpha^{b+i}) = \sum_{j=0}^{d-2} r_j(\alpha^{b+i})^j, \quad i = 0, 1, \ldots, d-2.$$

The conventional error-locator polynomial is $\Lambda(x) = \prod_{i=1}^{\nu}(1 - X_i x) = \Lambda_0 + \Lambda_1 x + \cdots + \Lambda_\nu x^\nu$, where $\Lambda_0 = 1$; the Welch–Berlekamp error locator polynomial is $W(x) = \prod_{i=1}^{\nu}(x - X_i) = W_0 + W_1 x + \cdots + x^\nu$. These are related by $\Lambda_i = W_{\nu-i}$. The conventional key equation can be written as (see 6.9)

$$\sum_{i=0}^{\nu} \Lambda_i S_{k-i} = 0, \quad k = \nu, \nu+1, \ldots, d-2.$$

Writing this in terms of coefficients of W, we have

$$\sum_{i=0}^{\nu} W_i S_{k+i} = 0, \quad k = 0, 1, \ldots, d-2-\nu,$$

or

$$\sum_{i=0}^{\nu} W_i \sum_{j=0}^{d-2} r_j \alpha^{j(b+k+i)} = 0.$$

Rearranging,

$$\sum_{j=0}^{d-2} r_j \left(\sum_{i=0}^{\nu} W_i \alpha^{ji} \right) \alpha^{j(k+b)} = 0, \quad k = 0, 1, \ldots, d-2-\nu. \tag{7.14}$$

Letting

$$f_j = r_j W(\alpha^j) \alpha^{jb}, \tag{7.15}$$

Equation (7.14) can be written as

$$\sum_{j=0}^{d-2} f_j \alpha^{jk} = 0, \quad k = 0, 1, \ldots, d-2-\nu,$$

which corresponds to the Vandermonde set of equations

$$\begin{bmatrix} 1 & 1 & \cdots & 1 & 1 \\ 1 & \alpha & \cdots & \alpha^{d-3} & \alpha^{d-2} \\ 1 & \alpha^2 & \cdots & \alpha^{2(d-3)} & \alpha^{2(d-2)} \\ \vdots & & & & \\ 1 & \alpha^{d-2-\nu} & \cdots & \alpha^{(d-2-\nu)(d-3)} & \alpha^{(d-2-\nu)(d-2)} \end{bmatrix} \begin{bmatrix} f_0 \\ f_1 \\ \vdots \\ f_{d-2} \end{bmatrix} = \mathbf{0}$$

with $(d-1-\nu) \times (d-1)$ matrix V. The bridge to the WB key equation is provided by the following lemma.

Lemma 7.3 *[86] Let V be a $m \times r$ matrix with $r > m$ having Vandermonde structure*

$$V = \begin{bmatrix} 1 & 1 & \cdots & 1 \\ u_1 & u_2 & \cdots & u_r \\ u_1^2 & u_2^2 & \cdots & u_r^2 \\ \vdots & & & \\ u_1^{m-1} & u_2^{m-1} & \cdots & u_r^{m-1} \end{bmatrix}$$

with the $\{u_i\}$ all distinct. For any vector z in the nullspace of V (satisfying $Vz = 0$), there exists a unique polynomial $N(x)$ of degree less than $r - m$ such that

$$z_i = \frac{N(u_i)}{F'(u_i)}, \quad i = 1, 2, \ldots, r,$$

where $F(x) = \prod_{i=1}^{r}(x - u_i)$.

Proof A vector $\mathbf{z}$ in the nullspace must satisfy

$$\sum_{i=1}^{r} u_i^j z_i = 0, \quad j = 0, 1, \ldots, m - 1. \tag{7.16}$$

Let $N(x)$ be a polynomial of degree $< r - m$. Then the highest degree of polynomials of the form

$$x^j N(x), \quad j = 0, 1, \ldots, m - 1$$

is less than $r - 1$. Now let us construct an interpolating function $\phi_j(x)$ such that for $u_1, u_2, \ldots, u_r$, $\phi_j(u_i) = u_i^j N(u_i)$, for each $j = 0, 1, \ldots, m - 1$. Using the Lagrange interpolating function (5.34), we can write

$$\phi_j(x) = \sum_{i=1}^{r} \frac{F(x)}{x - u_i} \frac{u_i^j N(u_i)}{F'(u_i)}, \quad j = 0, 1, \ldots, m - 1. \tag{7.17}$$

Since it is the case that $\phi_j(x) = x^j N(x)$ has degree less than $r - 1$, the coefficient of the monomial of degree $r - 1$ on the right-hand side of (7.17) must be equal to 0. Since the leading coefficient of $F(x)$ is 1, the leading coefficient of $F(x)/(x - u_i)$ is 1. Thus,

$$\sum_{i=1}^{r} \frac{u_i^j N(u_i)}{F'(u_i)} = 0, \quad j = 0, 1, \ldots, m - 1.$$

Thus, if $z_i = N(u_i)/F'(u_i)$, the nullspace relationship (7.16) is satisfied.

The dimension of the nullspace of V is $r - m$. The dimension of the space of polynomials of degree $< r - m$ is $r - m$. There must therefore be a one-to-one correspondence between vectors in the nullspace of V and the polynomials $N(x)$. Thus, $N(x)$ is unique. $\square$

Returning to the key equation problem, by this lemma, there exists a polynomial $N(x)$ of degree less than v such that $f_j = N(\alpha^j)/g_0'(\alpha^j)$, where

$$g_0(x) = \prod_{i=0}^{d-2}(x - \alpha^i).$$

Thus, from (7.15),

$$r_j W(\alpha^j) \alpha^{jb} = \frac{N(\alpha^j)}{g_0'(\alpha^j)}, \quad j = 0, 1, \ldots, d - 2.$$

This gives rise to a form of the key equation,

$$\boxed{N(\alpha^k) = r_k g_0'(\alpha^k) \alpha^{kb} W(\alpha^k), \quad k = 0, 1, \ldots, d - 2} \tag{7.18}$$

with $\deg(N(x)) < \deg(W(x)) \leq \lfloor (d-1)/2 \rfloor$. We call this the Dabiri–Blake (DB) form of the WB key equation. We can also write this in terms of the original generator polynomial $g(x)$:

$$\boxed{N(\alpha^k) = r_k g'(\alpha^{b+k}) \alpha^{b(2-d+k)} W(\alpha^k), \quad k = 0, 1, \ldots, d - 2.} \tag{7.19}$$

With $x_{i+1} = \alpha^i$ and $y_{i+1} = r_k g'(\alpha^{b+i})\alpha^{b(2-d+i)}$, this can be expressed in the form (7.13).

Example 7.4   For the same code and $R(x)$ as in Example 7.2, the (x_i, y_i) data are

i	1	2	3	4	5	6
x_i	1	α	α^2	α^3	α^4	α^5
y_i	α^9	α^8	0	α^{14}	0	1

$\square$

We will refer to the $N(x)$ and $W(x)$ derived using the DB method as $N_2(x)$ and $W_2(x)$.

7.3   Finding the Error Values

We begin with the key equation in the WB form, (7.12). Assuming that the error locator $W(x)$ has been found — as discussed in Section 7.4 — we consider here how to compute the error values Y_i corresponding to an error locator X_i; we denote this as $Y[X_i]$. For an error location in a message location, we have from (7.7) and (7.8)

$$r_k = p_k \alpha^k \sum_{i=1}^{\nu_1} \frac{Y[X_i]}{f(X_i)(\alpha^k - X_i)} = p_k \alpha^k \frac{N_1(\alpha^k)}{W_1(\alpha^k)}.$$

By definition,

$$\sum_{i=1}^{\nu} \frac{Y[X_i]}{f(X_i)(x - X_i)} = \frac{N_1(x)}{W_1(x)} = \frac{N_1(x)}{\prod_{i \in E_{cm}}(x - X_i)}, \tag{7.20}$$

where we use $E_{cm} = E_c \cup E_m$ to denote the set of all error locations. Multiplying both sides of (7.20) by $W(x)$ and evaluating at $x = X_k$, we obtain

$$\frac{Y[X_k]\prod_{i \neq k}(X_k - X_i)}{f(X_k)} = N_1(X_k),$$

since the factor $(x - X_k)$ in the denominator of (7.20) cancels the corresponding factor in $W_1(x)$, but all other terms in the sum are zero since they have factors of zero in the product.

Now taking the formal derivative, we observe that

$$W_1'(x) = \sum_{i \in E_{cm}} \prod_{j \neq i}(x - X_i)$$

so that $W_1'(X_k) = \prod_{j \neq k}(X_k - X_i)$. Thus,

$$Y[X_k] = f(X_k)\frac{N_1(X_k)}{W_1'(X_k)}. \tag{7.21}$$

When the error is in a check location, $X_j = \alpha^k$ for $k \in E_c$, we must revert to (7.10),

$$r_k = Y[X_j] + p_k \alpha^k \sum_{i=1}^{\nu_1} \frac{Y[X_i]}{f(X_i)(\alpha^k - X_i)} = Y[X_j] + p_k X_j \frac{N_1(X_j)}{W_1(X_j)}.$$

Thus, for $X_j = \alpha^k$,

$$Y[X_j] = r_k - p_k X_j \frac{N_1(X_j)}{W_1(X_j)}.$$

Both the numerator and the denominator are 0, so a "L'Hopital's rule" must be used. Using $N_1(x) = N_m(x)W_c(x)$ and $W_2(x) = W_m(x)W_c(x)$,

$$N_1'(X_j) = N_m(X_j)W_c'(X_j) + N_m'(X_j)W_c(X_j) = N_m(X_j)W_c'(X_j)$$

$$W_1'(X_j) = W_m(X_j)W_c'(X_j) + W_m'(X_j)W_c(X_j) = W_m(X_j)W_c'(X_j)$$

so $N_1'(X_j)/W_1'(X_j) = N_m(X_j)/W_m(X_j)$. The error value is thus

$$Y[X_j] = r_k - p_k X_j \frac{N_1'(X_j)}{W_1'(X_j)}. \tag{7.22}$$

Now consider the error values for the DB form of the WB equation, (7.18). It is shown in Exercise 7.6 that

$$g'(\alpha^{b+k})\alpha^{b(k+2-d)}p_k\alpha^k = \tilde{C} = \alpha^{b(d-2)}\prod_{i=0}^{d-3}(\alpha^{d-1} - \alpha^{i+1})$$

so that

$$\frac{N_2(\alpha^k)/W_2(\alpha^k)}{N_1(\alpha^k)/W_1(\alpha^k)} = \tilde{C}.$$

It is shown in Exercise 7.7 that $f(\alpha^k)g(\alpha^{b+k}) = -\tilde{C}\alpha^{b(d-1-k)}$. From these two facts we can express the error locators for the DB form as

$$Y[X_k] = -\frac{N_2(\alpha^k)\alpha^{b(d-1-k)}}{W_2'(\alpha^k)g(\alpha^{b+k})} = -\frac{N_2(X_k)X_k^{-b}\alpha^{b(d-1)}}{W_2'(X_k)g(X_k\alpha^b)} \quad \text{(message location)} \tag{7.23}$$

$$Y_k[X_k] = r_k - \frac{N_2'(\alpha^k)\alpha^{b(d-2-k)}}{W_2'(\alpha^k)g'(\alpha^{b+k})} = r_k - \frac{N_2'(X_k)X_k^{-b}\alpha^{b(d-2)}}{W_2'(X_k)g'(X_k\alpha^b)} \quad \text{(check location).} \tag{7.24}$$

7.4 Methods of Solving the WB Key Equation

The key equation problem can be expressed as follows: Given a set of *points* $(x_i, y_i), i = 1, 2, \ldots, m$ over some field $\mathbb{F}$, the problem of finding polynomials $N(x)$ and $W(x)$ with $\deg(N(x)) < \deg(W(x))$ satisfying

$$N(x_i) = W(x_i)y_i, \quad i = 1, 2, \ldots, m \tag{7.25}$$

is called a *rational interpolation problem*,[1] since in the case that $W(x_i) \neq 0$, we have

$$y_i = \frac{N(x_i)}{W(x_i)}.$$

A solution to the rational interpolation problem provides a pair $[N(x), W(x)]$ satisfying (7.25).

We present two different algorithms for solving the rational interpolation problem. Either of these algorithms can be used with the data from either of the two forms of the key equations derived in Section 7.2.

---

[1] Strictly speaking, this is a weak rational interpolation problem, since in the form it is written it does not have to address concerns when $W(x_i) = 0$.

7.4.1   Background: Modules

An additional algebraic structure is used in the algorithm below. In preparation for what follows, we pause to introduce this structure, which is a **module**. Modules are to rings what vector spaces are to fields. That is, they act like vector spaces, but they are built out of rings instead of fields. More formally, we have the following:

Definition 7.5 [84] A **module over a ring** R (or R-module) is a set M together with a binary operation (usually denoted as addition) and an operation of R on M called scalar multiplication with the following properties:

M1 M is an Abelian group under addition.

M2   For all $a \in R$ and $f, g \in M$, $a(f + g) = af + ag \in M$.

M3   For all $a, b \in R$ and all $f \in M$, $(a + b)f = af + bf \in M$.

M4   For all $a, b \in R$ and $f \in M$, $(ab)f = a(bf) \in M$.

M5   If 1 is the multiplicative identity in R, then $1f = f$ for all $f \in M$.

For $f, g \in M$ and $a, b \in R$, we say that $af + bg$ is an **R-linear combination** of f and g.

A **submodule** of a module M is a subset of M which is closed under addition and scalar multiplication by elements of R.   □

Thus, the structure appears to be exactly that of a vector space (see Section 2.4). However, there are a few important distinctions, as the following example shows.

Example 7.6   Let $R = \mathbb{F}[x, y, z]$, where $\mathbb{F}$ is some field and R is the ring of polynomials in the three variables x, y, and z. Let

$$\mathbf{f}_1 = \begin{bmatrix} y \\ -x \\ 0 \end{bmatrix} \quad \mathbf{f}_2 = \begin{bmatrix} z \\ 0 \\ -x \end{bmatrix} \quad \mathbf{f}_3 = \begin{bmatrix} 0 \\ z \\ -y \end{bmatrix}.$$

Let M be the module generated by R-linear combinations of $\mathbf{f}_1$, $\mathbf{f}_2$, and $\mathbf{f}_3$. We could denote this as $M = \langle \mathbf{f}_1, \mathbf{f}_2, \mathbf{f}_3 \rangle$. This set is minimal, in the sense that $\langle \mathbf{f}_i, \mathbf{f}_j \rangle$ does not generate M. However, they are linearly dependent, since

$$z\mathbf{f}_1 - y\mathbf{f}_2 + x\mathbf{f}_3 = \mathbf{0}.$$

We thus have a minimal generating set which is not linearly independent. This phenomenon cannot occur in any vector space.   □

Definition 7.7   If a module M over a ring R has a generating set which is R-linearly independent, then M is said to be a **free module**. The number of generating elements is the **rank** of the module.   □

Example 7.8   Let $R = \mathbb{F}[x]$ be a ring of polynomials and let $M = R^m$ be the module formed by columns of m polynomials. This is a free module. The standard basis for this module is

$$\mathbf{e}_1 = \begin{bmatrix} 1 \\ 0 \\ 0 \\ \vdots \\ 0 \end{bmatrix} \quad \mathbf{e}_2 = \begin{bmatrix} 0 \\ 1 \\ 0 \\ \vdots \\ 0 \end{bmatrix} \quad \cdots \quad \mathbf{e}_m = \begin{bmatrix} 0 \\ 0 \\ 0 \\ \vdots \\ 1 \end{bmatrix}.$$

□

7.4.2 The Welch–Berlekamp Algorithm

In this section, we describe a method of solving the rational interpolation problem which is structurally similar to the Berlekamp–Massey (BM) algorithm, in that it provides a sequence of solution pairs which are updated in the event that there is a discrepancy when a new point is considered. We are interested in a solution satisfying $\deg(N(x)) < \deg(W(x))$ and $\deg(W(x)) \le m/2$.

Definition 7.9 The **rank** of a solution $[N(x), W(x)]$ is defined as

$$\text{rank } [N(x), W(x)] = \max\{2 \deg(W(x)), 1 + 2 \deg(N(x))\}.$$

□

We construct a solution to the rational interpolation problem of rank $\le m$ and show that it is unique. By the definition of the rank, the degree of $N(x)$ is less than the degree of $W(x)$.

A polynomial expression for the interpolation problem (7.25) is useful. Let $P(x)$ be an interpolating polynomial such that $P(x_i) = y_i$, $i = 1, 2, \ldots, m$. For example, $P(x)$ could be the Lagrange interpolating polynomial,

$$P(x) = \sum_{i=1}^{m} y_i \frac{\prod_{k=1, k \neq i}^{m}(x - x_k)}{\prod_{k=1, k \neq i}^{m}(x_i - x_k)}.$$

By the evaluation homomorphism (see Section 5.3.1), the equation $N(x_i) = W(x_i)y_i$ is equivalent to

$$N(x) = W(x)P(x) \ (\text{mod } (x - x_i)).$$

Since this is true for each point (x_i, y_i) and since the polynomials $(x - x_i)$, $i = 1, 2, \ldots, m$ are pairwise relatively prime, by the ring isomorphism introduced in conjunction with the Chinese remainder theorem, we can write

$$N(x) = W(x)P(x) \ (\text{mod } \Pi(x)), \tag{7.26}$$

where

$$\Pi(x) = \prod_{i=1}^{m}(x - x_i).$$

Definition 7.10 Suppose $[N(x), W(x)]$ is a solution to (7.25) and that $N(x)$ and $W(x)$ share a common factor $f(x)$, such that $N(x) = n(x)f(x)$ and $W(x) = w(x)f(x)$. If $[n(x), w(x)]$ is also a solution to (7.25), the solution $[N(x), W(x)]$ is said to be **reducible**. A solution which has no common factors of degree > 0 which may be factored out leaving a solution is said to be **irreducible**.

□

It may be that an irreducible solution does have common factors of the form $(x - y_i)$, but which cannot be factored out while satisfying (7.26).

We begin with an statement regarding the existence of the solution.

Lemma 7.11 *There exists at least one irreducible solution to (7.26) with rank $\le m$.*

Interestingly, this proof makes no use of any particular algorithm to construct a solution — it is purely an existence proof.

Proof Let $S = \{[N(x), W(x)] : \text{rank } (N, W) \le m\}$ be the set of polynomials meeting the rank specification. For $[N(x), W(x)] \in S$ and $[M(x), V(x)] \in S$ and f a scalar value, define

$$\begin{aligned}
[N(x), W(x)] + [M(x), V(x)] &= [N(x) + M(x), W(x) + V(x)] \\
f[N(x), W(x)] &= [fN(x), fW(x)].
\end{aligned} \tag{7.27}$$

We thus make S into a module over $\mathbb{F}[x]$. The dimension of S is $m + 1$, since a basis for the $N(x)$ component is

$$\{1, x, \ldots, x^{\lfloor (m-1)/2 \rfloor}\} \quad (1 + \lfloor (m-1)/2 \rfloor \text{ dimensions})$$

and a basis for the $W(x)$ component is

$$\{1, x, \ldots, x^{\lfloor m/2 \rfloor}\} \quad (1 + \lfloor m/2 \rfloor \text{ dimensions})$$

so the dimension of the Cartesian product is $1 + \lfloor (m-1)/2 \rfloor + 1 + \lfloor m/2 \rfloor = m + 1$.

By (7.26) and by the division algorithm for every $[N(x), W(x)] \in S$ there exists a quotient $Q(x)$ and remainder $R(x)$ with $\deg(R(x)) < m$ such that

$$N(x) - W(x)P(x) = Q(x)\Pi(x) + R(x).$$

Now define the mapping $E : S \to \{h \in \mathbb{F}[x] | \deg(h) < m\}$ by

$$E([N(x), W(x)]) = R(x) \tag{7.28}$$

(the remainder polynomial). The dimension of the range of E is m. Thus, E is a linear mapping from a space of dimension $m + 1$ to a space of dimension m, so the dimension of its kernel is > 0. But the kernel is exactly the set of solutions to (7.26). There must therefore exist at least one solution to (7.26) with rank $\leq m$. $\qquad \square$

The Welch–Berlekamp algorithm finds a rational interpolant of minimal rank by building successive interpolants for increasingly larger sets of points. First, a minimal rank rational interpolant is found for the single point (x_1, y_1). This is used to construct a rational interpolant of minimal rank for the pair of points $\{(x_1, y_1), (x_2, y_2)\}$, and so on, until a minimal rank interpolant for the entire set of points $\{(x_1, y_1), (x_2, y_2), \ldots, (x_m, y_m)\}$ is found.

Definition 7.12 We say that $[N(x), W(x)]$ satisfy the interpolation(k) problem if

$$N(x_i) = W(x_i)y_i \quad i = 1, 2, \ldots, k. \tag{7.29}$$

$\qquad \square$

The Welch–Berlekamp algorithm finds a sequence of solutions $[N^{[k]}, W^{[k]}]$ of minimum rank satisfying the interpolation(k) problem, for $k = 1, 2, \ldots, m$. We can also express the interpolation(k) problem as

$$N(x) = W(x)P_k(x) \pmod{\Pi_k(x)},$$

where $\Pi_k(x) = \prod_{i=1}^{k}(x - x_i)$ and $P_k(x)$ is a polynomial that interpolates (at least) the first k points, $P_k(x_i) = y_i$, $i = 1, 2, \ldots, k$.

As with the BM algorithm, the Welch–Berlekamp algorithm propagates two solutions, using one of them in the update of the other. For the Welch–Berlekamp algorithm, the two sets of solution maintain the property that they are *complements* of each other, as defined here.

Definition 7.13 Let $[N(x), W(x)]$ and $[M(x), V(x)]$ be two solutions of interpolation(k) such that

$$\text{rank}\,[N(x), W(x)] + \text{rank}\,[M(x), V(x)] = 2k + 1$$

and

$$N(x)V(x) - M(x)W(x) = f\Pi(x)$$

for some scalar f. Then $[N(x), W(x)]$ and $[M(x), V(x)]$ are **complementary.** $\qquad \square$

The key results to construct the algorithm are presented in Lemmas 7.14 and 7.16.

Lemma 7.14 *Let $[N(x), W(x)]$ be an irreducible solution to the interpolation(k) problem with rank $\leq k$. Then there exists at least one solution to the interpolation(k) problem which is a complement of $[N(x), W(x)]$.*

Proof Define the set similar to that in Lemma 7.11,

$$S = \{[M(x), V(x)] | \text{rank } [M(x), V(x)] \leq 2k + 1 - \text{rank } (N(x), W(x))\}.$$

It may be verified that, under the operations defined in (7.27), S is a module of dimension $2k + 2 - \text{rank } (N(x), W(x))$. Let K be the kernel of the mapping E defined in (7.28). Since $\dim(\mathcal{R}(E)) = k$ (where $\mathcal{R}(E)$ is the range of E) and $\dim(S) = 2k + 1 - \text{rank } (N(x), W(x))$, we must have $\dim(K) = \dim(S) - \dim(\mathcal{R}(E)) = k + 1 - \text{rank } (N(x), W(x))$. We now show that there is an element $[M(x), V(x)] \in K$ which is not of the form $[g(x)N(x), g(x)W(x)]$. Let

$$T = \{[g(x)N(x), g(x)W(x)] : g \text{ is a polynomial such that}$$

$$\text{rank } [g(x)N(x), g(x)W(x)] \leq 2k + 1 - \text{rank } [N(x), W(x)]\}.$$

Then $T \subset S$. By the definitions, we have

$$\text{rank } [g(x)N(x), g(x)W(x)] \leq 2k + 1 - \text{rank } [N(x), W(x)]$$

and

$$\text{rank } [g(x)N(x), g(x)W(x)] = 2 \deg(g(x)) + \text{rank } [N(x), W(x)]$$

so that

$$\deg(g(x)) \leq k - \text{rank } [N(x), W(x)],$$

which therefore bounds the dimension of the subspace T. Since K has dimension $\geq k + 1 - \text{rank } [N(x), W(x)]$, there must be a point $[M(x), V(x)] \in K \backslash T$ such that

$$\text{rank } [N(x), W(x)] + \text{rank } [M(x), V(x)] \leq 2k + 1. \tag{7.30}$$

Since $[M(x), V(x)] \notin T$, $[M(x), V(x)]$ is not reducible to $[N(x), W(x)]$. We now need another lemma. □

Lemma 7.15 *If $[N(x), W(x)]$ is an irreducible solution to the interpolation(k) problem and $[M(x), V(x)]$ is another solution such that rank $[N(x), W(x)]$ + rank $[M(x), V(x)] \leq 2k$, then $[M(x), V(x)]$ can be reduced to $[N(x), W(x)]$.*

The proof of this lemma is developed in the exercises. Since we have argued that $[M(x), V(x)]$ is not reducible to $[N(x), W(x)]$, by this lemma, we must have that the inequality in (7.30) must be satisfied with equality:

$$rank \ [N(x), W(x)] + rank \ [M(x), V(x)] = 2k + 1.$$

Therefore, one of rank $[N(x), W(x)]$ and rank $[M(x), V(x)]$ is even and the other is odd. So it must be that either

$$2k + 1 = rank \ [N(x), W(x)] + rank \ [M(x), V(x)] = (1 + 2 \deg(N(x)) + 2 \deg(V(x)))$$

$$> 2 \deg(W(x)) + (1 + 2 \deg(M(x)))$$

(in which case $\deg(N(x)V(x)) = k$ and $\deg(W(x)M(x)) < k$) or

$$2k + 1 = rank \ [N(x), W(x)] + rank \ [M(x), V(x)] = 2 \deg(W(x)) + 1 + 2 \deg(M(x))$$

$$> 1 + 2 \deg(N(x)) + 2 \deg(V(x))$$

(in which case $\deg(M(x)W(x)) = k$ *and* $\deg(N(x)V(x)) < k$*) so that, in either case,*

$$\deg(N(x)V(x) - M(x)W(x)) = k.$$

Since $\Pi_k(x)$ *for the interpolation(k) problem has degree k, it must be the case that* $N(x)V(x) - M(x)W(x) = f\Pi_k(x)$ *for some scalar f.*

Lemma 7.16 *If* $[N(x), W(x)]$ *is an irreducible solution to the interpolation(k) problem and* $[M(x), V(x)]$ *is one of its complements, then for any* $a, b \in \mathbb{F}$ *with* $n \neq 0$*,* $[bM(x) - aN(x), bV(x) - aW(x)]$ *is also one of its complements.*

Proof Since $[N(x), W(x)]$ and $[M(x), V(x)]$ are solutions, it must be that

$$N(x) \equiv W(x)P_k(x) \pmod{\Pi_k(x)} \quad M(x) \equiv V(x)P_k(x) \pmod{\Pi_k(x)}.$$

Multiplying the first equation by a and the second equation by b and subtracting the first from the second yields

$$bM(x) - aN(x) \equiv (bV(x) - aW(x))P_k(x) \pmod{\Pi_k(x)}$$

so that $[bM(x) - aN(x), bV(x) - aW(x)]$ is a solution. We now show that it is complementary.

It is straightforward to show that $[bM(x) - aN(x), bV(x) - aW(x)]$ cannot be reduced to $[N(x), W(x)]$ (since $[M(x), V(x)]$ cannot be reduced to $[N(x), W(x)]$ by complementarity and Lemma 7.15). By Lemma 7.15, we must therefore have

$$\text{rank } [N(x), W(x)] + \text{rank } [bM(x) - aN(x), bV(x) - aW(x)] = 2k + 1.$$

$\square$

Lemma 7.15 also implies that there exists only one irreducible solution to the interpolation(k) problem with rank $\leq k$, and that this solution must have at least one complement.

We are now ready to state and prove the theorem describing the Welch–Berlekamp algorithm.

Theorem 7.17 *Suppose that* $[N^{[k]}, W^{[k]}]$ *and* $[M^{[k]}, V^{[k]}]$ *are two complementary solutions of the interpolation(k) problem. Suppose also that* $[N^{[k]}, W^{[k]}]$ *is the solution of lower rank. Let*

$$\begin{aligned} b_k &= N^{[k]}(x_{k+1}) - y_{k+1}W^{[k]}(x_{k+1}) \\ a_k &= M^{[k]}(x_{k+1}) - y_{k+1}V^{[k]}(x_{k+1}). \end{aligned} \tag{7.31}$$

(These are analogous to the discrepancies *of the BM algorithm.) If* $b_k = 0$ *(the discrepancy is 0, so no update is necessary), then*

$$[N^{[k]}(x), W^{[k]}(x)] \quad and \quad [(x - x_{k+1})M^{[k]}(x), (x - x_{k+1})V^{[k]}(x)]$$

are two complementary solutions of the interpolation(k + 1) problem, and $[N^{[k]}(x), W^{[k]}(x)]$ *is the solution of lower rank.*

If $b_k \neq 0$ *(the discrepancy is not 0, so an update is necessary), then*

$$[(x - x_{k+1})N^{[k]}(x), (x - x_{k+1})W^{[k]}(x)] \quad and \quad [b_kM^{[k]}(x) - a_kN^{[k]}(x), b_kN^{[k]} - a_kW^{[k]}(x)]$$

are two complementary solutions. The solution with lower rank is the solution to the interpolation(k + 1) problem.

Proof Since $[N^{[k]}(x), W^{[k]}(x)]$ and $[M^{[k]}(x), V^{[k]}(x)]$ are complementary,

$$\text{rank } [N^{[k]}(x), W^{[k]}(x)] + \text{rank } [M^{[k]}(x), V^{[k]}(x)] = 2k + 1$$

and

$$N^{[k]}(x)V^{[k]}(x) - M^{[k]}(x)W^{[k]}(x) = f \prod_{i=1}^{k}(x - x_i)$$

for some scalar f.

If $b_k = 0$: It is clear that $[N^{[k]}(x), W^{[k]}(x)]$ is a solution to the interpolation$(k + 1)$ problem. For $[(x - x_{k+1})M^{[k]}(x), (x - x_{k+1})V^{[k]}(x)]$, we must have

$$(x - x_{k+1})M^{[k]}(x) \equiv (x - x_{k+1})V^{[k]}(x)P_{k+1}(x) \pmod{\Pi_{k+1}(x)},$$

which is clearly true since $M^{[k]}(x) \equiv V^{[k]}(x)P_k(x) \pmod{\Pi_k(x)}$. When $x = x_{k+1}$, then both sides are 0. Since

$$\text{rank } [(x - x_{k+1})M^{[k]}(x), (x - x_{k+1})V^{[k]}(x)] = \text{rank } [M^{[k]}(x), V^{[k]}(x)] + 2$$

we have

$$\text{rank } [N^{[k]}(x), W^{[k]}(x)] + \text{rank } [(x - x_{k+1})M^{[k]}(x), (x - x_{k+1})V^{[k]}(x)] = 2k + 1 + 2$$

$$= 2(k + 1) + 1.$$

Furthermore,

$$(x - x_{k+1})N^{[k]}(x)V^{[k]}(x) - (x - x_{k+1})M^{[k]}(x)W^{[k]}(x) = f \prod_{i=1}^{k+1}(x - x_i)$$

so that $[N^{[k]}(x), W^{[k]}(x)]$ and $[(x - x_{k+1})M^{[k]}(x), (x - x_{k+1})V^{[k]}(x)]$ are complementary.

If $b_k \neq 0$: Since $[N^{[k]}(x), W^{[k]}(x)]$ satisfies

$$N^{[k]}(x) \equiv W^{[k]}(x)P_{k+1} \pmod{\Pi_k(x)} \tag{7.32}$$

it follows that

$$(x - x_{k+1})N^{[k]}(x) \equiv (x - x_{k+1})W^{[k]}(x)P_{k+1} \pmod{\Pi_{k+1}(x)}, \tag{7.33}$$

since it holds by (7.32) for the first k points and for the point (x_{k+1}, y_{k+1}), both sides of (7.33) are 0. Thus, $[(x - x_{k+1})N^{[k]}(x), (x - x_{k+1})W^{[k]}(x)]$ is a solution to the interpolation$(k + 1)$ problem.

That $[b_k M^{[k]}(x) - a_k N^{[k]}(x), b_k V^{[k]}(x) - a_k W^{[k]}(x)]$ is a solution to the interpolation(k) problem follows since

$$M^{[k]}(x) \equiv V^{[k]}(x)P_{k+1}(x) \pmod{\Pi_k(x)} \text{ and } N^{[k]}(x) \equiv W^{[k]}(x)P_{k+1}(x) \pmod{\Pi_k(x)}.$$

Multiplying the first of these equivalences by b_k and the second by a_k and subtracting gives the solution for the first k points.

To show that $[b_k M^{[k]}(x) - a_k N^{[k]}(x), b_k V^{[k]}(x) - a_k W^{[k]}(x)]$ is also a solution at the point (x_{k+1}, y_{k+1}), substitute a_k and b_k into the following to show that equality holds:

$$b_k M^{[k]}(x_{k+1}) - a_k N^{[k]}(x_{k+1}) = (b_k V^{[k]}(x_{k+1}) - a_k W^{[k]}(x_{k+1}))y_{k+1}.$$

It is clear from the inductive hypothesis that

$$\text{rank } [(x - x_{k+1})N^{[k]}(x), (x - x_{k+1})W^{[k]}(x)]$$

$$+ \text{rank } [b_k M^{[k]}(x) - a_k N^{[k]}(x), b_k V^{[k]}(x) - a_k W^{[k]}(x)] = 2(k + 1) + 1$$

and that

$$(x - x_{k+1})N^{[k]}(x)(b_k V^{[k]}(x) - a_k W^{[k]}(x))$$

$$- (b_k M^{[k]}(x) - a_k N^{[k]}(x))(x - x_{k+1})W^{[k]}(x) = f \prod_{i=1}^{k+1}(x - x_i)$$

for some scalar f. Hence these two solutions are complementary. $\qquad\square$

Based on this theorem, the Welch–Berlekamp rational interpolation function is shown in Algorithm 7.1.

Algorithm 7.1 Welch–Berlekamp Interpolation

Input: $(x_i, y_i), i = 1, \ldots, m$
Returns: $[N^{[m]}(x), W^{[m]}(x)]$ of minimal rank satisfying the interpolation problem.
Initialize:
$N^{[0]}(x) = 0; V^{[0]}(x) = 0; W^{[0]}(x) = 1; M^{[0]}(x) = 1;$
for $i = 0$ to $m - 1$
    $b_i = N^{[i]}(x_{i+1}) - y_{i+1}W^{[i]}(x_{i+1})$ (compute discrepancy)
    if($b_i = 0$) then (no change in $[N, W]$ solution)
        $N^{[i+1]}(x) = N^{[i]}(x); W^{[i+1]}(x) = W^{[i]}(x);$
        $M^{[i+1]}(x) = (x - x_{i+1})M^{[i]}(x); \quad V^{[i+1]}(x) = (x - x_{i+1})V^{[i]}(x)$
    else (update to account for discrepancy)
        $a_i = M^{[i]}(x_{i+1}) - y_{i+1}V^{[i]}(x_{i+1});$ (computeother discrepancy)
        $M^{[i+1]}(x) = (x - x_{i+1})N^{[i]}(x); \quad V^{[i+1]}(x) = (x - x_{i+1})W^{[i]}(x);$
        $N^{[i+1]}(x) = b_iM^{[i]}(x) - a_iN^{[i]}(x); \quad W^{[i+1]}(x) = b_iV^{[i]}(x) - a_iW^{[i]}(x);$
        if($\operatorname{rank}[N^{[i+1]}(x), W^{[i+1]}(x)] > \operatorname{rank}[M^{[i+1]}(x), V^{[i+1]}(x)]$) (swap for minimal rank)
            swap $[N^{[i+1]}(x), W^{[i+1]}(x)] \leftrightarrow [M^{[i+1]}(x), V^{[i+1]}(x)]$
    end (if)
    end (else)
end (for)

Example 7.18 Using the code and data from Example 7.2, the Welch–Berlekamp algorithm operates as follows. Initially, $N^{[0]}(x) = 0$, $W^{[0]}(x) = 1$, $M^{[0]}(x) = 1$, and $V^{[0]}(x) = 0$.

i	b_i	a_i	$N^{[i]}(x)$	$W^{[i]}(x)$	$M^{[i]}(x)$	$V^{[i]}(x)$	Swap?
0	α^7	1	α^7	1	0	$1 + x$	no
1	α^{10}	α^{10}	α^2	$\alpha^{10}x$	$\alpha^8 + \alpha^7 x$	$\alpha + x$	No
2	α^2	α^{12}	$\alpha^{11} + \alpha^9 x$	$\alpha^3 + \alpha^{12}x$	$\alpha^4 + \alpha^2 x$	$\alpha^{12} + \alpha^{10}x^2$	No
3	α^{12}	α^{10}	$\alpha^{11} + \alpha^9 x$	$\alpha^{13} + x + \alpha^7 x^2$	$\alpha^{14} + x + \alpha^9 x^2$	$\alpha^6 + \alpha^{14}x + \alpha^{12}x^2$	No
4	α^4	α^{11}	$\alpha^4 + \alpha^8 x + \alpha^{13}x^2$	$\alpha^{13} + \alpha^5 x + \alpha^9 x^2$	$1 + \alpha^4 x + \alpha^9 x^2$	$\alpha^2 + \alpha^{11}x + \alpha^{12}x^2 + \alpha^7 x^3$	No
5	α^2	0	$\alpha^2 + \alpha^6 x + \alpha^{11}x^2$	$\alpha^4 + \alpha^{13}x + \alpha^{14}x^2 + \alpha^9 x^3$	$\alpha^9 + \alpha^{11}x + \alpha^{13}x^2 + \alpha^{13}x^3$	$\alpha^3 + \alpha^9 x + \alpha^{12}x^2 + \alpha^9 x^3$	No

Using the Chien search, it can be determined that the error locator $W(x) = \alpha^4 + \alpha^{13}x + \alpha^{14}x^2 + \alpha^9 x^3$ has roots at α^4, α^9, and α^{12}. For the error location $X = \alpha^4$ (a check location), using (7.22) the error value is found to be

$$Y[\alpha^4] = r_4 - p_4 X \frac{N'(X)}{W'(X)} = 0 - \alpha^9 \alpha^4 \frac{N'(\alpha^4)}{W'(\alpha^4)} = \alpha^5.$$

For the error location $X = \alpha^9$ (a message location), using (7.21) the error value is found to be

$$Y[X] = f(X)\frac{N(X)}{W'(X)} = \alpha^2 \frac{N(\alpha^9)}{W'(\alpha^9)} = \alpha^7.$$

Similarly, for the error location $X = \alpha^{12}$, the error value is $Y[X] = \alpha^8$. The error polynomial is thus

$$E(x) = \alpha^5 x^4 + \alpha^7 x^9 + \alpha^8 x^{12}$$

and all errors are corrected.   □

Example 7.19 Using the same code and the data from Example 7.4, the Welch–Berlekamp algorithm operates as follows.

i	b_i	a_i	$N^{[i]}(x)$	$W^{[i]}(x)$	$M^{[i]}(x)$	$V^{[i]}(x)$	Swap?
0	α^9	1	α^9	1	0	$1+x$	No
1	α^{12}	α^{12}	α^6	$\alpha^{12}x$	$\alpha^{10}+\alpha^9 x$	$\alpha+x$	No
2	α^6	α^{14}	α^2+x	$\alpha^7+\alpha x$	$\alpha^8+\alpha^6 x$	$\alpha^{14}x+\alpha^{12}x^2$	No
3	α^3	α^{14}	$\alpha^6+\alpha^4 x$	$\alpha^6+\alpha^8 x+x^2$	$\alpha^5+\alpha^6 x+x^2$	$\alpha^{10}+\alpha^3 x+\alpha x^2$	No
4	α^{14}	α^2	$\alpha^5+\alpha^9 x+\alpha^{14}x^2$	$\alpha^{12}+\alpha^4 x+\alpha^8 x^2$	$\alpha^{10}+\alpha^{14}x+\alpha^4 x^2$	$\alpha^{10}+\alpha^4 x+\alpha^5 x^2+x^3$	No
5	α^3	0	$\alpha^{13}+\alpha^2 x+\alpha^7 x^2$	$\alpha^{13}+\alpha^7 x+\alpha^8 x^2+\alpha^3 x^3$	$\alpha^{10}+\alpha^{12}x+\alpha^{14}x^2+\alpha^{14}x^3$	$\alpha^2+\alpha^8 x+\alpha^{11}x^2+\alpha^8 x^3$	No

Using the Chien search, it can be determined that the error locator $W(x) = \alpha^{13} + \alpha^7 x + \alpha^8 x^2 + \alpha^3 x^3$ has roots at α^4, α^9, and α^{12}. For the error location $X = \alpha^4$ (a check location), the error value is found using (7.24) to be

$$Y[\alpha^4] = r_4 - \frac{N'(X)X^{-b}\alpha^{b(d-1)}}{W'(X)g'(X\alpha^b)} = 0 - \frac{N'(X)X^{-b}\alpha^{2(6)}}{W'(X)g'(X\alpha^2)} = \alpha^5.$$

For the error location $X = \alpha^9$ (a message location), the error value is found using (7.23) to be

$$Y[X] = \frac{N(X)X^{-b}\alpha^{b(d-1)}}{W'(X)g(X\alpha^b)} = \frac{N(\alpha^9)\alpha^{-18}\alpha^{2(6)}}{W'(\alpha^9)g(\alpha^9\alpha^2)} = \alpha^7.$$

Similarly, for the error location $X = \alpha^{12}$, the error value is $Y[X] = \alpha^8$. The error polynomial is thus

$$E(x) = \alpha^5 x^4 + \alpha^7 x^9 + \alpha^8 x^{12}$$

and all errors are corrected. □

7.4.3 A Modular Approach to the Solution of the WB Key Equation

In this section, we present an alternative approach to the solution of the WB key equation, due to [86], which makes use of modules and the concept of exact sequences. This solution is interesting theoretically because it introduces several important and powerful algebraic concepts. In addition, as shown in [86], it is suitable for representation in a parallel pipelined form for fast decoding.

The problem, again, is to find polynomials $N(x)$ and $W(x)$ satisfying the rational interpolation problem

$$N(x_i) = W(x_i)y_i, \quad i = 1, 2, \ldots, m \tag{7.34}$$

with $\deg(N(x)) < \deg(W(x))$ and $\deg(W(x))$ minimal. We observe that the set of solutions to (7.34), without regard to the degree requirements, can be expressed more abstractly as the kernel of the homomorphism

$$\phi_i : \mathbb{F}[x] \to \mathbb{F} \text{ defined by } \phi_i(w(x), n(x)) = n(x_i) - w(x_i)y_i. \tag{7.35}$$

Any pair of polynomials $(w(x), n(x))$ in the kernel of ϕ_i yields a solution to (7.34) at x_i.

By the Chinese remainder theorem, the equations in (7.34) can be collectively expressed as a congruence

$$N(x) \equiv W(x)P(x) \pmod{\Pi(x)}, \tag{7.36}$$

where $P(x)$ is any interpolating polynomial, $P(x_i) = y_i$, $i = 1, 2, \ldots, m$, and $\Pi(x) = \prod_{i=1}^{m}(x - x_i)$. Our approach is to develop a linear space of solutions $[w(x), n(x)]$ without regard to the minimality of degree, then to establish a means of selecting a point out of that space with minimal degree. The approach is made somewhat more general by defining a module as follows.

Definition 7.20 For fixed $D(x)$ and $G(x)$, let $\mathcal{M}$ be the module consisting of all pairs $[w(x), n(x)]$ satisfying

$$G(x)n(x) + D(x)w(x) \equiv 0 \pmod{\Pi(x)}. \tag{7.37}$$
□

The module $\mathcal{M}$ corresponds to the space of solutions of (7.36) when $G(x) = 1$ and $D(x) = -P(x)$.

Lemma 7.21 $\mathcal{M}$ *is a free $\mathbb{F}[x]$-module of rank 2 having a basis vectors*

$$[\Pi(x)\delta(x), \Pi(x)\gamma(x)] \quad [-G(x)/\lambda(x), D(x)/\lambda(x)],$$

where

$$\lambda(x) = GCD(G(x), D(x)), \quad (\lambda(x), \Pi(x)) = 1 \tag{7.38}$$

and

$$\delta(x)(D(x)/\lambda(x)) + \gamma(x)(G(x)/\lambda(x)) = 1. \tag{7.39}$$

Proof It is straightforward to verify that (7.37) holds for

$$[w(x), n(x)] = [-G(x)/\lambda(x), D(x)/\lambda(x)]$$

and for

$$[w(x), n(x)] = [\Pi(x)\delta(x), \Pi(x)\gamma(x)],$$

so these bases are in $\mathcal{M}$.

We must show that an arbitrary element $[w(x), n(x)] \in \mathcal{M}$ can be expressed as a $\mathbb{F}[x]$-linear combination of these basis vectors. Since $[w(x), n(x)] \in \mathcal{M}$, $G(x)n(x) + D(x)w(x) \equiv 0 \pmod{\Pi(x)}$, or

$$[w(x), n(x)] \begin{bmatrix} D(x) \\ G(x) \end{bmatrix} \equiv 0 \pmod{\Pi(x)}. \tag{7.40}$$

Consider the matrix

$$A = \begin{bmatrix} \delta(x) & \gamma(x) \\ -G(x)/\lambda(x) & D(x)/\lambda(x) \end{bmatrix}.$$

By (7.39), $\det(A) = 1$, so that A^{-1} is also a polynomial matrix. There therefore exist polynomials $n^*(x)$ and $w^*(x)$ such that

$$[w(x), n(x)] = [w^*(x), n^*(x)]A. \tag{7.41}$$

Substituting this into (7.40),

$$[w^*(x), n^*(x)] \begin{bmatrix} \delta(x) & \gamma(x) \\ -G(x)/\lambda(x) & D(x)/\lambda(x) \end{bmatrix} \begin{bmatrix} D(x) \\ G(x) \end{bmatrix} \equiv 0 \pmod{\Pi(x)},$$

or, using (7.39) again,

$$[w^*(x), n^*(x)] \begin{bmatrix} \lambda(x) \\ 0 \end{bmatrix} \equiv 0 \pmod{\Pi(x)}.$$

Thus, $w^*(x)\lambda(x) \equiv 0 \pmod{\Pi(x)}$, so that by (7.38) $\Pi(x)|w^*(x)$. Thus, there is a polynomial $\tilde{w}(x)$ such that $w^*(x) = \Pi(x)\tilde{w}(x)$. Equation (7.41) can thus be written as

$$[w(x), n(x)] = [\tilde{w}(x), n^*(x)] \begin{bmatrix} \delta(x)\Pi(x) & \gamma(x)\Pi(x) \\ -G(x)/\lambda(x) & D(x)/\lambda(x) \end{bmatrix} \overset{\triangle}{=} [\tilde{w}(x), n^*(x)]\Psi, \tag{7.42}$$

indicating that an arbitrary element $[n(x), w(x)]$ can be expressed as a $\mathbb{F}[x]$-linear combination of the basis vectors. □

It is convenient to represent the set of basis vectors for $\mathcal{M}$ as *rows* of a matrix. We use Ψ to represent a basis matrix. Then any point $[w(x), n(x)]$ can be represented as

$$[w(x), n(x)] = [a(x), b(x)]\Psi$$

for some $[a(x), b(x)] \in \mathbb{F}[x]^2$.

Lemma 7.22 *For any matrix* Ψ *whose rows form a basis of* $\mathcal{M}$, $\det(\Psi) = \alpha\Pi(x)$, *where* $\alpha \in \mathbb{F}$ *is not zero.*

Conversely, if the rows of $\Phi \in \mathbb{F}[x]^{2\times2}$ *are in* $\mathcal{M}$ *and* $\det\Phi = \alpha\Pi(x)$ *for some nonzero* $\alpha \in \mathbb{F}$, *then* Φ *is a basis matrix for* $\mathcal{M}$.

Proof For the matrix Ψ in (7.42),

$$\det(\Psi) = \frac{\Pi}{\lambda}[D\delta + G\gamma] = \Pi(x)$$

by (7.39). Let Ψ' be any other basis matrix. Then there must be a matrix T such that

$$\Psi' = T\Psi \quad \Psi = T^{-1}\Psi'.$$

Since T is invertible, it must be that $\det(T)$ is a unit in $\mathbb{F}[x]$, that is, $\det(T) \in \mathbb{F}$. Thus, $\det(\Psi') = \det(T\Psi) = \det(T)\det(\Psi) = \alpha\Pi(x)$.

To prove the converse statement, for a matrix Φ whose rows are in $\mathcal{M}$, there must be a matrix T such that $\Phi = T\Psi$. Then

$$\alpha\Pi(x) = \det(\Phi) = \det(T)\det(\Psi) = \det(T)\Pi(x)$$

so that $\det(T) = \alpha$, which is a unit. Thus, T is invertible and $\Psi = T^{-1}\Phi$. By this we observe that Φ must be a basis matrix. $\qquad\square$

Let us return to the question of finding the intersection of the modules which are the kernels of ϕ_i defined in (7.35). To this end, we introduce the notion of an exact sequence.

Definition 7.23 Let R be a ring [such as $\mathbb{F}[x]$] and let $\mathfrak{N}$, $\mathfrak{B}$, and $\mathfrak{R}$ be R-modules. Let f and g be module homomorphisms, $f : \mathfrak{N} \to \mathfrak{B}$ and $g : \mathfrak{B} \to \mathfrak{R}$. The sequence

$$\mathfrak{N} \xrightarrow{f} \mathfrak{B} \xrightarrow{g} \mathfrak{R}$$

is said to be **exact** if $\operatorname{im}(f) = \ker(g)$. $\qquad\square$

As an example, let $\mathcal{M}_i$ be the module of rank two that is the kernel of ϕ_i and let $\Psi_i(x)$ be a 2×2 basis matrix for the $\mathcal{M}_i$. Define $\psi_i(w(x), n(x)) = [w(x), n(x)]\Psi_i(x)$. Then

$$\mathbb{F}[x]^2 \xrightarrow{\psi_i} \mathbb{F}[x]^2 \xrightarrow{\phi_i} \mathbb{F}$$

is an exact sequence.

The main idea in the intersection-finding algorithm is embodied in the following lemma.

Lemma 7.24 *Let*

$$\mathfrak{R} \xrightarrow{\psi} \mathfrak{B} \xrightarrow{\phi_1} \mathfrak{R}$$

be exact and let $\phi_2 : \mathfrak{B} \to \mathfrak{R}'$ *be another module homomorphism. Then*

$$\ker(\phi_1) \cap \ker(\phi_2) = \psi(\ker(\phi_2 \circ \psi)).$$

Proof Consider the function $\phi_2 \circ \psi : \mathfrak{R} \to \mathfrak{R}'$. Since $\ker(\phi_2 \circ \psi) \subset \mathfrak{R}$, it follows that $\psi(\ker(\phi_2 \circ \psi)) \subset \operatorname{im}(\psi)$, which by exactness is equal to $\ker(\phi_1)$. Thus, $\psi(\ker(\phi_2 \circ \psi)) \subset \ker(\phi_1)$.

Furthermore, by definition, $\phi_2(\psi(\ker(\phi_2 \circ \psi))) = \{0\}$, that is, $\psi(\ker(\phi_2 \circ \psi)) \in \ker(\phi_2)$. Combining these, we see that

$$\psi(\ker(\phi_2 \circ \psi)) \subset \ker(\phi_1) \cap \ker(\phi_2). \tag{7.43}$$

By definition,

$$\phi_2 \circ \psi(\psi^{-1}(\ker(\phi_1) \cap \ker(\phi_2))) = \{0\}$$

so that

$$\psi^{-1}(\ker(\phi_1) \cap \ker(\phi_2)) \subset \ker(\phi_2 \circ \psi)$$

or, applying ψ to both sides,

$$\ker(\phi_1) \cap \ker(\phi_2) \subset \psi(\ker(\phi_2 \circ \psi)). \tag{7.44}$$

Combining (7.43) and (7.44), we see that

$$\ker(\phi_1) \cap \ker(\phi_2) = \psi(\ker(\phi_2 \circ \psi)).$$

$\square$

This lemma extends immediately: If $\mathfrak{N} \xrightarrow{\psi} \mathfrak{B} \xrightarrow{\phi_1} \mathfrak{R}$ is exact and $\phi_i : \mathfrak{B} \to \mathfrak{R}'$, $i = 1, 2, \ldots, m$ are module homomorphisms, then

$$\ker(\phi_1) \cap \ker(\phi_2) \cap \cdots \cap \ker(\phi_m) = \psi(\ker(\phi_2 \circ \psi) \cap \ker(\phi_3 \circ \psi) \cap \cdots \cap \ker(\phi_m \circ \psi)).$$

Consider the solution of the congruence

$$G_i n(x) + D_i w(x) \equiv 0 \pmod{x - x_i}, \quad i = 1, 2, \ldots, m \tag{7.45}$$

for given G_i and D_i. Define the homomorphisms for this problem as

$$\phi_i(w(x), n(x)) = G_i n(x_i) + D_i w(x_i) = [w(x_i), n(x_i)] \begin{bmatrix} D_i \\ G_i \end{bmatrix}, \tag{7.46}$$

and

$$\psi_i(w(x), n(x)) = \begin{cases} [w(x), n(x)] \begin{bmatrix} -G_i & D_i \\ (x - x_i) & 0 \end{bmatrix} & \text{if } D_i \neq 0 \\[12pt] [w(x), n(x)] \begin{bmatrix} -G_i & 0 \\ 0 & (x - x_i) \end{bmatrix} & \text{if } D_i = 0 \text{ and } G_i \neq 0. \end{cases} \tag{7.47}$$

The module of solutions of (7.45) for a particular value of i is denoted as $\mathcal{M}_i$.

Lemma 7.25 *For ϕ_i and ψ_i as just defined, the sequence*

$$\mathbb{F}[x]^2 \xrightarrow{\psi_i} \mathbb{F}[x]^2 \xrightarrow{\phi_i} \mathbb{F}$$

is exact.

Proof We consider the case that $D_i \neq 0$. By substitution of the elements $(w(x), n(x))$ from each row of the matrix defined in 7.47, $\Psi_i(x) = \begin{bmatrix} -G_i & D_i \\ (x - x_i) & 0 \end{bmatrix}$, into 7.46, it is clear that the rows are two elements of $\ker(\phi_i)$. Also, the determinant of the matrix is equal to $-D_i(x - x_i)$. Thus, by Lemma 7.22, $\Psi_i(x)$ is a basis matrix for the module $\mathcal{M}_i = \ker(\phi_)$.

The case when $D_i = 0$ follows similarly, making use of the fact that $D_i = 0$. $\square$

Each homomorphism ϕ_i can be written as

$$\phi_i(w(x), n(x)) = [w(x_i), n(x_i)] \begin{bmatrix} D_i \\ G_i \end{bmatrix}$$

so that (D_i, G_i) characterizes the homomorphism. Let $\phi_i^{[0]} = \phi_i$, $i = 1, 2, \ldots, m$ represent the initial set of homomorphisms, with initial parameters $(D_i^{[0]}, G_i^{[0]}) = (D_i, G_i)$. The superscript indicates the iteration number.

In the first step of the algorithm, a homomorphism ϕ_{j_1} is chosen from the set

$$\{\phi_1^{[0]}, \phi_2^{[0]}, \ldots, \phi_m^{[0]}\}$$

such that $D_i^{[0]} \neq 0$. (The second subscript in ϕ_{j_1} also denotes the iteration number.) The homomorphism ψ_{j_1} of 7.47, described by the matrix $\Psi_{j_1}^{[1]}(y)$, is formed,

$$\Psi_{j_1}^{[1]}(y) = \begin{bmatrix} -G_{j_1}^{[0]} & D_{j_1}^{[0]} \\ (x - x_{j_1}) & 0 \end{bmatrix}.$$

By Lemma 7.25, the sequence $\mathbb{F}[x]^2 \xrightarrow{\psi_{j_1}} \mathbb{F}[x]^2 \xrightarrow{\phi_{j_1}} \mathbb{F}[x]$ is exact. Now define

$$\phi_i^{[1]} = \phi_i^{[0]} \circ \psi_{j_1}. \tag{7.48}$$

Then from Lemma 7.24

$$\mathcal{M} = \psi_{j_1}(\ker(\phi_1^{[1]}) \cap \ker(\phi_2^{[1]}) \cap \cdots \cap \ker(\phi_m^{[1]})).$$

The interpolation problem is therefore equivalent to finding a basis for

$$\ker(\phi_1^{[1]}) \cap \ker(\phi_2^{[1]}) \cap \cdots \cap \ker(\phi_m^{[1]}). \tag{7.49}$$

We can write

$$\phi_i^{[1]}(w(x), n(x)) = [w(x_i), n(x_i)] \begin{bmatrix} -G_{j_1}^{[0]} & D_{j_1}^{[0]} \\ (x_i - x_{j_1}) & 0 \end{bmatrix} \begin{bmatrix} D_i^{[0]} \\ G_i^{[0]} \end{bmatrix} \tag{7.50}$$

$$= [w(x_i), n(x_i)] \Psi_{j_1}^{[1]}(x_i) \begin{bmatrix} D_i^{[0]} \\ G_i^{[0]} \end{bmatrix}$$

$$= [w(x_i), n(x_i)] \begin{bmatrix} D_{j_1}^{[0]} G_i^{[0]} - D_i^{[0]} G_{j_1}^{[0]} \\ D_i^{[0]}(x_i - x_{j_1}) \end{bmatrix} \triangleq [w(x_i), n(x_i)] \begin{bmatrix} D_i^{[1]} \\ G_i^{[1]} \end{bmatrix}. \tag{7.51}$$

Thus, the homomorphisms $\phi_i^{[1]}$ are defined by $(D_i^{[1]}, G_i^{[1]})$, where

$$\begin{bmatrix} D_i^{[1]} \\ G_i^{[1]} \end{bmatrix} = \Psi_{j_1}^{[1]}(x_i) \begin{bmatrix} D_i^{[0]} \\ G_i^{[0]} \end{bmatrix}. \tag{7.52}$$

When $i = j_1$, we have

$$\begin{bmatrix} D_{j_1}^{[1]} \\ G_{j_1}^{[1]} \end{bmatrix} = \begin{bmatrix} -G_{j_1}^{[0]} & D_{j_1}^{[0]} \\ (x_{j_1} - x_{j_1}) & 0 \end{bmatrix} \begin{bmatrix} D_{j_1}^{[0]} \\ G_{j_1}^{[0]} \end{bmatrix} = \begin{bmatrix} 0 \\ 0 \end{bmatrix}, \tag{7.53}$$

so that $\ker(\phi_{j_1}^{[1]}) = \mathbb{F}[x]^2$. (That is, $\phi_{j_1}^{[1]}$ maps all pairs of polynomials to 0.) This means that among the modules listed in (7.49) there is a trivial module, reducing the number of nontrivial modules to deal with by one. It also means that the equation is satisfied for index $i = j_1$.

At the next step, a single homomorphism $\phi_{j_2}^{[1]}$ is chosen from the set $\{\phi_1^{[1]}, \phi_2^{[1]}, \ldots, \phi_m^{[1]}\}$ such that $D_{j_2}^{[1]}$, defined by (7.52), is nonzero. The corresponding homomorphism ψ_{j_2} is also formed via its matrix representation,

$$\Psi_{j_2}^{[2]}(y) = \begin{bmatrix} -G_{j_2}^{[1]} & D_{j_2}^{[1]} \\ (x - x_{j_2}) & 0 \end{bmatrix}.$$

This choice of j_2 gives rise to a new set of homomorphisms $\{\phi_i^{[2]}\}$ by

$$\phi_i^{[2]} = \phi_i^{[1]} \circ \psi_{j_2}, \quad i = 1, 2, \ldots, m.$$

Then from (7.48),

$$\phi_i^{[2]} = \phi_i^{[0]} \circ \psi_{j_1} \circ \psi_{j_2}, \quad i = 1, 2, \ldots, m$$

so that

$$\phi_i^{[2]}(w(x), n(x)) = [w(x_i), n(x_i)]\Psi_{j_2}^{[2]}(x_i)\Psi_{j_1}^{[1]}(x_i) \begin{bmatrix} D_i^{[0]} \\ G_i^{[0]} \end{bmatrix} = [w(x_i), n(x_i)]\Psi^{[2]} \begin{bmatrix} D_i^{[1]} \\ G_i^{[1]} \end{bmatrix}$$

$$\triangleq [w(x_i), n(x_i)] \begin{bmatrix} D_i^{[2]} \\ G_i^{[2]} \end{bmatrix}.$$

From (7.53) it follows immediately that $G_{j_1}^{[2]} = D_{j_1}^{[2]} = 0$. It is also straightforward to show that

$$\begin{bmatrix} D_{j_2}^{[2]} \\ G_{j_2}^{[2]} \end{bmatrix} = \Psi_{j_2}^{[2]}(x_{j_2})\Psi_{j_1}^{[1]}(x_{j_2}) \begin{bmatrix} D_{j_2}^{[0]} \\ G_{j_2}^{[0]} \end{bmatrix} = \begin{bmatrix} 0 \\ 0 \end{bmatrix}.$$

Thus, $\ker(\phi_{j_1}^{[2]}) = \ker(\phi_{j_2}^{[2]}) = \mathbb{F}[x]^2$, and the equations corresponding to the indices j_1 and j_2 are satisfied. The number of nontrivial modules under consideration is again reduced by one. Furthermore, by Lemma 7.24,

$$\mathcal{M} = \psi_{j_1} \circ \psi_{j_2}(\ker(\phi_1^{[2]}) \cap \ker(\phi_2^{[2]}) \cap \cdots \cap \ker(\phi_m^{[2]})).$$

We continue iterating in this manner until iteration number $l \leq m$ at which the set of $D_i^{[l]} = 0$ for all $i = 1, 2, \ldots, m$. Now consider the set of homomorphisms $\{\phi_1^{[l]}, \phi_2^{[l]}, \ldots, \phi_m^{[l]}\}$. Define

$$\mathcal{M}^{[l]} = \ker(\phi_1^{[l]}) \cap \ker(\phi_2^{[l]}) \cap \cdots \cap \ker(\phi_m^{[l]}) \subset \mathbb{F}[x]^2$$

and let

$$\psi = \psi_{j_1} \circ \psi_{j_2} \circ \cdots \circ \psi_{j_l}.$$

By Lemma 7.24,

$$\mathcal{M} = \psi(\mathcal{M}^{[l]}).$$

By construction, $D_i^{[l]} = 0$ for $i = 1, 2, \ldots, m$. Since

$$\phi_i^{[l]}(w(x), n(x)) = G_i^{[l]} n(x_i) - D_i^{[l]} w(x_i), \quad i = 1, 2, \ldots, m,$$

the pair $(1, 0) \in \mathcal{M}^{[l]}$, which implies that $\psi(1, 0) \in \mathcal{M}$. We have thus found a solution to the interpolation problem! It remains, however, to establish that it satisfies the degree requirements. This is done by keeping track of how the homomorphism ψ is built.

We can write $\psi(w(x), n(x))$ as

$$\psi(w(x), n(x)) = (w(x), n(x)) \begin{bmatrix} -G_{j_l}^{[l-1]} & D_{j_l}^{[l-1]} \\ (x - x_{j_l}) & 0 \end{bmatrix} \begin{bmatrix} -G_{j_{l-1}}^{[l-2]} & D_{j_{l-1}}^{[l-2]} \\ (x - x_{j_{l-1}}) & 0 \end{bmatrix}$$

$$\cdots \begin{bmatrix} -G_{j_1}^{[0]} & D_{j_1}^{[0]} \\ (x - x_{j_1}) & 0 \end{bmatrix}.$$

Let

$$\Psi^1(x) = \Psi_{j_1}^{[1]}(x) = \begin{bmatrix} -G_{j_1} & D_{j_1} \\ (x - x_{j_1}) & 0 \end{bmatrix} \tag{7.54}$$

and

$$\Psi^i(x) = \prod_{p=1}^{i} \Psi_{j_p}^{[p]}(x) = \Psi_{j_i}^{[i]}(x)\Psi^{i-1}(x), \quad i = 2, 3, \ldots, l. \quad (7.55)$$

Use $\Psi(x) = \Psi^{[l]}(x)$. Then $\psi(w(x), n(x)) = [w(x), n(x)]\Psi(x)$. Let us write this as

$$\Psi(x) = \begin{bmatrix} \Psi_{1,1}(x) & \Psi_{1,2}(x) \\ \Psi_{2,1}(x) & \Psi_{2,2}(x) \end{bmatrix} = \begin{bmatrix} \psi(1,0) \\ \psi(0,1) \end{bmatrix}.$$

Our culminating lemma indicates that this construction produces the desired answer.

Lemma 7.26 *Let* $[\Psi_{1,1}(x), \Psi_{1,2}(x)]$ *be the image of* $(1, 0)$ *under the mapping* ψ. *That is,*

$$[\Psi_{1,1}(x), \Psi_{1,2}(x)] = \psi(1,0) = \psi_{j_1} \circ \psi_{j,2} \circ \cdots \circ \psi_{j_l}(1,0).$$

Then $[\Psi_{1,1}(x), \Psi_{1,2}(x)]$ *is a solution to the interpolation problem (7.34) and, furthermore,*

$$\deg(\Psi_{1,1}) < m/2 \quad \deg(\Psi_{1,2}) \leq m/2.$$

Proof The fact that $(\Psi_{1,1}, \Psi_{1,2})$ satisfies the interpolation equations has been shown by their construction. It remains to be shown that the degree requirements are met. The following conditions are established:

$$\deg(\Psi_{1,1}^{[i]}) \leq \left\lfloor \frac{i}{2} \right\rfloor \quad \deg(\Psi_{1,2}^{[i]}) \leq \left\lfloor \frac{i-1}{2} \right\rfloor$$

$$\deg(\Psi_{2,1}^{[i]}) \leq \left\lceil \frac{i}{2} \right\rceil \quad \deg(\Psi_{2,2}^{[i]}) \leq \left\lceil \frac{i-1}{2} \right\rceil$$

This is immediate when $i = 1$. The remainder are proved by induction. For example,

$$\deg(\Psi_{2,2}^{[i+1]}) = 1 + \deg(\Psi_{1,2}^{[i]}) \leq 1 + \lfloor (i-1)/2 \rfloor = \lceil i/2 \rceil.$$

This and the other inductive steps make use of the facts that

$$1 + \lfloor i/2 \rfloor = \lceil (i+1)/2 \rceil \quad \lfloor (i+1)/2 \rfloor = \lceil i/2 \rceil.$$

□

The solution to the WB equation can thus be computed using the following algorithm.

Algorithm 7.2 Welch–Berlekamp Interpolation, Modular Method, v. 1

---

1 **Input:** Points $(x_i, y_i), i = 1, 2, \ldots, m$.
   Returns: $N(x)$ and $W(x)$ satisfying $N(x_i) = W(x_i)y_i, i = 1, 2, \ldots, m$.

2 **Initialization:** Set $G_i^{[0]} = 1, D_i^{[0]} = -y_i, i = 1, 2, \ldots, m, \Psi^{[0]} = \begin{bmatrix} 1 & 0 \\ 0 & 1 \end{bmatrix}$.

3 for $s = 1$ to m

4 $\quad$ Choose j_s such that $D_{j_s}^{[s-1]} \neq 0$. If no such j_s, **break**.

5 $\quad$ for $k = 1$ to m (may be done in parallel)

6 $\quad\quad \begin{bmatrix} D_k^{[s]} \\ G_k^{[s]} \end{bmatrix} = \begin{bmatrix} -G_{j_s}^{[s-1]} & D_{j_s}^{[s-1]} \\ (x_k - x_{j_s}) & 0 \end{bmatrix} \begin{bmatrix} D_k^{[s-1]} \\ G_k^{[s-1]} \end{bmatrix}$

7 $\quad$ end (for)

8 $\quad \begin{bmatrix} \Psi_{1,1}^{[s]} & \Psi_{1,2}^{[s]} \\ \Psi_{2,1}^{[s]} & \Psi_{2,2}^{[s]} \end{bmatrix} = \begin{bmatrix} -G_{j_s}^{[s-1]} & D_{j_s}^{[s-1]} \\ (x - x_{j_s}) & 0 \end{bmatrix} \begin{bmatrix} \Psi_{1,1}^{[s-1]} & \Psi_{1,2}^{[s-1]} \\ \Psi_{2,1}^{[s-1]} & \Psi_{2,2}^{[s-1]} \end{bmatrix}$

9 end (for)

10 $W(x) = \Psi_{1,1}^{[s]}, N(x) = \Psi_{1,2}^{[s]}$.

As pointed out in the comment on line 5, computation of the new parameters G and D in line 6 may be done in parallel.

Example 7.27   For the (x_i, y_i) data of Example 7.2, the execution of the algorithm is as follows (using 1-based indexing):

$s=1$: $\{D_i^{[0]}\} = \{\alpha^7, \alpha^6, 0, \alpha^{12}, 0, \alpha^{13}\}$.   Choose: $j_1 = 1$. $\Psi^{[1]}(x) = \begin{bmatrix} 1 & \alpha^7 \\ 1+x & 0 \end{bmatrix}$ $s=2$: $\{D_i^{[1]}\}$

$= \{0, \alpha^{10}, \alpha^7, \alpha^2, \alpha^7, \alpha^5\}$.   Choose: $j_2 = 2$. $\Psi^{[2]}(x) = \begin{bmatrix} \alpha^{10}x & \alpha^2 \\ \alpha+x & \alpha^8 + \alpha^7 x \end{bmatrix}$ $s=3$: $\{D_i^{[2]}\} = \{0,0,\alpha^2,\alpha^4,\alpha^2,\alpha^{14}\}$.

Choose: $j_3 = 3$. $\Psi^{[3]}(x) = \begin{bmatrix} \alpha^3 + \alpha^{12}x & \alpha^{11} + \alpha^9 x \\ \alpha^{12}x + \alpha^{10}x^2 & \alpha^4 + \alpha^2 x \end{bmatrix}$ $s=4$: $\{D_i^{[3]}\} = \{0,0,0,\alpha^{12},\alpha^4,\alpha^2\}$. Choose: $j_4 = 4$.

$$\Psi^{[4]}(x) = \begin{bmatrix} \alpha^{13} + x + \alpha^7 x^2 & \alpha^{11} + \alpha^9 x \\ \alpha^6 + \alpha^{14}x + \alpha^{12}x^2 & \alpha^{14} + x + \alpha^9 x^2 \end{bmatrix}$$

$s=5$: $\{D_i^{[4]}\} = \{0,0,0,0,\alpha^4,0\}$. Choose: $j_5 = 5$.

$$\Psi^{[5]}(x) = \begin{bmatrix} \alpha^{13} + \alpha^5 x + \alpha^9 x^2 & \alpha^4 + \alpha^8 x + \alpha^{13}x^2 \\ \alpha^2 + \alpha^{11}x + \alpha^{12}x^2 + \alpha^7 x^3 & 1 + \alpha^4 x + \alpha^9 x^2 \end{bmatrix}$$

$s=6$: $\{D_i^{[5]}\} = \{0,0,0,0,0,\alpha^2\}$. Choose: $j_6 = 6$.

$$\Psi^{[6]}(x) = \begin{bmatrix} \alpha^4 + \alpha^{13}x + \alpha^{14}x^2 + \alpha^9 x^3 & \alpha^2 + \alpha^6 x + \alpha^{11}x^2 \\ \alpha^3 + \alpha^9 x + \alpha^{12}x^2 + \alpha^9 x^3 & \alpha^9 + \alpha^{11}x + \alpha^{13}x^2 + \alpha^{13}x^3 \end{bmatrix}.$$

At the end of the iteration, we take

$$W(x) = \Psi_{1,1}(x) = \alpha^4 + \alpha^{13}x + \alpha^{14}x^2 + \alpha^9 x^3 \quad N(x) = \Psi_{1,2}(x) = \alpha^2 + \alpha^6 x + \alpha^{11}x^2.$$

These are the same $(N(x), W(x))$ as were found in Example 7.18. The roots of $W(x)$ and the error values can be determined as before.   □

At the end of the algorithm, we have

$$\Psi(x) = \Psi^{[l]}(x).$$

This algorithm produces a $(D_i^{[s]}, G_i^{[s]})$ pairs satisfying

$$\begin{bmatrix} D_{j_u}^{[s]} \\ G_{j_u}^{[s]} \end{bmatrix} = \begin{bmatrix} 0 \\ 0 \end{bmatrix} \quad \text{for } u \leq s \leq l.$$

Thus, $\ker(\phi_{j_s}^{[l]}) = \mathbb{F}[x]^2$ for $s = 1, 2, \ldots, l$. By Lemma 7.24,

$$\ker(\phi_{j_1}^{[l]}) \cap \ker(\phi_{j_2}^{[l]}) \cap \cdots \cap \ker(\phi_{j_l}^{[l]}) = \psi(\mathbb{F}[x]^2). \tag{7.56}$$

Now consider $\psi(0,1) = (\Psi_{2,1}(x), \Psi_{2,2}(x))$ (that is, it is the second row of the matrix $\Psi(x)$). By (7.56), $\psi(0,1) \in \ker(\phi_{j_1}) \cap \ker(\phi_{j_2}) \cap \cdots \cap \ker(\phi_{j_l})$; that is, it solves all of the equations

$$D_{j_s}\Psi_{2,1}(x_{j_s}) + G_{j_s}\Psi_{2,2}(x_{j_s}) = 0 \quad s = 1, 2, \ldots, l. \tag{7.57}$$

Furthermore, we know by construction that the first row of the $\Psi(x)$ matrix satisfies the equations

$$D_{j_s}\Psi_{1,1}(x_{j_s}) + G_{j_s}\Psi_{1,2}(x_{j_s}) = 0 \quad s = 1, 2, \ldots, l. \tag{7.58}$$

(Note that these are the *original* (D_i, G_i) pairs which are not zero, not the modified $(D_i^{[l]}, G_i^{[l]})$ pairs.)

Like the Welch–Berlekamp algorithm, Algorithm 7.2 requires the propagation of four polynomials. However, we now show that it is possible to generate a solution using only two polynomials. This is done by showing how to compute the error values using only two elements in the $\Psi(x)$ matrix. We show how to compute the error values for the DB form of the key equation. (Extension to the WB form of the key equation is straightforward.)

Lemma 7.28 *[[86], p. 879] Define*

$$h(x) = \frac{g(\alpha^b x)}{\prod\limits_{s=1}^{l}(x - x_{j_s})}.$$

Then the error value corresponding to the location $x_i = \alpha^k$ is

$$Y[x_i] = \frac{\alpha^{b(d-1)} x_i^{-b} (-1)^l \prod\limits_{s=1}^{l-1} D_{j_s}^{[s-1]}}{\Psi'_{1,1}(x_i)\Psi_{2,1}(x_i)h(x_i)}. \tag{7.59}$$

Proof We consider separately the cases that the error is in a message location or a check location. Recall that the x_k, $k = 1, 2, \ldots, m$ defined in the interpolation problem represent check locations. Suppose first the error is in a message location, with locator x_i. From (7.54) and (7.55), we have

$$\det(\Psi(x)) = \Psi_{1,1}(x)\Psi_{2,2}(x) - \Psi_{1,2}(x)\Psi_{2,1}(x) = (-1)^l \prod\limits_{s=1}^{l} D_{j_s}^{[s-1]}(x - x_{j_s}). \tag{7.60}$$

By definition, the x_{j_s} are all in check locations, so the right-hand side of the equation is not zero at $x = x_i$. But since x_i is an error location, we must have $\Psi_{1,1}(x_i) = 0$. We thus obtain

$$\Psi_{1,2}(x_i) = -\frac{(-1)^l \prod\limits_{s=1}^{l} D_{j_s}^{[s-1]}(x_i - x_{j_s})}{\Psi_{2,1}(x_i)}. \tag{7.61}$$

Recalling that the error value for a message location is (see (7.23))

$$Y[x_i] = -\frac{N_2(x_i)x_i^{-b}\alpha^{b(d-1)}}{W'_2(x_i)g(x_i\alpha^b)} = \frac{\Psi_{1,2}(x_i)x_i^{-b}\alpha^{b(d-1)}}{\Psi'_{1,1}(x_i)g(x_i\alpha^b)}$$

and substituting from (7.61), the result follows.

Now consider the case that x_i is a check location. From (7.58), when $\Psi_{1,1}(x_i) = 0$, we must have $\Psi_{1,2}(x_i) = 0$. As observed in (7.57), $(\Psi_{2,1}(x), \Psi_{2,2}(x))$ satisfies the interpolation problem (7.18) for $\alpha^k \in \{x_{j_s}, s = 1, 2, \ldots, l\}$. The function $(h(x), h(x))$ satisfies it (trivially) for other values of α^k that are check locations, since it is zero on both sides of the interpolation equation. Thus, $(h(x)\Psi_{2,1}(x), h(x)\Psi_{2,2})(x))$ satisfies (7.18). Thus,

$$h(x_i)\Psi_{2,2}(x_i) = h(x_i)\Psi_{2,1}(x_i)r[x_i]g'(x_i\alpha^b)x_i^b\alpha^{b(2-d)}.$$

It can be shown that $\Psi_{2,1}(x_i) \neq 0$ and that $h(x_i) \neq 0$ (see Exercise 7.11), so that

$$r[x_i] = \frac{\Psi_{2,2}(x_i)x_i^{-b}\alpha^{b(d-2)}}{\Psi_{2,1}(x_i)g'(\alpha^b x_i)}.$$

Now substitute into (7.24):

$$
Y[x_i] = \frac{\Psi_{2,2}(x_i)x_i^{-b}\alpha^{b(d-2)}}{\Psi_{2,1}(x_i)g'(\alpha^b x_i)} - \frac{\Psi'_{1,2}(x_i)x_i^{-b}\alpha^{b(d-2)}}{\Psi'_{1,1}(x_i)g'(x_i\alpha^b)}
$$

$$
= \frac{(\Psi'_{1,1}(x_i)\Psi_{2,2}(x_i) - \Psi_{2,1}(x_i)\Psi'_{1,2}(x_i))x_i^{-b}\alpha^{b(d-2)}}{\Psi'_{1,1}(x_i)\Psi_{2,1}(x_i)g'(\alpha^b x_i)}.
$$

Since $\Psi_{1,1}(x_i) = 0$ and $\Psi_{1,2}(x_i) = 0$, we have

$$
(\Psi_{1,1}(x)\Psi_{2,2}(x) - \Psi_{1,2}(x)\Psi_{2,1}(x))'|_{x=x_i} = \Psi'_{1,1}(x_i)\Psi_{2,2}(x_i) - \Psi'_{1,2}(x_i)\Psi_{2,1}(x_i)
$$

which, in turn, using (7.60) is equal to

$$
(\det(\Psi(x)))'|_{x=x_i} = (-1)^l \prod_{\substack{s=1 \\ i\neq j_s}}^{l} D_{j_s}^{[s-1]}(x_i - x_{j_s}).
$$

We thus have

$$
Y[x_i] = \frac{x_i^{-b}\alpha^{b(d-2)}(-1)^l \prod_{\substack{s=1 \\ j_s\neq i}}^{l} D_{j_s}^{[s-1]}(x_i - x_{j_s})}{\Psi'_{1,1}(x_i)\Psi_{2,1}(x_i)g'(\alpha^b x_i)}.
$$

Since $g'(\alpha^b x_i) = \alpha^b \prod_{\substack{k=0 \\ k\neq i}}^{d-2}(\alpha^b x_i - \alpha^{b+k})$, we can write

$$
Y[x_i] = \frac{x_i^{-b}\alpha^{b(d-2)}(-1)^l \prod_{s=1}^{l} D_{j_s}^{[s-1]}}{\Psi'_{1,1}(x_i)\Psi_{2,1}(x_i)h(x_i)}.
$$

                                                       □

    Since by this lemma the only polynomials needed to compute the error values are $\Psi_{1,1}(x)$ and $\Psi_{2,1}(x)$ (the first column of $\Psi(z)$), we only need to propagate these. This gives rise to the following decoding algorithm.

Algorithm 7.3 Welch–Berlekamp Interpolation, Modular Method, v. 2

---

1 **Input:** Points (x_i, y_i), $i = 1, 2, \ldots, m$ from DB form of key equation.
   Returns: $\Psi_{2,1}(x)$ and $\Psi_{1,1}(x)$ which can be used to find error values.
2 **Initialization:** Set $G_i^{[0]} = 1, D_i^{[0]} = -y_i$, $i = 1, 2, \ldots, m$, $\Psi_{1,1}^{[0]} = 1$; $\Psi_{2,1}^{[0]} = 0$.
3 for $s = 1$ to m
4   Choose j_s such that $D_{j_s}^{[s-1]} \neq 0$. If no such j_s, **break**.
5   for $k = 1$ to m (may be done in parallel)
6       $\begin{bmatrix} D_k^{[s]} \\ G_k^{[s]} \end{bmatrix} = \begin{bmatrix} -G_{j_s}^{[s-1]} & D_{j_s}^{[s-1]} \\ (x_k - x_{j_s}) & 0 \end{bmatrix} \begin{bmatrix} D_k^{[s-1]} \\ G_k^{[s-1]} \end{bmatrix}$
7   end (for)
8     $\begin{bmatrix} \Psi_{1,1}^{[s]} \\ \Psi_{2,1}^{[s]} \end{bmatrix} = \begin{bmatrix} -G_{j_s}^{[s-1]} & D_{j_s}^{[s-1]} \\ (x - x_{j_s}) & 0 \end{bmatrix} \begin{bmatrix} \Psi_{1,1}^{[s-1]} \\ \Psi_{2,1}^{[s-1]} \end{bmatrix}$
9 end (for)

Example 7.29 For the (x_i, y_i) data in Example 7.4 (which form is necessary, since the method is based on the error values computed for the DB form), the algorithm operates as follows (using 1-based indexing).

$s = 1$. $\{D_i^{[0]}\} = \{\alpha^9, \alpha^8, 0, \alpha^{14}, 0, 1\}$. Choose: $j_1 = 1$. $(\Psi_{1,1}(x), \Psi_{2,1}(x)) = (1, 1 + x)$ $s = 2$. $\{D_i^{[1]}\} = \{0, \alpha^{12}, \alpha^9, \alpha^4, \alpha^9, \alpha^7\}$. Choose: $j_2 = 2$. $(\Psi_{1,1}(x), \Psi_{2,1}(x)) = (\alpha^{12}x, \alpha + x)$ $s = 3$. $\{D_i^{[2]}\} = \{0, 0, \alpha^6, \alpha^8, \alpha^6, \alpha^3\}$. Choose: $j_3 = 3$. $(\Psi_{1,1}(x), \Psi_{2,1}(x)) = (\alpha^7 + \alpha x, \alpha^{14}x + \alpha^{12}x^2)$ $s = 4$. $\{D_i^{[3]}\} = \{0, 0, 0, \alpha^3, \alpha^{10}, \alpha^8\}$. Choose: $j_4 = 4$. $(\Psi_{1,1}(x), \Psi_{2,1}(x)) = (\alpha^6 + \alpha^8 x + x^2, \alpha^{10} + \alpha^3 x + \alpha x^2)$ $s = 5$. $\{D_i^{[4]}\} = \{0, 0, 0, 0, \alpha^{14}, 0\}$. Choose: $j_5 = 5$. $(\Psi_{1,1}(x), \Psi_{2,1}(x)) = (\alpha^{12} + \alpha^4 x + \alpha^8 x^2, \alpha^{10} + \alpha^4 x + \alpha^5 x^2 + x^3)$ $s = 6$. $\{D_i^{[4]}\} = \{0, 0, 0, 0, 0, \alpha^3\}$. Choose: $j_6 = 6$. $(\Psi_{1,1}(x), \Psi_{2,1}(x)) = (\alpha^{13} + \alpha^7 x + \alpha^8 x^2 + \alpha^3 x^3, \alpha^2 + \alpha^8 x + \alpha^{11} x^2 + \alpha^8 x^3)$

The roots of $\Psi_{1,1}(x) = \alpha^{13} + \alpha^7 x + \alpha^8 x^2 + \alpha^3 x^3$ are at α^4, α^9, and α^{12}. Using (7.59) the error value are found to be α^5, α^7, and α^8, respectively. □

One last simplification is now developed for this algorithm. As we shall show, there are some computations which Algorithm 7.3 performs which turn out to be unnecessary. If we can postpone some of them until it is certain that they are needed, unnecessary computations can be avoided. This idea was originally suggested as using *queues* in ([34]).

Let

$$\Omega^s = \{k \in \{1, 2, \ldots, 2t\} : D_k^{[s]} = 0 \text{ and } G_k^{[s]} = 0\}$$

and let

$$\Sigma^s = \{k \in \{1, 2, \ldots, 2t\} : D_k^{[s]} = 0 \text{ and } G_k^{[s]} \neq 0\}.$$

For a $k \in \Sigma^2$, we can (by normalization if necessary) assume without loss of generality that $G_k^s = 1$.

Let j_s be such that $D_{s_j}^{[s-1]} \neq 0$ (that is, $j_s \notin \Sigma^{s-1}$ and $j_s \notin \Omega^{s-1}$) and let $k \in \Sigma^{s-1}$ such that $D_k^{[s-1]} = 0$ and $G_k^{[s-1]} = 1$. Then

$$\begin{bmatrix} D_k^{[s]} \\ G_k^{[s]} \end{bmatrix} = \begin{bmatrix} -G_{j_s}^{[s-1]} & D_{j_s}^{[s-1]} \\ (x_k - x_{j_s}) & 0 \end{bmatrix} \begin{bmatrix} 0 \\ 1 \end{bmatrix},$$

so that for all $k \in \Sigma^{s-1}$, $G_k^s = 0$ and $D_k^{[s]} = D_{j_s}^{[s-1]} \neq 0$. Hence $k \notin \Sigma^s$. Therefore, at the $(s + 1)$st step of the algorithm, if $\Sigma^{s-1} \neq \emptyset$, j_{s+1} can be chosen from Σ^{s-1}. So let $j_{s+1} \in \Sigma^{s-1}$. For $k \in \Sigma^{s-1}$ with $k \neq j_{s+1}$,

$$\begin{bmatrix} D_k^{[s+1]} \\ G_k^{[s+1]} \end{bmatrix} = \begin{bmatrix} 0 & 1 \\ (x_k - x_{j_{s+1}}) & 0 \end{bmatrix} \begin{bmatrix} D_k^{[s]} \\ 0 \end{bmatrix}$$

so that $D_k^{[s+1]} = 0$ and $G_k^{[s+1]} \neq 0$. From this, $k \in \Sigma^{s+1}$ and $j_{s+1} \in \Omega^{s+1}$.

Thus, the for loop in lines 5–7 of Algorithm 7.3 can exclude those values of k that are in $\Sigma^{s-1} \cup \Sigma^s \cup \Omega^s$, since over the next two iterations computations involving them are predictable (and eventually they may not need to be done at all). This leads to the following statement of the algorithm.

Algorithm 7.4 Welch–Berlekamp Interpolation, Modular Method, v. 3

---

1 **Input:** Points $(x_i, y_i), i = 1, 2, \ldots, m$.
  Returns: $\Psi_{2,1}(x)$ and $\Psi_{1,1}(x)$ which can be used to find error values.
2 **Initialization:** Set $\Sigma^0 = \Sigma^{-1} = \Omega^0 = \emptyset$, $G_i^{[0]} = 1$, $D_i^{[0]} = -y_i$, $i = 1, 2, \ldots, m$, $\Psi_{1,1}^{[0]} = 1$; $\Psi_{2,1}^{[0]} = 0$.
3 for $s = 1$ to m
4   If $\Sigma^{s-2} \neq \emptyset$ choose $j_s \in \Sigma^{s-2}$. Otherwise, choose j_s such that $D_{j_s}^{[s-1]} \neq 0$.
    If no such j_s, **break**.
5   for $k = 1$ to m such that $k \notin \Sigma^{s-2} \cup \Sigma^{s-1} \cup \Omega^{s-1}$ (may be done in parallel)
6   $$\begin{bmatrix} D_k^{[s]} \\ G_k^{[s]} \end{bmatrix} = \begin{bmatrix} -G_{j_s}^{[s-1]} & D_{j_s}^{[s-1]} \\ (x_k - x_{j_s}) & 0 \end{bmatrix} \begin{bmatrix} D_k^{[s-1]} \\ G_k^{[s-1]} \end{bmatrix}$$
7   end (for)

$$8 \quad \begin{bmatrix} \Psi_{1,1}^{[s]} \\ \Psi_{2,1}^{[s]} \end{bmatrix} = \begin{bmatrix} -G_{j_s}^{[s-1]} & D_{j_s}^{[s-1]} \\ (x - x_{j_s}) & 0 \end{bmatrix} \begin{bmatrix} \Psi_{1,1}^{[s-1]} \\ \Psi_{2,1}^{[s-1]} \end{bmatrix}$$

9   $\Sigma^{s-2} \leftarrow \Sigma^{s-1}$; Update Σ^s and Ω^s.

10 end (for)

7.5   Erasure Decoding with the WB Key Equation

In the event that some of the positions in $R(x)$ are erased, the algorithms can be modified as follows. Let the erasure locator polynomial be $\Gamma(x) = \prod_i (x - \alpha_i^e)$, where the e_i are in this case the erasure locations.

For the Welch–Berlekamp algorithm of Section 7.4.2, erasure/error decoding proceeds exactly as in the case of errors-only decoding, except that initial W polynomial is set equal to the erasure locator polynomial, $W^{[0]}(x) = \Gamma(x)$. The formulas for computing the error and erasure values are exactly the same as for errors-only decoding.

For the Dabiri–Blake decoding, Algorithm 7.2, think of $W(x)$ as consisting of two factors, one factor due to errors and the other due to erasures,

$$W(x) = W_1(x)\Gamma(x).$$

Then the interpolation problem is written as

$$N(x_i) = W(x_i)y_i = W_1(x_i)\Gamma(x_i)y_i.$$

Now let $\tilde{y}_i = \Gamma(x_i)y_i$ and run Algorithm 7.2 on the data $(x_i, \tilde{y}_i)$, except that the initialization $\Psi_{1,1}^{[0]}(x) = \Gamma(x)$ is performed. The error value computations are unchanged.

7.6   The Guruswami–Sudan Decoding Algorithm and Soft RS Decoding

The algebraic decoders presented to this point in the book are bounded distance decoders, meaning they are capable of decoding up to $t_0 = \lfloor (d_{\min} - 1)/2 \rfloor$ errors. In the remainder of this chapter, we discuss a list decoding approach to Reed–Solomon (and related) codes which is capable of decoding beyond t_0 errors. A *list decoder* generally returns several possible decoded messages. However, for many codes the size of the list is usually small, so that only one decoded message is usually returned. An extension of this decoding algorithm provides a means for *algebraic soft-decision* decoding of Reed–Solomon codes.

7.6.1   Bounded Distance, ML, and List Decoding

Consider an (n, k, d) Reed–Solomon code C. Three different decoding paradigms can be employed in decoding such codes, as illustrated in (Figure 7.2).

In **bounded distance (BD) decoding**, the following problem is solved: For a distance e such that $2e + 1 \le d_{\min}$, given a received vector $\mathbf{r}$, find a codeword $\mathbf{c} \in C$ which is within a Hamming distance e of $\mathbf{r}$. There exist many efficient algorithms for solving this (all of the algorithms in Chapter 6 are BD decoders), and for a t-error-correcting code the answer is unique when $t \ge e$. However, if $\mathbf{r}$ lies at a distance greater than $\lfloor (d_{\min} - 1)/2 \rfloor$ from any codeword, a decoding failure will result.

In **maximum likelihood (ML) decoding** (also known as **nearest codeword problem**), the codeword $\mathbf{c}$ which is closest to $\mathbf{r}$ is selected. Provided that the number of errors e satisfies $2e + 1 \le d_{\min}$, the ML and BD algorithms decode identically. However, ML decoding may be able to decode beyond $\lfloor (d_{\min} - 1)/2 \rfloor$ errors. The ML decoding problem, however, is computationally difficult in general [35].

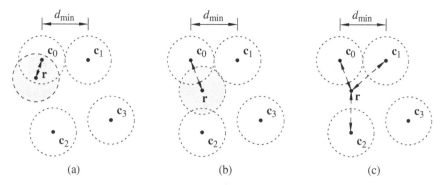

Figure 7.2: Comparing BD, ML, and list decoding. (a) BD decoding: codeword in same Hamming sphere as $\mathbf{r}$; (b) ML decoding: nearest codeword to $\mathbf{r}$ decoding (possibly beyond Hamming sphere); (c) List decoding: all codewords within a given Hamming distance of $\mathbf{r}$.

In **list decoding**, the problem is to find *all* codewords $\mathbf{c} \in C$ which are within a given distance e of the received word $\mathbf{r}$.

The Guruswami–Sudan (GS) algorithm is essentially a list-decoding algorithm, providing lists of all codewords within a distance t_m of the received word $\mathbf{r}$. Whereas the BD decoder is able to correct a fraction $\tau = \frac{1}{n}\frac{n-k}{2} = \frac{1-R}{2}$ of the errors, the GS algorithm is able to correct up to $t_{GS} = \lceil n - \sqrt{nk} - 1 \rceil$ errors, so that the fraction is (asymptotically) $\tau = 1 - \sqrt{R}$. Thus, the GS algorithm has better error-correction capability for every code rate R.

7.6.2 Error Correction by Interpolation

The motivating idea behind the GS decoding algorithm can be expressed as follows. Under Construction 1 of Reed–Solomon codes, a set of data points (x_i, c_i), $i = 1, \ldots, n$ are generated with a polynomial relationship $c_i = m(x_i)$ for some polynomial $m(x)$ which has at most degree $k - 1$. A set of points (x_i, c_i) are produced. The c_i are corrupted by some noise process, producing points (x_i, y_i) in which as many as e of the r_i are in error. The problem now is to fit a polynomial $p(x)$, of degree $< k$ through the data points, such that $p(x_i) = y_i$. However, since some of the points are in error, we seek an interpolating match only for $n - e$ of the data points, so $|\{i : p(x_i) = y_i\}| \geq n - e$. Then, based on this interpolating polynomial, the points in error are recovered. That is, if i is the index of a point in error, then we say that the recovered value is $\hat{r}_i = p(x_i)$.

The GS decoding is based generally on this idea of interpolation. The interpolating polynomial is constructed as a polynomial in *two* variables, $Q(x, y)$ which satisfies the interpolating condition $Q(x_i, y_i) = 0$. In addition to simply interpolating, an interpolation multiplicity m_i is introduced which defines the order of the interpolation at each point. This is roughly equivalent to specifying the value of the function and its $m_i - 1$ derivatives in the interpolating polynomial. This interpolation multiplicity improves the correction capability. Furthermore, as we will see in Section 7.6.8, we will see that the interpolating multiplicity can be used for soft-decision decoding of RS codes. From the bivariate polynomial $Q(x, y)$ the polynomials $p(x)$ are extracted by factorization, which will satisfy the property $p(x_i) = y_i$ for a sufficiently large number of locations (x_i, y_i). Then each polynomial $p(x)$ represents a possible transmitted codeword and the set of polynomials is the list of possible decoded codewords.

There are thus two main steps to the decoding algorithm:

The interpolation step The decoder constructs a two-variable polynomial

$$Q(x, y) = \sum_{i=0}^{d_x} \sum_{j=0}^{d_y} a_{i,j} x^i y^j \tag{7.62}$$

such that $Q(x_i, y_i) = 0$ for $i = 1, 2, \ldots, n$ (with a certain multiplicity of the zero, to be discussed below), and for which the "degree" (actually, the weighted degree) of $Q(x, y)$ is as small as possible.

Explaining and justifying this step will require a discussion of the concept of the degree of multivariable polynomials, which is presented in Section 7.6.3.

The problem can be set up and solved using straightforward linear algebra. However, a potentially more efficient (and interesting) algorithm due to Kötter [253] is presented in Section 7.6.5.2. An algorithm accomplishing the solution, which is an extension of the BM algorithm to vectors, is presented in Section 7.6.5.1.

The factorization step   The decoder then finds all factors of $Q(x, y)$ of the form $y - p(x)$, where $p(x)$ is a polynomial of degree v or less. This step produces the list of polynomials

$$\mathcal{L} = \{p_1(x), p_2(x), \ldots, p_L(x)\}$$

that agree with (x_i, y_i) in at least $n - t_m$ places. That is, $|\{i : p_j(x_i) = y_i\}| \geq n - t_m$ for every $p_j \in \mathcal{L}$.

An algorithm due to Roth and Ruckenstein [382] which performs the factorization by reducing it to single-variable factorization (amenable, e.g., to root-finding via the Chien search) is presented in Section 7.6.7.

The quantity t_m is the *designed decoding radius*. The larger t_m is, the more potential errors can be corrected. The quantity t_m depends in a nondecreasing way on m_i; that is $t_0 \leq t_1 \leq t_2 \cdots$, and there is a multiplicity m_0 such that $t_{m_0} = t_{m_0+1} = \cdots \overset{\triangle}{=} t_{GS}$ that describes the maximum error correction capability of the decoding algorithm.

7.6.3   Polynomials in Two Variables

In this section, we describe the concepts associated with polynomials in two variables which are necessary to understand the algorithm. We will see that for a polynomial $p(x)$ of degree v such that $(y - p(x))|Q(x, y)$ it is natural to consider the (univariate) polynomial $Q(x, p(x))$. For $Q(x, y)$ as in (7.62), this gives

$$Q(x, p(x)) = \sum_{i=0}^{d_x} \sum_{j=0}^{d_y} a_{i,j} x^i p(x)^j,$$

testpxy.cc

which is a polynomial in x of degree $d_x + vd_y$. It is thus natural to define the degree of $Q(x, y)$ as $d_x + vd_y$. This is called the $(1, v)$ **weighted degree** of $Q(x, y)$.

7.6.3.1   Degree and Monomial Order

For a polynomial in a single variable, the notion of degree is straightforward. For polynomials defined over multiple variables, however, there is some degree of flexibility available in defining the order of the polynomials. Various algorithms (and their complexity) depend on the particular order employed. (For a full discussion of the degree of multinomials, the reader is referred to [[83], Section 2.2].)

Let $\mathbb{F}$ be a field and let $\mathbb{F}[x, y]$ denote the commutative ring of polynomials in the variables x and y with coefficients from F. A polynomial $Q(x, y) \in \mathbb{F}[x, y]$ can be written as

$$Q(x, y) = \sum_{i,j \geq 0} a_{i,j} x^i y^j,$$

in which only a finite number of coefficients are nonzero.

Example 7.30 Let $\mathbb{F} = \mathbb{R}$ and let

$$Q(x, y) = 3x^3y + 4xy^3 + 5x^4.$$

Looking forward to the upcoming definitions, we ask the questions: What is the degree of $Q(x, y)$? What is the leading term of $Q(x, y)$? How is $Q(x, y)$ to be written with the terms ordered in increasing "degree"? □

To address the questions raised in this example, it will be convenient to impose an *ordering* on the set of monomials

$$\mathbb{M}[x, y] = \{x^i y^j : i, j \geq 0\} \subset \mathbb{F}[x, y].$$

That is, we want to be able to say when a monomial $x^{i_1}y^{j_1}$ is "less than" $x^{i_2}y^{j_2}$. Let $\mathbb{N}^2$ denote the set of pairs of natural numbers (pairs of non-negative integers).

Definition 7.31 A **monomial ordering** is a relation "$<$" on $\mathbb{M}[x, y]$ with the following properties.

MO1 For $(a_1, a_2) \in \mathbb{N}^2$ and $(b_1, b_2) \in \mathbb{N}^2$, if $a_1 \leq b_1$ and $a_2 \leq b_2$, then $x^{a_1}y^{a_2} \leq x^{b_1}y^{b_2}$. (That is, the monomial $x^{a_1}y^{a_2}$ "comes before" the monomial $x^{b_1}y^{b_2}$.)

MO2 The relation "$<$" is a total ordering. That is, if $\mathbf{a} = (a_1, a_2) \in \mathbb{N}^2$ and $\mathbf{b} = (b_1, b_2) \in \mathbb{N}^2$ are distinct, then either $x^{a_1}y^{a_2} < x^{b_1}y^{b_2}$ or $x^{b_1}y^{b_2} < x^{a_1}y^{a_2}$.

MO3 For any $(a_1, a_2), (b_1, b_2)$, and $(c_1, c_2) \in \mathbb{N}^2$, if $x^{a_1}y^{a_2} \leq x^{b_1}y^{b_2}$, then $x^{a_1}y^{a_2}x^{c_1}y^{c_2} \leq x^{b_1}y^{b_2}x^{c_1}y^{c_2}$. □

Of the many possible monomial orderings one might consider, those which will be most important in this development are the *weighted degree* (WD) monomial orderings. Each WD monomial order is characterized by a fixed pair $\mathbf{w} = (u, v)$ of non-negative integers where not both are 0. Then the $\mathbf{w}$-degree of the monomial $x^i y^j$ is defined as

$$\deg_{\mathbf{w}} x^i y^j = ui + vj.$$

The WD monomial order is sufficient to define a *partial order* on $\mathbb{M}[x, y]$. However, there may be ties under this order, since there are monomials $\phi_1(x, y)$ and $\phi_2(x, y)$ with $\phi_1(x, y) \neq \phi_2(x, y)$ with $\deg_{\mathbf{w}}\phi_1(x, y) = \deg_{\mathbf{w}}\phi_2(x, y)$, so that it is not yet an order. There are two common ways to break such ties.

Definition 7.32 In **w-lexicographic** (or **w-lex**) **order**, if $ui_1 + vj_1 = ui_2 + vj_2$, we say that $x^{i_1}y^{j_1} < x^{i_2}y^{j_2}$ if $i_1 < i_2$. In **w-reverse lexicographic** (or **w-revlex**) **order**, if $ui_1 + vj_1 = ui_2 + vj_2$, we say that $x^{i_1}y^{j_1} < x^{i_2}y^{j_2}$ if $i_1 > i_2$. These orderings are denoted by $<_{\mathrm{wlex}}$ and $<_{\mathrm{wrevlex}}$. □

Example 7.33 Let $\mathbf{w} = (1, 3)$. Let $\phi_1(x, y) = x^2y^3$; then $\deg_{\mathbf{w}}\phi_1 = 11$. Let $\phi_2(x, y) = x^8y$; then $\deg_{\mathbf{w}}\phi_2 = 11$, so there is a tie in the degree. Under **w-lex** order, $\phi_1(x, y) <_{\mathrm{wlex}} \phi_2(x, y)$. Under **w-revlex** order, $\phi_2(x, y) <_{\mathrm{wrevlex}} \phi_1(x, y)$. □

By a fixed monomial order $<$ a set of monomials $\{\phi_i\}$ can be uniquely ordered:

$$1 = \phi_0(x, y) < \phi_1(x, y) < \phi_2(x, y) < \cdots.$$

Example 7.34 Let $\mathbf{w} = (1, 3)$. Table 7.1 shows the first 30 monomials $\phi_j(x, y)$ ordered in **w**-revlex order, along with the **w**-degree of the monomial and the order index j. The first 30 monomials ordered in **w**-lex order are shown in Table 7.2. □

Table 7.1: Monomials Ordered Under $(1, 3)$-revlex Order

Monomial: $\phi_j(x,y)$	1	x	x^2	ax^3	y	x^4	xy	x^5	x^2y	x^6	x^3y	y^2	x^7	x^4y	xy^2
Weight: ($\mathbf{w}$-revlex):	0	1	2	3	3	4	4	5	5	6	6	6	7	7	7
j:	0	1	2	3	4	5	6	7	8	9	10	11	12	13	14

Monomial: $\phi_j(x,y)$	x^8	x^5y	x^2y^2	x^9	x^6y	x^3y^2	y^3	x^{10}	x^7y	x^4y^2	xy^3	x^{11}	x^8y	x^5y^2	x^2y^3
Weight: ($\mathbf{w}$-revlex):	8	8	8	9	9	9	9	10	10	10	10	11	11	11	11
j:	15	16	17	18	19	20	21	22	23	24	25	26	27	28	29

Table 7.2: Monomials Ordered Under $(1, 3)$-lex Order

Monomial: $\phi_j(x,y)$	1	x	x^2	y	x^3	xy	x^4	x^2y	x^5	y^2	x^3y	x^6	xy^2	x^4y	x^7
Weight: ($\mathbf{w}$-lex):	0	1	2	3	3	4	4	5	5	6	6	6	7	7	7
j:	0	1	2	3	4	5	6	7	8	9	10	11	12	13	14

Monomial: $\phi_j(x,y)$	x^2y^2	x^5y	x^8	y^3	x^3y^2	x^6y	x^9	xy^3	x^4y^2	x^7y	x^{10}	x^2y^3	x^5y^2	x^8y	x^{11}
Weight: ($\mathbf{w}$-lex):	8	8	8	9	9	9	9	10	10	10	10	11	11	11	11
j:	15	16	17	18	19	20	21	22	23	24	25	26	27	28	29

For purposes of characterizing the performance of the decoder, it is useful to know how many monomials there are up to a given weighted degree.

Lemma 7.35 *Let $C(v, l)$ be the number of monomials of weighted $(1, v)$-degree less than or equal to l. Then*

$$C(v,l) = \left(\left\lfloor \frac{l}{v} \right\rfloor + 1 \right) \left(l + 1 - \frac{v}{2} \left\lfloor \frac{l}{v} \right\rfloor \right). \tag{7.63}$$

Furthermore,

$$C(v,l) \geq \frac{l}{v} \frac{l+2}{2} > \frac{(l+1)^2}{2v}. \tag{7.64}$$

Example 7.36 Some values of $C(3, l)$ computed using (7.63) are

l	1	2	3	4	5	6	7	8	9	10	11
$C(3, l)$	2	3	5	7	9	12	15	18	22	26	30
Bound	0.67	1.5	2.67	4.17	6	8.17	10.67	13.5	16.67	20.17	24

These can be compared with the data in Table 7.1 or 7.2.   □

Proof For a fixed j_2, the monomials $x^{j_1}y^{j_2}$ of $(1, v)$-degree less than or equal to l is $l + 1 - vj_2$. The largest y-degree of a monomial of $(1, v)$-degree less than l is $\lfloor l/v \rfloor$. The total number of monomials of $(1, v)$-degree $\leq l$ is thus

$$C(v,l) = \sum_{j_2=0}^{\lfloor l/v \rfloor} (l + 1 - vj_2) = (l+1)\left(\left\lfloor \frac{l}{v} \right\rfloor + 1 \right) - \frac{v}{2}\left\lfloor \frac{l}{v} \right\rfloor \left(\left\lfloor \frac{l}{v} \right\rfloor + 1 \right)$$

$$= \left(\left\lfloor \frac{l}{v} \right\rfloor + 1 \right) \left(l + 1 - \frac{v}{2}\left\lfloor \frac{l}{v} \right\rfloor \right).$$

Define $r = l \pmod{v}$. Then

$$C(v,l) = \frac{(v\lfloor l/v \rfloor + v)(2l + 2 - v\lfloor l/v \rfloor)}{2v}$$

$$= \frac{(l - r + v)(2l + 2 - l + r)}{2v} = \frac{(l + (v - r))(l + (r + r))}{2v} > \frac{(l+1)^2}{2}. \quad\quad □$$

A polynomial $Q(x, y) = \sum_{i,j \geq 0} a_{i,j} x^i y^j$ with the monomials ordered by a fixed monomial ordering can be written uniquely as

$$Q(x, y) = \sum_{j=0}^{J} a_j \phi_j(x, y)$$

for some set of coefficients $\{a_j\}$, with $a_J \neq 0$. The integer J is called the **rank** of $Q(x, y)$, denoted rank $(Q(x, y))$. The monomial $\phi_J(x, y)$ is called the **leading monomial** of $Q(x, y)$, denoted $\text{LM}(Q(x, y))$. The coefficient a_J is called the **leading coefficient** of $Q(x, y)$. The weighted degree of the leading monomial of $Q(x, y)$ is called the **weighted degree** of $Q(x, y)$, or **w**-degree, denoted $\deg_{\mathbf{w}}(Q(x, y))$:

$$\deg_{\mathbf{w}}(Q(x, y)) = \deg_{\mathbf{w}} \text{LM}(Q(x, y)) = \max\{\deg_{\mathbf{w}} \phi_j(x, y) : a_j \neq 0\}.$$

We also say that the y-degree of $Q(x, y)$ is the degree of $Q(1, y)$ as a polynomial in y.

Example 7.37 Let $\mathbf{w} = (1, 3)$ and let $<$ be the **w**-revlex ordering. When

$$Q(x, y) = 1 + xy + x^4 y + x^2 y^3 + x + y + x^8 y$$

is written with monomials ordered in increasing degree under $<$, we have

$$Q(x, y) = 1 + x + y + xy + x^4 y + x^8 y + x^2 y^3.$$

The y-degree of $Q(x, y)$ is 3. The $\text{LM}(Q) = x^2 y^3$, rank $(Q) = 29$ (refer to Table 7.1) and $\deg_{\mathbf{w}}(Q) = 11$.
When $Q(x, y)$ is written under **w**-lex ordering,

$$Q(x, y) = 1 + x + y + xy + x^4 y + x^2 y^3 + x^8 y,$$

and $\text{LM}(Q) = x^8 y$ and rank $(Q) = 28$ (refer to Table 7.2). □

Having defined an order on monomials, this can be extended to a partial order on polynomials.

Definition 7.38 For two polynomials $P(x, y), Q(x, y) \in \mathbb{F}[x, y]$, we say that $P(x, y) < Q(x, y)$ if $\text{LM}(P(x, y)) < \text{LM}(Q(x, y))$. (This is a partial order on $\mathbb{F}[x, y]$, since distinct polynomials may have the same leading monomial.) □

7.6.3.2 Zeros and Multiple Zeros

In the GS decoder, we are interested in fitting an interpolating polynomial with a multiplicity of zeros. We define in this section what we mean by this.

We first make an observation about zeros at 0 of polynomials in one variable.

Definition 7.39 For $m \leq n$, the polynomial

$$Q(x) = a_m x^m + a_{m+1} x^{m+1} + \cdots + a_n x^n = \sum_{r=m}^{n} a_r x^r,$$

where $a_0 = a_1 = \cdots = a_{m-1} = 0$, is said to a zero of **order** or **multiplicity** m at 0. We write $\text{ord}(Q; 0) = m$. □

Let $\mathcal{D}_r$ denote the rth formal derivative operator (see Section 6.5.1). Then we observe that

$$Q(0) = \mathcal{D}_1 Q(0) = \cdots = \mathcal{D}_{m-1} Q(0) = 0.$$

So the order of a zero can be expressed in terms of derivative conditions in this case.

Let us generalize this result to zeros of order m at other locations. We say that $Q(x)$ has a zero of order m at α if $Q(x + \alpha)$ has a zero of order m at 0. This can be expressed using a kind of Taylor series, which applies over any field, known as **Hasse's theorem**.

Lemma 7.40 *[192] If $Q(x) = \sum_{i=0}^{n} a_i x^i \in \mathbb{F}[x]$, then for any $\alpha \in \mathbb{F}$,*

$$Q(x + \alpha) = \sum_{r=0}^{n} Q_r(\alpha) x^r,$$

where

$$Q_r(x) = \sum_{i=0}^{n} \binom{i}{r} a_i x^{i-r},$$

and where we take $\binom{i}{r} = 0$ if $r > i$.

The proof follows by straightforward application of the binomial theorem. $Q_r(x)$ is called the rth **Hasse derivative** of $Q(x)$. We will denote $Q_r(x)$ by $D_r Q(x)$. In the case that $\mathbb{F}$ is a field of characteristic 0, then

$$D_r Q(x) = Q_r(x) = \frac{1}{r!} \frac{d^r}{dx^r} Q(x), \qquad (7.65)$$

so that D_r does, in fact, act like a differentiating operator, but with a scaling factor of $1/r!$. We can write

$$Q(x + \alpha) = \sum_{r=0}^{n} D_r Q(\alpha) x^r.$$

Thus, if $Q(x)$ has a zero of order m at α, we must have the first m coefficients of this series equal to 0:

$$Q(\alpha) = D_1 Q(\alpha) = \cdots = D_{m-1} Q(\alpha) = 0.$$

Extending Definition 7.39, we have the following:

Definition 7.41 $Q(x)$ has a zero of **order** (or **multiplicity**) m at α if

$$Q(\alpha) = D_1 Q(\alpha) = \cdots = D_{m-1} Q(\alpha) = 0.$$

This is denoted as $\mathrm{ord}(Q; \alpha) = m$. $\square$

These concepts extend to polynomials in two variables.

Definition 7.42 Let $Q(x, y) \in \mathbb{F}[x, y]$ and let α and β be such that $Q(\alpha, \beta) = 0$. Then we say that Q has a **zero** at (α, β).

Let $Q(x, y) = \sum_{i,j \geq 0} a_{i,j} x^i y^j$. We say that Q has a **zero of multiplicity** m (or **order** m) at $(0, 0)$ if the coefficients $a_{i,j} = 0$ for all $i + j < m$. When Q has a zero of order m at $(0, 0)$, we write $\mathrm{ord}(Q; 0, 0) = m$.

Similarly, we say that $Q(x, y)$ has a zero of order m at (α, β), denoted as $\mathrm{ord}(Q; \alpha, \beta) = m$, if $Q(x + \alpha, y + \beta)$ has a zero of order m at $(0, 0)$. $\square$

Example 7.43 $Q(x, y) = x^4 y + x^3 y^2 + x^4 y^4$ has a zero of order 5 at $(0, 0)$.

$Q(x, y) = x + y$ has a zero of order 1 at $(0, 0)$.

$Q(x, y) = (x - \alpha)^4 (y - \beta) + (x - \alpha)^3 (y - \beta)^2 + (x - \alpha)^4 (y - \beta)^4$ has a zero of order 5 at (α, β). $\square$

We observe that a zero of order m requires that $\binom{m+1}{2} = m(m+1)/2$ coefficients are 0. For example, for a zero of order 3 at $(0,0)$, the $\binom{3+1}{2} = 6$ coefficients

$$a_{0,0}, a_{0,1}, a_{0,2}, a_{1,0}, a_{1,1}, a_{2,0}$$

are all zero.

Lemma 7.40 is extended in a straightforward way to two variables.

Lemma 7.44 *If $Q(x,y) = \sum_{i,j} a_{i,j} x^i y^j$, then*

$$Q(x+\alpha, y+\beta) = \sum_{r,s} Q_{r,s}(\alpha,\beta) x^r y^s,$$

where

$$Q_{r,s}(x,y) = \sum_i \sum_j \binom{i}{r}\binom{j}{s} a_{i,j} x^{i-r} y^{j-s}. \tag{7.66}$$

Again, the proof is by straightforward application of the binomial theorem. We will denote

$$Q_{r,s}(x,y) = D_{r,s}Q(x,y); \tag{7.67}$$

this is sometimes called the (r,s)th **Hasse (mixed partial) derivative** of $Q(x,y)$.

Based on this notation, we observe that if $\operatorname{ord}(Q; \alpha, \beta) = m$, then

$$D_{r,s}Q(\alpha,\beta) = 0 \text{ for all } r,s \text{ such that } r+s < m, \tag{7.68}$$

which is a total of $\binom{m+1}{2}$ constraints.

Example 7.45 We demonstrate some Hasse derivatives over $\mathbb{F} = GF(5)$.

$$D_{1,0}x = 1 \quad D_{1,0}y = 0$$
$$D_{0,1}x = 0 \quad D_{0,1}y = 1$$
$$D_{1,0}x^2 = \binom{2}{1}\binom{0}{0}x^{2-1}y^{0-0} = 2x$$
$$D_{2,0}x^5 = \binom{5}{2}\binom{0}{0}x^{5-2} = 10x^3 = 0 \quad \text{(over } GF(5))$$
$$D_{2,1}x^2y^3 = \binom{2}{2}\binom{3}{1}x^{2-2}y^{3-1} = 3y^2.$$

We note that $D_{r,s}$ acts very much like a partial differentiation operator, except for the division $1/r!s!$ suggested by (7.65). □

7.6.4 The GS Decoder: The Main Theorems

With the notation of the previous section, we can now describe the GS decoder in greater detail. For an (n,k) RS code over the field $\mathbb{F}$ with support set (see Section 6.2.1) $(x_1, x_2, \ldots, x_n)$ and a positive integer m, the GS(m) decoder accepts a vector $\mathbf{r} = (y_1, y_2, \ldots, y_n) \in \mathbb{F}^n$ as an input and produces a list of polynomials $\{p_1, p_2, \ldots, p_L\}$ as the output by the following two steps:

Interpolation step: The decoder constructs a nonzero two-variable polynomial of the form

$$Q(x, y) = \sum_{j=0}^{C} a_j \phi_j(x, y)$$

of minimal $(1, v)$-degree which has a zero of order m at each of the points (x_i, y_i), $i = 1, 2, \ldots, n$. Here, the $\phi_j(x, y)$ are monomials of the form $x^p y^q$, ordered according to the $(1, v)$-revlex monomial order such that $\phi_0 < \phi_1 < \cdots$.

Related to this step are two fundamental questions: Does such a polynomial exist? How can it be constructed?

Factorization step: The polynomial $Q(x, y)$ is factored by finding a set of polynomials $p(x)$ such that $y - p(x) | Q(x, y)$. We form the set of such polynomials, called the y-roots of $Q(x, y)$,

$$\mathcal{L} = \{p(x) \in \mathbb{F}[x] : (y - p(x)) | Q(x, y)\}.$$

Questions related to this step are: How does this relate to the error correction capability of the code? How is the factorization computed? How many polynomials are in $\mathcal{L}$?

As we will see, it is also possible to employ a different interpolation order m_i at each point (x_i, y_i). This is developed further in Section 7.6.8.

7.6.4.1 The Interpolation Theorem

We address the existence of the interpolating polynomial with the following theorem.

Theorem 7.46 *(The Interpolation Theorem) Let*

$$Q(x, y) = \sum_{i,j} a_{i,j} x^i y^j = \sum_{i=0}^{C} a_i \phi(x, y), \tag{7.69}$$

where the monomials are ordered according to an arbitrary monomial order. Then a nonzero $Q(x, y)$ polynomial exists that interpolates the points (x_i, y_i), $i = 1, 2, \ldots, n$ with multiplicity m at each point if

$$C = n \binom{m + 1}{2}. \tag{7.70}$$

Proof There is a zero of multiplicity m at (x_i, y_i) if

$$D_{r,s} Q(x_i, y_i) = 0 \text{ for all } (r, s) \text{ such that } 0 \le r + s < m. \tag{7.71}$$

Using the Hasse partial derivatives defined in (7.66) and (7.67), Equation (7.71) can be written as

$$\sum_k \sum_j \binom{k}{r} \binom{j}{s} a_{k,j} x_i^{k-r} y_i^{j-s} = 0 \quad i = 1, 2, \ldots, n, \text{ and } r + s < m. \tag{7.72}$$

There are $\binom{m+1}{2}$ linear homogeneous equations (constraints) for each value of i, for a total of $n \binom{m+1}{2}$ equations. If $C = n \binom{m+1}{2}$, then there are $C + 1$ variables $a_0, a_1, \ldots, a_C$ in (7.69). There must be at least one nonzero solution to the set of linear equations (7.71). $\square$

The solution to (7.72) can be computed using straightforward linear algebra, with complexity $O(C^3)$. Other algorithms are discussed in Section 7.6.5.

7.6.4.2 The Factorization Theorem

The main results regarding the factorization step are provided by the following lemma and theorem.

Lemma 7.47 *Let $Q(x_i, y_i)$ have zeros of multiplicity m at the points (x_i, y_i), $i = 1, 2, \ldots, n$. If $p(x)$ is a polynomial such that $y_i = p(x_i)$, then $(x - x_i)^m | Q(x, p(x))$.*

Proof To gain insight, suppose initially that $(x_i, y_i) = (0, 0)$, so $0 = p(0)$. Thus, we can write $p(x) = x\tilde{p}(x)$ for some polynomial $\tilde{p}(x)$. Then for

$$Q(x, y) = \sum_{i+j \geq m} a_{i,j} x^i y^j,$$

(where the sum is over $i + j \geq m$ since $Q(x, y)$ has zeros of multiplicity m) it follows that

$$Q(x, p(x)) = Q(x, x\tilde{p}(x)) = \sum_{i+j \geq m} a_{i,j} x^i (x\tilde{p}(x))^j,$$

which is divisible by x^m. This establishes the result for the point $(0, 0)$.

Now let (x_i, y_i) be a general input point with $y_i = p(x_i)$. Let $p^{(i)}(x) = p(x + x_i) - y_i$, so that $p^{(i)}(0) = 0$. Thus, $p^{(i)}(x) = x\tilde{p}^{(i)}(x)$ for some polynomial $\tilde{p}^{(i)}(x)$. Let $Q^{(i)}(x, y) = Q(x + x_i, y + y_i)$, so $Q^{(i)}(0, 0) = 0$. The problem has been shifted so that $Q^{(i)}(0, 0)$ and $p^{(i)}$ behave like the results above at $(0, 0)$. Thus, $x_i^m | Q^{(i)}(x, p^{(i)(x)})$. Shifting back gives the desired conclusion. □

Theorem 7.48 (The Factorization Theorem) *Let $Q(x, y)$ be an interpolating polynomial of $(1, v)$-weighted degree $\leq l$ such that $D_{r,s} Q(x_i, y_i) = 0$ for $i = 1, 2, \ldots, n$ and for all $r + s < m$. (That is, each (x_i, y_i) is interpolated up to order m.) Let $p(x)$ be a polynomial of degree at most v such that $y_i = p(x_i)$ for at least K_m values of i in $\{1, 2, \ldots, n\}$. If $mK_m > l$, then $(y - p(x)) | Q(x, y)$.*

Before proving this theorem, let us put it in context. If $p(x)$ is a polynomial of degree less than k, then $p(x)$ produces a codeword $\mathbf{c} \in C$ by the mapping

$$p(x) \to (p(x_1), p(x_2), \ldots, p(x_n)) \in C.$$

For this codeword, $y_i = p(x_i)$ for at least K_m places. Let $t_m = n - K_m$. Then $\mathbf{c}$ differs from the received vector $\mathbf{r} = (y_1, y_2, \ldots, y_m)$ in as many as t_m places. Thus, $p(x)$ identifies a codeword $\mathbf{c}$ at a distance no greater than t_m from $\mathbf{r}$. This codeword is a candidate to decode $\mathbf{r}$. So, if $p(x)$ agrees in at least K_m places, then by the factorization theorem, $p(x)$ is a y-root of $Q(x, y)$, and is therefore placed on the list of candidate decodings.

Proof Let $g(x) = Q(x, p(x))$. By the definition of the weighted degree, and by the fact that $Q(x, y)$ has $(1, v)$-weighted degree $\leq l$, $g(x)$ is a polynomial of degree at most l. By Lemma 7.47, $(x - x_i)^m | g(x)$ for each point such that $y_i = p(x_i)$. Let S be the set of points where there is agreement such that $y_i = p(x_i)$, that is, $S = \{i \in \{1, \ldots, n\} : y_i = p(x_i)\}$ and let

$$s(x) = \prod_{i \in S} (x - x_i)^m.$$

Then $s(x) | g(x)$. Since $|S| \geq K_m$ (by hypothesis), we have $\deg s(x) \geq mK_m$. We thus have a polynomial of degree $\geq mK_m$ dividing $g(x)$ which is of degree $< mK_m$. It must therefore be the case that $g(x)$ is identically 0, or $Q(x, p(x)) = 0$. Now think of $Q(x, y)$ as a polynomial in y with coefficients in $\mathbb{F}[x]$. Employ the division algorithm to divide by $(y - p(x))$:

$$Q(x, y) = (y - p(x))q(x, y) + r(x).$$

Evaluating at $y = p(x)$, we have

$$0 = Q(x, p(x)) = r(x)$$

so that $(y - p(x)) | Q(x, p(x))$.   □

The degree of $p(x)$ in Theorem 7.48 is at most v. Since $p(x)$ is to interpolate points as $y_i = p(x_i)$ and there is (by the Reed–Solomon encoding process) a polynomial relationship of degree $< k$ between the support set and the codewords, we must have $\deg p(x) < k$. We thus set

$$\boxed{v = k - 1.}$$

This establishes the weighted order to be used in the algorithm.

7.6.4.3 The Correction Distance

Let us now establish a connection between the correction distance t_m, the multiplicity m, and the maximum $(1, v)$-weighted degree l of $Q(x, y)$. The point of the interpolation theorem is that the number of variables in the interpolating polynomial must exceed the number of equations (constraints), which is $n \binom{m+1}{2}$. Recall from Lemma 7.35 that the number of monomials of weighted $(1, v)$-degree l is $C(v, l)$. So by the interpolation theorem (Theorem 7.46), we must have

$$n \binom{m+1}{2} < C(v, l). \tag{7.73}$$

By the Factorization Theorem (Theorem 7.48), we must also have

$$mK_m > l \quad \text{or} \quad mK_m \geq l + 1 \quad \text{or} \quad mK_m - 1 \geq l. \tag{7.74}$$

computekm.m
computekm.cc
floortest.m

Since $C(v, l)$ is increasing in its second argument, replacing the second argument with a larger value makes it larger. Thus, from (7.73) and (7.74), we have

$$C(v, mK_m - 1) > n \binom{m+1}{2}. \tag{7.75}$$

For $m \geq 1$, we will *define* K_m to be the smallest value for which (7.75) is true:

$$K_m = \min \left\{ K : C(v, mK - 1) > n \binom{m+1}{2} \right\}. \tag{7.76}$$

From the factorization theorem, K_m is the number of agreements between $\mathbf{y}$ and a codeword, so $t_m = n - K_m$ is the distance between $\mathbf{y}$ and a codeword; it is the error correction distance. For $m = 0$, we define K_m to be $n - t_0 = n - \lfloor (n-k)/2 \rfloor = \lceil (n+v+1)/2 \rceil$. As the following example shows, K_m is nonincreasing with m.

Example 7.49 Figure 7.3 shows K_m as a function of m for a $(32, 8)$ Reed–Solomon code. There is an immediate decrease with m for small values of m, followed by a long plateau. At $m = 120$, K_m decreases to its final value — there are no more decreases beyond that.   □

There is a multiplicity m_0 beyond which $K_{m_0} = K_{m_0+1} = \cdots$ — no further decreases are possible. We denote this as K_∞. Since K_m is nonincreasing with m, $t_m = n - K_m$ is nondecreasing with m. That is, increasing the multiplicity m can increase the error correction distance, up till the point $t_\infty = n - K_\infty$ is reached, which is the asymptotic decoding capability of the GS decoder.

We will denote

$$K_\infty = \lfloor \sqrt{vn} \rfloor + 1$$

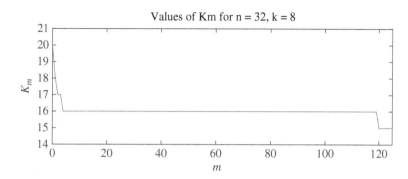

Figure 7.3: K_m as a function of m for a $(32, 8)$ Reed–Solomon code.

so that

$$t_\infty = n - K_\infty = n - 1 - \lfloor \sqrt{vn} \rfloor = n - 1 - \lfloor \sqrt{(k-1)n} \rfloor.$$

The following theorem indicates that the decoding distance of the GS decoder improves (or at least does not decrease) with increasing m. (As becomes evident below, the decoder algorithmic complexity increases with m, so this improved performance is obtained with higher complexity.)

Theorem 7.50 *[302]* K_m *is nonincreasing with m:*

$$K_0 \geq K_\infty \geq v + 1 \tag{7.77}$$

$$K_0 \geq K_1 \tag{7.78}$$

$$K_m \geq K_\infty \tag{7.79}$$

$$K_m \geq K_{m+1} \tag{7.80}$$

$$K_m = K_\infty \quad \text{for all sufficiently large } m. \tag{7.81}$$

Proof We will give only a partial proof. (The remaining results require bounds on $C(v, l)$ which are more fully developed in [302].) Proof of (7.77)[2]:

$$K_0 = \lceil (n + v + 1)/2 \rceil \geq \lfloor (n + v + 1)/2 \rfloor + 1$$

$$\geq \lfloor \sqrt{n(v+1)} \rfloor \qquad \text{(arithmetic–geometric inequality)}$$

$$\geq \lfloor \sqrt{nv} \rfloor + 1 = K_\infty.$$

Proof of (7.81): It must be shown that for all sufficiently large m

$$C(v, mK_\infty - 1) > n \binom{m+1}{2}. \tag{7.82}$$

Using the bound (7.63),

$$C(v, mK_\infty - 1) \geq \frac{m^2 K_\infty^2}{2v} = n \frac{m(m+1)}{2} \left(\frac{m}{m+1} \frac{K_\infty^2}{vn} \right).$$

---

[2] The arithmetic–geometric inequality states that for positive numbers $z_1, z_2, \ldots, z_m, (z_1 z_2 \cdots z_m)^{1/m} \leq \frac{1}{m}(z_1 + z_2 + \cdots + z_m)$; that is, the geometric mean is less than the arithmetic mean. Equality holds only in the case that all the z_i are equal.

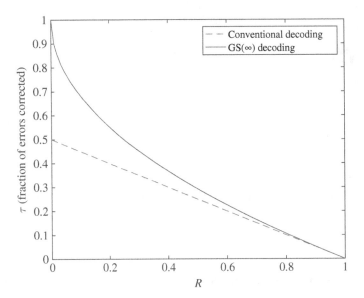

Figure 7.4: Fraction of errors corrected as a function of rate.

So (7.82) holds if $\frac{m}{m+1} \frac{K_\infty^2}{vn} > 1$, or when

$$m > \left(\frac{K_\infty^2}{vn} - 1 \right)^{-1}. \tag{7.83}$$

In order for the bound in (7.83) to make sense, the term on the right-hand side must be positive, which establishes the lower bound $K_\infty = \lfloor \sqrt{vn} \rfloor + 1$. Suppose it were the case that K_∞ were smaller, say, $K_\infty = \lfloor \sqrt{vn} \rfloor$. Then $(\lfloor \sqrt{vn} \rfloor /(vn) - 1)$ would be negative. Thus, $K_\infty = \lfloor \sqrt{vn} \rfloor + 1$ is the smallest possible value.   □

For an (n, k) decoder capable of correcting t errors, let $\tau = t/n$ denote the fraction of errors corrected and let $R = k/n$ denote the rate. For the conventional $t = t_0$ decoder, the fraction of errors corrected is (asymptotically) $\tau_0 = (1 - R)/2$. For the GS algorithm, $\tau_\infty = 1 - \sqrt{R}$ (asymptotically). Figure 7.4 shows the improvement in fraction of errors corrected as a function of rate. The increase in the decoding capability is substantial, particularly for low rate codes.

7.6.4.4   The Number of Polynomials in the Decoding List

The GS algorithm returns a list of polynomials $\mathcal{L} = \{p_1(x), p_2(x), \ldots, p_L(x)\}$. The transmitted codeword will be in $\mathcal{L}$ if the number of channel errors is $\leq t_m$. There may be other codewords as well, since this is a list decoding algorithm. How many polynomials can be in $\mathcal{L}$? (This material is drawn from [302].)

Recall that $Q(x, y)$ is a polynomial of $(1, v)$-weighted degree $\leq l$ and that the polynomials $p(x)$ are those such that $(y - p(x))|Q(x, y)$. The maximum number of such polynomials is thus the y-degree of $Q(x, y)$. We denote this number as L_m.

Let $B(v, L)$ be the rank of the polynomial y^L with respect to the $(1, v)$-weighted revlex order.

Example 7.51   Using Table 7.1, we have

$$
\begin{array}{c|cccccc}
L & 0 & 1 & 2 & 3 & 4 & 5 \\
B(3, L) & 0 & 4 & 11 & 21 & 34 & 50
\end{array}
$$

□

Then

$$L_m = \max \left\{ L : B(v,L) \le n \binom{m+1}{2} \right\}.$$

(Because if there is a y^{L_m} in a monomial, then $x^i y^{L_m}$ has rank $> m \binom{m+1}{2}$ for $i > 0$.) We will develop an analytical expression for L_m and a bound for it.

Lemma 7.52

$$B(v,L) = \frac{vL^2}{2} + \frac{(v+2)L}{2}. \tag{7.84}$$

Proof Note (e.g., from Table 7.1) that y^L is the last monomial of $(1,v)$-degree L in revlex order, so that

$$B(v,L) = |\{(i,j) : i + vj \le Lv\}| - 1. \tag{7.85}$$

Then we have the recursive expression

$$B(v,L) = (|\{(i,j) : i + vj \le (L-1)v\}| - 1) + |\{(i,j) : (L-1)v + 1 \le i + vj \le Lv\}|$$

$$= B(v,L-1) + vL + 1.$$

Then by induction,

$$B(v,L-1) + vL + 1 = \frac{v(L-1)^2}{2} + \frac{(v+2)(L-1)}{2} + vL + 1$$

$$= \frac{vL^2}{2} + \frac{(v+2)L}{2} = B(v,L).$$

$\square$

Define the function $r_B(x)$ as that value of L such that $B(v,L) \le x \le B(v,L+1)$. That is,

$$r_B(x) = \arg\max\{L \in \mathbb{N} : B(v,L) \le x\}.$$

Then $L_m = r_B \left(n \binom{m+1}{2} \right)$. Now we have a lemma relating r_B to $B(v,L)$.

Lemma 7.53 *If $B(v,x) = f(x)$ is a continuous increasing function of $x > 0$, taking integer values when x is integer, then*

$$r_B(x) = \lfloor f^{-1}(x) \rfloor.$$

More generally, if $g(x) \le B(v,x) \le f(x)$, where both f and g are continuous increasing functions of $x > 0$, then

$$\lfloor f^{-1}(x) \rfloor \le r_B(x) \le \lfloor g^{-1}(x) \rfloor. \tag{7.86}$$

Proof Let $L = r_B(x)$. By definition of $r_B(x)$, we have $B(v,L) \le x$. Invoking the inequalities associated with these quantities, we have

$$g(L) \le B(v,L) \le x < B(v,L+1) \le f(L+1).$$

Thus, $L \le g^{-1}(x)$ and $f^{-1}(x) < L + 1$. That is,

$$r_B(x) \le g^{-1}(x) \quad \text{and} \quad f^{-1}(x) < r_B(x) + 1,$$

or

$$f^{-1}(x) - 1 < r_B(x) \le g^{-1}(x).$$

Since $r_B(x)$ is integer valued, taking $\lfloor \cdot \rfloor$ Throughout, we obtain (7.86).   □

Using (7.84), we have $B(v, L) = f(L) = vL^2/2 + (v + 2)L/2$. If $f(L) = x$, then (using the quadratic formula)

$$f^{-1}(x) = \sqrt{\left(\frac{v+2}{2v}\right)^2 + \left(\frac{2x}{v}\right)} - \left(\frac{v+2}{2v}\right).$$

Using Lemma 7.53, we reach the conclusion:

Theorem 7.54

$$
\begin{aligned}
L_m &= r_B\left(n\binom{m+1}{2}\right) = \left\lfloor f^{-1}\left(n\binom{m+1}{2}\right)\right\rfloor \\
&= \left\lfloor \sqrt{\left(\frac{v+2}{2v}\right)^2 + \left(\frac{nm(m+1)}{v}\right)} - \left(\frac{v+2}{2v}\right)\right\rfloor.
\end{aligned}
\tag{7.87}
$$

computeLm.cc
computeLm.m

A convenient upper bound is (see Exercise 7.22)

$$L_m < \left(m + \frac{1}{2}\right)\sqrt{n/v}.$$

7.6.5 Algorithms for Computing the Interpolation Step

As observed in the proof of the Interpolation Theorem (Theorem 7.46), the interpolating polynomial can be found by solving the set of

$$C = n\binom{m+1}{2}$$

linear interpolation constraint equations with $> C$ unknowns, represented by (7.72). However, brute force numerical solutions (e.g., Gaussian elimination) would have complexity cubic in the size of the problem. In this section, we develop two other solutions which have, in principle, lower complexity.

The interpolation constraint operations in (7.68) act as *linear functionals*.

Definition 7.55 A mapping $D : \mathbb{F}[x, y] \to \mathbb{F}$ is said to be a **linear functional** if for any polynomials $Q(x, y)$ and $P(x, y) \in \mathbb{F}[x, y]$ and any constants $u, v \in \mathbb{F}$,

$$D(uQ(x, y) + vP(x, y)) = uDQ(x, y) + vDP(x, y).$$

   □

The operation

$$Q(x, y) \mapsto D_{r,s}Q(\alpha, \beta)$$

is an instance of a linear functional. We will recast the interpolation problem and solve it as a more general problem involving linear functionals: Find $Q(x, y)$ satisfying a set of constraints of the form

$$D_iQ(x, y) = 0, \quad i = 1, 2, \ldots, C,$$

where each D_i is a linear functional. For our problem, each D_i corresponds to some $D_{r,s}$, according to a particular order relating i to (r, s). (But other linear functionals could also be used, making this a more general interpolation algorithm.)

Let us write $Q(x, y) = \sum_{j=0}^{J} a_j\phi_j(x, y)$, where the $\phi_j(x, y)$ are ordered with respect to some monomial order, and where $a_C \neq 0$. The upper limit J is bounded by $J \leq C$, where C is given by (7.70). The operation of any linear functional D_i on Q is

$$D_iQ = \sum_{j=0}^{J} a_j D_i\phi_j(x, y) \triangleq \sum_{j=0}^{J} a_j d_{i,j}, \tag{7.88}$$

with coefficients $d_{i,j} = D_i\phi_j(x, y)$.

7.6.5.1 Finding Linearly Dependent Columns: The Feng–Tzeng Algorithm

The set of functionals $D_1, D_2, \ldots, D_C$ can be represented as the columns of a matrix $\mathcal{D}$,

$$\mathcal{D} = \begin{bmatrix} d_{1,0} & d_{1,1} & \cdots & d_{1,J} \\ d_{2,0} & d_{2,1} & \cdots & d_{2,J} \\ \vdots & & & \\ d_{C,0} & d_{C,1} & \cdots & d_{C,J} \end{bmatrix} \triangleq \begin{bmatrix} \mathbf{d}^{(0)} & \mathbf{d}^{(1)} & \cdots & \mathbf{d}^{(J)} \end{bmatrix} \in \mathbb{F}^{C \times (J+1)}. \tag{7.89}$$

Example 7.56 Over the field $GF(5)$, we desire to create a polynomial of minimal $(1,3)$-revlex rank through the following points, with the indicated multiplicities:

Point	Multiplicity
$(1,1)$	1
$(2,3)$	2
$(4,2)$	2

There are $1 + \binom{3}{2} + \binom{3}{2} = 1 + 3 + 3 = 7$ constraints. These constraints are (using the notation $Q_{r,s}$ introduced in (7.66))

$$Q_{0,0}(1,1) = 0$$
$$Q_{0,0}(2,3) = 0 \quad Q_{0,1}(2,3) = 0 \quad Q_{1,0}(2,3) = 0$$
$$Q_{0,0}(4,2) = 0 \quad Q_{0,1}(4,2) = 0 \quad Q_{1,0}(4,2) = 0.$$

With seven constraints, some linear combination of the first eight monomials listed in Table 7.1 suffices. These monomials are $1, x, x^2, x^3, y, x^4, xy$, and x^5. The polynomial we seek is

$$Q(x,y) = a_0 + a_1 x + a_2 x^2 + a_3 x^3 + a_4 y + a_5 x^4 + a_6 xy + a_7 x^5.$$

This polynomial should satisfy the constraints (using (7.67))

$$D_{0,0}1 = 1 \quad D_{0,0}x = 0 \quad D_{0,0}y = 1 \quad \cdots \quad D_{0,0}x^5 = 0$$
$$D_{1,0}1 = 0 \quad D_{1,0}x = 1 \quad D_{1,0}y = 0 \quad \cdots \quad D_{1,0}x^5 = 5x^4 = 0$$
$$D_{0,1}1 = 0 \quad D_{0,1}y = 1 \quad D_{0,1}y = 1 \quad \cdots \quad D_{0,1}x^5 = 0.$$

Now form a matrix $\mathcal{D}$ whose columns correspond to the eight monomials and whose rows correspond to the seven constraints.

$$\mathcal{D} = \begin{matrix} & \begin{matrix} 1 & x & x^2 & x^3 & y & x^4 & xy & x^5 \end{matrix} \\ \begin{matrix} Q_{0,0}(1,1): \\ Q_{0,0}(2,3): \\ Q_{0,1}(2,3): \\ Q_{1,0}(2,3): \\ Q_{0,0}(4,2): \\ Q_{0,1}(4,2): \\ Q_{1,0}(4,2): \end{matrix} & \begin{bmatrix} 1 & 1 & 1 & 1 & 1 & 1 & 1 & 1 \\ 1 & 2 & 2^2 & 2^3 & 3 & 2^4 & 2 \cdot 3 & 2^5 \\ 0 & 0 & 0 & 0 & 1 & 0 & 2 & 0 \\ 0 & 1 & 2 \cdot 2 & 3 \cdot 2^2 & 0 & 4 \cdot 2^3 & 3 & 5 \cdot 2^4 \\ 1 & 4 & 4^2 & 4^3 & 2 & 4^4 & 4 \cdot 2 & 4^5 \\ 0 & 0 & 0 & 0 & 1 & 0 & 4 & 0 \\ 0 & 1 & 2 \cdot 4 & 3 \cdot 4^2 & 0 & 4 \cdot 4^3 & 2 & 5 \cdot 4^4 \end{bmatrix} \end{matrix} \tag{7.90}$$

$\square$

The condition that all the constraints are simultaneously satisfied,

$$D_i Q(x,y) = 0, \quad i = 1, 2, \ldots, C$$

can be expressed using the matrix $\mathcal{D}$ as

$$
\mathcal{D}\begin{bmatrix} a_0 \\ a_1 \\ \vdots \\ a_J \end{bmatrix} = \mathbf{0} \quad \text{or} \quad \mathbf{d}^{(0)}a_0 + \mathbf{d}^{(1)}a_1 + \cdots + \mathbf{d}^{(J)}a_J = 0,
$$

so the columns of $\mathcal{D}$ are *linearly dependent*. The decoding problem can be expressed as follows:

> **Interpolation problem 1**: Determine the smallest J such that the first J columns of $\mathcal{D}$ are linearly dependent.

This is a problem in computational linear algebra, which may be solved by an extension of the BM algorithm known as the Feng–Tzeng algorithm. Recall that the BM algorithm determines the shortest linear-feedback shift register (LFSR) which annihilates a sequence of scalars. The Feng–Tzeng algorithm produces the shortest "LFSR" which annihilates a sequence of vectors.

We will express the problem solved by the Feng–Tzeng algorithm this way. Let

$$
A = \begin{bmatrix} a_{11} & a_{12} & \cdots & a_{1N} \\ a_{21} & a_{22} & \cdots & a_{2N} \\ \vdots & & & \\ a_{M1} & a_{M2} & \cdots & a_{MN} \end{bmatrix} = \begin{bmatrix} \mathbf{a}_1 & \mathbf{a}_2 & \cdots & \mathbf{a}_N \end{bmatrix}.
$$

The first $l + 1$ columns of A are linearly dependent if there exist coefficients $c_1, c_2, \ldots, c_l$, not all zero, such that

$$
\mathbf{a}_{l+1} + c_1 \mathbf{a}_l + \cdots + c_l \mathbf{a}_1 = \mathbf{0}. \tag{7.91}
$$

The problem is to determine the *minimum* l and the coefficients $c_1, c_2, \ldots, c_l$ such that the linear dependency (7.91) holds.

Let $C(x) = c_0 + c_1 x + \cdots + c_l x^l$, where $c_0 = 1$, denote the set of coefficients in the linear combination. Let $\mathbf{a}(x) = \mathbf{a}_0 + \mathbf{a}_1 x + \cdots + \mathbf{a}_N x^N$ be a representation of the matrix A, with $\mathbf{a}_0 = \mathbf{1}$ (the vector of all ones) and let $a^{(i)}(x) = a_{i,0} + a_{i,1}x + \cdots + a_{i,N}x^N$ be the ith row of $\mathbf{a}(x)$. We will interpret $C(x)\mathbf{a}(x)$ element by element; that is,

$$
C(x)\mathbf{a}(x) = \begin{bmatrix} C(x)a^{(1)}(x) \\ C(x)a^{(2)}(x) \\ \vdots \\ C(x)a^{(M)}(x) \end{bmatrix}.
$$

For $n = l + 1, l + 2, \ldots, N$, let $[C(x)\mathbf{a}(x)]_n$ denote the coefficient (vector) of x^n in $C(x)\mathbf{a}(x)$. That is,

$$
[C(x)\mathbf{a}(x)]_n = c_0 \mathbf{a}_n + c_1 \mathbf{a}_{n-1} + \cdots + c_l \mathbf{a}_{n-l} = \sum_{j=0}^{l} c_j \mathbf{a}_{n-j}.
$$

The problem to be solved can be stated as follows: Determine the minimum l and a polynomial $C(x)$ with $\deg C(x) \leq l$ such that $[C(x)\mathbf{a}(x)]_{l+1} = 0$.

The general flavor of the algorithm is like that of the BM algorithm, with polynomials being updated if they result in a discrepancy. The algorithm proceeds element-by-element through the matrix down the columns of the matrix. At each element, the discrepancy is computed. If the discrepancy is nonzero, previous columns on this row are examined to see if they had a nonzero discrepancy. If so, then the polynomial is updated using the previous polynomial that had the discrepancy. If there is no previous nonzero discrepancy on that row, then the discrepancy at that location is saved and the column is considered "blocked" — that is, no further work is done on that column and the algorithm moves to the next column.

Let $C^{(i-1,j)}(x) = c_0^{(i-1,j)} + c_1^{(i-1,j)}x + \cdots + c_{j-1}^{(i-1,j)}x^{j-1}$, with $c_0^{(i-1,j)} = 1$, be defined for each column j, where $j = 1, 2, \ldots, l+1$, and for $i = 1, 2, \ldots, M$, where each polynomial $C^{(i-1,j)}$ has the property that

$$[C^{(i-1,j)}(x)a^{(h)}(x)]_j = a_{h,j} + c_1^{(i-1,j)}a_{h,j-1} + \cdots + c_{j-1}^{(i-1,j)}a_{h,1} = 0 \quad \text{for } h \leq i - 1.$$

That is, in column j at position $(i-1, j)$ of the matrix and all previous rows there is *no* discrepancy. The initial polynomial for the first column is defined as $C^{(0,1)}(x) = 1$. The discrepancy at position (i, j) is computed as

$$d_{i,j} = [C^{(i-1,j)}(x)a^{(i)}(x)]_j = a_{i,j} + c_1^{(i-1,j)}a_{i,j-1} + \cdots + c_{j-1}^{(i-1,j)}a_{i,1}.$$

If $d_{i,j} = 0$, then no update to the polynomial is necessary and $C^{(i,j)}(x) = C^{(i-1,j)}(x)$. If, on the other hand, $d_{i,j} \neq 0$, then an update is necessary. If there is on row i a previous column u that had a nonzero discrepancy (that was not able to be resolved by updating the polynomial), then the polynomial is updated according to

$$C^{(i,j)}(x) = C^{(i-1,j)}(x) - \frac{d_{i,j}}{d_{i,u}}x^{j-u}C^{(u)}(x), \tag{7.92}$$

where u is the column where the previous nonzero discrepancy occurred and $C^{(u)}(x)$ is the polynomial which had the nonzero discrepancy in column u.

If there is a nonzero discrepancy $d_{i,j}$, but there is no previous nonzero discrepancy on that row, then that discrepancy is saved, the row at which the discrepancy occurred is saved, $\rho(j) = i$, and the polynomial is saved, $C^j(x) = C^{(i-1,j)}(x)$. The column is considered "blocked," and processing continues on the next column with $C^{(0,j+1)}(x) = C^{(i-1,j)}(x)$.

The following lemma indicates that the update (7.92) zeros the discrepancy.

Lemma 7.57 *If $d_{i,j} \neq 0$ and there is a previous polynomial $C^{(u)}(x)$ at column u, so that $C^{(u)}(x) = C^{(i-1,u)}(x)$ and $d_{i,u} \neq 0$, then the update (7.92) is such that*

$$[C^{(i,j)}(x)a^{(r)}(x)]_j = 0 \quad \text{for } r = 1, 2, \ldots, i.$$

Proof We have

$$[C^{(i,j)}(x)a^{(r)}(x)]_j = [C^{(i-1,j)}(x), a^{(r)}(x)]_j - \frac{d_{i,j}}{d_{i,u}}[C^{(u)}(x)a^{(r)}(x)x^{j-u}]_j$$

$$= [C^{(i-1,j)}(x), a^{(r)}(x)]_j - \frac{d_{i,j}}{d_{i,u}}[C^{(u)}(x)a^{(r)}(x)]_u$$

$$= \begin{cases} 0 - \frac{d_{i,j}}{d_{i,u}}0 & \text{for } r = 0, 1, \ldots, i-1 \\ d_{i,j} - \frac{d_{i,j}}{d_{i,u}}d_{i,u} & \text{for } r = i, \end{cases}$$

where the second equality follows from a result in Exercise 7.18. □

Algorithm 7.5 The Feng–Tzeng Algorithm

This representation is due to McEliece [302]
1 **Input:** A matrix A of size $M \times N$
2 **Output:** A polynomial C of minimal degree annihilating columns of A
3 **Initialize:** $s = 0$ (column counter)
4 $C = 1$ (C holds the current polynomial)

5   dsave = zeros(1,N) (holds nonzero discrepancies)

6   ρ = zeros(1,N) (holds row where nonzero discrepancy is)

7   **Begin:**

8   while(1) (loop over columns)

9       $s = s + 1; r = 0$; (move to beginning of next column)

10   columnblocked = 0;

11   while(1) (loop over rows in this column)

12          $r = r + 1$; (move to next row)

13          $d_{rs} = [C(x)a^{(r)}(x)]_s$ (compute discrepancy here using current poly.)

14   if($d_{rs} \neq 0$) (if nonzero discrepancy)

15   if(there is a u such that $\rho(u) = r$) (if a previous nonzero disc. on this row)

16                  $C(x) = C(x) - \frac{d_{rs}}{dsave(u)}C_u(x)x^{s-u}$; (update polynomial)

17   else (no previous nonzero discrepancy on this row)

18                  $\rho(s) = r$; (save row location of nonzero discrepancy)

19                  $C_s(x) = C(x)$; (save polynomial for this column)

20   dsave(s) = d_{rs}; (save nonzero discrepancy for this column)

21   columnblocked = 1; (do no more work on this column)

22   end (else)

23   end (if d_{rs})

24   if($r \geq M$ or columnblocked=1) break; end; (end of loop over row)

25   end (while (1))

26   if(columnblocked=0) break; end; (end loop over columns)

27 end (while(1))

28 End

testft.m
fengtzeng.m
invmodp.m

It can be shown that the polynomial $C(x)$ produced by this algorithm results in the *minimal* number of first columns of A which are linearly dependent [121].

Example 7.58   We apply the algorithm to the matrix $\mathcal{D}$ of (7.90) in Example 7.56. The following matrix outlines the steps of the algorithm.

$$
\begin{bmatrix}
1_a & \boxed{1}_b & 0 & 0 & 0 & 0 & 0 & 0 \\
0 & 1_c & \boxed{2}_d & 0 & \boxed{2}_h & 0 & \boxed{1}_m & 0 \\
0 & 0 & 0 & 0 & 1_i & 0 & \boxed{3}_n & 0 \\
0 & 0 & 1_e & \boxed{2}_f & 0 & \boxed{1}_j & 2_o & 0 \\
0 & 0 & 0 & 2_g & 0 & \boxed{4}_k & \boxed{1}_p & \boxed{1}_r \\
0 & 0 & 0 & 0 & 0 & 0 & 2_q & 0 \\
0 & 0 & 0 & 0 & 0 & 2_l & 0 & \boxed{2}_s
\end{bmatrix}
$$

The initially nonzero discrepancies are shown in this matrix; those which are in squares resulted in polynomials updated by (7.92) and the discrepancy was zeroed.

a: Starting with $C(x) = 1$, a nonzero discrepancy is found. There are no previous nonzero discrepancies on this row, so $C^{(1)}(x) = 1$ is saved and we jump to the next column.

b: Nonzero discrepancy found, but the polynomial was updated using previous nonzero discrepancy on this row (at a): $C(x) = 4x + 1$.

c: Nonzero discrepancy found and no update is possible. Save $C^{(2)}(x) = 4x + 1$ and the discrepancy and jump to next column.

d: Nonzero discrepancy found, but updated polynomial computed (using polynomial at c) $C(x) = 2x^2 + 2x + 1$.

e: Nonzero discrepancy found; no update possible. Save $C^{(3)}(x) = 2x^2 + 2x + 1$ and the discrepancy and jump to next column.

f: Update polynomial: $C(x) = x^3 + 3x^2 + 1$

g: Save $C^{(4)}(x) = x^3 + 3x^2 + 1$

h: Update polynomial: $C(x) = 2x^4 + 4x^3 + 3x^2 + 1$

i: Save $C^{(5)}(x) = 2x^4 + 4x^3 + 3x^2 + 1$

j: Update polynomial: $C(x) = 3x^5 + 3x^3 + 3x^2 + 1$

k: Update polynomial: $C(x) = x^5 + 4x^4 + 3x^3 + 1x^2 + 1$

l: Save $C^{(6)}(x) = x^5 + 4x^4 + 3x^3 + 1x^2 + 1$

m: Update polynomial $C(x) = x^6 + 4x^4 + 3x^3 + x^2 + 1$

n: Update polynomial $C(x) = 3x^5 + 3x^3 + 3x^2 + 1$

o: Update polynomial $C(x) = x^6 + 4x^5 + 3x^4 + 3x^3 + 3x^2 + 1$

p: Update polynomial $C(x) = 3x^6 + 3x^4 + 3x^2 + 1$

q: Save $C^{(7)}(x) = 3x^6 + 3x^4 + 3x^2 + 1$

r: Update polynomial $C(x) = 2x^7 + 4x^6 + 3x^2 + 1$

s: Update polynomial $C(x) = x^7 + 2x^5 + 4x^4 + 2x^2 + 1$

Returning to the interpolation problem of Example 7.56, we obtain from the coefficients of $C(x)$ the coefficients of the polynomial

$$Q(x, y) = 1 + 0x + 2x^2 + 4x^3 + 0y + 2x^4 + 0xy + x^5.$$

It can be easily verified that this polynomial satisfies the interpolation and multiplicity constraints specified in Example 7.56. □

The computational complexity goes as the cube of the size of the matrix. One view of this algorithm is that it is simply a restatement of conventional Gauss–Jordan reduction and has similar computational complexity.

7.6.5.2 Finding the Intersection of Kernels: The Kötter Algorithm

Let $\mathbb{F}_L[x, y] \subset \mathbb{F}[x, y]$ denote the set of polynomials whose y-degree is $\leq L$. (The variable y is distinguished here because eventually we will be looking for y-roots of $Q(x, y)$.) Then any $Q(x, y) \in \mathbb{F}_L[x, y]$ can be written in the form

$$Q(x, y) = \sum_{k=0}^{L} q_k(x) y^k$$

for polynomials $q_k(x) \in \mathbb{F}[x]$. $\mathbb{F}_L[x, y]$ is an $\mathbb{F}[x]$-module (see Section 7.4.1): for any polynomials $a(x)$ and $b(x)$ in $\mathbb{F}[x]$ and polynomials $Q(x, y)$ and $P(x, y)$ in $\mathbb{F}_L[x, y]$,

$$(a(x)P(x, y) + b(x)Q(x, y)) \in \mathbb{F}_L[x, y]$$

since the y-degree of the linear combination does not change.

For a linear functional D, we will generically write K_D as the kernel of D:

$$K_D = \ker D = \{Q(x, y) \in \mathbb{F}[x, y] : DQ(x, y) = 0\}.$$

For a set of linear functionals $D_1, D_2, \ldots, D_C$ defined on $\mathbb{F}_L[x, y]$, let $K_1, K_2, \ldots, K_C$ be their corresponding kernels, so that

$$K_i = \ker D_i = \{Q(x, y) \in \mathbb{F}[x, y] : D_i Q(x, y) = 0\}.$$

Then a solution to the problem

$$D_i Q(x, y) = 0 \quad \text{for all } i = 1, 2, \ldots, C \tag{7.93}$$

lies in the intersection of the kernels $K = K_1 \cap K_2 \cap \cdots \cap K_C$. We see that the interpolation problem can be expressed as follows:

Interpolation Problem 2: Determine the polynomial of minimal rank in K.

To find the intersection constructively, we will employ cumulative kernels, defined as follows: $\overline{K}_0 = \mathbb{F}_L[x, y]$ and

$$\overline{K}_i = \overline{K}_{i-1} \cap K_i = K_1 \cap \cdots \cap K_i.$$

That is, $\overline{K}_i$ is the space of solutions of the first i problems in (7.93). The solution of the interpolation is a polynomial of minimum $(1, v)$-degree in $\overline{K}_C$.

We will partition the polynomials in $\mathbb{F}_L[x, y]$ according to the exponent of y. Let

$$S_j = \{Q(x, y) \in \mathbb{F}_L[x, y] : \text{LM}(Q) = x^i y^j \text{ for some } i\}$$

be the set of polynomials whose leading monomial has y-degree j. Let $g_{i,j}$ be the minimal element of $\overline{K}_i \cap S_j$, where here and throughout the development "minimal" or "min" means minimal rank, with respect to a given monomial order. Then $\{g_{C,j}\}_{j=0}^L$ is a set of polynomials that satisfy all of the constraints (7.93).

The Kötter algorithm generates a sequence of sets of polynomials $(G_0, G_1, \ldots, G_C)$, where

$$G_i = (g_{i,0}, g_{i,1}, \ldots, g_{i,L}),$$

and where $g_{i,j}$ is a minimal element of $\overline{K}_i \cap S_j$. (That is, it satisfies the first i constraints and the y-degree is j.) Then the output of the algorithm is the element of G_C of minimal order in the set G_C which has polynomials satisfying all C constraints:

$$Q(x, y) = \min_{0 \le j \le L} g_{C,j}(x, y).$$

This satisfies all the constraints (since it is in $\overline{K}_C$) and is of minimal order.

We introduce a linear functional and some important properties associated with it. For a given linear functional D, define the mapping $[\cdot, \cdot]_D : \mathbb{F}[x, y] \times \mathbb{F}[x, y] \to \mathbb{F}[x, y]$ by

$$[P(x, y), Q(x, y)]_D = (DQ(x, y))P(x, y) - (DP(x, y))Q(x, y).$$

Lemma 7.59 *For all $P(x, y), Q(x, y) \in \mathbb{F}[x, y]$, $[P(x, y), Q(x, y)]_D \in \ker D$. Furthermore, if $P(x, y) > Q(x, y)$ (with respect to some fixed monomial order) and $Q(x, y) \notin K_D$, then rank $[P(x, y), Q(x, y)]_D = $ rank $P(x, y)$.*

Proof We will prove the latter statement of the lemma (the first part is in Exercise 7.19). For notational convenience, let $a = DQ(x, y)$ and $b = DP(x, y)$. (Recall that $a, b \in \mathbb{F}$.) If $a \ne 0$ and $P(x, y) > Q(x, y)$, then $[P(x, y), Q(x, y)]_D = aP(x, y) - bQ(x, y)$, which does not change the leading monomial, so that $\text{LM}[P(x, y), Q(x, y)]_D = \text{LM}P(x, y)$ and furthermore, rank $[P(x, y), Q(x, y)]_D = $ rank $P(x, y)$. $\square$

The algorithm is initialized with

$$G_0 = (g_{0,0}, g_{0,1}, \ldots, g_{0,L}) = (1, y, y^2, \ldots, y^L).$$

To form G_{i+1} given the set G_i, we form the set

$$J_i = \{j : D_{i+1}(g_{i,j}) \ne 0\}$$

as the set of polynomials in G_i which do not satisfy the $i + 1$st constraint. If J is not empty, then an update is necessary (i.e., there is a discrepancy). In this case, let j^* index the polynomial of minimal rank,

$$j^* = \arg \min_{j \in J_i} g_{i,j}$$

and let f denote the polynomial g_{i,j^*}:

$$f = \min_{j \in J_i} g_{i,j}. \tag{7.94}$$

The update rule is as follows:

$$g_{i+1,j} = \begin{cases} g_{i,j} & \text{if } j \notin J_i \\ [g_{i,j}, f]_{D_{i+1}} & \text{if } j \in J_i \text{ but } j \neq j^* \\ [xf, f]_{D_{i+1}} & \text{if } j = j^*. \end{cases} \tag{7.95}$$

The key theorem governing this algorithm is the following.

Theorem 7.60 *For $i = 0, \ldots, C$,*

$$g_{i,j} = \min\{g : g \in \overline{K}_i \cap S_j\} \quad \text{for } j = 0, 1, \ldots, L. \tag{7.96}$$

Proof The proof is by induction on i. The result is trivial when $i = 0$. It is to be shown that

$$g_{i+1,j} = \min\{g : g \in \overline{K}_{i+1} \cap S_j\} \quad \text{for } j = 0, 1, \ldots, L$$

is true, given that (7.96) is true. We consider separately the three cases in (7.95).

Case 1: $j \notin J_i$, so that $g_{i+1,j} = g_{i,j}$. The constraint $D_{i+1} g_{i,j} = 0$ is satisfied (since $j \notin J_i$), so $g_{i+1,j} = g_{i,j} \in K_{i+1}$. By the inductive hypothesis, $g_{i+1,j} \in \overline{K}_i \cap S_j$. Combining these, we have $g_{i+1,j} \in \overline{K}_{i+1} \cap S_j$. Since $g_{i,j}$ is minimal in $\overline{K}_i \cap S_j$, it must also be minimal in the set $\overline{K}_{i+1} \cap S_j$, since the latter is contained in the former.

Case 2: In this case,

$$g_{i+1,j} = [g_{i,j}, f]_{D_{i+1}} = (D_{i+1} g_{i,j}) f - (D_{i+1} f) g_{i,j},$$

which is a linear combination of f and $g_{i,j}$. Since both f and $g_{i,j}$ are in $\overline{K}_i$, $g_{i+1,j}$ is also in $\overline{K}_i$. By Lemma 7.59, $g_{i+1,j} \in K_{i+1}$. Combining these inclusions, $g_{i+1,j} \in \overline{K}_i \cap K_{i+1} = \overline{K}_{i+1}$.

By (7.94), rank $g_{i,j} > $ rank f, so that by Lemma 7.59, rank $g_{i+1,j} = $ rank $g_{i,j}$. Since $g_{i,j} \in S_j$, it follows that $g_{i+1,j} \in S_j$ also. And, since $g_{i+1,j}$ has the same rank as $g_{i,j}$, which is minimal in $\overline{K}_i \cap S_j$, it must also be minimal in the smaller set $\overline{K}_{i+1} \cap S_j$.

Case 3: In this case, the update is

$$g_{i+1,j} = [xf, f]_{D_{i+1}} = (D_{i+1} xf) f - (D_{i+1} f) xf,$$

which is a linear combination of f and xf. But $f \in \overline{K}_i$ by the induction hypothesis.

We must show that $xf \in \overline{K}_i$. Let $\tilde{f}(x, y) = xf(x, y)$. In Exercise 7.21, it is shown that, in terms of the Hasse partial derivatives of f and $\tilde{f}$,

$$\tilde{f}_{r,s}(x, y) = f_{r-1,s}(x, y) + x f_{r,s}(x, y). \tag{7.97}$$

If $f_{r-1,s}(x_j, y_j) = 0$ and $f_{r,s}(x_j, y_j) = 0$ for $j = 0, 1, \ldots, i$, then $\tilde{f}_{r,s}(x_j, y_j) = 0$, so $xf \in \overline{K}_i$. This will hold provided that the sequence of linear functionals $(D_0, D_1, \ldots, D_C)$ are ordered such that $D_{r-1,s}$ always precedes $D_{r,s}$.

Assuming this to be the case, we conclude that $f \in \overline{K}_i$ and $xf \in \overline{K}_i$, so that $g_{i+1,j} \in \overline{K}_i$. By Lemma 7.59, $g_{i+1,j} \in K_{i+1}$, so $g_{i+1,j} \in \overline{K}_i \cap K_{i+1} = \overline{K}_{i+1}$.

Since $f \in S_j$ (by the induction hypothesis), then $xf \in S_j$ (since multiplication by x does not change the y-degree). By Lemma 7.59, rank $g_{i+1,j}$ = rank xf, which means that $g_{i+1,j} \in S_j$ also.

Showing that $g_{i+1,j}$ is minimal is by contradiction. Suppose there exists a polynomial $h \in \overline{K}_{i+1} \cap S_j$ such that $h < g_{i+1,j}$. Since $h \in \overline{K}_i \cap S_j$, we must have $f \leq h$ and rank $g_{i+1,j}$ = rank xf. There can be no polynomial $f' \in S_j$ with rank $f <$ rank $f' <$ rank xf, so that it follows that $\mathrm{LM}(h) = \mathrm{LM}(f)$. By suitable normalization, the leading coefficients of h and f can be equated. Now let

$$\tilde{f} = h - f.$$

By linearity, $\tilde{f} \in \overline{K}_i$. By cancellation of the leading terms, $\tilde{f} < f$. Now $D_{i+1} h = 0$, since $h \in \overline{K}_{i+1}$, but $D_{i+1} f \neq 0$, since $j \in J_i$ in (7.94). Thus, we have a polynomial $\tilde{f}$ such that $\tilde{f} \in \overline{K}_i \backslash \overline{K}_{i+1}$ and $\tilde{f} < f$. But f was supposed to be the minimal element of $\overline{K}_i \backslash \overline{K}_{i+1}$, by its selection in (7.94). This leads to a contradiction: $g_{i+1,j}$ must be minimal. $\qquad\square$

Let us return to the ordering condition raised in Case 3. We must have an order in which $(r-1, s)$ precedes (r, s). This is accomplished when the (r, s) data are ordered according to $(m-1, 1)$ lex order:

$$(0,0), (0,1), \ldots, (0, m-1), (1,0), (1,1), \ldots, (1, m-2), \ldots, (m-1, 0).$$

At the end of the algorithm, we select the minimal element out of G_C as $Q_0(x, y)$.

Kötter's algorithm for polynomial interpolation is shown in Algorithm 7.6. This algorithm is slightly more general than just described: the point (x_i, y_i) is interpolated up to order m_i, where m_i can vary with i, rather than having a fixed order m at each point. There is one more explanation necessary, regarding line 19. In line 19, the update is computed as

$$
\begin{aligned}
g_{i,j} &= \Delta\, xf - (D_i xf) f = (D_{r,s} f(x_i, y_i) - D_{r,s} xf(x,y)|_{x=x_i, y=y_i}) f(x, y) \\
&= (x D_{r,s} f(x_i, y_i) - (D_{r-1,s} f(x_i, y_i) + x_i D_{r,s} f(x_i, y_i))) f(x, y) \quad \text{(using (7.97))} \\
&= (x D_{r,s} f(x_i, y_i) - x_i D_{r,s} f(x_i, y_i)) f(x, y) \quad \text{(since } D_{r-1,s} f(x_i, y_i) = 0) \\
&= D_{r,s} f(x_i, y_i)(x - x_i) f(x, y).
\end{aligned}
$$

Algorithm 7.6 Kötter's Interpolation for Guruswami–Sudan Decoder

---

1 **Input:** Points: $(x_i, y_i), i = 1, \ldots, n$; Interpolation order m_i; a $(1, v)$ monomial order; $L = L_m$
2 **Returns:** $Q_0(x, y)$ satisfying the interpolation problem.
3 **Initialize:** $g_j = y^j$ for $j = 0$ to L.
4 for $i = 1$ to n (go from $i - 1$st stage to ith stage)
5 $\quad C = (m_i + 1)m_i/2$ (compute number of derivatives involved)
6 $\quad$ for $(r, s) = (0, 0)$ to $(m_i - 1, 0)$ by $(m_i - 1, 1)$ lex order (from 0 to C)
7 $\qquad$ for $j = 0$ to L
8 $\qquad\quad \Delta_j = D_{r,s} g_j(x_i, y_i)$ (compute "discrepancy")
9 $\qquad$ end (for j)
10 $\qquad J = \{j : \Delta_j \neq 0\}$ (set of nonzero discrepancies)
11 $\qquad$ if($J \neq \emptyset$)
12 $\qquad\quad j^* = \arg\min\{g_j : j \in J\}$ (polynomial of least weighted degree)
13 $\qquad\quad f = g_{j^*}$
14 $\qquad\quad \Delta = \Delta_{j^*}$
15 $\qquad\quad$ for($j \in J$)
16 $\qquad\qquad$ if($j \neq j^*$)

17          $g_j = \Delta g_j - \Delta_j f$ (update without change in rank)

18   else if($j = j^*$)

19          $g_j = (x - x_i)f$ (update with change in rank)

20   end (if)

21   end (for j)

22   end (if J)

23   end (for (r,s))

24 end (for i)

25 $Q_0(x,y) = \min_j \{g_j(x,y)\}$ (least weighted degree)

---

testGS1.cc
kotter.cc

Example 7.61   The points $(1, \alpha^3), (\alpha, \alpha^4), (\alpha^2, \alpha^5), (\alpha^3, \alpha^7)$, and (α^4, α^8) are to be interpolated by a polynomial $Q(x, y)$ using the Kötter algorithm, where operations are over $GF(2^4)$ with $1 + \alpha + \alpha^4 = 0$. Use multiplicity $m = 1$ interpolation at each point and the $(1, 2)$-revlex order.

At each point, there is one constraint, since $m = 1$.

Initial: G_0: $g_0(x, y) = 1, g_1(x, y) = y, g_2(x, y) = y^2, g_3(x, y) = y^3, g_4(x, y) = y^4$.

$i = 0$: $(r, s) = (0, 0), (x_i, y_i) = (1, \alpha^3)$.

     Discrepancies: $\Delta_0 = g_0(1, \alpha^3) = 1, \ \Delta_1 = g_1(1, \alpha^3) = \alpha^3, \ \Delta_2 = g_2(1, \alpha^3) = \alpha^6, \ \Delta_3 = g_3(1, \alpha^3) = \alpha^9, \ \Delta_4 = g_4(1, \alpha^3) = \alpha^{12}. \ J = \{0, 1, 2, 3, 4\}, j^* = 0, f = 1, \Delta = 1.$

     G_1: $g_0 = 1 + x, g_1 = \alpha^3 + y, g_2 = \alpha^6 + y^2, g_3 = \alpha^9 + y^3, g_4 = \alpha^{12} + y^4$.

$i = 1$: $(r, s) = (0, 0), (x_i, y_i) = (\alpha, \alpha^4)$.

     Discrepancies: $\Delta_0 = \alpha^4, \Delta_1 = \alpha^7, \Delta_2 = \alpha^{14}, \Delta_3 = \alpha^8, \Delta_4 = \alpha^{13}. \ J = \{0, 1, 2, 3, 4\}, j^* = 0, f = 1 + x, \Delta = \alpha^4$.

     G_2: $g_0 = \alpha + \alpha^4 x + x^2, g_1 = \alpha^7 x + \alpha^4 y, g_2 = (\alpha^{11} + \alpha^{14} x) + \alpha^4 y^2, g_3 = (\alpha^3 + \alpha^8 x) + \alpha^4 y^3, g_4 = (\alpha^{12} + \alpha^{13} x) + \alpha^4 y^4$.

$i = 2$: $(r, s) = (0, 0), (x_i, y_i) = (\alpha^2, \alpha^5)$.

     Discrepancies: $\Delta_0 = \alpha^{13}, \Delta_1 = 0, \Delta_2 = \alpha^8, \Delta_3 = \alpha^6, \Delta_4 = \alpha^2. \ J = \{0, 2, 3, 4\}, j^* = 0, f = \alpha + \alpha^4 x + x^2, \Delta = \alpha^{13}$.

     G_3: $g_0 = \alpha^3 + \alpha^{11} x + \alpha^{10} x^2 + x^3, g_1 = \alpha^7 x + \alpha^4 y, g_2 = \alpha^8 x^2 + \alpha^2 y^2, g_3 = (\alpha^{14} + \alpha^7 x + \alpha^6 x^2) + \alpha^2 y^3, g_4 = (\alpha^{12} + \alpha x + \alpha^2 x^2) + \alpha^2 y^4$.

$i = 3$: $(r, s) = (0, 0), (x_i, y_i) = (\alpha^3, \alpha^7)$.

     Discrepancies: $\Delta_0 = \alpha^{14}, \Delta_1 = \alpha^{14}, \Delta_2 = \alpha^7, \Delta_3 = \alpha^2, \Delta_4 = \alpha^3. \ J = \{0, 1, 2, 3, 4\}, j^* = 1, f = \alpha^7 x + \alpha^4 y, \Delta = \alpha^{14}. \Delta = \alpha^{14}$.

     G_4: $g_0 = (\alpha^2 + \alpha^7 x + \alpha^9 x^2 + \alpha^{14} x^3) + \alpha^3 y, g_1 = (\alpha^{10} x + \alpha^7 x^2) + (\alpha^7 + \alpha^4 x)y, g_2 = (\alpha^{14} x + \alpha^7 x^2) + \alpha^{11} y + \alpha y^2, g_3 = (\alpha^{13} + \alpha^5 x + \alpha^5 x^2) + \alpha^6 y + \alpha y^3, g_4 = (\alpha^{11} + \alpha^5 x + \alpha x^2) + \alpha^7 y + \alpha y^4$.

$i = 4$: $(r,s) = (0,0)$, $(x_i, y_i) = (\alpha^4, \alpha^8)$.

Discrepancies: $\Delta_0 = \alpha^{11}, \Delta_1 = \alpha^7, \Delta_2 = \alpha^{11}, \Delta_3 = \alpha^2, \Delta_4 = \alpha^{10}$. $J = \{0,1,2,3,4\}$, $j^* = 0$, $f = (\alpha^2 + \alpha^7 x + \alpha^9 x^2 + \alpha^{14} x^3) + (\alpha^3)y$, $\Delta = \alpha^{11}$.

G_5: $g_0 = (\alpha^6 + \alpha^9 x + \alpha^5 x^2 + \alpha x^3 + \alpha^{14} x^4) + (\alpha^7 + \alpha^3 x)y$, $g_1 = (\alpha^9 + \alpha^8 x + \alpha^9 x^2 + \alpha^6 x^3) + (\alpha^{12} + x)y$, $g_2 = (\alpha^{13} + \alpha^{12} x + \alpha^{11} x^2 + \alpha^{10} x^3) + \alpha y + \alpha^{12} y^2$, $g_3 = (\alpha^{14} + \alpha^3 x + \alpha^6 x^2 + \alpha x^3) + \alpha y + \alpha^{12} y^3$, $g_4 = (\alpha^2 + \alpha^5 x + \alpha^6 x^2 + \alpha^9 x^3) + \alpha^8 y + \alpha^{12} y^4$.

Final: $Q_0(x,y) = g_1(x,y) = (\alpha^9 + \alpha^8 x + \alpha^9 x^2 + \alpha^6 x^3) + (\alpha^{12} + x)y$.

□

Example 7.62

Let C be a $(15,7)$ code over $GF(2^4)$ and let $m(x) = \alpha + \alpha^2 x + \alpha^3 x^2 + \alpha^4 x^3 + \alpha^5 x^4 + \alpha^6 x^5 + \alpha^7 x^6$ be encoded over the support set $(1, \alpha, \ldots, \alpha^{14})$. That is, the codeword is

$$(m(1), m(\alpha), m(\alpha^2), \ldots, m(\alpha^{14})).$$

The corresponding code polynomial is

$$c(x) = \alpha^6 + \alpha^{11} x + x^2 + \alpha^6 x^3 + \alpha x^4 + \alpha^{14} x^5 + \alpha^8 x^6 + \alpha^{11} x^7 + \alpha^8 x^8 + \alpha x^9$$
$$+ \alpha^{12} x^{10} + \alpha^{12} x^{11} + \alpha^{14} x^{12} + x^{13} + \alpha x^{14}.$$

Suppose the received polynomial is

$$r(x) = \alpha^6 + \alpha^9 x + x^2 + \alpha^2 x^3 + \alpha x^4 + \alpha^9 x^5 + \alpha^8 x^6 + \alpha^3 x^7 + \alpha^8 x^8 + \alpha x^9$$
$$+ \alpha^{12} x^{10} + \alpha^{12} x^{11} + \alpha^{14} x^{12} + x^{13} + \alpha x^{14}.$$

That is, the error polynomial is

$$e(x) = \alpha^2 x + \alpha^3 x^3 + \alpha^4 x^5 + \alpha^5 x^7.$$

For this code and interpolation multiplicity, let

$$t_m = 4 \quad L_m = 3.$$

The first decoding step is to determine an interpolating polynomial for the points

$$(1, \alpha^6), (\alpha, \alpha^9), (\alpha^2, 1), (\alpha^3, \alpha^2), (\alpha^4, \alpha), (\alpha^5, \alpha^9), (\alpha^6, \alpha^8), (\alpha^7, \alpha^3),$$
$$(\alpha^8, \alpha^8), (\alpha^9, \alpha), (\alpha^{10}, \alpha^{12}), (\alpha^{11}, \alpha^{12}), (\alpha^{12}, \alpha^{14}), (\alpha^{13}, 1), (\alpha^{14}, \alpha)$$

with interpolation multiplicity $m = 2$ at each point using the $(1, 6)$-revlex degree.

Using `testGS3`, the final set of interpolating polynomials $G_C = \{g_0, g_1, g_2, g_3\}$ can be shown to be

$$g_0(x, y) = (\alpha^{13} + \alpha x + \alpha^4 x^2 + \alpha^6 x^3 + \alpha^{13} x^4 + \alpha^{11} x^5 + \alpha^{10} x^6 + \alpha^8 x^8 + \alpha^8 x^9$$
$$+ \alpha^5 x^{10} + \alpha^9 x^{11} + \alpha^3 x^{12} + \alpha^6 x^{13} + \alpha^3 x^{14} + \alpha^2 x^{15} + \alpha^{10} x^{16} + \alpha^7 x^{17}$$
$$+ \alpha^{11} x^{18} + \alpha^8 x^{19} + \alpha^3 x^{20} + \alpha^{14} x^{21} + \alpha^{14} x^{22}) + (\alpha^6 + \alpha^5 x + \alpha^3 x^2 + \alpha^2 x^3$$
$$+ \alpha^{13} x^4 + \alpha^7 x^5 + \alpha^7 x^6 + x^7 + \alpha^7 x^8 + \alpha^{11} x^9 + \alpha^{14} x^{10} + \alpha^{12} x^{11} + \alpha^5 x^{12}$$
$$+ \alpha^8 x^{13} + \alpha^{13} x^{14} + \alpha^9 x^{15}) y + (\alpha^{13} + \alpha^9 x + \alpha^{11} x^2 + \alpha^7 x^3 + x^4 + \alpha^{10} x^5$$
$$+ \alpha^{11} x^6 + \alpha^5 x^7 + \alpha^5 x^8 + \alpha^7 x^9) y^2 + (1 + \alpha^2 x + \alpha^2 x^2 + \alpha^4 x^3) y^3$$

$$g_1(x, y) = (\alpha^{13} + \alpha^{13} x + \alpha^{14} x^2 + x^3 + \alpha^3 x^4 + \alpha^6 x^5 + \alpha^{12} x^6 + \alpha^{14} x^7 + \alpha^8 x^8 + \alpha^6 x^9$$
$$+ \alpha^8 x^{10} + \alpha^7 x^{11} + \alpha^{13} x^{12} + \alpha x^{13} + \alpha^{11} x^{14} + \alpha^{10} x^{15} + x^{16} + \alpha^9 x^{17} + \alpha^{14} x^{18}$$
$$+ \alpha^3 x^{19} + \alpha^3 x^{21}) + (\alpha^2 + \alpha^9 x + \alpha^{11} x^2 + \alpha x^3 + \alpha^{11} x^4 + \alpha^{10} x^5 + \alpha^5 x^6 + \alpha x^7$$
$$+ \alpha^6 x^8 + \alpha^{10} x^{10} + \alpha^7 x^{11} + \alpha^{10} x^{12} + \alpha^{13} x^{13} + \alpha^4 x^{14}) y + (\alpha^4 + \alpha^5 x + \alpha^{12} x^2$$
$$+ \alpha^{12} x^3 + \alpha^{11} x^4 + \alpha^5 x^5 + \alpha^7 x^6 + \alpha x^7) y^2 + (\alpha^{11} + \alpha x + \alpha^{14} x^2) y^3$$

$$g_2(x, y) = (\alpha^{13} + \alpha^{11} x + \alpha^5 x^2 + \alpha^{13} x^3 + \alpha^7 x^4 + \alpha^4 x^5 + \alpha^{11} x^6 + \alpha^{12} x^7 + \alpha^9 x^8$$
$$+ \alpha^4 x^9 + \alpha^{10} x^{10} + \alpha^5 x^{11} + \alpha^2 x^{12} + \alpha^{14} x^{13} + \alpha^6 x^{14} + \alpha^8 x^{15} + \alpha^{13} x^{16} + \alpha^7 x^{17}$$
$$+ \alpha^4 x^{18} + \alpha x^{19} + \alpha^7 x^{21}) + (1 + \alpha^7 x + \alpha^9 x^2 + \alpha^{14} x^3 + \alpha^9 x^4 + \alpha^8 x^5 + \alpha^3 x^6$$
$$+ \alpha^{14} x^7 + \alpha^4 x^8 + \alpha^8 x^{10} + \alpha^5 x^{11} + \alpha^8 x^{12} + \alpha^{11} x^{13} + \alpha^2 x^{14}) y + (\alpha^3 x + \alpha^7 x^2$$
$$+ \alpha^{10} x^3 + \alpha^6 x^4 + \alpha^3 x^5 + \alpha^{14} x^7 + x^8) y^2 + (\alpha^9 + \alpha^{14} x + \alpha^{12} x^2) y^3$$

$$g_3(x, y) = (\alpha^5 + \alpha^9 x + \alpha^{13} x^2 + \alpha^2 x^3 + \alpha x^4 + \alpha^{14} x^5 + \alpha^2 x^6 + \alpha x^7 + \alpha^{12} x^8$$
$$+ \alpha x^9 + \alpha^{14} x^{10} + \alpha^7 x^{11} + \alpha^9 x^{13} + \alpha^5 x^{14} + \alpha^5 x^{15} + \alpha^9 x^{16} + \alpha^{11} x^{17} + \alpha^3 x^{18}$$
$$+ \alpha^{13} x^{19}) + (\alpha^7 + \alpha^7 x + \alpha^8 x^2 + \alpha^{14} x^3 + x^4 + \alpha^{11} x^5 + \alpha^7 x^6 + \alpha^2 x^7 + \alpha^5 x^8$$
$$+ \alpha^{14} x^9 + \alpha^{12} x^{10} + \alpha^8 x^{11} + \alpha^5 x^{12} + \alpha^5 x^{13}) y + (\alpha^5 + \alpha x + \alpha^{10} x^2 + \alpha^{11} x^3$$
$$+ \alpha^{13} x^4 + \alpha^6 x^5 + \alpha^4 x^6 + \alpha^8 x^7) y^2 + (1 + \alpha^8 x) y^3$$

of weighted degrees 22, 20, 20, and 19, respectively. The one of minimal order selected is $Q(x, y) = g_3(x, y)$. ☐

The computational complexity of this algorithm, like the Feng–Tzeng algorithm, goes as the cube of the size of the problem, $O(m^3)$, with a rather large multiplicative factor. The cubic complexity of these problems makes decoding impractical for large values of m.

7.6.6 A Special Case: $m = 1$ and $L = 1$

We will see below how to take the interpolating polynomial $Q(x, y)$ and find its y-roots. This will handle the general case of arbitrary m. However, we treat here an important special case which occurs when $m = 1$ and $L = 1$. In this case, the y-degree of $Q(x, y)$ is equal to 1 and it is not necessary to employ a sophisticated factorization algorithm. This special case allows for conventional decoding of Reed–Solomon codes without computation of syndromes and without the error evaluation step.

When $L = 1$, let us write

$$Q(x, y) = P_1(x)y - P_0(x).$$

If it is the case that $P_1(x) | P_0(x)$, let

$$p(x) = \frac{P_0(x)}{P_1(x)}.$$

Then it is clear that $y - p(x)|Q(x,y)$, since

$$P_1(x)y - P_0(x) = P_1(x)(y - p(x)).$$

Furthermore, it can be shown that the $p(x)$ returned will produce a codeword within a distance $\leq \lfloor (n-k)/2 \rfloor$ of the transmitted codeword. Hence, it decodes up to the design distance.

   In light of these observations, the following decoding algorithm is an alternative to the more conventional approaches (e.g.: find syndromes; find error locator; find roots; find error values; or: find remainder; find rational interpolator; find roots; find error values).

Algorithm 7.7 Guruswami–Sudan Interpolation Decoder with $m = 1$ and $L = 1$

---

1 **Input:** Points: $(x_i, y_i), i = 1, \ldots, n$; a $(1, k-1)$ monomial order
2 **Returns:** $p(x, y)$ as a decoded codeword if it exists
3 **Initialize:** $g_0(x, y) = 1, g_1(x, y) = y$
4 for $i = 1$ to n
5     $\Delta_0 = g_0(x_i, y_i)$ (compute discrepancies)
6     $\Delta_1 = g_1(x_i, y_i)$
7     $J = \{j : \Delta_j \neq 0\}$ (set of nonzero discrepancies)
8   if$(J \neq \emptyset)$
9         $j^* = \arg\min\{g_j : j \in J\}$ (polynomial of min. weighted degree)
10        $f = g_{j^*}$
11        $\Delta = \Delta_{j^*}$
12   for$(j \in J)$
13   if$(j \neq j^*)$
14                $g_j = \Delta g_j - \Delta_j f$ (update without change in rank)
15   else if$(j = j^*)$
16                $g_j = (x - x_i)f$ (update with change in rank)
17   end(if)
18   end(for j)
19   end(if J)
20 end(for i)
21 $Q(x, y) = \min_j\{g_j(x, y)\}$ (least weighted degree)
22 Write $Q(x, y) = P_1(x)y - P_0(x)$
23 $r(x) = P_0(x) \mod P_1(x)$.
24 if$(r(x) = 0)$
25    $p(x) = P_0(x)/P_1(x)$.
26   if$(\deg p(x) \leq k - 1)$ then
27        $p(x)$ is decoded message
28   end(if)
29 else
30   Uncorrectable error pattern
31 end(if)

Example 7.63   Consider a $(5, 2)$ RS code over $GF(5)$, using support set $(0, 1, 2, 3, 4)$. Let $m(x) = 1 + 4x$. Then the codeword

$$(m(0), m(1), m(2), m(3), m(4)) = (1, 0, 4, 3, 2) \rightarrow c(x) = 1 + 4x^2 + 3x^3 + 2x^4.$$

Let the received polynomial be $r(x) = 1 + 2x + 4x^2 + 3x^3 + 2x^4$. The following table indicates the steps of the algorithm.

i	(x_i, y_i)	$g_0(x, y)$	$g_1(x, y)$
–	–	1	y
0	(0,1)	x	$4 + y$
1	(1,0)	$4x + x^2$	$(4 + 4x) + y$
2	(2,4)	$(2 + x + x^2) + 3y$	$(2 + 4 + 4x^2) + 3y$
3	(3,3)	$(4 + 4x + 3x^2 + x^3) + (1 + 3x)y$	$(3 + 4x + 3x^2) + (2 + 3x)y$
4	(4,2)	$(4 + 3x + 2x^2 + 4x^3 + x^4) + (1 + 4x + 3x^2)y$	$(3 + 4x + 3x^2) + (2 + 3x)y$

(An interesting thing happens at $i = 2$: It appears initially that $g_0(x, y) = (2 + x + x^2) + 3y$ is no longer in the set S_0, the set of polynomials whose leading monomial has y-degree 0, because a term with y appears in $g_0(x, y)$. However, the leading term is actually x^2. Similar behavior is seen at other steps.) At the end of the algorithm, we take

$$Q(x, y) = (2 + 3x)y + (3 + 4x + 3x^2) = (2 + 3x)y - (2 + x + 2x^2),$$

so that

$$p(x) = \frac{2 + x + 2x^2}{2 + 3x} = 1 + 4x,$$

which was the original message.

testGS5.cc
kotter1.cc

7.6.7 An Algorithm for the Factorization Step: The Roth–Ruckenstein Algorithm

We now consider the problem of factorization when the y-degree of $Q(x, y) \geq 1$. Having obtained the polynomial $Q(x, y)$ interpolating a set of data points (x_i, y_i), $i = 1, 2, \ldots, n$, the next step in the GS decoding algorithm is to determine all factors of the form $y - p(x)$, where $p(x)$ is a polynomial of degree $\leq v$, such that $(y - p(x))|Q(x, y)$. We have the following observation:

Lemma 7.64 $(y - p(x))|Q(x)$ if and only if $Q(x, p(x)) = 0$.

(This is analogous to the result in univariate polynomials that $(x - a)|g(x)$ if and only if $g(a) = 0$.)

Proof Think of $Q(x, y)$ as a polynomial in the variable y with coefficients over $\mathbb{F}(x)$. The division algorithm applies, so that upon division by $y - p(x)$, we can write

$$Q(x, y) = q(x, y)(y - p(x)) + r(x),$$

where the y-degree of $r(x)$ must be 0, since the divisor $y - p(x)$ has y-degree 1. Evaluating at $y = p(x)$, we see that $Q(x, p(x)) = r(x)$. Then $Q(x, p(x)) = 0$ if and only if $r(x) = 0$ (identically). □

Definition 7.65 A function $p(x)$ such that $Q(x, p(x)) = 0$ is called a y-**root** of $Q(x, y)$. □

The algorithm described in this section, the **Roth–Ruckenstein** algorithm [382], finds y-roots. (Another algorithm due to Gao and Shokrollahi [151] is also known to be effective for this factorization.)

The notation $\langle\langle Q(x, y) \rangle\rangle$ denotes the coefficient (polynomial) of the highest power of x that divides $Q(x, y)$. That is, if $x^m | Q(x, y)$ but $x^{m+1} \nmid Q(x, y)$, then

$$\langle\langle Q(x, y) \rangle\rangle = \frac{Q(x, y)}{x^m}.$$

Then

$$Q(x, y) = \langle\langle Q(x, y) \rangle\rangle x^m$$

for some $m \geq 0$.

Example 7.66 If $Q(x, y) = xy$, then $\langle\langle Q(x, y)\rangle\rangle = y$. If $Q(x, y) = x^2 y^4 + x^3 y^5$, then $\langle\langle Q(x, y)\rangle\rangle = y^4 + xy^5$. If $Q(x, y) = 1 + x^2 y^4 + x^3 y^5$, then $\langle\langle Q(x, y)\rangle\rangle = Q(x, y)$.   □

Let $p(x) = a_0 + a_1 x + a_2 x^2 + \cdots + a_v x^v$ be a y-root of $Q(x, y)$. The Roth–Ruckenstein algorithm will determine the coefficients of $p(x)$ one at a time. The coefficient a_0 is found using the following lemma.

Lemma 7.67 Let $Q_0(x, y) = \langle\langle Q(x, y)\rangle\rangle$. If $(y - p(x))|Q(x, y)$, then $y = p(0) = a_0$ is a root of the equation $Q_0(0, y) = 0$.

Proof If $(y - p(x))|Q(x, y)$, then $(y - p(x))|x^m Q_0(x, y)$ for some $m \geq 0$. But since $y - p(x)$ and x^m must be relatively prime, it must be the case that $(y - p(x))|Q_0(x, y)$, so that $Q_0(x, y) = T_0(x, y)(y - p(x))$ for some quotient polynomial $T_0(x, y)$. Setting $y = p(0)$, we have

$$Q_0(0, y) = Q_0(0, p(0)) = T_0(0, p(0))(p(0) - p(0)) = T_0(0, p(0))0 = 0.$$

□

From this lemma, the set of possible values of the coefficient a_0 of $p(x)$ are the roots of the polynomial $Q_0(0, y)$. The algorithm now works by inductively "peeling off" layers, leaving a structure by which a_1 can similarly be found, then a_2, and so forth. It is based on the following theorem, which defines the peeling off process and extends Lemma 7.67.

Theorem 7.68 Let $Q_0(x, y) = \langle\langle Q(x, y)\rangle\rangle$. Let $p_0(x) = p(x) = a_0 + a_1 x + \cdots + a_v x^v \in \mathbb{F}_v[x]$. For $j \geq 1$ define

$$p_j(x) = \frac{(p_{j-1}(x) - p_{j-1}(0))}{x} = a_j + \cdots + a_v x^{v-j} \qquad (7.98)$$

$$T_j(x, y) = Q_{j-1}(x, xy + a_{j-1}) \qquad (7.99)$$

$$Q_j(x, y) = \langle\langle T_j(x, y)\rangle\rangle. \qquad (7.100)$$

Then for any $j \geq 1$, $(y - p(x))|Q(x, y)$ if and only if $(y - p_j(x))|Q_j(x, y)$.

Proof The proof is by induction: We will show that $(y - p_{j-1}(x))|Q_{j-1}(x, y)$ if and only if $(y - p_j(x))|Q_j(x, y)$.

$\Rightarrow$: Assuming $(y - p_{j-1}(x))|Q_{j-1}(x, y)$, we write

$$Q_{j-1}(x, y) = (y - p_{j-1}(x))u(x, y)$$

for some quotient polynomial $u(x, y)$. Then from (7.99),

$$T_j(x, y) = (xy + a_{j-1} - p_{j-1}(x))u(x, xy + a_{j-1}).$$

Since $a_{j-1} - p_{j-1}(x) = -xp_j(x)$,

$$T_j(x, y) = x(y - p_j(x))u(x, xy + a_{j-1})$$

so that $(y - p_j(x))|T_j(x, y)$. From (7.100), $T_j(x, y) = x^m Q_j(x, y)$ for some $m \geq 0$, so $(y - p_j(x))|x^m Q_j(x, y)$. Since x^m and $y - p(x)$ are relatively prime, $(y - p_j(x))|Q_j(x, y)$.

$\Leftarrow$: Assuming $(y - p_j(x))|Q_j(x,y)$ and using (7.100), $(y - p_j(x))|T_j(x,y)$. From (7.99), $(y - p_j(x))|Q_{j-1}(x, xy + a_{j-1})$ so that

$$Q_{j-1}(x, xy + a_{j-1}) = (y - p_j(x))u(x,y) \tag{7.101}$$

for some quotient polynomial $u(x,y)$. Replace y by $(y - a_{j-1})/x$ in (7.101) to obtain

$$Q_{j-1}(x,y) = ((y - a_{j-1})/x - p_j(x))u(x, (y - a_{j-1})/x).$$

The fractions can be cleared by multiplying both sides by some sufficiently large power L of x. Then using the fact that $p_{j-1}(x) = a_{j-1} + xp_j(x)$, we obtain

$$x^L Q_{j-1}(x,y) = (y - p_{j-1}(x))v(x,y)$$

for some polynomial $v(x,y)$. Thus, $(y - p_{j-1}(x))|x^L Q_{j-1}(x,y)$ and so

$$(y - p_{j-1}(x))|Q_{j-1}(x,y).$$

$\square$

The following lemma is a repeat of Lemma 7.67 and is proved in a similar manner.

Lemma 7.69 *If* $(y - p(x))|Q(x,y)$, *then* $y = p_j(0)$ *is a root of the equation* $Q_j(0,y) = 0$ *for* $j = 0, 1, \ldots, v$.

Since $p_j(0) = a_j$, this lemma indicates that the coefficient a_j can be found by finding the roots of the equation $Q_j(0,y) = 0$.

Finally, we need a termination criterion, provided by the following lemma.

Lemma 7.70 *If* $y|Q_{v+1}(x,y)$, *then* $p(x) = a_0 + a_1 x + \cdots + a_v x^v$ *is a y-root of* $Q(x,y)$.

Proof Note that if $y|Q_{v+1}(x,y)$, then $Q_{v+1}(x,0) = 0$.

By the construction (7.98), $p_j(x) = 0$ for $j \geq v + 1$. The condition $y|Q_{v+1}(x,y)$ is equivalent to $(y - p_{v+1}(x))|Q_{v+1}(x,y)$. Thus, by Theorem 7.68, it must be the case that $(y - p(x))|Q(x)$. $\square$

The overall operation of the algorithm is outlined as follows.

```
for each a₀ in the set of roots of Q₀(0, y)
  for each a₁ in the set of roots of Q₁(0, y)
    for each a₂ in the set of roots of Q₂(0, y)
      ⋮
      for each aᵤ in the set of roots of Qᵤ(0, y)
        if Qᵤ(x, 0) = 0, then (by Lemma 7.70), p(x) = a₀ + a₁x + ⋯ + aᵤxᵘ is a y-root
        end for
      ⋮
    end for
  end for
end for
```

The iterated "for" loops (up to depth u) can be implemented using a recursive programming structure. The following algorithm uses a depth-first tree structure.

Algorithm 7.8 Roth–Ruckenstein Algorithm for Finding y-roots of $Q(x, y)$

---

1 **Input:** $Q(x, y)$, D (maximum degree of $p(x)$)
2 **Output:** List of polynomials $p(x)$ of degree $\leq D$ such that $(y - p(x)) \mid Q(x, y)$
3 **Initialization:** Set $p(x) = 0$, $u = \deg(p) = -1$, $D = $ maximum degree (set as internal global)
4 Set up linked list where polynomials are saved.
5 Set $v = 0$ (the number of the node; global variable)
6 Call `rothrucktree` $(Q(x, y), u, p)$

7 Function `rothrucktree` (Q, u, p):
8 **Input:** $Q(x, y)$, $p(x)$ and u (degree of p)
9 **Output:** List of polynomials
10 $v = v + 1$ (increment node number)
11 if($Q(x, 0) = 0$)
12   add $p(x)$ to the output list
13 end(if)
14 else if($u < D$) (try another branch of the tree)
15   R = list of roots of $Q(0, y)$
16   for each $\alpha \in R$
17      $Q_{new}(x, y) = Q(x, xy + \alpha)$ (shift the polynomial)
18      $p_{u+1} = \alpha$ (new coefficient of $p(x)$)
19   Call `rothrucktree` $(\langle\langle Q_{new}(x, y)\rangle\rangle, u + 1, p)$(recursive call)
20   end (for)
21 else (leaf of tree reached with nonzero polynomial)
22   (no output)
23 end (if)
24 end

Example 7.71   Let

$$Q(x, y) = (4 + 4x^2 + 2x^3 + 3x^4 + x^5 + 3x^6 + 4x^7) + (1 + 2x + 2x^2 + 3x^4 + 3x^6)y$$

$$+ (1 + x + 2x^2 + x^3 + x^4)y^2 + (4 + 2x)y^3$$

be a polynomial in $GF(5)[x, y]$. Figures 7.5 and 7.6 illustrate the flow of the algorithm with $D = 2$.

testGS2.cc
rothruck.cc
rothruck.h

- At Node 1, the polynomial $Q(0, y) = 4 + y + y^2 + 4y^3$ is formed (see Figure 7.5) and its roots are computed as $\{1, 4\}$ (1 is actually a repeated root).

- At Node 1, the root 1 is selected. Node 2 is called with $\langle\langle Q(x, xy + 1)\rangle\rangle$.

- At Node 2, the polynomial $Q(0, y) = 3 + 3y^2$ is formed, with roots $\{2, 3\}$.

- At Node 2, the root 2 is selected. Node 3 is called with $\langle\langle Q(x, xy + 2)\rangle\rangle$.

- At Node 3, the polynomial $Q(x, 0) = 0$, so the list of roots selected to this node $\{1, 2\}$ forms an output polynomial, $p(x) = 1 + 2x$.

- The recursion returns to Node 2, where the root 3 is selected, and Node 4 is called with $\langle\langle Q(x, xy + 3)\rangle\rangle$.

- At Node 4, the polynomial $Q(0, y) = 2 + 3y$ is formed, with roots $\{1\}$.

- At Node 4, the root 1 is selected. Node 5 is called with $\langle\langle Q(x, xy + 1)\rangle\rangle$.

- At Node 5, it is not the case that $Q(x, 0) = 0$. Since the level of the tree (3) is greater than D (2), no further searching is performed along this branch, so no output occurs. (However, if D had been equal to 3, the next branch would have been called with a root of 2 and a polynomial would have been found; the polynomial $p(x) = 1 + 3x + x^2 + 2x^3$ would have been added to the list.)

- The recursion returns to Node 1, where the root 4 is selected and Node 6 is called with $\langle\langle Q(x, xy + 4)\rangle\rangle$.

- At Node 6, the polynomial $Q(0, y) = 2 + y$ is formed, with root $\{3\}$. (See Figure 7.6.) Node 7 is called with $\langle\langle Q(x, xy + 3)\rangle\rangle$.

- At Node 7, the polynomial $Q(0, y) = 3 + y$ is formed, with root $\{2\}$. Node 8 is called with $\langle\langle Q(x, xy + 2)\rangle\rangle$.

- At Node 8, $Q(x, 0) = 0$, so the list of roots selected to this node $\{4, 3, 2\}$ forms an output polynomial $p(x) = 4 + 3x + 2x^2$.

The set of polynomials produced is $\{1 + 2x, 4 + 3x + 2x^2\}$. $\qquad\qquad\square$

Example 7.72 For the interpolating polynomial $Q(x, y)$ of Example 7.62, the Roth–Ruckenstein algorithm determines the following y-roots (see `testGS3.cc`):

$$p(x) \in \{\alpha + \alpha^2 x + \alpha^3 x^2 + \alpha^4 x^3 + \alpha^5 x^4 + \alpha^6 x^5 + \alpha^7 x^6,$$

$$\alpha^7 + \alpha^6 x + \alpha^{14} x^2 + \alpha^5 x^3 + \alpha^{10} x^4 + \alpha^{10} x^5 + \alpha^2 x^6,$$

$$\alpha^{12} + \alpha^{10} x + \alpha^{11} x^3 + \alpha^{13} x^4 + \alpha^{11} x^5 + \alpha^{11} x^6\} = \mathcal{L}.$$

Note that the original message $m(x)$ is among this list, resulting in a codeword a Hamming distance 4 away from the received $r(x)$. There are also two others (confer the fact that $L_m = 3$ was computed in Example 7.62). The other polynomials result in distances 5 and 6, respectively, away from $r(x)$. Being further than t_m away from $r(x)$, these can be eliminated from further consideration. $\qquad\qquad\square$

7.6.7.1 What to Do with Lists of Factors?

The GS algorithm returns the message $m(x)$ on its list of polynomials $\mathcal{L}$, provided that the codeword for $m(x)$ is within a distance t_m of the received vector. This is called the *causal* codeword. It may also return other codewords at a Hamming distance $\leq t_m$, which are called *plausible* codewords. Other codewords, at a distance $> t_m$ from $r(x)$ may also be on the list; these are referred to as *noncausal* codewords (i.e., codewords not caused by the original, true, codeword). We have essentially showed, by the results above, that all plausible codewords are in $\mathcal{L}$ and that the maximum number of codewords is $\leq L_m$.

In Example 7.72, it was possible to winnow the list down to a single plausible codeword. But in the general case, what should be done when there are multiple plausible codewords in $\mathcal{L}$? If the algorithm is used in conjunction with another coding scheme (in a concatenated scheme), it may be possible to eliminate one or more of the plausible codewords. Or there may be external ways of selecting a correct codeword from a short list. Another approach is to exploit *soft* decoding information, to determine using a more refined measure which codeword is closest to $r(x)$. But there is, in general, no universally satisfactory solution to this problem.

However, it turns out that for many codes, the number of elements in $\mathcal{L}$ is equal to 1: the list decoder may not actually return a list with more than one element in it. This concept has been explored in [302]. We summarize some key conclusions.

When a list decoder returns more than one plausible codeword, there is the possibility of a decoding failure. Let L denote the number of codewords on the list and let list L' denote the number of noncausal codewords. There may be a decoding error if $L' > 1$. Let P_E denote the probability of a decoding error. We can write

$$P_E < E[L'],$$

the *average* number of noncausal codewords on the list.

Now consider selecting a point at random in the space $GF(q)^n$ and placing a Hamming sphere of radius t_m around it. How many codewords of an (n, k) code, on average, are in this Hamming sphere?

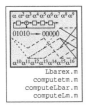

The "density" of codewords in the space is q^k/q^n. As we have seen (Section 3.3.1), the number of points in the Hamming sphere is

$$\sum_{s=0}^{t_m} \binom{n}{s} (q-1)^2.$$

Therefore, the average number of codewords in a sphere of radius t_m around a random point is

$$\overline{L}(t_m) = \frac{q^k}{q^n} \sum_{s=0}^{t_m} \binom{n}{s} (q-1)^2.$$

It can be shown [302] that $\overline{L}(t_m)$ is slightly less than a rigorous bound on the average number of noncausal codewords on the list.

Example 7.73   [302] For a $(32,8)$ RS code over $GF(32)$, we have the following results (only values of m are shown that lead to distinct values of t_m):

m	t_m	L_m	$\overline{L}(t_m)$
0	12	1	$1.36305e - 10$
1	14	2	$2.74982e - 07$
2	15	4	$1.02619e - 05$
4	16	8	0.000339205
120	17	256	0.00993659

Thus, while the list for $m = q$ may have as many as $L_4 = 8$ polynomials, the probability $\overline{L}(t_4)$ is very small — the list is very likely to contain only one codeword, which will be the causal codeword. It is highly likely that this code is capable of correcting up to 16 errors. (Actually, even for $m = 120$, the probability of more than codeword is still quite small; however, the computational complexity for $m = 120$ precludes its use as a practical decoding option.)   □

Example 7.74   [302] For a $(31,15)$ code over $GF(32)$, we have

m	t_m	L_m	$\overline{L}(t_m)$
0	8	1	$5.62584e-06$
3	9	4	0.000446534
21	10	31	0.0305164

It is reasonable to argue that the code can correct up to nine errors with very high probability.   □

7.6.8 Soft-Decision Decoding of Reed–Solomon Codes

The Reed–Solomon decoding algorithms described up to this point in the book have been *hard* decision decoding algorithms, making explicit use of the algebraic structure of the code and employing symbols which can be interpreted as elements in a Galois field. A long outstanding problem in coding theory has been to develop a *soft-decision* decoding algorithm for Reed–Solomon codes, which is able to exploit soft channel outputs without mapping it to hard values, while still retaining the ability to exploit the algebraic structure of the code. This problem was solved [251] by an extension of the GS algorithm which we call the Koetter–Vardy (KV) algorithm.[3]

---

[3] The name Koetter is simply a transliteration of the name Kötter.

Recall that the GS algorithm has a parameter m representing the interpolation multiplicity, m. For most of this chapter, a fixed multiplicity has been employed at each point. It is possible, however, to employ a different multiplicity at each point. (In fact, Algorithm 7.6 already handles multiple multiplicities.) In the KV algorithm, a mapping is found from posterior probabilities (soft information) to the multiplicities, after which the conventional interpolation and factorization steps of the GS are used to decode. (The mapping still results in some degree of "hardness," since probabilities exist on a continuum, while the multiplicities must be integers.) We present here their algorithm for *memoryless* channels; for further results on channels with memory and concatenated channels, the reader is referred to [251].

7.6.8.1 Notation

Recall (see Section 1.6) that a memoryless channel can be modeled as an input alphabet $\mathcal{X}$, an output alphabet $\mathcal{Y}$, and a set of $|\mathcal{X}|$ functions $f(\cdot|x) : \mathcal{Y} \to \mathbb{R}$. The channel input and output are conventionally viewed as a random variables X and Y. If Y is continuous, then $f(\cdot|x)$ is a probability density function (for example, for a Gaussian channel, $f(y|x)$ would be a Gaussian likelihood function). If Y is discrete, then $f(\cdot|x)$ is a probability mass function. The memoryless nature of the channel is reflected by the assumption that the joint likelihood factors,

$$f(y_1, y_2, \ldots, y_n | x_1, x_2, \ldots, x_n) = \prod_{i=1}^{n} f(y_i | x_i).$$

It is assumed that the X random variable is uniformly distributed (i.e., that each codeword is selected with equal probability). Given an observation $y \in \mathcal{Y}$, the probability that some $\alpha \in \mathcal{X}$ was transmitted is found using Bayes' theorem,

$$P(X = \alpha | Y = y) = \frac{f(y|\alpha)}{\sum_{x \in \mathcal{X}} f(y|x)},$$

where the assumption of uniformity of X is used.

For Reed–Solomon codes, the input alphabet is the field over which the symbols occur, $\mathcal{X} = GF(q)$. We have therefore $\mathcal{X} = \{\alpha_1, \alpha_2, \ldots, \alpha_q\}$, for some arbitrary ordering of the elements of $GF(q)$.

Let $\mathbf{y} = (y_1, y_2, \ldots, y_n) \in \mathcal{Y}^n$ be a vector of observations. We define the posterior probabilities

$$\pi_{i,j} = P(X = \alpha_i | Y = y_j), \quad i = 1, 2, \ldots, q, \quad j = 1, 2, \ldots, n$$

and form the $q \times n$ matrix Π with elements $\pi_{i,j}$. The matrix Π is called the **reliability matrix**. It is convenient below to use the notation $\Pi(\alpha, j)$ to refer the element in the row indexed by α and the column indexed by j. It is assumed that the reliability matrix is provided (somehow) as the input to the decoding algorithm.

A second matrix is also employed. Let M be a $q \times n$ *multiplicity matrix* with non-negative elements $m_{i,j}$, where $m_{i,j}$ is the interpolation multiplicity associated with the point (α_i, y_j). The key step of the algorithm to be described below is to provide a mapping from the reliability matrix Π to the multiplicity matrix M.

Definition 7.75 Let M be a multiplicity matrix with elements $m_{i,j}$. We will denote by $Q_M(x, y)$ the polynomial of minimal $(1, k-1)$-weighted degree that has a zero of multiplicity at least $m_{i,j}$ at the point (α_i, y_j) for every i, j such that $m_{i,j} \neq 0$. □

Recall that the main point of the interpolation theorem is that there must be more degrees of freedom (variables) than there are constraints. The number of constraints introduced by a multiplicity

$m_{i,j}$ is equal to $\binom{m_{i,j}+1}{2}$. The total number of constraints associated with a multiplicity matrix M is called the *cost of M*, denoted $C(M)$, where

$$C(M) = \frac{1}{2} \sum_{i=1}^{q} \sum_{j=1}^{n} m_{i,j}(m_{i,j} + 1).$$

As before, let $C(v, l)$ be the number of monomials of weighted $(1, v)$-degree less than or equal to l. Then by the interpolation theorem an interpolating solution exists if

$$C(v, l) > C(M).$$

Let $\mathcal{K}_v(x) = \min\{l \in \mathbb{Z} : C(v, l) > x\}$ be the smallest $(1, v)$-weighted degree which has the number of monomials of lesser (or equal) degree exceeding x. Then $\mathcal{K}_{k-1}(C(M))$ is the smallest $(1, k-1)$-weighted degree which has a sufficiently large number of monomials to exceed the cost $C(M)$. (Confer with K_m defined in (7.76).) By (7.64), for a given cost $C(M)$, we must have

$$\mathcal{K}_v(C(M)) < \sqrt{2vC(M)}. \tag{7.102}$$

It will be convenient to represent vectors in $GF(q)^n$ as indicator matrices over the reals, as follows. Let $\mathbf{v} = (v_1, v_2, \ldots, v_n) \in GF(q)^n$ and let $[\mathbf{v}]$ denote the $q \times n$ matrix which has $[\mathbf{v}]_{i,j} = 1$ if $v_j = \alpha_i$, and $[\mathbf{v}]_{i,j} = 0$ otherwise. That is,

$$[\mathbf{v}]_{i,j} = I_{\alpha_i}(v_j),$$

where $I_{\alpha_i}(v_j)$ is the indicator function, $I_{\alpha_i}(v_j) = \begin{cases} 1 & v_j = \alpha_i \\ 0 & \text{otherwise.} \end{cases}$

Example 7.76   In the field $GF(3)$, let $\mathbf{v} = (1, 2, 0, 1)$. The matrix representation is

$$[\mathbf{v}] = \begin{matrix} 0: \\ 1: \\ 2: \end{matrix} \begin{matrix} v_1 & v_2 & v_3 & v_4 \\ \begin{bmatrix} 0 & 0 & 1 & 0 \\ 1 & 0 & 0 & 1 \\ 0 & 1 & 0 & 0 \end{bmatrix} \end{matrix}.$$

$\square$

For two $q \times n$ matrices A and B, define the inner product

$$\langle A, B \rangle = tr(AB^T) = \sum_{i=1}^{q} \sum_{j=1}^{n} a_{i,j} b_{i,j}.$$

Now using this, we define the *score* of a vector $\mathbf{v} = (v_1, v_2, \ldots, v_n)$ with respect to a given multiplicity matrix M as

$$S_M(\mathbf{v}) = \langle M, [\mathbf{v}] \rangle.$$

The score thus represents the total multiplicities of all the points associated with the vector $\mathbf{v}$.

Example 7.77   If $M = \begin{bmatrix} m_{1,1} & m_{1,2} & m_{1,3} & m_{1,4} \\ m_{2,1} & m_{2,2} & m_{2,3} & m_{2,4} \\ m_{3,1} & m_{3,2} & m_{3,3} & m_{3,4} \end{bmatrix}$, then the score of the vector $\mathbf{v}$ from the last example is

$$S_M(\mathbf{v}) = m_{2,1} + m_{3,2} + m_{1,3} + m_{2,4}.$$

$\square$

7.6.8.2 A Factorization Theorem

Our key result is an extension of the factorization theorem for different multiplicities.

Theorem 7.78 *Let $C(M)$ be the cost of the matrix M (the number of constraints to satisfy). Let $\mathbf{c}$ be a codeword in a Reed–Solomon (n, k) code over $GF(q)$ and let $p(x)$ be a polynomial that evaluates to $\mathbf{c}$ (i.e., $\mathbf{c} = (p(x_1), p(x_2), \ldots, p(x_n))$ for code support set $\{x_1, x_2, \ldots, x_n\}$). If $S_M(\mathbf{c}) > \mathcal{K}_{k-1}(C(M))$, then $(y - p(x)) | Q_M(x, y)$.*

Proof Let $\mathbf{c} = (c_1, \ldots, c_n)$ be a codeword and let $p(x)$ be a polynomial of degree $< k$ that maps to the codeword: $p(x_j) = c_j$ for all x_j in the support set of the code. Let $g(x) = Q_M(x, p(x))$. We will show that $g(x)$ is identically 0, which will imply that $(y - p(x)) | Q_M(x, y)$.

Write $S_M(\mathbf{c}) = m_1 + m_2 + \cdots + m_n$. The polynomial $Q_M(x, y)$ has a zero of order m_j at (x_j, c_j) (by the definition of Q_M). By Lemma 7.47, $(x - x_j)^{m_j} | Q_M(x, p(x))$, for $j = 1, 2, \ldots, n$. Thus, $g(x) = Q_M(x, p(x))$ is divisible by the product

$$(x - x_1)^{m_1}(x - x_2)^{m_2} \cdots (x - x_n)^{m_n} \text{ having degree } m_1 + m_2 + \cdots + m_n = S_M(\mathbf{c}),$$

so that either $\deg(g(x)) \geq S_M(\mathbf{c})$, or $g(x)$ must be zero.

Since $\deg p(x) \leq k - 1$, the degree of $Q_M(x, p(x))$ is less than or equal to the $(1, k - 1)$-weighted degree of $Q_M(x, y)$. Furthermore, since $Q_M(x, y)$ is of minimal $(1, k - 1)$-degree, $\deg_{1,k-1} Q_M(x, y) \leq \mathcal{K}_{k-1}(C(M))$:

$$\deg g(x) \leq \deg_{1,k-1} Q_M(x, y) \leq \mathcal{K}_{k-1}(C(M)).$$

By hypothesis, we have $S_M(\mathbf{c}) > \mathcal{K}_{k-1}(C(M))$. Since we cannot have $\deg g(x) \geq S_M(\mathbf{c})$, we must therefore have $g(x)$ is zero (identically). As before, we write using the factorization theorem

$$Q(x, y) = (y - p(x))q(x, y) + r(x)$$

so that at $y = p(x)$, we have

$$Q(x, p(x)) = g(x) = 0 = 0q(x, y) + r(x)$$

so $r(x) = 0$, giving the stated divisibility. □

In light of (7.102), this theorem indicates that $Q_M(x, y)$ has a factor $y - p(x)$, where $p(x)$ evaluates to a codeword $\mathbf{c}$, if

$$S_M(\mathbf{c}) \geq \sqrt{2(k-1)C(M)}. \tag{7.103}$$

7.6.8.3 Mapping from Reliability to Multiplicity

Given a cost C, we define the set $\mathfrak{M}(C)$ as the set of all matrices with non-negative elements whose cost is equal to C:

$$\mathfrak{M}(C) = \left\{ M \in \mathbb{Z}^{q \times n} : m_{i,j} \geq 0 \text{ and } \frac{1}{2} \sum_{i=1}^{q} \sum_{j=1}^{n} m_{i,j}(m_{i,j} + 1) = C \right\}.$$

The problem we would address now is to select a multiplicity matrix M which maximizes the score $S_M(\mathbf{c})$ for a transmitted codeword $\mathbf{c}$ (so that the condition $S_M(\mathbf{c}) > \mathcal{K}_{k-1}(C(M))$ required by Theorem 7.78 is satisfied). Not knowing which codeword was transmitted, however, the best that can be hoped for is to maximize some function of a codeword chosen at random. Let $X = (X_1, X_2, \ldots, X_n)$ be a random transmitted vector. The score for this vector is $S_M(X) = \langle M, [X] \rangle$. We choose to maximize the *expected value* of this score,[4]

$$E[S_M(X)] = \sum_{\mathbf{x} \in \mathfrak{X}^n} S_M(\mathbf{x}) P(\mathbf{x})$$

with respect to a probability distribution $P(\mathbf{x})$. We adopt the distribution determined by the channel output (using the memoryless channel model),

$$P(\mathbf{x}) = P(x_1, x_2, \ldots, x_n) = \prod_{j=1}^{n} P(X_j = x_j | Y_j = y_j) = \prod_{j=1}^{n} \Pi(x_j, j), \qquad (7.104)$$

where Π is the reliability matrix. This would be the posterior distribution of X given the observations if the prior distribution of X were uniform over $GF(q)^n$. However, the X are, in fact, drawn from the set of codewords, so this distribution model is not accurate. But computing the optimal distribution function, which takes into account all that the receiver knows about the code locations, can be shown to be NP complete [251]. We therefore adopt the suboptimal, but tractable, stance.

The problem can thus be stated as: Select the matrix $M \in \mathfrak{M}$ maximizing $E[S_M(X)]$, where the expectation is with respect to the distribution P in (7.104). We will denote the solution as $M(\Pi, C)$, where

$$M(\Pi, C) = \arg \max_{M \in \mathfrak{M}(C)} E[S_M(X)].$$

We have the following useful lemma.

Lemma 7.79

$$E[S_M(X)] = \langle M, \Pi \rangle.$$

Proof

$$E[S_M(X)] = E \langle M, [X] \rangle = \langle M, E[X] \rangle$$

by linearity. Now consider the (i, j)th element:

$$E[X]_{i,j} = E[I_{\alpha_i}(X_j)] = (1)P(X_j = \alpha_i) + (0)P(X_j \neq \alpha_i) = P(X_j = \alpha_i) = \Pi(\alpha_i, j),$$

where the last equality follows from the assumed probability model in (7.104). $\square$

The following algorithm provides a mapping from a reliability matrix Π to a multiplicity matrix M.

Algorithm 7.9 Koetter–Vardy Algorithm for Mapping from Π to M

---

1 **Input:** A reliability matrix Π; a positive integer S indicating the number of interpolation points
2 **Output:** A multiplicity matrix M
3 **Initialization:** Set $\Pi^* = \Pi$ and $M = \mathbf{0}$.
4 Do:
5   Find the position (i, j) of the largest element $\pi^*_{i,j}$ of Π^*.
6   Set $\pi^*_{i,j} = \dfrac{\pi^*_{i,j}}{m_{i,j}+2}$
7   Set $m_{i,j} = m_{i,j} + 1$
8   Set $S = S - 1$
9 While $S > 0$

---

[4] More correctly, one might want to maximize $P(S_M(X) > \mathcal{K}_{k-1}(C(M)))$, but it can be shown that this computation is, in general, very complicated.

Let $\overline{M}$ be formed by normalizing the columns of M produced by this algorithm to sum to 1. It can be shown that $\overline{M} \to \Pi$ as $S \to \infty$. That is, the algorithm produces an integer matrix which, when normalized to look like a probability matrix, asymptotically approaches Π. Since one more multiplicity is introduced for every iteration, it is clear that the score increases essentially linearly with S and that the cost increases essentially quadratically with S.

Example 7.80

Suppose

$$\Pi = \begin{bmatrix} 0.1349 & 0.3046 & 0.2584 & 0.2335 \\ 0.2444 & 0.1578 & 0.1099 & 0.1816 \\ 0.2232 & 0.1337 & 0.2980 & 0.1478 \\ 0.1752 & 0.1574 & 0.2019 & 0.2307 \\ 0.2222 & 0.2464 & 0.1317 & 0.2064 \end{bmatrix}.$$

Figure 7.7 shows a plot of $\| \overline{M} - \Pi \|$ after S iterations as S varies up to 400 iterations. It also shows the score and the cost $\frac{1}{n}\langle M, \Pi \rangle$. The M matrix produced after 400 iterations, and its normalized equivalent, are

$$M = \begin{bmatrix} 13 & 31 & 26 & 23 \\ 25 & 16 & 11 & 18 \\ 22 & 13 & 30 & 15 \\ 17 & 16 & 20 & 23 \\ 22 & 25 & 13 & 21 \end{bmatrix} \quad \overline{M} = \begin{bmatrix} 0.1313 & 0.3069 & 0.2600 & 0.2300 \\ 0.2525 & 0.1584 & 0.1100 & 0.1800 \\ 0.2222 & 0.1287 & 0.3000 & 0.1500 \\ 0.1717 & 0.1584 & 0.2000 & 0.2300 \\ 0.2222 & 0.2475 & 0.1300 & 0.2100 \end{bmatrix}.$$

□

Some understanding of this convergence result — why M proportional to Π is appropriate — can be obtained as follows. We note that the cost $C(M)$ can be written as

$$C(M) = \frac{1}{2}(\langle M, M \rangle + \langle M, \mathbf{1} \rangle),$$

where $\mathbf{1}$ is the matrix of all ones. For sufficiently large M, $C(M)$ is close to $\frac{1}{2}\langle M, M \rangle$, which is (1/2) the Frobenius norm of M. For fixed norm $\langle M, M \rangle$, maximizing the expected score $\langle M, \Pi \rangle$ is accomplished (as indicated by the Cauchy–Schwartz inequality) by setting M to be proportional to Π.

7.6.8.4 The Geometry of the Decoding Regions

In the bound (7.103), write $S_M(\mathbf{c}) = \langle M, [\mathbf{c}] \rangle$ and $C(M) = \langle M, \Pi \rangle + \langle M, \mathbf{1} \rangle$; we thus see from Theorem 7.78 that the decoding algorithm outputs a codeword $\mathbf{c}$ if

$$\frac{\langle M, [\mathbf{c}] \rangle}{\sqrt{\langle M, M \rangle + \langle M, \mathbf{1} \rangle}} \geq \sqrt{k - 1}.$$

Asymptotically (as $S \to \infty$ and the normalized $\overline{M} \to \Pi$), we have

$$\frac{\langle \Pi, [\mathbf{c}] \rangle}{\sqrt{\langle \Pi, \Pi \rangle}} \geq \sqrt{k - 1} + o(1) \tag{7.105}$$

(where the $o(1)$ term accounts for the neglected $\langle \overline{M}, \mathbf{1} \rangle$ term).

Observe that for any codeword $\mathbf{c}$, $\langle [\mathbf{c}], [\mathbf{c}] \rangle = n$. Recall that in the Hilbert space $\mathbb{R}^{qn}$, the cosine of the angle β between vectors X and Y is

$$\cos \beta(X, Y) = \frac{\langle X, Y \rangle}{\sqrt{\langle X, X \rangle \langle Y, Y \rangle}}.$$

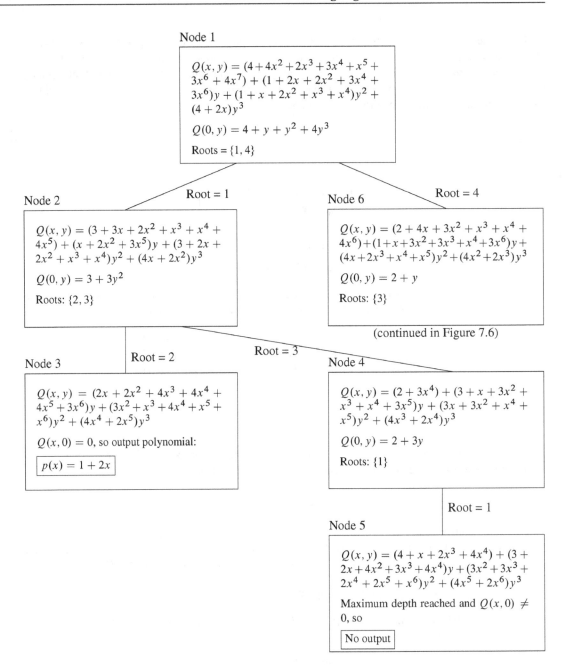

Figure 7.5: An example of the Roth–Ruckenstein Algorithm over $GF(5)$.

In light of (7.105), a codeword $\mathbf{c}$ is on the decoder list if

$$\frac{\langle \Pi, [\mathbf{c}] \rangle}{\sqrt{n \langle \Pi, \Pi \rangle}} \geq \sqrt{(k-1)/n} + o(1).$$

Asymptotically $(n \to \infty)$, the codeword is on the list if

$$\cos \beta([\mathbf{c}], \Pi) \geq \sqrt{R} + o(1).$$

Node 6

$$Q(x, y) = (2 + 4x + 3x^2 + x^3 + x^4 + 4x^6) + (1 + x + 3x^2 + 3x^3 + x^4 + 3x^6)y + (4x + 2x^3 + x^4 + x^5)y^2 + (4x^2 + 2x^3)y^3$$

$$Q(0, y) = 2 + y$$

Roots: $\{3\}$

Root = 3

Node 7

$$Q(x, y) = (3 + 2x^2 + 3x^3 + 4x^4 + 3x^5) + (1 + x^2 + 4x^3 + 2x^4 + x^5 + 3x^6)y + (4x^2 + x^3 + x^5 + x^6)y^2 + (4x^4 + 2x^5)y^3$$

$$Q(0, y) = 3 + y$$

Roots: $\{2\}$

Root = 2

Node 8

$$Q(x, y) = (x + 2x^3 + 3x^4 + 4x^6 + 2x^7)y + (4x^4 + x^5 + 4x^6 + 3x^7 + x^8)y^2 + (4x^7 + 2x^8)y^3$$

$Q(x, 0) = 0$, so output polynomial:

$$p(x) = 4 + 3x + 2x^2$$

Figure 7.6: An example of the Roth–Ruckenstein Algorithm over $GF(5)$ (cont'd).

The asymptotic decoding regions are thus cones in Euclidean space $\mathbb{R}^{qn}$: the central axis of the cone is the line from the origin to the point Π. Codewords which lie within an angle of $\cos^{-1}\sqrt{R}$ of the central axis are included in the decoding list of Π.

Each codeword lies on a sphere S of radius $\sqrt{\langle[\mathbf{c}], [\mathbf{c}]\rangle} = \sqrt{n}$. To contrast the KV algorithm with the GS algorithm, the GS algorithm would take a reliability matrix Π and project it (by some nonlinear means) onto the sphere S, and then determine the codewords within an angle of $\cos^{-1}\sqrt{R}$ of this projected point. Conventional decoding is similar, except that the angle of inclusion is $\cos^{-1}(1+R)/2$ and the decoding regions are nonoverlapping.

7.6.8.5 Computing the Reliability Matrix

We present here a suggested method for computing a reliability matrix for transmission using a large signal constellation.

Consider the constellation shown in Figure 7.8. Let the signal points in the constellation be $\mathbf{s}_0, \ldots, \mathbf{s}_{M-1}$ and let the received point be $\mathbf{r}$. Then the likelihood functions $f(\mathbf{r}|\mathbf{s}_i)$ can be computed. Rather than using all M points in computing the reliability, we compute using only the N largest likelihoods. From the N largest of these likelihoods (corresponding to the N closest points in Gaussian

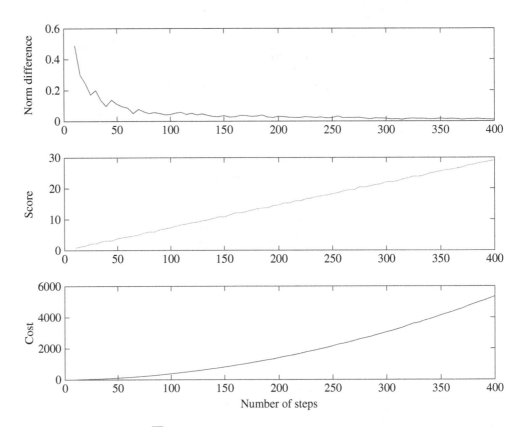

Figure 7.7: Convergence of $\overline{M}$ to Π, and the score and cost as a function of the number of iterations.

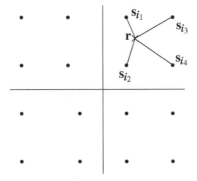

Figure 7.8: Computing the reliability function.

noise) $f(\mathbf{r}|\mathbf{s}_{i_1}), f(\mathbf{r}|\mathbf{s}_{i_2}), \ldots, f(\mathbf{r}|\mathbf{s}_{i_N})$, we form

$$P(\mathbf{r}|\mathbf{s}_{i_k}) = \frac{f(\mathbf{r}|\mathbf{s}_{i_k})}{\sum_{l=1}^{N} f(\mathbf{r}|\mathbf{s}_{i_l})}.$$

Using likelihoods computed this way, the authors of [251] have examined codes with a rate near 1/2 for a 256 QAM signal constellation. The soft-decision decoding algorithm achieved gains of up to 1.6 dB compared to conventional (hard-decision) decoding of the same RS codes.

7.7 Exercises

7.1 [84] Let M be a module over a ring R.

    (a) Show that the additive identity $0 \in M$ is unique.

    (b) Show that each $f \in M$ has a unique additive inverse.

    (c) Show that $0f = 0$, where $0 \in R$ on the left-hand side is the zero element in R and $0 \in M$ on the right-hand side is the additive identity element in M.

7.2 Show that an ideal $I \subset R$ is an R-module.

7.3 Show that if a subset $M \subset R$ is a module over R, then M is an ideal in R.

7.4 Let I be an ideal in R. Show that the quotient $M = R/I$ is an R-module under the quotient ring sum operation and the scalar multiplication defined for cosets $[g] \in R/I$ and $f \in R$ by $f[g] = [fg] \in R/I$.

7.5 Show that the expression leading to (7.19) is true, that is, $g_0'(\alpha^k)\alpha^{kb} = g'(\alpha^{b+k})\alpha^{b(2-d+k)}$.

7.6 Show that $g'(\alpha^{b+k})\alpha^{b(k+2-d)}p_k\alpha^k = \tilde{C}$ for $k = 0, 1, \ldots, d-2$, where $\tilde{C}$ is a constant, using the following steps. Let $g^{[r]}(x) = \prod_{i=0}^{r}(x - \alpha^i)$ and $p^{[r]}(x) = \prod_{i=1}^{r}(x - \alpha^i) = \sum_{k=0}^{r} p_k^{[r]} x^k$. (That is, these correspond to polynomials with $b = 0$.) You may prove the result by induction, using

$$g^{[r]}(\alpha^k)p_k^{[r]}\alpha^k = C^{[r]} = \prod_{i=0}^{r-1}(\alpha^{r+1} - \alpha^{i+1}), \quad k = 0, 1, \ldots, r$$

as the inductive hypothesis.

    (a) Show that $g^{[r]\prime}(\alpha^k) = g^{[r]\prime}(\alpha^{k-1})\frac{\alpha^{r+k-1} - \alpha^{r-1}}{\alpha^{k-1} - \alpha^r}$.

    (b) Show that $g^{[r+1]\prime}(\alpha^k) = \begin{cases} g^{[r]\prime}(\alpha^k)(\alpha^k - \alpha^{r+1}) & k = 0, 1, \ldots, r \\ g^{[r]}(\alpha^{r+1}) & k = r+1 \end{cases}$. *Hint*: $g^{[r+1]}(x) = g^{[r]}(x)(x - \alpha^{r+1})$.

    (c) Show that $p_k^{[r+1]} = \begin{cases} -p_0^{[r]}\alpha^{r+1} & k = 0 \\ p_{k-1}^{[r]} - \alpha^{r+1}p_k^{[r]} & k = 1, 2, \ldots, r. \\ 1 & k = r+1 \end{cases}$ *Hint*: $p^{[r+1]}(x) = p^{[r]}(x)(x - \alpha^{r+1})$.

    (d) Show that for the case $k = r + 1$, $g^{[r+1]\prime}(\alpha^{r+1})p_{r+1}^{[r+1]}\alpha^{r+1} = g^{[r+1]\prime}(\alpha^{r+1})\alpha^{r+1} = \prod_{i=0}^{r}\alpha^{r+2} - \alpha^{i+1} \triangleq C^{[r+1]}$.

    (e) For the case that $k = 0$, show (using the inductive hypothesis) that $g^{[r+1]\prime}(\alpha^0)p_0^{[r+1]}\alpha^0 = C^{[r+1]}$.

    (f) For the case that $k = 1, 2, \ldots, r$, show that $g^{[r+1]}(\alpha^k)p_k^{[r+1]}\alpha^k = C^{[r+1]}$.

    (g) Now extend to the case that $b \neq 0$. Let $g_0(x) = \prod_{i=0}^{d-2}(x - \alpha^i)$ and $g(x) = \prod_{i=b}^{b+d-2}$ and let $p_0(x) = \prod_{i=1}^{d-2}(x - \alpha^i)$ and $p(x) = \prod_{i=b+1}^{b+d-2}(x - \alpha^i)$. Show that $g_0'(x) = g'(\alpha^b x)\alpha^{-b(d-2)}$ and $p_{0k} = p_k\alpha^{b(k-d+2)}$. Conclude that

$$g'(\alpha^{b+k})p_k\alpha^{k+b(k-r)} = C\alpha^{br} = \tilde{C}.$$

    (h) Hence show that

$$\frac{N_2(\alpha^k)/W_2(\alpha^k)}{N_1(\alpha^k)/W_1(\alpha^k)} = \tilde{C}.$$

7.7 Show that $f(\alpha^k)g(\alpha^{b+k}) = -\tilde{C}\alpha^{b(d-1-k)}, k = d-1, \ldots, n-1$, where $\tilde{C}$ is defined in Exercise 7.6. This may be done as follows:

(a) Let $f_0(x) = \sum_{i=0}^{d-2} \frac{\alpha^i p_{0i}}{\alpha_j - x}$ and $g_0(x) = \prod_{i=0}^{d-2}(x - \alpha^i)$. Show that $f_0(x)g_0(x) = -\tilde{C}$. *Hint:* Lagrange interpolation.

(b) Show that $f(x) = x^{-b}f_0(x)\alpha^{b(d-2)}$ to conclude the result.

7.8 Show that (7.23) and (7.24) follow from (7.21) and (7.22) and the results of Exercises 7.6 and 7.7.

7.9 Work through the steps of Lemma 7.15.

(a) Explain why there must by polynomials $Q_1(x)$ and $Q_2(x)$ such that $N(x) - W(x)P(x) = Q_1(x)\Pi(x)$ and $M(x) - V(x)P(x) = Q_2(x)\Pi(x)$.

(b) Show that $(N(x)V(x) - M(x)W(x))P(x) = (M(x)Q_1(x) - N(x)Q_2(x))\Pi(x)$.

(c) Explain why $(\Pi(x), P(x))|N(x)$ and $(\Pi(x), P(x))|M(x)$. (Here, $(\Pi(x), P(x))$ is the GCD.)

(d) Show that

$$(N(x)V(x) - M(x)W(x))\frac{P(x)}{(\Pi(x), P(x))} = \frac{M(x)Q_1(x) - N(x)Q_2(x)}{\Pi(x), P(x)}\Pi(x)$$

and hence that $\Pi(x)|(N(x)V(x) - M(x)W(x))$.

(e) Show that $\deg(N(x)V(x) - M(x)W(x)) < k$. Hence conclude that $N(x)V(x) - M(x)W(x) = 0$.

(f) Let $d(x) = (W(x), V(x))$ (the GCD), so that $W(x) = d(x)w(x)$ and $V(x) = d(x)v(x)$ for relatively prime polynomials $v(x)$ and $w(x)$. Show that $N(x) = h(x)w(x)$ and $M(x) = h(x)v(x)$ for a polynomial $h(x) = N(x)/w(x) = M(x)/v(x)$.

(g) Show that $h(x)w(x) - d(x)w(x)P(x) = Q_1(x)\Pi(x)$ and $h(x)v(x) - d(x)v(x)P(x) = Q_2(x)\Pi(x)$.

(h) Show that there exist polynomials $s(x)$ and $t(x)$ such that $s(x)w(x) + t(x)v(x) = 1$. Then show that $h(x) - d(x)P(x) = (s(x)Q_1(x) + t(x)Q_2(x))\Pi(x)$.

(i) Conclude that $(h(x), d(x))$ is also a solution. Conclude that $\deg(w(x)) = 0$, so that only $(M(x), V(x))$ has been reduced.

7.10 [59] Explain how the Euclidean algorithm can be used to solve the rational interpolation problem (i.e., how it can be used to solve the WB key equation).

7.11 Show that when x_i is an error in a check location that $\Psi_{2,1}(x_i) \neq 0$ and that $h(x_i) \neq 0$. *Hint:* If $\Psi_{2,1}(x_i) = 0$, show that $\Psi_{2,2}(x_i)$ must also be zero; furthermore, we have $\Psi_{1,1}(x_i) = 0$, which implies $\Psi_{1,2}(x_i) = 0$. Show that this leads to a contradiction, since $(x - x_i)^2$ cannot divide $\det(\Psi(x))$.

7.12 Write down the monomials up to weight 8 in the $(1,4)$-revlex order. Compute $C(4,8)$ and compare with the number of monomials you obtained.

7.13 Write down the polynomials up to weight 8 in the $(1,4)$-lex order. Compute $C(4,8)$ and compare with the number of monomials you obtained.

7.14 Write the polynomial $Q(x,y) = x^5 + x^2y + x^3 + y + 1 \in GF(5)[x,y]$ with the monomials in $(1,3)$-revlex order. Write the polynomial with the monomials in $(1,3)$-lex order.

7.15 Let $Q(x,y) = 2x^2y + 3x^3y^3 + 4x^2y^4$. Compute the Hasse derivatives $D_{1,0}Q(x,y)$, $D_{0,1}Q(x,y)$, $D_{1,1}Q(x,y)$, $D_{2,0}Q(x,y)$, $D_{2,1}Q(x,y)$, and $D_{3,2}Q(x,y)$.

7.16 For a $(16,4)$ RS code over $GF(16)$, plot K_m as a function of m.

7.17 A polynomial $Q(x,y) \in GF(5)[x,y]$ is to be found such that:

$$Q(2,3) = 0 \quad D_{0,1}Q(2,3) = 0 \quad D_{1,0}Q(2,3) = 0$$

$$Q(3,4) = 0 \quad D_{0,1}Q(3,4) = 0 \quad D_{1,0}Q(3,4) = 0$$

(a) Determine the monomials that constitute $Q(x,y)$ in $(1,4)$-revlex order.

    (b) Determine the matrix $\mathcal{D}$ as in (7.89) representing the interpolation and multiplicity constraints for a polynomial.

7.18 In relation to the Feng–Tzeng algorithm, show that $[C(x)a^{(i)}(x)x^p]_n = [C(x)a^{(i)}(x)]_{n-p}$.

7.19 From Lemma 7.59, show that for $P(x,y), Q(x,y) \in \mathbb{F}[x,y]$, $[P(x,y), Q(x,y)]_D \in \ker D$.

7.20 Write down the proof to Lemma 7.40.

7.21 Show that (7.97) is true.

7.22 Bounds on L_m:

    (a) Show that

$$\left\lfloor \sqrt{\left(\frac{nm(m+1)}{v}\right)} - \left(\frac{v+2}{2v}\right) \right\rfloor \le r_B(nm(m+1)/2) \le \left\lfloor \sqrt{\frac{nm(m+1)}{v}} \right\rfloor.$$

    (b) Show that $L_m < (m + \frac{1}{2})\sqrt{n/v}$.

7.23 [302] Let $A(v,K)$ be the rank of the monomial x^K in $(1,v)$-revlex order. From Table 7.1, we have

$$
\begin{array}{cccccccc}
K & 0 & 1 & 2 & 3 & 4 & 5 \\
K(3,L) & 0 & 1 & 2 & 3 & 5 & 7
\end{array}
$$

    (a) Show that $A(v, K+1) = C(v,K)$.

    (b) Show that $A(v,K) = |\{(i,j) : i + vj < K\}|$.

    (c) Show that $B(L,v) = A(vL+1, v) - 1$.

    (d) Euler's integration formula [[247], Section 1.2.11.2, (3)] indicates that the sum of a function $f(k)$ can be represented in terms of an integral as

$$\sum_{k=0}^{n} f(k) = \int_0^n f(x)\,dx - \frac{1}{2}(f(n) - f(0)) + \int_0^n \left\{x - \frac{1}{2}\right\} f'(x)\,dx,$$

where $\{x\} = x - \lfloor x \rfloor$ is the fractional part of x. Based on this formula show that

$$A(v,K) = \frac{K^2}{2v} + \frac{K}{2} + \frac{r(v-r)}{2v}, \tag{7.106}$$

where $r = K \pmod v$.

    (e) Show the following bound:

$$\frac{K^2}{2v} < A(K,v) \le \frac{(K+v/2)^2}{2v}. \tag{7.107}$$

7.24 Bounds on K_m:

    (a) Show that

$$K_m = \left\lfloor r_A\left(n\binom{m+1}{2}\right)/m \right\rfloor + 1,$$

where

$$r_A(x) = \max\{K : A(v,K) \le x\}.$$

    (b) Show that

$$\lfloor \sqrt{vn(m+1)/m} - v/(2m) \rfloor + 1 \le K_m \le \lfloor \sqrt{vn(m+1)/m} \rfloor.$$

    (c) Hence show that asymptotically (as $m \to \infty$)

$$t_\infty = n - K_\infty = n - 1 - \lfloor \sqrt{vn} \rfloor.$$

7.8 References

The original Welch–Berlekamp algorithm appeared in [480]. In addition to introducing the new key equation, it also describes using different symbols as check symbols in a novel application to magnetic recording systems. This was followed by [34], which uses generalized minimum distance to improve the decoding behavior. The notation we use in Section 7.2.1 comes from this and from [320]. A comparison of WB key equations is in [317]. Our introduction to modules was drawn from [84]; see also [209, 218].

Our discussion of the DB form of the key equation, as well as the idea of "exact sequences" and the associated algorithms, is drawn closely from [86]. Other derivations of WB key equations are detailed in [284] and [320].

The development of the Welch–Berlekamp algorithm from Section 7.4.2 closely follows [284]. The modular form follows from [86]. Other related work is in [58] and [59].

The idea of list decoding goes back to [110]. The idea of this interpolating recovery is expressed in [480]. Work preparatory to the work here appears in [253] and was extended in [423], building in turn on [14], to decode beyond the RS design distance for some low rate codes. In particular, a form of Theorem 7.48 appeared originally in [14]; our statement and proof follows [172]. In [172], the restriction to low-rate codes was removed by employing higher multiplicity interpolating polynomials. The Feng–Tzeng algorithm appears in [121], which also shows how to use their algorithm for decoding up to the Hartmann–Tzeng and Roos BCH bounds. A preceding paper, [120] shows how to solve the multi-sequence problem using a generalization of the Euclidean algorithm, essentially producing a Gröbner basis approach. The algorithm attributed to Kötter [253] is clearly described in [302]. Other algorithms for the interpolation step are in [248] and in [327], which puts a variety of algorithms under the unifying framework of displacements.

The factorization step was efficiently expressed in [382]. The description presented of the Roth–Ruckenstein algorithm draws very closely in parts from the excellent tutorial paper [302]. Alternative factorization algorithms appear in [19, 121,154,495 in edits].

Chapter 8

Other Important Block Codes

8.1 Introduction

There are a variety of block codes of both historical and practical importance which are used either as building blocks or components of other systems, which we have not yet seen in this book. In this chapter, we introduce some of the most important of these.

8.2 Hadamard Matrices, Codes, and Transforms

8.2.1 Introduction to Hadamard Matrices

A Hadamard matrix of order n is an $n \times n$ matrix H_n of ± 1 such that

$$H_n H_n^T = nI.$$

That is, by normalizing H_n by $1/\sqrt{n}$ an orthogonal matrix is obtained. The distinct columns of H are pairwise orthogonal, as are the rows. Some examples of Hadamard matrices are:

$$H_1 = \begin{bmatrix} 1 \end{bmatrix} \quad H_2 = \begin{bmatrix} 1 & 1 \\ 1 & -1 \end{bmatrix} \quad H_4 = \begin{bmatrix} 1 & 1 & 1 & 1 \\ 1 & -1 & 1 & -1 \\ 1 & 1 & -1 & -1 \\ 1 & -1 & -1 & 1 \end{bmatrix}$$

$$H_8 = \begin{bmatrix} 1 & 1 & 1 & 1 & 1 & 1 & 1 & 1 \\ 1 & -1 & 1 & -1 & 1 & -1 & 1 & -1 \\ 1 & 1 & -1 & -1 & 1 & 1 & -1 & -1 \\ 1 & -1 & -1 & 1 & 1 & -1 & -1 & 1 \\ 1 & 1 & 1 & 1 & -1 & -1 & -1 & -1 \\ 1 & -1 & 1 & -1 & -1 & 1 & -1 & 1 \\ 1 & 1 & -1 & -1 & -1 & -1 & 1 & 1 \\ 1 & -1 & -1 & 1 & -1 & 1 & 1 & -1 \end{bmatrix}. \tag{8.1}$$

The operation of computing $\mathbf{r} H_n$, where $\mathbf{r}$ is a row vector of length n, is sometimes called computing the **Hadamard transform** of $\mathbf{r}$. As we show in Section 8.3.3, there are fast algorithms for computing the Hadamard transform which are useful for decoding certain Reed–Muller codes (among other things). Furthermore, the Hadamard matrices can be used to define some error-correction codes.

It is clear that multiplying a row or a column of H_n by -1 produces another Hadamard matrix. By a sequence of such operations, a Hadamard matrix can be obtained which has the first row and the first column equal to all ones. Such a matrix is said to be normalized.

Some of the operations associated with Hadamard matrices can be expressed using the Kronecker product.

Definition 8.1 The **Kronecker product** $A \otimes B$ of an $m \times n$ matrix A with a $p \times q$ matrix B is the $mp \times nq$ obtained by replacing every element a_{ij} of A with the matrix $a_{ij}B$. The Kronecker product is associative and distributive, but not commutative. $\square$

Error Correction Coding: Mathematical Methods and Algorithms, Second Edition. Todd K. Moon
© 2021 John Wiley & Sons, Inc. Published 2021 by John Wiley & Sons, Inc.
Companion website: www.wiley.com/go/Moon/ErrorCorrectionCoding

Example 8.2   Let

$$A = \begin{bmatrix} a_{11} & a_{12} & a_{13} \\ a_{21} & a_{22} & a_{23} \end{bmatrix} \quad \text{and} \quad B = \begin{bmatrix} b_{11} & b_{12} \\ b_{21} & b_{22} \end{bmatrix}.$$

Then

$$A \otimes B = \begin{bmatrix} a_{11}b_{11} & a_{11}b_{12} & a_{12}b_{11} & a_{12}b_{12} & a_{13}b_{11} & a_{13}b_{12} \\ a_{11}b_{21} & a_{11}b_{22} & a_{12}b_{21} & a_{12}b_{22} & a_{13}b_{21} & a_{13}b_{22} \\ a_{21}b_{11} & a_{21}b_{12} & a_{22}b_{11} & a_{22}b_{12} & a_{23}b_{11} & a_{23}b_{12} \\ a_{21}b_{21} & a_{21}b_{22} & a_{22}b_{21} & a_{22}b_{22} & a_{23}b_{21} & a_{23}b_{22} \end{bmatrix}.$$

□

Theorem 8.3   *The Kronecker product has the following properties [319, Chapter 9]:*

1. $A \otimes B \neq B \otimes A$ *in general. (The Kronecker product does not commute.)*

2. *For a scalar x, $(xA) \otimes B = A \otimes (xB) = x(A \otimes B)$.*

3. *Distributive properties:*
$$(A + B) \otimes C = (A \otimes C) + (B \otimes C).$$

$$A \otimes (B + C) = (A \otimes B) + (A \otimes C).$$

4. *Associative property: $(A \otimes B) \otimes C = A \otimes (B \otimes C)$.*

5. *Transposes: $(A \otimes B)^T = A^T \otimes B^T$.*

6. *Trace (for square A and B): $\mathrm{tr}(A \otimes B) = \mathrm{tr}(A)\mathrm{tr}(B)$.*

7. *If A is diagonal and B is diagonal, then $A \otimes B$ is diagonal.*

8. *Determinant, where A is $m \times m$ and B is $n \times n$: $\det(A \otimes B) = \det(A)^n \det(B)^m$.*

9. *The Kronecker product theorem:*

$$(A \otimes B)(C \otimes D) = (AC) \otimes (BD), \tag{8.2}$$

provided that the matrices are shaped such that the indicated products are allowed.

10. *Inverses: If A and B are nonsingular, then $A \otimes B$ is nonsingular and*

$$(A \otimes B)^{-1} = A^{-1} \otimes B^{-1}. \tag{8.3}$$

Returning now to Hadamard matrices, it may be observed that the Hadamard matrices in (8.1) have the structure

$$H_{2n} = H_2 \otimes H_n = \begin{bmatrix} H_n & H_n \\ H_n & -H_n \end{bmatrix}.$$

This works in general:

Theorem 8.4   *If H_n is a Hadamard matrix, then so is $H_{2n} = H_2 \otimes H_n$.*

Proof   By the properties of the Kronecker product,

$$H_{2n}H_{2n}^T = (H_2 \otimes H_n)(H_2 \otimes H_n)^T = H_2 H_2^T \otimes H_n H_n^T = (2I_2) \otimes (nI_n)$$
$$= 2n(I_2 \otimes I_n) = 2nI_{2n}.$$

□

This construction of Hadamard matrices is referred to as the Sylvester construction. By this construction, Hadamard matrices of sizes 1, 2, 4, 8, 16, 32, etc., exist. However, unless a Hadamard matrix of size 6 exists, for example, then this construction cannot be used to construct a Hadamard matrix of size 12. As the following theorem indicates, there is no Hadamard matrix of size 6.

Theorem 8.5 *A Hadamard matrix must have an order that is either 1, 2, or a multiple of 4.*

Proof [292, p. 44] Suppose without loss of generality that H_n is normalized. By column permutations, we can put the first three rows of H_n in the following form:

$$
\begin{array}{cccc}
\underbrace{\begin{matrix}1 & 1 & \cdots & 1\\ 1 & 1 & \cdots & 1\\ 1 & 1 & \cdots & 1\end{matrix}}_{i} &
\underbrace{\begin{matrix}1 & 1 & \cdots & 1\\ 1 & 1 & \cdots & 1\\ -1 & -1 & \cdots & -1\end{matrix}}_{j} &
\underbrace{\begin{matrix}1 & 1 & \cdots & 1\\ -1 & -1 & \cdots & -1\\ 1 & 1 & \cdots & 1\end{matrix}}_{k} &
\underbrace{\begin{matrix}1 & 1 & \cdots & 1\\ -1 & -1 & \cdots & -1\\ -1 & -1 & \cdots & -1\end{matrix}}_{l}
\end{array}
$$

For example, j is the number of columns such that the first two rows of H_n have ones while the third row has negative ones. Since the rows are orthogonal, we have

$$i+j-k-l=0 \qquad \text{(inner product of row 1 with row 2)}$$
$$i-j+k-l=0 \qquad \text{(inner product of row 1 with row 3)}$$
$$i-j-k+l=0 \qquad \text{(inner product of row 2 with row 3),}$$

which collectively imply $i=j=k=l$. Thus, $n=4i$, so n must be a multiple of 4. (If $n=1$ or 2, then there are not three rows to consider.) $\qquad\square$

This theorem does not exclude the possibility of a Hadamard matrix of order 12. However, it cannot be obtained by the Sylvester construction.

8.2.2 The Paley Construction of Hadamard Matrices

Another method of constructing Hadamard matrices is by the Paley construction, which employs some number-theoretic concepts. This allows, for example, creation of the Hadamard matrix H_{12}. While in practice Hadamard matrices of order 4^k are most frequently employed, the Paley construction introduces the important concepts of quadratic residues and the Legendre symbol, both of which have application to other error- correction codes.

Definition 8.6 For all numbers a such that $(a,p)=1$, the number a is called a **quadratic residue** modulo p if the congruence $x^2 \equiv a \pmod{p}$ has some solution x. That is to say, a is the square of some number, modulo p. If a is not a quadratic residue, then a is called a **quadratic nonresidue**. $\qquad\square$

If a is a quadratic residue modulo p, then so is $a+p$, so we consider as distinct residues only these which are distinct modulo p.

Example 8.7 The easiest way to find the quadratic residues modulo a prime p is to list the nonzero numbers modulo p, then square them.

Let $p=7$. The set of nonzero numbers modulo p is $\{1,2,3,4,5,6\}$. Squaring these numbers modulo p, we obtain the list $\{1^2,2^2,3^2,4^2,5^2,6^2\}=\{1,4,2,2,4,1\}$. So the quadratic residues modulo 7 are $\{1,2,4\}$. The quadratic nonresidues are $\{3,5,6\}$. The number 9 is a quadratic residue modulo 7, since $9=7+2$, and 2 is a quadratic residue.

Now let $p=11$. Forming the list of squares, we have

$$\{1^2,2^2,3^2,4^2,5^2,6^2,7^2,8^2,9^2,10^2\}=\{1,4,9,5,3,3,5,9,4,1\}.$$

The quadratic residues modulo 11 are $\{1,3,4,5,9\}$. $\qquad\square$

Theorem 8.8 *Quadratic residues have the following properties:*

1. *There are $(p-1)/2$ quadratic residues modulo p for an odd prime p.*

2. *The product of two quadratic residues or two quadratic nonresidues is always a quadratic residue. The product of a quadratic residue and a quadratic nonresidue is a quadratic nonresidue.*

3. *If p is of the form $4k+1$, then -1 is a quadratic residue modulo p. If p is of the form $4k+3$, then -1 is a nonresidue modulo p.*

The Legendre symbol is a number-theoretic function associated with quadratic residues.

Definition 8.9 Let p be an odd prime. The **Legendre symbol** $\chi_p(x)$ is defined as

$$\chi_p(x) = \begin{cases} 0 & \text{if } x \text{ is a multiple of } p \\ 1 & \text{if } x \text{ is a quadratic residue modulo } p \\ -1 & \text{if } x \text{ is a quadratic nonresidue modulo } p. \end{cases}$$

The Legendre symbol $\chi_p(x)$ is also denoted as $\left(\frac{x}{p}\right)$.   □

Example 8.10 Let $p = 7$. The Legendre symbol values are

x:	0	1	2	3	4	5	6
$\chi_7(x)$:	0	1	1	-1	1	-1	-1

When $p = 11$, the Legendre symbol values are

x:	0	1	2	3	4	5	6	7	8	9	10
$\chi_{11}(x)$:	0	1	-1	1	1	1	-1	-1	-1	1	-1

□

The key to the Paley construction of Hadamard matrices is the following theorem.

Lemma 8.11 *[292, p. 46] For any $c \not\equiv 0 \pmod{p}$, where p is an odd prime,*

$$\sum_{b=0}^{p-1} \chi_p(b)\chi_p(b+c) = -1. \tag{8.4}$$

Proof From Theorem 8.8 and the definition of the Legendre symbol, $\chi_p(xy) = \chi_p(x)\chi_p(y)$. Since $b = 0$ contributes nothing to the sum in (8.4), suppose $b \neq 0$. Let $z \equiv (b+c)b^{-1} \pmod{p}$. As b runs from $1, 2, \ldots, p-1$, z takes on distinct values in $0, 2, 3, \ldots, p-1$, but not the value 1. Then

$$\sum_{b=0}^{p-1} \chi_p(b)\chi_p(b+c) = \sum_{b=1}^{p-1} \chi_p(b)\chi_p(bz) = \sum_{b=1}^{p-1} \chi_p(b)\chi_p(b)\chi_p(z) = \sum_{b=1}^{p-1} \chi_p(b)^2 \chi_p(z)$$

$$= \sum_{z=0}^{p-1} \chi_p(z) - \chi_p(1) = 0 - \chi_p(1) = -1,$$

where the last equality follows since half of the numbers z from 0 to $p-1$ have $\chi_p(z) = -1$ and the other half $\chi_p(z) = 1$, by Theorem 8.8.   □

With this background, we can now define the Paley construction.

1. First, construct the $p \times p$ *Jacobsthal matrix* J_p, with elements q_{ij} given by $q_{ij} = \chi_p(j - i)$ (with zero-based indexing). Note that the first row of the matrix is $\chi_p(j)$, which is just the Legendre symbol sequence. The other rows are obtained by cyclic shifting. Note that each row and column of J_p sums to 0 since each row contains $(p - 1)/2$ elements of 1 and $(p - 1)/2$ elements of -1, and that $J_p + J_p^T = \mathbf{0}$.

2. Second, form the matrix

$$H_{p+1} = \begin{bmatrix} 1 & \mathbf{1}^T \\ \mathbf{1} & J_p - I_p \end{bmatrix},$$

where $\mathbf{1}$ is a column vector of length p containing all ones.

Example 8.12 Let $p = 7$. For the first row of the matrix, see Example 8.10.

$$J_7 = \begin{bmatrix} 0 & 1 & 1 & -1 & 1 & -1 & -1 \\ -1 & 0 & 1 & 1 & -1 & 1 & -1 \\ -1 & -1 & 0 & 1 & 1 & -1 & 1 \\ 1 & -1 & -1 & 0 & 1 & 1 & -1 \\ -1 & 1 & -1 & -1 & 0 & 1 & 1 \\ 1 & -1 & 1 & -1 & -1 & 0 & 1 \\ 1 & 1 & -1 & 1 & -1 & -1 & 0 \end{bmatrix} \quad H_8 = \begin{bmatrix} 1 & 1 & 1 & 1 & 1 & 1 & 1 & 1 \\ 1 & -1 & 1 & 1 & -1 & 1 & -1 & -1 \\ 1 & -1 & -1 & 1 & 1 & -1 & 1 & -1 \\ 1 & -1 & -1 & -1 & 1 & 1 & -1 & 1 \\ 1 & 1 & -1 & -1 & -1 & 1 & 1 & -1 \\ 1 & -1 & 1 & -1 & -1 & -1 & 1 & 1 \\ 1 & 1 & -1 & 1 & -1 & -1 & -1 & 1 \\ 1 & 1 & 1 & -1 & 1 & -1 & -1 & -1 \end{bmatrix}.$$

□

Example 8.13 We now show the construction of H_{12}. The 11×11 Jacobsthal matrix is

$$J_{11} = \begin{bmatrix} 0 & 1 & -1 & 1 & 1 & 1 & -1 & -1 & -1 & 1 & -1 \\ -1 & 0 & 1 & -1 & 1 & 1 & 1 & -1 & -1 & -1 & 1 \\ 1 & -1 & 0 & 1 & -1 & 1 & 1 & 1 & -1 & -1 & -1 \\ -1 & 1 & -1 & 0 & 1 & -1 & 1 & 1 & 1 & -1 & -1 \\ -1 & -1 & 1 & -1 & 0 & 1 & -1 & 1 & 1 & 1 & -1 \\ -1 & -1 & -1 & 1 & -1 & 0 & 1 & -1 & 1 & 1 & 1 \\ 1 & -1 & -1 & -1 & 1 & -1 & 0 & 1 & -1 & 1 & 1 \\ 1 & 1 & -1 & -1 & -1 & 1 & -1 & 0 & 1 & -1 & 1 \\ 1 & 1 & 1 & -1 & -1 & -1 & 1 & -1 & 0 & 1 & -1 \\ -1 & 1 & 1 & 1 & -1 & -1 & -1 & 1 & -1 & 0 & 1 \\ 1 & -1 & 1 & 1 & 1 & -1 & -1 & -1 & 1 & -1 & 0 \end{bmatrix}$$

and the Hadamard matrix is

$$H_{12} = \begin{bmatrix} 1 & 1 & 1 & 1 & 1 & 1 & 1 & 1 & 1 & 1 & 1 & 1 \\ 1 & -1 & 1 & -1 & 1 & 1 & 1 & -1 & -1 & -1 & 1 & -1 \\ 1 & -1 & -1 & 1 & -1 & 1 & 1 & 1 & -1 & -1 & -1 & 1 \\ 1 & 1 & -1 & -1 & 1 & -1 & 1 & 1 & 1 & -1 & -1 & -1 \\ 1 & -1 & 1 & -1 & -1 & 1 & -1 & 1 & 1 & 1 & -1 & -1 \\ 1 & -1 & -1 & 1 & -1 & -1 & 1 & -1 & 1 & 1 & 1 & -1 \\ 1 & -1 & -1 & -1 & 1 & -1 & -1 & 1 & -1 & 1 & 1 & 1 \\ 1 & 1 & -1 & -1 & -1 & 1 & -1 & -1 & 1 & -1 & 1 & 1 \\ 1 & 1 & 1 & -1 & -1 & -1 & 1 & -1 & -1 & 1 & -1 & 1 \\ 1 & 1 & 1 & 1 & -1 & -1 & -1 & 1 & -1 & -1 & 1 & -1 \\ 1 & -1 & 1 & 1 & 1 & -1 & -1 & -1 & 1 & -1 & -1 & 1 \\ 1 & 1 & -1 & 1 & 1 & 1 & -1 & -1 & -1 & 1 & -1 & -1 \end{bmatrix}. \qquad (8.5)$$

□

The following lemma establishes that the Paley construction gives a Hadamard matrix.

Lemma 8.14 *Let J_p be a $p \times p$ Jacobsthal matrix. Then $J_p J_p^T = pI - U$ and $J_p U = U J_p = \mathbf{0}$, where U is the matrix of all ones.*

Proof Let $P = J_p J_p^T$. Then

$$p_{ii} = \sum_{k=0}^{p-1} q_{ik}^2 = p - 1 \quad \text{(since } \chi_p^2(x) = 1 \text{ for } x \neq 0)$$

$$p_{ij} = \sum_{k=0}^{p-1} q_{ik} q_{jk} = \sum_{k=0}^{p-1} \chi_p(k-i)\chi_p(k-j)$$

$$= \sum_{b=0}^{p-1} \chi_p(b)\chi_p(b+c) = -1 \quad \text{(subs. } b = k - i, c = i - j, \text{ then use Lemma 8.11).}$$

Also, $J_p U = \mathbf{0}$ since each row contains $(p-1)/2$ elements of 1 and $(p-1)/2$ elements of -1.   □

Now

$$H_{p+1} H_{p+1}^T = \begin{bmatrix} 1 & \mathbf{1}^T \\ \mathbf{1} & J_p - I \end{bmatrix} \begin{bmatrix} 1 & \mathbf{1}^T \\ \mathbf{1} & J_p^T - I \end{bmatrix} = \begin{bmatrix} p+1 & \mathbf{0} \\ \mathbf{0} & U + (J_p - I)(J_p^T - I) \end{bmatrix}.$$

It can be shown that $J_p + J_p^T = \mathbf{0}$. So using Lemma 8.14, $U + (J_p - I)(J_p^T - I) = U + pI - U - J_p - J_p^T + I = (p+1)I$. So $H_{p+1} H_{p+1}^T = (p+1)I_{p+1}$.

8.2.3 Hadamard Codes

Let A_n be the binary matrix obtained by replacing the 1s in a Hadamard matrix with 0s, and replacing the -1s with 1s. We have the following code constructions:

- By the orthogonality of H_n, any pair of distinct rows of A_n must agree in $n/2$ places and differ in $n/2$ places. Deleting the left column of A_n (since these bits are all the same and do not contribute anything to the code), the rows of the resulting matrix form a code of length $n - 1$ called the **Hadamard code**, denoted $\mathcal{A}_n$, having n codewords and minimum distance $n/2$. This is also known as the **simplex code**.

- By including the binary-complements of all codewords in $\mathcal{A}_n$, we obtain the code $\mathcal{B}_n$ which has $2n$ codewords of length $n - 1$ and a minimum distance of $n/2 - 1$.

- Starting from A_n again, if we adjoin the binary complements of the rows of A_n, we obtain a code with code length n, $2n$ codewords, and minimum distance $n/2$. This code is denoted $\mathcal{C}$.

This book does not treat many nonlinear codes. However, if any of these codes are constructed using a Paley matrix with $n > 8$, then the codes are nonlinear. (The linear span of the nonlinear code is a quadratic residue code.) Interestingly, if the Paley Hadamard matrix is used in the construction of $\mathcal{A}_n$ or $\mathcal{B}_n$, then the codes are cyclic, but not necessarily linear. If the codes are constructed from Hadamard matrices constructed using the Sylvester construction, the codes are linear.

8.3 Reed–Muller Codes

Reed–Muller codes were among the first codes to be deployed in space applications, being used in the deep space probes flown from 1969 to 1977 [483, p. 149]. They were probably the first family of codes to provide a mechanism for obtaining a desired minimum distance. And, while they have been largely displaced by Reed–Solomon codes in volume of practice, they have a fast maximum likelihood decoding algorithm which is still very attractive. They are also used as components in several other systems. Furthermore, there are a variety of constructions for Reed–Muller codes which has made them useful in many theoretical developments.

8.3.1 Boolean Functions

Reed–Muller codes are closely tied to functions of Boolean variables and can be described as multinomials over the field $GF(2)$ [362]. Consider a Boolean function of m variables, $f(v_1, v_2, \ldots, v_m)$, which is a mapping from the vector space V_m of binary m-tuples to the binary numbers $\{0, 1\}$. Such functions can be represented using a *truth table*, which is an exhaustive listing of the input/output values. Boolean functions can also be written in terms of the variables.

Example 8.15 The table below is a truth table for two functions of the variables v_1, v_2, v_3, and v_4.

$$
\begin{array}{l}
v_4 = 0\ 0\ 0\ 0\ 0\ 0\ 0\ 0\ 1\ 1\ 1\ 1\ 1\ 1\ 1\ 1 \\
v_3 = 0\ 0\ 0\ 0\ 1\ 1\ 1\ 1\ 0\ 0\ 0\ 0\ 1\ 1\ 1\ 1 \\
v_2 = 0\ 0\ 1\ 1\ 0\ 0\ 1\ 1\ 0\ 0\ 1\ 1\ 0\ 0\ 1\ 1 \\
v_1 = 0\ 1\ 0\ 1\ 0\ 1\ 0\ 1\ 0\ 1\ 0\ 1\ 0\ 1\ 0\ 1 \\
\hline
f_1 = 0\ 1\ 1\ 0\ 1\ 0\ 0\ 1\ 1\ 0\ 0\ 1\ 0\ 1\ 1\ 0 \\
\hline
f_2 = 1\ 1\ 1\ 1\ 1\ 0\ 0\ 1\ 1\ 0\ 1\ 0\ 1\ 1\ 0\ 0
\end{array}
$$

It can be verified (using, e.g., methods from elementary digital logic design) that

$$f_1(v_1, v_2, v_3, v_4) = v_1 + v_2 + v_3 + v_4$$

and that

$$f_2(v_1, v_2, v_3, v_4) = 1 + v_1 v_4 + v_1 v_3 + v_2 v_3.$$

□

The columns of the truth table can be numbered from 0 to $2^m - 1$ using a base-2 representation with v_1 as the least-significant bit. Then without ambiguity, the functions can be represented simply using their bit strings. From Example 8.15,

$$\mathbf{f}_1 = (0110100110010110)$$

$$\mathbf{f}_2 = (1111100110101100).$$

The number of distinct Boolean functions in m variables is the number of distinct binary sequences of length 2^m, which is 2^{2^m}. The set M of all Boolean functions in m variables forms a vector space that has a basis

$$\{1, v_1, v_2, \ldots, v_m, v_1 v_2, v_1 v_3, \ldots, v_{m-1} v_m, \ldots, v_1 v_2 v_3 \cdots v_m\}.$$

Every function f in this space can be represented as a linear combination of these basis functions:

$$f = a_0 1 + a_1 v_1 + a_2 v_2 + \cdots + a_m v_m + a_{12} v_1 v_2 + \cdots + a_{12 \ldots m} v_1 v_2 \cdots v_m.$$

Functional and vector notation can be used interchangeably. Here are some examples of some basic functions and their vector representations:

$$1 \leftrightarrow \mathbf{1} = 1111111111111111$$

$$v_1 \leftrightarrow \mathbf{v}_1 = 0101010101010101$$

$$v_2 \leftrightarrow \mathbf{v}_2 = 0011001100110011$$

$$v_3 \leftrightarrow \mathbf{v}_3 = 0000111100001111$$

$$v_4 \leftrightarrow \mathbf{v}_4 = 0000000011111111$$

$$v_1 v_2 \leftrightarrow \mathbf{v}_1 \mathbf{v}_2 = 0001000100010001$$

$$v_1 v_2 v_3 v_4 \leftrightarrow \mathbf{v}_1 \mathbf{v}_2 \mathbf{v}_3 \mathbf{v}_4 = 0000000000000001.$$

As this example demonstrates, juxtaposition of vectors represents the corresponding Boolean "and" function, element by element. A vector representing a function can be written as

$$\mathbf{f} = a_0 \mathbf{1} + a_1 \mathbf{v}_1 + a_2 \mathbf{v}_2 + \cdots + a_m \mathbf{v}_m + a_{12} \mathbf{v}_1 \mathbf{v}_2 + \cdots + a_{12\ldots m} \mathbf{v}_1 \mathbf{v}_2 \cdots \mathbf{v}_m.$$

genrm.cc

8.3.2 Definition of the Reed–Muller Codes

Definition 8.16 [483, p. 151]   The binary Reed–Muller code $RM(r, m)$ of order r and length 2^m consists of all linear combinations of vectors $\mathbf{f}$ associated with Boolean functions f that are monomials of degree $\leq r$ in m variables.   □

Example 8.17   The $RM(1, 3)$ code has length $2^3 = 8$. The monomials of degree ≤ 1 are $\{1, v_1, v_2, v_3\}$, with associated vectors

$$\begin{aligned}
1 &\leftrightarrow \mathbf{1} = (1 \quad 1 \quad 1 \quad 1 \quad 1 \quad 1 \quad 1 \quad 1) \\
v_3 &\leftrightarrow \mathbf{v}_3 = (0 \quad 0 \quad 0 \quad 0 \quad 1 \quad 1 \quad 1 \quad 1) \\
v_2 &\leftrightarrow \mathbf{v}_2 = (0 \quad 0 \quad 1 \quad 1 \quad 0 \quad 0 \quad 1 \quad 1) \\
v_1 &\leftrightarrow \mathbf{v}_1 = (0 \quad 1 \quad 0 \quad 1 \quad 0 \quad 1 \quad 0 \quad 1).
\end{aligned}$$

It is natural to describe the code using a generator matrix having these vectors as rows.

$$G = \begin{bmatrix} 1 & 1 & 1 & 1 & 1 & 1 & 1 & 1 \\ 0 & 0 & 0 & 0 & 1 & 1 & 1 & 1 \\ 0 & 0 & 1 & 1 & 0 & 0 & 1 & 1 \\ 0 & 1 & 0 & 1 & 0 & 1 & 0 & 1 \end{bmatrix}. \tag{8.6}$$

This is an $(8, 4, 4)$ code; it is single-error correcting and double-error detecting. This is also the extended Hamming code (obtained by adding an extra parity bit to the $(7, 4)$ Hamming code).   □

Example 8.18   The $RM(2, 4)$ code has length 16 and is obtained by linear combinations of the monomials up to degree 2, which are

$$\{1, v_1, v_2, v_3, v_4, v_1 v_2, v_1 v_3, v_1 v_4, v_2 v_3, v_2 v_4, v_3 v_4\}$$

with the following corresponding vector representations:

$$\begin{aligned}
\mathbf{1} &= (1 \quad 1 \quad 1 \quad 1 \quad 1 \quad 1 \quad 1 \quad 1 \quad 1 \quad 1 \quad 1 \quad 1 \quad 1 \quad 1 \quad 1 \quad 1) \\[4pt]
\mathbf{v}_4 &= (0 \quad 0 \quad 0 \quad 0 \quad 0 \quad 0 \quad 0 \quad 0 \quad 1 \quad 1 \quad 1 \quad 1 \quad 1 \quad 1 \quad 1 \quad 1) \\
\mathbf{v}_3 &= (0 \quad 0 \quad 0 \quad 0 \quad 1 \quad 1 \quad 1 \quad 1 \quad 0 \quad 0 \quad 0 \quad 0 \quad 1 \quad 1 \quad 1 \quad 1) \\
\mathbf{v}_2 &= (0 \quad 0 \quad 1 \quad 1 \quad 0 \quad 0 \quad 1 \quad 1 \quad 0 \quad 0 \quad 1 \quad 1 \quad 0 \quad 0 \quad 1 \quad 1) \\
\mathbf{v}_1 &= (0 \quad 1 \quad 0 \quad 1 \quad 0 \quad 1 \quad 0 \quad 1 \quad 0 \quad 1 \quad 0 \quad 1 \quad 0 \quad 1 \quad 0 \quad 1) \\[4pt]
\mathbf{v}_3 \mathbf{v}_4 &= (0 \quad 0 \quad 0 \quad 0 \quad 0 \quad 0 \quad 0 \quad 0 \quad 0 \quad 0 \quad 0 \quad 0 \quad 1 \quad 1 \quad 1 \quad 1) \\
\mathbf{v}_2 \mathbf{v}_4 &= (0 \quad 0 \quad 0 \quad 0 \quad 0 \quad 0 \quad 0 \quad 0 \quad 0 \quad 0 \quad 1 \quad 1 \quad 0 \quad 0 \quad 1 \quad 1) \\
\mathbf{v}_2 \mathbf{v}_3 &= (0 \quad 0 \quad 0 \quad 0 \quad 0 \quad 0 \quad 1 \quad 1 \quad 0 \quad 0 \quad 0 \quad 0 \quad 0 \quad 0 \quad 1 \quad 1) \\
\mathbf{v}_1 \mathbf{v}_4 &= (0 \quad 0 \quad 0 \quad 0 \quad 0 \quad 0 \quad 0 \quad 0 \quad 0 \quad 1 \quad 0 \quad 1 \quad 0 \quad 1 \quad 0 \quad 1) \\
\mathbf{v}_1 \mathbf{v}_3 &= (0 \quad 0 \quad 0 \quad 0 \quad 0 \quad 1 \quad 0 \quad 1 \quad 0 \quad 0 \quad 0 \quad 0 \quad 0 \quad 1 \quad 0 \quad 1) \\
\mathbf{v}_1 \mathbf{v}_2 &= (0 \quad 0 \quad 0 \quad 1 \quad 0 \quad 0 \quad 0 \quad 1 \quad 0 \quad 0 \quad 0 \quad 1 \quad 0 \quad 0 \quad 0 \quad 1).
\end{aligned}$$

This is a $(16, 11)$ code, with minimum distance 4.   □

In general, for an $RM(r, m)$ code, the dimension is

$$k = 1 + \binom{m}{1} + \binom{m}{2} + \cdots + \binom{m}{r}.$$

The codes are linear, but not cyclic.

As the following lemma states, we can recursively construct an $RM(r + 1, m + 1)$ code — twice the length — from an $RM(r, m)$ and $RM(r + 1, m)$ code. In this context, the notation $(\mathbf{f}, \mathbf{g})$ means the *concatenation* of the vectors $\mathbf{f}$ and $\mathbf{g}$.

Lemma 8.19 $RM(r + 1, m + 1) = \{(\mathbf{f}, \mathbf{f} + \mathbf{g}) \text{ for all } \mathbf{f} \in RM(r + 1, m) \text{ and } \mathbf{g} \in RM(r, m)\}$.

Proof The codewords of $RM(r + 1, m + 1)$ are associated with Boolean functions in $m + 1$ variables of degree $\leq r + 1$. If $c(v_1, \ldots, v_{m+1})$ is such a function (i.e., it represents a codeword) we can write it as

$$c(v_1, \ldots, v_{m+1}) = f(v_1, \ldots, v_m) + v_{m+1} g(v_1, \ldots, v_m),$$

where f is a Boolean function in m variables of degree $\leq r + 1$, and hence represents a codeword in $RM(r + 1, m)$, and g is a Boolean function in m variables with degree $\leq r$, representing a Boolean function in $RM(r, m)$. The corresponding functions $\mathbf{f}$ and $\mathbf{g}$ are thus in $RM(r + 1, m)$ and $RM(r, m)$, respectively.

Now let $\tilde{f}(v_1, v_2, \ldots, v_{m+1}) = f(v_1, v_2, \ldots, v_m) + 0 \cdot v_{m+1}$ represent a codeword in $RM(r + 1, m + 1)$ and let $\tilde{g}(v_1, v_2, \ldots, v_{m+1}) = v_{m+1} g(v_1, v_2, \ldots, v_m)$ represent a codeword in $RM(r + 1, m + 1)$. The associated vectors, which are codewords in $RM(r + 1, m + 1)$, are

$$\tilde{\mathbf{f}} = (\mathbf{f}, \mathbf{f}) \quad \text{and} \quad \tilde{\mathbf{g}} = (\mathbf{0}, \mathbf{g}).$$

Their linear combination $(\mathbf{f}, \mathbf{f} + \mathbf{g})$ must therefore also be a codeword in $RM(r + 1, m + 1)$. □

We now use this lemma to compute the minimum distance of an $RM(r, m)$ code.

Theorem 8.20 *The minimum distance of $RM(r, m)$ is 2^{m-r}.*

Proof By induction. When $m = 1$, the $RM(0, 1)$ code is built from the basis $\{1\}$, giving rise to two codewords: it is the length-2 repetition code. In this case, $d_{\min} = 2$. The $RM(1, 1)$ code is built upon the basis vectors $\{1, v_1\}$ and has four codewords of length two: 00, 01, 10, 11. Hence $d_{\min} = 1$.

As an inductive hypothesis, assume that up to m and for $0 \leq r \leq m$ the minimum distance is 2^{m-r}. We will show that $d_{\min}$ for $RM(r, m + 1)$ is 2^{m-r+1}.

Let $\mathbf{f}$ and $\mathbf{f}'$ be in $RM(r, m)$ and let $\mathbf{g}$ and $\mathbf{g}'$ be in $RM(r - 1, m)$. By Lemma 8.19, the vectors $\mathbf{c}_1 = (\mathbf{f}, \mathbf{f} + \mathbf{g})$ and $\mathbf{c}_2 = (\mathbf{f}', \mathbf{f}' + \mathbf{g}')$ must be in $RM(r, m + 1)$.

If $\mathbf{g} = \mathbf{g}'$ then $d(\mathbf{c}_1, \mathbf{c}_2) = d((\mathbf{f}, \mathbf{f} + \mathbf{g}), (\mathbf{f}', \mathbf{f}' + \mathbf{g})) = d((\mathbf{f}, \mathbf{f}), (\mathbf{f}', \mathbf{f}')) = 2d(\mathbf{f}, \mathbf{f}') \geq 2 \cdot 2^{m-r}$ by the inductive hypothesis. If $\mathbf{g} \neq \mathbf{g}'$ then

$$d(\mathbf{c}_1, \mathbf{c}_2) = w(\mathbf{f} - \mathbf{f}') + w(\mathbf{g} - \mathbf{g}' + \mathbf{f} - \mathbf{f}').$$

Claim: $w(\mathbf{x} + \mathbf{y}) \geq w(\mathbf{x}) - w(\mathbf{y})$. Proof: Let w_{xy} be the number of places in which the nonzero digits of $\mathbf{x}$ and $\mathbf{y}$ overlap. Then $w(\mathbf{x} + \mathbf{y}) = (w(\mathbf{x}) - w_{xy}) + (w(\mathbf{y}) - w_{xy})$. But since $2w(\mathbf{y}) \geq 2w_{xy}$, the result follows.

By this result,

$$d(\mathbf{c}_1, \mathbf{c}_2) \geq w(\mathbf{f} - \mathbf{f}') + w(\mathbf{g} - \mathbf{g}') - w(\mathbf{f} - \mathbf{f}') = w(\mathbf{g} - \mathbf{g}').$$

But $\mathbf{g} - \mathbf{g}' \in RM(r - 1, m)$, so that $w(\mathbf{g} - \mathbf{g}') \geq 2^{m-(r-1)} = 2^{m-r+1}$. □

The following theorem is useful in characterizing the duals of RM codes.

Theorem 8.21 *For* $0 \le r \le m - 1$*, the* $RM(m - r - 1, m)$ *code is dual to the* $RM(r, m)$ *code.*

Proof [483, p. 154] Let **a** be a codeword in $RM(m - r - 1, m)$ and let **b** be a codeword in $RM(r, m)$. Associated with **a** is a polynomial $a(v_1, v_2, \ldots, v_m)$ of degree $\le m - r - 1$; associated with **b** is a polynomial $b(v_1, v_2, \ldots, v_m)$ of degree $\le r$. The product polynomial has degree $\le m - 1$, and thus corresponds to a codeword in the $RM(m - 1, m)$ code, with vector representation **ab**. Since the minimum distance of $RM(m - r - 1, m)$ is 2^{r-1} and the minimum distance of $RM(m - 1, m)$ is 2^{m-r}, the codeword **ab** must have even weight. Thus, $\mathbf{a} \cdot \mathbf{b} \equiv 0 \pmod 2$. From this, $RM(m - r - 1, m)$ must be a subset of the dual code to $RM(r, m)$. Note that

$$\dim(RM(r, m)) + \dim(RM(m - r - 1, m))$$

$$= 1 + \binom{m}{1} + \cdots + \binom{m}{r} + 1 + \binom{m}{1} + \binom{m}{2} + \cdots + \binom{m}{m - r - 1}$$

$$= 1 + \binom{m}{1} + \cdots + \binom{m}{r} + \binom{m}{m} + \binom{m}{m-1} + \binom{m}{m-2} + \cdots + \binom{m}{r+1}$$

$$= \sum_{i=0}^{m} \binom{m}{i} = 2^m.$$

By the theorem regarding the dimensionality of dual codes, Theorem 2.64, $RM(m - r - 1, m)$ must be the dual to $RM(r, m)$.   □

It is clear that the weight distribution of $RM(1, m)$ codes is $A_0 = 1$, $A_{2^m} = 1$, and $A_{2^{m-1}} = 2^{m+1} - 2$. Beyond these simple results, the weight distributions are more complicated.

8.3.3 Encoding and Decoding Algorithms for First-Order RM Codes

In this section, we describe algorithms for encoding and decoding $RM(1, m)$ codes, which are $(2^m, m + 1, 2^{m-1})$ codes. In Section 8.3.4, we present algorithms for more general RM codes.

8.3.3.1 Encoding $RM(1, m)$ Codes

Consider the $RM(1, 3)$ code generated by

$$\mathbf{c} = (c_0, c_1, \ldots, c_7) = \mathbf{m}G = (m_0, m_3, m_2, m_1) \begin{bmatrix} \mathbf{1} \\ \mathbf{v}_3 \\ \mathbf{v}_2 \\ \mathbf{v}_1 \end{bmatrix}$$

$$= (m_0, m_3, m_2, m_1) \begin{bmatrix} 1 & 1 & 1 & 1 & 1 & 1 & 1 & 1 \\ 0 & 0 & 0 & 0 & 1 & 1 & 1 & 1 \\ 0 & 0 & 1 & 1 & 0 & 0 & 1 & 1 \\ 0 & 1 & 0 & 1 & 0 & 1 & 0 & 1 \end{bmatrix}.$$

The columns of G consist of the numbers $(1, 0, 0, 0)$ through $(1, 1, 1, 1)$ in increasing binary counting order (with the least-significant bit on the right). This sequence of bit values can thus be obtained using a conventional binary digital counter. A block diagram of an encoding circuit embodying this idea is shown in Figure 8.1.

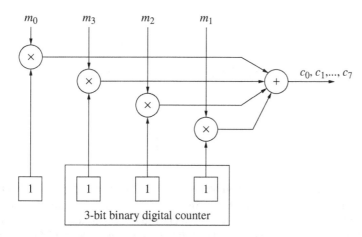

Figure 8.1: An encoder circuit for a $RM(1, 3)$ code.

8.3.3.2 Decoding $RM(1, m)$ Codes

The idea behind the decoder is to compare the received sequence $\mathbf{r}$ with every codeword in $RM(1, m)$ by means of correlation, then to select the codeword with the highest correlation. As we shall show, because of the structure of the code these correlations can be computed using a Hadamard transform. The existence of a fast Hadamard transform algorithms makes this an efficient decoding algorithm.

Let $\mathbf{r} = (r_0, r_1, \ldots, r_{2^m-1})$ be the received sequence, and let $\mathbf{c} = (c_0, c_1, \ldots, c_{2^m-1})$ be a codeword. We note that

$$\sum_{i=0}^{2^m-1} (-1)^{r_i}(-1)^{c_i} = \sum_{i=0}^{2^m-1} (-1)^{r_i+c_i} = \sum_{i=0}^{2^m-1} (-1)^{r_i \oplus c_i}$$
$$= \sum_{i=0}^{2^m-1} (-1)^{d(r_i, c_i)} = 2^m - 2d(\mathbf{r}, \mathbf{c}), \tag{8.7}$$

where $\oplus$ denotes addition modulo 2 and $d(r_i, c_i)$ is the Hamming distance between the arguments. A sequence which minimizes $d(\mathbf{r}, \mathbf{c})$ has the largest number of positive terms in the sum on the right of (8.7) and therefore maximizes the sum.

Let $\mathcal{F}(\mathbf{r})$ be the transformation that converts binary $\{0, 1\}$ elements of $\mathbf{r}$ to binary ± 1 values of a vector $\mathbf{R}$ according to

$$\mathcal{F}(\mathbf{r}) = \mathcal{F}(r_0, r_1, \ldots, r_{2^m-1}) = \mathbf{R} = ((-1)^{r_0}, (-1)^{r_1}, \ldots, (-1)^{r_{2^m-1}}).$$

We refer to $\mathbf{R}$ as the bipolar representation of $\mathbf{r}$. Similarly, define $\mathcal{F}(\mathbf{c}) = \mathbf{C} = (C_0, C_1, \ldots, C_{2^m-1})$. We define the correlation function

$$T = \text{cor}(\mathbf{R}, \mathbf{C}) = \text{cor}((R_0, R_1, \ldots, R_{2^m-1}), (C_0, C_1, \ldots, C_{2^m-1})) = \sum_{i=0}^{2^m-1} R_i C_i.$$

By (8.7), the codeword $\mathbf{c}$ which minimizes $d(\mathbf{r}, \mathbf{c})$ maximizes the correlation $\text{cor}(\mathbf{R}, \mathbf{C})$.

The decoding algorithm is summarized as: Compute $T_i = \text{cor}(\mathbf{R}, \mathbf{C}_i)$, where $\mathbf{C}_i = \mathcal{F}(\mathbf{c}_i)$ for each of the 2^{m+1} codewords, then select that codeword for which $\text{cor}(\mathbf{R}, \mathbf{C}_i)$ is the largest. The simultaneous computation of all the correlations can be represented as a matrix. Let $\mathbf{C}_i$ be represented as a *column* vector and let

$$H = \begin{bmatrix} \mathbf{C}_0 & \mathbf{C}_1 & \cdots & \mathbf{C}_{2^{m+1}-1} \end{bmatrix}.$$

Then all the correlations can be computed by

$$\mathbf{T} = \begin{bmatrix} T_0 & T_1 & \cdots & T_{2^{m+1}-1} \end{bmatrix} = \mathbf{R}H.$$

Recall that the generator matrix for the $RM(1, m)$ code can be written as

$$G = \begin{bmatrix} \mathbf{1} \\ v_m \\ v_{m-1} \\ \vdots \\ v_1 \end{bmatrix}.$$

We actually find it convenient to deal explicitly with those codewords formed as linear combinations of only the vectors $v_1, v_1, \ldots, v_m$, since $\mathbf{1} + \mathbf{c}$ complements all the elements of $\mathbf{c}$, which corresponds to negating the elements of the transform $\mathbf{C}$. We therefore deal with the $2^m \times 2^m$ matrix H_{2^m}. Let us examine one of these matrices in detail. For the $RM(1, 3)$ code with G as in (8.6), the matrix H_8 can be written as

$$H_8 = \begin{array}{c} \begin{array}{cccccccc} 0 & 1 & 2 & 3 & 4 & 5 & 6 & 7 \end{array} \\ \begin{bmatrix} 1 & -1 & 1 & -1 & 1 & -1 & 1 & -1 \\ 1 & 1 & -1 & -1 & 1 & 1 & -1 & -1 \\ 1 & -1 & -1 & 1 & 1 & -1 & -1 & 1 \\ 1 & 1 & 1 & 1 & -1 & -1 & -1 & -1 \\ 1 & -1 & 1 & -1 & -1 & 1 & -1 & 1 \\ 1 & 1 & -1 & -1 & -1 & -1 & 1 & 1 \\ 1 & -1 & -1 & 1 & -1 & 1 & 1 & -1 \end{bmatrix} \end{array}. \tag{8.8}$$

Examination of this reveals that, with this column ordering, column 1 corresponds to $\mathcal{F}(\mathbf{v}_1)$, column 2 corresponds to $\mathcal{F}(\mathbf{v}_2)$, and column 4 corresponds to $\mathcal{F}(\mathbf{v}_3)$. In general, the ith column corresponds to the linear combination of $i_1\mathbf{v}_1 + i_2\mathbf{v}_2 + i_3\mathbf{v}_3$, where i has the binary representation

$$i = i_1 + 2i_2 + 4i_3.$$

We write the binary representation as $i = (i_3, i_2, i_1)_2$. In the general case, for an $2^m \times 2^m$ Hadamard matrix, we place $\mathcal{F}\left(\sum_{j=1}^m i_j\mathbf{v}_j\right)$ in the ith column, where $i = (i_m, i_{m-1}, \ldots, i_1)_2$. The computation $\mathbf{R}H$ is referred to as the **Hadamard transform** of $\mathbf{R}$.

The decoding algorithm can be described as follows:

Algorithm 8.1 Decoding for $RM(1, m)$ Codes

---

1   **Input:** $\mathbf{r} = (r_0, r_1, \ldots, r_{2^m-1})$.
2   **Output:** A maximum-likelihood codeword $\hat{\mathbf{c}}$.
3   **Begin**
4   Find the bipolar representation $\mathbf{R} = \mathcal{F}(\mathbf{r})$.
5   Compute the Hadamard transform $\mathbf{T} = \mathbf{R}H_{2^m} = (t_0, t_1, \ldots, t_{2^m-1})$
6   Find the coordinate t_i with the largest magnitude
7   Let i have the binary expansion $(i_m, i_{m-1}, \ldots, i_1)_2$. ($i_1$ LSB)
8   if$(t_i > 0)$ ($\mathbf{1}$ is not sent)
9       $\hat{\mathbf{c}} = \sum_{j=1}^m i_j\mathbf{v}_j$
10 else ($\mathbf{1}$ is sent – complement all the bits)
11      $\hat{\mathbf{c}} = \mathbf{1} + \sum_{j=1}^m i_j\mathbf{v}_j$
12 end (if)
13 End

Example 8.22 For the $RM(1, 3)$ code, suppose the received vector is

$$\mathbf{r} = [1, 0, 0, 1, 0, 0, 1, 0].$$

The steps of the algorithm follow:

1. Compute the transform: $\mathbf{R} = [-1, 1, 1, -1, 1, 1, -1, 1]$.
2. Compute $\mathbf{T} = \mathbf{R}H = [2, -2, 2, -2, -2, 2, -2, -6]$.
3. The maximum absolute element occurs at $t_7 = -6$, so $i = 7 = (1, 1, 1)_2$.
4. Since $t_7 < 0$, $\mathbf{c} = \mathbf{1} + \mathbf{v}_1 + \mathbf{v}_2 + \mathbf{v}_3 = [1, 0, 0, 1, 0, 1, 1, 0]$.

$\square$

8.3.3.3 Expediting Decoding Using the Fast Hadamard Transform

The main step of the algorithm is the computation of the Hadamard transform $\mathbf{R}H$. This can be considerably expedited by using a *fast Hadamard transform*, applicable to Hadamard matrices obtained via the Sylvester construction. This transform is analogous to the fast Fourier transform (FFT), but is over the set of numbers ± 1. It is built on some facts from linear algebra.

As we have seen, Sylvester Hadamard can be built by

$$H_{2^m} = H_2 \otimes H_{2^{m-1}}. \tag{8.9}$$

This gives the following factorization.

Theorem 8.23 *The matrix* H_{2^m} *can be written as*

$$H_{2^m} = M_{2^m}^{(1)} M_{2^m}^{(2)} \cdots M_{2^m}^{(m)}, \tag{8.10}$$

where

$$M_{2^m}^{(i)} = I_{2^{m-i}} \otimes H_2 \otimes I_{2^{i-1}},$$

and where I_p *is a* $p \times p$ *identity matrix.*

Proof By induction. When $m = 1$ the result holds, as may be easily verified. Assume, then, that (8.10) holds for m. We find that

$$
\begin{aligned}
M_{2^{m+1}}^{(i)} &= I_{2^{m+1-i}} \otimes H_2 \otimes I_{2^{i-1}} \\
&= (I_2 \otimes I_{2^{m-i}}) \otimes H_2 \otimes I_{2^{i-1}} \quad \text{(by the structure of the identity matrix)} \\
&= I_2 \otimes (I_{2^{m-i}} \otimes H_2 \otimes I_{2^{i-1}}) \qquad\qquad \text{(associativity)} \\
&= I_2 \otimes M_{2^m}^{(i)} \qquad\qquad\qquad\qquad\qquad \text{(definition)}.
\end{aligned}
$$

Furthermore, by the definition, $M_{2^{m+1}}^{m+1} = H_2 \otimes I_{2^m}$. We have

$$
\begin{aligned}
H_{2^{m+1}} &= M_{2^{m+1}}^{(1)} M_{2^{m+1}}^{(2)} \cdots M_{2^{m+1}}^{(m+1)} \\
&= \left(I_2 \otimes M_{2^m}^{(1)} \right) \left(I_2 \otimes M_{2^m}^{(2)} \right) \cdots \left(I_2 \otimes M_{2^m}^{(m)} \right) (H_2 \otimes I_{2^m}) \\
&= (I_2^m H_2) \otimes \left(M_{2^m}^{(1)} M_{2^m}^{(2)} \cdots M_{2^m}^{(m)} \right) \quad \text{(Kronecker product theorem 8.2)} \\
&= H_2 \otimes H_{2^m}.
\end{aligned}
$$

$\square$

hadex.m

Example 8.24 By the theorem, we have the factorization

$$H_8 = M_8^{(1)} M_8^{(2)} M_8^{(3)} = (I_{2^2} \otimes H_2 \otimes I_{2^0})(I_{2^1} \otimes H_2 \otimes I_{2^1})(I_{2^0} \otimes H_2 \otimes I_{2^2}).$$

Straightforward substitution and multiplication show that this gives the matrix H_8 in (8.8).

Let $\mathbf{R} = [R_0, R_1, \ldots, R_7]$. Then the Hadamard transform can be written

$$\mathbf{T} = \mathbf{R} H_8 = \mathbf{R}(M_8^{(1)} M_8^{(2)} M_8^{(3)}) = \mathbf{R}(I_{2^2} \otimes H_2 \otimes I_{2^0})(I_{2^1} \otimes H_2 \otimes I_{2^1})(I_{2^0} \otimes H_2 \otimes I_{2^2}).$$

The matrices involved are

$$M_8^{(1)} = I_4 \otimes H_2 = \begin{bmatrix} 1 & 1 & & & & & & \\ 1 & -1 & & & & & & \\ & & 1 & 1 & & & & \\ & & 1 & -1 & & & & \\ & & & & 1 & 1 & & \\ & & & & 1 & -1 & & \\ & & & & & & 1 & 1 \\ & & & & & & 1 & -1 \end{bmatrix}$$

$$M_8^{(2)} = I_2 \otimes H_2 \otimes I_2 = \begin{bmatrix} 1 & 0 & 1 & 0 & & & & \\ 0 & 1 & 0 & 1 & & & & \\ 1 & 0 & -1 & 0 & & & & \\ 0 & 1 & 0 & -1 & & & & \\ & & & & 1 & 0 & 1 & 0 \\ & & & & 0 & 1 & 0 & 1 \\ & & & & 1 & 0 & -1 & 0 \\ & & & & 0 & 1 & 0 & -1 \end{bmatrix}$$

$$M_8^{(3)} = H_2 \otimes I_4 = \begin{bmatrix} 1 & & & & 1 & & & \\ & 1 & & & & 1 & & \\ & & 1 & & & & 1 & \\ & & & 1 & & & & 1 \\ 1 & & & & -1 & & & \\ & 1 & & & & -1 & & \\ & & 1 & & & & -1 & \\ & & & 1 & & & & -1 \end{bmatrix}.$$

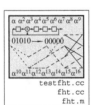

testfht.cc
fht.cc
fht.m

Let $\mathbf{P}^{[0]} = \mathbf{R}$ and let $\mathbf{P}^{[k+1]} = \mathbf{P}^{[k]} M_8^{(k+1)}$. The stages of transform can be written

$$\mathbf{T} = (\mathbf{R} M_8^{(1)}) M_8^{(2)} M_8^{(3)} = (\mathbf{P}^{(1)} M_8^{(2)}) M_8^{(3)} = \mathbf{P}^{(2)} M_8^{(3)} = \mathbf{P}^{(3)}.$$

Figure 8.2 shows the flow diagram corresponding to the matrix multiplications, where arrows indicate the direction of flow, arrows incident along a line imply addition, and the coefficients -1 along the horizontal branches indicate the gain along their respective branch. At each stage, the two-point Hadamard transform is apparent. (At the first stage, the operations of H_2 are enclosed in the box to highlight the operation.) The interleaving of the various stages by virtue of the Kronecker product is similar to the "butterfly" pattern of the FFT. $\quad\square$

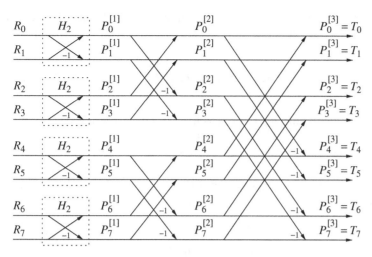

Figure 8.2: Signal flow diagram for the fast Hadamard transform.

The conventional computation of the Hadamard transform $\mathbf{R}H_{2^m}$ produces 2^m elements, each of which requires 2^m addition/subtraction operations, for a total complexity of $(2^m)^2$. The fast Hadamard transform has m stages, each of which requires 2^m addition/subtraction operations, for a total complexity of $m2^m$. This is still exponential in m (typical for maximum likelihood decoding), but much lower than brute force evaluation. Furthermore, as Figure 8.2 suggests, parallel/pipelined hardware architectures are possible.

The $RM(1,m)$ decoding algorithm employing the fast Hadamard transform is referred to as the "Green machine," after its developer at the Jet Propulsion Laboratory for the 1969 Mariner mission [483].

8.3.4 The Reed Decoding Algorithm for $RM(r,m)$ Codes, $r \geq 1$

Efficient decoding algorithms for general RM codes rely upon the concept of *majority logic* decoding, in which multiple estimates of a bit value are obtained, and the decoded value is that value which occurs in the majority of estimates. We demonstrate this first for a $RM(2,4)$ code, then develop a notation to extend this to other $RM(r,m)$ codes.

8.3.4.1 Details for an $RM(2,4)$ Code

Let us write the generator for the $RM(2,4)$ code as

$$
G = \left[\begin{array}{cccccccccccccccc}
1 & 1 & 1 & 1 & 1 & 1 & 1 & 1 & 1 & 1 & 1 & 1 & 1 & 1 & 1 & 1 \\
\hline
0 & 0 & 0 & 0 & 0 & 0 & 0 & 0 & 1 & 1 & 1 & 1 & 1 & 1 & 1 & 1 \\
0 & 0 & 0 & 0 & 1 & 1 & 1 & 1 & 0 & 0 & 0 & 0 & 1 & 1 & 1 & 1 \\
0 & 0 & 1 & 1 & 0 & 0 & 1 & 1 & 0 & 0 & 1 & 1 & 0 & 0 & 1 & 1 \\
0 & 1 & 0 & 1 & 0 & 1 & 0 & 1 & 0 & 1 & 0 & 1 & 0 & 1 & 0 & 1 \\
\hline
0 & 0 & 0 & 0 & 0 & 0 & 0 & 0 & 0 & 0 & 0 & 0 & 1 & 1 & 1 & 1 \\
0 & 0 & 0 & 0 & 0 & 0 & 0 & 0 & 0 & 0 & 1 & 1 & 0 & 0 & 1 & 1 \\
0 & 0 & 0 & 0 & 0 & 0 & 1 & 1 & 0 & 0 & 0 & 0 & 0 & 0 & 1 & 1 \\
0 & 0 & 0 & 0 & 0 & 0 & 0 & 0 & 0 & 1 & 0 & 1 & 0 & 1 & 0 & 1 \\
0 & 0 & 0 & 0 & 0 & 1 & 0 & 1 & 0 & 0 & 0 & 0 & 0 & 1 & 0 & 1 \\
0 & 0 & 0 & 1 & 0 & 0 & 0 & 1 & 0 & 0 & 0 & 1 & 0 & 0 & 0 & 1
\end{array}\right] = \left[\begin{array}{c}
\mathbf{1} \\
\hline
v_4 \\
v_3 \\
v_2 \\
v_1 \\
\hline
v_3 v_4 \\
v_2 v_4 \\
\vdots \\
v_1 v_2
\end{array}\right] = \left[\begin{array}{c}
G_0 \\
\hline
G_1 \\
\hline
G_2
\end{array}\right].
$$

We partition the 11 input bits to correspond to the rows of this matrix as

$$\mathbf{m} = (m_0, m_4, m_3, m_2, m_1, m_{34}, m_{24}, \ldots, m_{12}) = (\mathbf{m}_0, \mathbf{m}_1, \mathbf{m}_2).$$

Thus, the bits in $\mathbf{m}_0$ are associated with the zeroth-order term, the $\mathbf{m}_1$ bits are associated with the first-order terms, and the second-order terms are associated with $\mathbf{m}_2$. The encoding operation is

$$\mathbf{c} = (c_0, c_1, c_2, \ldots, c_{15}) = \mathbf{m}G = [\mathbf{m}_0, \mathbf{m}_1, \mathbf{m}_2] \begin{bmatrix} G_0 \\ G_1 \\ G_2 \end{bmatrix} = \mathbf{m}_0 G_0 + \mathbf{m}_1 G_1 + \mathbf{m}_2 G_2. \qquad (8.11)$$

The general operation of the algorithm is as follows: Given a received vector $\mathbf{r}$, estimates are first obtained for the highest-order block of message bits, $\mathbf{m}_2$. Then $\mathbf{m}_2 G_2$ is subtracted off from $\mathbf{r}$, leaving only lower-order codewords. Then the message bits for $\mathbf{m}_1$ are obtained, then are subtracted, and so forth.

The key to finding the message bits comes from writing *multiple* equations for the same quantity and taking a majority vote. Selecting coded bits from (8.11), we have

$$c_0 = m_0$$
$$c_1 = m_0 + m_1$$
$$c_2 = m_0 + m_2$$
$$c_3 = m_0 + m_1 + m_2 + m_{12}.$$

Adding these code bits together (modulo 2), we obtain an equation for the message bit m_{12}:

$$c_0 + c_1 + c_2 + c_3 = m_{12}.$$

We can similarly obtain three other equations for the message bit m_{12},

$$c_4 + c_5 + c_6 + c_7 = m_{12}$$
$$c_8 + c_9 + c_{10} + c_{11} = m_{12}$$
$$c_{12} + c_{13} + c_{14} + c_{15} = m_{12}.$$

Given the code bits $c_0, \ldots, c_{15}$, we could compute m_{12} four *independent* ways. However, the code bits are not available at the receiver, only the received bits $\mathbf{r} = (r_0, r_1, \ldots, r_{15})$. We use this in conjunction with the equations above to obtain four estimates of m_{12}:

$$\hat{m}_{12}^{(1)} = r_0 + r_1 + r_2 + r_3$$
$$\hat{m}_{12}^{(2)} = r_4 + r_5 + r_6 + r_7$$
$$\hat{m}_{12}^{(3)} = r_8 + r_9 + r_{10} + r_{11}$$
$$\hat{m}_{12}^{(4)} = r_{12} + r_{13} + r_{14} + r_{15}.$$

Expressions such as this, in which the check sums all yield the same message bit, are said to be *orthogonal*[1] on the message bit. From these four orthogonal equations, we determine the value of m_{12} by majority vote. Given $\hat{m}_{12}^{(i)}$, $i = 1, 2, 3, 4$, the decoded value $\hat{m}_{12}$ is

$$\hat{m}_{12} = \mathrm{maj}(\hat{m}_{12}^{(1)}, \hat{m}_{12}^{(2)}, \hat{m}_{12}^{(3)}, \hat{m}_{12}^{(4)}),$$

where $\mathrm{maj}(\cdots)$ returns the value that occurs most frequently among its arguments.

If errors occur such that only one of the $\hat{m}_{12}^{(i)}$ is incorrect, the majority vote gives the correct answer. If two of them are incorrect, then it is still possible to detect the occurrence of errors.

---

[1] This is a different usage from orthogonality in the vector-space sense.

It is similarly possible to set up multiple equations for the other second-order bits $m_{13}, m_{14}, \ldots, m_{34}$.

$$m_{13} = c_0 + c_1 + c_4 + c_5 \qquad m_{14} = c_0 + c_1 + c_8 + c_9$$

$$m_{13} = c_2 + c_3 + c_6 + c_7 \qquad m_{14} = c_2 + c_3 + c_{10} + c_{11}$$

$$m_{13} = c_8 + c_9 + c_{12} + c_{13} \qquad m_{14} = c_4 + c_5 + c_{12} + c_{13}$$

$$m_{13} = c_{10} + c_{11} + c_{14} + c_{15} \qquad m_{14} = c_6 + c_7 + c_{14} + c_{15}$$

$$m_{23} = c_0 + c_2 + c_4 + c_6 \qquad m_{24} = c_0 + c_2 + c_8 + c_{10}$$

$$m_{23} = c_1 + c_3 + c_5 + c_7 \qquad m_{24} = c_1 + c_3 + c_9 + c_{11}$$

$$m_{23} = c_8 + c_{10} + c_{12} + c_{14} \qquad m_{24} = c_4 + c_6 + c_{12} + c_{14}$$

$$m_{23} = c_9 + c_{11} + c_{13} + c_{15} \qquad m_{24} = c_5 + c_7 + c_{13} + c_{15}$$

$$m_{34} = c_0 + c_4 + c_8 + c_{12}$$
$$m_{34} = c_1 + c_5 + c_9 + c_{13}$$
$$m_{34} = c_2 + c_6 + c_{10} + c_{14}$$
$$m_{34} = c_3 + c_7 + c_{11} + c_{15}$$

(8.12)

Based upon these equations, majority logic decisions are computed for each element of the second-order block. These decisions are then stacked up to give the block

$$\hat{\mathbf{m}}_2 = (\hat{m}_{34}, \hat{m}_{24}, \hat{m}_{14}, \hat{m}_{23}, \hat{m}_{13}, \hat{m}_{12}).$$

We then "peel off" these decoded values to get

$$\mathbf{r}' = \mathbf{r} - \hat{\mathbf{m}}_2 G_2.$$

Now we repeat for the first-order bits. We have eight orthogonal check sums on each of the first-order message bits. For example,

$$m_1 = c_0 + c_1 \qquad m_1 = c_2 + c_3 \qquad m_1 = c_4 + c_5 \qquad m_1 = c_6 + c_7$$

$$m_1 = c_8 + c_9 \qquad m_1 = c_{10} + c_{11} \qquad m_1 = c_{12} + c_{13} \qquad m_1 = c_{14} + c_{15}$$

We use the bits of $\mathbf{r}'$ to obtain eight estimates,

$$m_1^{(1)} = r_0' + r_1' \qquad m_1^{(2)} = r_2' + r_3' \qquad m_1^{(3)} = r_4' + r_5' \qquad m_1^{(4)} = r_6' + r_7'$$

$$m_1^{(5)} = r_8' + r_9' \qquad m_1^{(6)} = r_{10}' + r_{11}' \qquad m_1^{(7)} = r_{12}' + r_{13}' \qquad m_1^{(8)} = r_{14}' + r_{15}'$$

then make a decision using majority logic,

$$\hat{m}_1 = \mathrm{maj}(m_1^{(1)}, m_1^{(2)}, \ldots, m_1^{(8)}).$$

Similarly, eight orthogonal equations can be written on the bits m_2, m_3, and m_4, resulting in the estimate $\hat{\mathbf{m}}_1 = (\hat{m}_1, \hat{m}_2, \hat{m}_3, \hat{m}_4)$.

Having estimated $\hat{\mathbf{m}}_1$, we strip it off from the received signal,

$$\mathbf{r}'' = \mathbf{r}' - \hat{\mathbf{m}}_1 G_1$$

and look for m_0. But if the previous decodings are correct,

$$\mathbf{r}'' = m_0 \mathbf{1} + \mathbf{e}.$$

Then m_0 is obtained simply by majority vote:

$$\hat{m}_0 = \text{maj}(r_0'', r_1'', \ldots, r_{15}'').$$

If at any stage there is no clear majority, then a decoding failure is declared.

Example 8.25   The computations described here are detailed in the indicated file. Suppose $\mathbf{m} = (00001001000)$, so the codeword is $\mathbf{c} = \mathbf{m}G = (0101011001010110)$. Suppose the received vector is $\mathbf{r} = (0101011011010110)$. The bit message estimates are

$$\hat{m}_{12}^{(1)} = r_0 + r_1 + r_2 + r_3 = 0 \qquad \hat{m}_{12}^{(2)} = r_4 + r_5 + r_6 + r_7 = 0$$
$$\hat{m}_{12}^{(3)} = r_8 + r_9 + r_{10} + r_{11} = 1 \qquad \hat{m}_{12}^{(4)} = r_{12} + r_{13} + r_{14} + r_{15} = 0$$

We obtain $\hat{m}_{12} = \text{maj}(0,0,1,0) = 0$. We similarly find

$$\hat{m}_{13} = \text{maj}(0,0,1,0) = 0 \quad \hat{m}_{14} = \text{maj}(1,0,0,0) = 0 \quad \hat{m}_{23} = \text{maj}(1,1,0,1) = 1$$
$$\hat{m}_{24} = \text{maj}(1,0,0,0) = 0 \quad \hat{m}_{34} = \text{maj}(1,0,0,0) = 0,$$

so that $\hat{\mathbf{m}}_2 = (001000)$. Removing this decoded value from the received vector, we obtain

$$\mathbf{r}' = \mathbf{r} - \hat{\mathbf{m}}_2 G_2 = \mathbf{r}' - \hat{\mathbf{m}}_2 \begin{bmatrix} \mathbf{v}_3\mathbf{v}_4 \\ \mathbf{v}_2\mathbf{v}_4 \\ \mathbf{v}_2\mathbf{v}_3 \\ \mathbf{v}_1\mathbf{v}_4 \\ \mathbf{v}_1\mathbf{v}_3 \\ \mathbf{v}_1\mathbf{v}_2 \end{bmatrix} = (0101010111010101).$$

At the next block, we have

$$\hat{m}_1 = \text{maj}(1,1,1,1,0,1,1,1) = 1 \quad \hat{m}_2 = \text{maj}(0,0,0,0,1,0,0,0) = 0$$
$$\hat{m}_3 = \text{maj}(0,0,0,0,1,0,0,0) = 0 \quad \hat{m}_4 = \text{maj}(1,0,0,0,0,0,0,0) = 0$$

so that $\hat{\mathbf{m}}_2 = (0001)$. We now remove this decoded block

$$\mathbf{r}'' = \mathbf{r}' - \hat{\mathbf{m}}_2 G_1 = \mathbf{r}' - \hat{\mathbf{m}}_2 \begin{bmatrix} \mathbf{v}_4 \\ \mathbf{v}_3 \\ \mathbf{v}_2 \\ \mathbf{v}_1 \end{bmatrix} = (0000000010000000).$$

rmdecex2.m

The majority decision is $\hat{m}_0 = 0$. The overall decoded message is

$$\hat{\mathbf{m}} = (\hat{m}_0, \hat{\mathbf{m}}_1, \hat{\mathbf{m}}_2) = (00001001000).$$

This matches the message sent. $\qquad\qquad\square$

8.3.4.2   A Geometric Viewpoint

Clearly, the key to employing majority logic decoding on an $RM(r,m)$ code is to find a description of the equations which are orthogonal on each bit. Consider, for example, the orthogonal equations for m_{34}, as seen in (8.12). Writing down the indices of the checking bits, we create the check set

$$S_{34} = \{\{0,4,8,12\}, \{1,5,9,13\}, \{2,6,10,14\}, \{3,7,11,15\}\}.$$

Now represent the indices in 4-bit binary,

$$S_{34} = \{\{(0000), (0100), (1000), (1100)\}, \{(0001), (0101), (1001), (1101)\},$$

$$\{(0010), (0110), (1010), (1110)\}, \{(0011), (0111), (1011), (1111)\}\}.$$

Within each subset there are pairs of binary numbers which are adjacent, differing by a single bit. We can represent this adjacency with a graph that has a vertex for each of the numbers from 0000 to 1111, with edges between those vertices that are logically adjacent. The graph for a code with $n = 3$ is shown in Figure 8.3(a). It forms a conventional three-dimensional cube. The graph for a code with $n = 4$ is shown in Figure 8.3(b); it forms a four-dimensional hypercube. The check set S_{34} can be represented as subsets of the nodes in the graph. Figure 8.4 shows these sets by shading the "plane" defined by each of the fours check subsets. Similarly, the check sets for each the bits m_{12}, m_{13}, etc., form a set of planes.

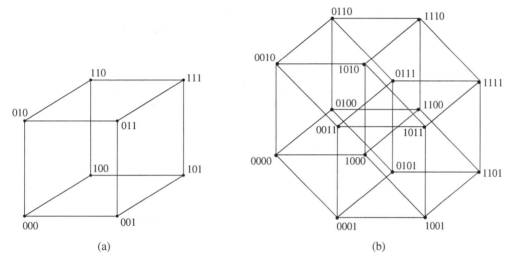

Figure 8.3: Binary adjacency relationships in (a) three and (b) four dimensions.

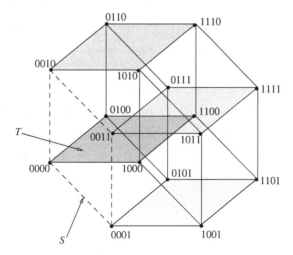

Figure 8.4: Planes shaded to represent the equations orthogonal on bit m_{34}.

With these observations, let us now develop the notation to describe the general situation. For a codeword $\mathbf{c} = (c_0, c_1, \ldots, c_{n-1})$, let the coordinate c_i be associated with the binary m-tuple P_i obtained by complementing the binary representation of the index i. For example, c_0 is associated with $P_0 = (1111)$ (since $0 = (0000)_2$) and c_6 is associated with $P_6 = (1001)$ (since $6 = (0110)_2$). We think of the P_i as points on the adjacency graph such as those shown in Figure 8.3.

Each codeword $\mathbf{c}$ in $RM(r, m)$ forms an incidence vector for a subset of the graph, selecting points in the graph corresponding to 1 bits in the codeword. For example, the codeword $\mathbf{c} = (0101011001010110)$ is an incidence vector for the subset containing the points $\{P_1, P_3, P_5, P_6, P_9, P_{11}, P_{13}, P_{14}\}$.

Let $I = \{1, 2, \ldots, m\}$. We represent the basis vectors for the $RM(r, m)$ code as subsets of I. For example, the basis vector $\mathbf{v}_1$ is represented by the set $\{1\}$. The basis vector $\mathbf{v}_2\mathbf{v}_3$ is represented by the set $\{2, 3\}$. The basis vector $\mathbf{v}_2\mathbf{v}_3\mathbf{v}_4$ is represented by $\{2, 3, 4\}$. With this notation, we now define the procedure for finding the orthogonal check sums for the vector $\mathbf{v}_{i_1}\mathbf{v}_{i_2}\cdots\mathbf{v}_{i_p}$ [483, p. 160].

1. Let $S = \{S_1, S_2, \ldots, S_{2^{m-p}}\}$ be the subset of points associated with the incidence vector $\mathbf{v}_{i_1}\mathbf{v}_{i_2}\cdots\mathbf{v}_{i_p}$.

2. Let $\{j_1, j_2, \ldots, j_{m-p}\}$ be the set difference $I - \{i_1, i_2, \ldots, i_p\}$. Let T be the subset of points associated with the incidence vector $\mathbf{v}_{j_1}\mathbf{v}_{j_2}\cdots\mathbf{v}_{j_{m-p}}$. The set T is called the *complementary subspace to S*.

3. The first check sum consists of the sum of the coordinates specified by the points in T.

4. The other check sums are obtained by "translating" the set T by the points in S. That is, for each $S_i \in S$, we form the set $T + S_i$. The corresponding check sum consists of the sum of the coordinates specified by this set.

Example 8.26   Checksums for $RM(2, 4)$. Let us find checksums for $\mathbf{v}_3\mathbf{v}_4 = (0000000000001111)$.

1. The subset for which $\mathbf{v}_3\mathbf{v}_4$ is an incidence vector contains the points

$$S = \{P_{12}, P_{13}, P_{14}, P_{15}\} = \{(0011)(0010)(0001)(0000)\}.$$

In Figure 8.4, the set S is indicated by the dashed lines.

2. The difference set is

$$\{j_1, j_2\} = \{1, 2, 3, 4\} - \{3, 4\} = \{1, 2\},$$

which has the associated vector $\mathbf{v}_1\mathbf{v}_2 = (0001000100010001)$. This is the incidence vector for the set

$$T = \{P_3, P_7, P_{11}, P_{15}\} = \{(1100)(1000)(0100)(0000)\}.$$

In Figure 8.4, the set T is the darkest of the shaded regions.

3. T represents the checksum $m_{34} = c_{12} + c_8 + c_4 + c_0$.

4. The translations of T by the nonzero elements of S are:

$$\text{by } P_{12} = (0011) \rightarrow \{(1111)(1011)(0111)(0011)\} = \{P_0, P_4, P_8, P_{12}\}$$
$$\text{by } P_{13} = (0010) \rightarrow \{(1110)(1010)(0110)(0010)\} = \{P_1, P_5, P_9, P_{13}\}$$
$$\text{by } P_{14} = (0001) \rightarrow \{(1101)(1001)(0101)(0001)\} = \{P_2, P_6, P_{10}, P_{14}\}.$$

These correspond to the checksums

$$m_{34} = c_{15} + c_{11} + c_7 + c_3$$
$$m_{34} = c_{14} + c_{10} + c_6 + c_2$$
$$m_{34} = c_{13} + c_9 + c_5 + c_1,$$

which are shown in the figure as shaded planes.

Figure 8.5 indicates the check equations for all of the second-order vectors for the $RM(2,4)$ code.

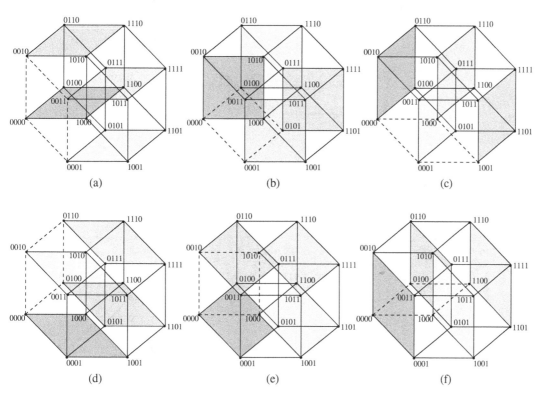

Figure 8.5: Geometric descriptions of parity check equations for second-order vectors of the $RM(2,4)$ code. (a) $\mathbf{v}_3\mathbf{v}_4$; (b) $\mathbf{v}_2\mathbf{v}_4$; (c) $\mathbf{v}_2\mathbf{v}_3$; (d) $\mathbf{v}_1\mathbf{v}_4$; (e) $\mathbf{v}_1\mathbf{v}_3$; (f) $\mathbf{v}_1\mathbf{v}_2$.

Now let us examine check sums for the first-order vectors.

1. For the vector $\mathbf{v}_4 = (0000000011111111)$ the set S is

$$S = \{P_8, P_9, P_{10}, P_{11}, P_{12}, P_{13}, P_{14}, P_{15}\}$$
$$= \{(0111), (0110), (0101), (0100), (0011), (0010), (0001), (0000)\}.$$

These eight points are connected by the dashed lines in Figure 8.6(a).

2. The difference set is

$$\{1, 2, 3, 4\} - \{4\} = \{1, 2, 3\},$$

which has the associated vector $\mathbf{v}_1\mathbf{v}_2\mathbf{v}_3 = (0000000100000001)$, which is the incidence vector for the set

$$T = \{P_7, P_{15}\} = \{(1000), (0000)\}.$$

The corresponding equation is $m_4 = c_8 + c_0$. The subset is indicated by the widest line in Figure 8.6(a).

3. There are eight translations of T by the points in S. These are shown by the other wide lines in the figure.

$\square$

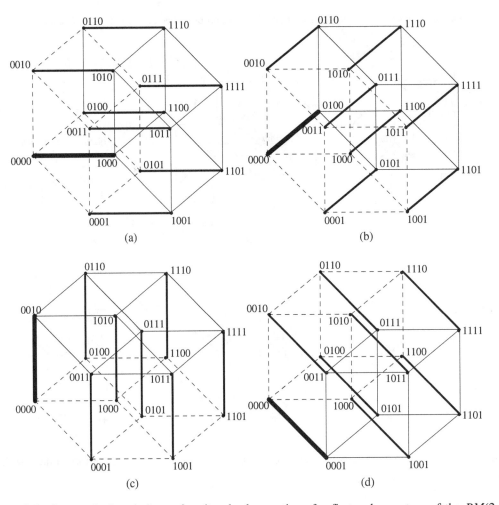

Figure 8.6: Geometric descriptions of parity check equations for first-order vectors of the $RM(2,4)$ code. (a) $\mathbf{v}_4$; (b) $\mathbf{v}_3$; (c) $\mathbf{v}_2$; (d) $\mathbf{v}_1$.

8.3.5 Other Constructions of Reed–Muller Codes

The $|\mathbf{u}|\mathbf{u}+\mathbf{v}|$ Construction The $|\mathbf{u}|\mathbf{u}+\mathbf{v}|$ introduced in Exercise 3.29 may be used to construct Reed–Muller codes. In fact,

$$RM(r,m) = \{[\mathbf{u}|\mathbf{u}+\mathbf{v}] : \mathbf{u} \in RM(r,m-1), \mathbf{v} \in RM(r-1,m-1)\}$$

having generator matrix

$$G_{RM}(r,m) = \begin{bmatrix} G_{RM}(r,m-1) & G_{RM}(r,m-1) \\ 0 & G_{RM}(r-1,m-1) \end{bmatrix}.$$

A Kronecker Construction Let $G_{(2,2)} = \begin{bmatrix} 1 & 1 \\ 0 & 1 \end{bmatrix}$. Define the m-fold Kronecker product of $G_{(2,2)}$ as

$$G_{(2^m,2^m)} = \underbrace{G_{(2,2)} \otimes G_{(2,2)} \otimes \cdots \otimes G_{(2,2)}}_{m \text{ operands}},$$

which is a $2^m \times 2^m$ matrix. Then the generator for the $RM(r, m)$ code is obtained by selecting from $G_{(2^m, 2^m)}$ those rows with weight greater than or equal to 2^{m-r}.

8.4 Building Long Codes from Short Codes: The Squaring Construction

There are several ways of combining short codes together to obtain codes with different properties. Among these are the $[\mathbf{u}|\mathbf{u} + \mathbf{v}]$ construction (outlined in Exercise 3.29) and concatenation (described in Section 10.6). In this section, we present another one, called the squaring construction [272, 292].

We begin by examining partitions of codes into cosets by subcodes. Let $C_0 = C$ be a binary linear (n, k_0) block code with generator G and let $C_1 \subset C_0$ be a (n, k_1) subcode of C_0. That is, C_1 is a subgroup of C_0. Recall that a coset of C_1 is a set of the form

$$\mathbf{c}_l + C_1 = \{\mathbf{c}_l + \mathbf{c} : \mathbf{c} \in C_1\},$$

where $\mathbf{c}_l \in C_0$ is a coset leader. We will take the nonzero coset leaders in $C \backslash C_1$. From Section 2.2.5, recall that C_0/C_1 forms a factor group, partitioning C_0 into $2^{k_0-k_1}$ disjoint subsets each containing 2^{k_1} codewords. Each of these subsets can be represented by a coset leader. The set of coset leaders is called the coset representative space. The coset representative for the coset C_1 is always chosen to be $\mathbf{0}$. Denote this coset representative space by $[C_0/C_1]$. The code C_1 and the set $[C/C_1]$ share only the zero vector in common, $C_1 \cap [C/C_1] = \mathbf{0}$.

Without loss of generality, let $G_0 = G$ be expressed in a form that k_1 rows of G_0 can be selected as a generator G_1 for C_1. The $2^{k_0-k_1}$ codewords generated by the remaining $k_0 - k_1$ rows of $G_0 \backslash G_1$ can be used as to generate representatives for the cosets in C/C_1. Let $G_{0\backslash 1} = G_0 \backslash G_1$ (that is, the set difference, thinking of the rows as individual elements of the set). The $2^{k_0-k_1}$ codewords generated by $G_{0\backslash 1}$ form a $(n, k - k_1)$ subcode of C_0.

Every codeword in C can be expressed as the sum of a codeword in C_1 and a vector in $[C_0/C_1]$. We denote this as

$$C_0 = C_1 \oplus [C_0/C_1] = \{\mathbf{u} + \mathbf{v} : \mathbf{u} \in C_1, \mathbf{v} \in [C_0/C_1]\}.$$

The set-operand sum $\oplus$ is called the *direct sum*.

Example 8.27 While the squaring construction can be applied to any linear block code, we demonstrate it here for a Reed–Muller code. Consider the $RM(1, 3)$ code with

$$G = G_0 = \begin{bmatrix} 1 & 1 & 1 & 1 & 1 & 1 & 1 & 1 \\ 0 & 0 & 1 & 1 & 0 & 0 & 1 & 1 \\ 0 & 0 & 0 & 0 & 1 & 1 & 1 & 1 \\ 0 & 1 & 0 & 1 & 0 & 1 & 0 & 1 \end{bmatrix}.$$

Let C_1 be the $(8, 3)$ code generated by the first $k_1 = 3$ rows of the generator G_0,

$$G_1 = \begin{bmatrix} 1 & 1 & 1 & 1 & 1 & 1 & 1 & 1 \\ 0 & 0 & 1 & 1 & 0 & 0 & 1 & 1 \\ 0 & 0 & 0 & 0 & 1 & 1 & 1 & 1 \end{bmatrix}.$$

The cosets in C/C_1 are

$$[0, 0, 0, 0, 0, 0, 0, 0] + C_1, [0, 1, 0, 1, 0, 1, 0, 1] + C_1.$$

The coset representatives are

$$[C_0/C_1] = \{[0, 0, 0, 0, 0, 0, 0, 0], [0, 1, 0, 1, 0, 1, 0, 1]\}$$

generated by the rows of the matrix

$$G_{0\backslash 1} = G_0 \backslash G_1 = [0, 1, 0, 1, 0, 1, 0, 1].$$

□

One-level squaring is based on C_1 and the partition C_0/C_1. Let $|C_0/C_1|^2$ denote the code $\mathfrak{C}_{0/1}$ of length $2n$ obtained by the squaring construction, defined as

$$\mathfrak{C}_{0/1} = |C_0/C_1|^2 = \{(\mathbf{a} + \mathbf{x}, \mathbf{b} + \mathbf{x}) : \mathbf{a}, \mathbf{b} \in C_1 \text{ and } \mathbf{x} \in [C_0/C_1]\}. \tag{8.13}$$

Since there are $2^{k_0 - k_1}$ vectors in $[C_0/C_1]$ and 2^{k_1} choices each for $\mathbf{a}$ and $\mathbf{b}$, there are $2^{k_0 - k_1} 2^{k_1} 2^{k_1} = 2^{k_0 + k_1}$ codewords in $\mathfrak{C}_{0/1}$. The code $\mathfrak{C}_{0/1}$ is thus a $(n, k_0 + k_1)$ code. Let

$$\mathbf{m} = [m_{1,0}, m_{1,1}, \ldots, m_{1,k_1 - 1}, m_{2,0}, m_{2,1}, \ldots, m_{2,k_1 - 1}, m_{3,0}, m_{3,1}, \ldots, m_{3,k_0 - k_1 - 1}]$$

be a message vector. A coded message of the form $\mathbf{c} = (\mathbf{a} + \mathbf{x}, \mathbf{b} + \mathbf{x})$ from (8.13) can be obtained by

$$\mathbf{c} = \mathbf{m} \begin{bmatrix} G_1 & 0 \\ 0 & G_1 \\ G_{0\backslash 1} & G_{0\backslash 1} \end{bmatrix} \triangleq \mathbf{m} \mathfrak{G}_{0/1}$$

so the matrix $\mathfrak{G}_{0/1}$ is the generator for the code. The minimum weight for the code is $d_{0/1} = \min(2d_0, d_1)$.

We can express the generator matrix $\mathfrak{G}_{0/1}$ in the following way. For two matrices M_1 and M_2 having the same number of columns, let $M_1 \oplus M_2$ denote the stacking operation

$$M_1 \oplus M_2 = \begin{bmatrix} M_1 \\ M_2 \end{bmatrix}.$$

This is called the matrix direct sum. Let I_2 be the 2×2 identity. Then

$$I_2 \otimes G_1 = \begin{bmatrix} G_1 & 0 \\ 0 & G_1 \end{bmatrix},$$

where $\otimes$ is the Kronecker product. We also have

$$\begin{bmatrix} 1 & 1 \end{bmatrix} \otimes G_{0\backslash 1} = \begin{bmatrix} G_{0\backslash 1} & G_{0\backslash 1} \end{bmatrix}.$$

Then we can write

$$\mathfrak{G}_{0/1} = I_2 \otimes G_1 \oplus \begin{bmatrix} 1 & 1 \end{bmatrix} \otimes G_{0\backslash 1}.$$

Example 8.28 Continuing the previous example, the generator for the code $|C_0/C_1|^2$ is

$$\mathfrak{G}_{0/1} = \begin{bmatrix} 1 & 1 & 1 & 1 & 1 & 1 & 1 & 1 & 0 & 0 & 0 & 0 & 0 & 0 & 0 & 0 \\ 0 & 0 & 1 & 1 & 0 & 0 & 1 & 1 & 0 & 0 & 0 & 0 & 0 & 0 & 0 & 0 \\ 0 & 0 & 0 & 0 & 1 & 1 & 1 & 1 & 0 & 0 & 0 & 0 & 0 & 0 & 0 & 0 \\ 0 & 0 & 0 & 0 & 0 & 0 & 0 & 0 & 1 & 1 & 1 & 1 & 1 & 1 & 1 & 1 \\ 0 & 0 & 0 & 0 & 0 & 0 & 0 & 0 & 0 & 0 & 1 & 1 & 0 & 0 & 1 & 1 \\ 0 & 0 & 0 & 0 & 0 & 0 & 0 & 0 & 0 & 0 & 0 & 0 & 1 & 1 & 1 & 1 \\ 0 & 1 & 0 & 1 & 0 & 1 & 0 & 1 & 0 & 1 & 0 & 1 & 0 & 1 & 0 & 1 \end{bmatrix}.$$

□

We can further partition the cosets as follows. Let C_2 be a (n, k_2) subcode of C_1 with generator G_2, with $0 \leq k_2 \leq k_1$. Then each of the $2^{k_0 - k_1}$ cosets $\mathbf{c}_l + C_1$ in the partition C_0/C_1 can be partitioned into $2^{k_1 - k_2}$ cosets consisting of the following codewords

$$\mathbf{c}_l + \mathbf{d}_p + C_2 = \{\mathbf{c}_l + \mathbf{d}_p + \mathbf{c} : \mathbf{c} \in C_2\}$$

for each l in $0, 1, 2, \ldots, 2^{k-k_1}$ and each p in $1, 2, \ldots, 2^{k_1-k_2}$, where $\mathbf{d}_p$ is a codeword in C_1 but not in C_2. This partition is denoted as $C/C_1/C_2$. We can express the entire code as the direct sum

$$C_0 = [C/C_1] \oplus [C_1/C_2] \oplus C_2.$$

Let $G_{1\backslash 2}$ denote the generator matrix for the coset representative space $[C_1/C_2]$. Then $G_{1\backslash 2} = G_1 \backslash G_2$.

Example 8.29 Let C_2 be generated by the first two rows of G_1, so

$$G_2 = \begin{bmatrix} 1 & 1 & 1 & 1 & 1 & 1 & 1 & 1 \\ 0 & 0 & 1 & 1 & 0 & 0 & 1 & 1 \end{bmatrix}.$$

There are two cosets in C_1/C_2,

$$[0,0,0,0,0,0,0,0] + C_2, [0,0,0,0,1,1,1,1] + C_2.$$

The set of coset representatives $[C_1/C_2]$ is generated by

$$G_{1\backslash 2} = G_1 \backslash G_2 = \begin{bmatrix} 0 & 0 & 0 & 0 & 1 & 1 & 1 & 1 \end{bmatrix}.$$

$\square$

Two-level squaring begins by forming the two one-level squaring construction codes $\mathfrak{C}_{0/1} = |C_0/C_1|^2$ and $\mathfrak{C}_{1/2} = |C_1/C_2|^2$, with generators $\mathfrak{G}_{0/1}$ and $\mathfrak{G}_{1/2}$, respectively, given by

$$\mathfrak{G}_{0/1} = \begin{bmatrix} G_1 & 0 \\ 0 & G_1 \\ G_{0\backslash 1} & G_{0\backslash 1} \end{bmatrix} \qquad \mathfrak{G}_{1/2} = \begin{bmatrix} G_2 & 0 \\ 0 & G_2 \\ G_{1\backslash 2} & G_{1\backslash 2} \end{bmatrix}. \tag{8.14}$$

Note that $\mathfrak{C}_{1/2}$ is a subcode (subgroup) of $\mathfrak{C}_{0/1}$. The coset representatives for $\mathfrak{C}_{0/1}/\mathfrak{C}_{1/2}$, which are denoted by $[\mathfrak{C}_{0/1}/\mathfrak{C}_{1/2}]$, form a linear code. Let $\mathfrak{G}_{\mathfrak{C}_{0/1}\backslash\mathfrak{C}_{1/2}}$ denote the generator matrix for the coset representatives $[\mathfrak{C}_{0/1}/\mathfrak{C}_{1/2}]$. Then form the code $\mathfrak{C}_{0/1/2} = |C_0/C_1/C_2|^4$ by

$$\mathfrak{C}_{0/1/2} = |C_0/C_1/C_2|^4 = \{(\mathbf{a}+\mathbf{x}, \mathbf{b}+\mathbf{x}) : \mathbf{a}, \mathbf{b} \in \mathfrak{C}_{1/2} \text{ and } \mathbf{x} \in [\mathfrak{C}_{0/1}/\mathfrak{C}_{1/2}]\}.$$

That is, it is obtained by the squaring construction of $\mathfrak{C}_{0/1}$ and $\mathfrak{C}_{0/1}/\mathfrak{C}_{1/2}$. The generator matrix for $\mathfrak{C}_{0/1/2}$ is

$$\mathfrak{G}_{0/1/2} = \begin{bmatrix} \mathfrak{G}_{1/2} & 0 \\ 0 & \mathfrak{G}_{1/2} \\ \mathfrak{G}_{\mathfrak{C}_{0/1}\backslash\mathfrak{C}_{1/2}} & \mathfrak{G}_{\mathfrak{C}_{0/1}\backslash\mathfrak{C}_{1/2}} \end{bmatrix}.$$

This gives a $(4n, k_0 + 2k_1 + k_2)$ linear block code with minimum distance

$$d_{0/1/2} = \min(4d_0, 2d_1, d_2).$$

Writing $\mathfrak{G}_{0/1}$ and $\mathfrak{G}_{1/2}$ as in (8.14), rearranging rows and columns and performing some simple row operations, we can write $\mathfrak{G}_{0/1/2}$ as

$$\mathfrak{G}_{0/1/2} = \begin{bmatrix} G_2 & 0 & 0 & 0 \\ 0 & G_2 & 0 & 0 \\ 0 & 0 & G_2 & 0 \\ 0 & 0 & 0 & G_2 \\ G_{0\backslash 1} & G_{0\backslash 1} & G_{0\backslash 1} & G_{0\backslash 1} \\ G_{1\backslash 2} & G_{1\backslash 2} & G_{1\backslash 2} & G_{1\backslash 2} \\ 0 & 0 & G_{1\backslash 2} & G_{1\backslash 2} \\ 0 & G_{1\backslash 2} & 0 & G_{1\backslash 2} \end{bmatrix},$$

which can be expressed as

$$\mathcal{G}_{0/1/2} = I_4 \otimes G_2 \oplus \begin{bmatrix} 1 & 1 & 1 & 1 \end{bmatrix} \otimes G_{0\backslash 1} \oplus \begin{bmatrix} 1 & 1 & 1 & 1 \\ 0 & 0 & 1 & 1 \\ 0 & 1 & 0 & 1 \end{bmatrix} \otimes G_{1\backslash 2}.$$

Note that

$$\begin{bmatrix} 1 & 1 & 1 & 1 \end{bmatrix} \quad \text{and} \quad \begin{bmatrix} 1 & 1 & 1 & 1 \\ 0 & 0 & 1 & 1 \\ 0 & 1 & 0 & 1 \end{bmatrix}$$

are the generator matrices for the zeroth- and first-order Reed–Muller codes of length 4.

More generally, let $C_1, C_2, \ldots, C_m$ be a sequence of linear subcodes of $C = C_0$ with generators G_i, minimum distance d_i, and dimensions $k_1, k_2, \ldots, k_m$ satisfying

$$C_0 \supseteq C_1 \supseteq \cdots \supseteq C_m$$

$$k \geq k_1 \geq \cdots \geq k_m \geq 0.$$

Then form the chain of partitions

$$C_0/C_1, C_0/C_1/C_2, \ldots, C_0/C_1/\cdots/C_m,$$

such that the code can be expressed as the direct sum

$$C_0 = [C/C_1] \oplus [C_1/C_2] \oplus \cdots \oplus [C_{q-1}/C_m].$$

Assume that the generator matrix is represented in a way that $G_0 \supseteq G_1 \cdots \supseteq G_m$. Let $G_{i\backslash i+1}$ denote the generator matrix for the coset representative space $[C_i/C_{i+1}]$, with

$$\text{rank}(G_{i\backslash i+1}) = \text{rank}(G_i) - \text{rank}(G_{i+1})$$

and $G_{i\backslash i+1} = G_i \backslash G_{i+1}$. Then higher-level squaring is performed recursively. From the codes

$$\mathcal{G}_{0/1/\cdots/m-1} \triangleq |C_0/C_1/\cdots/C_{m-1}|^{2^{m-1}}$$

and the code

$$\mathcal{G}_{1/2/\cdots/m} \triangleq |C_1/C_2/\cdots/C_m|^{2^{m-1}},$$

form the code

$$\mathcal{G}_{0/1/\cdots/m} \triangleq [C_0/C_1/\cdots/C_m]^{2^m}$$

$$= \{(\mathbf{a}+\mathbf{x}, \mathbf{b}+\mathbf{x}) : \mathbf{a}, \mathbf{b} \in \mathcal{G}_{1/2/\cdots/m}, \mathbf{x} \in [\mathcal{G}_{0/1/\cdots/m-1}/\mathcal{G}_{1/2/\cdots/m}]\}.$$

The generator matrix can be written (after appropriate rearrangement of the rows) as

$$\mathcal{G}_{0/1/\ldots/m} = I_{2^m} \otimes G_m \oplus \sum_{r=0}^{m} \oplus G_{RM}(r, m) \otimes G_{r\backslash r+1},$$

where $G_{RM}(r, m)$ is the generator of the $RM(r, m)$ code of length 2^m.

8.5 Quadratic Residue Codes

Quadratic residue codes are codes of length p, where p is a prime with coefficients in $GF(s)$, where s is a quadratic residue of p. They have rather good distance properties, being among the best codes known of their size and dimension.

We begin the construction with the following notation. Let p be prime. Denote the set of quadratic residues of p by Q_p and the set of quadratic nonresidues by N_p. Then the elements in $GF(p)$ are partitioned into sets as

$$GF(p) = Q_p \cup N_p \cup \{0\}.$$

As we have seen $GF(p)$ is cyclic. This gives rise to the following observation:

Lemma 8.30 *A primitive element of $GF(p)$ must be a quadratic nonresidue. That is, it is in N_p.*

Proof Let γ be a primitive element of $GF(p)$. We know $\gamma^{p-1} = 1$, and $p - 1$ is the smallest such power. Suppose γ is a quadratic residue. Then there is a number σ (square root) such that $\sigma^2 = \gamma$. Taking powers of σ, we have $\sigma^{2(p-1)} = 1$. Furthermore, the powers $\sigma, \sigma^2, \sigma^3, \ldots, \sigma^{2(p-1)}$ can be shown to all be distinct. But this contradicts the order p of the field. □

So a primitive element $\gamma \in GF(p)$ satisfies $\gamma^e \in Q_p$ if and only if e is even, and $\gamma^e \in N_p$ if and only if e is odd. The elements of Q_p correspond to the first $(p - 1)/2$ consecutive powers of γ^2; that is, Q_p is a cyclic group under multiplication modulo p, generated by γ^2.

The quadratic residue codes are designed as follows. Choose a field $GF(s)$ as the field for the coefficients, where s is a quadratic residue modulo p. We choose an extension field $GF(s^m)$ so that it has a primitive pth root of unity; from Lemma 5.54 we must have $p | s^m - 1$. (It can be shown [292, p. 519] that if $s = 2$, then p must be of the form $p = 8k \pm 1$.)

Let β be a primitive pth root of unity in $GF(s^m)$. Then the conjugates with respect to $GF(s)$ are

$$\beta^1, \beta^s, \beta^{s^2}, \beta^{s^3}, \ldots$$

The cyclotomic coset is $\{1, s, s^2, s^3, \ldots, \}$. Since $s \in Q_p$ and Q_p is a group under multiplication modulo p, Q_p is closed under multiplication by s. So all of the elements in the cyclotomic coset are in Q_p. Thus, Q_p is a cyclotomic coset or the union of cyclotomic cosets.

Example 8.31 Let $p = 11$, which has quadratic residues $Q_p = \{1, 3, 4, 5, 9\}$. Let $s = 3$. A field having a primitive 11th root of unity is $GF(3^5)$. Let $\beta \in GF(3^5)$ be a primitive 11th root of unity. The conjugates of β are:

$$\beta, \beta^3, \beta^9, \beta^{27} = \beta^5, \beta^{81} = \beta^4,$$

so the cyclotomic coset is

$$\{1, 3, 9, 5, 4\},$$

which is identical to Q_p. □

Now let β be a primitive pth root of unity in $GF(s^m)$. Because of the results above,

$$q(x) = \prod_{i \in Q_p} (x - \beta^i)$$

is a polynomial with coefficients in $GF(s)$. Furthermore,

$$n(x) = \prod_{i \in N_p} (x - \beta^i) \tag{8.15}$$

also has coefficients in $GF(s)$. We thus have the factorization

$$x^p - 1 = q(x)n(x)(x - 1).$$

Let R be the ring $GF(s)[x]/(x^p - 1)$.

Definition 8.32 [292, p. 481] For a prime p, the quadratic residue codes of length $\mathcal{Q}, \overline{\mathcal{Q}}, \mathcal{N}$, and $\overline{\mathcal{N}}$ are the cyclic codes (or ideals of R) with generator polynomials

$$q(x), \quad (x-1)q(x), \quad n(x), \quad (x-1)n(x),$$

respectively. The codes $\mathcal{Q}$ and N have dimension $\frac{1}{2}(p+1)$; the codes $\overline{\mathcal{Q}}$ and $\overline{N}$ have dimension $\frac{1}{2}(p-1)$.

The codes $\mathcal{Q}$ and $\mathcal{N}$ are sometimes called *augmented* QR codes, while $\overline{\mathcal{Q}}$ and $\overline{\mathcal{N}}$ are called *expurgated* QR codes. □

testQR.cc

Example 8.33 Let $p = 17$ and $s = 2$. The field $GF(2^8)$ has a primitive 17th root of unity, which is $\beta = \alpha^{15}$. The quadratic residues modulo 17 are $\{1, 2, 4, 8, 9, 13, 15, 16\}$. Then

$$q(x) = (x - \beta)(x - \beta^2)(x - \beta^4)(x - \beta^8)(x - \beta^9)(x - \beta^{13})(x - \beta^{15})(x - \beta^{16})$$
$$= 1 + x + x^2 + x^4 + x^6 + x^7 + x^8$$
$$n(x) = (x - \beta^3)(x - \beta^5)(x - \beta^6)(x - \beta^7)(x - \beta^{10})(x - \beta^{11})(x - \beta^{12})(x - \beta^{14})$$
$$= 1 + x^3 + x^4 + x^5 + x^8.$$

□

QR codes tend to have rather good distance properties. Some binary QR codes are the best codes known for their particular values of n and k. A bound on the distance is provided by the following.

Theorem 8.34 *The minimum distance d of the codes $\mathcal{Q}$ or $\mathcal{N}$ satisfies $d^2 \geq p$. If, additionally, $p = 4l - 1$ for some l, then $d^2 - d + 1 \geq p$.*

The proof relies on the following lemma.

Lemma 8.35 *Let $\tilde{q}(x) = q(x^n)$, where $n \in N_p$ (where the operations are in the ring R). Then the roots of $\tilde{q}(x)$ are in the set $\{\alpha^i, i \in N_p\}$. That is, $\tilde{q}(x)$ is a scalar multiple of $n(x)$. Similarly, $n(x^n)$ is a scalar multiple of $q(x)$.*

Proof Let ρ be a generator of the nonzero elements of $GF(p)$. From the discussion around Lemma 8.30, Q is generated by even powers of ρ and N_p is generated by odd powers of ρ.

Write $\tilde{q}(x) = \prod_{i \in Q_p}(x^n - \alpha^i)$. Let $m \in N_p$. Then for any $m \in N_p$,

$$\tilde{q}(\alpha^m) = \prod_{i \in Q_p}(\alpha^{mn} - \alpha^i).$$

But since $m \in N_p$ and $n \in N_p$, $mn \in Q_p$ (being both odd powers of ρ). So $\alpha^i = \alpha^{mn}$ for some value of i, so α^m is a root of $\tilde{q}(x)$. □

The effect of evaluation at $q(x^n)$ is to permute the coefficients of $q(x)$.

Proof of Theorem 8.34. [292, p. 483]. Let $a(x)$ be a codeword of minimum nonzero weight d in $\mathcal{Q}$. Then by Lemma 8.35, the polynomial $\tilde{a}(x) = a(x^n)$ is a codeword in $\mathcal{N}$. Since the coefficients of $\tilde{a}(x)$

Table 8.1: Extended Quadratic Residue Codes Q [292, 483]

n	k	d	n	k	d	n	k	d
8	4	4*	74	37	14	138	69	14–22
18	9	6*	80	40	16*	152	76	20
24	12	8*	90	45	18*	168	84	16–24
32	16	8*	98	49	16	192	96	16–28
42	21	10*	104	52	20*	194	97	16–28
48	24	12*	114	57	12–16	200	100	16–32
72	36	12	128	64	20			

*Indicates that the code is as good as the best known for this n and k.

are simply a permutation (and possible scaling) of those of $a(x)$, $\tilde{a}(x)$ must be a codeword of minimum weight in $\mathcal{N}$. The product $a(x)\tilde{a}(x)$ must be a multiple of the polynomial

$$\prod_{q \in Q_p}(x - \alpha^q) \prod_{n \in N_p}(x - \alpha^n) = \prod_{i=1}^{p-1}(x - \alpha^i) = \frac{x^p - 1}{x - 1} = \sum_{j=0}^{p-1} x^j.$$

Thus, $a(x)\tilde{a}(x)$ has weight p. Since $a(x)$ has weight d, the maximum weight of $a(x)\tilde{a}(x)$ is d^2. We obtain the bound $d^2 \geq p$.

If $p = 4k - 1$ then $n = -1$ is a quadratic nonresidue. In the product $a(x)\tilde{a}(x) = a(x)a(x^{-1})$ there are d terms equal to 1, so the maximum weight of the product is $d^2 - d + 1$. $\qquad\square$

Table 8.1 summarizes known distance properties for some augmented binary QR codes, with indications of best known codes. In some cases, d is expressed in terms of upper and lower bounds.

While general decoding techniques have been developed for QR codes, we present only a decoding algorithm for a particular QR code, the Golay code presented in the next section. Decoding algorithms for other QR codes are discussed in [292, 366, 365], and [108].

8.6 Golay Codes

Of these codes it was said, "The Golay code is probably the most important of all codes, for both practical and theoretical reasons." [292, p. 64]. While the Golay codes have not supported the burden of applications this alleged importance would suggest, they do lie at the confluence of several routes of theoretical development and are worth studying.

Let us take $p = 23$ and form the binary QR code. The field $GF(2^{11})$ has a primitive 23rd root of unity. The quadratic residues are

$$Q_p = \{1, 2, 3, 4, 6, 8, 9, 12, 13, 16, 18\}$$

and the corresponding generators for $\mathcal{Q}$ and $\mathcal{N}$ are

$$q(x) = \prod_{i \in Q_p}(x - \beta^i) = 1 + x + x^5 + x^6 + x^7 + x^9 + x^{11}$$

$$n(x) = 1 + x^2 + x^4 + x^5 + x^6 + x^{10} + x^{11}.$$

This produces a (23,12,7) code, the Golay code $\mathcal{G}_{23}$. It is straightforward to verify that this code is a perfect code: the number of points out to a distance $t = 3$ is equal to

$$V_2(23, 3) = \binom{23}{0} + \binom{23}{1} + \binom{23}{2} + \binom{23}{3} = 2^{11}.$$

This satisfies the Hamming bound. It is said that Golay discovered this code by observing this relationship in Pascal's triangle. Adding an extra overall parity bit to the (23, 12) code produces the Golay G_{24} (24,12,8) code.

The binary Golay code also has some interesting generator matrix representations. The generator matrix for the $\mathcal{G}_{24}$ code can be written as

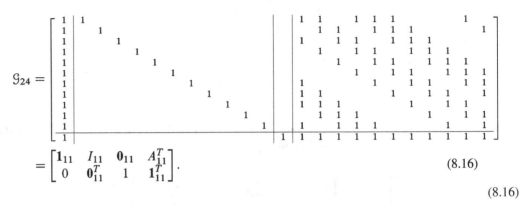

$$\mathcal{G}_{24} = \begin{bmatrix} \mathbf{1}_{11} & I_{11} & \mathbf{0}_{11} & A_{11}^T \\ 0 & \mathbf{0}_{11}^T & 1 & \mathbf{1}_{11}^T \end{bmatrix}. \tag{8.16}$$

$$\tag{8.16}$$

We note the following facts about $\mathcal{G}_{24}$.

- In this representation, the 11×11 A_{11}^T matrix on the upper right is obtained from the transpose of 12×12 Hadamard matrix of Paley type (8.5) by removing the first row and column of H_{12}, then replacing -1 by 1 and 1 by 0. Since the rows of H_{12} differ in six places, the rows of A_{11}^T differ by six places. Because of the identity block, the sum of any two rows of G has weight 8.

- If **u** and **v** are rows of G (not necessarily distinct), then wt($\mathbf{u} \cdot \mathbf{v}$) $\equiv 0$ (mod 2). So every row of G is orthogonal to every other row. Therefore, G is also the parity check matrix H of $\mathcal{G}_{24}$. Also G is dual to itself: $\mathcal{G}_{24} = \mathcal{G}_{24}^\perp$. Such a code is call **self-dual**.

- Every codeword has even weight: If there were a codeword **u** of odd weight then wt($\mathbf{u} \cdot \mathbf{u}$) = 1. Furthermore, since every row of the generator has weight divisible by 4, every codeword is even.

- The weight distributions for the (23, 12) and the (24, 12) codes are shown in Table 8.2.

8.6.1 Decoding the Golay Code

We present here two decoding algorithms for the Golay code. The first decoder, due to [108], is algebraic and is similar in spirit to the decoding algorithms used for BCH and Reed–Solomon codes. The second decoder is arithmetic, being similar in spirit to the Hamming decoder presented in Section 1.9.1.

Table 8.2: Weight Distributions for the $\mathcal{G}_{23}$ and $\mathcal{G}_{24}$ Codes [483]

$\mathcal{G}_{23}$:	i: 0	7	8	11	12	15	16	23
	A_i: 1	253	506	1288	1288	506	253	1

$\mathcal{G}_{24}$:	i: 0	8	12	16	24
	A_i: 1	759	2576	759	1

8.6.1.1 Algebraic Decoding of the $\mathcal{G}_{23}$ Golay Code

The algebraic decoder works similar to those we have seen for BCH codes. An algebraic syndrome is first computed, which is used to construct an error-locator polynomial. The roots of the error-locator polynomial determine the error locations, which for a binary code is sufficient for the decoding. Having minimum distance 7, $\mathcal{G}_{23}$ is capable of correcting up to three errors.

Let β be a primitive 23rd root of unity in $GF(2^{11})$. Recall that the quadratic residues modulo 23 are $Q_p = \{1, 2, 3, 4, 6, 8, 9, 12, 13, 16, 18\}$ and the generator polynomial is

$$g(x) = \prod_{i \in Q_p} (x - \beta^i).$$

Thus, β, β^3, and β^9 are all roots of $g(x)$, and hence of any codeword $c(x) = m(x)g(x)$. Let $c(x)$ be the transmitted codeword, and let $r(x) = c(x) + e(x)$ be the received polynomial. We define the syndrome as

$$s_i = r(\beta^i) = e(\beta^i).$$

If there are no errors, then $s_i = 0$ for $i \in Q_p$. Thus, for example, if $s_1 = s_3 = s_9 = 0$, no errors are detected. If there is a single error, $e(x) = x^{j_1}$, then

$$s_1 = \beta^{j_1}, \quad s_3 = \beta^{3j_1}, \quad s_9 = \beta^{9j_1}.$$

When this condition is detected, single-error correction can proceed.

Suppose there are two or three errors, $e(x) = x^{j_1} + x^{j_2} + x^{j_3}$. Let $z_1 = \beta^{j_1}$, $z_2 = \beta^{j_2}$, and $z_3 = \beta^{j_3}$ be the error locators, where $z_3 = 0$ in the case of only two errors. The syndromes in this case are

$$s_i = z_1^i + z_2^i + z_3^i.$$

Define the *error-locator* polynomial as

$$L(x) = (x - z_1)(x - z_2)(x - z_3) = x^3 + \sigma_1 x^2 + \sigma_2 x + \sigma_3,$$

where, by polynomial multiplication,

$$\sigma_1 = z_1 + z_2 + z_3$$

$$\sigma_2 = z_1 z_2 + z_1 z_3 + z_2 z_3$$

$$\sigma_3 = z_1 z_2 z_3.$$

The problem now is to compute the coefficients of the error-locator polynomial using the syndrome values. By substitution of the definitions, it can be shown that

$$s_9 + s_1^9 = \sigma_2 s_7 + \sigma_3 s_3^2 \qquad s_7 = s_1 s_3^2 + \sigma_2 s_5 + \sigma_3 s_1^4$$

$$s_5 = s_1^5 + \sigma_2 s_3 + \sigma_3 s_1^2 \qquad s_1^3 + s_3 = \sigma_3 + \sigma_2 s_1.$$

By application of these equivalences (see `golaysimp.m`), it can be shown that

$$D \triangleq (s_1^3 + s_3)^2 + \frac{s_1^9 + s_9}{s_1^3 + s_3} = (\sigma_2 + s_1^2)^3. \tag{8.17}$$

The quantity D thus has a cube root in $GF(2^{11})$. From (8.17), we obtain $\sigma_2 = s_1^2 + D^{1/3}$; similarly for σ_3. Combining these results, we obtain the following equations:

$$\sigma_1 = s_1 \qquad \sigma_2 = s_1^2 + D^{1/3} \qquad \sigma_3 = s_3 + s_1 D^{1/3}.$$

An example of the decoder is shown in `testGolay.cc`.

golaysimp.m

8.6.1.2 Arithmetic Decoding of the $\mathcal{G}_{24}$ Code

In this section, we present an arithmetic coder, which uses the weight structure of the syndrome to determine the error patterns.

Besides the generator matrix representation of (8.16), it is convenient to employ a systematic generator. The generator matrix can be written in the form

$$
G = \left[\begin{array}{cccccccccccc|cccccccccccc}
1 & & & & & & & & & & & & 1 & 1 & 1 & 1 & 1 & 1 & 1 & 1 & 1 & 1 & 1 & \\
& 1 & & & & & & & & & & & 1 & 1 & 1 & & 1 & 1 & 1 & & & & 1 & \\
& & 1 & & & & & & & & & & 1 & 1 & & 1 & 1 & 1 & & & & 1 & & 1 \\
& & & 1 & & & & & & & & & 1 & & 1 & 1 & 1 & & & 1 & & & 1 & 1 \\
& & & & 1 & & & & & & & & 1 & 1 & 1 & 1 & & & 1 & & & 1 & 1 & \\
& & & & & 1 & & & & & & & 1 & 1 & 1 & & & 1 & & 1 & 1 & & & 1 \\
& & & & & & 1 & & & & & & 1 & 1 & & & 1 & & 1 & 1 & & 1 & 1 & \\
& & & & & & & 1 & & & & & 1 & & & 1 & & 1 & 1 & & 1 & 1 & 1 & \\
& & & & & & & & 1 & & & & 1 & & 1 & & 1 & 1 & & 1 & 1 & 1 & & \\
& & & & & & & & & 1 & & & 1 & 1 & & 1 & 1 & & 1 & 1 & 1 & & & \\
& & & & & & & & & & 1 & & 1 & 1 & & 1 & 1 & & 1 & 1 & 1 & & & \\
& & & & & & & & & & & 1 & 1 & 1 & & 1 & 1 & & 1 & 1 & 1 & & & 1 \\
\end{array}\right]
$$

$$
= \begin{bmatrix} I_{12} & B \end{bmatrix}.
$$

It may be observed that B is orthogonal,

$$
B^T B = I.
$$

Let $\mathbf{r} = \mathbf{c} + \mathbf{e}$ and let $\mathbf{e} = (\mathbf{x}, \mathbf{y})$, where $\mathbf{x}$ and $\mathbf{y}$ are each vectors of length 12. Since the code is capable of correcting up to three errors, there are only a few possible weight distributions of $\mathbf{x}$ and $\mathbf{y}$ to consider:

$$
\begin{aligned}
\mathrm{wt}(\mathbf{x}) \le 3 \quad & \mathrm{wt}(\mathbf{y}) = 0 \\
\mathrm{wt}(\mathbf{x}) \le 2 \quad & \mathrm{wt}(\mathbf{y}) = 1 \\
\mathrm{wt}(\mathbf{x}) \le 1 \quad & \mathrm{wt}(\mathbf{y}) = 2 \\
\mathrm{wt}(\mathbf{x}) = 0 \quad & \mathrm{wt}(\mathbf{y}) = 3.
\end{aligned}
$$

Since the code is self-dual, the generator matrix is also the parity check matrix. We can compute a syndrome by

$$
\mathbf{s} = G\mathbf{r}^T = G(\mathbf{e}^T) = G[\mathbf{x}, \mathbf{y}]^T = \mathbf{x}^T + B\mathbf{y}^T.
$$

If $\mathbf{y} = \mathbf{0}$, then $\mathbf{s} = \mathbf{x}^T$. If $\mathbf{s}$ has weight ≤ 3, we conclude that $\mathbf{y} = \mathbf{0}$. The error pattern is $\mathbf{e} = (\mathbf{x}, \mathbf{0}) = (\mathbf{s}^T, \mathbf{0})$.

Suppose now that $\mathrm{wt}(\mathbf{y}) = 1$, where the error is in the ith coordinate of $\mathbf{y}$ and that $\mathrm{wt}(\mathbf{x}) \le 2$. The syndrome in this case is

$$
\mathbf{s} = \mathbf{x}^T + \mathbf{b}_i,
$$

where $\mathbf{b}_i$ is the ith column of B. The position i is found by identifying the position such that $\mathrm{wt}(\mathbf{s} + \mathbf{b}_i) = \mathrm{wt}(\mathbf{x}) \le 2$. Having thus identified i, the error pattern is $\mathbf{e} = ((\mathbf{s} + \mathbf{b}_i)^T, \mathbf{y}_i)$. Here, the notation $\mathbf{y}_i$ is the vector of length 12 having a 1 in position i and zeros elsewhere.

If $\mathrm{wt}(\mathbf{x}) = 0$ and $\mathrm{wt}(\mathbf{y}) = 2$ or 3, then $\mathbf{s} = \mathbf{b}_i + \mathbf{b}_j$ or $\mathbf{s} = \mathbf{b}_i + \mathbf{b}_j + \mathbf{b}_k$. Since B is an orthogonal matrix,

$$
B^T \mathbf{s} = B^T(B\mathbf{y}^T) = \mathbf{y}^T.
$$

The error pattern is $\mathbf{e} = (\mathbf{0}, (B^T \mathbf{s})^T)$.

Finally, if $\mathrm{wt}(\mathbf{x}) = 1$ and $\mathrm{wt}(\mathbf{y}) = 2$, let the nonzero coordinate of $\mathbf{x}$ be at index i. Then

$$B^T\mathbf{s} = B^T(\mathbf{x}^T + B\mathbf{y}^T) = B^T\mathbf{x}^T + B^T B\mathbf{y}^T = \mathbf{r}_i^T + \mathbf{y}^T,$$

where $\mathbf{r}_i$ is the ith row of B. The error pattern is $\mathbf{e} = (\mathbf{x}_i, (B^T\mathbf{s})^T + \mathbf{r}_i)$.

Combining all these cases together, we obtain the following decoding algorithm.

golayarith.m

Algorithm 8.2 Arithmetic Decoding of the Golay $\mathcal{G}_{24}$ Code

---

(This presentation is due to Wicker [483])

1 **Input:** $\mathbf{r} = \mathbf{e} + \mathbf{c}$, the received vector
2 **Output:** $\mathbf{c}$, the decoded vector
3 Compute $\mathbf{s} = G\mathbf{r}$ (compute the syndrome)
4 if $\mathrm{wt}(\mathbf{s}) \le 3$
5     $\mathbf{e} = (\mathbf{s}^T, \mathbf{0})$
6 else if $\mathrm{wt}(\mathbf{s} + \mathbf{b}_i) \le 2$ for some column vector $\mathbf{b}_i$
7     $\mathbf{e} = ((\mathbf{s} + \mathbf{b}_i)^T, \mathbf{y}_i)$
8 else
9   Compute $B^T\mathbf{s}$
10   if $\mathrm{wt}(B^T\mathbf{s}) \le 3$
11        $\mathbf{e} = (\mathbf{0}, (B^T\mathbf{s})^T)$
12   else if $\mathrm{wt}(B^T\mathbf{s} + \mathbf{r}_i^T) \le 2$ for some row vector $\mathbf{r}_i$
13        $\mathbf{e} = (\mathbf{x}_i, (B^T\mathbf{s})^T + \mathbf{r}_i)$
14   else
15   Too many errors: declare uncorrectable error pattern and stop.
16   end
17 end
18 $\mathbf{c} = \mathbf{r} + \mathbf{e}$

A MATLAB implementation that may be used to generate examples is in `golayarith.m`

8.7 Exercises

8.1   Verify items 1, 9, and 10 of Theorem 8.3.

8.2   Show that

$$\begin{bmatrix} 1 & 1 \\ 1 & -1 \end{bmatrix} \otimes H_n \quad \text{and} \quad H_n \otimes \begin{bmatrix} 1 & 1 \\ 1 & -1 \end{bmatrix}$$

are Hadamard matrices.

8.3   Prove the first two parts of Theorem 8.8.

8.4   Compute the quadratic residues modulo 19. Compute the values of the Legendre symbol $\chi_{19}(x)$ for $x = 1, 2, \ldots, 18$.

8.5   The Legendre symbol has the following properties. Prove them. In all cases, take $(a, p) = 1$ and $(b, p) = 1$.

    (a) $\chi_p(a) \equiv a^{(p-1)/2} \pmod{p}$. *Hint*: if $\chi_p(a) = 1$ then $x^2 \equiv a \pmod{p}$ has a solution, say x_0. Then $a^{(p-1)/2} \equiv x_0^{p-1}$. Then use Fermat's theorem.

    (b) $\chi_p(a)\chi_p(b) = \chi_p(ab)$.

    (c) $a \equiv b \pmod{p}$ implies that $\chi_p(a) = \chi_p(b)$.

    (d) $\chi_p(a^2) = 1$. $\chi_p(a^2 b) = \chi_p(b)$. $\chi_p(1) = 1$. $\chi_p(-1) = (-1)^{(p-1)/2}$.

8.6   Construct a Hadamard matrix of order 20.

8.7   Construct the Hadamard codes $\mathcal{A}_{20}$, $\mathcal{B}_{20}$, and $\mathcal{C}_{20}$. Which of these are linear codes? Which are cyclic?

8.8   Construct a generator and parity check matrix for $RM(2,4)$.

8.9   Show that $RM(r,m)$ is a subcode of $RM(r+1,m)$.

8.10 Show that $RM(0,m)$ is a repetition code.

8.11 Show that $RM(m-1,m)$ is a simple parity check code.

8.12 Show that if $\mathbf{c} \in RM(r,m)$, then $(\mathbf{c},\mathbf{c}) \in RM(r,m+1)$.

8.13 For each of the following received sequences received from $RM(1,3)$ codes, determine the transmitted codeword $\mathbf{c}$.

    (a) $\mathbf{r} = [1,0,1,0,1,1,0,1]$.

    (b) $\mathbf{r} = [0,1,0,0,1,1,1,1]$.

8.14 Prove that all codewords in $RM(1,m)$ have weight 0, 2^{m-1} or 2^m. *Hint*: By induction.

8.15 Show that the $RM(1,3)$ and $RM(2,5)$ codes are self-dual. Are there other self-dual RM codes?

8.16 For the $RM(1,4)$ code:

    (a) Write the generator G.

    (b) Determine the minimum distance.

    (c) Write down the parity checks for $\hat{m}_4$, $\hat{m}_3$, $\hat{m}_2$, $\hat{m}_1$ and $\hat{m}_0$.

    (d) Decode the received vector $\mathbf{r} = [0,1,1,1,0,1,1,0,1,0,0,1,1,0,0,1]$, if possible.

    (e) Decode the received vector $\mathbf{r} = [1,1,1,1,0,1,1,0,1,1,1,1,0,0,0,0]$, if possible.

    (f) Decode the received vector $\mathbf{r} = [1,1,1,1,0,0,1,1,0,1,0,1,1,0,1,0]$, if possible.

8.17 Verify the parity check equations for Figure 8.6(a) and (b).

8.18 For the inverse Hadamard transform:

    (a) Provide a matrix decomposition analogous to (8.10).

    (b) Draw the signal flow diagram for the fast inverse Hadamard computation.

    (c) Implement your algorithm in MATLAB.

8.19 Construct the generator for a $RM(2,4)$ code using the $[\mathbf{u}|\mathbf{u}+\mathbf{v}]$ construction.

8.20 Using the $[\mathbf{u}|\mathbf{u}+\mathbf{v}]$ construction show that the generator for a $RM(r,m)$ code can be constructed as

$$G = \begin{bmatrix} G_{RM}(r,m-2) & G_{RM}(r,m-2) & G_{RM}(r,m-2) & G_{RM}(r,m-2) \\ 0 & G_{RM}(r-1,m-2) & 0 & G_{RM}(r-1,m-2) \\ 0 & 0 & G_{RM}(r-1,m-2) & G_{RM}(r-1,m-2) \\ 0 & 0 & 0 & G_{RM}(r-2,m-2) \end{bmatrix}.$$

8.21 Construct the generator for a $RM(2,4)$ code using the Kronecker construction.

8.22 Let $G = \begin{bmatrix} 1 & 1 & 0 & 1 & 0 & 0 & 0 \\ 0 & 1 & 1 & 0 & 1 & 0 & 0 \\ 0 & 0 & 1 & 1 & 0 & 1 & 0 \\ 0 & 0 & 0 & 1 & 1 & 0 & 1 \end{bmatrix}$ be the generator for a $(7,4)$ Hamming code C_0. Let G_1 be formed from the first two rows of G. Let G_2 be formed from the first row of G.

    (a) Identify $G_{0\backslash 1}$ and the elements of $[C_0/C_1]$.

   (b) Write down the generator $\mathfrak{g}_{0/1}$ for the code $C_{0/1}$.

   (c) Write down the generator $\mathfrak{g}_{1/2}$ for the code $C_{1/2}$.

   (d) Write down the generator $\mathfrak{g}_{0/1/2}$ for the code $C_{0/1/2}$.

8.23 Quadratic residue code designs.

   (a) Find the generator polynomials for binary quadratic residue codes of length 7 and dimensions 4 and 3. Also, list the quadratic residues modulo 7 and compare with the cyclotomic coset for β.

   (b) Are there binary quadratic residue codes of length 11? Why or why not?

   (c) Find the generator polynomials for binary quadratic residue codes of length 23 and dimensions 12 and 11. Also, list the quadratic residues modulo 23 and compare with the cyclotomic coset for β.

8.24 Find quadratic residue codes with $s = 3$ of length 11 having dimensions 5 and 6.

8.25 Show that $n(x)$ defined in (8.15) has coefficients in $GF(s)$.

8.26 In decoding the Golay code, show that the cube root of D may be computed by finding $x = D^{1365}$.

8.27 Show that the Golay (24,12) code is self-dual.

8.28 Let $\mathbf{r} = [1, 1, 1, 1, 0, 1, 1, 1, 1, 1, 1, 0, 0, 0, 1, 1, 1, 0, 1, 0, 0, 1, 1, 1]$ be a received vector from a Golay $(24, 12)$ code. Determine the transmitted codeword using the arithmetic decoder.

8.29 Let $\mathbf{r} = [1, 1, 1, 0, 1, 1, 1, 1, 1, 1, 0, 0, 0, 1, 1, 1, 0, 1, 0, 0, 1, 1, 1]$ be the received vector from a Golay $(23, 12)$ code. Determine the transmitted codeword using the algebraic decoder.

8.8 References

This chapter was developed largely out of course notes based on [483] and closely follows it. The discussion of Hadamard matrices and codes is drawn from [292] and [483]. A more complete discussion on quadratic residues may be found in [325]. Considerably more detail about Reed–Muller codes is available in [292]. The Reed–Muller codes were first described in [321], with work by Reed immediately following [362] which reinforced the Boolean function idea and provided an efficient decoding algorithm. The graph employed in developing the Reed–Muller decoding orthogonal equations is an example of a Euclidean geometry $EG(m, r)$, a finite geometry. This area is developed and explored, giving rise to generalizations of the majority logic decoding, in [271, Chapter 8]. Chapter 7 of [271] also develops majority logic decoding for cyclic codes. Majority logic decoding can also be employed on convolutional codes [271, Chapter 13], but increasing hardware capabilities has made this less-complex alternative to the Viterbi algorithm less attractive.

The Golay codes are covered in lavish and fascinating detail in Chapters 2, 16, and 20 of [292]. Interesting connections between G_{24} and the 24-dimensional Leech lattice are presented in [79].

Another type of decoder which has worked well for the Golay code is an *error trapping decoder*. Such decoders employ the cycle structure of the codes, just as the Meggitt decoders do, but they simplify the number of syndromes the decoder must recognize. A thorough discussion of error trapping decoders is in [271] and [244]. Other Golay code decoders include conventional coset decoding; a method due to Berlekamp [458, p. 35]; and majority logic decoding [292].

Chapter 9

Bounds on Codes

Let C be an (n, k) block code with minimum distance d over a field with q elements with redundancy $r = n - k$. There are relationships that must be satisfied among the code length n, the dimension k, the minimum distance $d_{\min}$, and the field size q. We have already met two of these: the Singleton bound of Theorem 3.15,

$$d \leq n - k + 1 = r + 1,$$

and the Hamming bound of Theorem 3.17,

$$r \geq \log_q V_q(n, t),$$

where $V_q(n, t)$ is the number of points in a Hamming sphere of radius $t = \lfloor (d - 1)/2 \rfloor$,

$$V_q(n, t) = \sum_{i=0}^{t} \binom{n}{i} (q - 1)^i \tag{9.1}$$

(see (3.9)). In this chapter, we present other bounds which govern the relationships among the parameters defining a code. In this, we are seeking theoretical limits without regard to the feasibility of a code for any particular use, such as having efficient encoding or decoding algorithms. This chapter is perhaps the most mathematical of the book. It does not introduce any good codes or decoding algorithms, but the bounds introduced here have been of both historical and practical importance, as they have played a part in motivating the search for good codes and helped direct where the search should take place.

Definition 9.1 Let $A_q(n, d)$ be the maximum number of codewords in any code over $GF(q)$ of length n with minimum distance d. □

For a linear code the dimension of the code is $k = \log_q A_q(n, d)$.

Consider what happens as n gets long in a channel with probability of symbol error equal to p_c. The average number of errors in a received vector is np_c. Thus, in order for a sequence of codes to be asymptotically effective, providing capability to correct the increasing number of errors in longer codewords, the minimum distance must grow at least as fast as $2np_c$. We will frequently be interested in the relative distance and the rate k/n as $n \to \infty$.

Definition 9.2 For a code with length n and minimum distance d, let $\delta = d/n$ be the **relative distance** of the code. □

For a code with relative distance δ, the distance is $d \approx \lfloor \delta n \rfloor = \delta n + O(1)$.

Error Correction Coding: Mathematical Methods and Algorithms, Second Edition. Todd K. Moon
© 2021 John Wiley & Sons, Inc. Published 2021 by John Wiley & Sons, Inc.
Companion website: www.wiley.com/go/Moon/ErrorCorrectionCoding

Definition 9.3 Let[1]

$$\alpha_q(\delta) = \limsup_{n \to \infty} \frac{1}{n} \log_q A_q(n, \lfloor \delta n \rfloor). \tag{9.2}$$

For a linear code, $\log_q A_q(n, d)$ is the dimension of the code and $\frac{1}{n}\log_q A_q(n, d)$ is the code rate, so $\alpha_q(\delta)$ is the maximum possible code rate that an arbitrarily long code can have while maintaining a relative distance δ. We call this the **asymptotic rate**.   □

The functions $A_q(n, d)$ and $\alpha_q(\delta)$ are not known in general, but upper and lower bounds on these functions can be established. For example, the Singleton bound can be expressed in terms of these functions as

$$A_q(n, d) \le q^{n-d+1}$$

and, asymptotically,

$$\alpha_q(\delta) \le 1 - \delta.$$

plotbds.m
mcelieceg.m

Many of the bounds presented here are expressed in terms of $\alpha_q(\delta)$. A lower bound is the Gilbert–Varshamov bound (sometimes called the Varshamov–Gilbert bound). As upper bounds on $\alpha_q(\delta)$, we also have the Hamming and Singleton bounds, the Plotkin bound, the Elias bound, and the McEliece–Rodemich–Rumsey–Welch bound (in two forms). Figure 9.1 shows a comparison of the lower bound and these upper bounds. Codes exist which fall between the lower bound and the smallest of the upper bounds, that is, in the shaded region.

A function which figures into some of the bounds is the entropy function. The binary entropy function H_2 was introduced in Section 1.3. Here we generalize that definition.

Definition 9.4 Let $\rho = (q - 1)/q$. Define the entropy function H_q on $[0, \rho]$ by

$$H_q(x) = x\log_q(q - 1) - x\log_q x - (1 - x)\log_q(1 - x), \quad x \in (0, \rho]$$

and $H_q(0) = 0$.   □

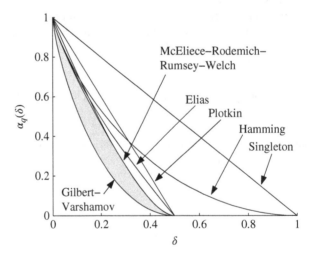

Figure 9.1: Comparison of lower bound (Gilbert–Varshamov) and various upper bounds.

---

[1] The lim sup is the least upper bound of the values that its argument function returns to infinitely often. Initially it may be helpful to think of lim sup as "sup" or "max."

The entropy and the number of points in the Hamming sphere are asymptotically related.

Lemma 9.5 *Let* $0 \le x \le \rho = (q-1)/q$*. Then*

$$\lim_{n \to \infty} \frac{1}{n} \log_q V_q(n, \lfloor xn \rfloor) = H_q(x). \tag{9.3}$$

Proof First we need a way to approximate the binomial. Stirling's formula (see Exercise 9.10) says that(see Box 9.1 for the o notation)

$$n! = \sqrt{2\pi n} \, n^n e^{-n}(1 + o(1)).$$

Thus,

$$\log n! = \log \sqrt{2\pi} + \left(n + \frac{1}{2}\right)\log n - n + o(1) = n \log n - n + O(\log n). \tag{9.4}$$

Now let $m = \lfloor xn \rfloor$. Then by (9.1),

$$V_q(n, m) = \sum_{i=0}^{m} \binom{n}{i}(q-1)^i.$$

The last term of the summation is the largest over this index range. Also, it is clear that

$$\sum_{i=0}^{m-1} \binom{n}{i}(q-1)^i \le m \binom{n}{m}(q-1)^m.$$

We thus obtain

$$\binom{n}{m}(q-1)^m \le V_q(n, m) \le (1+m) \binom{n}{m}(q-1)^m.$$

Take $\log_q$ throughout and divide through by n to obtain

$$\frac{1}{n}\log_q \binom{n}{m} + \frac{m}{n}\log_q(q-1) \le \frac{1}{n}\log_q V_q(n, m)$$

$$\le \frac{1}{n}\log_q(1+m) + \frac{1}{n}\log_q \binom{n}{m} + \frac{m}{n}\log_q(q-1). \tag{9.5}$$

As $n \to \infty$, $\frac{1}{n}\log_q(1+m) \to 0$. Using the fact that $\frac{m}{n} = x + o(1)$, we obtain

$$\lim_{n \to \infty} \frac{1}{n}\log_q V_q(n, m) = \lim_{n \to \infty} \frac{1}{n}\log_q \binom{n}{m} + \frac{m}{n}\log_q(q-1)$$

$$= \lim_{n \to \infty} \frac{1}{n}\log_q \binom{n}{m} + x\log_q(q-1) + o(1).$$

Using (9.4), we have

$$\lim_{n\to\infty} \frac{1}{n}\log_q V_q(n,m)$$

$$= \log_q n - \delta\log_q m - (1-\delta)\log_q(n-m) + \delta\log_q(q-1) + o(1)$$

$$= \log_q n - \delta\log_q \delta - \delta\log_q n - (1-\delta)\log_q(1-\delta) - (1-\delta)\log_q n$$

$$\quad + \delta\log_q(q-1) + o(1)$$

$$= -\delta\log_q \delta - (1-\delta)\log_q(1-\delta) + \delta\log_q(q-1) + o(1) = H_q(\delta) + o(1).$$

$\square$

9.1 The Gilbert–Varshamov Bound

The Gilbert–Varshamov bound is a lower bound on $A_q(n,d)$.

Theorem 9.6 *For natural numbers n and d, with $d \leq n$,*

$$A_q(n,d) \geq \frac{q^n}{V_q(n,d-1)}. \tag{9.6}$$

Proof [458] Let C be a code of length n and distance d with the maximum number of codewords. Then of all the q^n possible n-tuples, there is none with distance d or more to some codeword in C. (Otherwise, that n-tuple could be added to the code and C would not have had the maximum number of codewords.) Thus, the Hamming spheres of radius $d-1$ around the codewords cover all the n-tuples, so that the sum of their volumes is $\geq$ the number of points. That is,

$$|C|V_q(n,d-1) \geq q^n.$$

This is equivalent to (9.6). $\square$

For a linear code, the Gilbert–Varshamov bound can be manipulated as follows:

$$\log_q A_q(n,d) \geq n - \log_q V_q(n,d-1)$$

or

$$n - \log_q A_q(n,d) \leq \log_q V_q(n,d-1).$$

The correction capability satisfies $d = 2t + 1$. The redundancy can be written as $r = n - k = n - \log_q A_q(n,d)$. We obtain

$$r \leq \log_q V_q(n,2t). \tag{9.7}$$

The Gilbert–Varshamov bound can thus be viewed as an *upper bound* on the necessary redundancy for a code: there exists a t-error correcting q-ary code with redundancy r bounded as in (9.7).

The Gilbert–Varshamov bound also has an asymptotic form.

Theorem 9.7 *If $0 \leq \delta \leq \rho = (q-1)/q$, then*

$$\alpha_q(\delta) \geq 1 - H_q(\delta).$$

Proof [458] Using (9.2), (9.6), and Lemma 9.5, we have

$$\alpha_q(\delta) = \limsup_{n\to\infty} \frac{1}{n}\log_q A_q(n,\lfloor\delta n\rfloor) \geq \lim_{n\to\infty}\left(1 - \frac{1}{n}\log_q V_q(n,\delta n)\right) = 1 - H_q(\delta).$$

$\square$

The Gilbert–Varshamov bound is a lower bound: it should be possible to do at least as well as this bound predicts for long codes. However, for many years it was assumed that $\alpha_q(\delta)$ would, in fact, be equal to the lower bound for long codes, since no families of codes were known that were capable of exceeding the Gilbert–Varshamov bound as the code length increased. In 1982, a family of codes based on algebraic geometry was reported, however, which exceeded the lower bound [450]. Unfortunately, algebraic geometry codes fall beyond the scope of this book. (See [449] for a comprehensive introduction to algebraic geometry codes, or [457] or [351]. For mathematical background of these codes, see [421].)

9.2 The Plotkin Bound

Theorem 9.8 *Let C be a q-ary code of length n and minimum distance d. Then if d > ρn,*

$$A_q(n,d) \leq \frac{d}{d - \rho n}, \tag{9.8}$$

where $\rho = (q-1)/q$.

Proof [458] Consider a code C with M codewords in it. Form a list with the M codewords as the rows, and consider a column in this list. Let q_j denote the number of times that the jth symbol in the code alphabet, $0 \leq j < q$, appears in this column. Clearly, $\sum_{j=0}^{q-1} q_j = M$.

Let the rows of the table be arranged so that the q_0 codewords with the 0th symbol are listed first and call that set of codewords R_0, the q_1 codewords with the 1st symbol are listed second and call that set of codewords R_1, and so forth. Consider the Hamming distance between all $M(M-1)$ pairs of codewords, as perceived by this selected column. For pairs of codewords within a single set R_i, all the symbols are the same, so there is no contribution to the Hamming distance. For pairs of codewords drawn from different sets, there is a contribution of 1 to the Hamming distance. Thus, for each of the q_j codewords drawn from set R_j, there is a total contribution of $M - q_j$ to the Hamming distance between the codewords in R_j and all the other sets. Summing these up, the contribution of this column to the sum of the distances between all pairs of codewords is

$$\sum_{j=0}^{q-1} q_j(M - q_j) = M \sum_{j=0}^{q-1} q_j - \sum_{j=0}^{q-1} q_j^2 = M^2 - \sum_{j=0}^{q-1} q_j^2.$$

Now use the Cauchy–Schwartz inequality (see Box 9.2 and Exercise 9.6) to write

$$\sum_{j=0}^{q-1} q_j(M - q_j) \leq M^2 - \frac{1}{q}\left(\sum_{j=0}^{q-1} q_j\right)^2 = M^2\left(1 - \frac{1}{q}\right).$$

Now total this result over all n columns. There are $M(M-1)$ pairs of codewords, each a distance at least d apart. We obtain

$$M(M-1)d \leq n\left(1 - \frac{1}{q}\right)M^2 = n\rho M^2$$

or

$$M \leq \frac{d}{d - n\rho}.$$

Since this result holds for any code, since the C was arbitrary, it must hold for the code with $A_q(n,d)$ codewords. $\square$

Equivalently,

$$d \leq \frac{n\rho M}{M - 1}.$$

The Plotkin bound provides an upper bound on the distance of a code with given length n and size M.

BOX 9.2: The Cauchy–Schwartz Inequality

For our purposes, the Cauchy-Schwartz inequality can be expressed as follows (see [319] for extensions and discussions): Let $\mathbf{a} = (a_1, a_2, \ldots, a_n)$ and $\mathbf{b} = (b_1, b_2, \ldots, b_n)$ be sequences of real or complex numbers. Then

$$\left| \sum_{i=1}^{n} a_i b_i \right|^2 \leq \sum_{i=1}^{n} |a_i|^2 \sum_{i=1}^{n} |b_i|^2.$$

9.3 The Griesmer Bound

Theorem 9.9 *For a linear block (n,k) q-ary code C with minimum distance d,*

$$n \geq \sum_{i=0}^{k-1} \lceil d/q^i \rceil.$$

Proof Let $N(k,d)$ be the length of the shortest q-ary linear code of dimension k and minimum distance d. Let C be an $(N(k,d), k, d)$ code and let G be a generator matrix of the code. Assume (without loss of generality, by row and/or column interchanges and/or row operations) that G is written with the first row as follows:

$$G = \left[\begin{array}{ccc|ccc} 1 & 1 \quad \ldots \quad 1 & & 0 & 0 \quad \ldots \quad 0 \\ \hline & G_1 & & & G_2 & \end{array} \right],$$

where G_1 is $(k-1) \times d$ and G_2 is $(k-1) \times (N(k,d) - d)$. Claim: G_2 has rank $k-1$. Otherwise, it would be possible to make the first row of G_2 equal to 0 (by row operations). Then an appropriate input message could produce a codeword of weight $< d$, by canceling one of the ones from the first row with some linear combination of rows of G_1, resulting in a codeword of minimum distance $< d$.

Let G_2 be the generator for an $(N(k,d) - d, k-1, d_1)$ code C'. We will now determine a bound on d_1.

Now let $[\mathbf{u}_0 | \mathbf{v}]$ (the concatenation of two vectors) be a codeword in C,

$$[\mathbf{u}_0 | \mathbf{v}] = \mathbf{m}_0 G,$$

where $\mathbf{v} \in C'$ has weight d_1 and where $\mathbf{m}_0$ is a message vector with 0 in the first position,

$$\mathbf{m}_0 = [0, m_2, \ldots, m_k].$$

Let z_0 be the number of zeros in $\mathbf{u}_0$, $z_0 = d - \text{wt}(\mathbf{u}_0)$. Then we have

$$\text{wt}(\mathbf{u}_0) + d_1 = (d - z_0) + d_1 \geq d.$$

Let $\mathbf{m}_i = [i, m_2, \ldots, m_k]$, for $i \in GF(q)$, and let

$$\mathbf{u}_i = \mathbf{m}_i G.$$

Let z_i be the number of zeros in $\mathbf{u}_i$, $z_i = d - \text{wt}(\mathbf{u}_i)$. As i varies over the elements in $GF(q)$, eventually every element in $\mathbf{u}_i$ will be set to 0. Thus,

$$\sum_{i=0}^{q-1} z_i = d.$$

Writing down the weight equation for each i, we have

$$d_1 + d - z_0 \geq d$$

$$d_1 + d - z_1 \geq d$$

$$\vdots$$

$$d_1 + d - z_{q-1} \geq d.$$

Summing all these equations, we obtain

$$qd_1 + qd - d \geq qd$$

or

$$d_1 \geq \lceil d/q \rceil.$$

G_2 therefore generates an $(N(k,d) - d, k - 1)$ code with a minimum Hamming distance which is at least $\lceil d/q \rceil$. We conclude that

$$N(k-1, \lceil d/q \rceil) \leq N(k,d) - d.$$

Now we simply proceed inductively:

$$N(k,d) \geq d + N(k-1, \lceil d/q \rceil) \geq d + \lceil d/q^2 \rceil + N(k-2, \lceil d/q^2 \rceil)$$

$$\vdots$$

$$\geq \sum_{i=0}^{k-2} \lceil d/q^i \rceil + N(1, \lceil d/2^{k-1} \rceil)$$

$$\geq \sum_{i=0}^{k-1} \lceil d/q^i \rceil.$$

Since $N(k,d) < n$ for any actual code, the result follows. $\qquad\square$

9.4 The Linear Programming and Related Bounds

The linear programming bound takes the most development to produce of the bounds introduced so far. However, the tools introduced are interesting and useful in their own right. Furthermore, the programming bound technique leads to one of the tightest bounds known. We introduce first what is meant by linear programming, then present the main theorem, still leaving some definitions unstated. This is followed by the definition of Krawtchouk polynomials, the character (needed for a couple of key lemmas), and finally the proof of the theorem.

Let $\mathbf{x}$ be a vector, $\mathbf{c}$ a vector, $\mathbf{b}$ a vector, and A a matrix. A problem of the form

$$\begin{aligned} \text{maximize} \quad & \mathbf{c}^T \mathbf{x} \\ \text{subject to} \quad & A\mathbf{x} \leq \mathbf{b} \end{aligned} \tag{9.9}$$

(or other equivalent forms) is said to be a *linear programming problem*. The maximum quantity $\mathbf{c}^T\mathbf{x}$ from the solution is said to be the *value* of the linear programming problem.

Example 9.10   Consider the following problem:

$$\text{maximize } x_1 + x_2$$

$$\text{subject to } x_1 + 2x_2 \leq 10$$

$$\frac{15}{2}x_1 + 5x_2 \leq 45$$

$$x_1 \geq 0 \quad x_2 \geq 0.$$

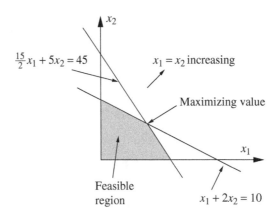

Figure 9.2: A linear programming problem.

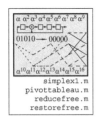

simplex1.m
pivottableau.m
reducefree.m
restorefree.m

Figure 9.2 illustrates the geometry. The shaded region is the *feasible region*, the region where all the constraints are satisfied. The function $x_1 + x_2$ increases in the direction shown, so that the point in the feasible region maximizing $x_1 + x_2$ is as shown.

The solution to this problem is $x_1 = 4$, $x_2 = 3$ and the value is $x_1 + x_2 = 7$.   □

The feasible region always forms a polytope and, due to the linear nature of the function being optimized, the solution is always found on a vertex or along an edge of the feasible region. Linear programming problems arise in a variety of applied contexts and algorithmic methods of solving them are well established. (See [319] and the references therein for an introduction.)

The linear programming bound applies to both linear and nonlinear codes.

Definition 9.11 Let C be a q-ary code with M codewords of length n. Define

$$A_i = \frac{1}{M} |\{(\mathbf{c}, \mathbf{d}) | \mathbf{c} \in C, \mathbf{d} \in C, d_H(\mathbf{c}, \mathbf{d}) = i\}|.$$

That is, A_i is the (normalized) number of codewords in the code at a distance i from each other. The sequence $(A_0, A_1, \ldots, A_n)$ is called the **distance distribution** of the code. For a linear code, the distance distribution is the weight distribution.   □

In Section 9.4.1, we will introduce a family of polynomials $K_k(x)$, known as *Krawtchouk polynomials*. The theorem is expressed in terms of these polynomials as follows.

Theorem 9.12 *[458]* (**Linear programming bound**)   *For a q-ary code of length n and minimum distance d*

$$A_q(n, d) \leq M,$$

where M is value of the linear programming problem

$$\text{maximize} \sum_{i=0}^{n} A_i$$

$$\text{subject to } A_0 = 1,$$

$$A_i = 0 \text{ for } 1 \leq i < d$$

$$\sum_{i=0}^{n} A_i K_k(i) \geq 0 \text{ for } k \in \{0, 1, \ldots, n\}$$

$$A_i \geq 0 \text{ for } i \in \{0, 1, \ldots, n\}.$$

Furthermore, if $q = 2$ and d is even, then we may take $A_i = 0$ for odd i.

Solution of the linear programming problem in this theorem not only provides a bound on $A_q(n, d)$, but also the distance distribution of the code.

Let us begin with an example that demonstrates what is involved in setting up the linear programming problem, leaving the $K_k(i)$ functions still undefined.

Example 9.13 Determine a bound on $A_2(14, 6)$ for binary codes.

Since $q = 2$, we have $A_1 = A_3 = A_5 = A_7 = A_9 = A_{11} = A_{13} = 0$. Furthermore, since the minimum distance is 6, we also have $A_2 = A_4 = 0$. All the A_i are ≥ 0. The condition $\sum_{i=0}^{n} A_i K_k(i) \geq 0$ in the theorem becomes

$$K_0(0) + K_0(6)A_6 + K_0(8)A_8 + K_0(10)A_{10} + K_0(12)A_{12} + K_0(14)A_{14} \geq 0$$

$$K_1(0) + K_1(6)A_6 + K_1(8)A_8 + K_1(10)A_{10} + K_1(12)A_{12} + K_1(14)A_{14} \geq 0$$

$$K_2(0) + K_2(6)A_6 + K_2(8)A_8 + K_2(10)A_{10} + K_2(12)A_{12} + K_2(14)A_{14} \geq 0 \qquad (9.10)$$

$$\vdots$$

$$K_{14}(0) + K_{14}(6)A_6 + K_{14}(8)A_8 + K_{14}(10)A_{10} + K_{14}(12)A_{12} + K_{14}(14)A_{14} \geq 0.$$

This problem can clearly be expressed in the form (9.9). $\qquad\square$

9.4.1 Krawtchouk Polynomials

The Krawtchouk polynomials mentioned above and used in the linear programming bound are now introduced.

Definition 9.14 The Krawtchouk polynomial $K_k(x; n, q)$ is defined by

$$K_k(x; n, q) = \sum_{j=0}^{k} (-1)^j \binom{x}{j} \binom{n-x}{k-j} (q-1)^{k-j},$$

where

$$\binom{x}{j} = \frac{x(x-1) \cdots (x-j+1)}{j!} \quad \text{for } x \in \mathbb{R}.$$

Usually, $K_k(x; n, q)$ is used in the context of a fixed n and q, so the abbreviated notation $K_k(x)$ is used. $\qquad\square$

krawtchouk.m

Some of the important properties of Krawtchouk polynomials are developed in Exercise 9.16.

9.4.2 Character

We also need the idea of a **character**.

Definition 9.15 Let $\langle G, + \rangle$ be a group and let $\langle T, \cdot \rangle$ be the group of complex numbers which have absolute value 1, with multiplication as the operation. A **character** is a homomorphism $\chi : G \to T$. That is, for all $g_1, g_2 \in G$,

$$\chi(g_1 + g_2) = \chi(g_1)\chi(g_2). \qquad (9.11)$$

If $\chi(g) = 1$ for every $g \in G$, then χ is called the **principal character**. $\qquad\square$

It is straightforward to show that $\chi(0) = 1$, where 0 is the identity of G.

The lemma which we need for our development is the following.

Lemma 9.16 *If χ is a character for $\langle G, + \rangle$, then*

$$\sum_{g \in G} \chi(g) = \begin{cases} |G| & \text{if } \chi \text{ is the principal character} \\ 0 & \text{otherwise.} \end{cases}$$

Proof If χ is principal, the first part is obvious.

Let h be an arbitrary element of G. Then

$$\chi(h) \sum_{g \in G} \chi(g) = \sum_{g \in G} \chi(h + g) = \sum_{k \in G} \chi(k),$$

where the first equality follows from the homomorphism (9.11) and the second equality follows since $h + g$ sweeps out all elements of G as g sweeps over all the elements of G. We thus have

$$(\chi(h) - 1) \sum_{g \in G} \chi(g) = 0.$$

Since h was arbitrary, then if χ is not principal it is possible to choose an $h \in G$ such that $\chi(h) \neq 1$. We must therefore have $\sum_{g \in G} \chi(g) = 0$.   □

Example 9.17   The character property of Lemma 9.16 is actually familiar from signal processing, under a slightly different guise. Let $G = \mathbb{Z}_n$, the set of integers modulo n, and let $\chi_l(g) = e^{-j2\pi lg/n}$ for $g \in G$. Then

$$\sum_{g \in G} \chi_l(g) = \sum_{i=0}^{n-1} e^{-j2\pi lg/n} = \begin{cases} n & l \equiv 0 \ (mod\ n) \\ 0 & \text{otherwise.} \end{cases}$$

Thus, $\chi_l(g)$ is principal if $l = 0$, and not principal if $l \neq 0$.   □

Now let G be the additive group in $GF(q)$. Let $\omega = e^{j2\pi/q}$ be a primitive qth root of unity in $\mathbb{C}$. We want to define a character by

$$\chi(g) = \omega^g$$

for $g \in GF(q)$, but g is not an integer. However, for the purposes of defining a character, we can *interpret* the elements of $GF(q)$ as integers. The only property we need to enforce is the homomorphism property, $\omega^{g_1 + g_2} = \omega^{g_1} \omega^{g_2}$, which will follow if we make the integer interpretation. Thus, we can interpret the alphabet over which a q-ary code exists as $\mathbb{Z}/q\mathbb{Z} \cong \mathbb{Z}_q$, which we will denote as Q.

Note that this character is not principal, so that, by Lemma 9.16,

$$\sum_{g \in Q} \omega^g = 0$$

or

$$\sum_{g \in Q \setminus \{0\}} \omega^g = -1. \tag{9.12}$$

Also note that

$$\sum_{g \in Q \setminus \{0\}} \omega^{0g} = (q - 1). \tag{9.13}$$

Let $\langle \mathbf{x}, \mathbf{y} \rangle$ be the conventional inner product (see Definition 2.60)

$$\langle \mathbf{x}, \mathbf{y} \rangle = \sum_{i=1}^{n} x_i y_i.$$

9.4.3 Krawtchouk Polynomials and Characters

We now present an important lemma which relates Krawtchouk polynomials and characters.

Lemma 9.18 *[458] Let ω be a primitive qth root of unity in $\mathbb{C}$ and let $\mathbf{x} \in Q^n$ be a fixed codevector with weight i. Then*

$$\sum_{\substack{\mathbf{y} \in Q^n: \\ wt(\mathbf{y}) = k}} \omega^{\langle \mathbf{x}, \mathbf{y} \rangle} = K_k(i).$$

Proof Assume that all the weight of $\mathbf{x}$ is in the first i positions,

$$\mathbf{x} = [x_1, x_2, \ldots, x_i, 0, 0, \ldots, 0],$$

with x_1 through x_i not equal to 0. In the vector $\mathbf{y}$ of weight k, choose positions $h_1, h_2, \ldots, h_k$ such that

$$0 < h_1 < h_2 < \cdots < h_j \leq i < h_{j+1} < \cdots < h_k \leq n$$

with $y_{h_k} \neq 0$. That is, the first j nonzero positions of $\mathbf{y}$ overlap the nonzero positions of $\mathbf{x}$. Let D be the set of all words of weight k that have their nonzero coordinates at these k fixed positions. Then

$$\sum_{\mathbf{y} \in D} \omega^{\langle \mathbf{x}, \mathbf{y} \rangle} = \sum_{\mathbf{y} \in D} \omega^{x_{h_1} y_{h_1} + \cdots + x_{h_j} y_{h_j} + 0 + \cdots + 0}$$

$$= \sum_{y_{h_1} \in Q \setminus \{0\}} \cdots \sum_{y_{h_k} \in Q \setminus \{0\}} \omega^{x_{h_1} y_{h_1} + \cdots + x_{h_j} y_{h_j} + 0 + \cdots + 0}$$

$$= \sum_{y_{h_1} \in Q \setminus \{0\}} \omega^{x_{h_1} y_{h_1}} \cdots \sum_{y_{h_j} \in Q \setminus \{0\}} \omega^{x_{h_j} y_{h_j}} \sum_{y_{h_{j+1}} \in Q \setminus \{0\}} \omega^0 \cdots \sum_{y_{h_k} \in Q \setminus \{0\}} \omega^0$$

$$= (-1)^j (q-1)^{n-j},$$

where the last equality follows from (9.12) and (9.13).

The set D may be chosen in $\binom{i}{j} \binom{n-i}{k-j}$ different ways for each fixed position j. We have

$$\sum_{\substack{\mathbf{y} \in Q^n: \\ wt(\mathbf{y}) = k}} \omega^{\langle \mathbf{x}, \mathbf{y} \rangle} = \sum_{\substack{\text{Different} \\ \text{choices of } D}} \sum_{\mathbf{y} \in D} \omega^{\langle \mathbf{x}, \mathbf{y} \rangle} = \sum_{j=0}^{k} \binom{i}{j} \binom{n-i}{k-j} \sum_{\mathbf{y} \in D} \omega^{\langle \mathbf{x}, \mathbf{y} \rangle}$$

$$= \sum_{j=0}^{k} \binom{i}{j} \binom{n-i}{k-j} (-1)^j (q-1)^{k-j} = K_k(i),$$

by the definition of the Krawtchouk polynomial. $\square$

The final lemma we need in preparation for proving the linear programming bound is the following.

Lemma 9.19 *Let $\{A_0, A_1, \ldots, A_n\}$ be the distance distribution of a code C of length n with M codewords. Then*

$$\sum_{i=0}^{n} A_i K_k(i) \geq 0.$$

Proof From Lemma 9.18 and the definition of A_i, we can write

$$\sum_{i=0}^{n} A_i K_k(i) = \sum_{i=0}^{n} \frac{1}{M} \sum_{\substack{(\mathbf{x},\mathbf{y}) \in \mathcal{C}^2: \\ d(\mathbf{x},\mathbf{y}) = i}} \sum_{\substack{\mathbf{z} \in C: \\ \mathrm{wt}(\mathbf{z}) = k}} \omega^{\langle \mathbf{x}-\mathbf{y}, \mathbf{z} \rangle}$$

$$= \frac{1}{M} \sum_{\substack{\mathbf{z} \in C: \\ \mathrm{wt}(\mathbf{z}) = k}} \sum_{(\mathbf{x},\mathbf{y}) \in \mathcal{C}^2} \omega^{\langle \mathbf{x}-\mathbf{y}, \mathbf{z} \rangle}$$

$$= \frac{1}{M} \sum_{\substack{\mathbf{z} \in C: \\ \mathrm{wt}(\mathbf{z}) = k}} \left(\sum_{\mathbf{x} \in C} \omega^{\langle \mathbf{x}, \mathbf{z} \rangle} \right) \left(\sum_{\mathbf{y} \in C} \omega^{-\langle \mathbf{y}, \mathbf{z} \rangle} \right)$$

$$= \frac{1}{M} \sum_{\substack{\mathbf{z} \in C: \\ \mathrm{wt}(\mathbf{z}) = k}} \left| \sum_{\mathbf{x} \in C} \omega^{\langle \mathbf{x}, \mathbf{z} \rangle} \right|^2 \geq 0.$$

□

We are now ready to prove the linear programming bound.

Proof of Theorem 9.12 Lemma 9.19 shows that the distance distribution must satisfy

$$\sum_{i=0}^{n} A_i K_k(i) \geq 0.$$

Clearly the A_i are nonnegative, $A_0 = 1$ and the $A_i = 0$ for $1 \leq i < d$ to obtain the distance properties. By definition, we also have $\sum_{i=0}^{n} A_i = M$, the number of codewords. Hence, any code must have its number of codewords less than the largest possible value of $\sum_{i=0}^{n} A_i = M$.

For binary codes with d even we may take the $A_i = 0$ for i odd, since any codeword with odd weight can be modified to a codeword with even weight by flipping 1 bit without changing the minimum distance of the code.   □

Example 9.20 Let us return to the problem of Example 9.13. Now that we know about the Krawtchouk polynomials, the inequalities in (9.10) can be explicitly computed. These become

$$k = 0: \quad 1 + A_6 + A_8 + A_{10} + A_{12} + A_{14} \geq 0$$
$$k = 1: \quad 14 + 2A_6 - 2A_8 - 6A_{10} - 10A_{12} - 14A_{14} \geq 0$$
$$k = 2: \quad 91 - 5A_6 - 5A_8 + 11A_{10} + 43A_{12} + 91A_{14} \geq 0$$
$$k = 3: \quad 364 - 12A_6 + 12A_8 + 4A_{10} - 100A_{12} - 364A_{14} \geq 0$$
$$k = 4: \quad 1001 + 9A_6 + 9A_8 - 39A_{10} + 121A_{12} + 1001A_{14} \geq 0$$
$$k = 5: \quad 2002 + 30A_6 - 30A_8 + 38A_{10} - 22A_{12} - 2002A_{14} \geq 0$$
$$k = 6: \quad 3003 - 5A_6 - 5A_8 + 27A_{10} - 165A_{12} + 3003A_{14} \geq 0$$
$$k = 7: \quad 3432 - 40A_6 + 40A_8 - 72A_{10} + 264A_{12} - 3432A_{14} \geq 0.$$

ipboundex.m

The other inequalities are duplicates, by symmetry in the polynomials. Also note that the $k = 0$ inequality is implicit in maximizing $A_6 + A_8 + \cdots + A_{14}$, so it does not need to be included. Solving the linear programming problem, we obtain the solution

$$A_6 = 42 \quad A_8 = 7 \quad A_{10} = 14 \quad A_{12} = 0 \quad A_{14} = 0.$$

Hence $A_2(14, 6) \leq 1 + 42 + 7 + 14 = 64$.   □

9.5 The McEliece–Rodemich–Rumsey–Welch Bound

The McEliece–Rodemich–Rumsey–Welch bound is a bound that is quite tight. It applies only to binary codes and is derived using the linear programming bound.

Theorem 9.21 *(The McEliece–Rodemich–Rumsey–Welch Bound) For a binary code,*

$$\alpha_2(\delta) \leq H_2\left(\frac{1}{2} - \sqrt{\delta(1-\delta)}\right), \quad 0 \leq \delta \leq \frac{1}{2}. \tag{9.14}$$

The proof is subtle and makes use of some properties of Krawtchouk polynomials introduced in Exercise 9.16, an extension of the linear programming bound in Exercise 9.17, as well as other properties that follow from the fact that Krawtchouk polynomials are orthogonal. What is provided here is a sketch; the reader may want to fill in some of the details.

Proof [303, 458] Let t be an integer in the range $1 \leq t \leq \frac{n}{2}$ and let a be a real number in $[0, n]$. Define the polynomial

$$\alpha(x) = \frac{1}{a - x}(K_t(a)K_{t+1}(x) - K_{t+1}(a)K_t(x))^2. \tag{9.15}$$

Because the $\{K_k(x)\}$ form an orthogonal set, they satisfy the Christoffel–Darboux formula

$$\frac{K_{k+1}(x)K_k(y) - K_k(x)K_{k+1}(y)}{y - x} = \frac{2}{k+1}\binom{n}{k}\sum_{i=0}^{k}\frac{K_i(x)K_i(y)}{\binom{n}{i}} \tag{9.16}$$

(see [319, p. 224] for an introduction, or a reference on orthogonal polynomials such as [427]). Using (9.16), Equation (9.15) can be written as

$$\alpha(x) = \frac{2}{t+1}\binom{n}{t}(K_t(a)K_{t+1}(x) - K_{t+1}(a)K_t(x))\sum_{k=0}^{t}\frac{K_k(a)K_k(x)}{\binom{n}{k}}. \tag{9.17}$$

Since $K_k(x)$ is a polynomial in x of degree k, it follows that $\alpha(x)$ is a polynomial in x of degree $2t + 1$. Then $\alpha(x)$ can also be written as a series in $\{K_k(x)\}$ as

$$\alpha(x) = \sum_{k=0}^{2t+1}\alpha_k K_k(x)$$

(since both are polynomials of degree $2t + 1$). Let $\beta(x) = \alpha(x)/\alpha_0 = 1 + \sum_{k=1}^{2t+1}\beta_k K_k(x)$. We desire to choose a and t such that $\beta(x)$ satisfies the conditions of the theorem in Exercise 9.17: $\beta_k \geq 0$ and $\beta(j) \leq 0$ for $j = d, d+1, \ldots, n$.

Note that if $a \leq d$, then by (9.15) $\alpha(j) \leq j$ for $j = d, d+1, \ldots, n$, so the only thing to be verified is whether $\alpha_i \geq 0$, $i = 1, \ldots, n$ and $\alpha_0 > 0$. This is established using the interlacing property of the roots of the Krawtchouk polynomials: $K_{t+1}(x)$ has $t + 1$ distinct real zeros on $(0, n)$. Denote these as $x_1^{(t+1)}, \ldots, x_{t+1}^{(t+1)}$, with $x_1^{(t+1)} < x_2^{(t+1)} < \cdots < x_{t+1}^{(t+1)}$. Similarly, $K_t(x)$ has t distinct real zeros on $(0, n)$, which we denote as $x_1^{(t)}, \ldots, x_t^{(t)}$ and order similarly. These roots are interlaced:

$$0 < x_1^{(t+1)} < x_1^{(t)} < x_2^{(t+1)} < x_2^{(t)} < \cdots < x_t^{(t)} < x_{t+1}^{(t+1)} < n.$$

(This interlacing property follows as a result of the orthogonality properties of the Krawtchouk polynomials; see [427].)

So choose t such that $x_1^{(t)} < d$ and choose a between $x_1^{(t+1)}$ and $x_1^{(t)}$ in such a way that $K_t(a) = -K_{t+1}(a) > 0$. Then $\alpha(x)$ can be written in the form $\alpha(x) = \sum c_{kl} K_k(x) K_l(x)$ where all the $c_{kl} \geq 0$. Thus, the $\alpha_i \geq 0$. It is clear that $\alpha_0 = -\frac{2}{t+1} \binom{n}{t} K_t(a) K_{t+1}(a) > 0$.

Thus, the theorem in Exercise 9.17 can be applied:

$$A_q(n,d) \leq \beta(0) = \frac{\alpha(0)}{\alpha_0} = \frac{(n+1)}{2a(t+1)} \binom{n}{t}. \tag{9.18}$$

We now invoke another result about orthogonal polynomials. It is known (see [427]) that as $n \to \infty$, if $t \to \infty$ in such a way that $t/n \to \tau$ for some $0 < \tau < \frac{1}{2}$, then $x_1^{(t)}/n \to \frac{1}{2} - \sqrt{\tau(1-\tau)}$. So let $n \to \infty$ and $d/n \to \delta$ in such a way that $t/n \to \frac{1}{2} - \sqrt{\delta(1-\delta)}$. Taking the logarithm of (9.18), dividing by n, and using the results of Lemma 9.5, the result follows. □

In [303], a slightly stronger bound is given (which we do not prove here):

$$\alpha_2(\delta) \leq \min_{0 \leq u \leq 1-2\delta} \{1 + g(u^2) - g(u^2 + 2\delta u - 2\delta)\}, \tag{9.19}$$

where

$$g(x) = H_2((1 - \sqrt{1-x})/2).$$

The bound (9.14) actually follows from this with $u = 1 - 2\delta$. For $0.273 \leq \delta \leq \frac{1}{2}$, the bounds (9.14) and (9.19) coincide, but for $\delta < 0.273$, (9.19) gives a slightly tighter bound.

Another bound is obtained from (9.19) when $u = 0$. This gives rise to the *Elias bound* for binary codes. In its more general form, it can be expressed as follows.

Theorem 9.22 (*Elias Bound*) *For a q-ary code,*

$$\alpha_q(\delta) \leq 1 - H_q(\rho - \sqrt{\rho(1-\delta)}) \quad 0 \leq \delta \leq \rho,$$

where $\rho = (q-1)/q$.

The Elias bound also has a nonasymptotic form: Let $r \leq \rho n$, where $\rho = (q-1)/q$. Then [458, p. 65]

$$A_q(n,d) \leq \frac{\rho n d}{r^2 - 2\rho n r + \rho n d} \frac{q^n}{V_q(n,r)}.$$

The value of r can be adjusted to find the tightest bound.

9.6 Exercises

9.1 Using the Hamming and Gilbert–Varshamov bounds, determine lower and upper bounds on the redundancy $r = n - k$ for the following codes:

(a) A single-error correcting binary code of length 7.
(b) A single-error correcting binary code of length 15.
(c) A triple-error correcting binary code of length 23.
(d) A triple-error correcting ternary code of length 23.
(e) A triple-error correcting 4-ary code of length 23.
(f) A triple-error correcting 16-ary code of length 23.

9.2 With $H_2(x) = -x\log_2 x - (1-x)\log_2(1-x)$, show that

$$2^{-nH_2(\lambda)} = \lambda^{n\lambda}(1-\lambda)^{n(1-\lambda)}.$$

9.3 With $H_2(x)$ as defined in the previous exercise, show that for any λ in the range $0 \le \lambda \le \frac{1}{2}$,

$$\sum_{i=0}^{\lambda n} \binom{n}{i} \le 2^{nH_2(\lambda)}.$$

Hint: Use the binomial expansion on $(\lambda + (1-\lambda))^n = 1$; truncate the sum up to λn and use the fact that $(\lambda/(1-\lambda))^i < (\lambda/(1-\lambda))^{\lambda n}$.

9.4 [45] Prove: In any set of M distinct nonzero binary words of length n having weight at most $n\lambda$, the sum of the weights W satisfies

$$W \ge n\lambda(M - 2^{nH_2(\lambda)})$$

for any $\lambda \in (0, 1/2)$. *Hint*: Use the fact that $\sum_{k=0}^{\lambda n} \binom{n}{k} \le 2^{nH_2(\lambda)}$. Then argue that for each λ there are at least $M - 2^{nH_2(\lambda)}$ words of weight exceeding $n\lambda$.

9.5 For binary codes, show that $A_2(n, 2l - 1) = A_2(n+1, 2l)$.

9.6 Using the Cauchy–Schwartz inequality, show that

$$\sum_{i=0}^{q-1} q_i^2 \ge \frac{1}{q}\left(\sum_{i=0}^{q-1} q_i\right)^2.$$

9.7 What is the largest possible number of codewords of a ternary ($q = 3$) code having $n = 13$ and $d = 9$?

9.8 Examine the proof of Theorem 9.8. Under what condition can equality be obtained in (9.8)?

9.9 Prove the asymptotic Plotkin bound:

$$\alpha_q(\delta) = 0 \quad \text{if } \rho \le \delta \le 1$$

$$\alpha_q(\delta) \le 1 - \delta/\rho \text{ if } 0 \le \delta \le \rho.$$

Hint: For the second part, let $n' = \lfloor (d-1)/\rho \rfloor$. Show that $1 \le d - \rho n' \le 1 + \rho$. Shorten a code of length n with M codewords to a code of length n' with M' codewords, both having the same distance. Show that $M' \ge q^{n'-n}M$ and apply the Plotkin bound.

9.10 [41, 183] Stirling's formula. In this problem, you will derive the approximation

$$n! \approx n^n e^{-n}\sqrt{2\pi n}.$$

(a) Show that

$$\int_1^n \log x \, dx = n \log n - n + 1.$$

(b) Use the trapezoidal rule, as suggested by Figure 9.3(a), to show that

$$\int_1^n \log x \, dx \ge \log n! - \frac{1}{2}\log n,$$

where the overbound is the area between the function $\log x$ and its trapezoidal approximation. Conclude that

$$n! \le n^n e^{-n}\sqrt{ne}.$$

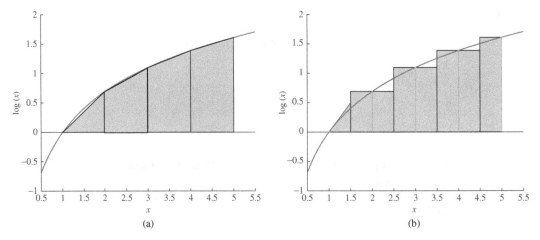

Figure 9.3: Finding Stirling's formula. (a) Under bound; (b) over bound.

(c) Using the integration regions suggested in Figure 9.3(b), show that

$$\int_1^n \log x \, dx \le \log n! + \frac{1}{8} - \frac{1}{2} \log n$$

and that

$$n! \ge n^n e^{-n} \sqrt{n} e^{7/8}.$$

In this integral approximation, for the triangular region, use a diagonal line tangent to the function at 1.

In the approximation

$$n! \approx n^n e^{-n} \sqrt{n} C, \qquad (9.20)$$

we thus observe that

$$e^{7/8} \le C \le e.$$

It will turn out that $C = \sqrt{2\pi}$ works as $n \to \infty$. To see this, we take a nonobvious detour. Define the function

$$I_k = \int_0^{\pi/2} \cos^k x \, dx.$$

(d) Show that $I_k = I_{k-2} - I_k/(k-1)$, and hence that $I_k = (k-1)I_{k-2}/k$ for $k \ge 2$. *Hint*: $\cos^k(x) = \cos^{k-2}(x)(1 - \sin^2 x)$.

(e) Show that $I_0 = \pi/2$ and $I_1 = 1$.

(f) Show that $I_{2k-1} > I_{2k} > I_{2k+1}$, and hence that

$$1 > \frac{I_{2k}}{I_{2k-1}} > \frac{I_{2k+1}}{I_{2k-1}}.$$

(g) Show that

$$1 > 2k \left[\frac{2k-1}{2k} \frac{2k-3}{2k-2} \cdots \frac{3}{2} \right]^2 \frac{\pi}{2} > \frac{2k}{2k+1}.$$

(h) Show that

$$1 > \pi k \left[\frac{(2k)!}{2^k k! 2^k k!} \right]^2 > \frac{2k}{2k+1}.$$

(i) Now substitute (9.20) for each factorial to show that

$$1 > \sqrt{\pi k} \left[\frac{(2k)^{2k} e^{-2k} \sqrt{2k} C}{2^{2k} k^k e^{-k} \sqrt{k} C k^k e^{-k} \sqrt{k} C} \right] > \sqrt{1 - \frac{1}{2k+1}}.$$

(j) Show that $C \to \sqrt{2\pi}$ as $k \to \infty$.

9.11 Show that asymptotically, the Hamming bound can be expressed as

$$\alpha_q(\delta) \leq 1 - H_q(\delta/2).$$

9.12 Use the Griesmer bound to determine the largest possible value of k for a $(13, k, 5)$ binary code.

9.13 Use the Griesmer bound to determine the largest possible value of k for a $(14, k, 9)$ ternary code.

9.14 Find a bound on the length of shortest triple-error correcting $(d = 7)$ binary code of dimension 5.

9.15 Let $d = 2^{k-1}$. Determine $N(k, d)$. Is there a code that reaches the bound? (*Hint*: simplex.)

9.16 Properties of Krawtchouk polynomials.

(a) Show that for $x \in \{0, 1, \ldots, k\}$,

$$\sum_{k=0}^{\infty} K_k(x) z^k = (1 + (q-1)z)^{n-x} (1-z)^x. \tag{9.21}$$

(b) Show that $K_k(x)$ is an orthogonal polynomial with weighting function $\binom{n}{i}(q-1)^i$, in that

$$\sum_{i=0}^{n} \binom{n}{i}(q-i)^i K_k(i) K_l(i) = \delta_{kl} \binom{n}{k}(q-1)^k q^n. \tag{9.22}$$

(c) Show that for $q = 2$,

$$K_k(x) = (-1)^k K_k(n-x).$$

(d) Show that

$$(q-1)^i \binom{n}{i} K_k(i) = (q-1)^k \binom{n}{k} K_i(k).$$

(e) Use this result to show another orthogonality relation:

$$\sum_{i=0}^{n} K_l(i) K_k(i) = \delta_{lk} q^n.$$

(f) One way to compute the Krawtchouk polynomials is to use the recursion

$$(k+1)K_{k+1}(x) = (k + (q-1)(n-k) - qx)K_k(x) - (q-1)(n-k+1)K_{k-1}(x),$$

which can be initialized with $K_0(x) = 1$ and $K_1(x) = n(q-1) - qx$ from the definition. Derive this recursion. *Hint*: Differentiate both sides of (9.21) with respect to z, multiply both sides by $(1 + (q-1)z)(1-z)$ and match coefficients of z^k.

(g) Another recursion is

$$K_k(x) = K_k(x-1) - (q-1)K_{k-1}(x) - K_{k-1}(x-1).$$

Show that this is true. *Hint*: In (9.21), replace x by $x - 1$.

9.17 [458] (Extension of Theorem 9.12) Theorem: Let $\beta(x) = 1 + \sum_{k=1}^{n} \beta_k K_k(x)$ be a polynomial with $\beta_i \geq 0$ for $1 \leq k \leq n$ such that $\beta(j) \leq 0$ for $j = d, d+1, \ldots, n$. Then $A_q(n, d) \leq \beta(0)$. Justify the following steps of the proof:

(a) $\sum_{i=d}^{n} A_i \beta(i) \leq 0$.

(b) $-\sum_{i=d}^{n} A_i \geq \sum_{k=1}^{n} \beta_k \sum_{i=d}^{n} A_k K_k(i)$

(c) $\sum_{k=1}^{n} \beta_k \sum_{i=d}^{n} A_k K_k(i) \geq -\sum_{k=1}^{n} \beta_k K_k(0)$.

(d) $-\sum_{k=1}^{n} \beta_k K_k(0) = 1 - \beta(0)$.

(e) Hence conclude that $A_q(n, d) \leq \beta(0)$.

(f) Now put the theorem to work. Let $q = 2$, $n = 2l + 1$ and $d = l + 1$. Let $\beta(x) = 1 + \beta_1 K_1(x) + \beta_2 K_2(x)$.

    a. Show that $\beta(x) = 1 + \beta_1(n - 2x) + \beta_2(2x^2 - 2nx + \frac{1}{2}n(n-1))$.

    b. Show that choosing to set $\beta(d) = \beta(n) = 0$ leads to $\beta_1 = (n+1)/2n$ and $\beta_2 = 1/n$.

    c. Show that the conditions of the theorem in this problem are satisfied.

    d. Hence conclude that $A_q(2l + 1, l + 1) \leq 2l + 2$.

9.18 Let χ be a character, $\chi : G \to T$. Show that $\chi(0) = 1$, where 0 is the identity of G.

9.19 Show that (9.17) follows from (9.15) and (9.16).

9.7 References

Extensive discussions of bounds appear in [292]. Our discussion has benefited immensely from [458]. The Hamming bound appears in [181]. The Singleton bound appears in [412]. The Plotkin bound appears in [342]. The linear programming bound was developed in [92].

An introduction to orthogonal polynomials is in [319]. More extensive treatment of general facts about orthogonal polynomials is in [427].

Chapter 10

Bursty Channels, Interleavers, and Concatenation

10.1 Introduction to Bursty Channels

The coding techniques introduced to this point have been appropriate for channels with independent random errors, such as a memoryless binary symmetric channel, or an AWGN channel. In such channels, each transmitted symbol is affected independently by the noise. We refer to the codes that are appropriate for such channels as random error correcting codes. However, in many channels of practical interest, the channel errors tend to be clustered together in "bursts." For example, on a compact disc (CD), a scratch on the media may cause errors in several consecutive bits. On a magnetic medium such as a hard disk or a tape, a blemish on the magnetic surface may introduce many errors. A wireless channel may experience fading over several symbol times, or a stroke of lightning might affect multiple digits. In a concatenated coding scheme employing a convolutional code as the inner code, a single incorrect decoding decision might give rise to a burst of decoding errors.

Using a conventional random error-correcting block code in a bursty channel leads to inefficiencies. A burst of errors may introduce several errors into a small number codewords, which therefore need strong correction capability, while the majority of codewords are not subjected to error and therefore waste error-correction capabilities.

In this chapter, we introduce techniques for dealing with errors on bursty channels. The straightforward but important concept of interleaving is presented. The use of Reed–Solomon codes to handle bursts of bit errors is described. We describe methods of concatenating codes. Finally, Fire codes are introduced, which is a family of cyclic codes specifically designed to handle bursts of errors.

Definition 10.1 In a sequence of symbols, a **burst** of length l is a sequence of symbols confined to l consecutive symbols of which the first and last are in error. □

For example, in the error vector

$$\mathbf{e} = (0\,0\,0\,0\,\underbrace{1\,1\,0\,1\,0\,1\,1\,0\,0\,1\,0\,0\,1\,0\,1}\,0\,0\,0\,0\,0\,0\,0\,)$$

is a burst of length 15.

A code C is said to have burst-error-correcting capability l if it is capable of correcting all bursts up to length l.

10.2 Interleavers

An **interleaver** takes a sequence of symbols and permutes them. At the receiver, the sequence is permuted back into the original order by a **deinterleaver**. Interleavers are efficacious in dealing with bursts of errors because, by shuffling the symbols at the receiver, a burst of errors appearing in close proximity may be broken up and spread around, thereby creating an effectively random channel.

A common way to interleave is with a **block interleaver**. This is simply an $N \times M$ array which can be read and written in different orders. Typically the incoming sequence of symbols is written into the

Error Correction Coding: Mathematical Methods and Algorithms, Second Edition. Todd K. Moon.
© 2021 John Wiley & Sons, Inc. Published 2021 by John Wiley & Sons, Inc.
Companion website: www.wiley.com/go/Moon/ErrorCorrectionCoding

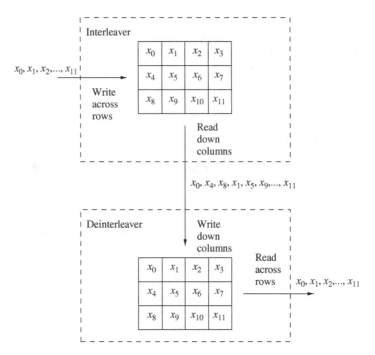

Figure 10.1: A 3×4 interleaver and deinterleaver.

interleaver in row order and read out in column order. Figure 10.1 shows a 3×4 interleaver. The input sequence $x_0, x_1, \ldots, x_{11}$ is read into the rows of array, as shown, and read off as the sequence

$$x_0, x_4, x_8, x_1, x_5, x_9, x_2, x_6, x_{10}, x_3, x_7, x_{11}.$$

Frequently, the width M is chosen to be the length of a codeword.

Example 10.2   We present here an application of interleaving. The UDP (user datagram protocol) internet protocol is one of the TCP/IP protocol suite which does not guarantee packet delivery, but experiences lower network latency. In this protocol, each packet carries with it a sequential packet number, so that any missing packets may be identified. Because of its lower latency, UDP is of interest in near real-time internet applications. Error correction coding can be used to significantly increase the probability that all packets are correctly received with only a moderate decrease in rate.

The data stream is blocked into message blocks of 249 bytes and the data are encoded with a (255, 249) Reed–Solomon code having $d_{\min} = 7$ and capable of correcting six erasures. The codewords are written into an $N \times 255$ matrix as rows and read out in column order. Each column is transmitted as a data packet of length N.

Suppose that the third packet associated with this interleaving block, corresponding to the third column, is lost in transmission, as suggested by the shading on this matrix.

$c_{1,1}$	$c_{1,2}$	$c_{1,3}$	...	$c_{1,255}$
$c_{2,1}$	$c_{2,2}$	$c_{2,3}$	...	$c_{2,255}$
$\vdots$	$\vdots$	$\vdots$	$\vdots$	$\vdots$
$c_{N,1}$	$c_{N,2}$	$c_{N,3}$	...	$c_{N,255}$

By the protocol, the fact that the third packet is lost is known. When the data are written into the matrix for deinterleaving, the missing column is left blank and recorded as an *erasure*. Then each of the N codewords is subjected to erasure decoding, recovering the lost byte in each codeword. For this code, up to six packets out of N may be lost in transmission (erased) and fully recovered at the receiver. □

In general, when a burst of length l is deinterleaved, it causes a maximum of $\lceil l/N \rceil$ errors to occur among the received codewords. If the code used can correct up to t errors, a decoding failure may occur if the burst length exceeds Nt.

The **efficiency** γ of an interleaver can be defined as the ratio of the length of the smallest burst of errors that exceeds the correction capability of a block code to the amount of memory in the interleaver. Based on our discussion, for the block interleaver the efficiency is

$$\gamma = \frac{Nt + 1}{NM} \approx \frac{t}{M}.$$

Another kind of interleaver is the **cross interleaver** or **convolutional interleaver** [361], which consists of a bank of delay lines of successively increasing length. An example is shown in Figure 10.2. This figure shows the input stream, and the state of the interleaver at a particular time as an aid in understanding its operation. The cross interleaver is parameterized by (M, D), where M is the number of delay lines and D the number of samples each delay element introduces. It is clear that adjacent symbols input to the interleaver are separated by MD symbols. If M is chosen to be greater than or equal to the length of the code, then each symbol in the codeword is placed on a different delay line. If a burst error of length l occurs, then $\lceil l/(MD + 1) \rceil$ errors may be introduced into the deinterleaved codewords. For a t-error-correcting code, a decoding failure may be possible when l exceeds $(MD + 1)t$. The total memory of the interleaver is $(0 + 1 + 2 + \cdots + (M - 1))D = DM(M - 1)/2$. The efficiency is thus

$$\gamma = \frac{(MD + 1)t + 1}{DM(M - 1)/2} \approx \frac{2t}{M - 1}.$$

Interleaver

Input: $\ldots, x_0, x_1, x_2, x_3, x_4, x_5, x_6, \ldots$

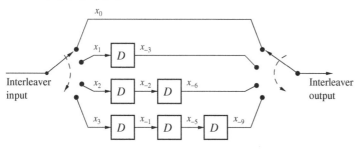

Output: $\ldots, x_0, x_{-3}, x_{-6}, x_{-9}, x_4, x_1, x_{-2}, x_{-5}, x_8, x_5, x_2, x_{-1}, \ldots$

Input: $\ldots, x_0, x_{-3}, x_{-6}, x_{-9}, x_4, x_1, x_{-2}, x_{-5}, x_8, x_5, x_2, x_{-1}, \ldots$

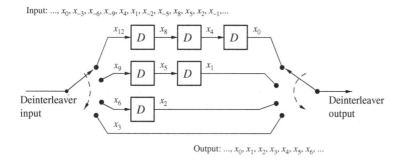

Output: $\ldots, x_0, x_1, x_2, x_3, x_4, x_5, x_6, \ldots$

Figure 10.2: A cross interleaver and deinterleaver system.

Comparison with the block interleaver shows that cross interleavers are approximately twice as efficient as block interleavers.

While block interleaving can be accomplished in a straightforward way with an array, for cyclic codes there is another approach. If C is a cyclic code of length n with generator $g(x)$, then the code obtained after interleaving with an $M \times n$ interleaver matrix is also cyclic, with generator polynomial $g(x^M)$. The encoding and syndrome computation can thus be implemented in conventional fashion using shift registers [271, p. 272].

10.3   An Application of Interleaved RS Codes: Compact Discs

By far the most common application of RS codes is to compact discs. The data on the CD is protected with a Reed–Solomon code, providing resilience to scratches on the surface of the disc. (Of course, scratches may still impede CD playback, as many listeners can attest, but these problems are more often the result of tracking problems with the read laser and not the problem of errors in the decoding stream read.) Because this medium is so pervasive, it is important to be familiar with the data representation. This presentation also brings out another important point. The error correction is only one aspect of the data processing that takes place. To be of practical value, error-correction coding must work as a component within a larger system design. In addition to basic error correction provided by Reed–Solomon codes, protection against burst errors due to scratches on the disc is provided by the use of a cross interleaver. The data stream is also formatted with an eight-to-fourteen modulation (EFM) code which prevents excessively long runs of ones. This is necessary because the laser motion control system employs a phase-locked loop (PLL) which is triggered by bit transitions. If there is a run of ones that is too long, the PLL may drift. Details on the data stream and the EFM code are in [211]. Our summary here follows [483].

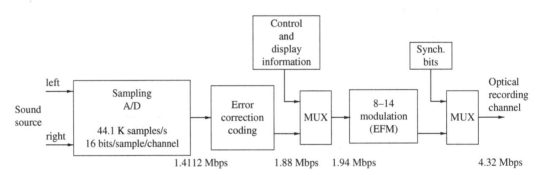

Figure 10.3: The CD recording and data formatting process.

The overall block diagram of the CD recording process is shown in Figure 10.3. The 1.41 Mbps sampled data stream passes through an error-correction system resulting in a data rate of 1.88 Mbps. The encoder system, referred to as CIRC, uses two interleaved, shortened, Reed–Solomon codes, C_1 and C_2. Both codes are built on codes over $GF(256)$. The 8-bit symbols of the field fit naturally with the 16-bit samples used by the A/D converter. However, the codes are significantly shortened: C_1 is a $(32, 28)$ code and C_2 is a $(28, 24)$ code. For every 24 input symbols there are 32 output symbols, resulting in a rate $R = 24/32 = 3/4$. Both codes have minimum distance 5.

Encoding The outer code, C_2, uses 12 16-bit samples to create 24 8-bit symbols as its message word. The 28-symbol codeword is passed through a $(28, 4)$ cross interleaver. The resulting 28 interleaved symbols are passed through the code C_1, resulting in 32 coded output symbols, as shown in Figure 10.4.

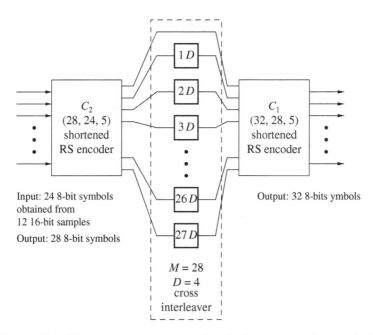

Figure 10.4: The error-correction encoding in the compact disc standard.

Decoding At the decoder (in the CD player), the data that reaches the CIRC decoder first passes through the outer decoder C_1. Since C_1 has minimum distance 5, it is capable of correcting two errors, or correcting one error and detecting two errors in the codeword, or detecting up to four errors. If the C_1 decoder detects a high-weight error pattern, such as a double error pattern or any error pattern causing a decoder failure, the decoder outputs 28 erased symbols. The deinterleaver spreads these erased symbols over 28 C_2 codewords, where the erasure correction capability of the C_2 code can be used.

The C_2 decoder can correct any combination of e errors and f erasures satisfying $2e + f < 5$. Since C_1 is likely to be able to produce error-free output, but will declare erasures when there seem to be too many errors for it to correct, the C_2 decoder is frequently built to be an erasures-only decoder. Since erasure decoding involves only straightforward linear algebra (e.g., Forney's algorithm) and does not require finding an error-locator polynomial, this can be a low-complexity decoder. In the rare event that a vector is presented having more than four erasures that C_2 is not able to correct the C_2 decoder outputs 24 erasures. In this case, the playback system uses an "error concealment" system which either mutes the corresponding 12 samples of music or performs some kind of interpolation.

The performance specifications for this code are summarized in Table 10.1.

10.4 Product Codes

Let C_1 be an (n_1, k_1) linear block code and let C_2 be an (n_2, k_2) linear block code over $GF(q)$. An $(n_1 n_2, k_1 k_2)$ linear code called the **product code**, denoted $C_1 \times C_2$, can be formed as diagrammed in Figure 10.5. A set of $k_1 k_2$ symbols is written into a $k_2 \times k_1$ array. Each of the k_2 rows of the array is (systematically) encoded using code C_1, forming n_1 columns. Each of the n_1 columns of the array is then (systematically) encoded using code C_2, forming an $n_2 \times n_1$ array. Because of linearity, it does not matter whether the encoding procedure is reversed (C_2 encoding followed by C_1 encoding).

Theorem 10.3 *If C_1 has minimum distance d_1 and C_2 has minimum distance d_2, then the product code $C_1 \times C_2$ has minimum distance $d_1 d_2$.*

Table 10.1: Performance Specification of the Compact Disc Coding System [211, p. 57]

Maximum completely correctable burst length	≈ 4000 bits (≈ 2.5 mm track length)
Maximum interpolatable burst length in the worst case	$\approx 12{,}300$ data bits (≈ 7.7 mm track length)
Sample interpolation rate	One sample every 10 hours at a bit error rate (BER) of 10^{-4}. 1000 samples per minute at BER of 10^{-3}
Undetected error samples (producing click in output)	Less than one every 750 hours at BER=10^{-3}. Negligible at BER$\leq 10^{-4}$
Code rate	$R = 3/4$
Implementation	One LSI chip plus one random-access memory of 2048 bytes.

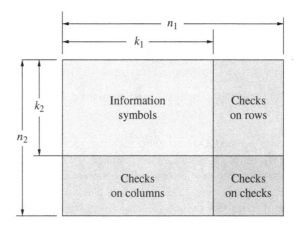

Figure 10.5: The product code $C_1 \times C_2$.

Proof The minimum weight cannot be less than $d_1 d_2$: Each nonzero row of the matrix in Figure 10.5 must have weight $\geq d_1$ and there must be at least d_2 nonzero rows.

To show that there is a codeword of weight $d_1 d_2$, let $\mathbf{c}_1$ be a codeword in C_1 of minimum weight and let $\mathbf{c}_2$ be a codeword in C_2 of minimum weight. Form an array in which all columns corresponding to zeros in $\mathbf{c}_1$ are zeros and all columns corresponding to ones in $\mathbf{c}_1$ are $\mathbf{c}_2$.   □

Using the Chinese remainder theorem it is straightforward to show [292, p. 570] that if C_1 and C_2 are cyclic and $(n_1, n_2) = 1$, then $C_1 \times C_2$ is also cyclic.

The product code construction can be iterated. For example, the code $C_1 \times C_2 \times C_3$ can be produced. It may be observed that by taking such multiple products, codes with large distance can be obtained. However, the rate of the product code is the product of the rates, so that the product code construction produces codes with low rate.

We do not present a detailed decoding algorithm for product codes here. However, decoding of codes similar to product codes is discussed in Chapter 14. Product codes are seen there to be an instance of turbo codes, so a turbo code decoding algorithm is used. However, we discuss here the burst-error-correction capability of product codes [271, p. 275]. Suppose C_1 has burst-error-correction capability l_1 and C_2 has burst-error-correction capability l_2. Suppose that the code is transmitted out of the matrix row by row. At the receiver the data are written back into an array in row-by-row order. A burst of length $n_1 l_2$ or less can affect no more than $l_2 + 1$ consecutive rows, since when the symbols are arranged into the array, each column is affected by a burst of length at most l_2. By decoding first on the columns, the burst can be corrected, so the burst correction capability of the product code is at least $n_1 l_2$. Similarly, it can be shown that bursts of length at least $n_2 l_1$ can be corrected, so the overall burst-error-correction capability of the code is $\max(n_1 l_2, n_2 l_1)$.

10.5 Reed–Solomon Codes

Reed–Solomon codes and other codes based on larger-than-binary fields have some intrinsic ability to correct bursts of binary errors. For a code over a field $GF(2^m)$, each coded symbol can be envisioned as a sequence of m bits. Under this interpretation, a (n, k) Reed–Solomon code over $GF(2^m)$ is a binary (mn, mk) code.

The RS code is capable of correcting up to t *symbols* of error. It does not matter that a single symbol might have multiple bits in error — it still is a single symbol error from the perspective of the RS decoder. A single symbol might have up to m bits in error. Under the best of circumstances then, when all the errors affect adjacent bits of a symbol, a RS code may correct up to mt bits in error. This means that RS codes are naturally effective for transmitting over bursty binary channels: since bursts of errors tend to cluster together, there may be several binary errors contributing to a single erroneous symbol. As an example [271, p. 278], a burst of length $3m + 1$ cannot affect more than four symbols, so a RS code capable of correcting 4 errors can correct any burst of length $3m + 1$. Or any burst of length $m + 1$ cannot affect more than 2 bytes, so the four-error-correcting code could correct up to two bursts of length $m + 1$. In general, a t-error-correcting RS code over $GF(2^m)$ can correct any combination of

$$\frac{t}{1 + \lfloor l + m - 2)/m \rfloor}$$

or fewer bursts of length l, or correcting a single burst up to length $(t - 1)m + 1$. And, naturally, it also corrects any combination of t or fewer random errors.

10.6 Concatenated Codes

Concatenated codes were proposed by Forney [126] as a means of obtaining long codes (as required by the Shannon channel coding theorem for capacity-approaching performance) with modest decoding complexity. The basic concatenation coding scheme is shown in Figure 10.6. The inner code is conventionally a binary code. The outer code is typically a (n_2, k_2) Reed–Solomon code over $GF(2^k)$. The outer code uses k_2 k-tuples of bits from the inner code as the message sequence. In the encoding, the outer code takes kk_2 bits divided into k-tuples which are employed as k_2 symbols in $GF(2^k)$ and encodes them as a Reed–Solomon codeword $(c_0, c_1, \ldots, c_{n_2})$. These symbols, now envisioned as k-tuples of binary numbers, are encoded by the inner encoder to produce a binary sequence transmitted over the channel.

The inner code is frequently a convolutional code. The purpose of the inner code is to improve the quality of the "superchannel" (consisting of the inner encoder, the channel, and the inner decoder) that

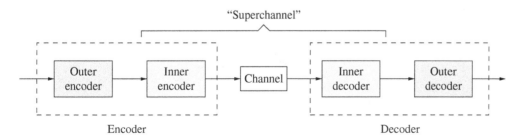

Figure 10.6: A concatenated code.

the outer RS code sees so that the RS code can be used very effectively. When the Viterbi decoder (the inner decoder) makes a decoding error, it typically involves a few consecutive stages of the decoding trellis, which results in a short burst of errors. The bursts of bit errors which tend to be produced by the inner decoder are handled by the RS decoder with its inherent burst-error-correction capability.

Example 10.4   [483, p. 432] Figure 10.7 shows the block diagram of a concatenated coding system employed by some NASA deep-space missions. The outer code is a (255, 223) Reed–Solomon code followed by a block interleaver. The inner code is a rate $1/2$ convolutional code, where the generator polynomials are

$$\text{Rate } 1/2\text{: } d_{\text{free}} = 10 \quad g_0(x) = 1 + x + x^3 + x^4 + x^6 \quad g_1(x) = 1 + x^3 + x^4 + x^5 + x^6.$$

The RS code is capable of correcting up to 16 8-bit symbols. The d_{free} path through the trellis traverses seven branches, so error bursts most frequently have length seven, which in the best case can be trapped by a single RS code symbol.

   To provide for the possibility of decoding bursts exceeding $16 \times 8 = 128$ bits, a symbol interleaver is placed between the RS encoder and the convolutional encoder. Since it is a symbol interleaver, burst errors which occupy a single byte are still clustered together. But bursts crossing several bytes are randomized. Block interleavers holding from 2 to 8 Reed–Solomon codewords have been employed. By simulation studies [177], it is shown that to achieve a bit error rate of 10^{-5}, with interleavers of sizes of 2, 4, and 8, respectively, an E_b/N_0 of 2.6, 2.45, and 2.35dB, respectively, are required. Uncoded BPSK performance would require 9.6dB; using only the rate $1/2$ convolutional code would require 5.1 dB, so the concatenated system provides approximately 2.5 dB of gain compared to the convolutional code alone.

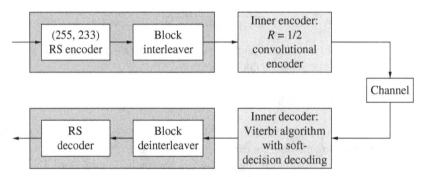

Figure 10.7: Deep-space concatenated coding system.

□

10.7   Fire Codes

10.7.1   Fire Code Definition

Fire codes, named after their inventor [124], are binary cyclic codes designed specifically to be able to correct a single burst of errors. They are designed as follows. Let $p(x)$ be an irreducible polynomial of degree m over $GF(2)$. Let ρ be the smallest integer such that $p(x)$ divides $x^\rho + 1$. ρ is called the *period* of $p(x)$. Let l be a positive integer such that $l \leq m$ and $\rho \,|\, 2l - 1$. Let $g(x)$ be the generator polynomial defined by

$$g(x) = (x^{2l-1} + 1)p(x). \tag{10.1}$$

Observe that the factors $p(x)$ and $x^{2l-1} + 1$ are relatively prime. The length n of the code is the least common multiple of $2l - 1$ and the period:

$$n = \text{LCM}(2l - 1, \rho)$$

and the dimension of the code is $k = n - m - 2l + 1$.

Example 10.5 Let $p(x) = 1 + x + x^4$. This is a primitive polynomial, so $\rho = 2^4 - 1 = 15$. Let $l = 4$ and note that $2l - 1 = 7$ is not divisible by 15. The Fire code has generator

$$g(x) = (x^7 + 1)(1 + x + x^4) = 1 + x + x^4 + x^7 + x^8 + x^{11}$$

with length and dimension

$$n = LCM(7, 15) = 105 \quad \text{and} \quad k = 94.$$

$\square$

The burst-error-correction capabilities of the Fire code are established by the following theorem.

Theorem 10.6 *The Fire code is capable of correcting any burst up to length l.*

Proof [271, p. 262] We will show that bursts of different lengths reside in different cosets, so they can be employed as coset leaders and form correctable error patterns. Let $a(x)$ and $b(x)$ be polynomials of degree $l_1 - 1$ and $l_2 - 1$, representing bursts of length l_1 and l_2, respectively,

$$a(x) = 1 + a_1 x + a_2 x^2 + \cdots + a_{l_1 - 2} x^{l_1 - 2} + x^{l_1 - 1}$$
$$b(x) = 1 + b_1 x + b_2 x^2 + \cdots + b_{l_2 - 2} x^{l_2 - 2} + x^{l_2 - 1},$$

with $l_1 \leq l$ and $l_2 \leq l$. Since a burst error can occur anywhere within the length of the code, we represent bursts as $x^i a(x)$ and $x^j b(x)$, where i and j are less than n and represent the starting position of the burst.

Suppose (contrary to the theorem) that $x^i a(x)$ and $x^j b(x)$ are in the same coset of the code. Then the polynomial

$$v(x) = x^i a(x) + x^j b(x)$$

must be a code polynomial in the code. We show that this cannot occur. Without loss of generality, take $i \leq j$. By the division algorithm, dividing $j - i$ by $2l - 1$, we obtain

$$j - i = q(2l - 1) + b \tag{10.2}$$

for some quotient q and remainder b, with $0 \leq b < 2l - 1$. Using this, we can write

$$v(x) = x^i (a(x) + x^b b(x)) + x^{i+b} b(x)(x^{q(2l-1)} + 1). \tag{10.3}$$

Since (by our contrary assumption) $v(x)$ is a codeword, it must be divisible by $g(x)$ and, since the factors of $g(x)$ in (10.1) are relatively prime, $v(x)$ must be divisible by $x^{2l-1} + 1$. Since $x^{q(2l-1)} + 1$ is divisible by $x^{2l-1} + 1$, it follows that $a(x) + x^b b(x)$ is either divisible by $x^{2l-1} + 1$ or is 0. Let us write

$$a(x) + x^b b(x) = d(x)(x^{2l-1} + 1) \tag{10.4}$$

for some quotient polynomial $d(x)$. Let δ be the degree of $d(x)$. The degree of $d(x)(x^{2l-1} + 1)$ is $\delta + 2l - 1$. The degree of $a(x)$ is $l_1 - 1 < 2l - 1$, so the degree of $a(x) + x^b b(x)$ must be established by the degree of $x^b b(x)$. That is, we must have

$$b + l_2 - 1 = 2l - 1 + \delta. \tag{10.5}$$

Since $l_1 \leq l$ and $l_2 \leq l$, subtracting l_2 from both sides of (10.5), we obtain

$$b \geq l_1 + \delta.$$

From this inequality we trivially observe that

$$b > l_1 - 1 \quad \text{and} \quad b > d.$$

Writing out $a(x) + x^b b(x)$, we have

$$a(x) + x^b b(x) = 1 + a_1 x + a_2 x^2 + \cdots + a_{l_1-2} x^{l_1-2} + x^{l_1-1}$$
$$+ x^b (1 + b_1 x + b_2 x^2 + \cdots + b_{l_2-2} x^{l_2-2} + x^{l_2-1})$$

so that x^b is one of the terms in $a(x) + x^b b(x)$. On the other hand, since $\delta < b < 2l - 1$, the expression $d(x)(x^{2l-1} + 1)$ from (10.4) does not have the term x^b, contradicting the factorization of (10.4). We must therefore have $d(x) = 0$ and $a(x) + x^b b(x) = 0$. In order to cancel the constant terms in each polynomial, we must have $b = 0$, so we conclude that

$$a(x) = b(x).$$

Since b must be 0, (10.2) gives

$$j - i = q(2l - 1). \tag{10.6}$$

Substituting this into (10.3), we obtain

$$v(x) = x^i b(x)(x^{j-i} + 1).$$

Now the degree $b(x)$ is $l_2 - 1 < l$, so $\deg(p(x)) < m = \deg(p(x))$. But since $p(x)$ is irreducible, $b(x)$ and $p(x)$ must be relatively prime. Therefore, since $v(x)$ is (assumed to be) a code polynomial, $x^{j-i} + 1$ must be divisible by $p(x)$ (since it cannot be divisible by $x^{2l-1} + 1$). Therefore, $j - i$ must be a multiple of ρ. By (10.6), $j - i$ must also be multiple of $2l - 1$. So $j - i$ must be a multiple of the least common multiple of $2l - 1$ and m. But this least common multiple is n. We now reach the contradiction which leads to the final conclusion: $j - i$ cannot be a multiple of n, since j and i are both less than n.

We conclude, therefore, that $v(x)$ is not a codeword, so the bursts $x^i a(x)$ and $x^j b(x)$ are in different cosets. Hence they are correctable error patterns. $\square$

10.7.2 Decoding Fire Codes: Error Trapping Decoding

There are several decoding algorithms which have been developed for Fire codes. We present here the **error trapping decoder**. Error trapping decoding is a method which works for many different cyclic codes, but is particularly suited to the structure of Fire codes.

Let $r(x) = c(x) + e(x)$ be a received polynomial. Let us recall that for a cyclic code, the syndrome may be computed by dividing $r(x)$ by $g(x)$, $e(x) = q(x)g(x) + s(x)$. The syndrome is a polynomial of degree up to $n - k - 1$,

$$s(x) = s_0 + s_1 x + \cdots + s_{n-k-1} x^{n-k-1}.$$

Also recall that if $r(x)$ is cyclically shifted i times to produce $r^{(i)}(x)$, the syndrome $s^{(i)}(x)$ may be obtained either by dividing $r^{(i)}(x)$ by $g(x)$, or by dividing $x^i s(x)$ by $g(x)$. Suppose that an l burst-error-correcting code is employed and that the errors occur in a burst confined to the l digits,

$$e(x) = e_{n-k-l} x^{n-k-l} + e_{n-k-l+1} x^{n-k-l+1} + \cdots + e_{n-k-1} x^{n-k-1}.$$

Then the syndrome digits $s_{n-k-l}, s_{n-k-l+1}, \ldots, s_{n-k-1}$ match the error values and the syndrome digits $s_0, s_1, \ldots, s_{n-k-l-1}$ are zeros.

If the errors occur in a burst of l consecutive positions at some other location, then after some number i of cyclic shifts, the errors are shifted to the positions $x^{n-k-l}, x^{n-k-l+1}, \ldots, x^{n-k-1}$ of $r^{(i)}(x)$. Then the corresponding syndrome $s^{(i)}(x)$ of $r^{(i)}(x)$ matches the errors at positions $x^{n-k-l}, x^{n-k-l+1}, \ldots, x^{n-k-1}$ of $r^{(i)}(x)$ and the digits at positions $x_0, x^1, \ldots, x^{n-k-l-1}$ are zeros. This fact allows us to "trap" the errors: when the condition of zeros is detected among the lower syndrome digits, we conclude that the shifted errors are trapped in the other digits of the syndrome register.

An error trapping decoder is diagrammed in Figure 10.8. The operation is as follows [271]:

1. With gate 1 and gate 2 open, the received vector $r(x)$ is shifted into the syndrome register, where the division by $g(x)$ takes place by virtue of the feedback connections, so that when $r(x)$ has been shifted in, the syndrome register contains $s(x)$. $r(x)$ is also simultaneously shifted into a buffer register.

2. Successive shifts of the syndrome register occur with gate 2 still open. When the left $n - k - l$ memory elements contain only zeros, the right l stages are deemed to have "trapped" the burst error pattern and error correction begins. The exact correction actions depends upon how many shifts were necessary.

   - If the $n - k - l$ left stages of the syndrome register are all zero after the ith shift for $0 \leq i \leq n - k - l$, then the errors in $e(x)$ are confined only to the parity check positions of $r(x)$, so that the message bits are error free. There is no need to correct the parity bits. In this case, gate 4 is open, and the buffer register is simply shifted out. If, for this range of shifts the $n - k - l$ left stages are never zero, then the error burst is not confined to the parity check positions of $r(x)$.

   - If the $n - k - l$ left stages of the syndrome register are all zero after the $(n - k - l + i)$th shift, for $1 \leq i \leq l$, then the error burst is confined to positions $x^{n-i}, \ldots, x^{n-1}, x^0, \ldots, x^{l-i-1}$ or $r(x)$. (This burst is contiguous in a cyclic sense.) In this case, $l - i$ right digits of the syndrome buffer register match the errors at the locations $x^0, x^1, \ldots, x^{l-i-1}$ of $r(x)$, which are parity check positions and the next i stages of the syndrome register match the errors at locations $x^{n-i}, \ldots, x^{n-2}, x^{n-1}$, which are message locations. The syndrome register is shifted $l - i$ times with gate 2 closed (no feedback) so that the errors align with the message digits in the buffer register. Then gate 3 and gate 4 are opened and the message bits are shifted out of the buffer register, being corrected by the error bits shifted out of the syndrome register.

   - If the $n - k - l$ left stages of the syndrome register are never all zeros by the time the syndrome register has been shifted $n - k$ times, the bits are shifted out of the buffer register with gate 4 open while the syndrome register is simultaneously shifted with gate 2 open. In the event that the $n - k - l$ left stages of the syndrome register become equal to all zeros, the digits in the l right stages of the syndrome register match the errors of the next l message bits. Gate 3 is then opened and the message bits are corrected as they are shifted out of the buffer register.

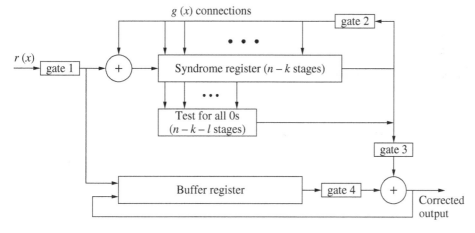

Figure 10.8: Error trapping decoder for burst-error-correcting codes [271, p. 260].

- If the $n - k - l$ left stages of the syndrome register are never all zeros by the time the k message bits have been shifted out of the buffer, an uncorrectable error burst has been detected.

10.8 Exercises

10.1 Let an (n, k) cyclic code with generator $g(x)$ be interleaved by writing its codewords into an $M \times n$ array, then reading out the columns. The resulting code is an (Mn, kn) code. Show that this code is cyclic with generator $g(x^M)$.

10.2 Let G_1 and G_2 be generator matrices for C_1 and C_2, respectively. Show that $G_1 \otimes G_2$ is a generator matrix for $C_1 \times C_2$, where $\otimes$ is the Kronecker product introduced in Chapter 8.

10.3 Let C_1 and C_2 be cyclic codes of length n_1 and n_2, respectively, with $(n_1, n_2) = 1$. Form the product code $C_1 \times C_2$. In this problem you will argue that $C_1 \times C_2$ is also cyclic. Denote the codeword represented by the matrix

$$
\mathbf{c} = \begin{bmatrix}
c_{00} & c_{01} & \cdots & c_{0\ n_2-1} \\
c_{10} & c_{11} & \cdots & c_{1\ n_2-1} \\
\vdots & & & \\
c_{n_1-1\ 0} & c_{n_1-1\ 1} & \cdots & c_{n_1-1\ n_2-1}
\end{bmatrix}
$$

by the polynomial

$$
c(x, y) = \sum_{i=0}^{n_1-1} \sum_{j=0}^{n_2-1} c_{ij} x^i y^j,
$$

where $c(x, y) \in \mathbb{F}[x]/(x^{n_1} - 1, y^{n_2} - 1)$. That is, in the ring where $x^{n_1} = 1$ and $y^{n_2} = 1$ (since the codes are cyclic). Thus, $xc(x, y)$ and $yc(x, y)$ represent cyclic shifts of the rows and columns, respectively, of $\mathbf{c}$.

(a) Show that there exists a function $I(i, j)$ such that for each pair (i, j) with $0 \le i < n_1$ and $0 \le j < n_2$, $I(i, j)$ is a unique integer in the range $0 \le I(i, j) < n_1 n_2$, such that

$$
I(i, j) \equiv i \pmod{n_1}
$$

$$
I(i, j) \equiv j \pmod{n_2}.
$$

(b) Using $I(i, j)$, rewrite $c(x, y)$ in terms of a single variable $z = xy$ by replacing each $x^i y^j$ by $z^{I(i,j)}$ to obtain the representation $d(z)$.

(c) Show that the set of code polynomials $d(z)$ so obtained is cyclic.

10.4 For each of the following (M, D) pairs, draw the cross interleaver and the corresponding deinterleaver. Also, for the sequence $x_0, x_1, x_2, \ldots$, determine the interleaved output sequence.

(a) $(M, D) = (2, 1)$ (c) $(M, D) = (3, 2)$

(b) $(M, D) = (2, 2)$ (d) $(M, D) = (4, 2)$

10.5 [271] Find a generator polynomial of a Fire code capable of correcting any single error burst of length 4 or less. What is the length of the code? Devise an error trapping decoder for this code.

10.9 References

The topic of burst-error-correcting codes is much more fully developed in [271] where, in addition to the cyclic codes introduced here, several other codes are presented which were found by computer search. Fire codes were introduced in [124]. The cross interleaver is examined in [361]. Error trapping decoding is also fully developed in [271]; it was originally developed in [246, 247, 314, 315, 388]. The CD system is described in [210]. A thorough summary is provided in [211]. Product codes are discussed in [292, chapter 18]. Application to burst error correction is described in [271]. Cyclic product codes are explored in [53, 274]. The interpretation of Reed–Solomon codes as binary (mn, mk) codes is discussed in [292]. Decoders which attempt binary-level decoding of Reed–Solomon codes are in [315] and references therein.

Chapter 11

Soft-Decision Decoding Algorithms

11.1 Introduction and General Notation

Most of the decoding methods described to this point in the book have been based on discrete field values, usually *bits* obtained by quantizing the output of the matched filter. However, the actual value of the matched filter output might be used, instead of just its quantization, to determine the reliability of the bit decision. For example, in BPSK modulation if the matched filter output is very near to zero, then any bit decision made based on only that output would have low reliability. A decoding algorithm which takes into account reliability information or uses probabilistic or likelihood values rather than quantized data is called a *soft-decision* decoding algorithm. Decoding which uses only the (quantized) received bit values and not their reliabilities is referred to as hard-decision decoding. As a general rule of thumb, soft-decision decoding can provide as much as 3 dB of gain over hard-decision decoding. In this short chapter, we introduce some of the most commonly used historical methods for soft-decision decoding, particularly for binary codes transmitted using BPSK modulation over the AWGN channel. Some modern soft-decision decoding techniques are discussed in the context of turbo codes (Chapter 14) and LDPC codes (Chapter 15) and polar codes (Chapter 17).

Some clarification in the terminology is needed. The algorithms discussed in the chapter actually provide *hard* output decisions. That is, the decoded values are provided without any reliability information. However, they rely on "soft" input decisions — matched filter outputs or reliabilities. They should thus be called soft-input hard-output algorithms. A soft-output decoder would provide decoded values accompanied by an associated reliability measure, or a probability distribution for the decoded bits. Such decoders are called soft-input, soft-output decoders. The turbo and LDPC decoders provide this capability.

Let C be a code and let a codeword $\mathbf{c} = (c_0, c_1, \ldots, c_{n-1}) \in C$ be modulated as the vector

$$\tilde{\mathbf{c}} = (\tilde{c}_0, \tilde{c}_1, \ldots, \tilde{c}_{n-1})$$

(assuming for convenience a one-dimensional signal space; modifications for two- or higher-dimensional signal spaces are straightforward). We will denote the operation of modulation — mapping into the signal space for transmission — by M, so that we can write

$$\tilde{\mathbf{c}} = \mathsf{M}(\mathbf{c}).$$

The modulated signal $\tilde{\mathbf{c}}$ is passed through a memoryless channel to form the received vector $\mathbf{r} = (r_0, r_1, \ldots, r_{n-1})$. For example, for an AWGN

$$r_i = \tilde{c}_i + n_i,$$

where $n_i \sim \mathcal{N}(0, \sigma^2)$, with $\sigma^2 = N_0/2$.

The operation of "slicing" the received signal into signal constellation values, the detection problem, can be thought of as an "inverse" modulation. We denote the "sliced" values as v_i. Thus,

$$v_i = \mathsf{M}^{-1}(r_i)$$

or

$$\mathbf{v} = \mathsf{M}^{-1}(\mathbf{r}).$$

Error Correction Coding: Mathematical Methods and Algorithms, Second Edition. Todd K. Moon
© 2021 John Wiley & Sons, Inc. Published 2021 by John Wiley & Sons, Inc.
Companion website: www.wiley.com/go/Moon/ErrorCorrectionCoding

If the r_i values are sliced into discrete detected values v_i and only this information is used by the decoder, then hard-decision decoding occurs.

Example 11.1 For example, if BPSK modulation is used, then $\tilde{c}_i = \mathsf{M}(c_i) = \sqrt{E_c}(2c_i - 1)$ is the modulated signal point. The received values are sliced into detected bits by

$$v_i = \mathsf{M}^{-1}(r_i) = \begin{cases} 0 & r_i < 0 \\ 1 & r_i \geq 0 \end{cases} \in \{0, 1\}.$$

In this case, as described in Section 1.5.7, there is effectively a BSC model between transmitter and receiver. Figure 11.1 illustrates the signal labels.

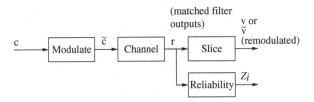

Figure 11.1: Signal labels for soft-decision decoding.

□

It is possible to associate with each sliced value v_i a *reliability* z_i, which indicates the quality of the decision. The reliabilities are ordered such that $z_i > z_j$ if the ith symbol is more reliable — capable of producing better decisions — than the jth symbol. If the channel is AWGN, then

$$z_i = |r_i| \in \mathbb{R}$$

can be used as the reliability measure, since the absolute log likelihood ratio

$$\left| \log \frac{p(r_i | c_i = 1)}{p(r_i | c_i = 0)} \right| \tag{11.1}$$

is proportional to $|r_i|$. Associated with each channel is a distance measure. For the BSC, the appropriate distance measure is the Hamming distance,

$$d_H(\mathbf{v}, \mathbf{c}) = \sum_{i=0}^{n-1} [v_i \neq c_i].$$

However, for soft-decision decoding over the AWGN, the Euclidean metric between the (soft) received vector and the transmitted codeword

$$d_E(\mathbf{r}, \tilde{\mathbf{c}}) = d_E(\mathbf{r}, \mathsf{M}(\mathbf{c})) = \|\mathbf{r} - \tilde{\mathbf{c}}\|^2$$

is more appropriate. (See Section 1.5 for further discussion.)

A key idea in soft-decision decoding is *sorting* the symbols in order of reliability. When the symbols are sorted in order of decreasing reliability, then the first sorted symbols are more likely to be correct than the last sorted symbols. The set of symbols which have the highest reliability (appearing first in the sorted list) are referred to as being in the most reliable positions and the set of symbols appearing at the end of the sorted list are said to be in the least reliable positions.

11.2   Generalized Minimum Distance Decoding

Recall (see Section 3.8) that an erasure-and-error decoder is capable of correcting twice as many erasures as errors. That is, a code with minimum Hamming distance d_{min} can simultaneously correct e errors and f erasures provided that $2e + f \leq d_{min} - 1$. The generalized minimum distance (GMD) decoder devised by Forney [127] makes use of this fact, deliberately erasing symbols which have the least reliability, then correcting them using an erasure-and-error decoder. The GMD decoding considers all possible patterns of up to $f \leq d_{min} - 1$ erasures in the least reliable positions. The decoder operates as follows.

Algorithm 11.1 Generalized Minimum Distance (GMD) Decoding

Initialize: For the (soft) received sequence $\mathbf{r} = (r_0, r_1, \ldots, r_{n-1})$, form
   the hard-decision vector $\mathbf{v} = (v_0, v_1, \ldots, v_{n-1})$ and the reliabilities $z_i = |r_i|$.
Sort the reliabilities to find the $d_{min} - 1$ least reliable positions
if d_{min} is even:
   for $j = 1$ to $d_{min} - 1$ by 2
      erase the j least reliable symbols in $\mathbf{v}$ to form amodified vector $\hat{\mathbf{v}}$
      Decode and Select the best codeword
else if d_{min} is odd:
   for $j = 0$ to $d_{min} - 1$ by 2
      erase the j least reliable symbols in $\mathbf{v}$ to form amodified vector $\hat{\mathbf{v}}$
      Decode and Select the best codeword
end if

Decode and Select the best codeword
   Decode $\hat{\mathbf{v}}$ using an erasures-and-errors decoding algorithmto obtain a codeword $\mathbf{c}$.
   Compute the soft-decision (e.g., Euclidean) distance betweenM($\mathbf{c}$) and $\mathbf{r}$, $d_E(\mathbf{r}, M(\mathbf{c}))$,
   and select the codeword with the best distance.

As discussed in Exercise 11.2, the correlation discrepancy λ can be computed instead of the distance.

Since hard-decision values are actually used in the erasures-and-errors decoding algorithm, an algebraic decoder can be used, if it exists for the particular code being decoded. (The Chase algorithms described below are also compatible with algebraic decoding algorithms.) Note that for d_{min} either even or odd, there are only $\lfloor (d_{min} + 1)/2 \rfloor$ different vectors that must be decoded.

While the GMD algorithm is straightforward and conceptually simple, justifying it in detail will require a bit of work, which follows in the next section.

11.2.1   Distance Measures and Properties

There are two theorems which will establish the correctness of the GMD algorithm, which will require some additional notation. We first generalize the concept of Hamming distance. In defining the Hamming distance between elements of a codeword $\mathbf{c}$ and another vector $\mathbf{v}$, there were essentially two "classes" of outcomes, those where v_i matches c_i, and those where v_i does not match c_i. We generalize this by introducing J *reliability classes* $C_1, C_2, \ldots, C_J$, each of which has associated with it two parameters β_{cj} and β_{ej} such that

$$0 \leq \beta_{cj} \leq \beta_{ej} \leq 1.$$

We also introduce the *weight* of the class, $\alpha_j = \beta_{ej} - \beta_{cj}$. Then β_{ej} is the "cost" when v_i is in class j and $v_i \neq c_i$, and β_{cj} is the "cost" when v_i is in class j and $v_i = c_i$. It is clear that $0 \leq \alpha_j \leq 1$.
   We write

$$d_G(v_i, c_i) = \begin{cases} \beta_{ej} & v_i \in C_j \text{ and } v_i \neq c_i \\ \beta_{cj} & v_i \in C_j \text{ and } v_i = c_i. \end{cases}$$

Then the *generalized distance* $d_G(\mathbf{v}, \mathbf{c})$ is defined as

$$d_G(\mathbf{v}, \mathbf{c}) = \sum_{i=0}^{n-1} d_G(v_i, c_i). \tag{11.2}$$

(Note that this is not a true distance, since it is not symmetric in $\mathbf{v}$ and $\mathbf{c}$.) Now let n_{cj} be the number of symbols received correctly (i.e., $v_i = c_i$) and put into class C_j. Let n_{ej} be the number of symbols received incorrectly (so that $v_i \neq c_i$) and put into class C_j. Then (11.2) can be written as

$$d_G(\mathbf{v}, \mathbf{c}) = \sum_{j=1}^{J} \beta_{cj} n_{cj} + \beta_{ej} n_{ej}. \tag{11.3}$$

Example 11.2   For conventional, errors-only decoding, there is only one reliability class, C_1, having $\beta_{c1} = 0$ and $\beta_{e1} = 1$, so $\alpha_1 = 1$. In this case, the generalized distance specializes to the Hamming distance.
   Introducing erasures introduces a second reliability class C_2 having $\beta_{c2} = \beta_{e2} = 0$, or $\alpha_2 = 0$. Symbols in the erasure class can be considered to be equally distant from all transmitted symbols.   □

   A class for which $\alpha_j = 1$ is said to be fully reliable.
   The first theorem provides a basis for declaring when the decoding algorithm can declare a correct decoded value.

Theorem 11.3 *[127] For a code having minimum distance $d_{\min}$, if $\mathbf{c}$ is sent and n_{cj} and n_{ej} are such that*

$$\sum_{j=1}^{J} [(1 - \alpha_j) n_{cj} + (1 + \alpha_j) n_{ej}] < d_{\min}, \tag{11.4}$$

then

$$d_G(\mathbf{v}, \mathbf{c}) < d_G(\mathbf{v}, \mathbf{c}')$$

for all codewords $\mathbf{c}' \neq \mathbf{c}$. That is, $\mathbf{v}$ is closer to $\mathbf{c}$ in the d_G measure than to all other codewords.

   Note that for errors-only decoding, this theorem specializes as follows: if $2n_{e1} < d_{\min}$, then $d_H(\mathbf{r}, \mathbf{c}) < d_H(\mathbf{r}, \mathbf{c}')$, which is the familiar statement regarding the decoding capability of a code, with n_{e1} the number of correctable errors. For erasures-and-errors decoding, the theorem specializes as follows: if $2n_{e1} + (n_{c2} + n_{e2}) < d_{\min}$, then $d_G(\mathbf{v}, \mathbf{c}) < d_G(\mathbf{v}, \mathbf{c}')$. Letting $f = n_{c2} + n_{e2}$ be the number of erasures, this recovers the familiar condition for erasures-and-errors decoding.

Proof   Let $\mathbf{c}'$ be any codeword not equal to $\mathbf{c}$. Partition the n symbol locations into sets such that

$$i \in \begin{cases} S_0 & \text{if } c_i = c'_i \\ S_{cj} & \text{if } c_i \neq c'_i \text{ and } v_i = c_i \text{ and } v_i \in C_j \\ S_{ej} & \text{if } c_i \neq c'_i \text{ and } v_i \neq c_i \text{ and } v_i \in C_j. \end{cases}$$

Clearly we must have $|S_{cj}| \leq n_{cj}$ and $|S_{ej}| \leq n_{ej}$.

- For $i \in S_0$, $d_G(v_i, c'_i) \geq 0 = d_H(c_i, c'_i)$.
- For $i \in S_{cj}$, $d_G(v_i, c'_i) = \beta_{ej} = d_H(c'_i, c_i) - 1 + \beta_{ej}$
- For $i \in S_{ej}$, $d_G(v_i, c'_i) \geq \beta_{cj} = d_H(c'_i, c_i) - 1 + \beta_{cj}$.

Summing both sides of these equalities/inequalities over $j = 1, \ldots, J$, we obtain

$$d_G(\mathbf{v}, \mathbf{c}') \geq d_H(\mathbf{c}, \mathbf{c}') - \sum_{i=0}^{n-1} [(1 - \beta_{ej})|S_{cj}| + (1 - \beta_{cj})|S_{ej}|]$$

$$\geq d_{\min} - \sum_{i=0}^{n-1} [(1 - \beta_{ej})n_{cj} + (1 - \beta_{cj})n_{ej})].$$

If, as stated in the hypothesis of the theorem,

$$d_{\min} > \sum_{j=1}^{J} [(1 - \beta_{ej} + \beta_{cj})n_{cj} + (1 - \beta_{cj} + \beta_{ej})n_{ej}],$$

then

$$d_G(\mathbf{v}, \mathbf{c}') > \sum_{j=1}^{J} n_{cj}\beta_{cj} + n_{ej}\beta_j = d_G(\mathbf{v}, \mathbf{c}). \qquad \square$$

This theorem allows us to draw the following conclusions:

- If generalized distance d_G is used as a decoding criterion, then no decoding error will be made when n_{cj} and n_{ej} are such that (11.4) is satisfied.

  Let us say that $\mathbf{c}$ is *within the minimum distance* of $\mathbf{v}$ if (11.4) is satisfied.

- The theorem also says that there can be at most one codeword within the minimum distance of any received word $\mathbf{v}$.

Thus, if by some means a codeword $\mathbf{c}$ can be found within the minimum distance of the received word $\mathbf{v}$, then it can be concluded that this is the decoded value.

The next theorem will determine the maximum number of different decoded values necessary and suggest how to obtain them.

Let the classes be ordered according to decreasing reliability (or weight), so that $\alpha_j \geq \alpha_k$ if $j < k$. Let

$$\boldsymbol{\alpha} = (\alpha_1, \alpha_2, \ldots, \alpha_J)$$

be the vector of all class weights. Let

$$R_b = \{0, 1, 2, \ldots, b\} \quad \text{and} \quad E_b = \{b + 1, b + 2, b + 3, \ldots, J\}.$$

Let

$$\boldsymbol{\alpha}_b = \{\underbrace{1, 1, \ldots, 1}_{b \text{ ones}}, 0, 0, \ldots, 0\}.$$

Theorem 11.4 *[127] Let the weights be ordered according to decreasing reliability. If*

$$\sum_{j=1}^{J} [(1 - \alpha_j)n_{cj} + (1 + \alpha_j)n_{ej}] < d_{\min},$$

then there is some integer b such that

$$2\sum_{j=1}^{b} n_{ej} + \sum_{i=b+1}^{J} (n_{cj} + n_{ej}) < d_{\min}.$$

Since erased symbols are associated with a class having $\alpha_j = 0$, which would occur last in the ordered reliability list, the import of the theorem is that if there is some codeword such that the inequality (11.4) is satisfied, then there must be some assignment in which (only) the least reliable classes are erased which will enable an erasures-and-errors decoder to succeed in finding that codeword.

Proof Let

$$f(\boldsymbol{\alpha}) = \sum_{j=1}^{J} [(1 - \alpha_j)n_{cj} + (1 + \alpha_j)n_{ej}].$$

Note that $f(\boldsymbol{\alpha}_b) = 2\sum_{j=1}^{b} n_{ej} + \sum_{j=b+1}^{J} (n_{cj} + n_{ej})$. The proof is by contradiction.

Suppose (contrary to the theorem) that $f(\boldsymbol{\alpha}_b) \geq d_{\min}$. Let

$$\lambda_0 = 1 - \alpha_1 \quad \lambda_b = \alpha_b - \alpha_{b+1} \quad 1 \leq b \leq J-1 \quad \lambda_J = \alpha_J.$$

By the ordering, $0 \leq \lambda_b \leq 1$ for $0 \leq b \leq J$, and $\sum_{b=0}^{J} \lambda_b = 1$.

Now let

$$\boldsymbol{\alpha} = \sum_{b=0}^{J} \lambda_b \boldsymbol{\alpha}_b.$$

Then

$$f(\boldsymbol{\alpha}) = f\left(\sum_{b=0}^{J} \lambda_b \boldsymbol{\alpha}_b\right) = \sum_{b=0}^{J} \lambda_b f(\boldsymbol{\alpha}_b) \geq d_{\min} \sum_{b=0}^{J} \lambda_b = d_{\min}.$$

Thus, if $f(\boldsymbol{\alpha}_b) \geq d$ for all b, then $f(\boldsymbol{\alpha}) \geq d_{\min}$. But the hypothesis of the theorem is that $f(\boldsymbol{\alpha}) < d_{\min}$, which is a contradiction. Therefore, there must be at least one b such that $f(\boldsymbol{\alpha}_b) < d_{\min}$. $\square$

Let us examine conditions under which an erasures-and-errors decoder can succeed. The decoder can succeed if there are apparently no errors and $d_{\min} - 1$ erasures, or one error and $d_{\min} - 3$ erasures, and so forth up to t_0 errors and $d_{\min} - 2t_0 - 1$ erasures, where t_0 is the largest integer such that $2t_0 \leq d_{\min} - 1$. These possibilities are exactly those examined by the statement of the GMD decoder in Algorithm 11.1.

11.3 The Chase Decoding Algorithms

In [60], three other soft-decision decoding algorithms were presented, now referred to as Chase-1, Chase-2, and Chase-3. These algorithms provide varying levels of decoder capability for varying degrees of decoder effort.

In the Chase-1 algorithm, *all* patterns of up to $d_{\min} - 1$ errors are added to the received signal vector $\mathbf{v}$ to form $\mathbf{w} = \mathbf{v} + \mathbf{e}$. Then $\mathbf{w}$ is decoded, if possible, and compared using a soft-decision metric to $\mathbf{r}$. The decoded codeword closest to $\mathbf{r}$ is selected. However, since all patterns of up to $d_{\min} - 1$ errors are used, this is very complex for codes of appreciable length or distance, so Chase-1 decoding has attracted very little interest.

In the Chase-2 algorithm, the $\lfloor d_{\min}/2 \rfloor$ least reliable positions are identified from the sorted reliabilities. The set E consisting of all errors in these $\lfloor d_{\min}/2 \rfloor$ least reliable positions is generated. Then the Chase-2 algorithm can be summarized as follows.

Algorithm 11.2 Chase-2 Decoder

Initialize: For the (soft) received sequence $\mathbf{r} = (r_0, r_1, \ldots, r_{n-1})$, form the hard-decision vector $\mathbf{v} = (v_0, v_1, \ldots, v_{n-1})$ and the reliabilities $z_i = |r_i|$.
Identify the $\lfloor d_{min}/2 \rfloor$ least reliable positions
Generate the set E of error vectors (one at a time, in practice)
for each $\mathbf{e} \in E$
   Decode $\mathbf{v} + \mathbf{e}$ using an errors-only decoder to produce the codeword $\mathbf{c}$
   Compute $d_E(\mathbf{r}, M(\mathbf{c}))$ and select the candidate codeword with the best metric.
end for

The Chase-3 decoder has lower complexity than the Chase-2 algorithm, and is similar to the GMD.

Algorithm 11.3 Chase-3 Decoder

Initialize: For the (soft) received sequence $\mathbf{r} = (r_0, r_1, \ldots, r_{n-1})$, form the hard-decision vector $\mathbf{v} = (v_0, v_1, \ldots, v_{n-1})$ and the reliabilities $z_i = |r_i|$.
Sort the reliabilities to find the $\lfloor d_{min} - 1 \rfloor$ least reliable positions

Generate a list of at most $\lfloor d_{min}/2 + 1 \rfloor$ sequences by modifying $\mathbf{v}$:
If d_{min} is even, modify $\mathbf{v}$ by complementing no symbols, then the least reliable symbol, then the three least reliable symbols, …, the d_{min-1} least reliable symbols.
If d_{min} is odd, modify $\mathbf{v}$ by complementing no symbols, then the two least reliable symbols, then the four least reliable symbols, …, the d_{min-1} least reliable symbols.
Decode each modified $\mathbf{v}$ into a codeword $\mathbf{c}$ using an error-only decoder.
Compute $d_E(\mathbf{r}, M(\mathbf{c}))$ and select the codeword that is closest.

11.4 Halting the Search: An Optimality Condition

The soft-decision decoding algorithms presented so far require searching over an entire list of candidate codewords to select the best. It is of interest to know if a given codeword is the best that is going to be found, without having to complete the search. In this section, we discuss an optimality condition appropriate for binary codes transmitted using BPSK which can be tested which establishes exactly this condition.

Let $\mathbf{r}$ be the received vector, with hard-decision values $\mathbf{v}$. Let $\mathbf{c} = (c_0, c_1, \ldots, c_{n-1})$ be a binary codeword in C and let $\tilde{\mathbf{c}} = (\tilde{c}_0, \tilde{c}_1, \ldots, \tilde{c}_{n-1})$ be its bipolar representation (i.e., for BPSK modulation), with $\tilde{c}_i = 2c_i - 1$. In this section, whenever we indicate a codeword $\mathbf{c}$, its corresponding bipolar representation $\tilde{\mathbf{c}}$ is also implied. We define the index sets $D_0(\mathbf{c})$ and $D_1(\mathbf{c})$ with respect to a codevector $\mathbf{c}$ by

$$D_0(\mathbf{c}) = \{i : 0 \le i < n \text{ and } c_i = v_i\} \quad \text{and} \quad D_1(\mathbf{c}) = \{i : 0 \le i < n \text{ and } c_i \ne v_i\}.$$

Let $n(\mathbf{c}) = |D_1(\mathbf{c})|$; this is the Hamming distance between the codeword $\mathbf{c}$ and the hard-decision vector $\mathbf{v}$.

It is clear from the definitions that $r_i \tilde{c}_i < 0$ if and only if $v_i \ne c_i$. In Exercise 11.2, the correlation discrepancy $\lambda(\mathbf{r}, \tilde{\mathbf{c}})$ is defined as

$$\lambda(\mathbf{r}, \tilde{\mathbf{c}}) = \sum_{i : r_i \tilde{c}_i < 0} |r_i|.$$

Based on the index sets just defined, λ can be expressed as

$$\lambda(\mathbf{r}, \tilde{\mathbf{c}}) = \sum_{i \in D_1(\mathbf{c})} |r_i|.$$

As discussed in Exercise 11.2, ML decoding seeks a codeword $\mathbf{c}$ such that $\lambda(\mathbf{r}, \tilde{\mathbf{c}})$ is minimized: a ML codeword $\mathbf{c}^*$ is one satisfying

$$\lambda(\mathbf{r}, \tilde{\mathbf{c}}^*) \leq \min_{\mathbf{c} \in C, \mathbf{c} \neq \mathbf{c}^*} \lambda(\mathbf{r}, \mathbf{c}).$$

While determining the minimum requires search over all $\mathbf{c} \in C$, we will establish a tight bound λ^* on $\min_{\mathbf{c} \in C, \mathbf{c} \neq \mathbf{c}^*} \lambda(\mathbf{r}, \mathbf{c})$ such that $\lambda(\mathbf{r}, \tilde{\mathbf{c}}) \leq \lambda^*$ represents a sufficient condition for the optimality of the candidate codeword in the list of candidate codewords generated by a reliability-based decoding algorithm such as those presented above.

Let the indices in $D_0(\mathbf{c})$ be written as

$$D_0(\mathbf{c}) = \{l_1, l_2, \ldots, l_{n-n(\mathbf{c})}\},$$

where the indices are ordered such that for $i < j$, the reliabilities are ordered as

$$|r_{l_i}| < |r_{l_j}|.$$

Let $D_0^{(j)}(\mathbf{c})$ denote the first j indices in the ordered set,

$$D_0^{(j)}(\mathbf{c}) = \{l_1, l_2, \ldots, l_j\}. \tag{11.5}$$

For $j \leq 0$, define $D_0^{(j)}(\mathbf{c}) = \emptyset$, and for $j \geq n - n(\mathbf{c})$, define $D_0^{(j)}(\mathbf{c}) = D_0(\mathbf{c})$.

Let w_i be the ith weight in the weight profile of the code C. That is, $w_0 = 0$, $w_1 = d_{\min}$, and $w_1 < w_2 < \cdots < w_m$ for some m. That is, w_m is the weight of the heaviest codeword in C. For a codeword $\mathbf{c} \in C$, define

$$G(\mathbf{c}, w_j) = \sum_{i \in D_0^{(q_j)}(\mathbf{c})} |r_i|$$

and

$$R(\mathbf{c}, w_j) = \{\mathbf{c}' \in C : d_H(\mathbf{c}, \mathbf{c}') < w_j\}.$$

The set $R(\mathbf{c}, w_j)$ is the set of codewords within a distance w_j of $\mathbf{c}$. When $j = 1$, $R(\mathbf{c}, w_1)$ is simply the codeword $\{\mathbf{c}\}$. When $j = 2$, $R(\mathbf{c}, w_2)$ is the codeword $\mathbf{c}$ and all codewords in C which are at a distance $d_{\min}$ from $\mathbf{c}$.

With this notation, we are now ready for the theorem.

Theorem 11.5 *[272, p. 404] Let $\mathbf{r}$ be the received vector, with corresponding hard-decision vector $\mathbf{v}$. For a codeword $\mathbf{c} \in C$ and a nonzero weight w_j in the weight profile of C, if the correlation discrepancy $\lambda(\mathbf{r}, M(\mathbf{c}))$ satisfies*

$$\lambda(\mathbf{r}, M(\mathbf{c})) \leq G(\mathbf{c}, w_j),$$

then the maximum likelihood codeword $\mathbf{c}_{\mathrm{ML}}$ for $\mathbf{r}$ is contained in $R(\mathbf{c}, w_j)$.

The theorem thus establishes a sufficient condition for $R(\mathbf{v}, w_j)$ to contain the maximum likelihood codeword for $\mathbf{r}$.

Proof Let $\mathbf{c}'$ be a codeword outside $R(\mathbf{c}, w_j)$. Then, by the definition of R, $d_H(\mathbf{c}, \mathbf{c}') \geq w_j$. The theorem is established if we can show that $\lambda(\mathbf{r}, M(\mathbf{c}')) \geq \lambda(\mathbf{r}, M(\mathbf{c}))$, since this would show that $\mathbf{c}'$ has lower likelihood than $\mathbf{c}$. Thus, no codeword outside $R(\mathbf{r}, w_j)$ is more likely than $\mathbf{c}$, so that the maximum likelihood codeword must be in $R(\mathbf{c}, w_j)$.

Define

$$n_{01} = |D_0(\mathbf{c}) \cap D_1(\mathbf{c}')| \quad \text{and} \quad n_{10} = |D_1(\mathbf{c}) \cap D_0(\mathbf{c}')|.$$

From the definitions of D_0 and D_1, it follows that $d_H(\mathbf{c}, \mathbf{c}') = n_{01} + n_{10}$. As we have just observed, we must also have

$$w_j \leq d_H(\mathbf{c}, \mathbf{c}') = n_{01} + n_{10}. \tag{11.6}$$

It also follows that

$$\begin{aligned} |D_1(\mathbf{c}')| &\geq |D_0(\mathbf{c}) \cap D_1(\mathbf{c}')| \geq w_j - n_{10} \\ &\geq w_j - |D_1(\mathbf{c})| \\ &= w_j - n(\mathbf{c}), \end{aligned} \tag{11.7}$$

where the first inequality is immediate from the nature of intersection, the second from (11.6), and the third from the definition of n_{10} and the intersection. Now we have

$$\begin{aligned} \lambda(\mathbf{r}, M(\mathbf{c})) = \sum_{i \in D_1(\mathbf{c})} |r_i| &\geq \sum_{i \in D_0(\mathbf{c}) \cap D_1(\mathbf{c}')} |r_i| \quad (\text{since } D_0(\mathbf{c}) \cap D_1(\mathbf{c}') \subset D_1(\mathbf{c}')) \\ &\geq \sum_{i \in D_0^{(w_j - n(\mathbf{c}))}(\mathbf{c})} |r_i| \quad (\text{by (11.7)}) \\ &= G(\mathbf{c}, w_j) \quad (\text{by definition}) \\ &\geq \lambda(\mathbf{c}, \mathbf{c}) \quad (\text{by hypothesis}). \end{aligned}$$

We thus have $\lambda(\mathbf{r}, \mathbf{c}') \geq \lambda(\mathbf{r}, \mathbf{c})$: no codeword outside $R(\mathbf{r}, w_j)$ is more likely than $\mathbf{c}$. Hence $\mathbf{c}_{ML}$ must lie in $R(\mathbf{r}, w_j)$. $\square$

For $j = 1$, this theorem says that the condition $\lambda(\mathbf{r}, M(\mathbf{c})) < G(\mathbf{c}, w_1)$ guarantees that $\mathbf{c}$ is, in fact, the maximum likelihood codeword. This provides a sufficient condition for optimality, which can be used to terminate the GMD or Chase algorithms before exhausting over all codewords in the lists these algorithms produce.

11.5 Ordered Statistic Decoding

The GMD and Chase algorithms make use of the least reliable symbols. By contrast, ordered statistic decoding [142] uses the *most* reliable symbols.

Let C be an (n, k) linear block code with $k \times n$ generator matrix

$$G = \begin{bmatrix} \mathbf{g}_0 & \mathbf{g}_1 & \cdots & \mathbf{g}_{n-1} \end{bmatrix}.$$

Let $\mathbf{r}$ be the received vector of matched filter outputs, with corresponding hard-decoded values $\mathbf{v}$. Let $\mathbf{z}$ denote the corresponding reliability values and let $\bar{\mathbf{z}} = (\bar{z}_0, \bar{z}_1, \ldots, \bar{z}_{n-1})$ denote the sorted reliability values, with $\bar{z}_0 \geq \bar{z}_1 \geq \cdots \geq \bar{z}_{n-1}$. This ordering establishes a permutation mapping π_1, with

$$\bar{\mathbf{z}} = \pi_1(\mathbf{z}).$$

In ordered statistic decoding, the columns of G are reordered by the permutation mapping to form a generator matrix G', where

$$G' = \pi_1(G) = \begin{bmatrix} \mathbf{g}'_0 & \mathbf{g}'_1 & \cdots & \mathbf{g}'_{n-1} \end{bmatrix}.$$

Now a *most reliable basis* for the codeword is obtained as follows. The first k linearly independent columns of G' (associated with the largest reliability values) are found. Then these k columns are used as the first k columns of a new generator matrix G'', in reliability order. The remaining $n - k$ columns of G'' are placed in decreasing reliability order. This ordering establishes another permutation mapping π_2, such that

$$G'' = \pi_2(G') = \pi_2(\pi_1(G)).$$

Applying π_2 to the ordered reliabilities $\bar{\mathbf{z}}$ results in another reliability vector $\tilde{\mathbf{z}}$,

$$\tilde{\mathbf{z}} = \pi_2(\bar{\mathbf{z}}) = \pi_2(\pi_1(\mathbf{z}))$$

satisfying

$$\tilde{z}_1 \geq \tilde{z}_2 \geq \cdots \geq \tilde{z}_k \text{ and } \tilde{z}_{k+1} \geq \tilde{z}_{k+2} \geq \cdots \geq \tilde{z}_n.$$

Now perform elementary row operations on G'' to obtain an equivalent generator matrix $\tilde{G}$ in systematic form,

$$\tilde{G} = \begin{bmatrix} 1 & 0 & \cdots & 0 & p_{1,1} & \cdots & p_{1,n-k} \\ 0 & 1 & \cdots & 0 & p_{2,1} & \cdots & p_{2,n-k} \\ \vdots & & & & & & \\ 0 & 0 & \cdots & 1 & p_{k,1} & \cdots & p_{k,n-k} \end{bmatrix} = \begin{bmatrix} I_k & P \end{bmatrix}.$$

Let $\tilde{C}$ denote the code generated by $\tilde{G}$. The code $\tilde{C}$ is equivalent to C (see Definition 3.7).

The next decoding step is to use the k most reliable elements of $\mathbf{v}$. Let us denote these as $\tilde{\mathbf{v}}_k = [\pi_2(\pi_1(\mathbf{v}))]_{1:k} = (\tilde{v}_1, \tilde{v}_2, \ldots, \tilde{v}_k)$. Since these are the most reliable symbols, these symbols should contain very few errors. Since $\tilde{G}$ is systematically represented, we will take these symbols as the message symbols for a codeword. The corresponding codeword $\tilde{\mathbf{c}}$ in $\tilde{C}$ is obtained by

$$\tilde{\mathbf{c}} = \tilde{\mathbf{v}}_k \tilde{G} \in \tilde{C}.$$

Finally, the codeword $\hat{\mathbf{c}}$ in the original code C can be obtained by unpermuting by both permutations:

$$\hat{\mathbf{c}} = \pi_1^{-1}(\pi_2^{-1}(\tilde{\mathbf{c}})) \in C.$$

This gives a single candidate decoded value. Then $\hat{\mathbf{c}}$ is compared with $\mathbf{r}$ by computing $d_E(\mathbf{r}, \mathsf{M}(\hat{\mathbf{c}}))$ (at least, this is the appropriate distance for the AWGN channel).

Now some additional search is performed. Fix a "search depth parameter" $l \leq k$. For each i in $1 \leq i \leq l$, make all possible changes of i of the k *most* reliable symbols in $\tilde{\mathbf{v}}_k$. Denote the modified vector as $\tilde{\mathbf{v}}'_k$. For each such $\tilde{\mathbf{v}}'_k$, find the corresponding codeword

$$\tilde{\mathbf{c}}' = \tilde{\mathbf{v}}'_k \tilde{G} \in \tilde{C}$$

and its corresponding codeword $\hat{\mathbf{c}}' = \pi_1^{-1}(\pi_2^{-1}(\tilde{\mathbf{c}}')) \in C$. Then compute $d_E(\mathbf{r}, \mathsf{M}(\tilde{\mathbf{c}}'))$. Select the codeword $\tilde{\mathbf{c}}'$ with the best metric. The number of codewords to try is $\sum_{i=0}^{l} \binom{k}{i}$.

The ordered statistic decoding algorithm is summarized below.

Algorithm 11.4 Ordered Statistic Decoding

Initialize: For the (soft) received sequence $\mathbf{r} = (r_0, r_1, \ldots, r_{n-1})$, form the hard-decision vector $\mathbf{v} = (v_0, v_1, \ldots, v_{n-1})$ and the reliabilities $z_i = |r_i|$.
Sort the reliabilities by π_1, such that

$$\bar{\mathbf{z}} = \pi_1(\mathbf{z})$$

such that $\bar{z}_0 \geq \bar{z}_1 \geq \cdots \geq \bar{z}_{n-1}$
Order the columns of G to produce $G'' = \pi_1(G)$.
Find the first k linearly independent columns of G'' and retain the order of the other columns. Let $G'''' = \pi_2(G'')$ have these first k linearly independent columns.
Reduce G'''' by row operations to produce $\tilde{G}$.
Let $\tilde{\mathbf{v}}_k = \pi_2(\pi_1(\mathbf{v}))_{1:k}$.
for $i = 0$ to l
     form all patterns of i errors and add them to the most reliable positions of $\tilde{\mathbf{v}}_k$ to form $\tilde{\mathbf{v}}_k''$
         for each such $\tilde{\mathbf{v}}_k''$, find $\tilde{\mathbf{c}}'' = \tilde{\mathbf{v}}_k''\tilde{G}$ and the corresponding $\hat{\mathbf{c}}'' = \pi_1^{-1}(\pi_2^{-1}(\tilde{\mathbf{c}}''))$
         for each $\hat{\mathbf{c}}''$, compute $d_E(\mathbf{r}, \mathsf{M}(\hat{\mathbf{c}}))$ and retain the codeword with the smallest distance.

When $l = k$, then the algorithm will compute a maximum likelihood decision, but the decoding complexity is $O(2^k)$. However, since the vector $\tilde{\mathbf{v}}_k$ contains the most reliable symbols, it is likely to have very few errors, so that making a change in only a small number of locations is likely to produce the ML codeword. It is shown in [142] (see also [272, p. 433]) that for most block codes of length up to $n = 128$ and rates $R \geq \frac{1}{2}$ that $i = \lfloor d_{\min}/4 \rfloor$ achieves nearly ML decoding performance.

11.6 Soft Decoding Using the Dual Code: The Hartmann Rudolph Algorithm

Where a code has a tractable dual code (e.g., a dual code of small dimension), an approach due to Hartmann and Rudolph for soft-input decoding may be useful [181, 192]. The Hartmann–Rudolph algorithm is a symbol-by-symbol decoding algorithm, analogous to the BCJR algorithm. It is also able to incorporate prior probabilities, making it a candidate for turboprocessing settings.

Let $\mathbf{c} = (c_0, \ldots, c_{n-1})$ be a codeword of an (n, k) linear block code C over $GF(2)$. Let $\mathbf{c}'_j = (c'_{j0}, \ldots, c'_{jn-1})$ denote the jth codeword of an $(n, n-k)$ dual code $C^\perp$. The codeword is transmitted over a memorlyless channel and a signal $\mathbf{r} = (r_0, \ldots, r_{n-1})$ is received. The posterior distribution for a single symbol is

$$P(c_m = s | \mathbf{r}) = \sum_{\mathbf{c} \in C : c_m = s} P(\mathbf{c} | \mathbf{r})$$

$$= \frac{1}{p(\mathbf{r})} \sum_{\mathbf{c} \in C : c_m = s} p(\mathbf{r} | \mathbf{c}) P(\mathbf{c}),$$

where $p(\mathbf{r})$ does not depend on the codeword, and will be neglected in what follows. To incorporate prior probabilities, we specifically do not assume equiprobable symbols, and write

$$P(\mathbf{c}) = \prod_{h=0}^{n-1} p_h,$$

where $p_h = P(c_h = 1)$. Let us denote $p(\mathbf{r} | \mathbf{c}) P(\mathbf{c})$ as $p(\mathbf{r}, \mathbf{c})$.

Let $\mathbf{e}_m$ be the vector of n elements with 1 in the mth position. Also, let $\delta_{x,y}$ be the function that is 1 when $x = y$ and is 0 otherwise. Then

$$P(c_m = s | \mathbf{r}) = \sum_{\mathbf{c} \in C} P(\mathbf{r}, \mathbf{c}) \delta_{0, \mathbf{c} \cdot \mathbf{e}_m - s}.$$

Here, $\mathbf{c} \cdot \mathbf{e}_m$ is the inner product over $GF(2)$. The $\delta_{0,x}$ function can be written in terms of a finite Fourier transform over $GF(2)$ as

$$\delta_{0,x} = \frac{1}{2} \sum_{t=0}^{1} (-1)^{tx},$$

where here we interpret (-1) as the primitive square root of unity. Write the joint probability $p(\mathbf{r}, \mathbf{c})$ in terms of an n-dimensional $GF(2)$ transform

$$p(\mathbf{r}, \mathbf{c}) = \frac{1}{2^n} \sum_{\mathbf{u} \in \{0,1\}^n} P(\mathbf{r}, \mathbf{u})(-1)^{\mathbf{u} \cdot \mathbf{c}},$$

where

$$P(\mathbf{r}, \mathbf{u}) = \sum_{\mathbf{v} \in \{0,1\}^n} p(\mathbf{r}, \mathbf{v})(-1)^{-\mathbf{u} \cdot \mathbf{v}}.$$

The transform summations are over all 2^n vectors with binary elements. Substituting these results, we obtain

$$P(c_m = s|\mathbf{r}) = \frac{1}{2^{n+1}} \sum_{\mathbf{c}\in C} \sum_{\mathbf{u}\in V_n} P(\mathbf{r}, \mathbf{u})(-1)^{\mathbf{u}\cdot\mathbf{c}} \sum_{t=0}^{1} (-1)^{t(\mathbf{c}\cdot\mathbf{e}_m - s)}$$

$$= \frac{1}{2^{n+1}} \sum_{t=0}^{1} (-1)^{st} \sum_{\mathbf{u}\in V_n} P(\mathbf{r}, \mathbf{u}) \sum_{\mathbf{c}\in C} (-1)^{\mathbf{c}\cdot(\mathbf{u}+t\mathbf{e}_m)}.$$

For a vector $\mathbf{v} \in C^perp$ and a vector $\mathbf{c} \in C$, $\mathbf{v} \cdot \mathbf{c} = 0$, so

$$\sum_{\mathbf{c}\in C} (-1)^{\mathbf{v}\cdot\mathbf{c}} = 2^k \quad \mathbf{v} \in C^{\perp}.$$

It can be argued that for a vector $\mathbf{v} \notin C^{\perp}$,

$$\sum_{\mathbf{c}\in C} (-1)^{\mathbf{v}\cdot\mathbf{c}} = 0.$$

We thus obtain

$$P(c_m = s|\mathbf{r}) = \frac{1}{2^{n-k+1}} \sum_{t=0}^{1} (-1)^{st} \sum_{\mathbf{c}'\in C^{\perp}} P(\mathbf{r}, \mathbf{c}' - t\mathbf{e}_m),$$

which we will write as

$$P(c_m = s|\mathbf{r}) = \frac{1}{2^{n-k+1}} \sum_{t=0}^{1} (-1)^{st} \sum_{j=0}^{M-1} F(\mathbf{r}, \mathbf{c}'_j - t\mathbf{e}_m),$$

where $M = 2^{n-k}$ is the number of codewords in the dual code.

Assuming a memoryless channel,

$$F(\mathbf{r}, \mathbf{u}) = \sum_{\mathbf{v}\in V_n} \prod_{\ell=0}^{n-1} p(r_\ell, v_\ell)(-1)^{-u_\ell v_\ell}$$

$$= \sum_{\mathbf{v}\in V_n} \prod_{\ell=0}^{n-1} p(r_\ell|v_\ell)P(v_\ell)(-1)^{-u_\ell v_\ell}$$

$$= \prod_{\ell=0}^{n-1} \sum_{i=0}^{1} p(r_\ell|i)P(v_\ell = i)(-1)^{-iu_\ell}.$$

We thus obtain

$$P(c_m = s|\mathbf{r}) = \frac{1}{2^{n-k+1}} \sum_{t=0}^{1} (-1)^{-st} \sum_{j=0}^{M-1} \prod_{\ell=0}^{n-1} p_\ell \sum_{i=0}^{1} (-1)^{-i(c'_{j\ell} - t\delta_{m\ell})} p(r_\ell|i).$$

The factor in front, of course, can be neglected. Let us write $p(r_\ell|i)p_\ell$ as $p(r_\ell; i)$. Expanding the sum over i,

$$P(c_m = s|\mathbf{r}) = \sum_{t=0}^{1} (-1)^{-st} \sum_{j=0}^{M-1} \prod_{\ell=0}^{n-1} (p(r_\ell; 0) + p(r_\ell; 1)(-1)^{c'_{j\ell} - t\delta_{m\ell}}).$$

Expanding the sum over t:

$$P(c_m = s | \mathbf{r}) = \sum_{j=0}^{M-1} \prod_{\ell=0}^{n-1} (P(r_\ell; 0) + P(r_\ell; 1)(-1)^{c'_{j\ell}})$$

$$+ (-1)^{-s} \sum_{j=0}^{M-1} \prod_{\ell=0}^{n-1} (P(r_\ell; 0) + P(r_\ell; 1)(-1)^{c'_{j\ell} - \delta_{m\ell}})$$

$$= \sum_{j=0}^{M-1} \prod_{\ell \neq m} (P(r_\ell; 0) + P(r_\ell; 1)(-1)^{c'_{j\ell}})(P(r_m; 0) + P(r_m; 1)(-1)^{c'_{jm}}) +$$

$$(-1)^{-s} \sum_{j=0}^{M-1} \prod_{\ell \neq m} (P(r_\ell; 0) + P(r_\ell; 1)(-1)^{c'_{j\ell} - 1})(P(r_m; 0) + P(r_m; 1)(-1)^{c'_{jm} - 1}).$$

Now consider the two cases $s = 0$ and $s = 1$:

$$P(c_m = 0 | \mathbf{r}) = 2P(r_m; 0) \sum_{j=0}^{M-1} \prod_{\ell \neq m} (P(r_\ell; 0) + P(r_\ell; 1)(-1)^{c'_{j\ell}}). \qquad (11.8)$$

$$P(c_m = 1 | \mathbf{r}) = 2P(r_m; 1) \sum_{j=0}^{M-1} (-1)^{c'_{jm}} \prod_{\ell \neq m} (P(r_\ell; 0) + P(r_\ell; 1)(-1)^{c'_{j\ell}}). \qquad (11.9)$$

11.7 Exercises

11.1 Show that for a signal transmitted over an AWGN, the absolute log likelihood ratio (11.1) is proportional to $|r_i|$.

11.2 Let $\tilde{\mathbf{c}}$ be a BPSK signal transmitted through an AWGN to produce a received signal $\mathbf{r}$.

(a) Show that, as far as ML decoding is concerned, $d_E(\mathbf{r}, \tilde{\mathbf{c}})$ is equivalent to $m(\mathbf{r}, \tilde{\mathbf{v}}) = \sum_{i=0}^{n-1} r_i \tilde{v}_i$, where $\tilde{v}_i = \begin{cases} -1 & v_i = 0 \\ 1 & v_i = 1. \end{cases}$

(b) Show that $m(\mathbf{r}, \tilde{\mathbf{v}})$ can be written as

$$m(\mathbf{r}, \tilde{\mathbf{v}}) = \sum_{i=0}^{n-1} |r_i| - 2\lambda(\mathbf{r}, \tilde{\mathbf{v}}),$$

where

$$\lambda(\mathbf{r}, \tilde{\mathbf{v}}) = \sum_{i : r_i \tilde{v}_i < 0} |r_i|.$$

Thus, minimizing $d_E(\mathbf{r}, \tilde{\mathbf{c}})$ is equivalent to minimizing $\lambda(\mathbf{r}, \tilde{\mathbf{v}})$. $\lambda(\mathbf{r}, \tilde{\mathbf{v}})$ is called the *correlation discrepancy*.

11.3 [272, p. 406] In this exercise, a sufficient condition for determining the optimality of a codeword based on two codewords is derived. Let $\mathbf{c}_1, \mathbf{c}_2 \in C$. Define

$$\delta_1 = w_1 - n(\mathbf{c}_1) \quad \delta_2 = w_1 - n(\mathbf{c}_2),$$

where $n(\mathbf{c}) = |\{i : 0 \leq i < n \text{ and } c_i \neq v_i\}|$ is the Hamming distance between $\mathbf{c}$ and $\mathbf{v}$, and w_i is the ith weight in the weight profile of the code. Assume that the codewords are ordered such that $\delta_1 \geq \delta_2$. Also define

$$D_{00} = D_0(\mathbf{c}_1) \cap D_0(\mathbf{c}_2) \quad D_{01} = D_0(\mathbf{c}_1) \cap D_1(\mathbf{c}_2).$$

Let $X^{(q)}$ denote the first q indices of an ordered index set X, as was done in (11.5). Define

$$I(\mathbf{c}_1, \mathbf{c}_2) = (D_{00} \cup D_{01}^{\lfloor (\delta_1 - \delta_2)/2 \rfloor})^{(\delta_1)}.$$

Also define

$$G(\mathbf{c}_1, w_1, \mathbf{c}_2, w_1) = \sum_{i \in I(\mathbf{c}_1, \mathbf{c}_2)} |r_i|.$$

Let $\mathbf{c}$ be the codeword among $\mathbf{c}_1, \mathbf{c}_2$, which has the smaller discrepancy.

Show that: If $\lambda(\mathbf{c}, \mathbf{c}) \leq G(\mathbf{c}_1, w_1, \mathbf{c}_2, w_1)$, then $\mathbf{c}$ is the maximum likelihood codeword for $\mathbf{r}$.

11.4 272 In GMD decoding, only $\lfloor (d_{min} + 1)/2 \rfloor$ erasure patterns in the $d_{min} - 1$ least reliable positions are examined. Explain why not all $d_{min} - 1$ possible erasure patterns are considered.

11.8 References

Generalized minimum distance decoding was presented first in [127]. The statement of the algorithm presented here follows [272]. The Chase decoding algorithms were presented in [60]; our statement of Chase-3 is essentially identical to that in [272]. Generalizations of the Chase algorithm presented in 141 circumscribe Chase-2 and Chase-3, and are capable of achieving bounded distance decoding. An iterative method of soft-decision decoding which is capable of finding the ML codeword is proposed in [244, 245]. Our discussion of the optimality criterion very closely follows [272, Section 10.3], which in turn is derived from [428]. Chapter 10 of [272], in fact, provides a very substantial discussion of soft-decision decoding, including topics not covered here such as reduced list syndrome decoding [415, 416], priority-first search decoding [27, 105, 188, 189, 460], and majority-logic decoding [255, 301]. Soft-decision decoding is also discussed in this book in Chapter 15 for LDPC codes, Chapter 12 using the trellis representation of codes, Chapter 7 for Reed–Solomon codes, Chapter 14 for turbo codes, and Chapter 17 for polar codes. Extensive work on algebraic soft decoding of BCH codes is presented in [240].

Part III

Codes on Graphs

Chapter 12

Convolutional Codes

12.1 Introduction and Basic Notation

Convolutional codes are linear codes that have additional structure in the generator matrix so that the encoding operation can be viewed as a filtering — or convolution — operation. Convolutional codes are widely used in practice, with several hardware implementations available for encoding and decoding. A convolutional encoder may be viewed as nothing more than a set of digital filters — linear, time-invariant systems — with the code sequence being the interleaved output of the filter outputs. Convolutional codes are often preferred in practice over block codes, because they provide excellent performance when compared with block codes of comparable encode/decode complexity. Furthermore, they were among the earliest codes for which effective soft-decision decoding algorithms were developed.

Whereas block codes take discrete blocks of k symbols and produce therefrom blocks of n symbols that depend only on the k input symbols, convolutional codes are frequently viewed as *stream codes*, in that they often operate on continuous streams of symbols not partitioned into discrete message blocks. However, they are still rate $R = k/n$ codes, accepting k new symbols at each time step and producing n new symbols. The arithmetic can, of course, be carried out over any field, but throughout this chapter and, in fact, in most of the convolutional coding literature, the field $GF(2)$ is employed.

We represent sequences and transfer functions as power series in the variable x.[1] A sequence $\{\ldots, m_{-2}, m_{-1}, m_0, m_1, m_2, \ldots\}$ with elements from a field $\mathbb{F}$ is represented as a formal **Laurent series** $m(x) = \sum_{l=-\infty}^{\infty} m_l x^l$. The set of all Laurent series over $\mathbb{F}$ is a field, which is usually denoted as $\mathbb{F}[[x]]$. Thus, $m(x) \in \mathbb{F}[[x]]$.

For multiple input streams, we use a superscript, so $m^{(1)}(x)$ represents the first input stream and $m^{(2)}(x)$ represents the second input stream. For multiple input streams, it is convenient to collect the input streams into a single (row) vector, as in

$$m(x) = \begin{bmatrix} m^{(1)}(x) & m^{(2)}(x) \end{bmatrix} \in \mathbb{F}[[x]]^2.$$

A convolutional encoder is typically represented as sets of digital (binary) filters.

Example 12.1 Figure 12.1 shows an example of a convolutional encoder. (Recall that the D blocks represent 1-bit storage devices, or D flip-flops.) The input information stream m_k passes through two filters (sharing memory elements) producing two output streams

$$c_k^{(1)} = m_k + m_{k-2} \quad \text{and} \quad c_k^{(2)} = m_k + m_{k-1} + m_{k-2}.$$

These two streams are interleaved together to produce the coded stream c_k. Thus, for every bit of input, there are two coded output bits, resulting in a rate $R = 1/2$ code.

It is conventional to assume that the memory elements are initialized with all zeros at the beginning of transmission.

For the input stream $\mathbf{m} = \{1, 1, 0, 0, 1, 0, 1\}$, the outputs are

$$\mathbf{c}^{(1)} = \{1, 1, 1, 1, 1, 0, 0, 0, 1\} \quad \text{and} \quad \mathbf{c}^{(2)} = \{1, 0, 0, 1, 1, 1, 0, 1, 1\}$$

---

[1] The symbol D is sometimes used instead of x. The Laurent series representation may be called the D-transform in this case.

Error Correction Coding: Mathematical Methods and Algorithms, Second Edition. Todd K. Moon
© 2021 John Wiley & Sons, Inc. Published 2021 by John Wiley & Sons, Inc.
Companion website: www.wiley.com/go/Moon/ErrorCorrectionCoding

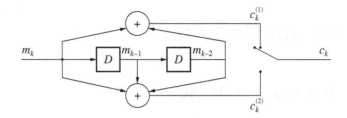

Figure 12.1: A rate $R = 1/2$ convolutional encoder.

and the interleaved stream is

$$\mathbf{c} = \{11, 10, 10, 11, 11, 01, 00, 01, 11\}$$

(where commas separate the pairs of outputs at a single input time). We can represent the transfer function from input $m(x)$ to output $c^{(1)}(x)$ as $g^{(1)}(x) = 1 + x^2$, and the transfer function from $m(x)$ to output $c^{(2)}(x)$ as $g^{(2)}(x) = 1 + x + x^2$. The information stream $\mathbf{m} = \{1, 1, 0, 0, 1, 0, 1\}$ can be represented as $m(x) = 1 + x + x^4 + x^6 \in GF(2)[[x]]$. The outputs are

$$c^{(1)}(x) = m(x)g_1(x) = (1 + x + x^4 + x^6)(1 + x^2) = 1 + x + x^2 + x^3 + x^4 + x^8$$

$$c^{(2)}(x) = m(x)g_2(x) = (1 + x + x^4 + x^6)(1 + x + x^2) = 1 + x^3 + x^4 + x^5 + x^7 + x^8. \qquad \square$$

A rate $R = k/n$ convolutional code has associated with it an encoder, a $k \times n$ matrix transfer function $G(x)$ called the *transfer function* matrix. For the rate $R = 1/2$ code of this example,

$$G_a(x) = \begin{bmatrix} 1 + x^2 & 1 + x + x^2 \end{bmatrix}.$$

The transfer function matrix of a convolutional code does not always have only polynomial entries, as the following example illustrates.

Example 12.2   Consider the convolutional transfer function matrix

$$G_b(x) = \begin{bmatrix} 1 & \frac{1+x+x^2}{1+x^2} \cdot \end{bmatrix}.$$

Since there is a 1 in the first column, the input stream appears explicitly in the interleaved output data; this is a *systematic* convolutional encoder.

A realization (in controller form) for this encoder is shown in Figure 12.2. For the input sequence $m(x) = 1 + x + x^2 + x^3 + x^4 + x^8$, the first output is

$$c^{(1)}(x) = m(x) = 1 + x + x^2 + x^3 + x^4 + x^8$$

and the second output is

$$c^{(2)}(x) = \frac{(1 + x + x^2 + x^3 + x^4 + x^8)(1 + x + x^2)}{1 + x^2}$$

$$= \frac{1 + x^2 + x^3 + x^4 + x^6 + x^8 + x^9 + x^{10}}{1 + x^2}$$

$$= 1 + x^3 + x^4 + x^5 + x^7 + x^8 + x^{10} + \cdots$$

as can be verified by long division, where the long division is set up to produce a power series (for an IIR filter) as

$$1 + x^2 \overline{)1 + x^2 + x^3 + x^4 + \; x^6 + \; x^8 + x^9 + x^{10}}$$

$\square$

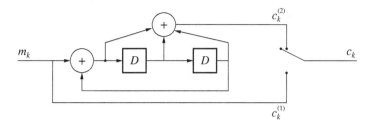

Figure 12.2: A systematic $R = 1/2$ encoder.

An encoder that has only polynomial entries in its transfer function matrix is said to be a **feedforward** encoder or an FIR encoder. An encoder that has rational functions in its transfer function matrix is said to be a **feedback** or IIR encoder.

For a rate $R = k/n$ code with $k > 1$, there are k input message sequences (usually obtained by splitting a single message sequence into k streams). Let

$$\mathbf{m}(x) = [m^{(1)}(x), m^{(2)}(x), \ldots, m^{(k)}(x)]$$

and

$$G(x) = \begin{bmatrix} g^{(1,1)}(x) & g^{(1,2)}(x) & \cdots & g^{(1,n)}(x) \\ g^{(2,1)}(x) & g^{(2,2)}(x) & \cdots & g^{(2,n)}(x) \\ \vdots & & & \\ g^{(k,1)}(x) & g^{(k,2)}(x) & \cdots & g^{(k,n)}(x) \end{bmatrix}. \tag{12.1}$$

The output sequences are represented as

$$\mathbf{c}(x) = [c^{(1)}(x), c^{(2)}(x), \ldots, c^{(n)}(x)] = \mathbf{m}(x)G(x).$$

A transfer function matrix $G(x)$ is said to be systematic if an identity matrix can be identified among the elements of $G(x)$. (That is, if by row and/or column permutations of $G(x)$, an identity matrix can be obtained.)

Example 12.3 For a rate $R = 2/3$ code, a systematic transfer function matrix might be

$$G_1(x) = \begin{bmatrix} 1 & 0 & \dfrac{x}{1+x^3} \\ 0 & 1 & \dfrac{x^2}{1+x^3} \end{bmatrix}, \tag{12.2}$$

with a possible realization as shown in Figure 12.3. This is based on the controller form of Figure 4.8. Another more efficient realization based on the observability form from Figure 4.9 is shown in Figure 12.4. In this case, only a single set of memory elements is used, employing linearity. With $m(x) = [1 + x^2 + x^4 + x^5 + x^7 + \cdots, x^2 + x^5 + x^6 + x^7 + \cdots]$, the output is

$$\mathbf{c}(x) = [1 + x^2 + x^4 + x^5 + x^7 + \cdots, x^2 + x^5 + x^6 + x^7 + \cdots, x + x^3 + x^5 + \cdots].$$

The corresponding bit sequences are

$$\{\{1, 0, 1, 0, 1, 1, 0, 1, \ldots\}, \{0, 0, 1, 0, 0, 1, 1, 1, \ldots\}, \{0, 1, 0, 1, 0, 1, 0, 1, \ldots,\}\}$$

which, when interleaved, produce the output sequence

$$\{100, 001, 110, 001, 100, 111, 010, 111, \ldots\}. \qquad \square$$

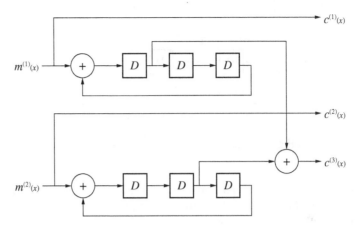

Figure 12.3: A systematic $R = 2/3$ encoder.

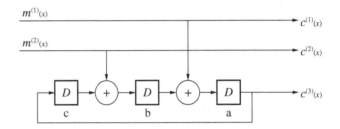

Figure 12.4: A systematic $R = 2/3$ encoder with more efficient hardware.

For feedforward encoders, it is common to indicate the connection polynomials as vectors of numbers representing the *impulse response* of the encoder, rather than polynomials. The transfer function matrix $G(x) = [1 + x^2, 1 + x + x^2]$ is represented by the vectors

$$\mathbf{g}^{(1)} = [101] \quad \text{and} \quad \mathbf{g}^{(2)} = [111].$$

These are often expressed compactly (e.g., in tables of codes) in octal form, where triples of bits are represented using the integers from 0 to 7. In this form, the encoder is represented using $g^{(1)} = 5, g^{(2)} = 7$.

For an impulse response $\mathbf{g}^{(j)} = [g_0^{(j)}, g_1^{(j)}, \ldots, g_r^{(j)}]$, the output at time i due to the input sequence m_i is

$$c_i = \sum_{l=0}^{r} m_{i-l} g_l^{(j)},$$

which is, of course, a convolution sum (hence the name of the codes). For an input sequence $\mathbf{m}$, the output sequence can be written as $\mathbf{c}^{(j)} = \mathbf{m} * \mathbf{g}^{(j)}$, where $*$ denotes discrete-time convolution. The operation of convolution can also be represented using matrices. Let $\mathbf{m} = [m_0, m_1, m_2, \ldots]$. Then for $\mathbf{g}^{(j)} = [g_0^{(j)}, g_1^{(j)}, \ldots, g_r^{(j)}]$, the convolution $\mathbf{c} = \mathbf{m} * \mathbf{g}^{(j)}$ can be represented as

$$\mathbf{c} = [m_0, m_1, \ldots, m_L] \begin{bmatrix} g_0^{(j)} & g_1^{(j)} & g_2^{(j)} & \cdots & g_r^{(j)} & & \\ & g_0^{(j)} & g_1^{(j)} & \cdots & g_{r-1}^{(j)} & g_r^{(j)} & \\ & & g_0^{(j)} & \cdots & g_{r-2}^{(j)} & g_{r-1}^{(j)} & g_r^{(j)} \\ & & & \ddots & \ddots & \ddots & \ddots & \ddots \end{bmatrix},$$

where empty entries in the matrix indicate zeros.

For a rate $1/2$ code, the operation of convolution and interleaving the output sequences is represented by the following generator matrix, where the columns of different matrices are interleaved:

$$G = \begin{bmatrix} g_0^{(1)} g_0^{(2)} & g_1^{(1)} g_1^{(2)} & g_2^{(1)} g_2^{(2)} & \cdots & g_r^{(1)} g_r^{(2)} & & \\ & g_0^{(1)} g_0^{(2)} & g_1^{(1)} g_1^{(2)} & \cdots & g_{r-1}^{(1)} g_{r-1}^{(2)} & g_r^{(1)} g_r^{(2)} & \\ & & g_0^{(1)} g_0^{(2)} & \cdots & g_{r-2}^{(1)} g_{r-2}^{(2)} & g_{r-1}^{(1)} g_{r-1}^{(2)} & g_r^{(1)} g_r^{(2)} \\ & & & \ddots & \ddots & \ddots & \ddots & \ddots \end{bmatrix}. \tag{12.3}$$

It is the shift (Toeplitz) structure of these generator matrices that gives rise to some of the desirable attributes of convolutional codes.

For a k-input, n-output code with impulse response vectors $\mathbf{g}^{(i,j)}$, $i = 1, 2, \ldots, k$ and $j = 1, 2, \ldots, n$, where $\mathbf{g}^{(i,j)}$ is the impulse response of the encoder connecting input i with output j, the output can be written as

$$c_t^{(j)} = \sum_{q=1}^{k} \sum_{l=0}^{r} m_{t-l}^{(q)} g_l^{(q,j)}, \quad j = 1, 2, \ldots, n.$$

A matrix description of these codes can also be given, but the transfer function matrix $G(x)$ is usually more convenient.

We always deal with *delay free* transfer function matrices, for which it is not possible to factor out a common multiple x^i from $G(x)$. That is, it is not possible to write $G(x) = x^i \tilde{G}(x)$ for some $i > 0$ and any $\tilde{G}(x)$.

12.1.1 The State

A convolutional encoder is a state machine. For both encoding and decoding purposes, it is frequently helpful to think of the *state diagrams* of the state machines, that is, a representation of the temporal relationships between the states portraying state/nextstate relationships as a function of the inputs and the outputs. For an implementation with v memory elements, there are 2^v states in the state diagram. (Box 12.1 summarizes basic definitions for graphs.) Another representation which is extremely useful is a graph representing the connections from states at one time instant to states at the next time instant. The graph is a bipartite graph, that is, a graph which contains two subsets of nodes, with edges running only between the two subsets. By stacking these bipartite graphs to show several time steps, one obtains a graph known as a *trellis*, so-called because of its resemblance to a trellis that might be used for decorative purposes in landscaping.

It may be convenient for some implementations to provide a table indicating the state/next state information explicitly. From the state/next state table the state/previous state information can be extracted.

Box 12.1: Graphs: Basic Definitions

Graph concepts are used throughout the remainder of the book. The following definitions summarize some graph concepts [486]. A **graph** G is a pair (V, E), where V is a nonempty finite set of **vertices** or **nodes** often called the vertex set and E is a finite family of unordered pairs of elements of V called **edges**. (A family is like a set, but some elements may be repeated.) In the graph here, the vertex set is $V = \{a, b, c, d\}$ and the edge family is $E = \{\{a, a\}, \{a, b\}, \{a, b\}, \{a, b\}, \{a, c\}, \{b, c\}, \{c, d\}, \{d, d\}\}$. A **loop** is an edge joining a vertex to itself. If the edge family is in fact a set (no repeated elements) and there are no loops, then the graph is a **simple graph.**

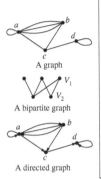

A graph

A bipartite graph

A directed graph

Two vertices of a graph G are **adjacent** if there is an edge joining them. We also say that adjacent nodes are **neighbors**. The two vertices are said to be **incident** to such an edge. Two distinct edges of a graph are adjacent if they have at least one vertex in common. The **degree** of a vertex is the number of edges incident to it.

The vertex set V of a **bipartite** graph can be split into two disjoint sets $V = V_1 \cup V_2$ in such a way that every edge of G joins a vertex of V_1 to a vertex of V_2.

A **walk** through a graph $G = (V, E)$ is a finite sequence of edges $\{v_0, v_1\}, \{v_1, v_2\}, \ldots, \{v_{m-1}, v_m\}$, where each $v_i \in V$ and each $\{v_i, v_j\} \in E$. The **length** of a walk is the number of edges in it. If all the edges are distinct, the walk is a **trail**; if all the vertices are also distinct (except possibly $v_0 = v_m$), the walk is a **path**. A path or trail is **closed** if $v_0 = v_m$. A closed path containing at least one edge is called a **circuit**. The **girth** of a graph is the number of edges in its shortest circuit.

A graph is **connected** if there is a path between any pair of vertices $v, w \in V$. A connected graph which contains no circuits is a **tree**. A node of a tree is a **leaf** if its degree is equal to 1.

A **directed graph** (digraph) G is a pair (V, E), where E is a finite family of *ordered pairs* of elements of V. Such graphs are frequently represented using arrows to represent edges. In the directed graph here, the edge set is $E = \{(a, a), (a, b), (b, a), (b, a), (a, c), (b, c), (c, d), (d, d)\}$.

Example 12.4 Consider again the convolutional encoder of Example 12.1 with transfer function matrix $G(x) = [1 + x^2, 1 + x + x^2]$. A realization and its corresponding state diagram are shown in Figure 12.5(a, b). The state is indicated as a pair of bits, with the first bit representing the least significant bit (lsb). The branches along the state diagram indicate input/output values. One stage of the trellis (corresponding to the transition between two time instants) is shown in Figure 12.5(c). Three trellis stages are shown in Figure 12.5(d). ☐

Example 12.5 For the rational systematic encoder with matrix transfer function

$$G(x) = \begin{bmatrix} 1 & 0 & \frac{x}{1+x^3} \\ 0 & 1 & \frac{x^2}{1+x^3} \end{bmatrix}, \tag{12.4}$$

with the circuit realization of Figure 12.4, the state diagram and trellis are shown in Figure 12.6. In the state diagram, the states are represented as integers from 0 to 7 using the numbers (a, b, c) corresponding to the registers shown on the circuit. (That is, the lsb is on the right of the diagram this time.) Only the state transitions are shown, not the inputs or outputs, as that would excessively clutter the diagram. The corresponding trellis is also shown, with the branches input/output information listed on the left, with the order of the listing corresponding to the sequence of branches emerging from the corresponding state in top-to-bottom order. ☐

12.2 Definition of Codes and Equivalent Codes

Having now seen several examples of codes, it is now time to formalize the definition and examine some structural properties of the codes. It is no coincidence that the code sequences $(c^{(1)}(x), c^{(2)}(x))$ are the same for Examples 12.1 and 12.2. The sets of sequences that lie in the range of the transfer function matrices $G_a(x)$ and $G_b(x)$ are identical: even though the encoders are different, they encode to the same code. (This is analogous to having different generator matrices to represent the same block code.)

We formally define a convolutional code as follows:

Definition 12.6 [[397], p. 94] A rate $R = k/n$ code over the field of rational Laurent series $F[[x]]$ over the field $\mathbb{F}$ is the image of an injective linear mapping of the k-dimensional Laurent series $\mathbf{m}(x) \in \mathbb{F}[[x]]^k$ into the n-dimensional Laurent series $\mathbf{c}(x) \in \mathbb{F}[[x]]^n$. ☐

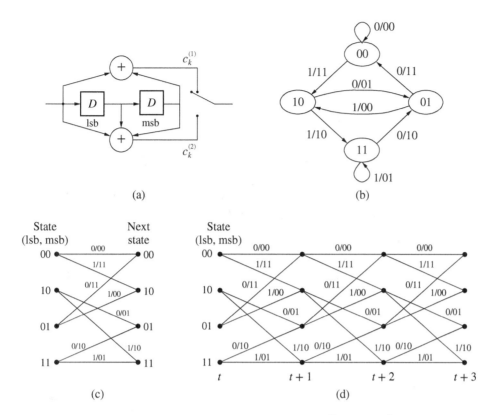

Figure 12.5: Encoder, state diagram, and trellis for $G(x) = [1 + x^2, 1 + x + x^2]$.(a) Encoder; (b) state diagram; (c) one stage of trellis; (d) three stages of trellis.

In other words, the convolutional code is the set $\{\mathbf{c}(x)\}$ of all possible output sequences as all possible input sequences $\{\mathbf{m}(x)\}$ are applied to the encoder. The code is the image set or (row) range of the linear operator $G(x)$, *not* the linear operator $G(x)$ itself.

Example 12.7 Let

$$G_2(x) = \begin{bmatrix} 1 & x^2 & x \\ x & 1 & 0 \end{bmatrix} \tag{12.5}$$

and note that

$$G_2(x) = \begin{bmatrix} 1 & x^2 \\ x & 1 \end{bmatrix} G_1(x) = T_2(x)G_1(x),$$

(where $G_1(x)$ was defined in (12.2)) and consider the encoding operation

$$m(x)G_2(x) = m(x) \begin{bmatrix} 1 & x^2 \\ x & 1 \end{bmatrix} G_1(x) = m'(x)G_1(x),$$

where

$$m'(x) = m(x) \begin{bmatrix} 1 & x^2 \\ x & 1 \end{bmatrix} = m(x)T_2(x).$$

Corresponding to each $m(x)$ there is a unique $m'(x)$, since $T_2(x)$ is invertible. Hence, as $m'(x)$ varies over all possible input sequences, $m(x)$ also varies over all possible input sequences. The set of output sequences $\{c(x)\}$ produced is the same for $G_2(x)$ as $G_1(x)$: that is, both encoders produce the same code.

Figure 12.7 shows a schematic representation of this encoder. Note that the implementation of both $G_1(x)$ (of Figure 12.4) and $G_2(x)$ have three 1-bit memory elements in them. The contents of these memory elements may

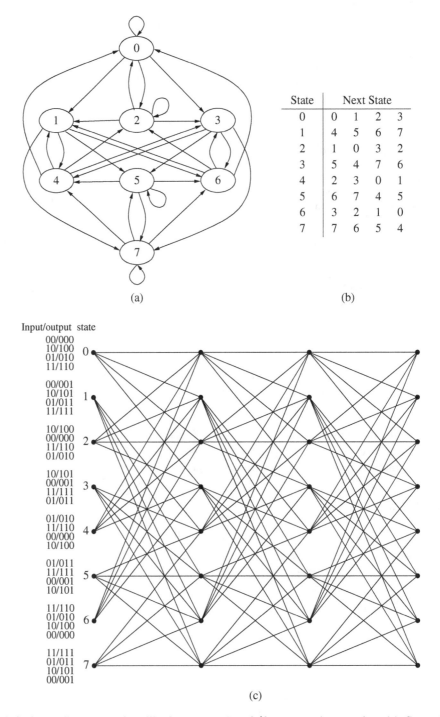

Figure 12.6: State diagram and trellis for a rate $R = 2/3$ systematic encoder. (a) State diagram; (b) State/next state information; (c) trellis.

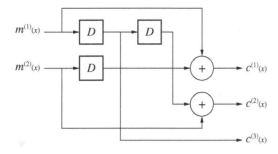

Figure 12.7: A feedforward $R = 2/3$ encoder.

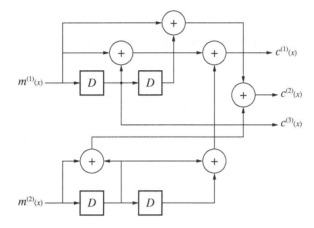

Figure 12.8: A less efficient feedforward $R = 2/3$ encoder.

be thought of as the *state* of the devices. Since these are binary circuits, there are $2^3 = 8$ distinct states in either implementation. □

Example 12.8 Another encoder for the code of Example 12.1 is

$$G_3(x) = \begin{bmatrix} 1+x & 1+x^2 & x \\ x+x^2 & 1+x & 0 \end{bmatrix}, \tag{12.6}$$

where, it may be observed,

$$G_3(x) = \begin{bmatrix} 1+x & 1+x^2 \\ x+x^2 & 1+x \end{bmatrix} G_1(x) = T_3(x)G_1(x).$$

The encoding operation

$$m(x)G_3(x) = m(x)T_3(x)G_1(x) = m'(x)G_1(x),$$

with $m'(x) = m(x)T_3(x)$, again results in the same code, since $T_3(x)$ is invertible.

The schematic for $G_3(x)$ in Figure 12.8 would require more storage blocks than either $G_1(x)$ or $G_2(x)$: it is not as efficient in terms of hardware. □

These examples motivate the following definition:

Definition 12.9 Two transfer function matrices $G(x)$ and $G'(x)$ are said to be **equivalent** if they generate the same convolutional code. Two transfer function matrices $G(x)$ and $G'(x)$ are equivalent if $G(x) = T(x)G'(x)$ for an *invertible* matrix $T(x)$. □

These examples also motivate other considerations: For a given a code, is there always a feedforward transfer matrix representation? Is there always a systematic representation? What is the "minimal" representation, requiring the least amount of memory? As the following section reveals, another question is whether the representation is catastrophic.

12.2.1 Catastrophic Encoders

Besides the hardware inefficiency, there is another fundamental problem with the encoder $G_3(x)$ of (12.6). Suppose that the input is

$$\mathbf{m}(x) = \begin{bmatrix} 0 & \frac{1}{1+x} \end{bmatrix},$$

where, expanding the formal series by long division,

$$\frac{1}{1+x} = 1 + x + x^2 + x^3 + \cdots$$

The input sequence thus has infinite Hamming weight. The corresponding output sequence is

$$\mathbf{c}(x) = m(x)G_3(x) = \begin{bmatrix} x & 1 & 0 \end{bmatrix},$$

a sequence with total Hamming weight 2. Suppose now that $\mathbf{c}(x)$ is passed through a channel and that *two* errors occur at precisely the locations of the nonzero code elements. Then the received sequence is exactly zero, which would decode (under any reasonable decoding scheme) to $\hat{\mathbf{m}}(x) = \begin{bmatrix} 0 & 0 \end{bmatrix}$. Thus, a *finite* number of errors in the channel result in an *infinite* number of decoder errors. Such an encoder is called a *catastrophic* encoder. It may be emphasized, however, that the problem is not with the code but the particular encoder, since $G_1(x)$, $G_2(x)$, and $G_3(x)$ all produce the same code, but $G_1(x)$ and $G_2(x)$ do not exhibit catastrophic behavior.

Letting $\text{wt}(c(x))$ denote the weight of the sequence $c(x)$, we have the following definition:

Definition 12.10 [[397], p. 97] An encoder $G(x)$ for a convolutional code is **catastrophic** if there exists a message sequence $\mathbf{m}(x)$ such that $\text{wt}(\mathbf{m}(x)) = \infty$ and the weight of the coded sequence $\text{wt}(\mathbf{m}(x)G(x)) < \infty$. □

To understand more of the nature of catastrophic codes, we introduce the idea of a right inverse of a matrix.

Definition 12.11 Let $k < n$. A **right inverse** of a $k \times n$ matrix G is a $n \times k$ matrix G^{-1} such that $GG^{-1} = I_{k,k}$, the $k \times k$ identity matrix. (This is not the same as the inverse, which cannot exist when G is not square.) A right inverse of G can exist only if G is full rank. □

Example 12.12   For $G_1(x)$ of (12.2), a right inverse is

$$G_1(x)^{-1} = \begin{bmatrix} 1 & 0 \\ 0 & 1 \\ 0 & 0 \end{bmatrix}.$$

For $G_2(x)$ of (12.5), a right inverse is

$$G_2(x)^{-1} = \begin{bmatrix} 1 & x \\ x & 1+x^2 \\ x^2 & 1+x+x^3 \end{bmatrix}.$$

For $G_3(x)$ of (12.6), a right inverse is

$$G_3(x)^{-1} = \frac{1}{1+x+x^3+x^4} \begin{bmatrix} 1+x & 1+x^2 \\ x+x^2 & 1+x \\ 0 & 0 \end{bmatrix}.$$

□

Note that $G_1(x)^{-1}$ and $G_2(x)^{-1}$ are *polynomial* matrices — they have only polynomial entries — while the right inverse $G_3(x)^{-1}$ has non-polynomial entries — some of its entries involve rational functions.

Example 12.13 It should be observed that right inverses are not necessarily unique. For example, the matrix $\left[1 + x^2, 1 + x + x^2\right]$ has the right inverses

$$\left[1 + x \ \ x\right]^T \quad \text{and} \quad \left[\frac{x}{x+1} \ \ 1\right]^T.$$

Of these, one has all polynomial elements. □

Definition 12.14 A transfer function matrix with only polynomial entries is said to be a **polynomial encoder** (i.e., it uses FIR filters). More briefly, such an encoder is said to be **polynomial**. A transfer function matrix with rational entries is said to be a **rational encoder** (i.e., it uses IIR filters), or simply **rational**. □

For an encoder $G(x)$ with right inverse $G(x)^{-1}$, the message may be recovered (in a theoretical sense when there is no noise corrupting the code — this is not a decoding algorithm!) by

$$\mathbf{c}(x)G(x)^{-1} = \mathbf{m}(x)G(x)G(x)^{-1} = \mathbf{m}(x). \tag{12.7}$$

Now suppose that $\mathbf{c}(x)$ has finite weight, but $\mathbf{m}(x)$ has infinite weight: from (12.7) this can only happen if one or more elements of the right inverse $G(x)^{-1}$ has an infinite number of coefficients, that is, they are rational functions. It turns out that this is a necessary and sufficient condition:

Theorem 12.15 *A transfer function matrix $G(x)$ is not catastrophic if and only if it has a right inverse $G(x)^{-1}$ having only polynomial entries.*

From the right inverses in Example 12.12, we see that $G_1(x)$ and $G_2(x)$ have polynomial right inverses, while $G_3(x)$ has non-polynomial entries, indicating that $G_3(x)$ is a catastrophic generator.

Definition 12.16 A transfer function matrix $G(x)$ is **basic** if it is polynomial and has a polynomial right inverse. □

$G_2(x)$ is an example of a basic transfer function matrix.

Example 12.17 Another example of a transfer function matrix for the code is

$$G_4(x) = \begin{bmatrix} 1 + x + x^2 + x^3 & 1 + x & x \\ x & 1 & 0 \end{bmatrix}. \tag{12.8}$$

The invariant factor decomposition (presented below) can be used to show that this is basic. However, for sufficiently small matrices finding a right inverse may be done by hand. We seek a polynomial matrix such that

$$\begin{bmatrix} 1 + x + x^2 + x^3 & 1 + x & x \\ x & 1 & 0 \end{bmatrix} \begin{bmatrix} a & d \\ b & e \\ c & f \end{bmatrix} = \begin{bmatrix} 1 & 0 \\ 0 & 1 \end{bmatrix}.$$

Writing out the implied equations, we have

$$a(1 + x + x^2 + x^3) + b(1 + x) + cx = 1 \quad ax + b = 0$$

$$d(1 + x + x^2 + x^3) + e(1 + x) + fx = 0 \quad dx + e = 1.$$

From the second, we obtain $b = ax$; substituting this into the first, we find $a(1 + x^3) + cx = 1$. By setting $c = x^2$ and $a = 1$, we can solve this using polynomials.

From the fourth equation, we obtain $e = 1 + dx$, so that from the third equation

$$d(1 + x + x^2 + x^3) + (1 + dx)(1 + x) + fx = 0$$

or $d(1 + x^3) + fx = 1 + x$. This yields $d = 1$ and $f = x^2 + 1$. This gives a polynomial right inverse, so $G_4(x)$ is basic. Note that the encoder requires four memory elements in its implementation.   □

Two *basic* encoders $G(x)$ and $G'(x)$ are equivalent if and only if $G(x) = T(x)G'(x)$, where

1. $T(x)$ is not only invertible (as required by mere equivalence),
2. But also $|\det(T(x))| = 1$,

so that when the right inverse is computed all the elements remain polynomial.

12.2.2   Polynomial and Rational Encoders

We show in this section that every rational encoder has an equivalent basic encoder. The implication is that it is sufficient to use only feedforward (polynomial) encoders to represent every code. There is, however, an important caveat: there may not be an equivalent basic (or even polynomial) *systematic* encoder. Thus, if a systematic coder is desired, it may be necessary to use a rational encoder. This is relevant because the very powerful behavior of turbo codes relies on good *systematic* convolutional codes.

Our results make use of the **invariant factor decomposition** of a matrix [[215], Section 3.7]. Let $G(x)$ be a $k \times n$ polynomial matrix. Then[2] $G(x)$ can be written as

$$G(x) = A(x)\Gamma(x)B(x),$$

where $A(x)$ is a $k \times k$ polynomial matrix and $B(x)$ is a $n \times n$ polynomial matrix and where $\det(A(x)) = 1$, $\det(B(x)) = 1$ (i.e., they are **unimodular matrices**); and $\Gamma(x)$ is the $k \times n$ diagonal matrix

$$\Gamma(x) = \begin{bmatrix} \gamma_1(x) & & & & & \\ & \gamma_2(x) & & & & \\ & & \gamma_3(x) & & & \mathbf{0}_{k,n-k} \\ & & & \ddots & & \\ & & & & \gamma_k(x) & \end{bmatrix}.$$

The nonzero elements $\gamma_i(x)$ of $\Gamma(x)$ are polynomials and are called the **invariant factors** of $G(x)$. (If any of the $\gamma_i(x)$ are zero, they are included in the zero block, so k is the number of nonzero elements.) Furthermore, the invariant factors satisfy

$$\gamma_i(x) \mid \gamma_{i+1}(x).$$

(Since we are expressing a theoretical result here, we won't pursue the algorithm for actually computing the invariant factor decomposition[3]); it is detailed in [215].

---

[2] The invariant factor decomposition has a technical requirement: The factorization in the ring must be unique, up to ordering and units. This technical requirement *is* met in our case, since the polynomials form a principal ideal domain, which implies unique factorization. See, e.g., [[144], chapter 32].

[3] The invariant factor decomposition can be thought of as a sort of singular value decomposition for modules.

Extending the invariant factor theorem to rational matrices, a rational matrix $G(x)$ can be written as

$$G(x) = A(x)\Gamma(x)B(x),$$

where $A(x)$ and $B(x)$ are again polynomial unimodular matrices and $\Gamma(x)$ is diagonal with rational entries $\gamma_i(x) = \alpha_i(x)/\beta_i(x)$, such that $\alpha_i(x)\alpha_{i+1}(x)$ and $\beta_{i+1}(x)$ $\beta_i(x)$.

Let $G(x)$ be a rational encoding matrix, with invariant factor decomposition $G(x) = A(x)\Gamma(x)B(x)$. Let us decompose $B(x)$ into the blocks

$$B(x) = \begin{bmatrix} G'(x) \\ B_2(x) \end{bmatrix},$$

where $G'(x)$ is $k \times n$. Then, since the last k columns of $\Gamma(x)$ are zero, we can write

$$G(x) = A(x) \begin{bmatrix} \frac{\alpha_1(x)}{\beta_1(x)} & & & \\ & \frac{\alpha_2(x)}{\beta_2(x)} & & \\ & & \ddots & \\ & & & \frac{\alpha_k(x)}{\beta_k(x)} \end{bmatrix} G'(x) \triangleq A(x)\Gamma'(x)G'(x).$$

Since $A(x)$ and $\Gamma'(x)$ are nonsingular matrices, $G(x)$ and $G'(x)$ are equivalent encoders: they describe the same convolutional code. But $G'(x)$ is polynomial (since $B(x)$ is polynomial) and since $B(x)$ is unimodular (and thus has a polynomial inverse) it follows that $G'(x)$ has a polynomial right inverse. We have thus proved the following:

Theorem 12.18 *Every rational encoder has an equivalent basic encoder.*

The proof of the theorem is constructive: To obtain a basic encoding matrix from a rational transfer function $G(x)$, compute the invariant factor decomposition $G(x) = A(x)\Gamma(x)B(x)$ and take the first k rows of $B(x)$.

12.2.3 Constraint Length and Minimal Encoders

Comparing the encoders for the code we have been examining, we have seen that the encoders for $G_1(x)$ or $G_2(x)$ use three memory elements, while the encoder $G_3(x)$ uses four memory elements. We investigate in this section aspects of the question of the smallest amount of memory that a code requires of its encoder.

Let $G(x)$ be a basic encoder (so that the elements of $G(x)$ are polynomials). Let

$$\nu_i = \max_j \deg(g_{ij}(x))$$

denote the maximum degree of the polynomials in row i of $G(x)$. This is the number of memory elements necessary to store the portion of a realization (circuit) of the encoder corresponding to input i. The number

$$\nu = \sum_{i=1}^{k} \nu_i \tag{12.9}$$

represents the total amount of storage required for all inputs. This quantity is called the **constraint length** of the encoder.

Note: In other sources (e.g., [483]), the constraint length is defined as the maximum number of bits in a single output stream that can be affected by any input bit (for a polynomial encoder). This is taken as the highest degree of the encoder plus one: $\nu = 1 + \max_{i,j} \deg(g_{i,j}(x))$. The reader should be aware that different definitions are used. Ours suits the current purposes.

We make the following definition:

Definition 12.19 A **minimal basic** encoder is a basic encoder that has the smallest constraint length among all equivalent basic encoders. □

   Typically, we are interested in minimal encoders: they require the least amount of hardware to build and they have the fewest evident states. We now explore the question of when an encoder is minimal basic.

   The first theorem involves a particular decomposition of the decoder matrix. We demonstrate first with some examples. Let $G(x) = G_2(x)$ from (12.2). Write

$$G_2(x) = \begin{bmatrix} 1 & x^2 & x \\ x & 1 & 0 \end{bmatrix} = \begin{bmatrix} x^2 & \\ & x \end{bmatrix} \begin{bmatrix} 0 & 1 & 0 \\ 1 & 0 & 0 \end{bmatrix} + \begin{bmatrix} 1 & 0 & x \\ 0 & 1 & 0 \end{bmatrix}. \tag{12.10}$$

As another example, when $G(x) = G_4(x)$ from (12.8)

$$\begin{aligned} G_4(x) &= \begin{bmatrix} 1 + x + x^2 + x^3 & 1 + x & x \\ x & 1 & 0 \end{bmatrix} \\ &= \begin{bmatrix} x^3 & \\ & x \end{bmatrix} \begin{bmatrix} 1 & 0 & 0 \\ 1 & 0 & 0 \end{bmatrix} + \begin{bmatrix} 1 + x + x^2 & 1 + x & x \\ 0 & 1 & 0 \end{bmatrix}. \end{aligned} \tag{12.11}$$

In general, given a basic encoder $G(x)$, we write it as

$$G(x) = \begin{bmatrix} x^{\nu_1} & & & \\ & x^{\nu_2} & & \\ & & \ddots & \\ & & & x^{\nu_k} \end{bmatrix} G_h + \tilde{G}(x) = \Lambda(x)G_h + \tilde{G}(x), \tag{12.12}$$

where G_h is a binary matrix with a 1 indicating the position where the highest degree term x^{ν_i} occurs in row i and each row of $\tilde{G}(x)$ contains all the terms of degree less than ν_i. Using this notation, we have the following:

Theorem 12.20 *[230] Let $G(x)$ be a $k \times n$ basic encoding matrix with constraint length ν. The following statements are equivalent:*

(a) $G(x)$ is a minimal basic encoding matrix.
(b) The maximum degree μ among the $k \times k$ subdeterminants of $G(x)$ is equal to the overall constraint length ν.
(c) G_h is full rank.

   To illustrate this theorem, consider the decomposition of $G_4(x)$ in (12.11). The 2×2 subdeterminants of $G_4(x)$ are obtained by taking the determinant of the two 2×2 submatrices of $G_4(x)$,

$$\det \begin{bmatrix} 1 + x + x^2 + x^3 & 1 + x \\ x & 1 \end{bmatrix} \quad \det \begin{bmatrix} 1 + x & x \\ 1 & 0 \end{bmatrix},$$

the maximum degree of which is 3. Also, we note that G_h is not full rank. Hence, we conclude that $G_4(x)$ is not a minimal basic encoding matrix.

Proof To show the equivalence of (b) and (c): Observe that the degree of a subdeterminant of $G(x)$ is determined by the $k \times k$ submatrices of $\Lambda(x)G_h$ (which have the largest degree terms) and not by $\tilde{G}(x)$. The degree of the determinants of the $k \times k$ submatrices of $G(x)$ are then determined by the subdeterminants of $\Lambda(x)$ and the $k \times k$ submatrices of G_h. Since $\det \Lambda(x) \neq 0$, if G_h is full rank, then at least one of its $k \times k$ submatrices has nonzero determinant, so that at least one of the determinants of the $k \times k$ submatrices of $\Lambda(x)G_h$ has degree μ equal to $\deg(\det(\Lambda(x))) = \nu$. On the other hand, if G_h is rank deficient, then none of the determinants of the submatrices of $\Lambda(x)G_h$ can be equal to the determinant of $\Lambda(x)$.

To show that (a) implies (b): Assume that $G(x)$ is minimal basic. Suppose that $\text{rank}(G_h) < k$. Let the rows of $G(x)$ be denoted by $\mathbf{g}_1, \mathbf{g}_2, \ldots, \mathbf{g}_k$, let the rows of G_h be denoted by $\mathbf{h}_1, \mathbf{h}_2, \ldots, \mathbf{h}_k$, and let the rows of $\tilde{G}(x)$ be denoted by $\tilde{\mathbf{g}}_1, \tilde{\mathbf{g}}_2, \ldots, \tilde{\mathbf{g}}_k$. Then the decomposition (12.12) is

$$\mathbf{g}_i = x^{\nu_i}\mathbf{h}_i + \tilde{\mathbf{g}}_i.$$

By the rank-deficiency there is a linear combination of rows of G_h such that

$$\mathbf{h}_{i_1} + \mathbf{h}_{i_2} + \cdots + \mathbf{h}_{i_d} = 0$$

for some $d \leq k$. Assume (without loss of generality) that the rows of $G(x)$ are ordered such that $\nu_1 \geq \nu_2 \geq \cdots \geq \nu_k$. The ith row of $\Lambda(x)G_h$ is $x^{\nu_i}\mathbf{h}_i$. Adding

$$x^{\nu_{i_1}}[\mathbf{h}_{i_2} + \mathbf{h}_{i_3} + \cdots + \mathbf{h}_{i_d}]$$

to the i_1st row of $\Lambda(x)G_h$ (which is $x^{\nu_i}\mathbf{h}_i$) reduces it to an all-zero row. Note that

$$x^{\nu_{i_1}}[\mathbf{h}_{i_2} + \mathbf{h}_{i_3} + \cdots + \mathbf{h}_{i_d}] = x^{\nu_{i_1}-\nu_{i_2}}x^{\nu_{i_2}}\mathbf{h}_{i_2} + x^{\nu_{i_1}-\nu_{i_3}}x^{\nu_{i_3}}\mathbf{h}_{i_3} + \cdots + x^{\nu_{i_1}-\nu_{i_d}}x^{\nu_{i_d}}\mathbf{h}_{i_d}.$$

Now consider computing $G'(x) = T(x)G(x)$, where $T(x)$ is the invertible matrix

$$T = \quad i_1: \quad \begin{bmatrix} 1 & & & & & & & & & & \\ & 1 & & & & & & & & & \\ & & \ddots & & & & & & & & \\ & & & 1 & \cdots & x^{\nu_{i_1}-\nu_{i_2}} & & x^{\nu_{i_1}-\nu_{i_3}} & \cdots & x^{\nu_{i_1}-\nu_{i_d}} & \\ & & & & \ddots & & & & & & \\ & & & & & 1 & & & & & \\ & & & & & & \ddots & & & & \\ & & & & & & & & & & 1 \end{bmatrix},$$

with an identity on the diagonal. This has the effect of adding

$$x^{\nu_{i_1}-\nu_{i_2}}\mathbf{g}_{i_2} + x^{\nu_{i_1}-\nu_{i_3}}\mathbf{g}_{i_3} + \cdots + x^{\nu_{i_1}-\nu_{i_d}}\mathbf{g}_{i_d}$$

to the i_1st row of $G(x)$, which reduces the highest degree of the i_1st row of $G(x)$ (because the term $x^{\nu_{i_1}}\mathbf{h}_{i_1}$ is eliminated) but leaves other rows of $G(x)$ unchanged. But $G'(x)$ is an equivalent transfer function matrix. We thus obtain a basic encoding matrix $G'(x)$ equivalent to $G(x)$ with an overall constraint length less than that of $G(x)$. This contradicts the assumption that $G(x)$ is minimal basic, which implies that G_h must be full rank. From the equivalence of (b) and (c), $\mu = \nu$.

Conversely, to show (b) implies (a): Let $G'(x)$ be a basic encoding matrix equivalent to $G(x)$. Then $G'(x) = T(x)G(x)$, where $T(x)$ is a $k \times k$ polynomial matrix with $\det T(x) = 1$. The maximum degree among the $k \times k$ subdeterminants of $G'(x)$ is equal to that of $G(x)$ (since $\det T(x) = 1$). Hence, $\text{rank}(G_h)$ is invariant over all equivalent basic encoding matrices. Since $\text{rank}(G_h)$ is less than or equal to the overall constraint length, if $\mu = \nu$, it follows that $G(x)$ is minimal basic. $\quad\square$

The proof is essentially constructive: given a non-minimal basic $G(x)$, a minimal basic encoder can be constructed by finding rows of G_h such that

$$\mathbf{h}_{i_1} + \mathbf{h}_{i_2} + \mathbf{h}_{i_3} + \cdots + \mathbf{h}_{i_d} = 0,$$

where the indices are ordered such that $v_{i_d} \geq v_{i_j}, 1 \leq j < d$, then adding

$$x^{v_{i_d}-v_{i_1}}\mathbf{g}_{i_1} + \cdots + x^{v_{i_d}-v_{i_{d-1}}}\mathbf{g}_{i_{d-1}}$$ (12.13)

to the i_dth row of $G(x)$.

Example 12.21 Let $G(x) = G_4(x)$, as before. Then

$$\mathbf{h}_1 = \begin{bmatrix} 1 & 0 & 0 \end{bmatrix} \quad \mathbf{h}_2 = \begin{bmatrix} 1 & 0 & 0 \end{bmatrix}$$

so that $\mathbf{h}_1 + \mathbf{h}_2 = 0$. We have $i_1 = 2$ and $i_2 = 1$. We thus add

$$x^{3-1}\mathbf{g}_2 = x^2 \begin{bmatrix} x & 1 & 0 \end{bmatrix} = \begin{bmatrix} x^3 & x^2 & 0 \end{bmatrix}$$

to row 1 of $G(x)$ to obtain the transfer function matrix

$$G_5(x) = \begin{bmatrix} 1+x+x^2 & 1+x+x^2 & x \\ x & 1 & 0 \end{bmatrix}$$

to obtain an equivalent minimal basic encoder. □

Comparing $G_5(x)$ with $G_2(x)$, we make the observation that minimal basic encoders are not unique.

As implied by its name, the advantage of a basic minimal encoder is that it is "smallest" in some sense. It may be built in such a way that the number of memory elements in the device is the smallest possible and the number of states of the device is the smallest possible. There is another advantage to minimal encoders: it can be shown that a minimal encoder is not catastrophic.

12.2.4 Systematic Encoders

Given an encoder $G(x)$, it may be turned into a systematic decoder by identifying a full-rank $k \times k$ submatrix $T(x)$. Then form

$$G'(x) = T(x)^{-1}G(x).$$

Then $G'(x)$ is of the form (perhaps after column permutations)

$$G'(x) = \begin{bmatrix} I_{k,k} & P_{k,n-k}(x) \end{bmatrix},$$

where $P_{k,n-k}(x)$ is a (generally) rational matrix. The outputs produced by $P_{k,n-k}$ — that is, the non-systematic part of the generator — are frequently referred to as the parity bits, or check bits, of the coded sequence.

Example 12.22 [230] Suppose

$$G(x) = \begin{bmatrix} 1+x & x & 1 \\ x^2 & 1 & 1+x+x^2 \end{bmatrix}$$

and $T(x)$ is taken as the first two columns:

$$T(x) = \begin{bmatrix} 1+x & x \\ x^2 & 1 \end{bmatrix} \quad T^{-1}(x) = \frac{1}{1+x+x^3}\begin{bmatrix} 1 & x \\ x^2 & 1+x \end{bmatrix}.$$

Then

$$G'(x) = T^{-1}(x)G(x) = \begin{bmatrix} 1 & 0 & \frac{1+x+x^2+x^3}{1+x+x^3} \\ 0 & 1 & \frac{1+x^2+x^3}{1+x+x^3} \end{bmatrix}.$$

□

Historically, polynomial encoders (i.e., those implemented using FIR filters) have been much more commonly used than systematic encoders (employing IIR filters). However, there are some advantages to using systematic codes. First, it can be shown that every systematic encoding matrix is minimal. Second, systematic codes cannot be catastrophic (since the data appear explicitly in the codeword).

For a given constraint length, the set of systematic codes with polynomial transfer matrices has generally inferior distance properties compared with the set of systematic codes with rational transfer matrices. In fact, it has been observed [[471], p. 252] that for large constraint lengths v, the performance of a polynomial systematic code of constraint length K is approximately the same as that of a nonsystematic code of constraint length $K(1 - k/n)$. (See Table 12.4) For example, for a rate $R = 1/2$ code, polynomial systematic codes have about the performance of nonsystematic codes of half the constraint length, while requiring exactly the same optimal decoder complexity. Because of these reasons, recent work in turbo codes has relied almost exclusively on systematic encoders.

12.3 Decoding Convolutional Codes

12.3.1 Introduction and Notation

Several algorithms have been developed for decoding convolutional codes. The one most commonly used is the Viterbi algorithm, which is a maximum likelihood sequence estimator (MLSE). A variation on the Viterbi algorithm, known as the soft-output Viterbi algorithm (SOVA), which provides not only decoded symbols but also an indication of the *reliability* of the decoded values, is presented in Section 12.11 in conjunction with turbo codes. Another decoding algorithm is the maximum a posteriori (MAP) decoder frequently referred to as the BCJR algorithm, which computes probabilities of decoded bits. The BCJR algorithm is somewhat more complex than the Viterbi algorithm, without significant performance gains compared to Viterbi decoders for convolutional codes. It is, however, ideally suited for decoding turbo codes, and so is also detailed in Chapter 14. It is also shown there that the BCJR and the Viterbi are fundamentally equivalent at a deeper level.

Suboptimal decoding algorithms are also occasionally of interest, particularly when the constraint length is large. These provide most of the performance of the Viterbi algorithm, but typically have substantially lower computational complexity. In Section 12.8, the stack algorithm (also known as the ZJ algorithm), Fano's algorithm, and the M-algorithm are presented as instances of suboptimal decoders.

To set the stage for the decoding algorithm, we introduce some notation for the stages of processing. Consider the block diagram in Figure 12.9. The time index is denoted by t, which indexes the times at which states are distinguished in the state diagram; there are thus k bits input to the encoder and n bits output from the encoder at each time step t.

- The information — message — data may have a sequence appended to drive the state to 0 at the end of some block of input. At time t there are k input bits, denoted as $m_t^{(i)}$ or $x_t^{(i)}$, $i = 1, 2, \ldots, k$. The set of k input bits at time t is denoted as $\mathbf{m}_t = (m_t^{(1)}, m_t^{(2)}, \ldots, m_t^{(k)})$ and those with the (optional) appended sequence are $\mathbf{x}_t$. An input sequence consisting of L blocks is denoted as $\mathbf{x}$:

$$\mathbf{x} = \{\mathbf{x}_0, \mathbf{x}_1, \ldots, \mathbf{x}_{L-1}\}.$$

- The corresponding coded output bits are denoted as $c_t^{(i)}$, $i = 1, 2, \ldots, n$, or collectively at time t as $\mathbf{c}_t$. The entire coded output sequence is $\mathbf{c} = \{\mathbf{c}_0, \mathbf{c}_1, \ldots, \mathbf{c}_{L-1}\}$.

- The coded output sequence is mapped to a sequence of M symbols selected from a signal constellation with Q points in some signal space, with $Q = 2^p$. We must have 2^{nL} (the number of coded bits in the sequence) equal to 2^{pM}, so that $M = nL/p$. For convenience in notation, we assume that $p = 1$ (e.g., BPSK modulation), so that $M = nL$.

  The mapped signals at time t are denoted as $a_t^{(i)}$, $i = 1, 2, \ldots, n$. The entire coded sequence is $\mathbf{a} = \{\mathbf{a}_0, \mathbf{a}_1, \ldots, \mathbf{a}_{L-1}\}$.

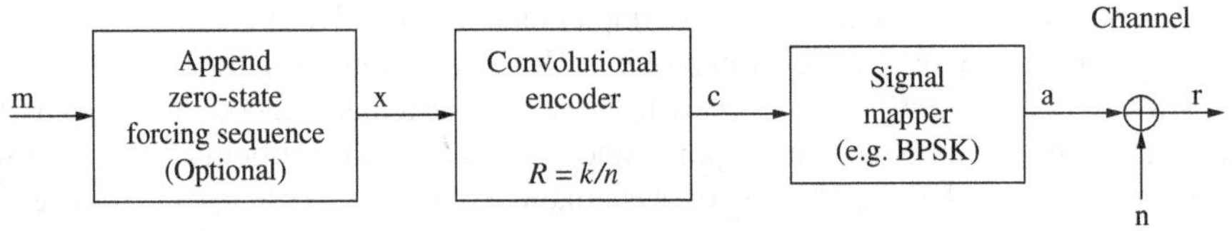

Figure 12.9: Processing stages for a convolutional code.

- The symbols $\mathbf{a}_t$ pass through a channel, resulting in a received symbol $r_t^{(i)}, i = 1, 2, \ldots, n$, or a block $\mathbf{r}_t$. We consider explicitly two channel models: an AWGN and a BSC. For the AWGN, we have

$$r_t^{(i)} = a_t^{(i)} + n_t^{(i)}, \quad \text{where } n_t^{(i)} \sim \mathcal{N}(0, \sigma^2), \text{ and where } \sigma^2 = \frac{N_0}{2}.$$

For the AWGN the received data are real- or complex-valued. For the BSC, the mapped signals are equal to the coded data, $\mathbf{a}_t = \mathbf{c}_t$. The received signal is

$$r_t^{(i)} = c_t^{(i)} \oplus n_t^{(i)}, \quad \text{where } n_t \sim \mathcal{B}(p_c),$$

where $\oplus$ denotes addition modulo 2 and p_c is the channel crossover probability and $\mathcal{B}(p_c)$ indicates a Bernoulli random variable. For both channels it is assumed that the $n_t^{(i)}$ are mutually independent for all i and t, resulting in a memoryless channel. We denote the likelihood function for these channels as $f(\mathbf{r}_t | \mathbf{a}_t)$. For the AWGN channel,

$$f(\mathbf{r}_t | \mathbf{a}_t) = \prod_{i=1}^{n} \frac{1}{\sqrt{2\pi}\sigma} \exp\left[-\frac{1}{2\sigma^2}(r_t^{(i)} - a_t^{(i)})^2\right]$$

$$= (\sqrt{2\pi}\sigma)^{-n} \exp\left[-\frac{1}{2\sigma^2}\|\mathbf{r}_t - \mathbf{a}_t\|^2\right],$$

where $\|\cdot\|^2$ denotes the usual Euclidean distance,

$$\|\mathbf{r}_t - \mathbf{a}_t\|^2 = \sum_{i=1}^{n} (r_t^{(i)} - a_t^{(i)})^2.$$

For the BSC,

$$f(\mathbf{r}_t | \mathbf{a}_t) = \prod_{i=1}^{n} p_c^{[r_t^{(i)} \neq a_t^{(i)}]} (1 - p_c)^{[r_t^{(i)} = a_t^{(i)}]} = p_c^{d_H(\mathbf{r}_t, \mathbf{a}_t)} (1 - p_c)^{n - d_H(\mathbf{r}_t, \mathbf{a}_t)}$$

$$= \left(\frac{p_c}{1 - p_c}\right)^{d_H(\mathbf{r}_t, \mathbf{a}_t)} (1 - p_c)^n,$$

where $[r_t^{(i)} \neq a_t^{(i)}]$ returns 1 if the indicated condition is true and $d_H(\mathbf{r}_t, \mathbf{a}_t)$ is the Hamming distance.

Since the sequence of inputs uniquely determines the sequence of outputs, mapped outputs, and states, the likelihood function can be equivalently expressed as $f(\mathbf{r}|\mathbf{c})$ or $f(\mathbf{r}|\mathbf{a})$ or $f(\mathbf{r}|\{\Psi_0, \Psi_1, \ldots, \Psi_L\})$.

- Maximizing the likelihood is obviously equivalent to minimizing the negative log likelihood. We deal with negative log-likelihood functions and throw away terms and/or factors that do not depend upon the conditioning values. For the Gaussian channel, since

$$-\log f(\mathbf{r}_t | \mathbf{a}_t) = +n \log \sqrt{2\pi}\sigma + \frac{1}{2\sigma^2}\|\mathbf{r}_t - \mathbf{a}_t\|^2,$$

we use

$$\|\mathbf{r}_t - \mathbf{a}_t\|^2 \tag{12.14}$$

as the "negative log-likelihood" function. For the BSC, since

$$-\log f(\mathbf{r}_t|\mathbf{a}_t) = -d_H(\mathbf{r}_t, \mathbf{a}_t) \log \frac{p_c}{1-p_c} - n\log(1-p_c),$$

we use

$$d_H(\mathbf{r}_t, \mathbf{a}_t) \tag{12.15}$$

as the "negative log-likelihood" (since $\log(p_c/(1-p_c)) < 0$).

More generally, the affine transformation

$$a[-\log f(\mathbf{r}_t|\mathbf{a}) - b] \tag{12.16}$$

provides a function equivalent for purposes of detection to the log- likelihood function for any $a > 0$ and any b. The parameters a and b can be chosen to simplify computations.

- The state at time t in the trellis of the encoder is denoted as Ψ_t. States are represented with integer values in the range $0 \le \Psi_t < 2^\nu$, where ν is the constraint length for the encoder. (We use 2^ν since we are assuming binary encoders for convenience. For a q-ary code, the number of states is q^ν.) It is always assumed that the initial state is $\Psi_0 = 0$.

- A sequence of symbols such as $\{\mathbf{x}_0, \mathbf{x}_1, \ldots, \mathbf{x}_l\}$ is denoted as $\mathbf{x}_0^l$.

- A sequence of states $(\Psi_0, \Psi_1, \ldots, \Psi_{t-1})$, representing a path through the trellis, is denoted as Ψ_0^{t-1}. Such a sequence of states is assumed to always denote a valid path through the trellis for the encoder.

- As suggested by Figure 12.10, quantities associated with the transition from state p to state q are denoted with $^{(p,q)}$. For example, the input which causes the transition from state $\Psi_t = p$ to the state $\Psi_{t+1} = q$ is denoted as $\mathbf{x}^{(p,q)}$. (If the trellis had different structure at different times, one might use the notation $\mathbf{x}_t^{(p,q)}$.) The code bits output sequence as a result of this state transition is $\mathbf{c}^{(p,q)}$ and the mapped symbols are $\mathbf{a}^{(p,q)}$.

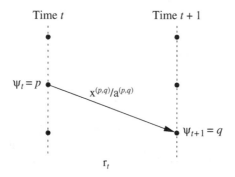

Figure 12.10: Notation associated with a state transition.

- Generalizing the idea of $\mathbf{x}^{(p,q)}$, a sequence of states Ψ_0^t corresponds to a sequence of inputs $\mathbf{x}_0, \mathbf{x}_1, \ldots, \mathbf{x}_{t-1}$, which takes the encoder through that sequence of states. This sequence of states is denoted as $\mathbf{x}(\Psi_0^t)$.

- Similarly, the sequence of coded outputs, and its corresponding sequence of modulated outputs produced along that sequence of states is denoted as $\mathbf{c}(\Psi_0^t)$ and $\mathbf{a}(\Psi_0^t)$, respectively.

12.3.2 The Viterbi Algorithm

The Viterbi algorithm was originally proposed by Andrew Viterbi [467], but its optimality as a maximum likelihood sequence decoder was not originally appreciated. In [128], it was established that the Viterbi algorithm computes the maximum likelihood code sequence given the received data. The Viterbi algorithm is essentially a shortest path algorithm, roughly analogous to Dijkstra's shortest path algorithm (see, e.g., [[400], p. 415]) for computing the shortest path through the trellis associated with the code. The Viterbi algorithm has been applied in a variety of other communications problems, including maximum likelihood sequence estimation in the presence of intersymbol interference [134] and optimal reception of spread-spectrum multiple access communication (see, e.g., [466]). It also appears in many other problems where a "state" can be defined, such as in hidden Markov modeling (see, e.g., [91]). See also [319] for a survey of applications. The decoder takes the input sequence $\mathbf{r} = \{\mathbf{r}_0, \mathbf{r}_1, \dots\}$ and determines an estimate of the transmitted data $\{\mathbf{a}_0, \mathbf{a}_1, \dots\}$ and from that an estimate of the sequence of input data $\{\mathbf{x}_0, \mathbf{x}_1, \dots\}$.

The basic idea behind the Viterbi algorithm is as follows. A coded sequence $\{\mathbf{c}_0, \mathbf{c}_1, \dots\}$, or its signal-mapped equivalent $\{\mathbf{a}_0, \mathbf{a}_1, \dots\}$, corresponds to a path through the encoder trellis through some sequence of states $\Psi_0, \Psi_1, \Psi_2, \dots$. Due to noise in the channel, the received sequence $\mathbf{r} = (\mathbf{r}_0, \mathbf{r}_1, \mathbf{r}_2, \dots)$ may not correspond exactly to a path through the trellis. The decoder finds a path through the trellis which is closest to the received sequence, where the measure of "closest" is determined by the likelihood function appropriate for the channel. In light of (12.14), for an AWGN channel the maximum likelihood path corresponds to the path through the trellis which is closest in *Euclidean* distance to $\mathbf{r}$. In light of (12.15), for a BSC the maximum likelihood path corresponds to the path through the trellis which is closest in *Hamming* distance to $\mathbf{r}$. Naively, one could find the maximum likelihood path by computing separately the path lengths of all of the possible paths through the trellis. This, however, is computationally intractable. The Viterbi algorithm organizes the computations in an efficient recursive form.

For an input $\mathbf{x}_t$ the output $\mathbf{c}_t$ depends on the state of the encoder Ψ_t, which in turn depends upon previous inputs. This dependency among inputs means that optimal decisions cannot be made based upon a likelihood function for a single time $f(\mathbf{r}_t|\mathbf{x}_t)$. Instead, optimal decisions are based upon an entire received *sequence* of symbols. The likelihood function to be maximized is thus $f(\mathbf{r}|\mathbf{x})$, where

$$f(\mathbf{r}|\mathbf{x}) = f(\mathbf{r}_0^{L-1}|\mathbf{x}_0^{L-1}) = f(\mathbf{r}_0, \mathbf{r}_1, \dots, \mathbf{r}_{L-1}|\mathbf{x}_0, \mathbf{x}_1, \dots, \mathbf{x}_{L-1}) = \prod_{t=0}^{L-1} f(\mathbf{r}_t|\mathbf{x}_t).$$

The fact that the channel is assumed to be memoryless is used to obtain the last equality. It is convenient to deal with the log- likelihood function,

$$\log f(\mathbf{r}|\mathbf{x}) = \sum_{t=0}^{L-1} \log f(\mathbf{r}_t|\mathbf{x}_t).$$

Consider a putative estimated information sequence $\hat{\mathbf{x}}_0^{t-1} = (\hat{\mathbf{x}}_0, \hat{\mathbf{x}}_1, \dots, \hat{\mathbf{x}}_{t-1})$, with corresponding modulated sequence $\hat{\mathbf{a}}_0^{t-1}$, resulting from the path $(\Psi_0, \Psi_1, \dots, \Psi_t) = \Psi_0^t$ which leaves the encoder in state $\Psi_t = p$ at time t. The log- likelihood function for this sequence is

$$\log f(\mathbf{r}_0^{t-1}|\hat{\mathbf{a}}_0^{t-1}) = \sum_{i=0}^{t-1} \log f(\mathbf{r}_i|\hat{\mathbf{a}}_i).$$

Let

$$M_{t-1}(p) = -\log f(\mathbf{r}_0^{t-1}|\hat{\mathbf{a}}_0^{t-1}) \tag{12.17}$$

denote the **path metric** for the path Ψ_0^t through the trellis defined by the information sequence $\hat{\mathbf{x}}_0^{t-1} = \mathbf{x}(\Psi_0^t)$ and terminating in state $\Psi_t = p$. The negative sign in this definition means that we seek to *minimize* the path metric (to maximize the likelihood).

Other notations are also used for the path metric. The path metric could also be denoted $M(\mathbf{r}_0^{t-1}|\Psi_0^t)$, where $\Psi_t = p$, which specifically indicates that the metric depends upon the path. Alternatively, the path metric could be denoted as $M(\mathbf{r}_0^{t-1}|\hat{\mathbf{x}}(\Psi_0^t))$, denoting that the metric depends on the sequence of inputs along the path Ψ_0^t. All of these represent the negative log likelihood (or simplifications discussed below). For the moment these latter notations are unduly heavy (although it will be used below), and the definition in (12.17) is used here.

Now let the sequence $\hat{\mathbf{x}}_0^t = (\hat{\mathbf{x}}_0, \hat{\mathbf{x}}_1, \ldots, \hat{\mathbf{x}}_t)$ be obtained by appending the input $\hat{\mathbf{x}}_t$ to $\hat{\mathbf{x}}_0^{t-1}$ and suppose the input $\hat{\mathbf{x}}_t$ is such that the state at time $t + 1$ is $\Psi_{t+1} = q$. The path metric for this longer sequence is

$$M_t(q) = -\sum_{i=0}^{t} \log f(\mathbf{r}_i|\hat{\mathbf{a}}_i) = -\sum_{i=0}^{t-1} \log f(\mathbf{r}_i|\hat{\mathbf{a}}_i) - \log f(\mathbf{r}_t|\hat{\mathbf{a}}_t) = M_{t-1}(p) - \log f(\mathbf{r}_t|\hat{\mathbf{a}}_t).$$

Let $\mu_t(\mathbf{r}_t, \hat{\mathbf{x}}_t) = -\log f(\mathbf{r}_t|\hat{\mathbf{a}}_t) = -\log f(\mathbf{r}_t|\mathbf{a}^{(p,q)})$ denote the negative log likelihood for this input, where $\hat{\mathbf{a}}_t$ is the output resulting from the input $\hat{\mathbf{x}}_t$ when the encoder is in state p at time t. As pointed out in (12.16), we could equivalently use

$$\mu_t(\mathbf{r}_t, \hat{\mathbf{x}}_t) = a[-\log f(\mathbf{r}_t|\hat{\mathbf{a}}^{(p,q)}) - b], \qquad (12.18)$$

for any $a > 0$. The quantity $\mu_t(\mathbf{r}_t, \hat{\mathbf{x}}_t)$ is called the **branch metric** for the decoder. Since $\hat{\mathbf{x}}_t$ moves the trellis from state p at time t to state q at time $t + 1$, we can write $\mu_t(\mathbf{r}_t, \hat{\mathbf{x}}_t)$ as $\mu_t(\mathbf{r}_t, \hat{\mathbf{x}}^{(p,q)})$. Then

$$M_t(q) = \sum_{i=0}^{t-1} \mu_i(\mathbf{r}_i, \hat{\mathbf{x}}_i) + \mu_t(\mathbf{r}_t, \hat{\mathbf{x}}_t) = M_{t-1}(p) + \mu_t(\mathbf{r}_t, \hat{\mathbf{x}}^{(p,q)}).$$

That is, the path metric along a path to state q at time t is obtained by adding the path metric to the state p at time $t - 1$ to the branch metric for an input which moves the encoder from state p to state q. (If there is no such input, then the branch metric is ∞.)

With this notation, we now come to the crux of the Viterbi algorithm: What do we do when paths merge? Suppose $M_{t-1}(p_1)$ is the path metric of a path ending at state p_1 at time t and $M_{t-1}(p_2)$ is the path metric of a path ending at state p_2 at time t. Suppose further that both of these states are connected to state q at time $t + 1$, as suggested in Figure 12.11. The resulting path metrics to state q are

$$M_{t-1}(p_1) + \mu_t(\mathbf{r}_t, \hat{\mathbf{x}}^{(p_1,q)}) \quad \text{and} \quad M_{t-1}(p_2) + \mu_t(\mathbf{r}_t, \hat{\mathbf{x}}^{(p_2,q)}).$$

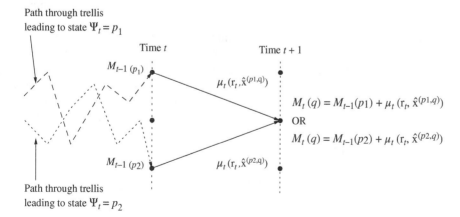

Figure 12.11: The Viterbi step: select the path with the best metric.

The governing principle of the Viterbi algorithm is this: To obtain the shortest path through the trellis, the path to state q must be the shortest possible. Otherwise, it would be possible to find a shorter path through the trellis starting from state q by finding a shorter path to state q. (This is Bellman's principle of optimality; see, e.g., [28].) Thus, when the two or more paths merge, the path with the *shortest* path metric is retained and the other path is eliminated from further consideration. That is,

$$M_t(q) = \min\{M_{t-1}(p_1) + \mu_t(\mathbf{r}_t, \hat{\mathbf{x}}^{(p_1,q)}), M_{t-1}(p_2) + \mu_t(\mathbf{r}_t, \hat{\mathbf{x}}^{(p_2,q)})\}$$

and the path with minimal length becomes the path to state q. This is called the *survivor path*.

Since it is not known at time $t < L$ which states the final path passes through, the paths to *each* state are found for each time. The Viterbi algorithm thus maintains the following data:

- A path metric to each state at time t.

- A path to each state at time t. (This may be efficiently represented by storing at each state and each time the state which is previous to it on the path leading to that state.)

Alternatively, the Viterbi algorithm could maintain the following data:

- A path metric to each state at time t.

- The sequence of inputs $\hat{\mathbf{x}}(\Psi_0^t)$ along the path leading to that state.

The Viterbi algorithm is thus summarized as follows:

1. Initialize the path metrics $M_{-1}(p)$. (For states p which can be valid starting states set $M_{-1}(p) = 0$. For states p which are invalid starting states set $M_{-1}(p) = \infty$; path extensions from those states will never be accepted by the Viterbi algorithm.)

2. For $t = 0, 1, \ldots, L - 1$: For each state q at time $t + 1$, find the path metric for each path to state q by adding the path metric $M_{t-1}(p)$ of each survivor path to state p at time t to the branch metric $\mu_t(\mathbf{r}_t, \hat{\mathbf{x}}^{(p,q)})$.

3. The survivor path to q is selected as that path to state q which has the smallest path metric.

4. Store the path and path metric to each state q.

5. Increment t and repeat until complete.

In the event that the path metrics of merging paths are equal, a random choice can be made with no negative impact on the likelihood.

More formally, there is the description in Algorithm 12.1. In this description, the path to state q is specified by listing for each state its predecessor in the graph. Other descriptions of the path are also possible. The algorithm is initialized reflecting the assumption that the initial state is 0 by setting the path metric at $\Psi_0 = 0$ to 0 and all other path metrics to ∞ (i.e., some large number), representing the assumption that the decoder starts in state 0. In this algorithm, Π_p denotes the path to state p.

The operations of extending and pruning that constitute the heart of the Viterbi algorithm are summarized as:

$$M_t(q) = \min_p[\underbrace{M_{t-1}(p) + \mu_t(\mathbf{r}_t, \hat{\mathbf{x}}^{(p,q)})}_{\text{Extend all paths at time t to state } q \ldots}]. \tag{12.19}$$

$$\underbrace{\phantom{M_t(q) = \min_p[M_{t-1}(p) + \mu_t(\mathbf{r}_t, \hat{\mathbf{x}}^{(p,q)})]}}_{\text{Then choose smallest cost}}$$

Algorithm 12.1 The Viterbi Algorithm

---

1. **Input:** A sequence $\mathbf{r}_0, \mathbf{r}_1, \ldots, \mathbf{r}_{L-1}$
2. **Output:** The sequence $\hat{\mathbf{x}}_0, \hat{\mathbf{x}}_1, \ldots, \hat{\mathbf{x}}_{L-1}$ which maximizes the likelihood $f(\mathbf{r}_0^{L-1}|\hat{\mathbf{x}}_0^{L-1})$.
3. **Initialize:** Set $M(0) = 0$ and $M(p) = \infty$ for $p = 1, 2, \ldots, 2^\nu - 1$ (initial path costs)
4.   Set $\Pi_p = \emptyset$ for $p = 0, 1, \ldots, 2^\nu - 1$ (initial paths)
5.   Set $t = 0$
6. Begin
7. For each state q at time $t + 1$
8.   Find the path metric for each path to state q:
9.   For each p_i connected to state q corresponding to input $\hat{\mathbf{x}}^{(p_i, q)}$, compute
         $m_i = M(p_i) + \mu_t(\mathbf{r}_t, \hat{\mathbf{x}}^{(p_i, q)}))$.
10.   Select the smallest metric $M(q) = \min_i m_i$ and the corresponding predecessor state p.
11.   Extend the path to state q: $\Pi_q = [\Pi_p \; q]$
12. end (for)
13. $t = t + 1$
14. if $t < L - 1$, goto line 6.
15. Termination:
16. If terminating in a known state (e.g. 0)
       Return the sequences of inputs along the path to that known state
17. If terminating in any state
       Find final state with minimal metric; Return the sequence of inputs along that path to that state.
18. End

Example 12.23   Consider the encoder

$$G(x) = \begin{bmatrix} x^2 + 1 & x^2 + x + 1 \end{bmatrix}$$

of Example 12.1, whose realization and trellis diagram are shown in Figure 12.5, passing the data through a BSC. When the data sequence

$$\mathbf{x} = \begin{bmatrix} 1, 1, 0, 0, 1, 0, 1, 0, \ldots \end{bmatrix}$$

$$= \begin{bmatrix} x_0, x_1, x_2, x_3, x_4, x_5, x_6, x_7, \ldots \end{bmatrix}$$

is applied to the encoder, the coded output bit sequence is

$$\mathbf{c} = \begin{bmatrix} 11, 10, 10, 11, 11, 01, 00, 01, \ldots \end{bmatrix}$$

$$= \begin{bmatrix} \mathbf{c}_0, \mathbf{c}_1, \mathbf{c}_2, \mathbf{c}_3, \mathbf{c}_4, \mathbf{c}_5, \mathbf{c}_6, \mathbf{c}_7, \ldots \end{bmatrix}.$$

For the BSC, we take the mapped data the same as the encoder output $\mathbf{a}_t = \mathbf{c}_t$. The output sequence and corresponding states of the encoder are shown here, where $\Psi_0 = 0$ is the initial state.

t	Input x_k	Output $\mathbf{c}_t$	State Ψ_{t+1}
0	1	11	1
1	1	10	3
2	0	10	2
3	0	11	0
4	1	11	1
5	0	01	2
6	1	00	1
7	0	01	2

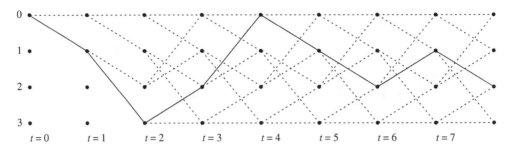

Figure 12.12: Path through trellis corresponding to true sequence.

The sequence of states through the trellis for this encoder is shown in Figure 12.12; the solid line shows the state sequence for this sequence of outputs. The path is

$$\Psi_0^7 = (0, 1, 3, 2, 0, 1, 2, 1, 2)$$

and the sequence of inputs is

$$\mathbf{x}(\Psi_0^7) = (1, 1, 0, 0, 1, 0, 1, 0).$$

The coded output sequence passes through a channel, producing the received sequence

$$\mathbf{r} = \begin{bmatrix} 11 & 10 & \underline{00} & 1\underline{0} & 11 & 01 & 00 & 01 & \ldots \end{bmatrix} = \begin{bmatrix} \mathbf{r}_0, \mathbf{r}_1, \mathbf{r}_2, \mathbf{r}_3, \mathbf{r}_4, \mathbf{r}_5, \mathbf{r}_6, \mathbf{r}_7, \ldots \end{bmatrix}.$$

The two underlined bits are flipped by noise in the channel.

The algorithm proceeds as follows:

$t = 0$: The received sequence is $\mathbf{r}_0 = 11$. We compute the metric to each state at time $t = 1$ by finding the (Hamming) distance between $\mathbf{r}_0$ and the possible transmitted sequence $\mathbf{c}_0$ along the branches of the first stage of the trellis. Since state 0 was known to be the initial state, we end up with only two paths, with path metrics 2 and 0, as shown here:

$$\mathbf{r}_0 = 11$$

At each state (with a path to it), these figures show the sequence of inputs leading to that state in brackets.

$t = 1$: The received sequence is $\mathbf{r}_1 = 10$. Again, each path at time $t = 1$ is simply extended, adding the path metric to each branch metric:

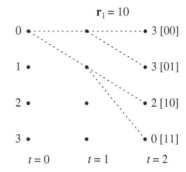

The memory of this encoder is $m = 2$. By $t = m = 2$, the set of paths has reached all states in the trellis.

$t = 2$: The received sequence is $\mathbf{r}_2 = 00$. Each path at time $t = 2$ is extended, adding the path metric to each branch metric of each path.

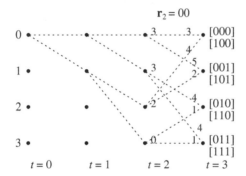

There are now multiple paths to each node at time $t + 1 = 3$. We select the path to each node with the best metric and eliminate the other paths. This gives the diagram as follows:

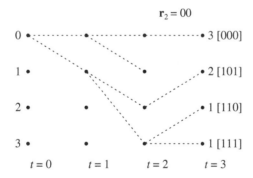

In general, for a convolutional code with memory m, the paths at time $t + 1 = m + 1$ begin to merge on the states, and the Viterbi algorithm begins to make its decisions about paths.

Another observation that can be made is that for a state p, the last $m = 2$ input bits along paths leading to the state are the binary representation of p. For example, for state $p = 1 = (01)_2$, all input bit sequences on paths leading to this state have their last 2 bits as 01. For the state $p = 3 = (11)_2$, all input bit sequences on paths leading to this state have their last 2 bits as 11. This fact is true for all times in this example. It is true in general *for feedforward (FIR) encoders*, and may not be true for recursive (IIR) encoders.

$t = 3$: The received sequence is $\mathbf{r}_3 = 10$. Each path at time $t = 3$ is extended, adding the path metric to each branch metric of each path.

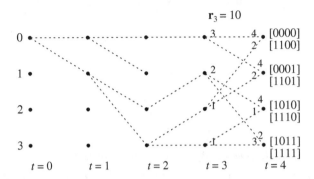

Again, the best path to each state is selected. We note that in selecting the best paths, some of the paths to some states at earlier times have no successors; these orphan paths are deleted now in our portrayal:

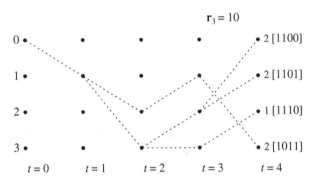

$t = 4$: The received sequence is $\mathbf{r}_4 = 11$. Each path at time $t = 4$ is extended, adding the path metric to each branch metric of each path.

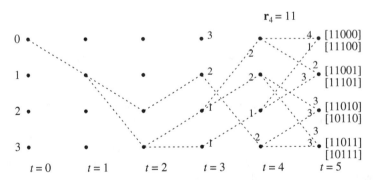

In this case, we note that there are multiple paths into state 3 which both have the same path metric; also there are multiple paths into state 2 with the same path metric. Since one of the paths must be selected, the choice can be made arbitrarily (e.g., at random). After selecting and pruning of orphan paths, we obtain:

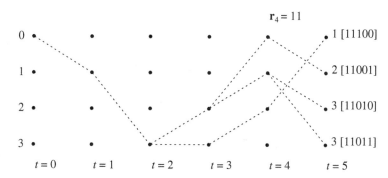

$t = 5$: The received sequence is $\mathbf{r}_5 = 01$.

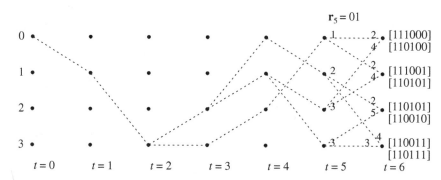

After selecting and pruning:

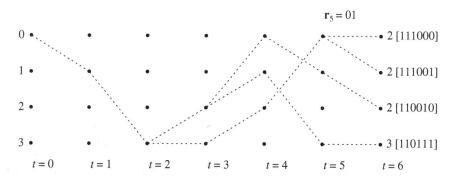

$t = 6$: The received sequence is $\mathbf{r}_6 = 00$.

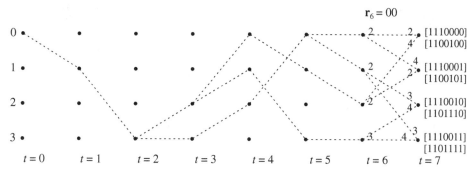

After selecting and pruning:

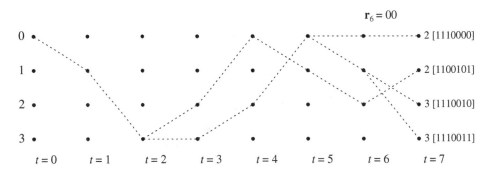

$t = 7$: The received sequence is $\mathbf{r}_7 = 01$.

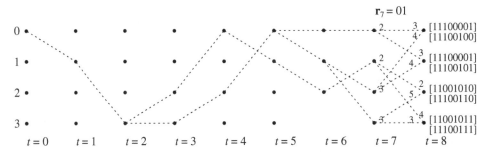

After selecting and pruning:

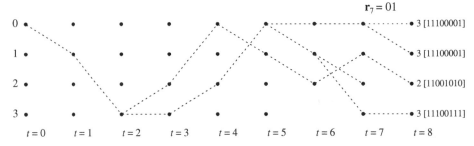

The decoding is finalized at the end of the transmission (the 16 received data bits) by selecting the state at the last stage having the lowest cost, traversing backward along the path so indicated to the beginning of the trellis, then traversing forward again along the best path, reading the input bits and decoded output bits along the path. This is shown with the solid line below; input/output pairs are indicated on each branch.

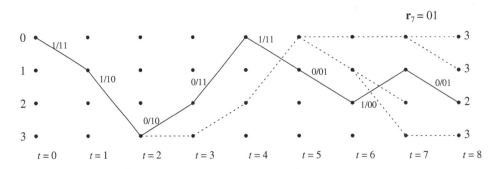

Note that the path through the trellis is the same as in Figure 12.12 and that the recovered input bit sequence is the same as the original bit sequence. Thus, out of this sequence of 16 bits, 2 bit errors have been corrected.   □

12.3.3   Some Implementation Issues

12.3.3.1   The Basic Operation: Add-Compare-Select

The basic operation of the Viterbi algorithm is Add-Compare-Select (ACS): Add the branch metric to the path metric for each path leading to a state; compare the resulting path metrics at that state; and select the better metric. A schematic of this idea appears in Figure 12.13. High-speed operation can be obtained in hardware by using a bank of 2^ν such ACS units in parallel. A variation on this theme, the compare-select-add (CSA) operation, is capable of somewhat improving the speed for some encoders. The algorithm employing CSA is called the *differential Viterbi algorithm*; see [143] for a description.

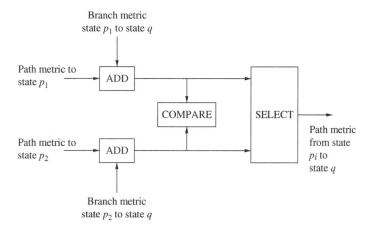

Figure 12.13: Add-compare-select operation.

12.3.3.2   Decoding Streams of Data: Windows on the Trellis

In convolutional codes, data are typically encoded in a stream. Once the encoding starts, it may continue indefinitely, for example, until the end of a file or until the end of a data transmission session. If such a data stream is decoded using the Viterbi algorithm as described above, the paths through the trellis would have to have as many stages as the code is long. For a long data stream, this could amount to an extraordinary amount of data to be stored, since the decoder would have to store 2^ν paths whose lengths grow longer with each stage. Furthermore, this would result in a large decoding latency: strictly speaking, it would not be possible to output *any* decoded values until the maximum likelihood path is selected at the end of the file.

Fortunately, it is not necessary to wait until the end of transmission. Consider the paths in Example 12.23. In this example, by $t = 4$, there is a single surviving path in the first two stages of the trellis. Regardless of how the Viterbi algorithm operates on the paths as it continues through the trellis, those first two stages could be unambiguously decoded.

In general, with very high probability there is a single surviving path some number of stages back from the "current" stage of the trellis. The initial stages of the survivor paths tend to merge if a sufficient decoding delay is allowed. Thus, it is only necessary to keep a "window" on the trellis consisting of the current stage and some number of previous stages. The number of stages back that the decoding looks to make its decision is called the **decoding depth**, denoted by Γ. At time t the decoder outputs a decision on the code bits $\mathbf{c}_{t-\Gamma}$. While it is possible to make an incorrect decoding decision on a finite decoding depth, this error, called the **truncation error**, is typically very small if the decoding depth is sufficiently large. It has been found (see, e.g., [129,197]) that if a decoding depth of about five to ten constraint lengths is employed, then there is very little loss of performance compared to using the full length due to truncation error.

It is effective to implement the decoding window using a circular queue of length Γ to hold the current window. As the window is "shifted," it is only necessary to adjust the pointers to the beginning and end of the window.

As the algorithm proceeds through the stream of data, the path metrics continue to accumulate. Overflow is easily avoided by periodically subtracting from all path metrics an equal amount (for example, the smallest path metric). The path metrics then show the differential qualities of each path rather than the absolute metrics (or their approximations), but this is sufficient for decoding purposes.

12.3.3.3 Output Decisions

When a decision about the output $\mathbf{c}_{t-\Gamma}$ is to be made at time t, there are a few ways that this can be accomplished [483]: Output $\mathbf{c}_{t-\Gamma}$ on a randomly selected survivor path; Output $\mathbf{c}_{t-\Gamma}$ on the survivor path with the best metric; Output $\mathbf{c}_{t-\Gamma}$ that occurs most often among all the survivor paths; Output $\mathbf{c}_{t-\Gamma}$ on any path. In reality, if Γ is sufficiently large that all the survivor paths have merged Γ decoding stages back, then the performance difference among these alternatives is very small.

When the decision is to be output, a survivor path is selected (using one of the methods just mentioned). Then it is necessary to determine the $\mathbf{c}_{t-\Gamma}$. There are a couple of ways of accomplishing this, the register exchange and the traceback.

In the *register exchange* implementation, an input register at each state contains the sequence of input bits associated with the surviving path that terminates at that state. A register capable of storing the $k\Gamma$ bits is necessary for each state. As the decoding algorithm proceeds, for the path selected from state p to state q, the input register at state q is obtained by copying the input register for state p and appending the k input bits resulting in that state transition. (Double buffering of the data may be necessary, so that the input registers are not lost in copying the information over.) When an output is necessary, the first k bits of the register for the terminating state of the selected path can be read immediately from its input register.

Example 12.24 For the decoding sequence of Example 12.23, the registers for the register exchange algorithm are shown here (boxed) for the first five steps of the algorithm.

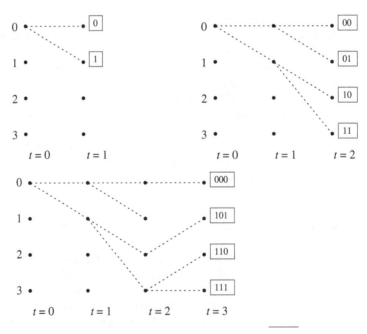

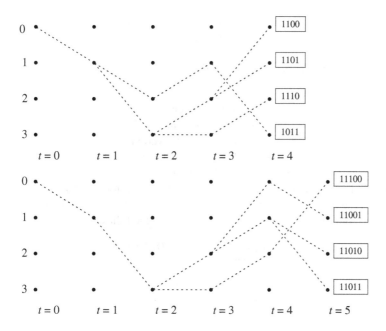

The number of initial bits all the registers have in common is the number of branches of the path that are shared by all paths. These common input bits are shown in bold above. In some implementations, it may be of interest to output only those bits corresponding to path branches which have merged.

In the *traceback* method, the path is represented by storing the *predecessor* to each state. This sequence of predecessors is traced back Γ stages. The state transition $\Psi_{t-\Gamma}$ to $\Psi_{t-\Gamma+1}$ determines the output $\mathbf{c}_{t-\Gamma}$ and its corresponding input bits $\mathbf{x}_{t-\Gamma}$.

Example 12.25 The table

t:	1	2	3	4	5	6	7	8
State				Previous State/Input				
0:	0/0	0/0	0/0	**2/0**	2/0	0/0	0/0	0/0
1:	**0/1**	0/1	2/1	2/1	**0/1**	0/1	**2/1**	0/1
2:	-	1/0	**3/0**	3/0	1/0	**1/0**	1/0	**1/0**
3:	-	**1/1**	3/1	1/1	1/1	3/1	1/1	3/1

shows the previous state traceback table which would be built up by the decoding of Example 12.23. For example, at time $t = 8$, the predecessor of state 0 is 2, the predecessor of state 1 is 0, and so forth. Starting from state 2 (having the lowest path cost), the sequence of states can be read off in reverse order from this table (the bold entries):

$$2 \rightarrow 1 \rightarrow 2 \rightarrow 1 \rightarrow 0 \rightarrow 2 \rightarrow 3 \rightarrow 1 \rightarrow 0.$$

Thus, the first state transition is from state 0 to state 1 and the input at that time is a 1.

The inputs for the entire sequence can also be read off, starting at the right, 11001010. □

In the traceback method, it is necessary to trace backward through the trellis once for each output. (As a variation on the theme, the predecessor to a state could be represented by the input bits that lead to that state.)

In comparing the requirements for these two methods, we note that the register exchange method requires shuffling registers among all the states at each time. In contrast, the traceback method requires no such shuffling, but it does require working back through the trellis to obtain a decision. Which is more efficient depends on the particular hardware available to perform the tasks. Typically, the traceback is regarded as faster but more complicated.

12.3.3.4 Hard and Soft Decoding; Quantization

Example 12.23 presents an instance of *hard-decision decoding*. If the outputs of a Gaussian channel had been used with the Euclidean distance as the branch metric, then *soft-decision* decoding could have been obtained. Comparing soft-decision decoding using BPSK over an AWGN with hard-decision decoding over a BSC, in which received values are converted to binary values with a probability of error of $p_c = Q(\sqrt{2E_b/N_0})$ (see Section 1.5.6), it has been determined that soft-decision decoding provides 2 to 3 dB of gain over hard-decision decoding.

For a hard-decision metric, $\mu_t(\mathbf{r}_t, \mathbf{x}^{(p,q)})$ can be computed and stored in advance. For example, for an $n = 2$ binary code, there are four possible received values, $00, 01, 10, 11$, and four possible transmitted values. The metric could be stored in a 4×4 array, such as the following:

$\mu_t(\mathbf{r}_t, \hat{\mathbf{x}}^{(p,q)})$	$\mathbf{r}_t = 00$	01	10	11
$\mathbf{x}^{(p,q)} = 00$	0	1	1	2
$\mathbf{x}^{(p,q)} = 01$	1	0	2	1
$\mathbf{x}^{(p,q)} = 10$	1	2	0	1
$\mathbf{x}^{(p,q)} = 11$	2	1	1	0

Soft-decision decoding typically requires more expensive computation than hard-decision decoding. Furthermore, soft-decision decoding cannot exactly precompute these values to reduce the ongoing decoding complexity, since $\mathbf{r}_t$ takes on a continuum of values. Despite these disadvantages, it is frequently desirable to use soft-decision decoding because of its superior performance. A computational compromise is to *quantize* the received value to a reasonably small set of values, then precompute the metrics for each of these values. By converting these metrics to small integer quantities, it is possible to efficiently accumulate the metrics. It has been found [196] that quantizing each $r_t^{(i)}$ into 3 bits (eight quantization levels) results in a loss in coding gain of around only 0.25 dB. It is possible to trade metric computation complexity for performance, using more bits of quantization to reduce the loss.

As noted above, if a branch metric μ is modified by $\tilde{\mu} = a\mu + b$ for any $a > 0$ and any real b, an equivalent decoding algorithm is obtained; this simply scales and shifts the resulting path metrics. In quantizing, it may be convenient to find scale factors which make the arithmetic easier.

A widely used quantizer is presented in Section 12.4.

Example 12.26 A 2-bit quantizer. In a BPSK-modulated system, the transmitted signal amplitudes are $a = 1$ or $a = -1$. The received signal r_t is quantized by a quantization function $Q[\cdot]$ to obtain quantized values

$$q_t = Q[r_t]$$

using quantization thresholds at ± 1 and 0, as shown in Figure 12.14, where the quantized values are denoted as $00, 01, 10$, and 11. These thresholds determine the regions $\mathcal{R}_q$. That is,

$$q_t = Q[r_t] = \begin{cases} 00 & \text{if } r_t \in \mathcal{R}_{00} = (-\infty, -1] \\ 01 & \text{if } r_t \in \mathcal{R}_{01} = (-1, 0] \\ 10 & \text{if } r_t \in \mathcal{R}_{10} = (0, 1] \\ 11 & \text{if } r_t \in \mathcal{R}_{11} = (1, \infty). \end{cases}$$

(This is not an optimal quantizer, merely convenient.) For each quantization bin, we can compute the likelihood that r_t falls in that region, given a particular input, as

$$P(q_t|a) = \int_{\mathcal{R}_{q_t}} f_R(r|a) \, dr.$$

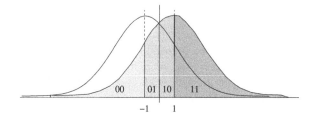

Figure 12.14: A 2-bit quantization of the soft-decision metric.

For example,

$$P(00|a = -1) = \int_{-\infty}^{-1} f_R(r| -1) \, dr = \frac{1}{2}.$$

Suppose the likelihoods for all quantized points are computed as follows.

$P(q_t|a)$ $q_t =$	00	01	10	11
$a = 1$	0.02	0.14	0.34	0.5
$a = -1$	0.5	0.34	0.14	0.02

The $-\log$ probabilities are

$-\log(P(q_t|a))$ $q_t =$	00	01	10	11
$a = 1$	3.9120	1.9661	1.0788	0.6931
$a = -1$	0.6931	1.0788	1.966	3.9120

The logarithms of these probabilities can be approximated as integer values by computing a transformation $a(\log P(q_t|a) - b)$. We use

$$-1.619(\log P(q_t|a) - \log P(00|1)),$$

where the factor $a = 1.619$ was found by a simple computer search and b was chosen to make the smallest value 0, resulting in the following metrics:

concodequant.m

$a(-\log(P(q_t|a) - b)$ $q_t =$	00	01	10	11
$a = 1$	5.211	2.061	0.624	0
$a = -1$	0	0.624	2.061	5.211

which can be rounded to

round $a(-\log(P(q_t|a) - b)$ $q_t =$	00	01	10	11
$a = 1$	5	2	1	0
$a = -1$	0	1	2	5

Although the signal is quantized into 2 bits, the metric requires 3 bits to represent it. With additional loss of coding gain, this could be reduced to 2 bits of metric (reducing the hardware required to accumulate the path metrics). For example, the first row of the metric table could be approximated as $3, 2, 1, 0$.

Note that, by the symmetry of the pdf and constellation, both rows of the table have the same values, so that in reality only a single row would need to be saved in an efficient hardware implementation. □

12.3.3.5   Synchronization Issues

The decoder must be synchronized with the stream of incoming data. If the decoder does not know which of the n symbols in a block initiates a branch of the trellis, then the data will be decoded with a very large number of errors. Fortunately, the decoding algorithm can detect this. If the data are correctly aligned with the trellis transitions, then with high probability, one (or possibly two) of the path metrics are significantly smaller than the other path metrics within a few stages of decoding. If this does not occur, the data can be shifted relative to the decoder and the decoding re-initialized. With at most n tries, the decoder can obtain symbol synchronization.

Many carrier tracking devices employed in communication systems experience a phase ambiguity. For a BPSK system, it is common that the phase is determined only up to $\pm\pi$, resulting in a sign change. For QPSK or QAM systems, the phase is often known only up to a multiple of $\pi/2$. The decoding algorithm can possibly help determine the absolute phase. For example, in a BPSK system if the all ones sequence is not a codeword, then for a given code sequence $\mathbf{c}$, $\mathbf{1} + \mathbf{c}$ cannot be a codeword. In this case, if decoding seems to indicate that no path is being decoded correctly (i.e., no path seems to emerge as a strong candidate compared to the other paths), then the receiver can complement all of its zeros and ones and decode again. If this decodes correctly, the receiver knows that it has the phase off by π. For a QPSK system, four different phase shifts could be examined to see when correct decoding behavior emerges.

12.4   Some Performance Results

Bit error rate characterization of convolutional codes is frequently accomplished by simulation and approximation. In this section, we present performance as a function of quantization, constraint length, window length, and codeword size. These results generally follow [196], but have been recomputed here.

Quantization of the metric was discussed in the previous section. In the results here, a simpler quantized metric is used. Assume that BPSK modulation is employed and that the transmitted signal amplitude a is normalized to ± 1. The received signal r is quantized to m bits, resulting in $M = 2^m$ different quantization levels, using uniformly spaced quantization thresholds. The distance between quantization thresholds is Δ. Figure 12.15 shows four-level quantization with $\Delta = 1$ and eight-level quantization using $\Delta = 0.5$ and $\Delta = \frac{1}{3}$. Rather than computing the log likelihood of the probability of falling in a decision region, in this approach the quantized q value itself is used as the branch metric if the signal amplitude 1 is sent, or the complement $M - q - 1$ is used if -1 is sent. The resulting integer branch metric is computed as shown in Table 12.1. This branch metric is clearly suboptimal, not being an affine transformation of the log likelihood. However, simulations have shown that it performs very close to optimal and it is widely used. Obviously, the performance depends upon the quantization threshold Δ employed. For the eight-level quantizer, the value $\Delta = 0.4$ is employed. For the 16-level quantizer, $\Delta = 0.25$ is used, and for the four-level quantizer, $\Delta = 1$ is used. We demonstrate below the dependence of the bit-error rate upon Δ.

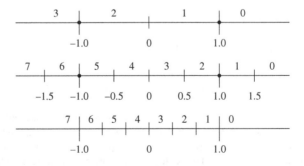

Figure 12.15: Quantization thresholds for four- and eight-level quantization.

Table 12.1: Quantized Branch Metrics Using Linear Quantization

Signal Amplitude	Quantization Level							
	0	1	2	3	4	5	6	7
	Branch Metric μ							
-1	7	6	5	4	3	2	1	0
1	0	1	2	3	4	5	6	7

Figure 12.16(a) shows the bit error rate as a function of SNR for codes with constraint lengths (here employing $K = 1 + \max \deg(g_j)$ as the constraint length) of $K = 3$, $K = 5$, and $K = 7$ using eight-level uniform quantization with $\Delta = 0.42$. The generators employed in this and the other simulations are the following:

K	$g_1(x)$	$g_2(x)$	d_{free}
3	$1 + x^2$	$1 + x + x^2$	5
4	$1 + x + x^3$	$1 + x + x^2 + x^3$	6
5	$1 + x^3 + x^4$	$1 + x + x^2 + x^4$	7
6	$1 + x^2 + x^4 + x^5$	$1 + x + x^2 + x^3 + x^5$	8
7	$1 + x^2 + x^3 + x^5 + x^6$	$1 + x + x^2 + x^3 + x^6$	10
8	$1 + x^2 + x^5 + x^6 + x^7$	$1 + x + x^2 + x^3 + x^4 + x^7$	10

The Viterbi decoder uses a window of 32 bits. As this figure demonstrates, the performance improves with the constraint length. Figure 12.16(b) shows 1-bit (hard) quantization for $K = 3$ through 8.

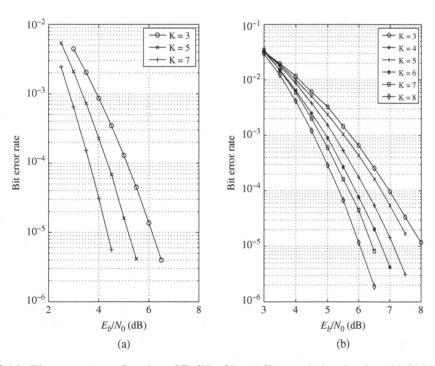

Figure 12.16: Bit error rate as a function of E_b/N_0 of $R = 1/2$ convolutional codes with 32 bit window decoding (following [196]). (a) Eight-level quantization, $K = 3, 5, 7$. (b) 1-bit (hard) quantization, $K = 3$ through 8.

Comparisons of the effect of the number of quantization levels and the decoding window are shown in Figure 12.17. In part (a), the performance of a code with $K = 5$ is shown with 2, 4, 8, and 16 quantization levels. As the figure demonstrates, there is very little improvement from 8 to 16 quantization levels; 8 is frequently chosen as an adequate performance/complexity tradeoff. In part (b), again a $K = 5$ code is characterized. In this case, the effect of the length of the decoding window is shown for two different quantization levels. With a decoding window of length 32, most of the achievable performance is attained.

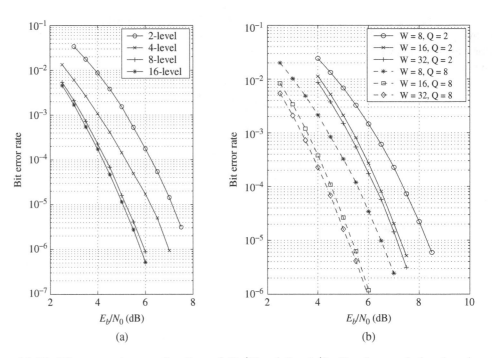

Figure 12.17: Bit error rate as a function of E_b/N_0 of $R = 1/2$, $K = 5$ convolutional code with different quantization levels and decoding window lengths (following [196]). (a) 2-, 4-, 8-, and 16-level quantization, decoding window 32; (b) Decoding window length $W = 8$, 16, and 32; quantization levels $Q = 2$ and 8.

Figure 12.18 shows the effect of the quantizer threshold spacing Δ on the performance for an eight-level quantizer with a $K = 5$, $R = 1/2$ code and a $K = 5$, $R = 1/4$ code. The plots are at SNRs of 3.3, 3.5, and 3.7 dB (reading from top to bottom) for the $R = 1/2$ code and 2.75, 2.98, and 3.19 dB (reading from top to bottom) for the $R = 1/4$ code. (These latter SNRs were selected to provide roughly comparable bit error rate for the two codes.) These were obtained by simulating, counting 20,000 bit errors at each point of data.

A convolutional code can be employed as a block code by simply truncating the sequence at a block length N (see Section 12.9). This truncation results in the last few bits in the codeword not having the same level of protection as the rest of the bits, a problem referred to as unequal error protection. The shorter the block length N, the higher the fraction of unequally protected bits, resulting in a higher bit error rate. Figure 12.19 shows BER for maximum likelihood decoding of convolutional codes truncated to blocks of length $N = 200$, $N = 2000$, as well as the "conventional" mode in which the codeword simply streams.

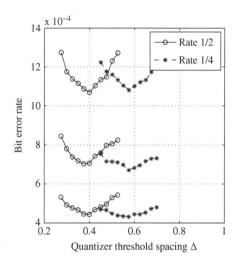

Figure 12.18: Viterbi algorithm bit error rate performance as a function of quantizer threshold spacing.

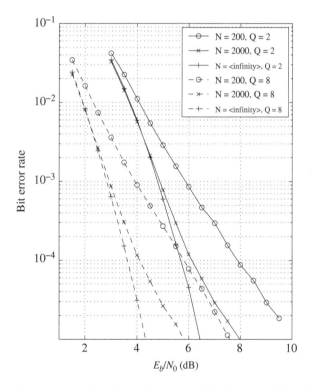

Figure 12.19: BER performance as a function of truncation block length, $N = 200$ and $N = 2000$, for two- and eight-level quantization.

12.5 Error Analysis for Convolutional Codes

While for block codes it is conventional to determine (or estimate) the probability of decoding a block incorrectly, the performance of convolutional codes is largely determined by the rate and the constraint length. It is not very meaningful to determine the probability of a block in error, since the block may be very long. It is more useful to explore the *probability of bit error*, or the *bit error rate*, which is the average number of message bits in error in a given sequence of bits divided by the total number of message bits in the sequence. We shall denote the bit error rate by P_b. In this section, we develop an upper bound for P_b [471].

Consider how errors can occur in the decoding process. The decision mechanism of the Viterbi algorithm operates when two paths join together. If two paths join together and the path with the lower (better) metric is actually the incorrect path, then an incorrect decision is made at that point. We call such an error a *node error* and say that the error event occurs at the place where the paths first diverged. We denote the probability of a node error as P_e. A node error, in turn, could lead to a number of input bits being decoded incorrectly.

Since the code is linear, it suffices to assume that the all-zero codeword is sent: With $d_H(\mathbf{r}, \mathbf{c})$ the Hamming distance between $\mathbf{c}$ and $\mathbf{r}$, we have $d_H(\mathbf{r}, \mathbf{c}) = d_H(\mathbf{r} + \mathbf{c}, \mathbf{c} + \mathbf{c}) = d_H(\mathbf{r} + \mathbf{c}, \mathbf{0})$. Consider the error events portrayed in Figure 12.20. The horizontal line across the top represents the all-zero path through the trellis. Suppose the path diverging from the all-zero path at a has a lower (better) metric when the paths merge at a'. This gives rise to an error event at a. Suppose that there are error events also at b and d. Now consider the path diverging at c: even if the metric is lower (better) at c', the diverging path from c may not ultimately be selected if its metric is worse than the path emerging at b. Similarly, the path emerging at d may not necessarily be selected, since the path merging at e may take precedence. This overlapping of decision paths makes the exact analysis of the bit error rate difficult. We must be content with bounds and approximations.

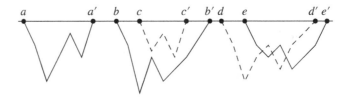

Figure 12.20: Error events due to merging paths.

The following example illustrates some of these issues.

Example 12.27   Consider again the convolutional code from Example 12.1, with

$$G(x) = \left[1 + x^2, 1 + x + x^2 \right].$$

Suppose that the input sequence is $\mathbf{x} = [0, 0, 0, 0, \ldots]$ with the resulting transmitted sequence $\mathbf{c} = [00, 00, 00, 00, \ldots]$, but that the received sequence after transmission through a BSC is $\mathbf{r} = [11, 01, 00, \ldots]$. A portion of the decoding trellis for this code is shown in Figure 12.21. After three stages of the trellis when the paths merge, the metric for the lower path (shown as a dashed line) is lower than the metric for the all-zero path (the solid line). Accordingly, the Viterbi algorithm selects the erroneous path, resulting in a node error at the first node. However, while the decision results in three incorrect branches on the path through the trellis, the input sequence corresponding to this selected path is $[1, 0, 0]$, so that only 1bit is incorrectly decoded due to this decision.

As the figure shows, there is a path of metric 5 which deviates from the all-zero path. The probability of incorrectly selecting this path is denoted as P_5. This error occurs when the received sequence has three or more errors (1s) in it. In general, we denote

$$P_d = \text{Probability of a decoding error on a path of metric } d.$$

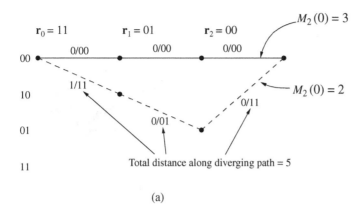

(a)

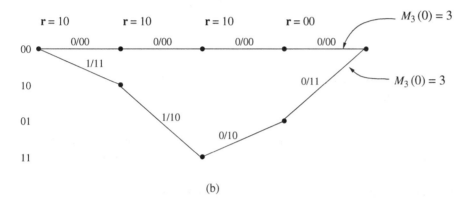

(b)

Figure 12.21: Two decoding examples. (a) Diverging path of distance 5; (b) diverging path of distance 6.

For a deviating path of odd weight, there will be an error if more than half of the bits are in error. The probability of this event for a BSC with crossover probability p_c is

$$P_d = \sum_{i=(d+1)/2}^{d} \binom{d}{i} p_c^i (1 - p_c)^{d-i} \quad \text{(with } d \text{ odd)}. \tag{12.20}$$

Suppose now the received signal is $\mathbf{r} = [10, 10, 10, 00]$. Then the trellis appears as in Figure 12.21(b). In this case, the path metrics are equal; one-half of the time the decoder chooses the wrong path. If the incorrect path is chosen, the decoded input bits would be $[1, 1, 0, 0]$, with 2 bits incorrectly decoded. The probability of the event of choosing the incorrect path in this case is P_6, where

$$P_d = \frac{1}{2} \binom{d}{d/2} p_c^{d/2} (1 - p_c)^{d/2} + \sum_{i=d/2+1}^{d} \binom{d}{i} p_c^i (1 - p_c)^{d-i} \quad \text{(with } d \text{ even)} \tag{12.21}$$

is the probability that more than half of the bits are in error, plus $\frac{1}{2}$ times the probability that exactly half the bits are in error. □

We can glean the following information from this example:

- Error events can occur in the decoding algorithm when paths merge together. If the erroneous path has lower (better) path metric than the correct path, the algorithm selects it.

- Merging paths may be of different lengths (number of stages).

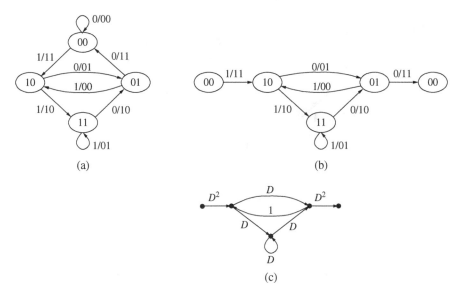

Figure 12.22: The state diagram and graph for diverging/remerging paths. (a) State diagram; (b) split state 0; (c) output weight irepresented by Di.

- This trellis has a shortest path of metric 5 (three stages long) which diverges from the all-zero path then remerges. We say there is an error path of metric 5. There is also an error path of metric 6 (four stages long) which deviates then remerges.

- When an error path is selected, the number of *input* bits that are erroneously decoded depends on the particular path.

- The probability of a particular error event can be calculated and is denoted as P_d.

- The error path of metric 5 was not disjoint of the error path of metric 6, since they both share a branch.

In the following sections, we first describe how to enumerate the paths through the trellis. Then bounds on the probability of node error and the bit error rate are obtained by invoking the union bound.

12.5.1 Enumerating Paths Through the Trellis

In computing (or bounding) the overall probability of decoder error, it is expedient to have a method of enumerating all the paths through the trellis. This initially daunting task is aided somewhat by the observation that, for the purposes of computing the probability of error, since the convolutional code is linear it is sufficient to consider only those paths which diverge from the all-zero path then remerge.

We develop a transfer function method which enumerates all the paths that diverge from the all-zero path then remerge. This transfer function is called the **path enumerator**. We demonstrate the technique for the particular code we have been examining.

Example 12.28   Figure 12.22(a) shows the state diagram for the encoder of Example 12.1. In Figure 12.22(b), the 00 state has been "split," or duplicated. Furthermore, the transition from state 00 to state 00 has been omitted, since we are interested only in paths which diverge from the 00 state. Any path through the graph in Figure 12.22(b) from the 00 node on the left to the 00 node on the right represents a path which diverges from the all-zero path then remerges. In Figure 12.22(c), the output codeword of weight i along each edge is represented using D^i. (For example, an output of 11 is represented by D^2; an output of 10 is represented by $D^1 = D$ and an output of 00 is represented by $D^0 = 1$.) For convenience the state labels have been removed.

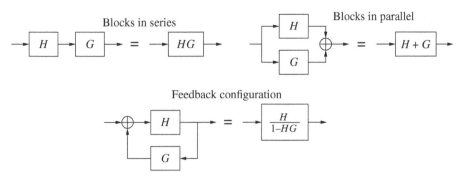

Figure 12.23: Rules for simplification of flow graphs.

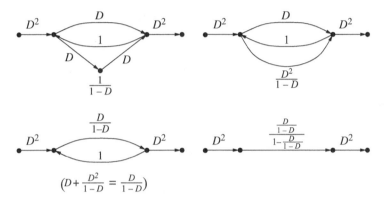

Figure 12.24: Steps simplifying the flow graph for a convolutional code.

The labels on the edges in the graph are to be thought of as transfer functions. We now employ the conventional rules for flow graph simplification as summarized in Figure 12.23.

- Blocks in series multiply the transfer functions.
- Blocks in parallel add the transfer functions.
- Blocks in feedback configuration employ the rule "forward gain over 1 minus loop gain."

(For a thorough discussion on more complicated flow graphs, see [294].) For the state diagram of Figure 12.22, we take each node as a summing node. The sequence of steps by successively applying the simplification rules is shown in Figure 12.24. Simplifying the final diagram, we find

$$T(D) = D^2 \frac{\frac{D}{1-D}}{1 - \frac{D}{1-D}} D^2 = \frac{D^5}{1 - 2D}.$$

To interpret this, we use the formal series expansion[4] (check by long division)

$$\boxed{\frac{1}{1-D} = 1 + D + D^2 + D^3 + \cdots .}$$

Expanding $T(D)$, we find

$$T(D) = D^5(1 + 2D + (2D)^2 + (2D)^3 + \cdots) = D^5 + 2D^6 + 4D^7 + \cdots + 2^k D^{k+5} + \cdots .$$

---

[4] A formal series is an infinite series that is obtained by symbolic manipulation, without particular regard to convergence.

Interpreting this, we see that we have:

- One diverging/remerging error path at metric 5 from the all-zero path;
- Two error paths of metric 6;
- Four error paths of metric 7, etc.

Furthermore, the shortest error path has metric 5.   □

Definition 12.29 The minimum metric of a path diverging from then remerging to the all-zero path is called the **free distance** of the convolutional code, and is denoted as d_{free}. The number of paths at that metric is denoted as $a(d_{\text{free}}) = N_{\text{free}}$.   □

The number of paths at a distance d is denoted as $a(d)$. In general, we write

$$T(D) = \sum_{d=d_{\text{free}}}^{\infty} a(d)D^d,$$

where $a(d_{\text{free}}) = N_{\text{free}}$.

Additional information about the paths in the trellis can be obtained with a more expressive transfer function. We label each path with three variables: D^i, where i is the output code weight; N^i, where i is the input weight; and L, to account for the length of the branch.

Example 12.30 Returning to the state diagram of Figure 12.22, we obtain the labeled diagram in Figure 12.25. Using the same rules for block diagram simplification as previously, the transfer function for this diagram is

$$T(D,N,L) = \frac{D^5 L^3 N}{1 - DLN(1 + L)}. \tag{12.22}$$

Expanding this as a formal series, we have

$$T(D,N,L) = D^5 L^3 N + D^6 L^4 (1 + L) N^2 + D^7 L^5 (1 + L)^2 N^3 + \cdots , \tag{12.23}$$

which has the following interpretation:

- There is one error path of metric 5 which is three branches long (from L^3) and one input bit is 1 (from N^1) along that path.

- There are two error paths of metric 6: one of them is four branches long and the other is five branches long. Along both of them, there are two input bits that are 1.

- There are four error paths of metric 7. One of them is five branches long; two of them are six branches long; and one is seven branches long. Along each of these, there are three input bits that are 1.

- Etc.   □

Clearly, we can obtain the simpler transfer function by $T(D) = T(D,N,L)|_{N=1,L=1}$. When we don't care to keep track of the number of branches, we write

$$T(D,N) = T(D,N,L)|_{L=1}.$$

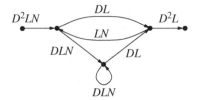

Figure 12.25: State diagram labeled with output weight, input weight, and branch length.

12.5.1.1 Enumerating on More Complicated Graphs: Mason's Rule

Some graphs are more complicated than the three rules introduced above can accommodate. A more general approach is Mason's rule [294]. Its generality leads to a rather complicated notation, which we summarize here and illustrate by example (not by proof) [483]. We will enumerate all paths from the 0 state to the 0 state in the state diagram shown in Figure 12.26.

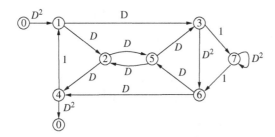

Figure 12.26: A state diagram to be enumerated.

A **loop** is a sequence of states which starts and ends in the same state, but otherwise does not enter any state more than once. We will say that a **forward loop** is a loop that starts and stops in state 0. A set of loops is **nontouching** if they have no vertices in common. Thus, $\{0, 1, 2, 4, 0\}$ is a forward loop. The loop $\{3, 6, 5, 3\}$ is a loop that does not touch this forward loop. The set of all forward loops in the graph is denoted as $L = \{L_1, L_2, \dots\}$. The corresponding set of path gains is denoted as $F = \{F_1, F_2, \dots\}$. Let $\mathcal{L} = \{\mathcal{L}_1, \mathcal{L}_2, \dots\}$ denote the set of loops in the graph that does *not* contain the vertex 0. Let $\mathcal{F} = \{\mathcal{F}_1, \mathcal{F}_2, \dots\}$ be the set of corresponding path gains. (Determining all the loops requires some care.) For the graph in Figure 12.26, the forward loops and their gains are

$$
\begin{aligned}
L_1 &: \{0, 1, 3, 7, 6, 5, 2, 4, 0\} & F_1 &= D^8 \\
L_2 &: \{0, 1, 3, 7, 6, 4, 0\} & F_2 &= D^6 \\
L_3 &: \{0, 1, 3, 6, 5, 2, 4, 0\} & F_3 &= D^{10} \\
L_4 &: \{0, 1, 3, 6, 4, 0\} & F_4 &= D^8 \\
L_5 &: \{0, 1, 2, 5, 3, 7, 6, 4, 0\} & F_5 &= D^8 \\
L_6 &: \{0, 1, 2, 5, 3, 6, 4, 0\} & F_6 &= D^{10} \\
L_7 &: \{0, 1, 2, 4, 0\} & F_7 &= D^6
\end{aligned}
$$

and the other loops and their gains are

$$
\begin{aligned}
\mathcal{L}_1 &: & \{1, 3, 7, 6, 5, 2, 4, 1\} & & \mathcal{F}_1 &= D^4 \\
\mathcal{L}_2 &: & \{1, 3, 7, 6, 4, 1\} & & \mathcal{F}_2 &= D^2 \\
\mathcal{L}_3 &: & \{1, 3, 6, 5, 2, 4, 1\} & & \mathcal{F}_3 &= D^6 \\
\mathcal{L}_4 &: & \{1, 3, 6, 4, 1\} & & \mathcal{F}_4 &= D^4 \\
\mathcal{L}_5 &: & \{1, 2, 5, 3, 7, 6, 4, 1\} & & \mathcal{F}_5 &= D^4 \\
\mathcal{L}_6 &: & \{1, 2, 5, 3, 6, 4, 1\} & & \mathcal{F}_6 &= D^6 \\
\mathcal{L}_7 &: & \{1, 2, 4, 1\} & & \mathcal{F}_7 &= D^2 \\
\mathcal{L}_8 &: & \{2, 5, 2\} & & \mathcal{F}_8 &= D^2 \\
\mathcal{L}_9 &: & \{3, 7, 6, 5, 3\} & & \mathcal{F}_9 &= D^2 \\
\mathcal{L}_{10} &: & \{3, 6, 5, 3\} & & \mathcal{F}_{10} &= D^4 \\
\mathcal{L}_{11} &: & \{7, 7\} & & \mathcal{F}_{11} &= D^2
\end{aligned}
$$

We also need to identify the *pairs* of nontouching loops in $\mathcal{L}$, the triples of nontouching loops in $\mathcal{L}$, etc., and their corresponding product gains. There are ten pairs of nontouching loops in $\mathcal{L}$:

$$
\begin{array}{llll}
(\mathcal{L}_2, \mathcal{L}_8) & \mathcal{F}_2\mathcal{F}_8 = D^4 & (\mathcal{L}_3, \mathcal{L}_{11}) & \mathcal{F}_3\mathcal{F}_{11} = D^8 \\
(\mathcal{L}_4, \mathcal{L}_8) & \mathcal{F}_4\mathcal{F}_8 = D^6 & (\mathcal{L}_4, \mathcal{L}_{11}) & \mathcal{F}_4\mathcal{F}_{11} = D^6 \\
(\mathcal{L}_6, \mathcal{L}_{11}) & \mathcal{F}_6\mathcal{F}_{11} = D^8 & (\mathcal{L}_7, \mathcal{L}_9) & \mathcal{F}_7\mathcal{F}_9 = D^4 \\
(\mathcal{L}_7, \mathcal{L}_{10}) & \mathcal{F}_7\mathcal{F}_{10} = D^6 & (\mathcal{L}_7, \mathcal{L}_{11}) & \mathcal{F}_7\mathcal{F}_{11} = D^4 \\
(\mathcal{L}_8, \mathcal{L}_{11}) & \mathcal{F}_8\mathcal{F}_{11} = D^4 & (\mathcal{L}_{10}, \mathcal{L}_{11}) & \mathcal{F}_{10}\mathcal{F}_{11} = D^6
\end{array}
$$

There are two **triplets** of nontouching loops in $\mathcal{L}$,

$$
(\mathcal{L}_4, \mathcal{L}_8, \mathcal{L}_{11}) \quad \mathcal{F}_4\mathcal{F}_8\mathcal{F}_{11} = D^8 \qquad (\mathcal{L}_7, \mathcal{L}_{10}, \mathcal{L}_{11}) \quad \mathcal{F}_7\mathcal{F}_{10}\mathcal{F}_{11} = D^8
$$

but no sets of four or more nontouching loops in $\mathcal{L}$.

With these sets collected, we define the **graph determinant** Δ as

$$
\Delta = 1 - \sum_{\mathcal{L}_i} \mathcal{F}_i + \sum_{(\mathcal{L}_i, \mathcal{L}_j)} \mathcal{F}_i\mathcal{F}_j - \sum_{(\mathcal{L}_i, \mathcal{L}_j, \mathcal{L}_k)} \mathcal{F}_i\mathcal{F}_j\mathcal{F}_k + \cdots,
$$

where the first sum is over all the loops in $\mathcal{L}$, the second sum is over all pairs of nontouching loops in $\mathcal{L}$, the third sum is over all triplets of nontouching loops in $\mathcal{L}$, and so forth.

We also define the **graph cofactor of the forward path** L_i, denoted as Δ_i, which is similar to the graph determinant except that all loops touching L_i are removed from the summations. This can be written as

$$
\Delta_i = 1 - \sum_{(L_i, \mathcal{L}_j)} \mathcal{F}_j + \sum_{(L_i, \mathcal{L}_j, \mathcal{L}_k)} \mathcal{F}_j\mathcal{F}_k - \sum_{(L_i, \mathcal{L}_j, \mathcal{L}_k, \mathcal{L}_l)} \mathcal{F}_j\mathcal{F}_k\mathcal{F}_l + \cdots
$$

With this notation we finally can express **Mason's rule** for the transfer function through the graph:

$$
T(D) = \frac{\sum_l F_l \Delta_l}{\Delta}, \tag{12.24}
$$

where the sum is over all forward paths.

For our example, we have

$$
\Delta_1 = 1 \quad \Delta_5 = 1
$$

(since there are no loops that do not contain vertices in the forward paths L_1 and L_5),

$$
\Delta_3 = \Delta_6 = 1 - \mathcal{F}_{11} = 1 - D^2
$$

(since L_3 and L_6 do not cross vertex 7 and so do not touch loop $\mathcal{L}_{11}$),

$$
\Delta_2 = 1 - \mathcal{F}_8 = 1 - D^2
$$

(since L_2 does not touch $\mathcal{L}_8$ but it does touch all other loops), and

$$
\Delta_4 = 1 - (\mathcal{F}_8 + \mathcal{F}_{11}) + \mathcal{F}_8\mathcal{F}_{11} = 1 - 2D^2 + D^4
$$

$$
\Delta_7 = 1 - (\mathcal{F}_9 + \mathcal{F}_{10} + \mathcal{F}_{11}) + (\mathcal{F}_{10}\mathcal{F}_{11}) = 1 - 2D^2 - D^4 + D^6.
$$

The graph determinant is

$$
\begin{aligned}
\Delta &= 1 - (D^4 + D^2 + D^6 + D^4 + D^4 + D^6 + D^2 + D^2 + D^2 + D^4 + D^2) \\
&\quad + (D^4 + D^8 + D^6 + D^6 + D^8 + D^4 + D^6 + D^4 + D^4 + D^6) - (D^8 + D^8) \\
&= 1 - 5D^2 + 2D^6.
\end{aligned}
$$

Finally, using (12.24), we obtain

$$
T(D) = \frac{2D^6 - D^{10}}{1 - 5D^2 + 2D^6}.
$$

12.5.2 Characterizing Node Error Probability P_e and Bit Error Rate P_b

We now return to the question of the probability of error for convolutional codes. Let P_j denote the set of all error paths that diverge from node j of the all-zero path in the trellis then remerge and let $\mathbf{p}_{i,j} \in P_j$ be one of these paths. Let $\Delta M(\mathbf{p}_{i,j}, 0)$ denote the difference between the metric accumulated along path $\mathbf{p}_{i,j}$ and the all-zero path. An error event at node j occurs due to path $\mathbf{p}_{i,j}$ if $\Delta M(\mathbf{p}_{i,j}, 0) < 0$. Letting $P_e(j)$ denote the probability of an error event at node j, we have

$$P_e(j) \leq \Pr\left[\bigcup_i \{\Delta M(\mathbf{p}_{i,j}, 0) \leq 0\} \right], \tag{12.25}$$

where the inequality follows since an error might not occur when $\Delta M(\mathbf{p}_{i,j}, 0) = 0$. The paths $\mathbf{p}_{i,j} \in P_j$ are not all disjoint since they may share branches, so the events $\{\Delta M(\mathbf{p}_{i,j}, 0) \leq 0\}$ are not disjoint. This makes (12.25) very difficult to compute exactly. However, it can be upper bounded by the union bound (see Box 1.1 in Chapter 1) as

$$P_e(j) \leq \sum_i \Pr(\Delta M(\mathbf{p}_{i,j}, 0) \leq 0). \tag{12.26}$$

Each term in this summation is now a *pairwise* event between the paths $\mathbf{p}_{i,j}$ and the all-zero path.

We develop expressions or bounds on the pairwise events in (12.26) for the case that the channel is memoryless. (For example, we have already seen that for the BSC, the probability P_d developed in (12.20) and (12.21) is the probability of the pairwise events in question.) For a memoryless channel, $\Delta M(\mathbf{p}_{i,j}, 0)$ depends only on those branches for which $\mathbf{p}_{i,j}$ is nonzero. Let d be the Hamming weight of $\mathbf{p}_{i,j}$ and let P_d be the probability of the event that this path has a lower (better) metric than the all-zero path. Let $a(d)$ be the number of paths at a distance d from the all-zero path. The probability of a node error event can now be written as follows:

$$P_e(j) \leq \sum_{d=d_{\text{free}}}^{\infty} \Pr(\text{error caused by any of the } a(d) \text{ incorrect paths at distance } d)$$

$$= \sum_{d=d_{\text{free}}}^{\infty} a(d) P_d. \tag{12.27}$$

Any further specification on $P_e(j)$ requires characterization of P_d. We show below that bounds on P_d can be written in the form

$$P_d < Z^d \tag{12.28}$$

for some channel-dependent function Z and develop explicit expressions for Z for the BSC and AWGN channel. For now, we simply express the results in terms of Z. With this bound, we can write

$$P_e(j) < \sum_{d=d_{\text{free}}}^{\infty} a(d) Z^d.$$

Recalling that the path enumerator for the encoder is $T(D) = \sum_{d=d_{\text{free}}}^{\infty} a(d) D^d$, we obtain a closed-form expression for the bound:

$$P_e(j) < T(D)|_{D=Z}. \tag{12.29}$$

The bound (12.29) is a bound on the probability of a node error. From this, a bound on the bit error rate can be obtained by enumerating the number of bits in error for each node error. The derivative

$$\frac{\partial}{\partial N} T(D, N)$$

brings exponents of N down as multipliers for each term in the series.

Example 12.31 For the weight enumerator of Example 12.28,

$$T(D,N) = D^5 N + 2D^6 N^2 + 4D^7 N^3 + \cdots,$$

we have

$$\frac{\partial}{\partial N} T(D,N) = (1)D^5 + (2)2D^6 N + (3)4D^7 N^2 + \cdots$$

so that a node error on the error path of metric 5 contributes 1 bit of error; a node error on either of the error paths of metric 6 contributes 2 bits of error, and so forth. □

The average number of bits in error along the branches of the trellis is

$$\left. \frac{\partial}{\partial N} T(D,N) \right|_{N=1, D=Z}.$$

For a rate $R = k/n$ code, each branch corresponds to k message bits, so that

$$P_b < \left. \frac{1}{k} \frac{\partial}{\partial N} T(D,N) \right|_{N=1, D=Z}. \tag{12.30}$$

An approximation on the probability of bit error can be obtained by retaining only the first term of the series in (12.30) and using the bound $P_d < Z^d$. To retain only the first term of the series, write

$$T(D,N) = D^{d_{\text{free}}}(N^{n_1} + N^{n_2} + \cdots) + \cdots.$$

Then

$$\left. \frac{\partial}{\partial N} T(D,N) \right|_{N=1} = D^{d_{\text{free}}}(n_1 + n_2 + \cdots) + \cdots.$$

The number $n_1 + n_2 + \cdots$ is the number of nonzero message bits associated with codewords of weight d_{free}. Let us denote this number as $b_{d_{\text{dfree}}} = n_1 + n_2 + \cdots$.

Example 12.32 Suppose

$$T(D,N) = D^6 N + D^6 N^3 + 3D^8 N + 5D^8 N^4 + \cdots.$$

Then there are two codewords of weight 6: one corresponding to a message of weight 1 and one corresponding to a message of weight 3. We could write

$$T(D,N) = D^6(N + N^3) + 3D^8 N + 5D^8 N^4 + \cdots.$$

Then $b_6 = 1 + 3 = 4$. □

Then the approximation is

$$P_b \approx \left. \frac{1}{k} b_{d_{\text{free}}} D^{d_{\text{free}}} \right|_{D=Z}. \tag{12.31}$$

A lower bound can be found as

$$P_b > \frac{1}{k} b_{d_{\text{free}}} P_{d_{\text{free}}}, \tag{12.32}$$

where $P_{d_{\text{dfree}}}$ is P_d at $d = d_{\text{free}}$.

Example 12.33 For

$$T(D,N) = \frac{D^5}{1 - 2DN} = D^5 N + 2D^6 N^2 + 4D^7 N^3 + \cdots$$

the derivative is

$$\frac{\partial}{\partial N} T(D,N) = D^5 + 4D^6 N + 12D^7 N^2 + \cdots$$

so the probability of error is approximated by

$$P_b \approx Z^5$$

or lower bounded by

$$P_b > P_5.$$

$\square$

12.5.3   A Bound on P_d for Discrete Channels

In this section, we develop a bound on P_d for discrete channels such as the BSC [[483], Section 12.3.1]. Let $p(r_i|1)$ denote the likelihood of the received signal r_i, given that the symbol corresponding to 1 was sent through the channel; similarly $p(r_i|0)$. Then

$$P_d = P(\Delta M(\mathbf{p}_{i,j}, 0) \leq 0 \quad \text{and} \quad d_H(\mathbf{p}_{i,j}, \mathbf{0}) = d)$$

$$= P[\sum_{i=1}^{d} \log P(r_i|1) - \sum_{i=1}^{d} \log P(r_i|0) \geq 0],$$

where $\{r_1, r_2, \ldots, r_d\}$ are the received signals at the d coordinates where $\mathbf{p}_{i,j}$ is nonzero. Continuing,

$$P_d = P\left[\sum_{i=1}^{d} \log \frac{p(r_i|1)}{p(r_i|0)} \geq 0\right] = P\left[\prod_{i=1}^{d} \frac{p(r_i|1)}{p(r_i|0)} \geq 1\right].$$

Let R' be the set of vectors of elements $\mathbf{r} = (r_1, r_2, \ldots, r_d)$ such that

$$\prod_{i=1}^{d} \frac{p(r_i|1)}{p(r_i|0)} \geq 1. \tag{12.33}$$

(For example, for $d = 5$ over the BSC, R' is the set of vectors for which 3 or 4 or 5 of the r_i are equal to 1.) The probability of any one of these elements is $\prod_{i=1}^{d} p(r_i|0)$, since we are assuming that all zeros are sent. Thus, the probability of any vector in R' is $\prod_{i=1}^{d} p(r_i|0)$. The probability P_d can be obtained by summing over all the vectors in R':

$$P_d = \sum_{\mathbf{r} \in R'} \prod_{i=1}^{d} p(r_i|0).$$

Since the left-hand side of (12.33) is ≥ 1, we have

$$P_d \leq \sum_{\mathbf{r} \in R'} \prod_{i=1}^{d} p(r_i|0) \left[\frac{p(r_i|1)}{p(r_i|0)}\right]^s$$

for any s such that $0 \leq s < 1$. The tightest bound is obtained by minimizing with respect to s:

$$P_d \leq \min_{0 \leq s < 1} \sum_{\mathbf{r} \in R'} \prod_{i=1}^{d} p(r_i|0) \left[\frac{p(r_i|1)}{p(r_i|0)}\right]^s = \min_{0 \leq s < 1} \sum_{\mathbf{r} \in R'} \prod_{i=1}^{d} p(r_i|0)^{1-s} p(r_i|1)^s.$$

This is made more tractable (and larger) by summing over the set R of *all* sequences $(r_1, r_2, \ldots, r_d)$:

$$P_d < \min_{0 \leq s < 1} \sum_{\mathbf{r} \in R} \prod_{i=1}^{d} p(r_i|0)^{1-s} p(r_i|1)^s.$$

The order of summation and product can be reversed, resulting in

$$P_d < \min_{0 \leq s < 1} \prod_{i=1}^{d} \sum_{r_i} p(r_i|0)^{1-s} p(r_i|1)^s.$$

This is known as the **Chernoff bound**. Let

$$Z = \min_{0 \le s < 1} \sum_{r_i} p(r_i|0)^{1-s} p(r_i|1)^s. \tag{12.34}$$

Then $P_d < Z^d$.

If the channel is symmetric, then by symmetry arguments the minimum must occur when $s = 1/2$. Then $Z = \sqrt{p(r_i|0)p(r_i|1)}$ and

$$P_d < \prod_{i=1}^{d} \sum_{r_i} \sqrt{p(r_i|0)p(r_i|1)}. \tag{12.35}$$

This bound is known as the **Bhattacharya bound**.

Example 12.34   Suppose the encoder with $T(D,N) = \frac{D^5 N}{1 - 2DN}$ is used in conjunction with an asymmetric channel having the following transition probabilities:

$P(r\|a)$	$a = 0$	$a = 1$
$r = 0$	0.98	0.003
$r = 1$	0.02	0.997.

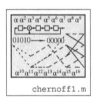

chernoff1.m

Then

$$Z = \min_{0 \le s < 1} \sum_{r_i} p(r_i|0)^{1-s} p(r_i|1)^s$$

$$= p(0|0)^{1-s} p(0|1)^s + p(1|0)^{1-s} p(1|1)^s$$

$$= (0.98)^{1-s}(0.003)^s + (0.02)^{1-s}(0.997)^s.$$

The minimum value can be found numerically as $Z = 0.1884$, which occurs when $s = 0.442$.

The node error probability can be bounded using (12.29) as

$$P_e(j) < \left. \frac{D^5 N}{1 - 2DN} \right|_{N=1, D=0.1884} = 3.8 \times 10^{-4}$$

and the bit error rate is bounded using (12.30) as

$$P_b < \left. \frac{1}{k} \frac{\partial}{\partial N} \frac{D^5 N}{1 - 2DN} \right|_{N=1, D=0.1884} = 6.1 \times 10^{-4}.$$

The approximate bit error rate from (12.31) is

$$P_b \approx \left. \frac{1}{k} b_{d_{\text{free}}} D^{d_{\text{free}}} \right|_{D=0.1884} = 2.4 \times 10^{-4},$$

where $d_{\text{free}} = 5$ and $b_{d_{\text{free}}} = 1$.   □

12.5.3.1   Performance Bound on the BSC

For the BSC with crossover probability p_c, (12.35) can be written as follows:

$$P_d < \prod_{i=1}^{d} \sum_{r_i} \sqrt{p(r_i|0)p(r_i|1)} = \prod_{i=1}^{d} (\sqrt{p(0|0)p(0|1)} + \sqrt{P(1|0)p(1|1)})$$

$$= \prod_{i=1}^{d} 2\sqrt{p_c(1-p_c)} = [4p_c(1-p_c)]^{d/2} = \sqrt{4p_c(1-p_c)}^d.$$

The expression Z in (12.28) is thus $Z = [4p_c(1-p_c)]^{1/2}$.

Let us now return to $P_e(j)$. Inserting this bound on P_d in (12.27), we obtain

$$P_e(j) < \sum_{d=d_{\text{free}}}^{\infty} a(d) P_d < \sum_{d=d_{\text{free}}}^{\infty} a(d) \sqrt{4 p_c (1 - p_c)}^d.$$

The closed-form expression for the bound on the probability of error is

$$P_e(j) < T(D)|_{D=\sqrt{4 p_c(1-p_c)}}. \tag{12.36}$$

The bound on the bit error rate of (12.30) is

$$P_b < \frac{1}{k} \frac{\partial}{\partial N} T(D,N)\bigg|_{N=1, D=\sqrt{4 p_c(1-p_c)}}. \tag{12.37}$$

A lower bound can be obtained using (12.32)

$$P_b > \frac{1}{k} b_{d_{\text{free}}} P_{d_{\text{free}}}, \tag{12.38}$$

where $P_{d_{\text{free}}}$ can be computed using (12.20) and (12.21).

12.5.4 A Bound on P_d for BPSK Signaling Over the AWGN Channel

Suppose that the coded bits $c_t^{(i)}$ are mapped to a BPSK signal constellation by $a_t^{(i)} = \sqrt{E_c}(2 c_t^{(i)} - 1)$, where E_c is the coded signal energy, with $E_c = R E_b$, and E_b is the energy per message bit. If the all-zero sequence is sent, then the sequence of amplitudes $(-\sqrt{E_c}, -\sqrt{E_c}, -\sqrt{E_c}, \ldots)$ is sent. A sequence which deviates from this path in d locations is at a squared distance $2 d E_c$ from it. Then P_d is the probability that a d-symbol sequence is decoded incorrectly, compared to the sequence for all-zero transmission. That is, it is the problem of distinguishing $\mathbf{p}_1 = (-\sqrt{E_c}, -\sqrt{E_c}, -\sqrt{E_c}, \ldots, -\sqrt{E_c})$ from $\mathbf{p}_2 = (\sqrt{E_c}, \sqrt{E_c}, \sqrt{E_c}, \ldots, \sqrt{E_c})$, where these vectors each have d elements. The Euclidean distance between these two points is

$$d_{\text{Euclidean}}(\mathbf{p}_1, \mathbf{p}_2) = 2[d E_c]^{1/2}.$$

The probability of a detection error is (see Section 1.5.4)

$$P_d = Q\left(\sqrt{\frac{2 d E_c}{N_0}}\right).$$

To express this in the form Z^d (for use in the bound (12.29)), use the bound $Q(x) < \frac{1}{2} e^{-x^2/2}$ (see Exercise 1.12). We thus obtain

$$P_d < \frac{1}{2} e^{-d E_c/N_0}.$$

Then (12.29) and (12.30) give

$$P_e(j) < \frac{1}{2} T(D)\bigg|_{D=e^{-E_c/N_0}} \qquad P_b < \frac{1}{2} \frac{1}{k} \frac{\partial}{\partial N} T(D,N)\bigg|_{N=1, D=e^{-E_c/N_0}}. \tag{12.39}$$

Another bound on the Q function is [468]

$$Q(\sqrt{x+y}) \le Q(\sqrt{x}) e^{-y/2}, \quad x \ge 0, y \ge 0. \tag{12.40}$$

Then

$$P_d = Q\left(\sqrt{\frac{2 d E_c}{N_0}}\right) = Q\left(\sqrt{\frac{2 d_{\text{free}} E_c}{N_0} + \frac{2(d - d_{\text{free}}) E_c}{N_0}}\right)$$

$$\le Q\left(\sqrt{\frac{2 d_{\text{free}} E_c}{N_0}}\right) e^{d_{\text{free}} E_c/N_0} e^{-d E_c/N_0} = Q\left(\sqrt{\frac{2 d_{\text{free}} E_c}{N_0}}\right) e^{d_{\text{free}} E_c/N_0} (e^{-E_c/N_0})^d.$$

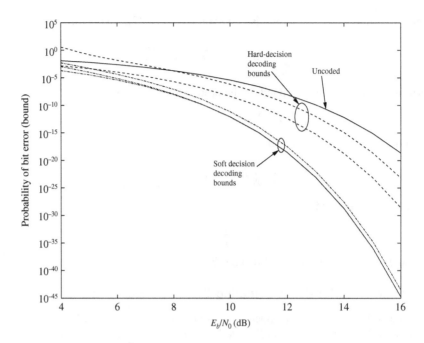

Figure 12.27: Performance of a $(2, 1)$ convolutional code with $d_{\text{free}} = 5$.

Then

$$P_e(j) \leq e^{d_{\text{free}} E_c / N_0} Q\left(\sqrt{\frac{2d_{\text{free}} E_c}{N_0}}\right) T(D) \Bigg|_{D = e^{-E_c / N_0}}$$

and

$$P_b \leq \frac{1}{k} e^{d_{\text{free}} E_c / N_0} Q\left(\sqrt{\frac{2d_{\text{free}} E_c}{N_0}}\right) \frac{\partial}{\partial N} T(D, N) \Bigg|_{N=1, D = e^{-E_c / N_0}}. \tag{12.41}$$

A lower bound can be obtained using (12.32)

$$P_b > \frac{1}{k} b_{d_{\text{free}}} Q\left(\sqrt{\frac{2d_{\text{free}} E_c}{N_0}}\right). \tag{12.42}$$

Example 12.35 For the $R = 1/2$ code of Example 12.1 with $d_{\text{free}} = 5$, Figure 12.27 shows the bounds on the probability of bit error of the code for both hard- and soft-decision decoders compared with uncoded performance.

For soft decoding, the lower bound and the upper bound of (12.41) approach each other for high signal-to-noise ratios, so the bounds are asymptotically tight. (The bound of (12.39) is looser.) Gains of approximately 4 dB at high SNR are evident for soft-decision decoding.

The hard-decision decoding bounds are clearly not as tight. Also, there is approximately 3 dB less coding gain for the hard-decision decoder. □

12.5.5 Asymptotic Coding Gain

The lower bound for the probability of bit error for the coded signal (using soft-decision decoding)

$$P_b > \frac{1}{k} a(d_{\text{free}}) n_{d_{\text{free}}} Q\left(\sqrt{\frac{2d_{\text{free}} E_c}{N_0}} \right)$$

can be approximated using the bound $Q(x) < \frac{1}{2} e^{-x^2/2}$ as

$$P_b \approx \frac{1}{k}\frac{1}{2} a(d_{\text{free}}) n_{d_{\text{free}}} e^{-d_{\text{free}} E_c/N_0}. \tag{12.43}$$

The probability of bit error for uncoded transmission is

$$P_b = Q\left(\sqrt{\frac{2E_b}{N_0}} \right) < \frac{1}{2} e^{-E_b/N_0}. \tag{12.44}$$

The dominant factor in (12.43) and (12.44) for large values of signal-to-noise ratio is determined by the exponents. Comparing the exponents in these two using $E_c = R E_b$, we see that the exponent in the probability of bit error for the coded case is a factor of Rd_{free} larger than the exponent for the uncoded case. The quantity

$$\gamma_{\text{soft}} = 10 \log_{10} R d_{\text{free}}$$

is called the *asymptotic coding gain* of the code. For sufficiently large SNR, performance essentially equivalent to uncoded performance can be obtained with γ dB less SNR when coding is employed. A similar argument can be made to show that the asymptotic coding gain for hard-decision decoding is

$$\gamma_{\text{hard}} = 10 \log_{10} \frac{R d_{\text{free}}}{2}.$$

This shows that asymptotically, soft-decision decoding is 3 dB better than hard-decision decoding.

As the SNR increases, the dominant term in computing the bit error rate is the first term in $T(x, N)$. As a result, the free distance has a very strong bearing on the performance of the code.

12.6 Tables of Good Codes

Unlike block codes, where many good codes have been found by exploiting the algebraic structure of the codes, good convolutional codes have been found mostly by computer search. As a result, good codes are known only for relatively short constraint lengths. The following tables [89, 261, 326, 331] provide the best known polynomial codes. It may be observed that all of these codes are nonsystematic. Tables 12.2 and 12.3 provide the best known polynomial codes.

There are separate tables for different rates. Within each table, different memory lengths L, are used, where

$$L = v + 1,$$

where $v = \max_{i,j} \deg(g_{ij}(x))$ is the degree of the highest polynomial. (This quantity is called in many sources the constraint length.) For the rate k/n codes with $k > 1$, L represents the largest degree and v represents the total memory.

Table 12.2: Best Convolutional Codes of Rates $R = 1/2$ and $R = 1/3$

$R = 1/2$ [261, 326]				$R = 1/3$ [261, 326]				
L	$g^{(1)}$	$g^{(2)}$	d_{free}	L	$g^{(1)}$	$g^{(2)}$	$g^{(3)}$	d_{free}
3	5	7	5	3	5	7	7	8
4	64	74	6	4	54	64	74	10
5	46	72	7	5	52	66	76	12
6	65	57	8	6	47	53	75	13
7	554	744	10	7	554	624	764	15
8	712	476	10	8	452	662	756	16
9	561	753	12	9	557	663	711	18
10	4734	6624	12	10	4474	5724	7154	20
11	4762	7542	14	11	4726	5562	6372	22
12	4335	5723	15	12	4767	5723	6265	24
13	42,554	77,304	16	13	42,554	43,364	77,304	24
14	43,572	56,246	16	14	43,512	73,542	76,266	26
15	56,721	61,713	18					
16	447,254	627,324	19					
17	716,502	514,576	20					

In these tables, the coefficients are represented using octal digits with the lsb on the right. Thus, $0 \to 000$, $1 \to 001$, $2 \to 010$, $3 \to 011$, and so forth. There may be trailing zeros on the right. For example, for the rate 1/4 code, the entry with $L = 5$ has generators $g_1 = 52$, $g_2 = 56$, $g_3 = 66$, and $g_4 = 76$. The corresponding bit values are

$$\mathbf{g}_1 = (101\ 010) \quad \mathbf{g}_2 = (101\ 110) \quad \mathbf{g}_3 = (110\ 110) \quad \mathbf{g}_4 = (111\ 110).$$

finddfree.cc

The first coefficient (on the left) is the first coefficient in the encoder.[5] Thus, the coded output streams are

$$c_t^{(1)} = m_t + m_{t-2} + m_{t-4} \qquad\qquad c_t^{(2)} = m_t + m_{t-2} + m_{t-3} + m_{t-4}$$

$$c_t^{(3)} = m_t + m_{t-1} + m_{t-3} + m_{t-4} \quad c_t^{(4)} = m_t + m_{t-1} + m_{t-2} + m_{t-3} + m_{t-4}$$

The program `finddfree` finds d_{free} for a given set of connection coefficients. It has been used to check these results. (Currently implemented only for $k = 1$ codes.)

Table 12.4 presents a comparison of d_{free} for systematic and nonsystematic codes (with polynomial generators), showing that nonsystematic codes have generally better distance properties. Results are even more pronounced for longer constraint lengths.

12.7 Puncturing

In Section 3.9, puncturing was introduced as a modification to block codes, in which one of the parity symbols is removed. In the context of convolutional codes, **puncturing** is accomplished by periodically removing bits from one or more of the encoder output streams [54]. This has the effect of increasing the rate of the code.

---

[5] To use the class `BinConvFIR`, the left bit must be interpreted as the LSB of a binary number. The function octconv returns an integer value that can be used directly in `BinConvFIR`.

Table 12.3: Best Convolutional Codes of Rates $R = 1/4$, $R = 2/3$, and $R = 3/4$

$R = 1/4$ [261, 326]

L	$g^{(1)}$	$g^{(2)}$	$g^{(3)}$	$g^{(4)}$	d_{free}
3	5	7	7	7	10
4	54	64	64	74	13
5	52	56	66	76	16
6	53	67	71	75	18
7	564	564	634	714	20
8	472	572	626	736	22
9	463	535	733	745	24
10	4474	5724	7154	7254	27
11	4656	4726	5562	6372	29
12	4767	5723	6265	7455	32
13	44,624	52,374	66,754	73,534	33
14	42,226	46,372	73,256	73,276	36

$R = 2/3$ [228, 331]

L	v	$g^{(1,1)}$ $g^{(2,1)}$	$g^{(1,2)}$ $g^{(2,2)}$	$g^{(1,3)}$ $g^{(2,3)}$	d_{free}
2	2	4	2	6	3
		2	4	4	
3	3	5	2	6	4
		1	4	7	
3	4	7	1	4	5
		2	5	7	
4	5	60	30	70	6
		14	40	74	
4	6	64	30	64	7
		30	64	74	
5	7	60	34	54	8
		16	46	74	
5	8	64	12	52	8
		26	66	44	
6	9	52	06	74	9
		05	70	53	
6	10	63	15	46	10
		32	65	61	

$R = 3/4$ [228, 331]

L	v	$g^{(1,1)}$ $g^{(2,1)}$ $g^{(3,1)}$	$g^{(1,2)}$ $g^{(2,2)}$ $g^{(3,2)}$	$g^{(1,3)}$ $g^{(2,3)}$ $g^{(3,3)}$	$g^{(1,4)}$ $g^{(2,4)}$ $g^{(3,4)}$	d_{free}
2	3	4	4	4	4	4
		0	6	2	4	
		0	2	5	5	
3	5	6	2	2	6	5
		1	6	0	7	
		0	2	5	5	
3	6	6	1	0	7	6
		3	4	1	6	
		2	3	7	4	
4	8	70	30	20	40	7
		14	50	00	54	
		04	10	74	40	
4	9	40	14	34	60	8
		04	64	20	70	
		34	00	60	64	

Example 12.36 Let the coded output sequence of a rate $R = 1/2$ code be

$$\mathbf{c} = (c_0^{(1)}, c_0^{(2)},\ c_1^{(1)}, c_1^{(2)},\ c_2^{(1)}, c_2^{(2)},\ c_3^{(1)}, c_3^{(2)},\ c_4^{(1)}, c_4^{(2)}, \ldots).$$

When the code is punctured by removing every fourth coded symbol, the punctured sequence is

$$\tilde{\mathbf{c}} = (c_0^{(1)}, c_0^{(2)},\ c_1^{(1)}, -,\ c_2^{(1)}, c_2^{(2)},\ c_3^{(1)}, -,\ c_4^{(1)}, c_4^{(2)}, \ldots).$$

The $-$ symbols merely indicate where the puncturing takes place; they are not transmitted. The punctured sequence thus produces three coded symbols for every two input symbols, resulting in a rate $R = 2/3$ code. $\square$

Decoding of a punctured code can be accomplished using the same trellis as the unpunctured code, but simply not accumulating any branch metric for the punctured symbols. One way this can be accomplished is by inserting symbols into the received symbol stream whose branch metric computation would be 0, then using conventional decoding.

Table 12.4: Comparison of Free Distance as a Function of Constraint Length for Systematic and
Nonsystematic Codes

$R = 1/2$ [326]			$R = 1/3$ [326]		
	Systematic	Nonsystematic		Systematic	Nonsystematic
L	d_{free}	d_{free}	L	d_{free}	d_{free}
2	3	3	2	5	5
3	4	5	3	6	8
4	4	6	4	8	10
5	5	7	5	9	12
6	6	8	6	10	13
7	6	10	7	12	15
8	7	10	8	12	16

The pattern of puncturing is often described by means of a **puncturing matrix** P. For a rate k/n code, the puncture matrix has n rows. The number of columns is the number of symbols over which the puncture pattern repeats. For example, for the puncturing of the previous example,

$$P = \begin{bmatrix} 1 & 1 \\ 1 & 0 \end{bmatrix}.$$

The element P_{ij} is 1 if the ith symbol is sent in the jth epoch of the puncturing period.

While the punctured code can be encoded as initially described — by encoding with the lower rate code then puncturing — this is wasteful, since computations are made which are promptly ignored. However, since the code obtained is still a convolutional code, it has its own trellis, which does not require any explicit puncturing.

Example 12.37 We demonstrate puncturing for the code which has been a *leitmotif* for this chapter, with generators $g^{(1)}(x) = 1 + x^2$ and $g^{(2)}(x) = 1 + x + x^2$. Puncturing is accomplished by deleting every other bit of the second output stream (as above). Four stages of the trellis for this punctured code are shown in Figure 12.28(a).

Now draw the trellis for the resulting $R = 2/3$ code by taking the input bits two at a time, or two stages in the original trellis, and think of this as representing a *single* transition of the new code. The resulting trellis is shown in Figure 12.28(b). □

Besides being used to increase the rate of the code, puncturing can sometimes be used to reduce decoding complexity. In decoding, each state must be extended to 2^k states at the next time. Thus, the decoding complexity scales exponentially with k. Given the trellis for an unpunctured code with rate $R = k/n$ with $k > 1$, if a trellis for an equivalent punctured code having $k' < k$ input bits can be found, then the decoding complexity can be decreased.

Suppose, for example, that the encoder having the trellis in Figure 12.28(b) is used. In decoding, four successor states must be examined for each state, so that the best of four paths to a state must be selected. However, we know that this encoder also has the trellis representation in Figure 12.28(a). Decoding on this trellis only has two successor states for each state. This results in only a two-way comparison, which can be done using a conventional add/compare/select circuit.

Of course, puncturing changes the distance properties of the code: a good rate $R = 2/3$ code is not necessarily obtained by puncturing a good $R = 1/2$ code. Tables of the best $R = 3/4$ and $R = 2/3$ codes obtainable by puncturing are presented in [54].

12.7.1 Puncturing to Achieve Variable Rate

Puncturing can also be used to generate codes of various rates using the same encoder. Such flexibility might be used, for example, to match the code to the channel in a situation in which the channel

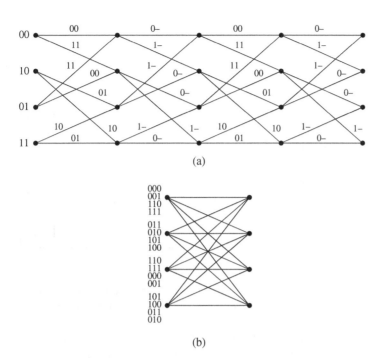

(a)

(b)

Figure 12.28: Trellises for a punctured code. (a) Trellis for initial punctured code; (b) trellis by collapsing two stages of the initial trellis into a single stage.

characteristics might change. Suppose that a rate $R = 1/2$ encoder is used as the "basic" code. As mentioned above, puncturing 1 bit out of every four results in a $R = 2/3$ code. Puncturing 3 out of every 8 bits results in a $R = 4/5$ code.

If the puncturing is done in such a way that bits punctured to obtain the $R = 2/3$ code are included among those punctured to obtain the $R = 4/5$ code, then the $R = 4/5$ codewords are embedded in the $R = 2/3$ codewords. These codewords are, in turn, embedded in the original $R = 1/2$ codewords. Such codes are said to be **rate-compatible punctured convolutional** (RCPC) codes. Assuming that all the RCPC codes have the same period (the same width of the P matrix), then the P matrix of a higher rate code is obtained simply by changing one or more of the 1–0 s. An RCPC code system can be designed so that the encoder and the decoder have the same structure for all the different rates. Extensive tables of codes and puncturing schedules which produce rate-compatible codes appear in [174]. Abbreviated tables appear in Table 12.5.

12.8 Suboptimal Decoding Algorithms for Convolutional Codes

While the Viterbi algorithm is an optimal decoding algorithm, its complexity grows as 2^v, exponentially with the number of states. However, it is known that better performance is obtained by codes with longer memory (constraint length). These two facts conflict: it may not be possible to build a decoder with a sufficiently long memory to achieve some desired level of performance.

The Viterbi algorithm also has fixed decoding costs, regardless of the amount of noise. It would be desirable to have an algorithm which is able to perform fewer computations when there is less noise, adjusting the amount of effort required to decode to the severity of the need.

In this section, we present two algorithms which address these problems. These algorithms have decoding complexity which is essentially *constant* as a function of constraint length. Furthermore, the less noisy the channel, the less work the decoders have to do, on average. This makes them typically very fast decoders. These positive attributes are obtained, however, at some price. These

Table 12.5: Best Known $R = 2/3$ and $R = 3/4$ Convolutional Codes Obtained by Puncturing a $R = 1/2$ Code [262]

Initial Code			Punctured Code			Initial Code			Punctured Code		
v	$g^{(0)}$	$g^{(1)}$	P	d_{free}	$N_{d_{\text{free}}}$	v	$g^{(0)}$	$g^{(1)}$	P	d_{free}	$N_{d_{\text{free}}}$
2	5	7	$\begin{bmatrix} 1 & 0 \\ 1 & 1 \end{bmatrix}$	3	1	2	5	7	$\begin{bmatrix} 1 & 0 & 1 \\ 1 & 1 & 0 \end{bmatrix}$	3	6
3	13	17	$\begin{bmatrix} 1 & 1 \\ 0 & 1 \end{bmatrix}$	4	3	3	13	17	$\begin{bmatrix} 1 & 1 & 0 \\ 1 & 0 & 1 \end{bmatrix}$	4	29
4	31	27	$\begin{bmatrix} 1 & 1 \\ 0 & 1 \end{bmatrix}$	4	1	4	31	27	$\begin{bmatrix} 1 & 0 & 1 \\ 1 & 1 & 0 \end{bmatrix}$	4	1
5	65	57	$\begin{bmatrix} 1 & 0 \\ 1 & 1 \end{bmatrix}$	6	19	5	65	57	$\begin{bmatrix} 1 & 0 & 0 \\ 1 & 1 & 1 \end{bmatrix}$	4	1
6	155	117	$\begin{bmatrix} 1 & 1 \\ 1 & 0 \end{bmatrix}$	6	1	6	155	117	$\begin{bmatrix} 1 & 1 & 0 \\ 1 & 0 & 1 \end{bmatrix}$	5	8

are *suboptimal* decoding algorithms: they do not always provide the maximum-likelihood decision. Furthermore, the decoding time and decoder memory required are random variables, depending on the particular received sequence.

In recent years, the availability of high-speed hardware has led to almost universal use of Viterbi decoding. However, there are still occasions where very long constraint lengths may be of interest, so these algorithms are still of value. Viterbi algorithms can be practically used on codes with constraint lengths up to about 10, while the sequential algorithms discussed here can be used with constraint lengths up to 50 or more.

The first algorithm is known as the **stack algorithm**, or the ZJ algorithm, after Zigangirov [511] and Jelinek [219]. The second algorithm presented is the **Fano algorithm** [113]. These are both instances of **sequential decoding** algorithms [489].

12.8.1 Tree Representations

While the Viterbi algorithm is based on a trellis representation of the code, the sequential algorithms are best understood using a tree representation. Figure 12.29 shows the tree for the convolutional code with generator $G(x) = \left[1 + x^2, 1 + x + x^2\right]$ whose state diagram and trellis are shown in Figure 12.5. At each instant of time, the input bit selects either the upper branch (input bit = 0) or the lower branch (input bit = 1). The output bits for the code are shown along the branches of the tree. By recognizing common states, it is possible to "fold" the tree back into a trellis diagram.

The tree shown in figure 12.29 is for an input sequence of length 4 in the "branching portion" of the tree, followed by a sequence of zeros which drives the tree back to the all-zero state in the "nonbranching" portion of the tree. The length of the codeword is L branches. Each path of length L from the root node to a leaf node of the tree corresponds to a unique convolutional codeword.

Since the size of the tree grows exponentially with the code length, it is not feasible to search the whole tree. Instead, a partial search of the tree is done, searching those portions of the tree that appear to have the best possibility of succeeding. The sequential decoding algorithms which perform this partial search can be described heuristically as follows: Start at the root node and follow the branches that appear to best match the noisy received data. If, after some decisions, the received word and the branch labels are not matching well, back up and try a different route.

12.8.2 The Fano Metric

As a general rule, paths of differing lengths are compared as the algorithm moves around the tree in these sequential decoding algorithms. A path of length five branches through the tree might be compared with a path of length twenty branches. A first step, therefore, is to determine an appropriate

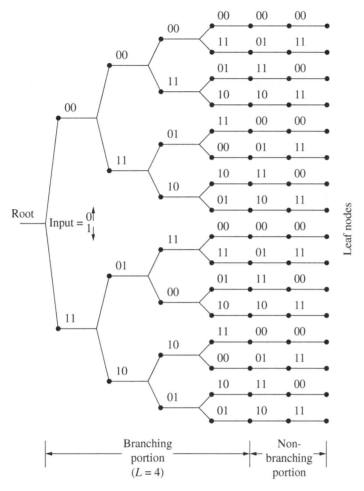

Figure 12.29: A tree representation for a rate $R = 1/2$ code.

metric for comparing different paths. The log-likelihood function used as the branch metric for the Viterbi algorithm is *not* appropriate to use for the sequential algorithm. This is because log-likelihood functions are biased against long paths.

Example 12.38 Suppose the transmitted sequence of a rate $R = 1/2$ code is

$$\mathbf{a} = [11, 10, 10, 11, 11, 01, 00, 01]$$

and the received sequence is

$$\mathbf{r} = [01, 10, 00, 11, 11, 01, 00, 01].$$

Using the Hamming distance as the path metric, this is to be compared with a partial path of one branch, $\tilde{\mathbf{a}}^{(1)} = [00]$ and a partial path of six branches, $\mathbf{a}^{(2)} = [11, 10, 10, 11, 11, 01]$. Letting $[\mathbf{r}]_i$ denote i branches of received data, we have

$$d_H([\mathbf{r}]_1, \mathbf{a}^{(1)}) = 1 \quad d_H([\mathbf{r}]_6, \mathbf{a}^{(2)}) = 2.$$

By not taking into account the fact that branches of different length are being compared, $\mathbf{a}_1$ appears to be better, since the Hamming distance is smaller. But intuitively, it seems that two errors out of 12 bits should be superior to one error out of 2 bits. □

The Fano metric is designed to take into account paths of different lengths. Let

$$\tilde{\mathbf{a}}^{(i)} = (\mathbf{a}_0^{(i)}, \mathbf{a}_1^{(i)}, \ldots, \mathbf{a}_{n_i-1}^{(i)})$$

be a partial input sequence of length n_i corresponding to a particular path through the tree, where each $\mathbf{a}_j^{(i)}$ consists of n bit symbols. Accordingly, let us write this as a vector of nn_i bits,

$$\tilde{\mathbf{a}}^{(i)} = (\mathbf{a}_0^{(i)}, \mathbf{a}_1^{(i)}, \ldots, \mathbf{a}_{n_i-1}^{(i)}) = (a_0^{(i)}, a_1^{(i)}, \ldots, a_{n_in-1}^{(i)}).$$

Assuming that each encoded bit occurs with equal probability, each sequence $\tilde{\mathbf{a}}^{(i)}$ occurs with probability

$$P(\tilde{\mathbf{a}}^{(i)}) = (2^{-k})^{n_i} = 2^{-Rnn_i}. \tag{12.45}$$

Suppose that there are M partial sequences to be compared, represented as elements of the set X,

$$X = \{\tilde{\mathbf{a}}^{(1)}, \tilde{\mathbf{a}}^{(2)}, \ldots, \tilde{\mathbf{a}}^{(M)}\}.$$

Let $n_{\max}$ be the longest of the partial sequences,

$$n_{\max} = \max(n_1, n_2, \ldots, n_M).$$

Let $\mathbf{r} = (\mathbf{r}_0, \mathbf{r}_1, \ldots, \mathbf{r}_{L-1})$ be a received sequence corresponding to a codeword and let

$$\tilde{\mathbf{r}} = (\mathbf{r}_0, \mathbf{r}_1, \ldots, \mathbf{r}_{n_{\max}-1})$$

be a "partial" sequence, starting at the beginning of $\mathbf{r}$, but extending only through $n_{\max}$ branches. (The tilde is used to represent partial sequences.) Each $\mathbf{r}_i$ consists of n symbols, so we can also write this as a vector of $nn_{\max}$ elements

$$\tilde{\mathbf{r}} = (r_0, r_1, \ldots, r_{nn_{\max}-1}).$$

From among the sequences in X, the optimal receiver chooses the $\tilde{\mathbf{a}}^{(i)}$ which maximizes

$$P(\tilde{\mathbf{a}}^{(i)}|\tilde{\mathbf{r}}) = \frac{P[\tilde{\mathbf{a}}^{(i)}]p(\tilde{\mathbf{r}}|\tilde{\mathbf{a}}^{(i)})}{p(\tilde{\mathbf{r}})}.$$

Assuming (as is typical) that the channel is memoryless, this can be written as

$$P(\tilde{\mathbf{a}}^{(i)}|\tilde{\mathbf{r}}) = \frac{P[\tilde{\mathbf{a}}^{(i)}] \prod_{j=0}^{n_i-1} p(\mathbf{r}_j|\mathbf{a}_j^{(i)}) \prod_{j=n_i}^{n_{\max}-1} p(\mathbf{r}_j)}{p(\tilde{\mathbf{r}})}, \tag{12.46}$$

where the second product arises since there are no known data associated with the sequence $\tilde{\mathbf{a}}^{(i)}$ for $j \geq n_i$. Canceling common terms in the numerator and denominator of (12.46), we obtain

$$P(\tilde{\mathbf{a}}^{(i)}|\tilde{\mathbf{r}}) = P[\tilde{\mathbf{a}}^{(i)}] \prod_{j=0}^{n_i-1} \frac{p(\mathbf{r}_j|a_j^{(i)})}{p(\mathbf{r}_j)}.$$

Taking the logarithm of both sides and using (12.45), we have

$$\log_2 P(\tilde{\mathbf{a}}^{(i)}|\tilde{\mathbf{r}}) = \sum_{j=0}^{n_i-1} [\log_2 p(\mathbf{r}_j|\mathbf{a}_j^{(i)}) - \log_2 p(\mathbf{r}_j)] - \log_2 Rnn_i.$$

Each $\mathbf{r}_j$ and $\mathbf{a}_j^{(i)}$ consists of n symbols, so we can write this as

$$\log_2 P(\tilde{\mathbf{a}}^{(i)}|\tilde{\mathbf{r}}) = \sum_{j=0}^{nn_i-1} [\log_2 p(r_j|a_j^{(i)}) - \log_2 p(r_j)] - \log_2 Rnn_i.$$

We use this as the *path metric* and denote it as

$$M(\tilde{\mathbf{a}}^{(i)}, \mathbf{r}) = \log_2 P(\tilde{\mathbf{a}}^{(i)} | \tilde{\mathbf{r}}).$$

The corresponding *branch metric* which is accumulated for each new symbol is

$$\boxed{\mu(r_j, a_j^{(i)}) = \underbrace{\log_2 P(r_j | a_j^{(i)}) - \log_2 P(r_j)}_{\text{ML metric}} \underbrace{- R.}_{\text{path length bias}}}$$

This metric is called the **Fano metric**. As indicated, the Fano metric consists of two parts. The first part is the same maximum likelihood metric used for conventional Viterbi decoding. The second part consists of a bias term which accounts for different path lengths. Thus, when comparing paths of different lengths, the path with the largest Fano metric is considered the best path, most likely to be part of the maximum likelihood path. If all paths are of the same length, then the path length bias becomes the same for all paths and may be neglected.

If transmission takes place over a BSC with transition probability p_c, then $P(r_j = 0) = P(r_j = 1) = \frac{1}{2}$. The branch length bias is

$$\log_2 \frac{1}{P(r_j)} - R = \log_2 2 - R = 1 - R,$$

which is > 0 for all codes of rate $R < 1$. The cumulative path length bias for a path of nn_i bits is $nn_i(1 - R)$: the path length bias increases linearly with the path length. For the BSC, the branch metric is

$$\mu(r_j, a_j) = \begin{cases} \log_2(1 - p_c) - \log_2 \frac{1}{2} - R = \log_2 2(1 - p_c) - R & \text{if } r_j = a_j \\ \log_2 p_c - \log_2 \frac{1}{2} - R = \log_2 2p_c - R & \text{if } r_j \neq a_j. \end{cases} \tag{12.47}$$

Example 12.39 Let us contrast the Fano metric with the ML metric for the data in Example 12.38, assuming that $p_c = 0.1$. Using the Fano metric, we have

$$M([00], \mathbf{r}) = \log_2(1 - p_c) + \log_2 p_c + 2(1 - 1/2) = -2.479$$

$$M([11, 10, 10, 11, 11, 01], \mathbf{r}) = 10\log_2(1 - p_c) + 2\log_2 p_c + 12(1 - 1/2) = -2.164.$$

Thus, the longer path has a better (higher) Fano metric than the shorter path. □

Example 12.40 Suppose that $R = 1/2$ and $p_c = 0.1$. Then from (12.47),

$$\mu(r_j, a_j) = \begin{cases} 0.348 & r_j = a_j \\ -2.82 & r_j \neq a_j. \end{cases}$$

It is common to scale the metrics by a constant so that they can be closely approximated by integers. Scaling the metric by $1/0.348$ results in the metric

$$\mu(r_j, a_j) = \begin{cases} 1 & r_j = a_j \\ -8 & r_j \neq a_j. \end{cases}$$

Thus, each bit a_j that agrees with r_j results in a $+1$ added to the metric. Each bit a_j that disagrees with r_j results in -8 added to the metric. □

A path with only a few errors (the correct path) tends to have a slowly increasing metric, while an incorrect path tends to have a rapidly decreasing metric. Because the metric decreases so rapidly, incorrect paths are not extended far before being effectively rejected.

For BPSK transmission through an AWGN , the branch metric is

$$\mu(r_j, a_j) = \log_2 p(r_j | a_j) - \log_2 p(r_j) - R,$$

where $p(r_j | a_j)$ is the PDF of a Gaussian r.v. with mean a_j and variance $\sigma_2 = N_0/2$ and

$$p(r_j) = \frac{p(r_j | a_j = 1) + p(r_j | a_j = -1)}{2}.$$

12.8.3 The Stack Algorithm

Let $\tilde{\mathbf{a}}^{(i)}$ represent a path through the tree and let $M(\tilde{\mathbf{a}}^{(i)}, \mathbf{r})$ represent the Fano metric between $\tilde{\mathbf{a}}^{(i)}$ and the received sequence $\mathbf{r}$. These are stored together as a pair $(M(\tilde{\mathbf{a}}^{(i)}, \mathbf{r}), \tilde{\mathbf{a}}^{(i)})$ called a stack entry.

In the stack algorithm, an ordered list of stack entries is maintained which represents all the partial paths which have been examined so far. The list is ordered with the path with the largest (best) metric on top, with decreasing metrics beneath. Each decoding step consists of pulling the top stack entry off the stack, computing the 2^k successor paths and their path metrics to that partial path, then rearranging the stack in order of decreasing metrics. When the top partial path consists of a path from the root node to a leaf node of the tree, then the algorithm is finished.

Algorithm 12.2 The Stack Algorithm

---

1 **Input:** A sequence $\mathbf{r}_0, \mathbf{r}_1, \ldots, \mathbf{r}_{L-1}$
2 **Output:** The sequence $\mathbf{a}_0, \mathbf{a}_1, \ldots, \mathbf{a}_{L-1}$
3 **Initialize:** Load the stack with the empty path with Fano path metric 0: $S = (\emptyset, 0)$.
4 Compute the metrics of the successors of the top path in the stack
5 Delete the top path from the stack
6 Insert the paths computed in step 4 into the stack, and
   rearrange the stack in order of decreasing metric values.
7 If the top path in the stack terminates at a leaf node of the tree, Stop.
   Otherwise, goto step 4.

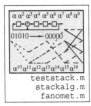

teststack.m
stackalg.m
fanomet.m

Example 12.41   The encoder and received data of Example 12.23 are used in the stack algorithm. We have

$$\mathbf{r} = \begin{bmatrix} 11 \ 10 \ \underline{00} \ \underline{10} \ 11 \ 01 \ 00 \ 01 \ \ldots \end{bmatrix}.$$

Figure 12.30 shows the contents of the stack as the algorithm progresses.

After 14 steps of the algorithm, the algorithm terminates with the correct input sequence on top. (The metrics here are not scaled to integers.)   □

A major part of the expense of the stack algorithm is the need to sort the metrics at every iteration of the algorithm. A variation on this algorithm due to Jelinek [219] known as the *stack bucket algorithm* avoids some of this complication. In the stack bucket algorithm, the range of possible metric values (e.g., for the data in Figure 12.30, the range is from 0.7 to -9.2) is partitioned into fixed intervals, where each interval is allocated a certain number of storage locations called a *bucket*. When a path

Step 1		Step 2		Step 3		Step 4		Step 5	
0.7	[1]	1.4	[11]	−1:1	[111]	−0:39	[1110]	0.31	[11100]
−5:6	[0]	−4:9	[10]	−1:1	[110]	−1:1	[110]	−1:1	[110]
		−5:6	[0]	−4:9	[10]	−4:9	[10]	−4:9	[10]
				−5:6	[0]	−5:6	[0]	−5:6	[0]
						−6:7	[1111]	−6	[11101]
								−6:7	[1111]

Step 6		Step 7		Step 8		Step 9	
−1:1	[110]	−2:2	[111000]	−1:5	[1110000]	−2:2	[111001]
−2:2	[111001]	−2:2	[111001]	−2:2	[111001]	−3:6	[1101]
−2:2	[111000]	−3:6	[1101]	−3:6	[1100]	−3:6	[1100]
−4:9	[10]	−3:6	[1100]	−3:6	[1101]	−3:9	[11100001]
−5:6	[0]	−4:9	[10]	−4:9	[10]	−3:9	[11100000]
−6	[11101]	−5:6	[0]	−5:6	[0]	−4:9	[10]
−6:7	[1111]	−6	[11101]	−6	[11101]	−5:6	[0]
		−6:7	[1111]	−6:7	[1111]	−6	[11101]
				−7:8	[1110001]	−6:7	[1111]
						−7:8	[1110001]

Step 10		Step 11		Step 12	
−3:6	[1100]	−2:9	[11001]	−2:2	[110010]
−3:6	[1101]	−3:6	[1101]	−3:6	[1101]
−3:9	[11100000]	−3:9	[11100001]	−3:9	[11100000]
−3:9	[11100001]	−3:9	[11100000]	−3:9	[11100001]
−4:6	[1110011]	−4:6	[1110010]	−4:6	[1110011]
−4:6	[1110010]	−4:6	[1110011]	−4:6	[1110010]
−4:9	[10]	−4:9	[10]	−4:9	[10]
−5:6	[0]	−5:6	[0]	−5:6	[0]
−6	[11101]	−6	[11101]	−6	[11101]
−6:7	[1111]	−6:7	[1111]	−6:7	[1111]
−7:8	[1110001]	−7:8	[1110001]	−7:8	[1110001]
		−9:2	[11000]	−8:5	[110011]
				−9:2	[11000]

Step 13		Step 14	
−1:5	[1100101]	−0:77	[11001010]
−3:6	[1101]	−3:6	[1101]
−3:9	[11100001]	−3:9	[11100000]
−3:9	[11100000]	−3:9	[11100001]
−4:6	[1110010]	−4:6	[1110011]
−4:6	[1110011]	−4:6	[1110010]
−4:9	[10]	−4:9	[10]
−5:6	[0]	−5:6	[0]
−6	[11101]	−6	[11101]
−6:7	[1111]	−6:7	[1111]
−7:8	[1110001]	−7:1	[11001011]
−7:8	[1100100]	−7:8	[1110001]
−8:5	[110011]	−7:8	[1100100]
−9:2	[11000]	−8:5	[110011]
		−9:2	[11000]

Figure 12.30: Stack contents for stack algorithm decoding example: metric, [input list].

is extended, it is deleted from its bucket and a new path is inserted as the top item in the bucket containing the metric interval for the new metric. Paths within buckets are *not* reordered. The top path in the nonempty bucket with the highest metric interval is chosen as the path to be extended. Instead of sorting, it only becomes necessary to determine which bucket new paths should be placed in. Unfortunately, the bucket approach does not always choose the best path, but only a "very good" path, to extend. Nevertheless, if there are enough buckets that the quantization into metric intervals is not too coarse, and if the received signal is not too noisy, then the top bucket contains only the best path. Any degradation from optimal is minor.

Another practical problem is that the size of the stack must necessarily be limited. For long codewords, there is always the probability that the stack fills up before the correct codeword is found. This is handled by simply throwing away the paths at the bottom of the stack. Of course, if the path that would ultimately become the best path is thrown away at an earlier stage of the algorithm, the best path can never be found. However, if the stack is sufficiently large, the probability that the correct path will be thrown away is negligible. Another possibility is to simply throw out the block where the frame overflow occurs and declare an erasure.

12.8.4   The Fano Algorithm

While the stack algorithm moves around the decoding tree, and must therefore save information about each path still under consideration, the Fano algorithm retains only one path and moves through the tree only along the edges of the tree. As a result, it does not require as much memory as the stack algorithm. However, some of the nodes are visited more than once, requiring recomputation of the metric values.

The general outline of the decoder is as follows. A threshold value T is maintained by the algorithm. The Fano decoder moves forward through the tree as long as the path metric at the next node (the "forward" node), denoted by M_F, exceeds the threshold and the path metric continues to increase (improve). The algorithm is thus a depth-first search. When the path metric would drop below the threshold if a forward move were made, the decoder examines the preceding node (the "backward" node, with path metric M_B). If the path metric at the backward node does not exceed the current threshold, then the threshold is reduced by Δ, and the decoder examines the next forward node. If the path metric at the previous node does exceed the threshold, then the decoder backs up and begins to examine other paths from that node. (This process of moving forward, then backward, then adjusting the threshold, and moving forward again is why nodes may be visited many times.) If all nodes forward of that point have already been examined, then the decoder once again considers backing up. Otherwise, the decoder moves forward on one of the remaining nodes.

Each time a node is visited for the first time (and if it is not at the end of the tree), the decoder "tightens" the threshold by the largest multiple of Δ such that the adjusted threshold does not exceed the current metric. (As an alternative, tightening is accomplished in some algorithms by simply setting $T = M_F$.)

Since the Fano algorithm does backtracking, the algorithm needs to keep the following information at each node along the path that it is examining: the path metric at the previous node, M_B; which of the 2^k branches it has taken; the input at that node; and also the state of the encoder, so that next branches in the tree can be computed. A forward move consists of adding this information to the end of the path list. A backward move consists of popping this information from the end of the path list. The path metric at the root node is set at $M_B = -\infty$; when the decoder backs up to that node, the threshold is always reduced and the algorithm moves forward again.

Figure 12.31 shows the flowchart for the Fano algorithm.

The number i indicates the length of the current path. At each node, all possible branches might be taken. The metric to each next node is stored in sorted order in the array P. At each node along the path, the number t_i indicates which branch number has been taken. When $t_i = 0$, the branch with the best metric is chosen, when $t_i = 1$ the next best metric is chosen, and so forth. The information stored about each node along the path includes the input, the state at that node, and t_i. (Recomputing the metric when backtracking could be avoided by also storing P at each node.)

The threshold is adjusted by the quantity Δ. In general, the larger Δ is, the fewer the number of computations are required. Ultimately, Δ must be below the likelihood of the maximum likelihood path, and so must be lowered to that point. If Δ is too small, then many iterations might be required to get to that point. On the other hand, if Δ is lowered in steps that are too big, then the threshold might be

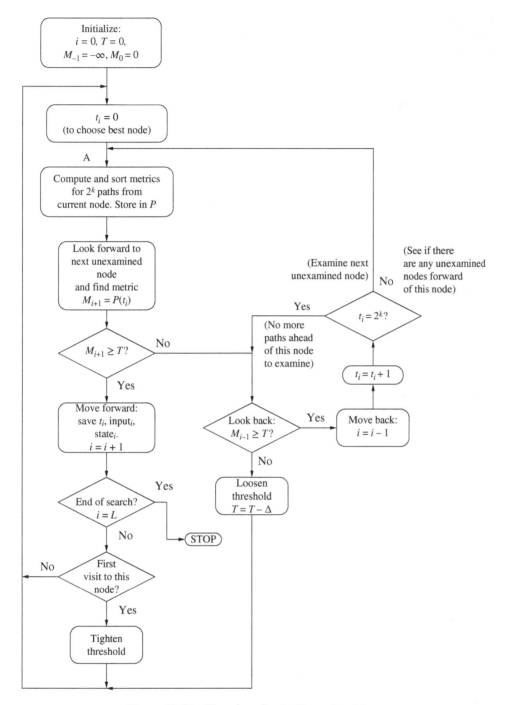

Figure 12.31: Flowchart for the Fano algorithm.

set low enough that other paths which are not the maximum likelihood path also exceed the threshold and can be considered by the decoder. Based on simulation experience [271], Δ should be in the range of $(2, 8)$ if unscaled metrics are used. If scaled metrics are used, then Δ should be scaled accordingly. The value of Δ employed should be explored by thorough computer simulation to ensure that it gives adequate performance.

Example 12.42 Suppose the same code and input sequence as in Example 12.23 is used. The following traces the execution of the algorithm when the scaled (integer) metric of Example 12.40 is used with $\Delta = 10$. The step number n is printed every time the algorithm passes through point A in the flow chart.

1. $n = 1$: $T = 0\ P = [2 - 16]\ t_0 = 0$
2. Look forward: $M_F = 2$
3. $M_F \geq T$. Move forward
4. First visit: Tighten T
5. $M_F = 2\ M_B = 0$ Node=[1]
6. $M = 2\ T = 0$

1. $n = 2$: $T = 0\ P = [4 - 14]\ t_1 = 0$
2. Look forward: $M_F = 4$
3. $M_F \geq T$. Move forward
4. First visit: Tighten T
5. $M_F = 4\ M_B = 2$ Node=[11]
6. $M = 4\ T = 0$

1. $n = 3$: $T = 0\ P = [-3 - 3]\ t_2 = 0$
2. Look forward: $M_F = -3$
3. $M_F < T$: Look back
4. $M_B = 2$
5. $M_B \geq T$: Move back
6. All forward nodes not yet tested. $t_1 = 1$
7. $M_F = -3\ M_B = 2$ Node=[1]
8. $M = 2\ T = 0$

1. $n = 4$: $T = 0\ P = [4 - 14]\ t_1 = 1$
2. Look forward: $M_F = -14$
3. $M_F < T$: Look back
4. $M_B = 0$
5. $M_B \geq T$: Move back
6. All forward nodes not yet tested. $t_0 = 1$
7. $M_F = -14\ M_B = 0$ Node=[]
8. $M = 0\ T = 0$

1. $n = 5$: $T = 0\ P = [2 - 16]\ t_0 = 1$
2. Look forward: $M_F = -16$
3. $M_F < T$: Look back
4. $M_B = -\infty$
5. $M_B < T$: $T = T - \Delta$

6. $M_F = -16$ $M_B = -\infty$ Node=[]
7. $M = 0$ $T = -10$

1. $n = 6$: $T = -10$ $P = [2 - 16]$ $t_0 = 0$
2. Look forward: $M_F = 2$
3. $M_F \geq T$. Move forward
4. $M_F = 2$ $M_B = 0$ Node=[1]
5. $M = 2$ $T = -10$

1. $n = 7$: $T = -10$ $P = [4 - 14]$ $t_1 = 0$
2. Look forward: $M_F = 4$
3. $M_F \geq T$. Move forward
4. $M_F = 4$ $M_B = 2$ Node=[11]
5. $M = 4$ $T = -10$

1. $n = 8$: $T = -10$ $P = [-3 - 3]$ $t_2 = 0$
2. Look forward: $M_F = -3$
3. $M_F \geq T$. Move forward
4. First visit: Tighten T
5. $M_F = -3$ $M_B = 4$ Node=[111]
6. $M = -3$ $T = -10$

1. $n = 9$: $T = -10$ $P = [-1 - 19]$ $t_3 = 0$
2. Look forward: $M_F = -1$
3. $M_F \geq T$. Move forward
4. First visit: Tighten T
5. $M_F = -1$ $M_B = -3$ Node=[1110]
6. $M = -1$ $T = -10$

1. $n = 10$: $T = -10$ $P = [1 - 17]$ $t_4 = 0$
2. Look forward: $M_F = 1$
3. $M_F \geq T$. Move forward
4. First visit: Tighten T
5. $M_F = 1$ $M_B = -1$ Node=[11100]
6. $M = 1$ $T = 0$

1. $n = 11$: $T = 0$ $P = [-6 - 6]$ $t_5 = 0$
2. Look forward: $M_F = -6$
3. $M_F < T$: Look back

4. $M_B = -1$

5. $M_B < T$: $T = T - \Delta$

6. $M_F = -6$ $M_B = -1$ Node=[11100]

7. $M = 1$ $T = -10$

1. $n = 12$: $T = -10$ $P = [-6 - 6]$ $t_5 = 0$

2. Look forward: $M_F = -6$

3. $M_F \geq T$. Move forward

4. First visit: Tighten T

5. $M_F = -6$ $M_B = 1$ Node=[111001]

6. $M = -6$ $T = -10$

1. $n = 13$: $T = -10$ $P = [-13 - 13]$ $t_6 = 0$

2. Look forward: $M_F = -13$

3. $M_F < T$: Look back

4. $M_B = 1$

5. $M_B \geq T$: Move back

6. All forward nodes not yet tested. $t_5 = 1$

7. $M_F = -13$ $M_B = 1$ Node=[11100]

8. $M = 1$ $T = -10$

1. $n = 14$: $T = -10$ $P = [-6 - 6]$ $t_5 = 1$

2. Look forward: $M_F = -6$

3. $M_F \geq T$. Move forward

4. First visit: Tighten T

5. $M_F = -6$ $M_B = 1$ Node=[111000]

6. $M = -6$ $T = -10$

1. $n = 15$: $T = -10$ $P = [-4 - 22]$ $t_6 = 0$

2. Look forward: $M_F = -4$

3. $M_F \geq T$. Move forward

4. First visit: Tighten T

5. $M_F = -4$ $M_B = -6$ Node=[1110000]

6. $M = -4$ $T = -10$

1. $n = 16$: $T = -10$ $P = [-11 - 11]$ $t_7 = 0$

2. Look forward: $M_F = -11$

3. $M_F < T$: Look back

4. $M_B = -6$

5. $M_B \geq T$: Move back

6. All forward nodes not yet tested. $t_6 = 1$

7. $M_F = -11\ M_B = -6$ Node=[111000]

8. $M = -6\ T = -10$

1. $n = 17$: $T = -10\ P = [-4 - 22]\ t_6 = 1$

2. Look forward: $M_F = -22$

3. $M_F < T$: Look back

4. $M_B = 1$

5. $M_B \geq T$: Move back

6. No more forward nodes

7. $M_B = -1$

8. $M_B \geq T$: Move back

9. All forward nodes not yet tested. $t_4 = 1$

10. $M_F = -22\ M_B = -1$ Node=[1110]

11. $M = -1\ T = -10$

1. $n = 18$: $T = -10\ P = [1 - 17]\ t_4 = 1$

2. Look forward: $M_F = -17$

3. $M_F < T$: Look back

4. $M_B = -3$

5. $M_B \geq T$: Move back

6. All forward nodes not yet tested. $t_3 = 1$

7. $M_F = -17\ M_B = -3$ Node=[111]

8. $M = -3\ T = -10$

1. $n = 19$: $T = -10\ P = [-1 - 19]\ t_3 = 1$

2. Look forward: $M_F = -19$

3. $M_F < T$: Look back

4. $M_B = 4$

5. $M_B \geq T$: Move back

6. All forward nodes not yet tested. $t_2 = 1$

7. $M_F = -19\ M_B = 4$ Node=[11]

8. $M = 4\ T = -10$

1. $n = 20$: $T = -10\ P = [-3 - 3]\ t_2 = 1$

2. Look forward: $M_F = -3$

3. $M_F \geq T$. Move forward

4. First visit: Tighten T

5. $M_F = -3\ M_B = 4$ Node=[110]

6. $M = -3\ T = -10$

1. $n = 21$: $T = -10$ $P = [-10 - 10]$ $t_3 = 0$
2. Look forward: $M_F = -10$
3. $M_F \geq T$. Move forward
4. First visit: Tighten T
5. $M_F = -10$ $M_B = -3$ Node=[1101]
6. $M = -10$ $T = -10$

1. $n = 22$: $T = -10$ $P = [-17 - 17]$ $t_4 = 0$
2. Look forward: $M_F = -17$
3. $M_F < T$: Look back
4. $M_B = -3$
5. $M_B \geq T$: Move back
6. All forward nodes not yet tested. $t_3 = 1$
7. $M_F = -17$ $M_B = -3$ Node=[110]
8. $M = -3$ $T = -10$

1. $n = 23$: $T = -10$ $P = [-10 - 10]$ $t_3 = 1$
2. Look forward: $M_F = -10$
3. $M_F \geq T$. Move forward
4. First visit: Tighten T
5. $M_F = -10$ $M_B = -3$ Node=[1100]
6. $M = -10$ $T = -10$

1. $n = 24$: $T = -10$ $P = [-8 - 26]$ $t_4 = 0$
2. Look forward: $M_F = -8$
3. $M_F \geq T$. Move forward
4. First visit: Tighten T
5. $M_F = -8$ $M_B = -10$ Node=[11001]
6. $M = -8$ $T = -10$

1. $n = 25$: $T = -10$ $P = [-6 - 24]$ $t_5 = 0$
2. Look forward: $M_F = -6$
3. $M_F \geq T$. Move forward
4. First visit: Tighten T
5. $M_F = -6$ $M_B = -8$ Node=[110010]
6. $M = -6$ $T = -10$

1. $n = 26$: $T = -10$ $P = [-4 - 22]$ $t_6 = 0$
2. Look forward: $M_F = -4$
3. $M_F \geq T$. Move forward

Table 12.6: Performance of Fano Algorithm on a Particular Sequence as a Function of Δ

Δ	Number of decoding steps	Correct decoding	Δ	Number of decoding steps	Correct decoding
1	158	Yes	7	31	No
2	86	Yes	8	31	No
3	63	No	9	31	No
4	47	No	10	27	Yes
5	40	Yes	11	16	No
6	33	No	12	16	No

4. First visit: Tighten T

5. $M_F = -4 \; M_B = -6$ Node=[1100101]

6. $M = -4 \; T = -10$

1. $n = 27$: $T = -10 \; P = [-2 - 20] \; t_7 = 0$

2. Look forward: $M_F = -2$

3. $M_F \geq T$. Move forward

4. First visit: Tighten T

5. $M_F = -2 \; M_B = -4$ Node=[11001010]

6. $M = -2 \; T = -10$

For this particular set of data, the value of Δ has a tremendous impact both on the number of steps the algorithm takes and whether it decodes correctly. Table 12.6 shows that the number of decoding steps decreases typically as Δ gets larger, but that the decoding might be incorrect for some values of Δ. □

In comparing the stack algorithm and the Fano algorithm, we note the following.

- The stack algorithm visits each node only once, but the Fano algorithm may revisit nodes.
- The Fano algorithm does not have to manage the stack (e.g., resort the metrics).

Despite its complexity, when the noise is low, the Fano algorithm tends to decode faster than the stack algorithm. However, as the noise increases, more backtracking might be required and the stack algorithm has the advantage. Overall, the Fano algorithm is usually selected when sequential decoding is employed.

12.8.5 Other Issues for Sequential Decoding

We briefly introduce some issues related to sequential decoding, although space precludes a thorough treatment. References are provided for interested readers.

12.8.5.1 Computational complexity

The computational complexity is a random variable, and so is described by a probability distribution. Discussions of the performance of the decoder appear in [129, 214, 218, 396].

12.8.5.2 Code design

The performance of a code decoded using the Viterbi algorithm is governed largely by the free distance d_{free}. For sequential decoding however, the codewords must have a distance that increases as rapidly as possible over the first few symbols of the codeword (i.e., the code must have a good **column distance function**) so that the decoding algorithm can make good decisions as early as possible. A large free distance and a small number of nearest neighbors are also important. A code having an optimum distance profile is one in which the column distance function over the first constraint length is better than all other codes of the same rate and constraint length. Tables of codes having optimum distance profiles are provided in [231]. Further discussion and description of the algorithms for finding these codes appear in [57, 225–229].

12.8.5.3 Variations on sequential decoding algorithms

In the interest of reducing the statistical variability of the decoding, or improving the decoder performance, variations on the decoding algorithms have been developed. In [69], a multiple stack algorithm is presented. This operates like the stack algorithm, except that the stack size is limited to a fixed number of entries. If the stack fills up before decoding is complete, the top paths are transferred to a second stack and decoding proceeds using these best paths. If this stack also fills up before decoding is complete, a third stack is created using the best paths, and so forth. In [112] and [220], hybrid algebraic/sequential decoding was introduced in which algebraic constraints are imposed across frames of sequentially decoded data. In [173], a generalized stack algorithm was proposed, in which more than one path in the stack can be extended at one time (as in the Viterbi algorithm) and paths merging together are selected as in the Viterbi algorithm. Compared to the stack algorithm, the generalized stack algorithm does not have buffer size variations as large and the error probability is closer to that of the Viterbi algorithm.

12.8.6 A Variation on the Viterbi Algorithm: The M Algorithm

For a trellis with a large number of states at each time instant, the Viterbi algorithm can be very complex. Furthermore, since there is only one correct path, most of the computations are expended in propagating paths that are not be used, but must be maintained to ensure the optimality of the decoding procedure. The M algorithm (see, e.g., [347]) is a suboptimal, breadth-first decoding algorithm whose complexity is parametric, allowing for more complexity in the decoding algorithm while decoding generally closer to the optimum.

A list of M paths is maintained. At each time step, these M paths are extended to $M2^k$ paths (where k is the number of input bits), and the path metric along each of these paths is computed just as for the Viterbi algorithm. The path metrics are sorted, then the best M paths are retained in preparation for the next step. At the end of the decoding cycle, the path with the best metric is used as the decoded value. While the underlying graphical structure for the Viterbi algorithm is a trellis, in which paths merge together, the underlying graphical structure for the M algorithm is a tree: the merging of paths is not explicitly represented, but better paths are retained by virtue of the sorting operation. The M-algorithm is thus a cross between the stack algorithm (but using all paths of the same length) and the Viterbi algorithm. If M is equal to the number of states, the M algorithm is nearly equivalent to the Viterbi algorithm. However, it is possible for M to be significantly less than the number of states with only modest loss of performance.

Another variation is the T-algorithm. It starts just like the M algorithm. However, instead of retaining only the best M paths, in the T algorithm all paths which are within a threshold T of the best path at that stage are retained.

12.9 Convolutional Codes as Block Codes and Tailbiting Codes

Convolutional codes may be used as block codes, in which a fixed number of bits is taken as the input bits, producing a fixed number of output bits. For a rate $R = k/n$ convolutional code in an encoder with memory v, there are various ways that this can be accomplished.

- (Direct truncation) Starting from a 0 initial state, a sequence of Lk bits can be input to the encoder, and Ln output bits are taken as the codeword. This produces an (Ln, Lk) block code. The encoder is left in a state determined by the input sequence, unknown in advance at the decoder. This straightforward method is referred to as *direct truncation*. The problem is that the full effect of the last bits v on the codeword are not seen, since the output is just truncated. The result is that these bits do not have the same error protection as earlier bits.

- (Zero tail). In order to let the latter bits propagate through the decoder and experience full code protection, a sequence of v bits can be input to the encoder after the Lk input bits are provided, taking $(L + v)n$ output bits from the decoder. All the bits have the same error protection. The decoder is left in the all-zero state, information which is used by the decoder. But the rate of the code is now,

$$\frac{kL}{(L+v)n} = \frac{k}{n} - \frac{k}{n}\frac{v}{L+v}.$$

The rate is reduced by the term $v/(L + v)$, which is called the rate loss.

A third alternative is to use a *tailbiting code*, in which the encoder starts and ends in the same state. While this state may not be known in advance by the decoder, knowing that the starting and ending starts are the same can be used by the decoder.

Consider a sequence of $L = kh$ bits $x_1, x_2, \ldots, x_L$ to be encoded. Tailbiting encoding can be achieved as follows:

1. Starting with the encoder in the all-zero state, encode the last v bits $x_{L-v+1}, \ldots, x_L$ and discard the encoder output. This places the encoder in some state Ψ.

2. Encode the entire sequence of bits $x_1, x_2, \ldots, x_L$, and use the sequence of kn bits as the codeword. As the last v bits are encoded, the encoder returns back to state Ψ.

The Viterbi algorithm decoder can exploit the fact that both the starting state and the ending state are the same (although not yet known).

There are different ways that the decoder can exploit the fact that the starting and ending states are the same. The optimum way is to use the Viterbi algorithm to decode 2^v times, starting successively in each state, and taking the path metric in the starting state. The path metric that is smallest out of all these trials determines the decoded sequence. This is quite expensive, requiring 2^v operations of the Viterbi algorithm over the entire codewords.

A less expensive approach, referred to as the Bar–David approach [285], operates as follows.

1. Choose an arbitrary state.

2. Decode using the Viterbi algorithm, selecting the state at the end with the best path metric.

3. If this ending state is the same as the starting state, then decoding is complete.

4. Otherwise, use the end state determined in step 2 as the new starting state. If this starting state has been tried before, return to step 2. Otherwise, return to step 1.

At signal-to-noise ratios high enough to produce usably low probability of error, the Bar-David approach may have less than a dB of penalty compared with the multiple Viterbi approach.

12.10 A Modified Expression for the Path Metric

In this section, we modify the expression for the path metric defined in (12.17), expressing the branch metric in terms of likelihood ratios. Looking ahead to the SOVA (Section 12.11), we will also incorporate prior probabilities into the path metric.

For the rate $R = k/n$ encoder, we assume here that $k = 1$, and that BPSK modulation is employed. The input bit x_t produces the coded sequence $\mathbf{c}_t \in \{0, 1\}^n$, which can be represented as signed quantities as $\tilde{\mathbf{c}}_t = 2\mathbf{c}_t - 1 \in \{-1, 1\}^n$. The corresponding modulated symbols, modulated with signal amplitude a, are $\mathbf{a}_t = 2\mathbf{c}_t - 1 = a\tilde{\mathbf{c}}_t \in \{-1, 1\}^n$. For an input bit $x_t \in \{0, 1\}$, denote $\tilde{x}_t \in \{-1, 1\}$, where $\tilde{x}_t = 2x_t - 1$. The received signal is $\mathbf{r}_t = \mathbf{a}_t + \mathbf{n}_t$, where each $\mathbf{n}_{t,i} \sim \mathcal{N}(0, \sigma^2)$, independently.

For a received sequence $\mathbf{r}_0^{t-1} = (\mathbf{r}_0, \mathbf{r}_1, \ldots, \mathbf{r}_{t-1})$, the path metric along the path determined by the state sequence $\Psi_0^t = (\Psi_0, \Psi_1, \ldots, \Psi_t)$, which terminates in state Ψ_t, is

$$M(\mathbf{r}_0^{t-1}|\Psi_0^t) = -\log[f(\mathbf{r}_0^{t-1}|\mathbf{a}(\Psi_0^t))P(x(\Psi_0^t))]. \tag{12.48}$$

It is similar to the path metric defined in (12.17), except that it includes the factor $P(x(\Psi_0^t))$, which is the prior probability of the sequence of inputs $x(\Psi_0^t)$. It is assumed that each bit is independent, so that

$$P(x(\Psi_0^t)) = P(x(\Psi_0^1))P(x(\Psi_1^2)) \cdots P(x(\Psi_{t-1}^t)).$$

Assuming a memoryless channel,

$$M(\mathbf{r}_0^{t-1}|\Psi_0^t) = -\left[\sum_{\ell=0}^{t-1} \log f(\mathbf{r}_\ell|\mathbf{a}(\Psi_\ell^{\ell+1})) + \log P(x(\Psi_\ell^{\ell+1}))\right]. \tag{12.49}$$

The path metric $M(\mathbf{r}_0^{t-1}|\Psi_0^t)$ can be extended along the path to the state Ψ_{t+1} at the next time as

$$M(\mathbf{r}_0^t|\Psi_0^{t+1}) = -\left[\sum_{\ell=0}^{t} \log f(\mathbf{r}_\ell|\mathbf{a}(\Psi_\ell^{\ell+1})) + \log P(x(\Psi_\ell^{\ell+1}))\right]$$

$$= -\left[\left(\sum_{\ell=0}^{t-1} \log f(\mathbf{r}_\ell|\mathbf{a}(\Psi_\ell^{\ell+1})) + \log P(x(\Psi_\ell^{\ell+1}))\right) + \log f(\mathbf{r}_t|\mathbf{a}(\Psi_t^{t+1})) + \log P(x(\Psi_t^{t+1}))\right]$$

$$= M(\mathbf{r}_0^{t-1}|\Psi_0^t) + \mu(\mathbf{r}_t, \Psi_t, \Psi_{t+1}),$$

where

$$\mu(\mathbf{r}_t, \Psi_t, \Psi_{t+1}) = -[\log f(\mathbf{r}_t|\mathbf{a}(\Psi_t^{t+1})) + \log P(x(\Psi_t^{t+1}))]$$

is the branch metric, incorporating information along the state transition from Ψ_t to Ψ_{t+1} and the log probability of the information symbol $x(\Psi_t^{t+1})$ which causes the transition. The branch metric can be further decomposed, assuming a memoryless channel, as

$$\mu(\mathbf{r}_t, \Psi_t, \Psi_{t+1}) = -\left[\sum_{j=1}^{n} \log f(\mathbf{r}_{t,j}|\mathbf{a}(\Psi_t^{t+1})_j) + \log P(x(\Psi_t^{t+1}))\right].$$

The posterior probability of the sequence $\mathbf{a}(\Psi_0^{t+1})$, given the sequence $\mathbf{r}_0^t$ can be expressed in terms of this metric as

$$P(\mathbf{a}(\Psi_0^{t+1})|\mathbf{r}_0^t) = \frac{f(\mathbf{r}_0^t|\mathbf{a}(\Psi_0^{t+1}))P(\mathbf{a}(\Psi_0^{t+1}))}{f(\mathbf{r}_0^t)} = \frac{\exp(-M(\mathbf{r}_0^t|\Psi_0^{t+1}))}{f(\mathbf{r}_0^t)}$$

or, more simply, $P(\mathbf{a}(\Psi_0^{t+1})|\mathbf{r}_0^t) \propto \exp(-M(\mathbf{r}_0^t|\Psi_0^{t+1}))$.

The metric (12.48) can modified to be expressed in terms of log probability ratios. Recalling that a metric may be transformed by affine transformations (recall (12.16), with $a > 0$), a new metric is created by multiplying the metric M by 2 and subtracting off a constant that does not depend on the path. Define the constants applicable at time t

$$C_{r,t}^j = -[\log f(\mathbf{r}_{t,j}|\tilde{\mathbf{c}}_{t,j} = +1) + \log f(\mathbf{r}_{t,j}|\tilde{\mathbf{c}}_{t,j} = -1)]$$

and

$$c_{u,t} = -[\log P(x_t = +1) + \log P(x_t = -1)].$$

These constants do not depend on the branch in the path taken, since they depend on all possible outputs across any branch. At time $t = 0$, assuming initial path metrics are 0, the path metric is simply the branch metric,

$$M(\mathbf{r}_0^0|\Psi_0^1) = -\left[\sum_{j=1}^{n} \log f(\mathbf{r}_{0,j}|\mathbf{a}(\Psi_0^1)_j) + \log P(x(\Psi_0^1))\right].$$

Form a new metric $M^*(\mathbf{r}_0^0|\Psi_0^1)$ by multiplying $M(\mathbf{r}_0^0|\Psi_0^1)$ by 2 and subtracting off the sum of the constants,

$$M^*(\mathbf{r}_0^0|\Psi_0^1) = 2M(\mathbf{r}_0^0|\Psi_0^1) - \sum_{j=1}^{n} C_{r,0}^j - c_{u,0}.$$

Consider the jth term of the likelihoods in this expression,

$$2f(\mathbf{r}_{0,j}|\mathbf{a}(\Psi_0^1)_j) - \log f(\mathbf{r}_{0,j}|\tilde{\mathbf{c}}_{0,j} = +1) + \log f(\mathbf{r}_{0,j}|\tilde{\mathbf{c}}_{0,j} = -1).$$

There are two cases to consider, when $\tilde{\mathbf{c}}(\Psi_0^1)_j = +1$ and $\tilde{\mathbf{c}}(\Psi_0^1)_j = -1$. In the first case, we find

$$2f(\mathbf{r}_{0,j}|\mathbf{a}(\Psi_0^1)_j) - C_{r,0}^j = \log f(\mathbf{r}_{0,j}|\tilde{\mathbf{c}}(\Psi_0^1) = +1) - \log f(\mathbf{r}_{0,j}|\tilde{\mathbf{c}}_{0,j} = -1)$$

$$= \log \frac{f(\mathbf{r}_{0,j}|\tilde{\mathbf{c}}_{0,j} = +1)}{f(\mathbf{r}_{0,j}|\tilde{\mathbf{c}}_{0,j} = -1)} = \tilde{\mathbf{c}}(\Psi_0^1)_j \log \frac{f(\mathbf{r}_{0,j}|\tilde{\mathbf{c}}_{0,j} = +1)}{f(\mathbf{r}_{0,j}|\tilde{\mathbf{c}}_{0,j} = -1)}.$$

In the case that $\tilde{\mathbf{c}}(\Psi_0^1)_j = -1$,

$$2f(\mathbf{r}_{0,j}|\mathbf{a}(\Psi_0^1)_j) - C_{r,0}^j = \log f(\mathbf{r}_{0,j}|\tilde{\mathbf{c}}(\Psi_0^1) = -1) - \log f(\mathbf{r}_{0,j}|\tilde{\mathbf{c}}_{0,j} = +1)$$

$$= -\log \frac{f(\mathbf{r}_{0,j}|\tilde{\mathbf{c}}_{0,j} = +1)}{f(\mathbf{r}_{0,j}|\tilde{\mathbf{c}}_{0,j} = -1)} = \tilde{\mathbf{c}}(\Psi_0^1)_j \log \frac{f(\mathbf{r}_{0,j}|\tilde{\mathbf{c}}_{0,j} = +1)}{f(\mathbf{r}_{0,j}|\tilde{\mathbf{c}}_{0,j} = -1)}.$$

In light of this, define

$$L_r(\mathbf{r}_{t,j}) = \log \frac{f(\mathbf{r}_{t,j}|\tilde{\mathbf{c}}_{t,j} = +1)}{f(\mathbf{r}_{t,j}|\tilde{\mathbf{c}}_{t,j} = -1)}.$$

Then

$$2f(\mathbf{r}_{0,j}|\mathbf{a}(\Psi_0^1)_j - C_{r,0}^j = \tilde{\mathbf{c}}(\Psi_0^1)_j L_r(\mathbf{r}_{0,j}).$$

Similarly, the term involving the prior probabilities,

$$2\log P(x(\Psi_0^1)) - c_{u,0} = \log \frac{P(\tilde{x}(\Psi_0^1) = +1)}{P(\tilde{x}(\Psi_0^1) = -1)} = \tilde{x}(\Psi_0^1)L_x(\tilde{x}(\Psi_0^1)),$$

where

$$L_x(\tilde{x}) = \frac{P(\tilde{x} = +1)}{P(\tilde{x} = -1)}.$$

The modified metric at $t = 0$ can thus be expressed as

$$M^*(\mathbf{r}_0^0|\mathbf{a}(\Psi_0^1)) = -\left[\sum_{j=1}^{n} \tilde{\mathbf{c}}(\Psi_0^1)_j L_r(\mathbf{r}_{0,j}) + \tilde{x}(\Psi_0^1)L_x(\tilde{x}(\Psi_0^1))\right].$$

Extending this forward in time, we find

$$M^*(\mathbf{r}_0^t|\mathbf{a}(\Psi_0^{t+1})) = M^*(\mathbf{r}_0^{t-1}|\mathbf{a}(\Psi_0^t)) - \left[\sum_{j=1}^{n} \tilde{c}(\Psi_t^{t+1})_j L_r(\mathbf{r}_{t,j}) + \tilde{x}(\Psi_t^{t+1}) L_x(\tilde{x}(\Psi_t^{t+1})) \right].$$

This metric, expressed now in terms of log-likelihood ratios instead of likelihoods, can be used in regular Viterbi algorithm. If it is assumed that each $L_x(\tilde{x}) = 0$ (equal prior probabilities), then this will give detection performance identical to the Viterbi algorithm using the previously defined metric.

As an example of the computation of $L_r(\mathbf{r}_{t,j})$, for an AWGN channel,

$$L_r(r) = \log \frac{\exp(-\frac{1}{2\sigma^2}(r-a)^2)}{\exp(-\frac{1}{2\sigma^2}(r+a)^2)} = \frac{2a}{\sigma^2} r.$$

The constant $L_c \overset{\triangle}{=} 2a/\sigma^2$ is referred to as the *channel reliability factor*. Using this, the metric can be expressed as

$$M^*(\mathbf{r}_0^t|\mathbf{a}(\Psi_0^{t+1})) = M^*(\mathbf{r}_0^{t-1}|\mathbf{a}(\Psi_0^t)) - \left[\sum_{j=1}^{n} \tilde{c}(\Psi_t^{t+1}) L_c \mathbf{r}_{t,j} + \tilde{x}(\Psi_t^{t+1}) L_x(\tilde{x}(\Psi_t^{t+1})) \right].$$

As above, the posterior probability can be expressed as

$$P(\mathbf{a}(\Psi_0^{t+1})|\mathbf{r}_0^t) \propto \exp\left(-\frac{1}{2} M(\mathbf{r}_0^t|\Psi_0^{t+1}) \right).$$

12.11   Soft Output Viterbi Algorithm (SOVA)

The SOVA is an alternative to the BCJR algorithm (introduced in Section 14.3.1) which accepts prior input probabilities and produces a sequence of estimated bits along with reliability information about them. It can be implemented so that it has lower computational complexity than the BCJR algorithm.

The key to SOVA is to keep track of the reliability of bits along the paths through the trellis as the Viterbi algorithm proceeds. Consider two paths through the trellis, Ψ_0^t and $\Psi_0'^t$, where $\Psi_t = \Psi_t' = p$, that is, both paths terminate at the same state p, with their corresponding metrics $M^*(\mathbf{r}_0^{t-1}\Psi_0^t)$ and $M^*(\mathbf{r}_0^t\Psi_0'^t)$. The putative sequences of information bits along these paths are $\hat{x}(\Psi_0^t)$ and $\hat{x}(\Psi_0'^t)$, which we will denote as $(\hat{x}_0, \hat{x}_1, \ldots, \hat{x}_{t-1})$ and $(\hat{x}_0', \hat{x}_1', \ldots, \hat{x}_{t-1}')$. The Viterbi algorithm will select one of these two paths, depending on which of $M^*(\mathbf{r}_0^{t-1}|\Psi_0^t)$ or $M^*(\mathbf{r}_0^{t-1}|\Psi_0'^t)$ is smaller. Of the two paths, let Ψ_0^t denote the correct path. Then if $M^*(\mathbf{r}_0^{t-1}|\Psi_0^t) < M^*(\mathbf{r}_0^{t-1}|\Psi_0'^t)$, the Viterbi algorithm selects the correct path.

Example 12.43 In the Viterbi decoding Example 12.23, at time step $t = 3$, the first time step when paths converge and decisions have to be made, the two paths leading to state 2 have state sequences $\Psi_0^3 = (0, 1, 3, 2)$ and $\Psi_0'^3 = (0, 0, 1, 2)$ (shown in solid lines in figure 12.32) with respective path metrics $M(\mathbf{r}_0^2|\Psi_0^3) = 1$ with $M(\mathbf{r}_0^2|\Psi_0'^3) = 4$, and corresponding bit sequences $\hat{x}(\Psi_0^3) = (1, 1, 0)$ and $\hat{x}(\Psi_0'^3) = (0, 1, 0)$. These two sequences agree on the last 2 bits (no information on these paths to distinguish between them), but they disagree on the first bit.   □

At times j such that $\hat{x}_j = \hat{x}_j'$, as far as either path is able to determine, this must be the value of the bit, $x_j = \hat{x}_j$. On the other hand, at times j such that $\hat{x}_j \neq \hat{x}_j'$, the presumption is that $\hat{x}_j$ is a better estimate of x_j than $\hat{x}_j'$. SOVA is based on the idea that the larger the value of $M^*(\mathbf{r}_0^{t-1}|\Psi_0'^t) - M^*(\mathbf{r}_0^{t-1}|\Psi_0^t)$, the more reliable the estimate. Define the metric difference between the paths as

$$\Delta_{t-1}(p) = \frac{1}{2}(M^*(r_0^{t-1}|\Psi_0'^t) - M^*(r_0^{t-1}|\Psi_0^t)) \quad \text{or} \quad \Delta_{t-1}(p) = (M(r_0^{t-1}|\Psi_0'^t) - M(r_0^{t-1}|\Psi_0^t))$$

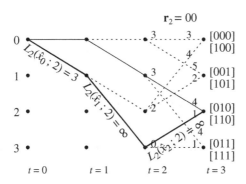

Figure 12.32: Computations of SOVA at $t = 3$ (see Example 12.23).

Between the two paths Ψ_0^t and Ψ'^t_0 (with $\Psi_t = \Psi'_t = p$) where Ψ_0^t is the correct path, the probability choosing the correct path is proportional to $\exp(-\frac{1}{2}M^*(\mathbf{r}_0^{t-1}|\Psi_0^t))$. More explicitly,

$$P(\text{choose correct path to state } p) = \frac{\exp\left(-\frac{1}{2}M^*(\mathbf{r}_0^{t-1}|\Psi_0^t)\right)}{\exp\left(-\frac{1}{2}M^*(\mathbf{r}_0^{t-1}|\Psi_0^t)\right) + \exp\left(-\frac{1}{2}M^*(\mathbf{r}_0^{t-1}|\Psi'^t_0)\right)} \qquad (12.50)$$

$$\times \frac{\exp\left(\frac{1}{2}M^*(\mathbf{r}_0^{t-1}|\Psi'^t_0)\right)}{\exp\left(\frac{1}{2}M^*(\mathbf{r}_0^{t-1}|\Psi'^t_0)\right)}$$

$$= \frac{\exp(\Delta_{t-1}(p))}{1 + \exp(\Delta_{t-1}(p))}$$

$$\overset{\triangle}{=} \pi_{t-1}(p). \qquad (12.51)$$

Similarly,

$$P(\text{choose incorrect path to state } p) = 1 - \pi_{t-1}(p) = \frac{1}{1 + \exp(\Delta_{t-1}(p))}.$$

The subscript on $\pi_{t-1}(p)$ indicates that this probability affects the bits $x_0, x_1, \ldots, x_{t-1}$.

In the SOVA algorithm, at each time step of the Viterbi algorithm a reliability probability $p_{t-1}(x_i; p)$ is assigned to each bit x_i along the survivor path, $i \in \Psi_0^t$, for the survivor path to each state p. The reliability probability is based upon (12.51) for bits that differ. These reliabilities are determined initially at the time that the Viterbi algorithm begins making decisions, when paths first merge. Let the memory of the convolutional encoder be v. As observed in Example 12.23, the first decision in the Viterbi algorithm results from the paths extending time to $t = v + 1$. For the sequence of estimated bits on the surviving path $\hat{x}(\Psi_0^m) = (\hat{x}_0, \hat{x}_1, \ldots, \hat{x}_m)$ to state p, the *initial* reliability probability $P_{\text{reliability}}$ is defined as follows:

$$p_v(\hat{x}_i; p) = \begin{cases} 1 & \text{if } \hat{x}_i = \hat{x}'_i \\ \frac{\exp(\Delta_v(p))}{1+\exp(\Delta_v(p))} & \text{if } \hat{x}_i \neq \hat{x}'_i \end{cases}, \quad i = 0, 1, \ldots, v.$$

For the entire sequence of bits on the surviving path to state p there is a reliability probability vector

$$\mathbf{p}_v(p) = (p_v(\hat{x}_0; p), p_v(\hat{x}_1; p), \ldots, p_v(\hat{x}_v; p)), \quad \text{for each state } p = 0, 1, \ldots, 2^v.$$

It will also be convenient to express this in terms of log probability ratios. Let

$$L_{t-1}(\hat{x}_i; p) = \log \frac{P_{t-1}(\hat{x}_i)}{1 - p_{t-1}(\hat{x}_i; p)}, i = 0, 1, \ldots, t-1.$$

This can be turned around with

$$p_{t-1}(\hat{x}_i;p) = \frac{\exp(L_{t-1}(\hat{x}_i;p)}{1 + \exp(L_{t-1}(\hat{x}_i;p))} \quad 1 - p_{t-1}(\hat{x}_i;p) = \frac{1}{1 + \exp(L_{t-1}(\hat{x}_i;p))}. \tag{12.52}$$

Initially, that is, at $t = v + 1$,

$$L_v(\hat{x}_i;p) = \begin{cases} \Delta_v(p) & \text{if } \hat{x}_i \neq \hat{x}'_i \\ \infty & \text{if } \hat{x}_i = \hat{x}'_i, \end{cases} \quad i = 0, 1, \dots, m.$$

There reliability (likelihood) vector for the sequence of bits on the path to state p,

$$\mathbf{L}_v(p) = (L_v(\hat{x}_0;p), L_v(\hat{x}_1;p), \dots, L_v(\hat{x}_v;p)).$$

Example 12.44 Return to $t = 2$ in Example 12.43,

$$\Delta_2 = M(\mathbf{r}_0^2|\Psi'^3_0) - M(\mathbf{r}_0^2|\Psi^3_0) = 3.$$

For the paths to state $p = 2$, the reliability probability is

$$p_2(2) = \frac{e^3}{1 + e^3} = 0.9526.$$

The reliability probability vector along the surviving path is

$$\mathbf{p}_2(2) = (0.9526, 1, 1),$$

and the corresponding reliability vector is

$$\mathbf{L}_2(2) = (3, \infty, \infty).$$

In the actual computation of the SOVA, similar computations are done for the paths to each state. □

For later times, $t > m + 1$, the reliability is determined by combining the previous reliability for a bit with the new reliability stemming from the new decision. Let Ψ^t_0 be the surviving path to state q at time t, and let the previous state be $\Psi_{t-1} = p$.

- For bits $\hat{x}_i$ on this surviving path with $\hat{x}_i \neq \hat{x}'_i$, the updated reliability probability is the probability the correct path is chosen and the current reliability, or that the incorrect path is chosen, and the complement of the current reliability:

$$p_{t-1}(\hat{x}_i;q) = p_{t-2}(\hat{x}_i;p)\pi_{t-1}(q)$$
$$+ (1 - p_{t-2}(\hat{x}_i;p))(1 - \pi_{t-1}(q))$$
$$= 0, 1, \dots, t-2 \text{ such that } \hat{x}_i \neq \hat{x}'_i, \quad q = 0, 1, \dots, 2^v - 1.$$

Using (12.52) at time $t - 2$, this becomes

$$p_{t-1}(\hat{x}_i;q) = \frac{\exp(L_{t-2}(\hat{x}_i;p) + \Delta_{t-1}(q)) + 1}{1 + \exp(\Delta_{t-1}(q)) + \exp(L_{t-2}(\hat{x}_i;p)) + \exp(\Delta_{t-1}(q) + \Delta_{t-1}(q))}$$

so that

$$L_{t-1}(\hat{x}_i;q) = \log\frac{p_{t-1}(\hat{x}_i;q)}{1 - p_{t-1}(\hat{x}_i;q)} = \log\frac{1 + \exp(L_{t-2}(\hat{x}_i;p) + \Delta_{t-1}(q))}{\exp(\Delta_{t-1}(q)) + \exp(L_{t-2}(\hat{x}_i;p))},$$
$$i = 0, 1, \dots, t-2 \text{ such that } \hat{x}_i \neq \hat{x}'_i, \quad q = 0, 1, \dots, 2^v - 1.$$

This function can be approximated as

$$L_{t-1}(\hat{x}_i;q) = \min(L_{t-2}(\hat{x}_i;p), \Delta_{t-1}(q)).$$

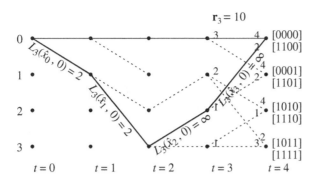

Figure 12.33: Computations of SOVA at $t = 4$.

- For bits on the surviving path with $\hat{x}_i = \hat{x}'_i$, the reliability remains unchanged:

$$L_{t-1}(\hat{x}_i; q) = L_{t-2}(\hat{x}_i; p)$$

$$i = 0, 1, \ldots, t-2 \text{ such that } \hat{x}_i \neq \hat{x}'_i, \quad q = 0, 1, \ldots, 2^v - 1.$$

For the reliability of $\hat{x}_{t-1}$ (the extension to the latest time), the reliability is as it was for the initial bits:

$$L_{t-1}(\hat{x}_{t-1}, q) = \begin{cases} \Delta_{t-1}(q) & \hat{x}_{t-1} \neq \hat{x}'_{t-1} \\ \infty & \hat{x}_{t-1} = \hat{x}'_{t-1}. \end{cases}$$

Example 12.45 Continuing example 12.43, at time step $t = 4$ the two paths to state $q = 0$ are $\Psi_0^4 = (0, 1, 3, 2, 0)$ and $\Psi'^4_0 = (0, 0, 0, 0, 0)$ with respective path metrics $M(\mathbf{r}_0^2 | \Psi_0^4) = 2$ with $M(\mathbf{r}_0^2 | \Psi'^3_0) = 4$, and corresponding bit sequences $\hat{x}(\Psi_0^4) = (1, 1, 0, 0)$ and $\hat{x}'(\Psi'^4_0) = (0, 0, 0, 0)$. These two sequences agree on the last 2 bits, but they disagree on the first bit. See Figure 12.33.

$$\Delta_3 = M(\mathbf{r}_0^3 | \Psi'^4_0) - M(\mathbf{r}_0^3 | \Psi_0^4) = 2.$$

For the paths to state $p = 2$, the reliability probability is

$$p_3(0) = \frac{e^2}{1 + e^2} = 0.881.$$

The reliability probability vector along the surviving path is

$$\mathbf{L}_3(0) = (\min(L_2(\hat{x}_0, 2), \Delta_3), \min(L_2(\hat{x}_1, 2), \Delta_3), \infty, \infty)$$

$$= (\min(3, 2), \min(3, 2), \infty, \infty) = (2, 2, \infty, \infty).$$ □

At each time step t of the Viterbi algorithm, the reliability of each bit along the path to each state must be updated. As t increases, this results in a large computational burden. But recall that as the Viterbi algorithm progresses, early branches in the path merge together (see, e.g., the trellis in Example 12.23, starting at time $t = 4$). As discussed with regard to running the VA on a window, taking a window length of approximately five constraint lengths is sufficient that with high probability paths will have merged, and it is not necessary to update the reliability of the bits earlier than this length. Let W denote the number of bits in a window that are used in the SOVA.

Also recall that for feedforward encoders with memory v, the last v bits in each putative bit sequence are the same, so it is not necessary to do an update computation over those bits. Regardless, let v' be the number of bits in putative bit sequences that agree in the range $t - v'$ to t.

In the SOVA algorithm, the following data structures are employed:

- A path metric M to each state at each time.

- For each state p, the sequence of input bits $\hat{x}_0^t(p)$ on the survivor path that state. (For a windowed Viterbi algorithm, the sequence of bits goes is x_{t-W}^t. Where $t - W < 0$, this is intended to denote x_0^t.)

- For each state p, the reliability sequence $\mathbf{L}(p)$ of the bits on the survivor path to state p. For a windowed Viterbi algorithm, the sequence of reliability values is for the bits in the window.

$$\mathbf{L}(p) = (L(\hat{x}_{t-W}, q), L(\hat{x}_{t-W+1}, q), \ldots, L(\hat{x}_t, q)).$$

In the algorithm below the reliability $L(\hat{x}_t, q)$ is denoted as $L_t(q)$.

Algorithm 12.3 The Soft Output Viterbi Algorithm

---

1   **Input:** A sequence $\mathbf{r}_0, \mathbf{r}_1, \ldots, \mathbf{r}_{L-1}$
2   **Output:** The sequence $\hat{x}_0, \hat{x}_1, \ldots, \hat{x}_{L-1}$ which maximizes the likelihood $f(\mathbf{r}_0^{L-1} | \hat{x}_0^{L-1})$, and a reliability measure of these bit estimates.
3   **Initialize:** Set $M(0) = 0$ and $M(p) = \infty$ for $p = 1, 2, \ldots, 2^v - 1$ (initial path costs)
4   Set $\hat{x}_0^{-1}(p) = \emptyset$ for $p = 0, 1, \ldots, 2^v - 1$
5   Set $t = 0$
6   Begin
7   For each state q at time $t + 1$
8   Find the path metric for each path to state q:
9   For each p_i connected to state q corresponding to input $\hat{\mathbf{x}}^{(p_i, q)}$, compute
     $m_i = M(p_i) + \mu_t(\mathbf{r}_t, \hat{\mathbf{x}}^{(p_i, q)})$
10   Select the smallest metric: $i_{\min} = \arg\min_i m_i$ and the largest metric $i_{\max} = \arg\max_i m_i$.
11   Set $M(q) = m_{i_{\min}}$.
12    $\Delta = m_{i_{\max}} - m_{i_{\min}}$
13   Extend the sequence of input bits on the survivor path and the other path to state q
     $\hat{x}_{t-W}^t(q) = (\hat{x}_{t-W}^{t-1}(p_{i_{\min}}), x^{(p_{i_{\min}}, q)})$ (survivor path)
     $\hat{x}_{t-W}^{\prime\prime t}(q) = (\hat{x}_{t-W}^{t-1}(p_{i_{\max}}), x^{(p_{i_{\max}}, q)})$ (other path)
14   Let $L_t(q) = +\infty$
15   For $j = t - W$ to $t - v''$ (Loop over the bit times in the window)
16   If($\hat{x}(j) \neq \hat{x}''(j)$) (Update the reliability)
17      $L_j(q) = \min(L_j(p_{i_{\min}}), \Delta)$
18   End
19   end (for)
20   end (for)
21   $t = t + 1$
20   if $t < L - 1$, goto line 6.
21   Termination:
22   If terminating in a known state (e.g. 0)
23   Return the sequences of inputs $\hat{x}_{t-W}^t(0)$ along the path to that known state
     and the reliability vector to that state $L_{t-W}^t(q)$
24   If terminating in any state
25   Find final state with minimal metric
26   Return the sequence of inputs along that path to that state
     and the reliability vector to that state.
27   End

12.12 Trellis Representations of Block and Cyclic Codes

In this section, we take a dual perspective to that of the previous section: we describe how linear block codes can be represented in terms of a trellis. Besides theoretical insight, the trellis representation can also be used to provide a means of soft-decision decoding that does not depend upon any particular algebraic structure of the code. These decoding algorithms can make block codes "more competitive with convolutional codes" [[273], p. 3].

12.12.1 Block Codes

We demonstrate the trellis idea with a $(7, 4, 3)$ binary Hamming code. Let

$$H = \begin{bmatrix} 1 & 1 & 1 & 0 & 1 & 0 & 0 \\ 1 & 1 & 0 & 1 & 0 & 1 & 0 \\ 1 & 0 & 1 & 1 & 0 & 0 & 1 \end{bmatrix} = \begin{bmatrix} \mathbf{h}_1 & \mathbf{h}_2 & \mathbf{h}_3 & \mathbf{h}_4 & \mathbf{h}_5 & \mathbf{h}_6 & \mathbf{h}_7 \end{bmatrix} \tag{12.53}$$

be the parity check matrix for the code. Then a column vector $\mathbf{x}$ is a codeword if and only if $\mathbf{s} = H\mathbf{x} = \mathbf{0}$; that is, the syndrome $\mathbf{s}$ must satisfy

$$\mathbf{s} = \begin{bmatrix} \mathbf{h}_1 & \mathbf{h}_2 & \mathbf{h}_3 & \mathbf{h}_4 & \mathbf{h}_5 & \mathbf{h}_6 & \mathbf{h}_7 \end{bmatrix} \begin{bmatrix} x_1 \\ x_2 \\ x_3 \\ x_4 \\ x_5 \\ x_6 \\ x_7 \end{bmatrix} = \sum_{i=1}^{7} \mathbf{h}_i x_i = \mathbf{0}.$$

We define the *partial syndrome* by

$$\mathbf{s}_{r+1} = \sum_{i=1}^{r} \mathbf{h}_i x_i = \mathbf{s}_r + \mathbf{h}_r x_r,$$

with $\mathbf{s}_1 = \mathbf{0}$. Then $\mathbf{s}_{n+1} = \mathbf{s}$.

A trellis representation of a code is obtained by using $\mathbf{s}_r$ as the state, with an edge between a state $\mathbf{s}_r$ and $\mathbf{s}_{r+1}$ if $\mathbf{s}_{r+1} = \mathbf{s}_r$ (corresponding to $x_r = 0$) or if $\mathbf{s}_{r+1} = \mathbf{s}_r + \mathbf{h}_r$ (corresponding to $x_r = 1$). Furthermore, the trellis is terminated at the state $\mathbf{s}_{n+1} = \mathbf{0}$, corresponding to the fact that a valid codeword has a syndrome of zero. The trellis has at most 2^{n-k} states in it.

Figure 12.34 shows the trellis for the parity check matrix of (12.53). Horizontal transitions correspond to $x_i = 0$ and diagonal transitions correspond to $x_i = 1$. Only those paths which end up at $\mathbf{s}_8 = \mathbf{0}$ are retained.

As may be observed, the trellis for a block code is "time-varying" — it has different connections for each section of the trellis. The number of states "active" at each section of the trellis also varies.

For a general code, the trellis structure is sufficiently complicated that it may be difficult to efficiently represent in hardware. There has been recent work, however, on families of codes whose trellises have a much more regular structure. These are frequently obtained by recursive constructions (e.g., based on Reed–Muller codes). Interested readers can consult [273].

12.12.2 Cyclic Codes

An alternative formulation of a trellis is available for a cyclic code. Recall that a cyclic code can be encoded using a linear feedback shift register as a syndrome computer. The sequence of possible states in this encoder determines a trellis structure which can be used for decoding. We demonstrate the idea again using a $(7, 4, 3)$ Hamming decoder, this time represented as a cyclic code with generator polynomial $g(x) = x^3 + x + 1$.

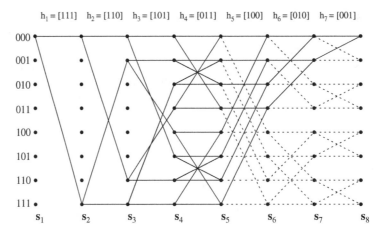

Figure 12.34: The trellis of a $(7, 4)$ Hamming code.

Figure 12.35 shows a systematic encoder. For the first $k = 4$ clock instants, switch 1 is closed (enabling feedback) and switch 2 is in position 'a'. After the systematic part of the data has been clocked through, switch 1 is opened and switch 2 is moved to position 'b'. The state contents then shift out as the coefficients of the remainder polynomial. Figure 12.36 shows the trellis associated with this encoder. For the first $k = 4$ bits, the trellis state depends upon the input bit. The coded output bit is equal to the input bit. For the last $n - k = 3$ bits, the next state is determined simply by shifting the current state. There are no input bits so the output is equal to the bit that is shifted out of the registers.

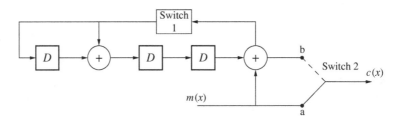

Figure 12.35: A systematic encoder for a $(7, 4, 3)$ Hamming code.

12.12.3 Trellis Decoding of Block Codes

Once a trellis for a code is established by either of the methods described above, the code can be decoded with a Viterbi algorithm. The time-varying structure of the trellis makes the indexing in the Viterbi algorithm perhaps somewhat more complicated, but the principles are the same. For example, if BPSK modulation is employed, so that the transmitted symbols are $a_i = 2c_i - 1 \in \{\pm 1\}$, and that the channel is AWGN, the branch metric for a path taken with input x_i is $(r_i - (2x_i - 1))^2$. Such soft-decision decoding can be shown to provide up to 2 dB of gain compared to hard decision decoding (see, for example, [[397], pp. 222–223]). However, this improvement does not come without a cost: for codes of any appreciable size, the number of states 2^{n-k} can be so large that trellis-based decoding is infeasible.

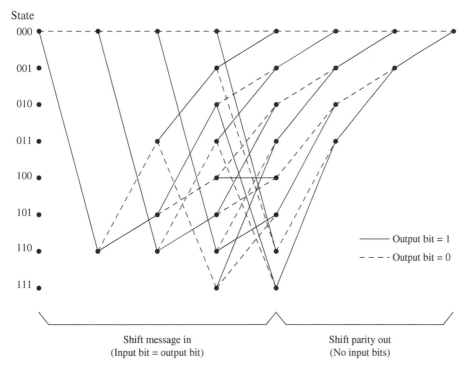

Figure 12.36: A trellis for a cyclically encoded (7,4,3) Hamming code.

Programming Laboratory 9: Programming Convolutional Encoders

Objective

In this lab, you are to create a program structure to implement both polynomial and systematic rational convolutional encoders.

Background

Reading: Sections 12.1 and 12.2.
Since both polynomial and systematic rational encoders are "convolutional encoders," they share many attributes. Furthermore, when we get to the decoding operations, it is convenient to employ one decoder which operates on data from either kind of encoder. As a result, it is structurally convenient to create a base class BinConv, then create two

derived classes, BinConvFIR and BinConvIIR. Since the details of the encoding operation and the way the state is determined differ, each of these classes employs its own encoder function. To achieve this, a virtual function encode is declared in the base class, which is then realized separately in each derived class.[6] Also, virtual member functions getstate and setstate are used for reading and setting the state of the encoder. These can be used for testing purposes; they are also used to build information tables that the decoder uses.

The declaration for the BinConv.h base class is shown here.

Algorithm 12.4 Base Class for Binary Convolutional Encoder
File: BinConv.h

---

[6] This is a tradeoff between flexibility and speed. In operation, the virtual functions are called via a pointer, so there is a pointer-lookup overhead associated with them. This also means that virtually called functions cannot be inline, even if they are very small. However, most of the computational complexity associated with these codes is associated with the decoding operation, which takes advantage of precomputed operations. So for our purposes, the virtual function overhead is not too significant.

The derived classes `BinConvFIR` and `BinConvIIR` are outlined here.

Algorithm 12.5 Derived classes for FIR and IIR Encoders
File: `BinConvFIR.h`
       `BinConvIIR.h`
       `BinConvFIR.cc`
       `BinConvIIR.cc`

Programming Part

1. Write a class `BinConvFIR` that implements convolutional encoding for a general polynomial encoder. That is, the generator matrix is of the form in (12.1), where each $g^{(i,j)}(x)$ is a polynomial. The class should have an appropriate constructor and destructor. The class should implement the virtual functions `encode`, `getstate`, and `setstate`, as outlined above.

verify that the impulse response is correct, that the `getstate` and `nextstate` functions work as expected, and that the state/nextstate table is correct. Use Figure 12.5.

The program `testconvenc.cc` may be helpful.

Algorithm 12.6 Test program for convolutional encoders
File: `testconvenc.cc`

(b) The polynomial transfer function

$$G(x) = \begin{bmatrix} x^2 + x + 1 & x^2 & 1 + x \\ x & 1 & 0 \end{bmatrix} \quad (12.54)$$

has the state diagram and trellis shown in Figure 12.37. Verify that for this encoder, the impulse response is correct, that the

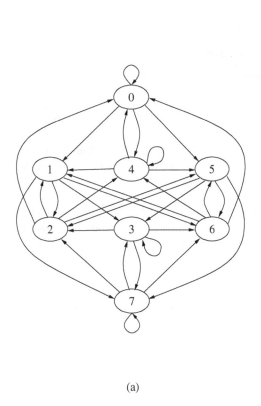

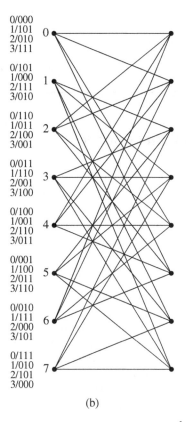

(a)   (b)

Figure 12.37 (a) State diagram and (b) trellis for the encoder in (12.54).

Test your encoder as follows:
(a) Using the encoder with transfer function

$$G(x) = \begin{bmatrix} 1 + x^2 & 1 + x + x^2 \end{bmatrix},$$

`getstate` and `nextstate` functions work as expected, and that the state/nextstate table is correct.

2. Write a class `BinConvIIR` that implements a systematic encoder (possibly employing IIR filters). The generator matrix is of the form

$$G(x) = \begin{bmatrix} & & \frac{p_1(x)}{q_1(x)} \\ & & \frac{p_2(x)}{q_2(x)} \\ & I & \vdots \\ & & \frac{p_k(x)}{q_k(x)} \end{bmatrix}$$

for polynomials $p_i(x)$ and $q_i(x)$.

Test your class using the recursive systematic encoder of (12.2), checking as for the first case. (You may find it convenient to find the samples of the impulse by long division.)

Programming Laboratory 10: Convolutional Decoders: The Viterbi Algorithm

Objective

You are to write a convolutional decoder class that decodes using both hard and soft metrics with the Viterbi algorithm.

Background

Reading: Section 12.3.

While there are a variety of ways that the Viterbi algorithm can be structured in C++, we recommend using a base class `Convdec.h` that implements that actual Viterbi algorithm and using a virtual function `metric` to compute the metric. This is used by derived classes `BinConvdec01` (for binary 0–1 data) and `BinConvBPSK` (for BPSK modulated data), where each derived class has its own metric function.

The base class `Convdec`

This class is a base class for all of the Viterbi-decoded objects.

Algorithm 12.7 The Base Decoder Class Declarations
File: `Convdec.h`
`Convdec.cc`

In this class, an object of type `BinConv` (which could be either an FIR or IIR convolutional encoder, if you have used the class specification in Lab 9) is passed in. The constructor builds appropriate data arrays for the Viterbi algorithm, placing them in the variables `prevstate` and `inputfrom`. A virtual member function `metric` is used by derived classes to compute the branch metric. The core of the algorithm is used in the member function `viterbi`, which is called by the derived classes. Some other functions are declared:

- `showpaths` — You may find it helpful while debugging to dump out information about the paths. This function (which you write) should do this for you.

- `getinpnow` — This function decodes the last available branch in the set of paths stored, based on the best most recent metric. If `adv` is asserted, the pointer to the end of the branches is incremented. This can be used for dumping out the decisions when the end of the input stream is reached.

- `buildprev` builds the state/previous state array, which indicates the connections between states of the trellis.

The derived class `BinConvdec01`

The first derived class is `BinConvdec01.h`, for binary 0–1 decoding using the Hamming distance as the branch metric.

Algorithm 12.8 Convolutional decoder for binary (0,1) data
File: `BinConvdec01.h`
`BinConvdec01.cc`

This class provides member data `outputmat`, which can be used for direct lookup of the output array given the state and the input. Since the output is, in general, a vector quantity, this is a three-dimensional array. It is recommended that space be allocated using `CALLOCTENSOR` defined in `matalloc.h`. The member variable `data` is used by the `metric` function, as shown. The class description is complete as shown here, except for the function `buildoutputmat`, which is part of the programming assignment.

The derived class `BinConvdecBPSK`

The next derived class is `BinConvdecBPSK.h`, for decoding BPSK-modulated convolutionally coded data using the Euclidean distance as the branch metric.

Algorithm 12.9   Convolutional decoder for BPSK data
File: `BinConvdecBPSK.h`
       `BinConvdecBPSK.cc`

As for the other derived class, space is provided for `outputmat` and `data`; the class is complete as presented here except for the function `buildoutputmat`.

Programming Part

1. Finish the functions in `Convdec.cc`.

2. Test the binary (0,1) `BinConvdec01` decoder for the encoder $G(x) = [1 + x^2, 1 + x + x^2]$ by reproducing the results in Example 12.23. The program `testconvdec` can help.

Algorithm 12.10   Test the convolutional decoder
File: `testconvdec.cc`

3. Test the convolutional decoder `BinConvdecBPSK` by modulating the $\{0, 1\}$ data. Again, `testconvdec` can help.

4. Determine the performance of the encoder $G(x) = \begin{bmatrix} 1 + x^2 & 1 + x + x^2 \end{bmatrix}$ by producing an error curve on the AWGN channel using BPSK modulation with a soft metric. Compare the soft metric performance with hard metric performance, where the BSC is modeled as having crossover probability $p_c = Q(\sqrt{2E_c/N_0})$. Compare the two kinds of coded performances with uncoded BPSK modulation. Also, plot the bound (12.41) and the approximation (12.43) on the same graph.

   How much coding gain is achieved? How do the simulation results compare with the theoretical bounds/approximations? How do the simulations compare with the theoretically predicted asymptotic coding gain? How much better is the soft-decoding than the hard-decoding?

5. Repeat the testing, but use the catastrophic code with encoder $G(x) = [1 + x, 1 + x^2]$. How do the results for the noncatastrophic encoder compare with the results for the catastrophic encoder?

12.13   Exercises

12.1   For the $R = 1/2$ convolutional encoder with

$$G(x) = \begin{bmatrix} 1 + x^2 + x^3 & 1 + x + x^3 \end{bmatrix} \tag{12.55}$$

(a) Draw a hardware realization of the encoder.

(b) Determine the convolutional generator matrix G.

(c) For the input sequence $\mathbf{m} = [1, 0, 1, 1, 0, 1, 1]$ determine the coded output sequence.

(d) Draw the state diagram. Label the branches of the state diagram with input/output values.

(e) Draw the trellis.

(f) What is the constraint length of the code?

(g) Determine the State/Next State table.

(h) Determine the State/Previous State table.

(i) Is this a catastrophic realization? Justify your answer.

(j) Determine the weight enumerator $T(D, N)$.

(k) What is d_{free}?

(l) Determine upper and lower bounds on P_b for a BSC using (12.37) and (12.38) and an approximation using (12.31). Plot as a function of the signal-to-noise ratio, where $p_c = Q(\sqrt{2E_c/N_0})$. Compare the bounds to uncoded performance.

(m) Determine upper and lower bounds on P_b for an AWGN channel using (12.41) and (12.42) and plot as a function of the signal-to-noise ratio.

(n) Determine the theoretical asymptotic coding gain for the BSC and AWGN channels. Compare with the results from the plots. Also, comment on the difference (in dB) between the hard and soft metrics.

(o) Express $G(x)$ as a pair of octal numbers using both leading 0 and trailing 0 conventions.

(p) Suppose the output of a BSC is $\mathbf{r} = [11, 11, 00, 01, 00, 00, 10, 10, 10, 11]$. Draw the trellis for the Viterbi decoder and indicate the maximum likelihood path through the trellis. Determine the maximum likelihood estimate of the transmitted codeword and the message bits. According to this estimate, how many bits of $\mathbf{r}$ are in error?

12.2 For the $R = 1/3$ convolutional coder with

$$G(x) = \begin{bmatrix} 1 + x & 1 + x^2 & 1 + x + x^2 \end{bmatrix}$$

(a) Draw a hardware realization of the encoder.

(b) Determine the convolutional generator matrix G.

(c) For the input sequence $\mathbf{m} = [1, 0, 1, 1, 0, 1, 1]$ determine the coded output sequence.

(d) Draw the state diagram. Label the branches of the state diagram with input/output values.

(e) Draw the trellis.

(f) What is the constraint length of the code?

(g) Determine the State/Next State table.

(h) Determine the State/Previous State table.

(i) Is this a catastrophic realization? Justify your answer.

(j) Determine the weight enumerator $T(D, N)$.

(k) What is d_{free}?

(l) Express $G(x)$ as a triplet of octal numbers.

12.3 Find a catastrophic encoder equivalent to $G(x) = \begin{bmatrix} 1 + x^2 & 1 + x + x^2 \end{bmatrix}$ and determine an infinite-weight message $m(x)$ that results in a finite-weight codeword for this catastrophic encoder.

12.4 Show that $G_4(x)$ defined in (12.8) is equivalent to $G_2(x)$ of (12.5).

12.5 Let $G(x)$ be the transfer function matrix of a basic convolutional code. Show that $G(x)$ is equivalent to a basic transfer function matrix $G'(x)$ if and only if $G'(x) = T(x)G(x)$, where $T(x)$ is a polynomial unimodular matrix.

12.6 Determine a polynomial systematic encoder transfer function matrix equivalent to

$$G(x) = \begin{bmatrix} 1 + x & x & 1 \\ x^2 & 1 & 1 + x + x^2 \end{bmatrix}.$$

12.7 For the transfer function matrices

$$G(x) = \begin{bmatrix} 1 + x & x & 1 \\ x^2 & 1 & 1 + x + x^2 \end{bmatrix} \quad \text{and} \quad G'(x) = \begin{bmatrix} 1 + x & x & 1 \\ 1 + x^2 + x^3 & 1 + x + x^2 + x^3 & 0 \end{bmatrix}$$

(a) Show that $G(x)$ is equivalent to $G'(x)$.

(b) Show that $G(x)$ is a minimal basic encoder matrix.

(c) Show that $G'(x)$ is not a minimal basic encoder matrix.

   (d) Using the procedure described in association with (12.13), determine a transfer function matrix $G''(x)$ which is a minimal basic encoding matrix equivalent to $G'(x)$, but different from $G(x)$.

12.8 For the code generated by

$$G(x) = \begin{bmatrix} \frac{1}{1+x+x^2} & \frac{x}{1+x^3} & \frac{1}{1+x^3} \\ \frac{x^2}{1+x^3} & \frac{1}{1+x^3} & \frac{1}{1+x^3} \end{bmatrix},$$

use elementary row operations to convert the generator matrix to systematic form. Draw a circuit realization of the systematic encoder.

12.9 Catastrophic codes.

   (a) For a rate $R = 1/2$ code, let $g_1(x) = 1 + x$, $g_2(x) = 1 + x^2$. Show that when $m(x) = \frac{1}{1+x}$ the transmitted sequence has finite weight. Determine $\mathrm{GCD}(g_1(x), g_2(x))$.

   (b) Motivated by this result, prove the following: For a rate $1/n$ code, if

$$\mathrm{GCD}[g_1(x), g_2(x), \ldots, g_n(x)] = 1,$$

then the code is noncatastrophic.

12.10 For the catastrophic code with generators $g_1(x) = 1 + x$, $g_2(x) = 1 + x^2$:

   (a) Draw the state diagram.

   (b) Determine the weight enumerator $T(D, N)$ for the code.

   (c) What is the minimum free distance of the code?

   (d) How is the catastrophic nature of the code evidenced in the weight enumerator?

12.11 For the generator $G(x) = \left[1 + x^2, 1 + x + x^2 + x^3\right]$:

   (a) Find the GCD of the generator polynomials.

   (b) Find an infinite-weight message sequence that generates a codeword of finite weight.

12.12 Prove that d_{free} is independent of the encoder realization, so that it is a property of the *code* and not of a particular *encoder* for the code.

12.13 Show that the formal series expansion

$$\frac{1}{1-x} = 1 + x + x^2 + x^3 + \cdots$$

is correct. Show the formal series expansions of

$$\frac{1}{1 - 2D} \quad \text{and} \quad \frac{D^5 L^3 N}{1 - DLN(1 + L)}.$$

12.14 Show that the expressions for P_d in (12.20) and (12.21) can be bounded by $P_d < [4p_c(1 - p_c)]^{d/2}$. *Hint*: Show that $\sum_{i=(d+1)/2}^{d} \binom{d}{i} p_c^i (1 - p_c)^{d-i} < \sum_{i=(d+1)/2}^{d} \binom{d}{i} p_c^{d/2} (1 - p_c)^{d/2}$.

12.15 For a BSC where $Z = \sqrt{4p_c(1 - p_c)}$, show that (12.28) can be replaced by $P_d < Z^{d+1}$ when d is odd. Using this result, show that (12.29) can be replaced by

$$P_e(j) < \frac{1}{2}[(1 + Z)T(Z) + (1 - Z)T(-Z)].$$

12.16 [195] An upper bound on d_{free}. Let K be the number of outputs determining the output of a rate $R = 1/n$ code (i.e., K is the constraint length). The code can be represented by a matrix such as that in (12.3), in which all rows are obtained by shifting the first row.

   (a) Show that for any binary linear code, if the codewords are arranged as the rows of a matrix, then any column is either all zeros or half zeros and half ones.

(b) Consider the set of all sequences of length no greater than L. Show that the code generated by these finite-length sequences has length $(K - 1 + L)n$ symbols. Also show that the average weight of all codewords (excluding the all-zero codeword) is $w_{av}(L) \leq 2^{L-1}(K - 1 + L)n/(2^L - 1)$.

(c) Argue that the code has a minimum distance between paths of $d_{free} \leq w_{av}(L)$.

12.17 Show that (12.22) and (12.23) are correct.

12.18 A code with $k = 1$ has weight enumerator $T(D, N) = \frac{D^5 N}{1 - 2ND}$. The codewords are passed through a BSC with $p_c = 0.01$. Compute upper and lower bounds on the node error probability and the bit-error rate for Viterbi decoding. Repeat this when the code is passed through an AWGN channel with $E_b/N_0 = 6$ dB.

12.19 For a rate $R = 1/2$ code, suppose the output sequence

$$\mathbf{c} = (c_0^{(1)}, c_0^{(2)}, \ c_1^{(1)}, c_1^{(2)}, \ c_2^{(1)}, c_2^{(2)}, \ c_3^{(1)}, c_3^{(2)}, \ c_4^{(1)}, c_4^{(2)}, \ c_5^{(1)}, c_5^{(2)}, \ldots)$$

is punctured as

$$\mathbf{c} = (c_0^{(1)}, c_0^{(2)}, -, c_1^{(2)}, \ c_2^{(1)}, -, \ c_3^{(1)}, c_3^{(2)}, -, c_4^{(2)}, \ c_5^{(1)}, -, \ldots).$$

Write down the puncture matrix P.

12.20 A binary-input/binary-output channel with input a and output r has transition probabilities

$$P(r = 0|a = 0) = 0.9 \quad P(r = 0|a = 1) = 0.3$$
$$P(r = 1|a = 0) = 0.1 \quad P(r = 1|a = 1) = 0.7.$$

(a) Determine the log likelihoods.

(b) Scale and shift these values to obtain a set of bit metrics that can be reasonably approximated with not more than 3 bits.

12.21 A channel has binary inputs and three outputs, 0 and 1, and E, where E denotes an erasure. When an erasure occurs, the symbol is known to be suspicious and does not influence the decoding process — it is erased. (It is a lot like a punctured bit.) This channel is called the *binary erasure channel*. The channel has transition probabilities

$$P(r = 0|a = 0) = 0.6 \quad P(r = E|a = 0) = 0.3 \quad P(r = 1|a = 0) = 0.1$$
$$P(r = 0|a = 1) = 0.2 \quad P(r = E|a = 1) = 0.2 \quad P(r = 1|a = 1) = 0.6.$$

(a) Determine the log-likelihood ratios.

(b) Scale and shift these values to obtain a set of bit metrics that can be reasonably approximated with not more than 3 bits, making sure that erased symbols do not contribute differentially to the path metric.

12.22 An AWGN with variance $\sigma^2 = 2$ is used with BPSK-modulated data sending signals with amplitudes $a = \pm 1$. The received signal r_t is quantized to four different values $q = Q[r]$ with quantization thresholds at ± 1.5 and 0.

(a) Determine the probabilities $P(q_t|a)$ and the log probabilities $-\log P(q_t|a)$.

(b) Determine a and b so that $a(-\log P(q_t|a) - b)$ can be approximated well by integers using at most 2 bits.

12.23 A binary input/binary output channel with input a and output r has

$$P(r = 0|a = 0) = 0.99999 \quad P(r = 0|a = 1) = 0.05$$
$$P(r = 1|a = 0) = 0.00001 \quad P(r = 1|a = 1) = 0.95.$$

(a) Determine Z in the Chernoff bound from (12.34).

(b) The input to this channel is coded using a convolutional code whose path enumerator is given by

$$T(D,N) = \frac{D^5 N}{1 - 2ND}.$$

Using (12.29), determine an upper bound on the node error probability $P_e(j)$. Using (12.30) and (12.31), determine an upper bound and an approximation on the bit error rate P_b.

12.24 (Chernoff bound.) Let $X_1, X_2, \ldots, X_n$ be independent random variables with densities $p_i(x)$ and moment generating functions $\phi_i(s) = E[e^{sX_i}]$. Let $Z = \sum_{i=1}^{n} X_i$, with moment generating function $\phi_Z(s)$. Using the following steps, show that

$$P(Z \geq \gamma) \leq e^{-s\gamma} \prod_{i=1}^{n} \phi_i(s)$$

for all $s \geq 0$ such that $\phi_i(s)$ exists.

(a) Let $\phi_Z(s)$ be the moment generating function for Z. Show that $\phi_Z(s) = \prod_{i=1}^{n} \phi_i(s)$.

(b) Show that $\int_{-\infty}^{\infty} e^{sz} f_Z(z)\, dz \geq \int_{\gamma}^{\infty} e^{sz} f_Z(z)\, dz$.

(c) Finish the proof.

12.25 Show that (12.40) is correct.

12.26 A RCPC based on a rate $R = 1/4$ convolutional code has puncturing period 8 and puncturing matrices

$$P_1 = \begin{bmatrix} 1 & 1 & 1 & 1 & 1 & 1 & 1 & 1 \\ 1 & 1 & 1 & 1 & 1 & 1 & 1 & 1 \\ 1 & 1 & 1 & 1 & 1 & 1 & 1 & 1 \\ 1 & 1 & 1 & 1 & 1 & 1 & 1 & 1 \end{bmatrix} \qquad P_2 = \begin{bmatrix} 1 & 1 & 1 & 1 & 1 & 1 & 1 & 1 \\ 1 & 0 & 1 & 0 & 1 & 0 & 1 & 0 \\ 0 & 0 & 0 & 0 & 0 & 0 & 0 & 0 \\ 0 & 0 & 0 & 0 & 0 & 0 & 0 & 0 \end{bmatrix}$$

$$P_3 = \begin{bmatrix} 1 & 1 & 1 & 1 & 0 & 1 & 1 & 1 \\ 1 & 0 & 0 & 0 & 1 & 0 & 0 & 0 \\ 0 & 0 & 0 & 0 & 0 & 0 & 0 & 0 \\ 0 & 0 & 0 & 0 & 0 & 0 & 0 & 0 \end{bmatrix}.$$

(a) Determine the actual rate when using the puncture matrix P_1. Also for P_2 and P_3.

(b) The generators for the convolutional code are $g^{(1)}(x) = 1 + x^3 + x^4$, $g^{(2)}(x) = 1 + x + x^2 + x^4$, $g^{(3)}(x) = 1 + x^2 + x^3 + x^4$, and $g^{(4)}(x) = 1 + x + x^3 + x^4$. Draw a convolutional encoder capable of transmitting at these three different rates.

12.27 Determine the branch Fano metric for binary transmission of a rate $R = 1/3$ code through a BSC with $p_c = 0.1$. Then scale the metric so it has nearly integer values. Repeat for $p_c = 0.05$ and $p_c = 0.001$.

12.28 For the asymmetric channel in Exercise 12.20, determine the Fano metric for a rate $R = 1/2$ code. Then shift and scale the metric so it has nearly integer values.

12.29 For the code with generator

$$G(x) = \begin{bmatrix} 1 + x^2 + x^3 & 1 + x + x^3 \end{bmatrix},$$

the sequence $\mathbf{r} = [11, 11, 11, 01, 11, 00, 00]$ is received through a BSC with $p_c = 0.125$. Using the stack algorithm, determine the transmitted sequence. Repeat using the Fano algorithm. (The Matlab code may prove very helpful.)

12.30 Draw a trellis representing the binary block code with parity check matrix

$$H = \begin{bmatrix} 0 & 0 & 0 & 1 & 1 & 1 \\ 0 & 1 & 1 & 0 & 0 & 1 \\ 1 & 0 & 1 & 0 & 1 & 0 \end{bmatrix}.$$

12.31 Draw a trellis representation for the cyclic code with generator $g(x) = x^3 + x^2 + 1$ that employs a systematic encoder.

12.14 References

Convolutional codes were introduced in 1955 by Elias [109]. Our presentation overall has benefited greatly from [397]. The discussion of structural properties comes from that source, which, in turn, closely follows [230]. This, in turn, builds on the landmark paper on the algebraic structure of convolutional codes [135]. Catastrophic codes were first discussed in [299]. The criterion for catastrophic codes in terms of the GCD of the generators appears in [299]. Extensive simulation studies of convolutional codes and error curves appears in [196]. The results here were computed by Ojas Chauhan.

The Viterbi algorithm was described in [467]. However, it was not until [128] that the Viterbi algorithm was shown to be a MLSE. This paper also presented the weight enumerator and the graph analysis associated with the performance of convolutional codes.

An important and still very relevant source on convolutional codes is [471]. This book presents random coding performance bounds for convolutional codes and shows that convolutional codes have a higher cutoff rate than block codes. A recent book dedicated to convolutional codes is [231]. Convolutional codes are also presented in most books on coding theory and digital communication theory.

Puncturing appears to have been first explored in [54]. Tail biting was introduced in [285]. Work on short tailbiting codes with many examples of good codes appears in [420]. Basic results regarding the structure of tailbiting trellises appears in [250]. The trellis representation of a block code was presented first in [20] and developed more fully in [488]. It has been the topic of a detailed monograph [273]. Readers interested in fully developed design methodologies should consult that source. A summary of this work is in [397].

The stack algorithm was explored in [511] and [219]. The genre of sequential decoding algorithms was explored early on in [489]. The Fano algorithm appeared first in [113]. The Fano metric received theoretical foundation as a maximum likelihood metric in [296]. A comparison of sequential decoding algorithms appears in [152,153]. A discussion of the performance of the M algorithm as a function of M and comparison with the Viterbi algorithm is summarized in [397].

Tailbiting codes approaches and their analyses are described in [285] and references therein.

The SOVA is presented in [176]. See also [140] and [178].

Chapter 13

Trellis-Coded Modulation

13.1 Adding Redundancy by Adding Signals

The error-correction codes studied up to this point in the book have added redundancy by increasing the number of coded symbols. If the channel is bandlimited so that the transmitted symbol rate is fixed, this results in a lower information transmission rate. In the very common case that the high transmission rate is of interest (in contrast to minimizing transmission power), this reduction in effective information rate is unfortunate. Up until the early 1970s it was believed that coding would not greatly benefit channels needing a spectral efficiency — the number of bits transmitted per channel use — exceeding 1.

In 1976, a new method of coding was introduced by Ungerboeck [452–455] which adds redundancy to the coded signal by increasing the number of symbols in the signal constellation employed in the modulation. If the average signal energy is fixed, having more signals in the signal constellation would tend to decrease the distance between points in the signal constellation. The key, therefore, is to combine the coding and modulation into a single unit which transmits only constrained *sequences* of symbols, and to employ a sequence detector (i.e., Viterbi algorithm) to detect the sequence. The combination of constrained symbol sequences and larger signal constellation gives rise to what is known as *trellis coded modulation*, or TCM.

13.2 Background on Signal Constellations

Because TCM is built upon signal constellations, we briefly review concepts related to signal constellations. For now, we restrict our attention to one- and two-dimensional signal constellations. (A review of the communications concepts in Section 1.4 may prove helpful.)

A *signal constellation* S is a discrete set of points, typically a subset of the real line $\mathbb{R}$ or the plane $\mathbb{R}^2$ (sometimes regarded as the complex plane). A one-dimensional constellation is used in what is often called *amplitude shift keying* (ASK). A one-dimensional constellation with two points $\pm\sqrt{E_b}$ is more frequently called BPSK (binary phase-shift keying). A two-dimensional constellation with all the points lying on a circle is referred to as phase-shift keying (PSK). The constellation is frequently expressed in terms of the number of points, such as 4-PSK, 8-PSK, or 16-PSK. QPSK — quaternary PSK — is a synonym for 4-PSK. Figure 13.1 shows examples of PSK constellations, scaled so that they all have the same signal energy E_s. The minimum distance between signal points is denoted as d_0. A two-dimensional constellation with points on a square grid is frequently referred to as quadrature-amplitude modulation (QAM). Figure 13.2 shows overlays of examples of QAM constellations, where the minimum distance between points is called d_0. (The 32-point and 128-point constellations are referred to as cross constellations, since the points are arranged in a cross; this reduces the average energy compared to rectangular constellations.) Other arrangements are also possible in two dimensions.

The *spectral efficiency* η of a constellation is the number of bits carried by each symbol. Assuming the bits are identically distributed, the average *symbol energy* E_s is the average of the squared distances of the constellation points from the origin. For example, for the 16-QAM constellation with minimum distance d_0,

$$E_s = \frac{1}{16}(4((d_0/2)^2 + (d_0/2)^2) + 8((d_0/2)^2 + (3d_0/2)^2) + 4((3d_0/2)^2 + (3d_0/2)^2))$$

$$= \frac{5d_0^2}{2}.$$

Error Correction Coding: Mathematical Methods and Algorithms, Second Edition. Todd K. Moon
© 2021 John Wiley & Sons, Inc. Published 2021 by John Wiley & Sons, Inc.
Companion website: www.wiley.com/go/Moon/ErrorCorrectionCoding

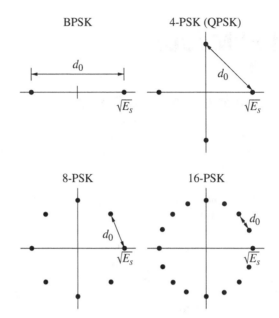

Figure 13.1: PSK signal constellations.

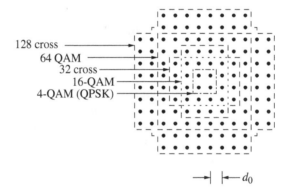

Figure 13.2: QAM signal constellations (overlaid).

Table 13.1 lists average energies and spectral efficiencies for various QAM constellations. Also shown is the average energy per bit, where $E_b = \frac{1}{\eta} E_s$. It may be computed that for a *square* constellation with M points,

$$E_s = \frac{M-1}{6} d_0^2. \tag{13.1}$$

The elements of a point $(a_1, a_2) \in \mathcal{S} \subset \mathbb{R}^2$ represent the amplitudes of two basis functions, which we denote as $\varphi_1(t)$ and $\varphi_2(t)$, which are assumed to be orthonormal (unit energy and orthogonal)

$$\int_{-\infty}^{\infty} \varphi_i^2(t)\, dt = 1 \quad \int_{-\infty}^{\infty} \varphi_1(t)\varphi_2(t)\, dt = 0.$$

Furthermore, shifts of the functions by the *symbol period* T are orthogonal,

$$\int_{-\infty}^{\infty} \varphi_i(t)\varphi_i(t - kT)\, dt = 0 \quad i = 1, 2, \text{ for all integer } k \neq 0.$$

Table 13.1: Average Energy Requirements for Some QAM Constellations

Constellation	Spectral Efficiency η (bits/symbol)	E_s	E_b
BPSK	1	$\frac{1}{4}d_0^2$	$\frac{1}{4}d_0^2$
QPSK	2	$\frac{1}{2}d_0^2$	$\frac{1}{4}d_0^2$
8PSK	3	$\frac{4}{6-2\sqrt{2}}d_0^2$	$\frac{4}{3(6-2\sqrt{2})}d_0^2$
16-QAM	4	$\frac{5}{2}d_0^2$	$\frac{5}{8}d_0^2$
32-cross	5	$5d_0^2$	d_0^2
64-QAM	6	$\frac{21}{2}d_0^2$	$\frac{7}{4}d_0^2$
128-cross	7	$\frac{41}{2}d_0^2$	$\frac{41}{14}d_0^2$
256-QAM	8	$\frac{85}{2}d_0^2$	$\frac{85}{16}d_0^2$

The time T is called the *symbol time*, or sometimes the baud interval. The number of symbols transmitted per second, $1/T$ is called the *symbol rate* or the *baud rate*.

The transmitted signal $s(t)$ is obtained by juxtaposing a sequence of scaled basis signals, each with their own amplitude representing the transmitted symbol

$$s(t) = \sum_k a_{1,k}\varphi_1(t - kT) + a_{2,k}\varphi_2(t - kT).$$

At the receiver, the received signal $r(t)$ is again projected back onto the signal constellation plane by matched filtering. Over each symbol interval, a point (r_1, r_2) is received, then the maximum likelihood (ML) detector without coding determines the constellation point nearest to (r_1, r_2).

13.3 TCM Example

With this background on signal constellations, consider the following three scenarios. In the first case, Figure 13.3(a), 2 bits select a single signal point in a QPSK constellation, resulting in $\eta = 2$ bits of information per transmitted symbol. In this QPSK constellation, the average signal energy is E_s, and the minimum squared distance between signals is $d_0^2 = 2E_s$. In the second case, $R = 2/3$ coding is used with the same QPSK constellation. The efficiency is reduced to $\eta = 4/3$ bits of information per transmitted symbol. The minimum squared distance in the second case is as in the first case $d_0^2 = 2E_s$. In the third case, 8-PSK modulation is employed on the coded bits, and again there are $\eta = 2$ bits of information per transmitted symbol. Thus, the larger signal constellation is able to attain the uncoded data rate. However, if the average signal energy E_s is the same for both the QPSK and 8-PSK, the symbol points are closer in the 8-PSK constellation. The minimum squared distance in this case is $d_0^2 = E_s(6 - 2\sqrt{2})/4$: approximately 4 dB additional signal energy would be required to make the minimum distance between 8-PSK points the same as the QPSK points. The problem of closer points can be overcome by combining the coding and the modulation.

Consider coded modulation with the 8-PSK signal constellation with points labeled as shown in Figure 13.4 [453]. (The rationale for the labeling by this partitioning mechanism is discussed below.) The points on the signal constellation correspond to elements of the sets labeled D_i. The signal point i as a binary number corresponds to the "set" of points D_i, with the least significant bit of i on the right. The minimum distance d_j at the jth partition between points in the constellation increases with j. The constellation is used with the rate $R = 2/3$ binary convolutional code, with the trellis as shown in Figure 13.5. The outputs of the convolutional coder are mapped to points in the signal constellation,

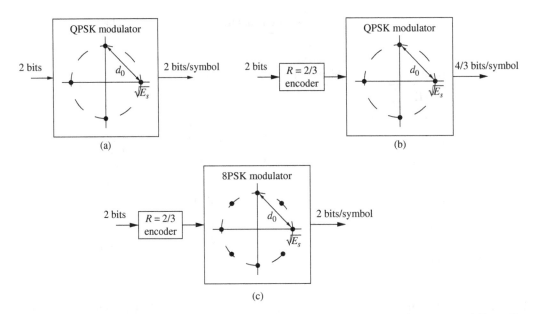

Figure 13.3: Three communication scenarios. (a) QPSK, no coding; (b) QPSK, $R = 2/3$ coding; (c) 8PSK, $R = 2/3$ coding.

resulting in a single 8-PSK symbol transmitted for each pair of input bits. We regard the convolutional encoder simply as a finite-state machine with a given number of states and specified state transitions, used to select points or subsets of the signal constellation. The combination of the convolutional coding followed by the mapping is indicated by the labeling of the trellis, with the sequence of outputs D_i corresponding to the sequence of branches read from top to bottom. Thus, for example, if the coder starts in the first state and the top branch is taken, the point in the set D_0 is transmitted; if the second branch is taken from the first state, the point in the set D_4 is transmitted, and so forth. The trellis structure imposes constraints on the *sequences* of symbols that can be transmitted. For example, starting from state 0, it is impossible to transmit the sequence (D_4, D_2). Thus, when determining the performance of the system, distances between sequences of symbols much be considered, rather than distances between individual points in the signal constellation.

The optimal decoding algorithm (Viterbi) finds a shortest path through the trellis, that is, a sequence of symbols in the trellis which is closest to the sequence observed at the receiver. Assuming that the channel is AWGN, the branch metric is related to the squared Euclidean distance between received signal points and transmitted signal points along a branch. As in the case of convolutional codes, the overall performance of the system is dominated by the shortest distance between two paths which diverge then come back together — errors which lead to the path metric exceeding half of this distance and result in selecting the incorrect path in the Viterbi algorithm.

Accordingly, let us find the shortest distance between two paths which diverge then remerge. One candidate to consider is the distance between the transmitted symbols (D_0, D_0) and the symbols along the path (D_4, D_1). The sequence is indicated in Figure 13.5 with a dotted line, remerging after two branches. The squared distance between the sequences is the sum of the squares of the distances, which can be determined with the help of the diagram in Figure 13.4:

$$d^2((D_0, D_0), (D_4, D_1)) = d^2(D_0, D_4) + d^2(D_0, D_1) = d_2^2 + d_0^2$$

$$= 4E_s + (2 - \sqrt{2})E_s = (6 - \sqrt{2})E_s.$$

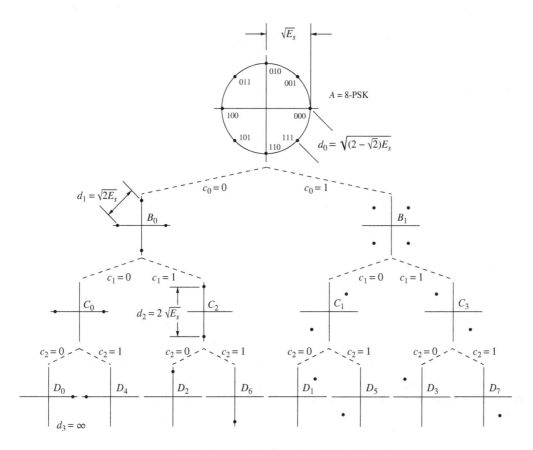

Figure 13.4: Set partitioning of an 8-PSK signal.

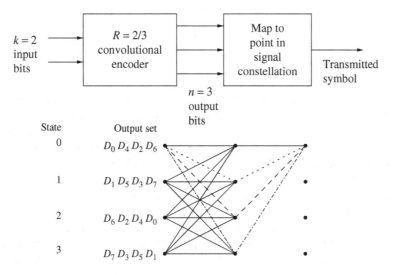

Figure 13.5: $R = 2/3$ trellis-coded modulation example.

A second path to consider is represented by the sequence (D_2, D_6), shown with dashed lines, with

$$d^2((D_0, D_0), (D_2, D_6)) = d^2(D_0, D_2) + D^2(D_0, D_6) = d_1^2 + d_1^2$$
$$= 2E_s + 2E_s = 4E_s.$$

A third path (dash-dot line) represented by (D_6, D_7) has

$$d^2((D_0, D_0), (D_6, D_7)) = d^2(D_0, D_6) + d^2(D_0, D_7) = d_1^2 + d_0^2$$
$$= 2E_s + (2 - \sqrt{2})E_s = (4 - \sqrt{2})E_s.$$

This is the minimum distance path between any sequences in the trellis.

The minimum distance between any sequences in the trellis for a code is called the *free Euclidean distance*. It is usually denoted as d_{free}. Thus, for this code

$$d_{\text{free}}^2 = (4 - \sqrt{2})E_s.$$

How does the performance of this coded scheme compare with uncoded 4-PSK that transmits information at the same rate? The quantity

$$\gamma = \left(\frac{E_{s,\text{uncoded}}}{E_{s,\text{coded}}} \right) \left(\frac{d_{\text{free,coded}}^2}{d_{\text{free,uncoded}}^2} \right) = \gamma_C \gamma_D$$

is called the **(asymptotic) coding gain** for the code. Here, $d_{\text{free,uncoded}}$ is the minimum distance between points in the original signal constellation and $d_{\text{free,coded}}$ is the free Euclidean distance between nearest sequences of the coded signal. The factor $\gamma_C = E_{s,\text{uncoded}}/E_{s,\text{coded}}$ is called the **constellation expansion factor**; it accounts for the average energy of the constellations — larger average energy in the coded constellation reduces the coding gain. The factor $\gamma_D = d_{\text{free,coded}}^2/d_{\text{free,uncoded}}^2$ is called the **increased distance factor**. In our case, the constellation expansion factor is 1 (the PSK constellations require the same energy per symbol) and we find the coding gain is

$$\gamma = \frac{(4 - \sqrt{2})E_s}{2E_s} = 1.29.$$

This is frequently expressed in dB, $\gamma_{\text{dB}} = 10\log_{10}(\gamma) = 10\log_{10}(1.29) = 1.1$ dB. Asymptotically (for high SNR), the coded 8-PSK scheme requires 1.1 dB less energy for (essentially) the same performance as the uncoded QPSK scheme.

There are other four-state convolutional coding schemes that can provide better coding performance. Consider the coding scheme shown in Figure 13.6. In this figure, there are two input bits. However, only one of them goes into the convolutional encoder, which is a rate $R = 1/2$ encoder. The two coded output bits are used to select one of four *sets* of constellation points, which are the sets denoted $C_0, C_1, C_2,$ and C_3 in Figure 13.4. Each set has two symbols. The other input bit is used to select one of the two points within a selected set. The result is that the pair of input bits can be used to select a single output symbol. The behavior of the convolutional code and the signal mapper is shown by the trellis of Figure 13.6. The sets selected by the output bits are listed to the left of the trellis. For example, from state 0, the output sets C_0 and C_2 can be selected, depending on which branch of the trellis is taken. The fact that C_0 actually consists of two points is shown as *parallel* paths in the trellis between state 0 and state 0. One of the paths corresponds to the point $D_0 \in C_0$; the parallel path corresponds to the point $D_4 \in C_0$. The parallel paths corresponding to C_2 are similarly labeled, and the other (unlabeled) parallel paths of the trellis have their corresponding symbol point assignments.

What is the minimum distance between diverging/remerging paths for this code? Let us consider the path (C_0, C_0, C_0) and the path (C_2, C_3, C_2), starting from state 0, indicated with dashed lines in

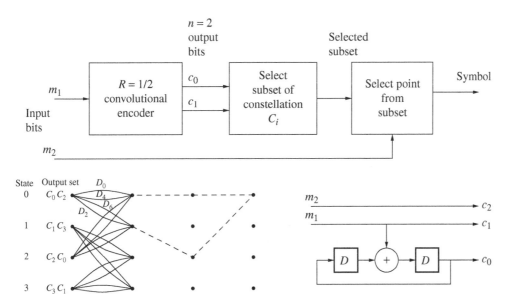

Figure 13.6: A TCM encoder employing subset selection and a four-state trellis.

Figure 13.6. In comparing distances between sets, the distance between the *nearest* points in the sets must be used. The squared distance is

$$d^2((C_0, C_0, C_0), (C_2, C_3, C_2)) = d^2(C_0, C_2) + d^2(C_0, C_3) + d^2(C_0, C_2)$$
$$= d_1^2 + d_0^2 + d_1^2 = (6 - \sqrt{2})E_s.$$

Is this the smallest distance between diverging/remerging paths? There is, in fact, another way that paths can diverge and remerge — through the parallel paths. Consider the distance between the path C_0 and C_0, where in one case the symbol D_0 is sent, and in the other case the symbol D_4 is sent. Then the distance is

$$d^2(D_0, D_4) = d_2^2 = 4E_s,$$

which is smaller than the last distance found and is, in fact, the smallest distance between diverging/remerging sequences.

The coding gain for this code compared to uncoded QPSK (transmitting information at the same rate) is

$$\gamma = \frac{4E_s}{2E_s} = 2,$$

a coding gain of 3 dB. It can be verified that this is the best possible coding gain for a TCM code having four states.

Let us now consider a convolutional encoder with eight states, with trellis and encoder as shown in Figure 13.7. The coder selects single subsets (the D_i). The minimum squared distance in this case is

$$d^2((D_0, D_0, D_0), (D_6, D_7, D_6)) = d_1^2 + d_0^2 + d_1^2 = 4.585E_s.$$

The coding gain relative to uncoded QPSK is

$$\gamma = \frac{4.585E_s}{2E_s} = 2.29 \quad \gamma_{dB} = 10\log_{10}\gamma = 3.6dB.$$

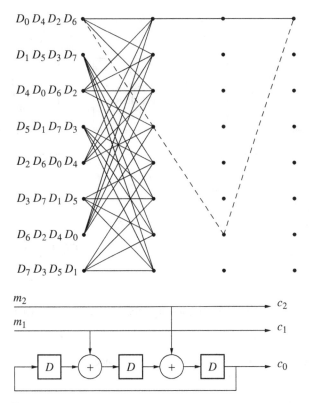

$$
\begin{array}{llll}
D_0\,D_4\,D_2\,D_6 & & & \\
D_1\,D_5\,D_3\,D_7 & & & \\
D_4\,D_0\,D_6\,D_2 & & & \\
D_5\,D_1\,D_7\,D_3 & & & \\
D_2\,D_6\,D_0\,D_4 & & & \\
D_3\,D_7\,D_1\,D_5 & & & \\
D_6\,D_2\,D_4\,D_0 & & & \\
D_7\,D_3\,D_5\,D_1 & & & \\
\end{array}
$$

Figure 13.7: An eight-state trellis for 8-PSK TCM.

From these examples, we may make the following observations:

- TCM relies on signal space enlargement to compensate for coding redundancy, resulting in equivalent data rates for coded data.

- The TCM concept combines convolutional coding with the signal mapping (modulation). Rather than optimizing the coding and modulation separately, TCM code design seeks a jointly optimum solution for coding and modulation.

- The finite-state machine structure imposed by the underlying convolutional code imposes constraints between sequences of symbols. The performance depends upon distances between *sequences* of symbols. By proper design, the reduced distance between symbols in the enlarged signal constellation or the additional average energy in the enlarged constellation can be more than compensated for by effective distance between sequences, resulting in net coding gain.

  While these examples have used convolutional codes, actually any finite state machine, even a nonlinear state machine, could be used to impose constraints on the sequences of allowed symbols.

- The (asymptotic) performance depends upon the minimum distance between diverging/remerging paths, where sums of squared Euclidean distances are used (in AWGN). This minimum distance is referred to as the free Euclidean distance of the code. The (asymptotic) coding gain in dB is computed as

$$
\gamma_{\mathrm{dB}} = 10\log_{10}\left(\frac{E_{s,\mathrm{uncoded}}}{E_{s,\mathrm{coded}}}\right)\left(\frac{d_{\mathrm{free,coded}}^2}{d_{\mathrm{free,uncoded}}^2}\right) = \gamma_{C,\mathrm{dB}} + \gamma_{D,\mathrm{dB}}.
$$

- The encoding architecture includes (in general) two stages. The first stage selects *sets* of points, based on the convolutional coder output. The second stage selects a single point for transmission from the set.

- The sets which are used in the TCM code can be obtained from a "set partitioning" process.

- The subset selection may give rise to parallel paths in the trellis; the number of parallel paths is the number of points in the set.

- Finding minimum distance requires consideration of distances between parallel paths, as well as other diverging/remerging paths through the trellis.

- As the number of states in the coder increases, increased coding gain is possible.

13.3.1 The General Ungerboeck Coding Framework

The general TCM idea is shown in Figure 13.8. We take $k = k_1 + k_2$ message bits as inputs. The first k_1 bits go into a rate $R = k_1/(k_1 + 1)$ convolutional encoder. The $k_1 + 1$ coded bits then select a subset of points. The remaining k_2 bits select a point from within the subset. The constellation must therefore have $2^{k_1+k_2+1}$ points in it.

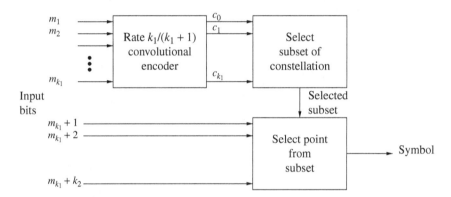

Figure 13.8: Block diagram of a TCM encoder.

In the first example above, $k_1 = 2$ and $k_2 = 0$ and the coder had four states. That is, we simply employ a rate 2/3 encoder, then use the output to select signal points. In the second example, $k_1 = 1$, $k_2 = 1$ and the encoder had four states. In the third example, $k_1 = 2$, $k_2 = 0$ and the encoder had eight states.

13.3.2 The Set Partitioning Idea

The problem now is how to determine the subsets of the signal constellation. An effective answer was developed by Ungerboeck, using what he called *set partitioning*. We recursively divide a constellation into subsets with increasing intraset distance. The Ungerboeck set partitioning rules [454] are summarized as follows:

- Signals in the lowest partition of the partition tree are assigned parallel transitions.

  This rule maximizes the distance between symbols assigned to parallel transitions in the trellis.

- State transitions that begin and end in the same state should be assigned subsets separated by the largest Euclidean distance.

This ensures that the total distance is at least the sum of the minimum distances between signals in these subsets.

For example, in the 8-PSK example, the 8-PSK constellation was partitioned into two 4-PSK constellations (the sets B_0 and B_1 in Figure 13.4).

- The signal points should be used equally often.

Furthermore, the partitioned constellation should produce subsets that have a higher minimum distance than the sets above it.

Figure 13.9 provides an example of set partitioning for a 16-QAM signal constellation. Figure 13.10 shows a partition for an amplitude shift-keyed system, 8-ASK, a one-dimensional constellation.

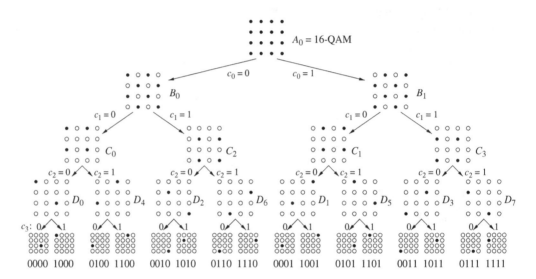

Figure 13.9: Set partitioning on a 16-QAM constellation.

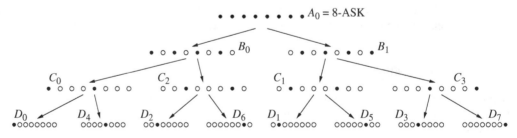

Figure 13.10: Partition for 8-ASK signaling.

13.4 Some Error Analysis for TCM Codes

13.4.1 General Considerations

The probability of error analysis for TCM codes starts out very similar to that of convolutional codes: We employ the union bound to express the probability of node error and bit error rate in terms of binary error probabilities, then develop expressions for those error probabilities. The problem is complicated, however, by the fact that TCM codes are not, in general, linear, even when the underlying state machine is a linear convolutional coder. Additional effort to bound the probability of error is therefore needed.

Denote the "correct" path through the trellis by $\mathbf{c}$. Let P_j denote the set of all paths that diverge from node j in the trellis and let $\mathbf{p}_{i,j} \in P_j$ be an incorrect path that diverges at node j, then remerges. Let $e_{i,j}$ be the event that $\mathbf{p}_{i,j}$ is chosen by the decoding (Viterbi) algorithm. The probability of a node error (i.e., the Viterbi algorithm chooses an incorrect path) at any node when $\mathbf{c}$ is the correct path is

$$P_{|\mathbf{c}} = \Pr\left(\bigcup_j \bigcup_i e_{i,j} | \mathbf{c}\right).$$

The average probability of error $\overline{P}_e$ is obtained by averaging over all correct paths,

$$\overline{P}_e = \sum_{\mathbf{c}} P(\mathbf{c}) P_{|\mathbf{c}} = \sum_{\mathbf{c}} P(\mathbf{c}) \Pr\left(\bigcup_j \bigcup_i e_{i,j} | \mathbf{c}\right),$$

where $P(\mathbf{c})$ is the probability of the path $\mathbf{c}$. Since the paths are not disjoint, the probability is difficult to compute, so the union bound is employed to obtain a somewhat simpler expression,

$$\overline{P}_e \le \sum_{\mathbf{c}} P(\mathbf{c}) \sum_j \Pr\left(\bigcup_i e_{i,j} | \mathbf{c}\right). \tag{13.2}$$

If the length l of the encoded sequence is very long, then it is probable that a node error eventually occurs. In fact, $\overline{P}_e \to 1$ as $l \to \infty$. A more interesting measure is the rate at which node errors occur. We denote

$$\overline{P} = \lim_{l \to \infty} \frac{1}{l} \overline{P}_e.$$

Averaged over an infinite trellis, every node has the same characteristics, so the dependence on an individual node j can be removed to write

$$\overline{P} \le \sum_{\mathbf{c}} P(\mathbf{c}) \Pr\left(\bigcup_i e_i | \mathbf{c}\right),$$

where e_i is the event that an error event starts at an arbitrary time unit.

We now employ the union bound again to write

$$\overline{P} \le \sum_{\mathbf{c}} P(\mathbf{c}) \sum_{e_i} \Pr(e_i | \mathbf{c}).$$

The probability $\Pr(e_i | \mathbf{c})$ is the probability of the error event e_i when $\mathbf{c}$ is sent. This is the probability of error for a *binary detection* problem. We denote this probability as $P_{\mathbf{c} \to e_i}$.

Now let d_{ci} denote the distance (metric) between the correct path $\mathbf{c}$ and the incorrect path corresponding to the error event e_i. The probability of the error event $P_{\mathbf{c} \to e_i}$ is a function of the distance d_{ci} between the correct path $\mathbf{c}$ and the error path e_i. We write the functional dependence in general as $P_{\mathbf{c} \to e_i} = P_{d_{ci}}$. The particular functional form depends on the particular channel. For example, for the AWGN channel,

$$P_{\mathbf{c} \to e_i} = P_{d_{ci}} = Q\left(\sqrt{\frac{d_{ci}^2 R E_b}{2 N_0}}\right). \tag{13.3}$$

We thus have

$$\overline{P} \le \sum_{\mathbf{c}} P(\mathbf{c}) \sum_{e_i} P_{d_{ci}}.$$

This sum can be rearranged as

$$\overline{P} \le \sum_{d_{ci}} A_{d_{ci}} P_{d_{ci}}, \tag{13.4}$$

where $A_{d_{ci}}$ is the average number of paths $\mathbf{p}_i$ that are at a distance d_{ci} from $\mathbf{c}$, and where the sum is over all the distances. The set of pairs $(d_{ci}, A_{d_{ci}})$ is known as the **distance spectrum** of the code [397, p. 124]. The smallest distance d_{ci} is the free distance of the code.

A lower bound on the probability of node error can be obtained by keeping only the first term of (13.4),

$$\overline{P} \ge A_{d_{\text{free}}} P_{d_{\text{free}}},$$

where d_{free} is the minimum of the distances between any correct sequence $\mathbf{c}$ and an incorrect sequence.

The discussion above applies to probability of a node error. Each node error causes a certain number of bit errors in the decoded message bits. Let $B_{d_{ci}}$ denote the average number of bit errors on error paths with distance d_{ci}. Since the trellis code encodes k bits per symbol, the average bit error rate is bounded by

$$\overline{P}_b \le \sum_{d_{ci}} \frac{1}{k} B_{d_{ci}} P(d_{ci}).$$

For an AWGN we have, using (13.3),

$$\overline{P} \le \sum_{d_{ci}} A_{d_{ci}} Q\left(\sqrt{\frac{d_{ci}^2 R E_b}{2N_0}}\right) \quad \overline{P} \ge A_{d_{\text{free}}} Q\left(\sqrt{\frac{d_{\text{free}}^2 R E_b}{2N_0}}\right)$$

$$\overline{P}_b \le \sum_{d_{ci}} \frac{1}{k} B_{d_{ci}} Q\left(\sqrt{\frac{d_{ci}^2 R E_b}{2N_0}}\right) \quad \overline{P}_b \ge \frac{1}{k} B_{d_{\text{free}}} Q\left(\sqrt{\frac{d_{\text{free}}^2 R E_b}{2N_0}}\right).$$

13.4.2   A Description of the Error Events

For the error analysis of convolutional codes (Section 12.5), it was not necessary to average over the set of correct code sequences $\mathbf{c}$, since it suffices to consider only the all zero codeword as the correct codeword. However, TCM is not necessarily a linear code. It may be necessary to consider average behavior over all correct paths. In this section, we introduce some notation to describe how this is done.

Consider the case illustrated in Figure 13.11, where the correct path $\mathbf{c}$ passes through the states $p = p_0 \to p_1 \to p_2 \to \cdots \to p_{L-1} \to p_L$ and the incorrect path $\mathbf{e}_i$ consists of the states $q = q_0 \to q_1 \to q_2 \to \cdots \to q_{L-1} \to q_L$, where $q_0 = p_0$ and $q_L = p_L$. To describe the error events corresponding to all error paths, we consider all paths $\mathbf{e}_i$ that deviate from the correct path. The 2-tuple sequence $(p_0, q_0) \to (p_1, q_1) \to \cdots \to (p_L, q_L)$ denotes the pair of paths

$$p_0 \to p_1 \to p_2 \to \cdots \to p_{L-1} \to p_L \text{ and } q_0 \to q_1 \to q_2 \to \cdots \to q_{L-1} \to q_L.$$

Let $\delta((p, q) \to (p_1, q_1))$ denote the squared distance accrued (the branch metric) when the correct path transitions from state p to state p_1 while the incorrect path transitions from state q to state q_1. If there is no transition $(p, q) \to (p_1, q_1)$, then $\delta((p, q) \to (p_1, q_1))$ is defined to be ∞. The cumulative squared distance along this path is

$$\sum_{l=1}^{L} \delta((p_{l-1}, q_{l-1}) \to (p_l, q_l)) \overset{\triangle}{=} d_{ci}^2,$$

where d_{ci}^2 is the squared interpath distance between the correct path $\mathbf{c}$ and the incorrect path $\mathbf{e}_i$.

We develop an algebraic expression for the set of interpath distances using a power-series-like notation. Let x be a "dummy" variable. The squared distance $\delta((p,q) \to (p_1,q_1))$ is represented as the monomial $x^{\delta((p,q) \to (p_1,q_1))}$. Using this notation, products of monomials accumulate distances in the exponent. Thus,

$$\prod_{l=1}^{L} x^{\delta((p_{l-1},q_{l-1}) \to (p_l,q_l))} = x^{\sum_{l=1}^{L} \delta((p_{l-1},q_{l-1}) \to (p_l,q_l))} = x^{d_{ci}^2}.$$

We assume that each transition $p \to p_1$ occurs with probability $1/2^k$ for a k-input TCM, which is the probability of the correct branch c.

We now define the **output transition matrix** associated with the encoder and decoder by

$$B_{(p,q),(p_1,q_1)} = [b_{(p,q),(p_1,q_1)}] = \frac{1}{2^k}[x^{\delta((p,q) \to (p_1,q_1))}] = \frac{1}{2^k}x^{d^2((p,q),(p_1,q_1))}.$$

The matrix B is indexed by all possible pairs of "from" states (p,q) and all possible pairs of "to" states (p_1,q_1). The elements of the matrix are monomials whose exponent is the squared branch metric.

Example 13.1 The trellis and encoder of Figure 13.12, having connection coefficients $g_0 = 5$, $g_1 = 4$, and $g_2 = 2$, are used with the 8-PSK partition shown in Figure 13.4. The following are some branch costs for this coder, assuming that the constellation is normalized so that $E_s = 1$.

$$\delta((0,0) \to (0,1)) = d^2(D_0,D_2) = 2 \qquad \delta((0,0) \to (0,2)) = d^2(D_0,D_4) = 4$$

$$\delta((0,1) \to (0,0)) = d^2(D_0,D_5) = 3.4 \qquad \delta((0,1) \to (0,1)) = d^2(D_0,D_7) = 0.6$$

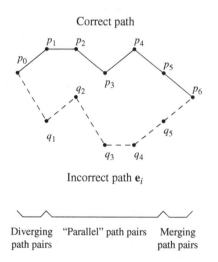

Figure 13.11: A correct path and an error path.

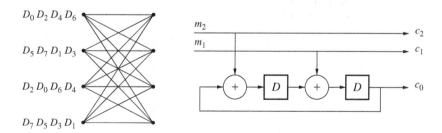

Figure 13.12: Example trellis for four-state code.

The corresponding output transition matrix B is

$$
B(x) = \frac{1}{4}
\begin{array}{c|cccccccccccccccc}
 & 00 & 01 & 02 & 03 & 10 & 11 & 12 & 13 & 20 & 21 & 22 & 23 & 30 & 31 & 32 & 33 \\
\hline
00 & 1 & x^2 & x^4 & x^2 & x^2 & 1 & x^2 & x^4 & x^4 & x^2 & 1 & x^2 & x^2 & x^4 & x^2 & 1 \\
01 & x^{3.4} & x^{0.6} & x^{0.6} & x^{3.4} & x^{3.4} & x^{3.4} & x^{0.6} & x^{0.6} & x^{0.6} & x^{3.4} & x^{3.4} & x^{0.6} & x^{0.6} & x^{0.6} & x^{3.4} & x^{3.4} \\
02 & x^2 & 1 & x^2 & x^4 & 1 & x^2 & x^4 & x^2 & x^2 & x^4 & x^2 & 1 & x^4 & x^2 & 1 & x^2 \\
03 & x^{0.6} & x^{3.4} & x^{3.4} & x^{0.6} & x^{3.4} & x^{3.4} & x^{0.6} & x^{0.6} & x^{3.4} & x^{0.6} & x^{0.6} & x^{3.4} & x^{0.6} & x^{0.6} & x^{3.4} & x^{3.4} \\
10 & x^{3.4} & x^{3.4} & x^{0.6} & x^{0.6} & x^{0.6} & x^{3.4} & x^{3.4} & x^{0.6} & x^{0.6} & x^{0.6} & x^{3.4} & x^{3.4} & x^{3.4} & x^{0.6} & x^{0.6} & x^{3.4} \\
11 & 1 & x^2 & x^4 & x^2 & x^2 & 1 & x^2 & x^4 & x^4 & x^2 & 1 & x^2 & x^2 & x^4 & x^2 & 1 \\
12 & x^{3.4} & x^{3.4} & x^{0.6} & x^{0.6} & x^{3.4} & x^{0.6} & x^{0.6} & x^{3.4} & x^{0.6} & x^{0.6} & x^{3.4} & x^{3.4} & x^{0.6} & x^{3.4} & x^{3.4} & x^{0.6} \\
13 & x^2 & 1 & x^2 & x^4 & 1 & x^2 & x^4 & x^2 & x^2 & x^4 & x^2 & 1 & x^4 & x^2 & 1 & x^2 \\
20 & x^2 & 1 & x^2 & x^4 & 1 & x^2 & x^4 & x^2 & x^2 & x^4 & x^2 & 1 & x^4 & x^2 & 1 & x^2 \\
21 & x^{3.4} & x^{3.4} & x^{0.6} & x^{0.6} & x^{3.4} & x^{0.6} & x^{0.6} & x^{3.4} & x^{0.6} & x^{0.6} & x^{3.4} & x^{3.4} & x^{0.6} & x^{3.4} & x^{3.4} & x^{0.6} \\
22 & 1 & x^2 & x^4 & x^2 & x^2 & 1 & x^2 & x^4 & x^4 & x^2 & 1 & x^2 & x^2 & x^4 & x^2 & 1 \\
23 & x^{3.4} & x^{3.4} & x^{0.6} & x^{0.6} & x^{0.6} & x^{3.4} & x^{3.4} & x^{0.6} & x^{0.6} & x^{0.6} & x^{3.4} & x^{3.4} & x^{3.4} & x^{0.6} & x^{0.6} & x^{3.4} \\
30 & x^{0.6} & x^{3.4} & x^{3.4} & x^{0.6} & x^{3.4} & x^{3.4} & x^{0.6} & x^{0.6} & x^{3.4} & x^{0.6} & x^{0.6} & x^{3.4} & x^{0.6} & x^{0.6} & x^{3.4} & x^{3.4} \\
31 & x^2 & 1 & x^2 & x^4 & 1 & x^2 & x^4 & x^2 & x^2 & x^4 & x^2 & 1 & x^4 & x^2 & 1 & x^2 \\
32 & x^{3.4} & x^{0.6} & x^{0.6} & x^{3.4} & x^{3.4} & x^{3.4} & x^{0.6} & x^{0.6} & x^{0.6} & x^{3.4} & x^{3.4} & x^{0.6} & x^{0.6} & x^{0.6} & x^{3.4} & x^{3.4} \\
33 & 1 & x^2 & x^4 & x^2 & x^2 & 1 & x^2 & x^4 & x^4 & x^2 & 1 & x^2 & x^2 & x^4 & x^2 & 1 \\
\end{array}
$$

□

For the output transition matrix, the $((p,p),(q,q))$ entry of the $B(x)^L$ is a polynomial in x whose exponents are all the distances between path pairs originating at (p,p) and terminating at (q,q); the coefficients of the polynomials are the average multiplicities of these distances. Thus, matrix multiplication can be used to keep track of the distances between paths. The $B(x)$ matrix can thus be used to compute the distance spectrum for a given encoder.

We now split $B(x)$ into matrices corresponding to branches which diverge from a common node, branches which are on a "parallel" path, and branches which merge to a common node, denoting these as $D(x)$, $P(x)$, and $M(x)$, respectively. Thus, the rows of $D(x)$ are indexed by values of (p,q) which are the same, the rows and columns of $P(x)$ are indexed by values of $(p,q), (p_1,q_1)$ which are pairwise distinct, and the columns of $M(x)$ are indexed by values of (p_1,q_1) which are the same.

Example 13.2   For the matrix $B(x)$ of Example 13.1, we have

$$
D(x) = \frac{1}{4}
\begin{array}{c|cccccccccccc}
 & 01 & 02 & 03 & 10 & 12 & 13 & 20 & 21 & 23 & 30 & 31 & 32 \\
\hline
00 & x^2 & x^4 & x^2 & x^2 & x^2 & x^4 & x^4 & x^2 & x^2 & x^2 & x^4 & x^2 \\
11 & x^2 & x^4 & x^2 & x^2 & x^2 & x^4 & x^4 & x^2 & x^2 & x^2 & x^4 & x^2 \\
22 & x^2 & x^4 & x^2 & x^2 & x^2 & x^4 & x^4 & x^2 & x^2 & x^2 & x^4 & x^2 \\
33 & x^2 & x^4 & x^2 & x^2 & x^2 & x^4 & x^4 & x^2 & x^2 & x^2 & x^4 & x^2 \\
\end{array}
$$

$$
P(x) = \frac{1}{4}
\begin{array}{c|cccccccccccc}
 & 01 & 02 & 03 & 10 & 12 & 13 & 20 & 21 & 23 & 30 & 31 & 32 \\
\hline
01 & x^{0.6} & x^{0.6} & x^{3.4} & x^{3.4} & x^{0.6} & x^{0.6} & x^{0.6} & x^{3.4} & x^{0.6} & x^{0.6} & x^{0.6} & x^{3.4} \\
02 & 1 & x^2 & x^4 & 1 & x^4 & x^2 & x^2 & x^4 & 1 & x^4 & x^2 & 1 \\
03 & x^{3.4} & x^{3.4} & x^{0.6} & x^{3.4} & x^{0.6} & x^{0.6} & x^{3.4} & x^{0.6} & x^{3.4} & x^{0.6} & x^{0.6} & x^{3.4} \\
10 & x^{3.4} & x^{0.6} & x^{0.6} & x^{0.6} & x^{3.4} & x^{0.6} & x^{0.6} & x^{0.6} & x^{3.4} & x^{3.4} & x^{0.6} & x^{0.6} \\
12 & x^{3.4} & x^{0.6} & x^{0.6} & x^{3.4} & x^{0.6} & x^{3.4} & x^{0.6} & x^{0.6} & x^{3.4} & x^{0.6} & x^{3.4} & x^{3.4} \\
13 & 1 & x^2 & x^4 & 1 & x^4 & x^2 & x^2 & x^4 & 1 & x^4 & x^2 & 1 \\
20 & 1 & x^2 & x^4 & 1 & x^4 & x^2 & x^2 & x^4 & 1 & x^4 & x^2 & 1 \\
21 & x^{3.4} & x^{0.6} & x^{0.6} & x^{3.4} & x^{0.6} & x^{3.4} & x^{0.6} & x^{0.6} & x^{3.4} & x^{0.6} & x^{3.4} & x^{3.4} \\
23 & x^{3.4} & x^{0.6} & x^{0.6} & x^{0.6} & x^{3.4} & x^{0.6} & x^{0.6} & x^{0.6} & x^{3.4} & x^{3.4} & x^{0.6} & x^{0.6} \\
30 & x^{3.4} & x^{3.4} & x^{0.6} & x^{3.4} & x^{0.6} & x^{0.6} & x^{3.4} & x^{0.6} & x^{3.4} & x^{0.6} & x^{0.6} & x^{3.4} \\
31 & 1 & x^2 & x^4 & 1 & x^4 & x^2 & x^2 & x^4 & 1 & x^4 & x^2 & 1 \\
32 & x^{0.6} & x^{0.6} & x^{3.4} & x^{3.4} & x^{0.6} & x^{0.6} & x^{0.6} & x^{3.4} & x^{0.6} & x^{0.6} & x^{0.6} & x^{3.4} \\
\end{array}
$$

$$
M(x) = \frac{1}{4}
\begin{array}{c}
\\
01 \\
02 \\
03 \\
10 \\
12 \\
13 \\
20 \\
21 \\
23 \\
30 \\
31 \\
32
\end{array}
\begin{array}{cccc}
00 & 11 & 22 & 33 \\
\left[\begin{array}{cccc}
x^{3.4} & x^{3.4} & x^{3.4} & x^{3.4} \\
x^{2} & x^{2} & x^{2} & x^{2} \\
x^{0.6} & x^{3.4} & x^{0.6} & x^{3.4} \\
x^{3.4} & x^{3.4} & x^{3.4} & x^{3.4} \\
x^{3.4} & x^{0.6} & x^{3.4} & x^{0.6} \\
x^{2} & x^{2} & x^{2} & x^{2} \\
x^{2} & x^{2} & x^{2} & x^{2} \\
x^{3.4} & x^{0.6} & x^{3.4} & x^{0.6} \\
x^{3.4} & x^{3.4} & x^{3.4} & x^{3.4} \\
x^{0.6} & x^{3.4} & x^{0.6} & x^{3.4} \\
x^{2} & x^{2} & x^{2} & x^{2} \\
x^{3.4} & x^{3.4} & x^{3.4} & x^{3.4}
\end{array}\right]
\end{array}.
$$

$\square$

With these matrices, we can now describe the set of all error events. An error path diverges from a node and only remerges at the end of the error event; in between the error path and the correct path are never in the same state at the same time step. The set of all metrics of error events of exactly L branches is computed by

$$
G_L(x) = D(x)P(x)^{L-2}M(x) \quad L \geq 2.
$$

This expression can be used to compute the distance spectrum for the code, although it becomes computationally infeasible for codes of even moderate numbers of states, due to the size of the matrices involved. (Algorithms based on the Viterbi algorithm are generally more efficient ways of actually computing the distance spectrum.) The rows and columns of the $G_L(x)$ matrix are indexed with (p, p) or (q, q) pairs. The $((p, p), (q, q))$ entry of G_L is an enumerator (or table) of all weighted distances between paths that start at the state p and end at the state q and have L branches. Note that

$$
\mathbf{1}^T G_L(x)\mathbf{1},
$$

where $\mathbf{1}$ is a vector of 2^ν 1s, is the sum of all the elements of the matrix, which contains all paths of length L from any state to any state.

Returning to (13.4), let us use the bound

$$
Q\left(\sqrt{\frac{d_{ci}^2 R E_b}{2N_0}}\right) \leq \frac{1}{2}\exp\left(-\frac{d_{ci}^2 R E_b}{4N_0}\right)
$$

(see Exercise 1.12) so that

$$
\overline{P} \leq \frac{1}{2}\sum_{d_{ci}} A_{d_{ci}}\exp\left(-\frac{d_{ci}^2 R E_b}{4N_0}\right).
$$

Since the elements of G_L tabulate all the distances between path segments of length L, this sum can be written as

$$
\overline{P} \leq \frac{1}{2}\frac{1}{2^\nu}\sum_{L=2}^{\infty}\mathbf{1}^T D(x)P(x)^{L-2}M(x)\mathbf{1}\Big|_{x=\exp(-RE_b/4N_0)}.
$$

This can be manipulated as

$$
\overline{P} \leq \frac{1}{2}\frac{1}{2^\nu}\mathbf{1}^T D(x)\sum_{i=0}^{\infty}P(x)^i M(x)\mathbf{1}\Big|_{x=\exp(-RE_b/4N_0)}
$$

$$
= \frac{1}{2}\frac{1}{2^\nu}\mathbf{1}^T D(x)(I - P(x))^{-1}M(x)\mathbf{1}\Big|_{x=\exp(-RE_b/4N_0)}, \tag{13.5}
$$

where we have used the matrix identity $(I - P)^{-1} = \sum_{i=0}^{\infty} P^i$, analogous to the identity for scalars $\frac{1}{1-p} = 1 + p + p^2 + p^3 + \cdots$. The identity holds when $\lambda_{\max} < 1$, the largest eigenvalue of $P(x)$. When the code is noncatastrophic and the SNR is sufficiently large, this is the case. The bound (13.5) is referred to as the transfer function bound. Computationally, actually computing this bound could be difficult, since it requires computing the inverse of a $(N^2 - N) \times (N^2 - N)$ matrix, where $N = 2^{\nu}$.

A tighter bound can be obtained (see, e.g., [397, p. 131]) by using a tight union bound for path differences up to a certain length, then employing the transfer function bound for the tail.

13.4.3 Known Good TCM Codes

Tables 13.2 through 13.5 describe TCM encoders which have been found by computer search [345, 452, 454]. The numbers g^i are connection polynomials in octal format. For example, the number $g = 23$ represents 10 011, with the LSB g_0 on the right. The connections are used with the systematic convolutional encoder circuit shown in Figure 13.13. The mapping from the outputs c_0, c_1, c_2 to the signal constellation is that of Figure 13.4, that is, with the points numbered consecutively around the circle. The asymptotic coding gain is with respect to QPSK, with minimum squared distance between signals of $2E_s$. The column $A_{d_{\text{free}}}$ is the average number of paths at distance d_{free}. The column $B_{d_{\text{free}}}$ is the average number of bit errors on those paths. The probability of a node error (selecting the wrong path) can be approximated by computing the probability of an error due to the shortest path (at distance d_{free} from the path corresponding to sending the all-zero sequence), scaled by the number of such paths:

$$P_e \approx A_{d_{\text{free}}} Q\left(\sqrt{\frac{d_{\text{free}}^2 R E_b}{2 N_0}} \right).$$

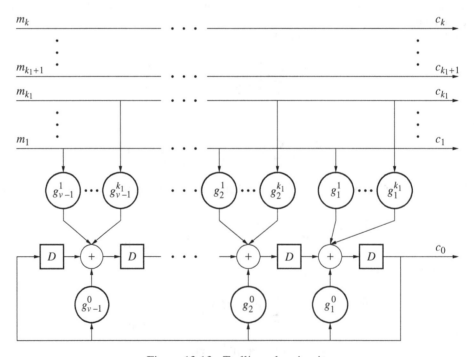

Figure 13.13: Trellis coder circuit.

Table 13.2: Maximum Free-Distance Trellis Codes for 8-PSK Constellation [345, 397, 454, 502]

$$\Delta_0 = 2\sin(\pi/8)$$

Number of States	g_0	g_1	g_2	$d^2_{\text{free}}/\Delta^2_0$	$A_{d_{\text{free}}}$	$B_{d_{\text{free}}}$	Asymptotic Coding Gain (dB) 8-PSK/4-PSK
4	5	2	–	4.00	1	1	3.0
8	11	2	4	4.59	2	7	3.6
8†	17	2	6	4.59	2	5	3.6
16	23	16	15	5.17	2.25	11.5	4.1
16†	27	4	12	5.17	2.25	7.5	4.1
32	45	16	34	5.76	4	22.25	4.6
32†	43	4	24	5.76	2.375	7.375	4.6
64	103	30	66	6.34	5.25	31.125	5.0
64†	147	12	66	6.34	3.25	14.8755	5.0
128	277	54	122	6.59	0.5	2.5	5.2
128†	277	54	176	6.59	0.5	2	5.2
256	435	72	130	7.52	1.5	12.25	5.8
256†	435	72	142	7.52	1.5	7.813	5.8
512	1525	462	360	7.52	0.313	2.75	5.8
512†	1377	304	350	7.52	0.0313	0.25	5.8
1024	2701	1216	574	8.10	1.32	10.563	6.1
1024†	2077	630	1132	8.10	0.2813	1.688	6.1
2048	4041	1212	330	8.34	3.875	21.25	6.2
4096	15,201	6306	4112	8.68	1.406	11.758	6.4
8192	20,201	12,746	304	8.68	0.617	2.711	6.4
32,768	143,373	70,002	47,674	9.51	0.25	2.5	6.8
131,072	616,273	340,602	237,374	9.85			6.9

Use point labeling (000), (001), (010), (011), (110), (111), (100), (101).

The probability of bit error is approximately

$$P_b \approx \frac{1}{k}B_{d_{\text{free}}}Q\left(\sqrt{\frac{d^2_{\text{free}}RE_b}{2N_0}}\right).$$

Another computer search [502] has yielded the improved 8-PSK designs also shown in Table 13.2. While the free distance is the same, the multiplicities $A_{d_{\text{free}}}$ and $B_{d_{\text{free}}}$ are smaller, resulting in smaller error probabilities. This uses the 8-PSK with the points around the constellation labeled in a different order, as noted in the table.

A table of good codes for 16-PSK is shown in Table 13.3. A table of good codes for one-dimensional amplitude modulated constellations is in Table 13.4. A table of good codes for 16-QAM and larger constellations is shown in Table 13.5. In these tables, the columns labeled Asymptotic Coding Gain show both the coded constellation and the constellation used for comparison. The circuit diagram corresponding to the 16-QAM and larger constellations is shown in Figure 13.14. An interesting feature about this structure is that it can be employed with larger signal constellations by using more uncoded bits. The 32-cross and 64-QAM constellations are shown in Figure 13.2. The set partition and assignment for most of these follow the pattern set in Figure 13.9. Also shown in Table 13.5 are connectors for another set of codes with generally lower $A_{d_{\text{free}}}$ and $B_{d_{\text{free}}}$ due to [502]. These are indicated with [†]. These use the labels shown below the table.

Table 13.3: Maximum Free-Distance Trellis Codes for 16-PSK Constellation [454]

	$\Delta_0 = 2\sin(\pi/16)$					
Number of States	g_0	g_1	g_2	$d_{\text{free}}^2/\Delta_0^2$	$A_{d_{\text{free}}}$	Asymptotic Coding Gain (dB) 16-PSK/8-PSK
4	5	2	–	1.324	4	3.54
8	13	4	–	1.476	4	4.01
16	23	4	–	1.628	8	4.44
32	45	10	–	1.910	8	5.13
64	103	24	–	2.000	2	5.33
128	203	24	–	2.000	2	5.33
256	427	176	374	2.085	8	5.51

Table 13.4: Maximum Free-Distance Trellis Codes for Amplitude Modulated (One-Dimensional) Constellations [454]

Number of States	g_0	g_1	$d_{\text{free}}^2/\Delta_0^2$	$A_{d_{\text{free}}}$	Asympt. Gain (dB) (Coded/Uncoded)	
					4-AM/ 2-AM	8-AM/4-AM
4	5	2	9.0	4	2.55	3.31
8	13	4	10.0	4	3.01	3.77
16	23	4	11.0	8	3.42	4.18
32	45	10	13.0	12	4.15	4.91
64	103	24	14.0	36	4.47	5.23
128	235	126	16.0	66	5.05	5.81
256	515	362	16.0	2	–	5.81

13.5 Decoding TCM Codes

Optimal decoding is accomplished using a Viterbi algorithm. The general outline is the same as for convolutional codes. However, in computing the branch metric associated with a received signal $\mathbf{r}_t$, the *nearest* point in the subset for that branch is used. For branches with parallel transitions (that is, whose subsets contain more than one point), it is necessary to compute the distance between $\mathbf{r}$ and every point in the subset.

In the second step, the signal point selected from each subset (in step 1) is used to determine a branch cost for a Viterbi algorithm using a squared distance measurement. The optimal sequence is that which has the minimum sum of squared distances along the trellis.

13.6 Rotational Invariance

A real digital receiver must typically estimate the phase of the received signal. For QAM signals, methods exist which can estimate the phase, but only up to a phase uncertainty of a multiple of $\pi/2$ radians. This introduces a $p\pi/2$ *phase ambiguity* (p an integer) which must be accommodated in the receiver. When TCM is employed, it may be possible to identify if the receiver has the correct decoding phase by examining the likelihoods computed by the Viterbi algorithm. If no path emerges as having significantly better likelihood than the others, than it is likely that the wrong phase has been selected. The receiver can adjust the phase by $\pi/2$ and try again. This procedure, however, takes additional synchronization time. Another approach is to transmit the information in such a way that it can be

Table 13.5: Encoder Connections and Coding Gains for Maximum Free-Distance QAM Trellis Codes [454, 502][†]

Number of States	g_0	g_1	g_2	g_3	d^2_{free}	$A_{d_{\text{free}}}$	$B_{d_{\text{free}}}$	16-QAM/ 8-PSK	32-cross/ 16-QAM	64-QAM/ 32-cross
								Asympt. Gain (dB) (Coded/Uncoded)		
4	5	2	–	–	4.0			4.4	3.0	2.8
8	11	2	4	–	5.0	3.656	18.313	5.3	4.0	3.8
8†	13	4	2	6	5.0	3.656	12.344			
16	23	4	16	–	6.0	9.156	53.5	6.1	4.8	4.6
16†	25	12	6	14	6.0	9.156	37.594			
32	41	6	10	–	6.0	2.641	16.063	6.1	4.8	4.6
32†	47	22	16	34	6.0	2	6			
64	101	16	64	–	7.0	8.422	55.688	6.8	5.4	5.2
64†	117	26	74	52	7.0	5.078	21.688			
128	203	14	42	–	8.0	36.36	277.367	7.4	6.0	5.8
128†	313	176	154	22	8.0	20.328	100.031			
256	401	56	304	–	8.0	7.613	51.953	7.4	6.0	5.8
256†	417	266	40	226	8.0	3.273	16.391			
512	1001	346	510	–	8.0			7.4	6.0	5.8

[†] Use the labeling shown here.

accurately recovered regardless of the $p\pi/2$ ambiguity. This can be accomplished by (1) using a TCM code which is invariant with respect to rotation; and (2) employing differential encoding of some of the bits.

Let $\mathbf{a} = (\mathbf{a}_0, \mathbf{a}_1, \mathbf{a}_2, \dots)$ be a sequence of complex coded symbols from a two-dimensional signal constellation. Let $\mathbf{a}^\phi$ be the sequence obtained by rotating each $\mathbf{a}_t$ by a fixed angle ϕ: $\mathbf{a}_t^\phi = e^{j\phi}\mathbf{a}_t$. We have the following:

Definition 13.3 A TCM code is **rotationally invariant** with respect to a rotation by ϕ if $\mathbf{a}^\phi$ is also a valid coded symbol sequence for every valid coded symbol sequence $\mathbf{a}$. □

Rotational invariance in TCM can be related to the trellis as follows. Let S denote the signal constellation and let S_i denote the set of subsets, at some level of signal partitioning, which are transmitted along the branches of the trellis. Assume that the partitioning is done such that, for each possible phase rotation, each subset S_i rotates into another S_j. Then the set of subsets is invariant under phase rotation. It turns out that this invariance holds automatically for one- and two-dimensional signal constellations [477]. (For example, consider the set partitions in Figures 13.4 and 13.9.) For such a rotational invariant set of subsets, we have the following.

Theorem 13.4 *[397, 477, 478] For each transition on the trellis from state i to state j associated with a subset A, let B denote the subset obtained when A is rotated by ϕ, as shown in Figure 13.15.*

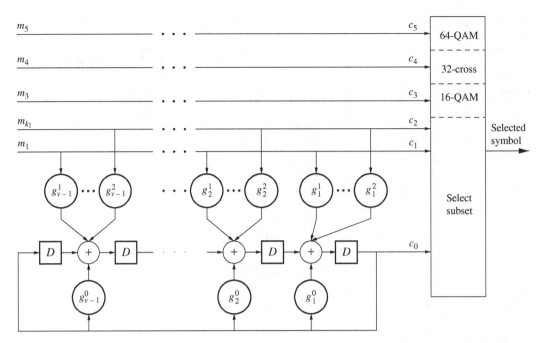

Figure 13.14: TCM encoder for QAM constellations.

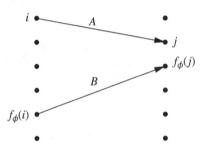

Figure 13.15: Mapping of edge (i, j) to edge $(f_\phi(i), f_\phi(j))$.

Then a TCM code is rotationally invariant with respect to a rotation by an angle ϕ if there exists a bijective function $f_\phi : S \to S$ with the property that B is the subset associated with the transition from $f_\phi(i)$ to state $f_\phi(j)$ (and so $f_\phi(i) \to f_\phi(j)$ is a valid state transition) when A is the subset associated with the transition from state i to state j.

Proof Let $i_1, i_2, i_3, \ldots$ denote a sequence of states on a valid path through the trellis. If the conditions of the theorem are satisfied, then $f_\phi(i_1), f_\phi(i_2), f_\phi(i_3), \ldots$ are also on a valid path, each branch selecting a rotated symbol. $\square$

It has been found that using a linear convolutional code as the state machine underlying the TCM cannot achieve rotational invariance [341]. Nonlinear trellis codes, however, have been found which can achieve rotational invariance [475, 476]. We present examples of such codes which are widely used in V.32 and V.33 industry standards, referring the interested reader to the literature [475, 476] for design methodologies. The V.32 standard [43] operates at bit rates of 9600 bits/second using a symbol rate of 2400 symbols/second (suitable for use on a standard telephone line) by achieving up to 4 bits per symbols. To do this, it uses a coded signal constellation with 32 points in it (the 32-cross

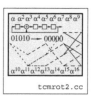

constellation). The V.33 standard [43] provides for data rates of up to 14,400 bits/second using 2400 symbols/second by carrying6 bits per symbol using a 128-point coded signal constellation. This code provides up to 4 dB of coding gain.

The encoder of Figure 13.16 is a nonlinear trellis encoder whose trellis is shown in Figure 13.17. In this figure, the input that gives rise to output subset D_i can be found by taking the two most significant bits of i. Thus, a branch transmitting D_5 is due to an input of $(\tilde{m}_2, \tilde{m}_1) = (1,0)$, since $5 = 101_2$. A branch transmitting D_7 is due to an input of $(\tilde{m}_2, \tilde{m}_1) = (1,1)$, etc. It can be shown that the code represented by this trellis is invariant, in the sense of Theorem 13.4. The corresponding labeled signals and the constellation partition are shown in Figure 13.18. We observe that the first 2 bits (labeled with the light font) are invariant with respect to $\pi/2$ rotations. However, the last three label bits *do* change with rotation. The code uses differential coding techniques to achieve invariance to the changes in the last 3 bits. The first stage of the encoder takes two input bits and differentially encodes them. The differentially encoded bits are used by the trellis coder.

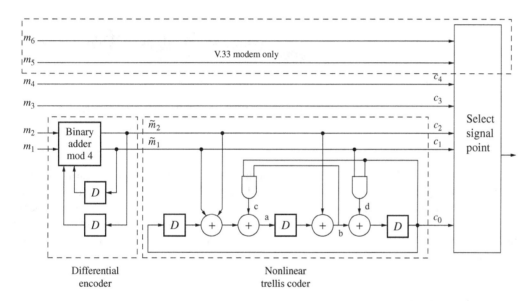

Figure 13.16: Encoder circuit for rotationally invariant TCM code.

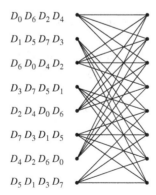

Figure 13.17: Trellis for the rotationally invariant code of Figure 13.16.

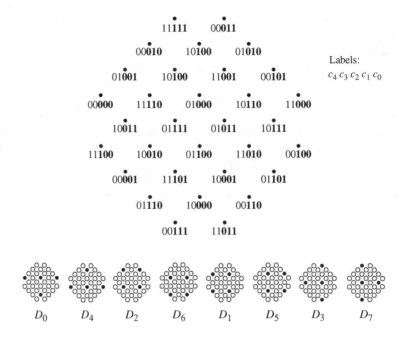

Figure 13.18: 32-Cross constellation for rotationally invariant TCM code.

The overall framework of invariance works as follows. If a transmitted signal point is rotated by some multiple of $\pi/2$, then the corresponding received signal point is identical in the first 2 bits. The last 3 bits differ because of the rotation. However, because the code is rotationally invariant, there is still a valid path through the trellis which can be used to decode this rotated sequence of symbols. The input bits for the rotated signals can be decoded. Then, since the bits are differentially encoded, so that the sequence of *differences* does not change when the signal sequence is rotated, the original bits can be recovered.

13.6.1 Differential Encoding

The **differential encoder** operates as follows. The input bits $m_{1,t}$ and $m_{2,t}$ are converted to an integer, $m_t = 2m_{2,t} + m_{1,t}$. The encoder keeps the previous outputs $\tilde{m}_{1,t-1}, \tilde{m}_{2,t-1}$, represented as an integer by $\tilde{m}_{t-1} = 2\tilde{m}_{2,t-1} + \tilde{m}_{1,t-1}$. Then the differential encoder computes

$$\tilde{m}_t = m_t + \tilde{m}_{t-1} \pmod{4}. \tag{13.6}$$

The initial memory of the differential encoder is assumed to be set at 0.

Given a received sequence of differentially encoded data $\tilde{m}_{1,t}, \tilde{m}_{2,t}$, the original data can be recovered as

$$m_t = \tilde{m}_t - \tilde{m}_{t-1} \pmod{4}. \tag{13.7}$$

Example 13.5 Suppose the sequence of input data $(m_{2,t}, m_{1,t})$ is

$$(01)(10)(11)(01)(10)(11)\dots$$

The differential encoding proceeds as in the following table.

$(m_{2,t}, m_{1,t})$	m_t	$(\tilde{m}_{2,t-1}, \tilde{m}_{1,t-1})$	$\tilde{m}_{t-1}$	$\tilde{m}_t = m_t + \tilde{m}_{t-1} \pmod 4$	$(\tilde{m}_{2,t}, \tilde{m}_{1,t})$
					$(0,0)$
$(0,1)$	1	$(0,0)$	0	1	$(0,1)$
$(1,0)$	2	$(0,1)$	1	3	$(1,1)$
$(1,1)$	3	$(1,1)$	3	2	$(1,0)$
$(0,1)$	1	$(1,0)$	2	3	$(1,1)$
$(1,0)$	2	$(1,1)$	3	1	$(0,1)$
$(1,1)$	3	$(0,1)$	1	0	$(0,0)$

□

13.6.2 Constellation Labels and Partitions

The sets D_i consist of points having the label i in the last three digits in binary notation (in bold font in Figure 13.18). Examination of the subsets in Figure 13.18 reveals that under rotation of $\pi/2$, the subset D_0 maps to D_7, and D_7 maps to D_4, and so forth. The sets map under $\pi/2$ rotations as

$$D_0 \to D_7 \to D_4 \to D_3 \to D_0$$
$$D_1 \to D_6 \to D_5 \to D_2 \to D_1. \tag{13.8}$$

Example 13.6 The sequence of bits

$$(11\ 01)(01\ 10)(11\ 11)(10\ 01)(00\ 10)(01\ 11)$$

is to be transmitted, where the 4-tuples represent $(m_{4,t}, m_{3,t}, m_{2,t}, m_{1,t})$. After differential encoding the second pair of bits (see the previous example), the sequence of bits $(m_4, m_3, \tilde{m}_2, \tilde{m}_1)$ is

$$(11\ 01)(01\ 11)(11\ 10)(10\ 11)(00\ 01)(01\ 00).$$

This sequence is presented to the nonlinear trellis coder (starting from state 0) resulting in the following output and path through the trellis.

state	input	output	subset	next state
000	1101	11**010**	D_2	010
010	0111	01**110**	D_6	000
000	1110	11**100**	D_4	011
011	1011	10**111**	D_7	101
101	0001	00**011**	D_3	101
101	0100	01**001**	D_1	110

Now suppose that at the receiver the sequence is received with a $\pi/2$ rotation, so that the points of the signal constellation correspond to the following bit patterns:

Received bits	Subset
11001	D_1
01101	D_5
11011	D_3
10100	D_4
00000	D_0
01110	D_6

$D_0\,D_6\,D_2\,D_4$

$D_1\,D_5\,D_7\,D_3$

$D_6\,D_0\,D_4\,D_2$

$D_3\,D_7\,D_5\,D_1$

$D_2\,D_4\,D_0\,D_6$

$D_7\,D_3\,D_1\,D_5$

$D_4\,D_2\,D_6\,D_0$

$D_5\,D_1\,D_3\,D_7$

Of course, the initial state in the trellis is not known initially, but would be discovered by the Viterbi algorithm. We make the following observations about these bits:

- The first 2 bits are unchanged by the rotation. This occurs because the symbol labels were created so that $p\pi/2$ rotations do not affect the first 2 bits.

- The subsets represented by the last 3 bits are obtained by rotating the transmitted subsets according to the cyclic translations of (13.8).

As shown, a valid path through the trellis can be found. However, it does not necessarily start with state 0. The Viterbi decoding algorithm must be prepared to start with any state. Furthermore, if the initial state is not zero, the differential decoder must be initialized with the data corresponding to the rotation which moves to the initial state. Since the path starts at state 7, the differential decoder is initialized with $(m_{2,-1}, m_{1,-1}) = (1, 1)$.

The sequence of input bits corresponding to this path is

$$(11\ 00)(01\ 10)(11\ 01)(10\ 10)(00\ 00)(01\ 11),$$

where the last 2 bits of the 4-tuple are differentially encoded. Using (13.7) to undo the effect of the differential decoding on those bits, we obtain the following:

$(\tilde{m}_{2,t}, m_{1,t})$	$\tilde{m}_t$	$(\tilde{m}_{2,t-1}, \tilde{m}_{1,t-1})$	$\tilde{m}_{t-1}$	$m_t = \tilde{m}_t - \tilde{m}_{t-1} \pmod 4$	$(m_{2,t}, m_{1,t})$
		(1,1)			
(0,0)	0	(1,1)	3	1	(0,1)
(1,0)	2	(0,0)	0	2	(1,0)
(0,1)	1	(1,0)	2	3	(1,1)
(1,0)	2	(0,1)	1	1	(0,1)
(0,0)	0	(1,0)	2	2	(1,0)
(1,1)	3	(0,0)	0	3	(1,1)

The decoded sequence is thus

$$(11\ 01)(01\ 10)(11\ 11)(10\ 01)(00\ 10)(01\ 11),$$

the same as transmitted originally. Thus, even though the signal constellation was rotated due to phase ambiguity, the decoder was invariant to such rotations. □

13.7 Multidimensional TCM

The TCM described up to this point has employed one- or two-dimensional signal constellations. However, there are several compelling reasons for dealing with constellations in more than two dimensions. After presenting some of these reasons, we present one of several possible frameworks for mathematical descriptions of signal constellations and their partitions in multiple dimensions using lattices and their cosets. These rather general descriptions are followed by an extended example, the code used in the V.34 (also known as V.fast) modem protocol.

We begin, however, with a discussion of how to obtain multiple dimensions using digital signaling. We detail the notation only with even-numbers of dimensions; modification to odd-numbers of dimensions is straightforward.

The $2L$-dimensional signal point $\mathbf{a} = (a_1, a_2, \ldots, a_{2L})$ can be transmitted by sending a sequence of L two-dimensional points over L signaling intervals

$$(a_1, a_2), (a_3, a_4), \ldots, (a_{2L-1}, a_{2L}).$$

If the uncoded multidimensional constellation is employed with an overall spectral efficiency of η bits/symbol, then there must be $2^{\eta L}$ symbols in the multidimensional constellation.

Example 13.7 Suppose that a signal is to be transmitted with $\eta = 4$ bits/symbol using a four-dimensional constellation. Then the two symbols required to carry the four coordinates must represent $2 \times 4 = 8$ bits, so that the constellation must have 2^8 points in it.

Now suppose that a TCM is used with a four-dimensional constellation with a $k/(k+1)$ convolutional encoder. There must be 2^9 points in the signal constellation.   □

Multidimensional TCM is similar to one- or two-dimensional TCM: k_1 out of k input bits are input into a rate $k_1/(k_1 + 1)$ trellis encoder. These bits are used to selected one of 2^{k_1+1} subsets of a $2L$-dimensional signal constellation. The remaining $k_2 = k - k_1$ input bits then select a single point out of the subset. This signal point is then transmitted by a sequence of L two-dimensional points. A difference from one- or two-dimensional TCM is that the trellis encoder circuit is used only every L symbol times.

13.7.1 Some Advantages of Multidimensional TCM

13.7.1.1 Energy expansion advantage

In one- or two-dimensional TCM, the rate $k_1/(k_1 + 1)$ encoder requires that the number of points in the signal constellation be doubled to preserve rate so that there must be $2^{\eta L+1}$ symbols in the constellation to transmit with a spectral efficiency of η bits/symbol. This roughly doubles the average signal energy, since the extra redundancy must be accommodated over a single symbol interval. This results in approximately a 3 dB penalty in γ_C.

However, in multiple dimensions there is only one redundant bit spread over L symbol times, so the energy penalty is reduced. The extra energy required to represent this larger signal constellation is shared among L transmitted symbols. For a four-dimensional signal constellation, the penalty in γ_C is 1.5 dB.

13.7.1.2 Sphere-packing advantages

To obtain the smallest average signal energy, it is desirable to pack the points of the signal constellation as closely as possible while maintaining minimum inter-symbol distance requirements. The problem of placing points in a signal constellation is thus an instance of the "sphere packing problem." This can be expressed in familiar terms in three dimensions as the problem of packing as many identical spherical oranges (maintaining at least a minimum distance between centers) as possible into a crate of given dimensions. It can be shown that if the oranges are stacked in layers with one orange resting over the interstices formed by the oranges in the layer below, then more oranges can be packed into the crate than if the oranges are stacked in "$\mathbb{Z}^3$" way, in a square lattice with the center of each orange over the center of the orange below it.

In higher dimensions it may be possible to stack points in such a way that the density is higher than simply stacking them on a multidimensional rectangular grid. This results in a lower average signal energy compared to the rectangular lattice $\mathbb{Z}^n$.

13.7.1.3 Spectral efficiency

If the channel has bandwidth to support η bits/symbol but not $\eta + 1$ bits/symbol, it may be possible to squeeze a little more out by using $\eta + \delta$ bits/symbol, for some rational number $0 < \delta < 1$. Using multidimensional constellations, it is possible to design transmission systems with such fractional spectral efficiencies.

13.7.1.4 Rotational invariance

For two-dimensional constellations, nonlinear trellis coders must be employed to obtain rotational invariance. However, linear encoders can be used in higher dimensional TCM.

13.7.1.5 Signal shape

Signal shape [133, 260] slightly reduces the average energy requirements even further by selectively using points of smaller energy. This is used in the V.34 modem, as described below.

13.7.1.6 Peak-to-average power ratio

Multidimensional constellations can be designed which have a lower peak-to-average power ratio.

13.7.1.7 Decoding speed

The first step in decoding is to determine the closest point in a subset to the received data. For many lattices, efficient algorithms exist for doing this (see, e.g., [80]). Furthermore, the state of the trellis must be advanced only every L received signals. These factors allow for higher speed decoding.

13.7.2 Lattices and Sublattices

While there are many ways of constructing multidimensional signal constellations, one very important way employs lattices and sublattices. We briefly introduce lattices here; extensive detail is presented in [79].

13.7.2.1 Basic Definitions

A lattice Λ is an (infinite) discrete periodic arrangement of points in $\mathbb{R}^m$. A signal constellation based on a lattice is obtained by selecting a finite number of points from the lattice, possibly with a translation, with the points usually selected in such a way as to minimize the average energy in the constellation.

A lattice may be described by a *generator matrix*[1] M, where

$$M = \begin{bmatrix} v_{11} & v_{12} & \cdots & v_{1m} \\ v_{21} & v_{22} & \cdots & v_{2m} \\ \vdots & & & \\ v_{n1} & v_{n2} & \cdots & v_{nm} \end{bmatrix}$$

with $m \geq n$, where, following convention, each *row* is a basis vector. Then the lattice is the set

$$\Lambda = \{\xi M : \xi \in \mathbb{Z}^n\};$$

that is, *integer* linear combinations of the basis vectors. Note that a lattice forms a group under addition.

It should be obvious that the generator is not unique. Two generator matrices M and $\tilde{M}$ define *equivalent* lattices if $\tilde{M} = cUMB$, where c is a nonzero constant, U is a matrix with integer entries and

---

[1] Not to be confused with the generator matrix for a linear block code.

$\det(U) = \pm 1$ (that is, U is unimodular), and B is orthogonal, $BB^T = I$. Equivalent lattices are essentially just rotated and/or scaled versions of each other.

Example 13.8 A portion of the lattice $\mathbb{Z}^2$, consisting of points (n_1, n_2) for $n_i \in \mathbb{Z}$, is shown in Figure 13.19(a). It has the generator $M = \begin{bmatrix} 1 & 0 \\ 0 & 1 \end{bmatrix}$. A 16-QAM constellation can be obtained, for example, by selecting 16 points of $\Lambda + (1/2, 1/2)$. The n-dimensional extensions of this lattice, denoted by $\mathbb{Z}^n$, are generated by the $n \times n$ identity matrix. □

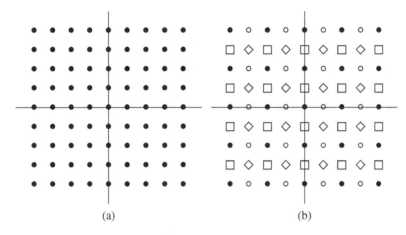

(a)   (b)

Figure 13.19: A portion of the lattice $\mathbb{Z}^2$ and its cosets. (a) $\mathbb{Z}^2$ lattice; (b) cosets of the lattice.

Example 13.9 The hexagonal lattice, known as the A_2 lattice, is shown in Figure 13.20(a). It can be generated by

$$M = \begin{bmatrix} 1 & 0 \\ \frac{1}{2} & \frac{\sqrt{3}}{2} \end{bmatrix}.$$

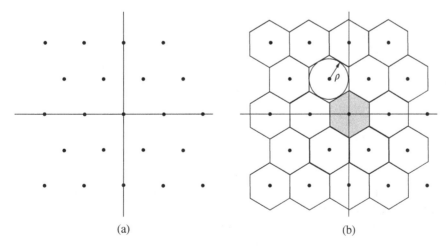

(a)   (b)

Figure 13.20: Hexagonal lattice. (a) Basic lattice; (b) the fundamental parallelotopes around the lattice points.

Not so obviously, the hexagonal lattice can also be generated by

$$M = \begin{bmatrix} 1 & -1 & 0 \\ 0 & 1 & -1 \end{bmatrix},$$

giving a two-dimensional lattice embedded in three dimensions.   □

Figure 13.20(b) shows that around each lattice point a circle (or, in general, a sphere) can be drawn which does not intersect with identical spheres around the other lattice points; we denote the radius of the largest such sphere by ρ. Also, around each point is a region known as the *fundamental parallelotope* (shown shaded). Associated with the generator is the *Gram matrix A*,

$$A = MM^T.$$

The determinant of the lattice generated by M is defined to be the determinant of the Gram matrix, $\det \Lambda = \det A$. The volume of the fundamental region of the lattice, or the *fundamental volume*, denoted by $V(\Lambda)$, is

$$V(\Lambda) = |\det(\Lambda)|^{1/2} = |\det(A)|^{1/2}.$$

Example 13.10   For the lattice $\Lambda = \mathbb{Z}^{2n}$ (even-numbered dimensions), the volume of the fundamental parallelotope is

$$V(\Lambda) = |\det(\Lambda)|^{1/2} = |\det(I)|^{1/2} = 1.$$

□

Example 13.11   For the A_2 lattice with minimum distance between points equal to 1, the volume of the fundamental parallelotope is

$$V(\Lambda) = |\det(\Lambda)|^{1/2} = \left[\det \begin{bmatrix} 1 & 0 \\ \frac{1}{2} & \frac{\sqrt{3}}{2} \end{bmatrix} \begin{bmatrix} 1 & \frac{1}{2} \\ 0 & \frac{\sqrt{3}}{2} \end{bmatrix}\right]^{1/2} = \sqrt{\frac{3}{4}}.$$

The hexagonal lattice has a smaller fundamental volume than the $\mathbb{Z}^2$ lattice with the same minimum distance. It thus packs points more efficiently into space.   □

Another relevant attribute of lattices is the *kissing number*, usually denoted by τ, which is the number of nearest neighbors a lattice point has. This has bearing in code design, since the asymptotic performance is governed by the number of nearest neighbors a point has. For the A_2 lattice the kissing number is $\tau = 6$. For the lattice $\mathbb{Z}^n$ the kissing number is $\tau = 2n$.

13.7.2.2 Common Lattices

Table 13.6 summarizes the attributes of the lattices described here.

D_4, also known as the checkerboard lattice, is the densest lattice in four dimensions [79, p. 9]. The lattice points are (u_1, u_2, u_3, u_4), where the u_i are integers and $u_1 + u_2 + u_3 + u_4$ is an even integer. The center $(0, 0, 0, 0)$ has the points $(\pm 1, \pm 1, 0, 0)$ and their permutations as nearest neighbors, so that the kissing number is $\tau = 24$. Any two distinct points must differ by at least one in at least two coordinates, or by twoin at least one coordinate, so the minimal distance between centers is $\sqrt{2}$, and $\rho = \sqrt{2}/2$. A generator matrix for this and other lattices mentioned here is provided in `lattstuff.m`.

Table 13.6: Attributes of Some Lattices

Name	Dimension	Kissing Number τ	Fundamental Volume $V(\Lambda)$	Lattice Coding Gain γ_{cg}	γ_{cg} (dB)
$\mathbb{Z}^n$	n	$2n$	1	1	0
A_2 (hexagonal)	2	6	$\sqrt{3}/2$	1.15	0.63
A_3 (face-centered cubic)	3	12	$\sqrt{2}/2$	1.26	1.00
D_4	4	24	0.5	$\sqrt{2}$	1.51
D_n	n (even)	$2n(n-1)$	$2^{(1-n/2)}$	$2^{(1-2/n)}$	$3.01(1-2/n)$
E_6	6	72	0.2165	1.6654	2.21
E_8	8	240	1/16	2	3.01
Λ_{16} (Barnes–Wall)	16	4320	2.33×10^{-4}	2.83	4.51
Λ_{24} (Leech)	24	196560	5.96×10^{-8}	4	6.02

The fundamental volume is computed for a lattice normalized so the minimum distance between points equal to 1.

E_8 provides the densest lattice packing in eight dimensions [79, p. 120]. The lattice can be described as follows: The set of points

$$\left\{ (u_1, u_2, \ldots, u_8) : \text{all } u_i \in \mathbb{Z} \text{ or all } u_i \in \mathbb{Z} + \frac{1}{2}, \text{and } \sum x_i \text{ is even} \right\}.$$

E_6 is the densest lattice in six dimensions [79, p. 125]. Points in this lattice are vectors in E_8 which are perpendicular to any A_2 sublattice V in E_8:

$$E_6 = \{x \in E_8 : x \cdot v = 0 \text{ for all } v \in V\};$$

another description is

$$E_6 = \{(x_1, \ldots, x_8) \in E_8 : x_1 + x_8 = x_2 + \cdots + x_7 = 0\}.$$

Another description for E_6 is over the Eisenstein integers, the set $\mathcal{E} = \{a + \omega b : a, b \in \mathbb{Z}, \omega = (-1 + i\sqrt{3})/2\}$. This uses the generator

$$M = \begin{bmatrix} \theta & 0 & 0 \\ 1 & -1 & 0 \\ 1 & 0 & -1 \end{bmatrix},$$

where $\theta = \sqrt{-3}$.

Λ_{16} is the Barnes–Wall lattice [[79], p. 129]. This lattice has strong connections with Reed–Muller codes of length 16.

Λ_{24} is the Leech lattice [79, p. 131]. What makes it remarkable is that it can be constructed in many ways, with many connections to block error-correcting codes. We mention only one. The lattice can be generated by all vectors of the form $\frac{1}{\sqrt{8}}(\mp 3, \pm 1^{23})$ (that is, 23 ones), where the ∓ 3 may be in any position, and the upper signs are taken on the set of coordinates, where the binary Golay $(24, 12)$ code is 1.

13.7.2.3 Sublattices and Cosets

A **sublattice** of a lattice is a lattice Λ' all of whose points lie in the lattice Λ. The sublattice is generated by a matrix M'.

As a subgroup of a group, there are cosets associated with a sublattice. A coset of a lattice Λ' is a translation $\Lambda' + \mathbf{p}$ of all points in Λ' by $\mathbf{p}$. The set of cosets of Λ produced by Λ' is denoted Λ/Λ'; since the lattice is an Abelian group, Λ/Λ' is a group. We can write the partition of Λ into cosets as

$$\Lambda = \Lambda' \cup \{\mathbf{p}_1 + \Lambda'\} \cup \{\mathbf{p}_2 + \Lambda'\} \cup \cdots \cup \{\mathbf{p}_{N-1} + \Lambda'\}$$

for some number N which is the number of cosets.

Example 13.12 Let $\Lambda = \mathbb{Z}^2$ and let $\Lambda' = 2\mathbb{Z}^2$. That is, the generator is

$$M' = 2M = 2 \begin{bmatrix} 1 & 0 \\ 0 & 1 \end{bmatrix}.$$

There are four cosets in this lattice, with the following shape designations in Figure 13.19(b):

$$S_0 = \Lambda' \text{ (denoted by } \bullet) \qquad S_1 = (1,0) + \Lambda' \text{ (denoted by } \circ)$$
$$S_2 = (0,1) + \Lambda' \text{ (denoted by } \square) \quad S_3 = (1,1) + \Lambda' \text{ (denoted by } \Diamond).$$

The set of lattices $\mathbb{Z}^2/2\mathbb{Z}^2$ is isomorphic to the group $\mathbb{Z}_2 \times \mathbb{Z}_2$. □

A **partition chain** of a lattice, denoted $\Lambda/\Lambda'/\Lambda''$ is the set obtained by partitioning Λ' and each of its cosets by Λ'', where Λ'' is a sublattice of Λ'.

A commonly used transformation is obtained by stacking 2×2 blocks of the form

$$R = \begin{bmatrix} 1 & -1 \\ 1 & 1 \end{bmatrix},$$

which represents a rotation of the lattice by $45°$ and a scaling by $\sqrt{2}$. The sublattice of Λ formed by this transformation is denoted $R\Lambda$.

Example 13.13 Figure 13.21(a) shows $\Lambda = \mathbb{Z}^2$. Figure 13.21(b) shows the cosets in the partition Λ/Λ', where $\Lambda = \mathbb{Z}^2$ and $\Lambda' = R\mathbb{Z}^2$, where the points in the cosets are designated as

$$\Lambda' = R\mathbb{Z}^2 \quad (\square)$$
$$\Lambda' + (1,0) \quad (\bullet).$$

Figure 13.21(c) shows the cosets in the partition chain $\Lambda/\Lambda'/\Lambda''$, where $\Lambda'' = R^2\Lambda = 2\mathbb{Z}^2$, where the points in the four cosets are designated as

$$\Lambda'' = R^2\mathbb{Z}^2 \quad (\square)$$
$$\Lambda'' + (1,0) \quad (\bullet)$$
$$\Lambda'' + (0,1) \quad (\circ)$$
$$\Lambda'' + (1,1) \quad (\Diamond).$$

This four-way partition creates the same partition as that in Figure 13.9. □

13.7.2.4 The Lattice Code Idea

Figure 13.22 shows the idea behind TCM on lattice cosets. It is very similar to TCM in general: a set of coded bits selects a coset (as a subset of the constellation), and a set of uncoded bits selects a point within the subset. The performance of the code is determined by the minimum distance between points in the coset (corresponding to parallel transitions in the trellis) and the minimum distance between diverging paths in the trellis of the encoder.

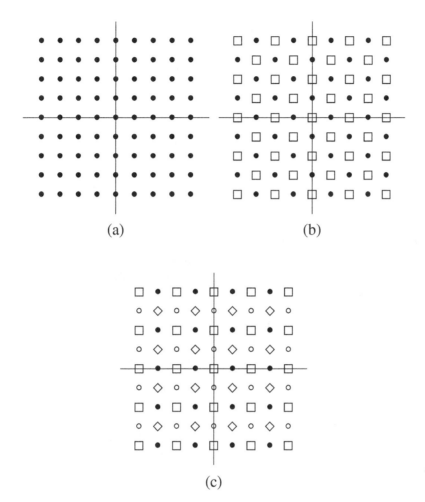

Figure 13.21: $\mathbb{Z}^2$ and its partition chain and cosets. (a) $\mathbb{Z}^2$; (b) cosets of $R\mathbb{Z}^2$; (c) Cosets of $R^2\mathbb{Z}^2$.

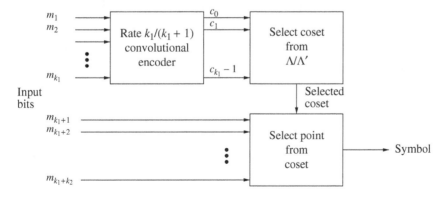

Figure 13.22: Block diagram for a trellis lattice coder.

13.7.2.5   Sources of Coding Gain in Lattice Codes

In addition to gains due to the distances between sequences obtained using trellis coding, the very shape of the lattice constellation contributes gains. Two sources of coding gain can be attributed to the use of lattices. The first is referred to as the *lattice coding gain*. The lattice coding gain for an n-dimensional lattice Λ is a measure of how much more effectively points are packed into Λ compared to the lattice $\mathbb{Z}^n$. Let Λ be a lattice that is normalized so that the minimum distance between points is equal to 1, and let the fundamental volume of Λ be $V(\Lambda)$. A rectangular lattice, a multiple of $\mathbb{Z}^n$, with this volume would have a minimum distance of $V(\Lambda)^{1/n}$. There is thus a gain in energy equal to the ratio of the square of the minimum distance of the lattice (which is 1) divided by the square of the minimum distance an equal-volume rectangular lattice would have. This is called the lattice coding gain, and is denoted by γ_{cg}:

$$\gamma_{cg} = \frac{1}{V(\Lambda)^{2/n}}.$$

Table 13.6 lists coding gains for the lattices described in the previous section.

The other source of coding gain provided by multidimensional constellations in general is called the *shape gain*, γ_s, which can be obtained by employing a nearly circular boundary on the constellation, instead of natural rectangular or cross boundaries such as shown in Figure 13.2. Figure 13.23(a) shows circular boundaries for constellations obtained using $\mathbb{Z}^2$; part (b) shows similar boundaries for constellations built from the A_2 lattice. Table 13.7 shows the comparison of the average energies for these constellations with the average energies for the constellations from Table 13.1. (Possible minor reductions in energy could also be obtained by slightly shifting the constellations, but this was not done.) As the table shows, there is efficiency gained by employing a constellation with a spherical boundary instead of a square or cross boundary. (There is also somewhat higher complexity in the decoder.) Gains of about 0.18 dB are possible compared with the square constellation. (The gain is not as large for the 32-point constellation, since the cross form is already an approximation to the circular constellation.) Also shown in Table 13.7 are the average signal energies and gains when an A_2 lattice with circular boundary is employed. The shape gain is independent of the lattice gain, so the overall gain is additive (on a dB scale) $(\gamma)_{dB} = (\gamma_s)_{dB} + (\gamma_{cg})_{dB}$.

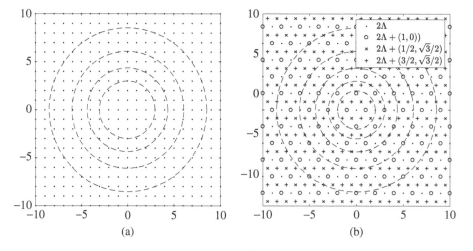

Figure 13.23: Lattice and circular boundaries for 16, 32, 64, 128, and 256-point constellations. (a) $\mathbb{Z}^2$ lattice; (b) A_2 lattice.

Table 13.7: Comparison of Average Signal Energy for Circular Boundary $\mathbb{Z}^2$ and A_2 Constellations with Regular QAM

M	E_s, Rect. Bdy., Rect. QAM (Table 13.1)	E_s, Circ. Bdy. Rect. QAM	Gain γ_s (dB)	E_s, Circ. Bdy. A_2 Lattice	Gain $\gamma_s \gamma_{cg}$ (dB)
64	10.5	10.19	0.13	8.85	0.74
128	20.5(CR)	20.41	0.02	17.68	0.64
256	42.5	40.79	0.18	35.26	0.81

The shape gain is for an N-dimensional constellation is

$$\gamma_s = \frac{(N/2)\text{Average energy for square 2-D lattice}}{\text{Average energy for circular lattice}}.$$

Let M_c denote the size of the two-dimensional signal constellation, and let $M_{c,N} = M_c^{N/2}$ denote the size of the N-dimensional constellation.

Assuming the minimum distance between points is $d_0 = 1$, the average energy for a circular $\mathbb{Z}^N$ (N even) constellation[2] C of is

$$E_{s,\text{circ}} = \frac{1}{M_{c,N}} \sum_{\mathbf{w}_i \in C} \|\mathbf{w}_i\|^2 \approx \frac{1}{M_{c,N}} \int_{\mathcal{V}} \|\mathbf{v}\|^2 d\mathbf{v},$$

where the summation is approximated by an integral and $\mathcal{V}$ is the volume of the spherical region containing the signal constellation. The number of points in the region can be approximated as

$$M_{c,N} \approx \int_{\mathcal{V}} d\mathbf{v}.$$

The N-dimensional volume element increment in this integral can be expressed in "polar" form as [41, pp. 242, 246]

$$d\mathbf{v} = \frac{N\pi^{N/2} r^{N-1}}{(N/2)!} dr$$

so that, with the radius of $\mathcal{V}$ equal to ρ,

$$M_{c,N} \approx \int_0^\rho \frac{N\pi^{N/2} r^{N-1}}{(N/2)!} dr = \frac{\pi^{N/2} \rho^N}{(N/2)!}. \tag{13.9}$$

Using the same volume element increment,

$$\int_{\mathcal{V}} \|\mathbf{v}\|^2 d\mathbf{v} = \int_0^\rho r^2 \frac{N\pi^{N/2} r^{N-1}}{(N/2)!} dr = \frac{\pi^{N+2} N \rho^{N+2}}{(N+2)(N/2)!}. \tag{13.10}$$

The average energy for the square lattice can be found using (13.1) as

$$E_{s,\text{square}} = \frac{M_c - 1}{6} = \frac{(M_{c,N})^{N/2}}{6} \approx \left[\int_{\mathcal{V}} d\mathbf{v} \right]^{N/2}.$$

Using (13.9) and (13.10), the shape gain is

$$\gamma_s \approx \frac{N/2 \left[\int_{\mathcal{V}} d\mathbf{v} \right]^{2/N}}{6 \int_{\mathcal{V}} \|\mathbf{v}\|^2 d\mathbf{v} / \int_{\mathcal{V}} d\mathbf{v}} = \frac{\pi(1 + N/2)}{6[(N/2)!]^{2/N}}.$$

---

[2] The results here hold even for other lattices; the fundamental volume cancels out of the ratio.

When $N = 2$, $\gamma = \pi/3 = 1.0472 = 0.2$ dB. This is apparent in Table 13.7 for $N = 256$. Stirling's approximation to $n!$ tells us[3]

$$n! \approx n^n e^{-n} \sqrt{2\pi n}.$$

Using Stirling's approximation, it can be shown that asymptotically, $\gamma_s \to \pi e/6 = 1.53$ dB.

13.7.2.6 Some Good Lattice Codes

Table 13.8 [397] lists some good codes that have been developed in the literature.

Table 13.8: Some Good Multidimensional TCM Codes [397]

Partition Λ/Λ'	d^2_{free}	Number of States	Asymptotic Coding Gain (dB)	$A_{d_{\text{free}}}$	Source
Four dimensions: Add 0.35 dB of shape gain					
$\mathbb{Z}^4/RD_4$	4	8	4.52	44	[?]
$\mathbb{Z}^4/RD_4$	4	16	4.52	12	[?]
$\mathbb{Z}^4/2\mathbb{Z}^4$	4	32	4.52	4	[?]
$\mathbb{Z}^4/2D_4$	5	64	6.28	72	[?]
$\mathbb{Z}^4/2D_4$	6	128	6.28	728	[454]
$D_4/2D_4$	6	16	4.77	152	[56]
$D_4/2D_4$	8	64	5.27	828	[56]
Eight dimensions: Add 0.76 dB of shape gain					
$\mathbb{Z}^8/E_8$	4	16	5.27	316	[?]
$\mathbb{Z}^8/E_8$	4	32	5.27	124	[?]
$\mathbb{Z}^8/E_8$	4	32	5.27	60	[?]
$\mathbb{Z}^8/RD_8$	4	128	5.27	28	[454]
RD_8/RE_8	8	32	6.02	> 500	[?]
RD_8/RE_8	8	64	6.02	316	[?]
RD_8/RE_8	8	128	6.02	124	[?]
E_8/RE_8	8	8	5.27	764	[56]
E_8/RE_8	8	16	5.27	316	[56]
E_8/RE_8	8	32	5.27	124	[56]
E_8/RE_8	8	64	5.27	60	[56]

13.8 Multidimensional TCM Example: The V.34 Modem Standard

In this section, we discuss the error-correction coding which is used for the V.34 modem standard. This modem is capable of transmitting up to 33.6 kB/second over the standard telephone system (on some lines). There are many technical aspects to this modem; space permits detailing only those related to the error-correction coding. A survey and pointers to the literature appears in [136]. However, we briefly summarize some of the aspects of the modem:

- The modem is adaptive in the symbol rate it employs and the size of the constellation. It is capable of sending at symbol rates of 2400, 2743, 2800, 3000, 3200, or 3429 symbols/second. (These peculiar-looking choices are rational multiples of the basic rate of 2400 symbols/second.)

---

[3] A very clear derivation of this appears in [180].

The symbol rate is selected by a line probing sequence employed during initialization which determines the available bandwidth.

- The modem is capable of transmitting variable numbers of bits per symbol. At the highest rate, 8.4 bits/symbols are carried. Rate is established at link initialization, and rate adjustments can occur during data transmission.

- Adaptive precoding [113, 139, 191, 450] and decision feedback equalization is also employed to compensate for channel dispersion.

- Shaping via shell mapping is employed, which provides modest gains in addition to the coding gains.

- Adaptive trellis coding is employed. The main code is a 16-state four-dimensional trellis code (to be described below). This code provides 4.66 dB of gain and is rotationally invariant. However, two other trellis codes are also included: a 32-state four-dimensional code with 4.5 dB of gain and a 64-state four- dimensional code providing 4.7 dB of gain. These codes are not described here.

Given the complexity of the modem, it is a technological marvel that they are so readily affordable and effective!

The trellis encoder for the modem is shown in Figure 13.24, with the corresponding trellis diagram in Figure 13.25.

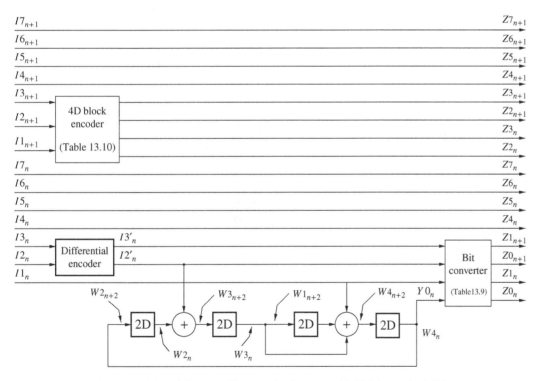

Figure 13.24: 16-State trellis encoder for use with V.34 standard [?].

The bit converter in the encoder supports the rotational invariance and is outlined in Table 13.9. The 4D block converter supports the shell shaping, controlling the selection of "inner" and "outer" constellation points. The operation is detailed below.

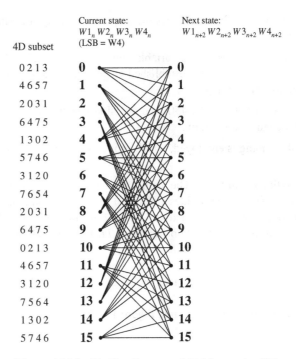

Figure 13.25: Trellis diagram of V.34 encoder [?].

Table 13.9: Bit Converter: Sublattice Partition of 4D Rectangular Lattice [?]

4D Sublattice (Subset)	$Y0_n$	$I1_n$	$I2_{n'}$	$I3_{n'}$	4D Types	$Z0_n$	$Z1_n$	$Z0_{n+1}$	$Z1_{n+1}$
0	0	0	0	0	(A, A)	0	0	0	0
	0	0	0	1	(B, B)	0	1	0	1
1	0	0	1	0	(C, C)	1	0	1	0
	0	0	1	1	(D, D)	1	1	1	1
2	0	1	0	0	(A, B)	0	0	0	1
	0	1	0	1	(B, A)	0	1	0	0
3	0	1	1	0	(C, D)	1	0	1	1
	0	1	1	1	(D, C)	1	1	1	0
4	1	0	0	0	(A, C)	0	0	1	0
	1	0	0	1	(B, D)	0	1	1	1
5	1	0	1	0	(C, B)	1	0	0	1
	1	0	1	1	(D, A)	1	1	0	0
6	1	1	0	0	(A, D)	0	0	1	1
	1	1	0	1	(B, C)	0	1	1	0
7	1	1	1	0	(C, A)	1	0	0	0
	1	1	1	1	(D, B)	1	1	0	1

To transmit η information bits per signaling interval using $2N = 4$-dimensional modulation, $N = 2$ signaling intervals are required. For uncoded transmission, $2^{\eta N}$ points in the signal constellation are necessary. For coded transmission, $2^{\eta N+1}$ points are necessary. The V.34 standard carries $\eta = 7$ bits per symbol, so 2^{15} points in the signal constellation are necessary. The V.34 standard does this using an interesting constellation. The four-dimensional constellation consists of the cross product of the 192-point constellation shown in Figure 13.26. The 192-point constellation contains a 128-point cross constellation in the *inner points*, plus an additional 64 *outer points*. The inner points can be used to transmit seven uncoded bits per symbol. The outer points are selected as close to the origin as possible (outside of the inner constellation) to minimize energy. Each of the A, B, C, and D sets has the same number of points. Also, a rotation of an outer point yields another outer point.

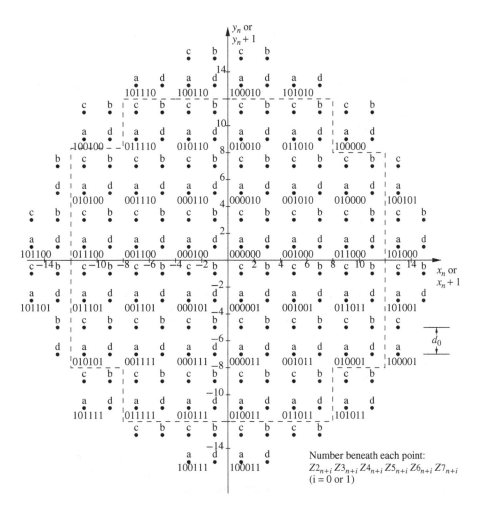

Figure 13.26: The 192-point two-dimensional constellation employed in the V.34 standard.

The 2^{15} points in the constellation are obtained by concatenating a pair of 192-point constellations (which would result in a 192^2 point constellation, but $192^2 > 2^{15}$), excluding those 4D points whose corresponding pair of two-dimensional points are both outer points. There are thus

$$192^2 - 64^2 = 2^{15}$$

points in this constellation. The inner points are used three-fourths of the time. By using the inner constellation more often, the average power is reduced compared to other (more straightforward) constellations. The average power of the constellation can be shown to be $28.0625d_0^2$, where d_0^2 is the minimum squared Euclidean distance (MSED) of the constellation. The peak power (which is also the peak power of the inner constellation) is $60.5d_0^2$.

The partition of the constellation proceeds through a sequence of steps which are illustrated in Figure 13.27.

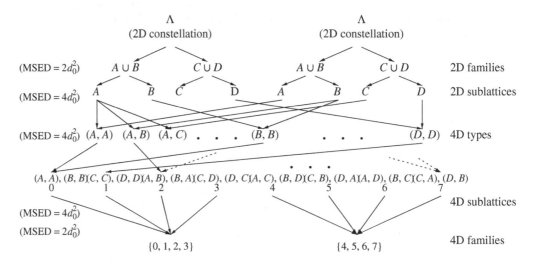

Figure 13.27: Partition steps for the V.34 signal constellation.

- Each constituent two-dimensional rectangular lattice is partitioned into two *families* $A \cup B$ and $C \cup D$, where the sublattice A is composed of those points in the constellation of Figure 13.26 labeled with the letter 'a,' and similarly for B, C, and D. The MSED between these two families is $2d_0^2$.

- The two-dimensional families are further partitioned into four sublattices A, B, C, and D, with MSED $4d_0^2$. The sublattices have the property that under a 90° counterclockwise rotation, sublattice A rotates to sublattice D. Collectively the sublattices rotate as

$$A \to D \to B \to C \to A. \tag{13.11}$$

- Sixteen four-dimensional *types* are defined by concatenating all pairs of two-dimensional sublattices. These types are $(A, A), (A, B), \ldots, (D, D)$. The MSED between the types is $4d_0^2$, the same as for the sublattices, since two of the same sublattices can be used in a type.

- The 16 types are grouped into 8 four-dimensional sublattices, denoted by $0, 1, \ldots, 7$, as denoted in Figure 13.27 and Table 13.9. The MSED between these sublattices is still $4d_0^2$, which may be verified as follows. The two first constituent two-dimensional sublattices in each four-dimensional sublattice are in $A \cup B$ or $C \cup D$, and likewise for the second two two-dimensional sublattices. Each of these thus have the minimum squared distance of the two-dimensional families, $2d_0^2$. Since there are two independent two-dimensional components, the MSED is $2d_0^2 + 2d_0^2$. It can be verified that the four-dimensional sublattices are invariant under 180° rotation.

- The eight sublattices are further grouped into two four-dimensional *families* $\bigcup_{i=0}^{3} i$ and $\bigcup_{i=4}^{7} i$, with MSED $2d_0^2$.

Combining the trellis of Figure 13.25 with the decomposition of Figure 13.27, the assignments of Table 13.9 satisfy the following requirements:

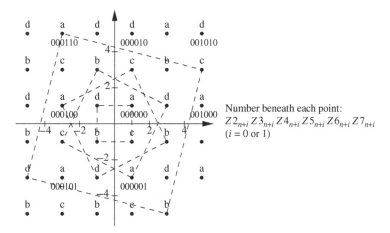

Number beneath each point:
$Z2_{n+i}\, Z3_{n+i}\, Z4_{n+i}\, Z5_{n+i}\, Z6_{n+i}\, Z7_{n+i}$
$(i = 0$ or $1)$

Figure 13.28: Orbits of some of the points under rotation: all points in an orbit are assigned the same bit pattern.

- The 4D sublattices associated with a transition from a state or to a state are all different, but all belong to the same family $\bigcup_{i=0}^{3} i$ or $\bigcup_{i=4}^{7} i$.

- The MSED between any two allowed sequences in the trellis is greater than $4d_0^2$. In combination with the first requirement, this means that the free distance of the code is established by the MSED of each 4D sublattice, $4d_0^2$. Compared to uncoded 128-point cross signal constellation with average energy $20.5d_0^2$, the asymptotic coding gain is

$$10\log_{10}\left(\frac{4d_0^2}{28.0625d_0^2} \Big/ \frac{d_0^2}{20.5d_0^2}\right) = 4.66 \text{ dB}.$$

- The assignment makes a rotationally invariant code (using just a linear trellis encoder). For a valid transition in the trellis from a state i to a state j, let X be the four-dimensional subset associated with the transition. Let Y be the four-dimensional subset that is obtained by rotating X by $90°$. Then Y is associated with the valid transition from the state $F(i)$ to the next state $F(j)$ for some function F. For this particular code, the function is:

$$F : W1_p W2_p W3_p W4_p \mapsto \overline{W1_p} W2_p \overline{W3_p} W4_p,$$

where the overbar denotes binary complementation. In combination with the fact that the sublattices are invariant with respect to $180°$ rotations, this makes the code rotationally invariant with respect to multiples of $90°$ rotations.

The encoding operation is now summarized. Fourteen bits, representing the information for two symbol periods, are presented to the encoder. These fourteen input bits are denoted by $(I1_n, \ldots, I7_n)$ and $(I1_{n+1}, \ldots, I7_{n+1})$, where the subscript n denotes bits or symbols associated with even-numbered symbols and $n+1$ denotes bits or symbols associated with odd-numbered symbols. We refer to the pair of symbol intervals at time n and time $n+1$ as a coding **epoch**. From these 14 bits, two symbols in the coding epoch are selected according to the following steps:

- The encoded bits $Y0_n, I1_n$, and $I2'_n$ select one of the eight four-dimensional sublattices. Then the nontrellis-encoded information bit $I3'_n$ selects one of the two four-dimensional types within the sublattice. This is done in such a way that the system is transparent to phase ambiguities of multiples of $90°$. To see this, consider a bit pattern $Y0_n I1_n I2'_n I3'_n$ and let X denote the associated

4D type from Table 13.9. Let $S2_1S3_1$, $S2_2S3_2$, $S2_3S3_3$ denote the bit pairs obtained when the bit pair $I2_n'I3_n'$ is advanced in the circular sequence

$$00 \rightarrow 11 \rightarrow 01 \rightarrow 10 \rightarrow 00. \tag{13.12}$$

Let X_1, X_2, and X_3 denote the types obtained by rotating X *counterclockwise* by successive multiples of 90°. Then the 4D types associated with the bit patterns $Y0_nI1_nS2_1S3_1$, $Y0_nI1_nS2_2S3_2$, and $Y0_nI1_nS2_3S3_3$ are X_1, X_2, and X_3, respectively.

Example 13.14   Let $Y0_nI1_nI2_n'I3_n' = 0010$. Then (from Table 13.9) the 4D type transmitted is $X = (C, C)$. When this is rotated 90°, the type is (see (13.11)) (A, A), corresponding to a transmitted sequence $Y0_nI1_nI2_n'I3_n' = 0000$. Note that the last 2 bits correspond to the succession of (13.12). □

To obtain rotational invariance, the bits $I2_nI3_n'$ are obtained as the output of a differential encoder, just as for the V.32 and V.33 standards presented in Section 13.6. The pair $(I3_n, I2_n)$ is converted to a number modulo 4 ($I2_n$ is the LSB), and the differential representation (13.6) is employed.

- The 4D block encoder serves the purpose of selecting points in the inner and outer constellation, ensuring that the outer constellation is not used for both the symbols in the coding epoch. The 4D block encoder takes the input bits $I1_{n+1}$, $I2_{n+1}$ and $I3_{n+1}$ and generates two pairs of output bits $(Z2_n, Z3_n)$ and $(Z2_{n+1}, Z3_{n+1})$ according to Table 13.10. The outputs (00) and (01) correspond to points in the inner constellation and the output 10 corresponds to points in the outer constellation. (See the labeling in Figure 13.26.) Each bit pair can be 00, 01, or 10, but they cannot both be 10.

Table 13.10: 4D Block Encoder [?]

$I1_{n+1}$	$I2_{n+1}$	$I3_{n+1}$	$Z2_n$	$Z3_n$	$Z2_{n+1}$	$Z3_{n+1}$
0	0	0	0	0	0	0
0	0	1	0	0	0	1
0	1	0	0	0	1	0
0	1	1	0	1	1	0
1	0	0	1	0	0	0
1	0	1	1	0	0	1
1	1	0	0	1	0	0
1	1	1	0	1	0	1

- There are 16 points in the outer group of a 2D lattice (such as A) or in either half of the inner part of a 2D subset. These sixteen points are indexed by the bits $Z4_pZ5_pZ6_pZ7_p$, where $p = n$ or $n + 1$.

- The bits $Z2_pZ3_pZ4_pZ5_pZ6_pZ7_p$ ($p = n$ or $n + 1$) select from a set of four points in the signal constellation. To ensure rotational invariance, the four rotations of a point are all assigned the same set of bits. Figure 13.28 shows the "orbits" of some of the points under rotation. The a, b, c, and d points in the orbit are all assigned the same label $Z2_pZ3_pZ4_pZ5_pZ6_pZ7_p$; then one of the points in the orbit is selected by $Z1_pZ0_p$. Since the bits $Z2_pZ3_pZ4_pZ5_pZ6_pZ7_p$ are rotationally invariant by labeling, and the bits $Z1_pZ0_p$ are invariant by differential encoding, the overall code is rotationally invariant.

The bits $Z0_pZ1_p \ldots Z7_p$ ($p = n$ or $n + 1$) are used to select two points in the signal constellation, corresponding to the two symbols sent in the coding epoch.

13.9 Exercises

13.1 Verify the energy per symbol E_s and the energy per bit E_b for BPSK signaling from Table 13.1. Repeat for 16-QAM and 32-cross signaling.

13.2 For each of the following signal constellations, determine a signal partition. Compute the minimum distance between signal points at each level of the tree.

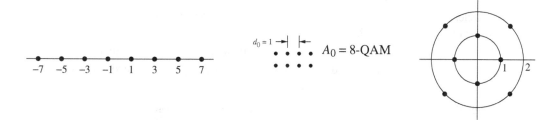

13.3 [483] The simple TCM encoder shown here

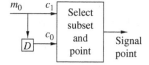

is used with the 8-PAM signal constellation shown in Exercise 13.2.

(a) Determine the trellis for the encoder.

(b) Determine a signal partitioning scheme which transmits 2 bits/symbol.

(c) Determine the squared minimum free distance for the coded system.

(d) Compute the asymptotic coding gain in dB for this system compared with an uncoded 4-PAM system.

(e) Determine the output transition matrix $B(x)$ for this code and determine the components $D(x)$, $P(x)$, and $M(x)$.

13.4 For the encoder shown here

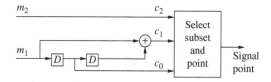

employed with an 8-PSK constellation partitioned as in Figure 13.4:

(a) Draw the trellis for the convolutional encoder.

(b) Draw the trellis for the trellis encoder, labeling the state transitions with the subsets from the constellation.

(c) Determine the minimum free distance between paths which deviate from the all-zero path, both for non-parallel paths and for parallel paths. Determine the minimum free distance for the code. Assume $E_s = 1$.

(d) Determine the coding gain of the system, compared with 4-PSK transmission.

13.5 The sequence of data $(m_{2,t}, m_{1,t})$ consisting of the pairs $(0,0), (1,0), (1,1), (1,1), (0,0), (0,1), (0,1)$ is applied to the encoder of Figure 13.16.

(a) Determine the differentially encoded sequence $(\tilde{m}_{2,t}, \tilde{m}_{1,t})$. Assume that the differential encoder starts with previous input 0.

(b) The sequence of inputs $(m_{4,t}, m_{3,t}, m_{2,t}, m_{1,t})$ consisting of the 4-tuples $(0,1,0,0), (1,1,1,0), (0,1,1,1), (1,0,1,1), (0,0,0,0), (1,1,0,1), (1,0,0,1)$ is presented to the encoder of Figure 13.16. Determine the sequence of output subsets and plot the corresponding path on the trellis, as in Example 13.6. Assume the encoder starts in state 0.

(c) Now take this sequence of output signals and rotate them by $\pi/2$. Determine the sequence of received signal points.

(d) Determine the state sequence decoded at the receiver. Assume the decoder is able to determine that state 7 is the starting state.

(e) Determine the sequence of input bits corresponding to this decoded sequence.

(f) Run the input bits through a differential decoder and verify that the decoded bits match the original sequence of transmitted bits.

13.6 The signal constellation below has 16 points, with the points on a hexagonal lattice with minimum distance between points equal to 1. Adjust the center location and the lattice points so that the constellation has minimum average signal energy. Compute the average signal energy E_s. Compare this average signal energy with a 16-QAM constellation having equal minimum distance. How much energy advantage is there for the hexagonal lattice (in dB)? What practical disadvantages might the hexagonal constellation have?

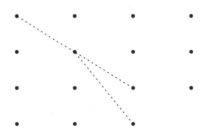

Programming Laboratory 11: Trellis-Coded Modulation Encoding and Decoding

Objective

In this laboratory, you will create an encoder and decoder for a particular TCM code.

Background

Reading: Section 13.3.

Programming Part

1) Construct an encoder to implement the trellis code for a four-state trellis with an 8-PSK signal constellation. Verify that it works as expected.

2) Construct a Viterbi decoder for the trellis code. Verify that it works as expected.

3) Make a plot of $P(e)$ as a function of SNR for the code. Compare $P(e)$ with $P(e)$ for uncoded 4-PSK. Plot the theoretical $P(e)$. Is the theoretical coding gain actually achieved?

13.10 References

The idea of combining coding and modulation can be traced at least back to 1974 [298]. It was developed into a mature technique by Ungerböck [456–459]. Important theoretical foundations were later laid by Forney [132–134, 140]. Rotationally invariant codes are described in [475, 476]. Additional work in this area appears in [339, 341, 478]. It was also mentioned in [454]. Rotational invariance also appears in [29, 451]

Our bound on the performance in Section 13.4 follows [397] very closely. See also [500]. A random coding bound is also presented there. Other analyses of the code performance appear in [40]. A thorough treatment of TCM appears in [272]. Theoretical foundations of coset codes appear in [130, 131].

TCM using lattices is described in [56]. An example of multidimensional TCM using an eight-dimensional lattice is described in [55]. Issues related to packing points in higher dimensional spaces and codes on lattices are addressed in [77–79, 81, 82]. The definitive reference related to sphere packings is [79]. The sphere-packing advantage as applied to data compression (vector quantization) is described in [278]. A trellis code in six dimensions based on the E_6 lattice is described in [313]. Lattices also have use in some computer algebra and cryptographic systems; in this context an important problem is finding the shortest vector in the lattice. For discussions and references, see [472, Chapter 16]. A concise but effective summary of lattice coding is presented in [11]. Extensive design results appear in [272, 344, 345].

Part IV

Iteratively Decoded Codes

Chapter 14

Turbo Codes

"Tell me how you decode and I'll be able to understand the code." When you have no particular gift for algebra, ... then think about the decoding side before the encoding one. Indeed, for those who are more comfortable with physics than with mathematics, decoding algorithms are more accessible than coding constructions, and help to understand them.

— Claude Berrou [37]

14.1 Introduction

Shannon's channel coding theorem implies strong coding behavior for random codes as the code block length increases, but increasing block length typically implies an exponentially increasing decoding complexity. Sequences of codes with sufficient structure to be easily decoded as the length increases were, until fairly recently, not sufficiently strong to approach the limits implied by Shannon's theorem. However, in 1993, an approach to error-correction coding was introduced which provided for very long codewords with only (relatively) modest decoding complexity. These codes were termed *turbo codes* by their inventors [38, 39]. They have also been termed parallel concatenated codes [194, 397]. Because the decoding complexity is relatively small for the dimension of the code, very long codes are possible, so that the bounds of Shannon's channel coding theorem become, for all practical purposes, achievable. Codes which can operate within a fraction of a dB of channel capacity are now possible. Since their announcement, turbo codes have generated considerable research enthusiasm leading to a variety of variations, such as turbo decoding of block codes and combined turbo decoding and equalization, which are introduced in this chapter. Actually, the turbo coding idea goes back somewhat earlier than the original turbo code announcement; the work of [276] and [277] also present the idea of parallel concatenated coding and iterative decoding algorithms.

The turbo code encoder consists of two (or more) systematic block codes which share message data via permuters (sometimes referred to as interleavers). In its most conventional realization, the codes are obtained from recursive systematic convolutional (RSC) codes — but other codes can be used as well. A key development in turbo codes is the *iterative* decoding algorithm. In the iterative decoding algorithm, decoders for each constituent encoder take turns operating on the received data. Each decoder produces an estimate of the probabilities of the transmitted symbols. The decoders are thus *soft* output decoders. Probabilities of the symbols from one encoder known as *extrinsic probabilities* are passed to the other decoder (in the symbol order appropriate for the encoder), where they are used as *prior probabilities* for the other decoder. The decoder thus passes probabilities back and forth between the decoders, with each decoder combining the evidence it receives from the incoming prior probabilities with the parity information provided by the code. After some number of iterations, the decoder converges to an estimate of the transmitted codeword. Since the output of one decoder is fed to the input of the next decoder, the decoding algorithm is called a turbo decoder: it is reminiscent of turbo charging an automobile engine using engine-heated air at the air intake. Thus, it is not really the *code* which is "turbo," but rather the decoding algorithm which is "turbo."

As an example of what turbo codes can achieve, Figure 14.1 shows the performance of a turbo code employing two RSC encoders with parity-producing transfer functions

$$G(x) = \frac{1 + x^4}{1 + x + x^2 + x^3 + x^4} \tag{14.1}$$

Error Correction Coding: Mathematical Methods and Algorithms, Second Edition. Todd K. Moon
© 2021 John Wiley & Sons, Inc. Published 2021 by John Wiley & Sons, Inc.
Companion website: www.wiley.com/go/Moon/ErrorCorrectionCoding

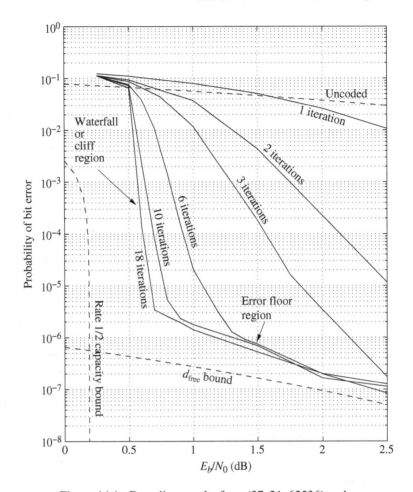

Figure 14.1: Decoding results for a $(37, 21, 65536)$ code.

in a rate $R = 1/2$ turbo code (i.e., it is punctured) with block length $N = 65536$ and permuter (with the permutation selected essentially at random). (The numerator and denominator polynomials are represented using the octal numbers $21 = 10\ 001$ and $37 = 11\ 111$, respectively, so this code is sometimes referred to as a $(37, 21, 65536)$ code.) The decoding performance for up to 18 decoding iterations is shown. Beyond 18 iterations, little additional coding gain is achieved. (These results were obtained by counting up to 100 bits in error.) We note that with 18 iterations of decoding, performance within about 0.5 dB of the BAWGN capacity limit is achieved by this code, at least for SNRs up to about 0.6 dB. However, an interesting phenomenon is observed at higher SNRs: while the decoding is still good, it fails to improve as dramatically as a function of SNR. At a certain SNR, the error curves nearly level off, so the improvement with increasing SNR is very modest. This phenomenon is referred to as the *error floor* and is discussed in Section 14.4. Briefly, it is due to the presence of low-weight codewords in the code. A bound due to the free distance of the convolutional coders is also shown in the plot, which indicates the slope of the error floor. The portion of the plot where the error plot drops steeply down as a function of SNR is referred to as the waterfall or cliff region.

In this chapter, we discuss the structure of the encoder, present various algorithms for decoding, and provide some indication of the structure of the codes that leads to their good performance and the error floor. We also introduce the idea of turbo equalization and the concept of EXIT analysis for the study of the convergence of the decoding algorithm.

14.2   Encoding Parallel Concatenated Codes

The conventional arrangement for the (unpunctured) turbo encoder is shown in Figure 14.2. It consists of two transfer functions representing the non-systematic components of RSC encoders called the *constituent encoders*, and a *permuter*, which permutes the input symbols prior to input to the second constituent encoder. (It is also possible to use more than two encoder blocks [98], but the principles remain the same, so for the sake of specific notation we restrict attention here to only two constituent encoders.) As discussed in Chapter 12, systematic convolutional codes typically work best when the encoder is a feedback (IIR) encoder, so the transfer function of each convolutional encoder is the rational function

$$G(x) = \frac{h(x)}{g(x)}.$$

Strictly speaking, there is no reason that both constituent transfer functions must be the same. However, it is conventional to use the same transfer function in each branch; research to date has not provided any reason to do otherwise.

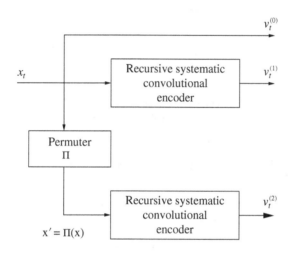

Figure 14.2: Block diagram of a turbo encoder.

A block of input symbols $\mathbf{x} = \{x_0, x_1, \ldots, x_{N-1}\}$ is presented to the encoder, where each x_i is in some alphabet $\mathcal{A}$ with $|\mathcal{A}|$ elements in it. These input symbols may include an appended zero-state forcing sequence, as in Figure 14.6, or it may simply be a message sequence, $\mathbf{x} = \mathbf{m} = \{m_0, m_1, \ldots, m_{N-1}\}$. In the encoder, the input sequence $\mathbf{x}$ is used three ways. First, it is copied directly to the output to produce the systematic output sequence $v_t^{(0)} = x_t$, $t = 0, 1, \ldots, N-1$. Second, the input sequence runs through the first RSC encoder with transfer function $G(x)$, resulting in a parity sequence $\{v_0^{(1)}, v_2^{(1)}, \ldots, v_{N-1}^{(1)}\}$. The combination of the sequence $\{v^{(0)}\}$ and the sequence $\{v_t^{(1)}\}$ results in a rate $R = 1/2$ (neglecting the length of the zero-forcing tail, if any) systematically encoded convolutionally encoded sequence. Third, the sequence $\mathbf{x}$ is also passed through a *permuter* or interleaver of length N, denoted by Π, which produces the permuted output sequence $\mathbf{x}' = \Pi(\mathbf{x})$. The sequence $\mathbf{x}'$ is passed through another convolutional encoder with transfer function $G(x)$ which produces the output sequence $\mathbf{v}^{(2)} = \{v_0^{(2)}, v_1^{(2)}, \ldots, v_{N-1}^{(2)}\}$. The three output sequences are multiplexed together to form the output sequence

$$\mathbf{v} = \{(v_0^{(0)}, v_0^{(1)}, v_0^{(2)}), (v_1^{(0)}, v_1^{(1)}, v_1^{(2)}), \ldots, (v_{N-1}^{(0)}, v_{N-1}^{(1)}, v_{N-1}^{(2)})\},$$

resulting in an overall rate $R = 1/3$ linear, systematic, block code. The code has two sets of parity information, $\mathbf{v}^{(1)}$ and $\mathbf{v}^{(2)}$ which, because of the interleaving, are fairly independent. In an ideal setting, the sets of parity bits would be exactly independent.

Frequently, in order to obtain higher rates, the filter outputs are punctured before multiplexing, as shown in Figure 14.3. Puncturing operates only on the parity sequences — the systematic bits are not punctured. The puncturing is frequently represented by a matrix, such as

$$P = \begin{bmatrix} 1 & 0 \\ 0 & 1 \end{bmatrix}.$$

The first column indicates which bits are output at the even output instants and the second column indicates which bits are output at the odd output instants. For example, this puncture matrix alternately selects the outputs of the encoding filters.

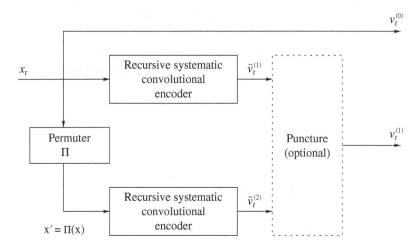

Figure 14.3: Block diagram of a turbo encoder with puncturing.

Example 14.1   Consider the transfer function $G(x) = \frac{1}{1+x^2}$ incorporated in the turbo encoder of Figure 14.4(a), with the trellis stage shown in Figure 14.4(b). Let the permuter be described by

$$\Pi = \{8, 3, 7, 6, 9, 0, 2, 5, 1, 4\}.$$

Then, for example, $x_0' = x_8$, $x_1' = x_3$, etc. Let the input sequence be

$$\mathbf{x} = [1, 1, 0, 0, 1, 0, 1, 0, 1, 1] = \mathbf{v}^{(0)}.$$

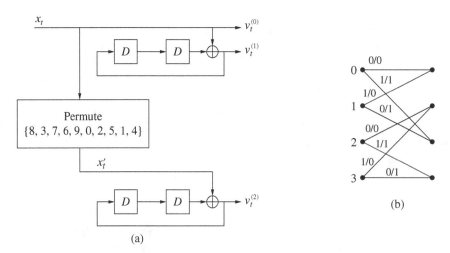

Figure 14.4: Example turbo encoder with $G(x) = 1/(1 + x^2)$.

Then the output of the first encoder is

$$\mathbf{v}^{(1)} = [\underline{1}, 1, \underline{1}, 1, \underline{0}, 1, \underline{1}, 1, \underline{0}, 0], \tag{14.2}$$

and the first encoder happens to be left in state 0 at the end of this sequence. The permuted bit sequence is

$$\mathbf{x}' = [1, 0, 0, 1, 1, 1, 0, 0, 1, 1]$$

and the output of the second encoder is

$$\mathbf{v}^{(2)} = [\underline{1}, 0, \underline{1}, 1, \underline{0}, 0, 0, \underline{0}, 1, \underline{1}]; \tag{14.3}$$

the second encoder is left in state 3. When the 3 bit streams are multiplexed together, the bit stream is

$$\mathbf{v} = [1, 1, 1, \ 1, 1, 0, \ 0, 1, 1, \ 0, 1, 1, \ 1, 0, 0, \ 0, 1, 0, \ 1, 1, 0, \ 0, 1, 0, \ 1, 0, 1, \ 1, 0, 1].$$

If the encoded bits are punctured, the underlined parity bits of (14.2) and (14.3) are retained. The resulting rate $R = 1/2$ encoded bit sequence is

$$\mathbf{v} = [1, 1, \ 1, 0, \ 0, 1, \ 0, 1, \ 1, 0, \ 0, 0, \ 1, 1, \ 0, 0, \ 1, 0, \ 1, 1].$$

□

It should be pointed out that there are also *serially* concatenated codes with iterative decoders. One such code is the repeat accumulate (RA) code, which is introduced in Section 16.2.

14.3 Turbo Decoding Algorithms

The multiplexed and encoded data $\mathbf{v}$ are modulated and transmitted through a channel, whose output is the received vector $\mathbf{r}$. The received data vector $\mathbf{r}$ is demultiplexed into the vectors $\mathbf{r}^{(0)}$ (corresponding to $\mathbf{v}^{(0)}$), $\mathbf{r}^{(1)}$ (corresponding to $\mathbf{v}^{(1)}$), and $\mathbf{r}^{(2)}$ (corresponding to $\mathbf{v}^{(2)}$).

The general operation of the turbo decoding algorithm is as follows, as summarized in Figure 14.5. The data $(\mathbf{r}^{(0)}, \mathbf{r}^{(1)})$ associated with the first encoder are fed to Decoder I. This decoder initially uses uniform priors on the transmitted bits and produces probabilities of the bits conditioned on the observed data. These probabilities are called the extrinsic probabilities, as described below. The output probabilities of Decoder I are permuted and passed to Decoder II, where they are used as "prior" probabilities in the decoder, along with the data associated with the second encoder, which is $\mathbf{r}^{(0)}$ (permuted) and $\mathbf{r}^{(2)}$. The extrinsic output probabilities of Decoder II are depermuted and passed back to become prior probabilities to Decoder I. The process of passing probability information back and forth continues until the decoder determines (somehow) that the process has converged, or until some maximum number of iterations is reached.

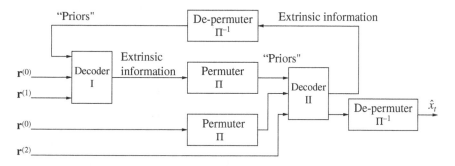

Figure 14.5: Block diagram of a turbo decoder.

The heart of the decoding algorithm is a soft-decision decoding algorithm which provides estimates of the posterior probabilities of each input bit. The algorithm most commonly used for the soft-decision decoding algorithm is the MAP algorithm, also commonly known as the BCJR algorithm. In Section 14.3.1, we describe this algorithm for the case of a general convolutional code. Then in Section 14.3.10, we describe modifications to the algorithm that apply to systematic codes, which sets the stage for the iterative turbo decoding algorithm. The MAP algorithm can also be expressed in a log-likelihood setting, as described in Section 14.3.12. A lower-complexity implementation of the MAP algorithm is discussed in Section 14.3.15. Another decoding algorithm, called the soft-output Viterbi algorithm (SOVA) is described in Section 12.11, which has even lower computational complexity (but slightly worse performance).

14.3.1   The MAP Decoding Algorithm

The maximum a posteriori (MAP) decoding algorithm suitable for estimating bit and/or state probabilities for a finite-state Markov system is frequently referred to as the BCJR algorithm, after Bahl, Cock, Jelenik, and Raviv who proposed it originally in [20]. The BCJR algorithm computes the posterior probability of symbols from Markov sources transmitted through discrete memoryless channels. Since the output of a convolutional coder passed through a memoryless channel (such as an AWGN channel or a BSC) forms a Markov source, the BCJR algorithm can be used for maximum *a posteriori* probability decoding of convolutional codes. In many respects, the BCJR algorithm is similar to the Viterbi algorithm. However, the Viterbi algorithm computes *hard decisions* — even if it is employing soft branch metrics — since a single path is selected to each state at each time. This result in an overall decision on an entire sequence of bits (or codeword) at the end of the algorithm, and there is no way of determining the reliability of the decoder decisions on the individual bits. Furthermore, the branch metric is based upon log-likelihood values; no prior information is incorporated into the decoding process. The BCJR algorithm, on the other hand, computes soft outputs in the form of posterior probabilities for each of the message bits. While the Viterbi algorithm produces the maximum likelihood *message sequence* (or codeword), given the observed data, the BCJR algorithm produces the *a posteriori* most likely sequence of message *bits*, given the observed data. (Interestingly, the sequence of bits produced by the MAP algorithm may not actually correspond to a continuous path through the trellis.) In terms of actual performance on convolutional codes, the distinction between the Viterbi algorithm and the BCJR algorithm is frequently insignificant, since the performance of the BCJR algorithm is usually comparable to that of the Viterbi algorithm and any incremental improvement offered by the BCJR algorithm is offset by its higher computational complexity. However, there are instances where the probabilities produced by the BCJR are important. For example, the probabilities can be used to estimate the *reliability* of decisions about the bits. This capability is exploited in the decoding algorithms of turbo codes. As a result, the BCJR algorithm lies at the heart of most turbo decoding algorithms.

We first express the decoding algorithm in terms of probabilities then, in Section 14.3.12, we present analogous results for likelihood ratio decoding. The probabilistic description is more general, being applicable to the case of nonbinary alphabets. However, it also requires particular care with normalization. Furthermore, there are approximations that can be made in association with the likelihood ratio formulation that can reduce the computational burden somewhat.

14.3.2   Notation

We present the BCJR algorithm here in the context of a $R = k/n$ convolutional coder. Consider the block diagram of Figure 14.6. The encoder accepts message symbols m_i coming from an alphabet $\mathcal{A}$ — most frequently, $\mathcal{A} = \{0, 1\}$ — which are grouped into k-tuples $\mathbf{m}_i = [m_i^{(0)}, \ldots, m_i^{(k-1)}]$. It is frequently convenient to employ convolutional encoders which terminate in a known state. To accomplish this, Figure 14.6 portrays the input sequence $\mathbf{m} = [\mathbf{m}_0, \mathbf{m}_1, \ldots, \mathbf{m}_{L-1}]$ passing through a system that appends a sequence of $\mathbf{x}_L, \mathbf{x}_{L+1}, \ldots, \mathbf{x}_{L+\nu-1}$, where ν is the constraint length (or memory)

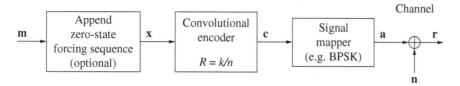

Figure 14.6: Processing stages for BCJR algorithm.

of the convolutional coder, which is used to drive the state of the encoder to 0. (For a polynomial encoder, the padding bits would be all zeros, but for the recursive encoder, the padding bits are a function of the state of the encoder after the last message bit m_{L-1} enters the encoder.) The sequence

$$\mathbf{x} = \left[\mathbf{m}, \mathbf{x}_L, \mathbf{x}_{L+1}, \ldots, \mathbf{x}_{L+v-1}\right]$$

forms the input to the $R = k/n$ convolutional encoder. We denote the actual length of the input sequence by N, so $N = L + v$ if the appended sequence is used, or $N = L$ if not. Each block $\mathbf{x}_i$ is in $\mathcal{A}^k$. The output of the encoder is the sequence of blocks of symbols

$$\mathbf{v} = \left[\mathbf{v}_0, \mathbf{v}_1, \ldots, \mathbf{v}_{N-1}\right],$$

where each block $\mathbf{v}_t$ contains the n output bits of the encoder for the tth input:

$$\mathbf{v}_t = \left[v_t^{(0)}, v_t^{(1)}, \ldots, v_t^{(n-1)}\right].$$

The encoder symbols $\mathbf{v}_t$ are mapped to a signal constellation (such as BPSK) to produce the output symbols $\mathbf{a}_t$. The dimension of the $\mathbf{a}_t$ depends on the dimension of the signal constellation. For example, if BPSK is employed, we might have $a_t^{(i)} \in \{\pm\sqrt{E_c}\}$, where $RE_b = E_c$, with $\mathbf{a}_t = [a_t^{(0)}, a_t^{(1)}, \ldots, a_t^{(n-1)}]$ and

$$a_t^{(i)} = \sqrt{E_c}(2v_t^{(i)} - 1), \quad i = 0, 1, \ldots, n-1. \tag{14.4}$$

We also use the notation

$$\tilde{v}_t^{(i)} = 2v_t^{(i)} - 1$$

to indicate the ± 1 modulated signals without the $\sqrt{E_c}$ scaling, so $a_t^{(i)} = \sqrt{E_c}\tilde{v}_t^{(i)}$.

The sequence of output symbols $\mathbf{a} = [\mathbf{a}_0, \mathbf{a}_1, \ldots, \mathbf{a}_{N-1}]$ passes through an additive white Gaussian noise (AWGN) channel to form the received symbol sequence

$$\mathbf{r} = [\mathbf{r}_0, \mathbf{r}_1, \ldots, \mathbf{r}_{N-1}],$$

where

$$\mathbf{r}_t = \mathbf{a}_t + \mathbf{n}_t, \quad t = 0, 1, \ldots, N-1,$$

and where $\mathbf{n}_i$ is a zero-mean Gaussian noise signal with variance $\sigma^2 = N_0/2$ in each component.

We denote the discrete time index as t. We denote the state of the encoder at time t by Ψ_t. There are $Q = 2^v$ possible states, where v is the constraint length of the encoder, which we denote as integers in the range $0 \leq \Psi_t < 2^v$. We assume that the encoder starts in state 0 (the all-zero state) before any message bits are processed, so that $\Psi_t = 0$ for $t \leq 0$. When the zero-forcing sequence is appended, the encoder terminates in state 0, so that $\Psi_N = 0$. Otherwise, it is assumed that the encoder could terminate in any state with equal probability. The sequence of states associated with the input sequence is $\{\Psi_0, \Psi_1, \ldots, \Psi_N\}$.

A portion of the trellis associated with the encoder is shown in Figure 14.7, portraying a state $\Psi_t = p$ at time t transitioning to a state $\Psi_{t+1} = q$ at time $t + 1$. The unique input $\mathbf{x}_t$ which causes this transition is denoted by $\mathbf{x}^{(p,q)}$. The corresponding mapped symbols $\mathbf{a}_t$ produced by this state transition are denoted by $\mathbf{a}^{(p,q)}$, with elements $a^{(0,p,q)}, a^{(1,p,q)}, \ldots, a^{(n-1,p,q)}$.

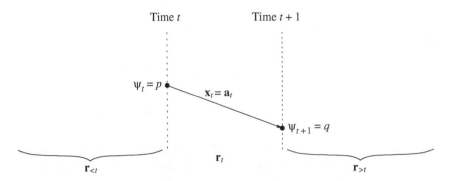

Figure 14.7: One transition of the trellis for the encoder.

Notationally, quantities with the time-index subscript $_t$ are often random variables or their realizations, (e.g., $\mathbf{a}_t$, $a_t^{(0)}$, or $\mathbf{x}_t$), whereas quantities without the time-index subscript are usually not random variables.

14.3.3 Posterior Probability

It is clear that the convolutional code introduces dependencies among the symbols $\{\mathbf{a}_t\}$. An optimal decoder should exploit these dependencies, examining the *entire* sequence of data to determine its estimates of the probabilities of the input bits. The goal of the decoder is thus: Determine the *a posteriori* probabilities of the input $P(\mathbf{x}_t = \mathbf{x}|\mathbf{r})$, that is, the probability that the input takes on some value $\mathbf{x}$ conditioned upon the entire received sequence $\mathbf{r}$. The BCJR algorithm provides an efficient way to compute these probabilities. The first step is to determine the probabilities of *state transitions*; once these are determined, finding the probabilities of the bits is straightforward.

The convolutional code introduces a Markov property into the probability structure: Knowledge of the state at time $t + 1$ renders irrelevant knowledge of the state at time t or previous times. To exploit this Markovity, we partition the observations into three different sets,

$$\mathbf{r} = \mathbf{r}_{<t} \cup \{\mathbf{r}_t\} \cup \mathbf{r}_{>t},$$

where $\mathbf{r}_{<t} = \{\mathbf{r}_l\colon l < t\}$ is the set of "prior" observations, $\mathbf{r}_t$ is the "current" observation, and $\mathbf{r}_{>t} = \{\mathbf{r}_l\colon l > t\}$ is the set of the future observations. Then the posterior probability of the transition ($\Psi_t = p$, $\Psi_{t+1} = q$) given the observed sequence $\mathbf{r}$ is

$$\begin{aligned}
P(\Psi_t = p, \Psi_{t+1} = q|\mathbf{r}) &= p(\Psi_t = p, \Psi_{t+1} = q, \mathbf{r})/p(\mathbf{r}) \\
&= p(\Psi_t = p, \Psi_{t+1} = q, \mathbf{r}_{<t}, \mathbf{r}_t, \mathbf{r}_{>t})/p(\mathbf{r}),
\end{aligned} \tag{14.5}$$

where P denotes a probability mass function and p denotes a probability density function. We now employ the conditioning factorization

$$\begin{aligned}
&P(\Psi_t = p, \Psi_{t+1} = q|\mathbf{r}) \\
&= p(\Psi_t = p, \Psi_{t+1} = q, \mathbf{r}_{<t}, \mathbf{r}_t)p(\mathbf{r}_{>t}|\Psi_t = p, \Psi_{t+1} = q, \mathbf{r}_{<t}, \mathbf{r}_t)/p(\mathbf{r}).
\end{aligned} \tag{14.6}$$

Because of the Markov property, we can rewrite the second probability in (14.6) as

$$p(\mathbf{r}_{>t}|\Psi_t = p, \Psi_{t+1} = q, \mathbf{r}_{<t}, \mathbf{r}_t) = p(\mathbf{r}_{>t}|\Psi_{t+1} = q), \tag{14.7}$$

since knowledge of the state at time $t + 1$ renders irrelevant knowledge about prior states or received data. The first factor in (14.6) can be factored further and the Markovity can exploited again:

$$\begin{aligned}
p(\Psi_t = p, \Psi_{t+1} = q, \mathbf{r}_{<t}, \mathbf{r}_t) &= p(\Psi_{t+1} = q, \mathbf{r}_t|\Psi_t = p, \mathbf{r}_{<t})p(\Psi_t = p, \mathbf{r}_{<t}) \\
&= p(\Psi_{t+1} = q, \mathbf{r}_t|\Psi_t = p)p(\Psi_t = p, \mathbf{r}_{<t}).
\end{aligned} \tag{14.8}$$

Substituting (14.7) and (14.8) into (14.6), we obtain

$$P(\Psi_t = p, \Psi_{t+1} = q | \mathbf{r}) = p(\Psi_t = p, \mathbf{r}_{<t}) p(\Psi_{t+1} = q, \mathbf{r}_t | \Psi_t = p) p(\mathbf{r}_{>t} | \Psi_{t+1} = q) / p(\mathbf{r}).$$

We denote the factors in this probability as follows:

$$\boxed{\alpha_t(p) = p(\Psi_t = p, \mathbf{r}_{<t})}$$

represents the probability of the observations up to time $t - 1$, with the state ending in state p at time t;

$$\boxed{\gamma_t(p, q) = p(\Psi_{t+1} = q, \mathbf{r}_t | \Psi_t = p)}$$

represents the probability of the transition from state p to state q, with the observation at time t; and

$$\boxed{\beta_{t+1}(q) = p(\mathbf{r}_{>t} | \Psi_{t+1} = q)}$$

is the probability of the future observed sequence $\mathbf{r}_{>t}$, given that it starts at state q at time $t + 1$. Thus, we have the posterior probability of the state transition

$$\boxed{P(\Psi_t = p, \Psi_{t+1} = q | \mathbf{r}) = \alpha_t(p)\gamma_t(p, q)\beta_{t+1}(q)/p(\mathbf{r}).} \tag{14.9}$$

We determine recursive techniques for efficiently computing α_t and β_t below.

Given the posterior probability of the state transitions, it is straightforward to determine the posterior probability of a bit $P(\mathbf{x}_t = \mathbf{x} | \mathbf{r})$. For each input value $\mathbf{x}$ in the input alphabet $\mathcal{A}$, let S_x denote the set of state transitions (p, q) which correspond to the input $\mathbf{x}_t = \mathbf{x}$:

$$S_x = \{(p, q) : \mathbf{x}^{(p,q)} = \mathbf{x}\}.$$

For example, for the trellis of Figure 14.4(b),

$$S_0 = \{(0, 0), (1, 2), (2, 1), (3, 3)\} \quad S_1 = \{(0, 2), (1, 0), (2, 3), (3, 1)\}.$$

(We assume for convenience that the trellis is time-invariant, but decoding on time-varying trellises is also possible.) The posterior probability of $\mathbf{x}_t = \mathbf{x}$ is then obtained by summing over all state transitions for which $\mathbf{x}$ is the input:

$$P(\mathbf{x}_t = \mathbf{x} | \mathbf{r}) = \sum_{(p,q) \in S_x} P(\Psi_t = p, \Psi_{t+1} = q | \mathbf{r}) = \frac{1}{p(\mathbf{r})} \sum_{(p,q) \in S_x} \alpha_t(p)\gamma_t(p, q)\beta_{t+1}(q), \tag{14.10}$$

for all $\mathbf{x} \in \mathcal{A}^k$. Up to this point, we have been including the factor $1/p(\mathbf{r})$ in all of our posterior probability computations. However, it is nothing more than a normalizing factor and does not need to be explicitly computed. Since $P(\mathbf{x}_t = \mathbf{x} | \mathbf{r})$ is a probability mass function, we have

$$\sum_{\mathbf{x} \in \mathcal{A}} P(\mathbf{x}_t = \mathbf{x} | \mathbf{r}) = 1.$$

Using this fact, we can compute (14.10) without finding $p(\mathbf{r})$ as follows. Let

$$\tilde{p}(\mathbf{x}_t = \mathbf{x} | \mathbf{r}) = \sum_{(p,q) \in S_x} \alpha_t(p)\gamma_t(p, q)\beta_{t+1}(q), \quad \mathbf{x} \in \mathcal{A}^k.$$

That is, $\tilde{p}(\mathbf{x}_t = \mathbf{x} | \mathbf{r})$ is the same as in $P(\mathbf{x}_t = \mathbf{x} | \mathbf{r})$, but without the factor $1/p(\mathbf{r})$. Then

$$P(\mathbf{x}_t = \mathbf{x} | \mathbf{r}) = \frac{\tilde{p}(\mathbf{x}_t = \mathbf{x} | \mathbf{r})}{\sum_{\mathbf{l} \in \mathcal{A}^k} \tilde{p}(\mathbf{x}_t = \mathbf{l} | \mathbf{r})}. \tag{14.11}$$

It is convenient to express this normalization using an operator. Define the scaling (or *normalization*) operator N_x by

$$\mathsf{N}_x f = \mathsf{N}_x f(\mathbf{x}) = \frac{f(\mathbf{x})}{\sum_{\mathbf{l} \in \mathcal{A}^k} f(\mathbf{l})}.$$

That is, the normalization of a function $f(\mathbf{x})$ is obtained by dividing $f(\mathbf{x})$ by the sum of $f(\mathbf{x})$, summed over the entire domain set of $\mathbf{x}$. The domain of $\mathbf{x}$ is implicit in this notation. Using the normalization notation, we have

$$P(\mathbf{x}_t = \mathbf{x} | \mathbf{r}) = \mathsf{N}_x \tilde{p}(\mathbf{x}_t = \mathbf{x} | \mathbf{r}) = \mathsf{N}_x \sum_{(p,q) \in S_x} \alpha_t(p) \gamma_t(p, q) \beta_{t+1}(q). \tag{14.12}$$

14.3.4   Computing α_t and β_t

Given $\alpha_t(p)$ for all states $p \in \{0, \ldots, Q-1\}$, the values of $\alpha_{t+1}(q)$ can be computed as follows:

$$\alpha_{t+1}(q) = p(\Psi_{t+1} = q, \mathbf{r}_{<t+1}) = p(\Psi_{t+1} = q, \mathbf{r}_t, \mathbf{r}_{<t}) \qquad \text{(definition of } \alpha_{t+1} \text{ and } \mathbf{r}_{<t+1})$$

$$= \sum_{p=0}^{Q-1} p(\Psi_{t+1} = q, \mathbf{r}_t, \Psi_t = p, \mathbf{r}_{<t}) \qquad \text{(compute marginal from joint)}$$

$$= \sum_{p=0}^{Q-1} p(\Psi_t = p, \mathbf{r}_{<t}) p(\Psi_{t+1} = q, \mathbf{r}_t | \Psi_t = p, \mathbf{r}_{<t}) \qquad \text{(conditioning factorization)}$$

$$= \sum_{p=0}^{Q-1} p(\Psi_t = p, \mathbf{r}_{<t}) p(\Psi_{t+1} = q, \mathbf{r}_t | \Psi_t = p) \qquad \text{(by Markovity)}$$

$$= \sum_{p=0}^{Q-1} \alpha_t(p) \gamma_t(p, q) \qquad \text{(definition of } \alpha \text{ and } \gamma).$$

That is,

$$\boxed{\alpha_{t+1}(q) = \sum_{p=0}^{Q-1} \alpha_t(p) \gamma_t(p, q).} \tag{14.13}$$

A backward recursion can similarly be developed for $\beta_t(p)$:

$$\beta_t(p) = p(\mathbf{r}_{>t-1} | \Psi_t = p) = p(\mathbf{r}_{>t}, \mathbf{r}_t | \Psi_t = p) \qquad \text{(definition of } \mathbf{r}_{>t-1})$$

$$= \sum_{q=0}^{Q-1} p(\mathbf{r}_{>t}, \mathbf{r}_t, \Psi_{t+1} = q | \Psi_t = p) \qquad \text{(marginal from joint)}$$

$$= \sum_{q=0}^{Q-1} p(\mathbf{r}_t, \Psi_{t+1} = q | \Psi_t = p) p(\mathbf{r}_{>t} | \mathbf{r}_t, \Psi_{t+1} = q, \Psi_t = p) \qquad \text{(conditioning factorization)} \quad (14.14)$$

$$= \sum_{q=0}^{Q-1} p(\mathbf{r}_t, \Psi_{t+1} = q | \Psi_t = p) p(\mathbf{r}_{>t} | \Psi_{t+1} = q) \qquad \text{(by Markovity)}$$

$$= \sum_{q=0}^{Q-1} \gamma_t(p, q) \beta_{t+1}(q) \qquad \text{(definition of } \gamma \text{ and } \beta).$$

That is,

$$\boxed{\beta_t(p) = \sum_{q=0}^{Q-1} \gamma_t(p,q)\beta_{t+1}(q).} \tag{14.15}$$

The α probabilities are computed starting at the beginning of the trellis with the set $\alpha_0(p), p = 0, 1, \ldots, Q-1$, and working forward through the trellis. This computation is called the *forward pass*. The β probabilities are computed starting at the end of the trellis with the set $\beta_N(p), p = 0, 1, \ldots, Q-1$, and working backward through the trellis. This computation is called the *backward pass*. Because the computation of α and β is such an essential part of the BCJR algorithm, it is sometimes also referred to as the *forward–backward* algorithm.

The recursions (14.13) and (14.15) are initialized as follows. Since the encoder is known to start in state 0, set all of the probability weight in state 0 for α_0:

$$[\alpha_0(0), \alpha_0(1), \ldots, \alpha_0(Q-1)] = [1, 0, \ldots, 0]. \tag{14.16}$$

If it is known that the encoder terminates in state 0, set

$$[\beta_N(0), \beta_N(1), \ldots, \beta_N(Q-1)] = [1, 0, \ldots, 0]. \tag{14.17}$$

Otherwise, since the encoder can terminate in any state with uniform probability, set

$$[\beta_N(0), \beta_N(1), \ldots, \beta_N(Q-1)] = [1/Q, 1/Q, \ldots, 1/Q]. \tag{14.18}$$

14.3.5 Computing γ_t

The transition probability $\gamma_t(p,q)$, or *branch metric* for the branch from $\Psi_t = p$ to $\Psi_{t+1} = q$, depends upon the particular distribution of the observations. For an AWGN channel, the branch metric can be computed as

$$\gamma_t(p,q) = p(\Psi_{t+1} = q, \mathbf{r}_t|\Psi_t = p) = \underbrace{p(\mathbf{r}_t|\Psi_t = p, \Psi_{t+1} = q)}_{\text{likelihood}}\underbrace{P(\Psi_{t+1} = q|\Psi_t = p)}_{\text{transition probability}}. \tag{14.19}$$

Knowing $\Psi_t = p$ and $\Psi_{t+1} = q$, that is, the beginning and ending of a state transition, completely determines and is determined by the output $\mathbf{a}^{(p,q)}$ and the corresponding input $\mathbf{x}^{(p,q)}$. The probability of the state transition (p,q) is thus equivalent to the probability of the input bit associated with it:

$$P(\Psi_{t+1} = q|\Psi_t = p) = P(\mathbf{x}_t = \mathbf{x}^{(p,q)}), \tag{14.20}$$

where $P(\mathbf{x}_t = \mathbf{x}^{(p,q)})$ is the *a priori* probability of the message symbol $\mathbf{x}_t$. In conventional binary coding, $P(\mathbf{x}_t = \mathbf{x})$ is usually equal to $1/2^k$; however, we will see below that it is helpful to use other interpretations.

The probability $p(\mathbf{r}_t|\Psi_t = p, \Psi_{t+1} = q)$ can be written as $p(\mathbf{r}_t|\mathbf{a}^{(p,q)})$. For the n-dimensional AWGN channel, this is simply the Gaussian likelihood,

$$p(\mathbf{r}_t|\mathbf{a}^{(p,q)}) = \frac{1}{(2\pi\sigma^2)^{n/2}} \exp\left[-\frac{1}{2\sigma^2}\|\mathbf{r}_t - \mathbf{a}^{(p,q)}\|^2\right], \tag{14.21}$$

where $\|\cdot\|^2$ is the conventional squared Euclidean metric,

$$\|\mathbf{x}\|^2 = \sum_{i=1}^{n} x_i^2.$$

Substituting (14.20) and (14.21) into (14.19), we obtain, for BPSK modulation,

$$
\begin{aligned}
\gamma_t(p, q) &= \frac{1}{(2\pi\sigma^2)^{n/2}} \exp\left[-\frac{1}{2\sigma^2} \|\mathbf{r}_t - \mathbf{a}^{(p,q)}\|^2\right] P(\mathbf{x}_t = \mathbf{x}^{(p,q)}) \\
&= \frac{1}{(2\pi\sigma^2)^{n/2}} \exp\left[-\frac{1}{2\sigma^2} \sum_{i=0}^{n-1} (r_t^{(i)} - \sqrt{E_c}\,\tilde{v}^{i,(p,q)})^2\right] P(\mathbf{x}_t = \mathbf{x}^{(p,q)}).
\end{aligned}
\tag{14.22}
$$

14.3.6 Normalization

Two different kinds of normalization are frequently used in computing the forward–backward algorithm. First, normalization is used to simplify the computation of the transition probability γ. Second, the normalization is used to numerically stabilize the computation of the αs and βs.

For some constant C, let $\gamma_t'(p, q) = C\gamma_t(p, q)$ and let $\alpha_t'(p)$ and $\beta_t'(p)$ be the corresponding forward and backward probabilities, defined by

$$
\alpha_{t+1}'(q) = \sum_p \alpha_t'(p)\gamma_t'(p, q)
$$

$$
\beta_{t+1}'(p) = \sum_q \gamma_t'(p, q)\beta_{t+1}'(q)
$$

with the same initialization for α_0' and β_N' as for the unnormalized case. At each stage of the propagation, an additional factor C accumulates, so that

$$
\alpha_t'(p) = C^t \alpha_t(p) \quad \beta_t'(p) = C^{N-t}\beta_t(p).
$$

When α' and β' are used in (14.11) or (14.34), the factor C cancels out, resulting in identical probability or likelihood values. Since the normalization constant C has no bearing on the detection problem, it may be chosen to simplify the computations. For example, using $C = 2^k(2\pi\sigma^2)^{n/2}$ in (14.22) yields the normalized branch metric

$$
\gamma_t'(p, q) = \left[\frac{P(\mathbf{x}_t = \mathbf{x}^{(p,q)})}{1/2^k}\right] \exp\left[-\frac{1}{2\sigma^2}\|\mathbf{r}_t - \mathbf{a}^{(p,q)}\|^2\right].
$$

If the prior probability $P(\mathbf{x}_t = \mathbf{x}^{(p,q)}) = 1/2^k$ for all t, then the factor in front is simply unity.

The propagation of α_t and β_t involves computing products and sums of small numbers. Without some kind of normalization there is a rapid loss in numerical precision in the forward and backward passes. It is therefore customary to normalize these probabilities. The forward probability $\alpha_t(p)$ and the backward probability $\beta_t(p)$ are replaced by $\alpha_t'(p)$ and $\beta_t'(p)$ which are normalized so that

$$
\sum_p \alpha_t'(p) = 1 \quad \sum_p \beta_t'(p) = 1
\tag{14.23}
$$

for each t. These normalized versions are propagated by

$$
\alpha_{t+1}'(q) = A_t \sum_{p=0}^{Q-1} \alpha_t'(p)\gamma_t(p, q)
$$

$$
\beta_t'(p) = B_t \sum_{q=0}^{Q-1} \gamma_t(p, q)\beta_{t+1}'(q),
$$

where A_t and B_t are chosen so that (14.23) is satisfied for each t. That is,

$$
\alpha_{t+1}'(q) = \frac{\sum_{p=0}^{Q-1} \alpha_t'(p)\gamma_t(p, q)}{\sum_{q=0}^{Q-1} \sum_{p=0}^{Q-1} \alpha_t'(p)\gamma_t(p, q)} = N_q \sum_{p=0}^{Q-1} \alpha_t'(p)\gamma_t(p, q)
$$

and

$$\beta'_t(p) = \mathsf{N}_p \sum_{q=0}^{Q-1} \gamma_t(p,q)\beta'_{t+1}(q).$$

The normalizations are

$$A_t = \frac{1}{\sum_{q=0}^{Q-1}\sum_{p=0}^{Q-1} \alpha'_t(p)\gamma_t(p,q)} \quad B_t = \frac{1}{\sum_{p=0}^{Q-1}\sum_{q=0}^{Q-1} \gamma_t(p,q)\beta'_{t+1}(q)}.$$

The relationship between the normalized and unnormalized versions is

$$\alpha'_t(p) = \left(\prod_{i=0}^{t} A_i\right)\alpha_t(p) \quad \beta'_t(p) = \left(\prod_{i=t}^{N-1} B_i\right)\beta_t(p).$$

When using α'_t and β'_t in (14.11) or (14.34) the products of the normalization factors cancel from the numerator and denominator. While the normalization does not affect the posterior probability computation mathematically, it does have a significant impact on the numerical performance of the algorithm.

14.3.7 Summary of the BCJR Algorithm

Algorithm 14.1 The BCJR (MAP) Decoding Algorithm, Probability Form

---

Initialize: Set α'_0 as in (14.16), and initialize β'_N as in (14.17) or (14.18).
For $t = 0, 1, \ldots, N-2$ propagate α':

$$\alpha'_{t+1}(q) = \mathsf{N}_q \sum_{p=0}^{Q-1} \alpha'_t(p)\gamma'_t(p,q).$$

For $t = N-1, N-2, \ldots, 1$ propagate β':

$$\beta'_t(p) = \mathsf{N}_p \sum_{q=0}^{Q-1} \gamma'_t(p,q)\beta'_{t+1}(q).$$

Compute the posterior probability for $\mathbf{x}_t$:

$$P(\mathbf{x}_t = \mathbf{x}|\mathbf{r}) = \mathsf{N}_x \sum_{(p,q)\in S_x} \alpha'_t(p)\gamma'_t(p,q)\beta'_{t+1}(q).$$

Example 14.2 Referring to Example 14.1, the sequence $\mathbf{x} = [1,1,0,0,1,0,1,0,1,1]$ is input to one of the convolutional encoders of Figure 14.4. The systematic and parity bits are multiplexed together to produce the coded sequence

$$\mathbf{v} = [1,1,\ 1,1,\ 0,1,\ 0,1,\ 1,0,\ 0,1,\ 1,1,\ 0,1,\ 1,0,\ 1,0].$$

The corresponding sequence of encoder states is

$$\mathbf{\Psi} = [0,2,3,3,3,1,2,3,3,1,0]. \tag{14.24}$$

The sequence $\mathbf{v}$ is BPSK modulated with amplitudes ± 1 and passed through an AWGN channel with $\sigma^2 = 0.45$, resulting in the received data

$$\begin{aligned}
\mathbf{r} = [&(2.53008, 0.731636)(-0.523916, 1.93052)(-0.793262, 0.307327)\ (-1.24029, 0.784426) \\
&(1.83461, -0.968171)(-0.433259, 1.26344)(1.31717, 0.995695)\ (-1.50301, 2.04413) \\
&(1.60015, -1.15293)(0.108878, -1.57889)].
\end{aligned} \tag{14.25}$$

Table 14.1: α_t' and β_t' Example Computations

Forward Pass

Direction of Processing→

q	α_0'	α_1'	α_2'	α_3'	α_4'	α_5'	α_6'	α_7'	α_8'	α_9'
0	**1**	$5.06e-7$	$9.74e-10$	$1.43e-5$	$1.36e-6$	$1.82e-4$	$5.31e-4$	$1.89e-8$	$7.21e-12$	$2.03e-7$
1	0	0	$1.92e-3$	$7.44e-3$	$1.81e-4$	**0.999**	$5.60e-8$	$3.56e-5$	$2.03e-7$	**0.999**
2	0	**0.999**	$5.05e-7$	$1.919e-3$	$7.45e-3$	$1.93e-8$	**0.999**	$5.31e-4$	$3.56e-5$	$1.03e-12$
3	0	0	**0.998**	**0.991**	**0.992**	$1.05e-4$	$1.05e-4$	**0.999**	**0.999**	$5.06e-6$

Backward Pass

Direction of Processing ←

p	β_1'	β_2'	β_3'	β_4'	β_5'	β_6'	β_7'	β_8'	β_9'	β_{10}'
0	$2.55e-3$	$2.41e-4$	$2.75e-6$	$4.15e-5$	0.127	$1.32e-3$	$1.08e-6$	$3.11e-4$	0.381	**1**
1	$2.61e-2$	$8.19e-3$	$3.23e-4$	0.127	**0.870**	$3.80e-6$	$8.14e-4$	0.381	**0.619**	0
2	$8.62e-2$	$2.85e-2$	$8.43e-3$	$2.85e-4$	$3.65e-4$	**0.996**	$1.32e-3$	$5.04e-4$	0	0
3	**0.885**	**0.963**	**0.991**	**0.872**	$2.50e-3$	$2.87e-3$	**0.998**	**0.618**	0	0

If a decision were made at this point based on the sign of the received signal, the detected bits would be

$$[1,1,\ 0,1,\ 0,1,\ 0,1,\ 1,0,\ 0,1,\ 1,1,\ 0,1,\ 1,0,\ 1,0],$$

where the underlined bit is in error.

The forward and backward passes are shown in Table 14.1. Note that the maximum probability states determined by the αs (shown in bold) correspond with the true state sequence of (14.24). The maximum likelihood sequence of states determined by the βs correspond with the true sequence of states from Ψ_{10} down to Ψ_2, but the maximum likelihood state determined by β_1 is $\hat{\Psi}_1 = 3$, whereas the true state is $\Psi_1 = 2$; the confusion arises because the $\mathbf{r}_1 = (-0.523916, 1.93052)$ decodes incorrectly, and the resulting sequence $(0,1)$ is a valid output transition on a state leading to $\Psi_2 = 3$.

As may be seen from the trellis in Figure 14.4, the input transition sets S_0 and S_1 are

$$S_0 = \{(0,0),(1,2),(2,1),(3,3)\} \quad S_1 = \{(0,2),(1,0),(2,3),(3,1)\}.$$

The input bit probabilities can be computed as follows for $t = 0$:

$$\tilde{p}(x_0 = 1|\mathbf{r}) = \alpha_0(0)\gamma_0(0,2)\beta_1(2) + \alpha_0(1)\gamma_0(1,0)\beta_1(0) + \alpha_0(2)\gamma_0(2,3)\beta_1(3)$$
$$+ \alpha_0(3)\gamma_0(3,1)\beta_1(1),$$

which results in $\tilde{p}(x_0 = 1|\mathbf{r}) = 0.00295$. Similarly, $\tilde{p}(x_0 = 0|\mathbf{r}) = 4.41 \times 10^{-11}$. After normalizing these, we find $P(x_0 = 0|\mathbf{r}) = 1.49 \times 10^{-8}$, $P(x_0 = 1|\mathbf{r}) = 0.999$. Table 14.2 shows the posterior bit probabilities (to three decimal places, so there is some roundoff in the probabilities near 1) and the posterior estimate of the bit sequence. Note that the estimated bit sequence matches the input sequence.

Table 14.2: Posterior Input Bit Example Computations

t:	0	1	2	3	4	5	6	7	8	9
$P(x_t = 0|\mathbf{r})$	$1.49e-8$	$1.64e-5$	1	1	$2.17e-6$	1	$3.31e-7$	1	$2.90e-8$	$1.25e-7$
$P(x_t = 1|\mathbf{r})$	1	1	$2.47e-6$	$2.58e-5$	1	$2.73e-5$	1	$7.55e-7$	1	1
$\hat{x}_t$	1	1	0	0	1	0	1	0	1	1

□

14.3.8   A Matrix/Vector Formulation

For notational purposes it is sometimes convenient to express the BCJR algorithm in a matrix formulation (although we do not use this further in this chapter). Let

$$
\boldsymbol{\alpha}_t = \begin{bmatrix} \alpha_t(0) \\ \alpha_t(1) \\ \vdots \\ \alpha_t(Q-1) \end{bmatrix} \quad \text{and} \quad \boldsymbol{\beta}_t = \begin{bmatrix} \beta_t(0) \\ \beta_t(1) \\ \vdots \\ \beta_t(Q-1) \end{bmatrix}
$$

be vectors of the forward and backward probabilities. Let G_t be the probability matrix with elements $g_{t,i,j}$ defined by

$$
g_{t,i,j} = \gamma_t(i,j).
$$

Then the forward update (14.13) can be expressed as

$$
\boldsymbol{\alpha}_{t+1} = G_t^T \boldsymbol{\alpha}_t.
$$

The backward update (14.15) can be expressed as

$$
\boldsymbol{\beta}_t = G_t \boldsymbol{\beta}_{t+1}.
$$

To compute (14.10), we need to define a matrix describing transitions in the trellis. Let $T(x)$ be defined with elements $t_{i,j}(x)$ by

$$
t_{i,j}(x) = \begin{cases} 1 & \text{if } (i,j) \text{ is a state transition with } x^{(i,j)} = x \\ 0 & \text{otherwise.} \end{cases}
$$

For example, for the trellis shown in Figure 14.4(b),

$$
T(0) = \begin{bmatrix} 1 & 0 & 0 & 0 \\ 0 & 0 & 1 & 0 \\ 0 & 1 & 0 & 0 \\ 0 & 0 & 0 & 1 \end{bmatrix} \quad T(1) = \begin{bmatrix} 0 & 0 & 1 & 0 \\ 1 & 0 & 0 & 0 \\ 0 & 0 & 0 & 1 \\ 0 & 1 & 0 & 0 \end{bmatrix}.
$$

Let $\odot$ denote the element-by-element product of two matrices. Then (14.10) can be expressed as

$$
P(x_t = x | \mathbf{r}) = \frac{1}{p(\mathbf{r})} \boldsymbol{\alpha}_t^T (T(x) \odot G_t) \boldsymbol{\beta}_{t+1}.
$$

14.3.9   Comparison of the Viterbi Algorithm and the BCJR Algorithm

It is interesting to contrast this update formula with the formula for updating the path metric in the Viterbi algorithm. In the Viterbi algorithm, the path metric is updated by *adding* the branch metric to the previous path metric. Then the *minimum* of the path metrics at a state is computed. In the BCJR case, the path metric $\alpha_t(p)$ is *multiplied* by the branch metric $\gamma_t(p, q)$, then the branch metrics are *summed* at each state. Mapping the operations

$$
\text{min} \leftrightarrow \text{sum} \quad \text{sum} \leftrightarrow \text{product}
$$

we obtain the equivalent algorithm. The Viterbi algorithm is sometimes referred to as a "min-sum" algorithm and the BCJR algorithm is referred to as a "sum-product" algorithm. (See [6] for other examples.)

14.3.10 The BCJR Algorithm for Systematic Codes

To finish setting the stage for turbo decoding, we now consider the specialization to the case that the convolutional encoder is a systematic $R = 1/2$ coder, and the signal mapper is BPSK, where, to be specific, we use the BPSK signal mapper in (14.4). The encoder output is now

$$\mathbf{v}_t = [v_t^{(0)}, v_t^{(1)}] = [x_t, v_t^{(1)}]$$

and the mapped signals are

$$\mathbf{a}_t = [a_t^{(0)}, a_t^{(1)}] = \sqrt{E_c}[2v_t^{(0)} - 1, 2v_t^{(1)} - 1] = \sqrt{E_c}[2x_t - 1, 2v_t^{(1)} - 1].$$

To denote the output corresponding to the transition from $\Psi_t = p$ to $\Psi_{t+1} = q$, we write

$$\mathbf{a}^{(p,q)} = [a^{(0,p,q)}, a^{(1,p,q)}] = \sqrt{E_c}[2x^{(p,q)} - 1, 2v^{(1,p,q)} - 1].$$

The received signal vector at time t is

$$\mathbf{r}_t = [r_t^{(0)}, r_t^{(1)}],$$

where

$$r_t^{(0)} = a_t^{(0)} + n_t^{(0)} \quad r_t^{(1)} = a_t^{(1)} + n_t^{(1)}.$$

The transition probability can be written

$$
\begin{aligned}
\gamma_t(p, q) &= p(\Psi_{t+1} = q, \mathbf{r}_t | \Psi_t = p) && \text{(definition)} \\
&= p(\mathbf{r}_t | \Psi_t = p, \Psi_{t+1} = q) P(\Psi_{t+1} = q | \Psi_t = p) && \text{(condition factorization)} \\
&= p(r_t^{(0)}, r_t^{(1)} | \Psi_t = p, \Psi_{t+1} = q) P(\Psi_{t+1} = q | \Psi_t = p) && \text{(definition of } \mathbf{r}_t) \\
&= p(r_t^{(0)}, r_t^{(1)} | \Psi_t = p, \Psi_{t+1} = q) P(x_t = x^{(p,q)}) && (x^{(p,q)} \text{ determines } \Psi_{t+1}).
\end{aligned}
$$
(14.26)

The conditioning on the state transition can be equivalently expressed as conditioning on the state and the input, since knowing the state and the input determines the next state unequivocally:

$$p(r_t^{(0)}, r_t^{(1)} | \Psi_t = p, \Psi_{t+1} = q) = p(r_t^{(0)}, r_t^{(1)} | \Psi_t = p, x_t = x^{(p,q)}).$$

But $r_t^{(0)}$ and $r_t^{(1)}$ are conditionally independent, given the input, since $r_t^{(0)}$ *depends on the input data and not on the state*. Thus,

$$
\begin{aligned}
p(r_t^{(0)}, r_t^{(1)} | \Psi_t = p, x_t = x^{(p,q)}) &= p(r_t^{(0)} | x_t = x^{(p,q)}) p(r_t^{(1)} | \Psi_t = p, \Psi_{t+1} = q) \\
&= p(r_t^{(0)} | a^{(0,p,q)}) p(r_t^{(1)} | a_t^{(1)} = a^{(1,p,q)}).
\end{aligned}
$$
(14.27)

Substituting (14.27) into (14.26), we obtain

$$\gamma_t(p, q) = p(r_t^{(0)} | x_t = x^{(p,q)}) p(r_t^{(1)} | a_t^{(1)} = a^{(1,p,q)}) P(x_t = x^{(p,q)}).$$
(14.28)

Now substitute (14.28) into (14.12):

$$P(x_t = x | \mathbf{r}) = \mathsf{N}_x \sum_{(p,q) \in S_x} \alpha_t(p) p(r_t^{(0)} | x_t) p(r_t^{(1)} | a_t^{(1)} = a^{(1,p,q)}) p(x_t = x^{(p,q)}) \beta_{t+1}(q).$$
(14.29)

In (14.29), since the sum is over elements in S_x, $P(x_t = x^{(p,q)})$ is constant and can be pulled out of the sum. Also, $p(r_t^{(0)} | x_t)$ does not depend on the state, and so can be pulled out of the sum. Thus,

$$
\begin{aligned}
P(x_t = x | \mathbf{r}) &= \mathsf{N}_x p(r_t^{(0)} | x_t = x) P(x_t = x) \left[\sum_{(p,q) \in S_x} \alpha_t(p) p(r_t^{(1)} | a_t^{(1)} = a^{(1,p,q)}) \beta_{t+1}(q) \right] \\
&= \mathsf{N}_x P_{s,t}(x) P_{p,t}(x) P_{e,t}(x).
\end{aligned}
$$
(14.30)

In (14.30), we refer to

$$P_{s,t}(x) = p(r_t^{(0)} | x_t = x)$$

as the *systematic probability*,

$$P_{p,t}(x) = P(x_t = x)$$

as the *prior probability*, and

$$P_{e,t}(x) = \sum_{(p,q) \in S_x} \alpha_t(p) p(r_t^{(1)} | a_t^{(1)} = a^{(1,p,q)}) \beta_{t+1}(q) \tag{14.31}$$

as the *extrinsic probability*. The word "extrinsic" means[1] "acting from the outside," or separate.
We now describe what the three different probabilities represent.

Prior The prior $P_{p,t}$ represents the information available about bits *before* any decoding occurs, arising from a source other than the received systematic or parity data. It is sometimes called *intrinsic* information, to distinguish it from the extrinsic information. In the iterative decoder, after the first iteration the "prior" is obtained from the other decoder.

Systematic The quantity $P_{s,t}^{(0)}$ represents the information about x_t explicitly available from the measurement of $r_t^{(0)}$. This is a posterior probability.

Extrinsic The extrinsic information $P_{e,t}$ is the information produced by the decoder based on the received sequence and prior information, but excluding the information from the received systematic bit $r_t^{(0)}$ and the prior information related to the bit x_t. It is thus the information that the code itself provides about the bit x_t.

From (14.13) and (14.15), we note that α_t and β_{t+1} do not depend on x_t, but only on received data at other times. Also note that $p(r_t^{(1)} | a_t^{(1)} = a^{(1,p,q)})$ does not depend on the received systematic information $r_t^{(0)}$. Thus, the extrinsic probability is, in fact, separate from the information conveyed by the systematic data about x_t. The extrinsic probability $P_{e,t}(x)$ conveys all the information about $P(x_t = x)$ that is available from the *structure of the code*, separate from information which is obtained from an observation of x_t (via $r_t^{(0)}$) or from prior information. This extrinsic probability is an important part of the turbo decoding algorithm; it is, in fact, the information passed between decoders to represent the "prior" probability.

14.3.11 Turbo Decoding Using the BCJR Algorithm

In the turbo decoding algorithm, the posterior probability computed by a previous stage is used as the prior for the next stage. Let us examine carefully which computed probability is to be used. For the moment, for simplicity of notation we ignore the permuters and the normalization.

We will show that the appropriate probability to pass between the decoders is the *extrinsic* probability by considering what would happen if the entire posterior probability $P(x_t = x | \mathbf{r})$ were used as the prior for the next decoding phase. Suppose we were to take the MAP probability estimate $P(x_t = x | \mathbf{r}) = P_{s,t}(x) P_{p,t}(x) P_{e,t}(x)$ of (14.30) computed by the first decoder and use it as the prior $P(x_t = x)$ for the second decoder. Then in the MAP decoding algorithm for the second decoder, the γ computation of (14.28) would be

$$\gamma_t(p,q) = p(r_t^{(0)} | x_t) p(r_t^{(2)} | a_t^{(2)} = a^{(2,p,q)}) P_{s,t}(x^{(p,q)}) P_{p,t}(x^{(p,q)}) P_{e,t}(x^{(p,q)}).$$

But recalling definition of $P_{s,t}$, we have

$$\gamma_t(p,q) = p(r_t^{(2)} | a_t^{(2)} = a^{(2,p,q)}) (P_{s,t}(x^{(p,q)}))^2 P_{p,t}(x^{(p,q)}) P_{e,t}(x^{(p,q)}). \tag{14.32}$$

---

[1] Webster's New World Dictionary.

We see that the initial prior information $P_{p,t}$ still appears in γ, even though we have already used whatever information it could provide. Furthermore, we see in (14.32) that the probability of the systematic information $P_{s,t}$ appears twice. If we were to continue this iteration between stages m times, $P_{s,t}$ would appear to the mth power, coming to yield an overemphasized influence. Thus, $P(x_t = x|\mathbf{r})$ is not the appropriate information to pass between the decoders.

Instead, we use the *extrinsic* probability $P_{e,t}$ as the information to pass between stages as the "prior" probability $P(x_t = x)$. Using this, γ_t is computed in the second decoder as

$$\gamma_t(p,q) = p(r_t^{(0)}|x_t)p(r_t^{(2)}|a_t^{(2)} = a^{(2,p,q)})P_{e,t}(x^{(p,q)}).$$

We now flesh out the details somewhat. Let the output of the encoder at time t be

$$\mathbf{v}_t = [x_t, v_t^{(1)}, v_t^{(2)}], \quad t = 0, 1, \ldots, N-1,$$

where $v_t^{(m)}$ is the output of encoder m, $m = 1, 2$. Also, let the received sequence be

$$\mathbf{r}_t = [r_t^{(0)}, r_t^{(1)}, r_t^{(2)}], \quad t = 0, 1, \ldots, N-1.$$

There are two MAP decoders employed in the BCJR algorithm, one for each constituent encoder. The first MAP decoder uses the input symbol sequence $\{(r_t^{(0)}, r_t^{(1)}), t = 0, 1, \ldots, N-1\}$, which we also denote (with some abuse of notation) as $(\mathbf{r}^{(0)}, \mathbf{r}^{(1)})$. The second MAP decoder uses the permuted received sequence $\{\Pi r_t^{(0)}\}$ and the received parity information from the second encoder $r_t^{(2)}$. Denote this information as $(\Pi\mathbf{r}^{(0)}, \mathbf{r}^{(2)})$. Let $P^{(0)}(x_t = x)$ denote the initial prior probabilities used by the first MAP decoder. Initially it is assumed that the symbols are equally likely. For binary signaling, $P^{(0)}(x_t = x) = 1/2$.

Let the extrinsic probability produced by decoder j, $j \in \{1, 2\}$, at the lth iteration be denoted by $P_{e,t}^{(l,j)}(x_t = x)$. Let the probability that is used as the prior probability in decoder j at the lth iteration be denoted by $P^{(l,j)}(x_t = x)$. Let M denote the number of iterations the decoder is to compute. The turbo decoding algorithm can be outlined as follows:

Algorithm 14.2 The Turbo Decoding Algorithm, Probability Form

1. Let $P^{(0,1)}(x_t = x) = P^{(0)}(x_t = x)$ (use the initial priors as the input to the first decoder).
2. For $l = 1, 2, \ldots, M$:
   (a) Using $P^{(l-1,1)}(x_t = x)$ as the prior $P(x_t = x)$, compute:
      - α and β using (14.13), (14.15), and (14.22) (or their normalized equivalents)
      - $P_{e,t}^{(l,1)}(x_t = x)$ using (14.31)
   (b) Let $P^{(l,2)}(x_t = x) = \Pi\left[P_{e,t}^{(l,1)}(x_t = x)\right]$
   (c) Using $P^{(l,2)}(x_t = x)$ as the prior $P(x_t = x)$ compute:
      - α and β using (14.13), (14.15), and (14.22) (or their normalized equivalents)
   (d) If not the last iteration:
      - Compute $P_{e,t}^{(l,2)}(x_t = x)$ using (14.31)
      - Let $P^{(l+1,1)}(x_t = x) = \Pi^{-1}\left[P_{e,t}^{(l,2)}(x_t = x)\right]$
   (e) Else if the last iteration:
      - Using $P^{(l,2)}(x_t = x)$ as the prior $P(x_t = x)$ compute (the permuted) $P(x_t = x|\mathbf{r})$ using (14.30).
      - Un-permute: $P(x_t = x|\mathbf{r}) = \Pi^{-1}\left[P(x_t = x|\mathbf{r})\right]$

In the iterative decoding algorithm, the "a priori" information used by a constituent decoder should be completely independent of the channel outputs used by that decoder. However, once the information is fed back around to the first decoder, it is reusing information obtained from the systematic bits used in the second decoder. Thus, the prior probabilities used are not truly independent of the channel outputs. However, since the convolutional codes have relatively short memories, the extrinsic probability for a bit x_t is only significantly affected by the received systematic bits close to x_t. Because of the interleaving employed, probability computations for x_t in the first decoder employ extrinsic probabilities that are, with high probability, widely separated. Thus, the dependence of the extrinsic probabilities on the systematic data for any given bit x_t is very weak.

14.3.11.1 The Terminal State of the Encoders

It is straightforward to append a tail sequence so that the terminal state of the first encoder is 0. However, due to interleaving, the state of the second encoder is not known. Discussions on how to drive the state of both encoders to zero are presented in [24, 224]. However, it has been found experimentally that ignorance of the terminal state of the second encoder leads to insignificant differences in decoder performance; it suffices to initialize β uniformly over the states in the decoder.

14.3.12 Likelihood Ratio Decoding

For encoders with a single binary input, the log-likelihood ratio is usually used in the detection problem. We denote log-likelihood ratios (or log-probability ratios of any sort) using the symbol λ. It is convenient to use the mapping from binary values $\{0, 1\}$ to signed binary values $\{1, -1\}$ defined by

$$\tilde{x}_t = 2x_t - 1.$$

For present purposes, we assume that the $\tilde{x}_t$ data are mapped to modulated signals by

$$a_t = \sqrt{E_c}\tilde{x}_t.$$

Let

$$\lambda(x_t|\mathbf{r}) = \log \frac{P(x_t = 1|\mathbf{r})}{P(x_t = 0|\mathbf{r})}, \tag{14.33}$$

where $\mathbf{r}$ is the entire observed sequence. Using (14.10), and noting that the $1/p(\mathbf{r})$ factor cancels in numerator and denominator, the likelihood ratio can be written

$$\lambda(x_t|\mathbf{r}) = \log \frac{\sum_{(p,q) \in S_1} \alpha_t(p)\gamma_t(p, q)\beta_{t+1}(q)}{\sum_{(p,q) \in S_0} \alpha_t(p)\gamma_t(p, q)\beta_{t+1}(q)}. \tag{14.34}$$

Assuming that systematic coding is employed and substituting (14.28) into (14.34), we obtain

$$\lambda(x_t|\mathbf{r}) = \log \frac{\sum_{(p,q) \in S_1} p(r_t^{(0)}|x_t)\alpha_t(p)\beta_{t+1}(q)}{\sum_{(p,q) \in S_0} p(r_t^{(0)}|x_t)\alpha_t(p)\beta_{t+1}(q)}$$

$$+ \log \frac{\sum_{(p,q) \in S_1} P(\Psi_{t+1} = q|\Psi_t = p)\alpha_t(p)\beta_{t+1}(q)}{\sum_{(p,q) \in S_0} P(\Psi_{t+1} = q|\Psi_t = p)\alpha_t(p)\beta_{t+1}(q)}$$

$$+ \log \frac{\sum_{(p,q) \in S_1} p(r_t^{(1)}|\Psi_t = p, \Psi_{t+1} = q)\alpha_t(p)\beta_{t+1}(q)}{\sum_{(p,q) \in S_0} p(r_t^{(1)}|\Psi_t = p, \Psi_{t+1} = q)\alpha_t(p)\beta_{t+1}(q)}$$

$$= \log \frac{p(r_t^{(0)}|x_t = 1)}{p(r_t^{(0)}|x_t = 0)} + \log \frac{P(x_t = 1)}{P(x_t = 0)}$$

$$+ \log \frac{\sum_{(p,q)\in S_1} p(r_t^{(1)}|\Psi_t = p, \Psi_{t+1} = q)\alpha_t(p)\beta_{t+1}(q)}{\sum_{(p,q)\in S_0} p(r_t^{(1)}|\Psi_t = p, \Psi_{t+1} = q)\alpha_t(p)\beta_{t+1}(q)}$$

$$\overset{\triangle}{=} \lambda_{s,t}^{(0)} + \lambda_{p,t} + \lambda_{e,t}. \tag{14.35}$$

The likelihood ratio is thus expressed as the *sum* of the log of the posterior probabilities for the systematic bits,

$$\lambda_{s,t}^{(0)} = \lambda(r_t^{(0)}|x_t) = \log \frac{p(r_t^{(0)}|x_t = 1)}{p(r_t^{(0)}|x_t = 0)},$$

plus the log-likelihood ratio of the prior probabilities,

$$\lambda_{p,t} = \log \frac{P(x_t = 1)}{P(x_t = 0)}$$

plus the *extrinsic information* $\lambda_{e,t}$,

$$\lambda_{e,t} = \log \frac{\sum_{(p,q)\in S_1} p(r_t^{(1)}|\Psi_t = p, \Psi_{t+1} = q)\alpha_t(p)\beta_{t+1}(q)}{\sum_{(p,q)\in S_0} p(r_t^{(1)}|\Psi_t = p, \Psi_{t+1} = q)\alpha_t(p)\beta_{t+1}(q)}$$

$$= \log \frac{\sum_{(p,q)\in S_1} p(r_t^{(1)}|a_t^{(1)} = a^{(1,p,q)})\alpha_t(p)\beta_{t+1}(q)}{\sum_{(p,q)\in S_0} p(r_t^{(1)}|a_t^{(1)} = a^{(1,p,q)})\alpha_t(p)\beta_{t+1}(q)}.$$

The extrinsic information $\lambda_{e,t}$ is the information that is passed from one decoder to the next as the turbo decoding algorithm progresses. This extrinsic information can be computed from (14.35) by

$$\lambda_{e,t} = \lambda(x_t|\mathbf{r}) - \lambda_{p,t} - \lambda_{s,t}^{(0)}. \tag{14.36}$$

Based on this, Figure 14.8 illustrates one way of implementing the turbo decoding. The conventional MAP output of the decoder (expressed in terms of log-likelihood ratio) is computed, from which the extrinsic probabilities are computed from (14.36).

We now examine some manipulations which can simplify the computation of some of these log likelihoods.

14.3.12.1 Log Prior Ratio $\lambda_{p,t}$

The log ratio of the priors

$$\lambda_{p,t} = \log \frac{P(x_t = 1)}{P(x_t = 0)}$$

can be solved for the prior probabilities. Since $P(x_t = 1) + P(x_t = 0) = 1$ and since

$$e^{\lambda_{p,t}} = \frac{P(x_t = 1)}{1 - P(x_t = 1)}$$

it is straightforward to show that

$$P(x_t = 1) = \frac{e^{\lambda_{p,t}}}{1 + e^{\lambda_{p,t}}} = \frac{1}{1 + e^{-\lambda_{p,t}}} \tag{14.37}$$

and

$$P(x_t = 0) = \frac{e^{-\lambda_{p,t}}}{1 + e^{-\lambda_{p,t}}} = \frac{1}{1 + e^{\lambda_{p,t}}}. \tag{14.38}$$

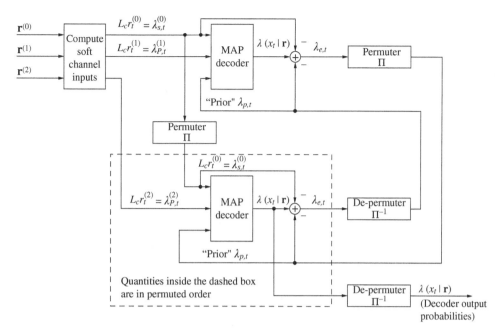

Figure 14.8: A log-likelihood turbo decoder.

For $x \in \{0, 1\}$ and $\tilde{x} = 2x - 1 \in \{-1, 1\}$, (14.37) and (14.38) can be combined together as

$$P(x_t = x) = P(\tilde{x}_t = \tilde{x})|_{\tilde{x}=2x-1} = \left[\frac{e^{-\lambda_{p,t}/2}}{1 + e^{-\lambda_{p,t}}} \right] e^{\tilde{x}\lambda_{p,t}/2}. \qquad (14.39)$$

The factor in brackets does not depend upon the value of x_t and so for many circumstances can be regarded as a constant.

14.3.12.2 Log Posterior $\lambda_{s,t}^{(0)}$

For an AWGN channel with variance σ^2 and BPSK modulation as in (14.4), $\lambda_{s,t}^{(0)}$ can be computed as

$$\lambda_{s,t}^{(0)} = \log \frac{p(r_t^{(0)}|a_t^{(0)} = \sqrt{E_c})}{p(r_t^{(0)}|a_t^{(0)} = -\sqrt{E_c})} = \log \frac{\exp \left[-\frac{1}{2\sigma^2}(r_t^{(0)} - \sqrt{E_c})^2 \right]}{\exp \left[-\frac{1}{2\sigma^2}(r_t^{(0)} + \sqrt{E_c})^2 \right]} = \frac{2\sqrt{E_c}r_t^{(0)}}{\sigma^2} = L_c r_t^{(0)}, \qquad (14.40)$$

where

$$L_c = \frac{2\sqrt{E_c}}{\sigma^2} = \frac{2\sqrt{RE_b}}{\sigma^2}$$

is the *channel reliability*, essentially just the signal-to-noise ratio. The quantity $\lambda_{s,t}^{(0)} = L_c r_t^{(0)}$ is often called the *soft channel input*. The posterior density can be expressed in terms of the channel reliability:

$$p(r_t^{(0)}|\tilde{x}_t = \tilde{x}) = C_1 \exp \left[-\frac{1}{2\sigma^2}(r_t^{(0)} - \tilde{x}\sqrt{E_c})^2 \right]$$

$$= C_2 \exp \left[-\frac{1}{2\sigma^2}r_t^{(0)2} \right] \exp \left[-\frac{1}{2\sigma^2}E_c \right] \exp \left[\frac{L_c}{2}r_t^{(0)}\tilde{x} \right] \qquad (14.41)$$

$$= C_3 \exp \left[\frac{L_c}{2}r_t^{(0)}\tilde{x} \right], \qquad (14.42)$$

where the C_i are constants which do not depend on $\tilde{x}$.

14.3.13 Statement of the Turbo Decoding Algorithm

Let us combine the equations from the last section together and express iterations of the turbo algorithm. Let $\lambda^{[l,j]}(x_t|\mathbf{r})$ denote the log-likelihood ratio computed at the lth iteration of the jth constituent encoder, $j \in \{1, 2\}$. Similarly, let $\lambda_{e,t}^{[l,j]}$ denote the extrinsic probability at the lth iteration for the jth decoder. The basic decomposition is described in (14.35). However, in light of the turbo principle, we replace the prior information $\lambda_{p,t}$ with the appropriate extrinsic information from the other decoder. Furthermore, we express the log posterior $\lambda_{s,t}^{(0)}$ in terms of the soft inputs $L_c r_t^{(0)}$.

Based on this notation, the turbo decoding algorithm (suppressing the permuter) can be expressed as

$$\lambda^{[l,1]}(x_t|\mathbf{r}) = \underbrace{L_c r_t^{(0)}}_{\substack{\text{channel input}}} + \underbrace{\lambda_{e,t}^{[l-1,2]}}_{\substack{\text{extrinsic from other} \\ \text{decoder used as prior}}} + \underbrace{\lambda_{e,t}^{[l,1]}}_{\substack{\text{new extrinsic}}}$$

$$\lambda^{[l,2]}(x_t|\mathbf{r}) = \underbrace{L_c r_t^{(0)}}_{\substack{\text{channel input}}} + \underbrace{\lambda_{e,t}^{[l,1]}}_{\substack{\text{extrinsic from other} \\ \text{decoder used as prior}}} + \underbrace{\lambda_{e,t}^{[l,2]}}_{\substack{\text{new extrinsic}}} \tag{14.43}$$

for $l = 1, 2, \ldots, M$, with $\lambda_{e,t}^{[0,2]} = 0$ to represent uniform prior probabilities.

14.3.14 Turbo Decoding Stopping Criteria

The turbo decoding algorithm is frequently run for a fixed number of iterations, which is determined by the worst-case noise degradation. Most codewords, however, are not corrupted by worst-case noise and therefore need fewer iterations to converge. A *stopping criterion* is a way of determining if the decoding algorithm has converged so that iterations can be terminated. A properly designed stopping criterion reduces the average number of iterations, while maintaining the same probability of bit error performance.

We introduce here three different stopping criteria.

14.3.14.1 The Cross Entropy Stopping Criterion

From (14.43), it follows that

$$\lambda^{[l,2]}(x_t|\mathbf{r}) - \lambda^{[l,1]}(x_t|\mathbf{r}) = \lambda_{e,t}^{[l,2]} - \lambda_{e,t}^{[l-1,2]}.$$

We define $\Delta_{e,t}^{[l]}(x_t|\mathbf{r}) = \lambda_{e,t}^{[l,2]} - \lambda_{e,t}^{[l-1,2]}$. From the likelihood $\lambda^{[l,j]}(x_t|\mathbf{r})$ of (14.43), the probability of a bit output can be computed as

$$P^{[l,j]}(\tilde{x}_t = \tilde{x}|\mathbf{r}) = \frac{e^{\tilde{x}\lambda^{[l,j]}}}{1 + e^{\tilde{x}\lambda^{[l,j]}}}. \tag{14.44}$$

Let $P^{[l,j]}(\tilde{\mathbf{x}}|\mathbf{r})$ denote the probability of the entire sequence $\tilde{\mathbf{x}}$,

$$P^{[l,j]}(\tilde{\mathbf{x}}|\mathbf{r}) = P^{[l,j]}(\tilde{x}_0, \tilde{x}_1, \ldots, \tilde{x}_{N-1}|\mathbf{r}).$$

Under the assumption that the elements in $\tilde{\mathbf{x}}$ are statistically independent, we have

$$P^{[l,j]}(\tilde{\mathbf{x}}|\mathbf{r}) = \prod_{k=0}^{N-1} P^{[l,j]}(\tilde{x}_k|\mathbf{r}).$$

We define the bit estimate at the lth iteration as $\hat{\tilde{x}}_t^{[l]} = \text{sign}(\lambda^{[l,2]}(x_t|\mathbf{r}))$.

Our first stopping criterion is based on the *cross entropy*, also known as the **relative entropy** or the **Kullback–Leibler distance** introduced in Section 1.12. The cross entropy between two probability distributions P and Q taking on values in some alphabet $\mathcal{A}$ is defined as

$$D(P||Q) = E_P\left[\log \frac{P}{Q}\right] = \sum_{x \in \mathcal{A}} P(x) \log \frac{P(x)}{Q(x)}. \qquad (14.45)$$

The cross entropy is a measure of similarity between the two distributions P and Q. From Lemma 1.18, we have that $D(P||Q) = 0$ if and only if $P = Q$, that is, if the distributions are identical.

We use the cross entropy as a measure of similarity between the distributions $P^{[l,2]}$ and $P^{[l,1]}$. Since convergence implies a fixed point of the turbo decoding iterations, at convergence we should have $P^{[l,2]} = P^{[l,1]}$. In practice, we determine convergence has occurred when the cross entropy becomes sufficiently small.

We denote the cross entropy at the lth iteration by $T(l)$:

$$T(l) = D(P^{[l,2]}||P^{[l,1]}) = E_{P^{[l,2]}(\tilde{\mathbf{x}})}\left[\log \frac{P^{[l,2]}(\tilde{\mathbf{x}})}{P^{[l,1]}(\tilde{\mathbf{x}})}\right],$$

where the expectation is with respect to the probability $P^{[l,2]}(\tilde{\mathbf{x}})$. Under the independence assumption,

$$T(l) = \sum_{k=0}^{N-1} E_{P^{[l,2]}(\tilde{x}_k)}\left[\log \frac{P^{[l,2]}(\tilde{x}_k)}{P^{[l,1]}(\tilde{x}_k)}\right]. \qquad (14.46)$$

From the definition of the expectation

$$E_{P^{[l,2]}(\tilde{x}_k)}\left[\log \frac{P^{[l,2]}(\tilde{x}_k)}{P^{[l,1]}(\tilde{x}_k)}\right] = P^{[l,2]}(\tilde{x}_k = 1) \log \frac{P^{[l,2]}(\tilde{x}_k = 1)}{P^{[l,1]}(\tilde{x}_k = 1)}$$

$$+ P^{[l,2]}(\tilde{x}_k = -1) \log \frac{P^{[l,2]}(\tilde{x}_k = -1)}{P^{[l,1]}(\tilde{x}_k = -1)}$$

and, using (14.44), it can be shown that

$$E_{P^{[l,2]}(\tilde{x}_k)}\left[\log \frac{P^{[l,2]}(\tilde{x}_k)}{P^{[l,1]}(\tilde{x}_k)}\right] = -\frac{\Delta_{e,k}^{[l]}}{1 + \exp[\lambda^{[l,2]}(x_k|\mathbf{r})]} + \log \frac{1 + \exp[-\lambda^{[l,1]}(x_k|\mathbf{r})]}{1 + \exp[-\lambda^{[l,2]}(x_k|\mathbf{r})]}. \qquad (14.47)$$

We now simplify this expectation using approximations which are accurate near convergence. We assume that the decisions do not change from among the different decoders, so

$$\text{sign}(\lambda^{[l,1]}(x_k|\mathbf{r})) = \text{sign}(\lambda^{[l,2]}(x_k|\mathbf{r})) = \hat{\tilde{x}}_k^{[l]}.$$

We invoke the approximation $\log(1 + x) \approx x$, which is true when $|x| \ll 1$. Then it can be shown (see Exercise 14.9) that

$$E_{P^{[l,2]}(\tilde{x}_k)}\left[\log \frac{P^{[l,2]}(\tilde{x}_k)}{P^{[l,1]}(\tilde{x}_k)}\right] \approx \exp(-\lambda^{[l,1]}\hat{\tilde{x}}_k^{[l]})(1 - \exp(-\hat{\tilde{x}}_k^{[l]}\Delta_{e,t}^{[l]})(1 + \hat{\tilde{x}}_k^{[l]}\Delta_{e,t}^{[l]})). \qquad (14.48)$$

Assuming further that $|\Delta_{e,t}^{[l]}| \ll 1$, we expand $\exp(-\hat{\tilde{x}}_k^{[l]}\Delta_{e,t}^{[l]})$ using the first two terms of its Taylor series expansion and write

$$E_{P^{[l,2]}(\tilde{x}_k)}\left[\log \frac{P^{[l,2]}(\tilde{x}_k)}{P^{[l,1]}(\tilde{x}_k)}\right] \approx \frac{(\hat{\tilde{x}}_k^{[l]}\Delta_{e,t}^{[l]})^2}{\exp(\lambda^{[l,1]}\hat{\tilde{x}}_k^{[l]})}.$$

Substituting this into (14.46), we obtain, using the fact that $(\hat{\tilde{x}}_k^{[l]})^2 = 1$,

$$T(l) \approx \sum_{k=0}^{N-1} \frac{(\Delta_{e,t}^{[l]})^2}{\exp(\lambda^{[l,1]}\hat{\tilde{x}}_k^{[l]})}.$$

Having found this approximate expression, we take as our stopping criterion: Stop if $T(l) <$ some threshold. Taking the threshold to be something in the range of $10^{-2}T(1)$ to $10^{-4}T(1)$ seems appropriate. For example, stopping when $T(l) < 10^{-3}T(1)$ is common.

It has been found experimentally that using this stopping criterion results in at most a few percent error degradation compared to a fixed number of iterations, with the amount of degradation being somewhat higher as the number of fixed iterations increases. At the same time, there is a significant decrease in the average number of iterations, with the amount of improvement being a function of the maximum number of iterations.

14.3.14.2   The Sign Change Ratio (SCR) Criterion

A stopping criterion which is simpler to compute than the cross entropy can be obtained as follows. Let $C(l)$ denote the number of changes of sign of $\lambda_{e,t}^{[l]}, t = 0, 1, \ldots, N-1$ compared with $\lambda_{e,t}^{[l-1]}$. Experimentally it has been found that if $C(l) < \epsilon N$, where ϵ is typically in the range of 0.005–0.03, then the stopping criterion performance is similar to that for the cross entropy criterion.

14.3.14.3   The Hard Decision Aided (HDA) Criterion

A third stopping criterion is obtained by comparing $\text{sign}(\lambda^{[l,2]}(x_t|\mathbf{r}))$ and $\text{sign}(\lambda^{[l-1,2]}(x_t|\mathbf{r}))$. When the signs are the same for all $t \in \{0, 1, \ldots, N-1\}$, then the decoding stops.

14.3.15   Modifications of the MAP Algorithm

14.3.15.1   The Max-Log-MAP Algorithm

The MAP algorithm is significantly more complex than the Viterbi algorithm, so that it is of interest to reduce the computational complexity of the MAP algorithm, if possible, even at the expense of some performance. In this section, we introduce the max-log-MAP algorithm, which propagates approximations to *logarithms* of the α and β probabilities. This not only avoids some potential roundoff properties, but also has lower complexity than the MAP algorithm. Unfortunately, the algorithm is only approximate, so that some performance is lost. A further modification which recovers the lost performance with a slight increase in computational complexity is then discussed.

Define

$$A_t(p) = \ln(\alpha_t(p)) \quad B_t(q) = \ln(\beta_t(q)) \quad \text{and} \quad \Gamma_t(p, q) = \ln(\gamma_t(p, q)).$$

Let us develop a recursion for computing $A_{t+1}(q)$. From (14.13), we have

$$A_{t+1}(q) = \ln(\alpha_{t+1}(q)) = \ln\left(\sum_{p=0}^{Q-1} \alpha_t(p)\gamma_t(p, q) \right)$$

$$= \ln\left(\sum_{p=0}^{Q-1} \exp\left[A_t(p) + \Gamma_t(p, q) \right] \right). \tag{14.49}$$

At this point, an approximation is made in the interest of developing a fast algorithm:

$$\ln\left(\sum_i e^{x_i} \right) \approx \max_i x_i. \tag{14.50}$$

Using this approximation in (14.49), we obtain

$$A_{t+1}(q) \approx \max_{p \in \{0,1,\ldots,Q-1\}} (A_t(p) + \Gamma_t(p, q)). \tag{14.51}$$

Thus, to find $A_{t+1}(q)$, we add a branch cost $\Gamma_t(p,q)$ to $A_t(p)$, then compute the maximum value of the result over all paths leading to state q. The selected path to state q can then be thought of as the survivor path. The result is exactly the same operation as the Viterbi algorithm! The computational complexity is thus essentially the same as for the Viterbi algorithm: for each pair of merging paths, two additions and one comparison are required, except that the branch cost Γ is a posterior probability for the log-MAP algorithm and is a likelihood for the Viterbi algorithm. In the max-log-MAP algorithm $A_t(p)$ provides the (approximation of the logarithm of the) most probable path through the trellis to state p, rather than the probability of *any* path through the trellis to state p.

The recursion for $B_t(q)$ is obtained as follows:

$$
\begin{aligned}
B_t(p) = \ln(\beta_t(p)) &= \ln\left(\sum_{q=0}^{Q-1} \gamma_t(p,q)\beta_{t+1}(q)\right) \\
&= \ln\left(\sum_{q=0}^{Q-1} \exp[\Gamma_t(p,q) + B_{t+1}(q)]\right) \\
&\approx \max_{q \in \{0,1,\ldots,Q-1\}}(\Gamma_t(p,q) + B_{t+1}(q)).
\end{aligned}
\tag{14.52}
$$

This amounts to a Viterbi algorithm working backward.

The branch metric $\Gamma_t(p,q)$ is computed using (14.28):

$$
\Gamma_t(p,q) = \ln(P(x_t = x^{(p,q)})) + \ln(p(r_t^{(0)}|x_t)) + \ln(p(r_t^{(1)}|a^{(1)} = a^{(1,p,q)})).
$$

Using (14.39) and (14.40) (and a similar expression for $p(r_t^{(1)}|x_t = 1)$) and throwing away unnecessary constants, we can write

$$
\Gamma_t(p,q) = \underbrace{\tilde{x}^{(p,q)}\frac{\lambda_{p,t}}{2}}_{\text{prior}} + \underbrace{\frac{L_c}{2}\tilde{x}^{(p,q)}r_t^{(0)}}_{\text{systematic}} + \underbrace{\frac{L_c}{2}\tilde{v}^{(1,p,q)}r_t^{(1)}}_{\text{parity}}.
\tag{14.53}
$$

The log posterior $\lambda(x_t|\mathbf{r})$ is, using (14.34),

$$
\begin{aligned}
\lambda(x_t|\mathbf{r}) &= \log\frac{\sum_{(p,q)\in S_1}\alpha_t(p)\gamma_t(p,q)\beta_{t+1}(q)}{\sum_{(p,q)\in S_0}\alpha_t(p)\gamma_t(p,q)\beta_{t+1}(q)} \\
&= \log\frac{\sum_{(p,q)\in S_1}\exp[A_t(p) + \Gamma_t(p,q) + B_{t+1}(q)]}{\sum_{(p,q)\in S_0}\exp[A_t(p) + \Gamma_t(p,q) + B_{t+1}(q)]} \\
&\approx \max_{(p,q)\in S_1}(A_t(p) + \Gamma_t(p,q) + B_{t+1}(q)) - \max_{(p,q)\in S_0}(A_t(p) + \Gamma_t(p,q) + B_{t+1}(q)).
\end{aligned}
\tag{14.54}
$$

This may be interpreted as follows [187, p. 132]: For each bit x_t, all the transitions from Ψ_t to Ψ_{t+1} are considered, grouped into those which might occur if $x_t = 1$ and those which might occur if $x_t = 0$. For each of these groups the transition which maximizes $A_t(p) + \Gamma_t(p,q) + B_{t+1}(q)$ is found, then the posterior log likelihood is computed based on these two optimal transitions.

If only the $A_t(p)$ values were needed, the max-log-MAP algorithm would have complexity essentially the same as the Viterbi algorithm; however, $B_t(p)$ must also be computed. It has been argued [469] that the complexity of the max-log-MAP algorithm is not more than three times that of the Viterbi algorithm. However, the storage requirements are higher, since the values of $A_t(p)$ and $B_t(p)$ must be stored. The storage can be reduced, however, at the expense of an increase in computational complexity [469, 470].

14.3.16 Corrections to the Max-Log-MAP Algorithm

The approximation (14.50) has been shown [380] to result in approximately 0.35 dB of degradation compared to exact decoding. Another algorithm is obtained by using the "Jacobian logarithm":

$$\ln(e^{x_1} + e^{x_2}) = \max(x_1, x_2) + \ln(1 + e^{-|x_1 - x_2|}). \tag{14.55}$$

Let us write this as

$$\ln(e^{x_1} + e^{x_2}) = \max(x_1, x_2) + f_c(\delta) = g(x_1, x_2),$$

where $\delta = |x_1 - x_2|$ and where $f_c(\delta)$ is the "correction" term. Since the $f_c(\delta)$ function depends upon only a single variable, it is straightforward to precompute it and determine its values in use by table lookup. It has been found [380] that sufficient accuracy can be obtained when only eight values of $f_c(\delta)$ are stored for values of δ between 0 and 5.

In order to handle multiple-term summations, the functions are composed as follows:

$$\ln\left(\sum_{i=1}^{I} e_{x_i}\right) = g(x_I, g(x_{I-1}, g(x_{I-2}, \ldots, g(x_3, g(x_2, x_1)) \cdots))).$$

If a lookup table for f_c is used, the computational complexity is only slightly higher than the max-log-MAP algorithm, but the decoding is essentially *exact*.

14.3.17 The Soft-Output Viterbi Algorithm

An alternative to the BCJR algorithm for turbo decoding is the SOVA. This is discussed in Section 12.11. A potential computational advantage of SOVA over BCJR is that BCJR has both forward and backward passes, while SOVA only has a forward pass, but then it propagates reliability information along surviving paths.

14.4 On the Error Floor and Weight Distributions

In this section, we discuss briefly two questions relating to the performance of turbo codes. These questions are: Why is there an error floor? and What makes turbo codes so effective? Other discussions along these lines appear in [397].

14.4.1 The Error Floor

As observed from the plot in Figure 14.1, there is an error floor associated with turbo codes, so that for moderate-to-high SNRs, the probability of error performance fails to drop off as rapidly as it does for low SNRs. This can be explained as follows. The probability of bit error for a turbo code can be approximated just as for convolutional codes. Thinking of the set of codes as block $(N/R, N)$ codes, there are 2^N codewords. Then the probability of bit error can be bounded as [397, p. 243]

$$P_b \leq \sum_{i=1}^{2^N - 1} \frac{w_i}{N} Q\left(\sqrt{\frac{2d_i R E_b}{N_0}}\right),$$

where w_i is the weight of the message sequence of the i th message and d_i is the Hamming weight of the codeword. Grouping together codewords of the same Hamming weight, the bound on the probability of bit error can be written as

$$P_b \leq \sum_{d=d_{\text{free}}}^{N/R} \frac{W_d}{N} Q\left(\sqrt{\frac{2dRE_b}{N_0}}\right) = \sum_{d=d_{\text{free}}}^{N/R} \frac{N_d \tilde{w}_d}{N} Q\left(\sqrt{\frac{2dRE_b}{N_0}}\right), \tag{14.56}$$

where N_d is the multiplicity of codewords of weight d, and

$$\tilde{w}_d = \frac{W_d}{N_d},$$

where W_d is the total weight of all message sequences whose codewords have weight d. Thus, $\tilde{w}_d$ is the average weight of the message sequences whose codewords have weight d. The quantity d_{free} is the free distance of the code, the minimum Hamming distance between codewords. The upper limit N/R of the summation comes from neglecting the length of the zero-forcing tail, if any.

As the SNR increases, the first term of the sum in (14.56) dominates. The asymptotic performance of the code is thus

$$P_b \approx \frac{N_{\text{free}} \tilde{w}_{\text{free}}}{N} Q\left(\sqrt{\frac{d_{\text{free}} 2RE_b}{N_0}} \right),$$

where N_{free} is the number of sequences at a distance d_{free} from each other and $\tilde{w}_{\text{free}}$ is the average weight of the message sequence causing the free-distance codewords. When plotted on a log–log scale (e.g., logarithmic probability with E_b/N_0 in dB), the slope of P_b is determined by d_{free}. If there is a small d_{free}, then the slope is small.

The error floor, which appears at higher SNRs, is thus ostensibly due to the presence of a small d_{free}, that is, due to low-weight codewords.

Why should there be low-weight codewords in a turbo code? We note first that the presence of a single 1 in the input sequence $\mathbf{x}$ can lead to many nonzero values in its parity sequence. If $x_t = 1$ for some t and $\mathbf{x}$ is zero at all other positions, then the encoder leaves the zero state when x_t arrives. Since the encoder is recursive, the remaining sequence of input zeros does not drive the encoder to the 0 state, so a sequence of 0s and 1s continues to be produced by the encoder. For example, for the encoder whose trellis is shown in Figure 14.4(b), a 1 followed by a string of 0s produces the parity sequence $\{1, 0, 1, 0, 1, 0, \dots\}$. This alternating sequence output is typical of many recursive encoders. Having a high-weight code sequence for a low-weight input is one reason why recursive encoders are used in turbo encoders. If $x_t = 1$ happens to occur near the end of the input sequence, then the parity sequence $\mathbf{v}^{(1)}$ has low weight. But the permuter may produce a sequence $\mathbf{x}'$ whose nonzero value occurs earlier, resulting in a parity sequence $\mathbf{v}^{(2)}$ of higher weight. From one point of view, this is one of the sources of strength of turbo encoders: if one of the parity sequences has low weight, then there is a reasonable probability that the other parity sequence has higher weight. There are thus codewords with high weight.

Consider now a low-weight input sequence $\mathbf{x}$ that results in a Low-weight parity sequence in $\mathbf{v}^{(1)}$. For example, a sequence of all zeros, followed by a single 1, so that $x_{N-1} = 1$. This would result in a parity sequence with $\text{wt}(\mathbf{v}^{(1)}) = 1$. More generally, there might be a single 1 appearing somewhere near the end of $\mathbf{x}$. This would result in a low-weight $\mathbf{v}^{(1)}$. When $\mathbf{x}$ is permuted, the resulting sequence may have the 1 appearing early in the sequence, causing the second encoder to leave the 0 state early on, after which, as mentioned, a parity sequence $\mathbf{v}^{(2)}$ of appreciable weight might be produced.

But circumstances may make it so that the second parity sequence also results in a low-weight codeword. In the first case, suppose that the parity sequence $\mathbf{v}^{(2)}$ is in fact a $\{1, 0\}$ alternating sequence, and that the parity sequences are now punctured with a puncturing phase that punctures all the 1s. All the weight from $\mathbf{v}^{(2)}$ is removed, so the weight of the codeword depends only upon the weight of $\mathbf{x}$ and $\mathbf{v}^{(1)}$, which may be very low.

A low-weight codeword could also be obtained another way. If the permuter is such that the single 1 appearing near the end of $\mathbf{x}$ also happens to appear near the end of $\mathbf{x}'$, then regardless of the puncturing, both $\mathbf{v}^{(1)}$ and $\mathbf{v}^{(2)}$ are low weight.

Thus, it may occur that a sequence $\mathbf{x}$ which produces a low-weight $\mathbf{v}^{(1)}$ can, after interleaving, produce a sequence $\mathbf{x}'$ which would also produce a low-weight $\mathbf{v}^{(2)}$. At this point in the state of the art, methods of designing encoders and/or permuter which completely avoid the low-weight codeword problem are unknown.

14.4.2 Spectral Thinning and Random Permuters

The difficulties of low-weight codewords notwithstanding, turbo codes are outstanding performers. This is because, while there are low weight codewords, there are not many of them! As mentioned, the permuter helps ensure that if one parity sequence has low weight, the other has higher weight with high probability.

The *distance spectrum* of a code is a listing of the (N_d, W_d) information as a function of the codeword weight d, where N_d, again, is multiplicity of codewords at weight d, and W_d is the total weight of the message sequences producing codewords of weight d. Turbo codes are said to have a *sparse* distance spectrum if the multiplicities of the lower-weight codewords is relatively small. Since each term in the probability bound in (14.56) is scaled by the multiplicity N_d, higher multiplicities result in more contribution to the probability of error, so that a higher SNR must be achieved before the probability of error term becomes negligible.

For example, for the $(37, 21, 65536)$ code, the distance spectrum computed using weight-2 message sequences, when the set of turbo codes is averaged over all possible permuters, is [397]

d	N_d	W_d
6	4.5	9
8	11	22
10	20.5	41
12	75	150

(This data was found using the algorithm described in [401].) Note that N_d increases relatively slowly with d. Convolutional codes, on the other hand, frequently are *spectrally dense*, meaning that N_d increases much more rapidly with d.

We now argue that the sparse distance spectrum is typical for long permuters. The argument is based on enumerating aspects of the weight behavior of the codes, averaged over the set of all possible random permuters. This argument is referred to as *random interleaving* [30, 397]. The sparse distance spectrum for turbo codes, compared to the distance spectrum of convolutional codes, is referred to as *spectral thinning*.

To characterize the weight spectrum, define the input redundancy weight enumerating function (IRWEF) $A(W, Z)$ [32]. The IRWEF $A(W, Z)$ is defined as

$$A(W, Z) = \sum_w \sum_z A_{w,z} W^w Z^z,$$

where $A_{w,z}$ is the number of codewords produced by message sequences $\mathbf{x}$ of weight w and parity sequences $\mathbf{v}^{(1)}$ and $\mathbf{v}^{(2)}$ of combined weight z. The quantities W and Z are formal variables used in the series expansion. Our interest here is not in the entire IRWEF $A(W, Z)$, but in the relationship between the low-weight codewords of the turbo code and $A_{w,z}$. This requires enumerating possible state sequences in the constituent encoders.

In the first encoder, a message sequence $\mathbf{x}$ of weight w gives rise to a sequence of states $\mathbf{\Psi}^{(1)}$. We say that a *detour* occurs in the state sequence if a contiguous sequence of states deviates from the zero state then returns to the zero state. Let n_1 denote the number of detours in $\mathbf{\Psi}^{(1)}$ and let l_1 denote the total length of the detours. Let $d_1 = w + z_1$ denote the weight of the message and first parity word. Similarly, the permuted sequence $\mathbf{x}'$ gives rise to a state sequence $\mathbf{\Psi}^{(2)}$ in the second encoder; we denote the number of detours and the total length of the detours in $\mathbf{\Psi}^{(2)}$ by n_2 and l_2, respectively. Let $d_2 = w + z_2$ denote the weight of the message and second parity word.

Example 14.3 Let $\mathbf{x} = [0, 1, 0, 0, 0, 1, 0, 0, 0, 0, 1, 0, 1]$ and the permuted bits $\mathbf{x}' = [1, 0, 0, 0, 1, 1, 0, 0, 0, 0, 1, 0, 0]$ be applied to the encoder of Example 14.1[2] . The parity sequences are

$$\mathbf{v}^{(1)} = [0, 1, 0, 1, 0, 0, 0, 0, 0, 0, 1, 0, 0] \quad \mathbf{v}^{(2)} = [1, 0, 1, 0, 0, 1, 0, 1, 0, 1, 1, 1, 1].$$

---

[2] The permuter is different from that example, since the length of the code is different.

Then $d_1 = 7$ and $d_2 = 12$. The combined weight of the parity bits is $z = 11$. The presence of this codeword contributes one codeword "count" to the coefficient $A_{4,11}$.

Figure 14.9 shows the state sequences for this codeword. The state sequence $\Psi^{(1)}$ has $n_1 = 2$ detours whose total length is $l_1 = 8$; the state sequence $\Psi^{(2)}$ has $n_2 = 2$ detours whose total length is $l_2 = 13$.

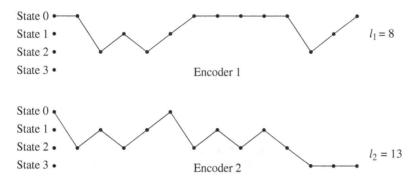

Figure 14.9: State sequences for an encoding example.

□

Suppose the permuter of length N is chosen at random, so there are $N!$ possible permuters. If we assume that a permuter is chosen according to a uniform distribution, then the probability of choosing any particular permuter is $1/N!$. Suppose the message sequence $\mathbf{x}$ has weight w. Then the permuted sequence $\mathbf{x}'$ also has weight w. Since all 1 bits of $\mathbf{x}$ are indistinguishable from each other, and similarly all 0 bits, there are $w!(N - w)!$ permuters out of the $N!$ that could all produce the same permuted sequence $\mathbf{x}'$. The probability that the mapping from $\mathbf{x}$ to $\mathbf{x}'$ occurs (where both have the same weight) is

$$\frac{w!(N - w)!}{N!} = \frac{1}{\binom{N}{w}}.$$

This is also the probability of occurrence of the codeword that results from the input sequences $\mathbf{x}$ and $\mathbf{x}'$.

Consider a sequence $\mathbf{x}$ of weight w, with corresponding encoder state sequences $\Psi^{(1)}$ and $\Psi^{(2)}$ and having parity weights z_1 and z_2. Since the particular codeword occurs with probability $1/\binom{N}{w}$, the contribution to A_{w,z_1+z_2}, averaged over all random permuters, is

$$\frac{1}{\binom{N}{w}}.$$

The sequence of zeros connecting any two distinct state sequence detours has no effect on either the weight of the message sequence or its parity sequence. The detours can be moved around within the state sequence, without changing their order, without changing their contribution to A_{w,z_1+z_2}. Enumerating all the possible ways that the detours can be moved around, there are

$$\binom{N - l_1 + n_1}{n_1}$$

distinct ways that the n_1 detours can be arranged, without changing their order. Each of these, therefore, results in a contribution to A_{w,z_1+z_2}.

Example 14.4 Figure 14.10 shows the different ways that $n_1 = 3$ detours (each of length 2, so that $l_1 = 6$) can be arranged, in order, in a sequence of length $N = 7$. There are

$$\binom{7 - 6 + 3}{3} = 4$$

different arrangements.

□

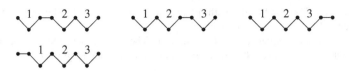

Figure 14.10: Arrangements of $n_1 = 3$ detours in a sequence of length $N = 7$.

This applies to the first constituent encoder. For the second constituent encoder, the number of possible arrangements depends on whether the encoder ends in the 0 state. If the second encoder ends in the 0 state, then there are

$$\binom{N - l_2 + n_2}{n_2}$$

ways that the detours in $\mathbf{\Psi}^{(2)}$ can be arranged in order, each of which contributes to the same $A_{w, z_1 + z_2}$. If the second encoder does not return to the 0 state, then the last of the n_2 "detours" is not a true detour. There are thus

$$\binom{N - l_2 + (n_2 - 1)}{n_2 - 1}$$

ways the detours can be arranged, each of which contributes a codeword count to $A_{w, z_1 + z_2}$.

The overall *average* contribution to $A_{w, z_1 + z_2}$ for a particular pattern of detours in $\mathbf{\Psi}^{(1)}$ and $\mathbf{\Psi}^{(2)}$ is

$$\frac{\binom{N - l_1 + n_1}{n_1} \binom{N - l_2 + n_2}{n_2}}{\binom{N}{w}} \tag{14.57}$$

if the last "detour" of the second encoder ends in the 0 state, or

$$\frac{\binom{N - l_1 + n_1}{n_1} \binom{N - l_2 + n_2 - 1}{n_2 - 1}}{\binom{N}{w}} \tag{14.58}$$

if the second encoder does not end in the 0 state.

Since our intent here is to explore codewords of low weight, we now assume that $n_1 \ll N$, $l_1 \ll N$, $n_2 \ll N$, $l_2 \ll N$, and $w \ll N$. (Because otherwise there would be either a large number of short detours or a few very long detours, either of which would be unlikely to result in codewords of low weight.) Under this assumption, the contribution to $A_{w, z_1 + z_2}$ of (14.57) can be approximated as

$$\frac{w!}{n_1! n_2!} N^{n_1 + n_2 - w} \tag{14.59}$$

and (14.58) can be approximated as

$$\frac{w!}{n_1! (n_2 - 1)!} N^{n_1 + n_2 - w - 1}. \tag{14.60}$$

Each detour in the state sequence must be caused by a message sequence whose weight is at least 2 (i.e., one message bit to deviate from the 0 state, and one message bit to return back to the 0 state), so $w \geq 2\max(n_1, n_2)$. In (14.59), as the block length (and permuter length) approaches ∞, the exponent $N^{n_1 + n_2 - w} \to 0$ unless $w = n_1 + n_2$ and $n_1 = n_2$. In (14.60), $N^{n_1 + n_2 - w - 1} \to 0$ as $N \to \infty$ for any values of n_1 and n_2. Thus, the following conditions must be met by the codeword in order for the codeword to contribute to $A_{w, z_1 + z_2}$:

1. The second encoder must terminate in the all-zero state.

2. Both encoders must make the same number of detours.

3. Each state detour is caused by a message sequence of weight 2.

If these conditions are not all met, then asymptotically $A_{w,z}$ receives no contribution from the codeword.

The result of this is that, for large enough N, $A_{w,z}$ for low-weight codewords is rather small: the conditions simply are not met very often. Thus, the distance spectrum for the code is "thinned."

One result of the thinned spectrum is that there are relatively few codewords of low weight, hence relatively few codewords near to other codewords. Thus, codewords selected at random will, with high probability, be decoded correctly. However, when errors occur, they tend to occur in clusters, since a decoding failure can cause several stages of the trellis to be corrupted in the BCJR algorithm. This observation is borne out in simulation: when the decoder is run for many iterations at low probability of error, most blocks are completely error free and errors, when they occur, tend to appear multiple times in the block.

14.4.3 On Permuters

The permuter is a key component of the turbo encoder, since it allows the extrinsic information passed into a decoder to be nearly independent of the observed data in the decoder. As we now argue, a rectangular permuter, which is probably the easiest from an implementation point of view, leads to degraded coder performance compared to a (pseudo-) random permuter, because it can lead to a large value of N_{free}. Thus, it is important to use an permuter which is closer to a true random permuter.

We observe that the permuted message sequence $\mathbf{x}' = \Pi\mathbf{x}$ has the same weight as the original message sequence $\mathbf{x}$. In the general case, the parity sequences $\mathbf{v}^{(1)}$ and $\mathbf{v}^{(2)}$ are different, however, because the inputs to the constituent convolutional encoders are different. Thus, if $\mathbf{v}^{(1)}$ is a low-weight parity sequence, it may be hoped that $\mathbf{v}^{(2)}$ has higher weight. However, if the permuted sequence $\mathbf{x}'$ not only has the same weight as $\mathbf{x}$, but is in fact equal to $\mathbf{x}$, and if $\mathbf{v}^{(1)}$ is low weight, then $\mathbf{v}^{(2)}$ has the same low weight, resulting in an overall low-weight codeword. Furthermore, as we show, a rectangular permuter provides the possibility for many such low-weight codewords, resulting in a large N_{free}.

We give a specific example based on a code using the transfer function in (14.1) in a rate $R = 1/2$ code. Suppose that a rectangular (or square) permuter is used in the turbo encoder, so that the message data $\mathbf{x}$ is written row by row, and read out column by column. Suppose, to be specific, that a 120×120 permuter is used, resulting in a block code of length $N = 120^2 = 14400$ [397]. As will be shown, $N_{\text{free}} = 28900$ for this code. When compared with the results for the $N = 65536$ code using a (pseudo-) random permuter, the performance is about $2\,\text{dB}$ worse at a probability of bit error of 10^{-5}. Some of the difference can be attributed to the shorter codeword length, but more significant is the fact that N_{free} is so large.

Consider a message sequence

$$\mathbf{x} = [\dots, 1, 0, 0, 0, 0, 1, 0, 0, \dots, 0, 1, 0, 0, 0, 0, 1, 0, \dots],$$

where there are zeros such that the four ones form a 6×6 square in the permuter, as shown in Figure 14.11. Thus, the permuted sequence $\mathbf{x}' = \Pi\mathbf{x}$ is equal to $\mathbf{x}$. The encoded parity sequence $\mathbf{v}^{(1)}$ has weight 4 after puncturing. Since $\mathbf{x}'$ is equal to $\mathbf{x}$, the parity sequence $\mathbf{v}^{(2)}$ also has weight 4. The entire codeword has weight $4 + 4 + 4 = 12$. There are $(120 - 5) \times (120 - 5) = 13325$ different positions where the square pattern can be placed in the permuter. There are also rectangular message patterns of size 11×6, 6×11, and 11×11 which also encode to sequences of weight 12. For the 6×11 and 11×6 patterns, the weight depends on the "phase" of the puncturing, depending on which parity sequence is punctured first, so only half of the positions result in the codeword of weight 12. There are thus

$$2 \times \frac{1}{2}(120 - 10) \times (120 - 5) = 12650$$

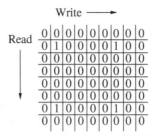

Figure 14.11: A 6×6 "square" sequence written into the 120×120 permuter.

different input sequences producing a weight-12 codeword. For the 11×11 pattern, the weight of both sequences is affected by which is punctured first. As a result, only one-fourth of the possible input patterns result in a weight-12 codeword, so there are $\frac{1}{4}(120 - 10) \times (120 - 10) = 3025$ different codewords producing this pattern. Adding this up, we see that there are 28900 weight-12 codewords.

It is clear that, for this example, increasing the size of the permuter only results in more minimum codeword patterns, resulting in a larger N_{free}. In fact, N_{free} grows roughly linearly with N, so the effective multiplicity N_{free}/N does not change significantly for larger rectangular permuters.

While this example was described for a particular code, the principles apply fairly generally. Attempts to design some kind of structured permuter to reduce the implementation complexity frequently destroys the very randomness needed to obtain good performance at low SNRs.

14.5 EXIT Chart Analysis

In this section, we introduce the extrinsic information transfer (EXIT) chart, a powerful method for analyzing iteratively decoded codes. While we present it here in the context of turbo codes, it can also be used for LDPC code analysis (see Section 15.8). The EXIT chart provides a means of characterizing a code which is both faster and more insightful than simulating the code. It reveals that there is a decoding threshold, an SNR below which correct decoding cannot be expected. EXIT analysis can also be used to search for good codes, or codes whose decoding converges quickly. It can also be used to approximate the probability of error in some regions of the curve.

The EXIT chart is expressed in terms of a likelihood ratio decoder. For our purposes, it will be convenient to use the labeling shown in Figure 14.12. The *a priori* information is labeled as A_i, $i = 1$ or 2, depending on which decoder is used. The extrinsic information is E_i, the decoder output information is D_i, and the soft input information is Z_i, with $D_i = Z_i + A_i + E_i$. We will also denote the transmitted information — the $\tilde{x}$ bits — as X. The key concept of the EXIT chart is measuring the amount of information that the prior A conveys about the transmitted data X and that the extrinsic information E conveys about the data information X. This information is measured using the *mutual information* in the form of $I(X; A_i)$ and $I(X; E_i)$. (Mutual information was introduced in Section 1.12.) To quantify these, it is necessary to model the distributions of the A_i and E_i data.

The soft output Z_i from the channel is obtained from the log-likelihood ratio

$$Z_i = \log \frac{p(r_t | \tilde{x}_t = 1)}{p(r_t | \tilde{x}_t = -1)}$$

(where r_t generically represents either systematic or parity information). Following (14.40), we have

$$Z = L_c r_t = L_c(\sqrt{E_c}\tilde{x}_t + n),$$

where $n \sim \mathcal{N}(0, \sigma^2)$, with $\sigma^2 = N_0/2$ and $L_c = 2\sqrt{E_c}/\sigma^2$. We can write

$$Z = \mu_Z \tilde{x}_t + n_Z,$$

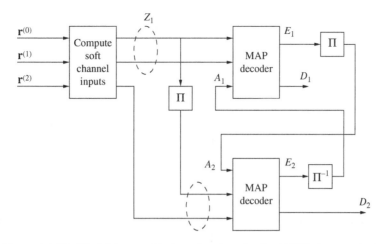

Figure 14.12: Variables used in iterative decoder for EXIT chart analysis.

where $\mu_Z = 2E_c/\sigma^2$ and $n_Z \sim \mathcal{N}(0, \sigma_Z^2)$, where

$$\sigma_Z^2 = 4E_c/\sigma^2 = 2\mu_Z.$$

That is, we have $\sigma_Z^2 = 2\mu_Z$. A Gaussian distribution having the variance twice the mean is said to be *consistent*.

We make the following assumptions for the analysis:

1. For sufficiently large permuters, the *a priori* values A_i are fairly uncorrelated from their respective channel observations Z_i over many iterations.

2. The probability density functions of the extrinsic information E_i — which are the prior inputs for the next decoder — approach Gaussian distributions with increasing iterations.

Mutual Information Between X and A Under these assumptions, we model the *a priori* probability input A_i to an encoder as

$$A_i = \mu_A \tilde{x}_t + n_A, \tag{14.61}$$

where n_A is an independent Gaussian random variable with variance σ_A^2 and zero mean. We assume that A_i is also consistent, so $\sigma_A^2 = 2\mu_A$. Then the conditional pdf of A can be written as

$$p_{A|X}(y|\tilde{x}) = \frac{1}{\sqrt{2\pi}\sigma_A} \exp\left[-\frac{1}{2\sigma_A^2}(y - (\sigma_A^2/2)\tilde{x})^2\right]. \tag{14.62}$$

Using the Kullback–Leibler distance introduced in (14.45), the mutual information $I(X;A)$ can be computed as (see Section 1.12)

$$I(X;A) = D(p_{XA}\|p_X p_A) = \int p_{XA}(\tilde{x}, y)\log_2 \frac{p_{XA}(\tilde{x}, y)}{p_X(\tilde{x})p_A(y)}d\tilde{x}dy,$$

where p_{XA} is the joint probability distribution of $\tilde{x}$ and A, and p_X and p_A are the marginal distributions. We assume that the $\tilde{x}$ occurs with equal probability for $\tilde{x} \in \{\pm 1\}$ and that, as mentioned, A is conditionally Gaussian. Then

$$I(X;A) = \int p_{A|X}(y|\tilde{x})p_X(\tilde{x})\log_2 \frac{p_{A|X}(y|\tilde{x})p_X(\tilde{x})}{p_X(\tilde{x})p_A(y)}d\tilde{x}dy$$

$$= \frac{1}{2} \int_{-\infty}^{\infty} \sum_{\tilde{x} \in \{\pm 1\}} p_{A|X}(y|\tilde{x}) \log_2 \frac{2p_A(y|\tilde{x})}{p_{A|X}(y|1) + p_{A|X}(y|-1)} \, dy \qquad (14.63)$$

$$= 1 - \int_{-\infty}^{\infty} \frac{e^{-\frac{1}{2\sigma_A^2}(y - \sigma_A^2/2)^2}}{\sqrt{2\pi}\sigma_A} \log_2(1 + e^{-y}) \, dy. \qquad (14.64)$$

We will denote this as $I_A(\sigma_A) \triangleq I(X;A)$. Since this is information regarding a binary-valued random variable, we have the limits $0 \le I(X;A) \le 1$. We will furthermore define the function $J(\sigma) = I_A(\sigma_A)|_{\sigma_A = \sigma}$. Since this is mutual information, it can be shown that $J(\sigma)$ is a monotonic function of σ, so that there is an inverse:

$$\sigma_A = J^{-1}(I_A). \qquad (14.65)$$

Mutual Information Between X and E We can similarly write the mutual information between X and E. Following (14.63), we have

$$I_E = I(X;E) = \frac{1}{2} \int_{-\infty}^{\infty} \sum_{\tilde{x} \in \{\pm 1\}} p_{E|X}(y|\tilde{x}) \log_2 \frac{2p_{E|X}(y|\tilde{x})}{p_{E|X}(y|1) + p_{E|X}(y|-1)} \, dy, \quad 0 \le I_E \le 1. \qquad (14.66)$$

In this case, we do not consider E to be a Gaussian random variable. Instead, to compute I_E, a simulated channel is used to produce data which are passed through a stage of the decoder. Then, the extrinsic output of the decoder is used to estimate $p_E(y|\tilde{x})$ by creating a histogram of the extrinsic outputs. This estimated density is numerically integrated to produce I_E in (14.66). In this simulation, the parameter σ_A corresponding to some value of I_A via (14.65) is selected, and a Gaussian input vector A is generated according to (14.61), which is then passed through the BCJR algorithm at some SNR E_b/N_0. There is thus some functional relationship between I_A, E_b/N_0, and I_E, denoted abstractly as

$$I_E = T(I_A, E_b/N_0)$$

or, for a fixed E_b/N_0, simply as

$$I_E = T(I_A).$$

This function T denotes the "transfer" of information from the prior information A at the input of a decoder to the extrinsic information E at the output of the decoder, which, in the turbo decoding scheme, is then used as the prior input at the next decoder.

Figure 14.13 illustrates the qualitative shape of the function $T(I_A)$ for various values of SNR. As the SNR increases, the I_E available at the output of the decoder increases.

14.5.1 The EXIT Chart

The plot in Figure 14.13 shows the mutual information I_E at the output of a single decoder as a function of the mutual information I_A at the input of the decoder. Let us now consider how this curve affects an iterative decoder. The extrinsic information E_1 at the output of the first decoder is permuted and used as the prior information A_2 at the next decoder. Let $I_{A_1}^{[n]}$ denote the mutual information $I(X;A_1)$ at the nth iteration of first the decoder, starting with zero *a priori* knowledge $I_{A_1}^{[0]} = 0$. Similarly let $I_{E_1}^{[n]} = I(X;E_1)$ denote the mutual information $I(X;E_1)$ at the output of the first decoder at the nth iteration, $I_{E_1}^{[n]} = T_1(I_{A_1}^{[n]})$. This is forwarded to the next decoder to become $I_{A_2}^{[n]} = I_{E_1}^{[n]}$. This passes through the second decoder to become $I_{E_2}^{[n]} = T_2(I_{A_2}^{[n]})$, which in turn is passed back to the first decoder as the prior, $I_{A_1}^{[n+1]} = I_{E_2}^{[n]}$. (Note that interleaving or de-interleaving does not change the mutual information.)

To portray this iteration graphically, the mutual information function $I_{E_1} = T(I_{A_1})$ is reflected across the line $y = x$ and plotted, so that the abscissa and ordinate of the plot are interchanged. Then

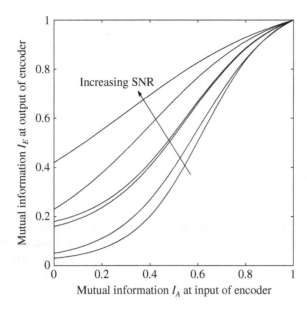

Figure 14.13: Qualitative form of the transfer characteristic $I_E = T(I_A)$.

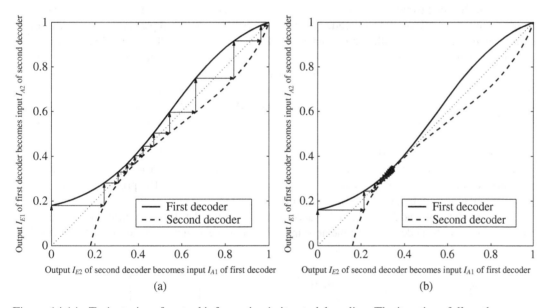

Figure 14.14: Trajectories of mutual information in iterated decoding. The iterations follow the arrows. (a) Decoding above threshold; (b) decoding below threshold. The decoder cannot get past the pinchoff point.

starting at $I_{A_1}^{[0]} = 0$, each ordinate becomes an abscissa for the next iteration. Figure 14.14(a) shows the information decoding in a sequence of decoding steps, following the arrows. Ultimately (in this case), a point is reached where $I_A = 1$. If the prior information about a bit is sufficiently close to 1, then we conclude that the prior information is sufficient to accurately decode the bit. Thus, in this case, the decoder iterates until a correct decoding occurs. There is a "channel" or gap between the two curves in Figure 14.14(a). The decoding proceeds by walking through this channel.

Figure 14.14(b) shows how the iterative decoding process can break down. In this case, $T(I_A)$ is plotted for a lower SNR, producing a function $T(I_A)$ which crosses the $y = x$ line. As a result, the iterations get stuck at the crossover point. The decoder is unable to "exit" the channel in the EXIT chart.

Clearly, there is a threshold phenomenon taking place: for a sufficiently large SNR, after a sufficiently large number of iterations the decoder is able to decode correctly. For a sufficiently small SNR, the "channel" in the graph shuts down. The decoder never reaches the point that there is sufficient information about X in the extrinsic information to be able to correctly decode, no matter how many times the decoder iterates.

Clearly, the farther the EXIT chart is from the line $y = x$, the faster the I_A will converge to 1. When the EXIT chart remains above the line $y = x$, convergence occurs. However, if it remains too near the $y = x$ line, then convergence is slowed. Such a line, having a derivative with value nearly equal to 1, is said to be "flat."

The EXIT chart reveals something fundamental about the iterative decoding process. As the SNR approaches the threshold, the number of decoding iterations must increase, because each step through the EXIT chart is smaller. This behavior occurs independent of the particular decoding algorithm used and regardless of the fact that there are cycles in the associated factor graph. Decoding near capacity seems to be intrinsically difficult.

14.6   Block Turbo Coding

While the turbo code examples up to this point in the chapter have employed convolutional codes as their constituent codes, other block codes may also be used. As an example, Figure 14.15 illustrates a turbo coder built using parallel concatenated BCH codes in what is called Turbo BCH coding. One particular structure for the permuter is suggested in Figure 14.16. In this case, message data are written into a $k_2 \times k_1$ matrix. Data are read out in row order and passed to encoder 1, and data are read out in column order — constituting a permuted order — and passed through encoder 2. This framework is highly suggestive of the product codes introduced in Section 10.4, except that there is no portion of the codeword corresponding to the "parity on parity" that is present in a conventional product code. (Compare Figure 14.16 with Figure 10.5.)

Decoding of block turbo decoding proceeds as for the convolutional code: a decoder is used for each constituent code which produces a soft output in the form of an extrinsic probability, which is permuted (or de-permuted) and passed into the other decoder as a prior. The primary difficulty, then, is how to obtain soft output decoders for the codes.

Soft decoding of each code can be accomplished using the BCJR algorithm on the trellis representation for the code. To make the description explicit, we assume transmission over an AWGN.

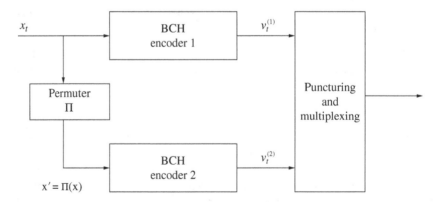

Figure 14.15: Turbo BCH encoding.

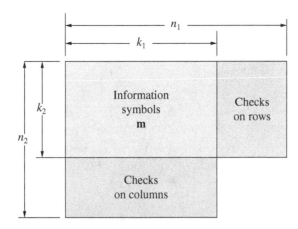

Figure 14.16: Structure of a particular implementation of a parallel concatenated code.

To make the description even more explicit, consider the trellis representation for the cyclically encoded $(7, 4, 3)$ Hamming code with generator $g(x) = x^3 + x + 1$, shown in Figure 14.17 (and also originally in Figure 12.36). Unlike convolutional codes, where each branch of the trellis may convey several bits of systematic and/or parity information, each branch of the block code trellis carries only 1 bit of information, either message bits (for the first k stages) or parity bits (for the last $n - k$ stages). The transition probability $\gamma_t(p, q)$ is thus simplified compared to (14.28) and (14.53). We can write the transition probability as (neglecting uninformative factors)

$$\gamma_t(p, q) = \underbrace{\exp\left[\tilde{x}^{(p,q)} \frac{\lambda(\tilde{x}_t)}{2}\right]}_{\text{prior}} \underbrace{\exp\left[r_t \tilde{x}^{(p,q)} \frac{L_c}{2}\right]}_{\text{message or parity}}.$$

The likelihood ratio can then be computed as

$$\lambda(x_t | \mathbf{r}) = \log \frac{\sum_{(p,q) \in S_1} \alpha_t(p) \gamma_t(p, q) \beta_{t+1}(q)}{\sum_{(p,q) \in S_0} \alpha_t(p) \gamma_t(p, q) \beta_{t+1}(q)} \tag{14.67}$$

$$= \log \frac{\sum_{(p,q) \in S_1} e^{\lambda(\tilde{x}_t)/2} e^{r_t L_c/2} \alpha_t(p) \beta_{t+1}(q)}{\sum_{(p,q) \in S_0} e^{-\lambda(\tilde{x}_t)/2} e^{-r_t L_c/2} \alpha_t(p) \beta_{t+1}(q)}$$

$$= \lambda(\tilde{x}_t) + L_c r_t + \log \frac{\sum_{(p,q) \in S_1} \alpha_t(p) \beta_{t+1}(q)}{\sum_{(p,q) \in S_0} \alpha_t(p) \beta_{t+1}(q)} \tag{14.68}$$

$$= \lambda_{p,t} + \lambda_{s,t} + \lambda_{e,t}, \tag{14.69}$$

where $\lambda_{p,t} = \lambda(\tilde{x}_t)$ is the prior information, $\lambda_{s,t} = L_c r_t$ is the channel information, and

$$\lambda_{e,t} = \log \frac{\sum_{(p,q) \in S_1} \alpha_t(p) \beta_{t+1}(q)}{\sum_{(p,q) \in S_0} \alpha_t(p) \beta_{t+1}(q)}$$

is the extrinsic information. Note that, unlike the convolutional coded case, the extrinsic information depends only on α and β probabilities and not on any parity bits transmitted with the systematic bits along a branch. Given $\gamma_t(p, q)$, the computation of the α and β probabilities is identical to that for turbo codes based on convolutional codes.

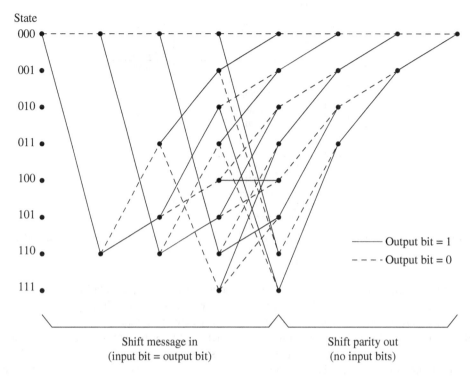

State

Figure 14.17: A trellis for a cyclically encoded $(7, 4, 3)$ Hamming code.

14.7 Turbo Equalization

14.7.1 Introduction to Turbo Equalization

In this section, we introduce a decoding technique applicable to a channel model which differs significantly from other channel models used throughout this book. Because of the close connection of turbo equalization with turbo decoding, it is deemed to be an appropriate topic to include here. In the rest of the book, the channel model has been a discrete memoryless model, specifically, an additive noise channel in which the received signal r_t is simply the transmitted signal s_t corrupted by additive noise (typically either Gaussian or Bernoulli): $r_t = s_t + n_t$. In this section, however, we consider the case that the channel has a response characterized by a transfer function $H(z) = h_0 + h_1 z^{-1} + \cdots + h_L z^{-L}$, so that the received signal is

$$r_t = \left(\sum_{i=0}^{L} s_{t-i} h_i \right) + n_t.$$

Such a channel could arise, for example, in a multipath environment or bandlimited channel.

The degradation of the received signal due to the channel can be severe, so that it is important to compensate in some way for the effect of the channel. Over the years, considerable work has been done on receivers for such channels. Various approaches include the following:

1. Linear equalization with a fixed filter $\tilde{H}(z)$, so that $r(z)\tilde{H}(z)$ "looks" a lot like the transmitted signal $s(z)$. The equalizer filter can be designed according to several criteria, such as zero forcing (cancel all interference, but neglect the influence of noise) or minimum mean-square error (minimize the average interference energy) [353].

2. Decision feedback equalization, a technique in which decisions on previous outputs are fed back to cancel their influence in the received signal [353].

3. Adaptive linear equalizers and decision feedback techniques, in which the receiver adaptively estimates the coefficients for the receiver (see, e.g., [353]).

4. Maximum likelihood sequence estimation (MLSE), in which the channel is regarded as having a state determined by the previous L bits, and a Viterbi decoder is used to decode [353].

5. Maximum a posteriori decoding, similar to MLSE, except that the MAP (or BCJR) algorithm is run. The latter two methods are arguably optimal, but run into computational difficulties because the number of states grows exponentially with the length L of the channel response. (Conventional turbo equalization also suffers from this problem.)

6. Suboptimal variations and interpolations of these ideas (such as [407]).

Until recently, most work in this area employed a nearly tacit separation principle: the equalization and detection was followed by the error-correction decoding. However, the advent of turbo decoding algorithms has led to the development of *turbo equalization*, in which the channel impairments and the error correction are dealt with in an iterated structure.

14.7.2 The Framework for Turbo Equalization

A key observation is that if a convolutional encoder at the transmitter is followed by a permuter, then the convolutive effects experienced as the signal traverses through the channel act like a second convolutional encoder, so the overall scheme acts like a serially concatenated code, with a permuter between them. It is thus amenable to turbo decoding. Figure 14.18 shows the general framework for a system that can employ turbo decoding. The permuter serves to decorrelate the values, so that extrinsic information computed in the decoder is nearly independent of the input values and can be used as a prior. In practice, the length of the permuter is on the order of the length of the channel response.

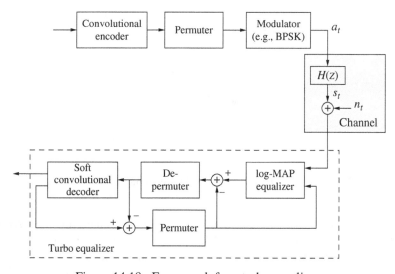

Figure 14.18: Framework for a turbo equalizer.

In the turbo decoder, the channel response is first accounted for using a MAP equalizer, which produces information about the bits in the form of log-likelihood ratios, $\lambda(x_t|\mathbf{r})$. The prior information is subtracted, leaving an extrinsic information that is passed through the permuter and on to the convolutional decoder, where it is employed as a prior probability. The output of the decoder is again bit information in the form of log-likelihood ratios $\lambda(x_t|\mathbf{r})$. The prior information associated with this is subtracted off, then the resulting extrinsic information is sent back to the equalizer for another iteration.

All elements of this equalizer should by now be familiar, with the possible exception of the MAP equalizer, which is described via an example.

Suppose ± 1-valued bits emerging from the convolutional encoder are denoted as $\tilde{v}_t$ (where, for the moment, we simply think of these as a string of bits, without regard to which are message bits and which are parity bits). The modulated bits are $a_t = \sqrt{E_c}\tilde{v}_t$. Suppose that the channel has length $L = 2$, so that the received signal can be written as

$$r_t = h_0 \sqrt{E_c}\tilde{v}_t + h_1 \sqrt{E_c}\tilde{v}_{t-1} + h_2 \sqrt{E_c}\tilde{v}_{t-2}.$$

We now form the trellis associated with this channel by defining the state at time t to be the L *previous* bits $(\tilde{v}_{t-1}, \tilde{v}_{t-2})$. Figure 14.19 shows the trellis associated with this channel. At a state $p = (\tilde{v}_{t-1}, \tilde{v}_{t-2})$ at time t, with the input $\tilde{v}_t = \tilde{v}^{(p,q)}$ leading to the state $q = (\tilde{v}_t, \tilde{v}_{t-1})$ at time $t + 1$, let the channel output (excluding the noise) be denoted as

$$s_t(p,q) = h_0 \sqrt{E_c}\tilde{v}_t + h_1 \sqrt{E_c}\tilde{v}_{t-1} + h_2 \sqrt{E_c}\tilde{v}_{t-2}.$$

Then for AWGN, the likelihood function is

$$p(r_t|s_t(p,q)) = C \exp\left[-\frac{1}{2\sigma^2}(r_t - s_t)^2\right].$$

Based on this, a transition probability suitable for use with the MAP algorithm is

$$\gamma_t(p,q) = p(r_t|s_t(p,q))P(\tilde{v}_t = \tilde{v}^{(p,q)}).$$

This can be subjected to the usual simplifications (e.g., expressed in log form, unimportant terms ignored, etc.).

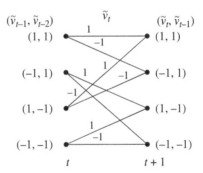

Figure 14.19: Trellis associated with a channel with $L = 2$.

Once the transition probability $\gamma_t(p,q)$ is established, the remainder of the MAP or log-MAP algorithm follows exactly as outlined in Section 14.3.12. The resulting decoder produces log likelihoods $\lambda(\tilde{v}_t|\mathbf{r})$, from which the extrinsic probabilities can be extracted for use in the convolutional decoder.

It is typical for turbo equalizers to have several dB of improvement compared to non-turbo equalizers. For a comparative study, we refer the reader to [187].

Of course, computing the transition probability, and hence the MAP decoding, requires knowledge of the channel coefficients $\{h_0, h_1, \ldots, h_L\}$. A variety of methods of estimating these are known. Many signals are prefaced with a training sequence which can be used to establish linear equations for computing the coefficients, using, for example, a minimum mean-squared error or least-squares criterion. Channel coefficients can also be estimated "blindly" by averaging out the unknown bits using an EM (expectation/maximization) type algorithm (see, e.g., [407]). Once transmission has begun, previous bits can be used to re-estimate the channel coefficients if the channel is time-varying.

Programming Laboratory 12: Turbo Code Decoding

Objective

In this laboratory, you will finalize the decoding algorithms for the probabilistic form of the BCJR algorithm and use this to construct a turbo decoder.

Background

Reading: Sections 14.2 and 14.3.

Programming Part

1. Using the class definitions and declarations shown in Algorithm 14.3, complete the function alpha-beta to compute α and β using the forward and backward passes. Use normalized computations. Verify that α and β are computed correctly using the program testbcjr, comparing the results with Example 14.2.

Algorithm 14.3 BCJR Algorithm
File: BCJR.h
BCJR.cc
testbcjr.cc

2. Use your BCJR algorithm in conjunction with testturbodec2 to reproduce (part of) the data shown in Figure 14.1 for a $(37, 21, 65536)$ turbo code. *Note*: Do not take the SNR too large, or the computations will take excessively long.

Algorithm 14.4 Test the turbo decoder
File: testturbodec2.cc

As currently implemented, the permuter is a very simple random permuter.

14.8 Exercise

14.1 A convolutional encoder uses the parity generator $G(x) = \frac{1}{1+x+x^2}$. The length of the input sequence is 10. The permuter is described by the sequence $\Pi = \{9, 4, 2, 7, 0, 6, 1, 8, 3, 5\}$.

(a) Draw the block diagram for the turbo encoder and the trellis for the convolutional code.

(b) The sequence $\mathbf{x} = [1, 1, 0, 0, 1, 0, 1, 0, 1, 1]$ is input to the turbo encoder. Determine the output sequences $\mathbf{v}^{(0)}$, $\mathbf{v}^{(1)}$, $\mathbf{v}^{(2)}$, and $\mathbf{v}$.

(c) The sequence is punctured to obtain a rate $R = 1/2$ code by taking the even bits of $\mathbf{v}^{(1)}$ and the odd bits of $\mathbf{v}^{(2)}$. Determine the output sequence $\mathbf{v}$ now.

14.2 [178] This exercise is meant to introduce concepts related to turbo decoding.

(a) Let r_t be the output of an AWGN channel. Suppose that BPSK modulation is employed. Let the transmitted signal s_t have energy E_b, where $s_t = \sqrt{E_b}\tilde{x}_t$ and $\tilde{x}_t \in \{\pm 1\}$. Let

$$\lambda(\tilde{x}_t|r_t) = \log \frac{P(\tilde{x}_t = 1|r_t)}{P(\tilde{x}_t = -1|r_t)}.$$

Show that

$$\lambda(\tilde{x}_t|r_t) = L_c r_t + \lambda(\tilde{x}_t), \tag{14.70}$$

where $L_c = 2\sqrt{E_b}/\sigma^2$ and $\lambda(\tilde{x}_t) = \log \frac{P(\tilde{x}=1)}{P(\tilde{x}=-1)}$.

(b) Suppose that the signal s_t is sent independently through two different channels, so the received values are

$$r_t^{(1)} = s_t + n_t^{(1)}$$

$$r_t^{(2)} = s_t + n_t^{(2)},$$

where $n_t^{(1)}$ and $n_t^{(2)}$ are independent. Show that

$$\lambda(\tilde{x}_t | r_t^{(1)}, r_t^{(2)}) = L_{c_1} r_t^{(1)} + L_{c_2} r_t^{(2)} + \lambda(\tilde{x}_t). \tag{14.71}$$

(c) Now consider the simple (3,2,2) parity check code shown in Figure 14.20(a). The parity check p_i^- (across the rows) is defined by

$$p_i^- = \tilde{x}_{i1} \oplus \tilde{x}_{i2}$$

and the parity check for the $p_i^|$ (down the columns) is defined by

$$p_i^| = \tilde{x}_{1i} \oplus \tilde{x}_{2i},$$

where $\oplus$ is the $GF(2)$ addition defined by

$$1 \oplus 1 = 1 \quad 1 \oplus -1 = -1 \quad -1 \oplus 1 = -1 \quad -1 \oplus -1 = 1. \tag{14.72}$$

Explain why $\lambda(\tilde{x}_{12} \oplus p_1^- | r)$ is extrinsic information for the bit $\tilde{x}_{11}$. (Here the conditioning on r denotes conditioning based on the entire set of received codeword data.) Denote this extrinsic information as $\lambda_e(\tilde{x}_{11})^-$, that is, the likelihood ratio of the extrinsic information using the horizontal code parity checks.

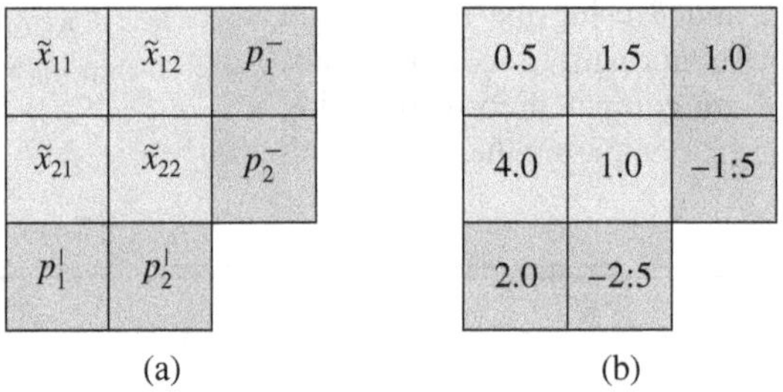

$\tilde{x}_{11}$	$\tilde{x}_{12}$	p_1^-
$\tilde{x}_{21}$	$\tilde{x}_{22}$	p_2^-
$p_1^|$	$p_2^|$	

0.5	1.5	1.0
4.0	1.0	-1:5
2.0	-2:5	

                             (a)   (b)

Figure 14.20: Example for a $(3, 2, 2)$ parity check code. (a) A simple $(3, 2, 2)$ parity check code; (b) received values $L_c r_t$.

Note that, using the $\boxplus$ operator defined as

$$\lambda(\tilde{x}_1) \boxplus \lambda(\tilde{x}_2) = \lambda(\tilde{x}_1 \oplus \tilde{x}_2)$$
$$= 2 \tanh^{-1}(\tanh(\lambda(\tilde{x}_1/2)) \tanh(\lambda(\tilde{x}_2/2)))$$
$$\approx \text{sign}(\lambda(\tilde{x}_1)) \text{sign}(\lambda(\tilde{x}_2)) \min(|\lambda(\tilde{x}_1)|, |\lambda(\tilde{x}_2)|),$$

we can write

$$\lambda_e(\tilde{x}_{11})^- = \lambda(\tilde{x}_{12} \oplus p_1^- | r) = \lambda(\tilde{x}_{12} | r) \boxplus \lambda(p_1^- | r). \tag{14.73}$$

(d) Suppose the channel input values $L_c r_t$ are as shown in Figure 14.20(b). Using (14.73) and the approximate formula for the $\boxplus$ (above), determine the extrinsic information for $\tilde{x}_{11}, \tilde{x}_{12}, \tilde{x}_{21}$, and $\tilde{x}_{22}$ using the horizontal parity bits p_i^-. That is, determine $\lambda_e(\tilde{x}_{11})^-$, $\lambda_e(\tilde{x}_{12})^-$, $\lambda_e(\tilde{x}_{21})^-$, and $\lambda_e(\tilde{x}_{22})^-$. Assume uniform priors. Computing this extrinsic information constitutes the horizontal stage of decoding.

For example, for $\tilde{x}_{11}$, we have

$$\lambda_e(\tilde{x}_{11})^- = \lambda(\tilde{x}_{12} \oplus p_1^- | r) = \lambda(\tilde{x}_{12} | r) \boxplus \lambda(p_1^- | r)$$
$$= (L_c r_{12} + \lambda(\tilde{x}_{12})) \boxplus \lambda(p_1^- | r) \quad \text{(using, e.g., (14.70))}$$
$$= L_c r_{12} \boxplus \lambda(p_1^- | r) \quad \text{(assuming uniform priors)}$$
$$= 1.5 \boxplus 1.0 \approx 1.0.$$

These likelihoods are available from $L_c r_t$ in Figure 14.20(b). Show that the extrinsic information $\lambda_e(\tilde{x}_{ij})^-$ is as shown here:

+1.0	+0.5
−1.0	−1.5

(e) For the second stage of decoding, determine the extrinsic information after the first vertical decoding using the information from the first (horizontal) extrinsic information as the prior. For example,

$$\lambda_e(x_{11})^| = \lambda(\tilde{x}_{21} \oplus p_1^|\,|r) = \lambda(\tilde{x}_{21}|r) \boxplus \lambda(p_1^|\,|r)$$

$$= (L_c r_{21} + \lambda_e(\tilde{x}_{21})^-) \boxplus \lambda(p_1^|\,|r)$$

$$= (4 + (-1)) \boxplus 2.0 \approx 2.0.$$

Show that $\lambda_e(\tilde{x}_{11})^|$, $\lambda_e(\tilde{x}_{12})^|$, $\lambda_e(\tilde{x}_{21})^|$, and $\lambda_e(\tilde{x}_{22})^|$ are as shown here:

+2.0	+0.5
−1.5	−2.0

This completes the vertical stage of decoding.

(f) The overall information after a horizontal and a vertical stage is

$$\lambda(\tilde{x}_{i,j}|r, -, |) = L_c r_{ij} + \lambda_e(\tilde{x}_{ij})^- + \lambda_e(\tilde{x}_{ij})^|.$$

The addition is justified by (14.71), since after this first complete round the three terms in the sum are independent. Show that this information is as shown here:

+3.5	+2.5
+4.0	−2.5

(g) Decoding can be accomplished by taking the sign of the total likelihoods. Determine the decoded values after this round of decoding.

(h) If iteration continues, the information $\lambda_e(\tilde{x}_{ij})^|$ is used as the prior for the next horizontal stage. Show that at the next stage, the extrinsic information is

+1.0	+1.0
−1.0	−1.5

(If iteration continues, then the independence assumption no longer holds, but is invoked anyway.)

14.3 Suppose that a $R = k/n$ convolutionally encoded sequence is passed through a BSC with channel crossover probability p_c. Determine the transition probability $\gamma_t(p, q)$ for this channel.

14.4 In Example 14.2:

(a) Compute α_1' and α_2' using the received data $\mathbf{r}$ in the example.

(b) Compute β_9' and β_8' using the received data $\mathbf{r}$ in the example.

(c) Using the data provided in Table 14.1, compute $P(x_0 = 0|\mathbf{r})$ and $P(x_1 = 0|\mathbf{r})$.

14.5 Show that the log likelihood of the sequence $\log p(\mathbf{r}) = \log p(\mathbf{r}_0^{N-1})$ can be written as

$$\log p(\mathbf{r}_0^{N-1}) = \log \sum_{\text{all valid } p} \alpha_N'(p) - \sum_{i=0}^{N} A_i.$$

14.6   Given the log-probability ratio $\lambda = \log(P(X = 1)/P(X = 0))$, determine $P(X = 1)$ and $P(X = 0)$. Show that $P(X = x)$ can be written as $P(X = x) = [e^{-\lambda/2}/(1 + e^{-\lambda})]e^{\tilde{x}\lambda/2}$, where $\tilde{x} = 2x - 1$.

14.7   Show that (14.40) is correct.

14.8   Show that (14.47) is correct.

14.9   Show that (14.48) is correct. *Hint*: Consider separately the cases

$$\hat{\tilde{x}}_k = 1,$$

$$\lambda^{[l,1]}(x_k|\mathbf{r}) \gg 0, \lambda^{[l,2]}(x_k|\mathbf{r}) \gg 0,$$

and

$$\hat{\tilde{x}}_k = -1.$$

$$\lambda^{[l,1]}(x_k|\mathbf{r}) \ll 0, \lambda^{[l,2]}(x_k|\mathbf{r}) \ll 0.$$

14.10   (Examination of the approximation (14.50).) Let $x_1 = 1$ and make a plot of x_2 vs. $\log(e^{x_1} + e^{x_2}) - x_2$ for x_2 in the range $[1, 20]$. Comment on where the approximation becomes particularly accurate.

14.11   Show that (14.55) is correct.

14.12   Show how to obtain the approximation (14.59) from (14.57).

14.13   Show how (14.64) follows from (14.62) and (14.63).

14.14   The EXIT chart can be used to estimate the bit error rate after an arbitrary number of iterations. Using $D = Z + A + E$:

(a)   Argue that D is Gaussian distributed with variance σ_D^2 and mean $\sigma_D^2/2$, where

$$\sigma_D^2 = \sigma_Z^2 + \sigma_A^2 + \sigma_E^2.$$

(b)   Show that the probability of bit error is therefore $P_b \approx Q(\mu_d/\sigma_D)$.

(c)   Show that

$$P_b \approx Q\left(\frac{\sqrt{8RE_b/N_0 + J^{-1}(I_A)^2 + J^{-1}(I_E)^2}}{2} \right).$$

14.9   References

Turbo codes were originally described in [38, 39]; their decoding algorithm was somewhat different than that described here, since they used a Gaussian random variable to represent the extrinsic probability passed between the decoders. The original BCJR algorithm appears in [20]. The α and β probabilities are also fundamental in hidden Markov models; see, for example, [91, 346, 359]. The presentation here benefited from the discussion in [25], [397], and [187]. The latter reference provides an extensive comparison between the various decoding algorithms presented here as well as a wealth of information about turbo code performance and tradeoff studies. Several tutorial expositions are also available; see, for example, [413]. A discussion of the weight distributions of turbo codewords appears in [31, 32]. Discussion on the structure of the codewords appears in [379], while some discussion of design issues appears in [31]. The paper [97] provides suggested tables of encoder polynomials and suggests that the feedback coefficients for the encoder should be a primitive polynomial.

The discussion on spectral thinning was drawn from [397], as was the discussion on interleaving. For more on distance spectrum of turbo codes, see [335]. A more extensive treatment of interleaving, discussing several different structured approaches to permuter, appears in [194, Chapter 3] and [12, 13, 102, 429]. See also [23, 88, 238, 430] for discussions on interleaving.

The EXIT chart analysis is discussed in [440] and references therein.

Our discussion of the cross entropy stopping criterion is drawn from [178]. The other stopping criteria are described in [405, 406]; see also [491], [501], [5], and [408].

The max-log-MAP algorithm appeared first in [380]. The SOVA algorithm is widely attributed to [176]. It is also described in [175, 178]. The essential equivalence of the SOVA and max-log-MAP algorithm is discussed in [140].

Turbo block codes are discussed in [178]. Extensive simulation results of Turbo BCH codes appear in [187]. For an alternative viewpoint based upon the Chase algorithm, see [357] or [358].

On turbo equalization, see [451]. For an extensive, self-contained introduction to turbo equalization, see [249]. The book [187] provides detailed examples of turbo equalization. An example of turbo equalization using LDPC codes combined with blind estimation of the channel coefficients is in [170].

An excellent resource on material related to turbo codes, LDPC codes, and iterative decoding in general is the February 2001 issue of the *IEEE Transactions on Information Theory*, which contains many articles in addition to those articles cited here.

Chapter 15

Low-Density Parity-Check Codes: Introduction, Decoding, and Analysis

15.1 Introduction

Low-density parity-check (LDPC) codes, quite simply, are linear block codes whose parity check matrices are sparse, that is, only a small fraction of the elements in the parity check matrices are nonzero. A graphical representation of these codes called a Tanner graph leads to decoding algorithms of fairly low complexity. These decoding algorithms can incorporate soft channel information and run iteratively. LDPC codes have excellent performance — among the best codes known — and have been adopted in modern communication standards, such as IEEE 802.16, IEEE 802.20, IEEE 802.3, and DBV-S2.

On the negative side, LDPC codes have higher *encode* complexity than turbo codes, being generically quadratic in the code dimension. This can be mitigated using variations on LDPC codes such as repeat-accumulate (RA) codes, or LDPC convolutional codes.

It is a curious twist of history that LDPC codes should have been largely unnoticed for so long. LDPC codes were originally proposed in 1962 by Gallager [148, 149]. At that time, the codes might have been overlooked because contemporary investigations in concatenated coding overshadowed LDPC codes and because the hardware of the time could not support effective decoder implementations. As a result, LDPC codes remained largely unstudied for over thirty years, with only scattered references to them appearing in the literature, such as [297, 437, 486, 487, 517]. This began to change with the work of MacKay [92, 291–293]. LDPC codes have been proved to be capable of closely approaching the channel capacity. In fact, the proof of the distance properties of LDPC codes demonstrates such strong performance for these codes that it has been termed a "semiconstructive proof of Shannon's noisy channel coding theorem" [288, p. 400]. In particular, using random coding arguments, MacKay showed that LDPC code ensembles can approach the Shannon capacity limit exponentially fast in the length of the code. (See also [375].)

These two chapters on LDPC codes are intended to highlight several significant aspects of LDPC codes, with some focus on decoding algorithms and elements of code design. The field of LDPC codes, however, has grown far beyond the reach of two chapters. (IEEE Xplore has well over 10,000 papers devoted to this, an area for research and application that is still very active.)

15.2 LDPC Codes: Construction and Notation

We use N to denote the length of the code and K to denote its dimension and $M = N - K$.[1] Throughout this chapter, binary LDPC codes are primarily considered (although can be constructed

---

[1] In other chapters, n, k, and m are used to describe the code. In this chapter, we use N, K, and M to describe the sizes, reserving n, k, and m (lower case) as indices.

Error Correction Coding: Mathematical Methods and Algorithms, Second Edition. Todd K. Moon.
© 2021 John Wiley & Sons, Inc. Published 2021 by John Wiley & Sons, Inc.
Companion website: www.wiley.com/go/Moon/ErrorCorrectionCoding

over other fields). Denote the rows of the parity check matrix by

$$H = \begin{bmatrix} \mathbf{h}_1^T \\ \mathbf{h}_2^T \\ \vdots \\ \mathbf{h}_M^T \end{bmatrix}.$$

The equation $\mathbf{h}_m^T \mathbf{c} = 0$ is a linear parity check on the codeword $\mathbf{c}$. For a vector $\mathbf{v}$, the *check* is computed by $z_m = \mathbf{h}_m^T \mathbf{v}$; obviously, $\mathbf{v}$ is a codeword if and only if $z_m = 0$ for all $m = 1, 2, \ldots, M$.

For a code specified by a parity check matrix H, it is expedient for encoding purposes to determine the corresponding generator matrix G. A systematic generator matrix may be found as follows. Using Gaussian elimination with column pivoting as necessary (with binary arithmetic) determine an $M \times M$ matrix H_p^{-1} so that

$$H_{\text{systematic}} = H_p^{-1} H = \begin{bmatrix} I & -H_2 \end{bmatrix}.$$

(If such a matrix H_p does not exist, then H is rank deficient, $r = \text{rank}(H) < M$. In this case, modify H by truncating the linearly dependent rows. The corresponding code has $R = K/N > (N - M)/N$, so it is a higher rate code than the dimensions of H would suggest.) Having found $H_{\text{systematic}}$, form

$$G = \begin{bmatrix} H_2^T \\ I \end{bmatrix}.$$

makegenfromA.m
gaussj2.m

Then $GH^T = \mathbf{0}$, so G is a generator matrix for H. While H may be sparse, neither the systematic generator G nor $H_{\text{systematic}}$ is necessarily sparse.

Informally, a matrix is said to be *sparse* if a small fraction of its elements are nonzero. Typically, the "small fraction" is much less than $\frac{1}{2}$.

Definition 15.1 A **low-density parity-check code** is linear block code which has a very sparse parity check matrix.

For reasons to be made clear below, in addition, the parity check matrix should also be such that no two columns have more than one row in which elements in both columns are nonzero. (This corresponds to no cycles of length four in the Tanner graph.) □

The *weight* of a binary vector is the number of nonzero elements in it. The column weight of a column of a matrix is the weight of the column; similarly for *row weight*. An LDPC parity check matrix is regular if the column weights are all the same and the row weights are all the same.

To generate a regular LDPC code, a column weight w_c is selected (typically a small integer such as $w_c = 3$) and values for N (the block length) and M (the redundancy) are selected. Then an $M \times N$ matrix H is generated which has weight w_c in each column and row weight w_r in each row. Attaining uniform row weight w_r requires that $w_c N = w_r M$. This structure says that every bit participates in w_c checks and each check involves w_r bits. Such a regular code is called a (w_c, w_r, N) code (or a (w_c, w_r) code, if a sequence of codes of increasing length N is considered). The *design rate* of a regular (w_c, w_r) code is $R = 1 - w_c/w_r$, provided that all the rows are linearly independent. (Because rows may be linearly dependent, the actual rate may be somewhat higher than the design rate.) Gallager showed that the minimum distance of a typical regular LDPC code increases linearly with N provided that $w_c \geq 3$. The parity check matrix need not be regular; codes having varying column weights may be superior to regular codes. Irregular codes are introduced in Section 15.9.

Several constructive techniques for constructing parity check matrices are discussed in Chapter 16, but LDPC parity check matrices H may be generated at random with the appropriate column and row weights (although there are some restrictions on column overlap which should be met, as discussed in

Section 15.10). We thus have, in constructive fulfillment of Shannon's original proof, a random code that may be easily decoded.

Example 15.2 The parity check matrix

$$H = \begin{bmatrix} 1 & 1 & 1 & 0 & 0 & 1 & 1 & 0 & 0 & 1 \\ 1 & 0 & 1 & 0 & 1 & 1 & 0 & 1 & 1 & 0 \\ 0 & 0 & 1 & 1 & 1 & 0 & 1 & 0 & 1 & 1 \\ 0 & 1 & 0 & 1 & 1 & 1 & 0 & 1 & 0 & 1 \\ 1 & 1 & 0 & 1 & 0 & 0 & 1 & 1 & 1 & 0 \end{bmatrix} \tag{15.1}$$

has column weight $w_c = 3$ and row weight $w_r = 6$. The italicized elements are explained below. (Strictly speaking, H is not a sparse matrix, since more than half of its elements are nonzero. However, it was chosen as a small matrix to illustrate the concept of a random matrix with fixed-weight columns. Space considerations preclude explicit presentation of more realistic parity check matrices.)

For a codeword $\mathbf{c} = [c_1, c_2, \ldots, c_{10}]$, the parity check constraints from each row require that

$$c_1 + c_2 + c_3 + c_6 + c_7 + c_{10} = 0,$$
$$c_1 + c_3 + c_5 + c_6 + c_8 + c_9 = 0,$$

etc. The corresponding checks are

$$z_1 = c_1 + c_2 + c_3 + c_6 + c_7 + c_{10}, \quad z_2 = c_1 + c_3 + c_5 + c_6 + c_8 + c_9, \quad \text{etc.}$$

Thus, bits c_1, c_2, c_3, c_6, c_7, and c_{10} participate in check z_1. Also, from H it may be observed that bit c_1 is involved in checks z_1, z_2, and z_5. (The italicized elements of H are discussed below.)   □

Example 15.3 One way to construct a (w_c, w_r) parity check matrix is as follows. Construct the matrix H_0,

$$H_0 = \begin{bmatrix} \underbrace{1\ 1\ \cdots\ 1}_{w_r} & & & \\ & \underbrace{1\ 1\ \cdots\ 1}_{w_r} & & \\ & & \ddots & \\ & & & \underbrace{1\ 1\ \cdots\ 1}_{w_r} \end{bmatrix}$$

with $N/w_r = M/w_c$ rows and N columns. This defines a $(1, w_r)$ regular parity-check code, but one having minimum distance 2 (why?). Then we form H by stacking permutations of H_0,

$$H = \begin{bmatrix} \pi_1(H_0) \\ \pi_2(H_0) \\ \pi_3(H_0) \\ \vdots \\ \pi_{w_c}(H_0) \end{bmatrix},$$

where each $\pi_i(H_0)$ denotes a matrix obtained by permuting the columns of H_0. Obviously, the choice of the permutations determines the distance structure of the code. However, a random choice of permutation will, on average, produce a good code. (This is an instance of the *concentration principle*, which essentially states that a random code will, with high probability, have behavior like the average code.) Gallager showed that if each permutation is chosen at random out of the $N!$ possible permutations, then the average minimum distance increases linearly with N. Such codes are called good codes. This is thus a rather constructive way of achieving Shannon's original idea of random codes. While the code is increasing in size, the column and row weight are fixed, which means that the decoding complexity (per iteration) remains fixed.   □

Example 15.4 An example of an LDPC parity check matrix for a $(3, 4)$-regular LDPC code due to Gallager [149] is

$$
H = \begin{bmatrix}
1 & 1 & 1 & 1 & 0 & 0 & 0 & 0 & 0 & 0 & 0 & 0 & 0 & 0 & 0 & 0 & 0 & 0 & 0 & 0 \\
0 & 0 & 0 & 0 & 1 & 1 & 1 & 1 & 0 & 0 & 0 & 0 & 0 & 0 & 0 & 0 & 0 & 0 & 0 & 0 \\
0 & 0 & 0 & 0 & 0 & 0 & 0 & 0 & 1 & 1 & 1 & 1 & 0 & 0 & 0 & 0 & 0 & 0 & 0 & 0 \\
0 & 0 & 0 & 0 & 0 & 0 & 0 & 0 & 0 & 0 & 0 & 0 & 1 & 1 & 1 & 1 & 0 & 0 & 0 & 0 \\
0 & 0 & 0 & 0 & 0 & 0 & 0 & 0 & 0 & 0 & 0 & 0 & 0 & 0 & 0 & 0 & 1 & 1 & 1 & 1 \\
1 & 0 & 0 & 0 & 1 & 0 & 0 & 0 & 1 & 0 & 0 & 0 & 1 & 0 & 0 & 0 & 0 & 0 & 0 & 0 \\
0 & 1 & 0 & 0 & 0 & 1 & 0 & 0 & 0 & 1 & 0 & 0 & 0 & 0 & 0 & 0 & 1 & 0 & 0 & 0 \\
0 & 0 & 1 & 0 & 0 & 0 & 1 & 0 & 0 & 0 & 0 & 0 & 1 & 0 & 0 & 0 & 1 & 0 & 0 \\
0 & 0 & 0 & 1 & 0 & 0 & 0 & 0 & 0 & 0 & 1 & 0 & 0 & 0 & 1 & 0 & 0 & 0 & 1 & 0 \\
0 & 0 & 0 & 0 & 0 & 0 & 0 & 1 & 0 & 0 & 0 & 1 & 0 & 0 & 0 & 1 & 0 & 0 & 0 & 1 \\
1 & 0 & 0 & 0 & 0 & 1 & 0 & 0 & 0 & 0 & 0 & 1 & 0 & 0 & 0 & 0 & 0 & 1 & 0 & 0 \\
0 & 1 & 0 & 0 & 0 & 0 & 1 & 0 & 0 & 0 & 1 & 0 & 0 & 0 & 0 & 1 & 0 & 0 & 0 & 0 \\
0 & 0 & 1 & 0 & 0 & 0 & 0 & 1 & 0 & 0 & 0 & 0 & 1 & 0 & 0 & 0 & 0 & 0 & 1 & 0 \\
0 & 0 & 0 & 1 & 0 & 0 & 0 & 0 & 1 & 0 & 0 & 0 & 0 & 1 & 0 & 0 & 1 & 0 & 0 & 0 \\
0 & 0 & 0 & 0 & 1 & 0 & 0 & 0 & 0 & 1 & 0 & 0 & 0 & 0 & 1 & 0 & 0 & 0 & 0 & 1
\end{bmatrix}.
$$

It can be shown that there are 13 linearly independent rows. The dimension of the code is thus $20 - 13 = 7$, so we have a $(20, 7)$ code with actual rate $R = 0.35$. □

In many LDPC codes, N is taken to be quite large (such as $N > 10{,}000$) while the column weight is held at around 3 or 4, so the density of ones in the matrix is quite low. (A column weight of $w_c = 2$ has been found to be ineffective [288].)

Since the H matrix is sparse, it can be represented efficiently using lists of its nonzero locations.

In this notation, bits are typically indexed by n or n' (e.g., $c_{n'}$) and the checks are typically indexed by m or m' (e.g., z_m). The set of bits that participate in check z_m (i.e., the nonzero elements on the mth row of H) is denoted

$$
\mathcal{N}(m) = \{n : H_{mn} = 1\}.
$$

The mth check can be computed as

$$
z_m = \sum_{n \in \mathcal{N}(m)} c_n
$$

(where the sum is modulo 2). The notation $|\mathcal{N}(m)|$ indicates the number of elements in the set $\mathcal{N}(m)$.

The set of checks in which bit c_n participates (i.e., the nonzero elements of the nth column of H) is denoted

$$
\mathcal{M}(n) = \{m : H_{mn} = 1\}.
$$

For a regular LDPC code, $|\mathcal{M}_n| = w_c$.

Example 15.5 For the parity check matrix H of (15.1),

$$
\mathcal{N}(1) = \{1, 2, 3, 6, 7, 10\}, \quad \mathcal{N}(2) = \{1, 3, 5, 6, 8, 9\}, \quad \text{etc.}
$$

$$
\mathcal{M}(1) = \{1, 2, 5\}, \quad \mathcal{M}(2) = \{1, 4, 5\}, \quad \text{etc.}
$$

□

15.3   Tanner Graphs

Associated with a parity check matrix H is a graph called the *Tanner graph*, whose nodes can be partitioned into two sets, with edges only between those two sets. The first set of nodes consists of N nodes representing the N bits of a codeword. Nodes in this set are called "variable" nodes or (for binary codes) "bit" nodes. The second set of nodes consists of M nodes, called "check" nodes (or "constraint" nodes), representing the parity constraints. The graph has edges only between variable nodes and check nodes, with an edge between the nth bit node and the mth check node if and only if the nth bit is involved in the mth check, that is, if $H_{mn} = 1$. (A graph such as this, consisting of two distinct sets of nodes and having edges only between the nodes in different sets, is called a *bipartite* graph.) Figure 15.1 illustrates the graph for H from Example 15.2.

The check nodes are designated as C_m, $i = 1, \ldots, M$. The variable nodes are designated as V_n, $n = 1, \ldots, N$. Sometimes the nodes will be designated simply by the index, such as a check node m or a variable node n. The set $\mathcal{N}(m)$ (introduced above) can be viewed as the set of variable nodes V_n that are neighbors on the Tanner graph to check node C_m, and the set $\mathcal{M}(n)$ can be viewed as the set of check nodes C_m that are neighbors on the Tanner graph to variable node V_n.

The Tanner graph is used below to develop insight into decoding algorithms for LDPC codes. The iterative decoding algorithm can be viewed as passing information around on the Tanner graph of the code. This information may be log-likelihood ratios or probabilities.

At a high level, the decoding is suggested by Figure 15.2. There are "decoders" at the variable nodes which take inputs from the channel and messages coming from the check nodes and process them to produce messages sent to the check nodes. There are "decoders" at the check nodes which take messages from the variable nodes and process them to send them back to the variable nodes. Between these nodes there is an interleaving operation, representing the connections in the parity check matrix. Decoding works by "sloshing" messages back forth in this graph until either the codeword is determined to be correct, or some fixed number of iterations has been reached.

In Figure 15.1, a series of edges has been indicated with bold lines: $V_1 \ C_1 \ V_2 \ C_5 \ V_1$. In these four edges there is a path that forms a cycle in the graph. Such cycles are problematic for decoding, particularly short cycles such as this one, since information sent out by the message-passing decoder comes back after some steps to the node that sent it. This results in biases in the decoding algorithm. A shortest possible cycle in a graph is 4 (as in this graph). In general, the shortest cycle in a bipartite graph is called the *girth* of the graph. This graph has girth 4.

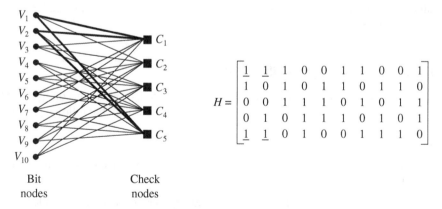

Figure 15.1: Bipartite graph associated with the parity check matrix H. (The bold edges correspond to a cycle of length four, as discussed below.)

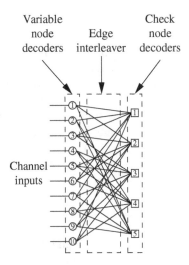

Figure 15.2: Structure of LDPC decoding.

The condition that leads to a girth 4 in the Tanner graph can be identified from the parity check matrix. Two columns that have two or more ones in common produce a cycle of length 4. In the H matrix shown in Figure 15.1, the elements of the parity check matrix H corresponding to the cycle are highlighted. A parity check matrix in which no two columns have more than one 1 position in common (that is, do not have girth 4) are said to satisfy the *row-column* constraint, referred to as the RC constraint. Designs of LDPC codes often seek to satisfy the RC constraint as a first-order consideration in the design.

15.4 Decoding LDPC Codes

Several decoding algorithms are developed in this chapter. The presentation develops decoding first using log-likelihood ratios in a step-by-step way to develop intuition into decoding (Section 15.4.1). This is followed (Section 15.4.2) by decoding using probabilities. Several variations on decoding follow, most still using the idea of moving information around on the Tanner graph.

ldpcdecoder.cc
ldpctest2.cc

C++ code for most of these decoders accompanies this book. (For memory efficiency, different decoding algorithms share memory, so running multiple decoding algorithms in parallel would require modification of the code.)

15.4.1 Decoding Using Log-Likelihood Ratios

We first present decoding using log-likelihood ratios. This method, or variations on it, is used in most implementations of LDPC decoding. The development proceeds through the following steps:

- Log-likelihood ratios.
- Parity check probabilities: the tanh rule. This analysis will produce the decoding that occurs at the check nodes.
- Repeat codes. This analysis will produce the decoding that occurs at the variable nodes.
- Putting the check node computations and the variable node computations together, we obtain the overall LDPC decoding algorithm.

15.4.1.1 Log-Likelihood Ratios

Let b be a random variable taking values in $\{0, 1\}$. The log-probability ratio, often referred to as a log-likelihood ratio (LLR), of b is

$$L_b = \log \frac{P(b = 0)}{P(b = 1)}.$$

The sign of the LLR L_b corresponds to a decision value:

$$\text{if } L_b > 0 \text{ then } b = 0 \text{ is more probable;}$$

$$\text{if } L_b < 0 \text{ then } b = 1 \text{ is more probable.}$$

The magnitude $|L_b|$ provides a measure of reliability: the larger $|L_b|$, the more confidence may be placed on the decision.

By straightforward algebra, it is possible to convert the LLR back to a probability:

$$P(b = 0) = \frac{1}{1 + e^{-L_b}} = \frac{e^{L_b}}{1 + e^{L_b}} \quad P(b = 1) = \frac{1}{1 + e^{L_b}}.$$

We consider now the situation of sending a bit $b \in \{0, 1\}$ through a channel with output y, and look for the log of the posterior probabilities, which is denoted as L_{post},

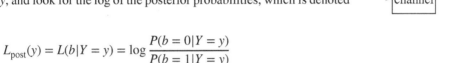

$$L_{\text{post}}(y) = L(b|Y = y) = \log \frac{P(b = 0|Y = y)}{P(b = 1|Y = y)}$$

$$= \log \frac{P(Y = y|b = 0)P(b = 0)}{P(Y = y|b = 1)P(b = 1)} = \underbrace{\log \frac{P(b = 0)}{P(b = 1)}}_{\substack{\text{a priori LLR} \\ L_A}} + \underbrace{\log \frac{P(Y = y|b = 0)}{P(Y = y|b = 1)}}_{\substack{\text{channel information} \\ \text{(likelihood ratio)} \\ L_{\text{CH}}(y)}}$$

$$= L_A + L_{CH}(y).$$

Here, L_A denotes the *a priori* likelihood, and $L_{CH}(y)$ denotes the channel information. In many instances, the prior probabilities on the bits are assumed to be equiprobable, so $L_A = 0$ and $L_{\text{post}}(y) = L_{\text{CH}}(y)$.

15.4.1.2 Log-Likelihood Ratio of the Sum of Bits

We now consider the situation where 2 bits, b_1 and b_2 are added in $GF(2)$ to produce

$$z = b_1 \oplus b_2$$

and develop the LLR. First,

$$P(z = 0) = P(b_1 \oplus b_2 = 0) = P(b_1 = 0)P(b_2 = 0) + P(b_1 = 1)P(b_2 = 1). \tag{15.2}$$

Similarly,

$$P(z = 1) = P(b_1 \oplus b_2 = 1) = P(b_1 = 1)P(b_2 = 0) + P(b_1 = 0)P(b_2 = 1).$$

Let

$$L_1 = \log \frac{P(b_1 = 0)}{P(b_1 = 1)} \quad \text{and} \quad L_2 = \log \frac{P(b_2 = 0)}{P(b_2 = 1)}$$

so

$$P(b_1 = 0) = \frac{e^{L_1}}{1 + e^{L_1}} \quad \text{and} \quad P(b_2 = 0) = \frac{e^{L_2}}{1 + e^{L_2}}.$$

Using (15.2),

$$P(z = 0) = \frac{e^{L_1}e^{L_2}}{(1 + e^{L_1})(1 + e^{L_2})} + \frac{1}{(1 + e^{L_1})(1 + e^{L_2})} = \frac{1 + e^{L_1 + L_2}}{(1 + e^{L_1})(1 + e^{L_2})}$$

and similarly,

$$P(z = 1) = \frac{e^{L_1} + e^{L_2}}{(1 + e^{L_1})(1 + e^{L_2})}. \tag{15.3}$$

Then

$$L_z = \log \frac{P(z = 0)}{P(z = 1)} = \log \frac{1 + e^{L_1 + L_2}}{e^{L_1} + e^{L_2}}.$$

This computation is important enough that several notations are used to denote it. One notation is the chk function:

$$\text{chk}(L_1, L_2) = \log \frac{1 + e^{L_1 + L_2}}{e^{L_1} + e^{L_2}}.$$

That is, $L_z = \text{chk}(L_1, L_2)$. Another notation is $\boxplus$, where

$$L_1 \boxplus L_2 \triangleq \text{chk}(L_1, L_2) = \log \frac{1 + e^{L_1 + L_2}}{e^{L_1} + e^{L_2}}.$$

The $\boxplus$ notation is suggestive of the fact that the bits b_1 and b_2 are added, so the $\boxplus$ gives the LLR of the sum.

Algebraically it can be shown that this likelihood ratio can be written in terms of tanh functions as

$$\log \frac{1 + e^{L_1 + L_2}}{e^{L_1} + e^{L_2}} = 2\tanh^{-1}(\tanh(L_1/2)\tanh(L_2/2)).$$

Summarizing these different notations:

$$\boxed{\text{chk}(L_1, L_2) = L_1 \boxplus L_2 = 2\tanh^{-1}(\tanh(L_1/2)\tanh(L_2/2)) = \log \frac{1 + e^{L_1 + L_2}}{e^{L_1} + e^{L_2}}.} \tag{15.4}$$

This operation is also referred to as the "tanh rule."

The probability can be inductively extended to multiple bits. Let $b_1, b_2, \ldots, b_d$ be independent $\{0, 1\}$ random variables, with

$$L_i = \log \frac{P(b_i = 0)}{P(b_i = 1)}$$

and let $z = b_1 \oplus b_2 \oplus \cdots \oplus b_d$. Then

$$L_z = \log \frac{P(z = 0)}{P(z = 1)}$$

can be computed as

$$\boxed{L_z \triangleq \text{chk}(L_1, L_2, \ldots, L_d) \triangleq L_1 \boxplus L_2 \boxplus \cdots \boxplus L_d = 2\tanh^{-1}\left(\prod_{i=1}^{d} \tanh(L_i/2)\right).}$$

15.4.1.3 Decoding: Message from a Check Node to a Variable Node

This parity computation is now applied to decoding at a check node of a Tanner graph. Consider a check node with four connections to variable nodes V_1, V_2, V_3, and V_4, which also designate the bit values, as shown in Figure 15.3. The check node represents the parity constraint to be satisfied

$$V_1 \oplus V_2 \oplus V_3 \oplus V_4 = 0. \tag{15.5}$$

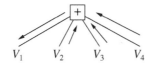

Figure 15.3: A check node with four connections.

To develop some intuition about parity nodes, consider first the case when the values of most of the bits are definitely known, such that

$$P(V_2 = 1) = 1 \quad P(V_3 = 0) = 1 \quad P(V_4 = 0) = 1.$$

What can be said about V_1? By (15.5), V_1 should satisfy the equation

$$V_1 = V_2 \oplus V_3 \oplus V_4,$$

so, with the given values, $V_1 = 1$, that is,

$$P(V_1 = 1) = 1 \oplus 0 \oplus 0.$$

We can think of the parity node taking "messages" — here bit values — from the variable nodes V_2, V_3, and V_4, and computing a "message" to variable node V_1 telling it the bit value that it "ought" to be in order to satisfy the parity constraint.

Now consider the situation when probabilities are "softened", with

$$P(V_2 = 1) = 0.8 \quad P(V_3 = 1) = 0.15 \quad P(V_4 = 1) = 0.23.$$

These probabilities form the messages sent from their respective variable nodes to the check node. The log-likelihood information for these bits is

$$L_2 = \log \frac{P(V_2 = 0)}{P(V_2 = 1)} = \log \frac{0.2}{0.8} = -1.4$$

$$L_3 = \log \frac{0.85}{0.15} = 1.7 \quad L_4 = \log \frac{0.77}{0.23} = 1.2.$$

Using both the $\boxplus$ notation and the tanh notation, the value that V_1 should have, based on the values of the other bits, is determined by

$$L_1 = \log \frac{P(V_1 = 0)}{P(V_1 = 1)} = \log \frac{P(V_2 \oplus V_3 \oplus V_4 = 0)}{P(V_2 \oplus V_3 \oplus V_4 = 1)}$$

$$= L_2 \boxplus L_3 \boxplus L_4$$

$$= 2\tanh^{-1}(\tanh(L_2/2)\tanh(L_3/2)\tanh(L_4/2)) \quad = -0.4616.$$

Since L_1 is less than 0, this favors that $V_1 = 1$, in fact

$$P(V_1 = 1) = \frac{1}{1 + e^{-0.4616}} = 0.6134.$$

In this probabilistic case, the check node sends a message to variable node V_1 indicating what value V_1 should probably be in order to satisfy the parity condition at the check node.

In this computation, of all the nodes connected to the check node, one is singled out for an outgoing log-likelihood message and the remaining nodes send their log-likelihood messages that are used to compute the log-likelihood message. This "leave one out" computation is typical of computations in LDPC decoding.

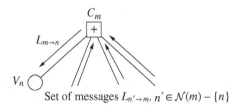

Figure 15.4: The message from check node C_m to variable node V_n.

We now develop some more general notation to express this concept on the Tanner graph associated with a code. Let $\mathcal{N}(m)$ denote the set of variable nodes that are neighbors of check node C_m on the graph (that is, the set of ns that are neighbors to node m). The log-likelihood message that C_m sends to variable V_n is computed using the messages coming from all the neighbors of C_m, except the variable node V_n. This set of neighbors can be denoted as $\mathcal{N}(m) - \{n\}$. Let $L_{n' \to m}$ be the "message," on a Tanner graph, here a LLR, which is sent from variable node $V_{n'}$ to check node C_m. Then the message that check node C_m sends to variable node V_n is

$$
\begin{aligned}
L_{m \to n} &= \boxplus_{n' \in \mathcal{N}(m) - \{n\}} L_{n' \to m} \\
&= 2\tanh^{-1} \left(\prod_{n' \in \mathcal{N}(m) - \{n\}} \tanh(L_{n' \to m}/2) \right).
\end{aligned}
\tag{15.6}
$$

In words: The message that check node C_m sends to variable V_n is determined as the tanh rule (or the $\boxplus$ rule) applied to all the messages that C_m receives from its neighbors except V_n. This rule is portrayed in Figure 15.4.

15.4.1.4 Log Likelihood of Repeated Observations About a Bit

Consider now a situation in which information about a single bit $b \in \{0, 1\}$ is conveyed by d measured values $\mathbf{y} = (y_1, y_2, \ldots, y_d)$, where each measurement is independent of the other measurements, and we want to fuse these measurements together to obtain information about b. Each measurement is described by a likelihood equation $p(y_\ell|b)$, or by a LLR

$$
L(y_\ell|b) = \log \frac{p(y_\ell|b=0)}{p(y_\ell|b=1)}.
$$

This situation may arise, for example, in a repetition code, where a channel is used d times independently to convey information about b. We will see below that this will be analogous to the decoding at a variable node.

The log posterior ratio using all the measurements is

$$
L(b|\mathbf{y}) = \log \frac{P(b=0|\mathbf{y})}{P(b=1|\mathbf{y})}.
$$

Assuming the bits are equally probable, the conditioning can be turned around using Bayes rule and this can be written as

$$
\begin{aligned}
L(b|\mathbf{y}) &= \log \frac{P(b=0|\mathbf{y})p(\mathbf{y})/P(b=0)}{P(b=1|\mathbf{y})p(\mathbf{y})/P(b=1)} = \log \frac{P(\mathbf{y}|b=0)}{P(\mathbf{y}|b=1)} = \log \frac{\prod_{\ell=1}^d p(y_\ell|b=0)}{\prod_{\ell=1}^d p(y_\ell|b=1)} \\
&= \sum_{\ell=1}^d \log \frac{P(y_\ell|b=0)}{P(y_\ell|b=1)} \triangleq \sum_{\ell=1}^d L(y_\ell|b),
\end{aligned}
$$

where the product in the first line results from the independence of the measurements.

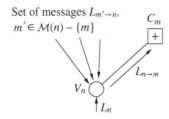

Figure 15.5: The message from variable node V_n to check node C_m.

The point of this argument is that with d independent measurements, the log likelihoods are simply added together, essentially providing an average of the information from each measurement. If there is more net negative likelihood than positive likelihood, then collectively the measurements suggest that $b = 1$, otherwise they suggest that $b = 0$.

15.4.1.5 Decoding: Message from a Variable Node to a Check Node

Consider now a variable node V_n that has neighboring check nodes $\mathcal{M}(n)$ (the set of check nodes m that are neighbors to variable node n) and a channel input node with channel log likelihood, L_n. In words: The information that check node V_n sends to its neighboring variable node C_m, $L_{n \to m}$ is obtained by adding the messages from all of its neighbors except C_m (including the channel input),

$$L_{n \to m} = L_n + \sum_{m' \in \mathcal{M}(n) - \{m\}} L_{m' \to n}. \tag{15.7}$$

This is suggested by Figure 15.5. At the variable node, the addition is regular addition of real numbers, instead of the specialized log likelihood sum $\boxplus$ which is used at the check nodes. In this computation, again there is the "leave one out" theme.

The sum total of all the information about a bit at a variable node V_n is obtained by adding all of the log-likelihood ratios from *all* of its neighboring check nodes and the channel input likelihood, L_n. Denote this as a message from variable node V_n to "out":

$$L_{n \to \text{out}} = L_n + \sum_{m' \in \mathcal{M}(n)} L_{m' \to n}. \tag{15.8}$$

15.4.1.6 Inputs to the LDPC Decoding Algorithm

The inputs to the LDPC decoding algorithm are the channel posterior probabilities. This is described here for the example of transmission 1 bit per transmitted symbol (e.g., BPSK). Let the transmitted bits be $\mathbf{b} = (b_1, b_2, \ldots, b_N)$, and let the received signal be $\mathbf{y} = (y_1, \ldots, y_N)$. Assuming equally likely priors and a memoryless channel, the posterior likelihood ratios are computed as

$$L_n = \log \frac{p(y_n | b_n = 0)}{p(y_n | b_n = 1)} = \log \frac{P(b_n = 0 | y_n) p(y_n) / P(b_n = 0)}{P(b_n = 1 | y_n) p(y_n) / P(b_n = 1)} = \log \frac{P(b_n = 0 | y_n)}{P(b_n = 1 | y_n)}. \tag{15.9}$$

These log likelihoods are referred to as the *channel log likelihood ratios*.

The channel log-likelihood ratios are used as the inputs to the overall decoding algorithm. Initially, the messages that are sent from a variable node V_n to a check node, $L_{n \to m}$ are formed using channel log-likelihood ratios. That is, initially

$$L_{n \to m} = L_n = \log \frac{P(b_n = 0 | y_n)}{P(b_n = 1 | y_n)} \quad \text{for all } m \in \mathcal{M}(n).$$

As the algorithm progresses, these messages change to incorporate information from other bits about the parity information. As the algorithm progresses, it becomes approximately true that

$$L_{n \to m} = \log \frac{P(b_n = 0 | \mathbf{y})}{P(b_n = 1 | \mathbf{y})}.$$

Example 15.6 (**AWGN channel with binary transmission**). Suppose that BPSK transmission is used, where signal amplitude a represents a bit $= 0$, and the signal amplitude $-a$ represents a bit $= 1$, and where $|a| = \sqrt{E_c}$. A transmitted signal amplitude can thus be represented as $s_i = (1 - 2c_i)a$. The energy per bit is $E_c = RE_b$. Let the received signal be

$$\mathbf{y} = \mathbf{s} + \mathbf{n},$$

where $\mathbf{n} = (n_1, n_2, \ldots, n_N)$, where $n_i \sim \mathcal{N}(0, \sigma^2)$, with $\sigma^2 = N_0/2$. Assuming equiprobable bits, the channel posterior probability is

$$P(b_n = 1 | y_n) = \frac{p(y_n | b_n = 1)}{p(y_n | b_n = 0) + p(y_n | b_n = 1)} = \frac{1}{1 + e^{2ay_n/\sigma^2}}. \tag{15.10}$$

Then

$$L_n = \log \frac{p(y_n | b_n = 0)}{p(y_n | b_n = 1)} = \log \frac{\exp(-1/(2\sigma^2)(y_n - a)^2)}{\exp(-1/(2\sigma^2)(y_n + a)^2)} = \frac{2a}{\sigma^2} y_n. \tag{15.11}$$

The constant $2a/\sigma^2$ is the channel reliability, denoted by L_c:

$$L_c = \frac{2a}{\sigma^2}.$$

Suppose $a = -1$ (a negative number represents 0), then L_c is negative. In this case, the larger (more positive) y_n is, the more negative L_n is, corresponding to a higher probability that $b_n = 1$.

By contrast, if $a = 1$ (positive number represents 0), then L_c is positive, and the more positive y_n is, the more positive L_n is, corresponding to a higher probability that $b_n = 0$. □

Example 15.7 **BSC channel** with crossover probability p. In this case, $y_n \in \{0, 1\}$, with

$$P(c_n = c | y_n) = (1 - p)^{[c_n = y_n]} p^{[c_n \neq y_n]},$$

using the Iverson notation, where [condition] = 1 if the condition is true, and 0 otherwise. Then

$$L_n = (-1)^{y_n} \log \left(\frac{1 - p}{p} \right). \tag{□}$$

Example 15.8 (**Binary Erasure Channel (BEC)**) Let E denote that the bit is erased. Since

$$P(b_n = b | y_n) = \begin{cases} 1 & \text{if } y_n = b \\ \frac{1}{2} & \text{if } y_n = \mathsf{E} \\ 0 & \text{if } y_n = (1 - b). \end{cases}$$

Then

$$L_n = \begin{cases} +\infty & \text{if } y_n = 0 \\ -\infty & \text{if } y_n = 1 \\ 0 & \text{if } y_n = \mathsf{E}. \end{cases} \qquad \square$$

15.4.1.7 Terminating the Decoding Algorithm

The LDPC decoding algorithm iterates between [passing messages from check nodes to variable nodes] and [passing messages from variable nodes to check nodes] until some stopping condition is met. One way to determine the stopping condition is to form bits from the output likelihood,

$$\hat{b}_i = \begin{cases} 0 & \text{if } L_{i \to \text{out}} > 0 \\ 1 & \text{if } L_{i \to \text{out}} < 0 \end{cases} \tag{15.12}$$

then seeing if the detected codeword satisfies parity,

$$H\hat{\mathbf{b}} = \mathbf{0}.$$

If so, then the algorithm can stop with this decoded codeword.

Another stopping condition is to set a maximum number of iterations and to stop when a maximum number of iterations is reached. The best estimate of the codeword obtained using (15.12) is returned, which may be correct in many positions.

15.4.1.8 Summary of Decoding: The Belief Propagation Algorithm

The steps of passing messages from check nodes to variable nodes and from variable nodes to check nodes are combined together for the overall LDPC decoding algorithm. At each check node, the "leave one out" computation is performed, in succession, leaving out the message from each neighboring variable node in turn. At each variable node, the "leave one out" computation is performed, in succession, leaving out the message from each variable node in turn. This is established in the following formal description. The notation is as follows:

- N: number of variable nodes (length of code).

- K: number of input bits (dimension of code).

- M: number of check nodes $= N - K$.

- n: index on variable nodes.

- m: index on check nodes.

- $\mathcal{N}(m)$: set of variable nodes (the set of n indices) which are neighbors to check node m.

- $\mathcal{M}(n)$: set of check nodes (the set of m indices) which are neighbors to variable node n.

- $\mathcal{N}(m) - \{n\}$: the neighbors to V_m, excluding n.

- $L_{m'\to n}$: The message (log probability ratio) from check node m' to variable node n.

- $L_{n'\to m}$: The message (log probability ratio) from variable node n' to check node m.

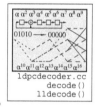

```
ldpcdecoder.cc
         decode()
       lldecode()
```

Algorithm 15.1 Log-Likelihood Belief Propagation Decoding Algorithm for Binary LDPC Codes

Input:
Description of the parity check matrix using $\mathcal{N}(m)$ and $\mathcal{M}(n)$.
The channel log likelihoods L_n,
Maximum # of iterations, MAXITER
Output: Estimate of codeword
Initialization: For each n, and for each $m \in \mathcal{M}(n)$, set

$$L_{n\to m} = L_n$$

Check Node to Variable Node Step (horizontal step):
for each check node m
  for each variable node $n \in \mathcal{N}(m)$
    Compute the message from C_m to V_n by

$$L_{m\to n} = 2\tanh^{-1}\left(\prod_{n'\in\mathcal{N}(m)-\{n\}} \tanh(L_{n'\to m}/2)\right)$$

  end **for**
end **for**
Variable Node to Check Node Step (vertical step)
for each variable node n

for each check node $m \in \mathcal{M}(n)$
  Compute the message from V_n to C_m by

$$L_{n \to m} = L_n + \sum_{m' \in \mathcal{M}(n)-\{m\}} L_{m' \to n}.$$

  Also compute the output likelihoods

$$L_{n \to \text{out}} = L_n + \sum_{m' \in \mathcal{M}(n)} L_{m' \to n}.$$

  end **for**
end **for**
for each n, decide $\hat{c}_n = 1$ if $L_{n \to \text{out}} < 0$.

Check Parity:
if $H\hat{c} = \mathbf{0}$ then **return** $\hat{c}$.
Otherwise, if # iterations < MAXITER, goto **Check Node to Variable Node Step**
Else **return** $\hat{c}$ and an indication of coding failure.

Example 15.9   The message vector $\mathbf{m} = \begin{bmatrix} 1 & 0 & 1 & 0 & 1 \end{bmatrix}^T$ is encoded using a systematic generator G derived from (15.1) to obtain the code vector

$$\mathbf{b} = \begin{bmatrix} 0 & 0 & 0 & 1 & 0 & 1 & 0 & 1 & 0 & 1 \end{bmatrix}^T. \tag{15.13}$$

Then $\mathbf{b}$ is mapped to a signal constellation with amplitude $a = -2$ to obtain the vector

$$\mathbf{t} = \begin{bmatrix} -2 & -2 & -2 & 2 & -2 & 2 & -2 & 2 & -2 & 2 \end{bmatrix}^T,$$

which is transmitted through an AWGN channel with $\sigma^2 = 2$. The vector

$$\mathbf{y} = \begin{bmatrix} -0.63 & -0.83 & -0.73 & -0.04 & 0.1 & 0.95 & -0.76 & 0.66 & -0.55 & 0.58 \end{bmatrix}^T$$

is received. Using (15.10), it is found that the channel posterior probabilities are

$$P(\mathbf{c} = 1|\mathbf{y}) = \begin{bmatrix} 0.22 & 0.16 & 0.19 & 0.48 & 0.55 & 0.87 & 0.18 & 0.79 & 0.25 & 0.76 \end{bmatrix}^T. \tag{15.14}$$

If, ignoring the fact that the information is coded, these posterior probabilities were converted to a binary vector by thresholding the probabilities in (15.14) at 0.5, the estimated vector

$$\hat{\mathbf{c}} = \begin{bmatrix} 0 & 0 & 0 & \underline{0} & \underline{1} & 1 & 0 & 1 & 0 & 1 \end{bmatrix}$$

would be obtained, which differs from the original code vector at the two underlined locations. However, note that at the error locations, the channel posterior probability is only slightly different than the threshold 0.5, so that the bits only "weakly" decode to the values 0 and 1, respectively. Other bits more strongly decode to their true values. These weak and strong indications are exploited by a soft-decision decoder.

Converting the received values to log-likelihood ratios, use the channel reliability $L_c = 2a/\sigma^2 = 2$ to find the channel log likelihoods

$$\mathbf{L}_n = (-L_c)\mathbf{y} = \begin{bmatrix} 1.3 & 1.7 & 1.5 & 0.08 & -0.2 & -1.9 & 1.5 & -1.3 & 1.1 & -1.2 \end{bmatrix}.$$

The initial messages $L_{n \to m}$ (expressed as a matrix) is

$$L_{n \to m} = \begin{bmatrix} 1.3 & 1.7 & 1.5 & & & -1.9 & 1.5 & & & -1.2 \\ 1.3 & & 1.5 & & -0.2 & -1.9 & & -1.3 & 1.1 & \\ & & 1.5 & 0.08 & -0.2 & & 1.5 & & 1.1 & -1.2 \\ & 1.7 & & 0.08 & -0.2 & -1.9 & & -1.3 & & -1.2 \\ 1.3 & 1.7 & & 0.08 & & & 1.5 & -1.3 & 1.1 & \end{bmatrix}.$$

(Note that there are only values computed for elements where the parity check matrix is nonzero.)

Iteration 1: After the first iteration, the messages $L_{m \to n}$ (expressed as a matrix) and the messages $L_{n \to m}$ and $L_{n \to \text{out}}$ are

$$L_{m \to n} = \begin{bmatrix} 0.21 & 0.17 & 0.19 & & & -0.16 & 0.18 & & & -0.22 \\ -0.027 & & -0.024 & & 0.15 & 0.02 & & 0.026 & -0.03 & \\ & & 0.0013 & 0.021 & -0.0083 & & 0.0013 & & 0.0017 & -0.0016 \\ & 0.0018 & & 0.03 & -0.012 & -0.0016 & & -0.0021 & & -0.0023 \\ -0.01 & -0.0083 & & -0.14 & & & -0.0088 & 0.0097 & -0.011 & \end{bmatrix}$$

$$L_{n \to m} = \begin{bmatrix} 1.2 & 1.7 & 1.4 & & & -1.9 & 1.5 & & & -1.2 \\ 1.5 & & 1.6 & & -0.22 & -2.1 & & -1.3 & 1.1 & \\ & & 1.6 & -0.031 & -0.064 & & 1.7 & & 1.1 & -1.4 \\ & 1.8 & & -0.041 & -0.06 & -2 & & -1.3 & & -1.4 \\ 1.4 & 1.8 & & 0.13 & & & 1.7 & -1.3 & 1.1 & \end{bmatrix}$$

$$L_{n \to \text{out}} = \begin{bmatrix} 1.4 & 1.8 & 1.6 & -0.011 & -0.072 & -2 & 1.7 & -1.3 & 1.1 & -1.4 \end{bmatrix}.$$

The estimated bits $\hat{\mathbf{c}}$ and corresponding parity $H\hat{\mathbf{c}}$ are

$$\hat{\mathbf{c}} = \begin{bmatrix} 0 & 0 & 0 & 1 & 1 & 1 & 0 & 1 & 0 & 1 \end{bmatrix} \quad \mathbf{z} = \begin{bmatrix} 0 & 1 & 1 & 1 & 0 \end{bmatrix}.$$

Since the parities do not all check, two more iterations are required:

Iteration 2:

$$L_{m \to n} = \begin{bmatrix} 0.2 & 0.16 & 0.18 & & & -0.15 & 0.18 & & & -0.21 \\ -0.033 & & -0.03 & & 0.19 & 0.027 & & 0.036 & -0.041 & \\ & & -0.0002 & 0.0085 & 0.0042 & & -0.00019 & & -0.00027 & 0.00022 \\ & -0.00032 & & 0.011 & 0.0077 & 0.0003 & & 0.0004 & & 0.00038 \\ -0.018 & -0.016 & & -0.17 & & & -0.016 & 0.02 & -0.023 & \end{bmatrix}$$

$$L_{n \to m} = \begin{bmatrix} 1.2 & 1.6 & 1.4 & & & -1.9 & 1.5 & & & -1.2 \\ 1.5 & & 1.6 & & -0.19 & -2.1 & & -1.3 & 1.1 & \\ & & 1.6 & -0.083 & -0.0055 & & 1.7 & & 1 & -1.4 \\ & 1.8 & & -0.085 & -0.009 & -2 & & -1.3 & & -1.4 \\ 1.4 & 1.8 & & 0.1 & & & 1.7 & -1.3 & 1.1 & \end{bmatrix}$$

$$L_{n \to \text{out}} = \begin{bmatrix} 1.4 & 1.8 & 1.6 & -0.074 & -0.0013 & -2 & 1.7 & -1.3 & 1 & -1.4 \end{bmatrix}$$

$$\hat{\mathbf{c}} = \begin{bmatrix} 0 & 0 & 0 & 1 & 1 & 1 & 0 & 1 & 0 & 1 \end{bmatrix} \quad \mathbf{z} = \begin{bmatrix} 0 & 1 & 1 & 1 & 0 \end{bmatrix}.$$

Iteration 3:

$$L_{m \to n} = \begin{bmatrix} 0.2 & 0.16 & 0.18 & & & -0.15 & 0.17 & & & -0.21 \\ -0.028 & & -0.025 & & 0.18 & 0.022 & & 0.03 & -0.035 & \\ & & -4.4e-05 & 0.0007 & 0.011 & & -4.2e-05 & & -6.1e-05 & 4.9e-05 \\ & -9.9e-05 & & 0.0017 & 0.016 & 9.2e-05 & & 0.00013 & & 0.00012 \\ -0.014 & -0.012 & & -0.17 & & & -0.012 & 0.015 & -0.017 & \end{bmatrix}$$

$$L_{n \to m} = \begin{bmatrix} 1.2 & 1.6 & 1.4 & & & -1.9 & 1.5 & & & -1.2 \\ 1.5 & & 1.6 & & -0.17 & -2 & & -1.3 & 1.1 & \\ & & 1.6 & -0.087 & -0.0029 & & 1.7 & & 1 & -1.4 \\ & 1.8 & & -0.088 & -0.008 & -2 & & -1.3 & & -1.4 \\ 1.4 & 1.8 & & 0.082 & & & 1.7 & -1.3 & 1.1 & \end{bmatrix}$$

$$L_{n \to \text{out}} = \begin{bmatrix} 1.4 & 1.8 & 1.6 & -0.086 & 0.0077 & -2 & 1.7 & -1.3 & 1 & -1.4 \end{bmatrix}$$

$$\hat{\mathbf{c}} = \begin{bmatrix} 0 & 0 & 0 & 1 & 0 & 1 & 0 & 1 & 0 & 1 \end{bmatrix} \quad \mathbf{z} = \begin{bmatrix} 0 & 0 & 0 & 0 & 0 \end{bmatrix}.$$

At this point, all the parities check and the codeword is corrected decoded. $\qquad\qquad \square$

15.4.1.9   Messages on the Tanner Graph

As pointed out above, the decoding algorithm can be viewed as passing messages on the Tanner graph associated with the code. This view can be emphasized by unfolding the bipartite graph as suggested in Figure 15.6.

If the Tanner graph could actually be unfolded this way, as a tree, then the belief propagation decoding algorithm would be optimal. However, as shown in Figure 15.7, using V_1 as an example node, there exists a cycle in the graph:

$$V_1 \rightarrow C_1 \rightarrow V_2 \rightarrow C_5 \rightarrow V_1.$$

This means that as information propagates through the graph through multiple iterations, information emerging from a variable node (such as V_1) will eventually come back to V_1. This means that the estimated probabilities are not independent of information coming from other nodes. As the decoding algorithm develops, the information will be biased by information previously at the node, not formed by collecting independently from other nodes in the graph. Since independence was an important assumption in deriving the decoding at both the check nodes and the variable nodes, the decoding at both check and variable nodes becomes biased.

Another view of the iterative nature of the decoding algorithm is shown in Figure 15.8. Duplicating the Tanner graph in multiple stages to show the flow of information, in the iterative decoding information passes from the bit (or variable) nodes to the check nodes, then from check nodes to bit nodes, then to check nodes, and so forth. As indicated by the dashed line in this portrayal, information emerging from the first bit eventually (after two full iterations) finds its way back to the first bit node.

15.4.2   Decoding Using Probabilities

While the log-likelihood approach to decoding is frequently used in implementations of LDPC decoding algorithm, there is insight and understanding to be gained by also considering the decoding from a probabilistic standpoint. There may also be some computational advantages.

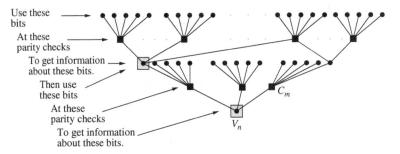

Figure 15.6: A parity check tree associated with the Tanner graph.

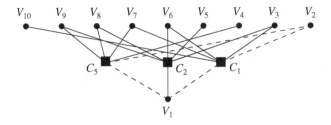

Figure 15.7: A portion of the Tanner graph for the example code, with node for V_1 as a root, showing a cycle.

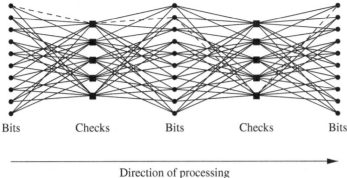

Figure 15.8: Processing information through the graph determined by H. The dashed line illustrates a cycle of length 4.

15.4.2.1 Probability of Even Parity: Decoding at the Check Nodes

Just as the likelihood ratio-based decoding started by considering the probability of the sum of bits, so does the probability-based decoding.

Lemma 15.10 *(Gallager's Lemma) Let $b_1, b_2, \ldots, b_d$ be independent bits, with $P(b_i = 1) = p_i$. Then*

$$P(b_1 \oplus b_2 \oplus \cdots \oplus b_d = 1) = \frac{1 - \prod_{i=1}^{d}(1 - 2p_i)}{2}.$$

and

$$P(b_1 \oplus b_2 \oplus \cdots \oplus b_d = 0) = \frac{1 + \prod_{i=1}^{d}(1 - 2p_i)}{2}.$$

Proof The proof is inductive. The formulas are easily verified with $d = 1$. Assume the result is true for $d - 1$, that is,

$$P(b_1 \oplus b_2 \oplus \cdots \oplus b_{d-1} = 1) = \frac{1 - \prod_{i=1}^{d-1}(1 - 2p_i)}{2}.$$

Denote this quantity as W_{d-1}. Then

$$P(b_1 \oplus b_2 \oplus \cdots \oplus b_d = 1) = W_{d-1}P(b_d = 0) + (1 - W_{d-1})P(b_d = 1)$$

$$W_{d-1}(1 - p_d) + (1 - W_{d-1})p_d = W_{d-1}(1 - 2p_d) + p_d$$

$$= \frac{(1 - 2p_d) + \prod_{i=1}^{d}(1 - 2p_i)}{2} + \frac{2p_d}{2} = \frac{1 - \prod_{i=1}^{d}(1 - 2p_i)}{2}.$$

$\square$

Gallager's lemma is used for decoding at a check node. To repeat a previous example, suppose that at a check node

$$V_1 \oplus V_2 \oplus V_3 \oplus V_4 = 0$$

with $p_2 = P(V_2 = 1), p_3 = P(V_3 = 1)$, and $p_4 = P(V_4 = 1)$ given. Then since

$$V_1 = V_2 \oplus V_3 \oplus V_4,$$

using Gallager's lemma,

$$P(V_1 = 1) = P(V_2 \oplus V_3 \oplus V_4 = 1) = \frac{1 - (1 - 2p_2)(1 - 2p_3)(1 - 2p_4)}{2}.$$

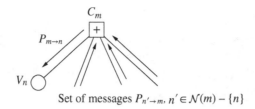

Figure 15.9: Probabilistic message from check node m to variable nodes n.

More generally, let $P_{n \to m}(b)$ denote the message from variable node V_n to check node C_m, representing the probability that the bit is equal to b (conditioned on channel measurement and ultimately parity constraints):

$$P_{n \to m}(b) \approx P(V_n = b).$$

The message that check node m sends to variable node V_n is computed by the probability that V_n is 1, based on the parity constraint and the probabilities of other variable nodes connected to C_m, as shown in Figure 15.9 By Gallager's lemma, this is

$$P_{m \to n}(1) = \frac{1 - \prod_{n' \in \mathcal{N}(m)-\{n\}}(1 - 2P_{n' \to m}(1))}{2},$$

$$P_{m \to n}(0) = \frac{1 + \prod_{n' \in \mathcal{N}(m)-\{n\}}(1 - 2P_{n' \to m}(1))}{2}.$$

One way to implement this is as follows. Let

$$\delta q_{m,n'} = P_{n' \to m}(0) - P_{n' \to m}(1) = 1 - 2P_{n' \to m}(1).$$

Compute the leave-one-out product

$$\delta r_{mn} = \prod_{n' \in \mathcal{N}(m)-\{n\}} \delta q_{m,n'}.$$

Then

$$P_{m \to n}(1) = \frac{1 - \delta r_{mn}}{2} \quad P_{m \to n}(0) = \frac{1 + \delta r_{mn}}{2}.$$

15.4.2.2   Probability of Independent Observations Decoding at a Variable Node

Consider now that d independent observations $\mathbf{y} = (y_1, \ldots, y_d)$ are available about a bit b. Then

$$P(b = 1|\mathbf{y}) = \frac{p(\mathbf{y}|b = 1)P(b = 1)}{p(\mathbf{y})} = \frac{p(\mathbf{y}|b = 1)}{p(\mathbf{y}|b = 0)P(b = 0) + p(\mathbf{y}|b = 1)P(b = 1)}$$

$$= \frac{\prod_{i=1}^{d} p(y_i|b = 1)}{p(\mathbf{y}|b = 0)P(b = 0) + p(\mathbf{y}|b = 1)P(b = 1)}$$

and similarly,

$$P(b = 0|\mathbf{y}) = \frac{p(\mathbf{y}|b = 0)P(b = 0)}{p(\mathbf{y})} = \frac{\prod_{i=1}^{d} p(y_i|b = 1)}{p(\mathbf{y}|b = 0)P(b = 0) + p(\mathbf{y}|b = 1)}.$$

The denominators in $P(b = 1|\mathbf{y})$ and $P(b = 0|\mathbf{y})$ are identical. As a result, assuming 0 and 1 are equiprobable, the probability can be computed by first computing the numerators as

$$q'(1) = \prod_{i=1}^{d} p(y_i|b = 1) \quad \text{and} \quad q'(0) = \prod_{i=1}^{d} p(y_i|b = 0)$$

then forming the normalizing factor

$$\alpha = \frac{1}{q'(1) + q'(0)}$$

to that

$$P(b = 1|\mathbf{y}) = \alpha q'(1) \quad \text{and} \quad P(b = 0|\mathbf{y}) = \alpha q'(0).$$

As applied to decoding at a variable node, let $P_{m' \to n}(b)$ be messages (bit probabilities) sent from check node m' to variable node n, and let $P_n(b)$ be the channel information there. The probability message that variable node n sends to check node m is determined by the product of all the bit probabilities from check nodes adjacent to variable node n, except for the check node m to which the message is being sent. That is,

$$P_{n \to m}(1) = \alpha P_n(1) \prod_{m' \in \mathcal{M}(n) - \{m\}} P_{m' \to n}(1)$$

$$P_{n \to m}(0) = \alpha P_n(0) \prod_{m' \in \mathcal{M}(n) - \{m\}} P_{m' \to n}(0),$$

where α is chosen as a normalization constant such that

$$P_{n \to m}(0) + P_{n \to m}(1) = 1.$$

Also at variable node n, a message incorporating all the information from *all* check nodes and the channel information is computed:

$$P_{n \to \text{out}}(b) = \alpha P_n(b) \prod_{m' \in \mathcal{M}(n)} P_{m' \to n}(b), \quad b = 0, 1,$$

where again α is a normalization constant such that

$$P_{n \to \text{out}}(0) + P_{n \to \text{out}}(1) = 1.$$

The inputs to the probability decoding algorithm are the channel probabilities,

$$P_n(1) = \frac{1}{1 + e^{L_n}}.$$

For the AWGN channel and BPSK modulation,

$$P_n(1) = L_c y_n$$

with $L_c = 2a/\sigma^2$.

```
ldpcdecoder.cc
probdecode()
```

Algorithm 15.2 Probability Belief Propagation Decoding Algorithm for Binary LDPCCodes

---

Input:
    Description of the parity check matrix using $\mathcal{N}(m)$ and $\mathcal{M}(n)$.
    The channel log likelihoods $P_n(1)$,
    Maximum # of iterations, MAXITER
Output: Estimate of codeword
Initialization: For each n, and for each $m \in \mathcal{M}(n)$, set

$$P_{n \to m}(1) = P_n(1), \quad P_{n \to m}(0) = 1 - P_n(1).$$

Check Node to Variable Node Step (horizontal step):
for each check node m
    for each variable node $n \in \mathcal{N}(m)$

Compute the message from C_m to V_n:

$$\delta r_{mn} = \prod_{n' \in \mathcal{N}(m)-\{n\}} P_{n' \to m}(0) - P_{n' \to m}(1)$$

$$P_{m \to n}(1) = \frac{1 - \delta r_{mn}}{2} \quad P_{m \to n}(0) = \frac{1 + \delta r_{mn}}{2}.$$

end **for**
end **for**

Variable Node to Check Node Step (vertical step):
for each variable node n
    for each check node $m \in \mathcal{M}(n)$
        Compute the message from V_n to C_m by

$$P_{n \to m}(1) = \alpha P_n(1) \prod_{m' \in \mathcal{M}(n)-\{m\}} P_{m' \to n}(1).$$

$$P_{n \to m}(0) = \alpha P_n(0) \prod_{m' \in \mathcal{M}(n)-\{m\}} P_{m' \to n}(0),$$

where α is such that $P_{n \to m}(1) + P_{n \to m}(0) = 1$.
Also compute the output probabilities

$$P_{n \to \text{out}}(1) = \alpha P_n(1) \prod_{m' \in \mathcal{M}(n)} P_{m' \to n}(1).$$

$$P_{n \to \text{out}}(0) = \alpha P_n(0) \prod_{m' \in \mathcal{M}(n)} P_{m' \to n}(0),$$

where α is such that $P_{n \to \text{out}}(0) + P_{n \to \text{out}}(1) = 1$.
end **for**
end **for**
for each n, decide $\hat{c}_n = 1$ if $P_{n \to \text{out}} > \frac{1}{2}$.

Check Parity:
if $H\hat{c} = 0$ then **return** $\hat{c}$.
Otherwise, if # iterations < MAXITER, goto **Check Node to Variable Node Step**
Else **return** $\hat{c}$ and an indication of coding failure.

This algorithm is properly called the *sum–product algorithm*, since it decodes using only sums and products. The log- likelihood-based algorithm is also sometimes referred to as the sum–product algorithm, because it is (ideally) numerically equivalent to this algorithm.

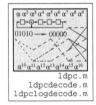

ldpc.m
ldpcdecode.m
ldpclogdecode.m

A fundamental difference between the log-likelihood ratio-based decoder and the probability decoder is that the probability decoder requires computing probabilities for both 0 and 1 outcomes. This requires essentially twice the amount of memory, and twice as many computations (at the level of the loops in the algorithm). However, no complicated functions such as logarithms or tanh need to be computed. Further variations on decoding are developed which provide other tradeoffs in complexity.

Example 15.11 For the parity check matrix (15.1) of Example 15.9, the decoding proceeds as follows:

Initialization: Set $P_{n \to m}(b) = p_n(b)$ from (15.14)

$$P_{n \to m}$$

$$\begin{bmatrix} 0.22 & 0.16 & 0.19 & & & 0.87 & 0.18 & & & 0.76 \\ 0.22 & & 0.19 & & 0.55 & 0.87 & & 0.79 & 0.25 & \\ & & 0.19 & 0.48 & 0.55 & & 0.18 & & 0.25 & 0.76 \\ & 0.16 & & 0.48 & 0.55 & 0.87 & & 0.79 & & 0.76 \\ 0.22 & 0.16 & & 0.48 & & & 0.18 & 0.79 & 0.25 & \end{bmatrix}.$$

Iteration 1: Check Node to Variable Node Computation:

$$P_{m \to n}(1)$$

$$
\begin{bmatrix}
0.45 & 0.46 & 0.45 & & & 0.54 & 0.45 & & & 0.56 \\
0.51 & & 0.51 & & 0.46 & 0.49 & & 0.49 & 0.51 & \\
& & 0.5 & 0.49 & 0.5 & & 0.5 & & 0.5 & 0.5 \\
& 0.5 & & 0.49 & 0.5 & 0.5 & & 0.5 & & 0.5 \\
0.5 & 0.5 & & 0.54 & & & 0.5 & 0.5 & 0.5 &
\end{bmatrix}.
$$

Iteration 1: Variable Node to Check Node Computation:

$$P_{n \to m}(1)$$

$$
\begin{bmatrix}
0.23 & 0.16 & 0.19 & & & 0.87 & 0.18 & & & 0.76 \\
0.19 & & 0.16 & & 0.56 & 0.89 & & 0.79 & 0.25 & \\
& & 0.17 & 0.51 & 0.52 & & 0.16 & & 0.26 & 0.8 \\
& 0.14 & & 0.51 & 0.51 & 0.88 & & 0.78 & & 0.8 \\
0.19 & 0.14 & & 0.47 & & & 0.15 & 0.79 & 0.26 &
\end{bmatrix}
$$

$$P_{n \to \text{out}}(1)$$

$$
\begin{bmatrix}
0.19 & 0.14 & 0.17 & 0.5 & 0.52 & 0.88 & 0.16 & 0.78 & 0.26 & 0.8
\end{bmatrix}
\tag{15.15}
$$

$$
\hat{\mathbf{c}} = \begin{bmatrix} 0 & 0 & 0 & 1 & 1 & 1 & 0 & 1 & 0 & 1 \end{bmatrix} \quad \mathbf{z} = \begin{bmatrix} 0 & 1 & 1 & 1 & 0 \end{bmatrix}.
$$

At the end of the first iteration, the parity check condition is not satisfied. The algorithm runs through two more iterations (not shown here). At the end, the decoded value

$$
\hat{\mathbf{c}} = \begin{bmatrix} 0 & 0 & 0 & 1 & 0 & 1 & 0 & 1 & 0 & 1 \end{bmatrix}
$$

is obtained, which exactly matches the transmitted code vector $\mathbf{c}$ of (15.13).   □

15.4.2.3 Computing the Leave-One-Out Product

The leave-one-out computation is an important computation in both the likelihood and probabilistic formulation. In this section, we consider how to efficiently compute these products in a numerically stable way.

Given real numbers a, b, c, d, and e, it is desired to compute the products

$$bcde \quad acde \quad abde \quad abce \quad abcd.$$

An obvious efficient way to compute this is to compute the overall product $abcde$ (4 multiplications) then compute successive quotients

$$\frac{abcde}{a} \quad \frac{abcde}{b} \quad \frac{abcde}{c} \quad \frac{abcde}{d} \quad \frac{abcde}{e},$$

an additional five operations, for a total of 9 operations. In general, with n operands, there will be $2n - 1$ multiplications/divisions. Computing this way introduces difficulties if a factor is near 0 — the overall product is near 0, and division by a small number is numerically problematic. If one of the factors is 0, then this method fails.

A superior approach does not require any division operations (but it does require a few more computations). This is done by using a table called the forward/backward table (not to be confused with the forward/backward algorithm used in turbo code decoding). The forward table is formed by successive products in the forward direction, and the backward table is formed by successive products in the reverse direction, as shown below.

Forward Products	Backward Products
$f_0 = a$	$b_0 = e$
$f_1 = ab$	$b_1 = de$
$f_2 = abc$	$b_2 = cde$
$f_3 = abcd$	$b_3 = bcde$

Then the leave-one-out products are computed as

$$bcde = b_3 \quad acde = f_0 b_2 \quad abde = f_1 b_1 \quad abcd = b_3.$$

With n operands, there are $2(n-2)$ products to form the forward/backward table, and $n-2$ additional products, for a total of $3n-6$. No divisions are required.

This method can also be used for a leave-one-out sum, or, significantly, for a leave-one-out min operation (used for the min-sum algorithm below).

15.4.2.4 Sparse Memory Organization

Operations in the decoding algorithm only rely on data corresponding to nonzero elements of the parity check matrix H, which is sparse. In general, the parity check matrix may be very sparse, such as 3 nonzero elements in each column of a 1000×6000 parity check matrix. It makes no sense in terms of memory efficiency to allocate space for all the elements of H, since most of this would be unused space. In this section, a method is described that exploits the sparseness of the matrix.

Let w_c denote the maximum column weight of H. The number of elements to be stored is no more than $w_c N$. In the representation here, think of all the elements "floating" to the top of a matrix. For example, for a check-to-variable message matrix,

$$L_{m \to n}$$

$$
\begin{bmatrix}
0.21 & 0.17 & 0.19 & & & -0.16 & 0.18 & & & -0.22 \\
-0.027 & & -0.024 & & 0.15 & 0.02 & & 0.026 & -0.03 & \\
& & 0.0013 & 0.021 & -0.0083 & & 0.0013 & & 0.0017 & -0.0016 \\
& 0.0018 & & 0.03 & -0.012 & -0.0016 & & -0.0021 & & -0.0023 \\
-0.01 & -0.0083 & & -0.14 & & & -0.0088 & 0.0097 & -0.011 &
\end{bmatrix}
$$

the floated matrix is

$$\tilde{L}_{m \to n}$$

$$
\begin{bmatrix}
0.21 & 0.17 & 0.19 & 0.021 & 0.15 & -0.16 & 0.18 & 0.026 & -0.03 & -0.22 \\
-0.027 & 0.0018 & -0.024 & 0.03 & -0.0083 & 0.02 & 0.0013 & -0.0021 & 0.0017 & -0.0016 \\
-0.01 & -0.0083 & 0.0013 & -0.14 & -0.012 & -0.0016 & -0.0088 & 0.0097 & -0.011 & -0.0023
\end{bmatrix}.
$$

In this representation:

- Column operations (variable node to check node step) are easy: just work down the column.

- Row operations (check node to variable node step) requires more care. An array na is introduced with an integer value for each column n. This denotes the "number of elements above" the element being indexed that have been used in previous computations. As the elements in a column are used, the row index skips down to row na[n]. The counter is incremented as it is used:

```
// Check node to variable node computation
for(m = 0; m < M; m++) {  // for each check
   // work over nonzero elements of this row
   for(l = 0; l < Nmlen[m]; l++) {
      n = Nm[m][l];
      tanhstuff[l] = tanh(Lntom[na[n]][n]/2);
   }
   // compute leave-one-out products on tanh stuff
   forbackprobs(tanhstuff,Nmlen[m],poutprobsLL);
   for(l = 0; l < Nmlen[m]; l++) { // for each n on this row
      n = Nm[m][l];
      Lmton[n][na[n]++] = 2*atanh(poutprobsLL[l]);
//                   ^
// Note the increment
   }
}
```

15.4.3 Variations on Decoding Algorithms: The Min-Sum Decoder

The complexity of the check node to variable node computation, with its $\boxplus$ operations, has motivated several variations in an attempt to reduce computational complexity. (By contrast, the variable node to check node computation, being only additions, remain unchanged in these lower-complexity variations.)

15.4.3.1 The $\boxplus$ Operation and the $\phi(x)$ Function

In this section, we introduce the function $\phi(x)$, which provides yet another representation of the $\boxplus$ operation. This will be instrumental in several of the variations on the decoding algorithm. We consider the $\boxplus$ operator for two messages, L_1 and L_2:

$$L_1 \boxplus L_2 = 2\tanh^{-1}(\tanh(L_1/2)\tanh(L_2/2)).$$

Noting that tanh and $\tanh^{-1}$ are odd functions, for any real x,

$$\tanh(x) = \text{sign}(x)\tanh(|x|) \quad \text{and} \quad \tanh^{-1}(x) = \text{sign}(x)\tanh^{-1}(|x|).$$

This observation motivates representing L_1 and L_2 in terms of sign and magnitude,

$$L_1 = \alpha_1\beta_1 \quad L_2 = \alpha_2\beta_2,$$

where

$$\alpha_i = \text{sign}(L_i) \quad \beta_i = |L_i|, \quad i = 1, 2.$$

Using the odd symmetry of the functions, we can now write

$$L_1 \boxplus L_2 = \alpha_1\alpha_2 2\tanh^{-1}(\tanh(\beta_1/2)\tanh(\beta_2/2)).$$

Now interpose the composed functions $\log^{-1}(\log(\cdot))$ (where $\log^{-1}(x)$ is just an alias of e^x). Then

$$L_1 \boxplus L_2 = (\alpha_1\alpha_2)2\tanh^{-1}\log^{-1}(\log(\tanh(\beta_1/2)\tanh(\beta_2/2)))$$

$$= (\alpha_1\alpha_2)2\tanh^{-1}\log^{-1}(\log(\tanh(\beta_1/2)) + \log(\tanh(\beta_2/2))). \qquad (15.16)$$

Define the function

$$\phi(x) = -\log(\tanh(x/2)) = \log\frac{e^x + 1}{e^x - 1}.$$

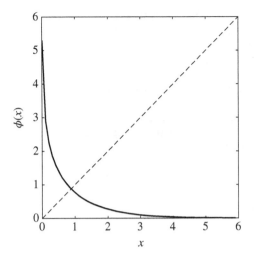

Figure 15.10: The function $\phi(x)$.

This function is plotted in figure 15.10. Since the function is symmetric across the line, $y = x$, $\phi(x)$ is its own inverse:

$$\phi(\phi(x)) = x$$

so that

$$\phi(x) = \phi^{-1}(x) = 2\tanh^{-1}(\log^{-1}(-x)).$$

Substituting these expressions for $\phi(x)$ in (15.16), we obtain

$$L_1 \boxplus L_2 = (\alpha_1 \alpha_2)\phi(\phi(\beta_1) + \phi(\beta_2)). \tag{15.17}$$

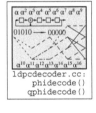

ldpcdecoder.cc:
  phidecode()
  qphidecode()

If the ϕ function is able to be rapidly evaluated (such as by table lookup), this reduces the $\boxplus$ operation to table lookups, addition, another table lookup, and keeping track of signs (which can be done using bit arithmetic). This thus has reduced complexity compared to computing the $\boxplus$ operator using log, tanh, and $\tanh^{-1}$ function, at the expense of storing the table for $\phi(x)$.

Additional simplifications are possible. Since the $\phi(x)$ is rapidly decreasing with x, in the sum $\phi(\beta_1) + \phi(\beta_2)$, the term with the smallest value of β_i will be the largest and may largely dominate the sum, so that

$$\phi(\beta_1) + \phi(\beta_2) \approx \phi(\min(\beta_1, \beta_2)).$$

Using this approximation in (15.17),

$$L_1 \boxplus L_2 \approx (\alpha_1 \alpha_2)\phi(\phi(\min(\beta_1, \beta_2))) = \alpha_1 \alpha_2 \min(\beta_1, \beta_2).$$

That is, the $\boxplus$ operation can be approximated by the message L_i having the least reliability, $\min(|L_1|, |L_2|)$. Recalling that the $\boxplus$ operation provides information about the parity of bits represented by L_1 and L_2, this makes sense: the less certainty there is about the value of a bit in a parity computation, the less certainty there can be in the information about the parity.

This insight is now applied to the message $L_{m \to n}$. Each of the messages $L_{n' \to m}$, $n' \in \mathcal{N}(m)$, is represented in sign/magnitude form using

$$\alpha_{n'm} = \text{sign}(L_{n' \to m}) \quad \text{and} \quad \beta_{n'm} = |L_{n' \to m}|.$$

Then (using sums and products over n' as an abbreviation for $n' \in \mathcal{N}(m) - \{n\}$), and using the notations above,

$$
\begin{aligned}
L_{m \to n} &= \left(\prod_{n'} a_{n'm} \right) 2\tanh^{-1}\log^{-1}\left(\sum_{n'} \log\tanh(\beta_{n'm}/2) \right) \\
&= \left(\prod_{n'} a_{n'm} \right) \phi\left(\sum_{n'} \phi(\beta_{n'm}) \right).
\end{aligned} \tag{15.18}
$$

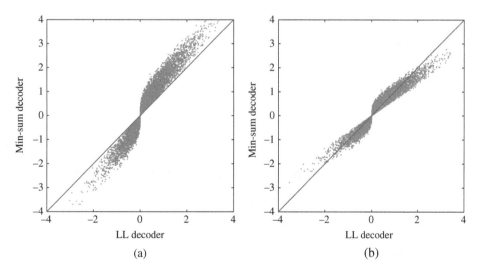

Now approximating the sum as above,

$$
\sum_{n'} \phi(\beta_{n'm}) \approx \min_{n'} \phi(\beta_{n'm}),
$$

we obtain the **min-sum** decoder rule:

$$
L_{m \to n, \text{min sum}} = \left(\prod_{n'} \alpha_{n'm} \right) \phi(\phi(\min_{n'} \beta_{n'm})) = \left(\prod_{n'} \alpha_{n'm} \right) \min_{n'} \beta_{n'm}. \tag{15.19}
$$

When this formulation is used, the decoder is called a *min-sum* decoder: it computes a *min* at the check nodes and *sum* at the variable nodes.

15.4.3.2 Attenuated and Offset Min-Sum Decoders

Figure 15.11(a) shows a scatter plot of message $L_{m \to n}$ computed using (15.6) compared with using (15.19). As the figure shows, the min-sum decoder message tends to overestimate its values compared with the LL decoder. The approximation can be improved by scaling back the values using

$$
L_{m \to n, \text{min sum scaled}} = \left(\prod_{n'} \alpha_{n'm} \right) \phi(\phi(\min_{n'} \beta_{n'm})) = \left(\prod_{n'} \alpha_{n'm} \right) c_{\text{scale}} \min_{n'} \beta_{n'm},
$$

where c_{scale} is a number less than 1. It may be found, for example, by generating Q messages (e.g., $Q \approx 10{,}000$), denoted here as $L_{m \to n}(i)$ and $L_{m \to n, \text{min sum scaled}}(i)$ for message numbers $i = 1, 2, \dots, Q$ by

Figure 15.11: Comparison between LL-based computing and min-sum computing for check to variable node computation. (a) Original comparison; (b) scaled comparison.

decoding typically using the all-0 codeword and choosing c_{scale} to minimize

$$\sum_{i=1}^{q} (L_{m \to n}(i) - L_{m \to n, \text{min sum scaled}}(i))^2,$$

which leads to

$$c_{scale} = \frac{\sum_{i=1}^{Q} L_{m \to n}(i) L_{m \to n, \text{min sum scaled}}(i)}{\sum_{i=1}^{Q} L_{m \to n, \text{min sum scaled}}(i)^2}.$$

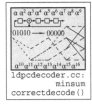

Figure 15.11(b) shows the scatterplot comparison after scaling, where $c_{scale} = 0.6248$ when the signal-to-noise ratio is $1\,\text{dB}$. In hardware implementations, c_{scale} may be set to 0.5 to make the multiplication simpler.

    Another way to modify the min-sum decoder is to subtract an offset c_{offset} from each message, while imposing the constraint that the message must be nonnegative. This results in the message

$$L_{m \to n, \text{min sum, offset}}$$

$$= \left(\prod_{n'} \alpha_{n'm}\right) \phi(\phi(\min_{n'} \beta_{n'm})) = \left(\prod_{n'} \alpha_{n'm}\right) \max[\min_{n'} \beta_{n'm} - c_{offset}, 0].$$

15.4.4   Variations on Decoding Algorithms: Min-Sum with Correction

The min-sum decoder loses performance compared to the sum-product algorithm. In this section, we consider better approximations to the $\boxplus$ operator which still have low computational difficulty. Define the function

$$\max^*(x, y) = \log(e^x + e^y).$$

Consider this function when $x > y$:

$$\max^*(x, y) = \log(e^x(1 + e^{y-x})) = x + \log(1 + e^{y-x}).$$

As x increases (compared to y), this becomes closer and closer to x. Similarly, if $y > x$, $\max^*(x, y) = y + \log(1 + e^{x-y})$. In either case, we have that

$$\max^*(x, y) \approx \max(x, y).$$

The exact value can be seen to be

$$\max^*(x, y) = \max(x, y) + \log(1 + e^{-|x-y|}). \tag{15.20}$$

We now consider expressing the $\boxplus$ operation in terms of the $\max^*$ function and related functions. From (15.4),

$$L_1 \boxplus L_2 = \log(1 + e^{L_1 + L_2}) - \log(e^{L_1} + e^{L_2})$$
$$= \max^*(0, L_1 + L_2) - \max^*(L_1, L_2).$$

Using (15.20), it follows that

$$L_1 \boxplus L_2 = \max(0, L_1 + L_2) - \max(L_1, L_2) + s(L_1, L_2), \tag{15.21}$$

where $s(x, y)$ is a correction term,

$$s(x, y) = \log(1 + e^{-|x+y|}) - \log(1 + e^{-|x-y|}).$$

Observe that $s(x, y)$ is odd in both its arguments, so that

$$s(x, y) = \text{sign}(x)\text{sign}(y)s(|x|, |y|).$$

By checking the various cases (such as $L_2 > 0, L_1 > L_2$; $L_1 > 0, L_2 > 0$; $L_1 < 0, L_2 < L_1$; etc.), it is straightforward to show that

$$\max(0, L_1 + L_2) - \max(L_1, L_2) = \text{sign}(L_1)\text{sign}(L_2)\min(|L_1|, |L_2|).$$

Using these facts in (15.21), we obtain

$$L_1 \boxplus L_2 = \text{sign}(L_1)\text{sign}(L_2)\min(|L_1|, |L_2|) + s(L_1, L_2)$$
$$= \text{sign}(L_1)\text{sign}(L_2)[\min(|L_1|, |L_2|) + s(|L_1|, |L_2|)]$$

This is an exact expression, but would require computing $s(x, y)$, which is no easier than computing the $\boxplus$ function so an approximation is desirable. Figure 15.12(a) shows a plot of $s(x, y)$. There is a cross-shaped ridge region where $s(x, y)$ takes its highest values, from which it slopes down. Figure 15.12(b) shows an approximation $\tilde{s}(x, y)$, with the same qualitative features, where

$$\tilde{s}(x, y) = \begin{cases} c & \text{if } |x+y| < 2 \text{ and } |x-y| > 2|x+y| \\ -c & \text{if } |x-y| < 2 \text{ and } |x+y| > 2|x-y| \\ 0 & \text{otherwise.} \end{cases}$$

In this representation, $c = 0.5$. In this computation, the numbers involved are powers of 2, so that multiplications can be performed using simple bit shift operations. The output is quantized to only two nonzero values, with the range determined by a simple computation. Figure 15.12(c) shows the function $L_1 \boxplus L_2$ computed using the exact $s(x, y)$, and 15.12(d) shows the approximation computed using the approximation $\tilde{s}(x, y)$. These plots show that the same qualitative shape is obtained in the approximation, but with some effects of quantization.

15.4.4.1 Approximate min* Decoder

Another complexity-reducing computation at the check nodes is called the approximate min* decoder, or a-min* decoder. It is based on the following idea. Suppose that a check node is connected to w_c variable nodes. To compute a single message $L_{m \to n}$ (15.6) requires $(w_c - 1)$ $\boxplus$ operations. Sending a separate message to each of the w_c neighbors requires $w_c(w_c - 1)$ $\boxplus$ operations. (The forward/backward computation does not reduce this.) The a-min* decoder provides a method in which only w_c $\boxplus$ operations are needed at each check node.

```
ldpcdecoder.cc:
aminstardecode()
```

Recall from Section 15.4.3.1 that the smallest reliability has the dominant effect on the $\boxplus$ operation. That is, larger reliabilities have a less significant effect on the $\boxplus$ operation than smaller reliabilities.

Let

$$n_{\min} = \arg \min_{n' \in \mathcal{N}(m)-\{n\}} |L_{n' \to m}|$$

denote the variable node with smallest reliability. The message sent to variable node $n_{\min}$ is the usual one:

$$L_{m \to n_{\min}} = \boxplus_{n' \in \mathcal{N}(m)-\{n_{\min}\}} L_{n' \to m}$$

($w_c - 2$ $\boxplus$ operations). The message sent to the other variable nodes is the $\boxplus$ of all incoming messages (adjusted for their sign).

$$L_{m \to n}(\text{approximate}) = \left(\prod_{n' \in \mathcal{N}(m)-\{n\}} \alpha_{n'm} \right) \left| \boxplus_{n' \in \mathcal{N}(m)} L_{n' \to m} \right|$$

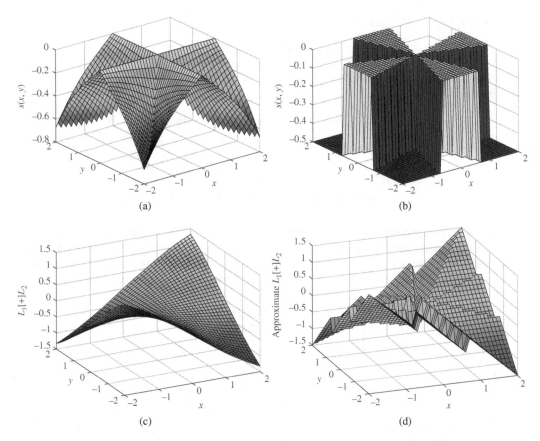

Figure 15.12: $s(x,y)$, the approximation $\tilde{s}(x,y)$, $L_1 \boxplus L_2$, and the approximation using $\tilde{s}(x,y)$. (a) $s(x,y)$; (b) $\tilde{s}(x,y)$; (c) exact $L_1 \boxplus L_2$; (d) approximate $L_1 \boxplus L_2$.

The $\boxplus$ in this case is computed over all variable nodes in $\mathcal{N}(m)$ – the leave-one-out computation is not done. This is not the correct message, since the message $L_{m\to n}$ should not include the message $L_{n\to m}$. But since $L_{n\to m}$ is not the smallest (and therefore most significant) message that might be included, the effect of the error is generally small. Since $L_{m\to n}$(approximate) can be computed as

$$|L_{m\to n}(\text{approximate})| = |L_{m\to n_{\min}} \boxplus L_{n_{\min}\to m}|,$$

the message sent to all other (non-minimum) nodes can be computed using just a single addition $\boxplus$ operation.

The computations can also be organized in an efficient way which does not require finding the $n_{\min}$ first. To explain this, note first that ∞ is an identity for the $\boxplus$ operation: $\infty \boxplus x = x$. As an example of this, $\infty \boxplus \infty = \infty$. (In code, some indicator of the ∞ concept has to be represented.) This is used in association with the initialization of the routine. In the implementation of the a-min* algorithm, $\boxplus$ operations are computed as the algorithm proceeds. When a message with smaller reliability than any previously seen is encountered (which might not yet be the smallest), it is saved. If it turns out not to be the smallest, then it is $\boxplus$-ed in at the next iteration. If a message does not have smaller reliability than any encountered previously, it is immediately $\boxplus$-ed in.

Algorithm 15.3 a-Min* Algorithm for Check Node Computation

Function `a-min*` (m, $\{L_{n \to m}\}$)
% a-min* operation at a check node;

1   **Inputs:** m = this check node index; $L_{n \to m}$ =messages from adjacent variable nodes. **Outputs:** $\{L_{m \to n}\}$: messages from this check node to adjacent variable nodes.

3   **Initialize:** $|L_{n_{\min} \to m}| = \infty, |L_{m \to n_{\min}}| = \infty, s = 1$

4   **for** $n \in \mathcal{N}(m)$ **do**   % for each neighboring variable node

5       $s = s \cdot \text{sign}(L_{n \to m})$ % accumulate all signs

6   **if** $|L_{n \to m}| < |L_{n_{\min} \to m}|$ **then**   % New smallest incoming message found

7          $|L_{m \to n_{\min}}| = |L_{m \to n_{\min}}| \boxplus |L_{n_{\min} \to m}|$ % $\boxplus$ thesaved message (not the min)

8          $n_{\min} = n$ % Save index of least reliable message found so far

9          $|L_{n_{\min} \to m}| = |L_{n \to m}|$ % save this least reliable so far

      end

10   **else**

11         $|L_{m \to n_{\min}}| = |L_{m \to n_{\min}}| \boxplus |L_{n \to m}|$ % Not min: $\boxplus$ this message immediately

      end

   end

12    $|L_{m \to *}| = |L_{m \to n_{\min}}| \boxplus |L_{n_{\min} \to m}|$ % $\boxplus$ all the messages for message to all other nodes

13   **for** $n \in \mathcal{N}(m)$ **do**   % for each neighboring variable node

14   **if** $n = n_{\min}$ **then**

15         $L_{m \to n} = s \cdot \text{sign}(L_{n \to m}) \cdot |L_{n \to n_{\min}}|$ % message to leastreliable node

      end

16   **else**

17         $L_{m \to n} = s \cdot \text{sign}(L_{n \to m}) \cdot |L_{m \to *}|$ % message to all other nodes

      end

   end

ldpcdecoder.cc:
rcbpdecode()

15.4.4.2 The Reduced Complexity Box-Plus Decoder

Another quantization of the check node computation is provided by the reduced complexity box-plus (RCBP) decoder. The basic check node computation is operating on incoming messages a and b is

$$\text{chk}(a, b) = a \boxplus b = 2 \tanh^{-1}(\tanh(a/2) \tanh(b/2)).$$

If 6-bit quantization is used, integer values of in the range -32 to 31 are obtained. If a quantization interval of $\Delta = 0.5$ is used (which is convenient as it can be represented with a bit shift) message values a or b are in the range -16 to 15.75.

We have seen that the sign information can be factored out,

$$a \boxplus b = \text{sign}(a)\text{sign}(b)2 \tanh^{-1}(\tanh(|a|/2) \tanh(|b|/2)).$$

Leaving out the sign bit, the remaining 5 bits of the integer range is 0 to 31, corresponding to values from 0 to 15.5.

Let r and c be integer indices used to look up values in a lookup table T representing the $\boxplus$ operator for positive operands. Let Δ be a quantization step size, and define the table as

$$T(r, c) = |\text{quantize}(\text{chk}(r\Delta + \Delta/2, c\Delta + \Delta/2))|.$$

The "quantize" operation may be performed (for example) by dividing by Δ and rounding down. A step size of $\Delta = 0.5$ has been found to give good performance. The 32×32 table can be further reduced using some properties of the $\boxplus$ function. In the first place, it is clear that $a \boxplus b) = b \boxplus a$, so the lookup table satisfies the same symmetry $T(r,c) = T(c,r)$. Also the table is monotonic nondecreasing, so that if $r' > r$ then $T(r',c) \geq T(r,c)$. Also, the $\boxplus$ function is continuous, so that its quantized version in T increases by unit steps where it increases.

Example 15.12 As an example of the computation, consider a 6×6 table with $\Delta = 1.33$, whose values (after dividing by Δ and truncating) are in the table below

$$T = \begin{bmatrix} 0 & 0 & 0 & 0 & 0 & 0 \\ 0 & 0 & 1 & 1 & 1 & 1 \\ 0 & 1 & 1 & 2 & 2 & 2 \\ 0 & 1 & 2 & 2 & 3 & 3 \\ 0 & 1 & 2 & 3 & 3 & 4 \\ 0 & 1 & 2 & 3 & 4 & 4 \end{bmatrix}$$

Observe that in the first column, there is only one value; in the second column, there is one transition; in the third column, there are two transitions; in the fourth column, there are three transitions, etc. As the column number increases, the number of changes is nondecreasing. □

For efficiency of storage, the information in T may be represented using a run-length coding down each column, starting from the diagonal element (since the table is symmetric). The run-length coding for column c is stored in a list of information called $\mathbf{v}_c$. The first element in the list is the value $T(c,c)$. The next element is the number of times that element is repeated (including the diagonal). If there are more elements down the column, then the number of times it is repeated is appended to the list. (There is no need to indicate what the number is, because it will always be exactly one more than the previous number.)

Example 15.13 For the T matrix above, the column information is as follows:

$$\mathbf{v}_0 = (0, 6)$$
$$\mathbf{v}_1 = (0, 1, 4)$$
$$\mathbf{v}_2 = (1, 1, 3)$$
$$\mathbf{v}_3 = (2, 1, 2)$$
$$\mathbf{v}_4 = (3, 1, 1)$$
$$\mathbf{v}_5 = (4, 1).$$

□

Since the number of transitions in a column (generally) increases with column number, but since later columns start further down the column (since they start on the diagonal), this results in an efficient representation.

For a full quantizer with a table of size 32×32, the column information is

$$\mathbf{v}_0 = (0, 32)$$
$$\mathbf{v}_1 = (0, 2, 29)$$
$$\mathbf{v}_c = (c-1, 3, 29-c), \quad 2 \leq 2 \leq 29$$
$$\mathbf{v}_c = (c-1, 2 - \delta(c-31)), \quad 30 \leq c \leq 31.$$

Here, $\delta(\cdot)$ is the Kronecker δ function. The structure makes it possible to represent the table with simple if statements. Assuming that $r \geq c$ (that is, representing the lower half of the table) with $d = r - c$, the logic can be expressed as follows:

$$c = 0 : \quad T(r,c) = 0$$

$$c = 1 : \quad T(r,c) = \begin{cases} 0 & \text{if } d = 0 \text{ or } 1 \\ 1 & \text{if } d > 1 \end{cases}$$

$$c = 2, \dots, 29 : \quad T(r,c) = \begin{cases} c-1 & \text{if } d = 0 \text{ or } 1 \text{ or } 2 \\ c & d > 2 \end{cases}$$

$$c = 30 : \quad T(r,c) = 29$$

$$c = 31 : \quad T(r,c) = 30.$$

This logic can be summarized as follows in a way amenable to implementation in digital logic.

Algorithm 15.4 Quantize the chk Function

Function T (r,c) % Quantize the $\boxplus$ function
Enforce: $r > c$
Output: $T(r,c)$
$d = r - c;$
if $c > 1$ **then**
    $T = (c-1) + (d > 2);$
end
else % $c = 0$ or $c = 1$
    $T = (d > 1) \cdot (c == 1);$
end

The quantized $\boxplus$ operation can be computed as follows:

$$a \boxplus b \approx \Delta[T(\text{floor}(a/\Delta), \text{floor}(b/\Delta))] + \Delta/2.$$

The performance of the quantized $\boxplus$ operation is compared with $\boxplus$ in figure 15.13 for different values of c, along with the percent error. The overall percent error across all different values of c is 2.64%.

An efficient decoding can be obtained using the logic of the a-min* decoder but replacing the $\boxplus$ computation with the quantized $\boxplus$ operation.

showchktable.m

15.4.4.3 The Richardson–Novichkov Decoder

The Richardson–Novichkov decoder provides another approximation to the ϕ function in the check node decoder computation in (15.18) based on integer representations. The magnitude of the check node message is

$$|L_{m \to n}| = \phi\left(\sum_{n' \in \mathcal{N}(m) - \{n\}} \phi(\beta_{n'm}) \right),$$

where β is a real number (such as a message $|L_{n' \to m}|$) and where

$$\phi(\beta) = \log\left(\frac{e^\beta + 1}{e^\beta - 1} \right).$$

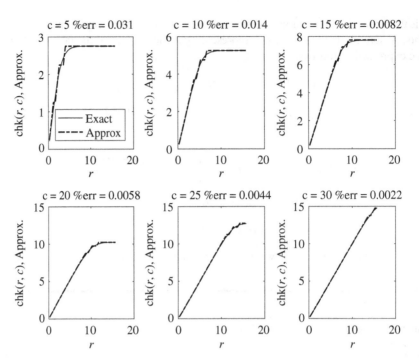

Figure 15.13: Comparison of ⊞ and its RCBP quantization.

For large β, $\log(1 \pm e^{-\beta}) \approx \pm e^{-\beta}$, so

$$\phi(\beta) \approx 2e^{-\beta}.$$

This approximation is shown (along with the exact $\phi(\beta)$ function) in figure 15.14. As is clear from the figure, the approximation is fairly accurate for $\beta > 2 \approx 2$. Since $\phi(\beta)$ is its own inverse, another approximation to $\phi(\beta)$, denoted as $\hat{\phi}^{-1}$ is

$$\hat{\phi}^{-1}(\beta) = -\ln(\beta/2),$$

which is accurate for $\beta < \ln 2$.

    Now another approximation is introduced which uses integer values. Let δ be a scale factor (as discussed below) and let b be an integer such that $\beta = \delta b$ (approximately). The integer b will represent the value of β. Define the function

$$\phi_\delta(b) = \log\left(\frac{1 + e^{-\delta b}}{1 - e^{-\delta b}}\right).$$

Using the approximation from above, write

$$\hat{\phi}_\delta(b) = 2e^{-\delta b} \quad \text{and} \quad \hat{\phi}_\delta^{-1}(b) = -\frac{1}{\delta}\ln(b/2). \qquad (15.22)$$

Using the particular value $\delta = \ln(2)$, the latter can be expressed as

$$\hat{\phi}_\delta^{-1}(b) = -\log_2(b/2). \qquad (15.23)$$

    The check node message is now expressed in terms of ϕ_δ and its approximations. Let $b_{n'm}$ denote the integerized representation of $\beta_{n'm}$. Then using (15.22) and (15.23), the check node message can be

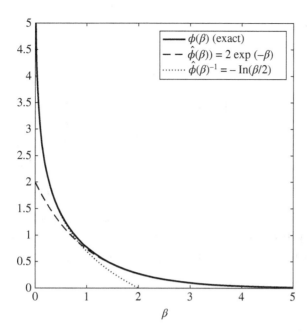

Figure 15.14: Approximations to the $\phi(\beta)$ function for the Richardson–Novichkov decoder.

written

$$|L_{m\to n}| \approx \phi_\delta^{-1}\left(\sum_{n\in\mathcal{N}(m)-\{n\}} \phi_\delta(b_{n'm})\right)$$

$$\approx -\log_2\left(\sum_{n\in\mathcal{N}(m)-\{n\}} \exp(-\delta b_{n'm})\right)$$

$$= -\log_2\left(\sum_{n\in\mathcal{N}(m)-\{n\}} \exp(-\ln(2)b_{n'm})\right)$$

$$= -\log_2\left(\sum_{n\in\mathcal{N}(m)-\{n\}} 2^{-b_{n'm}}\right).$$

The inner part of the computation $2^{-b_{n'm}}$ can be achieved using bit shift operations.

To compensate for the approximations, the algorithm can be tuned by introducing constants C_1 and C_2, and expressly noting that integer values are used. Let $[\cdot]$ denote the integer part of its argument. Then the integer message is expressed as

$$|L_{m\to n}| = C_1 - \left[\log_2\left(\sum_{n\in\mathcal{N}(m)-\{n\}} 2^{-b_{n'm}} + C_2\right)\right].$$

Further detail is provided in [371].

15.4.5 Hard-Decision Decoding

The decoders above are soft-decision decoders. But there are instances where a hard-decision decoder is of interest, such as in very high-speed communications that can afford to lose some of the error-correction capability of the code, or when the channel is well-modeled as a BSC. We present in this section several approaches to hard-decision decoding.

15.4.5.1 Bit Flipping

We illustrate the notion of bit flipping with an example.

Let

$$H = \begin{bmatrix} 1 & 1 & 1 & 0 & 0 & 1 & 1 & 0 & 0 & 1 \\ 1 & 0 & 1 & 0 & 1 & 1 & 0 & 1 & 1 & 0 \\ 0 & 0 & 1 & 1 & 1 & 0 & 1 & 0 & 1 & 1 \\ 0 & 1 & 0 & 1 & 1 & 1 & 0 & 1 & 0 & 1 \\ 1 & 1 & 0 & 1 & 0 & 0 & 1 & 1 & 1 & 0 \end{bmatrix}$$

be a parity check matrix and let $\mathbf{r} = \begin{bmatrix} 0 & 1 & 0 & 1 & 0 & 1 & 0 & 1 & 0 & 1 \end{bmatrix}$ be a received vector (over a BSC). The syndrome is

$$\mathbf{s} = \mathbf{r}H^T = \begin{bmatrix} 1 & 0 & 0 & 1 & 1 \end{bmatrix} \quad \text{(computations in } GF(2)\text{)}.$$

There are three parity conditions (rows of H) which are not satisfied. Now consider for each bit the number of unsatisfied parity checks it is involved in:

bit 1: 2 checks (1st and 5th)   bit 2: 3 checks (1st, 4th, and 5th)

bit 3: 1 check (1st)   bit 4: 2 checks (4th and 5th)   etc.

Summarizing, we get the following number of unsatisfied checks for the received bits:

Number of unsatisfied checks for each bit: $\begin{bmatrix} 2 & 3 & 1 & 2 & 1 & 2 & 2 & 2 & 1 & 2 \end{bmatrix}$.

Note that this list can be obtained by interpreting $\mathbf{s}$ as a vector in $\mathbb{Z}$ (integers) and computing $\mathbf{s}H^T$, now doing the arithmetic over the integers. From this list, the second bit is involved in the most unsatisfied checks. Flip the second bit to produce the modified received vector:

$$\hat{\mathbf{r}} = \begin{bmatrix} 0 & 0 & 0 & 1 & 0 & 1 & 0 & 1 & 0 & 1 \end{bmatrix}.$$

```
ldpcdecoder.c:
bitflip1decode()
```

Compute the syndrome again:

$$\mathbf{s} = \hat{\mathbf{r}}H^T \bmod 2 = \begin{bmatrix} 0 & 0 & 0 & 0 & 0 \end{bmatrix}.$$

In this case, a codeword is obtained.

In general, in bit flipping, decoding syndromes are computed, and the number of unsatisfied checks that each bit is involved in is computed. For bits involved in too many checks, flip the bit. Then repeat.

The computations are detailed as follows using both matrix notation and the notation of the data structures associated with the parity check matrix. For an input binary vector $\mathbf{r}$:

Algorithm 15.5 Bit Flipping Decoder

---

1. Set $\hat{\mathbf{r}} = \mathbf{r}$.

2. Compute the syndrome $\mathbf{s} = \hat{\mathbf{r}}H^T$, computations in $GF(2)$.
   That is, for $m = 1, 2, \ldots, M$ compute

   $$s_m = \bigoplus_{n \in \mathcal{N}(m)} r_n \quad \text{(modulo 2 addition)}$$

   If $\mathbf{s} = \mathbf{0}$, stop.

3. Compute $\mathbf{f} = \mathbf{s}H$, computations in $\mathbb{Z}$. That is, for $n = 1, 2, \ldots, N$ compute

   $$f_n = \sum_{m \in \mathcal{M}(m)} s_m \quad \text{(integer addition)}$$

   This computes the number of unsatisfied checks that each bit is involved in.

4. For those elements of $\mathbf{f}$ greater than some threshold, flip the corresponding bits in $\hat{\mathbf{r}}$. (As a variation on this step, flip the bits involved in the largest number of unsatisfied checks.)

5. Repeat from step 2 (up to some number of times).

15.4.5.2 Gallager's Algorithms A and B

Another hard decoding algorithm is Gallager's Algorithm A. Let the channel be a BSC(p_0). Let $y_n \in \{0, 1\}$ denote the channel input. Decoding is as follows:

```
ldpcdecoder.c:
galAbitflipdecode()
```

Algorithm 15.6 Gallager Algorithm A Bit Flipping Decoder

Initialization Elements in the initial matrix $B_{n \to m}$ corresponding to nonzero elements in the parity check matrix are set to y_n. That is, for each $n = 0, 1, \dots, N - 1$,

$$B_{n \to m} = y_n \text{ for } m \in \mathcal{M}(n)$$

Check Node to Variable Node: The message $B_{m \to n}$ is the parity of the adjacent variable (bit) nodes, except the node the parity is being sent to, in the usual leave-one-out fashion:

$$B_{m \to n} = \bigoplus_{n' \in \mathcal{N}(m) - \{n\}} B_{n' \to m} \quad \text{(modulo 2 addition)}$$

Variable Node Computation: Set $B_{n \to m} = y_n$ (the channel input bits) unless all of the incoming messages $B_{m' \to n}$ disagree with y_n. That is,

$$B_{n \to m} = \begin{cases} y_n & \text{if } \exists m' \in \mathcal{M}(n) - m \text{ such that } B_{m' \to n} = y_n \\ 1 - y_n & \text{otherwise (that is, all the } B_{m' \to n} \text{ disagree with } y_n) \end{cases}$$

Decoding Decision The decision about the bit c_n is based on $B_{n \to m}$. If $|\mathcal{M}(n)|$ is even, then $\hat{c}_n = 1$ if the majority of the bits in the set

$$\{B_{n \to m} : m \in \mathcal{M}(n)\} \cup \{y_n\}$$

are equal to 1.
If $|\mathcal{M}(n)|$ is odd, then $\hat{c}_n = 1$ if the majority of the bits in the set $\{B_{n \to m} : m \in \mathcal{M}(n)\}$ are equal to 1.

Gallager's Algorithm B is similar to Algorithm A. The check node computation is identical. At the variable node, if among the messages $B_{m \to n}$ there are at least b values that disagree with y_n, then the message $B_{n \to m}$ is set to $1 - y_n$. Otherwise, $B_{n \to m} = y_n$. (Gallager Algorithm A is the same as Gallager Algorithm B with $b = 1$.) Gallager showed that for a regular (w_c, w_v) code, the optimum value of b is the smallest integer b such that

$$\frac{1 - p_0}{p_0} \leq \left[\frac{1 + (1 - 2p)^{w_c - 1}}{1 - (1 - 2p)^{w_c - 1}} \right]^{2b - d_v + 1},$$

where p_0 is the crossover probability for the BSC and p is the message error rate. It has been shown [15, p. 21, Chapter 3] that Gallager Algorithm B is the best possible binary message-passing algorithm for regular LDPC codes.

Example 15.14 For the parity check matrix from (15.1), let the received data be

$$\mathbf{y} = \begin{bmatrix} 0 & 1 & 0 & 1 & 0 & 1 & 0 & 1 & 0 & 1 \end{bmatrix}.$$

The initial $B_{n \to m}$ is

$$B_{n \to m} = \begin{bmatrix} \underline{0} & \underline{1} & 0 & 0 & 0 & \underline{1} & 0 & 0 & 0 & \underline{1} \\ 0 & 0 & \underline{0} & 0 & \underline{0} & \underline{1} & 0 & \underline{1} & \underline{0} & 0 \\ 0 & 0 & \underline{0} & \underline{1} & 0 & 0 & 0 & 0 & 0 & \underline{1} \\ 0 & \underline{1} & 0 & \underline{1} & \underline{0} & \underline{1} & 0 & \underline{1} & 0 & \underline{1} \\ \underline{0} & \underline{1} & 0 & \underline{1} & 0 & 0 & \underline{0} & \underline{1} & \underline{0} & 0 \end{bmatrix}.$$

(Underlined elements correspond to nonzero elements in the parity check matrix.) The message $B_{m \to n}$ is

$$
B_{m \to n} = \begin{bmatrix}
\underline{1} & 0 & \underline{1} & 0 & 0 & \underline{0} & \underline{1} & 0 & 0 & \underline{0} \\
0 & 0 & \underline{0} & 0 & \underline{0} & \underline{1} & 0 & \underline{1} & \underline{0} & 0 \\
0 & 0 & \underline{0} & \underline{1} & 0 & 0 & \underline{0} & 0 & 0 & \underline{1} \\
0 & \underline{0} & 0 & \underline{0} & \underline{1} & \underline{0} & 0 & \underline{0} & \underline{0} & 0 \\
\underline{1} & 0 & 0 & \underline{0} & 0 & 0 & \underline{1} & 0 & \underline{1} & 0
\end{bmatrix}.
$$

The message $B_{n \to m}$ is

$$
B_{n \to m} = \begin{bmatrix}
\underline{0} & \underline{0} & 0 & 0 & 0 & \underline{1} & 0 & 0 & 0 & \underline{1} \\
\underline{1} & 0 & \underline{0} & 0 & \underline{0} & \underline{0} & 0 & \underline{0} & 0 & 0 \\
0 & 0 & \underline{0} & \underline{0} & \underline{0} & 0 & \underline{1} & 0 & 0 & \underline{0} \\
0 & \underline{0} & 0 & \underline{1} & \underline{0} & \underline{1} & 0 & \underline{1} & \underline{0} & \underline{1} \\
\underline{0} & \underline{0} & 0 & \underline{1} & 0 & 0 & \underline{0} & \underline{1} & 0 & 0
\end{bmatrix}.
$$

The column sums (used to determine if a majority of messages are 1) are

$$
\begin{bmatrix} 1 & 0 & 0 & 2 & 0 & 2 & 1 & 2 & 0 & 2 \end{bmatrix}.
$$

Based on a majority (out of 3 values), the decoded values are

$$
\hat{\mathbf{c}} = \begin{bmatrix} 0 & 0 & 0 & 1 & 0 & 1 & 0 & 1 & 0 & 1 \end{bmatrix}.
$$

This is a codeword which satisfies all parities, so decoding is done.   □

15.4.5.3   Weighted Bit Flipping

Let $\mathbf{c} \in \{0, 1\}^N$ denote a codeword, and let $\tilde{\mathbf{c}} \in \{-1, 1\}^N$ denote the bits of the codeword represented as ± 1 values, $\tilde{c}_i = 1 - 2c_i$. Let the codeword be BPSK modulated and passed through an AWGN channel to produce $\mathbf{y} = \tilde{\mathbf{c}} + \mathbf{z}$, where $z_i \sim \mathcal{N}(0, \sigma^2)$. Some reliability of the received bit can be determined by $|y_n|$ — smaller values are less reliable.

In this ± 1 representation of bits, parity can be checked by multiplication. For example,

$$
\prod_{n \in \mathcal{M}(m)} \tilde{c}_n
$$

computes the parity associated with check m. When these bits satisfy the parity check, then this product is equal to 1.

Weighted bit flipping (WBF) deals with a function termed an *inversion function*, formed as follows. Let $\mathbf{x} = (x_1, \ldots, x_n) \in \{-1, 1\}^N$, and let

$$
\Delta_n^{(\text{WBF})}(\mathbf{x}) = \sum_{m \in \mathcal{M}(n)} \beta_m \prod_{n' \in \mathcal{N}(m)} x_{n'}.
$$

This is the weighted sum of all the parity products over all the parities that bit n is involved in. Here, β_m is the reliability, determined as the smallest absolute received value of the bits associated with check m:

$$
\beta_m = \min_{n' \in \mathcal{N}(m)} |y_{n'}|.
$$

The function $\Delta_n^{(\text{WBF})}(\mathbf{x})$ can be viewed as a measure of reliability of $\mathbf{x}$. Smaller values — due either to small β or to unsatisfied parities (resulting in the product being negative) — indicate less desirable bit configurations than large values.

A variation on this inversion function is used in modified weighted bit flipping algorithm (MWBF) which employs the received value as

$$\Delta_n^{(\text{MWBF})}(\mathbf{x}) = \alpha|y_n| + \sum_{m \in \mathcal{M}(n)} \beta_m \prod_{n' \in \mathcal{N}(m)} x_{n'}.$$

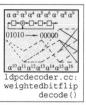

ldpcdecoder.cc:
weightedbitflip
decode()

Using either $\Delta^{(\text{WBF})}(\mathbf{x})$ or $\Delta^{(\text{MWBF})}(\mathbf{x})$, the bit flipping works by identifying the bit index n having smallest $\Delta_n(\mathbf{x})$ (indicative of the least unreliable bit). The decoding algorithm can be summarized as follows.

Algorithm 15.7 Weighted Bit Flipping Decoder

Step 1 Initialization (for BPSK over AWGN): For $n = 1, \ldots, N$, let $x_n = \text{sign}(y_n)$. (Quantize the received data to bit values). Let $\mathbf{x} = (x_1, \ldots, x_N)$.

Step 2 If all parities are satisfied, exit. That is: If $\prod_{n \in \mathcal{N}(m)} x_n = 1$ for $m = 1, \ldots, M$, then exit.

Step 3 Find the least reliable bit position: $\ell = \arg \min_{n \in [1,N]} \Delta_n(\mathbf{x})$. Flip the corresponding bit $x_\ell \to -x_\ell$.

Step 4 If the maximum number of iterations is not exceeded, goto step 2. Otherwise, return $\mathbf{x}$ and indicate decoding failure.

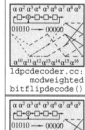

ldpcdecoder.cc:
modweighted
bitflipdecode()

ldpcdecoder.cc:
grad1bitflip
decode()

15.4.5.4 Gradient Descent Bit Flipping

Let the bits of a codeword be represented by $\mathbf{x} = (x_1, x_2, \ldots, x_N) \in \{+1, -1\}^N$. Assuming BPSK modulation, let the transmitted signal be

$$s_n = ax_n$$

ldpcdecoder.cc:
grad2bitflip
decode()

for some amplitude a. The signal received through an AWGN is

$$y_n = s_n + v_n$$

The likelihood function is

$$\exp\left[-\left(\sum_{n=1}^N (y_n - ax_n)^2\right)/2\sigma^2\right]$$

$$= \exp\left[-\left(\sum_{n=1}^N y_n^2\right)/2\sigma^2\right] \exp\left[-\left(\sum_{n=1}^N x_n y_n\right)/2\sigma^2\right] \exp\left[-a^2\left(\sum_{n=1}^N x_n^2\right)/2\sigma^2\right].$$

Taking a logarithm and neglecting noninformative terms, the term

$$\sum_{n=1}^N x_n y_n$$

may be regarded as the likelihood function. A codeword $\mathbf{x}$ is sought that maximizes this correlation.

To enforce the fact that $\mathbf{x}$ needs to be a codeword, consider the product

$$\prod_{n \in \mathcal{N}(m)} x_n$$

for $m = 1, \ldots, M$. This is equal to 1 when the bits satisfy the mth parity constraint.

For gradient descent bit flipping, we define an objective function combining both the likelihood consideration and the parity consideration,

$$f(\mathbf{x}) = \sum_{i=1}^N x_i y_i + \sum_{m=1}^M \prod_{n' \in \mathcal{N}(m)} x_{n'}. \tag{15.24}$$

The function $f(\mathbf{x})$ is maximized when the likelihood is maximized and when all the constraints are satisfied (the product is equal to 1). Thus, decoding can be posed as the problem

$$\hat{\mathbf{x}} = \arg \max_{\mathbf{x} \in \{-1,1\}^N} f(\mathbf{x}). \tag{15.25}$$

This may equivalently be expressed as a minimization problem

$$\hat{\mathbf{x}} = \arg \min_{\mathbf{x} \in \{-1,1\}^N} -f(\mathbf{x}). \tag{15.26}$$

Under the gradient-based bit flipping algorithms, the solution is approached using gradient-based information. It is natural to think of maximizing, as in (15.25), in which case the operation is gradient ascent. But the literature frequently refers to gradient *descent*, in which case the problem (15.26) is solved using gradient descent.

With the intent of doing maximization or minimization, the partial derivative of (15.24) is computed as

$$\frac{\partial}{\partial x_n} f(\mathbf{x}) = y_n + \sum_{m \in \mathcal{M}(n)} \prod_{n' \in \mathcal{N}(m) \setminus n} x_{n'}.$$

The product of x_n and this partial derivative is

$$x_n \frac{\partial}{\partial x_n} f(\mathbf{x}) = x_n y_n + \sum_{m \in \mathcal{M}(n)} \prod_{n' \in \mathcal{N}(m)} x_{n'}.$$

Let s be a small real number and consider the first-order Taylor expansion

$$f(x_1, \ldots, x_n + s, \ldots, x_N) \approx f(\mathbf{x}) + s \frac{\partial}{\partial x_n} f(\mathbf{x}).$$

It is desired to choose s to increase this function. When $\frac{\partial}{\partial x_n} f(\mathbf{x}) > 0$, s should be > 0. When $\frac{\partial}{\partial x_n} f(\mathbf{x}) < 0$, s should be < 0. In light of this, if $x_n \frac{\partial}{\partial x_n} f(\mathbf{x}) < 0$, then flipping x_n by setting $x_n \to -x_n$ is likely to increase the objective function. A reasonable way to determine which bit position n to flip is to choose the position at which the absolute value of the partial derivative is the largest. We formulate the function

$$\Delta_n^{(GD)}(\mathbf{x}) = x_n y_n + \sum_{m \in \mathcal{M}(n)} \prod_{n' \in \mathcal{N}(m)} x_{n'}.$$

ldpcdecoder.cc:
DC1decode()

15.4.6 Divide and Concur Decoding

In this section, an alternative approach to decoding is described which differs from the message-passing paradigm of previous sections.

15.4.6.1 Summary of the Divide and Concur Algorithm

The divide and concur (DC) algorithm is a flexible meta-algorithm that has been applied to a variety of problems such as the Boolean satisfiability problem. As shown below, it maps very well onto the problem of decoding. Because of its power and flexibility, it merits broader acquaintance among the general information-processing community.

A problem described by N parameters is decomposed into a set of $M + 1$ constraint subproblems, each of which involves some subset of all the parameters (with overlap among the subsets). (The $M + 1$ looks ahead to the decoding problem, where there are M parity constraints, and an additional subproblem associated with an energy constraint.) Let $\mathcal{I}_N = \{0, 1, \ldots, N - 1\}$ denote the set of indices associated with the parameters, $\mathcal{I}_M = \{0, 1, \ldots, M - 1\}$ denote the set of indices associated with the subproblems (the parity subproblems in the decoding case), and $\mathcal{I}_M^+ = \{0, 1, \ldots, M\}$ (including the energy constraint subproblem in the decoding case). Let $\mathcal{I}_m$ denote the set of indices of parameters associated with the mth subproblem. In the decoding problem,

$$\mathcal{I}_m = \begin{cases} \mathcal{N}_m & \text{for } m \in \mathcal{I}_M \\ \mathcal{I}_N & \text{for } m = M. \end{cases}$$

Let $\mathcal{I}_n$ be the set of indices of subproblems associated with the nth variable. For the decoding problem,

$$\mathcal{I}_n = \mathcal{M}_n \cup M.$$

Information about the subproblems may be represented in a matrix $\mathbf{r}$, which contains a *replica* of each of the parameters for each subproblem. The subset of parameters associated with the mth subproblem is denoted as $\mathbf{r}_{(m)} = \{r_{mn}, n \in \mathcal{I}_m\}$. These may be thought of as a subset of elements on the mth row of the matrix $\mathbf{r}$. For each parameter n, let $\mathbf{r}_{[n]}$ denote the set of replicas of variable r_n across the subproblems, $\mathbf{r}_{[n]} = \{r_{mn}, m \in \mathcal{I}_n\}$. These may be thought of as a subset of the elements of the nth column of $\mathbf{r}$.

The operation of DC is illustrated in Figure 15.15. Each subproblem is represented by a constraint set $\mathcal{P}_m$ and a local solution is found for each subproblem by projecting its subset of parameters onto its constraint set $\mathcal{P}_m$. This is called the *divide* step, since the parameters as separately projected (divided). In Figure 15.15(a), there are two replicas $\mathbf{r}_{(0)}$ and $\mathbf{r}_{(1)}$. These replicas are projected onto their constraint sets. The "divide" projection operation associated with the mth constraint, denoted as $P_D^m : \mathbb{R}^{|\mathcal{I}_m|} \to \mathbb{R}^{|\mathcal{I}_m|}$ for $m \in \mathcal{I}_M$, produces the vector in $\mathbb{R}^{|\mathcal{I}_m|}$ that is closest to $\mathbf{r}_{(m)}$ which satisfies the mth constraint:

$$\tilde{\mathbf{r}}_{(m)} = P_D^m(\mathbf{r}_{(m)}) \triangleq \arg \min_{\substack{\tilde{\mathbf{r}}_{(m)} : \tilde{\mathbf{r}}_{(m)} \text{ satisfies} \\ \text{constraint } m}} \| \tilde{\mathbf{r}}_{(m)} - \mathbf{r}_{(m)} \|^2.$$

The set of all the divide projections is denoted as $P_D(\mathbf{r}) : \mathbb{R}^{(M+1) \times N} \to \mathbb{R}^{(M+1) \times N}$, which operates as follows: For each $m \in \mathcal{I}_M$, compute $P_D^m(\mathbf{r}_{(m)})$ as a row vector, then stack into the appropriate columns to form the matrix $P_D(\mathbf{r})$.

It has been found that using the projected values directly can result in the algorithm getting trapped at parameters that are not the best. Instead, an *overshoot* is used. As shown in Figure 15.15(a), there is a vector $P_D^m(\mathbf{r}_{(m)}) - \mathbf{r}_{(0)}$ (shown as an arrow). The overshoot is computed as

$$\mathbf{r}_{(m)} + 2[P_D^m(\mathbf{r}_{(m)}) - \mathbf{r}_{(m)}],$$

which moves two times the direction of $P_D^m(\mathbf{r}_{(m)}) - \mathbf{r}_{(m)}$ away from $\mathbf{r}_{(m)}$. The overshoot computation is shown in Figure 15.15(b). Collectively, each of these overshoot values are collected together in the rows of a matrix (placed into appropriate columns) denoted as $\mathbf{r} + 2[P_D(\mathbf{r}) - \mathbf{r}]$.

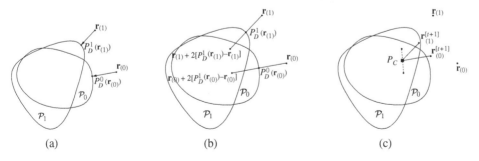

Figure 15.15: Steps in the DC algorithm. (a) Projection of $\mathbf{r}_{[0]}$ and $\mathbf{r}_{[1]}$ onto $\mathcal{P}_0$ and $\mathcal{P}_1$; (b) $\mathbf{r}_{(m)} + 2(P_D^m(\mathbf{r}_{(m)}) - \mathbf{r}_{(m)})$ (Overshoot); (c) concur projection, and results of difference map.

After projection and overshoot on each subproblem, there may be different values for the parameters (different values on different rows of column n of the matrix), so the different solutions to the subproblems are combined together in the *concur* step. For each variable n, the concur projection $P_C^n : \mathbb{R}^{|\mathcal{I}_n|} \to \mathbb{R}$ associated with the nth variable projects to a value in which all the replicas associated with parameter n (that is, in column n) concur. For each n this results in a scalar value

$$b_n = P_C^n((\mathbf{r} + 2[P_D(\mathbf{r}) - \mathbf{r}])_{[n]}).$$

The set of all concur projections for all $n \in \mathcal{I}_N$, denoted as $P_C(\mathbf{r}) : \mathbb{R}^{(M+1)\times N} \to \mathbb{R}^{(M+1)\times N}$, operates as follows: For each $n \in \mathcal{I}_N$, compute b_n, then replicate these to form a column vector with values at indices $m' \in \mathcal{I}_n$. These columns are stacked to form the matrix $P_C(\mathbf{r})$. The concur step is illustrated in figure 15.15(c) as the square block that is the average of the two overshoot points.

Following the concur step, the updated parameter value is obtained by removing from the concurrence value in each row the original difference vector $P_d^{(m)}(\mathbf{r}_{(m)}) - \mathbf{r}_{(m)}$, resulting in an update rule known as the *difference map* [170, 171]

$$\mathbf{r}^{[t+1]} = P_C(\mathbf{r}^{[t]} + 2[P_D(\mathbf{r}^{[t]}) - \mathbf{r}^{[t]}]) - [P_D(\mathbf{r}^{[t]}) - \mathbf{r}^{[t]}]. \tag{15.27}$$

This is illustrated in Figure 15.15(c).

The update rule in (15.27) is actually a simplification of a more general update rule proposed by [170, 171],

$$\mathbf{r}^{[t+1]} = \mathbf{r}^{[t]} + \beta[P_C(P_D(\mathbf{r}^{[t]})) - P_D(f_C(\mathbf{r}^{[t]}))],$$

where $f_s(\mathbf{r}^{[t]}) = (1 + \gamma_s)P_s(\mathbf{r}^{[t]}) - \gamma_s \mathbf{r}^{[t]}$ for $s = C$ or D, with $\gamma_C = -1/\beta$ and $\gamma_D = 1/\beta$. While β can be tuned for performance, the update rule (15.27) takes $\beta = 1$.

After a single iteration of the difference map update, the replicas $\mathbf{r}_{(m)}^{[t+1]}$ may not satisfy the constraints of the subproblems, so the process is iterated, repeating the divide, concur, and difference map steps until convergence. It can be shown that if there is a fixed point $\mathbf{r}^*$ such that $\mathbf{r}^{[t+1]} = \mathbf{r}^{[t]}$, then it corresponds to a solution to the problem, where the solution is found from $P_D(\mathbf{r}^*)$ or $P_C(\mathbf{r}^* + 2[P_D(\mathbf{r}^*) - \mathbf{r}^*])$.

It has been shown that for many problems the difference map update may be less likely to get caught in non-optimum traps than other update rules, such as updating according to

$$\mathbf{r}^{[t+1]} = P_C(P_D(\mathbf{r}^{[t]})).$$

15.4.6.2 DC Applied to LDPC Decoding

In applying DC to decoding, there are N parameters which are the decoded bit values, and $M + 1$ constraints. The first M constraints are the parity constraints associated with the M rows of the parity check matrix. The $(M + 1)$st constraint is that the codeword should correspond with the received information.

In the development here, BPSK modulation is assumed here, but higher order modulation can be accommodated. A codeword $\mathbf{c} = [c_0, c_1, \ldots, c_{N-1}]^T$, with $c_i \in \{0, 1\}$, is also represented as $\mathbf{x} = [x_0, x_1, \ldots, x_{N-1}]^T$ with $x_n = 1 - 2c_n$. The transmitted vector is $\mathbf{s} = (s_0, s_1, \ldots, s_{N-1})$, where

$$s_n = \begin{cases} a & c_n = 0 \\ -a & c_n = 1 \end{cases} = ax_n.$$

Denote the received data as $\mathbf{y}$. The log-likelihood ratios are

$$L_n = \log\left(\frac{p(y_n|x_n = 1)}{p(y_n|x_n = -1)}\right);$$

$L_n > 0$ indicates that $x_n = 1$ (that is, $c_n = 0$) is more probable. Recall from (15.11) that for the AWGN channel the LLR can be expressed as

$$L_n = \frac{2a}{\sigma^2} y_n, n \in \mathcal{I}_N.$$

These log-likelihood ratios are collected into a vector

$$\boldsymbol{\ell} = \begin{bmatrix} L_0 & L_1 & \cdots & L_{N-1} \end{bmatrix}^T.$$

A negative "energy" term is defined which measures the similarity between estimated ± 1 bit values $\{\hat{x}_n\}$ and the log-likelihood ratios

$$E = -\sum_{n=1}^{N} L_n \hat{x}_n = -\boldsymbol{\ell}^T \hat{\mathbf{x}}. \tag{15.28}$$

The smaller (more negative) E is, the more similar $\hat{\mathbf{x}}$ is to $\mathbf{y}$. In the DC algorithm, one of the constraints is to choose a decoding vector $\hat{\mathbf{x}}$ to make the energy as negative as possible. More precisely, a threshold is set, and values are selected to make the negative energy less than that threshold.

As suggested by [497], rather than using the log-likelihood ratios directly, a sort of signed probability is used as the information for the algorithm. First, compute the bit probabilities according to

$$p_n = \frac{e^{L_n}}{1 + e^{L_n}} \in (0, 1)$$

and then map these into

$$\tilde{p}_n = 2p_n - 1 \in (-1, 1).$$

If $\tilde{p}_n > 0$, then it is more probable that $x_n = 1$.

Example 15.15 For the $(10, 5)$ code with the data in Example 15.9, the signed probability vector is

$$\tilde{\mathbf{p}} = \begin{bmatrix} 0.56 & 0.68 & 0.62 & 0.04 & -0.10 & -0.74 & 0.64 & -0.58 & 0.50 & 0.52 \end{bmatrix}.$$

$\square$

Data associated with the algorithm is represented in the $(M + 1) \times N$ matrix $\mathbf{r}$ (or its sparsely represented equivalent) whose nonzero elements are in positions corresponding to the nonzero elements of the parity check matrix for the code, with elements r_{mn}, with an additional row to represent the replicas associated with the energy constraint.

As above, let $\mathbf{r}_{(m)}$ denote the (row) vector of data associated with the mth constraint. For $m = 0, 1, \ldots, M - 1$, $\mathbf{r}_{(m)} = \{r_{mn}, n \in \mathcal{N}(m)\}$, that is, the data from the mth row of the $\mathbf{r}$ matrix associated with the variable nodes connected to the mth check. For $m = M$, the data from the mth row of $\mathbf{r}$ is associated with the energy constraint.

Let $\mathbf{r}_{[n]}$ denote the vector of data associated with the nth variable, $\mathbf{r}_{[n]} = \{r_{mn}, n \in \mathcal{I}_n\}$.

Example 15.16 For the example above, the initial $\mathbf{r}$ is

$$\mathbf{r}^{[0]} = \begin{bmatrix} 0.56 & 0.68 & 0.62 & & & -0.74 & 0.64 & & & -0.52 \\ 0.56 & & 0.62 & & -0.1 & -0.74 & & -0.58 & 0.5 & \\ & & 0.62 & 0.04 & -0.1 & 0 & 0.64 & & 0.5 & -0.52 \\ & 0.68 & & 0.04 & -0.1 & -0.74 & & -0.58 & & -0.52 \\ 0.56 & 0.68 & & 0.04 & & & 0.64 & -0.58 & 0.5 & \\ 0.56 & 0.68 & 0.62 & 0.04 & -0.1 & -0.74 & 0.64 & -0.58 & 0.5 & -0.52 \end{bmatrix}. \tag{15.29}$$

Then, for example,

$$\mathbf{r}_{(0)} = [0.56, 0.68, -0.74, 0.64, -0.52]$$

is the data associated with the first parity constraint, and

$$\mathbf{r}_{(M)} = [0.56, 0.68, 0.62, 0.04, -0.1, -0.74, 0.64, -0.58, 0.5, -0.52)$$

is associated with the energy constraint, and

$$\mathbf{r}_{[0]} = \begin{bmatrix} 0.56 \\ 0.56 \\ 0.56 \\ 0.56 \end{bmatrix}$$

is associated with variable $n = 0$.   □

We present first the overall algorithm, making use of the divide projections P_D and concur projection P_C which are explained below.

Algorithm 15.8 Divide and Concur LDPC Decoder

---

1. **Initialization:** Given likelihoods L_n, form ℓ and compute $p_n = e^{L_n}/(1 + e^{L_n})$ and $\tilde{p}_n = 2p_n - 1$. Fill the replicant matrix $\mathbf{r}^{[0]}$ according to $r_{mn}^{[0]} = \tilde{p}_n$ for $m \in \mathcal{I}_n$. Let $t = 0$.

2. Compute the overshoot

$$\mathbf{q}^{[t]} = \mathbf{r}^{[t]} + 2[P_D(\mathbf{r}^{[t]}) - \mathbf{r}^{[t]}] \tag{15.30}$$

   Here, $P_D(\cdot)$ is the divide projection operator, discussed below.

3. Compute the belief information at each variable node using the concur projection,

$$b_n(t) = P_C^n(\mathbf{q}_{[n]}^{[t]}) = \frac{1}{|\mathcal{I}_n|} \sum_{m \in \mathcal{I}_n} q_{mn}^{[t]} \qquad n \in \mathcal{I}_N.$$

   and form a bit from this by

$$\hat{c}_n = \begin{cases} 1 & b_n(t) < 0 \\ 0 & b_n(t) > 0. \end{cases}$$

   From these bits form $\hat{\mathbf{c}}^{[t]}$. If parities all check, then output $\hat{\mathbf{c}}$ as the decoded codeword.

4. Otherwise form the matrix $P_C(\mathbf{q}^{[t]})$ by duplicating $b_n(t)$ across the rows of the matrix and compute

$$\mathbf{r}^{[t+1]} = P_C(\mathbf{q}^{[t]}) - [P_D(\mathbf{r}^{[t]}) - \mathbf{r}^{[t]}]$$

15.4.6.3   The Divide Projections

Parity Constraints Let

$$c_m(\mathbf{r}_{(m)}) = \text{sat}$$

denote that the data in $\mathbf{r}_{(m)}$ satisfy the parity constraint. This is determined as follows: Form $h_{mn} = \text{sign}(r_{mn})$, where $\text{sign}(r) = 1$ if $r > 0$ and $\text{sign}(r) = -1$ if $r < 0$. The $\{h_{mn}\}$, representing signed bits, satisfy parity if

$$\prod_{n \in \mathcal{N}(m)} h_{mn} = 1,$$

that is, if there are an *even* number of −1s among them. Thus,

$$c_m(\mathbf{r}_{(m)}) = \text{sat} \leftrightarrow \prod_{n \in \mathcal{N}(m)} \text{sign}(r_{mn}) = 1.$$

For the vector $\mathbf{r}_{(m)}$, $m \in \mathcal{I}_M$, the projection $P_D^m(\mathbf{r}_{(m)})$ computes a vector $\tilde{\mathbf{r}}_{(m)}$ nearest to $\mathbf{r}_{(m)}$ which satisfies the mth parity constraint,

$$\tilde{\mathbf{r}}_{(m)} = P_D^m(\mathbf{r}_{(m)}) \triangleq \arg \min_{\tilde{\mathbf{r}}_{(a)} \,:\, c_m(\tilde{\mathbf{r}}_{(m)}) = \text{sat}} \|\tilde{\mathbf{r}}_{(m)} - \mathbf{r}_{(m)}\|^2, \quad m = 1, 2, \ldots, M, \tag{15.31}$$

where $\|\cdot\|^2$ is the squared Euclidean norm. The projection operation (15.31) is computed as follows.

- Let $h_{mn} = \text{sign}(r_{mn})$. Let $\mathbf{h}_m$ denote the vector consisting of the elements of h_{mn}.
- If $\mathbf{h}_m$ contains an even number of −1s, then set $P_D^m(\mathbf{r}_{(m)}) = \mathbf{h}_m$ and return.
- If $\mathbf{h}_m$ does not contain an even number of −1s (a change is necessary), then let $v = \arg \min_{n \in \mathcal{N}_m} |r_{mn}|$. It is the index of the smallest element whose flipped value produces a vector satisfying parity. (If there are multiple indices with minimum value, select one at random.)

  Flip h_{mv} by $h_{mv} \to -h_{mv}$. Then set $P_D^m(\mathbf{r}_{(m)}) = \mathbf{h}_m$ and return.

Energy Constraint In the DC algorithm, one of the constraints (goals) will be to make the negative energy as small as possible, indicating that $\mathbf{y}$ is similar to $\hat{\mathbf{x}}$. The constraint is imposed that

$$-\sum_{n=1}^{N} L_n \hat{x}_i \text{sign}(a) \leq E_{\max}, \tag{15.32}$$

where $E_{\max}$ is a parameter of the decoding algorithm. It is reported [497] that a good choice is $E_{\max} = -(1 + \epsilon) \sum_{n=1}^{N} |L_n|$, where $0 < \epsilon \ll 1$. The computed energy can never actually achieve this, but this aspirational bound works well, and in any event achievement of the bound is not used to determine convergence.

The projection onto this constraint is done as follows.

- If the energy constraint (15.32) is already satisfied by $\mathbf{r}_{(M)}$, then $P_D^M(\mathbf{r}_{(M)}) = \mathbf{r}_{(M)}$.
- Otherwise, find the vector $\mathbf{h}$ which is the closest vector to $\mathbf{r}_{(M)}$ and satisfies the energy constraint:

$$\mathbf{h} = \arg \min_{\mathbf{h}\,:\,-\boldsymbol{\ell}^T \mathbf{h} \leq E_{\max}} \|\mathbf{r}_{(M)} - \mathbf{h}\|_2^2.$$

The solution to this inequality-constrained optimization problem is found as follows. Form the Lagrangian

$$\mathcal{L} = \|\mathbf{r}_{(M)} - \mathbf{h}\|^2 - 2\lambda(\boldsymbol{\ell}^T \mathbf{h} - E_{\max}).$$

Computing the gradient and setting it to 0 yields

$$\frac{\partial \mathcal{L}}{\partial \mathbf{h}} = -2\mathbf{r}_{(M)} + 2\mathbf{h} - 2\lambda \boldsymbol{\ell} = 0$$

so

$$\mathbf{h} = \mathbf{r}_{(M)} + \lambda \boldsymbol{\ell}.$$

The Lagrange multiplier λ is selected so that

$$-\mathbf{h}^T \boldsymbol{\ell} = E_{\max},$$

which leads to

$$\mathbf{h} = \mathbf{r}_{(M)} - \frac{\boldsymbol{\ell}(\boldsymbol{\ell}^T \mathbf{r}_{(M)} + E_{\max})}{\boldsymbol{\ell}^T \boldsymbol{\ell}}.$$

Thus, in this case,

$$P_D^M(\mathbf{r}_{(M)}) = \mathbf{r}_{(M)} - \frac{\boldsymbol{\ell}(\boldsymbol{\ell}^T \mathbf{r}_{(M)} + E_{\max})}{\boldsymbol{\ell}^T \boldsymbol{\ell}}.$$

Example 15.17 For the $\mathbf{r}^{[0]}$ in (15.29), the divide step gives

$$P_D(\mathbf{r}^{[0]}) = \begin{bmatrix} 1 & 1 & 1 & & & -1 & 1 & & & -1 \\ 1 & & 1 & & \underline{1} & -1 & & -1 & 1 & \\ & & 1 & 1 & -1 & & 1 & & 1 & -1 \\ & 1 & & 1 & -1 & -1 & & -1 & & -1 \\ 1 & 1 & & \underline{-1} & & & 1 & -1 & 10.0 & \\ 0.91 & 1.1 & 1 & 0.062 & -0.16 & -1.3 & 1.1 & -0.95 & 0.81 & -0.85 \end{bmatrix}.$$

Underlined elements are flipped in the parity projection. □

15.4.6.4 The Concur Projection

For each $n \in \mathcal{I}_N$, there are $|\mathcal{I}_n|$ replicas of the information r_{mn}. In the concur projection, these $|\mathcal{I}_n|$ replicas are combined together in a concurrence b_n which is closest to all of the replicas:

$$b_n = \arg\min_r \sum_{m \in \mathcal{I}_n} (r - r_{mn})^2.$$

Taking the derivative with respect to r and solving yields

$$b_n = \frac{1}{|\mathcal{I}_n|} \sum_{m \in \mathcal{I}_n} r_{mn},$$

so the concur projection P_C^n simply averages across the information in column n. As mentioned above, these projected values (scalars) can be replicated along columns and then stacked to form the projection matrix.

Example 15.18 The concur projection is applied to the overshoot $\mathbf{q}^{[t]} = 2P_D(\mathbf{r}^{[t]}) - \mathbf{r}^{[t]}$, so this is computed first. The overshoot is

$$\mathbf{q}^{[t]} = \begin{bmatrix} 1.4 & 1.3 & 1.4 & & & -1.3 & 1.4 & & & -1.5 \\ 1.4 & & 1.4 & & 2.1 & -1.3 & & -1.4 & 1.5 & \\ & & 1.4 & 2.0 & -1.9 & & 1.4 & & 1.5 & -1.5 \\ & 1.3 & & 2.0 & -1.9 & -1.3 & & -1.4 & & -1.5 \\ 1.4 & 1.3 & & -2.0 & & & 1.4 & -1.4 & 1.5 & \\ 1.3 & 1.6 & 1.4 & 0.085 & -0.21 & -1.8 & 1.5 & -1.3 & 1.1 & -1.2 \end{bmatrix}.$$

Its concur projection is

$$P_C(2P_D(\mathbf{r}^{[0]}) - \mathbf{r}^{[0]}) = \begin{bmatrix} 1.4 & 1.4 & 1.4 & & & -1.4 & 1.4 & & & -1.4 \\ 1.4 & & 1.4 & & -0.48 & -1.4 & & -1.4 & 1.4 & \\ & & 1.4 & 0.49 & -0.48 & & 1.4 & & 1.4 & -1.4 \\ & 1.4 & & 0.49 & -0.48 & -1.4 & & -1.4 & & -1.4 \\ 1.4 & 1.4 & & 0.49 & & & 1.4 & -1.4 & 1.4 & \\ 1.3 & 1.4 & 1.4 & 0.49 & -0.48 & -1.4 & 1.4 & -1.4 & 1.4 & -1.4 \end{bmatrix}.$$

This does not satisfy all the parities, so the parameters are updated for the next iteration. The updated parameters are

$$\mathbf{r}^{[t+1]} = P_C(2P_D(\mathbf{r}^{[0]}) - \mathbf{r}^{[0]}) - (P_D(\mathbf{r}^{[0]}) - \mathbf{r}^{[0]})$$

$$= \begin{bmatrix} 0.96 & 1.1 & 1 & & & -1.1 & 1 & & & -0.92 \\ 0.96 & & 1 & & -1.6 & -1.1 & & -0.97 & 0.91 & \\ & & 1 & -0.47 & 0.42 & & 1 & & 0.91 & -0.92 \\ & 1.1 & & -0.47 & 0.42 & -1.1 & & -0.97 & & -0.92 \\ 0.96 & 1.1 & & 1.5 & & & 1 & -0.97 & 0.91 & \\ 1 & 0.93 & 0.98 & 0.47 & -0.42 & -0.86 & 0.97 & -1.0 & 1.1 & -1.1 \end{bmatrix}.$$

$\square$

15.4.6.5 A Message-Passing Viewpoint of DC Decoding

The DC decoding algorithm can be interpreted as a message-passing algorithm. Let $r_{mn}^{[t]}$ be interpreted as a message from variable node n to message node m, $d_{n\to m}(t)$. Let the overshoot $q_{mn}^{[t]}$ from (15.30) be interpreted as the message from check node m to variable node n:

$$d_{n\to m}(t) = r_{mn}^{[t]} \quad d_{m\to n}(t) = q_{mn}^{[t]}.$$

Note that

$$P_D(\mathbf{r}^{[t]}) - \mathbf{r}^{[t]} = \frac{1}{2}[\mathbf{q}^{[t]} - \mathbf{r}^{[t]}]$$

so that the updated message is

$$d_{n\to m}(t+1) = b_n(t) - \frac{1}{2}[d_{m\to n}(t) - d_{n\to m}(t)].$$

15.4.7 Difference Map Belief Propagation Decoding

Difference Map Belief Propagation (DMBP) decoding combines ideas from belief propagation (BP) decoding with the difference map from DC decoding. The decoder described here is a variation on min-sum decoding. Recall that the min-sum decoding messages can be computed using the (by now familiar) leave-one-out rule

$$L_{m\to n} = \prod_{n'\in\mathcal{N}(m)} |L_{n'\to m}| \prod_{n'\in\mathcal{N}(m)} \text{sign}(L_{n'\to n}). \tag{15.33}$$

Example 15.19 Consider the use of the min-sum decoding algorithm at a check node m having four adjacent variable nodes, where three of the messages $L_{n'\to m}$ are positive and one is negative. The outgoing messages $L_{m\to n'}$ computed by (15.33) will have three negative messages and one positive message.

Since the parity check is, in reality, connected to an even number of negative nodes — even parity — the presence of three computed negative messages in some sense overshoots the correct answer. $\square$

In the standard min-sum decoding rule, the variable node computation uses the sum of the channel information and the messages from check nodes (using leave-one-out computation). For DMBF propagation, the check node computation is more of an average, and includes all incoming messages (no leave-one-out):

$$b_n(t) = Z\left(L_n + \sum_{m \in \mathcal{M}_n} L_{m \to m}(t)\right).$$

(15.34)

Z is a decoder parameter which may be tuned to optimize decoder performance. Typical values are $Z = 0.35$ or $Z = 0.45$.

Because of the overshoot, an final step is to adjust the message for the next step by

$$L_{n \to m}(t+1) = b_n(t) - \frac{1}{2}[L_{m \to n}(t) - L_{n \to m}(t)].$$

(15.35)

ldpcdecoder.cc:
DMBPdecode()

The DMBP decoder is summarized below.

Algorithm 15.9 Difference Map Belief Propagation Decoder

---

1. **Initialization:** Set $t = 0$. Set $L_{n \to m}(t) = L_n$ for $m \in \mathcal{M}_n$, where L_n is the channel log likelihood.

2. **Compute messages from checks to variables:** Compute $L_{m \to n}$ using (15.33).

3. **Compute bit probabilities and bit estimates:** Compute $b_n(t)$ using (15.34). Set $\hat{c}_n = 1$ if $b_n(t) < 0$ and $\hat{c}_n = 0$ if $b_n(t) > 0$. If these bits satisfy all parities ($H\hat{c} = 0$), output $\hat{c}$ as the decoded codeword and return.

4. **Compute messages from variable nodes to check nodes** using (15.35).

---

ldpcdecoder.cc:
LPdecode()

15.4.8   Linear Programming Decoding

Linear programming decoding is an interesting alternative to other decoders, providing some interesting theoretical insight, although possibly at the expense of some computational complexity. The presentation here is rather leisurely, with examples to illustrate the general concept.

15.4.8.1   Background on Linear Programming

Before turning to the decoding question, we summarize briefly the linear programming (LP) problem. A LP problem has a linear objective function of the vector $\mathbf{x} \in \mathbb{R}^n$ to maximized or minimized, subject to linear inequality constraints

$$\text{minimize } \mathbf{d}^T \mathbf{x}$$

$$\text{subject to } \mathbf{a}_i^T \mathbf{x} \le b_i \quad i = 1, 2 \dots, m.$$

A LP problem may also include some linear equality constraints

$$\text{minimize } \mathbf{d}^T \mathbf{x}$$

$$\text{subject to } \mathbf{a}_i^T \mathbf{x} \le b_i \quad i = 1, 2 \dots, m$$

$$\mathbf{f}_i^T \mathbf{x} = e_i \quad i = 1, 2, \dots, n.$$

This form can be expressed as

$$\text{minimize } \mathbf{d}^T \mathbf{x}$$

$$\text{subject to } A\mathbf{x} \le \mathbf{b}$$

$$F\mathbf{x} = \mathbf{e}.$$

(Here $\preceq$ means element-by-element inequality: each element of $A\mathbf{x}$ is less than the corresponding element of $\mathbf{b}$.) A LP problem may also have lower and upper bounds on the variables, as in

$$
\begin{aligned}
\text{minimize} \quad & \mathbf{d}^T\mathbf{x} \\
\text{subject to} \quad & A\mathbf{x} \preceq \mathbf{b} \\
& F\mathbf{x} = \mathbf{e} \\
& \mathbf{lb} \preceq \mathbf{x} \preceq \mathbf{ub},
\end{aligned}
\tag{15.36}
$$

where the matrix F (typically wide) represents relationships between variables. In the LP decoding problem described below, the linear inequality constraint $H\mathbf{x} \preceq \mathbf{b}$ is absent.

All of these forms are essentially interchangeable by introduction of appropriate auxiliary variables.

Example 15.20 Consider the problem

$$
\text{minimize} \quad \begin{bmatrix} -1 & -1.5 \end{bmatrix} \begin{bmatrix} x_1 \\ x_2 \end{bmatrix}
$$

$$
\text{subject to } x_1 + x_2 \le 3
$$

$$
x_1 + 2x_2 \le 4
$$

$$
x_1 \ge 0 \quad x_2 \ge 0.
$$

The feasible region, points that satisfy the constraints, are shown in the shaded region in Figure 15.16.

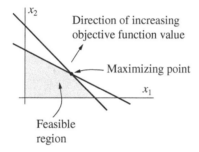

Figure 15.16: Linear programming problem.

$\square$

As this example illustrates, the linear constraints cause the feasible region to be a *polytope* in $\mathbb{R}^n$ (a geometric object with flat sides). The linear objective function means that there a direction along which the function decreases. Typically, the optimal solutions lies on a vertex of the polytope (unless the direction of increase is orthogonal to a face of the polytope, in which case any point on that face is optimum).

Once the problem is expressed as an LP problem, such as the $\mathbf{d}$, H, $\mathbf{b}$, F, and $\mathbf{e}$ and lower and upper bounds of (15.36), the problem is typically solved by calling a library function such as the `glpk` (the Gnu linear programming kit) in C or `linprog` in MATLAB.

LP problems arise in a variety of disciplines, so there is a huge body of literature related to them, and many algorithms for solving LP problems. The *simplex algorithm* essentially moves from vertex to vertex on the polytope in the direction of increase. For typical problems the simplex algorithm runs with moderate computational complexity, but there are pathological problems whose computational complexity is exponential in the number of variables. There are alternative algorithms known as *interior point methods* which have guaranteed polynomial performance. These operate (essentially) using a Newton-type algorithm with barrier constraints to ensure the constraints.

Background on LP can be found in many places, such as [398] or [318].

15.4.8.2 Formulation of the Basic LP Decoding Algorithm

Let y_n be a signal received through a channel, and let c_n be the corresponding bit, transmitted through a channel, such as BPSK or a BSC, which is assumed memoryless. The maximum likelihood rule chooses, for each $n = 0, 1, \ldots, N-1$, the value of the bit $\hat{c}_n$ that maximizes $P(y_n|c_n = \hat{c}_n)$. From the difference

$$L_n = \log P(y_n|c_n = 0) - \log P(y_n|c_n = 1) = \log \frac{P(y_n|c_n = 0)}{P(y_n|c_n = 1)},$$

the ML rule indicates

$$\begin{cases} \text{if } L_n > 0, \text{ decide } \hat{c}_n = 0 \\ \text{if } L_n < 0, \text{ decide } \hat{c}_n = 1. \end{cases}$$

This rule can be written as: choose $\hat{c}_n \in \{0, 1\}$ to minimize $J_n = L_n\hat{c}_n$: If $L_n < 0$, then selecting $\hat{c}_n = 1$ produces a smaller value of J_n; if $L_n > 0$, then selecting $\hat{c}_n = 0$ produces a smaller value of J_n. Extending this across N independent uses of the channel results in the following objective function:

$$J = \sum_{n=0}^{N-1} L_n\hat{c}_n.$$

This leads to the (incomplete) optimization problem

$$\underset{\hat{\mathbf{c}} \in \{0,1\}^N}{\text{minimize}} \sum_{n=0}^{N-1} L_n\hat{c}_n. \tag{15.37}$$

Example 15.21   For a BPSK channel where a bit $c_n = 0$ is transmitted with amplitude a and a bit $c_n = 1$ is transmitted with amplitude $-a$,

$$L_n = \log \frac{\exp\left(-\frac{1}{2\sigma^2}(y_n - a)^2\right)}{\exp\left(-\frac{1}{2\sigma^2}(y_n + a)^2\right)} = \frac{2a}{\sigma^2}y_n \triangleq L_c y_n.$$

Thus, $J = L_c \sum_{n=0}^{N-1} y_n\hat{c}_n$.
   For a BSC, if $y_n = 0$, then

$$L_n = \log \frac{P(y_n = 0|c_n = 0)}{P(y_n = 0|c_n = 1)} = \log \frac{1-p}{p} > 0.$$

If $y_n = 1$, then

$$L_n = \log \frac{P(y_n = 1|c_n = 0)}{P(y_n = 1|c_n = 0)} = \log \frac{p}{1-p} < 0.$$

Since these costs are fixed, they can be rescaled to

$$L_n = \begin{cases} +1 & \text{if } y_n = 0 \\ -1 & \text{if } y_n = 1. \end{cases}$$

□

The minimization problem in (15.37) is obviously incomplete, since $\hat{\mathbf{c}}$ is not yet constrained to be a codeword. For decoding a codeword, the ML principle can be restated as

$$\text{minimize} \sum_{n=0}^{N-1} L_n\hat{c}_n \tag{15.38}$$
$$\text{subject to } \hat{\mathbf{c}} \in \mathcal{C},$$

where $\mathcal{C}$ is the set of codewords. This is merely a restatement of the ML decoding rule, requiring a search over all codewords, so there is nothing new here yet.

We will now introduce some geometry, however, that turns this decoding rule into a LP problem. The complexity of this linear programming problem is still too high, so the problem is further relaxed to a LP problem that is easier to solve.

For a code $\mathcal{C}$, with its 2^N codewords, define the *codeword polytope* as the convex hull of all possible codewords,

$$\text{poly}(\mathcal{C}) = \left\{ \mathbf{w} \in \mathbb{R}^N : \mathbf{w} = \sum_{\mathbf{c} \in \mathcal{C}} \lambda_{\mathbf{c}} \mathbf{c}, \lambda_{\mathbf{c}} \geq 0, \sum_{\mathbf{c} \in \mathcal{C}} \lambda_{\mathbf{c}} = 1 \right\}.$$

Figure 15.17 illustrates a polytope in $\mathbb{R}^3$. The vertices of the polytope poly(C) correspond exactly to the codewords of $\mathcal{C}$. Every point in poly($\mathcal{C}$) corresponds to a vector $\hat{\mathbf{c}}$, with components determined by $\hat{c}_i = \sum_{\mathbf{c}} \lambda_{\mathbf{c}} c_i$. The ML decoding problem can be expressed as

$$\text{minimize} \sum_{n=1}^{N-1} L_n \hat{c}_n$$

$$\text{subject to } \hat{\mathbf{c}} \in \text{poly}(\mathcal{C}).$$

This is a *linear programming* problem. For each codeword $\mathbf{c} \in \mathcal{C}$, let $d_{\mathbf{c}}$ be the scalar

$$d_{\mathbf{c}} = \sum_{n=0}^{N-1} L_n c_n.$$

Then the LP problem can be expressed as

$$\text{minimize} \sum_{\mathbf{c} \in \mathcal{C}} \lambda_{\mathbf{c}} d_{\mathbf{c}}$$

$$\text{subject to } \lambda_{\mathbf{c}} \geq 0 \text{ for each } \lambda_{\mathbf{c}}$$

$$\sum_{\mathbf{c} \in \mathcal{C}} \lambda_{\mathbf{c}} = 1.$$

The vector $\lambda \in \mathbb{R}^{2^N}$ whose elements are the $\lambda_{\mathbf{c}}$ providing the minimum likelihood is sought. Solution of this LP problem gives the ML solution. However, since there are 2^N variables, the computational complexity is of the same order as the ML problem in (15.38). We therefore seek to relax some of the constraints to reduce the complexity.

15.4.8.3 LP Relaxation

In this section, the statement of general principles is accompanied by a specific example based on a Hamming $(7, 4)$ code with parity check and generator matrices

$$H = \begin{bmatrix} 1 & 0 & 0 & 1 & 1 & 0 & 1 \\ 0 & 1 & 0 & 1 & 0 & 1 & 1 \\ 0 & 0 & 1 & 0 & 1 & 1 & 1 \end{bmatrix} \quad G = \begin{bmatrix} 1 & 1 & 0 & 1 & 0 & 0 & 0 \\ 1 & 0 & 1 & 0 & 1 & 0 & 0 \\ 0 & 1 & 1 & 0 & 0 & 1 & 0 \\ 1 & 1 & 1 & 0 & 0 & 0 & 1 \end{bmatrix}$$

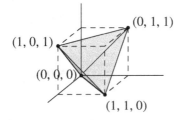

Figure 15.17: Polytope of the codewords $(0, 0, 0), (0, 1, 1), (1, 1, 0), (1, 0, 1)$.

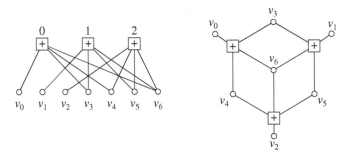

Figure 15.18: Tanner graph for the Hamming $(7,4)$ code.

and Tanner graph shown in Figure 15.18. The variable nodes adjacent to each check node are described by the sets

$$\mathcal{N}(0) = \{0,3,4,6\} \quad \mathcal{N}(1) = \{1,3,5,6\} \quad \mathcal{N}(2) = \{2,4,5,6\}.$$

At each check node of the Tanner graph for the code, define a *local code*, which is the set of binary vectors that have even weight at that check node. For example, for the Hamming code at check node 0, the local code has even parity on the bits in the set $\mathcal{N}(0) = \{0,3,4,6\}$. Possible codewords for this local code are (the S notation is described below)

$$
\begin{array}{ccccccccl}
0 & * & * & 0 & 0 & * & 0 & \quad S = \emptyset & \\
1 & * & * & 1 & 0 & * & 0 & \quad S = \{0,3\} & \\
1 & * & * & 0 & 1 & * & 0 & \quad S = \{0,4\} & \\
0 & * & * & 1 & 1 & * & 0 & \quad S = \{3,4\} & \\
\end{array}
$$

$$
\begin{array}{ccccccccl}
1 & * & * & 0 & 0 & * & 1 & \quad S = \{0,6\} & \\
0 & * & * & 1 & 0 & * & 1 & \quad S = \{3,6\} & \\
0 & * & * & 0 & 1 & * & 1 & \quad S = \{4,6\} & \quad (15.39) \\
1 & * & * & 1 & 1 & * & 1 & \quad S = \{0,3,4,6\} & \\
\end{array}
$$

where $*$ denotes locations where a local codeword can be either 0 or 1. The global code (that is, the original code $\mathcal{C}$) is the intersection of the local codes associated with each check node. Each check node determines a local codeword polytope as the convex hull of convex combinations of local codewords.

For check node m, the set of adjacent variable nodes is $\mathcal{N}(m)$. Define subsets $S \subset \mathcal{N}(m)$ that contain an even number of variable nodes. Each set S corresponds to the set of local codewords determined by setting

$$
c_n = \begin{cases} 1 & n \in S \\ 0 & n \in \mathcal{N}(m) \text{ but } n \notin S. \end{cases}
$$

In (15.39), each set of local code words is associated with an S set.

Collecting together the S set for each check node, form

$$E_m = \{S \subseteq \mathcal{N}(m) : |S| \text{even}\}, \quad m = 0, 1, \ldots, M.$$

For the Hamming code,

$$E_0 = \{\emptyset, \{0,3\}, \{0,4\}, \{3,4\}, \{0,6\}, \{3,6\}, \{4,6\}, \{0,3,4,6\}\}$$

$$E_1 = \{\emptyset, \{1,3\}, \{1,5\}, \{3,5\}, \{1,6\}, \{3,6\}, \{5,6\}, \{1,3,5,6\}\}$$

$$E_2 = \{\emptyset, \{2,4\}, \{2,5\}, \{4,5\}, \{2,6\}, \{4,6\}, \{5,6\}, \{2,4,5,6\}\}.$$

Let κ_m denote the number of S-sets in E_m,

$$\kappa_m = \sum_{i=0}^{\lfloor |\mathcal{N}(m)|/2 \rfloor} \binom{|\mathcal{N}(m)|}{2i} \qquad (15.40)$$

and let $\kappa = \sum_{j=0}^{M-1} \kappa_j$. In our example, $\kappa_0 = \kappa_1 = \kappa_2 = 8$ and $\kappa = 24$.

To set up a LP problem, for each S in each E_m, introduce an indicator variable $w_{m,S}$ which describes a codeword, where $w_{m,S} = 1$ indicates that S is the set of bits in $\mathcal{N}(m)$ that are equal to 1. The variable $w_{m,S}$ can be interpreted as indicating that the codeword satisfies check m using the configuration S.

For the Hamming code example the set of these indicator variables is

$$m = 0 : \quad w_{0,\emptyset}, w_{0,\{0,3\}}, w_{0,\{0,4\}}, w_{0,\{3,4\}}, w_{0,\{0,6\}}, w_{0,\{3,6\}}, w_{0,\{4,6\}}, w_{0,\{0,3,4,6\}}$$

$$m = 1 : \quad w_{1,\emptyset}, w_{1,\{1,3\}}, w_{1,\{1,5\}}, w_{1,\{3,5\}}, w_{1,\{1,6\}}, w_{1,\{3,6\}}, w_{1,\{5,6\}}, w_{1,\{1,3,5,6\}}$$

$$m = 2 : \quad w_{2,\emptyset}, w_{2,\{2,3\}}, w_{2,\{2,5\}}, w_{2,\{4,5\}}, w_{2,\{2,6\}}, w_{2,\{4,6\}}, w_{2,\{5,6\}}, w_{2,\{2,4,5,6\}}.$$

As indicator variables, these must satisfy the constraints (bounds)

$$0 \leq w_{m,S} \leq 1 \quad \text{for all } S \in E_m. \tag{15.41}$$

There are κ of these constraints.

As an example, suppose that the codeword is $\mathbf{c} = (0, 0, 0, 1, 1, 1, 0)$. Then the indicator variables associated with this codeword are

$$w_{0,\{3,4\}} = 1 \quad w_{1,\{3,5\}} = 1 \quad w_{2,\{4,5\}} = 1$$

and all other $w_{j,S} = 0$. That is, the codeword satisfies check $m = 0$ because $c_3 \oplus c_4 = 0$, and check $m = 1$ since $c_3 \oplus c_5 = 0$, and check $m = 2$ because $c_4 \oplus c_5 = 1$.

For a given codeword, each parity check m is satisfied by exactly one even-sized subset of nodes in $\mathcal{N}(m)$. This introduces a constraint on the $w_{m,S}$ variables:

$$\sum_{S \in E_m} w_{m,S} = 1, \quad m = 0, 1, \ldots, M - 1. \tag{15.42}$$

(The number of constraints here is M.)

For our example problem, these constraints are

$$w_{0,\emptyset} + w_{0,\{0,3\}} + w_{0,\{0,4\}} + w_{0,\{3,4\}} + w_{0,\{0,6\}} + w_{0,\{3,6\}} + w_{0,\{4,6\}} + w_{0,\{0,3,4,6\}} = 1$$

$$w_{1,\emptyset} + w_{1,\{1,3\}} + w_{1,\{1,5\}} + w_{1,\{3,5\}} + w_{1,\{1,6\}} + w_{1,\{3,6\}} + w_{1,\{5,6\}} + w_{1,\{1,3,5,6\}} = 1 \tag{15.43}$$

$$w_{2,\emptyset} + w_{2,\{2,4\}} + w_{2,\{2,5\}} + w_{2,\{4,5\}} + w_{2,\{2,6\}} + w_{2,\{4,6\}} + w_{2,\{5,6\}} + w_{2,\{2,4,5,6\}} = 1.$$

For each $m = 0, 1, \ldots, M - 1$, the set of indicator variables can be stacked to form a vector $\mathbf{w}_j$ of length κ_j such as, in our example

$$\mathbf{w}_0 = \begin{bmatrix} w_{0,\emptyset} \\ w_{0,\{0,3\}} \\ \vdots \\ w_{0,\{0,3,4,6\}} \end{bmatrix}_{8 \times 1}.$$

Let $\hat{c}_n$ denote the variable (bit) node value. As a softened bit value, each must satisfy the constraint (bound)

$$0 \leq \hat{c}_n \leq 1 \quad n = 0, 1, \ldots, N - 1. \tag{15.44}$$

The bit value $\hat{c}_n$ must belong to the local codeword polytope associated with check node m, so that for all $n \in \mathcal{N}(m)$,

$$\hat{c}_n = \sum_{S \in E_m \text{such that } n \in S} w_{n,S}. \tag{15.45}$$

(The number of constraints here is $\sum_{m=0}^{M-1} |\mathcal{N}_m(m)|$.)

In our example problem, these constraints are as follows:

$m = 0:$

$$\hat{c}_0 = \sum_{S \in E_0 : 0 \in S} w_{0,S} = w_{0,\{0,3\}} + w_{0,\{0,4\}} + w_{0,\{0,6\}} + w_{0,\{0,3,4,6\}}$$

$$\hat{c}_3 = \sum_{S \in E_0 : 3 \in S} w_{0,S} = w_{0,\{0,3\}} + w_{0,\{3,4\}} + w_{0,\{3,6\}} + w_{0,\{0,3,4,6\}}$$

$$\hat{c}_4 = \sum_{S \in E_0 : 4 \in S} w_{0,S} = w_{0,\{0,4\}} + w_{0,\{3,4\}} + w_{0,\{4,6\}} + w_{0,\{0,3,4,6\}}$$

$$\hat{c}_6 = \sum_{S \in E_0 : 6 \in S} w_{0,S} = w_{0,\{0,6\}} + w_{0,\{3,6\}} + w_{0,\{4,6\}} + w_{0,\{0,3,4,6\}}$$

$m = 1:$

$$\hat{c}_1 = \sum_{S \in E_1 : 1 \in S} w_{1,S} = w_{1,\{1,3\}} + w_{1,\{1,5\}} + w_{1,\{1,6\}} + w_{1,\{1,3,5,6\}}$$

$$\hat{c}_3 = \sum_{S \in E_1 : 3 \in S} w_{1,S} = w_{1,\{1,3\}} + w_{1,\{3,5\}} + w_{1,\{3,6\}} + w_{1,\{1,3,5,6\}}$$

$$\hat{c}_5 = \sum_{S \in E_1 : 5 \in S} w_{1,S} = w_{1,\{1,5\}} + w_{1,\{3,5\}} + w_{1,\{5,6\}} + w_{1,\{1,3,5,6\}}$$

$$\hat{c}_6 = \sum_{S \in E_1 : 6 \in S} w_{1,S} = w_{1,\{1,6\}} + w_{1,\{3,6\}} + w_{1,\{5,6\}} + w_{1,\{1,3,5,6\}}$$

$m = 2:$

$$\hat{c}_2 = \sum_{S \in E_2 : 2 \in S} w_{2,S} = w_{2,\{2,4\}} + w_{2,\{2,5\}} + w_{2,\{2,6\}} + w_{2,\{2,4,5,6\}}$$

$$\hat{c}_4 = \sum_{S \in E_2 : 4 \in S} w_{2,S} = w_{2,\{2,4\}} + w_{2,\{4,5\}} + w_{2,\{4,6\}} + w_{2,\{2,4,5,6\}}$$

$$\hat{c}_5 = \sum_{S \in E_2 : 5 \in S} w_{2,S} = w_{2,\{2,5\}} + w_{2,\{4,5\}} + w_{2,\{5,6\}} + w_{2,\{2,4,5,6\}}$$

$$\hat{c}_6 = \sum_{S \in E_2 : 6 \in S} w_{2,S} = w_{2,\{2,6\}} + w_{2,\{4,6\}} + w_{2,\{5,6\}} + w_{2,\{2,4,5,6\}}$$

There are $N + \kappa$ variables, which are the $\hat{c}_n$ and the κ set indicator variables. The solution vector $\mathbf{x}$ (to be found) has the structure

$$\mathbf{x} = \begin{bmatrix} \hat{\mathbf{c}} \\ \mathbf{w}_0 \\ \mathbf{w}_1 \\ \vdots \\ \mathbf{w}_{M-1} \end{bmatrix}_{(N+\kappa) \times 1} .$$

Collectively a point such as this is denoted (with slight abuse of notation) as $(\hat{\mathbf{c}}, \mathbf{w})$ (that is, the codeword information, and the parity indicator variables).

Corresponding to $\mathbf{x}$ is a $\mathbf{d}$ vector in the LP notation of (15.36)

$$\mathbf{d} = \begin{bmatrix} L_c \mathbf{y} \\ \mathbf{0}_{\kappa_0 \times 1} \\ \mathbf{0}_{\kappa_1 \times 1} \\ \vdots \\ \mathbf{0}_{\kappa_{M-1} \times 1} \end{bmatrix}.$$

For the example problem of the $(7,4)$ Hamming code, there are $7 + 3 \times 8 = 31$ variables and $3 \times 4 + 3 = 15$ equality constraints.

The objective function (to be minimized) $\sum_{n=0}^{N-1} L_n \hat{c}_n$ can now be expressed as $\mathbf{d}^T \mathbf{x}$. This leads to the LP expressed as

$$\text{minimize} \qquad \mathbf{d}^T \mathbf{x}$$

$$\text{subject to (15.42)} \quad (M \text{ constraints})$$

$$(15.45) \quad \left(\sum_{m=0}^{M-1} |\mathcal{N}_m(m)| \text{ constraints} \right)$$

$$(15.41) \quad (\kappa \text{ bounds})$$

$$(15.44) \quad (N \text{ bounds})$$

The lower and upper bounds in (15.36) are 0 and 1 vectors, respectively. Other than the bounds, there are no inequality constraints in (15.36). The equality constraints (15.42) and (15.45) can be represented using the F matrix

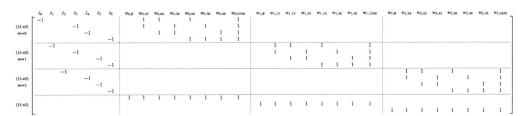

and corresponding $\mathbf{e}$ vector

$$\mathbf{e} = \begin{bmatrix} 0\ 0\ 0\ 0 & 0\ 0\ 0\ 0 & 0\ 0\ 0\ 0 & 1\ 1\ 1 \end{bmatrix}.$$

Using this notation the LP for decoding is

$$\text{minimize } \mathbf{d}^T \mathbf{x}$$

$$\text{subject to } F\mathbf{x} = \mathbf{e}$$

$$\mathbf{0} \leq \mathbf{x} \leq \mathbf{1}.$$

The number of indicator variables, $w_{m,S}$, is given by κ, which depends on the number of combinations in (15.40). Being combinatorial, this number grows very quickly. Figure 15.19 shows that κ_m increases exponentially with $|\mathcal{N}(m)|$. Thus, while linear programming can be used for arbitrary linear codes, it is practical only for codes having $|\mathcal{N}(m)|$ small, such as LDPC codes.

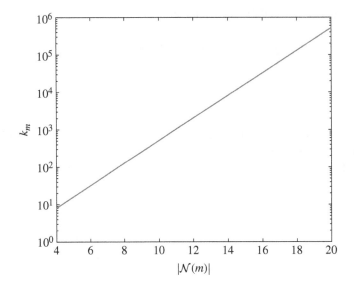

Figure 15.19: Number of constraints κ_m as a function of $|\mathcal{N}(m)|$.

15.4.8.4 Examples and Discussion

In the examples below, assume (for convenience) $L_c = 1$.

- The received data vector is $\mathbf{y} = [1, 1, 1, -1, -1, -1, 1]^T$. Form the vector

$$\mathbf{d} = \begin{bmatrix} L_c\mathbf{y} \\ \mathbf{0}_{8\times1} \\ \mathbf{0}_{8\times1} \\ \mathbf{0}_{8\times1} \end{bmatrix}.$$

Using this and the matrix F above in a linear programming function results in the solution vector

$$\mathbf{x} = \begin{bmatrix} 0 & 0 & 0 & 1 & 1 & 1 & 0 | 0 & 0 & 0 & 1 & 0 & 0 & 0 & 0 | 0 & 0 & 0 & 1 & 0 & 0 & 0 & 0 | 0 & 0 & 0 & 1 & 0 & 0 & 0 & 0 \end{bmatrix}.$$

From this, we observe that the decoded codeword is $\hat{\mathbf{c}} = (0, 0, 0, 1, 1, 1, 0)$, and that

$$w_{0,\{3,4\}} = 1 \quad w_{1,\{3,5\}} = 1 \quad w_{2,\{4,5\}} = 1$$

(as expected).

The value of the objective function is $\mathbf{d}^T\mathbf{x} = -3$.

- Introducing an error, let $\mathbf{y} = [1, 1, 1, -1, -1, \underline{1}, 1]^T$. Using this to form the first 7 elements of $\mathbf{d}$ (leaving zeros in the other positions of $\mathbf{d}$) yields the codeword $\hat{\mathbf{c}} = (0, 0, 0, 1, 1, 1, 0)$ (as expected), with the $w_{j,S}$ values as before.

The value of the objective function is $\mathbf{d}^T\mathbf{x} = -1$.

Observe that in both of these examples, the solution vector produced integer values for both the elements of $\hat{\mathbf{c}}$ and $w_{m,S}$. These are examples of an *integral point*, a point $(\hat{\mathbf{c}}, \mathbf{w})$ in the polytope whose values are all integers. It is straightforward to show that if $(\hat{\mathbf{c}}, \mathbf{w})$ is an integral point, then $\mathbf{c}$ is a codeword. Also, if $\hat{\mathbf{c}}$ is a codeword, then there is a corresponding $\mathbf{w}$ representing the parity information about $\hat{\mathbf{c}}$ such that $(\hat{\mathbf{c}}, \mathbf{w})$ is an integral point.

- Now let the certainty of the erroneous term be even higher by letting $\mathbf{y} = [1, 1, 1, -1, -1, \underline{2}, 1]^T$. This received vector strongly suggests that $\hat{c}_6 = 0$. Calling the LP solver gives the solution

$$\mathbf{x} = \left[0\ 0\ 0\ 0.6667\ 0.6667\ 0\ 0.6667 \,\middle|\, 0\ 0\ 0\ 0.3333\ 0\ 0.3333\ 0.3333\ 0 \,\middle|\, 0.3333\ 0\ 0\ 0\ 0\ 0.6667\ 0\ 0 \,\middle|\, 0.3333\ 0\ 0\ 0\ 0\ 0.6667\ 0\ 0 \right].$$

This vector does meet all the constraints, but the elements are not integral values. Thresholding this vector would suggest that $\hat{\mathbf{c}} = (0, 0, 0, 1, 1, 0, 1)$, which is not a codeword.

The value of the objective function is $\mathbf{d}^T\mathbf{x} = -0.6667$.

This example illustrates an important property about LP decoding. If the solution vector is an integral point, then the $\hat{\mathbf{c}}$ portion of it is guaranteed to be the ML codeword, and if the solution vector is *not* an integral point, then $\hat{\mathbf{c}}$ is not a codeword. This is referred to as the *ML certificate property*. Finding a nonintegral point can be used to declare decoder failure.

This does not mean that if $\mathbf{x}$ is an integral point that it is guaranteed to be the true (transmitted) codeword, since noise can cause the received vector to be in the basin of attraction of another codeword.

In characterizing the performance of a code and decoder using simulation, it is often useful to assume the all-zero codeword is transmitted. It can be shown that the probability that the LP decoder fails is independent of what codeword is transmitted, so that nothing is lost evaluating using the all-zero codeword.

The LP decoder is of theoretical interest, but for codes of any appreciable size, the decoding complexity is too large to be practical.

15.4.9 Decoding on the Binary Erasure Channel

The general belief propagation decoder described in Section 15.4.1 or 15.4.2 applies to the BEC, but it is interesting to examine the dynamics of the decoding. The algorithm here is referred to as a peeling decoder, since it peels off one erased bit after the other.

Example 15.22 Consider the $(7, 4)$ Hamming code with Tanner graph shown in Figure 15.20(a). The received signal vector is

$$\mathbf{y} = \begin{bmatrix} 1 & ? & 0 & ? & 0 & ? & 0 \end{bmatrix},$$

where ? denotes an erased value. In the figure, solid lines show edges connected to 1, dotted lines show edges connected to 0, and heavy dashed lines show edges connected to erasures.

Before formally stating the decoding algorithm, consider the messages at check node 0. There are four incoming messages, with values 0, 0, 1, and an erasure. Since the parity of all messages must be even, it must be that the erased bit at v_3 is a 1. This 1 can be propagated back through the graph.

In light of this observation, here is a statement of the peeling algorithm.

1. **Initialization:** Send messages from each variable node to its connected message nodes. At the check nodes, record the parity of the unerased messages. Delete the variable nodes of known bits and edges from those nodes to the corresponding check nodes.
   The result of this initialization is shown in Figure 15.20(b), with edges deleted and parity values at each check node.

2. **Decoding:** Select, if possible, a check node with only one edge remaining (coming from an erased variable node). Based on the parity of that node, determine the erased bit value, and send the bit value to the variable node. Then delete the check node and its edge.
   In Figure 15.20(b), the check node with a single remaining edge is circled, check node 0.
   Based on the parity at check node 0, variable node v_3 is determined to be a 1. After propagating this value throughout the graph and deleting the edges and variable nodes, the graph appears as in Figure 15.20(c). Note that the parity at check node 1 is now updated to 1.
   In this figure, the next node with a single edge is also circled, check node 2.
   Based on the parity at check node 2, variable node v_5 is determined to be 0. After propagating this value throughout the graph and deleting the edges and variable nodes, the graph appears as in Figure 15.20(d).

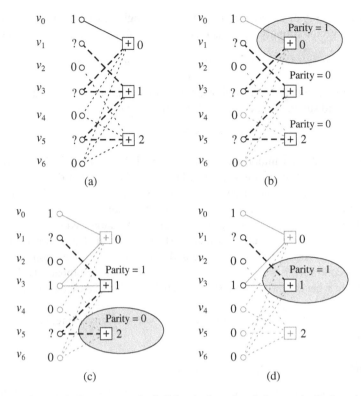

Figure 15.20: Hamming code Tanner graph. Solid = 1, dotted = 0, heavy dashed = erasure. (a) Tanner graph; (b) graph with deleted edges; (c) after one erasure corrected; (d) after two erasures corrected.

In Figure 15.20(d), the check node with a single remaining edge (the last check node) is circled, check node 1.

From the parity at check node 1, it can be determined that variable node $v_1 = 1$. Node v_1 and the edges connected to it are deleted.

The decoded codeword is thus

$$\hat{\mathbf{c}} = \begin{bmatrix} 1 & 1 & 0 & 1 & 0 & 0 & 0 \end{bmatrix}.$$

3. **Termination:** If the remaining graph is empty, the codeword has been successfully determined. If the graph is not empty (i.e., there are check nodes that have multiple erased edges still connected to them), then declare a decoding failure.

The peeling algorithm was explained in a sequential fashion, but it can also be expressed in a conventional belief propagation mode.   □

15.4.10   BEC Channels and Stopping Sets

The peeling algorithm helps provide insight into the random error correction capability of LDPC codes over the BEC channel. Let $\mathcal{G}$ be the Tanner graph associated with a linear block code. Let $\mathcal{V}$ be a subset of the variable nodes of $\mathcal{G}$ and let $\mathcal{C}$ be a subset of the check nodes of G that is a neighbor set of $\mathcal{V}$, that is, each check node in $\mathcal{C}$ is connected to at least one variable node in $\mathcal{V}$. A set $\mathcal{V}$ of variable nodes is called a *stopping set* of $\mathcal{G}$ if each check node in a neighbor set $\mathcal{C}$ of $\mathcal{V}$ is connected to at least two variable nodes in V (all of the neighbors of the variable nodes in a stopping set are connected to this set twice) [93]. Figure 15.21(a) illustrates the idea of a stopping set — neighbors of variables connected multiple times — and Figure 15.21(b) illustrates a Tanner graph in which nodes $\{v_0, v_4, v_6\}$ form a stopping set.

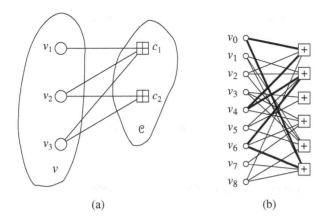

Figure 15.21: Stopping sets. (a) Idea of stopping sets; (b) stopping set $\{v_0, v_4, v_6\}$ on a $(9, 3)$ example code [442].

Recall that in the peeling decoder for the BEC channel, when a check node is connected to only one erased bit then that erased bit can be determined by the parity constraints. (The peeling algorithm is simply one way to organize the message-passing algorithm, so this insight applies more generally to erasure decoding.) In light of this, suppose that a set of erased variables E is equal to a stopping set $\mathcal{V}$; that is, all of the variables associated with the nodes in $\mathcal{V}$ are erased. Then since there are multiple connections of the check nodes to these variable nodes, these erased bits cannot be corrected.

It is clear that the union of two or more stopping sets is a stopping set. The union of all stopping sets is said to be the maximum stopping set. Any erasure pattern (of more than one erasure) occurring in the maximum stopping set cannot be recovered. Perhaps more interesting is a set of variable nodes $\mathcal{V}_{\text{ssf}}$ which is *stopping-set-free*, in that neighboring check nodes are not connected to more than one variable node in the stopping-set-free set. Then all patterns of errors in the stopping-set-free set can be decoded. A stopping set of minimum size in $\mathcal{G}$ is called a *minimum stopping set*, which we denote here as $\mathcal{V}_{\text{min}}$. Code symbols which are erased corresponding to the variables in $\mathcal{V}_{\text{min}}$ are unrecoverable. In order for a code to have large random-erasure correction capability (e.g., capable of correcting any pattern of erasures), it is necessary to have large minimum stopping sets.

There is an interesting relationship between minimum stopping sets and the row weight of a regular LDPC code.

Lemma 15.23 *Let H be the RC-constrained parity-check code of a regular (j, k) LPDC code. Then the size of the minimum possible stopping set is $j + 1$. (That is, there are no minimum stopping sets of size $\leq j$).*

Proof Let $\mathcal{E} = \{n_1, n_2, \ldots, n_t\}$ be a pattern of t erasures, with $0 \leq t \leq g$. For an erasure at any location, say $n_\ell \in \mathcal{E}$, since the column weight of H is j, then there are j rows of H that all check location n_ℓ; denote the set of these rows as $H_\ell = \{\mathbf{h}_{m_1}, \mathbf{h}_{m_2}, \ldots, \mathbf{h}_{m_j}\}$. Consider another erasure location in $\mathcal{E}$, say, $n_{\ell'}$. By the RC condition, there will not be two (or more) rows in H_ℓ that also check $n_{\ell'}$. This is true for any $\ell' \neq \ell$, so the other $t - 1$ erasures in $\mathcal{E}$ can be checked by at most $t - 1$ rows in H_ℓ. Therefore, there is at least one row in H_ℓ that checks one erased symbol n_ℓ and $k - 1$ other non-erased symbols. Thus, erasure n_ℓ can thus be recovered. Since this applies to any n_ℓ in $\mathcal{E}$, every erasure in $\mathcal{E}$ can be recovered. Hence every erasure pattern of up to j erasures can be recovered, and there is no minimum stopping set of size $\leq j$.

Now consider an erasure pattern $\mathcal{E} = \{n_1, n_2, \ldots, n_{j+1}\}$ of $j + 1$ erasures. Consider the j rows in H_ℓ that check the erased symbol n_ℓ. The erasure pattern could be such that each of the other j erasures are checked separately by the rows of H_ℓ, so that each row of H_ℓ checks two erasures. In this situation, $\mathcal{E}$

corresponds to a stopping set of size $j + 1$. Therefore, the minimum possible stopping set of a regular (j, k) code is $j + 1$.   □

It can be shown that for regular (j, k) codes, the sizes of minimum stopping sets with girths 4, 6, and 8 are 2, $j + 1$, and $2j$, respectively [329, 330]. This indicates that cycles of girth 4 are particularly deleterious to code performance, and many of the code design algorithms specifically avoid this. (It is also easy to detect cycles of girth 4, so this makes the design methods feasible.)

It has also been shown that [443] that a code with minimum distance $d_{\min}$ contains stopping sets of size $d_{\min}$. So a code having good random erasure capability must have large minimum distance.

15.5   Why Low-Density Parity-Check Codes?

Gallager showed that for random LDPC codes, the minimum distance $d_{\min}$ between codewords increases with N when column and row weights are held fixed [148, p. 5], that is, as they become increasingly sparse. Sequences of LDPC codes as $N \to \infty$ have been proved to reach channel capacity [288]. LDPC codes thus essentially act like the random codes used in Shannon's original proof of the channel coding theorem.

The decoding algorithm is tractable, at least on a per-iterations basis. As observed, the decoding algorithm has complexity linearly proportional to the length of the code. Thus, we get the benefit of a random code, but without the exponential decoding complexity usually associated with random codes. These codes fly in the face of the now outdated conventional coding wisdom, that there are "few known constructive codes that are good, fewer still that are practical, and none at all that are both practical and very good" [288, p. 399]. It is the extreme sparseness of the parity check matrix for LDPC codes that makes the decoding particularly attractive. The low-density nature of the parity check matrix thus, fortuitously, contributes both to good distance properties and the relatively low complexity of the decoding algorithm.

For finite length (but still long) codes, excellent coding gains are achievable as we briefly illustrate. Figure 15.22(a) shows the BPSK probability of error performance for two LDPC codes, a rate 1/2 code with $(N, K) = (20,000, 10,000)$ and a rate 1/3 code with $(N, K) = (15,000, 5000)$ from [286], compared with uncoded BPSK. These plots were made by adding simulated Gaussian noise to a codeword then iterating the message-passing algorithm up to 1000 times. The minimum number of blocks codewords

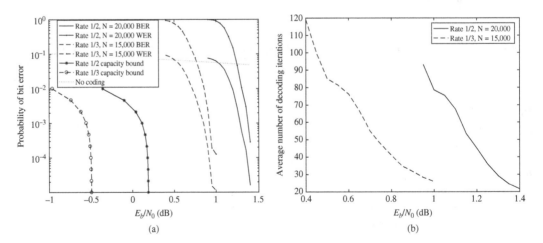

Figure 15.22: Illustration of the decoding performance of LPDC codes and the number of iterations to achieve decoding. (a) Performance for a rate 1/2 and a rate 1/3 code; (b) average number of decoding iterations.

at each SNR was 2000 . In all cases, the errors counted in the probability of error are detected errors; in no case did the decoder declare a successful decoding that was erroneous. (This is not always the case. We have found that for very short codes, the decoder may terminate with the condition $H\hat{\mathbf{c}} = \mathbf{0}$, but $\hat{\mathbf{c}}$ is erroneous. However, for long codes, decoding success essentially means correct decoding.) For both of these codes the performance is within about 1.5 dB of the Shannon channel capacity.

Figure 15.22(b) shows the *average* number of iterations for correctly decoded codewords to complete the decoding. (The peak number of iterations, not shown, would reach to the maximum set of 1000 in the case that the codeword is not found.) As the SNR decreases, the number of decoding iterations increases — additional work is required as the noise increases. At lower SNR, the number of iterations is around 100. The high number of iterations suggests a rather high potential decoding complexity, even though each iteration is readily computed. As suggested by EXIT chart analysis, as the decoding threshold is approached, the number of iterations must increase.

There are, of course, some potential disadvantages to LDPC codes. First, the best code performance is obtained for very long codes (as predicted by the channel coding theorem). This long block length, combined with the need for iterative decoding, introduces latency which may be unacceptable in many applications. Second, since the G matrix is not necessarily sparse, the encoding operation may have complexity $O(N^2)$. Some progress in reducing complexity is discussed in Section 15.11, and also using variations such as RA codes.

LDPC codes have an error floor, just as turbo codes do. Considerable effort has been devoted to designing codes with low error floors.

15.6 The Iterative Decoder on General Block Codes

There initially seems to be nothing impeding the use of the sum-product decoder for a general linear block code: it simply relies on the parity check matrix. This would mean that there is a straightforward iterative soft decoder for every linear block code. For example, Figure 15.23 shows the use of the soft decoder on a $(7,4)$ Hamming code. The soft decoding works better than conventional hard decoding by about 1.5 dB.

However, for larger codes a serious problem arises. Given a generator matrix G, the corresponding H matrix that might be found for it is not likely to be very sparse, so the resulting Tanner graph has

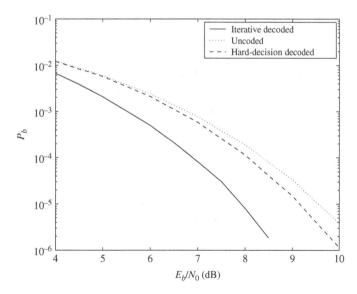

Figure 15.23: Comparison of hard-decision Hamming decoding and sum-product (iterative) decoding.

many cycles in it. In fact, a threshold is reached at some density of the parity check matrix at which the decoder seems to break down completely. Also, the problem of finding the sparsest representation of a matrix is as computationally difficult (NP-complete) as performing a ML decoding, so there is not much hope of taking a given H matrix and finding its sparsest equivalent to be used for decoding.

15.7 Density Evolution

Having described LDPC codes and the decoding, we now turn our attention to some analytical techniques associated with the codes. Density evolution is an analytical technique which has been used to understand limits of performance of LDPC decoders. It also provides a tool which can be used in the design of families of LDPC codes, since their performance can be predicted using density evolution much more rapidly than the performance can be simulated. Density evolution analysis introduces the idea of a channel threshold, above which the code performs well and below which the probability of error is non-negligible. This provides a single parameter characterizing code performance which may be used to gauge the performance compared to the ultimate limit of the channel capacity.

In density evolution, we make a key assumption that the block length $N \to \infty$, under which it is assumed there are no cycles in the Tanner graph. Since the code is linear and we have assumed a symmetric channel, it suffices for this analysis to assume that the all-zero codeword $\mathbf{c} = \mathbf{0}$ is sent. We also assume that the LDPC code is regular, with $|\mathcal{M}_n| = w_c$ and $|\mathcal{N}_m| = w_r$ for each n and m.

The analysis is essentially performed over ensembles of variable and check nodes, as the particular structure is drawn at random (respecting the assumption that there are no cycles in the Tanner graph.)

Let $L_{n \to m}^{[\ell]}$ and $L_{m \to n}^{[\ell]}$ denote the messages at variable and check nodes at decoding iteration ℓ.

Local Convention: We assume furthermore that a bit of zero is mapped to a signal amplitude of $+\sqrt{E_c}$ (i.e., $0 \to 1$ and $1 \to -1$). Based on this convention, the received signal is $y_n = \sqrt{E_c} + v_n$, where $v_n \sim \mathcal{N}(0, \sigma^2)$. In the log-likelihood decoding algorithm, the initial LLR is

$$L_{n \to m}^{[0]} = \frac{2\sqrt{E_c}}{\sigma^2} y_n = \frac{2\sqrt{E_c}}{\sigma^2} (\sqrt{E_c} + v_n),$$

which is Gaussian. The mean and variance of $L_{n \to m}^{[0]}$ are

$$m^{[0]} = E[L_{n \to m}^{[0]}] = \frac{2E_c}{\sigma^2} \quad \text{var}(L_{n \to m}^{[0]}) = \frac{4E_c}{\sigma^2} = 2m^{[0]}.$$

That is, the variance is equal to twice the mean. Thus,

$$L_{n \to m}^{[0]} \sim \mathcal{N}(m^{[0]}, 2m^{[0]}).$$

A Gaussian random variable having the property that its variance is equal to twice its mean is said to be **consistent**. Consistent random variables are convenient because they are described by a single parameter.

Clearly, the initial $L_{n \to m}^{[0]}$ are Gaussian, but at other iterations the $L_{n \to m}^{[\ell]}$ are not Gaussian. However, since the variable node computation involves a sum of incoming messages (see (15.7)), a central limit argument can be made that it should tend toward Gaussian. Furthermore, numerical experiments confirm that they are fairly Gaussian. Let $m^{[\ell]}$ denote the mean of $L_{n \to m}^{[\ell]}$. (This does not depend on the node n, so this is an ensemble average.)

The messages sent from check nodes, $L_{m \to n}[\ell]$, are nongaussian (e.g., computed using the tanh rule), but again numerical experiments confirm that they can be approximately represented by Gaussians. Let $\mu^{[\ell]} = E[L_{m \to n}^{[\ell]}]$ denote the mean of a randomly chosen $L_{m \to n}^{[\ell]}$ (or the average over an ensemble of codes). Under the assumption that the nodes are randomly chosen and that the code is regular, we also assume that the mean does not depend on m or n. In the interest of analytical tractability, *we assume that all messages are not only Gaussian, but consistent* so

$$L_{m \to n}^{[\ell]} \sim \mathcal{N}(\mu^{[\ell]}, 2\mu^{[\ell]}) \quad L_{n \to m}^{[\ell]} \sim \mathcal{N}(m^{[\ell]}, 2m^{[\ell]}).$$

Density evolution analysis tracks the parameters of these Gaussian random variables through the decoding process. By the tanh rule (15.6),

$$\tanh\left(\frac{L_{m\to n}^{[\ell]}}{2}\right) = \prod_{n'\in\mathcal{N}(m)\setminus\{n\}} \tanh\left(\frac{L_{n'\to m}^{[\ell]}}{2}\right).$$

Taking the expectation of both sides, we have

$$E\left[\tanh\left(\frac{L_{m\to n}^{[\ell]}}{2}\right)\right] = E\left[\prod_{n'\in\mathcal{N}(m)\setminus\{n\}} \tanh\left(\frac{L_{n'\to m}^{[\ell]}}{2}\right)\right]. \qquad (15.46)$$

Now define the function

$$\Psi(x) = E[\tanh(y/2)] \text{where } y \sim \mathcal{N}(x, 2x)$$

$$= \frac{1}{\sqrt{4\pi x}} \int_{-\infty}^{\infty} \tanh(y/2) e^{-(y-x)^2/(4x)}\, dy,$$

which is plotted in Figure 15.24 compared with the function $\tanh(x/2)$. The $\Psi(x)$ function is monotonic and looks roughly like $\tanh(x/2)$ stretched out somewhat.[2]

psifunc.m

Using the Ψ function, we can write (15.46) as

$$\Psi(\mu^{[\ell]}) = (\Psi(m^{[\ell]}))^{w_r-1}. \qquad (15.47)$$

Taking expectations of both sides of (15.7), we obtain

$$m^{[\ell]} = \frac{2E_c}{\sigma^2} + (w_c - 1)\mu^{[\ell-1]}.$$

Substituting this into (15.47), we obtain

$$\Psi(\mu^{[\ell]}) = \left(\Psi\left(\frac{2E_c}{\sigma^2} + (w_c - 1)\mu^{[\ell-1]}\right)\right)^{w_r-1},$$

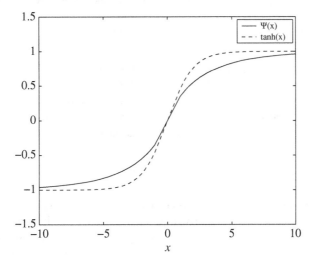

Figure 15.24: The function $\Psi(x)$ compared with $\tanh(x/2)$.

---

[2] It has been found [73] that $\Psi(x)$ can be closely approximated by $\Psi(x) \approx 1 - e^{-0.4527x^{0.86}+0.0218}$.

or

$$\mu^{[\ell]} = \Psi^{-1} \left(\left(\Psi \left(\frac{2E_c}{\sigma^2} + (w_c - 1)\mu^{[\ell-1]} \right) \right)^{w_r - 1} \right). \qquad (15.48)$$

The recursion is initialized with $\mu^{[0]} = 0$. The dynamics are completely determined by the row weight w_r, the column weight w_c, and the SNR E_c/σ^2.

This equation describes how the mean log-likelihood messages from a check node change with time. (Again, under the assumptions that there are no cycles in the Tanner graph, and that the Gaussian assumptions are valid.) If the decoding algorithm converges to a decoded value, the random variables $L_{m \to n}^{[\ell]}$ should become more and more certain — since the all-zero codeword is assumed — that is, larger and larger. Then, since the messages are assumed Gaussian, the probability of a message less than 0 (that is, incorrectly decoded) becomes small as the number of iterations increases.

For some values of SNR, the mean $\mu^{[\ell]}$ converges to a small fixed point. The Gaussian pdf it represents would thus have both positive and negative outcomes, meaning that the messaged $L_{m \to n}^{[\ell]}$ represented by this distribution could have negative values, or that (recalling that the all-zero codeword is assumed) there is a non-negligible probability that there are decoding errors. On the other hand, for some values of SNR, the mean $\mu^{[\ell]}$ tends to infinity. The pdf has all of its probability on positive values. Thus, for a sufficiently large number of iterations the decoder would decode correctly.

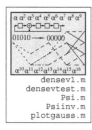

densev1.m
densevtest.m
Psi.m
Psiinv.m
plotgauss.m

Example 15.24 Let $w_c = 4$ and $w_r = 6$, resulting in a $R = 1 - 4/6 = 1/3$ code. Recall that $E_c = RE_b$ and $\sigma^2 = N_0/2$, so that $E_c/\sigma^2 = 2RE_b/N_0$. Let $E_b/N_0 = 1.72$ dB. Then the iteration (15.48) achieves a fixed point at $\mu^* = \lim_{l \to \infty} \mu^{[\ell]} = 0.3155$. The corresponding density $\mathcal{N}(0.3155, 0.631)$ is shown using dashed lines in Figure 15.25(a). The mean is small enough that there is a high probability that $\lambda^{[\ell]} < 0$ for any iteration; hence, decoding errors are probable. In Figure 15.25(b), the mean value is shown as a function of iterations. When $E_b/N_0 = 1.72$ dB, after about 20 iterations the mean has converged to its value of 0.3155.

When $E_b/N_0 = 1.764$ dB, the mean (15.48) tends to ∞: $\mu^{[\ell]} \to \infty$ as $l \to \infty$. Figure 15.25(a) shows the distributions for iterations 507 through 511. Clearly, for high iteration numbers, the decoder is almost certain to decode correctly. After about 507 iterations, the mean quickly increases.

Figure 15.25(b) shows the mean values $\mu^{[\ell]}$ as a function of the iteration number ℓ for various SNRs. For sufficiently small SNR, the mean converges to a finite limit, implying a nonzero probability of error. As the SNR increases, the mean "breaks away" to infinity after some number of iterations, where the number of iterations required decreases with increasing SNR. At 1.72, 1.75, and 1.76 dB, the means converge to finite values. However, for a slight increase of SNR to 1.764 dB, the mean breaks away (after about 500 iterations). For another slight increase to 1.765 dB, the breakaway happens at about 250 iterations.   □

threshtab.m

As this example shows, there is a value of E_b/N_0 above which reliable decoding can be expected ($\mu^{[\ell]} \to \infty$) and below which it cannot. This is called the *threshold* of the decoder. Table 15.1 [73] shows thresholds for regular LDPC codes of various rates, as well as channel capacity at that rate. (*Note*: The recursion (15.48) is sensitive to numerical variation.) The thresholds are shown both in terms of E_b/N_0 and in terms of a channel standard deviation σ_τ, where

$$\frac{2RE_b}{N_0} = \frac{1}{\sigma_\tau^2}.$$

As the table shows, there is a tendency toward decrease (improvement) in the E_b/N_0 threshold as the rate of the code decreases. However, even within a given rate, there is variation depending on the values of w_c and w_r. It appears that values of $w_c > 3$ generally raise the threshold. Note that, since the analysis does not take cycles in the graph into account, this has nothing to do with problems in the decoding algorithm associated with cycles; it is an intrinsic part of the structure of the code.

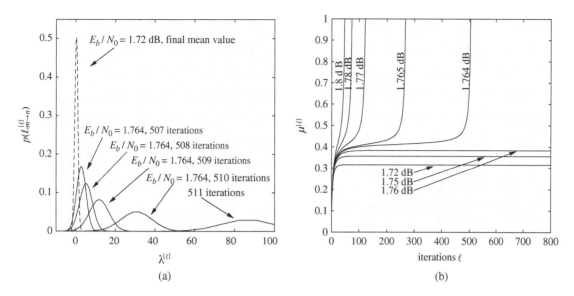

Figure 15.25: Behavior of density evolution for a $R = 1/3$ code. (a) The pdf of $L_{m \to n}^{[\ell]}$ for $E_b/N_0 = 1.72$ (final), and $E_b/N_0 = 1.764$ (various iterations); (b) the mean of the pdf of $L_{m \to n}^{[\ell]}$ as a function of iteration ℓ for different values of E_b/N_0.

Table 15.1: Threshold Values for Various LDPC Codes for the Binary AWGN Channel

w_c	w_r	Rate	Threshold σ_τ	Threshold E_b/N_0 (dB)	Capacity (dB)	Gap (dB)
3	12	0.75	0.6297	2.2564	1.6264	0.63
3	9	2/3	0.7051	1.7856	1.0595	0.7261
4	10	0.6	0.7440	1.7767	0.6787	1.098
3	6	0.5	0.8747	1.1628	0.1871	0.9757
4	8	0.5	0.8323	1.5944	0.1871	1.4073
5	10	0.5	0.7910	2.0365	0.1871	1.8494
3	5	0.4	1.0003	0.9665	-0.2383	1.2048
4	6	1/3	1.0035	1.7306	-0.4954	2.226
3	4	0.25	1.2517	1.0603	-0.7941	1.8544

15.8 EXIT Charts for LDPC Codes

Recall from Section 14.5 that an EXIT chart is a method for representing how the mutual information between the decoder output and the transmitted bits changes over turbo decoding iterations. EXIT charts can also be established for LDPC codes, as we now describe.

Consider the fragments of a Tanner graph in Figure 15.26. In these fragments, there are bit-to-check messages and check-to-bit messages, denoted as $\mu_{B \to C}$ and $\mu_{C \to B}$, respectively, where the messages are the log-likelihood ratios. Let $r_{mn}^{[\ell]}(x)$ and $q_{mn}^{[\ell]}(x)$ denote the probabilities computed in the horizontal and vertical steps of Algorithm 15.1, respectively, at the ith iteration of the algorithm. Using the original probability-based decoding algorithm of Algorithm 15.2, the messages from bit nodes (n) to check

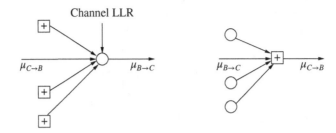

Figure 15.26: A portion of a Tanner graph, showing messages from bits to checks and from checks to bits.

nodes (m) or back are

$$C \to B : \mu_{C \to B} = \log \frac{r_{mn}(1)}{r_{mn}(0)}$$

$$B \to C : \mu_{B \to C} = \log \frac{q_{mn}(1)}{q_{mn}(0)}.$$

Let X denote the original transmitted bits. The mutual information (see Section 1.12) between a check-to-bit message $\mu_{C \to B}$ and the transmitted data symbol for that bit X is denoted as $I(X, \mu_{C \to B}) = I_{C \to B}$. The iteration number ℓ may also be indicated, as in $I_{C \to B}^{[\ell]}$. The actual mutual information is computed experimentally as follows. Histograms of the message data $\mu_{C \to B}^{[\ell]}$ are used to estimate the probability distribution. These histograms are obtained from the outputs $\log r_{mn}(1)/r_{mn}(0)$ of *all* the check nodes in the Tanner graph. (Alternatively a single node could be used, by sending the codeword multiple times through the channel with independent noise.) These histograms are normalized to form estimated probability density functions, here denoted $\hat{p}(\mu)$, of the random variable $\mu_{C \to B}$. Then these estimated density functions are used in the mutual information integral (1.43) wherever $p(y| - a)$ appears. Because of symmetry, the likelihood $p(y|a)$ is computed using $\hat{p}(-\mu)$. The numerical evaluation of the integral then gives the desired mutual information.

In a similar way, the mutual information between a bit-to-check message $\mu_{B \to C}$ and the transmitted data symbol for that bit X, $I(X, \mu_{B \to C}) = I_{B \to C}$, is computed from the histograms of the outputs $\log q_{mn}(1)/q_{mn}(0)$ to estimate the densities in (1.43).

ldpcsim.mat
exit1.m
loghist.m

The first trace of the EXIT chart is now formed by plotting $I_{C \to B}^{[\ell]}, I_{B \to C}^{[\ell+1]}$ for values of the iteration number ℓ as the decoding algorithm proceeds. The horizontal axis is thus the check-to-bit axis. The second trace of the EXIT chart uses $I_{B \to C}^{[\ell+1]}$ as the independent variable, but plotted on the vertical axis, with $I_{C \to B}^{[\ell+1]}$ — that is, the mutual information at the *next* iteration — on the horizontal axis. The "transfer" of information in the EXIT chart results because the check-to-bit message at the output of the $\ell + 1$th stage becomes the check-to-bit message at the input of the next stage.

exit3.m
dotrajectory.m

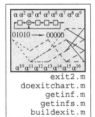

exit2.m
doexitchart.m
getinf.m
getinfs.m
buildexit.m

Example 15.25 Figure 15.27 shows the density estimated from the histogram of the log-likelihood ratios $L = \log r_{mn}(1)/r_{mn}(0)$ for a (15,000, 10,000) LDPC code at an SNR of 1.6 dB for various iterations of the algorithm. At iteration 0, the log likelihoods from the received signal data are plotted. At the other iterations, the log likelihoods of the bit-to-check information are plotted. Observe that the histogram has a rather Gaussian appearance (justifying the density evolution analysis of Section 15.7) and that as the iterations proceed, the mean becomes increasingly negative. The decoder thus becomes increasingly certain that the transmitted bits are 0.

Figure 15.28 shows the mutual information as a function of decoder iteration number for bit-to-check and check-to-bit information for various SNRs. Perhaps the most interesting is for an SNR of 0.4 dB: after an initial increase in information, the decoder stalls and no additional increases occur. The EXIT chart is essentially obtained by eliminating the iteration number parameter from these two plots and plotting them against each other.

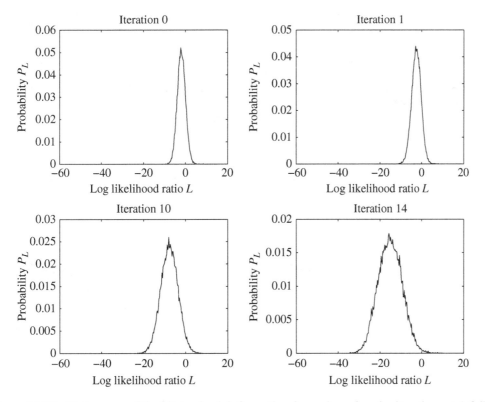

Figure 15.27: Histograms of the bit-to-check information for various decoder iterations at 1.6 dB.

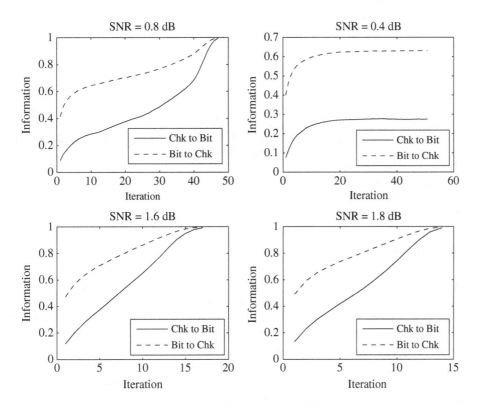

Figure 15.28: Decoder information at various signal-to-noise ratios.

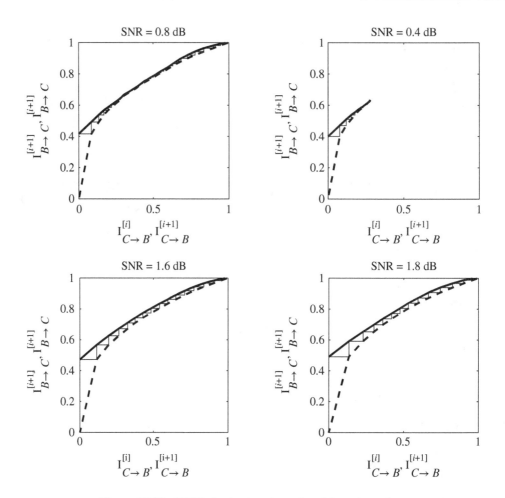

Figure 15.29: EXIT charts at various signal-to-noise ratios.

Figure 15.29 shows the EXIT chart for this code at various SNRs. The solid bold line plots the points $(I_{C \to B}^{[\ell]}, I_{B \to C}^{[\ell+1]})$ and the dashed bold line plots the points $(I_{B \to C}^{[\ell+1]}, I_{C \to B}^{[\ell+1]})$, with the horizontal axis representing $I_{C \to B}$ and the vertical axis representing $I_{B \to C}$. The narrow solid line plots the progress of the decoding algorithm: the decoder essentially follows the stair-step pattern between the two traces of the plot. At an SNR of 0.8 dB, the code is fairly close to the decoding threshold, so it takes many iterations for the decoder to pass through the channel. At an SNR of 0.4 dB, the decoder is below the decoding threshold: the information is not able to make it through the channel. At an SNR of 1.2 dB, the channel is open somewhat wider, so fewer decoding iterations are required, and at 1.8 dB the channel is open wider still.   □

15.9   Irregular LDPC Codes

Regular LDPC codes, good as they may be, can by improved upon by using irregular LDPC code [283]. An irregular (or nonuniform) LDPC code has a very sparse parity check matrix in which the column weight (resp. row weight) may vary from column to column (resp. row to row). Considering that the results in Table 15.1 suggest that for the same rate, different column/row weights perform differently, the ability to allocate weights flexibly provides potentially useful design capability. In fact, the best known LDPC codes are irregular; gains of up to 0.5 dB compared to regular codes are attainable [282, 373]. In this section, we present some results of the design of irregular codes. This is followed by a sketch of the density evolution analysis which leads to these results.

15.9.1 Degree Distribution Pairs

The distribution of the weights of the columns and rows of the parity check matrix is described as follows. We let λ_i represent the fraction of *edges* emanating from a variable node in the Tanner graph for the code and let ρ_i represent the fraction of edges emanating from a check node. Let d_v denote the maximum number of edges connected to a variable node and let d_c be the maximum number of edges connected to a check node. The polynomial

$$\lambda(x) = \sum_{i=2}^{d_v} \lambda_i x^{i-1}$$

represents the distribution of variable node weights and

$$\rho(x) = \sum_{i=2}^{d_c} \rho_i x^{i-1}$$

represents the distribution of check node weights. These are called the variable node and check node distributions, respectively. The degree distributions satisfy $\lambda(1) = 1$ and $\rho(1) = 1$. The pair $(\lambda(x), \rho(x))$ is called a *degree distribution pair*. For example, for the $(3, 6)$ regular code, $\lambda(x) = x^2$ and $\rho(x) = x^5$.

The number of variable nodes of degree i is (see Exercise 15.12)

$$N \frac{\lambda_i}{\sum_{j \geq 2} \lambda_j / j} = N \frac{\lambda_i}{\int_0^1 \lambda(x)\, dx}. \tag{15.49}$$

The total number of edges emanating from all nodes is

$$E = N \sum_{i \geq 2} i \frac{\lambda_i / i}{\int_0^1 \lambda(x)\, dx} = N \frac{1}{\int_0^1 \lambda(x)\, dx}. \tag{15.50}$$

Similarly, the number of check nodes of degree i is

$$N \frac{\rho_i / i}{\sum_{j \geq 2} \rho(j)/j} = N \frac{\rho_i / i}{\int_0^1 \rho(x)\, dx}$$

and the total number of edges is

$$E = M \frac{1}{\int_0^1 \rho(x)\, dx}. \tag{15.51}$$

Equating (15.50) and (15.51) we find

$$\frac{M}{N} = \frac{\int_0^1 \rho(x)\, dx}{\int_0^1 \lambda(x)\, dx}.$$

Under the assumption that the corresponding check equations are all linearly independent, the rate of the code is

$$R(\lambda, \rho) = \frac{N - M}{N} = 1 - \frac{\int_0^1 \rho(x)\, dx}{\int_0^1 \lambda(x)\, dx}.$$

Example 15.26 Suppose $\lambda_3 = 0.5$ and $\lambda_4 = 0.5$ and $N = 1000$. Then

$$\lambda(x) = 0.5x^2 + 0.5x^3$$

and there are

$$N\frac{0.5/3}{0.5/3 + 0.5/4} = 571$$

(rounding) variable nodes of degree 3 and

$$N\frac{0.5/4}{0.5/3 + 0.5/4} = 429$$

variable nodes of degree 4, for a total of

$$E = 571 \cdot 3 + 429 \cdot 4 = 3426$$

edges in the graph. □

15.9.2 Density Evolution for Irregular Codes

We now summarize how the density evolution is described for these irregular codes. We present the highlights of the technique, leaving aside some technicalities which are covered in [?]. In the current analysis, a more explicit representation of the distribution of the messages is needed than the consistent Gaussian approximation made in Section 15.7.

The decoder algorithms can be summarized as

$$L_{m\to n}^{[\ell]} = 2\tanh^{-1}\left(\prod_{n'\in\mathcal{N}_m\setminus\{n\}}\tanh\left(\frac{L_{n\to m}^{[\ell-1]}}{2}\right)\right) \tag{15.52}$$

$$L_{n\to m}^{[\ell]} = L_n^{[0]} + \sum_{m'\in\mathcal{M}_n\setminus\{m\}} L_{m'\to n}^{[\ell]}. \tag{15.53}$$

Write (15.52) as

$$\tanh\frac{L_{m\to n}^{[\ell]}}{2} = \prod_{n'\in\mathcal{N}_m\setminus n}\tanh(\frac{L_{n'\to m}^{[\ell-1]}}{2})$$

and take the log of both sides. In doing this, we have to be careful about the signs. Therefore, we will separate out the sign,

$$\left(\text{sgn}(L_{m\to n}^{[\ell]}), \log\left|\tanh\frac{L_{m\to n}^{[\ell]}}{2}\right|\right) = \sum_{n\in\mathcal{N}_m\setminus\{n\}}\left(\text{sgn}(L_{n'\to m}^{[\ell-1]}), \log\left|\tanh\frac{L_{n'\to m}^{[\ell-1]}}{2}\right|\right). \tag{15.54}$$

We employ here a somewhat different definition of the sgn function:

$$\text{sgn}(x) = \begin{cases} 0 & x > 0 \\ 0 & \text{with probability } \frac{1}{2} \text{ if } x = 0 \\ 1 & \text{with probability } \frac{1}{2} \text{ if } x = 0 \\ 1 & x < 0 \end{cases}$$

so that sgn(x) = 1 means that x < 0. Then the sum for the signs is performed in $\mathbb{Z}_2$ and the sum for the magnitude is the ordinary sum in $\mathbb{R}$.

Now let γ be the function

$$\gamma(x) : [-\infty, +\infty] \to \{0, 1\} \times [0, \infty]$$

(where by {0, 1} we designate GF(2) with elements 0 and 1) defined by

$$\gamma(x) = (\gamma_1(x), \gamma_2(x)) = (\text{sgn}(x), \log\tanh(|x/2|)). \tag{15.55}$$

Then (15.54) is

$$\gamma(L_{m\to n}^{[\ell]}) = \sum_{n' \in \mathcal{N}_m \setminus \{n\}} \gamma(L_{n'\to m}^{[\ell-1]})$$

so we can express (15.52) as

$$L_{m\to n}^{[\ell]} = \gamma^{-1}\left(\sum_{n' \in \mathcal{N}_m \setminus \{n\}} \gamma(L_{n'\to m}^{[\ell-1]}) \right). \tag{15.56}$$

Equation (15.56) has the feature that the product is converted to a sum; in the analysis below this is useful because sums of independent random variables have convolved distributions.

We describe the evolution in terms of distribution functions: Let $\mathcal{F}$ denote the space of right-continuous, nondecreasing functions F_z defined on $\mathbb{R}$, such that for $F_z \in \mathcal{F}$, $\lim_{x\to-\infty} F_z(x) = 0$ and $\lim_{x\to\infty} F_z(x) \leq 1$, allowing for the possibility of a point probability mass at ∞: $P(z = \infty) = 1 - \lim_{x\to\infty} F_z(x)$. A function $F_z \in \mathcal{F}$ represents the usual cumulative distribution function of the random variable z: $F_z(x) = P(z \leq x)$. We define the left limit of F_z as $F_z^-(x) = \lim_{y\uparrow x} F_z(y)$, so that $1 - F_z^-(x) = P(z \geq x)$. Derivatives (more precisely, Radon–Nikodyn derivatives [41]) of the distribution functions are probability densities.

Suppose we have a random variable z with distribution F_z. We wish to describe the distribution of the random variable $\gamma(z) = (\gamma_1(z), \gamma_2(z))$, with γ defined in (15.55). Note that any function $G(s,x)$ defined over $\{0,1\} \times [0,\infty)$ can be written as

$$G(s,x) = I_{s=0} G^0(x) + I_{s=1} G^1(x),$$

where $I_{s=a}$ is the indicator (or characteristic) function:

$$I_{s=a} = \begin{cases} 1 & \text{if } s = a \\ 0 & \text{if } s \neq a. \end{cases}$$

Using this notation, we define the distribution of $\gamma(z)$ as

$$\Gamma(F_z)(s,x) = I_{s=0}\Gamma_0(F_z)(x) + I_{s=1}\Gamma_1(F_z)(x), \tag{15.57}$$

where

$$\Gamma_0(F_z)(x) = 1 - F_z^-(-\log\tanh(x/2)) = P(z \geq -\log\tanh(x/2))$$

and

$$\Gamma_1(F_z)(x) = F_z(\log\tanh(x/2)) = P(z \leq \log\tanh(x/2)).$$

It can be shown that

$$\lim_{x\to\infty} \Gamma_0(F_z)(x) - \lim_{x\to\infty}\Gamma_1(F_z)(x) = P(z = 0).$$

The function Γ has an inverse: for a function

$$G(s,x) = I_{s=0}G^0(x) + I_{s=1}G^1(x),$$

define Γ^{-1} by

$$\Gamma^{-1}(G)(x) = I_{x>0}G^0(-\log\tanh(x/2)) + I_{x<0}G^1(-\log\tanh(-x/2)) \tag{15.58}$$

and

$$\Gamma^{-1}(G)(0) = \lim_{x\to\infty} G^0(x).$$

It can be verified that $\Gamma^{-1}(\Gamma(F)) = F$ for all $F \in \mathcal{F}$.

For notational convenience, Γ and Γ^{-1} are also applied to densities, where it is to be understood that the notation is a representation of the operation applied to the associated distributions.

Let G and H be two distributions,

$$G = I_{s=0}G^0 + I_{s=1}G^1 \quad H = I_{s=0}H^0 + I_{s=1}H^1.$$

Let $\otimes$ denote the operation of convolution on distribution functions. Then we define the convolution $\otimes$ on G and H by

$$G \otimes H = I_{s=0}((G^0 \otimes H^0) + (G^1 \otimes H^1)) + I_{s=1}((G^0 \otimes H^1) + (G^1 \otimes H^0)).$$

Again for notational convenience we allow the convolution operator to act on densities, where it is to be understood that it applies to the associated distributions. We denote repeated convolution as $\otimes$:

$$\underbrace{G \otimes G \otimes \cdots \otimes G}_{p \text{ factors}} = G^{\otimes p}.$$

Let $P^{[\ell]}$ and $Q^{[\ell]}$ be the densities of the random variables $L_{n\to m}^{[\ell]}$ and $L_{m\to n}^{[\ell]}$, respectively. The corresponding distribution functions are denoted $\int P^{[\ell]}$ and $\int Q^{[\ell]}$.

Let the graph associated with the code have the distribution pair (λ, ρ),

$$\lambda(x) = \sum_{i\geq2} \lambda_i x^{i-1} \quad \rho(x) = \sum_{i\geq2} \rho_i x^{i-1}.$$

Recall that the fraction of edges connected to a variable node of degree i is λ_i and the fraction of edges connected to a check node is ρ_i. Thus, a randomly chosen edge in the graph is connected to a check node of degree i with probability ρ_i. Therefore, with probability ρ_i, the sum in (15.56) has $(i-1)$ terms, corresponding to the edges connecting check m with its neighbors except bit n. We now invoke the independence assumption, that these neighboring nodes are independent. Combining (15.56) with the definition of the Γ function, we obtain

$$Q^{[\ell]} = \Gamma^{-1}\left(\sum_{i\geq2} \rho_i[\Gamma(P^{[l-1]})]^{\otimes(i-1)}\right).$$

We use the shorthand notation for this

$$Q^{[\ell]} = \Gamma^{-1}\rho(\Gamma(P^{[\ell-1]})). \tag{15.59}$$

(This explains the definition $\sum_{i\geq2} \rho_i x^{i-1}$, with the exponent $i-1$.) The recursion for $P^{[\ell]}$ is straightforward, since only sums are involved:

$$P^{[\ell]} = P_0 \otimes \sum_{i\geq2} \lambda_i[Q^{[\ell]}]^{\otimes(i-1)}.$$

Again we use the shorthand notation

$$P^{[\ell]} = P_0 \otimes \lambda(Q^{[\ell]}). \tag{15.60}$$

Combining (15.59) and (15.60), we obtain the overall recursion,

$$P^{[\ell]} = P_0 \otimes \lambda(\Gamma^{-1}(\rho(\Gamma(P^{[\ell-1]})))). \tag{15.61}$$

15.9.3 Computation and Optimization of Density Evolution

It can be shown that the recursion (15.61) always converges to some fixed distribution, although it may be the distribution with its probability mass at ∞. It can further be shown that the probability of error is a nonincreasing function of the iteration number l.

The convolutions implied in (15.61) can be efficiently computed by quantizing the distributions and employing an FFT for fast convolution. This corresponds to a quantized message-passing algorithm, which is suboptimal compared to exact message passing. Any decoding threshold σ_τ thus obtained is therefore a lower bound on the actual threshold.

The basic problem is to choose coefficients $\{\eta_i\}$ and $\{\rho_i\}$ so that the decoding threshold σ_τ is as large as possible. The basic outline for the computation is as follows. Starting with a given degree distribution pair $(\eta(x), \rho(x))$, an error probability ϵ and a maximum number of iterations L is selected. From this, a maximum admissible channel parameter σ is selected, which is the largest channel parameter such that the error probability after L iterations is less than ϵ. Then a *hill climbing* approach is used. A small change to the degree distribution pair is introduced. If the change leads to a target error probability after L iterations, or if the maximum admissible channel parameter is larger, then the new degree distribution pair is accepted, otherwise the old degree distribution pair is retained. The hill climbing process repeats until some termination criterion is satisfied.

Clearly, there is a very large search space. Some acceleration of the search process can be obtained by limiting the scope of the search. It has been found that very good degree distribution pairs exist with only a few nonzero terms. In particular, it suffices to allow only two or three nonzero check node degrees (which may be chosen consecutively) and to limit the nonzero variable node degrees to 2, 3, or d_v.

A variation on this density evolution concept has been used to design rate $R = 1/2$ codes which (theoretically) perform to within 0.0045 dB of the capacity limit [72]. Simulations of actual codes with block lengths $N = 10^7$ indicate that the actual performance is within 0.04 dB of capacity. So, while the analysis and design are somewhat idealized, the theory matches the practice rather well.

Table 15.2 shows results of this design procedure for rate 1/2 codes. The parameter d_v is the maximum variable node degree.

Table 15.2: Degree Distribution Pairs for $R = 1/2$ Codes for Binary Transmission over an AWGN [?, p. 623]. σ_τ is the decoding threshold, also expressed as (E_b/N_0) (dB)

d_v:	4	5	6	7	8	9	10	11	12
λ_2	0.38354	0.32660	0.33241	0.31570	0.30013	0.27684	0.25105	0.23882	0.24426
λ_3	0.04327	0.11960	0.24632	0.41672	0.28395	0.28342	0.30938	0.29515	0.25907
λ_4	0.57409	0.18393	0.11014				0.00104	0.03261	0.01054
λ_5		0.36988							0.05510
λ_6			0.3112						
λ_7				0.43810					
λ_8					0.41592				0.01455
λ_9						0.43974			
λ_{10}							0.43853		0.01275
λ_{11}								0.43342	
λ_{12}									0.40373
ρ_5	0.24123								
ρ_6	0.75877	0.78555	0.76611	0.43810	0.22919	0.01568			
ρ_7		0.21445	0.23389	0.56190	0.77081	0.85244	0.63676	0.43011	0.25475
ρ_8						0.13188	0.36324	0.56989	0.73438
ρ_9									0.01087
σ_τ	0.9114	0.9194	0.9304	0.9424	0.9497	0.9540	0.9558	0.9572	0.9580
E_b/N_0 (dB)	0.8058	0.7299	0.6266	0.5153	0.4483	0.4090	0.3927	0.3799	0.3727
Gap (dB)	0.6187	0.5428	0.4395	0.3282	0.2612	0.2219	0.2056	0.1928	0.1856

15.9.4 Using Irregular Codes

The procedure outlined above determines a degree distribution pair $(\eta(x), \rho(x))$. This can be used to construct an actual code as follows. Choose a code length N (usually quite large). Determine the number of variable nodes N_i having i edges and the number of check nodes M_i having i edges. Randomly generate a matrix H having the given column and row weights. Some iteration of this is probably necessary to avoid cycles of length 4 in the graph (and possibly other short cycles). Then the decoding algorithms described above apply to this parity check matrix without any change.

15.10 More on LDPC Code Construction

sparseHno4.m

It is straightforward to generate random LDPC codes: simply generate columns of H at random having the appropriate weight. However, there are some practicalities to be dealt with. First, if the rows of H are not linearly independent, some rows can be eliminated, which serves to *increase* the rate of the code by decreasing the redundancy. Second, it is important to reduce the number of cycles in the graph associated with the code. Therefore, eliminating or regenerating columns which would contribute to short cycles is advised. It can be seen that when two columns of H have an overlap of more than 1 bit (as in the italicized elements of (15.1)) there is a cycle of length 4 in the iterated graph. For large N, this is a very easy condition to check for and eliminate in the random generation process. With somewhat more work, longer cycles can be detected and removed.

Besides such random constructions, there have been more recent constructions which attempt to introduce additional structure into the parity check matrix and/or the generator matrix. These techniques are outlined in Chapter 16.

15.11 Encoding LDPC Codes

While LDPC codes have an efficient decoding algorithm, with complexity linear in the code length, the *encoding* efficiency is quadratic in the block length, since it requires multiplication by the generator matrix which is not sparse. This complexity is in contrast to the turbo code case, which has linear encode complexity. However, as we present here [374], it is possible to encode with a reasonable complexity, provided that some preprocessing is performed prior to encoding.

Before encoding, we perform the following preprocessing steps. By row and column permutations, we bring the parity check matrix into the form indicated in Figure 15.30, where the upper right corner can be identified as a lower triangular matrix. Because it is obtained only by permutations, the parity check matrix is still sparse. We denote the permutation/decomposition of the parity check matrix as H, where

$$H = \begin{bmatrix} A & B & T \\ C & D & E \end{bmatrix}$$

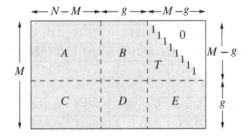

Figure 15.30: Result of permutation of rows and columns on parity check matrix.

and say that H is in *approximate lower triangular* form. We say that g is the *gap* of this representation. T is a $(M - g) \times (M - g)$ lower triangular matrix with ones along the diagonal and hence is invertible. Now multiply H on the left by the matrix

$$\begin{bmatrix} I & \mathbf{0} \\ -ET^{-1} & I \end{bmatrix}.$$

This amounts to doing Gaussian elimination to clear the matrix E, which produces the form

$$\tilde{H} = \begin{bmatrix} I & \mathbf{0} \\ -ET^{-1} & I \end{bmatrix} H = \begin{bmatrix} A & B & T \\ -ET^{-1}A + C & -ET^{-1}B + D & \mathbf{0} \end{bmatrix}.$$

Note that $\tilde{H}$ is the parity check matrix for an equivalent code.

For a message vector $\mathbf{m}$ of length K, we write the codeword as

$$\mathbf{c} = \begin{bmatrix} \mathbf{m} \\ \mathbf{p}_1 \\ \mathbf{p}_2 \end{bmatrix},$$

where $\mathbf{p}_1$ and $\mathbf{p}_2$ represent parity information. The parity check equation $\tilde{H}\mathbf{c} = \mathbf{0}$ gives rise to two equations,

$$A\mathbf{m} + B\mathbf{p}_1 + T\mathbf{p}_2 = \mathbf{0} \tag{15.62}$$

$$(-ET^{-1}A + C)\mathbf{m} + (-ET^{-1}B + D)\mathbf{p}_1 = \mathbf{0}. \tag{15.63}$$

Letting $X = (-ET^{-1}B + D)$ and assuming for the moment that X is nonsingular, we have from (15.63)

$$\mathbf{p}_1 = -X^{-1}(-ET^{-1}A + C)\mathbf{m}.$$

The $g \times (N - M)$ matrix $-X^{-1}(-ET^{-1}A + C)$ can be precomputed and saved, so that $\mathbf{p}_1$ can be computed with a complexity of $O(g(N - M))$. The complexity can be further reduced, as is outlined below.

Once $\mathbf{p}_1$ is known, then $\mathbf{p}_2$ can be obtained from (15.62) by

$$\mathbf{p}_2 = -T^{-1}(A\mathbf{m} + B\mathbf{p}_1).$$

Note that since T^{-1} is lower triangular, $\mathbf{p}_2$ can be found by backsubstitution.

If it turns out that X is singular, then columns of $\tilde{H}$ can be permuted to obtain a nonsingular X.

The process of computing $\mathbf{p}_1$ and $\mathbf{p}_2$ constitutes the encoding process. The steps for the computation as well as their computational complexity are outlined here (assuming that the preprocessing steps have already been accomplished). For the sake of clarity, intermediate variables are used to show the steps which may not be necessary in a final implementation.

Steps to compute $\mathbf{p}_1 = -X^{-1}(-ET^{-1}A + C)\mathbf{m}$:

Operation	Comment	Complexity
$\mathbf{x}_1 = A\mathbf{m}$	Multiplication by a sparse matrix	$O(N)$
$\mathbf{x}_2 = T^{-1}\mathbf{x}_1$	Solve $T\mathbf{x}_2 = \mathbf{x}_1$ by backsubstitution (T is sparse)	$O(N)$
$\mathbf{x}_3 = -E\mathbf{x}_2$	Multiplication by a sparse matrix	$O(N)$
$\mathbf{x}_4 = C\mathbf{m}$	Multiplication by a sparse matrix	$O(N)$
$\mathbf{x}_5 = \mathbf{x}_3 + \mathbf{x}_4$	Addition	$O(N)$
$\mathbf{p}_1 = -X^{-1}\mathbf{x}_5$	Multiplication by dense $g \times g$ matrix	$O(g^2)$

Steps to compute $\mathbf{p}_2 = -T^{-1}(A\mathbf{m} + B\mathbf{p}_1)$.

Operation	Comment	Complexity
$\mathbf{x}_1 = A\mathbf{m}$	Multiplication by sparse matrix (already done)	0
$\mathbf{x}_6 = B\mathbf{p}_1$	Multiplication by sparse matrix	$O(N)$
$\mathbf{x}_7 = \mathbf{x}_1 + \mathbf{x}_6$	Addition	$O(N)$
$\mathbf{p}_2 = -T^{-1}\mathbf{x}_7$	Solve $T\mathbf{p}_2 = \mathbf{x}_7$ by backsubstitution (T is sparse)	$O(N)$

The overall algorithm is $O(N + g^2)$. Clearly, the smaller g (the "gap") can be made, the lower the complexity of the algorithm. A heuristic greedy search method for performing the initial permutations is described in [374].

15.12   A Variation: Low-Density Generator Matrix Codes

As a variation on the LDPC theme, it is interesting to consider low-density generator matrix (LDGM) codes. These are codes in which the generator matrix G is very sparse. Let $G = \begin{bmatrix} I \\ P \end{bmatrix}$ be a very sparse generator in systematic form. Then the corresponding parity check matrix $H = \begin{bmatrix} -P & I \end{bmatrix}$ is also very sparse, so the code is amenable to decoding using the sum-product algorithm. The LDGM code is thus straightforward to encode and decode.

However, it is clear that since G is very sparse the code has low-weight codewords, which results in a significant error floor. For this reason, LGDM codes have not been of as much interest. It has been shown, however, that a straightforward concatenation of two LGDM codes (which is still easy to encode) has good performance when used with an iterative decoder between the concatenated stages [162].

Programming Laboratory 13: Programming an LDPC Decoder

Objective

You are to implement the decoding algorithm for the low-density parity-check code, as described in Algorithm 15.2, and test it using (1) a small code, to verify that your algorithm is working correctly and (2) a couple of long codes.

Background

Reading: Sections 15.2 and 15.4.

Because the parity check matrix for a long code would be huge if explicitly represented, it is important to represent only the nonzero elements of the sparse matrix. To store a sparse matrix in a file, the following format is used.

```
N M
maxcolweight maxrowweight
colwt colwt colwt ... colwt
rowwt rowwt rowwt ... rowwt
M1(1) M1(2) M1(3) ...
```

```
M2(1) M2(2) M2(3) ...
...
N1(1) N1(2) N1(3) N1(4) N1(5) N1(6) ...
N2(1) N2(2) N2(3) N2(4) N2(5) N2(6) ...
...
```

In this file representation, N and M are the N and M parameters for the code, where $M = N - K$, maxcolweight and maxrowweight represent the maximum weight of the columns (typically 3) and maxrowweight represents the maximum weight of the rows. The list colwt colwt colwt ... colwt is the list the column weights of each of the N columns of H. The list rowwt rowwt ... rowwt is the list of the row weights of each of the M rows of H. Then the list M1(1) M1(2) M1(3) ... is the list of the data $\mathcal{M}_1$, that is, the checks that bit 1 participates in (representing the first column of H). The other M data describe the other columns of H. Then N1(1) N1(2) ... describe $\mathcal{N}_1$, the set of bits that participate in check 1, and so forth. As an example, the description of the H matrix of (15.1) provided in the file Asmall.txt.

Since the matrices for real codes are very large, it important to use a sparse representation in the internal computer representation as well. That is, rather than allocate space for a $M \times N$ matrix to represent H, you only need to allocate space for a $w_c \times N$ matrix or a $M \times w_r$ matrix (depending on how you do your internal representation).

There are a variety of ways in which you can represent the sparse data. It takes some work, however, to represent the data in such a way that you can access data in both row-oriented and column-oriented ways, since both directions are used in the vertical and horizontal steps. We describe here one method to sparsely represent the data.

Think of the sparse elements in the H matrix "floating" to the top of the matrix. With this representation, it is easy to access down the column to do a vertical step. Here is the computation of the pseudoposteriors:

```
// Vertical step:
// Work across the columns
for(n = 0; n < N; n++) {
    prod0 = 1-pn[n];  prod1 = pn[n];
    // pn represents the channel posterior
    // compute the pseudoposteriors
    // Now work down each column
    for(l = 0; l < Mnlen[n]; l++) {
        prod0 *= r0[l][n];  prod1 *= r1[l][n];
    }
    alpha = 1/(prod0 + prod1);
    q0p[n] = alpha*prod0;  q1p[n] = alpha*prod1;
}
```

However, when doing the horizontal step, it is necessary to keep track of which row the compressed data come from. This is done by counting the number of nonzero elements above an element, in an array called na ("number above"). The na array is set to zero initially (for every iteration). As the elements in a column are used, the row indexing into the "compressed" matrix skips down to row na[column]. The following code shows the horizontal step implemented this way:

```
// Make sure na[] is set to zero before this step
// Horizontal step:
for(row = 0; row < M; row++) {
    // Copy the data on this row into a
    // temporary array of deltaq values
    for(l = 0; l < Nmlen[row]; l++) {
        // for each nonzero value on this row
        idx = Nm[row][l];
        deltaq[l] = 1-2*q1[na[idx]][idx];
        // compute delta q
    }
    // Work over nonzero elements of
    // this row, taking products
    for(l = 0; l < Nmlen[row]; l++) {
        prod = 1;
        for(k = 0; k < Nmlen[row]; k++) {
            if(k==l) continue;  // skip when k==l
            prod *= deltaq[k];
        }
        // assign the product back into
```

```
        // sparse structure
        idx = Nm[row][l];
        r1[na[idx]][idx] = (1-prod)/2;  // r1 value
        r0[na[idx]++][idx] = (1+prod)/2; // r0 value
    }
}
```

Assignment

1) Complete the class `ldpcdec` by finishing the details on the `decode` member function. Test the decode function using the `ldpctest1` program, which uses the 5×10 parity check matrix represented in `Asmall.txt`. You should obtain numerical results similar to those in Example 15.11.

Algorithm 15.10 LDPC class declaration and definition
File: `ldpcdec.h`
     `ldpcdec.cc`
     `galtest.cc`

For debugging purposes, it may be helpful to compare with a MATLAB version of the decoder. Note, however, that this implementation does *not* treat the sparse matrices efficiently, and so will have trouble scaling to larger codes.

Algorithm 15.11 MATLAB code to test LDPC decoding
File: `ldpc.m`
     `ldpcdecode.m`

2) Using the program `ldpctest1`, produce the probability of error plot and average number of decoding iterations plot as in the chapter for a rate 1/3 and a rate 1/2 code, defined in A1-2.txt and `A1-3.txt`.

Algorithm 15.12 Make performance plots for LDPC codes
File: `galtest1.cc`
     `A1-2.txt`
     `A1-3.txt`

Numerical Considerations

Because the probabilities eventually tend toward either 0 or 1, some of the computations can be somewhat sensitive. Suppose that the numbers p'_0 and p'_1 are to be normalized to form probabilities according to

$$p_0 = \frac{p'_0}{p'_0 + p'_1} \quad p_1 = \frac{p'_1}{p'_0 + p'_1}.$$

Suppose also that $p'_0 > p'_1$. Then the probabilities can be computed as

$$p_0 = \frac{1}{1 + \frac{p'_1}{p'_0}} \qquad p_1 = \frac{\frac{p'_1}{p'_0}}{1 + \frac{p'_1}{p'_0}}.$$

This is a stable way of numerically computing the result. If $p'_1 > p'_0$, then the result can similarly be written in terms of the ratio p'_0/p'_1.

15.13 Exercise

15.1   Determine a low-density parity check matrix for the $(n, 1)$ repetition code. Show that there are no cycles of girth 4 in the Tanner graph.

15.2   Let H be a binary matrix whose columns are formed from the $\binom{m}{2}$ m-tuples of weight 2. Determine the minimum nonzero weight of a code that has H as its parity check matrix. Show that there are no cycles of girth 4 in the Tanner graph.

15.3   Let $h(x) = 1 + x + x^3 + x^7$ by a parity check polynomial. Form a 15×15 parity check matrix by the cyclical shifts of the coefficients of $h(x)$. Show that there are no cycles of length 4 in the Tanner graph. What is the dimension of the code represented by this matrix?

15.4   For the parity check matrix

$$A = \begin{bmatrix} 1 & 1 & 0 & 1 & 0 & 0 & 0 \\ 0 & 1 & 1 & 0 & 1 & 0 & 0 \\ 0 & 0 & 1 & 1 & 0 & 1 & 0 \\ 0 & 0 & 0 & 1 & 1 & 0 & 1 \end{bmatrix}$$

(a) Construct the Tanner graph for the code.
(b) Determine the girth of the minimum-girth cycle.
(c) Determine the number of cycles of length 6.
(d) Determine a generator matrix for this code.
(e) Express the $\mathcal{N}$ and $\mathcal{M}$ lists describing this parity check matrix.

15.5   Let $\{c_1, \dots, c_n\}$ be independent bits, $c_i \in \{0, 1\}$ and let $\lambda_i(c) = \log \frac{P(c_i=1)}{P(c_i=0)}$. Let $z = \sum_{i=1}^{n} c_i$ be the parity check of the c_i. Let

$$\lambda(z) = \log \frac{P(z = 1)}{P(z = 0)}$$

be the likelihood ratio of the parity check.

(a) Show that

$$\tanh\left(-\frac{\lambda(z)}{2}\right) = \prod_{i=1}^{n} \tanh\left(\frac{-\lambda_i(c)}{2}\right).$$

This is the tanh rule (with the sign switched from the form in the chapter). Thus,

$$\lambda(z) = -2 \tanh^{-1}\left(\prod_{i=1}^{n} \tanh\left(\frac{-\lambda_i(c)}{2}\right)\right). \tag{15.64}$$

(b) Let

$$f(x) = \log \frac{e^x + 1}{e^x - 1}, \quad x > 0.$$

Show that $f(f(x)) = x$ for $x > 0$.

(c) Plot $f(x)$.

(d) Let $\sigma_z = -\prod_{i=1}^{n} \text{sign}(-\lambda_i(c))$ be the product of the signs of the bit likelihoods. Show that (15.64) can be written as

$$\text{sign}(-\lambda(z)) = \prod_{i=1}^{n} \text{sign}(-\lambda_i(c))$$

$$\tanh(|\lambda(z)/2|) = \prod_{i=1}^{n} \tanh(|\lambda_i(c)|/2). \qquad (15.65)$$

(e) Show that (15.65) can be written as

$$\lambda(z) = \sigma_z f\left(\sum_{i=1}^{n} f(|\lambda_i(c)|) \right).$$

Hint: $\tanh(z/2) = \frac{e^z-1}{e^z+1}$.

(f) Show that if c_k is equally likely to be 0 or 1, then $\lambda(z) = 0$. Explain why this is reasonable.

(g) Explain why $\lambda(z) \approx -(-1)^{\hat{z}}|\lambda_{\min}(c)|$, where $|\lambda_{\min}(c)| = \min_i |\lambda_i(c)|$.

15.6 Let $\mathbf{a}_m$ be the mth row of a parity check matrix H and let z_m be the corresponding parity check. That is, for some received vector $\mathbf{e}$, $z_m = \mathbf{e}\mathbf{a}_m^T$. Let $\mathbf{a}_m$ be nonzero in positions $i_1, i_2, \ldots, i_p$, so that

$$z_m = e_{i_1} + e_{i_2} + \cdots + e_{i_p}.$$

Assume that each e_i is 1 with probability p_c. Let $z_m(w)$ be the sum of the first w terms in z_m and let $p_z(w)$ be the probability that $z_m(w) = 1$.

(a) Show that $p_z(w+1) = p_z(w)(1-p_c) + (1-p_z(w))p_c$, with initial condition $p_z(0) = 0$.

(b) Show that $p_z(w) = \frac{1}{2} - \frac{1}{2}(1-2p_c)^w$.

15.7 [288] Hard-decision decoding on the BSC. Let H be the $m \times n$ parity check matrix for a code and let $\mathbf{r}$ be a binary-valued received vector. A simple decoder can be implemented as follows:

Set $\hat{\mathbf{c}} = \mathbf{r}$ (initial codeword guess)
[*] Let $\mathbf{z} = \hat{\mathbf{c}}A^T$ (mod 2) (compute checks)
If $\mathbf{z} = \mathbf{0}$, end. (everything checks — done)
Evaluate the vote vector $\mathbf{v} = \mathbf{z}A$ (not modulo 2), which counts for each bit the number of unsatisfied checks to which it belongs. The bits of $\hat{\mathbf{c}}$ that get the most votes are viewed as the most likely candidates for being wrong. So flip all bits $\hat{\mathbf{c}}$ that have the largest vote.
Go to [*]

(a) Let $\mathbf{r} = [1,0,1,0,1,0,0,1,0,1]$. Compute $\mathbf{s}$, $\mathbf{v}$, and the updated $\hat{\mathbf{c}}$ using the parity check matrix in (15.1). Is the decoding complete at this point?

(b) Repeat for $\mathbf{r} = [1,0,1,0,1,1,0,1,0,1]$. Continue operation until correct decoding occurs.

(c) Show that $\mathbf{v} = \hat{\mathbf{s}}A$ counts the number of unsatisfied checks.

(d) Some analysis of the algorithm. We will develop an expression for the average number of bits changed in an iteration. Let w_r be the row weight of H (assumed fixed) and w_c be the column weight (assumed fixed). Determine the largest possible number of votes w a check can be involved in.

(e) Let $\mathbf{e}$ be the (binary) error vector. Let bit l of $\mathbf{e}$ participate in check z_m (that is, $H_{ml} = 1$). Show that when $e_l = 0$, the probability that bit l receives a vote of w is $a = P(\text{vote}_l = w | e_l = 0) = [p_z(w_r - 1)]^w$, where $p_z(w)$ is the function defined in Exercise 15.6.

(f) Show that when $e_l = 1$, the probability that this bit receives the largest possible number of votes w is the probability $b = P(\text{vote}_l = w | e_l = 1) = [1 - p_z(w_r - 1)]^w$.

(g) Show that $P(e_l = 0 | \text{vote}_l = w) \propto a(1 - p_c)$ and $P(e_l = 1 | \text{vote}_l = w) \propto bp_c$, where p_c is the crossover probability for the channel.

(h) Hence show that the expected change in the weight of the error vector when a bit is changed after one round of decoding is $(a(1 - p_c) - bp_c)/(a(1 - p_c) + bp_c)$.

15.8 [149] Consider a sequence of m independent bits in which the jth bit is 1 with probability p_j. Show that the probability that an even number of the bits in the sequence are 1 is $(1 + \prod_{j=1}^{m}(1 - 2p_j))/2$. (For an expression when all the probabilities are the same, see Exercise 3.3.)

15.9 The original Gallager decoder: Let P_{il} be the probability that in the ith parity check the lth bit of the check is equal to 1, $i = 1, 2, \ldots, w_c$, $l = 1, 2, \ldots, w_r$. Show that

$$\frac{P(c_n = 0 | \mathbf{r}, \{z_m = 0, m \in \mathcal{M}_n\})}{P(c_n = 1 | \mathbf{r}, \{z_m = 0, m \in \mathcal{M}_n\})} = \frac{1 - P(c_n = 1 | \mathbf{r})}{P(c_n = 1 | \mathbf{r})} \prod_{i=1}^{w_c} \frac{1 + \prod_{l=1}^{w_r-1}(1 - 2P_{il})}{1 - \prod_{l=1}^{w_r-1}(1 - 2P_{il})}.$$

Use Exercise .15.8.

15.10 Suppose that each bit is checked by $w_c = 3$ checks, and that w_r bits are involved in each check. Let $p_0 = p_c$ be the probability that a bit is received in error.

(a) Suppose that r_n is received incorrectly (which occurs with probability p_0). Show that a parity check on this bit is unsatisfied with probability $(1 + (1 - 2p_0)^{w_r-1})/2$.

(b) Show that the probability that a bit in the first tier is received in error and then corrected is $p_0((1 + (1 - 2p_0)^{w_r-1})/2)^2$.

(c) Show that the probability that a bit in the first tier is received correctly and then changed because of unsatisfied parity checks is $(1 - p_0)((1 - (1 - 2p_0)^{w_r-1})/2)^2$.

(d) Show that the probability of error p_1 of a digit in the first tier after applying the decoding process is

$$p_1 = p_0 - p_0 \left[\frac{1 + (1 - 2p_0)^{w_r-1}}{2} \right]^2 + (1 - p_0) \left[\frac{1 - (1 - 2p_0)^{w_r-1}}{2} \right]^2$$

and that after i steps the probability of error of processing a digit in the ith tier is

$$p_{i+1} = p_0 - p_0 \left[\frac{1 + (1 - 2p_i)^{w_r-1}}{2} \right]^2 + (1 - p_0) \left[\frac{1 - (1 - 2p_i)^{w_r-1}}{2} \right]^2.$$

15.11 A bound on the girth of a graph. The girth of a graph is the length of the smallest cycle. In this exercise, you will develop a bound on the girth. Suppose a regular LDPC code of length n has m parity checks, with column weight w_c and row weight w_r. Let $2l$ be the girth of the associated Tanner graph.

(a) Argue that for any node, the neighborhood of edges on the graph of depth $l - 1$ forms a tree (i.e., the set of all edges up to $l - 1$ edges away), with nodes of odd depth having "out-degree" w_r and nodes of even depth having "out-degree" w_c.

(b) Argue that the number of nodes at even depths of the tree should be at most equal to n, and that the number of nodes at odd depths is equal to m.

(c) Determine the number of nodes at depth 0 (the root), at depth 2, at depth 4, at depth 6, and so forth. Conclude that the total number of nodes at even depth is

$$1 + w_c(w_r - 1) \frac{[(w_c - 1)(w_r - 1)]^{\lfloor l/2 \rfloor} - 1}{(w_c - 1)(w_r - 1) - 1}.$$

This number must be less than or equal to n. This yields an upper bound on l.

15.12 (Irregular codes) Show that (15.49) is true.

15.13 Show that $\sum_{j\geq2}\lambda_j/j = \int_0^1 \lambda(x)\,dx$.

15.14 Draw the Tanner graph for a $(4,1)$ RA code with three input bits with an interleaver $\Pi = (6, 12, 8, 2, 3, 4, 10, 1, 9, 5, 11, 7)$.

15.14 References

Many references appear throughout this chapter; see especially Section 15.1. Tanner graphs and codes built using graphs are discussed in [432]. On the analysis of LDPC codes, the paper [375] is highly recommended, which uses density evolution. Density evolution is also discussed in [73] (our discussion comes from there) and from [26]. See also [106]. The EXIT chart for turbo codes was presented in [438, 439].

The discussion of irregular LDPC codes comes from [373]. See also [282].

One of the potential drawbacks to LDPC codes is the large number of decoding iterations that may be required, resulting in increased latency and decoding hardware complexity. An approach to reduce the number of iterations is presented in [61, 85], in which the messages around a cycle in the Tanner graph establish an eigenvalue problem or a least-squares problem.

Bit flipping was proposed originally in Gallager [149] and has been extensively examined since then [171,221,254,263,373]. The gradient descent bit flipping is presented in [473], from which discussion on WBF and MWBF is drawn.

The presentation on many of the decoding algorithms in sections 15.4 and 15.5 is deeply indebted to the extensive survey in William E. Ryan and Shu Lin, *Channel Codes: Classical and Modern* (Cambridge University Press, 2009), Chapter 5. The reduced complexity bit box-plus decoder is described in M. Viens and W.E. Ryan, "A Reduced-Complexity Box-Plus Decoder for LDPC Codes," *Fifth Interntional Symposium on Turbo Codes and Related Topcics*, pp. 151–156, September 2008, and M. Viens, *A Reduced-Complexity Iterative Decoder for LDPC Codes*, M.S. Thesis, ECE Department, University of Arizona, December 2007.

Discussion of the WBF was presented in [254] and MWBF was presented in [505]. These were discussed with gradient descent bit flipping in [473]. See also [171, 222, 263].

The DC algorithm for decoding is discussed in [497]. Divide and concur, in general, appeared in [170, 171].

Linear programming decoding is discussed in [117]. In addition to decoding, this paper discusses pseudocodewords and fractional distance, which provide a way to lower bound the minimum distance of a code.

Another approach to decoding is to use multiple decoding stages, with simple, fast decoders used in early stages, and more complicated decoders used for later stages only if the earlier stages produce a decoding failure. This can result in a decoder with low average decoding complexity but excellent performance. Multistage decoding is discussed in [497].

Despite the breadth of coverage of decoding algorithms here, there are still additional algorithms in the literature. For example: "Algorithm E" of [375] is a low complexity algorithm for a discrete alphabet with erasures; a reduced complexity decoder of [62]; an "eigenmessage" approach which accounts for cycles in the Tanner graph [316].

Our discussion of encoding comes from [374]. Another class of approaches is based on iterative use of the decoding algorithm in the encoding process. This could allow for the same hardware to be used for both encoding and decoding. These approaches are described in [179]. Using the sum-product decoder on general matrices is explored in [314]. An excellent resource on material related to turbo codes, LDPC codes, and iterative decoding in general is the February 2001 issue of the *IEEE Transactions on Information Theory*, which contains many articles in addition to those articles cited here. Interesting results on the geometry of the iterative decoding process are in [208].

Stopping sets are described in [93]. RA codes are presented in [223]. Our presentation has benefited from the discussion in [26].

Chapter 16

Low-Density Parity-Check Codes: Designs and Variations

16.1 Introduction

This chapter builds on the LDPC foundations of the previous chapter to present ideas related to the analysis of LDPC codes and several design methodologies.

The chapter begins (Section 16.2) with a description of repeat- accumulate (RA) and irregular repeat-accumulate (IRA) codes, codes which have low encode complexity and good performance.

LDPC convolutional codes (LDPCCC) are presented in Section 16.3. These are LDPC codes which have a convolutional structure which provides for low encode complexity.

Then several design methodologies are presented, starting with a generalization of cyclic codes known as quasi-cyclic (QC) codes (Section 16.4). Many of the LDPC designs are based on QC codes. These designs provide connections between some of the coding and field theory of earlier chapters to LDPC codes.

The chapter continues (Section 16.7) with a description of ensembles of LDPC codes. The presentation here is merely descriptive, but these ensembles are used sometimes in design algorithms. Code design using progressive edge growth (PEG) is then described (Section 16.8) and protograph and multi-edge- type LDPC codes (Section 16.9).

Trapping sets have been explored as causing error floors in LDPC codes. Trapping sets are examined briefly in Section 16.10.

Attention then turns to importance sampling in Section 16.11. This is a topic not directly related to LDPC codes, but seemed appropriate to include here. Simulation is often used to characterize the performance of codes. For strong codes (such as LDPC codes), doing the simulation can take a very long time. Importance sampling is a method of simulation than can (properly applied) reduce the simulation time by many orders of magnitude. The discussion here presents the basic ideas and methods to apply these to error correction coding. This is still an area of research, so applying the principles may take some creativity.

The chapter concludes with an introduction to fountain codes in Section 16.12. These are not, strictly speaking, low- density parity-check codes. But the encoding operations make use of simple parity-type computations, so they are in some ways similar to LDPC codes.

16.2 Repeat-Accumulate Codes

A regular RA code encoder consists of three trivial encoding blocks, as shown in Figure 16.1.

1. The outer code is an $(n, 1)$ repetition code. These are the simplest known error correction codes, having good distance properties but very low rate.

2. A pseudorandom interleaver (permuter) Π.

3. The inner code is a rate-1 recursive convolutional code with generator $G(x) = \frac{1}{1+x}$. This acts as an accumulator, because the output is the mod-2 sum (accumulation) of the inputs.

Error Correction Coding: Mathematical Methods and Algorithms, Second Edition. Todd K. Moon
© 2021 John Wiley & Sons, Inc. Published 2021 by John Wiley & Sons, Inc.
Companion website: www.wiley.com/go/Moon/ErrorCorrectionCoding

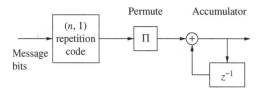

Figure 16.1: A repeat-accumulate encoder.

Suppose that a *systematic* RA code is employed, in which the original message bits are transmitted along with the accumulator output. This linear code would have a parity check matrix, which, in turn, would have a Tanner graph representation.

Example 16.1   [[26], p. 623] Consider a systematic RA code on $K = 2$ message bits with a $(3, 1)$ repetition code. The interleaver (permuter) is $\Pi = (1, 4, 6, 2, 3, 5)$. The operation of the code is as follows. Two message bits, m_1 and m_2, arrive at the encoder and are replicated three times:

$$m_1, m_1, m_1, m_2, m_2, m_2.$$

These bits pass through the interleaver (permuter), which produces the output sequence

$$m_1, m_2, m_2, m_1, m_1, m_2.$$

Then the accumulator produces the running sum output:

$$p_1 = m_1, \quad p_2 = m_2 + p_1, \quad p_3 = m_2 + p_2, \quad p_4 = m_1 + p_3, \quad \cdots \tag{16.1}$$
□

The p_i information (that is, the accumulator outputs) form the codeword $\mathbf{c} = (p_1, p_2, \dots, p_6)$. Bits in this codeword are modulated, transmitted, and received.

The Tanner graph for such a code is shown in Figure 16.2. The variable nodes of the graph have been split into the (systematic) message bits and the parity bits to help distinguish the structure of the graph. The sequence of accumulator computations (16.1) are reflected in the lower part of the graph (connected to the parity bit nodes).

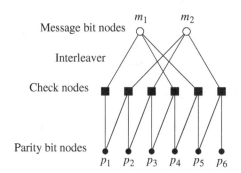

Figure 16.2: The Tanner graph for a $(3, 1)$ RA code with two input bits.

The Tanner graph can be interpreted as follows. Reading left-to-right, the first check node constrains the parity bit to be equal to the first bit, m_1. Each succeeding check node constrains the parity bit to be the sum of the previous parity bit and the next input, where the input sequence is determined by the interleaver. This does not define a regular code, since each message bit is connected to n check nodes and the parity bits are connected to one or two check nodes.

Once we observe the structure of the RA code on the Tanner graph, we may also observe that, regardless of the length N of the code, the Tanner graph retains its sparseness. Each parity bit node is connected to no more than two check nodes and each message bit node is connected to n check nodes.

Sometimes RA codes are transmitted systematically, in which the original bits are sent as well. In this case, the message bits are sent along with the parity information. The codeword in the example above would be

$$\mathbf{c} = (m_1, m_2, p_1, p_2, p_3, p_4, p_5, p_6).$$

The RA encoder may also be understood in terms of parity check and generator matrices. This will be demonstrated using the example above, then generalized to other encoders with other parameters. Writing the accumulator equations (16.1) in vector form, we have

$$\begin{bmatrix} p_1 & p_2 & p_3 & p_4 & p_5 & p_6 \end{bmatrix} = \begin{bmatrix} m_1 & m_2 + p_1 & m_2 + p_2 & m_1 + p_3 & m_1 + p_4 & m_2 + p_5 \end{bmatrix}$$

$$= \begin{bmatrix} m_1 & m_2 \end{bmatrix} \begin{bmatrix} 1 & 0 & 0 & 1 & 1 & 0 \\ 0 & 1 & 1 & 0 & 0 & 1 \end{bmatrix}$$

$$+ \begin{bmatrix} p_1 & p_2 & p_3 & p_4 & p_5 & p_6 \end{bmatrix} \begin{bmatrix} 0 & 1 & 0 & 0 & 0 & 0 \\ 0 & 0 & 1 & 0 & 0 & 0 \\ 0 & 0 & 0 & 1 & 0 & 0 \\ 0 & 0 & 0 & 0 & 1 & 0 \\ 0 & 0 & 0 & 0 & 0 & 1 \\ 0 & 0 & 0 & 0 & 0 & 0 \end{bmatrix}.$$

Moving the term on the right involving p_i to the other side, we obtain

$$\begin{bmatrix} p_1 & p_2 & p_3 & p_4 & p_5 & p_6 \end{bmatrix} \begin{bmatrix} 1 & 1 & 0 & 0 & 0 & 0 \\ 0 & 1 & 1 & 0 & 0 & 0 \\ 0 & 0 & 1 & 1 & 0 & 0 \\ 0 & 0 & 0 & 1 & 1 & 0 \\ 0 & 0 & 0 & 0 & 1 & 1 \\ 0 & 0 & 0 & 0 & 0 & 1 \end{bmatrix} = \begin{bmatrix} m_1 & m_2 \end{bmatrix} \begin{bmatrix} 1 & 0 & 0 & 1 & 1 & 0 \\ 0 & 1 & 1 & 0 & 0 & 1 \end{bmatrix}.$$

Let the matrix on the left be called H_p^T and the matrix on the right be H_m^T. Then stacking things up, we obtain

$$\begin{bmatrix} m_1 & m_2 & p_1 & p_2 & p_3 & p_4 & p_5 & p_6 \end{bmatrix} \begin{bmatrix} H_m^T \\ H_p^T \end{bmatrix} = \mathbf{0}.$$

The matrix

$$H = \begin{bmatrix} H_m & H_p \end{bmatrix}$$

is thus observed to be a parity check matrix for the codeword

$$\begin{bmatrix} m_1 & m_2 & p_1 & p_2 & p_3 & p_4 & p_5 & p_6 \end{bmatrix}.$$

A generator matrix corresponding to this parity check matrix is

$$G = \begin{bmatrix} I & H_m^T H_p^{-T} \end{bmatrix},$$

where H_p^{-T} can be seen to be

$$H_p^{-T} = \begin{bmatrix} 1 & 1 & 1 & 1 & 1 & 1 \\ 0 & 1 & 1 & 1 & 1 & 1 \\ 0 & 0 & 1 & 1 & 1 & 1 \\ 0 & 0 & 0 & 1 & 1 & 1 \\ 0 & 0 & 0 & 0 & 1 & 1 \\ 0 & 0 & 0 & 0 & 0 & 1 \end{bmatrix}.$$

The action of the generator on an input message vector $\begin{bmatrix} m_1 & m_2 \end{bmatrix}$ is that H_u^T duplicates the message bits (3 times each) then randomly interleaves them into 6 different positions. The matrix H_p^{-T} computes across its columns the cumulative sum of the sequence of inputs in the row vector applied to its left.

More generally, in the parity check matrix $H = \begin{bmatrix} H_m & H_p \end{bmatrix}$, H_m is a $nK \times K$ matrix with column weight n and row weight 1, and H_p is a $nK \times nK$ matrix with 1s on the diagonal and upper diagonal

$$H_p = \begin{bmatrix} 1 & 0 & 0 & \cdots & 0 & 0 \\ 1 & 1 & 0 & \cdots & 0 & 0 \\ 0 & 1 & 1 & \cdots & 0 & 0 \\ 0 & 0 & 1 & \cdots & 0 & 0 \\ 0 & 0 & 0 & \cdots & 1 & 1 \end{bmatrix}.$$

16.2.1 Decoding RA Codes

Decoding of RA codes using message passing, just as for other LDPC codes. Unless the RA code is systematic, the variable nodes in the graph are distinguished as two types: the parity bit nodes, corresponding to the observed channel information, and the message bit nodes, corresponding to the unobserved message bits. The major steps are outlined in Figure 16.3.

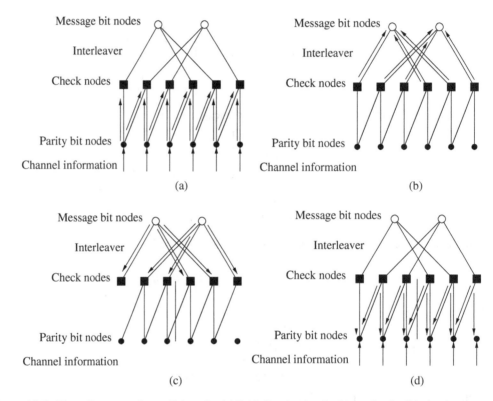

Figure 16.3: Decoding steps for an RA code. (a) Initialization/parity bit to check; (b) check to message; (c) message to check; (d) check to parity bit.

Algorithm 16.1 Repeat Accumulate Decoding

Initialization: The input to the decodingalgorithm is the channel information (just as for LDPC codes), whichis copied as the message to each check node.

Check node to message bit messages At the check nodes, theusual check node to variable node computation (e.g., ⊞ operations) is performed to send messages to the message bits. Atthe first check node, involved in only 1 bit, the message to thebit node is simply passed through.

Message bit to check bit messages The usual variable nodeleave-one-out computation (e.g., sum of likelihood messages) isperformed at the message bits to pass information back to the checknodes.

Check node to parity bit messages The usual check nodecomputation is performed.

For systematic RA codes, the decoding is identical to the decoding algorithms described above for LDPC codes.

16.2.2 Irregular RA Codes

The RA encoder structure presented above can be generalized to an irregular repeat-accumulate structure [223]. The structure is shown in Figure 16.4. There are K input bits. Instead of repeating all K bits an equal number of times, we choose fractions $f_2, f_3, \ldots, f_q$ such that

$$\sum_{i=2}^{q} f_i = 1.$$

For a block of a total of K bits, a subset $f_2 K$ bits is repeated two times, the next subset of $f_3 K$ bits is repeated three times, and so forth. These repeated bits pass through a pseudorandom interleaver and the output is divided into M subsets to form the parity bits. There are d_1 bits in the first group, d_2 bits in the second group, and so on, up to d_M bits in the last group. These are added together to form the parity information. Furthermore, the parity check nodes are generalized so that parity p_i connects to a sum of d_i of the repeated message bit nodes. In this figure, the accumulator structure is on the top of the Tanner graph. Assignment of the code parameters (e.g., the fractions $f_2, f_3, \ldots, f_q$) can be optimized using density evolution, so that the decoding SNR threshold can be minimized.

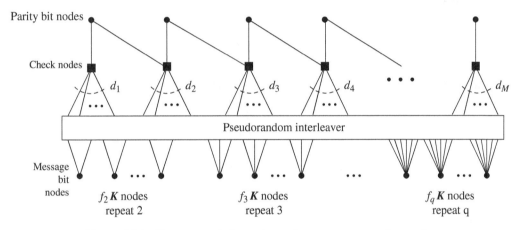

Figure 16.4: Tanner graph for an irregular repeat-accumulate code.

Example 16.2 Let $K = 2$, $f_2 = 0.5$, $f_3 = 0.5$, $M = 3$ and $d_1 = 2$, $d_2 = 2$, $d_3 = 1$. The Tanner graph for this encoder is shown in Figure 16.5.

The operation of the Tanner graph can be expressed as

$$[p_1 \ p_2 \ p_3] = [m_1 \ m_2] \begin{bmatrix} 1 & 1 & 0 \\ 1 & 1 & 1 \end{bmatrix} + [p_1 \ p_2 \ p_3] \begin{bmatrix} 0 & 1 & 0 \\ 0 & 0 & 1 \\ 0 & 0 & 0 \end{bmatrix}$$

or

$$[p_1 \ p_2 \ p_3] \begin{bmatrix} 1 & 1 & 0 \\ 0 & 1 & 1 \\ 0 & 0 & 1 \end{bmatrix} = [m_1 \ m_2] \begin{bmatrix} 1 & 1 & 0 \\ 1 & 1 & 1 \end{bmatrix}$$

Calling the matrix on the left H_p and the matrix on the right H_m (as before), these equations can be stacked as

$$[m_1 \ m_2 \ p_1 \ p_2 \ p_3] \begin{bmatrix} H_m^T \\ H_p^T \end{bmatrix} = \mathbf{0}.$$

□

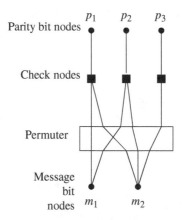

Figure 16.5: Example Tanner graph for an irregular repeat-accumulate code.

In general, the parity check matrix has the same structure as for the RA code, but H_m has column weighs $Kf_2, Kf_3, \ldots, Kf_q$, and row weights $d_1, d_2, \ldots, d_M$. The matrix H_p representing the accumulator is as for the RA codes.

Let

$$\bar{q} = \frac{1}{K} \sum_{j=1}^{K} Kf_j$$

denote the average repetition rate of the message bits and let

$$\bar{d} = \frac{1}{M} \sum_{j=1}^{M} d_j$$

be the average of the degrees. Then for nonsystematic IRA codes, the rate is

$$R = \frac{\bar{d}}{\bar{q}}$$

(in the example above the rate is $R = 2/3$). For systematic IRA codes, the rate is

$$R = \frac{\bar{d}}{\bar{d} + \bar{q}}$$

(in the example above, it the message bits are also sent to make a systematic code the rate is $2/5$).

While an irregular RA code is simply a special case of an irregular LDPC code, it has an important advantage: it can be very efficiently encoded. The RA codes thus provide an instance of a code which has linear encode complexity and linear decode complexity, while still achieving excellent decoding performance.

16.2.3 RA Codes with Multiple Accumulators

The flexibility provided by IRA structures can be further enhanced with encoding structures that employ multiple accumulators. It has been shown, for example, that designs with lower error floors can be obtained.

A structure known as the irregular repeat-accumulate-accumulate (IRAA) is shown in Figure 16.6, in which the IRA structure is followed by a permutation Π and another accumulator. If the output is

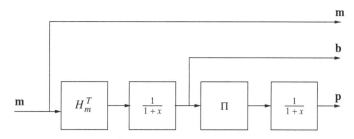

Figure 16.6: An IRAA encoder.

taken to be systematic and both **b** and **p** (the doubly accumulated bits), then the parity check equations are

$$\mathbf{m}H_m^T + \mathbf{b}H_p^T = \mathbf{0} \quad \text{(regular IRA)}$$

$$\mathbf{b}\Pi^T + \mathbf{p}H_p^T = \mathbf{0} \quad \text{(permute parity and accumulate)}$$

That is, the **b** vector is the same as the IRA decoder above. Then these bits are permuted and pass through another accumulator.

16.3 LDPC Convolutional Codes

Encoding LDPC codes based on simply multiplying a message vector times a generator matrix has computational complexity $O(N^2)$, and the hardware can be complex due to the usual irregularity of the structure of G. LDPCCC, like the more traditional convolutional codes, offer low encode complexity, while still retaining the benefits typically associated with LDPC codes.

Let $\mathbf{u}_i = (u_{i,1}, u_{i,2}, \ldots, u_{i,b})$ be a block of b input bits. A sequence of input data over $t + 1$ blocks is

$$\mathbf{u}_{[0,t]} = \begin{bmatrix} \mathbf{u}_0 & \mathbf{u}_1 & \mathbf{u}_2 & \cdots & \mathbf{u}_t \end{bmatrix}.$$

Each block $\mathbf{u}_i$ is encoded to produce an encoded block of length c

$$\mathbf{v}_i = \begin{bmatrix} v_{i,1} & v_{i,2} & v_{i,3} & \cdots & v_{i,c} \end{bmatrix},$$

where each $v_{i,j}$ is a bit. The encoding is systematic, so that the first b bits are the input bits and the last $c - b$ bits are parity bits. That is, each $\mathbf{v}_i$ can be written as

$$\mathbf{v}_i = \begin{bmatrix} \mathbf{v}_i(s) & \mathbf{v}_i(p) \end{bmatrix}$$

with $\mathbf{v}_i(s) = \mathbf{u}_i$. Considering these are convolutional codes, an infinite stream of bits $\mathbf{u}_{[0,\infty]}$ is input and an infinite stream of coded bits $\mathbf{v}_{[0,\infty]}$ is produced. Let $H_{[0,\infty]}$ be the infinite parity check matrix associated with the convolutional code. The coded sequence must satisfy the parity check equation

$$\mathbf{v}_{[0,\infty]} H_{[0,\infty]}^T = \mathbf{0}. \tag{16.2}$$

For an LDPCCC, a section of the parity check matrix has the form

$$H_{[t,t']}^T = \begin{bmatrix} H_0(t)^T & H_1(t+1)^T & \cdots & H_M(t+M)^T & & & \\ & H_0(t+1)^T & H_1(t+2)^T & \cdots & H_M(t+M+1)^T & & \\ & & \ddots & \ddots & & \ddots & \\ & & & H_0(t')^T & H_1(t'+1)^T & \cdots & H_M(t'+M+1)^T \end{bmatrix}.$$

Each block $H_i(t)$ has the following properties:

- $H_i(t)^T$ is of size $c \times (c - b)$.
- $H_0(t)^T$ has full rank for all t.
- $H_M(t)$ for at least one value of t.

Also, the matrix repeats after some number of block rows.

Example 16.3   An example of an H^T matrix is given here.

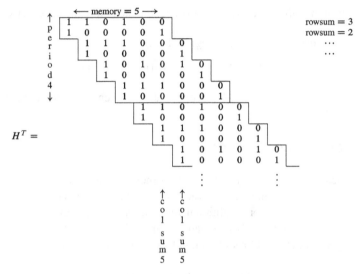

In this case, each block is of size 2×1 ($c = 2, b = 1$). The number of columns along a block row is $M + 1 = 5$. □

The parity check equation (16.2) applied over a block of data leads to

$$\mathbf{v}_t H_0(t)^T + \mathbf{v}_{t-1} H_1(t)^T + \cdots + \mathbf{v}_{t-M} H_M(t)^T = 0.$$

At time t, the previous blocks $\mathbf{v}_{t-1}, \ldots, \mathbf{v}_{t-M}$ are known. Moving the known blocks to the other side and writing

$$\mathbf{v}_t H_0(t)^T = \begin{bmatrix} \mathbf{u}_t & \mathbf{v}_t(p) \end{bmatrix} \begin{bmatrix} H_s \\ H_p \end{bmatrix},$$

where H_s is $b \times (c - b)$ and H_p is $(c - b) \times (c - b)$, we can write

$$\mathbf{v}_t(p) H_p = -\mathbf{u}_t H_s - \mathbf{v}_{t-1} H_1(t)^T - \cdots - \mathbf{v}_{t-M} H_M(t)^T.$$

Since H_p is full rank, the parity bits can be obtained.

To be a low-density parity check matrix, a column of H must be low density, which means that the weight of each column of H should be much less than $(c - b)(M + 1)$.

Parity check matrices can be found by computer search, or by stacking parity check matrix blocks from an LDPC code. For example, consider the 5×10 parity check matrix on the left of (16.3). This can be partitioned as shown with the line. The lower partition is stacked above the upper partition, as shown on the right of (16.3). This construction can be repeated indefinitely. This gives a convolutional encoder with row weight 4, column weight 2, and period 5 [386, Section 15.5].

$$
\begin{bmatrix}
1 & 1 & 1 & 1 & 0 & 0 & 0 & 0 & 0 & 0 \\
1 & 0 & 0 & 0 & 1 & 1 & 1 & 0 & 0 & 0 \\
0 & 1 & 0 & 0 & 1 & 0 & 0 & 1 & 1 & 0 \\
0 & 0 & 1 & 0 & 0 & 1 & 0 & 1 & 0 & 1 \\
0 & 0 & 0 & 1 & 0 & 0 & 1 & 0 & 1 & 1
\end{bmatrix}
\rightarrow
\begin{bmatrix}
1 & 1 & & & & & & & \\
1 & 0 & 0 & 0 & & & & & \\
0 & 1 & 0 & 0 & 1 & 0 & & & \\
0 & 0 & 1 & 0 & 0 & 1 & 0 & 1 & \\
0 & 0 & 0 & 1 & 0 & 0 & 1 & 0 & 1 & 1 \\
& & & & 1 & 1 & 0 & 0 & 0 & 0 & 0 & 0 \\
& & & & & & 1 & 1 & 1 & 0 & 0 & 0 \\
& & & & & & & & 0 & 1 & 1 & 0 \\
& & & & & & & & & & 0 & 1
\end{bmatrix}
\qquad (16.3)
$$

16.4 Quasi-Cyclic Codes

QC codes are a class of linear codes generalizing the cyclic codes introduced in Chapter 4. QC codes have encoding complexity linear in the size of the code (as opposed to quadratic complexity for typical block codes). While they are of general interest, the particular interest here is due to the fact that some QC codes may have a low-density parity matrix, that is, some QC codes are LDPC codes. Methods of constructing such parity check matrices are described in sections below.

16.4.1 QC Generator Matrices

Let $\mathbf{v}_1, \mathbf{v}_2, \ldots, \mathbf{v}_t$ be binary row vectors, each of length b, where

$$
\mathbf{v}_j = \begin{bmatrix} v_{j,1} & v_{j,2} & v_{j,3} & \cdots & v_{j,b} \end{bmatrix}.
$$

Let $\mathbf{v}^{(1)}$ denote the vector obtained by cyclically shifting $\mathbf{v}_j$ one place to the right:

$$
\mathbf{v}_j^{(1)} = \begin{bmatrix} v_{j,b} & v_{j,1} & v_{j,2} & \cdots & v_{j,b-1} \end{bmatrix}.
$$

Form the vector $\mathbf{v}$ of length bt by stacking up the $\mathbf{v}_j$ vectors,

$$
\mathbf{v} = \begin{bmatrix} \mathbf{v}_1 & \mathbf{v}_2 & \cdots & \mathbf{v}_t \end{bmatrix}
$$

and let $\mathbf{v}^{(1)}$ denote the stack of the cyclic shifts $\mathbf{v}_j^{(1)}$,

$$
\mathbf{v}^{(1)} = \begin{bmatrix} \mathbf{v}_1^{(1)} & \mathbf{v}_2^{(1)} & \cdots & \mathbf{v}_t^{(1)} \end{bmatrix}.
$$

This vector is called the *t-sectionalized cyclic shift of* $\mathbf{v}$. With this notation, we define a *quasi-cyclic code* C_{qc} with parameters b, k, and t as a (tb, k) linear block code if every t-sectionalized cyclic shift of a codeword in C_{qc} is also a codeword in C_{qc}. Clearly, if $t = 1$, a conventional cyclic code is obtained.

A *circulant* $b \times b$ matrix is one for which each row is a right cyclic shift of the row above it. An example of a circulant matrix is

$$
\begin{bmatrix}
1 & 0 & 1 & 0 & 0 \\
0 & 1 & 0 & 1 & 0 \\
0 & 0 & 1 & 0 & 1 \\
1 & 0 & 0 & 1 & 0 \\
0 & 1 & 0 & 0 & 1
\end{bmatrix}.
$$

The first row of a circulant matrix is called its *generator*.

The generator matrix of a QC code is a $c \times t$ block matrix, where each block is a $b \times b$ circulant matrix. In systematic form,

$$G = \begin{bmatrix} G_1 \\ G_2 \\ \vdots \\ G_c \end{bmatrix} = \begin{bmatrix} G_{1,1} & G_{1,2} & \cdots & G_{1,t-c} & I & 0 & \cdots & 0 \\ G_{2,1} & G_{2,2} & \cdots & G_{2,t-c} & 0 & I & \cdots & 0 \\ \vdots & \vdots & \ddots & \vdots & \vdots & \vdots & \ddots & \vdots \\ G_{c,1} & G_{c,2} & \cdots & G_{c,t-c} & 0 & 0 & \cdots & I \end{bmatrix}$$
$$= \begin{bmatrix} P & I_{cb} \end{bmatrix}$$

(16.4)

Each block of G, including each $G_{i,j}$ and the identities I and the 0s, is a $b \times b$ circulant matrix.

Example 16.4   [386, p, 134] A generator matrix for a (20, 10) code with $b = 5$, $c = 2$, and $t = 4$ is

$$G_{\text{qc,sys}} = \left[\begin{array}{ccccc|ccccc|ccccc|ccccc}
1 & 0 & 1 & 0 & 0 & 1 & 0 & 0 & 0 & 1 & 1 & 0 & 0 & 0 & 0 & 0 & 0 & 0 & 0 & 0 \\
0 & 1 & 0 & 1 & 0 & 1 & 1 & 0 & 0 & 0 & 0 & 1 & 0 & 0 & 0 & 0 & 0 & 0 & 0 & 0 \\
0 & 0 & 1 & 0 & 1 & 0 & 1 & 1 & 0 & 0 & 0 & 0 & 1 & 0 & 0 & 0 & 0 & 0 & 0 & 0 \\
1 & 0 & 0 & 1 & 0 & 0 & 0 & 1 & 1 & 0 & 0 & 0 & 0 & 1 & 0 & 0 & 0 & 0 & 0 & 0 \\
0 & 1 & 0 & 0 & 1 & 0 & 0 & 0 & 1 & 1 & 1 & 0 & 0 & 0 & 1 & 0 & 0 & 0 & 0 & 0 \\
\hline
1 & 1 & 0 & 0 & 0 & 0 & 1 & 0 & 1 & 0 & 0 & 0 & 0 & 0 & 0 & 1 & 0 & 0 & 0 & 0 \\
0 & 1 & 1 & 0 & 0 & 0 & 0 & 1 & 0 & 1 & 0 & 0 & 0 & 0 & 0 & 0 & 1 & 0 & 0 & 0 \\
0 & 0 & 1 & 1 & 0 & 1 & 0 & 0 & 1 & 0 & 0 & 0 & 0 & 0 & 0 & 0 & 0 & 1 & 0 & 0 \\
0 & 0 & 0 & 1 & 1 & 0 & 1 & 0 & 0 & 1 & 0 & 0 & 0 & 0 & 0 & 0 & 0 & 0 & 1 & 0 \\
1 & 0 & 0 & 0 & 1 & 1 & 0 & 1 & 0 & 0 & 0 & 0 & 0 & 0 & 0 & 0 & 0 & 0 & 0 & 1
\end{array} \right]$$

□

Encoding is done using the usual vector/matrix multiplication. Let the message vector $\mathbf{m}$ be partitioned into c blocks of b bits as

$$\mathbf{m} = \begin{bmatrix} \mathbf{m}_1 & \mathbf{m}_2 & \cdots & \mathbf{m}_c \end{bmatrix} = \begin{bmatrix} m_1 & m_2 & \cdots & m_{cb} \end{bmatrix},$$

where the elements of $\mathbf{m}_i$ are

$$\mathbf{m}_i = \begin{bmatrix} m_{(i-1)b+1} & m_{(i-1)b+2} & \cdots & m_{ib} \end{bmatrix}.$$

The systematically encoded QC codeword is

$$\mathbf{c} = \mathbf{m}G = \mathbf{m}_1 G_1 + \mathbf{m}_2 G_2 + \cdots + \mathbf{m}_c G_c = \begin{bmatrix} \mathbf{p}_1 & \mathbf{p}_2 & \cdots & \mathbf{p}_{t-c} & \mathbf{m}_1 & \mathbf{m}_2 & \cdots & \mathbf{m}_c \end{bmatrix},$$

where

$$\mathbf{p}_j = \mathbf{m}_1 G_{1,j} + \mathbf{m}_2 G_{2,j} + \cdots + \mathbf{m}_c G_{c,j}.$$

(16.5)

This operation can be accomplished efficiently by utilizing the cyclic structure of the generator. For the subblock $G_{i,j}$ in the generator (16.4), let $\mathbf{g}_{i,j}$ denote its generator (first row), and let $\mathbf{g}_{i,j}^{(\ell)}$ denote its right cyclic shift, where $\mathbf{g}_{i,j}^{(0)} = \mathbf{g}_{i,j}$.

The vector/matrix product terms in (16.5) can be expressed using generators as

$$\mathbf{m}_i G_{i,j} = m_{(i-1)b+1} \mathbf{g}_{i,j}^{(0)} + m_{(i-1)b+2} \mathbf{g}_{i,j}^{(1)} + \cdots + m_{ib} \mathbf{g}_{i,j}^{(b-1)}.$$

This computation can be efficiently realized using hardware as shown in Figure 16.7(a). This hardware is referred to as a cyclic shift register adder accumulator (CSRAA). The hardware works as follows:

- The b-bit feedback shift register at the top is loaded with the generator $\mathbf{g}_{c,j} i^{(b-1)}$, the $(b-1)$st right cyclic shift of the generator $\mathbf{g}_{c,j}$ of the circulant $G_{c,j}$.

- The message bits are shifted in, starting at the last message bit m_{cb}. The circuitry forms the product $m_{cb}\mathbf{g}_{c,j}^{(b-1)}$, which is placed into the b-bit accumulator (at the bottom).

- The shift register at the top is shifted left, producing $\mathbf{g}_{c,j}^{(b-2)}$, and the next message bit m_{cb-1} is shifted in. The product $m_{cb-1}\mathbf{g}_{c,j}^{(b-2)}$ is accumulated into the accumulator.

- This process continues, cyclically shifting the top register while shifting in message bits until the first bit of $\mathbf{m}_c$ and accumulating the products into the accumulator, which is $m_{(c-1)b+1}$. At this point, the accumulator contains the product $\mathbf{u}_c G_{c,j}$.

- Now the feedback shift register is loaded with the generator $\mathbf{g}_{c,j}^{(b-1)}$, the $(b-1)$-times right-shifted generator and the next b bits are shifted in. After these b shifts, the accumulator contains the product $\mathbf{u}_{c-1}G_{c-1,j} + \mathbf{u}_c G_{c,j}$.

- The process continues inputting $\mathbf{c}_{c-2}, \mathbf{c}_{c-3}, \ldots, \mathbf{c}_1$, initializing the top buffer, in turn, with $\mathbf{g}_{c-2,j}^{(b-1)}, \mathbf{g}_{c-3,j}^{(b-1)}, \ldots, \mathbf{g}_{1,j}^{(b-1)}$.

- After the process finishes, the register contains $\mathbf{p}_j$ from (16.5). The encoding complexity (as measured by "ticks of the clock") is the length of the message, since the whole message is clocked in.

The operation of computing $\mathbf{p}_j$ can be performed in parallel to compute the set $\mathbf{p}_1, \mathbf{p}_2, \ldots, \mathbf{p}_{t-c}$, essentially duplicating the CSRAA for each block. This is shown in Figure 16.7(b).

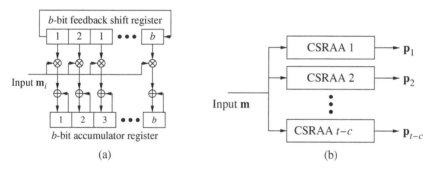

Figure 16.7: Encoding QC codes. (a) cyclic shift register adder accumulator (CSRAA); (b) parallelizing the CRSAA.

16.4.2 Constructing QC Generator Matrices from QC Parity Check Matrices

In the sections below, QC low-density parity check matrices will be constructed. This raises the question: given a QC parity check matrix, how can a QC generator matrix be produced so that the low-complexity encoding techniques described in the previous section can be employed? This question is addressed in this section.

Let

$$
H = \begin{bmatrix}
A_{0,0} & A_{0,1} & \cdots & A_{0,t-1} \\
A_{1,0} & A_{1,1} & \cdots & A_{1,t-1} \\
\vdots & & & \\
A_{t-c-1,0} & A_{t-c-1,1} & \cdots & A_{t-c-1,t-1}
\end{bmatrix}
$$

be a $(t-c)b \times tb$ binary matrix, where each $A_{i,j}$ is a $b \times b$ circulant matrix. A QC code C_{QC} is formed by the nullspace of this matrix. It may happen that the rank of H is equal to number of rows $(t-c)b$; in this case, H is said to be full rank and the code is a (tb, cb) code. If H is not full rank, then the dimension of the code is larger than cb.

16.4.2.1 Full Rank Case

In finding a corresponding generator matrix, we consider first the case that H is full rank. Assume that the columns of H are arranged such that the left $(t-c)b \times (t-c)b$ matrix D,

$$D = \begin{bmatrix} A_{0,0} & A_{0,1} & \cdots & A_{0,t-c-1} \\ A_{1,0} & A_{1,1} & \cdots & A_{1,t-c-1} \\ \vdots & & & \\ A_{t-c-1,0} & A_{t-c-1,1} & \cdots & A_{t-c-1,t-c-1} \end{bmatrix}$$

has rank $(t-c)b$. A generator G corresponding to the parity check matrix H must satisfy $HG^T = \mathbf{0}$. Imposing the condition that G is to be circulant of the form (16.4), let $\mathbf{g}_{i,j}$ be the generator of the circulant block $G_{i,j}$. Let $\mathbf{0}_b = (0, 0, \ldots, 0)$ be an all-zero (row) b-tuple and let $\mathbf{u}_b = (1, 0, \ldots, 0)$ be the unit (row) b-tuple with 1 in the first position. The first row of the block row G_i of G in (16.4) is

$$\mathbf{g}_i = \begin{bmatrix} \mathbf{g}_{i,0} & \mathbf{g}_{i,1} & \cdots & \mathbf{g}_{i,t-c-1} & \mathbf{0}_b & \cdots & \mathbf{0}_b & \mathbf{u}_b & \mathbf{0}_b & \cdots & \mathbf{0}_b \end{bmatrix},$$

where the $\mathbf{u}_b$ is in block $(t-c+i)$. From the condition that $HG^T = \mathbf{0}$, it follows that $H\mathbf{g}_i^T = \mathbf{0}$. Let $\mathbf{z}_i$ be the $(t-c)b \times 1$ vector

$$\mathbf{z}_i = \begin{bmatrix} \mathbf{g}_{i,0} & \mathbf{g}_{i,1} & \cdots & \mathbf{g}_{i,t-c-1} \end{bmatrix}.$$

Let M_{t-c+i} denote the $(t-c+i)$th column of circulant blocks H,

$$M_{t-c+i} = \begin{bmatrix} A_{0,t-c+i} \\ A_{1,t-c+i} \\ \vdots \\ A_{t-c-1,t-c+i} \end{bmatrix},$$

where $0 \leq i < c$, so that M_{t-c+i} is a column of H not included in D. The product $H\mathbf{g}_i^T = \mathbf{0}$ can be expressed as

$$D\mathbf{z}_i^T + M_{t-c+i}\mathbf{u}_b^T = \mathbf{0}. \tag{16.6}$$

Since D is a $(t-c)b \times (t-c)b$ (square) matrix and full rank, it has an inverse and (16.6) can be solved for $\mathbf{z}_i^T$ as

$$\mathbf{z}_i^T = D^{-1} M_{t-c+i}\mathbf{u}_b^T.$$

Solving this for $i = 0, 1, \ldots, c-1$ gives $\mathbf{z}_0, \mathbf{z}_1, \ldots, \mathbf{z}_{c-1}$. Breaking each of these into b-blocks gives the set of generators $g_{i,j}$ of $G_{i,j}$ of G.

16.4.2.2 Non-Full Rank Case

Let $r = \text{rank}(H)$, where $r < (t-c)b$. Find the number of block columns of H such that these ℓ columns form a submatrix having rank r. The columns of H can be reordered to form a $(t-c)b \times tb$ matrix H^* such that the first ℓ block columns of H^* form an array D^*, where the columns are now labeled such that

$$D^* = \begin{bmatrix} A_{0,0} & A_{0,1} & \cdots & A_{0,\ell-1} \\ A_{1,0} & A_{1,1} & \cdots & A_{1,\ell-1} \\ \vdots & & & \\ A_{t-c,0} & A_{t-c,1} & \cdots & A_{t-c,\ell-1} \end{bmatrix}.$$

Each $A_{i,j}$ is a $b \times b$ circulant matrix. The code that is the nullspace of H^* is equivalent to the code what is the nullspace of H (same distance properties). D^* is a matrix that has rank r, so there are r linearly independent columns and $b\ell - r$ linearly dependent columns.

The generator is a $(tb - r) \times tb$ matrix that has the following form:

$$G = \begin{bmatrix} Q \\ G^* \end{bmatrix}, \tag{16.7}$$

where Q is $(\ell b - r) \times tb$ and G^* is $(t - \ell)b \times tb$ that can be expressed in systematic circulant form

$$G^* = \begin{bmatrix} G_{0,0} & G_{0,1} & \cdots & G_{0,\ell-1} & I & \mathbf{0} & \cdots & \mathbf{0} \\ G_{1,0} & G_{1,1} & \cdots & G_{1,\ell-1} & \mathbf{0} & I & \cdots & \mathbf{0} \\ \vdots & & & & & & & \\ G_{t-\ell,0} & G_{t-\ell,1} & \cdots & G_{t-\ell,\ell-1} & \mathbf{0} & \mathbf{0} & \cdots & I \end{bmatrix}.$$

Here, each $G_{i,j}$ and I and $\mathbf{0}$ are $b \times b$, and each $G_{i,j}$ is circulant with generator $\mathbf{g}_{i,j}$. As in the full rank case, let

$$\mathbf{z}_i = \begin{bmatrix} \mathbf{g}_{i,0} & \mathbf{g}_{i,1} & \cdots & \mathbf{g}_{i,\ell-1} \end{bmatrix}.$$

Let

$$M_{t-\ell+i} = \begin{bmatrix} A_{0,t-\ell+i} \\ A_{1,t-\ell+i} \\ \vdots \\ A_{t-c,t-\ell+i} \end{bmatrix}, \quad 0 \le i \le \ell - 1$$

be column $t - \ell + i$ of H^*. The equation $H^* G^T = \mathbf{0}$ implies (for the i block row) that

$$D^* \mathbf{z}_i + M_{t-\ell+i} \mathbf{u}_b^T = \mathbf{0}. \tag{16.8}$$

Setting the elements of $\mathbf{z}_i$ to 0 that correspond to the linearly dependent columns of D^* (resulting in r elements of $\mathbf{z}_i$ to solve for), (16.8) can be solved for the remaining elements of $\mathbf{z}_i$. This gives the generators of the $G_{i,j}$ in G^*.

The matrix Q in (16.7) must satisfy $H^* Q = \mathbf{0}$. This can be done by exploiting the structure of the circulant matrices in D^*. Since D^* is not full rank, some of the circulant matrices in D^* will have rank less than b. Let d_0 be the number of linearly dependent columns (out of b) in the first block column of D^*, let d_1 be the number of linearly independent columns in the second block column of D^*, and so on up to $d_{\ell-1}$. Then

$$d_0 + d_1 + \cdots + d_{\ell-1} = \ell b - r.$$

If a $b \times b$ circulant matrix has rank ρ less than b, then any ρ columns of the matrix are linearly independent, and the other $b - \rho$ columns are linearly dependent. Using this fact, take the last $b - d_j$ columns of the jth block column of D^* as linearly independent columns, for $j = 0, 1, \ldots, \ell - 1$. Now the matrix Q can be put in the form

$$Q = \begin{bmatrix} Q_0 \\ Q_1 \\ \vdots \\ Q_{\ell-1} \end{bmatrix} = \begin{bmatrix} Q_{0,0} & Q_{0,1} & \cdots & Q_{0,\ell-1} & \mathbf{0}_{0,0} & \mathbf{0}_{0,1} & \cdots & \mathbf{0}_{0,t-\ell-1} \\ Q_{1,0} & Q_{1,1} & \cdots & Q_{1,\ell-1} & \mathbf{0}_{1,0} & \mathbf{0}_{1,1} & \cdots & \mathbf{0}_{1,t-\ell-1} \\ \vdots & & & & & & & \\ Q_{\ell-1,0} & Q_{\ell-1,1} & \cdots & Q_{\ell-1,\ell-1} & \mathbf{0}_{\ell-1,0} & \mathbf{0}_{\ell-1,1} & \cdots & \mathbf{0}_{\ell-1,t-\ell-1} \end{bmatrix}.$$

Here, each $\mathbf{0}_{i,j}$ is a $d_i \times b$ matrix of zeros and $Q_{i,j}$ is a $d_i \times b$ partial circulant matrix, formed by cyclically shifting its first row $d_i - 1$ times. From this matrix form the first row of Q_i as

$$\mathbf{q}_i = (\mathbf{w}_i, \mathbf{0}) = (q_{i,0}, q_{i,1}, \ldots, q_{i,lb-1}, 0, 0, \ldots, 0),$$

where there are $(t - \ell)b$ zeros. The ℓb bits of $\mathbf{w}_i$ correspond to the ℓb columns of D^*. The $\ell b - r$ bits that correspond to the linearly dependent columns of D^* are set to have the form

$$(\mathbf{0}_0, \ldots, \mathbf{0}_{i-1}, \mathbf{u}_i, \mathbf{0}_{i+1}, \ldots, \mathbf{0}_{\ell-1}),$$

where $\mathbf{0}_e$ is a row of d_e zeros and $\mathbf{u}_i$ (here) is the unit row vector $\mathbf{u}_i = (1, 0, \ldots, 0)$ with d_i elements. The number of unknown elements in $\mathbf{w}_i$ to be determined is thus r. The requirement that $H^* Q^T = \mathbf{0}$ gives rise to the equation

$$
D^* \mathbf{w}_i^T =
\begin{bmatrix}
A_{0,0} & A_{0,1} & \cdots & A_{0,\ell-1} \\
A_{1,0} & A_{1,1} & \cdots & A_{1,\ell-1} \\
\vdots & & & \\
A_{t-c-1,0} & A_{t-c-1,1} & \cdots & A_{t-c-1,\ell-1}
\end{bmatrix}
\begin{bmatrix}
q_{i,0} \\
q_{i,1} \\
\vdots \\
q_{i,\ell b-1}
\end{bmatrix}
= \mathbf{0}.
$$

Finding a nonzero in the nullspace gives the vector $\mathbf{w}_i$, which can be broken up into $\ell - 1$ components $\mathbf{w}_{i,0}, \mathbf{w}_{i,1}, \ldots, \mathbf{w}_{i,\ell-1}$, each of length b. Each partial circulant $Q_{i,j}$ of Q is then obtained by shifting $\mathbf{w}_{i,j}$ as its generator and shifting $d_i - 1$ times.

Once G is obtained, it can be used with a CSRAA circuit as in Figure 16.7 for an efficient encoding operation.

16.5 Construction of LDPC Codes Based on Finite Fields

In the early days of LDPC codes, the parity check matrices of LDPC codes were selected at random. More recently, however, several approaches to designing parity-check codes have been developed. Many of these make use of finite field theory, thus providing some interesting interplay between classical field-based codes such as BCH and RS codes and more modern LDPC codes. In this section, we consider a few of these design techniques.

In the Galois field $GF(q)$, where $q = p^s$ for some prime p, let α be primitive. Then all of the nonzero elements of the field can be represented as powers of α. For each nonzero element of the field α^i, $0 \le i \le q - 2$, form vector $\mathbf{z}(\alpha_i)$, known as the *location vector* of α^i, as

$$
\mathbf{z}(\alpha^i) = (z_0, z_1, \ldots, z_{q-1}),
$$

where the ith element is 1 and all other elements are 0. Clearly if $i \ne j$, then $\mathbf{z}(\alpha^i) \ne \mathbf{z}(\alpha^j)$ — the nonzero elements appear in different locations.

Let δ be a nonzero element of $GF(q)$, say $\delta = \alpha^j$. The location vector $\mathbf{z}(\delta)$ is nonzero only at position j. The location vector $\mathbf{z}(\alpha\delta)$ is nonzero at position $j + 1$ (modulo $q - 1$), where the nonzero location wraps around the end of the location vector. In general, $\mathbf{z}(\alpha^i \delta)$ is a right cyclic shift of $\mathbf{z}(\delta)$ by i positions, and $\mathbf{z}(\alpha^{q-1}\delta) = \mathbf{z}(\delta)$. Now form a matrix with rows

$$
A =
\begin{bmatrix}
\mathbf{z}(\delta) \\
\mathbf{z}(\alpha\delta) \\
\vdots \\
\mathbf{z}(\alpha^{q-2}\delta)
\end{bmatrix}.
$$

This is a $(q - 1) \times (q - 1)$ circulant matrix. Since there is only one 1 on each row, A is a permutation matrix, referred to as a circulant permutation matrix (CPM). The matrix A is also referred to as the $(q - 1)$-fold matrix dispersion of δ over $GF(2)$. The matrix A is a function of δ, so it would be more explicit to write $A = A(\delta)$. It is clear that for different field elements δ and γ in $GF(q)$, $A(\delta) \ne A(\gamma)$.

Consider now a matrix an $m \times n$ matrix W over $GF(q)$, defined as

$$
W =
\begin{bmatrix}
\mathbf{w}_0 \\
\mathbf{w}_1 \\
\vdots \\
\mathbf{w}_{m-1}
\end{bmatrix}
=
\begin{bmatrix}
w_{0,0} & w_{0,1} & \cdots & w_{0,n-1} \\
w_{1,0} & w_{1,1} & \cdots & w_{1,n-1} \\
\vdots & & & \\
w_{m-1,0} & w_{m-1,1} & \cdots & w_{m-1,n-1}
\end{bmatrix}.
$$

The matrix W is to be designed to satisfy two constraints:

1. Consider the row $\mathbf{w}_i$. The multiplication $\alpha^k \mathbf{w}_i$ produces a row that shuffles the elements in $GF(q)$ around, as does the product $\alpha^\ell \mathbf{w}_i$. The first constraint is that for any row, $0 \le i \le m$ and any $k \ne \ell$ with $0 \le k, \ell \le q-2$, $\alpha^k \mathbf{w}_i$ and $\alpha^\ell \mathbf{w}_i$ differ in at least $n-1$ positions. This constraint precludes the possibility that $\mathbf{w}_i = 0$ in more than one position (because in such zero positions both $\alpha^k \mathbf{w}_i$ and $\alpha^\ell \mathbf{w}_i$ would be 0).

2. For rows $\mathbf{w}_i$ and $\mathbf{w}_j$, $\alpha^k \mathbf{w}_i$ and $\alpha^\ell \mathbf{w}_j$ differ in at least $n-1$ positions for $0 \le i, j \le m-1$, $i \ne j$ and $0 \le k, \ell \le q-2$. This constraint implies that $\mathbf{w}_i$ and $\mathbf{w}_j$ differ in at least $n-1$ positions.

Matrices over $GF(q)$ satisfying these two constraints are said to satisfy the *α-multiplied row constraint*. A construction of a matrix satisfying the α-multiplied row constraint is given in Section 16.5.1.

For a matrix W as above, a potential parity check matrix is obtained by replacing each nonzero $GF(q)$ element by its $(q-1) \times (q-1)$ CPM, and replacing each 0 $GF(q)$ element by $(q-1) \times (q-1)$ matrix of 0s, resulting in

$$H_{\text{disp}} = \begin{bmatrix} A_{0,0} & A_{0,1} & \cdots & A_{0,n-1} \\ A_{1,0} & A_{1,1} & \cdots & A_{1,n-1} \\ \vdots & & & \\ A_{m-1,0} & A_{m-1,1} & \cdots & A_{m-1,n-1} \end{bmatrix}.$$

H_{disp} is a $m(q-1) \times n(q-1)$ binary matrix. From the first constraint above, there is at most one zero in each row of W, and so at most one block of zeros in each block row of H_{disp}. By the second constraint above, for any two block rows of H_{disp} there is at most one place where they have the same cyclic permutation matrix. At any other place on any two rows, the two cyclic permutation matrices are different. It follows that H_{disp} satisfies the RC-constraint described in Section 15.3.

For any pair of integer (g, r), $1 \le g \le m$ and $1 \le r \le n$, let $H_{\text{disp}}(g, r)$ be a $g \times r$ submatrix of H_{disp}, forming a $g(q-1) \times r(q-1)$ matrix over $GF(2)$. This also satisfies the RC constraint. The nullspace of this matrix is a binary linear code of length $r(q-1)$ with rate at least $(r-g)/r$. It can be shown that this code has minimum distance at least $g+2$ (for even g) or $g+1$ (for odd g).

This construction motivates the search for α-multiplied row-constrained matrices such as W, from which a parity check matrix can be formed by matrix dispersion. Several such methods are developed in Sections 16.5.1 through 16.5.5. The general pattern in each case is the same. A method of constructing a matrix W is obtained, an H matrix is obtained by replacing elements of W with a matrix dispersion, and then a submatrix is obtained. The descriptions are summarized as code construction recipes.

The codes constructed by these techniques tend to have good distance properties, such as being close to Shannon channel capacity, or having low error floors.

16.5.1 I. Construction of QC-LDPC Codes Based on the Minimum-Weight Codewords of a Reed–Solomon Code with Two Information Symbols

This method is presented in [386, Section 11.3] and [100]. Consider a $(q-1, 2)$ RS $(q-1, 2)$ RS code C_{RS2} over the field $GF(q)$ having minimum distance $q-2$ with a generator polynomial $g(x)$ whose roots are $\alpha, \alpha^2, \ldots, \alpha^{q-3}$, where α is primitive: $\alpha^{q-1} = 1$. Since the minimum distance is $q-2$, the minimum weight nonzero codeword has weight $q-2$. The polynomials

$$c_1(x) = 1 + x + x^2 + \cdots + x^{q-2} = \sum_{j=0}^{q-2} x^j = \frac{x^{q-1} - 1}{x^n \, 1}$$

and

$$c_2(x) = 1 + \alpha x + \alpha^2 x^2 + \cdots + \alpha^{q-2} x^{q-2} = \frac{\alpha^{q-1} x^{q-1} - 1}{\alpha x - 1}$$

have $\alpha, \alpha^2, \ldots, \alpha^{q-2}$ as roots, so they are both code polynomials in the code. The corresponding codewords are

$$\mathbf{c}_1 = (1, 1, \ldots, 1) \quad \mathbf{c}_2 = (1, \alpha, \ldots, \alpha^{q-2}),$$

each having weight $q - 1$. Form the weight-$(q - 2)$ codeword as the difference

$$\mathbf{w}_0 = \mathbf{c}_2 - \mathbf{v}_1 = (0, \alpha - 1, \alpha^2 - 1, \ldots, \alpha^{q-2} - 1).$$

Now form the $(q - 1) \times (q - 1)$ matrix $W^{(1)}$ by cyclic shifts of $\mathbf{w}_0$,

$$W^{(1)} = \begin{bmatrix} \mathbf{w}_0 \\ \mathbf{w}_1 \\ \vdots \\ \mathbf{w}_{q-2} \end{bmatrix} = \begin{bmatrix} 0 & \alpha - 1 & \alpha^2 - 1 & \cdots & \alpha^{q-2} - 1 \\ \alpha^{q-2} - 1 & 0 & \alpha - 1 & \cdots & \alpha^{q-3} - 1 \\ \vdots & & & & \\ \alpha - 1 & \alpha^2 - 1 & \alpha^3 - 1 & \cdots & 0 \end{bmatrix}.$$

Each row and column of $W^{(1)}$ contains exactly one 0, with the 0 elements each lying on the main diagonal of $W^{(1)}$. Since C_{RS2} is cyclic, each of the rows of $W^{(1)}$ is a codeword of C_{RS2}, each of minimum weight. Any two rows of $W^{(1)}$ differ in $q - 1$ positions. Furthermore, any $\alpha^k \mathbf{w}_i$ and $\alpha^\ell \mathbf{w}_i$ are also minimal weight codewords, where $0 \le i < q - 1, 0 \le k < q - 1, 0 \le \ell < q - 1$ with $k \ne \ell$. Both such codewords have 0 at position i and so must differ at the other $q - 2$ positions. The rows of $W^{(1)}$ thus satisfy the α-multiplied row constraint 1. For rows i and j with $i \ne j$, $\alpha^k \mathbf{w}_i$ and $\alpha^\ell \mathbf{w}_k$ are two different minimum-weight codewords in C_{RS2} which differ in at least $q - 2$ places. So $W^{(1)}$ also satisfies the α-multiplied row constraint 2.

By replacing each element in $W^{(1)}$ by its $(q - 1)$-fold matrix dispersion, a $(q - 1)^2 \times (q - 1)^2$ block circulant matrix is obtained,

$$H^{(1)} = \begin{bmatrix} \mathbf{0} & A_{0,1} & \cdots & A_{0,q-2} \\ A_{0,q-2} & \mathbf{0} & A_{0,1} & \cdots & A_{0,q-3} \\ \vdots & & & & \\ A_{0,1} & A_{0,2} & \cdots & \mathbf{0} \end{bmatrix}.$$

From its construction, $H^{(1)}$ has the following properties:

1. Each row (and column) has only one zero block matrix.

2. These zero block matrices lie down the main diagonal.

3. Each block row is a cyclic shift of the block row above it.

4. Each of the cyclic permutation matrices in each row are different from each other.

5. $H^{(1)}$ satisfies the RC constraint and has row weight and column weight equal to $q - 2$.

Now submatrices can be selected to establish codes of different sizes. For a pair of integers (g, r), with $1 \le g, r < q$, let $H^{(1)}(g, r)$ be a $g \times r$ block submatrix of $H^{(1)}$. It will also satisfy the RC constraint. If the submatrix $H^{(1)}(g, r)$ is chosen to exclude the diagonal of $H^{(1)}$, then $H^{(1)}(g, r)$ has constant weight g in each column and constant weight r in each row. The nullspace of $H^{(1)}(g, r)$ is a code of rate at least $(r - g)/r$.

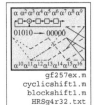

```
gf257ex.m
cyclicshift1.m
blockshift1.m
HRSg4r32.txt
```

Example 16.5 [386, p 489] Let $q = 257$ (prime) and consider the $(256, 2)$ RS code over $GF(q)$. The matrix $W^{(1)}$ is of size 256×256. The matrix formed by the matrix dispersion is of size $256^2 \times 256^2 = 65{,}536 \times 65{,}536$. Then for various values of (g, r) codes of different sizes can be obtained. For example, when $g = 4$, $r = 32$ the H matrix is of size 1024×8192, corresponding to a $(8192, 7171)$ code of rate 0.875. If the submatrix is taken from above or below the diagonal, the code is regular, with column weight 4 and row weight 32. By simulation it can be determined, for example, that at a probability of bit error or $P_b = 10^{-6}$, it is approximately 1 dB away from Shannon channel capacity.

Taking $g = 4$ and $r = 64$ gives a $(16384, 15363)$ code of rate 0.9376, which performs 0.75 dB away from capacity at $P_b = 10^{-6}$.   □

16.5.2 II. Construction of QC-LDPC Codes Based on a Special Subclass of RS Codes

This method is presented in [386, Section 11.4].

For a finite field $GF(q)$, let α be primitive. Let m be the largest prime factor of $q - 1$, and let $q - 1 = cm$. Then $\beta = \alpha^c$ is an element of $GF(q)$ of order m. The set

$$\mathcal{G}_m = \{\beta^0 = 1, \beta, \ldots, \beta_{m-1}\}$$

is a cyclic subgroup of the nonzero elements of $GF(q)$. Form the Vandermonde matrix

$$W^{(2)} = \begin{bmatrix} \mathbf{w}_0 \\ \mathbf{w}_1 \\ \vdots \\ \mathbf{w}_{m-1} \end{bmatrix} = \begin{bmatrix} 1 & 1 & 1 & \cdots & 1 \\ 1 & \beta & \beta^2 & \cdots & \beta^{m-1} \\ 1 & \beta^2 & \beta^4 & \cdots & \beta^{2(m-1)} \\ \vdots & & & & \\ 1 & \beta^{m-1} & \beta^{2(m-1)} & \cdots & \beta^{(m-1)^2} \end{bmatrix}.$$

Since $\beta^m = 1$, powers of β in this matrix are taken modulo m. Taking any t consecutive rows ($1 \leq t \leq m$) of $W^{(2)}$ produces a matrix that can be considered a parity check matrix for an $(m, m - t)$ RS code, whose generator polynomial has t consecutive powers of β as roots. $W^{(2)}$ has the following properties:

1. Except for the first row, all the elements of a row are different, forming all the elements of the cyclic subgroup $\mathcal{G}_m$. Similarly for all the elements in the columns of $W^{(2)}$ (except the first column).

2. Any two rows have only the first entries the same; the elements in the other $m - 1$ positions are different between any two rows. Similarly for the column structure.

Because of these two properties, it can be shown that $W^{(2)}$ satisfies the α-multiplied row constraints 1 and 2. $W^{(2)}$ can thus be used as the base matrix for array dispersion. Replace each element of $W^{(2)}$ by its multiplicative $(q - 1)$-fold matrix dispersion to obtain the $(q - 1) \times (q - 1)$ matrix of cyclic permutation matrices:

$$H^{(2)} = \begin{bmatrix} A_{0,0} & A_{0,1} & \cdots & A_{0,m-1} \\ A_{1,0} & A_{1,1} & \cdots & A_{1,m-1} \\ \vdots & & & \\ A_{m-1,0} & A_{m-1,1} & \cdots & A_{m-1,m-1} \end{bmatrix}.$$

$H^{(2)}$ contains no 0-blocks. As before, for any pair integers (g, r) with $1 \leq g, r \leq m$, a submatrix $H^{(2)}(g, r)$ can be extracted to use as a parity check matrix of size $(q - 1)g \times (q - 1)r$.

Example 16.6 [386, 497] For the field $GF(2^7)$, $q - 1 = 127$ is itself a prime and can be used as the prime factor, so $m = 127$. The matrix $W^{(2)}$ is of size 127×127 and $H^{(2)}$ is of size $127^2 \times 127^2$. For $(g, r) = (4, 40)$, for example, results in a parity check matrix $H^{(2)}(4, 40)$ of size 508×5080, which produces a $(5080, 4575)$ code with rate 0.9006. □

There is another related way to construct LDPC codes. Suppose $q - 1$ can be factored as $q - 1 = \ell t m$, where as before m is the largest prime factor of $q - 1$. Let $\beta = \alpha^{\ell t}$ (an element of order m in $GF(q)$) and let $\delta = \alpha^\ell$ (an element of order tm). The sets

$$G_m = \{\beta^0 = 1, \beta, \ldots, \beta^{m-1}\} \quad \text{and} \quad G_{tm} = \{\delta^0 = 1, \delta, \ldots, \delta^{tm-1}\}$$

are cyclic subgroups of the nonzero elements of $GF(q)$, and G_m is a subgroup of G_{tm}.

For an element $\delta^i \in G_{tm}$, define the location vector $\mathbf{z}(\delta^i)$ as the binary tm-tuple

$$\mathbf{z}(\delta^i) = (z_0, z_1, \ldots, z_{tm-1}),$$

where all elements are zero except $z_i = 1$. $\mathbf{z}(\delta^i)$ is referred to as the G_{tm}-location vector of δ^i. Let $\sigma \in G_{tm}$. Form the $tm \times tm$ dispersion matrix A^* over G_{tm} with the G_{tm}-location vectors of $\sigma, \delta\sigma, \ldots, \delta^{tm-1}\sigma$. This is a cyclic permutation matrix.

Since G_m is a cyclic subgroup of G_{tm}, $W^{(2)}$ satisfies δ-multiplied row constraints 1 and 2. Now, instead of replacing elements of $W^{(2)}$ with the $(q-1)$-fold dispersions (as above), replace each element of $W^{(2)}$ with is tm-fold dispersion to produce the $tm^2 \times tm^2$ matrix

$$H^{(3)} = \begin{bmatrix} A^*_{0,0} & A^*_{0,1} & \cdots & A^*_{0,m-1} \\ A^*_{1,0} & A^*_{1,1} & \cdots & A^*_{1,m-1} \\ \vdots & & & \\ A^*_{m-1,0} & A^*_{m-1,1} & \cdots & A^*_{m-1,m-1} \end{bmatrix}.$$

As before, for any (g, r), $H^{(3)}(g, r)$ can be formed as a submatrix of size $gtm \times rtm$, having column and row weights g and r, respectively.

Example 16.7 [386, p. 499] For the field $GF(2^{10})$, factor $2^{10} - 1 = 1023$ as $1023 = 3 \times 11 \times 31$. Ler $m = 31, l = 11, t = 3$. Let α be primitive in $GF(2^{10})$ and $\beta = \alpha^{33}, \delta = \alpha^{11}$. Then

$$G_{31} = \{\beta^0 = 1, \beta, \ldots, \beta^{30}\} \quad \text{and} \quad G_{93} = \{\delta^0 = 1, \delta, \ldots, \delta^{92}\}.$$

Form $W^{(2)}$ with elements from G_{31}. Then replace each element by its 93-fold matrix dispersion, resulting in $H^{(3)}$ of size 2883×2883.   □

16.5.3 III. Construction of QC-LDPC Codes Based on Subgroups of a Finite Field

This is based on [[386], Section 11.5] and [418]. Let p be prime and let $q = p^m$. Let α be primitive in $GF(q)$. Then (as described in Chapter 5), the elements $\alpha^0, \alpha, \ldots, \alpha^{m-1}$ are linearly independent and $GF(q)$ can be expressed as a vector space over these basis vectors so that any $\alpha^i \in Gf(q)$ can be written as

$$\alpha^i = c_{i,0}\alpha^0 + c_{i,1}\alpha^1 + \cdots + c_{i,m-1}\alpha^{m-1}$$

with $c_{i,j} \in GF(p)$. Now take a subset of these basis elements to form $\{\alpha^0, \alpha, \alpha^2, \ldots, \alpha^{t-1}\}$ and generate the additive subgroup G_1 of $GF(q)$ by linear combinations of this restricted set of basis elements. For every element $\beta_i \in G_1$,

$$\beta_i = c_{i,0}\alpha^0 + c_{i,1}\alpha + \cdots + c_{i,t-1}\alpha^{t-1}$$

with $c_{i,j} \in GF(p)$. Since each coefficient can be chosen independently, the subgroup G_1 has p^t elements. Write $G_1 = \{\beta_0 = 1, \beta_1, \ldots, \beta_{p^t-1}\}$. Similarly, form the complementary subset of basis elements $\{\alpha^t, \alpha^{t+1}, \ldots, \alpha^{m-1}\}$ and form the additive subgroup G_2 using these elements as the basis. An element $\delta_i \in G_2$ can be expressed as

$$\delta_i = c_{i,t}\alpha^t + c_{i,t+1}\alpha^{t+1} + \cdots + c_{i,m-1}\alpha^{m-1}.$$

This subgroup has p^{m-t} elements in it. Write $G_2 = \{\delta_0 = 0, \delta_1, \ldots, \delta_{p^{m-t}-1}\}$. By this construction the two subgroups satisfy $G_1 \cap G_2 = \{0\}$.

Based on this additive group structure, for $\delta_i \in G_2$, form the coset with coset leader δ_i,

$$\delta_i + G_1 = \{\delta_i, \delta_i + \beta_1, \ldots, \delta_i + \beta_{p^t-1}\}.$$

There are p^{m-t} such cosets which form a partition of $GF(q)$; two such cosets of G_1 are disjoint.

These cosets are now used to form a $p^{m-t} \times p^t$ matrix $W^{(4)}$ by

$$W^{(4)} = \begin{bmatrix} \mathbf{w}_0 \\ \mathbf{w}_1 \\ \mathbf{w}_2 \\ \vdots \\ \mathbf{w}_{p^{m-t}-1} \end{bmatrix} = \begin{bmatrix} 0 & \beta_1 & \cdots & \beta_{p^t-1} \\ \delta_1 & \delta_1 + \beta_1 & \cdots & \delta_1 + \beta_{p^t-1} \\ \delta_2 & \delta_2 + \beta_1 & \cdots & \delta_2 + \beta_{p^t-1} \\ \vdots & & & \\ \delta_{p^{m-t}-1} & \delta_{p^{m-t}-1} + \beta_1 & \cdots & \delta_{p^{m-t}-1} + \beta_{p^t-1} \end{bmatrix}.$$

Since the cosets of G_1 are disjoint, different rows $\mathbf{w}_i$ and $\mathbf{w}_j$ differ in all positions. Based on this, it can be argued that $W^{(4)}$ satisfies the α-multiplied row constraints 1 and 2.

Replace each element of $W^{(4)}$ by its $(q-1)$-fold matrix dispersion to construct a matrix $H^{(4)}$, in the pattern established in the sections above. For any pair (g, r), a submatrix $H^{(4)}(g, r)$ of size $(q-1)g \times (q-1)r$ can be extracted and used as a parity check matrix.

16.5.4 IV. Construction of QC-LDPC Codes Based on Subgroups of the Multiplicative Group of a Finite Field

The set of integers $\{0, 1, \ldots, p-1\}$ forms a field $GF(p)$ when p is prime. For an element $i \in GF(p)$, its location vector with respect to the additive group is the unit p-tuple

$$\mathbf{z}(i) = (z_0, z_1, \ldots, z_{p-1}),$$

where all elements are 0 except $z_i = 1$. Location vectors for different elements of $GF(p)$ are obviously different. The location vector for $\mathbf{z}(k + 1)$ is the right cyclic shift of $\mathbf{z}(k)$, with $\mathbf{z}(0)$ the right cyclic shift of $\mathbf{z}(p-1)$. For a $k \in GF(p)$, form a matrix A with the location vectors $\mathbf{z}(k), \mathbf{z}(k + 1), \ldots, \mathbf{z}(k + p - 1)$ (operations modulo p). A is a cyclic permutation matrix, called the *additive p-fold matrix of the element k*.

Now form the $p \times p$ matrix of elements of $GF(p)$ as

$$W^{(6)} = \begin{bmatrix} \mathbf{w}_0 \\ \mathbf{w}_1 \\ \vdots \\ \mathbf{w}_{p-1} \end{bmatrix} = \begin{bmatrix} 0 \cdot 0 & 0 \cdot 1 & 0 \cdot 2 & \cdots & 0 \cdot (p-1) \\ 1 \cdot 0 & 1 \cdot 1 & 1 \cdot 2 & \cdots & 1 \cdot (p-1) \\ \vdots & & & & \\ (p-1) \cdot 0 & (p-1) \cdot 1 & (p-1) \cdot 2 & \cdots & (p-1) \cdot (p-1) \end{bmatrix}$$

(operations modulo p). $W^{(6)}$ has the following structural properties:

1. $\mathbf{w}_0$ has all 0 elements.

2. For any other row, all elements on the row are distinct, forming the p elements of $GF(p)$; similarly for the elements of the columns.

3. Any two distinct rows have the 0 element in the first position, and differ in the other $p - 1$ positions.

Now construct a matrix $H^{(6)}$ by replacing each element of $W^{(6)}$ by its additive p-fold matrix dispersion, resulting in the $p^2 \times p^2$ matrix

$$H^{(6)} = \begin{bmatrix} A_{0,0} & A_{0,1} & \cdots & A_{0,p-1} \\ A_{1,0} & A_{1,1} & \cdots & A_{1,p-1} \\ \vdots & & & \\ A_{p-1,0} & A_{p-1,1} & \cdots & A_{p-1,p-1} \end{bmatrix},$$

where each $A_{i,j}$ is a cyclic permutation matrix.

For any pair (g, r), let $H^{(6)}(g, r)$ be the $g(p-1) \times r(r-1)$ submatrix of $H^{(6)}$.

Example 16.8   [[386], p. 508] Let $p = 73$. The matrix $H^{(6)}$ composed of the cyclic permutation matrices of dispersions of location vector with respect to the additive group of $GF(73)$ results in a matrix $H^{(6)}$ of size $73^2 \times 73^2$. Taking $(g, r) = (6, 72)$ results in a parity check matrix $H^{(6)}(g, r)$ of size 438×5256.   □

16.5.5   Construction of QC-LDPC Codes Based on Primitive Elements of a Field

Let α be primitive in $GF(q)$, where q is the power of a prime. Factor $q - 1$ as powers of primes as

$$q - 1 = p_1^{k_1} p_2^{k_2} \cdots p_t^{k_t}.$$

Let $K = \phi(q - 1)$ be the number of primitive elements in $GF(q)$, where ϕ is the Euler's totient function. Write these primitive elements as $\{\alpha^{j_1}, \alpha^{j_2}, \ldots, \alpha^{j_K}\}$. Let $j_0 = 0$. Form the matrix

$$W^{(7)} = \begin{bmatrix} \alpha^{j_0-j_0} - 1 & \alpha^{j_1-j_0} - 1 & \cdots & \alpha^{j_K-j_0} - 1 \\ \alpha^{j_0-j_1} - 1 & \alpha^{j_1-j_1} - 1 & \cdots & \alpha^{j_K-j_1} - 1 \\ \vdots & & & \\ \alpha^{j_0-j_K} - 1 & \alpha^{j_1-j_K} - 1 & \cdots & \alpha^{j_K-j_K} - 1 \end{bmatrix}.$$

It can be shown that $W^{(7)}$ satisfies the α-constrained row constraints 1 and 2.

Now form $H^{(7)}$ by replacing element of $W^{(7)}$ by its $(q - 1)$-fold matrix dispersion to obtain an RC-constrained $(K + 1)(q - 1) \times (K + 1)(q - 1)$ matrix. Then a parity check matrix can be formed for any (g, r) by taking a $g(q - 1) \times r(q - 1)$ submatrix.

Example 16.9   [[386], p. 512] For the field $GF(2^6)$, factor $2^6 - 1 = 63$ as 9×7. This field has 36 primitive elements. Then $H^{(7)}$ has size $37 \cdot 63 \times 37 \cdot 63$. With $(g, r) = (6, 37)$, a matrix $H^{(7)}(6, 37)$ of size 378×2331 is obtained.   □

16.6   Code Design Based on Finite Geometries

A Euclidean geometry (EG) over $GF(q)$ consists of a set of points, Lines, and other geometric objects, where the elements of the points are drawn from $GF(q)$. For an integer m and a field $GF(q)$, the EG over $GF(q)$, denoted as $EG(m, q)$, consists of points, lines, and flats. Basic concepts of EG are defined below with examples from $EG(2, 4)$ to illustrate the concepts and develop intuition.

In this section, some elements of EG are presented, followed by an example construction in which the incidence structure of the geometry is exploited. A more exhaustive summary of code designs based on finite geometries is presented in [386].

16.6.1   Rudiments of Euclidean Geometry

16.6.1.1   Points in $EG(m, q)$

Each point in $EG(m, q)$ is an m-tuple over $GF(q)$, so there are q^m points in the geometry.

Example 16.10   Points in $EG(3, 4)$
For the field $GF(4)$ with elements $0, 1, \beta, \beta^2$, where β is an element of order 3, and $m = 3$, there are $4^4 = 256$ points:

$$\begin{array}{llll} \mathbf{p}_0 = (0,0,0,0) & \mathbf{p}_1 = (0,0,0,1) & \mathbf{p}_2 = (0,0,0,\beta) & \mathbf{p}_3 = (0,0,0,\beta^2) \\ \mathbf{p}_4 = (0,0,1,0) & \mathbf{p}_5 = (0,0,1,1) & \mathbf{p}_6 = (0,0,1,\beta) & \mathbf{p}_7 = (0,0,1,\beta^2) \\ \mathbf{p}_8 = (0,0,\beta,0) & \mathbf{p}_9 = (0,0,\beta,1) & \mathbf{p}_{10} = (0,0,\beta,\beta) & \mathbf{p}_{11} = (0,0,\beta,\beta^2) \\ \vdots & \vdots & \vdots & \vdots \\ \mathbf{p}_{252} = (\beta^2,\beta^2,\beta^2,0) & \mathbf{p}_{252} = (\beta^2,\beta^2,\beta^2,1) & \mathbf{p}_{254} = (\beta^2,\beta^2,\beta^2,\beta) & \mathbf{p}_{255} = (\beta^2,\beta^2,\beta^2,\beta^2) \end{array}$$

□

Example 16.11   **Points in** $EG(2,4)$: This is 2-tuples over $GF(4)$. These are listed as 2-tuples and with a suggestive "geometric" representation.

$$
\begin{array}{llll}
\mathbf{p}_0 = (0,0) & \mathbf{p}_1 = (0,1) & \mathbf{p}_2 = (0,\beta) & \mathbf{p}_3 = (0,\beta^2) \\
\mathbf{p}_4 = (1,0) & \mathbf{p}_5 = (1,1) & \mathbf{p}_6 = (1,\beta) & \mathbf{p}_7 = (1,\beta^2) \\
\mathbf{p}_8 = (\beta,0) & \mathbf{p}_9 = (\beta,1) & \mathbf{p}_{10} = (\beta,\beta) & \mathbf{p}_{11} = (\beta,\beta^2) \\
\mathbf{p}_{12} = (\beta^2,0) & \mathbf{p}_{13} = (\beta^2,1) & \mathbf{p}_{14} = (\beta^2,\beta) & \mathbf{p}_{15} = (\beta^2,\beta^2)
\end{array}
$$

The 16 points in $EG(2,4)$ form a vector space. Recall that $GF(16)$ can be constructed as a vector space over $GF(4)$. There is thus an isomorphism between $EG(2,4)$ and $GF(16)$, which we denote as

$$EG(2,4) \Leftrightarrow GF(16).$$

More generally, the isomorphism between $EG(m,q)$ and $GF(q^m)$ is denoted as

$$EG(m,q) \Leftrightarrow GF(q^m).$$

By this isomorphism the q^m points in $EG(m,q)$ can be identified with the points in $GF(q^m)$.

Example 16.12   Let $GF(2^4)$ be generated by the polynomial $1 + x + x^4$, with α primitive, and consider $GF(2^4)$ as an extension field of $GF(2^2) = \{0,1,\beta,\beta^2\}$, with $\beta = \alpha^5$. The points in $GF(16)$ are identified with points in $EG(2,4)$ in the following table.

Power representation	Polynomial representation	Vector representation	$GF(2^4)$ as ext. of $GF(4)$	Vector representation	$EG(2,4)$ point
$0 = \alpha^{-\infty}$	0	(0000)	0	(0,0)	$\mathbf{p}_0$
$1 = \alpha^0$	1	(1000)	1	(1,0)	$\mathbf{p}_4$
α	α	(0100)	α	(0,1)	$\mathbf{p}_1$
α^2	α^2	(0010)	$\beta + \alpha$	$(\beta,1)$	$\mathbf{p}_9$
α^3	α^3	(0001)	$\beta + \beta^2\alpha$	(β,β^2)	$\mathbf{p}_{11}$
α^4	$1+\alpha$	(1100)	$1 + \alpha$	(1,1)	$\mathbf{p}_5$
α^5	$\alpha+\alpha^2$	(0110)	β	$(\beta,0)$	$\mathbf{p}_8$
α^6	$\alpha^2+\alpha^3$	(0011)	$\beta\alpha$	$(0,\beta)$	$\mathbf{p}_2$
α^7	$1+\alpha\ \ +\alpha^3$	(1101)	$\beta^2 + \beta\alpha$	(β^2,β)	$\mathbf{p}_{14}$
α^8	$1+\ \ \alpha^2$	(1010)	$\beta^2 + \alpha$	$(\beta^2,1)$	$\mathbf{p}_{13}$
α^9	$\alpha\ \ \ +\alpha^3$	(0101)	$\beta + \beta\alpha$	(β,β)	$\mathbf{p}_{10}$
α^{10}	$1+\alpha+\alpha^2$	(1110)	β^2	$(\beta^2,0)$	$\mathbf{p}_{12}$
α^{11}	$\alpha+\alpha^2+\alpha^3$	(0111)	$\beta^2\alpha$	$(0,\beta^2)$	$\mathbf{p}_3$
α^{12}	$1+\alpha+\alpha^2+\alpha^3$	(1111)	$1 + \beta^2\alpha$	$(1,\beta^2)$	$\mathbf{p}_7$
α^{13}	$1\ \ \ +\alpha^2+\alpha^3$	(1011)	$1 + \beta\alpha$	$(1,\beta)$	$\mathbf{p}_6$
α^{14}	$1\ \ \ \ \ \ \ +\alpha^3$	(1001)	$\beta^2+\beta^2\alpha$	(β^2,β^2)	$\mathbf{p}_{15}$

We will use the terms "point" notation and the "field" notation interchangeably.

16.6.1.2 Lines in $EG(m,q)$

A line in $EG(m,q)$ is the set of points $\{\mathbf{p}_0 + \gamma\mathbf{p}, \gamma \in GF(q)\}$, that is, as γ sweeps over all values in $GF(q)$, where $\mathbf{p} \neq 0$. (That is, in the notation below, $\gamma\mathbf{p}$ is intended to denote the set of values as γ sweeps over its field.) Each line in $EG(m,q)$ has q distinct points on it.

Example 16.13   Lines through the origin in $EG(2,4)$. Let the field $GF(4)$ have the values $\gamma \in \{0,1,\beta,\beta^2\}$, where $\beta = \alpha^5$ and α is primitive in $GF(16)$. In the list below, points are shown both as 2-tuples in $GF(4)^2$, and as isomorphically labeled points in $GF(16)$.

$$\mathbf{p} = (1,0) : \mathcal{L} = \{\gamma(1,0)\} = \{(0,0),(1,0),(\beta,0),(\beta^2,0)\}$$
$$= \{\gamma\alpha^0\} = \{0,1,\beta,\beta^2\}$$
$$\mathbf{p} = (0,1) : \mathcal{L} = \{\gamma(0,1)\} = \{(0,0),(0,1),(0,\beta),(0,\beta^2)\}$$
$$= \{\gamma\alpha\} = \{0,\alpha,\alpha^6,\alpha^{11}\}$$
$$\mathbf{p} = (1,1) : \mathcal{L} = \{\gamma(1,1)\} = \{(0,0),(1,1),(\beta,\beta),(\beta^2,\beta^2)\}$$
$$= \{\gamma\alpha^4\} = \{0,\alpha^4,\alpha^9,\alpha^{14}\}$$
$$\mathbf{p} = (\beta,1) : \mathcal{L} = \{\gamma(\beta,1)\} = \{(0,0),(\beta,1),(\beta^2,\beta),(1,\beta^2)\}$$
$$= \{\gamma\alpha^2\} = \{0,\alpha^2,\alpha^7,\alpha^{12}\}$$
$$\mathbf{p} = (\beta^2,1) : \mathcal{L} = \{\gamma(\beta^2,1)\} = \{(0,0),(\beta^2,1),(1,\beta),(\beta,\beta^2)\}$$
$$= \{\gamma\alpha^8\} = \{0,\alpha^8,\alpha^{13},\alpha^3\}$$

The lines defined by these four points $\mathbf{p}$ cover all the points in $EG(2,4)$. (Color versions of this page can be viewed at wileywebpage or `https://github.com/tkmoon/eccbook/colorpages`.) □

More generally, lines are of the form $\{\mathbf{p}_0 + \beta\mathbf{p}, \beta \in GF(q)\}$, where $\mathbf{p} \neq 0$.

Example 16.14   Lines through $\mathbf{p}_0 = (1,1) = \alpha^4$ in $EG(2,4)$. (Color versions of this page can be viewed at wileywebpage or `https://github.com/tkmoon/eccbook/colorpages`.)

$$\mathbf{p} = (1,0) : \mathcal{L} = \{(1,1) + \gamma(1,0)\} = \{(1,1),(0,1),(\beta^2,1),(\beta,1)\}$$
$$= \{\alpha^4 + \gamma(1)\} = \{\alpha^4,\alpha,\alpha^8,\alpha^2\}$$
$$\mathbf{p} = (0,1) : \mathcal{L} = \{(1,1) + \gamma(0,1)\} = \{(1,1),(1,0),(1,\beta^2),(1,\beta)\}$$
$$= \{\alpha^4 + \gamma\alpha\} = \{\alpha^4,1,\alpha^{12},\alpha^{13}\}$$
$$\mathbf{p} = (1,1) : \mathcal{L} = \{(1,1) + \gamma(1,1)\} = \{(1,1),(0,0),(\beta^2,\beta^2),(\beta,\beta)\}$$
$$= \{\alpha^4 + \gamma\alpha^4\} = \{\alpha^4,0,\alpha^{14},\alpha^9\}$$
$$\mathbf{p} = (\beta,1) : \mathcal{L} = \{(1,1) + \gamma(\beta,1)\} = \{(1,1),(\beta^2,0),(\beta,\beta^2),(0,\beta)\}$$
$$= \{\alpha^4 + \gamma\alpha^2\} = \{\alpha^4,\alpha^{10},\alpha^3,\alpha^6\}$$
$$\mathbf{p} = (\beta^2,1) : \mathcal{L} = \{(1,1) + \gamma(\beta^2,1)\} = \{(1,1),(\beta,0),(0,\beta^2),(\beta^2,\beta)\}$$
$$= \{\alpha^4 + \gamma\alpha^8\} = \{\alpha^4,\alpha^5,\alpha^{11},\alpha^7\}$$

□

If $\mathbf{p}_0 \neq 0$, the lines $\{\beta\mathbf{p}\}$ and $\{\mathbf{p}_0 + \beta\mathbf{p}\}$ do not have any common points. These may be considered to be parallel lines.

Example 16.15   In $EG(2,4)$, let $\mathbf{p} = (1,1) = \alpha^4$ and consider the lines defined with different values of $\mathbf{p}_0$. (Color versions of this page can be viewed at wileywebpage or `https://github.com/tkmoon/eccbook/colorpages`.)

$$\mathbf{p}_0 = (0,0) : \mathcal{L} = \{\gamma(1,1)\} = \{(0,0),(1,1),(\beta,\beta),(\beta^2,\beta^2)\}$$
$$= \{\gamma\alpha^4\} = \{0,\alpha^4,\alpha^9,\alpha^{14}\}$$
$$\mathbf{p}_0 = (\beta,\beta^2) : \mathcal{L} = \{(\beta,\beta^2) + \gamma(1,1)\} = \{(\beta,\beta^2),(\beta^2,\beta),(0,1),(1,0)\}$$
$$= \{\alpha^3 + \gamma\alpha^4\} = \{\alpha^3,\alpha^7,\alpha,1\}$$
$$\mathbf{p}_0 = (0,\beta) : \mathcal{L} = \{(0,\beta) + \gamma(1,1)\} = \{(0,\beta),(1,\beta^2),(\beta^2,1),(\beta,0)\}$$
$$= \{\alpha^6 + \gamma\alpha^4\} = \{\alpha^6,\alpha^{12},\alpha^8,\alpha^5\}$$
$$\mathbf{p}_0 = (0,\beta^2) : \mathcal{L} = \{(0,\beta^2) + \gamma(1,1)\} = \{(0,\beta^2),(1,\beta),(\beta,1),(\beta^2,0)\}$$
$$= \{\alpha^{11} + \gamma\alpha^4\} = \{\alpha^{11},\alpha^{13},\alpha^2,\alpha^{10}\}$$

□

In general, there are q^{m-1} such parallel lines having the same direction $\mathbf{p}$, with different offsets $\mathbf{p}_0$. (In the example above, $q^{m-1} = q^{2-1} = 4$.) The set of such parallel lines is referred to as a *parallel bundle*. There are

$$K_p = \frac{q^m - 1}{q - 1}$$

parallel bundles. (In $EG(2,4)$ there are five parallel bundles.) These will be denoted as $\mathcal{P}_1, \mathcal{P}_2, \ldots, \mathcal{P}_{K_p}$, each consisting of q^{m-1} lines. Each parallel bundle contains all the q^m points in $EG(m,q)$. In each parallel bundle, there is one line passing through the origin.

We discussed placing a footnote indicating that a color page would be available at some web page

Let $\mathbf{p}_1$ and $\mathbf{p}_2$ be two linearly independent points, that is, points such that $\beta_1\mathbf{p}_1 + \beta_2\mathbf{p}_2 \neq 0$ unless $\beta_1 = \beta_2 = 0$. Then the lines $\{\mathbf{p}_0 + \beta\mathbf{p}_1\}$ and $\{\mathbf{p}_0 + \beta\mathbf{p}_2\}$ have only one point in common, the point $\mathbf{p}_0$.

Example 16.16   In $EG(2,4)$, let $\mathbf{p}_0 = (\beta, \beta^2) = \alpha^3$, $\mathbf{p}_1 = (1,0) = 1$ and $\mathbf{p}_2 = (\beta, \beta) = \alpha^9$.

$$\mathcal{L} = \{(\beta, \beta^2) + \gamma(1,0)\} = \{(\beta, \beta^2), (\beta^2, \beta^2), (0, \beta^2), (1, \beta^2)\}$$
$$= \{\alpha^3 + \gamma(1)\} = \{\alpha^3, \alpha^{14}, \alpha^{11}, \alpha^{12}\}$$
$$\mathcal{L} = \{(\beta, \beta^2) + \gamma(\beta, \beta)\} = \{(\beta, \beta^2), (0,1), (1,0), (\beta^2, \beta)\}$$
$$= \{\alpha^3 + \gamma\alpha^9\} = \{\alpha^3, \alpha, 1, \alpha^7\}$$

The only point in common on these two lines is (β, β^2). (Color versions of this page can be viewed at wileywebpage or `https://github.com/tkmoon/eccbook/colorpages`.) □

Some basic facts about points and lines can be summarized as follows:

- Any two points are connected by exactly one line.
- Two lines either have exactly one point in common (intersect), or they have no points in common (disjoint; parallel).
- Let $\mathbf{p}$ be a point in $EG(m,q)$, and $\mathcal{L}$ a line in $EG(m,q)$. If $\mathbf{p}$ is a point on $\mathcal{L}$, we say that $\mathcal{L}$ passes through $\mathbf{p}$.
- There are $(q^m - 1)/(q-1)$ lines passing through any point $\mathbf{p}$.
- If two lines have a common point $\mathbf{p}$, we say they intersect at $\mathbf{p}$.
- There are

$$q^{m-1}\frac{q^m - 1}{q - 1}$$

lines in $EG(m,q)$.

16.6.1.3 Incidence vectors in $EG^*(m,q)$

$EG^*(m,q)$ is the *subgeometry* of $EG(m,q)$ obtained by removing from $EG(m,q)$ the origin and all lines passing through the origin. $EG^*(m,q)$ has $q^m - 1$ points and $(q^{m-1} - 1)(q^m - 1)/(q-1)$ lines.

The finite geometry structure will now be endowed with an incidence vector structure, to be able to define sparse matrices. Let $\mathcal{L}$ be a line in $EG^*(m,q)$ (not passing through the origin). Define the incidence vector

$$\mathbf{v}_{\mathcal{L}} = (v_0, v_1, \ldots, v_{q^m - 2})$$

with elements 0 or 1 corresponding to the $q^m - 1$ nonzero points

$$(\alpha^0 = 1, \alpha^1, \alpha^2, \ldots, \alpha^{q^m - 1}),$$

where α is primitive in $GF(q^m)$, where $v_i = 1$ if and only if α^i is a point on $\mathcal{L}$. The weight of any incidence vector in $EG(m,q)$ is q (that is, there are q points on the line).

Example 16.17   For the line

$$\mathcal{L} = \{(\beta, \beta^2) + \gamma(1,1)\} = \{(\beta, \beta^2), (\beta^2, \beta), (0,1), (1,0)\} = \{\alpha^3 + \gamma\alpha^4\} = \{\alpha^3, \alpha^7, \alpha, 1\}$$

in $EG^*(2,4)$, the incidence vector is

$$\mathbf{v}_{\mathcal{L}} = (1,1,0,1,0,0,0,1,0,0,0,0,0,0,0).$$

□

We discussed placing a footnote indicating that a color page would be available at some web page

For a line $\mathcal{L} = (\alpha^{j_1}, \alpha^{j_2}, \ldots, \alpha^{j_q})$, the incidence vector $\mathbf{v}_{\mathcal{L}}$ is 1 only at locations j_i. The product $\alpha^t \mathcal{L}$ means the product of α^t with each point of $\mathcal{L}$. For $\mathcal{L}$ as above,

$$\alpha^t \mathcal{L} = \{\alpha^{j_1+t}, \alpha^{j_2+t}, \ldots, \alpha^{j_q+t}\}$$

$\alpha^t \mathcal{L}$ is a line for $0 \leq t \leq q^m - 2$. The set of these lines is said to form a *cyclic class*. The incidence vector $\mathbf{v}_{\alpha^t \mathcal{L}}$ is the incidence vector $\mathbf{v}_{\mathcal{L}}$ shifted to the right by t places.

Each cyclic class has $q^m - 1$ lines in it, and there are

$$K_c = \frac{q^m - 1}{q - 1}$$

cyclic classes. These classes are denoted as $S_1, S_2, \ldots, S_{K_c}$.

Example 16.18 In $EG^*(2, 4)$, a cyclic class is as follows.

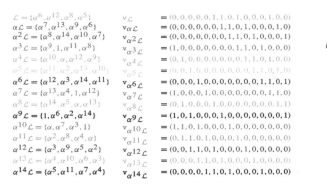

There are 15 lines in this cyclic class, and $EG^*(2, 4)$ has only this $K_c = 1$ cyclic class. (Color versions of this page can be viewed at wileywebpage or `https://github.com/tkmoon/eccbook/colorpages`.) □

16.6.2 A Family of Cyclic EG-LDPC Codes

Material in this section is drawn from [[386], chapter 10]. The incidence vectors of a cyclic class S_i can be used to form a sparse matrix. For each class S_i of lines in $EG^*(m, q)$, $1 \leq i \leq K_c$, form a $(q^m - 1) \times (q^m - 1)$ matrix H_i with incidence vectors $\mathbf{v}_{\mathcal{L}}, \mathbf{v}_{\alpha \mathcal{L}}, \ldots, \mathbf{v}_{\alpha^{q^m-2} \mathcal{L}}$ as rows. This produces a matrix with row and column weight equal to q.

Example 16.19 For the cyclic class in Example 16.18 the H matrix is

$$H_i = \begin{bmatrix} 0 & 0 & 0 & 0 & 0 & 1 & 1 & 0 & 1 & 0 & 0 & 0 & 1 & 0 & 0 \\ 0 & 0 & 0 & 0 & 0 & 0 & 1 & 1 & 0 & 1 & 0 & 0 & 0 & 1 & 0 \\ 0 & 0 & 0 & 0 & 0 & 0 & 0 & 1 & 1 & 0 & 1 & 0 & 0 & 0 & 1 \\ 1 & 0 & 0 & 0 & 0 & 0 & 0 & 0 & 1 & 1 & 0 & 1 & 0 & 0 & 0 \\ 0 & 1 & 0 & 0 & 0 & 0 & 0 & 0 & 0 & 1 & 1 & 0 & 1 & 0 & 0 \\ 0 & 0 & 1 & 0 & 0 & 0 & 0 & 0 & 0 & 0 & 1 & 1 & 0 & 1 & 0 \\ 0 & 0 & 0 & 1 & 0 & 0 & 0 & 0 & 0 & 0 & 0 & 1 & 1 & 0 & 1 \\ 1 & 0 & 0 & 0 & 1 & 0 & 0 & 0 & 0 & 0 & 0 & 0 & 1 & 1 & 0 \\ 0 & 1 & 0 & 0 & 0 & 1 & 0 & 0 & 0 & 0 & 0 & 0 & 0 & 1 & 1 \\ 1 & 0 & 1 & 0 & 0 & 0 & 1 & 0 & 0 & 0 & 0 & 0 & 0 & 0 & 1 \\ 1 & 1 & 0 & 1 & 0 & 0 & 0 & 1 & 0 & 0 & 0 & 0 & 0 & 0 & 0 \\ 0 & 1 & 1 & 0 & 1 & 0 & 0 & 0 & 1 & 0 & 0 & 0 & 0 & 0 & 0 \\ 0 & 0 & 1 & 1 & 0 & 1 & 0 & 0 & 0 & 1 & 0 & 0 & 0 & 0 & 0 \\ 0 & 0 & 0 & 1 & 1 & 0 & 1 & 0 & 0 & 0 & 1 & 0 & 0 & 0 & 0 \\ 0 & 0 & 0 & 0 & 1 & 1 & 0 & 1 & 0 & 0 & 0 & 1 & 0 & 0 & 0 \end{bmatrix}. \tag{16.9}$$

□

We discussed placing a footnote indicating that a color page would be available at some web page

Then for some k, $1 \leq k \leq K_c$ stack the H_i for $1 \leq i \leq k$ to form a matrix H of size $k(q^m - 1) \times (q^m - 1)$

$$H_{EG,k}^{(1)} = \begin{bmatrix} H_1 \\ H_2 \\ \vdots \\ H_{K_c} \end{bmatrix}.$$

$H_{EG,k}^{(1)}$ has column weight kq and row weight q.

Now we can invoke the geometric structure of lines in $EG^*(m, q)$. The rows of $H_{EG,k}^{(1)}$ correspond to lines, and no two lines have more than one point in common. It follows, therefore, that no two rows (or two columns) have more than one component in common. Thus, $H_{EG,k}^{(1)}$ satisfies the RC constraint and has no four-cycles in its Tanner graph. The nullspace of H is an LDPC code. From the cyclic structure of the lines and the incidence vectors, H is the parity check matrix of a cyclic code. To find the generator polynomial, express the rows of $H_{EG,k}^{(1)}$ as polynomials. For example, the first row in (16.9) has the polynomial

$$x^5 + x^6 + x^8 + x^{12}.$$

Let $h(x)$ be the greatest common divisor of the row polynomials of $H_{EG,k}^{(1)}$, and let $h^*(x)$ be the reciprocal polynomial of $h(x)$. The generator polynomial for the EG-LDPC code is

$$g(x) = \frac{x^{q^m-1} - 1}{h^*(x)}.$$

Example 16.20 As an example of this construction, consider codes built on $EG^*(2, q)$, which has $q^2 - 1$ points and $q^2 - 1$ lines. There is a single cyclic class, S. The circulant matrix $H_{EG,k}^{(1)}$ produces a cyclic code of length $2^q - 1$. If $q = 2^s$, then the code can be shown to have the following parameters:

- Length $N = 2^{2^s} - 1$.

- Number of parity bits: $3^s - 1$.

- Minimum distance: $2^s + 1$.

$\square$

16.6.3 Construction of LDPC Codes Based on Parallel Bundles of Lines

Let K_p be the number of parallel bundles of lines, $K_p = (q^m - 1)/(q - 1)$, each consisting of q^{m-1} parallel lines. Let $\mathcal{L}$ be a line in $EG(m, q)$ (possibly passing through the origin). Define an incidence vector now as

$$\mathbf{v}_{\mathcal{L}} = (v_{-\infty}, v_0, v_1, \ldots, v_{q^m-2})$$

representing all the points in $EG(m, q)$, $\alpha^{-\infty} = 0, \alpha^0 = 1, \alpha, \ldots, \alpha^{q^m-2}$, where $v_j \in \{0, 1\}$ and $v_j = 1$ only if α^j is a point in $\mathcal{L}$. The weight of $\mathbf{v}_{\mathcal{L}}$ is q.

For each parallel bundle P_i of lines in $EG(m, q)$, with $1 \leq i \leq K_p$ form a $q^{m-1} \times q^m$ matrix $H_{i,p}$ whose rows are the incidence vectors for the lines in $\mathcal{P}_i$. $H_{i,p}$ has column weight 1 and row weight q. For a number k, $1 \leq k \leq K_p$ stack these $H_{i,p}$ to form the matrix

$$H_{EG,k}^{(2)} = \begin{bmatrix} H_{1,p} \\ H_{2,p} \\ \vdots \\ H_{k,p} \end{bmatrix}.$$

The column and row weights of $H_{EG,k}^{(2)}$ are k and q, respectively.

16.6.4 Constructions Based on Other Combinatoric Objects

Several LDPC constructions have been reported based on combinatoric objects.

Constructions based on Kirkman triple systems are reported in [233, 234], which produce $(3, k)$-regular LDPC codes whose Tanner graph is free of four-cycles for any k.

Constructions based on Latin rectangles are reported in [464], with reportedly low encode and decode complexity.

Designs based on Steiner 2-designs are reported in [463], [236], and [388]. See also [465].

High rate LDPC codes based on constructions from unital designs are reported in [235].

Constructions based on disjoint difference sets permutation matrices for use in conjunction with the magnetic recording channel are reported in [417].

16.7 Ensembles of LDPC Codes

In the analysis and design of LDPC codes, an important analysis tool is to discuss ensembles of LDPC codes and to examine, for example, average performance these ensembles of codes. Historically this hearkens back to Shannon's idea of establishing capacity by computing average performance over an ensemble of (block) codes [404], but in the case of LDPC codes some specific theorems have been proven. To describe these theorems, we need some notation. Let K denote some particular LDPC code (examples of such configurations will be given below). Let $P_e^N(\ell; K)$ denote the probability of decoding error for a code of length N at the ℓth iteration of a message-passing decoding algorithm. Obviously, for different codes the error will be different — some codes will be good and some codes will be bad. The ensemble approach to LDPC code analysis looks at the *average* of $P_e^N(\ell; K)$ over all different configurations of codes:

$$P_e^N(\ell) = E_K[P_e^N(\ell; K)].$$

The efficacy of this approach is determined by the following theorems [375].

Concentration Theorem The performance of individual codes in the ensemble converges exponentially fast (in N) to $P_e^N(\ell)$ as $N \to \infty$.

> The relevance of this theorem is that when performance of the ensemble is established, pretty much any code selected at random (or by some construction technique) from the ensemble will have that performance.

Convergence to the Cycle-free case It has been discussed that cycles in the Tanner graph affect the decoding by introducing biases into what would otherwise be an ML detector. Defining $P_e^\infty(\ell)$ as the probability of error given that there are no cycles of length 2ℓ or less (e.g., the cycles have no effect up to iteration ℓ), then this theorem says that $P_e^N(\ell)$ converges to P_e^∞ as $N \to \infty$.

> Practically what this means is that for analysis of long codes (ideally, as the block length $N \to \infty$), the effect of cycles can be neglected.

Density Evolution The probability $P_e^\infty(\ell)$ (on ensembles of codes) can be calculated through a process called density evolution.

> This means that aspects of performance of codes can be analyzed by density evolution instead of by simulation, which leads to insight and significant computational savings. Density evolution is discussed in Section 15.7.

A Tanner graph ensemble is a description of conventional LDPC codes in terms of connectivity at variable and check nodes. These are described here in terms of increasing generality: regular ensembles; irregular ensembles; and ensembles of multiple-edge types.

16.7.1 Regular ensembles

A regular ensemble describes sets of regular LDPC codes. A (j, k) ensemble is the set of all Tanner graphs of length N where each variable node is of degree j and each check node is of degree k. Figure 16.8 illustrates the idea. There are N variable nodes, each having j *sockets* to which edges can be connected, for a total of jN sockets (edges). There are jN/k check nodes, each having k sockets. Any variable node socket can connect to any check node socket. A Tanner graph is formed by connecting each variable node socket to exactly one check node socket, so there are $(jN)!$ different Tanner graphs, each representable by a permutation on jN elements. Multiple graphs might correspond to the same parity check matrix, and many parity check matrices might represent the same code, so the relationship between the permutations and the codes is complicated.

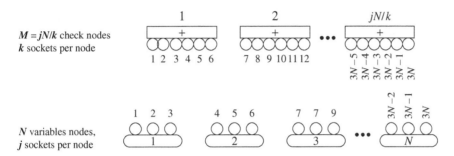

Figure 16.8: $(3, 6)$ Ensemble.

16.7.2 Irregular Ensembles

In an irregular ensemble, different variable and check nodes may have different numbers of sockets. The concept is illustrated with an example.

Figure 16.9 illustrates $N = 12$ variable nodes and $M = 8$ check nodes. Six of the variable nodes have two sockets (that is, will connect to two edges), four of the variable nodes have three sockets, and so forth. In this figure, any socket from a variable node can connect to any socket from a check node.

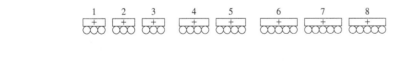

Figure 16.9: Illustrating an irregular ensemble.

It is common to describe the allocation of different degrees using fractions. The table below (on the left) shows the fraction Λ_i of variable nodes (out of $N = 12$ variable nodes) that have i sockets and the table below (on the right) shows the fraction P_i of check nodes (out of $M = 8$ check nodes) that have i sockets. This description is said to provide a *node perspective* definition. The tables also provide the fraction λ_i of edges (out of a total of 32 edges) which connect to variable nodes of degree i (on the left) and the fraction ρ_i of edges (out of 32 edges) which connect to check nodes of degree i (on the right). This is said to provide an *edge perspective* definition of the Tanner graph.

VN Deg:		2	3	4
Λ_i: Fraction of variable nodes with this VN degree		$\frac{1}{2}$	$\frac{1}{3}$	$\frac{1}{6}$
λ_i: Fraction of edges connected to VN of this degree		$\frac{3}{8}$	$\frac{3}{8}$	$\frac{1}{4}$

CN Deg		3	4	5
P_i: Fraction of check nodes with this CN degree		$\frac{3}{8}$	$\frac{1}{4}$	$\frac{3}{8}$
ρ_i: Fraction of edges connected to CN of this degree		$\frac{9}{32}$	$\frac{8}{32}$	$\frac{15}{32}$

It is also common to summarize this information using a generating function representation (think z-transform), using the polynomial

$$\Lambda(x) = \sum_i \Lambda_i x^{i-1}$$

to represent the distribution of variable node degrees, and

$$P(x) = \sum_i P_i x^{i-1}$$

to represent the distribution of check node degrees, and

$$\lambda(x) = \sum_i \lambda_i x^{i-1}$$

to represent the fractions of edges connected to variable nodes, and

$$\rho(x) = \sum_i \rho_i x^{i-1}$$

to represent the fractions of edges connected to check nodes. For the example in the tables above,

$$\Lambda(x) = \frac{1}{2}x + \frac{1}{3}x^2 + \frac{1}{6}x^3 \quad P(x) = \frac{3}{8}x^2 + \frac{1}{4}x^3 + \frac{3}{8}x^4$$

$$\lambda(x) = \frac{3}{8}x + \frac{3}{8}x^2 + \frac{1}{4}x^3 \quad \rho(x) = \frac{9}{32}x^2 + \frac{8}{32}x^3 + \frac{15}{32}x^4.$$

The total number of edges is

$$E = N \sum_i \Lambda_i = M\Lambda(1)$$

$$= M \sum_i P_i = MP(1).$$

The average number of edges per variable node and the average number of edges per check nodes are

$$\bar{d}_v = \frac{E}{N} = \frac{1}{\sum_i \lambda_i/i} \quad \text{and} \quad \bar{d}_c = \frac{E}{M} = \frac{1}{\sum_i \rho_i/i},$$

respectively. The relationships between the node perspective and the edge perspective for variable and check nodes are

$$\Lambda_i = \frac{\bar{d}_v \lambda_i}{i} \quad P_i = \frac{\bar{d}_c \rho_i}{i}.$$

Observe that

$$\int_0^1 \lambda(x)\,dx = \sum_i \lambda_i/i \quad \text{and} \quad \int_0^1 \rho(x)\,dx = \sum_i \rho_i/i,$$

so that

$$\bar{d}_v = \frac{1}{\int_0^1 \lambda(x)\,dx}, \quad \bar{d}_c = \frac{1}{\int_0^1 \rho(x)\,dx}, \quad \text{and} \quad E = \frac{N}{\int_0^1 \lambda(x)\,dx} = \frac{M}{\int_0^1 \rho(x)\,dx}$$

and

$$\Lambda_i = \frac{\lambda_i/i}{\int_0^1 \lambda(x)\,dx} \quad P_i = \frac{\rho_i/i}{\int_0^1 \rho(x)\,dx}.$$

16.7.3 Multi-edge-type Ensembles

Multi-edge-type (MET) ensembles generalize the notion of irregular ensembles by introducing the notion of a socket *type*. These provide a finer degree of specification on the nature of the ensemble. MET ensembles are general enough that they capture most interesting code sets related to LDPC codes, such as regular and irregular codes, RA and IRA codes, and protograph codes. In a MET ensemble, the sockets at the variable nodes and check nodes are each assigned a *type*, and edges can be placed only on sockets of the same type.

As an example of such an ensemble, consider Figure 16.10. In this ensemble, variable nodes have either two sockets, three sockets, or eight sockets, occurring with probabilities $\frac{1}{2}$, $\frac{1}{3}$, and $\frac{1}{6}$, respectively. Check nodes have either six or seven sockets, occurring with probabilities $\frac{1}{3}$ and $\frac{2}{3}$, respectively. Furthermore, the ensemble is restricted so that degree-3 variable nodes only connect to degree-7 check nodes. This is done by introducing another *edge type*. In the figure, there is an edge type that can connect circular sockets to each other, and another edge type that connects triangular sockets to each other.

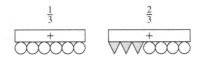

Figure 16.10: An example MET ensemble.

To describe the ensembles with multiple-edge types, a representation similar to the generating functions $\lambda(x)$ above is used. Let m_t denote the number of edge types. The variables $x_1, x_2, \ldots, x_{m_t}$ are used. Let $\mathbf{x} = x_1 x_2 \cdots x_{m_t}$. The MET degree type of a check node is a vector of nonnegative integers of length m_t, $\mathbf{d} = (d_1, d_2, \ldots, d_{m_t})$. The notation $\mathbf{x}^{\mathbf{d}}$ is used to represent $\prod_{i=1}^{m_t} x_i^{d_i}$. Let $R_{\mathbf{d}}$ denote the fraction of check nodes (out of N) that have MET degree $\mathbf{d}$. The ensemble of check nodes is described by the multinomial

$$R(\mathbf{x}) = \sum_{\mathbf{d}} \mathbf{x}^{\mathbf{d}}.$$

In Figure 16.10, the MET degrees are $(6, 0)$ and $(3, 4)$. The ensemble of check nodes is described by

$$R(\mathbf{x}) = \frac{1}{3} x_1^6 + \frac{2}{3} x_1^4 x_2^3.$$

For variable nodes in MET ensemble, yet another degree of generalization is employed. The bits associated with a variable node may be modeled as having been received from different kinds of channels, such as erasure channels, AWGN channels, BSC, or having been punctured. Let m_r denote the number of different channels in the communications model. The convention in the literature is to let channel 0 denote the puncturing channel (which may be thought of as an erasure channel with probability of erasure equal to 1). Let $\mathbf{b} = b_0 b_1 \cdots, b_{m_r}$ denote the received degree for each channel type and let $\mathbf{r} = r_0 r_1 \cdots r_{m_r}$ denote the variables corresponding to the received distribution.

The notation $\mathbf{r}^{\mathbf{b}}$ is used to denote $\prod_{i=0}^{m_r} r_i^{b_i}$. Let $L_{\mathbf{b},\mathbf{d}}$ denote the fraction of variable nodes (out of N) that have MET degree $\mathbf{d}$ and received degree $\mathbf{r}$. Then the ensemble of MET variable nodes is described by

$$L(\mathbf{r},\mathbf{x}) = \sum_{\mathbf{b},\mathbf{d}} L_{\mathbf{b},\mathbf{d}} \mathbf{r}^{\mathbf{b}} \mathbf{x}^{\mathbf{d}}.$$

In Figure 16.10, assuming there is only one channel type, $m_r = 1$, associated with variable r, the ensemble of variable nodes is described by

$$L(\mathbf{r},\mathbf{x}) = \frac{1}{2}rx_1^2 + \frac{1}{3}rx_2^3 + \frac{1}{6}rx_1^8.$$

Designs based on MET are described in [377].

16.8 Constructing LDPC Codes by Progressive Edge Growth (PEG)

PEG is a method of building Tanner graphs with large girth. PEG is described in [203, 494][1] and [[386], Section 12.6]. In general, PEG starts with a set of variable nodes and a set of edge nodes, with no edges between them. Working sequentially through the variable nodes, the algorithm adds edges to a variable node until the degree reaches some specified degree.

Let $G = (V_v, V_c)$ be a bipartite graph, where $V_v = \{v_0, v_1, \ldots, v_{N-1}\}$ is the set of variable nodes and $V_c = \{c_0, c_1, \ldots, c_{M-1}\}$ is the set of check nodes. Let λ_i be the length of the shortest cycle passing through v_n. This is called the *local girth* of v_n. The girth of the entire graph is, of course, the smallest of these $\min_{0 \le n < N} \lambda_n$. The PEG approach is greedy, in that it maximizes the local girth of every variable node. Let d_n denote the number of check nodes connected to variable node v_n, and let $D = \{d_0, d_1, \ldots, d_{N-1}\}$ be the degree profile.

Figure 16.11 represents paths through the bipartite Tanner graph G as a tree with a sequence of layers, where a layer consists of a sublayer of variable nodes and a sublayer of check nodes. This tree rooted at variable node v_n is denoted as $\mathcal{R}_n$. The distance between nodes in the graph is the shortest path between nodes. Paths on the tree $\mathcal{R}_n$ alternate between variable nodes and check nodes, and each path on $\mathcal{R}_n$ terminates on a check node. The distance from v_n to a variable node at level ℓ is 2ℓ; the distance from v_n to a variable node at level ℓ is $2\ell + 1$. When a tree $\mathcal{R}_n$ is traversed, it is traversed breadth first. That is, the edges $(v_n, c_{n_1}), (v_n, c_{n_2}), \ldots, (v_n, c_{n_{d_{v_n}}})$ are visited at the 0-th level of the tree. Then the edges that connect from these 0-level check nodes to the variable nodes in the first level are traversed next, and so forth.

If there is an edge in the Tanner graph $\mathcal{G}$ that connects a check node at level ℓ of the tree $\mathcal{R}_n$ to the root of the tree v_n, then this edge creates a cycle of length $2\ell + 1$ in $\mathcal{G}$.

Let $N_n^{(\ell)}$ denote the set of check nodes in G connected to v_n within a distance of $2\ell + 1$. $N_n^{(\ell)}$ is referred to as the neighborhood within depth ℓ of v_n. In Figure 16.11, $|N_n^{(0)}| = 2$ and $|N_n^{(1)}| = 4$. Let $\overline{N}_n^{(\ell)}$ denote the complement of $N_n^{(\ell)}$ with respect to the set of check nodes: $\overline{N}_n^{(\ell)} = V_c \backslash N_n^{(\ell)}$.

Assume that a partially connected Tanner graph has been constructed in which the trees have been built for variable nodes $v_0, v_1, \ldots, v_{n-1}$, producing a partially connected Tanner graph. Edges are grown from the variable node d_1 to d_n check nodes, one edge at a time. Suppose $k - 1 < d_n$ edges have been added to v_n. Before the kth edge is added to v_n, construct a path tree $\mathcal{R}_n$ with v_n as root, based on

---

[1] C++ code by [203] is available at http://www.inference.org.uk/mackay/PEG_ECC.html.

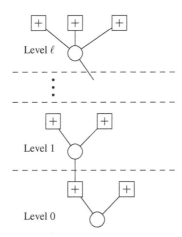

Figure 16.11: Notation for the PEG algorithm.

the current partially connected Tanner graph. This tree is grown until it reaches a level, call it the ℓth level, such that either:

1. The tree cannot grow further, but the number of check nodes $|N_n^{(\ell)}|$ is less than M.

   In this case, not all check nodes can be reached from v_n under the current partially connected Tanner graph. Choose a check node $c_m \in \overline{N}_n^{(\ell)}$ of smallest degree and connect v_n and c_m with a new edge (adding the edge to the partially connected Tanner graph).

   or

2. $\overline{N}_n^{(\ell)} \neq \emptyset$ (there are still unconnected check nodes), but $\overline{N}^{(\ell+1)} = \emptyset$ (at the next level there would be no unconnected check nodes).

   In this case, all the check nodes may be reached from v_n. Choose the check node c_j at the $(\ell + 1)$st level, and add a new edge to connect v_n to c_m. Adding an edge creates a cycle of length $2(\ell + 2)$. But choosing this at the largest level maximizes the local girth of the node v_n.

The algorithm may be summarized as follows:

Algorithm 16.2 Progressive Edge Growth [203]

Input:
  N (number of variable nodes), M (number of check nodes),
  D (degree distribution for variable nodes)
Output: PEG-grown parity check matrix
for $n = 0$ to $N - 1$ **do**
  for $k = 0$ to $d_n - 1$ **do**
    if $k = 0$ **then**
      Add the edge (v_n, c_m) to the Tanner graph, where c_k is
      a check node of lowest degree in the current partial Tanner graph
    else
      Grow a path tree $\mathcal{R}_n$ from root v_n to a level (call it ℓ)
      such that either $|\mathcal{N}_n^{(\ell)}|$ stops increasing (thefirst case above);
      or at level $\ell + 1$, $\bar{N}_n^{(\ell+1)} = \emptyset$.
      Find the check node c_k in $\bar{N}_n^{(\ell)}$ of lowerdegree, and add the edge
      (v_n, c_k) to the current partial Tanner graph.
    end if
  end for k
end for n

Given a variable node degree distribution, this provides an effective way of creating a useful parity check matrix for it.

Example 16.21   For the check node degree distribution

$$\lambda(x) = 0.5x + 0.4x^2 + 0.1x^9$$

the degree distribution can be expressed as an input to the PEG program as

```
3
2  3  10
0.5  0.4  0.1
```

A rate $R = 1/2$ code with $N = 4000$ can be produced invoking the software

```
MainPEG -numM 2000 -numN 4000 -codeName PEGN4000.txt -degFileName test-
deg2.deg
```

This produces a description of the parity check matrix in `PEGN4000.txt` which can be used by `ldpctest1` or `ldpctest2`. The code found by PEG has girth 8. The performance of the code is shown in Figure 16.12.   □

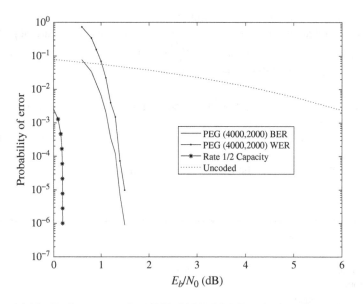

Figure 16.12: Performance of a $(4000, 2000)$ LDPC code founding using PEG.

There is a modification to the PEG algorithm related to how cycles connect to other nodes in a graph. Consider a cycle of length t in a Tanner graph, a sequence of variable and check nodes such as $S = (v_1, c_1, v_2, c_2, \ldots, v_t, c_t)$. At a variable node v_n, there are at least two check nodes it is connected to, an "incoming" check node and an "outgoing" check node in the cycle. If the degree of the node $d_n > 2$, then that node is also connected to other nodes. For such a cycle, form the quantity

$$\epsilon = \sum_{i=1}^{t} d_i - 2.$$

This is the total number of edges that connect this cycle S to other nodes in the Tanner graph. The quantity is called the *approximate cycle extrinsic message degree* (ACE). When ACE is larger, there are more messages coming from outside the cycle into the cycle to ameliorate the effect of the cycle. It has been observed that larger ACE tends to improve the performance of LDPC codes by decreasing the error floor. The modification to the PEG algorithm seeks to increase ACE. In the case that $\overline{N}_n^{(\ell)} \neq \emptyset$ but $\overline{N}_n^{(\ell+1)} = \emptyset$. In this case, adding a node will create a cycle. The modification applies when there is more than one candidate check node of minimal degree. In this case, for each such candidate check node, the node is checked to see what is the ACE that results for the cycle produced by adding it to the Tanner graph. The node producing the largest ACE is the one selected.

16.9 Protograph and Multi-Edge-Type LDPC Codes

Protograph LDPC codes are a way of imposing some structure on the design of LDPC parity check matrices while still maintaining considerable flexibility. The main idea is that a small prototype graph is established, referred to as a *protograph*. Then nodes in the graph are expanded by a factor of Q, that is, each node is repeated Q times. Edges between repeated nodes are also duplicated, not directly, but using a permuting structure. The idea is explained by means of an example. Begin with an adjacency matrix for the protograph which begins with two check nodes and three variable nodes,

$$B = \begin{bmatrix} 2 & 0 & 1 \\ 1 & 1 & 1 \end{bmatrix}. \tag{16.10}$$

This matrix has a feature not seen in other adjacency matrices, having an element greater than 1. This corresponds to multiple edges in the graph. The graph corresponding to this adjacency matrix is shown in Figure 16.13(a).

Figure 16.13(b) shows the concept of expansion by Q. In this figure, each node is duplicated $Q = 3$ times. The bold lines are suggestive of the repetition of connections. The edges between the repeated

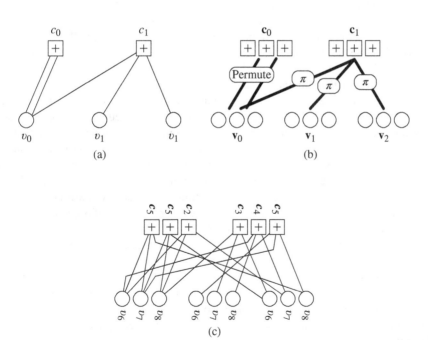

Figure 16.13: Graphs related to protograph description of LDPC code. (a) Initial protograph from adjacency matrix in (16.10); (b) repeating nodes $Q = 3$ times, and permutations of repeated edges; (c) detailed Tanner graph derived from protograph.

variable nodes and the repeated check nodes are permuted by a $Q \times Q$ permutation (or circulant) matrix, whose column sum is the number of edges between variable and edge in the original protograph.

Figure 16.13(c) fills in the sketch of the expansion with the detailed Tanner graph.

The parity check matrix corresponding to this construction is

$$H = \begin{bmatrix} 1 & 1 & 0 & 0 & 0 & 0 & 0 & 0 & 1 \\ 0 & 1 & 1 & 0 & 0 & 0 & 1 & 0 & 0 \\ 1 & 0 & 1 & 0 & 0 & 0 & 0 & 1 & 0 \\ 0 & 0 & 1 & 0 & 1 & 0 & 1 & 0 & 0 \\ 1 & 0 & 0 & 0 & 0 & 1 & 0 & 1 & 0 \\ 0 & 1 & 0 & 1 & 0 & 0 & 0 & 0 & 1 \end{bmatrix}.$$

This has two block rows (from the original 2 check nodes) and three block columns (from the original 3 variable nodes), each block of which has a permutation or circulant matrix. The column sum of the (1,1) block of H is two, corresponding to the 2 at the corresponding position in B.

A general approach to the design of protograph codes is as follows. Select the desired rate and the number of nodes N_p in the protograph. This determines the number of check nodes in the protograph. Determine a degree distribution for the protograph. Choose an expansion factor. Then choose cyclic permutation matrices (more or less at random) to connect the expanded variable nodes with the expanded check nodes. When there are multiple edges (as in the example above), the connection matrix may be viewed as a sum of that many cyclic permutation matrices.

Protograph architecture can lead to some potential parallel operations in hardware-based decoders. See the references at the end of the chapter.

16.10   Error Floors and Trapping Sets

The concept of error floors was described for turbo codes in Section 14.4. In many modern communication and storage systems, probability of *word* errors below 10^{-12} are desired, so the problem of error floors becomes increasingly important. In [289], the error floors were attributed to "near codewords" in the graph — configurations that message-passing decoding algorithms converge to (or return to periodically) that are not codewords — which are erroneous. As an example of how this can happen, consider the subgraph of a Tanner graph in Figure 16.14(a). In this figure, check nodes which are satisfied are indicated with □. Each of these is connected to two variable nodes (degree-2 check nodes), which, in turn, are connected to an unsatisfied check node, indicated with ■. These unsatisfied check nodes are connected to only a single variable node. Suppose that the all-zero codeword is sent, but that all of the variable nodes in the subgraph are (erroneously) equal to 1, then the check nodes are all satisfied. In the message-passing algorithm, there is no message sent from the unsatisfied check nodes ■ ("leave-one-out"), so the erroneous bits never change. The decoding algorithm thus converges to, and gets stuck at, a situation that is not a codeword (since not all checks are satisfied). The other subfigures in Figure 16.14 give other examples of trapping set graphs.

This leads to the definition of a *trapping set*. A (w, v) trapping set is a set of w variable nodes associated with a subgraph of a Tanner graph that has v odd-degree check nodes (for which there are v unsatisfied checks; indicated with ■) and an arbitrary number of even-degree check nodes (indicated with □). Trapping sets are associated with near codewords. The performance of the message-passing decoder in the low-SNR region is determined by the number of different trapping sets, and their structure, rather than the minimum distance of the code.

Actually, the situation with trapping sets is somewhat more complicated than suggested by the discussion above. It has been found that there are different kinds of trapping behavior.

1. A *stable trapping set* is one for which, once reached, the decoder remains fixed there, no matter how many iterations it performs.

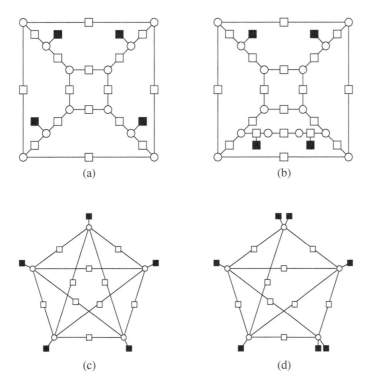

Figure 16.14: Subgraphs associated with trapping sets. ○ = variable nodes. ■ = unsatisfied check nodes. □ = incorrectly satisfied check nodes. (a) $(12, 4)$ trapping set; (b) $(14, 4)$ trapping set; (c) $(5, 5)$ trapping set; (d) $(5, 7)$ trapping set.

    For example, with a stable $(12, 4)$ trapping set the decoder has 12 bits in error, no matter how long the decoder runs.

2. A *periodically oscillating trapping set* is when the decoding algorithm cycles deterministically through a number of different error patterns. Once the message-passing decoder falls into a such a cycle, it cannot escape.

    For example, there may be a $(6, 18)$ and $(7, 18)$ trapping set pair, and the decoder alternates between these on successive decoding iterations.

3. More complicated, in an *aperiodic oscillating trapping set*, as the message-passing decoder proceeds, the number of erroneous bits varies in a random fashion, but no matter how many decoding iterations are computed a correct solution is never reached.

16.11   Importance Sampling

Determining the probability of error for a coded system by Monte Carlo (MC) methods (that is, by simulation) can be challenging, especially when the probability of error is very small. For a probability of error of P_b, approximately $10/P_b$ bits must be simulated to achieve a probability of bit error estimate accurate to about 10%. For example, if a code has a bit error probability of 10^{-8}, at least 10^8 bits must be simulated before even a single error may be seen. To reduce the variance of the estimate, it is advised to simulate an order of magnitude (or more) more than this. For codes having complicated or iterated decoding algorithms, this can be very time-consuming. The problem only becomes more difficult as systems requirements push word error rates below 10^{-12}. Importance sampling (IS) is a method of reducing the complexity of conventional MC simulation by reducing the variance of the estimated probabilities of error. Extensive simulation may still be necessary, but in some instances, when IS is properly applied, the simulation runtime may be reduced by many orders of magnitude using IS.

IS is not, strictly, related to LDPC codes. It is relevant in communications generally, and has been broadly applied. But this section is placed in this chapter because modern LDPC-coded systems are designed for very low rates where the advantages of IS can be especially important.

This section introduces the general principles of IS and applies them to communication systems. There has been much work in applying IS to coded systems, but this is still an area of research. This chapter points to some of the work in this area. While IS applies generally to estimating probability of error, this discussion is placed in the chapter on LDPC codes for two reasons. First, many LDPC codes are designed to have very low error probabilities, at rates below which their performance can be simulated. Also, the structure of LDPC codes provides mechanisms for the application of IS.

16.11.1 Importance Sampling: General Principles

Let $g(\mathbf{x})$ be a function to be integrated over $\mathbb{R}^n$, where for convenience we assume $g(\mathbf{x}) \geq 0$ for all $\mathbf{x} \in \mathbb{R}^n$, let $f(\mathbf{x})$ be a probability density function, and consider the following integral:

$$P = \int_{\mathbb{R}^n} g(\mathbf{x})f(\mathbf{x}) \, d\mathbf{x} = E_f[g(\mathbf{x})]. \tag{16.11}$$

(The subscript on the expectation E indicates the distribution with respect to which the expectation is computed.) In one dimension ($n = 1$) numerical evaluation is often straightforward using standard numerical integration routines. As the dimension n increases, the definite integral may become even more difficult to evaluate. More generally, the integral

$$\int_\Omega g(\mathbf{x}) \, d\mathbf{x}$$

over a domain $\Omega \subset \mathbb{R}^n$ may be considered to be of the form (16.11) by introducing a pdf $u(\mathbf{x})$ which is uniform over Ω, so that

$$\int_\Omega g(\mathbf{x}) \, d\mathbf{x} = \int_{\mathbb{R}^n} g(\mathbf{x})u(\mathbf{x}) \, d\mathbf{x} = E_u[g(\mathbf{x})].$$

Returning to (16.11), let $\mathbf{x}_1, \mathbf{x}_2, \ldots, \mathbf{x}_L$ samples drawn according to the distribution $f(\mathbf{x})$, which we denote a $\mathbf{x}_i \sim f, i = 1, 2, \ldots, L$. The integral (16.11) is approximated as the *sample average*

$$\hat{P}_{MC} = \frac{1}{L} \sum_{i=1}^{L} g(\mathbf{x}_i).$$

By the law of large numbers, this sample average converges to the expectation, so

$$\hat{P} \to P \text{ as } L \to \infty.$$

This is said to be the *Monte Carlo* (MC) approximation to the integral. Even though the integral (16.11) is deterministic, the approximation is a random variable (due to the random samples). The variance can be computed as follows:

$$E_f[\hat{P}_{MC}] = \frac{1}{L} \sum_{i=1}^{L} E_f[g(\mathbf{x}_i)] = \frac{1}{L} L E_f[g(\mathbf{x}_i)] = P.$$

(That is, $\hat{P}_{MC}$ is an unbiased estimate.)

$$E_f[\hat{P}_{MC}^2] = \frac{1}{L^2} E_f \left[\sum_{i=1}^{L} g(\mathbf{x}_i)^2 + \sum_{i \neq j} g(\mathbf{x}_i)g(\mathbf{x}_j) \right]$$

$$= \frac{1}{L^2} [L E_f[g(\mathbf{x})^2] + (L^2 - L) E_f[g(\mathbf{x})]^2].$$

Then

$$\text{var}(\hat{P}_{MC}) = E_f[\hat{P}_{MC}^2] - E_f[\hat{P}_{MC}]^2 = \frac{1}{L}[E_f[g(\mathbf{x})^2] - P^2]. \qquad (16.12)$$

IS is used to evaluate integrals using averages of random samples, as in the MC method above, but introduces another degree of freedom by using a different density $q(\mathbf{x})$, known as the *sample distribution* or the *proposal distribution*. This may result in a reduction of the variance of the approximation (compared to the $\text{var}(P_{MC})$), or may be easier to draw samples from. Let $q(\mathbf{x})$ be a pdf over $\mathbb{R}^n$ (the domain of integration) and write the integral (16.11) as

$$P = \int_{\mathbb{R}^n} g(\mathbf{x}) f(\mathbf{x}) \frac{q(\mathbf{x})}{q(\mathbf{x})} \, d\mathbf{x} = \int_{\mathbb{R}^n} \frac{f(\mathbf{x})}{q(\mathbf{x})} g(\mathbf{x}) q(\mathbf{x}) \, d\mathbf{x}$$

$$= \int_{\mathbb{R}^n} w(\mathbf{x}) g(\mathbf{x}) q(\mathbf{x}) \, d\mathbf{x} = E_q[w(\mathbf{x}) g(\mathbf{x})],$$

where

$$w(\mathbf{x}) = \frac{f(\mathbf{x})}{q(\mathbf{x})}$$

is the *weight function*. Again the integral is expressed as an expectation, but of the weighted function $w(\mathbf{x})g(\mathbf{x})$ and with respect to the density q.

The integral may be approximated as follows: Draw $\tilde{\mathbf{x}}_i \sim q$, $i = 1, 2, \ldots, L$. Form the sample average

$$\hat{P}_{IS} = \frac{1}{L} \sum_{i=1}^{L} w(\tilde{\mathbf{x}}_i) g(\tilde{\mathbf{x}}_i).$$

Again by the law of large numbers, this sample average converges to the expectation,

$$\hat{P}_{IS} \to P \text{ as } L \to \infty.$$

The mean and variance of this approximation are $E[\hat{P}_{IS}] = P$ (the approximation is unbiased) and, reasoning as in the MC case,

$$\text{var}(\hat{P}_{IS}) = \frac{1}{L}[E_q[w(\mathbf{x})^2 g(\mathbf{x})^2] - E_q[w(\mathbf{x}) g(\mathbf{x})]^2]$$

$$= \frac{1}{L}\left[\int_{\mathbb{R}^n} w(\mathbf{x})^2 g(\mathbf{x})^2 q(\mathbf{x}) \, d\mathbf{x} - P^2\right] = \frac{1}{L}\left[\int_{\mathbb{R}^n} w(\mathbf{x}) g(\mathbf{x})^2 f(\mathbf{x}) \, d\mathbf{x} - P^2\right].$$

The variance can be estimated by

$$\widehat{\text{var}}(\hat{P}_{IS}) = \frac{1}{L}\left[\frac{1}{L} \sum_{i=1}^{L} w(\tilde{\mathbf{x}}_i)^2 g(\tilde{\mathbf{x}}_i)^2 - \hat{P}^2\right].$$

Since the importance sample estimate is unbiased for any choice of sample distribution q, it may be selected with consideration to the variance of the estimate. It is natural to select a distribution $q(\cdot)$ which minimizes $\text{var}(\hat{P}_{IS})$. The optimum sample distribution, which causes $\text{var}(\hat{P}_{IS})$ to be 0, is

$$q^*(\mathbf{x}) = \frac{g(\mathbf{x}) f(\mathbf{x})}{\int_{\mathbb{R}^n} g(\mathbf{x}) f(\mathbf{x}) \, d\mathbf{x}} = \frac{g(\mathbf{x}) f(\mathbf{x})}{P}. \qquad (16.13)$$

With this sample distribution, $w(\mathbf{x}) = \frac{\int_{\mathbb{R}^n} g(\mathbf{x}) f(\mathbf{x}) \, d\mathbf{x}}{g(\mathbf{x})}$, resulting in a variance

$$\text{var}(\hat{P}_{MS}) = \frac{1}{N}\left[\int_{\mathbb{R}^n} \frac{\int_{\mathbb{R}^n} g(\mathbf{x}) f(\mathbf{x}) \, d\mathbf{x}}{g(\mathbf{x})} g(\mathbf{x})^2 f(\mathbf{x}) \, d\mathbf{x} - P^2\right] = 0.$$

The optimal sample distribution q^* is a theoretical concept, since it requires knowing the value of P, which is unknown, being the value of the integral which is desired in the first place. Even if q^* could be obtained, it may be difficult to sample from. But the optimal distribution is of interest, because it teaches that a good (if not optimal) sample distribution should draw samples where $g(\mathbf{x})f(\mathbf{x})$ is large. This is sensible, since in approximating an integral with a finite number of points it is prudent to apply those points where the function being integrated makes the largest contribution to the integral.

The number of samples needed to achieve a precision $\epsilon = \sigma_{\hat{P}}/P$ is

$$L = \left\lceil \frac{v}{\epsilon^2 P^2} \right\rceil,$$

where $v = \text{var}[1_E(x)w(x)]$, and where $1_E(x)$ is the indicator function defined below.

Selecting a good sample distribution q is the "art" of IS [414]. A good q can provide significant speedup, while a poorly chosen q can actually result in the simulation runtime being longer.

For nonoptimal sampling, the IS variance gain γ is the ratio of the variance for the MC approximation and the IS approximation, with the same number of points N,

$$\gamma = \frac{\text{var}(\hat{P}_{MS})}{\text{var}(\hat{P}_{IS})} = \frac{E_f[g(\mathbf{x})^2] - P^2}{\int_{\mathbb{R}^n} w(\mathbf{x})g(\mathbf{x})^2 f(\mathbf{x}) \, d\mathbf{x} - P^2}.$$

Regardless of the sampling distribution selected, the estimate is unbiased. Even suboptimal sampling distributions can be practically effective, resulting in a significantly reduced variance, and a corresponding reduction in the number of samples needed to obtain a given variance.

16.11.2   Importance Sampling for Estimating Error Probability

In this section, we apply the general principles of IS from above to problems of estimating probability of error. This is done by a series of example.

Example 16.22   In this first example, we consider the problem of uncoded binary communication, in which a signal $s = \pm 1$ is sent in AWGN. Suppose, to be specific that $s = -1$ transmitted. The received signal is

$$y = s + n, \tag{16.14}$$

where $n \sim \mathcal{N}(0, \sigma^2)$. Assuming equally probable symbols there is a decision threshold $\tau_0 = 0$ and the optimal decision rule is

$$\hat{s} = \begin{cases} 1 & \text{if } y > \tau_0 \\ -1 & \text{if } y < \tau_0. \end{cases}$$

Given that $s = -1$ is sent, the error region where an incorrect decision is made is

$$E = \{y \in \mathbb{R} : y > \tau_0\}.$$

The probability of detection error, P_E, can be expressed as

$$P_E = P(\text{error}|s = -1) = P(y \in E|s = -1) = \int_E f_y(y|s = -1) \, dy,$$

Let $1_E(y)$ denote the indicator function

$$1_E(y) = \begin{cases} 1 & y \in E \\ 0 & y \notin E. \end{cases}$$

Then

$$P_E = \int_{-\infty}^{\infty} 1_E(y) f_y(y|s = -1) \, dy.$$

This integral is analogous to the integral in (16.11), where the function is $g(y) = 1_E(y)$ and is recognized as an expectation,

$$P_E = E_{f(y|s=-1)}[1_E(y)].$$

(This is an application of the principle that the expectation of an indicator function is a probability.) Because of the additive signal model, $f_y(y|s=-1) = f_n(y+1) = \mathcal{N}(-1, \sigma^2)$. The situation is indicated in Figure 16.15(a) (where $\sigma^2 = 0.3$). The probability of error is the shaded region under the Gaussian curve. The error region E is also shaded.

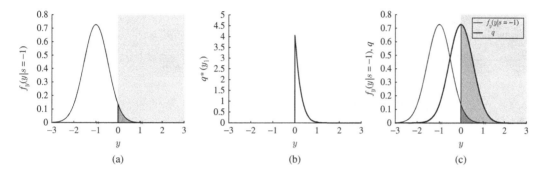

Figure 16.15: Probability of error for a BPSK detection problem using MC and IS sampling. (a) Distribution for Monte Carlo integration; (b) optimal sampling distribution for this problem; (c) distribution for IS integration.

Conventional Sampling (MC)

Let $y_1, y_2, \ldots, y_L$ be samples of a signal drawn according to the distribution $f_y(y|s=-1) = \mathcal{N}(-1, \sigma^2)$. Then the expectation can be approximated by the sum

$$\hat{P}_{E,MC} \approx \frac{1}{L} \sum_{i=1}^{L} 1_E(y_i) = \frac{1}{L}(\text{number of } y_i \text{ greater than } 0).$$

This is simply a description of the conventional way of estimating the probability of error by a MC simulation. This can be described as follows:

1. Generate noise samples $n_1, n_2, \ldots, n_L$, where each $n_i \sim \mathcal{N}(0, \sigma^2)$.
2. Produce the "received" signals $y_i = s + n_i$ (with $s = -1$ in this example).
3. Count how many of the y_i are greater than 0, and divide by the count by L.

By the law of large numbers, $\hat{P}_{E,MC} \to P_E$ as $N \to \infty$. Figure 16.15(a) illustrates the practical problem with this approach. When a point y_i is drawn, with high probability it falls in the unshaded region (correct), so it contributes nothing to the error count. To get a low variance (accurate) estimate many samples must be counted, which means that L must be very large.

Using $g(y) = 1_E(y)$ and $g(y)^2 = 1_E(y)$, using (16.12) the variance of the MC estimate is

$$\text{var}(\hat{P}_{E,MS}) = \frac{1}{L}(P_E - P_E^2).$$

Importance Sampling (IS)

We will now express this problem using IS. Let q denote a sample distribution, and write the probability of error as

$$P_E = \int_{-\infty}^{\infty} 1_E(y) f_y(y|s=-1) \frac{q(y)}{q(y)} \, dy = \int_{-\infty}^{\infty} \frac{f_y(y|s=-1)}{q(y)} 1_E(y) q(y) \, dy$$

$$= \int_{-\infty}^{\infty} w(y) 1_E(y) q(y \, dy = E_q[1_E(y) w(y)].$$

Here, $q(y)$ is a sampling distribution and

$$w(y) = \frac{f_y(y|s=-1)}{q(y)}$$

is a weight function.

How should the sample distribution q be selected? From (16.13), the optimal sample distribution is

$$q^*(y) = \frac{1_E(y) f(y|s=-1)}{\int_{-\infty}^{\infty} 1_E(y') f(y'|s=-1) \, dy'} = \frac{1_E(y) f(y|s=-1)}{P_E},$$

which would give $\text{var}(\hat{P}_{E,IS}) = 0$, if it could be computed, which it can't since it requires knowing P_E. This optimal sampling distribution is shown in Figure 16.15(b). While it would not be difficult to approximate q^* (for example, using an exponential function), a common approach that generalizes well is as follows.

What is observed from Figure 16.15(b) is that the optimal sampling distribution places more weight in the E region than the original density $f_y(y|s=-1)$. Given the additive nature of the signal (16.14), a readily obtainable sampling distribution is obtained by shifting the noise toward the decision boundary. Let $\tilde{n}$ be a "shifted,'' or "mean translated,'' noise $\tilde{n} = n + \zeta$, so

$$\tilde{n} \sim \mathcal{N}(\zeta, \sigma^2)$$

for some shift ζ. Then $f_{\tilde{n}}(y) = f_n(y - \zeta)$. This shifted noise will be referred to as the IS noise. Let the observation with this shifted noise be

$$\tilde{y} = s + \tilde{n}.$$

The pdf of $\tilde{y}$ (given $s = -1$) is

$$f_{\tilde{y}}(\tilde{y}|s=-1) = f_{\tilde{n}}(\tilde{y} - s)|_{s=-1} = f_n(\tilde{y} - \zeta - s)|_{s=-1} = f_n(\tilde{y} - \zeta + 1).$$

This is used as the sample distribution:

$$q(y) = f_{\tilde{n}}(y - s)|_{s=-1} = f_n(y - \zeta + 1).$$

The original distribution $f(y|s=-1) = \mathcal{N}(-1, \sigma^2)$ has been replaced by a sample distribution $q(y) = \mathcal{N}(\zeta - 1, \sigma^2)$. Figure 16.15(c) shows the sampling distribution q with the shift $\zeta = 1$. In this figure, q is shifted so that its mean lies at the point of the decision threshold τ_0. Half of the samples drawn using q fall in the region E.

This is an instance of *mean translation* , in which the sample distribution is obtained by translating the mean of the original pdf in the integral. (Another alternative would be to use a sample distribution with larger variance, but mean translation is more common in communication problems.)

In this example, in which $f(y|s=-1) = \mathcal{N}(-1, \sigma^2)$ is replaced by $\mathcal{N}(\zeta - 1, \sigma^2)$, we say that ζ is a new bias point, and the shift amount $\zeta - 1$ is the bias. The selection $\zeta = 1$ is a *dominant point* [387].

Using this sample density, the IS estimate of P_E is computed as follows:

1. Generate noise samples $\tilde{n}_1, \tilde{n}_2, \ldots, \tilde{n}_N$, with each $\tilde{n}_i \sim \mathcal{N}(\zeta, \sigma^2)$.

2. Produce the IS received signals $\tilde{y}_i = s + \tilde{n}_i$ (with $s = -1$ in this example).

3. Compute the weight function

$$w(\tilde{y}_i) = \frac{\mathcal{N}(\tilde{y}_i; 0, \sigma^2)}{\mathcal{N}(\tilde{y}_i; \zeta - 1, \sigma^2)} = \frac{\exp[-\frac{1}{2\sigma^2} \tilde{y}_i^2]}{\exp[-\frac{1}{2\sigma^2} (\tilde{y}_i - \zeta + 1)^2]}, \quad i = 1, 2, \ldots, N.$$

4. Compute

$$\hat{P}_{E,IS} = \frac{1}{N} \sum_{i=1}^{N} 1_E(\tilde{y}_i) w(\tilde{y}_i),$$

that is, count how many IS received signals fall in the error region, *weighted by the weight function*, then divide by N.

It is evident from Figure 16.15(c) that there will be many more $\tilde{y}_i$ that fall in the error region E compared to drawing $y_i \sim f_y(y|s = -1)$, but each of these error counts is weighted by $w(\tilde{y}_i)$, which is a small number, so the net contribution to P_E works out to give an unbiased estimate.

The variance of this estimator is

$$\text{var}(\hat{P}_{E,IS}) = \frac{1}{L}\left[\int_{-\infty}^{\infty} w(y)^2 1_E(y) q(y)\, dy - P_E^2\right] = \frac{1}{L}\left[\int_{-\infty}^{\infty} w(y) f_y(y|s=-1)\, dy - P_E^2\right].$$

This can be estimated by

$$\widehat{\text{var}}(\hat{P}_{E,IS}) = \frac{1}{L}\left[\frac{1}{L}\sum_{i=1}^{L} w(\tilde{y}_i)^2 1_E(\tilde{y}_i) - \hat{P}_{E,IS}^2\right].$$

The variance gain is

$$\gamma = \frac{\text{var}(\hat{P}_{E,MS})}{\text{var}(\hat{P}_{E,IS})} = \frac{P_E - P_E^2}{\int_{-\infty}^{\infty} w(y) f_y(y|s=-1) - P_E^2} \approx \frac{\hat{P}_{E,IS} - \hat{P}_{E,IS}^2}{\frac{1}{N}\sum_{i=1}^{N} w^2(\tilde{y}_i) 1_E(\tilde{y}_i) - \hat{P}_{E,IS}^2}. \qquad (16.15)$$

A simulation was performed to demonstrate some aspects of this problem (see Table 16.1). For different values of shift ζ, $N = 1,00,000$ symbols were generated and the probability of error was estimated using MC and IS methods. This was repeated 10 times. The variance of the different estimates using MC and IS methods were computed. These estimated variances are displayed, along with the value of γ computed using (16.15). In this simulation $\sigma^2 = 0.1$. The true probability of error is $P_E = Q(2/(2\sigma)) = 0.00782$. Some observations from this experiment:

- The IS method is much more accurate than the MC method, as seen by comparing the %error columns. The % error for the IS in almost every instance less than 1%, while for the MC method the errors are much higher, ranging up to 20%.

Table 16.1: IS Simulation Results

ζ	$\hat{P}_{E,MC}$	%Err_{MC}	$\hat{P}_{E,IS}$	%Err_{IS}	$\text{Var}(\hat{P}_{E,MC})$	$\text{Var}(\hat{P}_{E,IS})$	$\dfrac{\text{Var}(\hat{P}_{E,MC})}{\text{Var}(\hat{P}_{E,IS})}$	γ
0.5	0.00094	−20.0969	0.000794419	−1.49707	6.88444e−09	1.48479e−10	46.3666	64.3651
0.6	0.00073	6.73324	0.000781498	0.153668	7.05e−09	5.15492e−11	136.762	110.176
0.7	0.00097	−23.9298	0.000778427	0.546093	8.71667e−09	1.34966e−11	645.84	173.329
0.8	0.00081	−3.48778	0.000779367	0.425995	1.45e−09	1.4428e−11	100.499	246.936
0.9	0.00086	−9.87591	0.000781537	0.148749	1.78178e−08	1.75635e−11	1014.48	315.327
1	0.00088	−12.4312	0.00077407	1.10276	5.06778e−09	2.07852e−11	243.816	357.96
1.1	0.00082	−4.7654	0.00077946	0.414091	3.08444e−09	1.28797e−11	239.481	354.914
1.2	0.00091	−16.264	0.000777432	0.673217	1.30711e−08	2.1317e−11	613.177	313.076
1.3	0.00071	9.28849	0.000777043	0.722907	2.57333e−09	4.031e−11	63.8385	245.394
1.4	0.00071	9.28849	0.000775506	0.919295	8.91222e−09	1.00685e−10	88.5157	168.927
1.5	0.00096	−22.6522	0.000779201	0.447142	5.67111e−09	2.01995e−10	28.0755	108.621
1.6	0.00084	−7.32066	0.000783985	−0.164008	1.085e−08	1.15386e−10	94.032	63.0629
1.7	0.00084	−7.32066	0.000788395	−0.727431	1.004e−08	2.86059e−10	35.0977	33.0292
1.8	0.00077	1.62273	0.000773905	1.12386	9.97889e−09	3.30281e−10	30.2133	15.4904
1.9	0.00078	0.345104	0.000797485	−1.88882	8.35556e−09	9.59689e−10	8.70653	7.11057
2	0.00086	−9.87591	0.000759019	3.02565	6.96556e−09	1.218e−09	5.71885	2.8325

- The ratio of the estimated variances $\text{var}(\hat{P}_{E,MC})/\text{var}(\hat{P}_{E,IS})$ (where the variances are estimated over 10 different estimates) is not exactly the same as γ, but they are generally within an order of magnitude of each other.

- Both of these measures achieve their highest value with the shift $\zeta = 1$. $\gamma = 358$ there — the variance using IS is approximately 350 times better than using MC.

These result suggest that the shift ζ should be selected so that the shifted pdf q has its mode (peak value) at the decision threshold. This is portrayed in Figure 16.15(c).

Figure 16.16(a) shows the best IS gain γ (for the best ζ) as a function of the noise variance. As the noise variance σ^2 decreases (SNR increases), γ increases. The figure also shows the probability of error P_E. There is a fortuitous benefit indicated: as P_E decreases, it would take more iterations to estimate P_E well; the increase in γ offsets the number of iterations that would be required.

Figure 16.16(b) illustrates another aspect of IS. As the noise variance increases, the shift ζ increases. Intuitively, as the noise distribution broadens, the sample distribution is pushed further into the error region E.

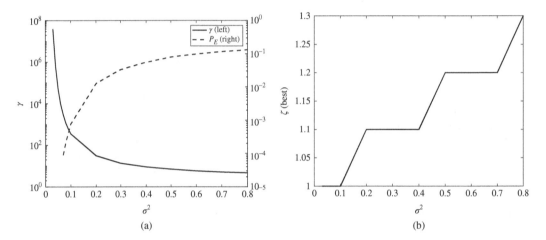

Figure 16.16: Best gain and shift ζ for an importance sampling example. (a) γ and P_E as a function of σ^2. P_E decreases when γ increases; (b) z as a function of σ^2.

□

Example 16.23   Now consider the situation where there are three possible signals, $s \in \{-1, 0, 1\}$, and assume that $s = 0$ is sent. As before, $y = s + n$ and $n \sim \mathcal{N}(0, \sigma^2)$. The decision regions are

$$\hat{s} = \begin{cases} -1 & \text{if } y < \tau_0 = -.5 \\ 1 & \text{if } y > \tau_1 = 0.5 \\ 0 & \text{if } \tau_0 < y < \tau_1. \end{cases}$$

With $s = 0$ sent, the error region is

$$E = \{y \in \mathbb{R} : y < \tau_0 \text{ or } y > \tau_1\}.$$

The probability of error is $P_E = \int_{-\infty}^{\infty} 1_E(y) f_y(y|s = 0) \, dy$. The region of integration is shown in Figure 16.17(a).

The optimal sampling distribution q^* is shown in Figure 16.17(b). It puts all of its weight in the region E. As before, computing this and drawing from this would require knowing P_E. Instead, a tractable sample distribution is obtained by a Gaussian mixture

$$\tilde{n} \sim 0.5\mathcal{N}\left(\frac{1}{2}, \sigma^2\right) + 0.5\mathcal{N}\left(-\frac{1}{2}, \sigma^2\right),$$

as shown in Figure 16.17(c).

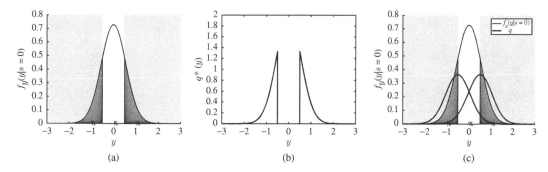

Figure 16.17: Probability of error for three-symbols detection problem using MC and IS sampling. (a) Distribution for Monte Carlo integration; (b) optimal sampling distribution q^* for this problem; (c) distribution for IS integration. □

Before proceeding with the next communications-related example, consider the description of hyperspherical surfaces. Let K be a $d \times d$ covariance matrix (symmetric, positive definite), thought of as the covariance of AWGN of an observation $\mathbf{x}$ with density $\mathcal{N}(\mathbf{x}; \mathbf{0}, K)$. Let $\tilde{K} = K/n$, so the covariance $\tilde{K}$ decreases with n. The density corresponding to $\tilde{K}$ is $\mathcal{N}(\mathbf{x}; \mathbf{0}; K/n)$.

Let $R(\mathbf{x}) = \frac{1}{2}\mathbf{x}^T K^{-1} \mathbf{x}$. The set of points $S = \{\mathbf{x} \in \mathbb{R}^d : \frac{1}{2}\mathbf{x}^T K^{-1}\mathbf{x} = c\}$ is a hyperellipsoid centered at $\mathbf{0}$ (think, roughly, of the shape of American football). Such a surface could represent the set of points where a zero-mean Gaussian with covariance K takes on a constant value:

$$\{\mathbf{x} \in \mathbb{R}^d : \mathcal{N}(\mathbf{x}; \mathbf{0}, K) = c'\}.$$

Moving constants to the other side and taking a logarithm, this set can be expressed in terms of the representation S.

With this background, consider the way of generating a random outcome for points near the set S.

1. Pick a point uniformly at random on a hypersphere of radius ρ. This may be done by drawing $\mathbf{u} \sim \mathcal{N}(0, I_d)$, then normalize by $\mathbf{u} \leftarrow \rho\mathbf{u}/\|\mathbf{u}\|$.

2. Add a Gaussian random number with covariance $\tilde{K}$,

$$\tilde{\mathbf{n}} \sim \mathcal{N}(\mathbf{0}, \tilde{K})$$

$$\mathbf{y} = \mathbf{u} + \tilde{\mathbf{n}}.$$

Figure 16.18 shows the draws (the dots in the plane), where $K = \sigma^2 I_2$ with $\sigma^2 = 1$ for $n = 0.5, 1$, and 2. As n increases, the random samples cluster more tightly around the circle of radius ρ. To be useful in IS, the pdf of data so generated is needed. This is described as follows.

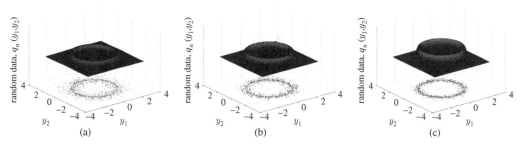

Figure 16.18: Points chosen at random on a circle of radius $\rho = 2$ with Gaussian noise added of covariance $\tilde{K} = K/n$, where $K = \sigma^2 I_2$ with $\sigma^2 = 1$. (a) $n = 0.5$; (b) $n = 1$; (c) $n = 2$.

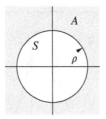

Figure 16.19: An example constraint set A.

Let A be an arbitrary closed set (for example, the set A shown in Figure 16.19). Let

$$r = \min_{\mathbf{x} \in A} R(\mathbf{x}).$$

If, as in the figure, A is the region outside a circle (or hypersphere) of radius ρ, and $K = \sigma^2 I_d$, then

$$r = \frac{1}{2\sigma^2} \rho^2.$$

It has been shown [51] that the pdf of the data generated around the hypersphere of radius ρ is

$$q_n(\mathbf{y}) = \mathcal{N}(\mathbf{y}\sqrt{n}; \mathbf{0}, K) n^{d/2} \exp(-nr) \frac{\Gamma\left(\frac{d}{2}\right) \sqrt{2}^{\frac{d}{2}-1}}{\sqrt{r}^{\frac{d}{2}-1}} \frac{I_{\frac{d}{2}-1}(n\sqrt{2r} \, \|K^{-(1/2)}\mathbf{y}\|)}{(n \, \|K^{-1/2}\mathbf{y}\|)^{\frac{d}{2}-1}}. \tag{16.16}$$

The pdfs are also plotted in Figure 16.18. They have the form of the "rim of a volcano" of radius ρ, with the steepness and concentration of the rim depending on n.

Example 16.24   [51] Let $X = (X_1, X_2) \sim \mathcal{N}(\mathbf{0}, \sigma^2 I)$ be a two-dimensional random variable. Let A be the exterior to a disk of radius $\rho = 10$. Then

$$r = \min_{\mathbf{x} \in A} \frac{1}{2}\mathbf{x}^T K^{-1}\mathbf{x} = \frac{1}{2\sigma^2}\rho^2 = 50.$$

The probability that $X \in A$ can be computed as

$$P = \int_{10}^{\infty} z \exp\left(-\frac{z^2}{2}\right) \, dz = \exp(-50) = 1.93 \times 10^{-22}.$$

If this were determined using MC techniques by picking points at random using conventional MC estimation, on the order of 10^{24} instances would need to be generated at random to obtain accurate results.

    However, this can be determined using IS with far fewer samples by translating the mean to a point chosen at random on a circle of radius 10, as described by the pdf (16.16). Let $\mathbf{u}$ be uniform on the circle of radius 10, let $\mathbf{n} \sim \mathcal{N}(0, \sigma^2 I_2)$ and $\tilde{\mathbf{y}} = \mathbf{u} + \mathbf{n}$. Using $n = 1$, $\sigma^2 = 1$, $d = 2$, and $K = \sigma^2 I_2$, using (16.16) the weight function is

$$w(\mathbf{y}) = \frac{\mathcal{N}(\mathbf{y}; \mathbf{0}, \sigma^2 I_2)}{q_1(\mathbf{y})} = \frac{\exp(50)}{I_0(10 \, \|\mathbf{y}\|)},$$

where $I_0(\cdot)$ is the modified Bessel function of order 0. Using this to form the estimate

$$\hat{P} = \frac{1}{L} \sum_{i=1}^{L} 1_{\|\tilde{\mathbf{y}}_i\| > 10} \frac{\exp(50)}{I_0(10 \, \|\tilde{\mathbf{y}}_i\|)},$$

results in an accurate estimate with relatively small L. For example, on a run with $L = 10{,}000$, a value $\hat{P} = 1.919 \times^{-22}$ was obtained, an error of about 0.5%.   □

The point of this is that when there are multiple possible outcomes which could occur at some distance from the transmitted point s, it may be possible to use this circular distribution idea to do a mean translation.

Example 16.25   We now return to a communication example. In this example, the constellation is in d dimensions with $2d + 1$ points consisting of the $\mathbf{s}_0 = \mathbf{0}$ point and points of the form

$$\pm\mathbf{s}_i = \begin{bmatrix} 0 \\ \vdots \\ \pm 1 \\ \vdots \\ 0 \end{bmatrix}, \quad i = 1, 2, \ldots, d,$$

where the ± 1 amplitude occurs in coordinate i. The constellation is portrayed in $d = 2$ dimensions in Figure 16.20(a), where the points are

$$\begin{bmatrix} 1 \\ 0 \end{bmatrix} \quad \begin{bmatrix} -1 \\ 0 \end{bmatrix} \quad \begin{bmatrix} 0 \\ 1 \end{bmatrix} \quad \begin{bmatrix} 0 \\ -1 \end{bmatrix}.$$

Observations are of the form

$$\mathbf{y} = \mathbf{s} + \mathbf{n},$$

where $\mathbf{n} \sim \mathcal{N}(\mathbf{0}, \sigma^2 I_d)$. Given that $\mathbf{s}_0 = \mathbf{0}$ is sent, an error occurs if the absolute value of any coordinate exceeds 0.5. The true probability of error given $\mathbf{s}_0$ is sent is

$$P_E = 1 - (1 - 2Q(1/(2\sigma)))^d.$$

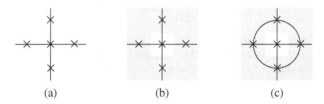

(a)   (b)   (c)

Figure 16.20: Example constellation. (a) Constellation; (b) error region; (c) spherical offset.

For IS there are some options to consider for a sample density q.

- (a) One potential sample density shifts the noise in one dimension, always in the positive direction, $\tilde{\mathbf{n}} \sim \mathcal{N}(\zeta \mathbf{e}_1, \sigma^2)$, where $\mathbf{e}_1$ is the unit vector with 1 in the first component and ζ is an offset size, e.g., $\zeta = 1$.

- (b) Another potential sample density uses a Gaussian mixture density in each of the $2d$ directions

$$\tilde{\mathbf{n}} \sim \frac{1}{2d} \sum_{i=1}^{d} \mathcal{N}(+\zeta \mathbf{s}_i, \sigma^2 I_d) + \mathcal{N}(-\zeta \mathbf{s}_i, \sigma^2).$$

  This shifts the mean in the direction of one of the actual signal points.

- (c) A third potential sample density picks a point at random on the d-dimensional hypersphere of radius ζ, then uses this as the mean of a d-dimensional Gaussian density, as described above to produce the noise signal $\tilde{\mathbf{n}}$.

The IS received signal is now

$$\tilde{\mathbf{y}} = \mathbf{s}_0 + \tilde{\mathbf{n}}.$$

A critical aspect of the IS is the weight function. For a sample $\tilde{\mathbf{y}}_i$, this is computed for each of the three different cases above as follows.

- (a) One-dimensional shift:

$$w(\tilde{\mathbf{y}}_i) = \frac{\mathcal{N}(\tilde{\mathbf{y}}_i - \mathbf{s}_0; \mathbf{s}_0, \sigma^2 I_d)}{\mathcal{N}(\tilde{\mathbf{y}}_i - \mathbf{s}_0; \zeta\mathbf{s}_1, \sigma^2 I_d)}.$$

- (b) Gaussian mixture over the dimensions:

$$w(\tilde{\mathbf{y}}_i) = \frac{\mathcal{N}(\tilde{\mathbf{y}}_i - \mathbf{s}; \sigma^2 I_d)}{\frac{1}{2d}\sum_{i=1}^d \mathcal{N}(\tilde{\mathbf{y}}_i - \mathbf{s}_i - \mathbf{s}; \zeta\mathbf{s}_i, \sigma^2 I_d) + \mathcal{N}(\tilde{\mathbf{y}}_i + \mathbf{s}_i - \mathbf{s}; -\zeta\mathbf{s}_i, \sigma^2 I_d)}.$$

- (c) Circular selection:

$$w(\tilde{\mathbf{y}}_i) = \frac{\mathcal{N}(\tilde{\mathbf{y}}_i - \mathbf{s}; \sigma^2 I_d)}{q_n(\tilde{\mathbf{y}}_i)},$$

where $q_n(\tilde{\mathbf{y}}_i)$ is in (16.16).

is5.m

A simulation was established which draws $L = 500$ samples and estimates the probability of error using MC and each of the three IS approaches described above. Each of these simulations was repeated 10 times so that the variance of P_E could be estimated. The ratio of these variances, as well as the IS gain γ, is computed for each of the IS methods.

In the simulation, various values of ζ can be tried. A value of $\zeta = 0.5$ is generally selected as producing the highest variance ratio.

A sample of results is shown in Table 16.2 for $d = 2$ dimensions and $n = 1$. The P_E estimates are taken from the first of the 10 estimates produced. As the table shows, the MC estimates of the probability of error are far from the true values (because of the small number of iterations), while the IS methods are better. The IS1 method (bias in one direction only) did not fare as well as the method that use the Gauss mixture or the spherical model. The Gauss mixture model appeared to have lower variance, and hence better variance ratios. □

Example 16.26 (See, for example, [474].) Let C be an (N, K) linear code with minimum distance d_{min}. Assume the coded bits c_i are mapped via BPSK modulation to signal components $s_i = 2c_i - 1 \in \{-1, 1\}$. We will call the n-dimensional symbols obtained from code words as the coded symbols. The all-zero codeword thus maps to the coded symbol signal $\mathbf{s}_0 = (-1, -1, \ldots, -1)$. The squared minimum Euclidean distance between modulated codewords is $4d_{min}$.

Let $\mathbf{y} = (y_1, y_2, \ldots, y_n)$ be a vector in the received signal space. If $\mathbf{y} = \mathbf{s} = (s_1, s_2, \ldots, s_N)$ is the vector corresponding to a coded symbol, then $\mathbf{y}$ lies on the N-dimensional hypersphere S_1 centered at the origin satisfying

$$y_1^2 + y_2^2 + \cdots + y_N^2 = N. \tag{16.17}$$

The points $\mathbf{y}$ corresponding to codewords of minimum Hamming distance from the coded symbol $\mathbf{s}_0$ lie on the N-dimensional hypersphere S_0 centered at $\mathbf{s}_0$ satisfying

$$(y_1 + 1)^2 + (y_2 + 1)^2 + \cdots + (y_N + 1)^2 = 4d_{min}. \tag{16.18}$$

Coded symbols closest to $\mathbf{s}_0$ lie on the intersection of S_0 and S_1, which is an $(N-1)$-dimensional hypersphere, as suggested by Figure 16.21(a), designated as $S_{0\cap1}$. Figure 16.21(b) illustrates the same concept from a side view. The idea for IS is that points lying on the sphere $S_{0\cap1}$ are reasonable points to use as translated means in an IS setting. Since those points may not in general be known, an effective approach to IS may be to use the hypersphere sample idea above to select points at random in $S_{0\cap1}$.

Expanding (16.17) and (16.18) and subtracting yields the equation

$$y_1 + y_2 + \cdots + y_N = 2d_{min} - N. \tag{16.19}$$

Equation (16.19) describes the (hyper)plane upon which the intersection $S_{0\cap1}$ lies. Let $\mathbf{1} = (1, 1, \ldots, 1)^T \in \mathbb{R}^N$. Equation (16.19) can be written as

$$\mathbf{1}^T(\mathbf{y} - \mathbf{p}) = 0,$$

Table 16.2: MC and IS Comparison for Digital Communication for Various IS Mean Translation Schemes

σ^2	ζ	P_E (true)	P_E (MC)	P_E (IS1)	P_E (IS2)	P_E (IS3)	Var (MC)	Var (IS1)	Var (IS2)	Var (IS3)	Var (MC)/ Var (IS1)	Var (MC)/ Var (IS2)	Var (MC)/ Var (IS3)	γ (IS1)	γ (IS2)	γ (IS3)
0.02	0.5	8.1×10^{-4}	0.002	1.9×10^{-4}	8.5×10^{-4}	8.3×10^{-4}	1.9×10^{-6}	3.1×10^{-10}	2.7×10^{-9}	8.6×10^{-9}	6	730	226	1200	328	160
0.05	0.5	0.05	0.036	0.036	0.047	0.047	1.7×10^{-4}	5.5×10^{-4}	5.2×10^{-6}	1.9×10^{-6}	0.3	33	88	0.13	7	7

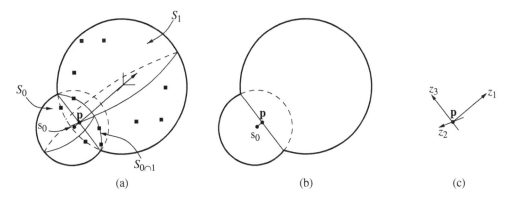

Figure 16.21: Geometry of coded symbol points. (a) The sphere of codewords around $\mathbf{0}$, and the sphere of codewords around $\mathbf{s}_0$; (b) side view of two spheres; (c) plane in $\mathbb{R}^{N-1}$ on which intersecting hypersphere lies.

where

$$
\mathbf{y} = \begin{bmatrix} y_1 \\ y_2 \\ \vdots \\ y_N \end{bmatrix} \qquad
\mathbf{p} = \begin{bmatrix} \dfrac{2d_{\min}}{N} - 1 \\[6pt] \dfrac{2d_{\min}}{N} - 1 \\[6pt] \vdots \\[6pt] \dfrac{2d_{\min}}{N} - 1 \end{bmatrix}.
$$

$\mathbf{1}$ is the normal to the plane, and $\mathbf{p}$ is a point on the plane from which the normal vector emerges. Let $\tilde{\mathbf{y}} = \mathbf{y} - \mathbf{p}$ represent points on the plane, with $\mathbf{p}$ as the origin.

Further algebraic manipulation of (16.17) and (16.18) shows that

$$
\left(y_1 - \left(\frac{2d_{\min}}{N} - 1\right)\right)^2 + \cdots + \left(y_N - \left(\frac{2d_{\min}}{N} - 1\right)\right)^2 = 4d_{\min}\left(1 - \frac{d_{\min}}{N}\right). \tag{16.20}
$$

This is an equation for the (hyper)sphere $S_{0\cap1}$ centered at $\mathbf{p} = (2d_{\min}/N - 1)\mathbf{1}$ with squared radius $4d_{\min}\left(1 - \frac{d_{\min}}{N}\right)$.

To use this geometry for IS, randomly selected points on the hypersphere $S_{0\cap1}$ are used as the location to which the means are shifted. This is done as follows.

1. An orthogonal coordinate system with axes $z_1, z_2, \ldots, z_N$ is established, where the z_1 axis lies in the $(1, 1, \ldots, 1)$ direction, and the $z_2, \ldots, z_N$ directions lie on the plane (16.19).

   This may be done as follows. In $N = 3$ dimensions form a matrix

   $$
   T = \begin{bmatrix} 1 & 1 & 0 \\ 1 & 0 & 1 \\ 1 & 0 & 0 \end{bmatrix}.
   $$

   This generalizes in obvious ways to larger values of N.
   Do Gram–Schmidt processes to obtain orthonormalized columns

   $$
   Q = \begin{bmatrix} 1/\sqrt{N} & q_{12} & q_{13} \\ 1/\sqrt{N} & q_{22} & q_{23} \\ 1/\sqrt{N} & q_{32} & q_{33} \end{bmatrix}.
   $$

   For a point $\tilde{\mathbf{y}}$ on the plane centered at $\mathbf{p}$, let

   $$
   \tilde{\mathbf{y}} = Q \begin{bmatrix} z_1 \\ z_2 \\ z_3 \end{bmatrix}
   $$

or

$$\mathbf{z} = Q^T \tilde{\mathbf{y}}.$$

For example, in $N = 3$ dimensions,

$$\begin{bmatrix} z_1 \\ z_2 \\ z_3 \end{bmatrix} = \begin{bmatrix} 1/\sqrt{N} & 1/\sqrt{N} & 1/\sqrt{N} \\ q_{21} & q_{22} & q_{23} \\ q_{31} & q_{32} & q_{33} \end{bmatrix} \begin{bmatrix} \tilde{y}_1 \\ \tilde{y}_2 \\ \tilde{y}_3 \end{bmatrix} = Q^T \tilde{\mathbf{r}}.$$

The vector $\mathbf{z} = \begin{bmatrix} 1 \\ 0 \\ 0 \end{bmatrix}$ (in z coordinates) corresponds to the vector $\frac{1}{\sqrt{N}} \mathbf{1}$ (in $\tilde{y}$ coordinates). The vectors $\mathbf{z} = \begin{bmatrix} 0 \\ 1 \\ 0 \end{bmatrix}$ and $\mathbf{z} = \begin{bmatrix} 0 \\ 0 \\ 1 \end{bmatrix}$ corresponds to vectors which are orthogonal.

Thus, the variables $z_2, z_3, \ldots, z_N$ are coordinates on the plane.

2. For a radius $2d_{\min}\sqrt{1 - \frac{d_{\min}}{N}}$, generate points $(z_2, z_3, \ldots, z_N)$ on the hypersphere (16.20) at random

$$(z_2, z_3, \ldots, z_N) \sim \mathcal{N}(\mathbf{0}, I_{N-1})$$

$$(z_2, z_3) \leftarrow 2d_{\min}\sqrt{1 - \frac{d_{\min}}{n}}(z_2, z_3) / \| (z_2, z_3) \| .$$

3. Transform this back to $\tilde{\mathbf{y}}$ coordinates.

$$\tilde{\mathbf{y}} = Q\mathbf{z}$$

and then to $\mathbf{y}$ coordinates,

$$\mathbf{y} = \tilde{\mathbf{y}} + \mathbf{p}.$$

4. Add noise on to this:

$$\tilde{\mathbf{n}} = \mathbf{y} + \mathcal{N}(\mathbf{0}, K/n),$$

where $K = \sigma^2 I_n$.

5. The received signal is

$$\tilde{\mathbf{y}} = \mathbf{s}_0 + \tilde{\mathbf{n}}.$$

The sample distribution to be used in computing the weight function for IS is

$$q_n(z_1, \ldots, z_N) = \frac{1}{(2\pi)^{N/2} \det(K)^{1/2}} \sqrt{n}^N \exp\left(-\frac{1}{2\sigma^2} n \sum_{i=1}^{N} (z_i)^2\right) \exp(-nr)$$

$$\times \frac{\Gamma(\frac{N-1}{2})\sqrt{2}^{(N-3)/2}}{\sqrt{r}^{(N-3)/2}} \frac{I_{(N-3)/2}\left(n\sqrt{2r}\sqrt{\sum_{i=2}^{N} z_i^2}/\sigma\right)}{\left(n/\sigma\sqrt{\sum_{i=2}^{N} z_i^2}\right)^{(N-3)/2}},$$

where $K = \sigma^2 I_N$, $r = \frac{1}{2\sigma^2}\rho^2$, and ρ is near the size of the radius $2\sqrt{d_{\min}(1 - d_{\min}/N)}$. $\qquad \square$

16.11.3 Importance Sampling for Tanner Trees

In this section, another set of points to use for mean translation is discussed that provides an approach suitable for codes defined on Tanner trees. The work begins with single parity-check codes, then combines these together for more general codes. See [493].

16.11.3.1 Single Parity-Check Codes

Consider a single $(N, N - 1)$ parity-check code with codewords satisfying

$$c_1 \oplus c_2 \oplus \cdots \oplus c_N = 0.$$

By symmetry, we will study the situation when the all-zero codeword is sent. In this section, this is mapped to the symbol $\mathbf{s}_0 = (s_1, s_2, \ldots, s_N) = (1, 1, \ldots, 1)$. Let $y_n = s_n + v_n$, where v_n is AWGN with variance σ^2. By symmetry, decoding at variable node 1 is considered. Decoding can be accomplished using one iteration of a message-passing algorithm using the tanh rule. Let $\ell_n = L_c y_n$, where L_c is the channel parameter $2/\sigma^2$. Let $M(\ell_2, \ldots, \ell_N) = 2\tanh^{-1}\left(\prod_{n=2}^{N} \tanh(\ell_n/2)\right)$. The message at variable node 1 is computed as

$$m_1 = \ell_1 + M(\ell_2, \ldots, \ell_N).$$

Having computed m_1, a decision is made as

$$\hat{c}_1 = \begin{cases} 0 & m_1 > 0 \\ 1 & m_1 < 0. \end{cases}$$

Points $(y_1, y_2, \ldots, y_N)$ such that $\ell_1 + M(\ell_2, \ldots, \ell_N) < 0$ form an error set E, and points such that $\ell_1 + M(\ell_2, \ldots, \ell_N) = 0$ form the decision boundary, denoted as ∂E. Points lying below the boundary decode to 1 (error); points lying above the boundary decode to 0 (correct). Figure 16.22 shows this decision boundary for $N = 3$. The boundary forms a saddle surface consisting of nearly planar surfaces delimited by the planes $y_2 \pm y_3 = 0$. This nearly planar structure follows since, as discussed in Section 15.4.3.1,

$$M(\ell_2, \ldots, \ell_N) \approx \prod_{n=2}^{N} \operatorname{sign}(\ell_n) \min(|\ell_2|, \ldots, |\ell_N|).$$

Of particular interest are the two surfaces closest to the transmitted point $(1, 1, 1)$, denoted as $\partial E^{(2)}$ and $\partial E^{(3)}$, where

$$\partial E^{(2)} = \partial E \cap \{|y_2| \leq y_3\} \quad \text{and} \quad E^{(3)} = \partial E \cap \{|y_3| \leq y_2\}.$$

The boundary $\partial E^{(2)}$ can be approximated by points such that

$$\ell_1 + \operatorname{sign}(\ell_2)\operatorname{sign}(\ell_3)|\ell_2| = \ell_1 + \ell_2 = 0.$$

The $+$ sign appears because $\operatorname{sign}(\ell_3) = 1$ on $\partial E^{(2)}$. Similarly the boundary $\partial E^{(2)}$ can be approximated by

$$\ell_1 + \ell_3 = 0.$$

The error region E is partitioned into two regions

$$E^{(2)} = E \cap \{y_2 \leq y_3\} \quad \text{and} \quad E^{(3)} = E \cap \{y_3 \leq y_2\},$$

suggested by the shading in Figure 16.22.

Let $P_{E^{(2)}}$ and $P_{E^{(3)}}$ be the error probabilities in the two regions $E^{(2)}$ and $E^{(3)}$,

$$P_{E^{(2)}} = P((y_1, y_2, y_2) \in E \text{ and } y_2 \geq y_3) \quad P_{E^{(3)}} = P((y_1, y_2, y_2) \in E \text{ and } y_2 \leq y_3)$$

and the overall probability of error is

$$P_E = P_{E^{(2)}} + P_{E^{(3)}}. \tag{16.21}$$

By symmetry, only $P_{E^{(2)}}$ needs to be computed, and $P_E = 2P_{E^{(2)}}$.

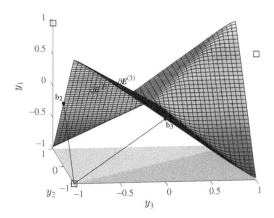

Figure 16.22: Decision boundary for $(3, 2)$ single parity check coding ($\sigma = 0.1$). Squares denote codewords.

For IS, the points on the two planar surfaces closest to the transmitted point $(1, 1, 1)$ are used as the dominant points, where

$$\mathbf{b}_2 = (0, 0, 1) \in \partial E^{(2)} \quad \text{and} \quad \mathbf{b}_3 = (0, 1, 0) \in E^{(3)}.$$

That is, the mean is shifted in the IS simulation so that instead of transmitting $\mathbf{s}_0$ either the point $\mathbf{b}_2$ or the point $\mathbf{b}_3$ is transmitted. (That is, the mean is shifted by $\mathbf{b}_2 - \mathbf{s}_0$.)

The densities in the IS weight function are

$$f(\tilde{\mathbf{y}}) \sim \mathcal{N}(\tilde{\mathbf{y}}; \mathbf{s}_0; \sigma^2 I) \quad \tilde{f}(\tilde{\mathbf{y}}) \sim \mathcal{N}(\tilde{\mathbf{y}}; \mathbf{b}_2; \sigma_2 I)$$

so that

$$w(\tilde{\mathbf{y}}) = \frac{f(\tilde{\mathbf{y}})}{\tilde{f}(\tilde{\mathbf{y}})} = \exp\left[-\frac{\|\tilde{\mathbf{y}} - \mathbf{s}_0\|^2 - \|\tilde{\mathbf{y}} - \mathbf{b}_2\|^2}{2\sigma^2}\right] = \exp\left[\frac{1}{\sigma^2}(\tilde{y}_1 + \tilde{y}_2 - 1)\right]. \tag{16.22}$$

The IS estimate of the probability of error is as follows. Select a number of iterations L. For each iteration i, draw $\tilde{\mathbf{y}}_i = \mathbf{b}_2 + \mathbf{n}$, where $\mathbf{n} \sim \mathcal{N}(\mathbf{0}, \sigma^2 I)$. Then compute the log-likelihood ratios $\boldsymbol{\ell} = \tilde{\mathbf{y}} L_c$, where $L_c = 2/\sigma^2$. Compute

$$m_1 = \ell_1 + M(\ell_2, \ldots, \ell_N).$$

If m_1 is < 0 (decoding error) and $\tilde{y}_2 < \tilde{y}_3$ (so the error falls in $E^{(2)}$), accumulate the weighted error. The error estimate $\hat{P}_{E^{(2)}}$ is thus

$$\hat{P}_{E^{(2)}} = \frac{1}{L} \sum_{i=1}^{L} 1_{E^{(2)}}(\tilde{\mathbf{y}}_i) w(\tilde{\mathbf{y}}_i).$$

Then by (16.21),

$$\hat{P}_E = 2\hat{P}_{E^{(2)}}.$$

From Figure 16.22, it can be seen that the distance from the codeword $(1, 1, \ldots, 1)$ to the dominant point $\mathbf{b}_2$ is $\sqrt{2}$. By the union bound, an upper bound on the probability of error can thus be obtained as

$$P_E \leq (N - 1)Q\left(\frac{\sqrt{2}}{\sigma}\right). \tag{16.23}$$

IS can be generalized to single parity checks in N dimensions. The error region E is defined as

$$E = \{\mathbf{y} \in \mathbb{R}^N : \ell_1 + M(\ell_2, \ldots, \ell_N) < 0\}.$$

Table 16.3: IS Simulation Results for Single Parity-Check Codes of Length N. (See [493])

N	E_b/N_0 (dB)	σ	$\hat{P}_b$ (MC)	$\hat{P}_b$ (IS)	$\hat{P}_b$ (bound)
3	3	0.2739	2.2×10^{-7}	2.41×10^{-7}	2.41×10^{-7}
3	20	0.0866	—	7.3×10^{-60}	6.04×10^{-60}
20	10	0.2294	—	6.30×10^{-9}	6.72×10^{-9}
20	20	0.0725	—	1.22×10^{-83}	1.18×10^{-83}

This is partitioned into disjoint regions

$$E^{(k)} = E \cap \{\mathbf{y}|\ell_k \leq \ell_i \forall i = 2, \ldots, N\}, k = 2, \ldots, N.$$

The bias points for each of these regions is given by

$$\mathbf{b}_k = (0, 1, 1, 0^{k\,\text{th}}, 1, \ldots, -1), \quad k = 2, 3, \ldots, N$$

and the importance weight function is the same as (16.22).

By symmetry, it is still sufficient to estimate only $\hat{P}_{E^{(2)}}$. The overall probability of error estimate is then

$$\hat{P}_E = (N - 1)\hat{P}_{E^{(2)}},$$

and the error bound is given by (16.23).

Some results of applying this to single parity-check codes of length $N = 3$ and $N = 20$ are shown in Table 16.3. The MC result (conventional simulation) is obtained using 10^8 codewords simulated. MC results are computed only for the $N = 3$ code at $E_b/N_0 = 10$ dB, since the probabilities of error are far too small in the other cases in the table. The IS results were obtained with 10,000 codewords at $N = 3$ and $E_b/N_0 = 10$ dB, and 2000 iterations otherwise. (There was, of course, some variance in the IS results, so different results are obtained with every simulation run. At longer lengths and higher SNR, the MC methods tend to overestimate the probability of bit error, dominated by a small number of received vectors with large weight.)

spcxiaryan1.m

16.11.3.2 Symmetric Tanner Trees

The methods presented above are now extended to *symmetric* Tanner trees, which are trees in which all nodes on the same layer have identical connection degrees. The notation (d_v, d_c, ℓ) is used, where ℓ is the number of layers (with root at layer 0), d_c is the check node degree, and d_v is the variable node degree, except that root has degree $d_v - 1$ and the leaves have degree 1. Figure 16.23(a) shows

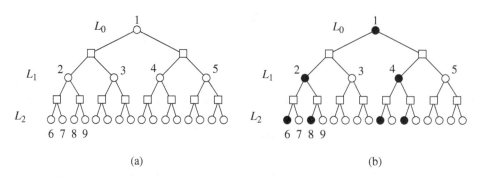

(a)   (b)

Figure 16.23: A $(3, 2, 2)$ tree and labeling for a particular boundary. (a) Tree; (b) indication of variable nodes for the $\partial E^{(2,4,6,8,14,16)}$ boundary.

a $(3, 3, 2)$ degree. Trees such as this can be obtained by "unfolding" a bipartite graph representing a code, then eliminating nodes duplicated by this unfolding process. At node v_1 the decision boundary is described by

$$\ell_1 + M(\ell_2, \ell_3) + M(\ell_4, \ell_5) = 0.$$

Define a boundary set $\partial E^{(2,4)} = \partial E \cap \{|\ell_2| \le \ell_3\} \cap \{|\ell_4| \le \ell_5\}$. As for the single parity-check code case this set is approximated for large SNR by the plane

$$\ell_1 + \ell_2 + \ell_4 = 0.$$

The dominant point associated with this boundary is

$$\mathbf{b}^{(2,4)} = (0, 0, 1, 0, 1).$$

The error subset corresponding to $\mathbf{b}^{(2,4)}$ is

$$E^{(2,4)} = E \cap \{\ell_2 \le \ell_3\} \cap \{\ell_4 \le \ell_5\}.$$

Observe that by symmetry, other error regions that could have been chosen are $E^{(2,5)}, E^{(3,4)}, E^{(3,5)}$, each yielding the same performance. The selected subset $E^{(2,4)}$ thus has a multiplicity of 4.

In actual decoding, the channel messages ℓ_2 through ℓ_5 are replaced by decoded messages passed up from the layer below, which we denote as $\hat{\ell}_2$ through $\hat{\ell}_5$, where

$$\hat{\ell}_2 = \ell_2 + M(\ell_6, \ell_7) \quad \hat{\ell}_4 = \ell_4 + M(\ell_{14}, \ell_{17}).$$

Thinking in terms of the variables used in each of these tanh rules, for sufficiently large SNR, there is a linear approximation to a decision boundary given by

$$\ell_1 + \ell_2 + \ell_4 + \ell_6 + \ell_8 + \ell_{14} + \ell_{16} = 0, \tag{16.24}$$

which corresponds to a boundary region

$$\partial E^{(2,4,6,8,14,16)} = \partial E^P(2,4) \cap \{|\ell_6| \le \ell_7\} \cap \{|\ell_8| \le \ell_9\} \cap \{|\ell_{14}| \le \ell_{15}\} \cap \{|\ell_{16}| \le \ell_{17}\}$$

(The subset $E^{(2,4,6,8,14,16)}$ has a multiplicity of 16.) The dominant point associated with the boundary $\partial E^{(2,4,6,8,14,16)}$ is denoted as $\mathbf{b}^{(2,4,6,8,14,16)}$ in which b_k is 0 if ℓ_k appears in (16.24), and is 1 otherwise, for $k = 1, \ldots, 21$. The nodes with $b_k = 0$ are said to be biased. The biased variable nodes associated with this boundary are indicated in Figure 16.23(b) with shading. For brevity in the discussion below, $\partial E^{(2,4,6,8,14,16)}$ will be denoted simply as E'.

In general, to do IS simulation for a (d_v, d_c, l) tree:

1. Find the set of biased (colored) variable nodes.

   (a) Shade variable node 1 (the root of the tree).

   (b) For each shaded variable node in the current layer, locate all check nodes connected from below, and for each of these check nodes, shade the left variable node in the next layer.

   (c) Move down to the next layer, and repeat step (b) until the last layer is reached.

   (d) Form a bias vector with 0 in the biased variable positions.

The number of bias (shaded) variables is

$$n_b = 1 + (d_v - 1) + (d_v - 1)^2 + \cdots + (d_v - 1)^l.$$

The number of symmetric error subsets is

$$N_E = (d_c - 1)^{n_b - 1}.$$

Table 16.4: IS Simulation Results for a $(3, 6, 3)$ Decoding Tree. $\epsilon = 10\%$ [493]

E_b/N_0 (dB)	$\hat{P}_b$ (MC)	$\hat{P}_b$ (MC)	P_b (bound)	$\hat{L}_\epsilon$
3	8.6×10^{-5}	8.75×10^{-5}	0.0137	10^5
4	6.9×10^{-7}	6.76×10^{-7}	2.5×10^{-5}	27,000
6	—	8.75×10^{-14}	4.36×10^{-13}	5300
8	—	1.56×10^{-25}	2.53×10^{-25}	2300
10	—	1.07×10^{-44}	1.168×10^{-44}	2000
12	—	2.94×10^{-75}	3.02×10^{-75}	2400

The error region E' is given by

$$E' = \cap_{v \neq v_1} \{\hat{\ell}_v \leq \hat{\ell}_{v'}, \forall v' \in C(v)\} \cap E,$$

where $C(v)$ is the set of variable nodes having the same parent as v. For example, in Figure 16.23, $C(v_2) = \{v_2, v_3\}$.

With these preliminaries, $\hat{P}_{E'}$ can be obtained from an IS simulation for E', and the error probability is computed from

$$\hat{P}_E = N_E \hat{P}_{E'}.$$

Since the distance from s_0 to E' is $\sqrt{n_b}$, the probability of error can also be bounded, as in the single parity case, by

$$P_E \leq N_e Q\left(\frac{\sqrt{n_b}}{\sigma}\right). \tag{16.25}$$

Table 16.4 (copied from [493]) illustrates performance for a $(3, 6, 3)$ code. The column $\hat{P}_b$ (MC) shows the results for conventional probability of error simulations, which can only be computed for relatively high bit error rates. The column P_b (bound) shows the bound computed using (16.25). For higher SNRs, this provides a good estimate of the error. Also shown is the estimated number of IS codewords to be generated to estimate the probability of error within $\epsilon = 10\%$ error.

16.11.3.3 General Trees

As the previous subsections illustrated, if a tree is symmetric then the error probability can be estimated using only one error subset, since all error subsets have equivalent error performance by symmetry. While general trees do not have the same global symmetries, local symmetries may be used to reduce complexity.

Consider the tree shown in Figure 16.24(a), with a subset $E^{(2,4)}$ represented by the shaded variable nodes. Equivalent subsets correspond to $E^{(2,5)}$, $E^{(3,4)}$, and $E^{(3,5)}$, so $E^{(2,4)}$ has multiplicity 4, since

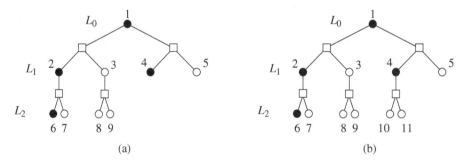

(a)   (b)

Figure 16.24: Trees which are not symmetric. (a) Variable nodes 2 and 3 and nodes 4 and 5 isormophically interchangeable; (b) variable nodes 2 and 3 isormophically interchangeable.

nodes 2 and 3 and nodes 4 and 5 can be swapped to produce isomorphic trees. Selecting $E^{(2,4)}$ as the representative, it can be further partitioned into $E^{(2,4,6)}$ and $E^{(2,4,7)}$, each having multiplicity 8. By contrast, in Figure 16.23(b), a subtree has been added to variable node 4, so that 4 and 5 cannot be isomorphically interchanged. In this case, the four subsets $E^{(2,4)}$, $E^{(2,5)}$, $E^{(3,4)}$, and $E^{(3,5)}$ are not symmetric. However, the sets $E^{(2,4)}$ and $E^{(2,5)}$ may both be selected, each having multiplicity 2. These can be further partitioned into subsets $E^{(2,4,6,10)}$ and $E^{(2,5,6)}$, having multiplicities eight and four, respectively.

In general, as this example illustrates, the procedure for dealing with an arbitrary tree is to identify isomorphisms among variable nodes connected above to the same check node, then determine representative subsets with their multiplicities. This proceeds from the top layer down to the bottom layer.

16.11.3.4 Importance Sampling for LDPC Codes

To apply these ideas to an LDPC code (or other linear block code), the Tanner graph is unfolded into a tree, continuing the unfolding process until all variable and check nodes have been considered. Figure 16.25(a) illustrates a Tanner graph for a $(9, 3)$ code which (since one of the check equations is redundant) represents a rate 4/9 code. The initial unfolding of this Tanner graph using v_1 as the root is the tree shown in Figure 16.25(b). Because the code is finite, as the unfolding proceeds, some of the variable nodes are duplicated. In this example, nodes v_2, v_3, v_6, and v_8 are duplicated. These duplicated nodes are an indication of cycles in the Tanner graph. Since the IS technique developed here is based on analysis on trees, it does not take the cycles into account. To apply the analysis, the duplicates must be removed, which results in a performance underestimate (that is, estimates worse performance than actually occurs). When a duplicated variable node is removed from a tree, the check nodes connected to it must also be removed. The tree pruned based on these principles, in which four duplicated variable nodes on the right and their connected check nodes are removed, is shown in Figure 16.25(c). This tree happens to be identical to the tree in Figure 16.24. The probability of error can be estimated to be $8P_{E^{(2,4,6)}}$, where $P_{E^{(2,4,6)}}$ is the probability for the error subset $E^{(2,4,6)}$, which has multiplicity 8. For high SNR, the performance can be bounded as $P_E \leq 8Q\left(\frac{\sqrt{4}}{\sigma}\right)$, where the 4 is the number of biased variable nodes.

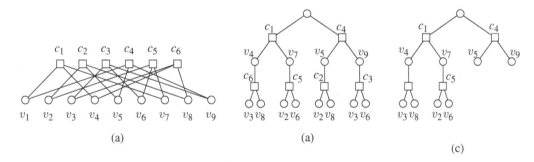

Figure 16.25: Tanner graph for $(9, 3)$ regular code, and its unfolding into a tree. (a) Tanner graph for the code; (b) unfolded tree; (c) pruned unfolded tree.

While this procedure was fairly straightforward for this short example code, complications arise for longer codes. Longer codes have more ways that structural complexity can occur in the tree. Also, the performance is underestimated due to removal of cycles. Despite this, the IS method can be used to obtain effective upper bounds on performance.

16.12 Fountain Codes

A digital fountain is an analogy drawn from a sprinkling water fountain. When you fill a cup from a water fountain, you do not care which particular drops of water fall in, but only that the cup fills with enough water. With a digital fountain, data packets may be obtained from one or more servers, and once enough packets are obtained (from whatever source) that an original file, transmission can end. Which particular packets are obtained does not matter [312]. In an ideal that is not quite attained, for a message that would require receipt of k packet of data, a digital fountain receiver can receive *any k* packets and be able to quickly reconstruct the desired message. In practice, some overhead is incurred, so that it is necessary to receive $(1 + \epsilon)k$ packets. A fountain code is a means of representing the data in a way that provides the capabilities of a digital fountain.

A digital fountain can be used, for example, to create efficient **multicast**, in which a number of users desire to download the same file, at roughly the same time. (Think of streaming a newly released movie, or a software update.) If packets are sent uncoordinated (not in a fountain sense) and packets are subject to loss, when users request retransmission (as in an ARQ protocol), there could be an explosion of feedback. Using fountain-coded data can prevent the need for retransmission: each user simply collects enough packets to reconstruct its data.

There are several ways of implementing digital fountains. They are not all, strictly speaking, LDPC codes, but many of the ideas are related to Tanner graphs.

16.12.1 Conventional Erasure Correction Codes

Erasure correction codes, such as Reed–Solomon codes, can be used to implement a digital fountain. A code of minimum distance d can recover up to $d - 1$ erasures. The RS codes are MDS (see Section 6.2.4). Encoding/decoding is conceptually straightforward, but can incur undesirable computational complexity. The decode (and encode) complexity is $O(k^2)$, which may be too much for moderate to long values of k. The codes below trade off some rate (they are not minimum-distance separable) for lower computational complexity.

16.12.2 Tornado Codes

Tornado codes are based on Tanner-like graphs. A tornado code encoder is a cascade of $s + 1$ rate $1/(1 + \beta)$ LDPC encoders, followed by a rate $1 - \beta$ erasure correcting code (such as a Reed–Solomon code). Let B_0 be the bipartite graph shown in Figure 16.26(a). There are K message bits on the left and βK, $0 < \beta < 1$ check bits on the right. While this looks like a Tanner graph for an LDPC code, it operates somewhat differently. Associated with this graph is a code $C(B)$, in which each check bit on the right is computed simply as the modulo-2 ($\oplus$) sum of its neighboring bits on the left. For this stage there are K bits in, and $K + \beta K = K(1 + \beta)$ bits out, with the message bits appearing systematically, to produce the codeword $(x_1, x_2, \ldots, x_k, c_1, \ldots, c_{\beta K})$.

If there is an erasure on a message bit, it is recovered using the code structure suggested by Figure 16.26(b). Knowing the other message bits and the check bits, a bit can be recovered, as for bit x_3 in the figure. In general, decoding of message bits can be accomplished using an algorithm analogous to the peeling algorithm of Section 15.4.9. To protect the check bits, an additional layer of check bits can be added, as shown in Figure 16.26(c). Decoding of bits not in the last check layer proceeds from right to left.

In general, construct a family of codes $C(B_0), C(B_1), \ldots, C(B_m)$ from a family of graphs $B_0, \ldots, B_m$, where B_i has $\beta^i K$ left nodes and $\beta^{i+1} K$ right nodes. The sequence of coded bits terminates with an erasure correcting code C of rate $1 - \beta$, with $\beta^{m+1} K$ message bits input and $K\beta^{m+2}/(1 - \beta)$ check bits, for which it is known how to recover from the random loss of a fraction of up to β of its bits with high probability. (This final erasure code may be, for example, a Reed–Solomon code.) This is portrayed in Figure 16.26(d). The overall code $C(B_0, B_1, \ldots, B_m, C)$ has K message bits and

$$\sum_{i=1}^{m+1} \beta^i K + \frac{\beta^{m+2} K}{(1 - \beta)} = \frac{K\beta}{1 - \beta}$$

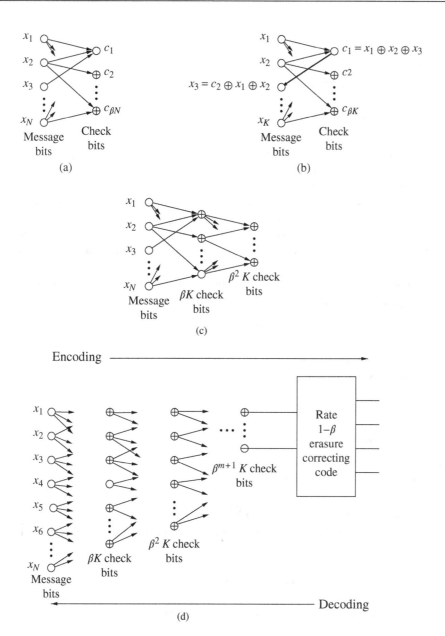

Figure 16.26: Graph defining Tornado codes. (a) One stage of code graph; (b) decoding an erased value; (c) two stages of check bits; (d) overall Tornado code with $m + 1$ stages.

check bits. The overall rate is

$$R = \frac{K}{K\beta/(1 - \beta)} = 1 - \beta.$$

Encoding proceeds left to right, computing checks, then checks on checks, and so on, then through the erasure correcting code. Decoding proceeds right to left, first decoding using the erasure correcting code to correct any missing check bits at the last stage, then propagating back through the layers of checks until the message bits are decoded.

The key to an effective Tornado code is to select the degree distributions at each graph $B_0, \ldots, B_m$ that makes it possible to correct a fraction $\beta(1 - \epsilon)$ of erasures with high probability. This is described in [282]. The connections between the left and right nodes of each node are chosen sparsely, so that the encode and decode complexity is linear in the size of the code. The end result is that this construction is able to recover a message from a random set of $K(1 + \epsilon)$ coordinate locations (codeword bits) with high probability, and with a decode complexity that is linear in the number of message bits.

16.12.3 Luby Transform Codes

Luby transform (LT) codes are *rateless*, which means practically that they more nearly achieve the idea of collecting drops of water (data) until the cup (packet) is full. "The decoder can recover an exact copy of the transmitted data from any set of the generated encoding symbols that are in aggregate only slightly longer in length than the original data. No matter what the loss is on the erasure channel, encoding symbols can be generated as needed and sent over the erasure channel until a sufficient number have arrived at the decoder in order to recover the data" [281].

There is a degree distribution associated with the message nodes which ensures the properties described above. The encoding process for LT codes is as follows. To generate an encoding symbol:

- Randomly choose the degree d of the encoding symbol from a degree distribution.
- Choose d random distinct input symbols.
- The parity packet is the modulo-2 sum of the d neighbors.

To do the decoding the decoder needs to know the degree and set of neighbors of each encoding symbol. This might be accomplished, for example, by employing the same random number generator initiated with the same seed at both the encode and decode side.

Design of degree distributions is described in [281].

16.12.4 Raptor Codes

Raptor codes [410] introduce some pre-coding to the LT code which reduces the encode–decode complexity. The basic idea is as follows:

- K input symbols are encoded by an (N, K) linear block code C.
- These N symbols are then encoded with an LT code, having a degree distribution represented by $\Omega(x)$ on the N symbols.

The raptor code is characterized by the parameters $(K, C, \Omega(x))$.

Raptor codes relax the LT code requirement that all K input symbols are recoverable, requiring that only a constant fraction of the input symbols be recoverable.

16.13 References

RA codes were introduced in [94]. IRA codes were introduced in [223]. See also [373]. IRA codes having structure to reduce hardware complexity, such as QC structure in H_m, have been investigated; see, e.g., [433, 506, 508]. IRAA codes are described in [503], where it is shown that the error floor may be lower while the waterfall region is worse. A variation on multiple accumulator codes is the family of accumulate-repeat-accumulate codes [3, 4]. These encoders add an accumulator to a subset of the input bits. These accumulated bits (or some puncturing of them) are then passed into the usual permuter/accumulator stage.

Encoding hardware of QC codes are discussed in [267], which also discusses how to find the generator from a QC parity check matrix and cites literature on QC LDPC codes. More on QC LDPC codes can be found in [63, 64, 258, 259].

Discussion of matrix dispersions was drawn from [386], which, in turn, draws from [66, ?].

EG-LDPC codes can be traced back to the 1960s [107, 384, 385]. More recently, see [254]. For a discussion of polynomial theory related to these computations, see [246].

PEG was presented in [203]. The improvement to produce larger ACE was proposed in [494]. An alternative to PEG for creating Tanner graphs is a trellis-based method for removing short cycles from a Tanner graph, presented in [256].

There are many other algorithms for LDPC design. For example, a *superposition* approach has been investigated which replaces each element of matrix satisfying the RC constraint with other matrices (analogous to replacing elements of a $GF(q)$ matrix with a matrix dispersion). These approaches are described in [495, 496]. An family of approaches is based on combinatorial objects known as *combinatorial designs* [10, 232, 257].

Several LDPC constructions have been reported based on combinatoric objects.

Constructions based on Kirkman triple systems are reported in [233, 234], which produce $(3, k)$-regular LDPC codes whose Tanner graph is free of four-cycles for any k.

Constructions based on Latin rectangles are reported in [464], with reportedly low encode and decode complexity.

Designs based on Steiner 2-designs are reported in [463], [236], and [388]. See also [465].

High-rate LDPC codes based on constructions from unital designs are reported in [235].

Constructions based on disjoint difference sets permutation matrices for use in conjunction with the magnetic recording channel are reported in [417].

LDPCCC are presented in [118, 355].

Protograph designs were introduced in [370, 441] and were further developed in [96] and [95]. Discussions of efficient decoder architectures appear in [237, 372].

A generalization of protograph codes is the MET codes. In these codes, groups of repeated nodes may be combined to share permutation matrices on edges emanating from them. These are discussed in [368, 377]. For more recent work, see, e.g., [217]. For some design work using MET, see [198].

Discussion of error floors follows [[386], Section 15.3] and [183]. Because of the importance of low error floors, there has been a lot of research studying the problem and seeking code designs that mitigate the effect. [369] describes some experimental ways of looking for error floors and some analytic tools for estimating the effect of error floors. Because the error floor phenomenon is associated with low error rates, it is difficult to evaluate using software decoders, so decoding hardware is used for some of these studies [504, 507]. Design studies are in [503]. Analysis of trapping sets is in [308]. There has also been some work on modified decoding algorithms to avoid the problem of trapping sets [186]. An algorithm for approximately identifying trapping sets is given in [199].

Another analysis technique is based on absorbing sets, which are combinatorial and hence do not depend on the particular decoder [101]. These have been used with IS to obtain good probability of error estimates in the error floor region.

Importance sampling in communication is surveyed generally in [213]. The excellent survey paper [414] provides intuitive explanations and a large number of references, placing the mean translation methods described here in context with other methods such as variance scaling. [280] is "improved" using mean translation techniques. [51] describes efficient estimators using the Gaussian mixture and spherical bias idea. Using this spherical idea for block codes is described in [474]. Another mean translation idea for block codes is described in [492], where it is applied to single parity codes then generalized to more general linear block codes. See also [419], [387]. The paper [75] goes into some depth on using trapping sets as dominant points for IS. This may be the recommended method for IS simulation of LDPC codes.

Tornado codes are detailed in [282], including how to design the degree distributions for each bipartite graph to achieve high decoding probability.

Part V

Polar Codes

Chapter 17

Polar Codes

17.1 Introduction and Preview

Polar codes, invented by Erdal Arıkan, are the first family of codes proven to achieve Shannon channel capacity. The codes have low encoding and decoding complexity: for a code of length N, both the encoding and the decoding complexity is $O(N \log N)$. Unlike many modern codes such as turbo codes or LDPC codes, decoding is noniterative. There are explicit code design algorithms and there is great flexibility in selection of the rate for virtually any rate below the channel capacity.

As an introduction, Figure 17.1 highlights some aspects of the probability of error performance of polar codes. In Figure 17.1(a), frame error rates and bit error rates for a rate $R = 1/2$ code of a "moderate" length of $N = 2048$ are shown. The red line shows the performance of the basic "successive cancellation" (SC) decoder, the $O(N \log N)$ decoder originally proposed. This is described in Section 17.4.7. Also shown is the result of list decoding for list sizes of $L = 2, 16$, and 32. List decoding provides some improvement over SC decoding, particularly at low SNRs. However, at larger SNRs, the performance is essentially the same for all list sizes. List decoding can be easily concatenated with a CRC code, producing *modified polar codes*. As the figure shows, the performance of the modified polar code improves with list size, reaching a frame error rate (FER) of about 10^{-5} for only 2 dB. The list decoding complexity, using the algorithm described in Section 17.9, is $O(LN \log N)$.

Figure 17.1(b) provides some more results, comparing polar code decoding with a rate $R = 0.84$ (2048, 1723) LDPC code used in the 10GBASE-T standard (black line). With SC decoding of a (2048, 1723) polar code (blue line), the performance is inferior to the LDPC code. Comparable results can be obtained using a longer (32768, 27568) code. Because polar decoding is noniterative, this may be comparable to LDPC decoding in terms of complexity. Using list decoding (magenta line), even the much shorter (2048, 1723) polar code performs at the same level as the LDPC code.

We present in this introductory section the basic idea of polarization. The ideas touched on here are fleshed out in the remainder of this chapter. Let W denote a channel that accepts binary inputs. In Figure 17.2(a), the channel W is used twice, once with input u_0 and a second time with input u_1. (These uses may be in succession, such as sending multiple bits down a single channel.) The channel outputs are denoted y_0 and y_1. The mutual information between u_0 and y_0 is denoted I^0 and the mutual information between u_1 and y_1 is denoted as I^1. Since the same channel is used for each transmission, we have $I^0 = I^1 = I(W)$, where $I(W)$ is the mutual information associated with the channel W. In this case, the two uses of the channel are equally reliable.

In Figure 17.2(b), we use the W twice again, but over the first W we send $u_0 \oplus u_1$ and over the second W we send u_1. Let I_c^0 now denote the mutual information between u_0 and the collective output (y_0, y_1) in this coded scenario and let I_c^1 denote the mutual information between u_1 and the collective output (y_0, y_1, u_0). u_1 appears in (influences) both y_0 and y_1, so that we have a little bit more information about u_1 than we do about u_0. And since $u_1 \oplus u_0$ scrambles u_0 by u_1, there is a little less information about u_0 than in the original transmission setting. Hence, with details to be developed below,

$$I_c^0 < I(W) < I_c^1.$$

By this simple coding scheme, we have artificially created a channel I_c^1 which is better than it was without coding, at the same time creating a channel I_c^0 which is worse than without coding.

Error Correction Coding: Mathematical Methods and Algorithms, Second Edition. Todd K. Moon
© 2021 John Wiley & Sons, Inc. Published 2021 by John Wiley & Sons, Inc.
Companion website: www.wiley.com/go/Moon/ErrorCorrectionCoding

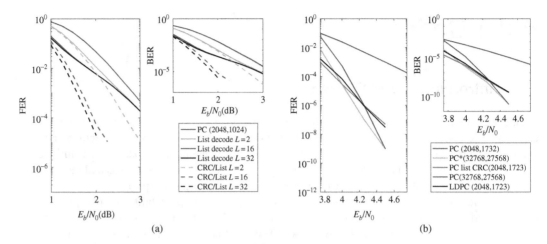

Figure 17.1: Error correction performance of polar codes compared with an LDPC code of the same rate. (a) Results for a (2048,1024) polar code, with list decoding (see [431]); (b) comparison of $R = 0.84$ polar codes with LDPC code of same rate (see [391]). (Color versions of the page can be found at wileywebpage or `https://github.com/tkmoon/eccbook/colorpages`).

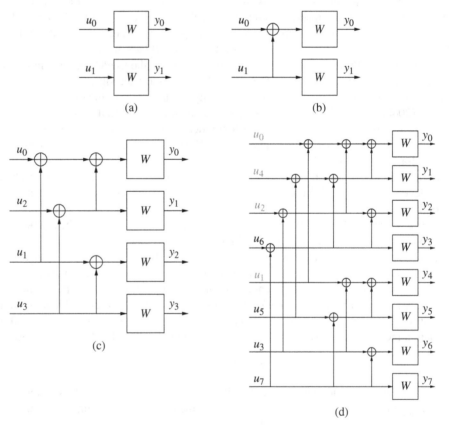

Figure 17.2: Basic ideas of polarization. (a) Two uses of the channel W; (b) simple coding and two channel uses; (c) recursively applying the coding construction, $N = 4$; (d) recursively applying the coding construction, $N = 8$ with some bits frozen.

The coding construction can be applied recursively, as in Figure 17.2(c) which shows $N = 4$ (note the particular input order, which is discussed below), and in Figure 17.2(d) which shows $N = 8$. As this recursive construction is repeated and N becomes large, some of the bit channels become a lot better, eventually becoming so good they are nearly perfect. At the same time, some of the channels become a lot worse, becoming so bad they cannot carry any reliable information. This is what is meant by *polarizing*. Significantly, the proportion of the nearly perfect channels approaches the channel capacity of the channels W, which is $I(W)$. In polar coding, to transmit at rate $R = K/N$, select the K best channels to transmit information and "freeze" the remaining $N - K$ bits to 0. In Figure 17.2(d), the frozen bits are indicated with gray, so u_3, u_5, u_6, and u_7 are unfrozen "information" bits.

This chapter develops the basic ideas of polarization, describes how to do encoding (both for nonsystematic and systematic representations), how to design polar codes, how to do successive cancellation decoding and simplified successive cancellation decoding, and how to do efficient list decoding and modified polar codes. The basic theorems describing how polarization happens are stated and proved.

As the chapter begins, the development of the polar coding idea is deliberately leisurely, presenting major ideas first for codes of length $N = 2$ to build some concrete understanding, then generalizing to codes of larger length.

17.2 Notation and Channels

A sequence $x_0, x_1, \ldots, x_{N-1}$ may be written as x_0^{N-1}. Note that the convention of 0-based indexing is employed throughout this chapter.[1] The subsequence $x_i, x_{i+1}, \ldots, x_j$ may be written as x_i^j. If $j < i$, then x_i^j is an empty sequence. The notation $x_{i,\text{even}}^j$ denotes the subsequence with even indices, and $x_{i,\text{odd}}^j$ denotes the subsequence with odd indices. For example,

$$x_0^3 = (x_0, x_1, x_2, x_3) \quad x_{0,\text{even}}^3 = (x_0, x_2) \quad x_{0,\text{odd}}^3 = (x_1, x_3).$$

The notation $x_{\neg j}$ denotes the sequence x_0^{N-1} (the range understood by context) with the jth element removed:

$$x_{\neg j} = (x_0, x_1, \ldots, x_{j-1}, \ x_{j+1}, \ldots, x_{N-1}).$$

If $\mathcal{A}$ is a subset of $\{0, 1, \ldots, N - 1\}$, then $u_{\mathcal{A}}$ denotes the subsequence $(u_i : i \in \mathcal{A})$.

To say that a sequence u_0^{N-1} is equal to a sequence $\hat{u}_0^{N-1}$ means that they are equal element-by-element:

$$u_0^{N-1} = \hat{u}_0^{N-1} \leftrightarrow u_i = \hat{u}_i \quad \forall i \in 0, 1, \ldots, N - 1.$$

Random variables are denoted with upper-case letters, such as U_1 or X_1. Particular outcome values of random variables are denoted by corresponding lower-case letters, such as u_1 or x_1.

A *discrete memoryless channel* accepts inputs from a discrete alphabet $\mathcal{X}$ and produces outputs from a discrete alphabet $\mathcal{Y}$. The channel is *memoryless* if the conditional probability distribution of the output y given some input x, $p(y|x)$, at some time depends only on the input at that time and is conditionally independent of channel inputs or outputs at other times. A channel which is discrete and memoryless is denoted as a DMC. A channel for which $\mathcal{X} = \{0, 1\}$ (or some other binary-valued alphabet) is referred to as a binary DMC, or B-DMC. In this chapter, work on polar codes is largely restricted to B-DMCs.

Let $W : \mathcal{X} \to \mathcal{Y}$ denote a B-DMC, where the input alphabet is $\mathcal{X} = \{0, 1\}$ and $\mathcal{Y}$ is an output alphabet depending on the channel. For example, for a binary erasure channel (BEC), $\mathcal{Y} = \{0, 1, ?\}$. Channel transition probabilities are denoted as $W(y|x)$ for $x \in \mathcal{X}, y \in \mathcal{Y}$. The notation W^N (with

---

[1] Readers interested in one-based indexing may refer to [16].

superscripted N) is used to denote N uses of (or copies of) the channel, with $W^N : \mathcal{X}^N \to \mathcal{Y}^N$. Due to the memoryless nature of the channels,

$$W^N(y_0^{N-1}|x_0^{N-1}) = \prod_{i=0}^{N-1} W(y_i|x_i).$$

Definition 17.1 A B-DMC $W : \mathcal{X} \to \mathcal{Y}$ is *symmetric* if there exists a permutation $\pi : \mathcal{Y} \to \mathcal{Y}$ such that $\pi = \pi^{-1}$ and $W(y|0) = W(\pi(y)|1)$ for all $y \in \mathcal{Y}$. □

Examples of symmetric channels include the binary symmetric channel and the BEC.

For a symmetric channel $W : \mathcal{X} \to \mathcal{Y}$, with $X \in \mathcal{X}$ and $Y \in \mathcal{Y}$, denote the mutual information as $I(X;Y)$ as $I(W)$. For a binary symmetric channel with symmetric probabilities on the input $P(X = 0) = P(X = 1) = \frac{1}{2}$, the mutual information is (see (1.38))

$$I(W) = \sum_{y \in \mathcal{Y}} \sum_{x \in \mathcal{X}} \frac{1}{2} W(y|x) \log \frac{W(y|x)}{\frac{1}{2} W(y|0) + \frac{1}{2} W(y|1)}. \tag{17.1}$$

Recall that for symmetric channels with equiprobable inputs — as in this case — this mutual information is the channel capacity (see (1.41)).

The uncoded input (random) bits will be denoted as $(U_0, \ldots, U_{N-1}) = U_0^{N-1}$, with realizations $(u_0, \ldots, u_{N-1}) = u_0^{N-1}$ which are coded using a linear code to produce the bits $(x_0, \ldots, x_{N-1}) = x_0^{N-1}$. These code bits are conveyed through the channel to produce measurements $y_0, \ldots, y_{N-1} = y_0^{N-1}$. The input bits are assumed to be binary, independent, identically distributed with equal probability.

17.3 Channel Polarization, $N = 2$ Channel

Channel polarization constructs out of N independent copies of a B-DMC W (or N independent uses of a single channel) another set of N channels that exhibit a *polarization effect*, which is that as N becomes large the set of capacities of the synthesized channels tend either toward 0 or 1 for almost all of the synthetic channels.

In this section, we consider in detail the case when $N = 2$. Despite its apparent simplicity, this case uncovers many of the issues that surface for larger values of N. Specifically, we consider the following aspects of the coding problem for the $N = 2$ case:

- Encoding and the encoding matrix (Section 17.3.1).
- The channels synthesized by the polarization process via channel combining and channel splitting, and the mutual information associated with these channels (Section 17.3.2).
- The transition probabilities associated with these channels (Section 17.3.3).
- An example using BECs (Section 17.3.4).
- Successive cancellation decoding (Section 17.3.5).
- Using the polarized channels for improved coded performance (Section 17.3.7).

In later sections these issues will be extended to the case that $N > 2$.

17.3.1 Encoding

With $N = 2$ copies of W, the input bits are u_0 and u_1. The input bits are encoded into bits x_0 and x_1 by (see Figure 17.3(a))

$$\begin{aligned} x_0 &= u_0 \oplus u_1 \\ x_1 &= u_1, \end{aligned} \tag{17.2}$$

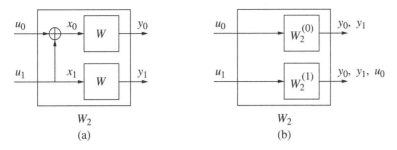

Figure 17.3: First stage of the construction of the polar transform. (a) The basic building block; (b) representation in terms of the channels $W_2^{(0)}$ and $W_2^{(1)}$.

where $\oplus$ denotes addition in $GF(2)$. This transformation is invertible, since given x_0 and x_1,

$$u_0 = x_0 \oplus x_1$$
$$u_1 = x_1.$$

The codeword (x_0, x_1) is transmitted through the channels W^2, with channel outputs (y_0, y_1). This structure, comprising coding and channel transmission, creates the channel

$$W_2 : u_0, u_1 \mapsto y_0, y_1.$$

(The subscript on W_2 denotes the synthesized channel.)

The encoding operation in (17.2) can be expressed in terms of an $\mathbb{F}_2$ generator matrix

$$G_2 = \begin{bmatrix} 1 & 0 \\ 1 & 1 \end{bmatrix}$$

with encoding as $\mathbf{x} = \mathbf{u}G_2$, where $\mathbf{u} = \begin{bmatrix} u_0 & u_1 \end{bmatrix}$ is a row vector. For later use, this matrix will also be referred to as F,

$$F = \begin{bmatrix} 1 & 0 \\ 1 & 1 \end{bmatrix}. \tag{17.3}$$

17.3.2 Synthetic Channels and Mutual Information

Since X_0 and X_1 are independent, the mutual information between the joint channel input X_0, X_1 and the joint channel output Y_0, Y_1 is

$$I(X_0, X_1; Y_0, Y_1) = 2I(X_0; Y_0) = 2I(W). \tag{17.4}$$

Since X_0, X_1 is in one-to-one invertible correspondence with U_0, U_1,

$$I(X_0, X_1; Y_0, Y_1) = I(U_0, U_1; Y_0, Y_1). \tag{17.5}$$

Recall that the chain rule for information is (1.40)

$$I(X_1, \ldots, X_n; Y) = \sum_{i=1}^{n} I(X_i; Y | X_{i-1}, X_{i-2}, \ldots, X_1).$$

As applied to (17.5), the chain rule indicates that

$$I(U_0, U_1; Y_0, Y_1) = I(U_0; Y_0, Y_1) + I(U_1; Y_0, Y_1 | U_0). \tag{17.6}$$

Recalling that (see (1.39))

$$I(U_1; Y_0, Y_1 | U_0) = H(U_1 | U_0) - H(U_1 | Y_0, Y_1, U_0),$$

since U_0 and U_1 are independent, the second term of (17.6) can be written as $I(U_1; Y_0, Y_1, U_0)$, so that

$$I(U_0, U_1; Y_0, Y_1) = I(U_0; Y_0, Y_1) + I(U_1; Y_0, Y_1, U_0) \qquad \boxed{\begin{array}{c} \\ I(U_0, U_1; Y_0, Y_1) \!\!\!< \!\!\begin{array}{l} I(U_0; Y_0, Y_1) \\ I(U_0; Y_0, Y_1, U_0) \end{array} \end{array}} \tag{17.7}$$

Combining this with (17.4),

$$2I(W) = \underbrace{I(U_0; Y_0, Y_1)}_{W_2^{(0)} \text{channel}} + \underbrace{I(U_1; Y_0, Y_1, U_0)}_{W_2^{(1)} \text{channel}}. \tag{17.8}$$

The first term on the right represents the mutual information on some channel having input U_0 and output (Y_0, Y_1). The second term on the right represents the mutual information on some channel having input U_1 and output (Y_0, Y_1, U_0). The first of these channels is denoted as $W_2^{(0)}$ and the second of these channels is denoted as $W_2^{(1)}$. That is,

$$\begin{aligned} W_2^{(0)} &: U_0 \mapsto (Y_0, Y_1) \\ W_2^{(1)} &: U_1 \mapsto (Y_0, Y_1, U_0). \end{aligned} \tag{17.9}$$

This is suggested by Figure 17.3(b). The mutual information for these channels is denoted $I(W_2^{(0)})$ and $I(W_2^{(1)})$, where

$$I(W_2^{(0)}) = I(U_0; Y_0, Y_1) \quad \text{and} \quad I(W_2^{(1)}) = I(U_1; Y_0, Y_1, U_0).$$

The channels $W_2^{(0)}$ and W_2^1 are "synthetic" channels, produced as a result of the linear operations on the inputs and the actual channels used. These channels are sometimes referred to as *bit channels*. $W_2^{(0)}$ and $W_2^{(1)}$ are "split" from the combined channel W^2, so the perception of these channels from W^2 is called the *splitting phase*. It should be understood that the two diagrams in Figure 17.3 are simply two representations for exactly the same thing, based on the equivalence in (17.7). Thus, the encoding of the $W_2^{(0)}$ and $W_2^{(1)}$ channels is performed as in Figure 17.3(a). The result of this encoding can be considered to result in the channels in Figure 17.3(b).

In terms of input and output spaces, recall that $\mathcal{X} = \{0, 1\}$ denotes the input space, and $\mathcal{Y}$ denotes the output space, with $W : \mathcal{X} \to \mathcal{Y}$. Then from (17.9),

$$\begin{aligned} W_2^{(0)} &: \mathcal{X} \to \mathcal{Y}^2 \\ W_2^{(1)} &: \mathcal{X} \to \mathcal{Y}^2 \times \mathcal{X}. \end{aligned}$$

The outputs of the channels are considered to be vector outputs, from $\mathcal{Y}^2$ in the case of $W_2^{(0)}$, and from $\mathcal{Y}^2 \times \mathcal{X}$ in the case of $W_2^{(1)}$. As the number of channels N increases, the size of the vector output increases as well. The mutual information of interest between channel input and channel output is between the scalar input $u_i \in \mathcal{X}$ and the vector output of the respective channel.

Notation note: Later, when we generalize to more than $N = 2$ channels, we will talk about the synthetic channels $W_N^{(i)}$, where $0 \le i < N$. When i is thought of as an integer, it will be enclosed in parentheses. It will also be convenient at times to express i in binary, as in $3 = 011_2$. When the upper index is expressed in binary, it is not enclosed in parentheses. We may thus write $W_8^{(3)} = W_8^{011}$. When the binary index is used, the subscript N may not be used, since it can be inferred by the number of bits n in the upper index, and $N = 2^n$. Obviously for $N = 2$ and $i = 0$ or $i = 1$ there is no distinction between the integer representation and the binary notation.

The W channel has $I(W) = I(U_1; Y_1)$. The $W_2^{(1)}$ channel with $I(W_2^{(1)}) = I(U_1; Y_0, Y_1, U_0)$ has input U_1 and output Y_1 and it has additional outputs U_0, Y_0, which cannot decrease the amount of information conveyed by the channel. Thus,

$$I(W_2^{(1)}) \geq I(W). \tag{17.10}$$

In light of (17.8), it must be the case that $I(W_2^{(0)}) \leq I(W)$. Combining these together,

$$\boxed{I(W_2^{(0)}) \leq I(W) \leq I(W_2^{(1)}).} \tag{17.11}$$

This inequality embodies the concept of channel polarization: one of the synthesized bit channels has higher mutual information than the other one. As we will see, this polarization tendency is amplified as the basic encoding building block is recursively applied.

The nature of these synthetic channels merits some discussion. The variables y_0 and y_1 are the measured outputs of real channels. The channel $W_2^{(0)} : U_0 \mapsto (Y_0, Y_1)$ is a "bonafide" channel: u_0 is input to a channel, and observations $Y_0 = y_0$ and $Y_1 = y_1$ are available from the channel. By contrast, the channel $W_2^{(1)} : U_1 \mapsto Y_0, Y_1, U_0$ is conceptually more problematic, since $U_0 = u_0$ is not actually observed at the receiver (being an input to the coding system). The $W_2^{(1)}$ channel can by synthesized, however, by first processing the output of $W_2^{(0)}$ to obtain an estimate $\hat{u}_0$ of u_0. This is used to synthesize the channel $W_2^{(1)}$ with outputs $y_0, y_1, \hat{u}_0$.

How does the use of $\hat{u}_0$ in this synthetic receiver compare with the performance obtained if u_0 were actually known in forming the $W_2^{(1)}$ channel? To explore this, consider two receivers, a "genie-aided receiver," that is, a conceptual receiver with more information than is physically possible, and an "implementable" receiver, which only uses received values y_0 and y_1. We will show that these two receivers have identical *block error* performance.

The genie-aided receiver works as follows: The receiver first computes an estimate $\tilde{u}_0$ as a function ϕ_0 of the W_0^0 channel outputs (for some appropriate decoder function ϕ_0):

$$\tilde{u}_0 = \phi_0(y_0, y_1).$$

Following this, the genie provides the true value u_0, and the genie-aided receiver then computes an estimate $\tilde{u}_1$ as a function of the W_2^1 channel outputs:

$$\tilde{u}_1 = \phi_1(y_0, y_1, u_0).$$

In determining the probability of error, the detected symbol $\tilde{u}_0$ and the genie-aided detected symbol $\tilde{u}_1$ are used.

The implementable receiver, on the other hand, first estimates u_0 as

$$\hat{u}_0 = \phi_0(y_0, y_1).$$

The implementable receiver then estimates u_1 by

$$\hat{u}_1 = \phi_1(y_0, y_1, \hat{u}_0).$$

The symbols $\hat{u}_0$ and $\hat{u}_1$ are used to determine the probability of error.

The probability of decoding a block correctly is the probability that $P((\tilde{u}_0, \tilde{u}_1) = (u_0, u_1))$ in the genie-aided case and $P((\hat{u}_0, \hat{u}_1) = (u_0, u_1))$ in the implementable case. Since the implementable receiver uses only an estimate of u_0, it would seem the genie-aided receiver should exhibit better performance. But as we show, they exhibit the same probability of block decoder error.

- Suppose the genie-aided receiver correctly detects u_0 (so $\tilde{u}_0 = u_0$). Then the probability of a *block* decoder error $P((\tilde{u}_0, \tilde{u}_1) \neq (u_0, u_1))$ is the probability $P(\tilde{u}_1 \neq u_1)$.

  In the case that the implementable receiver correctly detects u_0, so $\hat{u}_0 = u_0$, the probability of the block error for the implementable receiver is the probability $P(\hat{u}_1 \neq u_1)$.

- If the genie-aided receiver incorrectly estimates u_0, so $\tilde{u}_0 \neq u_0$, then a block error is already committed, so $P((\tilde{u}_0, \tilde{u}_1) \neq (u_0, u_1)) = P(\tilde{u}_0 \neq u_0)$, the probability of this incorrect estimate.

  The same holds for the implementable receiver.

Thus, the synthesized channels $W_2^{(0)}$ and $W_2^{(1)}$ can be regarded as true channels for the purposes of analysis. For implementation, of course, the implementable receivers are used.

17.3.3 Synthetic Channel Transition Probabilities

The synthetic channel transition probabilities are the transition probabilities for the synthetic channels $W_2^{(0)}$ and $W_2^{(1)}$, or, more generally, for the channels $W_N^{(i)}$, $0 \leq i < N$. Understanding these probabilities will help explain the channel polarization, and will be used in the likelihood functions used for decoding.

Collectively the pair of channels $(W_2^{(0)}, W_2^{(1)})$ is denoted as $W_2(y_0, y_1 | u_0, u_1)$. The transition probability for this joint channel can be written as

$$
\begin{aligned}
W_2(y_0, y_1 | u_0, u_1) &= W^2(y_0, y_1 | (u_0, u_1) G_2) = W^2(y_0, y_1 | (u_0 \oplus u_1, u_1)) \\
&= W(y_0 | u_0 \oplus u_1) W(y_1 | u_1),
\end{aligned}
\tag{17.12}
$$

where $W(y|x)$ denotes the transition probability for the channel W, and where the last equality follows because the channel W is memoryless. The synthetic channel probabilities are $W_2^{(0)}(y_0, y_1 | u_0)$ and $W_2^{(1)}(y_0, y_1, u_0 | u_1)$. These transition probabilities are computed using the laws of probability (assuming that the bits are equally likely to be 0 or 1) as

$$
\begin{aligned}
W_2^{(0)}(y_0, y_1 | u_0) &= \sum_{u_1 \in \mathcal{X}} W_2(y_0, y_1 | u_0, u_1) P(u_1) = \frac{1}{2} \sum_{u_1 \in \mathcal{X}} W_2(y_0, y_1 | u_0, u_1) \\
W_2^{(1)}(y_0, y_1, u_0 | u_1) &= W_2(y_0, y_1 | u_0, u_1) P(u_0) = \frac{1}{2} W_2(y_0, y_1 | u_0, u_1),
\end{aligned}
\tag{17.13}
$$

which can be written using (17.12) as

$$
\begin{aligned}
W_2^{(0)}(y_0, y_1 | u_0) &= \frac{1}{2} \sum_{u_1 \in \mathcal{X}} W(y_0 | u_0 \oplus u_1) W(y_1 | u_1) \\
W_2^{(1)}(y_0, y_1, u_0 | u_1) &= \frac{1}{2} W(y_0 | u_0 \oplus u_1) W(y_1 | u_1).
\end{aligned}
\tag{17.14}
$$

Abstractly, a pair of channels (W, W) has been transformed by (17.14) to a pair of new channels $(W_2^{(0)}, W_2^{(1)})$. This transformation is denoted as

$$
(W, W) \mapsto (W_2^{(0)}, W_2^{(1)}).
\tag{17.15}
$$

17.3.4 An Example with $N = 2$ Using the Binary Erasure Channel

The BEC is simple enough that the concepts introduced above can be explicitly computed. The results for the BEC will form a framework for more general results for other channels.

Consider the case when W is the BEC with erasure probability p, that is, W is BEC(p), so that $W : \mathcal{X} \to \mathcal{Y}$ can be described as

$$
Y = \begin{cases} X & \text{with probability } 1 - p \\ ? & \text{with probability } p, \end{cases}
$$

where ? denotes an erasure. This channel has capacity $I(W) = 1 - p$. The synthetic channels $W_2^{(0)}$ and $W_2^{(1)}$ are formed from this erasure channel. The $W_2^{(0)}$ channel with input u_0 has output

$$(y_0, y_1) = \begin{cases} (u_0 \oplus u_1, u_1) & \text{w.p. } (1-p)^2 & \text{(neither channel erases)} & \checkmark \text{(case 1)} \\ (?, u_1) & \text{w.p. } p(1-p) & \text{(the } y_0 \text{ channel erases)} & \textbf{✗} \text{(case 2)} \\ (u_0 \oplus u_1, ?) & \text{w.p. } (1-p)p & \text{(the } y_1 \text{ channel erases)} & \textbf{✗} \text{(case 3)} \\ (?, ?) & \text{w.p. } p^2 & \text{(both channels erase)} & \textbf{✗} \text{(case 4)}. \end{cases}$$

A check $\checkmark$ denotes a successful transmission from which both u_0 and u_1 can be recovered (a successful block transmission) and a $\textbf{✗}$ denotes an erasure.

- In case 1, from y_1 the input u_1 is available, from which u_0 can be extracted from $u_0 = y_0 \oplus y_1$.
- In case 2, u_0 cannot be recovered — the information is erased.
- In case 3, neither u_0 nor u_1 can be recovered — the information is erased.
- And, obviously, in case 4 the information is erased.

Collectively across the outputs (y_0, y_1) there is no erasure with probability $(1-p)^2$ and there is an erasure of some sort with probability $1 - (1-p)^2 = 2p - p^2$. We denote the probability of erasure for this channel $W_2^{(0)}$ (with the block output) as $p_2^{(0)} = 2p - p^2$. That is, $W_2^{(0)}$ is a BEC($p_2^{(0)}$) channel. Let $g(p)$ denote this function:

$$p_2^{(0)} = g(p) = 2p - p^2. \tag{17.16}$$

For $p \in (0, 1)$ (specifically, $p \neq 0$ or 1), $2p - p^2 > p$. This confirms that $I(W_2^{(0)}) < I(W)$.

Considering now the synthetic channel $W_2^{(1)}$ with input u_1, the possible outputs at the genie-aided receiver are

$$(y_0, y_1, u_0) = \begin{cases} (u_0 \oplus u_1, u_1, u_0) & \text{w. p. } (1-p)^2 & \text{(neither channel erases)} & \checkmark \text{(case 1)} \\ (?, u_1, u_0) & \text{w.p. } p(1-p) & \text{(} y_0 \text{ channel erases)} & \checkmark \text{(case 2)} \\ (u_0 \oplus u_1, ?, u_0) & \text{w.p. } (1-p)p & \text{(} y_1 \text{ channel erases)} & \checkmark \text{(case 3)} \\ (?, ?, u_0) & \text{w.p. } p^2 & \text{(both channels erase)} & \textbf{✗} \text{(case 4)}. \end{cases}$$

Because the genie-aided receiver provides u_0, it is possible to recover (u_0, u_1) in all cases except case 4. The probability of an erasure on the block is thus p^2. Thus, $W_2^{(1)}$ is a BEC channel with probability of erasure $p_2^{(1)} = p^2$. Let $h(p)$ denote the function

$$p_2^{(1)} = h(p) = p^2. \tag{17.17}$$

Since $p_2^{(1)} = p^2 \leq p$ (see Figure 17.4) and $I(W_2^{(1)}) = 1 - p_2^{(1)}$, this confirms the inequality in (17.10) that $I(W_2^{(1)}) > I(W)$. The inequality is strict unless $p = 0$ or 1, so that in all interesting channels, the synthetic channel $W_2^{(1)}$ improves performance compared to the channel W.

17.3.5 Successive Cancellation Decoding

The first decoding algorithm proposed for polar codes is called *successive cancellation* (SC). The basic idea is that bits are decoded in a particular order and previously estimated bits are used in the likelihood computation of new bits.

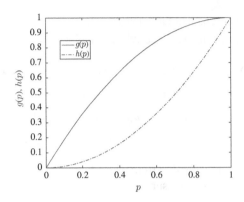

Figure 17.4: $g(p)$ and $h(p)$ for $p \in [0, 1]$, showing that $g(p) > h(p)$.

The basic computations of bit likelihoods are similar to those used for decoding LDPC codes using log-likelihood ratios (LLRs), as discussed in Section 15.4.1. However, to make a stand-alone presentation and to put the notation in the context of this chapter, the concepts are reviewed here.

The decoding is based on likelihood ratios for the different channels. Consider first the channel $W_2^{(0)}$, with transition probabilities $W_2^{(0)}(y_0, y_1 | u_0)$. Let

$$\lambda_2^{(0)}(y_0, y_1) = \frac{W_2^{(0)}(y_0, y_1 | u_0 = 0)}{W_2^{(0)}(y_0, y_1 | u_0 = 1)} \tag{17.18}$$

denote a likelihood ratio for the bit u_0 as a function of the received values (y_0, y_1). It will be convenient to deal with a log likelihood ratio

$$L_2^{(0)}(y_0, y_1) = \log \lambda_2^{(0)}(y_0, y_1) = \log \frac{W_2^{(0)}(y_0, y_1 | u_0 = 0)}{W_2^{(0)}(y_0, y_1 | u_0 = 1)}. \tag{17.19}$$

Then the decision about u_0 is formulated according to

$$\hat{u}_0 = \begin{cases} 0 & L_2^{(0)}(y_0, y_1) \geq 0 \\ 1 & L_2^{(0)}(y_0, y_1) < 0 \end{cases} \stackrel{\triangle}{=} \phi_0(y_0, y_1).$$

Note that, since $W_2^{(0)}$ is considered to have output (y_0, y_1), this decision is based on both channel observations, not just the channel output y_0. Computing the log-likelihood ratio is discussed below.

For the $W_2^{(1)}$ channel, the log-likelihood ratio is

$$L_2^{(1)}(y_0, y_1, u_0) = \log \frac{W_2^{(1)}(y_0, y_1, u_0 | u_1 = 0)}{W_2^{(1)}(y_0, y_1, u_0 | u_1 = 1)}. \tag{17.20}$$

Note that this likelihood ratio depends on u_0. In successive cancellation decoding, the u_0 that is used is the $\hat{u}_0$ obtained from the likelihood ratio in the first step. As N becomes large, a reliable decision for u_0 is highly probable, so it is reasonable to use it in following computations. The decision about u_1 is formulated as

$$\hat{u}_1 = \begin{cases} 0 & L_2^{(1)}(y_0, y_1, \hat{u}_0) \geq 0 \\ 1 & L_2^{(1)}(y_0, y_1, \hat{u}_1) < 0 \end{cases} \stackrel{\triangle}{=} \phi_1(y_0, y_1, \hat{u}_0).$$

17.3.5.1 Log-Likelihood Ratio Computations

We now consider how to compute the LLRs in (17.19) and (17.20). The conditioning can be turned around using Bayes rule and the assumed equiprobable nature of the bits. From (17.18), write

$$\lambda_2^{(0)}(y_0, y_1) = \frac{W_2^{(0)}(y_0, y_1 | u_0 = 0)}{W_2^{(0)}(y_0, y_1 | u_0 = 1)} = \frac{P(u_0 = 0 | y_0, y_1) P(y_0, y_1) / P(u_0 = 0)}{P(u_0 = 1 | y_0, y_1) P(y_0, y_1) / P(u_0 = 1)}$$

$$= \frac{P(u_0 = 0 | y_0, y_1)}{P(u_0 = 1 | y_0, y_1)}.$$

Consider the basic building block shown in Figure 17.3(a). From this encoding structure, reading left to right,

$$x_0 = u_0 \oplus u_1$$

$$x_1 = u_1.$$

These equations can be turned around as

$$u_0 = x_0 \oplus x_1$$

$$u_1 = u_0 \oplus x_0.$$

We first obtain the likelihood of u_0 and corresponding estimate $\hat{u}_0$ based on channel-corrupted measurements of x_0 and x_1. Assuming that the input bits are equiprobable, the log-likelihood ratio for x_i conditioned on its channel observation y_i is

$$\log \frac{P(x_i = 0 | y_i)}{P(x_i = 1 | y_i)} = \log \frac{W(y_i | x_i = 0)}{W(y_i | x_i = 1)} \triangleq L_{y_i}, \tag{17.21}$$

and turning that around,

$$P(x_i = 0 | y_i) = \frac{e^{L_{y_i}}}{1 + e^{L_{y_i}}} \quad P(x_i = 1 | y_i) = \frac{1}{1 + e^{L_{y_i}}} \tag{17.22}$$

Since $u_0 = x_0 \oplus x_1$ and the channel is memoryless, the probability $P(u_0 = 0 | y_0, y_1)$ is

$$P(u_0 = 0 | y_0, y_1) = P(x_0 \oplus x_1 = 0 | y_0, y_1)$$

$$= P(x_0 = 0 | y_0, y_1) P(x_1 = 0 | y_0, y_1) + P(x_0 = 1 | y_0, y_1) P(x_1 = 1 | y_0, y_1). \tag{17.23}$$

Using the probabilities in terms of the LLRs in (17.22),

$$P(u_0 = 0 | y_0, y_1) = \frac{e^{L_{y_0}} e^{L_{y_1}}}{(1 + e^{L_{y_0}})(1 + e^{L_{y_1}})} + \frac{1}{(1 + e^{L_{y_0}})(1 + e^{L_{y_1}})}$$

$$= \frac{1 + e^{L_{y_0} + L_{y_1}}}{(1 + e^{L_{y_0}})(1 + e^{L_{y_1}})}.$$

Similarly,

$$P(u_0 = 1 | y_0, y_1) = \frac{e^{L_{y_0}} + e^{L_{y_1}}}{(1 + e^{L_{y_0}})(1 + e^{L_{y_1}})}.$$

The log-likelihood ratio for u_0 is thus

$$L_2^{(0)}(y_0, y_1) = \log \frac{P(u_0 = 0 | y_0, y_1)}{P(u_0 = 1 | y_0, y_1)} = \log \frac{1 + e^{L_{y_0} + L_{y_1}}}{e^{L_{y_0}} + e^{L_{y_1}}}.$$

Readers familiar with LDPC codes will recognize that this is the computation that takes place at a check node in the LDPC decoding algorithm. This computation is important enough that it goes by several notations in the literature. It is sometimes called the chk function, and it may be computed using the tanh function. Since this computes the likelihood on the "upper" branch of the basic encoding operation, this will also be referred to as the "upper" decoder. Symbolically, since it does the decoding on the branch that involves a *sum* $x_0 = u_0 \oplus u_1$, we will also denote the computation as $s(L_{y_0}, L_{y_1})$. Another notation used is $\boxplus$. Collecting all these synonyms, we have

$$
\begin{aligned}
L_2^{(0)}(y_0, y_1) &= \log \frac{P(u_0 = 0|y_0, y_1)}{P(u_0 = 1|y_0, y_1)} = \log \frac{1 + e^{L_{y_0} + L_{y_1}}}{e^{L_{y_0}} + e^{L_{y_1}}} = \text{chk}(L_{y_0}, L_{y_1}) \\
&= 2 \tanh^{-1}(\tanh(L_{y_0}/2)\tanh(L_{y_1}/2)) = s(L_{y_0}, L_{y_1}) \\
&= L_{y_0} \boxplus L_{y_1}.
\end{aligned}
\tag{17.24}
$$

The computation is suggested by Figure 17.5(a). The brown lines indicate the path over which the information into the sum s flows, moving from right to left.

Once $L_2^{(0)}(y_0, y_1)$ is computed, an estimate of the bit u_0 is obtained as

$$
\hat{u}_0 = \begin{cases} 0 & L_2^{(0)}(y_0, y_1) \geq 0 \\ 1 & L_2^{(0)}(y_0, y_1) < 0. \end{cases}
$$

With $\hat{u}_0$ on hand (and assumed to be correct) there are two equations related to u_1,

$$
u_1 = x_1
$$

$$
u_1 = \hat{u}_0 \oplus x_0,
$$

observed in channel outputs y_1 and y_0, respectively. Then

$$
L_2^{(1)}(y_0, y_1|\hat{u}_0) \triangleq \log \frac{P(u_1 = 0|y_0, y_1, \hat{u}_0)}{P(u_1 = 1|y_0, y_1, \hat{u}_0)} = \log \frac{P(y_0, y_1|u_1 = 0, \hat{u}_0)}{P(y_0, y_1|u_1 = 1, \hat{u}_0)}
$$

(assuming equal priors)

$$
= \log \frac{P(y_0|u_1 = 0, \hat{u}_0)P(y_1|u_1 = 0, \hat{u}_0)}{P(y_0|u_1 = 1, \hat{u}_0)P(y_1|u_1 = 1, \hat{u}_0)}
$$

(memoryless channels)

$$
= \log \frac{P(\hat{u}_0 \oplus x_0 = 0|y_0)}{P(\hat{u}_0 \oplus x_0 = 1|y_0)} + \log \frac{P(x_1 = 0|y_1)}{P(x_1 = 1|y_1)}
$$

(assuming equal priors).

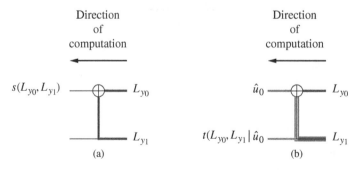

Figure 17.5: Successive cancellation on $N = 2$ channels. (a) Upper log-likelihood ratio computation; (b) lower log-likelihood ratio computation. Color versions of this plot are available at wileywebpage or https://gitghub/tkmoon/eccbook/colorpages

The second term is recognized as L_{y_1} from (17.21). The first term is

$$\log \frac{P(\hat{u}_0 \oplus x_0 = 0 | y_0)}{P(\hat{u}_0 \oplus x_0 = 1 | y_0)} = \begin{cases} L_{y_0} & \text{if } \hat{u}_0 = 0 \\ -L_{y_0} & \text{if } \hat{u}_0 = 1, \end{cases}$$

so that

$$L_2^{(1)}(y_0, y_1 | \hat{u}_0) = \begin{cases} L_{y_1} + L_{y_0} & \text{if } \hat{u}_0 = 0 \\ L_{y_1} - L_{y_0} & \text{if } \hat{u}_0 = 1. \end{cases}$$

This will be denoted variously as

$$L_2^{(1)}(y_0, y_1 | \hat{u}_0) = L_{y_1} \overset{\hat{u}_0}{\pm} L_{y_0} = L_{y_1} + L_{y_0}(1 - 2\hat{u}_0). \tag{17.25}$$

As a sum, this is analogous to the computation that takes place at the variable node of a log-likelihood-based LDPC decoder. Let $t(L_{y_0}, L_{y_1} | \hat{u}_0) = L_2^{(1)}$ be the log-likelihood ratio in (17.25). (The t may be suggested by the fact that u_1 goes straight *through* to x_1.) Since $L_2^{(1)}$ is on the lower branch, this is also referred to as the lower decoding. Thus, the *lower* computation computes $t(L_{y_0}, L_{y_1} | \hat{u}_0) = L_2^{(1)}$. The computation is portrayed in Figure 17.5(b). The brown lines indicate the path over which the channel likelihoods L_{y_0} and L_{y_1} are conveyed. From the upper computation, there is an estimate of the bit $\hat{u}_0$, portrayed with the green line. Then the likelihood produces the lower (t) output, conveyed on the cyan line. While visually this does introduce some confusion, because the lower line carries both likelihood information L_{y_1} as an input (brown) and the lower computation t as an output (cyan), the computation that is actually done is very simple.

17.3.5.2 Computing the Log-Likelihood Function with Lower Complexity

The chk (or ⊞ or tanh-rule) computation of (17.24) involves either tanh or logarithmic/exponential computations. In implementation, it is desirable to reduce the computational complexity. One way to do this is using an approximation:

$$x \boxplus y \approx \text{sign}(x)\text{sign}(y)\min(|x|, |y|). \tag{17.26}$$

The approximation is illustrated in Figure 17.6. The approximation is seen to be a piecewise linear/constant approximation to the decoding function. Using this approximation has a negligible effect on the code performance (see [392]).

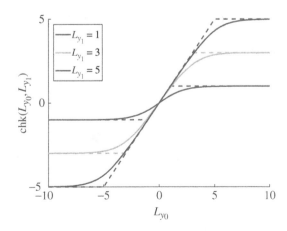

Figure 17.6: Comparison of tanh rule (solid lines) with (17.26) (dashed lines).

17.3.6 Tree Representation

The encoder for $N = 2$, shown in Figure 17.3(a) and repeated in Figure 17.7(a) can be represented as a tree. The inputs u_0 and u_1 are associated with nodes, indicated in black, and the adder and its associated parallel edge are combined into a single block, as shown in Figure 17.7(b). This block and its two connections (y_0 and y_1) are represented with a single node, indicated in black in Figure 17.7(c). The encoder is thus represented as a binary tree, whose leaf nodes correspond to the bits u_0 and u_1 and whose root node incorporates all the inputs or, more precisely, all the log-likelihood functions L_{y_i}. This tree is shown rotated with the root node at the top in Figure 17.7(d). In the decoding algorithm, each v node recursively performs a computation appropriate to its position in the tree and the sequence in the algorithm and sends a message to its children, first the left node then the right. Then, upon receiving messages from its children, it sends a message to its parent node.

For the $N = 2$ decoder, the sequence of steps is as follows:

- The root node, v in Figure 17.7(d), computes $L_{y_0} \boxplus L_{y_1}$ and sends this as the message to its left child:

$$\alpha_{v_l} = L_{y_0} \boxplus L_{y_1}.$$

- The left node v_l is in this case a leaf node. The computation at a leaf node is to determine the bit value based on the incoming message α_{v_l}. For a nonfrozen bit, this is done by quantizing the incoming message, that is, converting it to a bit value,

$$\hat{u}_0 = \begin{cases} 0 & \alpha_{v_l} \geq 0 \\ 1 & \alpha_{v_l} < 0. \end{cases}$$

  This estimated bit value is the message sent to the parent of v_l:

$$\beta_{v_l} = \hat{u}_0.$$

- The root node performs another computation, which is the likelihood in (17.25) and sends this to its right child:

$$\alpha_{v_r} = L_{y_1} + L_{y_0}(1 - 2\beta_{v_l}).$$

- The right node v_r is again a leaf node, which quantizes its incoming message α_{v_r}.

For $N = 2$, this completes the decoding.

From this perspective, the SC is seen to be a depth-first traversal of the tree representing the encoding operation, with likelihood messages sent leafward and bit messages sent rootward in the traversal.

The encoding diagram shows that there is an asymmetry, so that 1 bit is decoded before another in SC. By contrast, the abstraction of the tree representation hides the asymmetry, since all leaf nodes appear equivalent in the tree, but this asymmetry must be taken into account in the order in which the bits are decoded.

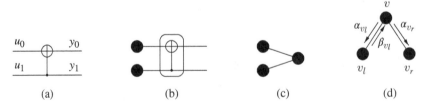

Figure 17.7: Tree representation of the encoding. (a) Encoder $N = 2$; (b) converting to a tree; (c) converted to a tree; (d) rotated with the root node at the top.

17.3.7 The Polar Coding Idea

Continuing the case when $N = 2$, we examine now the idea of polar coding. With this small value of N the details will not yet be clear, but the main idea can now be conveyed, with details to be fleshed out later. Based on the inequalities in (17.11), of the two synthetic channels $W_2^{(0)}$ and $W_2^{(1)}$, the $W_2^{(1)}$ channel, which carries information about u_1, is superior. A simple-minded rate 1/2 coding scheme can be devised as follows: Set u_0 to some arbitrary value $\bar{u}_0$ known to both transmitter and receiver. This bit is said to be *frozen*. Then encode the single bit u according to

$$\begin{bmatrix} x_0 & x_1 \end{bmatrix} = \begin{bmatrix} \bar{u}_0 & u \end{bmatrix} G_2$$

and transmit this two-component vector over the channel. Since this sends u through the more reliable $W_2^{(1)}$ channel, this transmits u more reliably than it would have been without coding, albeit at the cost of a rate 1/2 code.

At the decoder, the value of the frozen bits is known *a priori*, so it is not necessary to threshold the log-likelihood functions to decode them.

At this point, this does not seem like a reliable way to encode information. But we will see that as N increases, a fraction of the synthetic channels become increasingly reliable. Using only these reliable channels allows codewords, each of whose elements are transmitted using reliable channels, to be reliably transmitted.

Here, with $N = 2$, the only possible code rates are 1 (use both bits), $\frac{1}{2}$ (freeze 1 bit), and 0 (freeze both bits). But as we will see, as N increases, it becomes possible to finely tune the rate of the code. The ability to tune the rate is another advantage of polar codes compared to many other block codes.

In order to exploit the polar coding idea, it will be necessary to identify which of the N synthetic channels have high capacity. This is the *code design problem*, which is discussed in Section 17.6.

17.4 Channel Polarization, $N > 2$ Channels

We now show how to go from 2 to 4 channels, then describe the general construction to go from $N/2$ to N channels.

17.4.1 Channel Combining: Extension from $N / 2$ to N channels.

The next level of recursion is obtained by making two copies of the W_2 channel to create the channel $W_4 : \mathcal{X}^4 \to \mathcal{Y}^4$.

- Start with two copies of W_2, with inputs now called v_0 through v_3 and outputs y_0 through y_3, as shown in Figure 17.8(a).
- Combine the two $W_2^{(0)}$ channels (the inputs to the $\oplus$ operators of the W_2s) using inputs v_0 and v_2 to create the "0" channel and the "1" channel of $W_2^{(0)}$, as shown in Figure 17.8(b). This gives channels which can be denoted as

$$(W_2^0)^0 = W_4^{00} = W_4^{(0)} \quad \text{and} \quad (W_2^0)^1 = W_4^{01} = W_4^{(1)}.$$

The $W_4^{(0)}$ channel acts according to

$$W_4^{(0)} : u_0 \mapsto y_0, y_1, y_2, y_3 \tag{17.27}$$

and the $W_4^{(1)}$ channel acts according to

$$W_4^{(1)} : u_1 \mapsto y_0, y_1, y_2, y_3, u_0. \tag{17.28}$$

- Combine the two $W_2^{(1)}$ channels (the inputs of the W_2s that don't have $\oplus$ operators) with inputs v_1 and v_3 to create the "0" and "1" channels of $W_2^{(1)}$, as shown in Figure 17.8(c). This gives channels which can be denoted as

$$(W_2^1)^0 = W_4^{10} = W_4^{(2)} \quad \text{and} \quad (W_2^1)^1 = W_4^{11} = W_4^{(3)}.$$

The $W_4^{(2)}$ and $W_4^{(3)}$ channels act according to

$$W_4^{(2)} : u_2 \mapsto y_0, y_1, v_0, y_2, y_3, v_2 \tag{17.29}$$

$$W_4^{(3)} : u_3 \mapsto y_0, y_1, v_0, y_2, y_3, v_2, u_2. \tag{17.30}$$

The pair (v_0, v_2) is informationally equivalent to knowing (u_0, u_1). Making this substitution in (17.30) and reordering the sequence of outputs, we have

$$W_4^{(2)} : u_2 \mapsto y_0, y_1, y_2, y_3, u_0, u_1$$

$$W_4^{(3)} : u_3 \mapsto y_0, y_1, y_2, y_3, u_0, u_1, u_2.$$

This completes the construction of the W_4 channel, as indicated in Figure 17.8(c).

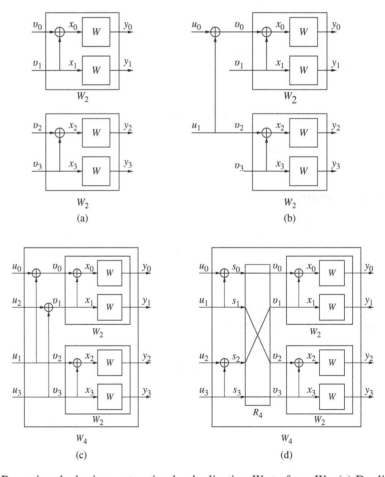

Figure 17.8: Repeating the basic construction by duplicating W_2 to form W_4. (a) Duplication of W_2; (b) creation of $W_4^{(0)}$ and $W_4^{(1)}$; (c) creation of $W_4^{(2)}$ and $W_4^{(3)}$; (d) reordering the inputs of W_4.

There is a natural representation of the exponents in the binary and integer representation, for example, $(W_2^0)^0 = W_4^{00} = W_4^{(0)}$. The least significant bit (on the right) indicates the most recent synthetic channel created.

As drawn in Figure 17.8(c), the inputs are in the order u_0, u_2, u_1, u_3. These can be redrawn in order as shown in Figure 17.8(d). In this case, there is a permutation block R_4 which reorders the inputs. Denoting the inputs to the permutation as $s_0, \ldots, s_3$ and the outputs as $v_0, \ldots, v_3$, the permutation is

$$s_0 \leftrightarrow v_0 \quad s_1 \leftrightarrow v_2 \quad s_2 \leftrightarrow v_1 \quad s_3 \leftrightarrow v_3. \tag{17.31}$$

Another representation of the encoder in Figure 17.9 has all the inputs in order, but interchanges the initial $\oplus$s and R_4 to place all the $\oplus$s together. This involves another permutation block B_4 which turns out in the general case to be a bit-reverse permutation.

The encoding operation can be written in terms of a generator matrix. This will be developed in two steps. First, consider the vector of values after the bit reverse permutation. Then

$$(x_0, x_1, x_2, x_3) = (u_0, u_2, u_1, u_3) \begin{bmatrix} 1 & 0 & 0 & 0 \\ 1 & 1 & 0 & 0 \\ 1 & 0 & 1 & 0 \\ 1 & 1 & 1 & 1 \end{bmatrix}.$$

This matrix can be written as the Kronecker product of the F matrix of (17.3) with itself, denoted $F^{\otimes 2}$. To put the u_i values in the order there is a permutation matrix, B_4. The overall encoding operation is

$$(x_0, x_1, x_2, x_3) = (u_0, u_1, u_2, u_3) \begin{bmatrix} 1 & 0 & 0 & 0 \\ 0 & 0 & 1 & 0 \\ 0 & 1 & 0 & 0 \\ 0 & 0 & 0 & 1 \end{bmatrix} \begin{bmatrix} 1 & 0 & 0 & 0 \\ 1 & 1 & 0 & 0 \\ 1 & 0 & 1 & 0 \\ 1 & 1 & 1 & 1 \end{bmatrix} = (u_0, u_1, u_2, u_3)(B_4 F^{\otimes 2})$$

$$= (u_0, u_1, u_2, u_3) \begin{bmatrix} 1 & 0 & 0 & 0 \\ 1 & 0 & 1 & 0 \\ 1 & 1 & 0 & 0 \\ 1 & 1 & 1 & 1 \end{bmatrix} \overset{\triangle}{=} (u_0, u_1, u_2, u_3)G_4. \tag{17.32}$$

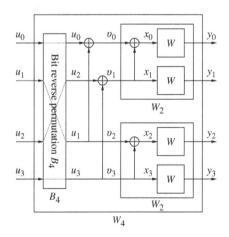

Figure 17.9: Another representation of W_4.

Generalizing now to arbitrary $N = 2^n$, the recursion to go from $W_{N/2}$ to W_N is shown in Figure 17.10(a). Two copies of the channel $W_{N/2}$ are used. Incoming bits are permuted by a permuter R_N. The input bits are added pairwise to form $s_{2i} = u_{2i} \oplus u_{2i+1}$. The odd-indexed values are $s_{2i+1} = u_{2i+1}$. The permutation operator R_N acts on s_0^{N-1} to produce $v_0^{N-1} = (s_0, s_2, \ldots, s_{N-2}, s_1, s_3, \ldots, s_{N-1})$. The encoding can also be written as shown in Figure 17.10(b). Based on the operations described in this figure, the encoder matrix is

$$G_N = R_N(F \otimes I_{N/2})(I_2 \otimes G_{N/2}).$$

By the properties of the Kronecker product (see Section 8.2.1),

$$G_N = R_N(F \otimes G_{N/2}).$$

Proceeding recursively using $G_{N/2} = R_{N/2}(F \otimes G_{N/4})$,

$$G_N = R_N(F \otimes (R_{N/2}(F \otimes G_{N/4})) = R_N(I_2 \otimes R_{N/2})(F^{\otimes 2} \otimes G_{N/4}),$$

where the latter follows from the Kronecker product theorem $(AC) \otimes (BD) = (A \otimes B)(C \otimes D)$ with $A = I_2$, $C = F$, $B = R_{N/2}$ and $D = F \otimes G_{N/4}$. Continuing, we find

$$G_N = B_N F^{\otimes n}, \tag{17.33}$$

where $F^{\otimes n}$ is the n-fold Kronecker product of F with itself, defined recursively as $F^{\otimes 1} = F$ and

$$F^{\otimes n} = \begin{bmatrix} F^{\otimes n-1} & \mathbf{0} \\ F^{\otimes n-1} & F^{\otimes n-1} \end{bmatrix} \tag{17.34}$$

and

$$B_N = R_N(I_2 \otimes B_{N/2}). \tag{17.35}$$

For example, the B_8 permutation matrix performs the following Permutations:

$$u_0 \leftrightarrow u_0 \quad u_1 \leftrightarrow u_4 \quad u_2 \leftrightarrow u_2 \quad u_3 \leftrightarrow u_6 \quad u_4 \leftrightarrow u_1 \quad u_5 \leftrightarrow u_5 \quad u_6 \leftrightarrow u_3 \quad u_7 \leftrightarrow u_7. \tag{17.36}$$

This permutation can be understood as follows. For an index j in u_j, express the index as an n-bit binary number. Then the permuted index is obtained from writing the binary number in bit-reversed order. Writing (17.36) in binary form,

$$u_{000} \leftrightarrow u_{000} \quad u_{001} \leftrightarrow u_{100} \quad u_{010} \leftrightarrow u_{010} \quad u_{011} \leftrightarrow u_{110}$$

$$u_{100} \leftrightarrow u_{001} \quad u_{101} \leftrightarrow u_{101} \quad u_{110} \leftrightarrow u_{011} \quad u_{111} \leftrightarrow u_{111}.$$

In Appendix 17.A it is shown that, in general, B_N is the bit-reversal permutation matrix and furthermore that

$$B_N F^{\otimes n} = F^{\otimes n} B_N.$$

Summarizing, the encoding operation can be expressed as

$$\boxed{x_0^{N-1} = (u_0^{N-1})B_N F^{\otimes n},}$$

where B_N is an N-bit bit-reverse permutation and $F^{\otimes n}$ is the n-fold Kronecker product defined by

$$F^{\otimes n} = F \otimes F^{\otimes n-1} \quad \text{with} \quad F^{\otimes 1} = F.$$

As is apparent from the structure shown in Figure 17.11, the encoder simply pushes data from left to right across the graph: there are $\log_2 N$ stages, each of which has $N/2$ adders in it, so the overall encoding complexity is $O(N \log_2 N)$.

The presence of the bit-reverse permutation matrix B_N obviously does not affect the distance properties of the code. Some implementations do not include it. When the bit-reverse permutation is not included, the encoder is said to be in *natural order*.

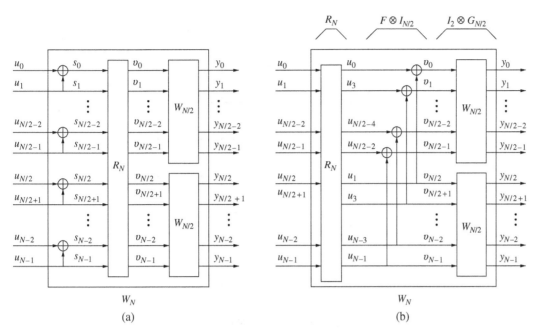

Figure 17.10: General recursion to go from two $W_{N/2}$ channels to W_N. (a) Basic form of general recursion to go from two $W_{N/2}$ channels to W_N; (b) alternative form for the recursion.

17.4.2 Pseudocode for Encoder for Arbitrary N

Algorithm 17.1 shows pseudocode for the $O(N \log_2 N)$-complexity encoder described above. It takes into account which bits are frozen (as discussed below) and performs the bit-reverse permutation.

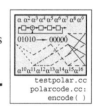

Algorithm 17.1 Polar Code Encoding

Function `PolarEncode`(u)
 % Encoding a binary message vector u of length K
 Input: u binary message vector of length K
1 Merge the information bits u_0^K into a message word $\tilde{u}_0^{N-1}$, setting the frozen bits to 0, in
   bit-reversed order
 % Compute $\tilde{u}_0^{N-1} F^{\otimes n}$ in place:
2 skipr $= 1$ % offset of RHS of adder equation, and number of addergroups
3 stepl $= 2$ % left index steps
4 ninaddergroup $= N/2$ % number of adders in group in current level
5 lindexstart $= 0$ % starting index of addergroup
6 **for** n1 $= 0, 1, \ldots, n - 1$ **do** for each level
7   **for** i2 $= 0, 1, \ldots,$ skipr $- 1$ **do**
8   lindex = lindexstart
9   **for** i1 $= 0, 1, \ldots,$ ninaddergroup $- 1$ **do**
10         $\tilde{u}[\text{lindex}] = \tilde{u}[\text{lindex}] \oplus \tilde{u}[\text{lindx} + \text{skipr}]$
11   lindx+ = stepl
12   **end**
13   lindexstart++
14   **end**
15   skipr $= 2 \cdot$ skipr
16   stepl $= 2 \cdot$ stepl
17   ninaddergruop = ninaddergroup/2
18   lindexstart $= 0$
19 **end**

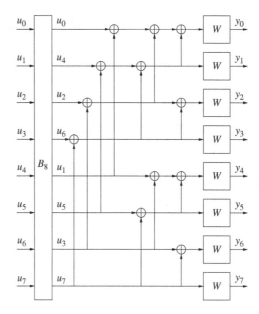

Figure 17.11: The channel W_8.

Figure 17.11 shows the channel combining for $N = 8$.

17.4.3 Transition Probabilities and Channel Splitting

The transition probabilities for the joint channels are expressed in terms of the iterated channel usage as

$$W_N(y_0^{N-1}|u_0^{N-1}) = W^N(y_0^{N-1}|u_0^{N-1}G_N).$$

In the case when $N = 4$, referring to Figure 17.9, since the two W_2 channels are independent, the joint transition probability for the W_4 channel is

$$W_4(y_0^3|u_0^3) = W_2(y_0, y_1|u_0 \oplus u_1, u_2 \oplus u_3)W_2(y_2, y_3|u_1, u_3). \qquad (17.37)$$

The conditioning argument in the first W_2 can be stacked up as

$$(u_0 \oplus u_1, u_2 \oplus u_3) = (u_0, u_2) \oplus (u_1, u_3).$$

On the right-hand side of this equation, since the indices in the first vector are even and the indices in the second vector are odd, this can be written as

$$(u_0 \oplus u_1, u_2 \oplus u_3) = u_{0,\text{even}}^3 \oplus u_{0,\text{odd}}^3.$$

Equation (17.37) can thus be written as

$$W_4(y_0^3|u_0^3) = W_2(y_0^1|u_{0,\text{even}}^3 \oplus u_{0,\text{odd}}^3)W_2(y_2^3|u_{0,\text{odd}}^3).$$

In general, following this model, referring to Figure 17.10, the transition probabilities for W_{2N} are

$$W_{2N}(y_0^{2N-1}|u_0^{2N-1}) = W_N(y_0^{N-1}|u_{0,\text{even}}^{N-1} \oplus u_{0,\text{odd}}^{N-1})W_N(y_N^{2N-1}|u_{0,\text{odd}}^{N-1}). \qquad (17.38)$$

We develop recursive expressions for the channel conditional probabilities for the synthetic channels $W_{2N}^{(i)}$ in terms of the probabilities for the channels $W_N^{(i)}$. These probabilities are used in decoding, and help explain the nature of polarization. Generalizing (17.13) to N channels, straightforward application of the laws of probability yields, for $0 \le i < N$,

$$
\begin{aligned}
W_N^{(i)}(y_0^{N-1}, u_0^{i-1} | u_i) &= \sum_{u_{i+1}^{N-1} \in \mathcal{X}^{N-1-i}} W_N(y_0^{N-1} | u_0^{N-1}) P(u_{\neg i}) \\
&= \frac{1}{2^{N-1}} \sum_{u_{i+1}^{N-1} \in \mathcal{X}^{N-1-i}} W_N(y_0^{N-1} | u_0^{N-1}).
\end{aligned}
\tag{17.39}
$$

In words, and somewhat more abstractly, this expression says that a normalized sum over bit sequences $u_{i+1}^{N-1} \in \mathcal{X}^{N-1-i}$ of $W_N(y_0^{N-1} | u_0^{N-1})$ gives a closed-form probability expression $W_N^{(i)}(y_0^{N-1}, u_0^{i-1} | u_i)$, where the probability is conditioned on the first bit u_i not summed out, and the summed probability is joint with the bits u_0^{i-1} prior to u_i. The argument y_0^{N-1} (whatever it may be) is not changed in the summation.

Example 17.2 When $N = 4$, (17.39) gives:

$$
i = 0 : \quad W_4^{(0)}(y_0^3 | u_0) = \frac{1}{2^{4-1}} \sum_{u_1^3 \in \mathcal{X}^3} W_4(y_0^3 | u_0^3)
$$

$$
i = 1 : \quad W_4^{(0)}(y_0^3, u_0 | u_1) = \frac{1}{2^{4-1}} \sum_{u_2^3 \in \mathcal{X}^2} W_4(y_0^3 | u_0^3)
$$

$$
i = 2 : \quad W_4^{(0)}(y_0^3, u_0^1 | u_2) = \frac{1}{2^{4-1}} \sum_{u_3 \in \mathcal{X}} W_4(y_0^3 | u_0^3)
$$

$$
i = 3 : \quad W_4^{(0)}(y_0^3, u_0^2 | u_3) = \frac{1}{2^{4-1}} W_4(y_0^3 | u_0^3).
$$

As i increases, the probability is a function jointly on "previous" symbols u_0^{i-1}. This will be an important aspect of successive cancellation decoding. $\qquad\square$

The recursive construction of W_{2N} provides for recursive computation of the channel transition probabilities, generalizing the relation in (17.14).

Theorem 17.3 *The probabilities $W_{2N}^{(2i)}$ and $W_{2N}^{(2i+1)}$ can be expressed in terms of the probabilities W_N^i as*

$$
W_{2N}^{(2i)}(y_0^{2N-1}, u_0^{2i-1} | u_{2i})
$$

$$
= \frac{1}{2} \sum_{u_{2i+1} \in \mathcal{X}} W_N^{(i)}(y_0^{N-1}, u_{0,even}^{2i-1} \oplus u_{0,odd}^{2i-1} | u_{2i} \oplus u_{2i+1}) W_N^{(i)}(y_N^{2N-1}, u_{0,odd}^{2i-1} | u_{2i+1})
\tag{17.40}
$$

$$
W_{2N}^{(2i+1)}(y_0^{2N-1}, u_0^{2i} | u_{2i+1})
$$

$$
= \frac{1}{2} W_N^{(i)}(y_0^{N-1}, u_{0,even}^{2i-1} \oplus u_{0,odd}^{2i-1} | u_{2i} \oplus u_{2i+1}) W_N^{(i)}(y_N^{2N-1}, u_{0,odd}^{2i-1} | u_{2i+1})
\tag{17.41}
$$

for $0 \le i < N$.

Proof For (17.40):

$$W_{2N}^{(2i)}(y_0^{2N-1}, u_0^{2i-1}|u_{2i}) = \frac{1}{2^{2N-1}} \sum_{u_{2i+1}^{2N-1} \in \mathcal{X}^{2(N-i)-1}} W_{2N}(y_0^{2N-1}|u_0^{2N-1})$$

(basic rules of probability)

$$= \frac{1}{2^{2N-1}} \sum_{u_{2i+1,even}^{2N-1}} \sum_{u_{2i+1,odd}^{2N-1}} W_N(y_0^{n-1}|u_{0,even}^{2N-1} \oplus u_{0,odd}^{2N-1}) W_N(y_N^{2N-1}|u_{0,odd}^{2N-1})$$

(using (17.38))

$$= \frac{1}{2} \sum_{u_{2i+1} \in \mathcal{X}} \sum_{u_{2i+2,odd}^{2N-1} \in \mathcal{X}^{N-1-i}} W_N(y_N^{2N-1}|u_{0,odd}^{2N-1})$$

$$+ \sum_{u_{2i+2,even}^{2N-1} \in \mathcal{X}^{N-1-i}} W_N(y_0^{N-1}|u_{0,even}^{2N-1} \oplus u_{0,odd}^{2N-1})$$

(split the indices of summation)

$$= (*).$$

Consider the final sum in (*), $\sum_{u_{2i+2,even}^{2N-1} \in \mathcal{X}^{N-1-i}} W_N(y_0^{N-1}|u_{0,even}^{2N-1} \oplus u_{0,odd}^{2N-1})$: For any fixed value of $u_{0,even}^{2N-1}$, as $u_{2i+2,odd}^{2N-1}$ ranges over $\mathcal{X}^{N-1-i}$, the conditioning quantity $u_{0,even}^{2N-1} \oplus u_{0,odd}^{2N-1}$ also ranges over $\mathcal{X}^{N-1-i}$. Comparing this result with (17.39), we see that the summation equals

$$\sum_{u_{2i+2,even}^{2N-1} \in \mathcal{X}^{N-1-i}} W_N(y_0^{N-1}|u_{0,even}^{2N-1} \oplus u_{0,odd}^{2N-1}) = W_N^{(i)}(y_0^{N-1}, u_{0,even}^{2i-1} \oplus u_{0,odd}^{2i-1}|u_{2i} \oplus u_{2i+1}).$$

Similarly, in the middle sum of (*), as $u_{2i+2,odd}^{2N-1}$ ranges over $\mathcal{X}^{N-1-i}$, (17.39) shows that this is equal to $W_N^i(y_N^{2N-1}, u_{0,odd}^{2i-1}|u_{2i})$.

For (17.41):

$$W_{2N}^{(2i+1)}(y_0^{2N-1}, u_0^{2i}|u_{2i+1}) = \frac{1}{2^{2N-1}} \sum_{u_{2i+2}^{2N-1} \in \mathcal{X}^{2(N-i)}} W_{2N}(y_0^{2N-1}|u_0^{2N-1})$$

$$= \frac{1}{2} \sum_{u_{2i+2,odd}^{2N-1} \in \mathcal{X}^{N-i}} \frac{1}{2^{N-1}} W_N(y_N^{2N-1}|u_{0,odd}^{2N-1})$$

$$\sum_{u_{2i+2}^{2N-1} \in \mathcal{X}^{N-i}} \frac{1}{2^{N-1}} W_N(y_0^{N-1}|u_{0,even}^{2N-1} \oplus u_{0,odd}^{2N-1}).$$

Applying (17.39) to the inner and outer summations yields (17.41). □

Example 17.4 Setting $N = 1$ in (17.40) and (17.41) yields

$$W_2^{(0)}(y_0^1|u_0) = \frac{1}{2} \sum_{u_1 \in \mathcal{X}} W_1^{(0)}(y_0|u_0 \oplus u_1) W_1^0(y_1|u_1)$$

$$W_2^{(1)}(y_0^1, u_0|u_1) = \frac{1}{2} W_1^{(0)}(y_0|u_0 \oplus u_1) W_1^{(0)}(y_1|u_1),$$

which is the same as (17.14).

When $N = 2$:

$$i = 0: \quad W_4^{(0)}(y_0^3|u_0) = \frac{1}{2} \sum_{u_1 \in \mathcal{X}} W_2^{(0)}(y_0^1|u_0 \oplus u_1) W_2^0(y_2^3|u_1)$$

$$i = 1: \quad W_4^{(2)}(y_0^3, u_0^1|u_2) = \frac{1}{2} \sum_{u_3 \in \mathcal{X}} W_2^{(1)}(y_0^1, u_0 \oplus u_1|u_2 \oplus u_3) W_2^{(1)}(y_2^3, u_1|u_3)$$

$$i = 0: \quad W_4^{(1)}(y_0^3, u_0|u_1) = \frac{1}{2} W_2^{(0)}(y_0^1, |u_0 \oplus u_1) W_2^{(0)}(y_2^3|u_1)$$

$$i = 1: \quad W_4^{(3)}(y_0^3, u_0^2|u_3) = \frac{1}{2} W_2^{(1)}(y_0^1, u_0 \oplus u_1|u_2 \oplus u_3) W_2^{(1)}(y_2^3, u_1|u_3).$$

$\square$

The formulas (17.40) and (17.41) are abstractly represented by the expression

$$(W_N^{(i)}, W_N^{(i)}) \mapsto (W_{2N}^{(2i)}, W_{2N}^{(2i+1)}),$$

which generalizes (17.15).

Figure 17.12 illustrates the channel construction process. Starting from a channel $W = W_1$ at level 0, each node $W_N^{(i)}$ in the tree gives birth to two nodes $W_{2N}^{(2i)}$ and $W_{2N}^{(2i+1)}$. In Figure 17.12, the node $W_N^{(i)}$ is also portrayed as $W^{b_1 b_2 \ldots b_n}$, where $b_1 b_2 \ldots b_n$ is the binary representation of i, and the length n of the sequence implicitly represents $N = 2^n$. Given a channel at level n at index $b_1 b_2 \ldots b_n$, the tree connects to a channel at level $n + 1$ at index $b_1 b_2 \ldots b_n 0$ on the upper branch, and to a channel at index $b_1 b_2 \ldots b_n 1$ on the lower branch. The root at level $n = 0$ is indexed by an empty sequence.

The decomposition into split channels $W_N^{(i)}$ can also be expressed in terms of information theory, generalizing the result in (17.7). For example, for $N = 4$, successively applying the chain rule of

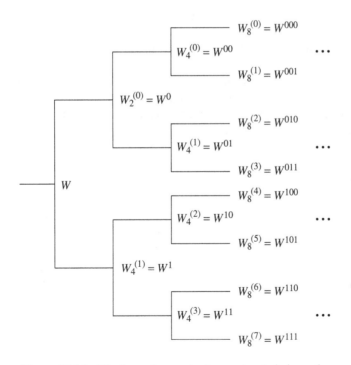

Figure 17.12: The tree of recursively constructed channels.

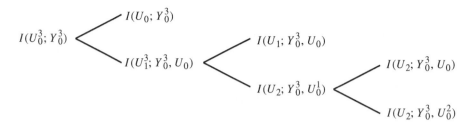

Figure 17.13: Tree decomposition of the information in the W_4 channels.

information to $I(U_0^3; Y_0^3)$ yields

$$
\begin{aligned}
I(U_0^3; Y_0^3) &= I(U_0; Y_0^3) + I(U_1^3; Y_0^3 | U_0) \\
&= I(U_0; Y_0^3) + I(U_1; Y_0^3 | U_0) + I(U_2^3; Y_0^3 | U_0, U_1) \\
&= I(U_0; Y_0^3) + I(U_1; Y_0^3 | U_0) + I(U_2; Y_0^3 | U_0, U_1) + I(U_3; Y_0^3 | U_0, U_1, U_2).
\end{aligned}
\tag{17.42}
$$

Again using the conditional independence among the U_i, this can be written as

$$
I(Y_0^3; Y_0^3) = I(U_0; Y_0^3) + I(Y_1; Y_0^3, Y_0) + I(Y_2; Y_0^3, Y_0, U_1) + I(U_3; Y_0^3, U_0, U_1, U_2).
$$

These four terms correspond to the channels $W_4^{(0)}$, $W_4^{(1)}$, $W_4^{(2)}$, and $W_4^{(3)}$. The decomposition (17.42) suggests a tree representation, as shown in Figure 17.13, where the leaf nodes of the tree correspond to the four channels.

17.4.4   Channel Polarization Demonstrated: An Example Using the Binary Erasure Channel for $N > 2$

In this section, we provide an example analogous to that of Section 17.3.4 for the BEC with $N = 4$. Recall that in that section the synthetic channels $W_2^{(0)}$ and $W_2^{(1)}$ could be interpreted as BEC channels with transition probabilities $p_2^{(0)}$ and $p_2^{(1)}$, respectively. In this section, we generalize beyond this result to further demonstrate polarization.

Let W be a BEC(p) channel. For the channel $W_4^{(0)} : u_0 \mapsto y_0^3$, the table below shows different output values, where $\bullet$ indicates that y_i has been received as transmitted and ? indicates that a y_i is an erasure. The symbol ✓ indicates that the received data are sufficient to decode u_0^3 and ✗ indicates that the received data are insufficient to decode u_0^3,

(y_0, y_1, y_2, y_3)

$u_0 \oplus u_1 \oplus u_2 \oplus u_3$	$u_2 \oplus u_3$	$u_1 \oplus u_3$	u_3		
$\bullet$	$\bullet$	$\bullet$	$\bullet$	w.p. $(1-p)^4$	✓
?	$\bullet$	$\bullet$	$\bullet$	w.p. $p(1-p)^3$	✗
$\bullet$	?	$\bullet$	$\bullet$	w.p. $(1-p)p(1-p)^2$	✗
$\bullet$	$\bullet$	?	$\bullet$	w.p. $(1-p)^2 p(1-p)$	✗
$\bullet$	$\bullet$	$\bullet$	?	w.p. $(1-p)^3 p$	✗
?	?	$\bullet$	$\bullet$	w.p. $p^2(1-p)^2$	✗
?	$\bullet$	?	$\bullet$	w.p. $(1-p)p(1-p)p$	✗
?	$\bullet$	$\bullet$	?	w.p. $p(1-p)^2 p$	✗
$\bullet$	?	?	$\bullet$	w.p. $(1-p)p^2(1-p)$	✗
$\bullet$	?	$\bullet$	?	w.p. $(1-p)p(1-p)p$	✗
$\bullet$	$\bullet$	?	?	w.p. $(1-p)^2 p^2$	✗

$=$

etc.

As this table shows, there is an erasure precluding the possibility of accurate decoding in every case except the first, so the overall erasure probability for the $W_4^{(0)}$ channel is

$$p_4^{(0)} = 1 - (1-p)^4 = 4p - 6p^2 + 4p^3 - p^4.$$

This probability can be understood another way. The second polarization $W_4^{(0)}$ operation operates on the probabilities produced by the first polarization operation using a $W_2^{(0)}$ channel, so, recalling that $p_2^{(0)} = g(p)$, where $g(p)$ is defined in (17.16),

$$p_4^{(0)} = g(g(p)) = g(2p - p^2) = 2(2p - p^2) - (2p - p^2)^2 = 4p - 6p^2 + 4p^3 - p^4.$$

Also consider the various $W_4^{(1)}$ channel outputs.

$(y_0, y_1, y_2, y_3, u_0)$

$u_0 \oplus u_1 \oplus u_2 \oplus u_3$	$u_2 \oplus u_3$	$u_1 \oplus u_3$	u_3	u_0	w.p.	decodable?
•	•	•	•	•	$(1-p)^4$	✓
?	•	•	•	•	$p(1-p)^3$	✓
•	?	•	•	•	$p(1-p)^3$	✓
•	•	?	•	•	$p(1-p)^3$	✓
•	•	•	?	•	$p(1-p)^3$	✓
?	?	•	•	•	$p^2(1-p)^2$	✓
?	•	•	?	•	$p^2(1-p)^2$	✓
?	•	•	?	•	$p^2(1-p)^2$	✗
•	?	?	•	•	$p^2(1-p)^2$	✗
•	?	•	?	•	$p^2(1-p)^2$	✗
•	•	?	?	•	$p^2(1-p)^2$	✗
?	?	?	•	•	$p^3(1-p)$	✗
?	?	•	?	•	$p^3(1-p)$	✗
?	•	?	?	•	$p^3(1-p)$	✗
•	?	?	?	•	$p^3(1-p)$	✗
?	?	?	?	•	p^4	✗

(17.43)

The probability of a block erasure is

$$p_4^{(1)} = 4p^2(1-p)^2 + 4p^3(1-p) + p^4 = p^4 - 4p^3 + 4p^2.$$

This can be computed more simply since this is the probability of a $W_2^{(1)}$ BEC channel acting on a $W_2^{(0)}$ BEC channel. Recalling that $p_2^{(1)} = h(p)$, where $h(p)$ is defined in (17.17),

$$p_4^{(1)} = h(g(p)) = (2p - p^2)^2 = p^4 - 4p^3 + 4p^2.$$

Forming a table similar to (17.43) for the $W_4^{(2)}$ channel, it is determined that there is a block erasure for the individual erasure patterns

$$(?, ?, •, •), (•, •, ?, ?), (?, ?, ?, •), (?, ?, •, ?), (•, ?, ?, ?), (?, ?, ?, ?),$$

which results in a block erasure probability

$$p_4^{(2)} = 2p^2(1-p)^2 + 4p^3(1-p) + p^4 = 2p^2 - p^4.$$

This can also be computed as

$$p_4^{(2)} = g(h(p)) = 2p^2 - p^4.$$

For the $W_4^{(3)}$ channel it is straightforward to show that

$$p_4^{(3)} = h(h(p)) = p^4.$$

These BEC channel probabilities are conveniently represented on a tree, as in Figure 17.14. This duplication pattern can be repeated, duplicating $p_4^{(0)}$ to obtain $p_8^{(0)}$ and $p_8^{(1)}$; and duplicating $p_4^{(1)}$ to obtain $p_8^{(2)}$ and $p_8^{(3)}$, and so forth. The BEC erasure probabilities for $N = 2^3$ are

$$p_8^{(0)} = g(g(g(p)))\ p_8^{(1)} = h(g(g(p)))\ p_8^{(2)} = g(h(g(p)))\ p_8^{(3)} = h(h(g(p)))$$

$$p_8^{(4)} = g(g(h(p)))\ p_8^{(5)} = h(g(h(p)))\ p_8^{(6)} = g(h(h(p)))\ p_8^{(7)} = h(h(h(p))).$$

Figure 17.15 shows the effect of continuing to repeat the polarization construction multiple times. The vertical axis is mutual information, recalling that for a BEC $I(W(p)) = 1 - p$. As the code length increases, many of the channels approach a mutual information = 1 and become "good" channels. Many of the channels approach a mutual information of 0 and become "bad" channels. There are a few channels whose performance remains mediocre, neither "good" nor "bad."

This effect can be further explored as follows. The following MATLAB function computes $g(p) = p^2$ and $h(p) = 2p - p^2$ for each p in a vector passed in:

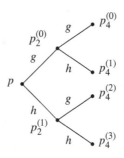

Figure 17.14: Computing the synthetic BEC erasure probabilities on a tree.

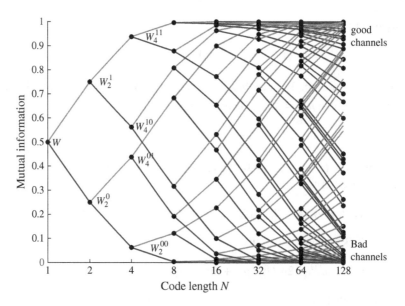

Figure 17.15: Polarization effect for the BEC channel.

```
function pout = polarize(pin)
% polarize.m:  For each probability in pin,
% compute the W^0 and W^1
% probabilities for a BEC and return them in pout

pout = [];
for p = pin     % for each p passed in
   pout = [pout p^2 2*p - p^2];  % compute g(p) and h(p)
end
```

For example, when this is called as `polarize(.3)`, the output is `0.09 0.51`. The effect of repeated polarization is obtained by repeated function calls, for example,

```
polarize(polarize(0.3))
```

yields [`0.0081 0.1719 0.2601 0.7599`]. Repeating this eight times (eight polarization iterations)

```
polarize(polarize(polarize(polarize(polarize(polarize(polarize
```

```
   (.3)))))))
```

produces 256 probability outputs. These are plotted in the order $p_{256}^{(0)}$ to $p_{256}^{(255)}$ in Figure 17.16(a), and more revealingly in sorted order in Figure 17.16(b). The polarization effect become evident: There are channels for which the synthetic probability $p_N^{(i)}$ is near 1 (and hence the capacity is near 0 bit), and channels for which the synthetic probability is near 0 (and hence the capacity is near 1). There are also some mediocre channels. The effect of polarization is further demonstrated in Figure 17.16(c), which plots the sorted probabilities $p_{2^{16}}^i$ for 16 iterations. The channel polarization effect is more complete in this case: the fraction of mediocre channels is smaller (a more abrupt transition from probability 0 to probability 1), and the railed probabilities are closer to 0 and 1. As the number of polarization iterations increases, this effect becomes increasingly strong.

How many of these "good" channels are there? Let $\epsilon > 0$ be a threshold, and consider the fraction of channels whose probability is less than ϵ. For example, take $\epsilon = 0.1$. The fraction of probabilities less than ϵ,

$$\frac{\#(\text{channel probabilities} < \epsilon)}{\#(\text{number of channels})}$$

is the fraction of channels that are "good" at the ϵ level. For the eight-iteration probabilities of Figure 17.16(b), this fraction is 0.605 for $\epsilon = 0.1$. For the 16-iteration probabilities of Figure 17.16(c), this fraction is 0.6807. As the number of polarization iterations increases, this fraction of "good" channel approaches a limit of 0.7.

The channel polarization effect demonstrated in these figures indicates how reliable communication can be obtained. Out of all the communication channels available in this iterated scheme, only the best channels are used for communication. The fraction of "good" channels (having probability below some threshold ϵ) approaches the channel capacity of the channel. For the BEC of this example, $I(W) = 1 - p$. For $p = 0.3$, with 16 iterations the fraction good channels at ϵ-level 0.1 is already $0.6807/0.7$, or 86.5% of capacity.

The nature of the BEC channel makes it easy to compute the parameters of the synthesized channels. For other channels (such as BSC or AWGN), computing $I(W_N)$ is more difficult, and analysis will resort to bounds. This is done in Section 17.5.

17.4.5 Polar Coding

As Figure 17.16 suggests, there is a set of channels which has low crossover probability (high capacity) and other channels with high crossover probability (low capacity). In the encoding operation, each input bit u_i corresponds to a different channel $W_N^{(i)}$. Thus, in the encoding operation expressed in terms

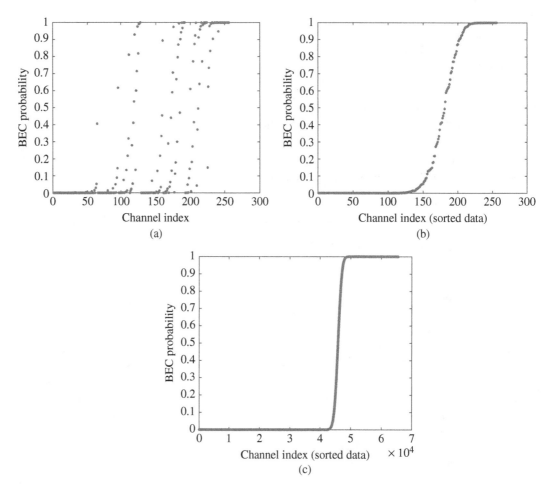

Figure 17.16: BEC probability for polarized channels, $p = 0.3$. (a) Unsorted probabilities, 8 iterations; (b) sorted probabilities, 8 iterations; (c) sorted probabilities, 16 iterations.

of the generator matrix,

$$x_0^{N-1} = u_0^{N-1} G_N, \tag{17.44}$$

the i rows of G_N correspond to encoding into the channel $W_N^{(i)}$.

Let $\mathcal{A}$ denote an arbitrary subset of $\{0, 1, \ldots, N - 1\}$, where the elements of $\mathcal{A}$ select the high-capacity channels to be used and let $\mathcal{A}^c$ denote its set complement. Let $G_N(\mathcal{A})$ denote the submatrix of G_N formed by the rows with indices in $\mathcal{A}$. Also, let $u_{\mathcal{A}}$ denote the elements of **u** with indices in $\mathcal{A}$. The encoding operation (17.44) can be expressed as

$$x_0^{N-1} = u_{\mathcal{A}} G_N(\mathcal{A}) \oplus u_{\mathcal{A}^c} G_N(\mathcal{A}^c). \tag{17.45}$$

Equation (17.45) represents the polar coding operation: The set $\mathcal{A}$ indexes the set of channels selected for transmission (i.e., having high capacity). Thus, $\mathcal{A}$ is referred to as the *information set*. The bits in $u_{\mathcal{A}}$ are the bits that are encoded for transmission. The bits in $u_{\mathcal{A}^c}$ are *frozen* — not used to transmit information, and known to both the transmitter and the receiver.

Since $u_{\mathcal{A}} G_N(\mathcal{A})$ produces a subgroup of $\mathbb{F}_2^N$, adding the offset $u_{\mathcal{A}^c} G_N(\mathcal{A}^c)$ produces a *coset* of this subgroup. The polar code is therefore said to be a *coset code*, that is, a linear code offset by a vector.

Let $K = |\mathcal{A}|$. A polar code (more generally, a coset code) is specified by the parameter list $(N, K, \mathcal{A}, u_{\mathcal{A}^c})$. The rate of the code is $R = K/N$. The vector $u_{\mathcal{A}^c} \in \mathcal{X}^{N-K}$ is called the set of *frozen bits*.

Example 17.5 For encoding with the G_4 matrix in (17.32), suppose that $\mathcal{A} = \{1, 3\}$ and $u_{\mathcal{A}} = (0, 1)$. The encoding operation of this $(4, 2, \{1, 3\}, (0, 1))$ code is represented with

$$x_0^3 = (u_1, u_3) \begin{bmatrix} 1 & 0 & 1 & 0 \\ 1 & 1 & 1 & 1 \end{bmatrix} + (0, 1) \begin{bmatrix} 1 & 0 & 0 & 0 \\ 1 & 1 & 0 & 0 \end{bmatrix}.$$

$\square$

In the decoding operation, bits which are frozen do not need to be decoded, so $\hat{u}_i = u_i$ if $i \in \mathcal{A}^c$. Nevertheless, the likelihood function computations leading to such bits u_i are usually performed since these likelihood functions are usually needed for decoding other bits.

17.4.6 Tree Representation

Given the recursive structure of the polar code, it is natural to use a tree to represent it. We demonstrate the general principles for an encoder with $N = 8$.

Figure 17.17(a) shows the encoding structure with the input bits in bit-reverse permuted order, as in Figure 17.11. Bits that are frozen are indicated in gray font; bits that are unfrozen (u_5, u_6, and u_7) are in black font. The outputs y_i are indicated to show the order (even though the channels are not shown). In Figure 17.17(b), the structure is the same, but the inputs have been reordered so that the bits are numbered sequentially, rather than in bit-reverse order. Note that the output sequence is reordered. In Figure 17.17(c), the input bits are represented with colored nodes. The black nodes represent unfrozen bits and the white nodes represent frozen bits. Also, the adders in each stage have been grouped together with boxes. These boxes will represent nodes in the tree.

In Figure 17.17(d), the first stage of converting the groups to nodes in the tree is accomplished. The nodes are colored according to the frozen nature of their children. A node whose children are all frozen (white) is a white node. A node whose children are all unfrozen (black) is a black node. A node whose children are partially frozen and partially unfrozen is gray. This replacement of groups with nodes on the tree continues in Figure 17.17(e). As before, parent of a node which is gray is gray. The completed tree is portrayed in Figure 17.17(f).

The decoding algorithm passes messages along the edges of the tree. For some edges, the messages passed are vectors (not scalars). In the representations of the tree in Figure 17.17, thickness of the line suggests that the closer to the root, the bigger the vector that is conveyed along the edge. A message along an edge with multiple components is denoted using indexing using, e.g., $[i]$, such as $\alpha_v[i]$.

Figure 17.18(a) shows the tree rotated by $90°$ to portray the root at the top of the tree, as is conventional. Figure 17.18(b) shows a labeling of a typical node v. The parent of the node is denoted p_v, its children are v_l and v_r. The message to node v from its parent is denoted α_v; the message of node v to its parent is β_v. Similarly, messages to and from its left and right children are, respectively, α_{v_l}, β_{v_l}, α_{v_r}, and β_{v_r}, as shown.

17.4.7 Successive Cancellation Decoding

In Section 17.3.5, we met SC for $N = 2$, based on likelihood ratio and log-likelihood ratio computations. In this section, we extend these concepts to arbitrary N.

The log-likelihood function is used in the decoding algorithms. Based on the recursive nature of the channel transition function, this can also be computed recursively. Let

$$\lambda_N^{(i)}(y_0^{N-1}, \hat{u}_0^{i-1}) = \frac{W_N^{(i)}(y_0^{N-1}, \hat{u}_0^{i-1}|u_i = 0)}{W_N^{(i)}(y_0^{N-1}, \hat{u}_0^{i-1}|u_i = 1)} \tag{17.46}$$

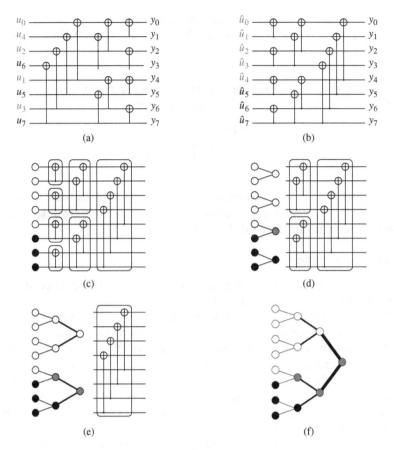

Figure 17.17: A tree representation of the decoder structure. (a) Basic encoding structure; (b) basic encoding structure, sequential bit order; (c) identifying frozen and unfrozen nodes, and the groupings of adders; (d) first stage of converting groupings into nodes, with nodes colored to match colorings of children; (e) next stage of converting groupings into nodes; (f) final stage of converting groupings into nodes.

and let

$$L_N^{(i)}(y_0^{N-1}, \hat{u}_0^{i-1}) = \log \lambda_N^{(i)}(y_0^{N-1}, \hat{u}_0^{i-1}).$$

This likelihood ratio can be used to estimate the value of the bit u_i using the function h_i defined as

$$h_i(y_0^{N-1}, \hat{u}_0^{i-1}) = \begin{cases} 0 & \text{if } L_N^{(i)}(y_0^{N-1}, \hat{u}_0^{i-1}) \geq 0 \\ 1 & \text{otherwise.} \end{cases} \tag{17.47}$$

For decoding, if $i \in \mathcal{A}^c$ (the set of frozen bits), then the decoded value is the frozen bit value. Otherwise, it is determined by the h function:

$$\hat{u}_i = \begin{cases} u_i & i \in \mathcal{A}^c \\ h_i(y_0^{N-1}, \hat{u}_0^{i-1}) & i \in \mathcal{A}. \end{cases} \tag{17.48}$$

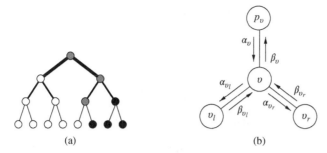

Figure 17.18: Rotated tree and messages in the tree. (a) Rotating the tree to put the root node at the top; (b) a portion of a tree, showing messages passed in a local decoder.

The two aspects of decoding for frozen and nonfrozen bits described in (17.47) and (17.48) are summarized in the decoding function $\tilde{h}$, defined as

$$\hat{u}_i = \tilde{h}(y_0^{N-1}, \hat{u}_0^{i-1}) = \begin{cases} u_i & i \in \mathcal{A}^c \\ h(y_0^{N-1}, \hat{u}_0^{i-1}) & i \in \mathcal{A} \end{cases}$$

Note that $\hat{u}_i$ depends on the previously estimated values $\hat{u}_0^{i-1}$. This is the essence of SC: bits are estimated in order $\hat{u}_0, \hat{u}_1, \hat{u}_2, \ldots, \hat{u}_{N-1}$, with the estimate $\hat{u}_i$ being based upon previously determined bits. Under thepolarization idea, since the polarized channels used are assumed to be good, each of the previously determined bits $\hat{u}_0^{i-1}$ are assumed to be good.

The formulas (17.40) and (17.41) allow the likelihood ratios (17.46) to be recursively expressed in terms of likelihood ratios of subsequences of the received data.

Theorem 17.6 *The likelihood ratio (17.46) can be written recursively in terms of likelihood ratio for smaller values of N:*

$$\lambda_N^{(2i)}(y_0^{N-1}, \hat{u}_0^{2i-1}) = \frac{\lambda_{N/2}^{(i)}(y_0^{N/2-1}, \hat{u}_{0,even}^{2i-1} \oplus \hat{u}_{0,odd}^{2i-1})\lambda_{N/2}^{(i)}(y_{N/2}^{N-1}, \hat{u}_{0,odd}^{2i-1}) + 1}{\lambda_{N/2}^{(i)}(y_0^{N/2-1}, \hat{u}_{0,even}^{2i-1} \oplus \hat{u}_{0,odd}^{2i-1}) + \lambda_{N/2}^{(i)}(y_{N/2}^{N-1}, \hat{u}_{0,odd}^{2i-1})} \qquad (17.49)$$

$$\lambda_N^{(2i+1)}(y_0^{N-1}, \hat{u}_0^{2i-1}) = [\lambda_{N/2}^{(i)}(y_0^{N/2-1}, \hat{u}_{0,even}^{2i-1} \oplus \hat{u}_{0,odd}^{2i-1})]^{1-2\hat{u}_{2i-1}} \lambda_{N/2}^{(i)}(y_{N/2}^{N-1}, \hat{u}_{0,odd}^{2i-1}). \qquad (17.50)$$

Proof For (17.49), substituting $i \to 2i$ in (17.46) then employing (17.40) gives

$$\lambda_N^{(2i)}(y_0^{N-1}|\hat{u}_0^{2i-1}) = \frac{W_N^{(2i)}(y_0^{N-1}\hat{u}_0^{2i-1}|u_{2i} = 0)}{W_N^{(2i)}(y_0^{N-1}, \hat{u}_0^{2i-1}|u_{2i} = 1)}$$

$$= \frac{W_{N/2}^{(i)}(a|0 \oplus 0)W_{N/2}^{(i)}(b|0) + W_{N/2}^{(i)}(a|0 \oplus 1)W_{N/2}^{(i)}(b|1)}{W_{N/2}^{(i)}(a|1 \oplus 0)W_{N/2}^{(i)}(b|0) + W_{N/2}^{(i)}(a|1 \oplus 1)W_{N/2}^{(i)}(b|1)}$$

(from (17.40) with $a = (y_0^{N/2-1}, \hat{u}_{0,even}^{2i-1} \oplus \hat{u}_{0,odd}^{2i-1})$ and $b = (y_{N/2}^{N-1}, u_{0,odd}^{2i-1})$)

$$= \frac{\dfrac{W_{N/2}^{(i)}(a|0)}{W_{N/2}^{(i)}(a|1)} \dfrac{W_{N/2}^{(i)}(b|0)}{W_{N/2}^{(i)}(b|1)} + 1}{\dfrac{W_{N/2}^{(i)}(a|1)}{W_{N/2}^{(i)}(a|1)} \dfrac{W_{N/2}^{(i)}(b|0)}{W_{N/2}^{(i)}(b|1)} + \dfrac{W_{N/2}^{(i)}(a|0)}{W_{N/2}^{(i)}(a|1)} \dfrac{W_{N/2}^{(i)}(b|1)}{W_{N/2}^{(i)}(b|1)}} \dfrac{W_{N/2}^{(i)}(a|1)W_{N/2}^{(i)}(b|1)}{W_{N/2}^{(i)}(a|1)W_{N/2}^{(i)}(b|1)}$$

$$= \frac{\lambda_{N/2}^{(i)}(y_0^{N/2-1}, \hat{u}_{0,even}^{2i-1} \oplus \hat{u}_{0,odd}^{2i-1})\lambda_{N/2}^{(i)}(y_{N/2}^{N-1}, \hat{u}_{0,odd}^{2i-1}) + 1}{\lambda_{N/2}^{(i)}(y_0^{N/2-1}, \hat{u}_{0,even}^{2i-1} \oplus \hat{u}_{0,odd}^{2i-1}) + \lambda_{N/2}^{(i)}(y_{N/2}^{N-1}, \hat{u}_{0,odd}^{2i-1})} = (17.49)$$

For (17.50), substituting $i \to 2i + 1$ in (17.46) and employing (17.41) gives

$$
\lambda_N^{(2i+1)}(y_0^{N-1}|\hat{u}_0^{2i}) = \frac{W_N^{(2i+1)}(y_0^{N-1}, \hat{u}_0^{2i}|u_{2i+1} = 0)}{W_N^{(2i+1)}(y_0^{N-1}, \hat{u}_0^{2i}|u_{2i+1} = 1)}
$$

$$
= \frac{W_{N/2}^{(i)}(y_0^{N/2-1}, \hat{u}_{0,\text{even}}^{2i-1} \oplus \hat{u}_{0,\text{odd}}^{2i-1}|\hat{u}_{2i} \oplus 0)}{W_{N/2}^{(i)}(y_0^{N/2-1}, \hat{u}_{0,\text{even}}^{2i-1} \oplus \hat{u}_{0,\text{odd}}^{2i-1}|\hat{u}_{2i} \oplus 1)} \; \frac{W_{N/2}^{(i)}(y_{N/2}^{N-1}, \hat{u}_{0,\text{odd}}^{2i-1}|0)}{W_{N/2}^{(i)}(y_{N/2}^{N-1}, \hat{u}_{0,\text{odd}}^{2i-1}|1)}.
$$

If $\hat{u}_{2i} = 0$, then the first ratio is a likelihood ratio; if $\hat{u}_{2i} = 1$, the first ratio is the reciprocal of a likelihood ratio, so

$$
\lambda_N^{(2i+1)}(y_0^{N-1}|\hat{u}_0^{2i}) = [\lambda_{N/2}^{(i)}(y_0^{N/2-1}|\hat{u}_{0,\text{even}}^{2i-1} \oplus \hat{u}_{0,\text{odd}}^{2i-1})]^{1-2\hat{u}_{2i}} \lambda_{N/2}^{(i)}(y_{N/2}^{N-1}|\hat{u}_{0,\text{odd}}^{2i-1}) = (17.50).
$$
□

It will be convenient to express these formulas using log likelihoods. Equation (17.49) can be written as

$$
L_N^{(2i)}(y_0^{N-1}|\hat{u}_0^{2i-1}) = \frac{\exp[L_{N/2}^{(i)}(y_0^{N/2-1}|\hat{u}_{0,\text{even}}^{2i-1} \oplus \hat{u}_{0,\text{odd}}^{2i-1}) + L_{N/2}^{(i)}(y_{N/2}^{N-1}|\hat{u}_{0,\text{odd}}^{2i-1})] + 1}{\exp[L_{N/2}^{(i)}(y_0^{N/2-1}|\hat{u}_{0,\text{even}}^{2i-1} \oplus \hat{u}_{0,\text{odd}}^{2i-1})] + \exp[L_{N/2}^{(i)}(y_{N/2}^{N-1}|\hat{u}_{0,\text{odd}}^{2i-1})]}
$$

$$
= \boxed{\text{chk}(L_{N/2}^{(i)}(y_0^{N/2-1}|\hat{u}_{0,\text{even}}^{2i-1} \oplus \hat{u}_{0,\text{odd}}^{2i-1}), L_{N/2}^{(i)}(y_{N/2}^{N-1}|\hat{u}_{0,\text{odd}}^{2i-1}))} \tag{17.51}
$$

$$
= \boxed{L_{N/2}^{(i)}(y_0^{N/2-1}|\hat{u}_{0,\text{even}}^{2i-1} \oplus \hat{u}_{0,\text{odd}}^{2i-1}) \boxplus L_{N/2}^{(i)}(y_{N/2}^{N-1}|\hat{u}_{0,\text{odd}}^{2i-1})}. \tag{17.52}
$$

To use other notations, this is the s or "upper" computation, also computable using the tanh rule. Also,

$$
\boxed{L_N^{(2i+1)}(y_0^{N-1}|\hat{u}_0^{2i}) = L_{N/2}^{(i)}(y_{N/2}^{N-1}|\hat{u}_{0,\text{odd}}^{2i-1}) \overset{\hat{u}_{2i}}{\pm} L_{N/2}^{(i)}(y_0^{N/2-1}|\hat{u}_{0,\text{even}}^{2i-1} \oplus \hat{u}_{0,\text{odd}}^{2i-1}).} \tag{17.53}
$$

This is the t or "lower" computation.

These recursions end with $L_2^{(0)}$ and $L_2^{(1)}$, which are computed using the formulas for $N = 2$ in (17.24) and (17.25).

In all of these computations, whether (17.52) or (17.53) is used depends on whether the likelihood is for an even-numbered bit or an odd-numbered bit.

17.4.8 SC Decoding from a Message Passing Point of View on the Tree

Conventional SC decoding can be expressed as message passing on the tree introduced in Section 17.4.6. For a node v in the tree, let d_v denote the depth of the tree, where $d_v = 0$ for the root node. The operations that take place at node v are said to constitute a decoder.

When a non-leaf decoder v is activated, it computes the message

$$
\alpha_{v_l}(i) = \alpha_v[2i] \boxplus \alpha_v[2i + 1] \quad \text{for } i = 0, 1, \ldots, 2^{n-d_v-1} - 1 \tag{17.54}
$$

and sends α_{v_l} to its left child v_l. This implements (17.52). The decoder at v then waits until it receives the codeword β_{v_l} from v_l. This corresponds to the bits that are sent toward the output. Node v then calculates the messages

$$
\alpha_{v_r}[i] = \alpha_v[2i](1 - 2\beta_{v_l}[i]) + \alpha_v[2i + 1]
$$

$$
= \alpha_v[2i + 1] \overset{\beta_{v_l}[i]}{\pm} \alpha_v[2i] \qquad \text{for } i = 0, 1, \ldots, 2^{n-d_v-1} - 1 \tag{17.55}
$$

and sends it to its right child v_r. This implements (17.53). The local decoder at v then waits until it receives the codeword β_{v_r} from v_r. Node v then calculates the message to its parent as

$$\beta_v[2i] = \beta_{v_l}[i] \oplus \beta_{v_r}[i]$$
$$\beta_v[2i + 1] = \beta_{v_r}[i] \qquad \text{for } i = 0, 1, \ldots, 2^{n-d_v-1} - 1$$

and sends this to p_v. This computes the bit addition/copying operations. At this point, the computations in the set of nodes V_v terminate as these local decoders will never be activated again through the rest of the decoding.

When v is a leaf node, the local decoder at v takes the incoming message (log likelihood) and thresholds it to obtain a bit if it is not frozen, or uses the frozen value if it is frozen. This bit forms the message to the parent of v.

17.4.9 A Decoding Example with $N = 4$

In this section, we demonstrate how the decoding works with $N = 4$, illustrating the flow of information both on the encoding diagram and also in the tree. The two different perspectives inform the overall process. While the computations are identical, the different perspectives might lead to different implementations.

The log-likelihood formulas developed above are applied to decoding when $N = 4$. The processing steps are summarized in Figure 17.20. Before these computations, the LLRs $L_{y_i}, i = 0, 1, \ldots, N - 1$ are computed.

Step 4-0 $i = 0$ using (17.52), Figure 17.20(a):

$$L_4^{(0)}(y_0^3) = L_2^{(0)}(y_0^1) \boxplus L_2^{(0)}(y_2^3).$$

To compute this, $L_2^{(0)}(y_0^1)$ and $L_2^0(y_2^3))$ are recursively computed as

$$L_2^{(0)}(y_0^1) = L_{y_0} \boxplus L_{y_1} \qquad L_2^{(0)}(y_2^3) = L_{y_2} \boxplus L_{y_3}.$$

In Figure 17.20(a), the computations are shown using the brown lines leading from the likelihoods of the received values (on the right) to the input symbols (on the left). These computations produce the estimate $\hat{u}_0 = \tilde{h}(L_4^{(0)}(y_0^3))$ (the green dot).

On the tree in Figure 17.19(b), the messages are as follows:

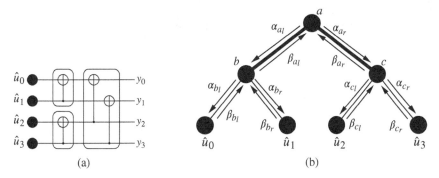

Figure 17.19: Encoder for $N = 4$ and its associated tree. (a) Encoder illustrating node groupings; (b) decoding tree for $N = 4$ with messages labeled.

Node a has the incoming messages (not shown in the figure)

$$\alpha_v = (L_{y_0}, L_{y_1}, L_{y_2}, L_{y_3}).$$

The message that node a sends to its left child b is the vector (see (17.54))

$$\alpha_{a_l} = (\alpha_a[0] \boxplus \alpha_a[1], \alpha_a[2] \boxplus \alpha_a[3]) = (L_{y_0} \boxplus L_{y_1}, L_{y_2} \boxplus L_{y_3}) = (L_2^{(0)}(y_0^1), L_2^{(0)}(y_2^3)).$$

The message that node b sends to its left child is

$$\alpha_{b_l} = \alpha_{a_l}[0] \boxplus \alpha_{a_l}[1] = L_4^{(0)}(y_0^3) = L_{y_0} \boxplus L_{y_1} \boxplus L_{y_2} \boxplus L_{y_3}.$$

At node $\hat{u}_0$, a leaf node, the bit value is determined and transmitted back as the message that $\hat{u}_0$ sends to its parent b,

$$\beta_{b_l} = \tilde{h}(\alpha_{b_l}) = \hat{u}_0.$$

Step 4-1 $i = 1$ using (17.53), Figure 17.20(b):

$$L_4^{(1)}(y_0^3|\hat{u}_0) = L_2^{(0)}(y_2^3) \overset{\hat{u}_0}{\pm} L_2^{(0)}(y_0^1).$$

The sum/difference of the likelihoods $L_2^{(0)}(y_2^3)$ and $L_2^{(0)}(y_0^1)$ (both already computed in Step 4-0, brown lines) are controlled by $\hat{u}_0$ (computed in Step 4-0, green line) to produce the cyan line and the estimate $\hat{u}_1 = \tilde{h}(L_4^{(1)}(y_0^3|\hat{u}_0))$ (green dot).

Observe that the order of the bits decoded is numeric order: first u_0, then u_1, etc., even that is not the order they appear on the graph.

In terms of the tree, the message that b sends to its right child is

$$\alpha_{b_r} = \alpha_{a_l}[1] \overset{\beta_{b_l}}{\pm} \alpha_{a_l}[0] = L_4^{(1)}(y_0^3|\hat{u}_0).$$

At node $\hat{u}_1$, a leaf node, the bit value is determined and transmitted back as the message that $\hat{u}_1$ sends to its parent b:

$$\beta_{b_r} = \tilde{h}(\alpha_{b_r}) = \hat{u}_1.$$

At this point, the subtree rooted at node b is complete, so it can send a message back to its parent. This message is based on the pair of bits from this subtree,

$$\beta_{a_l} = (\hat{u}_0 \oplus \hat{u}_1, \hat{u}_1).$$

Step 4-2 $i = 2$ using (17.52), Figure 17.20(c):

$$L_4^{(2)}(y_0^3|\hat{u}_0^1) = L_2^{(1)}(y_0^1, \hat{u}_0 \oplus \hat{u}_1) \boxplus L_2^{(1)}(y_2^3, \hat{u}_1).$$

The log-likelihood functions $L_2^{(1)}(y_0^1|\hat{u}_0 \oplus \hat{u}_1)$ and $L_2^{(1)}(y_2^3|\hat{u}_1)$ are computed using (17.25):

$$L_2^{(1)}(y_0^1|\hat{u}_0 \oplus \hat{u}_1) = L_{y_1} \overset{\hat{u}_0 \oplus \hat{u}_1}{\pm} [L_{y_0}] \quad L_2^{(1)}(y_2^3|\hat{u}_1) = L_{y_3} \overset{\hat{u}_1}{\pm} L_{y_2}.$$

The sum $\hat{u}_0 \oplus \hat{u}_1$ (green lines) is used to control the sum/difference in $L_2^{(1)}(y_0^1, \hat{u}_0 \oplus \hat{u}_1)$. Also, $\hat{u}_1$ (green line) is used to control $L_2^{(1)}(y_2^3, \hat{u}_1)$. These are then used in a $\boxplus$ computation to produce $\hat{u}_2$:

$$\hat{u}_2 = \tilde{h}(L_4^{(2)}(y_0^3, \hat{u}_0^1)).$$

In terms of the tree, the message that a sends to its right child c is the vector

$$\alpha_{a_r} = (L_2^{(1)}(y_0^1|\hat{u}_0 \oplus \hat{u}_1), L_2^{(1)}(y_2^3|\hat{u}_1)).$$

The message that c sends to its left child is

$$\alpha_{c_l} = \alpha_{a_r}[0] \boxplus \alpha_{a_r}[1] = L_4^{(2)}(y_0^3|\hat{u}_0^1).$$

At node $\hat{u}_2$, a leaf node, the bit value is determined and transmitted back as the message that $\hat{u}_2$ sends to its parent c:

$$\beta_{c_l} = \tilde{h}(\alpha_{c_l}) = \hat{u}_1.$$

Step 4-3 $i = 3$ using (17.53), Figure 17.20(d):

$$L_4^{(3)}(y_0^3|\hat{u}_0^2) = L_1^{(1)}(y_2^3|\hat{u}_1) \overset{\hat{u}_2}{\pm} L_2^{(1)}(y_0^1|\hat{u}_0 \oplus \hat{u}_1).$$

Using previously computed $L_1^{(1)}(y_2^3|\hat{u}_1)$ and $L_2^{(1)}(y_0^1|\hat{u}_0 \oplus \hat{u}_1)$, compute the sum/difference controlled by $\hat{u}_2$.

In terms of the tree, the message that c sends to its right child is

$$\alpha_{c_r} = \alpha_{a_r}[0] \overset{\hat{u}_2}{\pm} \alpha_{a_r}[1] = L_4^{(3)}(y_0^3, \hat{u}_0^2).$$

At this point there is no need to send further information back up the tree.

17.4.10 A Decoding Example with $N = 8$

The example in this section provides a larger illustration of the successive cancellation algorithm with $N = 8$ and details some data structures which can be used for an efficient decoding algorithm, that require only $O(N)$ space.

The decoding tree labeled with the message is shown in Figure 17.21. Figure 17.22 illustrates the encoding operation. On the left, the input bits are numbered using an index j. After passing through a bit reverse permutation, the bits are numbered using an index i, which is listed in numerical order. The decoding proceeds *in numerical order* of j, $j = 0, 1, \ldots, N - 1$. This means that the order of i is 0, 4, 2, 6, 1, 5, 3, 7. Decoding operations are performed once per bit in this order. LLRs are propagated from right to left. As bits are determined, they are propagated left to right as necessary. This general rule is tempered by the fact that it is not necessary at every step to propagate the LLRs all the way from the far right-hand side, nor is it necessary to propagate all the bits all the way to the far right-hand side.

As described above, the LLR computations involve two types. For the "upper" branches of the basic blocks, the LLR computation involves the s function. For the "lower" branches of the basic blocks, the LLR computation involve the t function. In the examples, results of computing s are shown using brown lines and results of computing t are shown using cyan lines. Known bits and values propagated from bits are shown using green lines.

There are two overall steps to the algorithm for each j: LLR computation, which proceeds from right to left in the encoding diagram, and from top to bottom in the tree representation, and bit propagation

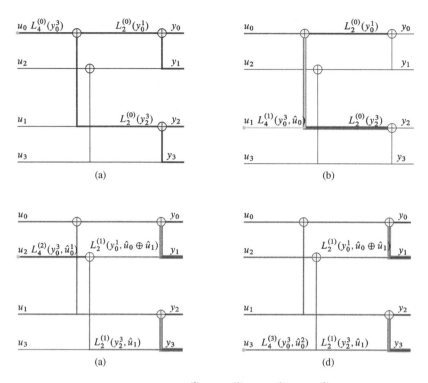

Figure 17.20: Decoding steps for $N = 4$. (a) $L_4^{(0)}$; (b) $L_4^{(1)}$; (c) $L_4^{(2)}$; (d) $L_4^{(3)}$. (Color versions of the page can be found at wileywebpage or `https://github.com/tkmoon/eccbook/colorpages`.)

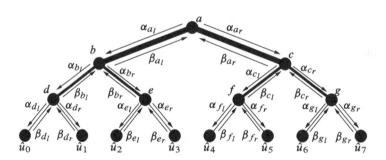

Figure 17.21: Decoding tree for $N = 8$ with messages labeled.

in which bit values on the left are propagated as far to the right in the encoding diagram and from bottom to top in the tree, as needed for future computations.

There are two simple data structures used in the decoding algorithm. The first is an array of length $2N - 1$ which contains the LLR values. The last N values, LLR(N-1), ..., LLR($2N - 2$) (using 0-based indexing) hold the channel input LLRs L_{y_i}, $i = 0, 1, \ldots, N - 1$. The other LLR values contain results of LLR computations (either s or t computations), *varying in position depending on which bit is being decoded*. This makes for a memory-efficient implementation.

There is also an array BITS of size $2 \times (N - 1)$ which hold bit information propagating back through the network. A BITS whose first index is 0, such as BITS(0,0), corresponds to an *upper* branch going into a $\oplus$. A BITS whose first index is 1, such as BITS(1,0), corresponds to a *lower* branch going into a $\oplus$. The second index in BITS indicates which LLR value the bit is associated with. As bits become available, they are propagated to the right to populate the BITS data. Like the LLR data

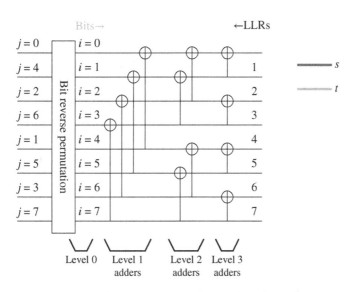

Figure 17.22: The structure used for the decoding example.

structure, the bit values are reused as possible for efficiency in storage. (Data structures described here are based on code derived from [459].)

We now describe the algorithm in detail, referring to Figures 17.23, 17.24 and 17.25. The description unfolds as the various aspects of the algorithm are uncovered. 0-based indexing is used is used throughout.

$j = 0, i = 0$ Figure 17.23(a, b).

Update LLR Using (17.52),

$$\underbrace{L_8^{(0)}(y_0^7) = L_4^{(0)}(y_0^3) \boxplus L_4^{(0)}(y_4^7),}_{\text{LLR}(0)}$$

where

$$\underbrace{L_4^{(0)}(y_0^3)}_{\text{LLR}(1)} = \underbrace{L_2^{(0)}(y_0^1)}_{\text{LLR}(3)} \boxplus \underbrace{L_2^{(0)}(y_2^3)}_{\text{LLR}(4)}$$

$$\underbrace{L_4^{(0)}(y_4^7)}_{\text{LLR}(2)} = \underbrace{L_2^{(0)}(y_4^5)}_{\text{LLR}(5)} \boxplus \underbrace{L_2^{(0)}(y_6^7)}_{\text{LLR}(6)}$$

and the L_2 quantities are each computed using the chk computation in (17.24). The tree indicated with brown lines propagates log-likelihood information from the received values to the node 0. In the figure, the shaded $\oplus$s indicate that computations take place at those nodes, s (i.e., chk) computations in this case since these are all upper branches. After propagating to the left, a bit value $\hat{u}_0$ is computed (indicated by the green dot).

The LLR for this bit, $L_8^{(0)}$ at level 0, is contained in LLR(0). At the next level, LLR values are in LLR(1) and LLR(2). At the next level, LLR values are in LLR(3) through LLR(6), and the input level on the right LLR values are in LLR(7) through LLR(14). In general, at a level number level (from 0 on the left to through n on the right) the LLR values associated with that level have indexes ranging from $2^{\text{level}} - 1$ through $2^{\text{level}+1} - 2$.

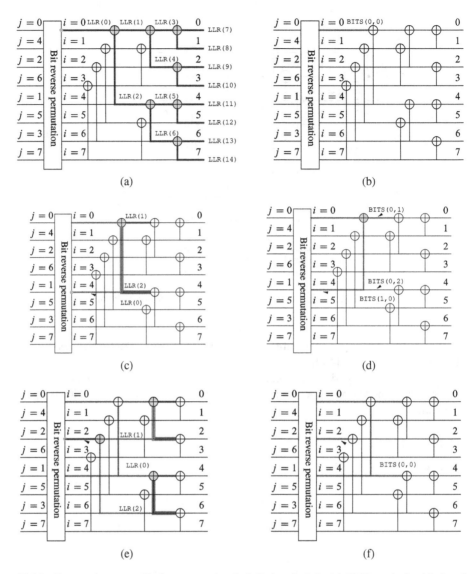

Figure 17.23: Successive cancellation steps, $j = 0, 1, 2$, $i = 0, 4, 2$. (a) LLR path for bit $j = 0$. $i = 0$, level1 $= 3$; (b) bit propagation, $j = 0, i = 0$; (c) LLR path for bit $j = 1$. $i = 4$, level1 $= 1$; (d) bit propagation $j = 1$. $i = 4$, level0 $= 2$; (e) LLR path for bit $j = 2, i = 2$. level1 $= 2$; (f) bit propagation $j = 2, i = 2$. (Color versions of the page can be found at wileywebpage or `https://github.com/tkmoon/eccbook/colorpages`.).

In terms of messages on the tree in Figure 17.21, the message that node a computes and sends to its left child b is the vector

$$\alpha_{a_l} = (L_{y_0} \boxplus L_{y_1}, L_{y_2} \boxplus L_{y_3}, L_{y_4} \boxplus L_{y_5}, L_{y_6} \boxplus L_{y_7})$$
$$= (L_2^{(0)}(y_0^1), L_2^{(0)}(y_2^3), L_2^{(0)}(y_4^5), L_2^{(0)}(y_6^7)).$$

The message that node b sends to its left child d is the vector

$$\alpha_{b_l} = (\alpha_{a_l}[0] \boxplus \alpha_{a_l}[1]), \alpha_{a_l}[2] \boxplus \alpha_{a_l}[3]) = (L_4^{(0)}(y_0^3), L_4^{(0)}(y_4^7)).$$

The message that node d sends to its left child $\hat{u}_0$ is

$$\alpha_{d_l} = \alpha_{b_l}[0] \boxplus \alpha_{b_l}[1] = L_8^{(0)}(y_0^7).$$

At node $\hat{u}_0$, a child node, the bit is estimated and its value is passed up to the parent node,

$$\beta_{d_l} = \tilde{h}(\alpha_{d_l}) = \hat{u}_0.$$

Update Bits At this point, there are no bits to be added to the bit just found. The presence of this bit is indicated with a green line on the graph. The bit value just obtained in stored in `BITS(0,0)`. The first index indicates that this is an "upper" bit into an adder. The second index indicates that this value is associated with the first ("zeroth") element on the graph, corresponding to `LLR(0)`.

Observations: For future reference, when $i < N/2$, the MSB of i is 0 (the LSB of j is 0; j is even), the line is in the the top half of the figure, there is a $\oplus$ immediately connected to it (a Level 1 adder in Figure 17.22) whose other input is not yet known. So there is no further propagation of the bits. Save the bit value in `BITS(0,0)`. Furthermore, at the next time step, j is odd, the LSB of j is 1, the MSB of i is 1, and we get the line connected to the other input of the Level 1 adder.

The number of levels into the tree for which the likelihood is recursively computed is 3 in this case — it was necessary to go all the way to the root of the tree (the input likelihoods).

$j = 1, i = 4$ Figure 17.23(c, d).

Update LLR Using (17.53),

$$L_8^{(1)}(y_0^7|\hat{u}_0^0) = L_4^{(0)}(y_4^7) \overset{\hat{u}_0}{\pm} L_4^{(0)}(y_0^3),$$

where $L_4^{(0)}(y_4^7)$ and $L_4^{(0)}(y_0^3)$ are already available in `LLR(2)` and `LLR(1)`, respectively, from the previous step, as indicated with the brown lines coming in from the right. These combine with the estimated bit $\hat{u}_0$ into the $\oplus$ (shaded) to compute the LLR shown on the cyan line, a lower branch.

There is potential confusion in the figure, since the lower line on the $\oplus$ is both an input (from `LLR(2)`) and an output `LLR(0)`. This is a visual portrayal of the fact that L_{y_0} is an input connected to the lower terminal in the $\oplus$, and $L_8^{(1)}$ is an output connected to the lower terminal in the $\oplus$. In order to show both lines, the brown line is portrayed with greater width.

The bit determined by $L_8^{(1)}$ is stored in `BITS(1,0)`, where the first index 1 indicates that the bit came from a lower t computation.

Observations: For this bit it is not necessary to go any further into the tree than a level 1 adder to get the LLR information. Note that at the previous step, when $j = 0$ and $i = 0$, the MSB of i was 0. At the present step, when $j = 1$ and $i = 4$, the MSB of i is 1, and both inputs to the adder at level 1 are available to compute the needed LLR. If the first bit (MSB) of i is 1, then information from the upper branch computed at the previous value of j (with MSB $i = 0$ there) is available to compute at an $\oplus$ at level 1.

As stated, it was only necessary to go to Level 1 of the tree. The depth of the tree necessary is determined by a variable `level1`, which may be determined as follows. Write down the binary representation of the index i. Then `level1` is the index of the first 1 in the representation starting with the MSB of i, or `level1 = n` if $i = 0$. It is only necessary to compute LLRs from level `level1` down to 1. Higher levels are *inactive*. This results in a savings of computation.

In the code provided, the `level1` is computed in the same function that computes the bit-reversal of j.

For this computation at $i = 4$ (level1 = 1), the LLR was computed using a lower (t). In general, the t computation is performed at the highest level for that step, and LLR computations at lower levels use the upper (s) formula.

In terms of messages on the tree, the message that node d send to its right child $\hat{u}_1$ is

$$\alpha_{d_r} = \alpha_{b_l}[1] \overset{\hat{u}_0}{\pm} \alpha_{b_l}[1].$$

At $\hat{u}_1$ the bit is detected and the message is sent back

$$\beta_{d_r} = \tilde{h}(\alpha_{d_r}) = \hat{u}_1.$$

All the children of d have sent their messages, so d can send the message to its parent, which consists of a pair of bits

$$\beta_{b_l} = (\hat{u}_0 \oplus \hat{u}_1, \hat{u}_1).$$

Update Bits The shaded $\oplus$ in Figure 17.23(d) has both inputs available since BITS(0,0) contains the upper value computed when $i = 0$ and the bit value just computed is available, stored in BITS(1,0). The sum is computed and stored in BITS(0,1). The index 0 here indicates that this is a bit on an upper branch, and the 1 indicates that this corresponds to the same branch as LLR(1) (compare with Figure 17.23(c)).

The function that computes these bit sums also propagates bit values forward for use in further bit computations. Thus, the value BITS(0,2) is assigned, equal to BITS(1,0). Note that BITS(0,2) is on the same line as LLR(2).

When bits are propagated to the right (that is, $i \geq N/2$) the number of levels to propagate the bits is determined by the level0 variable. level0 is the index of the first 0 in the binary representation of i, starting with the MSB. The highest level to propagate to through level0 - 1. In this case, bits are propagated through the Level 1 adders.

$j = 2$, $i = 2$ Figure 17.23(e, f).

Update LLR With $i = 010$, level1=2. Using (17.52),

$$\text{LLR}(0) = L_8^{(2)}(y_0^7|\hat{u}_0^1) = L_4^{(1)}(y_0^3|\hat{u}_{0,\text{even}}^1 \oplus \hat{u}_{0,\text{odd}}^1) \boxplus L_4^{(1)}(y_4^7|\hat{u}_{0,\text{odd}}^1)$$

$$= L_4^{(1)}(y_0^3|\hat{u}_0 \oplus \hat{u}_1) \boxplus L_4^{(1)}(y_4^7|\hat{u}_1).$$

The $L_4^{(1)}$ are not available, so they must be computed at the level1 = 2 adders, using (17.53):

$$\text{LLR}(1) = L_4^{(1)}(y_0^3|\hat{u}_0 \oplus \hat{u}_1) = L_2^{(0)}(y_2^3) \overset{\hat{u}_0 \oplus \hat{u}_1}{\pm} L_2^{(0)}(y_0^1)$$

$$\text{LLR}(2) = L_4^{(1)}(y_4^7|\hat{u}_1) = L_2^{(0)}(y_6^7) \overset{\hat{u}_1}{\pm} L_2^{(0)}(y_4^5).$$

These are both lower (t) computations.

Note that the output values LLR(1) and LLR(2) are on different lines than previously. Specifically, in Figure 17.23(a), LLR(1) and LLR(2) were on lines $i = 0$ and $i = 4$. Since those values of i have been used (above) and are not needed now, it is permissible to reuse these memory locations, so LLR(1) and LLR(2) are reassociated with lines $i = 2$ and $i = 6$. With two levels of LLR computation, we see that the first level (level 2) is lower (t), and the second (level = 1) is upper (s).

In terms of the decoding tree, the message that node b sends to its right child e is the vector

$$\alpha_{b_r} = (\alpha_{a_l}[1] \overset{\hat{u}_0 \oplus \hat{u}_1}{\pm} \alpha_{a_l}[0], \alpha_{a_l}[3] \overset{\hat{u}_1}{\pm} \alpha_{a_l}[2]) = (L_4^{(1)}(y_0^3, \hat{u}_0 \oplus \hat{u}_1), L_4^{(1)}(y_4^7, \hat{u}_1)).$$

The message that node e sends to its left child is

$$\alpha_{e_l} = \alpha_{b_r}[0] \boxplus \alpha_{b_r}[1].$$

At the leaf node $\hat{u}_2$, the bit is detected and sent back

$$\beta_{e_l} = \tilde{h}(\alpha_{e_l}) = \hat{u}_2.$$

Update Bits In general, lines for $i < N/2$ occur in the in the top half of the structure (where the MSB $= 0$), and are connected immediately to a $\oplus$ at level 1. Since to this point the other input of the adder (from a corresponding line where the MSB) is not done yet, no bit propagation is accomplished. All the update bits stage is to save the current bit estimate $\hat{u}_1$ into BITS(0,0) in preparation for the next step.

$j = 3$, $i = 6$ Figure 17.24(a, b).

Update LLR Using (17.53),

$$L_8^{(3)}(y_0^7|\hat{u}_0^2) = L_4^{(1)}(y_4^7|\hat{u}_1) \overset{\hat{u}_2}{\pm} L_4^{(1)}(y_0^3|\hat{u}_0 \oplus \hat{u}_1).$$

Both of the $L_4^{(1)}$ values are available from the previous step, so only a single level of computation is necessary. (The number of levels is level1 = 1.)

In terms of messages on the tree, the message that node e sends to its right child $\hat{u}_3$ is

$$\alpha_{e_r} = \alpha_{b_r}[1] \overset{\alpha}{\underset{b_r}{\pm}}[0] = L_8^{(3)}(y_0^j 7, \hat{u}_0^2).$$

The leaf node $\hat{u}_3$ detects the bit and sends it back to its parent

$$\beta_{e_r} = \tilde{h}(\alpha_{e_r}) = \hat{u}_3.$$

The children of node e have now sent their messages, so e can send the message to its parent, which is a pair of bits

$$\beta_{b_r} = (\hat{u}_2 \oplus \hat{u}_3, \hat{u}_3).$$

And now the children of node b have sent their messages, so b can send the message to its parent, which consists of 4 bits

$$\beta_{a_l} = (\hat{u}_0 \oplus \hat{u}_1, \hat{u}_1, \hat{u}_2 \oplus \hat{u}_3, \hat{u}_3).$$

Update Bits level0=3, so bits are propagated through the Level 2 adders. The current bit $\hat{u}_3$ is stored in BITS(1,0), and is added to BITS(0,0) which is presently associated with $\hat{u}_2$ from that last step $i = 2$, to produce BITS(1,1). The bit in BITS(1,0) is also propagated forward into BITS(1,2) (on the same line as LLR(2)).

At the next level, the bits output of the two shaded $\oplus$s are stored in BITS(0,3) and BITS(0,5). Also, the bits in BITS(1,1) and BITS(1,2) are propagated forward as BITS(0,4) and BITS(0,6). (These bits are never used.)

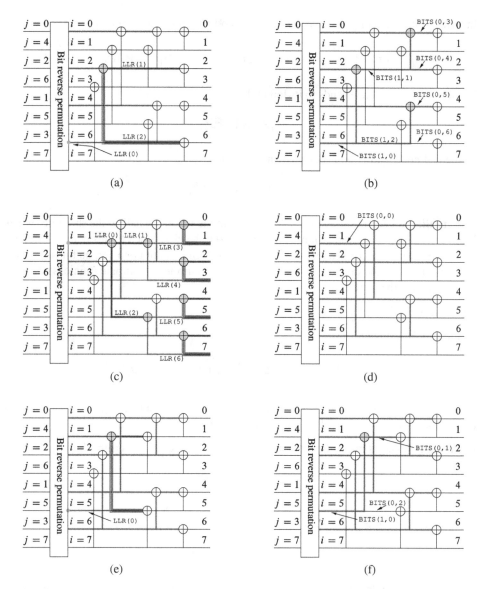

Figure 17.24: Successive cancellation steps, $j = 3, 4, 5$, $i = 6, 1, 5$. (a) LLR path for bit $j = 3, i = 6$. `level1` = 1; (b) bit propagation for bit $j = 3, i = 6$. `level0` = 3; (c) LLR path for bit $j = 4, i = 1$. `level1` = 3; (d) bit propagation $j = 4, i = 1$; (e) LLR path for bit $j = 5, i = 5$. `level1` = 1; (f) bit propagation $j = 5, i = 5$. `level0` = 2. (Color versions of the page can be found at wileywebpage or `https://github.com/tkmoon/eccbook/colorpages`.).

Observations: Examination of this result reveals that there are two kinds of computation here: those that produce "lower" bits `BITS(1,*)` and those that produce "upper" bits `BITS(0,*)`. The number of levels of lower bit computation is `level0-2`. This is followed by one level of upper bit computation at level `level0-1`.

$j = 4, i = 1$ Figure 17.24(c, d).

Update LLR `level1` = 3. From (17.52),

$$L_8^{(4)}(y_0^7 | \hat{u}_0^3) = L_4^{(2)}(y_0^3 | (\hat{u}_0, \hat{u}_2) \oplus (\hat{u}_1, \hat{u}_3)) \boxplus L_4^{(2)}(y_4^7 | \hat{u}_1, \hat{u}_3).$$

Neither of the $L_4^{(2)}$ are available. From (17.52) again,

$$\underbrace{L_4^{(2)}(y_0^3|(\hat{u}_0, \hat{u}_2) \oplus (\hat{u}_1, \hat{u}_3))}_{\text{LLR(1)}} = \underbrace{L_2^{(1)}(y_0^1|(\hat{u}_0 \oplus \hat{u}_1) \oplus (u_2 \oplus u_3))}_{\text{LLR(3)}} \boxplus \underbrace{L_2^{(1)}(y_2^3|\hat{u}_2 \oplus \hat{u}_3)}_{\text{LLR(4)}},$$

$$\underbrace{L_4^{(2)}(y_4^7, (\hat{u}_1, \hat{u}_3))}_{\text{LLR(2)}} = \underbrace{L_2^{(1)}(y_4^5|\hat{u}_1 \oplus \hat{u}_3)}_{\text{LLR(5)}} \boxplus \underbrace{L_2^{(1)}(y_6^7|\hat{u}_3)}_{\text{LLR(6)}}.$$

At level 3, a lower (t) is computation performed, reassociating the values `LLR(3)`, `LLR(4)`, `LLR(5)`, and `LLR(6)`. At level 2, upper (s) computations are performed, and then another at level 1.

In terms of the tree, the message that node a sends to its right child c is the vector

$$\alpha_{a_r} = (L_{y_1} \overset{\hat{u}_{0,\text{even}} \oplus \hat{u}_{0,\text{odd}}}{\pm} L_{y_0}, L_{y_3} \overset{\hat{u}_2 \oplus \hat{u}_3}{\pm} L_{y_2}, L_{y_5} \overset{\hat{u}_1 \oplus \hat{u}_3}{\pm} L_{y_4}, L_{y_7} \overset{\hat{u}_3}{\pm} L_{y_6}))$$

$$= (L_2^{(1)}(y_0^1|\hat{u}_{0,\text{even}} \oplus \hat{u}_{0,\text{odd}}), L_2^{(1)}(y_2^3|\hat{u}_2 \oplus \hat{u}_3), L_2^{(1)}(y_4^5|\hat{u}_1 \oplus \hat{u}_3), L_2^{(1)}(y_6^7|\hat{u}_3)).$$

The message that node c sends its left child f is the vector

$$\alpha_{c_l} = (\alpha_{a_r}[0] \boxplus \alpha_{a_r}[1], \alpha_{a_r}[2] + \alpha_{a_r}[3]) = (L_4^{(2)}(y_0^3|(\hat{u}_0, \hat{u}_2) \oplus (\hat{u}_1, \hat{u}_3)), L_4^{(2)}(y_4^7|(\hat{u}_1, \hat{u}_3)).$$

The message that node f sends its left child is the vector

$$\alpha_{f_l} = \alpha_{c_l}[0] \boxplus \alpha_{c_l}[1] = L_8^{(4)}(y_0^7, \hat{u}_0^3).$$

At the leaf node, the bit is detected and sent to its parent

$$\beta_{f_l} = \tilde{h}(\alpha_{f_l}) = \hat{u}_4.$$

Update Bits Since $i < N/2$, no bit updates are computed.

$j = 5, i = 5$ Figure 17.24(e, f).

Update LLR `level1=1`. Using (17.53),

$$L_8^{(5)}(y_0^7|\hat{u}_0^4) = L_4^{(2)}(y_4^7|\hat{u}_0^3) \overset{\hat{u}_4}{\pm} L_4^{(2)}(y_0^3|\hat{u}_{0,\text{even}}^3 \oplus \hat{u}_{0,\text{odd}}^3).$$

Both of the $L_4^{(2)}$ are available, so this lower (t) does not require any additional levels.

In terms of the tree, the message that node f computes and sends its right child $\hat{u}_5$ is

$$\alpha_{f_r} = \alpha_{c_l}[3] \overset{\beta_{f_l}}{\pm} \alpha_{c_l}[2] = L_4^{(2)}(y_0^3, (\hat{u}_0, \hat{u}_2) \oplus (\hat{u}_1, \hat{u}_3)) \boxplus L_4^{(2)}(y_4^7, (\hat{u}_1, \hat{u}_3)).$$

At the leaf node $\hat{u}_5$ the bit is detected and sent up

$$\beta_{f_r} = \tilde{h}(\alpha_{f_r}) = \hat{u}_5.$$

At this point, node f has received messages from both of its children and its sends a message to its parents consisting of 2 bits

$$\beta_{c_l} = (\hat{u}_4 \oplus \hat{u}_5, \hat{u}_5).$$

Update Bits There are two levels. According to the rules described for $i = 6$, there are no lower bits computed, and 1 level of upper bits computed at level 1, including propagating a bit forward.

$j = 6$, $i = 3$ Figure 17.25(a, b).

Update LLR `level1=1`. Using (17.52),

$$L_8^{(6)}(y_0^7|\hat{u}_0^5) = L_4^{(3)}(y_0^3|(\hat{u}_0 \oplus \hat{u}_1, \hat{u}_2 \oplus \hat{u}_3, \hat{u}_4 \oplus \hat{u}_5)) \boxplus L_4^{(3)}(y_4^7|(\hat{u}_1, \hat{u}_3, \hat{u}_5)).$$

The $L_4^{(3)}$ must be computed. Using (17.53),

$$\underbrace{L_4^{(3)}(y_0^3|(\hat{u}_0 \oplus \hat{u}_1, \hat{u}_2 \oplus \hat{u}_3, \hat{u}_4 \oplus \hat{u}_5))}_{\text{LLR(1)}}$$

$$= L_2^{(1)}(y_2^3|\hat{u}_2 \oplus \hat{u}_3) \overset{\hat{u}_4 \oplus \hat{u}_5}{\pm} L_2^{(1)}(y_0^1|\hat{u}_0 \oplus \hat{u}_1 \oplus \hat{u}_2 \oplus \hat{u}_3),$$

$$\underbrace{L_4^{(3)}(y_4^7|(\hat{u}_1, \hat{u}_3, \hat{u}_5))}_{\text{LLR(2)}} = L_2^{(1)}(y_6^7|\hat{u}_3) \overset{\hat{u}_5}{\pm} L_2^{(1)}(y_4^5|\hat{u}_1 \oplus \hat{u}_3).$$

The $L_2^{(1)}$ values are available from the $j = 4$ step.

In terms of the tree, the message that node c sends to its right child g is the vector

$$
\begin{aligned}
\alpha_{c_r} &= (\alpha_{a_r}[1] \overset{\hat{u}_4 \oplus \hat{u}_5}{\pm} \alpha_{a_r}[0], \alpha_{a_r}[3] \overset{\hat{u}_5}{\pm} \alpha_{a_r}[2]) \\
&= (L_4^{(3)}(y_0^3, (\hat{u}_0 \oplus \hat{u}_1, \hat{u}_2 \oplus \hat{u}_3, \hat{u}_4 \oplus \hat{u}_5)), L_4^{(3)}(y_4^7, (\hat{u}_1, \hat{u}_3, \hat{u}_5))).
\end{aligned}
\tag{17.56}
$$

The message that g sends to its left node $\hat{u}_6$ is

$$\alpha_{g_l} = \alpha_{c_r}[0] \boxplus \alpha_{c_r}[1] = L_8^{(6)}(y_0^7, \hat{u}_0^5).$$

At the leaf node $\hat{u}_6$ the bit is detected and sent up

$$\beta_{\beta_l} = \tilde{h}(\alpha_{g_l}) = \hat{u}_6.$$

Update Bits Since $i < N/2$, no bit propagation.

$j = 7$, $i = 7$ Figure 17.25(c).

Update LLR `level1=1`. Using (17.53),

$$L_8^{(7)}(y_0^7|\hat{u}_0^6) = L_4^{(3)}(y_4^7|(\hat{u}_1, \hat{u}_3, \hat{u}_5)) \overset{\hat{u}_6}{\pm} L_4^{(3)}(y_0^3|(\hat{u}_0 \oplus \hat{u}_1, \hat{u}_2 \oplus \hat{u}_3, \hat{u}_4 \oplus \hat{u}_5)).$$

The $L_4^{(3)}$ are available from step $j = 6$.

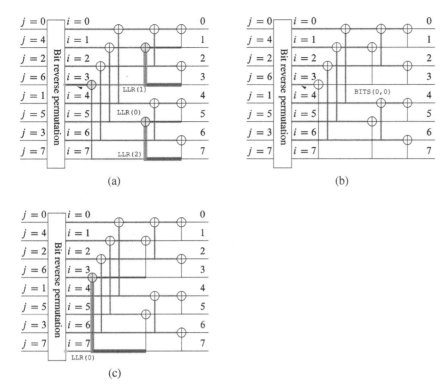

Figure 17.25: Successive cancellation steps, $j = 6, 7, i = 3, 7$. (a) LLR path for bit $j = 6, i = 3$. level1 = 2; (b) bit propagation $j = 6, i = 3$; (c) LLR path for bit $j = 7, i = 7$. level1 = 1. (Color versions of the page can be found at wileywebpage or `https://github.com/tkmoon/eccbook/colorpages`.).

In terms of the tree, the message that node g sends to its right child $\hat{u}_7$ is

$$\alpha_{g_r} = \alpha_{c_r}[1] \overset{\hat{u}_6}{\pm} \alpha_{c_r}[0] = L_8^{(7)}(y_0^y|\hat{u}_0^6).$$

The bit is detected, but there is no need to send a message back:

$$\hat{u}_7 = \tilde{h}(\alpha_{g_r}).$$

Update Bits Since all bits have been estimated, there is no need to propagate bits, so no computation is performed.

17.4.11 Pseudo-Code Description of Successive Cancellation Algorithm

Combining the observations above, the successive cancellation algorithm is set forth in Algorithm 17.2.

Algorithm 17.2 Successive Cancellation Decoder

Function SCPolarDecode(**y**)
% Decode polar coded data from a Gaussian channel
% Derived from code by Harish Vangala then of (Monash University)
%
Input: **y** received vector of length N
1 computeLLR(**y**, LLR + N − 1)   % compute log-likelihood ratios and put into last N
   positions of LLR array
2 **for** $j = 0, 1, \ldots, N - 1$ **do** % For each bit position
3 $\quad$ (i, level1, level0) = bitreverse(j, n)   % i is bit-reversed of j
   $\quad$ % level1 = index of first 1 in binary representation of i. level0 = index of first 0 in
   $\quad\quad$ binary representation of i
4 $\quad$ updateLLR(i, level1)   % Compute LLR at bit j, right to left
5 $\quad$ LLRtobit(j, i)   % Convert LLR to bit in bitsout[i], using code design
6 $\quad$ LLRfinal[i] = LLR[0]   % save the likelihood (optional)
7 $\quad$ updateBITS(bitsout[j], i, level0)   % Push the bits right
8 **end**

Function updateLLR(*i, level1*)
% Update the LLR at (reversed) bit i using level1, pushing LLRs from right to left
Input: i bit-reversed bit index, level1 index of 1st 1 in i
9 **if** $i = 0$ **then**
10 $\quad$ nextlevel = n % No "lower" computations for first iteration
11 **else**
12 $\quad$ % At the deepest level of the tree for this i, do the LLR "lower" t computation
13 $\quad$ lastlevel = level1
14 $\quad$ start = $2^{\text{level1}-1} - 1$
15 $\quad$ end = $2^{\text{level1}} - 1$
16 $\quad$ **for** index = start, start + 1, $\ldots$, end − 1 **do**
17 $\quad\quad$ LLR[index] = LLRlower(BITS[0][index], LLR[end + 2(index −
   $\quad\quad$ start)], LLR[end + 2(index − start) + 1])
18 $\quad$ **end**
19 $\quad$ nextlevel = level1 - 1
20 **end**

% Do the other levels of the tree with "upper" s computations
21 **for** level = nextlevel, nextlevel − 1, $\ldots$, 1 **do**
22 $\quad$ start = $2^{\text{level}-1} - 1$
23 $\quad$ end = $2^{\text{level}} - 1$
24 $\quad$ **for** index = start, $\ldots$, end − 1 **do**
25 $\quad\quad$ LLR[index] =
   $\quad\quad$ LLRupper(LLR[end + 2(index − start)], LLR[end + 2(index − start) + 1]
26 $\quad$ **end**
27 **end**

Function `updateBITS` (*latestbit, i, level0*)
% Push estimated bits from left to right
Input: latestbit is most recent bit estimate; i is (bit reversed) bit number; level0 is index of
　　　0 in i

28 **if** $i = N - 1$ **then** % Nothing more to do on last step
29 　| return
30 **else if** $i < N/2$ **then** % bit lines in the top half
31 　|
32 　| BITS[0][0] = latestbit　　　　　　　% Just save the bit for next step
33 **else**
34 　| lastlevel = level0
35 　| BITS[1][0] = latestbit
36 　| **for** level1 $= 1, \ldots,$ lastlevel $- 2$ **do**
37 　| 　| start $= 2^{\text{level}-1} - 1$
38 　| 　| end $= 2^{\text{level}} - 1$
39 　| 　| **for** index $=$ start$, \ldots,$ end $- 1$ **do**
40 　| 　| 　| BITS[1][end $+ 2($index $-$ start$)$] = BITS[0][index] $\oplus$ BITS[1][index]
41 　| 　| 　| BITS[1][end $+ 2($index $-$ start$) + 1$] = BITS[1][index] % propagate
42 　| 　| **end**
43 　| **end**
44 　| **if** level0 $= n$ **then return**
　　　　　　　　　　% Don't need to compute upper bits here
45 　| level = lastlevel - 1;
46 　| start $= 2^{\text{level}-1} - 1$
47 　| end $= 2^{\text{level}} - 1$
48 　| **for** index $=$ start$, \ldots,$ end $- 1$ **do**
49 　| 　| BITS[0][end $+ 2($index $-$ start$)$] = BITS[0][index] $\oplus$ BITS[1][index]
50 　| 　| BITS[0][end $+ 2($index $-$ start$) + 1$] = BITS[1][index]
51 　| **end**
52 **end**

Function `LLRupper` (*LLR1, LLR2*)
% Compute the likelihood for the "upper" part, using log-based computation
Input: LLR1: LLR input from upper branch; LLR2: LLR input from lower branch
Output: Returns log likelihood

53 **return** logdomainsum($LLR1 + LLR2, LLR1$) $-$ logdomainsum($LLR1, LLR2$)

Function `LLRlower` (*bit, LLR1, LLR2*)
% Compute the likelihood for the "lower" part, using log-based computation
Input: bit: input bit; LLR1: LLR input from upper branch; LLR2: LLR input from lower branch
Output: Returns log likelihood

54 **if** *bit* $= 0$ **then**
55 　| **return** $LLR1 + LLR2$
56 **else**
57 　| **return** $LLR2 - LLR1$
58 **end**

Function `logdomainsum` (*x, y*)
Output: Returns log likelihood

59 **if** $y > x$ **then**
60 　| **return** $y + \log(1 + \exp(x - y))$
61 **else**
62 　| **return** $x + \log(1 + \exp(y - x))$
63 **end**

17.5   Some Theorems of Polar Coding Theory

This section formalizes and generalizes the ideas that have been developed informally in this chapter.

17.5.1 $I(W)$ and $Z(W)$ for general B-DMCs

The informal development above presented examples using the BEC. We generalize this to other channels. For a B-DMC channel W there are two parameters of interest related to polar coding. The first is the symmetric capacity already introduced,

$$I(W) = \sum_{y \in \mathcal{Y}} \sum_{x \in \mathcal{X}} \frac{1}{2} W(y|x) \log_2 \frac{W(y|x)}{\frac{1}{2}W(y|0) + \frac{1}{2}W(y|1)}. \tag{17.57}$$

By the channel coding theorem, $I(W)$ represents the Shannon channel capacity when W is a symmetric channel, the highest rate at which information can reliably transmitted through the channel by using equiprobable selection of input data $x \in \mathcal{X}$.

Example 17.7   Recall that

- For the $BEC(p)$ channel, $I(W) = 1 - p$;
- For the $BSC(p)$ channel, $I(W) = 1 - H_2(p)$.   □

The second parameter of interest is the *Battacharyya parameter*. For a binary channel $W : \mathcal{X} \to \mathcal{Y}$, the Battacharyya parameter is defined as

$$Z(W) = \sum_{y \in \mathcal{Y}} \sqrt{W(y|0)W(y|1)}. \tag{17.58}$$

For channels with a continuum of outputs such as a Gaussian channel,

$$Z(W) = \int_{y \in \mathcal{Y}} \sqrt{W(y|0)W(y|1)}.$$

The Battacharyya parameters may be thought of as a measure of the distance between the pmf (or pdf) $W(y|0)$ and the pmf (or pdf) $W(y|0)$.

Example 17.8

- For the BEC(p) channel it is straightforward to show that

$$Z(W) = p.$$

- For the BSC(p) channel,

$$Z(W) = \sqrt{4p(1 - p)}.$$

□

As suggested by these examples, when $Z(W)$ is small, the channel is reliable (p is small). As discussed in Section 17.5.5, the Battacharyya parameter is an upper bound on the probability of error in maximum likelihood (ML) decoding. A small Battacharyya parameter corresponds to a low probability of error for ML decoding. Figure 17.26 shows $Z(W)$ for $0 \le p \le 0.5$ for the BEC and the BSC channels. Qualitatively, $Z(W)$ for these two channels is similar, in that they both start at $Z(W) = 0$ and increase

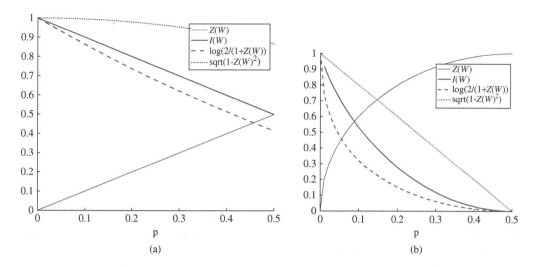

Figure 17.26: $Z(W)$, $I(W)$ and the bounds from (17.59) and (17.60). (a) BEC; (b) BSC.

monotonically with p (for $p \in [0, 0.5]$). We will find that we can use $Z(W)$ for a general channel where previously we used p.

There is a tradeoff between the information $I(W)$ and $Z(W)$: If $Z(W)$ is near 0 or 1, then $I(W)$ is near 1 or 0, respectively. These intuitions are quantified by the following theorem:

Theorem 17.9 *For any B-DMC channel W,*

$$I(W) \geq \log_2 \frac{2}{1 + Z(W)} \tag{17.59}$$

$$I(W) \leq \sqrt{1 - Z(W)^2}. \tag{17.60}$$

Proof of this theorem is given in Section 17.5.5. Figure 17.26 shows $Z(W)$, $I(W)$, and the bounds (17.59) and (17.60) for the BEC and BSC.

17.5.2 Channel Polarization

In this section, we formalize and generalize results that were developed more informally in the previous sections. We first abstract the notation used in the polarization recursion equations (17.40) and (17.41).

- Let W be shorthand for $W_N^{(i)}$.
- Let y_0 be shorthand for the set of data $(y_0^{N-1}, u_{0,\text{even}}^{2i-1} \oplus u_{0,\text{odd}}^{2i-1})$.
- Let y_1 be shorthand for $(y_N^{2N-1}, u_{0,\text{odd}}^{2i-1})$.
- Let u_0 be shorthand for u_{2i}.
- Let u_1 be shorthand for u_{2i+1}.
- Let W^0 be shorthand for $W_{2N}^{(2i)}$.
- Let W^1 be shorthand for $W_{2N}^{(2i+1)}$.
- Let $\mathsf{F}(\mathsf{y}_0, \mathsf{y}_1) = (y_0^{2N-1}, u_0^{2i-1})$, that is, a pooling of the data in y_0 and y_1.

Using this notation, (17.40) can be written as

$$W^0(F(y_0, y_1)|u_0) = \frac{1}{2} \sum_{u_1} W(y_0|u_0 \oplus u_1)W(y_1|u_1) \tag{17.61}$$

and (17.41) can be written as

$$W^1(F(y_0, y_1), u_0|u_1) = \frac{1}{2}W(y_0|u_0 \oplus u_1)W(y_1|u_1). \tag{17.62}$$

Under this shorthand, the mapping $(W_N^{(i)}, W_N^{(i)}) \mapsto (W_{2N}^{(2i)}, W_{2N}^{(2i+1)})$ in the sense of (17.40) and (17.41) is expressed as

$$(W, W) \mapsto (W^0, W^1). \tag{17.63}$$

That is, two independent copies of a channel W, whose channel transition probabilities are functions of independent data y_0 and y_1, produce two new channels W^0 and W^1, which are functions of the pool of the data $F(y_0, y_1)$ in the first case, and that pool and the input u_0 in the second case.

Let the input and output spaces of W and outputs be denoted by $\mathcal{X}$ and $\tilde{\mathcal{Y}}$, so $W : \mathcal{X} \to \tilde{\mathcal{Y}}$. Let $W^0 : \mathcal{X} \to \tilde{\mathcal{Y}} \times \tilde{\mathcal{Y}}$. Denote $\tilde{\mathcal{Y}} \times \tilde{\mathcal{Y}}$ by $\mathcal{Y}^0$. Then

$$W^0 : \mathcal{X} \to \mathcal{Y}^0$$

and

$$W^1 : \mathcal{X} \to \mathcal{Y}^0 \times \mathcal{X}.$$

Example 17.10   Recall from (17.9) that

$$W_2^{(0)} : U_0 \mapsto Y_0, Y_1.$$

Taking $W = W_2^{(0)}$, we have $\mathcal{X} = \{0, 1\}$ and $\tilde{\mathcal{Y}} = \mathcal{Y} \times \mathcal{Y}$, the space of the two outputs Y_0, Y_1.

From (17.27) and (17.28),

$$W_4^{(0)} : U_0 \mapsto (Y_0, Y_1, Y_2, Y_3)$$

$$W_4^{(1)} : U_1 \mapsto (Y_0, Y_1, Y_2, Y_3, X).$$

Taking $W^0 = W_4^{(0)}$ and $W^1 = W_4^{(1)}$, we see that $\mathcal{Y}^0$ is the space $\tilde{\mathcal{Y}} \times \tilde{\mathcal{Y}}$ and $\mathcal{Y}^1 = \mathcal{Y}^0 \otimes \mathcal{X}$.   □

The following theorem formalizes and generalizes the observation about polarization made in (17.10).

Theorem 17.11   *Suppose* $(W, W) \mapsto (W^0, W^1)$. *Then*

$$I(W^0) + I(W^1) = 2I(W) \tag{17.64}$$

$$I(W^0) \leq I(W^1). \tag{17.65}$$

Proof   Let $U_0, U_1 \in \mathcal{X}$ be independent and let $(X_0, X_1) = (U_0 \oplus U_1, U_1)$. Let $(Y_0, Y_1) \in \tilde{\mathcal{Y}}$. Then for $U_0 \in \mathcal{X}$,

$$I(W^0) = I(U_0; Y_0, Y_1)$$

and

$$I(W^1) = I(U_1; Y_0, Y_1, U_0).$$

Since U_0 and U_1 are independent, $I(U_1; Y_0, Y_1, U_0)$ is equal to $I(U_1; Y_0, Y_1|U_0)$. By the chain rule,

$$I(\mathsf{W}^0) + I(\mathsf{W}^1) = I(U_0; Y_0, Y_1) + I(U_1; Y_0, Y_1|U_0) = I(U_0, U_1; Y_0, Y_1).$$

Since (X_0, X_1) and (U_0, U_1) are in a one-to-one, onto relationship,

$$I(U_0, U_1; Y_0, Y_1) = I(X_0, X_1; Y_0, Y_1).$$

Now note that $I(X_0, X_1; Y_0, Y_1) = I(X_0; Y_0) + I(X_1; Y_1) = 2I(\mathsf{W})$. This proves (17.64).
    To prove (17.65),

$$I(\mathsf{W}^1) = I(U_1; Y_0, Y_1, U_0) = I(U_1; Y_1) + I(U_1; Y_0, U_0|Y_1) \quad \text{(chain rule)}$$
$$= I(\mathsf{W}) + I(U_1; Y_0, U_0|Y_1).$$

This shows that $I(\mathsf{W}^1) \geq I(\mathsf{W})$. In light of (17.64) it must be the case that $I(\mathsf{W}^0) \leq I(\mathsf{W}^1)$. $\qquad\square$

    It can be shown that $I(\mathsf{W}^0) = I(\mathsf{W}^1)$ if and only if $I(\mathsf{W})$ equals 0 or 1.
    In Sections 17.3.4 and 17.4.4 it was demonstrated that for a BEC(p) channel W, the result of combining and splitting to produce channels W^0 and W^1 is that channels W^0 and W^1 are BEC($2p - p^2$) and BEC(p^2), respectively. The following theorem formalizes this and extends beyond BEC channels.

Theorem 17.12 *Suppose $(\mathsf{W}, \mathsf{W}) \mapsto (\mathsf{W}^0, \mathsf{W}^1)$ in the sense of (17.61) and (17.62). Then*

$$Z(\mathsf{W}^0) \leq 2Z(\mathsf{W}) - Z(\mathsf{W})^2 \tag{17.66}$$

$$Z(\mathsf{W}^1) = Z(\mathsf{W})^2 \tag{17.67}$$

$$Z(\mathsf{W}^0) \geq Z(\mathsf{W}) \geq Z(\mathsf{W}^1), \tag{17.68}$$

where $Z(\mathsf{W})$ is the Battacharyya parameter for the channel W (17.58).

    The proof of this theorem is provided in Appendix 17.C.
    The inequalities in (17.68) show that the W^1 channel, that is, the $W_{2N}^{(2i+1)}$ channel, i.e., the "odd" channel, is better than the $W_{2N}^{(2i)}$ channel, or the "even" channel. As a result, as the combining and splitting operations are recursively applied polarization happens.
    As we have seen in the examples, for the BEC channel, the result (17.66) holds with equality. For other channels, $Z(\mathsf{W}^0)$ is merely bounded by $2Z(\mathsf{W}) - Z(\mathsf{W})^2$.
    Less abstractly, (17.64) and (17.68) can be expressed as

$$I(W_{2N}^{(2i)}) + I(W_{2N}^{(2i+1)}) = 2I(W_N^{(i)}) \tag{17.69}$$

$$Z(W_{2N}^{(2i)}) + Z(W_{2N}^{(2i+1)}) \leq 2Z(W_N^{(i)}). \tag{17.70}$$

    Recall the discussion in the context of Figure 17.16, in which it was shown numerically that the channels $W_N^{(i)}$ polarize: most have capacity going to either 0 or 1, with a vanishingly small fraction in between. Let $\delta > 0$. As $N \to \infty$, channels with $I(W_N^{(i)}) < \delta$ are "bad." Channels with $I(W_N^{(i)}) > 1 - \delta$ are "good." Channels with $I(W_N^{(i)}) \in [\delta, 1 - \delta)$ are "ugly"[2] . The key polarization theorem is that the fraction of channels with $I(W_N^{(i)}) > 1 - \delta$ goes to $I(\mathsf{W})$, that is, the channel capacity. This theorem is formally stated and proved in the next section.

---

[2] The language here is due to Emre Telatar. See [437].

17.5.3 The Polarization Theorem

The polarization theorem establishes the main tenet of polar coding theory: the fraction of good channels approaches $I(W)$, the fraction of bad channels approaches $1 - I(W)$, so the fraction of ugly channels approaches 0, as $N \to \infty$.

Theorem 17.13 *[16, Theorem 1]* (**The Polarization Theorem**) *For any B-DMC W, the channels* $\{W_N^{(i)}\}$ *polarize in the sense that, for any fixed* $\delta \in (0, 1)$, *as* $N \to \infty$ *through powers of 2, the fraction of channels* $W_N^{(i)}$, $i \in \{0, 1, \dots, N - 1\}$ *for which* $I(W_N^{(i)}) \in (1 - \delta, 1]$ *goes to* $I(W)$ *and the fraction of channels for which* $I(W_N^{(i)}) \in [0, \delta)$ *goes to* $1 - I(W)$.

By this theorem, as the channels polarize into "good" and "bad" channels, and the "ugly" channels are squeezed out as $N \to \infty$.

17.5.4 A Few Facts About Martingales

The proof of the polarization theorem makes use of some martingale theory. In preparation for the proof, we briefly present a few facts about this important class of random processes.

Definition 17.14 [411, Section 6.8] A random sequence $\{X_0, X_1, X_2, \dots\}$ with $E[|X[k]|] < \infty$ is a *martingale* if

$$E[X_k | X_{k-1}, X_{K-2}, \dots, X_0] = X_{k-1} \quad \text{for all } k \ge 1.$$

Such a random sequence is said to be *supermartingale* if

$$E[X_k | X_{k-1}, X_{k-2}, \dots, X_0] \le X_{k-1}.$$

A random sequence Y_k with $E[|Y_k|] < \infty$ is martingale with respect to sequence X_k if

$$E[Y_k | X_{k-1}, X_{k-2}, \dots, X_0] = Y_{k-1} \quad \text{for all } k \ge 1. \qquad \square$$

Martingales and supermartingales enjoy a convergence property that says that the martingale or supermartingale sequence $\{X_n\}$ is a uniformly integrable sequence and it converges almost everywhere to an integrable random variable X_∞. (see [71, Theorem 9.4.5, Theorem 9.4.6]). An implication of this (see [71, Theorem 4.5.4]) is that

$$\lim_{n \to \infty} E[X[n]] = E[\lim_{n \to \infty} X[n]],$$

that is, taking limits and expectations can be interchanged.

Let $\{X_0, X_1, X_2, \dots\}$ be a martingale sequence. Then by definition

$$E[X_1 | X_0] = X_0. \qquad (17.71)$$

Taking expectations again and using the rule of iterated expectation,[3]

$$E[E[X_1 | X_0]] = E[X_1].$$

In combination with (17.71), $E[X_1] = E[X_0]$.

---

[3] The rule of iterated expectations says $E[E[X|Y]] = E[X]$.

Repeating this at the next sample instant,

$$E[X_2 | X_1, X_0] = X_1.$$

Using iterated expectation again,

$$E[E[X_2 | X_1, X_0] = E[X_2]$$

and by martingale property this is also $E[X_1] = E[X_0]$, so that $E[X_2] = E[X_0]$. Proceeding inductively, $E[X_n] = E[X_0]$, $n = 1, 2, \ldots$.

17.5.5 Proof of the Polarization Theorem

Proof The tree in Figure 17.12 can be associated with a random process. Let B_n be 0 or 1 with equal probability, that is, Bernoulli(1/2), and let $b_1 b_2 \ldots b_n$ be a sequence of outcomes of these random values. Define a random process of channels $\{K_n, n \geq 0\}$ as follows: Begin at the root $K_0 = W$. For $n \geq 0$, when $K_n = W^{b_1 b_2 \cdots b_n}$, the next node K_{n+1} is randomly set to $W^{b_1 b_2 \cdots b_n 0}$ or $W^{b_1 b_2 \cdots b_n 1}$, with equal probability. The node $W^{b_1 b_2 \cdots b_n}$ represents $W_N^{(i)}$, where $N = 2^n$ and $b_1 b_2 \ldots b_n$ is the binary representation of the number i. Given a sequence of bits $b_1 \ldots b_n$, defining a node on the tree in Figure 17.12 its successor nodes are $b_1 \ldots b_n 0$ and $b_1 \ldots b_n 1$, representing channels $W_{2N}^{(2i)}$ and $W_{2N}^{(2i+1)}$, respectively.

Associated with this random process of channels, define the real random processes $I_n = I(K_n)$ and $Z_n = Z(K_n)$, the information and Battacharyya parameter, respectively, associated with the channel K_n.

At the root of the tree, $I_0 = I(W)$ and $Z_0 = Z(W)$, which are not random variables.

We will show the following:

- I_n is a martingale sequence which has a limit I_∞ such that $E[I_\infty] = I_0$.

- Z_n is a supermartingale which has a limit Z_∞.

- Based on Theorem 17.12, we will show that Z_∞ takes on values either 0 or 1.

- From this it follows that I_∞ takes on values of either 0 or 1, from which we can determine the fraction of channel on which it takes on the value 1.

Given a sequence of bits $b_1 b_2 \ldots b_n$ defining a node on the tree in Figure 17.12 and its associated random process $\{I_n, n \geq 0\}$,

$$E[I_{n+1} | b_1, \ldots, b_n] = I(W^{b_1 b_n 0}) P(B_{n+1} = 0) + I(W^{b_1 b_n 1}) P(B_{n+1} = 1)$$

$$= I(W_{2N}^{(2i)}) P(B_{n+1} = 0) + I(W_{2N}^{(2i+1)}) P(B_{n+1} = 1)$$

$$= \frac{1}{2} (I(W_{2N}^{(2i)}) + I(W_{2N}^{(2i+1)}))$$

$$= I(W^{b_1 \cdots b_n}) = I(W_N^{(i)}),$$

where the last equality follows from (17.69). Thus, $\{I_n, n \geq 0\}$ is a martingale with respect to the sequence $\{b_n, n \geq 0\}$. By the results in Section 17.5.4, the martingale converges to a limit I_∞ such that $E[I_\infty] = E[I_0]$. Since $I_0 = I(W)$ (not random), $E[I_\infty] = I_0$.

Now consider the random process $\{Z_n, n \geq 0\}$. Given a sequence of bits $b_1 \ldots b_n$ defining a node on the tree,

$$E[Z_{n+1} | b_1, \ldots, b_n] = Z(W^{b_1 \cdots b_n 0}) P(b_{n+1} = 0) + Z(W^{b_1 \cdots b_n 1}) P(b_{n+1} = 1)$$

$$= \frac{1}{2} Z(W^{b_1 \cdots b_n 0}) + \frac{1}{2} Z(W^{b_1 \cdots b_n 0}) \leq Z(W^{b_1 \cdots b_n}) = Z_n,$$

where the inequality follows from (17.70). Thus, $\{Z_n\}$ is a supermartingale with respect to $b_1, \ldots, b_n$. Z_n converges to a limit Z_∞ so that $E[|Z_n - Z_\infty|] \to 0$ as $n \to \infty$. Since

$$E[|Z_n - Z_\infty|] = E[|Z_n - Z_{n+1} + Z_{n+1} - Z_\infty|] \leq E[|Z_n - Z_{n+1}|] + E[|Z_{n+1} - Z_\infty|] \to 0,$$

it must be that $E[|Z_n - Z_{n+1}|] \to 0$. By Theorem 17.12 and the construction of the tree, either $Z_{n+1} \leq 2Z_n - Z_n^2$ (from (17.66)) or $Z_{n+1} = Z_n^2$ (from (17.67)), each possibility occurring with probability $1/2$. Hence

$$E[|Z_{n+1} - Z_n|]$$
$$= E[|Z_{n+1} - Z_n| \mid Z_{n+1} = Z_n^2] P(Z_{n+1} = Z_n^2)$$
$$\quad + E[|Z_{n+1} - Z_n| \mid Z_{n+1} \neq Z_n^2] P(Z_{n+1} \neq Z_n^2)$$
$$\geq \frac{1}{2} E[|Z_n^2 - Z_n|] \geq 0.$$

Since the LHS converges to 0, $E[Z_n(Z_n - 1)] \to 0$, so that $E[Z_\infty(1 - Z_\infty)] \to 0$. This implies that $Z_\infty = 0$ or $Z_\infty = 1$. By the convergence properties of martingales, this is with probability 1.

Using the fact that Z_∞ is equal to 0 or 1 with probability 1 and using the inequalities in Theorem 17.9 implies that $I_\infty = 1 - Z_\infty$ w.p. 1. Since $E[I_\infty] = I_0$ and

$$E[I_\infty] = 1(P(I_\infty) = 1) + 0P(I_\infty) = I_0,$$

it follows that $P(I_\infty) = I_0 = I(W)$. $\square$

17.5.6 Another Polarization Theorem

In [437], another approach to proving polarization is presented, based on insights from BEC channels.

Let $W_N^{(i)}$, $0 \leq i < N$ denote a $\mathrm{BEC}(p_N^{(i)})$ channel. Let $I(W_N^{(i)})$ denote the information associated with the channel $W_N^{(i)}$, where for the BEC $I(W_N^{(i)}) = 1 - p_N^{(i)}$. Following the pattern in Section 17.3.4, the two children channels $W_{2N}^{(2i)}$ and $W_{2N}^{(2i+1)}$ are $\mathrm{BEC}(p_N^{(2i)})$ and $\mathrm{BEC}(p_N^{(2i+1)})$ channels. For notational simplicity, we will refer to $W_N^{(i)}$, $W_{2N}^{(2i)}$, and $W_{2N}^{(2i+1)}$ as W, W', and W'', respectively, with BEC channel parameters p, p', and p'', respectively. Then

$$p' = g(p) = 2p - p^2 \qquad p'' = h(p) = p^2.$$

We define the *ugliness of a* $\mathrm{BEC}(p)$ *channel* W by

$$\mathrm{ugly}(W) = \sqrt{4p(1-p)}.$$

This is a measure of how close the channel parameter p is to 0 or 1, or equivalently, how close the mutual information $I(W)$ is to 1 or 0 (respectively). A channel which is mediocre is one which has larger ugliness.

For a BEC channel W with parameter p and with ugliness $\mathrm{ugly}(W) = \sqrt{4p(1-p)}$, the ugliness of its two children W' and W'' is

$$\mathrm{ugly}(W'') = \sqrt{4p^2(1-p^2)} = \mathrm{ugly}(W_N^{(i)})\sqrt{p(1+p)}$$

and

$$\mathrm{ugly}(W') = \sqrt{4(2p - p^2)(1 - 2p + p^2)}$$
$$= \sqrt{4p(2-p)(1-p)^2} = \mathrm{ugly}(W)\sqrt{(2-p)(1-p)}.$$

The average ugliness of the two children is thus

$$\frac{1}{2}\mathrm{ugly}(W') + \frac{1}{2}\mathrm{ugly}W'' = \mathrm{ugly}(W)\frac{1}{2}[\sqrt{p(1+p)} + \sqrt{(2-p)(1-p)}].$$

By symmetry arguments (replacing $p \rightarrow 1 - p$) it is argued that the function involving the square roots is maximized when $p = \frac{1}{2}$, leading to

$$\frac{1}{2} \text{ugly}(W') + \frac{1}{2} \text{ugly} W'' \leq \text{ugly}(W) \sqrt{\frac{3}{4}}.$$

So, whatever the ugliness of W, on average its children are less ugly.

For a tree with root at W with ugliness $\text{ugly}(W)$, the average ugliness one level away is, as shown, less than or equal to $\sqrt{3/4} \text{ugly}(W)$. Inductively, the average ugliness n levels from the root is $\leq (3/4)^{n/2} \text{ugly}(W)$.

A channel W_N is said to be ϵ-mediocre if $I(W_N) \in (\epsilon, 1 - \epsilon)$, that is, its information neither close to 0 nor close to 1. *The fraction of ϵ-mediocre channels at level n of polarization* is defined as

$$\mu_n(\epsilon) = \frac{1}{2^n} \sum_{i=0,1,\ldots,2^n-1} [I(W_{2^n}^{(i)}) \in (\epsilon, 1 - \delta)],$$

where $[x]$ denote the indicator function

$$[x] = \begin{cases} 1 & \text{if } x \text{ is true} \\ 0 & \text{otherwise.} \end{cases}$$

For the BEC channel,

$$\mu_n(\epsilon) = \frac{1}{2^n} \sum_{i=0,1,\ldots,2^n-1} [p_N^{(i)} \in (\epsilon, 1 - \delta)].$$

Another measure of interest is the *fraction of good channels at level ϵ*, the fraction of channels whose information exceeds $1 - \epsilon$:

$$\gamma_n(\epsilon) = \frac{1}{2^n} \sum_{i=0,1,\ldots,N-1} [I(W_N^{(i)}) \geq \epsilon] = \frac{1}{2^n} \sum_{i=0,1,\ldots,N-1} [p_N^{(i)} \leq 1 - \epsilon].$$

The following theorem shows that the fraction of mediocre channels approaches 0, and the fraction of good channels approaches the BEC channel capacity $1 - p$:

Theorem 17.15 *For any $\epsilon > 0$ and any channel $W = BEC(p)$, the fraction of ϵ-mediocre channels vanishes:*

$$\lim_{n \to \infty} \mu_n(\epsilon) = 0. \tag{17.72}$$

Furthermore,

$$\lim_{n \to \infty} \gamma_n(\epsilon) = 1 - p. \tag{17.73}$$

Proof From the discussion above,

$$\frac{1}{2^n} \sum_{i=0,1,\ldots,N-1} \text{ugly}(W_{2^n}^{(i)}) \leq \left(\frac{3}{4}\right)^{n/2} \text{ugly}(W).$$

If $p_N^{(i)} \in (\epsilon, 1 - \epsilon)$, then

$$\text{ugly}(W_N^{(i)}) / \sqrt{4\epsilon(1 - \epsilon)} \geq 1,$$

so that

$$[p_N^{(i)} \in (\epsilon, 1 - \epsilon)] \leq \text{ugly}(W_N^{(i)} / \sqrt{4\epsilon(1 - \epsilon)}).$$

Thus,

$$\mu_n(\epsilon) = \frac{1}{2^n} \sum_{i=0,1,\ldots,N-1} [p_{2^n}^{(i)} \in (\epsilon, 1-\epsilon)] \le \left(\frac{3}{4}\right)^{n/2} / \sqrt{4\epsilon(1-\epsilon)},$$

so $\lim_{n\to\infty} \mu_n(\epsilon) = 0$.

Since for large n almost all channels at level n are either good or bad, and since the average erasure probability is preserved at each generation, it must be that the fraction of good channels approaches $1-p$. $\square$

This theorem would seem to establish the polarization as desired. But consider the probability of block errors under polar coding. Let $R < I(W)$ and let $K = NR$ be the number of channels used (unfrozen) and let $\mathcal{A}_K$ be an unfrozen set with K elements. Then for each $i \in \mathcal{A}_K$, $p_N^{(i)} < \epsilon$. The probability of block error is upper bounded by

$$\sum_{i \in \mathcal{A}_K} p_N^{(i)} \le N\epsilon.$$

That is, as N gets large, the bound on the probability of block error seems to go up, even though any individual channel has low probability. A stronger polarization theorem is needed, one in which $\epsilon \ll 1/N$. This is provided by the following.

Theorem 17.16 *Let $W = \text{BEC}(p)$. For any $\delta > 0$ let $\epsilon_n = 2^{-n^{\frac{1}{2}-\delta}}$. Then the fraction of ϵ_n-good channels approaches $1-p$:*

$$\lim_{n\to\infty} \gamma_n(\epsilon_n) = 1 - p.$$

Proof A channel $W_N^{(i)} = W_N^{b_1\ldots b_n}$ at level n (where $N = 2^n$) is said to be ϵ-tainted if it has an ϵ-mediocre ancestor $W_N^{b_1\ldots b_i}$ at any generation $i \in [\sqrt{n}, n]$. The fraction of tainted channels at generation n is upper bounded by

$$\sum_{j=\sqrt{n}}^{n} \mu_j(\epsilon) \le \frac{1}{\sqrt{4\epsilon(1-\epsilon)}} \sum_{j=\sqrt{n}}^{n} \left(\frac{3}{4}\right)^{j/2} \le K(\epsilon)\left(\frac{3}{4}\right)^{\sqrt{n}/2}$$

for some constant K that may depend on ϵ.

For small ϵ, the transformation $p_N^{(i)} \to p_{2N}^{(2i)}$ and $p_N^{(i)} \to p_{2N}^{(2i+1)}$ do not jump between $[0, \epsilon]$ and $[1-\epsilon, 1]$. So if ϵ is small and if $W_N^{b_1\ldots b_n}$ is ϵ-untainted, then all its ancestors $\{W^{(i)}, i \in [\sqrt{n}, n]\}$ are the same type, that is, all of the ancestors in generations $j \in [\sqrt{n}, n]$ are all either good or bad.

Another measure is *luck*. A channel $W_N^{(i)} = W_N^{b_1\ldots b_n}$ is said to be ϵ-*unlucky* if $\{b_i, i \in [\sqrt{n}, n]$ has an (unlucky) share of 1s:

$$\sum_{i=\sqrt{n}}^{n} [b_i = 1] < \left(\frac{1}{2} - \epsilon\right)n.$$

As n gets large, the fraction of ϵ-unlucky channels vanishes.

Let $p^{(i)} = p^{b_1\ldots b_n}$ denote an ϵ-good, ϵ-untainted, ϵ-lucky channel. The fraction of such channels approaches $1-p$ as n gets large. For such a channel, trace its ancestors in generations $i \in [\sqrt{n}, n]$. At each generation i next generational step, either the next generation satisfies

$$p^{b_1\ldots b_i b_{i+1}} = (p^{b_1\ldots b_i})^2$$

or

$$p^{b_1\ldots b_i b_{i+1}} = p^{b_1\ldots b_i}(2 - p^{b_1\ldots b_i}) \le 2p^{b_1\ldots b_i} = e^{-\epsilon'} p^{b_1\ldots b_i},$$

where $\epsilon' = 1/\log_2(1/\epsilon)$. Since the channel is untainted, the inequalities continue as

$$p^{b_1 \ldots b_i b} \leq (p^{b_1 \ldots b_i})^{1-\epsilon'}.$$

Taking logs of both of these,

$$\log_2 \frac{1}{p^{b_1 \ldots b_i b_{i+1}}} \geq \log_2 \frac{1}{p^{b_1 \ldots b_i}} \times \begin{cases} 2 & b_{i+1} = 1 \\ 1 - \epsilon' & b_{i+1} = 0. \end{cases}$$

Taking another log,

$$\log_2 \log_2 \frac{1}{p^{b_1, \ldots, b_i b_{i+1}}} \geq \log_2 \log_2 \frac{1}{b^{b_1 \ldots b_i}} + \begin{cases} 1 & b_{i+1} = 1 \\ -\epsilon'' & b_{i+1} = 0 \end{cases} \quad \text{where } \epsilon'' = -\log_2(1 - \epsilon').$$

Chaining these inequalities from $i = \sqrt{n}$ to $n - 1$ gives

$$\log_2 \log_2 \frac{1}{p^{b_1 \ldots b_n}} \geq \log_2 \log_2 \frac{1}{\epsilon} + \left(\frac{1}{2} - \epsilon\right) n - n\epsilon'' \geq \left(\frac{1}{2} - \delta\right) n \quad \text{for small enough } \epsilon.$$

Exponentiating,

$$-\log_2 p^{b_1 \ldots b_n} \geq 2^{(1/2-\delta)t} = N^{1/2-\delta}.$$

This proves the stronger version of the polarization result.

$\square$

17.5.7 Rate of Polarization

It is also of interest how rapidly polarization can happen, that is, how quickly polarization takes hold as N increases. Let $P_e(N, R)$ denote the *block* error probability for a rate R code with $R < I(W)$. One result is given here, without proof. (See the reference for proof and discussion.)

Theorem 17.17 *[18] Let W be a B-DMC. For any fixed rate $R < I(W)$ and constant $\beta < \frac{1}{2}$, for $N = 2^n$, $n \geq 0$, the block error probability for polar cancellation decoding at block length N satisfies*

$$P_e(N, R) = O(2^{-N^\beta})$$

that is, the probability of block error goes down as 2^{-N^β}.

17.5.8 Probability of Error Performance

In this section, we derive a bound on the probability of block error. The bound is expressed in terms of the Z function, specifically the function

$$Z(W_N^{(i)}) \triangleq \sum_{y_0^{N-1} \in \mathcal{Y}^N} \sum_{u_0^{i-1} \in \mathcal{X}^i} \sqrt{W_N^{(i)}(y_0^{N-1}, u_0^{i-1} | 0) W_N^{(i)}(y_0^{N-1}, u_0^{i-1} | 1)}. \tag{17.74}$$

For an $(N, K, \mathcal{A}, u_{\mathcal{A}^c})$ code, let $P_e(N, K, \mathcal{A}, u_{\mathcal{A}^c})$ denote the probability of block error, where each data vector $u_{\mathcal{A}} \in \mathcal{X}^K$ is sent with probability 2^{-K}, that is,

$$P_e(N, K, \mathcal{A}, u_{\mathcal{A}^c}) = \sum_{u_{\mathcal{A}} \in \mathcal{X}^K} \frac{1}{2^K} \sum_{y_0^{N-1} \in \mathcal{Y}^N : \hat{u}_0^{N-1} \neq u_0^{N-1}} W_N(y_0^{N-1} | u_0^{N-1}).$$

The average of this probability of error over all frozen bit sequences $u_{\mathcal{A}^c}$ is denoted $P_e(N, K, \mathcal{A})$:

$$P_e(N, K, \mathcal{A}) = \frac{1}{2^{N-K}} \sum_{u_{\mathcal{A}^c} \in \mathcal{X}^{N-k}} P_e(N, K, \mathcal{A}, u_{\mathcal{A}^c}).$$

The performance is bounded as follows:

Theorem 17.18 *For any B-DMC W and any choice of the parameters* $(N, K, \mathcal{A})$*,*

$$P_e(N, K, \mathcal{A}) \le \sum_{i \in \mathcal{A}} Z(W_N^{(i)}). \tag{17.75}$$

Proof Let u_0^{N-1} be an input sequence and y_0^{N-1} be its corresponding received value. Let $\hat{u}_0^{N_1}(u_0^{N_1}, y_0^{N-1})$ denote the SC-decoded block. Since the SC decoder always correctly decodes the frozen bits, we are interested in the error event

$$\mathcal{E} = \{(u_0^{N-1} \in \mathcal{X}^N, y_0^{N-1} \in \mathcal{Y}^N : \hat{u}_{\mathcal{A}^c}(u_0^{N-1}, y_0^{N-1}) \ne u_{\mathcal{A}}\}.$$

The probability of block error can be expressed in terms of this error event:

$$P_e(N, K, \mathcal{A}) = P(\mathcal{E}).$$

The error event $\mathcal{E}$ can be decomposed into events related to individual decoding errors. Let $\mathcal{B}_i$ be the event of a first decoding error at the i step of SC decoding:

$$\mathcal{B} = \{u_0^{N-1} \in \mathcal{X}^N, y_0^{N-1} \in \mathcal{Y}^N : u_0^{i-1} = \hat{u}_0^{i-1}(u_0^{N-1}, y_0^{N-1}, u_i \ne \hat{u}_i(u_0^{N-1}, y_0^{N-1}))\}.$$

Then $\mathcal{E} = \cup_{i \in \mathcal{A}} \mathcal{B}_i$. The set $\mathcal{B}_i$ can be written as

$$\mathcal{B}_i = \{u_0^{N-1} \in \mathcal{X}^N, y_0^{N-1} \in \mathcal{Y}^N : u_0^{i-1} = \hat{u}_0^{i-1}(u_0^{N-1}, y_0^{N-1}), u_i \ne h_i(y_0^{N-1}, u_0^{i-1})\}$$

$$\subset \{u_0^{N-1} \in \mathcal{X}^N, y_0^{N-1} \in \mathcal{Y}^N : u_i \ne h_i(y_0^{N-1})\}$$

$$\subset \{u_0^{N-1} \in \mathcal{X}^N, y_0^{N-1} \in \mathcal{Y}^N : W_N^{(i-1)}(y_0^{N-1}, u_0^{i-1} | u_i)\}$$

$$\le W_N^{(i-1)}(y_0^{N-1}, u_0^{i-1} | u_0 \oplus 1) \overset{\triangle}{=} \mathcal{E}_i.$$

Then $\mathcal{E} = \bigcup_{i \in \mathcal{A}} \mathcal{E}_i$, so by the union bound

$$P(\mathcal{E}) \le \sum_{i \in \mathcal{A}} P(\mathcal{E}_i).$$

Using the notation

$$[C] = \begin{cases} 1 & C \text{ is true} \\ 0 & C \text{ is not true} \end{cases}$$

the constituent probabilities in this sum can be bounded as follows:

$$P(\mathcal{E}_i) = \sum_{u_0^{N-1} \in \mathcal{X}^N, y_0^{N-1} \in \mathcal{Y}^N} \frac{1}{2^N} W_N(y_0^{N-1} | x_0^{N-1})[(u_0^{N-1}, y_0^{N-1}) \in \mathcal{E}_i]$$

$$\le \sum_{u_0^{N-1} \in \mathcal{X}^N, y_0^{N-1} \in \mathcal{Y}^N} \frac{1}{2^N} W_N(y_0^{N-1} | x_0^{N-1}) \sqrt{\frac{W_N^{(i)}(y_0^{N-1}, u_0^{i-1} | u_i \oplus 1)}{W_N^{(i)}(y_0^{N-1}, u_0^{i-1} | u_i)}} \tag{17.76}$$

$$= \sum_{y_0^{N-1}} \frac{1}{2} \sum_{u_i} \sum_{u_0^{i-1}} \frac{1}{2^{N-1}} \sum_{u_{i+1}^{N-1}} W_N(y_0^{N-1}|u_0^{N-1}) \sqrt{\frac{W_N^{(i)}(y_0^{N-1}, u_0^{i-1}|u_i \oplus 1)}{W_N^{(i)}(y_0^{N-1}, u_0^{i-1}|u_i)}} \quad (17.77)$$

$$= Z(W_N^{(i)})), \quad (17.78)$$

where the inequality (17.76) follows since for every sequence in $\mathcal{E}_i$ the ratio in the square root ≥ 1 by definition. The result (17.75) follows. $\qquad\square$

17.6 Designing Polar Codes

The design of a polar code consists of selecting the set $\mathcal{A}^c$, that is, the bits that are frozen in the encoding/decoding process. We will refer to the design as selecting the frozen set $\mathcal{F} = \mathcal{A}^c$. In principle, all that needs to be done to design good polar codes is to select the K best synthetic channels out of the N channels, to achieve a rate $R = K/N$ codes, where "best" here means the lowest values of $Z(W_N^{(i)})$, since that will result in the lowest bound (17.75) on the probability of block error. For BEC channels, this is easily accomplished since $Z(W_N^{(i)})$ can be recursively computed using (17.67) by (17.66) with equality

$$Z(W_N^{(2i)}) = 2Z(W_{N/2}^{(i)}) - Z(W_{N/2}^{(i)})^2 \quad Z(W_N^{(2i+1)}) = Z(W_{N/2}^{(i)})^2.$$

For a channel of specified length N, these N values can be easily computed, and the largest (worst) values are placed in the frozen bit set $\mathcal{F}$.

But for non-BEC channels, there is rarely a closed-form formula to compute $Z_N^{(i)}(W)$. In this section, we select methods from [462], in which four polar code design methodologies were compared. They showed that, under proper selection, these four methodologies produce codes with essentially the same performance. As a result, rather than presenting more complicated methods, we select a pair of methods.

An important consideration in polar code design is to recall that polar codes are *not* universal: a polar code is ideally designed for a particular channel, for example, at a particular SNR. If the code designed for one SNR is used in a channel with a different SNR, then the performance may degrade. The SNR at which a polar code is designed is called its *design SNR*.

Practically, however, once a code is designed for some particular SNR, it may be used over a range of SNRs (see, e.g., [431]). It is not necessary, therefore, to keep a separate code design for every single operating point in the channel.

A practical approach described by [462] is as follows:

1. Consider a set of SNRs $\{S_1, S_2, \ldots, S_m\}$ that cover the range of SNRs of interest in the channel.

2. For each SNR S_i, design a polar code (i.e., select $\mathcal{F}$ for the code).

3. Examine the bit error rate or block error rate as a function of SNR for each of these designed polar codes.

4. From this examination, select the single code (if possible) that best suits the application.

17.6.1 Code Design by Battacharyya Bound

This approach to code design operates by assuming that whatever the channel, the bound on the Battacharyya parameters in (17.67) and (17.66) is sufficiently tight to be used for code design.

The algorithm is initialized with the Battacharyya parameter appropriate for the channel. For a BEC(p) channel, simply set $z = p$. For a BSC(p), set $z = \sqrt{4p(1-p)}$. For an AWGN channel with SNR RE_b/N_0 dB, set $S = 10^{RE_b/N_0/10}$ and initialize with $z = e^{-S}$.

This results in the following algorithm.

testpolardesign.cc
polarcode.cc:
designBhatt2()

Algorithm 17.3 Design of Polar Codes Using Bhattacharrya Parameter

Function `DesignBhatt2`(*N, K, designSNRdB*)

% Design a polar code using the Bhattacharrya parameter at a particular design SNR

Input: N: Code length; K: Code dimension; designSNRdB

Output: $\mathcal{F} \subset \{0, 1, \ldots, N-1\}$, with $|\mathcal{F}| = N - K$

1 **Initialize** Allocate z, a vector of length N

2 designSNR = $10^{\text{designSNRdB}/10}$

3 $z[0] = -$designSNR $n = \log_2 N$ % number of levels

4

5 **for** $j = 1, 2, \ldots, n$ **do** For each level

6 $\quad$ $u = 2^j$

7 $\quad$ **for** $t = 0$ *to* $u/2 - 1$ **do**

8 $\quad\quad$ $T = z[t]$

9 $\quad\quad$ $z[t] = 2T - T^2$ % lower channel (bound)

10 $\quad\quad$ $z[u/2 + t] = T^2$ % upper channel (exact)

11 $\quad$ **end**

12 **end**

13 $\mathcal{F}$ = indices of the $N - K$ greatest elements of z

14 **return** $\mathcal{F}$

The indices of the $N - K$ greatest elements can be obtained, of course, by sorting the elements and retaining the sort order, then selecting the best $N - K$ indices of the sorted data.

17.6.2 Monte Carlo Estimation of $Z(W_N^{(i)})$

The expression in (17.77) can be written as

$$Z(W_N^{(i)}) = \sum_{y_0^{N-1}} \frac{1}{2^{N-1}} \sum_{u_{i+1}^{N-1}} W_N(y_0^{N-1}|u_0^{N-1}) \sqrt{\frac{W_N^{(i)}(y_0^{N-1}, u_0^{i-1}|u_i \oplus 1)}{W_N^{(i)}(y_0^{N-1}, u_0^{i-1}|u_i)}}.$$

Recognize this as an expectation with respect to the distribution $W_N(y_0^{N-1}|u_0^{N-1})$ of the quantity

$$\sqrt{\frac{W_N^{(i)}(y_0^{N-1}, u_0^{i-1}|u_i \oplus 1)}{W_N^{(i)}(y_0^{N-1}, u_0^{i-1}|u_i)}}. \tag{17.79}$$

This expectation can be approximated via Monte Carlo techniques, generating sequences u_0^{N-1} and y_0^{N-1} according to the governing distribution, and computing (17.79). Fortunately, the argument of the square root in (17.79) is computed by the successive cancellation decoder, which operates with $O(N \log N)$ complexity.

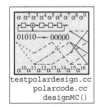

testpolardesign.cc
polarcode.cc
designMC()

Practically, since $Z(W_N^{(i)})$ is related to the probability of error (see (17.103)), a Monte Carlo simulation can be based on the estimated probability of bit error. This leads to the very heuristically plausible algorithm: simulate the probability of error on each of the bits separately, then select the K bits with the smallest probability of error.

Since the polar code is linear, it suffices to simulate the all-zero code transmission.

Algorithm 17.4 Design of Polar Codes Using Monte Carlo Simulation

---

Function `DesignMC` (*N, K, M, designSNRdB*)
% Design a polar code at a particular design SNR using Monte Carlo Simulation of Bits
Input: N: Code length; K: Code dimension; M: number of bits to simulation; designSNR:
 design SNR
Output: $\mathcal{F} \subset \{0, 1, \ldots, N-1\}$, with $|\mathcal{F}| = N - K$
1 Initialize c, a vector of length N and set all elements to 0
2 **for** $i = 0, 1, \ldots, N - 1$ **do**
3 $\quad$ Unfreeze bit i
4 $\quad$ **for** $m = 0, 1, \ldots, M - 1$ **do**
5 $\quad\quad$ Generate a modulated vector from an all-zero codeword
6 $\quad\quad$ Decode the modulated codeword, and count the number of bits in location i
7 $\quad$ **end**
8 **end**
9 $\mathcal{F}$ = indices of the $N - K$ largest error counts

---

17.7 Perspective: The Channel Coding Theorem

In the proof of the channel coding theorem, Shannon used the ideas of:

1. Random code selection;

2. Joint asymptotic equipartition property (AEP) between the transmitted codeword and the received sequence;

3. And ML decoding.

Random coding was important to Shannon's proof, because it provided a tool for proof which allowed him to step over the details of identifying a particular good code while proving that a good code exists. Recent coding successes, such as LDPC codes and turbo codes have made use of the random coding idea, such as via interleavers or pseudorandom connections between variable nodes and check nodes. While this has been effective, it is not necessarily required for good coding performance.

Joint AEP is more central to the coding theorem, because it guarantees that the received sequence is jointly typical with the transmitted codeword, with high probability. Under joint AEP, the set of all pairs of transmitted codewords/received sequences can be divided into two sets: the jointly typical set, where the mutual information between the input and output sequences is close to capacity, and the non-jointly typical set, where the mutual information between the input and output sequences is lower.

Joint AEP is related to channel polarization: selecting the good channels which result from polarization, the codewords from the jointly typical set can be reliably transmitted over the nearly noiseless channels created by channel polarization. Polar coding is thus a constructive instance of joint AEP.

17.8 Systematic Encoding of Polar Codes

The encoding described in Section 17.4 is not systematic. However, systematic encoding for polar codes has been found, and (surprisingly) it has been shown to have superior bit error performance to nonsystematic encoding, although the word error rate is the same.

17.8.1 Polar Systematic Encoding via the Encoder Graph

As a preface to the discussion of systematic polar encoding, it may be helpful to review a couple of points about linear coding. Recall that for a linear code, a codeword is a point in the row space of the generator matrix G, so that in $\mathbf{x} = \mathbf{z}G$, $\mathbf{x}$ is a codeword, regardless of the particular values in $\mathbf{z}$. One way to do encoding might be to take a message vector $\mathbf{u}$, place it into K elements of the codeword $\mathbf{x}$, then find a vector $\mathbf{z}$ which fill in the remaining $N - K$ elements of $\mathbf{x}$ in such a way that $\mathbf{x}$ is in the row space of G. If $\mathbf{z}$ can be found via linear operations from $\mathbf{u}$ in such a way that the message symbols appear explicitly in $\mathbf{x}$, then systematic encoding has been achieved. This is an alternative to the method of doing systematic encoding discussed in Section 3.2, in which the form of the generator G is modified to achieve systematic encoding.

This viewpoint is essentially the way systematic encoding may be achieved for polar codes. This will be described first using an example for a code of length $N = 8$ and dimension $K = 4$. For the moment, ignore the bit reverse permutation on the bits. Let the frozen bits be represented by the vector

$$\mathbf{f} = \begin{bmatrix} 0 & 0 & 0 & -1 & 0 & -1 & -1 & -1 \end{bmatrix},$$

where the -1 locations indicate unfrozen bits, and the frozen bits take on the other values indicated (0s in this case). That is, the set of unfrozen bits is $\mathcal{A} = \{3, 5, 6, 7\}$. Let the message bits be $\mathbf{u} = [u_0, u_1, u_2, u_3]$. The systematic codeword for this message places these message bits in the unfrozen locations and fills in the frozen bits with x_i values, to be determined, such that the $\mathbf{x}$ so formed is in the row space of the generator G.

Let the vector operating on G be denoted by $\mathbf{z}$. $\mathbf{z}$ is formed by placing 0 in the frozen locations, with other elements in the unfrozen locations determined to satisfy the relationship $\mathbf{x} = \mathbf{z}G$.

Specifically, consider as an example the message vector $\mathbf{u} = [1, 0, 0, 1]$. Then the encoding relationship is

$$\begin{bmatrix} x_0 & x_1 & x_2 & 1 & x_4 & 0 & 0 & 1 \end{bmatrix} = \begin{bmatrix} 0 & 0 & 0 & z_3 & 0 & z_5 & z_6 & z_7, \end{bmatrix} G \tag{17.80}$$

where (still neglecting the bit reverse permutation)

$$G = F^{\otimes 3} = \begin{bmatrix} 1 & 0 & 0 & 0 & 0 & 0 & 0 & 0 \\ 1 & 1 & 0 & 0 & 0 & 0 & 0 & 0 \\ 1 & 0 & 1 & 0 & 0 & 0 & 0 & 0 \\ 1 & 1 & 1 & 1 & 0 & 0 & 0 & 0 \\ 1 & 0 & 0 & 0 & 1 & 0 & 0 & 0 \\ 1 & 1 & 0 & 0 & 1 & 1 & 0 & 0 \\ 1 & 0 & 1 & 0 & 1 & 0 & 1 & 0 \\ 1 & 1 & 1 & 1 & 1 & 1 & 1 & 1 \end{bmatrix}.$$

The number of unknowns in $\mathbf{x}$ is $|\mathcal{A}^c| = N - K$ and the number of unknowns in $\mathbf{z}$ is always $|\mathcal{A}| = K$, so the total number of unknowns in $\mathbf{x}$ and $\mathbf{y}$ is N. Rearranging the equations in (17.80) results in N equations in N unknowns.

There is a method for solving for the unknowns in (17.80) with $O(N \log N)$ complexity and memory $O(N \log N)$ [460]. As we have seen, because of the Kronecker structure of G, (17.80) can be represented using the now-familiar encoder graph shown in Figure 17.27. In the figure, the inputs z_i are on the left and the outputs x_i are on the right. The x_is from the unfrozen codeword bits are indicated, and the z_is that are zeros from the frozen portion are shown. Observe that for each horizontal line, either z_i or x_i is known.

In Figure 17.27, each horizontal line is labeled with ℓ_i. Along each line there are $n = 3$ *potential* positions for adders. For example, line ℓ_0 has three adders along it. Line ℓ_7 has no adders along it. Consider the binary representation of i in comparison with ℓ_i. For ℓ_7, $i = 7 = 111_2$ (with the MSB

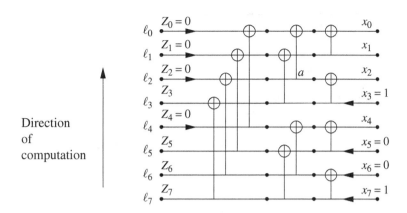

Direction
of
computation

Figure 17.27: Calculations for systematic polar encoding.

on the left). This line has no adders. For ℓ_6, $i = 6 = 110_2$. This line has adders in position 3. For ℓ_0, $i = 000_2$, and this has adders in each region. A binary 1 in a position corresponds to "no adder" in the corresponding position along the line and a binary 0 in a position corresponds to placing an adder in its corresponding position along the line. The recursive structure of the graph and of binary numbers ensures that this observation is true for any $N = 2^n$.

Along each line ℓ_i there are $n + 1 = 4$ computational nodes, each denoted by a •, representing the input z_i, the output x_i, and $n - 1$ interior computational nodes between the adder regions. The algorithm makes use of $N(n + 1) = N(\log_2 N + 1)$ storage representing the • locations. For each horizontal line ℓ_i, the computation of the $n + 1$ nodes on it involves only nodes from the same horizontal line and nodes below it. Significantly, along each line ℓ_i, either the left node (z_i) or the right node (x_i) is known. By performing bottom-up computation (the "direction of computation" shown), the unknown x_i and z_i values can be determined.

Continuing our example, examining Figure 17.27,

$$z_7 = x_7 = 1$$

$$z_6 = x_6 \oplus x_7$$

$$z_5 = x_5 \oplus x_7$$

$$x_4 = z_4 \oplus z_6 \oplus x_5$$

$$z_3 = x_3 \oplus x_7$$

$$x_2 = z_2 \oplus z_6 \oplus x_3$$

$$x_1 = z_1 \oplus z_5 \oplus x_3$$

$$x_0 = z_0 \oplus z_4 \oplus a \oplus x_1.$$

All N unknowns are easily solved for.

In general terms, the computation proceeds as follows. For bit number $i = N - 1$ down to 0, if i is unfrozen, then computation proceeds from right to left. If i is frozen, then computation proceeds from left to right. Computations at each node involves either copying from the appropriate adjacent node, or adding the adjacent node to the node from a line below it, to compute the value at each • along each line ℓ_i. More specifically, the encoding proceeds as shown in Algorithm 17.5.

polarcode.cc
encodesyst ()

Algorithm 17.5 Polar Code Systematic Encoder

Function encodesyst (u)
% Systematically encode the K-bit vector in u
Input: u: the bit string to be encoded
Output: Codeword and Vector $\mathbf{x}$ with solution of (17.80)

1 **Initialize** Form matrix $B \in \mathbb{F}_2^{N\times(n+1)}$ of zeros
2   For $i \in \mathcal{A}^c$, set $B[i][0] = 0$
3   For $i \in \mathcal{A}$, set $B[i][n] = u_j$ % fill in message bits sequentially
    for $i = N-1, N-2, \ldots, 0$ **do** % For each line from the bottom to the top
       if $i \in \mathcal{A}$ **then** % If not frozen, start on right side and move left
4
5            $s = n - 1$
6            $\delta = -1$.
7   **else**
8   % If frozen, start on left side and move right
           $s = 1 \; \delta = 1$
9   **end**
10   Denote the binary representation of $i = b_0 b_1 \ldots b_{n-1}$, with b_0 the MSB
11       $t = s$
12   **for** $j = 0, 1, \ldots, n-1$ **do** % For each level needing computation
13
14            $\ell = \min(t, t - \delta)$
15   **if** $b_\ell == 0$ **then** % If there is an adder at this branch
16
17                $\kappa = 2^{n-1-\ell}$
18                $B[i][t] = B[i][t-\delta] \oplus B[i+\kappa][t-\delta]$
19   **else**
20   % No adder on this branch – just copy over
               $B[i][t] = B[i][t-\delta]$
21   **end**
           $t = t + \delta$ % that is, $t = s + j * \delta$
22   **end**
23 **end**
    Copy out $\mathbf{x} = B[:][n]$ in bit reverse order

The encoding complexity is $O(N \log_2 N)$, counting one operation for every exclusive-OR. The memory size is $O(N \log_2 N)$ (a memory location for each $\bullet$ in the graph).

While the complexity is only $O(N \log_2 N)$, the encoding algorithm is strictly sequential, proceeding in the direction of computation. This sequential order limits throughput compared to parallel implementations.

17.8.2 Polar Systematic Encoding via Arıkan's Method

Systematic encoding of polar codes can be expressed more formally, leading to another algorithm for encoding. For a code of length N, let G be a $N \times N$ generator matrix over a field $\mathbb{F}$, let $\mathbf{u} \in \mathbb{F}^N$, $\mathbf{x} \in \mathbb{F}^N$, and denote the encoding operation as $\mathbf{x} = \mathbf{z}G$ for some vector $\mathbf{z}$ to be determined. Let $\mathcal{B} \subset \{0, 1, \ldots, N-1\}$ be a subset of indices with $|\mathcal{B}| = |\mathcal{A}|$. Ultimately we will take $\mathcal{B} = \mathcal{A}$, but we start with a more general formulation. The vector $\mathbf{x}$ consists of two parts, the systematic information, $\mathbf{x}_\mathcal{B} = \mathbf{u}$, and the other information in $\mathbf{x}_{\mathcal{B}^c}$. The vector $\mathbf{z}$ is decomposed into a portion corresponding to the unfrozen bits and the frozen bits by $\mathbf{z}_\mathcal{A}$ and $\mathbf{z}_{\mathcal{A}^c}$. Then the encoding

$$\mathbf{x} = \mathbf{z}_\mathcal{A} G_\mathcal{A} + \mathbf{z}_{\mathcal{A}^c} G_{\mathcal{A}^c}, \tag{17.81}$$

where G_A and G_{A^c} a submatrices having *rows* indexed by A and A^c, respectively, further divides as

$$\mathbf{x}_B = \mathbf{u} = \mathbf{z}_A G_{AB} + \mathbf{z}_{A^c} G_{A^c B} \tag{17.82}$$

$$\mathbf{x}_{B^c} = \mathbf{z}_A G_{AB^c} + \mathbf{z}_{A^c} G_{A^c B^c}. \tag{17.83}$$

Since $\mathbf{x}_B$ is known in (17.82), solve as

$$\mathbf{z}_A = (\mathbf{u} - \mathbf{z}_{A^c} G_{A^c B}) G_{AB}^{-1}. \tag{17.84}$$

This can now be substituted in (17.83) to determine $\mathbf{x}_{B^c}$. (The method of Section 17.8.1 takes $\mathbf{z}_{A^c} = \mathbf{0}$ and simultaneously and efficiently solves for $\mathbf{z}_A$ and $\mathbf{x}_{B^c}$.)

For polar codes $G = F^{\otimes n}$ and B is taken to be equal to A. Then the recursive structure of G it possible to efficiently compute G_{AA}^{-1} in (17.84). With care, this can be done with slightly less memory than the method of Section 17.8.1, but at higher computational cost.

17.8.3 Systematic Encoding: The Bit Reverse Permutation

The discussion of systematic encoding of polar codes has neglected the bit reverse permutation. Including now the bit reverse permutation, the encoding is written as

$$\mathbf{x} = \mathbf{z} B_N F^{\otimes n},$$

where B_N is the bit reverse permutation matrix. The matrices commute so that $B_N F^{\otimes n} = F^{\otimes n} B_N$. The methods described above provide a solution to the equation $\mathbf{x} = \mathbf{z} F^{\otimes n}$. Multiplying both sides on the right by B_N thus gives the encoding including the bit reverse permutation.

17.8.4 Decoding Systematically Encoded Codes

The usual encoding operation is $\mathbf{x} = \mathbf{u}G$, and the usual decoder takes the codeword information (via the channel) and returns the message vector $\mathbf{u}$. In the systematic case, the encoding operation is $\mathbf{x} = \mathbf{z}G$, where $\mathbf{x}$ has systematic information about $\mathbf{u}$ within it. Calling the usual decoder would return the vector $\mathbf{z}$. To extract the codeword and its contained message $\mathbf{u}$, it is necessary to *re-encode* the vector $\mathbf{z}$ using G. From this, $\mathbf{u}$ can be extracted.

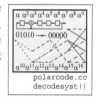

polarcode.cc
decodesyst()

17.8.5 Flexible Systematic Encoding

While the systematic encoder of Section 17.8.1 has low complexity, it is distinctly sequential and hence not amenable to parallel processing, since the processing proceeds from the bottom to the top of the encoding graph. In this section, we present a systematic encoder which is amenable to parallel implementation.

Let the information set be $A = \{a_0, a_1, \ldots, a_{k-1}\}$, ordered as $a_0 < a_1 < \cdots < a_{k-1}$. The systematic encoder not only contains the input bits $\mathbf{u}$ explicitly, but in the order of A. An encoder diagram for an $(8, 5)$ code is shown in Figure 17.28 with $A = \{3, 4, 5, 6, 7\}$, where the bit-reverse permutation is not used. Based on this figure, the encoder process is as follows:

1. The input vector $\mathbf{u} = (u_0, u_1, \ldots, u_{k-1})$ is formed into the $\mathbf{v}_I = (v_{I,0}, v_{I,1}, \ldots, v_{I,n-1})$ of length n by setting $v_{i,a_i} = u_i$ for $i = 0, 1, \ldots, k - 1$. The remaining $n - k$ elements of $\mathbf{v}_I$ are set to 0.

2. Compute $\mathbf{v}_{II} = \mathbf{v}_I F^{\otimes n}$.

3. Form the vector $\mathbf{v}_{III}$ be setting elements not in A to 0.

4. Compute $\mathbf{x} = \mathbf{v}_{III} F^{\otimes n}$.

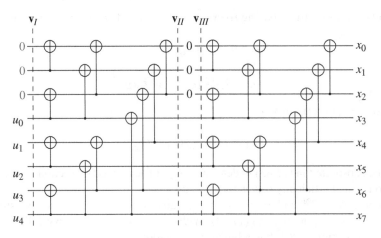

Figure 17.28: A systematic encoder for an $(8,5)$ polar code [390].

Since multiplication by $F^{\otimes n}$ can be done in parallel, this encoder is parallelizable. The computational complexity is $O(2\,N\log_2 N)$.

The remainder of this section explains why this operation works. Let $\mathcal{E}(\mathbf{u})$ denote the encoding operation just described. Let G be an $k\times n$, rank k, encoding matrix. The encoding operation is linear, and so it can be written as

$$\mathcal{E}(\mathbf{u}) = \mathbf{u}\Pi G$$

for an invertible $k\times k$ matrix Π. The encoding operation $\mathcal{E}$ is systematic if there are a set of indices $\mathcal{A} = \{a_0, a_1, \ldots, a_{k-1}\}$, which we can identify as the information bits, such that restricting $\mathcal{E}(\mathbf{u})$ to the indices in $\mathcal{A}$ is equal to $\mathbf{u}$. We assume, as before, that the indices in $\mathcal{A}$ are ordered, $a_0 < a_1 < \cdots < a_{k-1}$ so that in $\mathcal{E}(\mathbf{u})$ the u_i appears before u_j if $i < j$.

One way to do systematic encoding is to take k linearly independent columns of G and to take Π as the inverse of the $k\times k$ submatrix of G.

Let E be the $k\times n$ matrix with elements

$$E_{i,j} = \begin{cases} 1 & \text{if } j = a_i \\ 0 & \text{otherwise.} \end{cases} \tag{17.85}$$

Example 17.19   For the $(8,5)$ polar code whose encoder is shown in Figure 17.28,

$$E = \begin{bmatrix} 0 & 0 & 0 & 1 & 0 & 0 & 0 & 0 \\ 0 & 0 & 0 & 0 & 1 & 0 & 0 & 0 \\ 0 & 0 & 0 & 0 & 0 & 1 & 0 & 0 \\ 0 & 0 & 0 & 0 & 0 & 0 & 1 & 0 \\ 0 & 0 & 0 & 0 & 0 & 0 & 0 & 1 \end{bmatrix}.$$

□

The polar encoding operation, not necessarily systematic (excluding the bit-reverse permutation) can be expressed in terms of a generator matrix G, where

$$G = EF^{\otimes n}.$$

That is, E selects the rows of G associated with the information (unfrozen) bits.

Applying E to the right of a length-k vector $\mathbf{u}$ produces a vector $\mathbf{v}_I$ of length n,

$$\mathbf{v}_I = \mathbf{u}E,$$

where $v_{I,a_j} = u_j$. This is Step 1 of the encoding algorithm above. The next step of decoding is

$$\mathbf{v}_{II} = \mathbf{v}_I F^{\otimes n} = \mathbf{u} E F^{\otimes n}.$$

Step 3 of the algorithm produces

$$\mathbf{v}_{III} = \mathbf{v}_{II} E^T E,$$

producing a vector in which elements indexed by $\mathcal{A}$ are the same and the other elements are set to 0. Step 4 of the algorithm produces

$$\mathbf{x} = \mathbf{v}_{III} F^{\otimes n} = \mathbf{u} \underbrace{E F^{\otimes n} E^T}_{\Pi} \underbrace{E F^{\otimes n}}_{G}.$$

The encoding is systematic if the elements of $\mathbf{x}$ restricted to the indices of $\mathcal{A}$ are equal to the elements of $\mathbf{u}$:

$$\mathbf{x} E^T = \mathbf{u}.$$

Thus, we need to show that

$$E F^{\otimes n} E^T E F^{\otimes n} E^T = I.$$

A matrix is said to be an *involution* if multiplication of the matrix by itself yields the identity matrix. Proof that the encoding is systematic amounts to showing that $E F^{\otimes n} E^T$ is an involution.

The following example shows that not every polar-type code produces an involution.

Example 17.20   For a code with length $N = 4$, let $\mathcal{A}_1 = \{0, 1, 3\}$. The associated E matrix is

$$E_1 = \begin{bmatrix} 1 & 0 & 0 & 0 \\ 0 & 1 & 0 & 0 \\ 0 & 0 & 0 & 1 \end{bmatrix} \quad E_1^T = \begin{bmatrix} 1 & 0 & 0 \\ 0 & 1 & 0 \\ 0 & 0 & 0 \\ 0 & 0 & 1 \end{bmatrix} \quad F^{\otimes n} = \begin{bmatrix} 1 & 0 & 0 & 0 \\ 1 & 1 & 0 & 0 \\ 1 & 0 & 1 & 0 \\ 1 & 1 & 1 & 1 \end{bmatrix}$$

and

$$E_1 F^{\otimes n} E_1^T = \begin{bmatrix} 1 & 0 & 0 \\ 1 & 1 & 0 \\ 1 & 1 & 1 \end{bmatrix}$$

so

$$(E_1 F^{\otimes n} E_1^T)(E_1 F^{\otimes n} E_1^T) = \begin{bmatrix} 1 & 0 & 0 \\ 0 & 1 & 0 \\ 1 & 0 & 1 \end{bmatrix}.$$

For information set $\mathcal{A}_1$, the encoding process does *not* produce a systematically encoded code!

By contrast, let $\mathcal{A}_2 = \{1, 2, 3\}$ and

$$E_2 = \begin{bmatrix} 0 & 1 & 0 & 0 \\ 0 & 0 & 1 & 0 \\ 0 & 0 & 0 & 1 \end{bmatrix} \quad E_2^T = \begin{bmatrix} 0 & 0 & 0 \\ 1 & 0 & 0 \\ 0 & 1 & 0 \\ 0 & 0 & 1 \end{bmatrix}$$

and

$$E_2 F^{\otimes n} E_2^T = \begin{bmatrix} 1 & 0 & 0 \\ 1 & 1 & 0 \\ 1 & 1 & 1 \end{bmatrix}$$

and

$$(E_2 F^{\otimes n} E_2^T)(E_2 F^{\otimes n} E_2^T) = \begin{bmatrix} 1 & 0 & 0 \\ 0 & 1 & 0 \\ 0 & 0 & 1 \end{bmatrix}.$$

For information set $\mathcal{A}_2$, the encoding process *does* produce a systematically encoded code! $\mathcal{A}_2$ would be an appropriate information set for systematic encoding.   □

We now explore conditions under which an involution occurs. This will be examined first from the point of view of the set $\mathcal{A}$. This will then be related to polar codes via the polar code design process.

17.8.6 Involutions and Domination Contiguity

Definition 17.21 Let i and j be integers such that $0 \le i, j < N$, and let the binary representations of i and j be

$$i = (i_0, i_1, \dots, i_{n-1}) \quad j = (j_0, j_1, \dots, j_{n-1}).$$

We save that *i binary dominates* , denoted by $i \succeq j$ if and only if $i_\ell \ge j_\ell$ for $0 \le \ell < n$.

That is, $i \succeq j$ iff the support of the binary representation of i (the indices ℓ for which $i_\ell = 1$) contains the support of the binary representation of j.   □

Definition 17.22 A set of indices $\mathcal{A} \subset \{0, 1, \dots, N-1\}$ is *domination contiguous* if for all $h, j \in \mathcal{A}$ and for all $0 \le i < n$ such that $h \succeq i$ and $i \succeq j$ it holds that $i \in \mathcal{A}$. That is,

If $h, j \in \mathcal{A}$ and $h \succeq i \succeq j$ then $i \in \mathcal{A}$.   □

Example 17.23 Let $N = 4$ and let $\mathcal{A} = \{0, 1, 3\}$, as in Example 17.20. In binary representation,

$$\mathcal{A} = \{(00), (01), (11)\}.$$

Let $h = 3 = (11)$ and $j = 1 = (01)$. Then $h \succeq j$. If $i = 2 = (10)$, then $h \succeq i \succeq j$, but $i \notin \mathcal{A}$. So this set $\mathcal{A}$ is not domination contiguous.

Now let

$$\mathcal{A} = \{1, 2, 3\} = \{(01), (10), (11)\}.$$

With $h = 3 = (11)$ and $j = 1 = (01)$ and $i = 2 = (10)$, it is clear that $h \succeq i \succeq j$. This set *is* domination contiguous □

Theorem 17.24 *[390, Theorem 1] Let the information set $\mathcal{A} \subseteq \{0, 1, \dots, N-1\}$ be domination contiguous. Let E be defined as in (17.85). Then $EF^{\otimes n} E^T$ is an involution: $(EF^{\otimes n} E^T)(EF^{\otimes n} E^T) = I$.*

The proof relies on the following lemma.

Lemma 17.25 *The elements of the matrix $F^{\otimes n}$ satisfy*

$$(F^{\otimes n})_{i,j} = \begin{cases} 1 & i \succeq j \\ 0 & \textit{otherwise.} \end{cases}$$

Proof It is clear from (17.34) that the upper right $(N/2) \times (N/2)$ block is 0. Elements in these locations have i_{n-1} (the most-significant bit) equal to 0 and j_{n-1} equal to 0.

For the other three blocks of (17.34), $i \succeq j$ iff $(i \bmod 2^{n-1}) \succeq (j \bmod 2^{n-1})$. Since each of the remaining blocks all have the same structure it suffices to consider the claim for the lower left block.

Continuing this reduction recursively, it suffices to consider the 2×2 block F for which verification is straightforward. $\qquad\square$

Proof *of theorem* **17.24.** For $0 \leq p, q, r < k$, let $h = a_p$, $i = a_q$ and $j = a_r$. It is matter of checking indices to verify that

$$(EF^{\otimes n}E^T)_{p,q} = (F^{\otimes n})_{h,i}$$

$$(EF^{\otimes n}E^T)_{q,r} = (F^{\otimes n})_{i,j}$$

so that

$$((EF^{\otimes n}E^T)(EF^{\otimes n}E^T))_{p,r} = \sum_{q=0}^{k-1} (EF^{\otimes n}E^T)_{p,q}(EF^{\otimes n}E^T)_{q,r}$$

$$= \sum_{i \in \mathcal{A}} (F^{\otimes n})_{h,i}(F^{\otimes n})_{i,j}.$$

To show that an identity is obtained, it must be shown that this sum (modulo 2) is equal to 1 if $h = j$, and 0 otherwise. That is, when $h = j$ there must be an odd number of $i \in \mathcal{A}$ for which

$$h \succeq i \text{ and } i \succeq j, \tag{17.86}$$

and if $h \neq j$ there must be an even number of i satisfying (17.86). This is examined on a case-by-case basis.

1. If $h = j$, then the only possible i satisfying (17.86) is $i = h = j$, so there are an odd number (one) of such i.

2. If $h \neq j$ and $h \not\succeq j$ there are zero values of i satisfying (17.86), which is an even number of values.

3. If $h \neq j$ and $h \succeq j$, then the support of j is properly contained in the support of h. To retain binary domination, the number of bit positions that are eligible for changing between h and j are those ℓ for which $j_\ell = 0$ and $h_\ell = 1$. The total number of possible i satisfying (17.86) is $2^{w(h)-w(j)}$, where $w(h)$ and $w(j)$ are the weight of the binary representations of h and j, respectively. Since $\mathcal{A}$ is dominant contiguous, each of these possible i are in $\mathcal{A}$, which means there are an even number of i satisfying (17.86).

$\qquad\square$

17.8.7 Polar Codes and Domination Contiguity

The previous section provided conditions on the information set, namely, domination contiguity, that ensured that systematic encoding occurs. In this section, conditions related to the polarized channels are established that relate to domination contiguity.

Definition 17.26

A channel $W : \mathcal{X} \to \mathcal{Y}$ is *upgraded* with respect to a channel $Q : \mathcal{X} \to \mathcal{Z}$ if there exists a channel $\Phi : \mathcal{Y} \to \mathcal{Z}$ such that concatenating Φ to W results in Q. This means that

$$Q(z|x) = \sum_{y \in \mathcal{Y}} \Phi(z|y)W(y|x).$$

The statement "W is upgraded with respect to Q" is denoted as $W \succeq Q$. $\qquad\square$

Recall from the data-processing inequality of information theory (see Section 1.12.2) that concatenating channels cannot improve the mutual information from input to output. In light of this, in this definition, in order for W followed by Φ to be equal to Q, W must be in some way superior to, that is, "upgraded relative to," Q.

"Upgraded relative to" is transitive: if Q_1 is upgraded relative to Q_2 and Q_2 is upgraded relative to Q_3, then Q_1 is upgraded relative to Q_3. To see this, let Φ_1 be such that the concatenation of Q_1 and Φ_1 results in Q_2, and let Φ_2 be such that the concatenation of Q_2 and Φ_2 results in Q_3. Then the concatenation of Φ_1 and Φ_2 (in that order) to Q_1 results in Q_3.

Lemma 17.27 *[390, Lemma 3] Let $W : \mathcal{X} \to \mathcal{Y}$ be a B-DMC channel. Let $W^0 : \mathcal{X} \to \mathcal{Y}^2$ and $W^1 : \mathcal{Y}^2 \otimes \mathcal{X}$ as in Section 17.5.2. Then $W^1 \succeq W^0$.*

Proof We have (see (17.61) and (17.62))

$$W^0(y_0, y_1|u_0) = \frac{1}{2} \sum_{u_1 \in 0,1} W(y_0|u_0 \oplus u_1)W(y_1|u_1)$$

and

$$W^1(y_0, y_1, u_0|u_1) = \frac{1}{2} W(y_0|u_0 \oplus u_1)W(y_1|u_1).$$

Let $\Phi : \mathcal{Y}^2 \times \mathcal{X} \to \mathcal{Y}^2$ be the channel that maps (y_0, y_1, u_0) to (y_0, y_1) with probability 1, so the transition probabilities are

$$\Phi(\tilde{y}_0, \tilde{y}_1|u_0, y_1, u_0) = \begin{cases} 1 & \tilde{y}_0 = y_0, \tilde{y}_1 = y_1 \\ 0 & \text{otherwise.} \end{cases}$$

Then the transition probabilities for the concatenation of W^1 and Φ are

$$\sum_{y_0, y_1, u_0} \Phi(\tilde{y}_0, \tilde{y}_1|y_0, y_1, u_0)\frac{1}{2} W(y_0|u_0 \oplus u_1)W(y_1|u_1)$$

$$= \frac{1}{2}[W(y_0|u_1)W(y_1|u_1) + W(y_0|1 \oplus u_1)W(y_1|u_1)] = W^0(y_0, y_1|u_0).$$

$\square$

The polar transformation preserves the relationship of being upgraded:

Lemma 17.28 *Let $W : \mathcal{X} \to \mathcal{Y}$ and $Q : \mathcal{X} \to \mathcal{Z}$ be two symmetric B-DMC channels such that $W \succeq Q$ and let (W^0, W^1) and (Q^0, Q^1) be polarizations of these channels. Then*

$$W^0 \succeq Q^0 \quad \text{and} \quad W^1 \succeq Q^1. \tag{17.87}$$

Proof By the upgrade relationship, write $Q(y|x) = \sum_{z \in \mathcal{Y}} \Phi(y|z)W(z|x)$. The polarized channel Q^0 can be written as

$$Q^0(y_0, y_1|u_0) = \frac{1}{2} \sum_{u_1 \in \mathcal{X}} Q(y_0|u_0 \oplus u_1)Q(y_1|u_1)$$

$$= \frac{1}{2} \sum_{u_1 \in \mathcal{X}} \left(\sum_{y_0' \in \mathcal{Y}} \Phi(y_0|y_0')W(y_0'|u_0 \oplus u_1) \right) \left(\sum_{y_1' \in \mathcal{Y}} \Phi(y_1|y_1')W(y_1'|u_1) \right)$$

$$= \sum_{(y_0', y_1') \in \mathcal{Y}^2} \Phi(y_0|y_0')\Phi(y_1|y_1')\frac{1}{2} \sum_{u_1 \in \mathcal{X}} W(y_0'|u_0 \oplus u_1)W(y_1'|u_1)$$

$$= \sum_{(y_0', y_1') \in \mathcal{Y}^2} \Phi(y_0|y_0')\Phi(y_1|y_1')W^0(y_0', y_1'|u_0),$$

so $W^0 \succeq Q^0$. It can be similarly shown that $W^1 \succeq Q^1$.

$\square$

The key lemma is the following.

Lemma 17.29 *Let $W : \mathcal{X} \to \mathcal{Y}$ be a symmetric B-DMC. For indices i, j with $0 \leq i, j < N$, if $i \geq j$ then $W_N^{(i)} \succeq W_N^{(j)}$.*

Proof For $N = 2$, the result follows from Lemma 17.27 if $i > j$, or from the fact that $W \succeq W$ if $i = j$. Proceeding inductively for $n = \log_2 N = 2, 3, \ldots$, suppose that

$$W_{N/2}^{(\lfloor i/2 \rfloor)} \succeq W_{N/2}^{(\lfloor j/2 \rfloor)}.$$

Considering $W_N^{(i)}$ and $W_N^{(j)}$, if the least significant bits (LSBs) of i and j are the same then (17.87) applies, with W and Q in the lemma being $W_{N/2}^{(\lfloor i/2 \rfloor)}$ and $W_{N/2}^{(\lfloor j/2 \rfloor)}$, respectively, and $W_N^{(i)}$ being W^0 or W^1, depending on the parity of i.

If i and j have different LSBs, then the LSB of i must be 1 and the LSB of j must be 0. Then

$$W_N^{(i)} = (W_{N/2}^{(\lfloor i/2 \rfloor)})^1 \succeq W_{N/2}^{(\lfloor i/2 \rfloor)}$$

and

$$W_N^{(j)} = (W_{N/2}^{(\lfloor j/2 \rfloor)})^0 \succeq W_{N/2}^{(\lfloor j/2 \rfloor)}.$$

By the transitivity of $\succeq$,

$$W_N^{(i)} \succeq W_N^{(j)}.$$

$\square$

The next piece relates the upgrade relationship and the Battacharyya parameter.

Lemma 17.30 *Let W and Q be channels with $W \succeq Q$. Then*

$$Z(W) \leq Z(Q).$$

Proof

$$Z(Q) = \sum_{y \in \mathcal{Y}} \sqrt{Q(y|0)Q(y|1)} = \sum_{y \in \mathcal{Y}} \sqrt{\sum_{y_1 \in \mathcal{Y}} \Phi(y|y_1)W(y_1|0) \sum_{y_2 \in \mathcal{Y}} \Phi(y|y_2)W(y_2|0)},$$

where the second equality follows from the upgrade relationship between W and Q.

Inside the square root, we can write

$$\left[\sum_{y_1 \in \mathcal{Y}} (\sqrt{\Phi(y|y_1)W(y_1|0)})^2 \right]^{1/2}$$

and recognize this as the norm of vector with components $\sqrt{\Phi(y|y_1)W(y_1|0)}$, and similarly for the other terms inside the square root. Applying the Cauchy–Schwartz inequality gives

$$Z(Q) \geq \sum_{y_1 \in \mathcal{Y}} \sqrt{W(y_2|0)W(y_2|1)} \sum_y \Phi(y|y_1) = Z(W).$$

$\square$

Combining Lemmas 17.29 and 17.30, if $i \geq j$ then $Z(W_N^{(i)}) \leq Z(W_N^{(j)})$.

Recall that in Section 17.6.1, polar codes were designed by selecting the K channels having the smallest Battacharyya parameter. Under this design, if the inequality $Z(W_N^{(i)}) \leq Z(W_N^{(j)})$ when $i \geq j$ and $i \neq j$, then if $j \in \mathcal{A}$, then it must also be the case that $i \in \mathcal{A}$. This ensures that $\mathcal{A}$ is domination contiguous according to Definition 17.22 so that, by Theorem 17.24, the encoder is systematic.

If it turns out that under the numerical precision employed in the polar code design $Z(W_N^{(i)}) = Z(W_N^{(j)})$ for some i and j, it may turn out that $j \in \mathcal{A}$ but $i \notin \mathcal{A}$ in a way that makes $\mathcal{A}$ not domination contiguous. In this case, the design can be altered (with no practical effect on performance) by removing j from $\mathcal{A}$ and putting in i. If other design criteria are used (such as selecting the channels having the smallest bit error rate), similar tweaks will ensure systematic encoding with negligible performance penalties.

17.8.8 Modifications for Polar Codes with Bit-Reverse Permutation

The discussion about systematic decoding was expressed for encoders that do not employ bit-reverse permutation, so the generator matrix is $G = EF^{\otimes n}$, where E selects the rows corresponding to the information bits in $\mathcal{A}$. If the bit-reverse permutation is used, the generator matrix is $G = EB_N F^{\otimes n}$. Given an information set $\mathcal{A}$ for unpermuted encoding, define the set of bit-reversed active rows by applying the bit-reverse operation on each $a_i \in \mathcal{A}$ to define a set $\overleftarrow{\mathcal{A}}$. These elements can be ordered as

$$\overleftarrow{\mathcal{A}} = \{\beta_j\}_{j=0}^{k-1}, \quad 0 \le \beta_0 < \beta_1 < \cdots < \beta_{k-1} < n.$$

Define $\overleftarrow{E}$ similar to E:

$$(\overleftarrow{E})_{i,j} = \begin{cases} 1 & \text{if } j = \beta_i \\ 0 & \text{otherwise.} \end{cases}$$

The generator can now be written as $G = \overleftarrow{E}F^{\otimes n}$, and the encoding operation for the reversed code can be expressed as

$$\mathcal{E}(\mathbf{u}) = \mathbf{u}\overleftarrow{E}F^{\otimes n}\overleftarrow{E}^T \overleftarrow{E}F^{\otimes n}.$$

Encoding is systematic if

$$(\overleftarrow{E}F^{\otimes n}\overleftarrow{E}^T)(\overleftarrow{E}F^{\otimes n}\overleftarrow{E}^T) = I.$$

The point now is that, by the definition of domination contiguous, if $\mathcal{A}$ is domination contiguous, then so is $\overleftarrow{\mathcal{A}}$.

17.9 List Decoding of Polar Codes

Despite the remarkable properties of polar codes, such as low encode and decode complexity, explicit construction algorithms, and provable asymptotically good performance, finite-length polar codes are not as strong as some other modern codes of similar length, such as LDPC or turbo codes. Part of this is due to the fact that the successive cancellation decoding leaves some performance on the table, and part due to the fact that the capacity-achieving performance is asymptotic, so finite-length polar codes are not necessarily capacity achieving. Practice improvements can be obtained by improving the decoding using list decoding.

The idea behind list decoding of polar codes is that instead of producing a single decoded codeword as SC cancellation does, a list decoder considers up to L decoding paths concurrently. Let $\hat{u}_0^i$ denote a sequence of decisions about the bits u_0^i. When the next (unfrozen) bit u_{i+1} is to be decoded, the decoding path is split into two paths, each of which has $\hat{u}_0^i$ as a prefix. One new path has $\hat{u}_{i+1} = 0$ and the other new path has $\hat{u}_{i+1} = 1$. (No splitting of paths occurs for frozen bits.) This splitting is accomplished by "cloning" a path: duplicating the path $\hat{u}_0^i$, then adding to the two paths the values of $\hat{u}_{i+1} = 0$ or 1.

Obviously this doubling of paths cannot continue indefinitely, so after doubling the paths the decoder selects among the L most likely paths. At the end of decoding, the most probable path is selected from the L remaining paths.

The list decoding idea is portrayed in Figure 17.29, where $N = 4$, $L = 4$, and all bits are unfrozen. Figure 17.29(a): the first unfrozen bit u_0 can be either 0 or 1, producing two paths. Figure 17.29(b): the second unfrozen bit u_1 can be either 0 or 1, producing four paths; no need to prune yet. Figure 17.29(c): With the third bit u_2, eight paths would be produced. Figure 17.29(d): the eight paths are pruned to $L = 4$ paths by selecting the L most likely paths. Pruned paths are indicated in gray. Figure 17.29(e): For the fourth bit u_3, unpruned bits are extended, producing eight paths. Figure 17.29(f): Pruned back

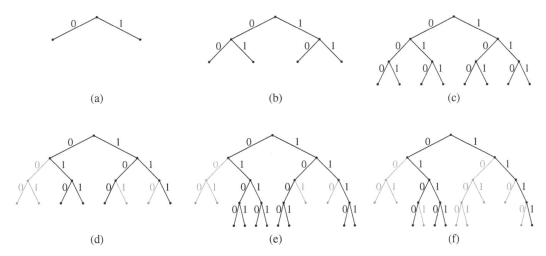

Figure 17.29: Evolution of paths in list decoding. Following [431].

to four best paths. At this point in the decoding algorithm, the path having the best likelihood is selected, resulting in the decoded sequence $\hat{u}_0^3$.

The likelihoods are computed for list decoding using the same formulas (17.40) and (17.41) as for successive cancellation, but here they are re-expressed in terms of a *layer* parameter λ, $0 \le \lambda \le n$, where the number of bits associated with a layer is $\Lambda = 2^\lambda$. Rewriting (17.40) and (17.41) using this notation,

$$
\underbrace{W_\lambda^{(2i)}(y_0^{\Lambda-1}, u_0^{2i-1} | u_{2i})}_{\text{branch } \beta}
$$

$$
= \frac{1}{2} \sum_{u_{2i+1} \in \mathcal{X}} \underbrace{W_{\lambda-1}^{(i)}(y_0^{\Lambda/2-1}, u_{0,\text{even}}^{2i-1} \oplus u_{0,\text{odd}}^{2i-1} | u_{2i} \oplus u_{2i+1})}_{\text{branch } 2\beta} \underbrace{W_{\lambda-1}^{(i)}(y_{\Lambda/2}^{\Lambda-1}, u_{0,\text{odd}}^{2i-1} | u_{2i+1})}_{\text{branch } 2\beta+1} \tag{17.88}
$$

$$
\underbrace{W_\lambda^{(2i+1)}(y_0^{\Lambda-1}, u_0^{2i} | u_{2i+1})}_{\text{branch } \beta}
$$

$$
= \frac{1}{2} \underbrace{W_{\lambda-1}^{(i)}(y_0^{\Lambda/2-1}, u_{0,\text{even}}^{2i-1} \oplus u_{0,\text{odd}}^{2i-1} | u_{2i} \oplus u_{2i+1})}_{\text{branch } 2\beta} \underbrace{W_{\lambda-1}^{(i)}(y_{\Lambda/2}^{\Lambda-1}, u_{0,\text{odd}}^{2i-1} | u_{2i+1})}_{\text{branch } 2\beta+1} \tag{17.89}
$$

for $0 \le 2i < \Lambda$. The meaning of the β annotations is explained below.

17.9.1 The Likelihood Data Structure P

The list decoder employs some data structures to keep track of the likelihoods, bits, and the various paths. The first data structure is the P data structure, which keeps track of the likelihood functions for the various paths.

Example 17.31 To understand the data structures associated with list decoding, we will return to decoding with $N = 4$, with the encoding portrayed and labeled as in Figure 17.30. and write out the likelihoods $W_2^{(0)}$, $W_2^{(1)}$, $W_2^{(2)}$, $W_2^{(3)}$, recalling that now the subscript $_2$ refers to the level λ, not the number of elements at that level, which is 2^λ.

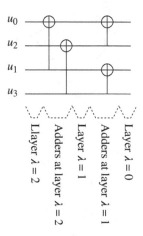

Figure 17.30: Encoder for $N = 4$.

Using (17.88) and (17.89)

$$i = 0 \quad W_2^{(0)}(y_0^3 | u_0) = \frac{1}{2} \sum_{u_1} W_1^{(0)}(y_0^1 | u_0 \oplus u_1) W_1^{(0)}(y_2^3 | u_1)$$

$$i = 1 \quad W_2^{(1)}(y_0^3, u_0 | u_1) = \frac{1}{2} W_1^{(0)}(y_0^1 | u_0 \oplus u_1) W_1^{(0)}(y_2^3 | u_1)$$

$$i = 2 \quad W_2^{(2)}(y_0^3, u_0^1 | u_2) = \frac{1}{2} \sum_{u_3} W_1^{(1)}(y_0^1, u_0 \oplus u_1 | u_2 \oplus u_3) W_1^{(1)}(y_2^3, u_1, | u_3)$$

$$i = 3 \quad W_2^{(3)}(y_0^3, u_0^2 | u_3) = \frac{1}{2} W_1^{(1)}(y_0^1, u_0 \oplus u_1 | u_2 \oplus u_3) W_1^{(1)}(y_2^3, u_1 | u_3). \tag{17.90}$$

Continuing recursively, the components that are needed for $i = 0$ are $W_1^{(0)}(y_0^1 | u_0 \oplus u_1)$ and $W_1^{(0)}(y_2^3 | u_1)$. Representing the conditioning argument as b (from which these functions can be evaluated), these can be computed as

$$W_1^{(0)}(y_0^1 | b) = \frac{1}{2} \sum_{u_1} W_0^{(0)}(y_0) | b \oplus u_1) W_0^{(0)}(y_1 | u_1)$$

$$W_1^{(0)}(y_2^3 | b) = \frac{1}{2} \sum_{u_1} W_0^{(0)}(y_2 | b \oplus u_1) W_0^{(0)}(y_3 | u_1).$$

In turn, these quantities depend on $W_0^{(0)}(y_0 | u)$, $W_0^{(0)}(y_1 | u)$, $W_0^{(0)}(y_2 | u)$, and $W_0^{(0)}(y_3 | u)$, for $u = 0$ or 1. The quantities needed to compute for $i = 0$ can be stacked into a data structure that has one function in its first block, two functions in its second block, and four functions in its third block, as shown:

$$
\begin{array}{cccccccc}
\lambda = 2 & & \lambda = 1 & & & \lambda = 0 & & \\
\beta = 0 & \beta = 0 & \beta = 1 & \beta = 0 & \beta = 1 & \beta = 2 & \beta = 3 \\
i = 0: & \left[W_2^{(0)}(y_0^3 | b)\right] & \left[W_1^{(0)}(y_0^1 | b)\right] & \left[W_1^{(0)}(y_2^3 | b)\right] & \left[W_0^{(0)}(y_0) | b)\right. & \left. W_0^{(0)}(y_1 | b)\right] & \left[W_0^{(0)}(y_2 | b)\right. & \left. W_0^{(0)}(y_3 | b)\right]
\end{array}
\tag{17.91}
$$

Similarly, when $i = 1$, the values needed to compute $W_2^{(1)}(y_0^3, u_0 | u_1)$ in (17.90) can be stacked up as

$$
\begin{array}{cccccccc}
\lambda = 2 & & \lambda = 1 & & & \lambda = 0 & & \\
\beta = 0 & \beta = 0 & \beta = 1 & \beta = 0 & \beta = 1 & \beta = 2 & \beta = 3 \\
i = 1: & \left[W_2^{(1)}(y_0^3, u_0 | b)\right] & \left[W_1^{(0)}(y_0^1 | b) \quad W_1^{(0)}(y_2^3 | b)\right] & \left[W_0^{(0)}(y_0) | b) \quad W_0^{(0)}(y_1 | b) \quad W_0^{(0)}(y_2 | b) \quad W_0^{(0)}(y_3 | b)\right]
\end{array}
\tag{17.92}
$$

The index β portrayed in (17.91) and (17.92) is called the *branch number*. β indexes the values of the arguments to the W functions. As seen in (17.88) and (17.89), the arguments are of the form $(y_0^{\Lambda/2 - 1}, u_{0,\text{even}}^{2i-1} \oplus u_{0,\text{odd}}^{2i-1})$ are associated with index 2β. Arguments of the form $(y_{\Lambda/2}^{\Lambda - 1}, u_{0,\text{odd}}^{2i-1})$

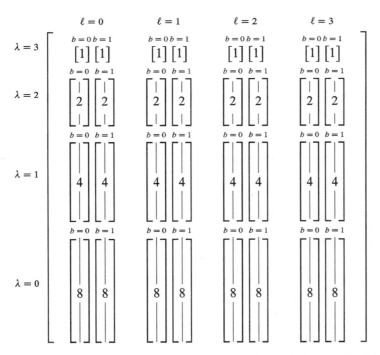

Figure 17.31: Data structure P used in list decoding with $N = 8$, $n = 3$, $L = 4$. Numbers in the braces indicate the dimension of the array.

are associated with with index $2\beta + 1$. As the example illustrates, the range of branch numbers at level λ is

$$0 \le \beta < 2^{n-\lambda}.$$

For the list decoding algorithm a data structure P is created for each path ℓ such that

$$P_\lambda^\ell[\beta][b] = W_\lambda^{(i)}(y_{(\text{range})}u_{(\text{range})}|b) \quad \text{on path } \ell, \tag{17.93}$$

where the range of indices of y and u are determined by the particular value of β. The data structure P thus can be considered an "array of arrays," a four-dimensional object with real values containing the W values. The outer array dimension is of size $(n + 1) \times L$, corresponding to the $n + 1$ different values of λ and the L different paths in the list. Then the dimension of the array P_λ^ℓ is of size $2^{n-\lambda} \times 2$, where the first index is for β and the second index is for the values of the conditioning argument $b \in \{0, 1\}$. A picture of the data structure for $N = 8$, $n = 3$, and $L = 4$ is shown in Figure 17.31.

17.9.2 Normalization

Since the likelihoods are small numbers, as they are propagated through the layers using (17.88) and (17.89), the numbers may be small enough to cause loss of numeric precision. Note that

$$W_n^{(i)}(y_0^{N-1}, \hat{u}_0^{i-1}|b) = 2P(y_0^{N-1}, \hat{u}_0^{i-1}, u_i = b) \quad \text{with } P(U_i = b) = 1/2$$

$$\le 2P(\hat{u}_0^{i-1}, \hat{u}_i = b) = 2^{-i}.$$

For codes having length N of any appreciable length, the numbers lose numerical precision. This problem of underflow can be mitigated by normalizing the likelihoods. The normalization is done in a way that preserves the relative ranking of the likelihoods, even though the absolute values lose their meaning. In the algorithms here, we set

$$P_\lambda^\ell[\beta][b] \leftarrow \frac{P_\lambda^\ell[\beta][b]}{\max\limits_{\beta,b} P_\lambda^\ell[\beta][b]}.$$

17.9.3   Code to Compute P

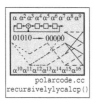

polarcode.cc
recursivelylycalcp()

Algorithm 17.6 shows code to compute the likelihoods in the data structure P. This function is called as recursivelyCalcP(n, i), where n is the highest layer number and i is the bit index. Recursive calls are determined by the binary structure of i (just as in SC) in line 3. Line 7 returns a pointer P_λ to the $2^{n-\lambda} \times 2$ that holds the likelihood data W_λ for path ℓ, and similarly for $P_{\lambda-1}$. Also, C_λ gets the pointer to the array of bits needed for the update of P_λ. The actual update of the likelihoods according to (17.88) and (17.89) for the upper and lower likelihood computations is in lines 10–23.

Algorithm 17.6 Polar List Decoder: Recursively Calculate P

Function recursivelyCalcP(λ, i)
% For each active path, calculate the likelihood to bit $i, P_n^\ell(i)$, pushing likelihood from the right to the left. See reference [431], alg 10.
Input: layer λ and bit index i
1 **if** $\lambda = 0$ **then return**; % Recursion stopping condition
2 set $\psi \leftarrow \lfloor i/2 \rfloor$
  % Recurse into lower levels if needed, as determined by parity of i
3 **if** $i \mod 2 = 0$ **then** recursivelyCalcP$(\lambda - 1, \psi)$
  % Do the calculation from (17.88) and (17.89)
4 set $\sigma \leftarrow 0$ % Prepare to get the scaling factor
5 **for** $\ell = 0, 1, \ldots, L - 1$ **do** % For each active path
6 | **if** activePath$[\ell]$ = false **then continue**
7 | P_λ = getArrayPointer_P(λ, ℓ) % Get pointers to P data for this layer and path
8 | $P_{\lambda-1}$ = getArrayPointer_P(λ, ℓ)
9 | C_λ = getArrayPointer_C(λ, ℓ) % Get pointers to C (bit) data for this layer and path
10 | **for** $\beta = 0, 1, \ldots, 2^{n-\lambda} - 1$ **do** % For each "branch" at this level
11 | **if** $i \mod 2 = 0$ **then** % Apply (17.88)
12 | **for** $u' \in \{0, 1\}$ **do**
13 | $P_\lambda[\beta][u'] \leftarrow \frac{1}{2} \sum_{u'' \in \{0,1\}} P_{\lambda-1}[2\beta][u' \oplus u'']P_{\lambda-1}[2\beta + 1][u'']$
14 | set $\sigma \leftarrow \max(\sigma, P_\lambda[\beta][u'])$
15 | **end**
16 | **else**
       % Else apply (17.89)
17 | set $u'' \leftarrow C_\lambda[\beta][0]$ % Get the bit that controls this "lower" computation
18 | **for** $u'''' \in \{0, 1\}$ **do**
19 | $P_\lambda[\beta][u''''] \leftarrow \frac{1}{2}P_{\lambda-1}[2\beta][u'' \oplus u'''']P_{\lambda-1}[2\beta + 1][u'''']$
20 | set $\sigma \leftarrow \max(\sigma, P_\lambda[\beta][u''])$
21 | **end**
22 | **end**
23 | **end**
24 **end**

  % Normalize the probabilities by σ
25 **for** $\ell = 0, 1, \ldots, L - 1$ **do**
26 | **if** activePath$[\ell]$ = false **then continue**
27 | $P_\lambda \leftarrow$ getArrayPointer_P(λ, ℓ)
28 | **for** $\beta = 0, 1, \ldots, 2^{n-\lambda} - 1$ **do**
29 | **for** $u \in \{0, 1\}$ **do**
30 | $P_\lambda[\beta][u] \leftarrow P_\lambda[\beta][u]/\sigma$
31 | **end**
32 | **end**
33 **end**

17.9.4 The Bits Data Structure C

The data structure C contains the bits necessary for likelihood computation. Because of SC, at bit index i, it is not necessary to retain all of the previous bits at indices $< i$, since their effect is propagated into the encoding system.

At each layer λ, the data that is saved is preserved in an array C_λ. As more data arrive, the C_λ fill up.

Example 17.32 For a code with $N = 4$, consider a "path," that is, a sequence of message bits $\pi = (u_0, u_1, u_2, u_3) = (0, 1, 1, 0)$. We consider each of these in sequence, placing dots • on the encoding diagram to indicate the data involved. We show the data in the bit arrays C_2, C_1, and C_0 as it arrives.

- $u_0 = 0$. With only a single input, no additions are computed.

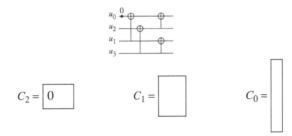

C_2 contains the most recent bit u_0. There is insufficient data for C_1 or C_2 to be populated.

- $u_1 = 1$. C_2 contains the two most recent bits of information, u_0 and u_1. There is now sufficient information to compute values at the output of the adders at layer $\lambda = 2$. These output location are shown with •s.

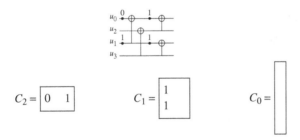

The left column of C_1 contains the outputs of adders at layer 2.

- $u_2 = 1$. The information from u_0 and u_1 are now represented at the $\lambda = 1$ level in C_1, and u_0 and u_1 are no longer needed in C_2, leaving C_2 free to store u_2. There is not sufficient data to propagate u_2 through adders yet, so C_1 is unchanged.

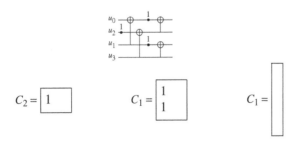

- $u_3 = 0$. C_2 now contains u_2 and u_3. There is sufficient information to push u_2, u_3 through the adders at level $\lambda = 2$. Furthermore, there is information for the adders at level $\lambda = 1$, so the final output can be computed into C_0.

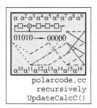

$$u_0 \quad u_2 \quad u_1 \quad u_3$$

$$C_2 = \boxed{\begin{array}{cc} 1 & 0 \end{array}} \qquad C_1 = \boxed{\begin{array}{cc} 1 & 1 \\ 1 & 0 \end{array}} \qquad C_0 = \boxed{\begin{array}{c} 0 \\ 1 \\ 1 \\ 0 \end{array}}.$$

□

As shown in this example, a data structure C_λ is associated with each path in the list, where C_λ has the bit data at layer λ. Except for the C_n data, the C_λ arrays contain the results of the additions of the encoder, so the bit sequence in the path is not explicitly saved. Instead, as the bit data gets pushed to the right, a codeword is formed and stored in C_0. Extraction of the message bits after the decoding is complete requires unencoding this codeword. This introduces additional complexity, but means that the decoder produces both the message bits and the codeword.

The list decoder keeps a set of data analogous to the C_λ data in this example for each of the L decoding paths. The algorithm allocates data $C_\lambda^\ell[\beta][b]$ of the same size as the P data, but containing bit values instead of real values.

Consider now the cloning of the path $\hat{u}_0^i$ to form $\hat{u}_0^{i+1}$ for $\hat{u}_{i+1} = 0$ and $\hat{u}_{i+1} = 1$. When cloning a path, the information associated with $\hat{u}_0^i$ — all the previous bits — is preserved. The data on the path that is common to both is pooled together in the lower λ values of C_λ.

17.9.5   Code to Compute C

Algorithm 17.7 shows code to update the bits for each path. Like the code to calculate P, pointers to the bit data at levels λ and $\lambda - 1$ are extracted for path ℓ. The actual bit propagation is in lines 6 through 9, with line 7 pushing bits to the right through an adder, and line 8 simply copying bits over on the lower line, paralleling the adder output.

```
polarcode.cc
recursively
UpdateCalcC()
```

Algorithm 17.7 Polar List Decoder: Recursively Calculate C

Function `recursivelyCalcC(`λ, i`)`

%For each active path, push the bit i to the next lower level to\the right. See reference [431], alg 11.**Input:** layer λ and bit index i

%i will be odd, or there is no computation to be done in theencoding graphs

1 set $\psi \leftarrow \lfloor i/2 \rfloor$

2 **for** $\ell = 0, 1, \ldots, L - 1$ **do**   % For each active path

3   **if** activePath$[\ell]$ = false **then** continue

4   C_λ = getArrayPointer_C(λ, ℓ) % Getpointers to C data for this layer and path

5     $C_{\lambda-1}$ = getArrayPointer_C$(\lambda - 1, \ell)$

6   **for** $\beta = 0, 1, \ldots, 2^{n-\lambda} - 1$ **do**   % For each "branch" at this level

7        $C_{\lambda-1}[2b][\psi \bmod 2] \leftarrow C_\lambda[\beta][0] \oplus C_\lambda[\beta][1]$ % propagate bits through an adder to next lower level

8        $C_\lambda - 1][2\beta + 1][2\beta + 1][\psi \bmod 2] \leftarrow C_\lambda[\beta][1]$ % copy bits on other branch to next lower level

9   **end**

10 **end**

11 **if** $\psi \bmod 2 = 1$ **then** Parity is odd, so propagate to next lower layer

12   recursivelyUpdateC$(\lambda - 1, \psi$

13 **end**

17.9.6 Supporting Data Structures

In addition to the P and C data structures there are some supporting data structures that support efficient operations, such as pooling of data in paths, keeping track of paths, and so forth. These supporting data structures are briefly summarized here.

- inactivePathIndices: A stack of path indices in $\{0, 1, \ldots, L-1\}$ which are inactive. Initialized with this whole list.

- activePath: A vector of booleans of length L indicating which paths are active. (activePath and inactivePathIndices are different representations of the same information.)

- pathIndextoArrayIndex: $(n+1) \times L$ array which indicates which of the P_λ and C_λ matrices is associated with path ℓ at level λ. This is an important data structure which enables the pooling of data when paths are split.

  For a given layer λ and path index ℓ, the probability array corresponding to this layer and path are in the P data structure pointed to by

  $$\text{arrayPointer\_P}[\lambda][\text{pathIndexToArrayIndex}[\lambda][\ell],$$

  and similarly for the C data.

- arrayReferenceCount: $(n+1) \times L$ array indicating how many time the P_λ and C_λ are used. When pooling of data in a path occurs, this count is incremented. When a path is killed, this count is decremented. This supports the pooling of data. That is, the value arrayReferenceCount$[\lambda][s]$ denotes the number of paths current using the array pointed to by arrayPointer_P$[\lambda][s]$.

- inactiveArrayIndices: An array of $n+1$ stacks, indicating the array indices that are inactive at each level.

17.9.7 Code for Polar List Decoding

polarcodes.cc
listdecode()

The remainder of the code listings are provided in this section. Some explanations are provided in the example below.

Algorithm 17.8 Polar List Decoder: Main Loop

Function SCLdecode (**y**)
% Main decoder loop of successive cancellation list decoder. See reference [431], alg 12
Input: Received vector **y**
Output: Decoded codeword $\hat{\mathbf{c}}$

% Initialize data structures and likelihoods at level $\lambda = 0$
1 buildDataStructures()   % Done only **once** during construction of decoder object
2 initializeDataStructures()   % Do for each call of this function
3 ;$\ell \leftarrow$ assignInitialPath()   % Get path number
4 $P_0 \leftarrow$ getArrayPointer_P$(0, \ell)$
5 **for** $\beta = 0, 1, \ldots, N-1$ **do**
6 | $P_0[\beta][0] \leftarrow W(y_\beta|0), \quad P_0[\beta][1] \leftarrow W(y_\beta|1)$
7 **end**

% Main Loop: Loop over each bit number i in sequence

8 **for** $i = 0, 1, \ldots, N - 1$ **do**

9   recursivelyCalcP(n,i)   % Calculate all likelihoods for this i, right to left

10   **if** u_i *is frozen* **then**   % if this bit is frozen, assign bit to frozen value

11   **if** *activePath*[ℓ] = *false* **then continue**

12        $C_n \leftarrow$ getArrayPointer_C(n,ℓ)

13   set C_n][$i \mod 2$] to the frozen value of u_i

14   **else**

15   continuePaths_UfrozenBit(i)

16   **end**

17   **if** $i \mod 2 = 1$ **then**

18   recursivelyUpdateC(n, i)   % Push the bits left to right

19   **end**

    % Return the codeword in the list with the highest likelihood

20     $\ell' \leftarrow 0, p' \leftarrow 0$

21   **for** $\ell = 0, 1, \ldots, L - 1$ **do**

22   **if** *activePath*[ℓ] = *false* **then continue**

23        $C_n \leftarrow$ getArrayPointer_C(n, ℓ)

24        $P_n \leftarrow$ getArrayPointer_p(n, ℓ)

25   **if** $P_n[0][C_n[0][1]] > p'$ **then**

26           $\ell' \leftarrow \ell, p' \leftarrow P_n[0][C_n[0][1]]$

27   **end**

28   **end**

29   set $C_0 \leftarrow$ getArrayPointer_C($0, \ell'$)

30 **end**

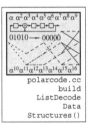

polarcode.cc
build
ListDecode
Data
Structures()

Algorithm 17.9 Polar List Decoder: Build Polar Code List Decoder Data Structures

---

Function `buildDataStuctures()`

% Build the data structures for the list decoder. Should appear in the constructor. See reference [431], alg 5

1 inactivePathIndices $\leftarrow$ **new** stack of capacity L

2 activePath $\leftarrow$ boolean array of size L

3 arraypointer_P $\leftarrow$ **new** $(n + 1) \times L$ arrays of pointers to (2-d arrays of pointers to doubles)

4 arrayPointer_C $\leftarrow$ **new** $(n + 1) \times L$ arrays of pointers to (2-d arrays of pointers to bits)

5 pahtIndexToArrayIndex $\leftarrow$ new$(n + 1) \times L$ array of integers

6 inactiveArrayIndices $\leftarrow$ **new** array of size $n + 1$ whose elements are stacks with capacity L

7 arrayReferenceCount $\leftarrow$ **new** $(n + 1) \times L$ array of integers

% Allocate space for the other two dimensions of arraypointer_P and arraypointer_P

8 **for** $\lambda = 0, 1, \ldots, n$ **do**

9   **for** $s = 0, 1, \ldots, L - 1$ **do**

10   arrayPointer_P[λ][s] $\leftarrow$ **new** $2^{n-\lambda} \times 2$ array of doubles

11   arrayPointer_C[λ][s] $\leftarrow$ **new** $2^{n-\lambda} \times 2$ array of bits

12   **end**

13   probForks $\leftarrow$ double array of size $L \times 2$ % Used to sort most likely paths

14   contForks $\leftarrow$ boolean array of size $L \times 2$ % Flag which paths are kept

15 **end**

Algorithm 17.10 Polar List Decoder: Initialize Data Structures

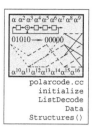
```
polarcode.cc
initialize
ListDecode
Data
Structures()
```

1 **Function** `initializeDataStuctures()`
2 % Initialize the data structures for the list decoder.Done for each decoded codeword. See reference [431], alg 5
3
4 **clearstack**(inactivePathIndices)
5 **for** $\lambda = 0, 1, \ldots, n$ **do**
6   **clearstack**(inactiveArrayIndices[λ])
7   **for** $s = 0, 1, \ldots, L-1$ **do**
8   arrayReferenceCounter[λ][s] $\leftarrow 0$
9   **push**(inactiveArrayIndices[λ], s)
10   **end**
11 **end**
12 **for** $\ell = 0, 1, \ldots, L-1$ **do**
13   activePath[ℓ] $\leftarrow$ False
14   **push**(inactivePathIndices, ℓ)
15 **end**

Algorithm 17.11 Polar List Decoder: Assign Initial Path

```
polarcode.cc
assign
initial
path()
```

Function `assignInitialPath()`
% Assign the initial path: grab the first available path, and associate an array with that path index. See reference [431], alg 6
1
Output: Index ℓ of the initial path
2 $\ell \leftarrow$ **pop**(inactivePathIndices)
3 activePath[ℓ] $\leftarrow$ true
% Associate an array at each level to this path index
4 **for** $\lambda = 0, 1, \ldots, n$ **do**
5    $s \leftarrow$ **pop**(inactiveArrayIndices[λ])
6   pathIndextoArrayIndex[λ][ℓ] $\leftarrow s$
7   arrayReferenceCount[λ][s] $\leftarrow 1$
8 **end**
9 **Return** ℓ

Algorithm 17.12 Polar Code Decoder: Clone a Path, Sharing Data in C and P

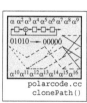
```
polarcode.cc
clonePath()
```

Function `clonePath()`
% Grabs a new path, then associates with that path to path ℓ.See reference [431], alg 7
Input: Index ℓ of path to clone
Output: Index ℓ' of copy
1 $\ell' \leftarrow$ **pop**(inactivePathIndices)
2 activePath[ℓ'] $\leftarrow$ true
% Make ℓ' reference the same arrays as ℓ
3 **for** $\lambda = 0, 1, \ldots, n$ **do**
4    $s \leftarrow$ **pop**(inactiveArrayIndices[λ])
5   pathIndextoArrayIndex[λ][ℓ'] $\leftarrow s$
6   arrayReferenceCount[λ][s]++
7 **end**
8 **Return** ℓ'

polarcode.cc
killPath()

Algorithm 17.13 Polar List Decoder: Kill a Path

Function killPath(ℓ) % Kill a path by decrementing reference counts. See reference [431], alg 8.
Input: Index ℓ of path to kill
1 activePath[ℓ] $\leftarrow$ false
2 **push**(inactivePathIndices, ℓ)
   % Disassociate array with path index
3 **for** $\lambda = 0, 1, \ldots, n$ **do**
4 | $s \leftarrow$ pathIndexToArrayIndex[λ][ℓ]
5 | arrayReferenceCount[λ][s]$-$
6 | **if** arrayReferencescount[λ][s] $= 0$ **then**
7 | | **push**(inactiveArrayIndices[λ], s)
8 | **end**
9 **end**

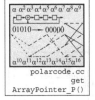

polarcode.cc
get
ArrayPointer_P()

Algorithm 17.14 Polar List Decoder: Get Pointer P_λ^ℓ

Function getArrayPointer_P(λ, ℓ)
% Return a pointer to the $2^{n-\lambda} \times 2$ matrix pointed to by P_λ^ℓ. See reference [431], alg 9.
Input: layer λ and path index ℓ
Output: Pointer to P_λ^ℓ, the $2^{n-\lambda} \times 2$ probability pair array
1 $s \leftarrow$ pathIndexToArrayIndex[λ][ℓ]
2 **if** arrayReferenceCount[λ][s] $= 1$ **then**
3 | $s' \leftarrow s$
4 **else**
5 | $s' \leftarrow$ **pop**(inactiveArrayIndices[λ]
6 | Copy the contents of the $2^{n-\lambda} \times 2$ array pointedto by arrayPointer_P[λ][s] into that pointed to by arrayPointer_P[λ][s'].
7 | Also copy the contents of the $2^{n-\lambda} \times 2$ array pointed to by arrayPointer_C[λ][s] into that pointed to by arrayPointer_C[λ][s'].
8 **end**
9 **return** arrayPointer_P[λ][s']

---

polarcode.cc
getArrayPointer_C()

Algorithm 17.15 Polar List Decoder: Get Pointer C_λ^ℓ

Function getArrayPointer_C(λ, ℓ)
% Return a pointer to the $2^{n-\lambda} \times 2$ matrix pointed to by C_λ^ℓ. See reference [431], alg 9.
Input: layer λ and path index ℓ
Output: Pointer to C_λ^ℓ, the $2^{n-\lambda} \times 2$ probability pair array
1 $s \leftarrow$ pathIndexToArrayIndex[λ][ℓ]
2 **if** arrayReferenceCount[λ][s] $= 1$ **then**
3 | $s' \leftarrow s$
4 **else**
5 | $s' \leftarrow$ **pop**(inactiveArrayIndices[λ]
6 | Copy the contents of the $2^{n-\lambda} \times 2$ array pointed to by arrayPointer_P[λ][s] into that pointed toby arrayPointer_P[λ][s'].
7 | Also copy the contents of the $2^{n-\lambda} \times 2$ array pointed to by arrayPointer_C[λ][s] into that pointed toby arrayPointer_C[λ][s'].
8 **end**
9 **return** arrayPointer_C[λ][s']

Algorithm 17.16 Polar List Decoder: Continue Paths for Unfrozen Bit

---

Function `continuePathsUnfrozenBit(i)`
% Find the L most likely paths, kill those that don't pass, and clone remaining paths as necessary to end up with L paths. See reference [431], alg 13.
Input: bit index i
1 nactivepath $\leftarrow 0$
% Store likelihood for each bit value u_i for each active path
2 **for** $\ell = 0, 1, \dots, L - 1$ **do**
3   **if** activePath$[\ell]$ = true **then**
4         $P_m \leftarrow$ getArrayPointer_P$[n, \ell]$
5   ProbForks$[\ell][0] \leftarrow P_m[0][0]$ % save likelihood for $u_i = 0$
6   ProbForks$[\ell][0] \leftarrow P_m[0][1]$ % save likelihood for $u_i = 1$
7   nactivepath $\leftarrow$ nactivepath $+ 1$
8   **else**
9   probForks$[\ell][0] \leftarrow -1$
10   probForks$[\ell][1] \leftarrow -1$
11   **end**
12 **end**

$\rho \leftarrow$ min(2nactivepath, L)
Populate the boolean matrix contForks such that contForks$[\ell][b]$ is true iff probForks$[\ell][b]$ is one of the ρ largest entriesin probForks.
% (The present implementation uses a quicksort algorithm to do this, but it is possible in principle to do this in $O(L)$ time.)

% Kill off noncontinuing paths
13 **for** $\ell = 0, 1, \dots, L - 1$ **do**
14   **if** activePath$[\ell]$ = false **then** continue
15   **if** contForks$[\ell][0]$ = false *and* contForks$[\ell][1]$ = false **then**
16   killPath(ℓ);
17   **end**
18 **end**

% Then, continue relevant paths and duplicate if necessary
19 **for** $\ell = 0, 1, \dots, L - 1$ **do**
20   **if** contForks$[\ell][0]$ = false *and* contForks$[\ell][1]$ = false **then** **continue**; % if both forks are bad or invalid
21     $C_n \leftarrow$ getArrayPointer_C(n, ℓ)
22   **if** contForks$[\ell][0]$ = true *and*contForks$[\ell][1]$ = true **then**
       % Both forks are good: clone paths
23   set $C_m[0][i \mod 2] \leftarrow 0$
24        $\ell' \leftarrow$ clonePath(ℓ)
25        $C_m \leftarrow$ getArrayPointer_C(n, ℓ')
26   set $C_m[i \mod 2] \leftarrow 1$
27   **else**
       % Exactly one fork is good
28   **if** contForks$[\ell][0]$ = *true* **then**
29   set $C_m[0][i \mod 2] \leftarrow 0$
30   **else**
31   set $C_m[0][i \mod 2] \leftarrow 1$
32   **end**
33   **end**
34 **end**

17.9.8   An Example of List Decoding

In this section, the different data structures presented in the previous sections are combined to show how the pieces work together. At various stages in the decoding algorithm, the example shows the contents of the C data structure, the paths represented by the data structures, and the encoding diagram with •s to show the locations that the data in C represent. Also shown is a description of the supporting data structures. The P data structure, showing the computed likelihoods, is not portrayed. The portrayal here is conceptual, and figures may not correspond exactly to values in an actual run of the algorithm.

- After initialization.

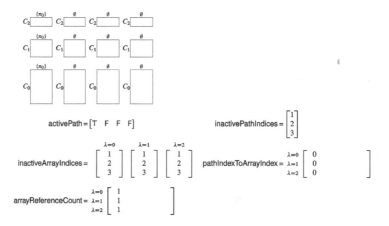

There is one active path π_0 which is assigned to the first C_2, C_1, and C_0 arrays by the **assignInitialPath** function. However, the path is empty (and not shown) since no data have been processed yet.

- At the end of the main loop with $i = 0$.

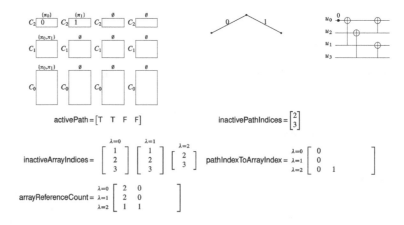

There are two active paths $\pi_0 = 0$ and $\pi_1 = 1$, where π_1 is cloned from π_0 using **clonePath**. These two paths are created in **continuePaths_UnfrozenBit** and the call to **getArrayPointer_C**.

Note that element **pathIndexToArrayIndex**[2][1] = 1. This means that path π_1 (the second path) refers to the second column of C_2. This is only referenced once. The other two $C\lambda$ components are shared with the path π_0, which are referred to twice.

- At the end of the main loop with $i = 1$.

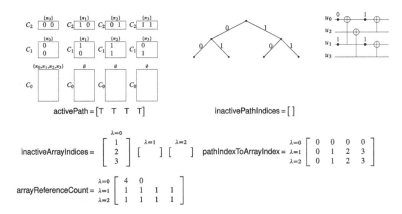

There are four active paths, $\pi_0 = 00$, $\pi_1 = 10$, $\pi_2 = 01$, and $\pi_3 = 11$. The path π_2 is the result of applying clonePath to the former π_0. After this, a unique C_2 is obtained by the call to getArrayPointer_C.

- $i = 2$, just after calling killPath in the continuePaths_UnFrozenBit function.

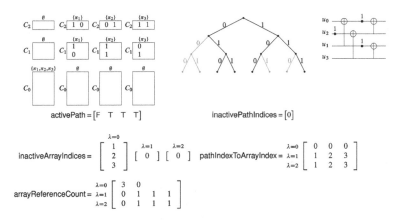

At this point π_0 has been killed leaving the active paths as $\pi_1 = 10$, $\pi_2 = 01$, and $\pi_3 = 11$. The first block of both C_2 and C_1 are free as a result of killing π_0.

- $i = 2$, at end of iteration.

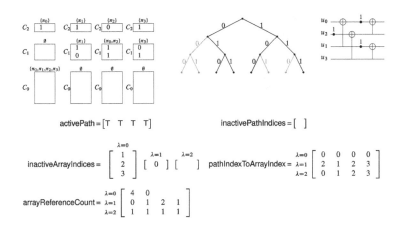

There are again four active paths, $\pi_0 = 011$, $\pi_1 = 100$, $\pi_2 = 010$, and $\pi_3 = 111$. The current π_0 is a result of applying clonePath to the former π_2. This results in π_0 and π_2 sharing the C_1 array, but π_0 get its own C_2 array in getArrayPointer_C. The path π_1 is a continuation of the former π_1.

- $i = 3$, end of main loop

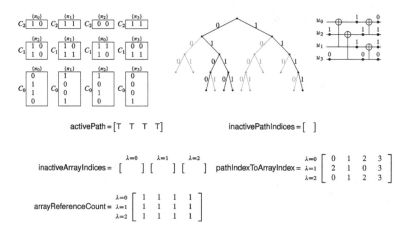

At the end of the main loop with $i = 3$, there are four active paths $\pi_0 = 0110$, $\pi_1 = 0111$, $\pi_2 = 0100$, and $\pi_3 = 1111$. The previous π_1 has been killed, a path was cloned and split into two paths (the former π_0 split into π_0 and π_1). The call to recursivelyUPdateC has resulted in private copies of C_2, C_1, and C_0 for each path.

At the end of this iteration, the *codewords* corresponding to the each path of input bits is stored in the C_0 arrays.

17.9.9 Computational Complexity

The size of the data structure associated with each path is $O(N)$. Each time a decoding path is split into two, the P data for path ℓ is duplicated. The number of splits is $O(NL)$. A naive implementation, the splitting and duplication would thus have a computational complexity of $O(N) \cdot O(NL) = O(LN^2)$. This would make the computational complexity impractical unless N is too small to be useful. However, a couple of observations can reduce the computational complexity. First, the cost of duplicating the data in P or C (when a path splits) at layer λ is proportional to $2^{n-\lambda}$. So the larger λ is, the less the cost to duplicate.

The other cost-saving aspect is that the larger P_λ or C_λ data is, less frequently it is accessed. This is illustrated in the following example.

Example 17.33   Consider the decoding algorithm detailed in Figures 17.23 through 17.25. The LLRs, the lines on which they are computed, and the smallest layer number at which the update occurs, are summarized as follows:

1. Figure 17.23a: ($j = 0$) LLR(7) – LLR(14), lines 0 – 7 layer 0.

2. Figure 17.23c: ($j = 1$) LLR(0) line 4, layer 3.

3. Figure 17.23e: ($j = 2$) LLR(1) ,LLR(0) lines 2, 6 layer 2.

4. Figure 17.24a: ($j = 3$), LLR(0), line 6, layer 3.

5. Figure 17.24c: ($j = 4$) LLR(3), LLR(4), LLR(5), LLR(6), lines 1, 3, 5, 7, layer 1.

6. Figure 17.24e: ($j = 5$) LLR(), line 5, layer 3.

7. Figure 17.25a: ($j = 6$) LLR(1), LLR(0), lines 3, 7, layer 2.

8. Figure 17.25c: ($j = 7$) LLR() line 7, layer 3.

□

Generalizing from this example, layer λ is accessed every $2^{n-\lambda}$ increments of j. The bigger the data in P_λ and C_λ (from smaller λ), the less often it is accessed.

These observations are used in a decoding algorithm as follows. At a given stage of decoding, data shared by more than one decoding path is "flagged" as belonging to more than one decoding path. This is done with the arrayReferenceCount array. When a decoding path needs access to an array it is sharing with another path, a copy is made.

17.9.10 Modified Polar Codes

It has been found in simulation that when a decoding error occurs (that is, the path with the ML is not the path for the correct codeword), the path corresponding to the transmitted codeword is, in fact, a member of the final list. It was simply not selected because another path had higher likelihood. If it were possible to know, somehow, what the correct codeword is, it could have been correctly decoded.

This is done (with high probability) using a simple concatenated coding scheme as follows. Choose a length r of a CRC code, such as $r = 8$ or $r = 16$. Of the K unfrozen bits that are available to transmit data on, send information on $K - r$ of them, and use the last r unfrozen bits to hold the CRC parity information. This does result in a slight reduction in rate, since the rate is now $(K - r)/N$, instead of K/N.

In decoding, the selection is refined as follows. If at least one path has a correct CRC, then paths having incorrect CRC are removed from further consideration, and the path having the highest likelihood among those with the correct CRC is selected. Otherwise, in the hope to minimize the number of bits in error, the codeword with the highest likelihood is selected.

List decoding is obviously more complex than SC decoding. Modified polar codes can also be used provide a mechanism for obtaining low probability and lower average decoding complexity. The concept is called a two-step list decoder and is shown in Figure 17.32. The received data are first decoded using a fast (non-list-based) decoder, such as SC or simplified successive cancellation (SSC). Most of the time this will decode correctly, as can be verified by examining the CRC. If there is not a valid CRC, which happens infrequently, then a more complex list-based decoder can be called which will do a better job with the decoding. The two-step decoder provides approximately the same throughput as the fast decoder, with essentially the same performance as the list decoder.

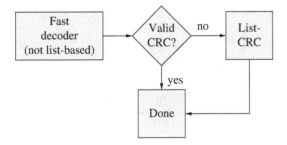

Figure 17.32: A two-step list decoder.

17.10 LLR-Based Successive Cancellation List Decoding

As noted in Section 17.9.2, likelihood computation is subject to underflow. This problem was mitigated with the likelihood-based list decoder using normalization. Another way of addressing underflow is to use log likelihoods, but it has been determined that in hardware implementations, preserving numerical accuracy requires a different number of bits per word at different levels. Further numerical improvement can be obtained using log- likelihood ratio decoding. This has been shown to be area efficient in hardware implementations and numerically stable. But there is a problem in list decoding, where the top L most likely children (paths) out of $2L$ paths of different parents must be chosen. What is needed is a *path metric*, computing the likelihood along the entire path of bits. This path metric is established in the following theorem.

Theorem 17.34 *[22, Theorem 1] For a path ℓ having bits $\hat{u}_0(\ell), \hat{u}_1(\ell), \ldots, \hat{u}_i(\ell)$ and bit number $i \in 0, 1, \ldots, N-1$, define the path metric as*

$$PM_\ell^{(i)} = \sum_{j=0}^{i} \ln(1 + \exp[-(1 - 2\hat{u}_j(\ell))L_N^{(j)}[\ell]]), \qquad (17.94)$$

where

$$L_N^{(i)}[\ell] = \ln\left(\frac{W_N^{(i)}(y_0^{N-1}, \hat{u}_0^{i-1}[\ell]|0)}{W_N^{(i)}(y_0^{N-1}, \hat{u}_0^{i-1}[\ell]|1)}\right)$$

is the log-likelihood ratio of the bit u_i given the channel output y_0^{N-1} and the past trajectory of the path $\hat{u}_0^{i-1}[\ell]$.

Furthermore, if the bits are equally probable $\{0, 1\}$ for any pair of paths ℓ_1, ℓ_2,

$$W_N^{(i)}(y_0^{N-1}, \hat{u}_0^{i-1}[\ell_1]|\hat{u}_i[\ell_1]) < W_N^{(i)}(y_0^{N-1}, \hat{u}_0^{i-1}[\ell_2]|\hat{u}_i[\ell_2])$$

if and only if

$$PM_{\ell_1}^{(i)} > PM_{\ell_2}^{(i)}.$$

That is, comparing bits along a path using the likelihood computed along that path is equivalent to the path metric. However, the path metric is computed using LLRs, in a numerically stable way.

Proof Define the likelihood ratio

$$\begin{aligned}
\Lambda_\lambda^{(i)}[\ell] &= \frac{W_\lambda^{(i)}(y_0^{N-1}, \hat{u}_0^{i-1}[\ell]|u_i = 0)}{W_\lambda^{(i)}(y_0^{N-1}, \hat{u}_0^{i-1}[\ell]|u_i = 1)} \\
&= \frac{P(y_0^{N-1}, \hat{u}_0^{i-1}[\ell], u_i = 0)/P(u_i = 0)}{P(y_0^{N-1}\hat{u}_0^{i-1}[\ell], u_i = 1)/P(u_i = 1)} = \frac{P(y_0^{N-1}, \hat{u}_0^{i-1}[\ell], u_i = 0)}{P(y_0^{N-1}, \hat{u}_0^{i-1}[\ell], u_i = 1)},
\end{aligned}$$

assuming, as usual, equal prior probabilities on the bits. Note that $L_\lambda^{(i)}[\ell] = \ln \Lambda_\lambda^{(i)}[\ell]$.

The joint probability of the observation and the bits $\hat{u}_0^{i-1}[\ell]$ can be expressed as

$$
\begin{aligned}
P(y_0^{N-1}, \hat{u}_0^{i-1}[\ell]) &= \sum_{\hat{u}_i[\ell] \in \{0,1\}} P(y_0^{N-1}, \hat{u}_0^{i-1}[\ell], \hat{u}_i[\ell]) \\
&= P(y_0^{N-1}, \hat{u}_0^{i-1}[\ell], \hat{u}_i[\ell] = 0) + P(y_0^{N-1}, \hat{u}_0^{i-1}[\ell], \hat{u}_i[ell] = 1) \\
&= \begin{cases} P(y_0^{N-1}, \hat{u}_0^{i-1}[\ell], \hat{u}_i = 1)(1 + \Lambda_\lambda^{(i)}[\ell]) & \hat{u}_i = 1 \\ P(y_0^{N-1}, \hat{u}_0^{i-1}[\ell], \hat{u}_i = 0)(1 + (\Lambda_\lambda^{(i)}[\ell])^{-1}) & \hat{u}_i = 0 \end{cases} \\
&= P(y_0^{N-1}, \hat{u}_0^{i-1}[\ell], \hat{u}_i[\ell])(1 + (\Lambda_\lambda^{(i)}[\ell])^{-(1-2\hat{u}_i)}).
\end{aligned}
$$

Moving the factor to the other side, we have

$$
P(y_0^{N-1}, \hat{u}_0^i[\ell]) = (1 + (\Lambda_\lambda^{(i)}[\ell])^{-(1-2\hat{u}_i[\ell])})^{-1} P(y_0^{N-1}, \hat{u}_0^{i-1}[\ell]).
$$

Repeated application of this for $i-1, i-2, \ldots, 0$ yields

$$
P(y_0^{N-1}, \hat{u}_0^i[\ell]) = \prod_{j=0}^{i} (1 + (\Lambda_\lambda^{(j)})^{-(1-2\hat{u}_j[\ell])})^{-1} P(y_0^{N-1}).
$$

Dividing both sides of this by $P(y_0^{N-1})$ gives the posterior probability

$$
P(\hat{u}_0^i[\ell]|y_0^{N-1}) = \prod_{j=0}^{i} (1 + (\Lambda_\lambda^{(j)})^{-(1-2\hat{u}_j)})^{-1}.
$$

Taking the negative log of this and expressing in terms of $L_\lambda^{(i)}[\ell]$, we obtain

$$
-\ln P(\hat{u}_0^i[\ell]|y_0^{N-1}) = \mathsf{PM}_\ell^{(i)},
$$

which establishes the conclusion of the theorem. □

```
listdecodeLLR()
clonepathllr()
getArrayPointer
_llr()
getArrayPointer
_Cllr()
recursivelyCalc
llr()
recursivelyUpdate
Cllr()
continuePaths
_UnFrozenBitllr()
findMostProbable
Pathllr()
```

17.10.1 Implementation Considerations

The implementation provided follows the same outline as the likelihood-based list decoder, with a new data structure **pathmetric** associated with each path. This is cloned and copied just like an element of the P data structure.

17.11 Simplified Successive Cancellation Decoding

Even the efficient decoding algorithm described in Section 17.4.7 is limited when it comes to very high-speed hardware and software implementations. One limitation is that the decoding is sequential, so bit $i+1$ cannot be decoded until bit i has been decoded. This limits the throughput rate of polar codes. The throughput has been shown to be approximately $0.5fR$, where f is the decoder clock frequency and R is the code rate [265]. In this section, we describe approaches to simplified successive decoding which can be used for very high-speed decoding by decoding at the level of *constituent codes* instead of at the bit level. Throughput achieved by this SSC decoding is between two and twenty times faster than conventional SC decoding, depending on the code length [7].

Central to the simplification is the tree structure identified in Section 17.4.6. In addition to the notation introduced in that section, we introduce some additional notation related to trees here. Let the leaves of the tree be indexed by the integers $0, 1, \ldots, 2^n - 1$. If v is a leaf node of the tree, let $\ell(v)$ denote the index of the leaf node, so $\ell(v) \in 0, 1, \ldots, 2^n - 1$. For a node v, let V_v denote the set of nodes of the subtree rooted at v. Let $\mathcal{I}_v$ be the set of the indices of all the leaf nodes that are descendants of node v,

$$\mathcal{I}_v = \{\ell(u) : u \in V_v \text{ and } u \text{ is a leaf node}\}.$$

Example 17.35 To illustrate this notation, consider the tree labeled in Figure 17.33. For this tree:

$$\mathcal{I}_b = \{0,1,2,3\} \quad V_b = \{b,d,e,0,1,2,3\} \quad \mathcal{I}_c = \{4,5,6,7\} \quad V_c = \{c,f,g,4,5,6,7\}$$

$$\mathcal{I}_d = \{0,1\} \quad V_d = \{d,0,1\} \quad \mathcal{I}_e = \{2,3\} \quad V_e = \{e,2,3\}$$

$$\mathcal{I}_f = \{4,5\} \quad V_f = \{f,4,5\} \quad \mathcal{I}_g = \{6,7\} \quad V_g = \{g,6,7\}. \qquad \qquad \square$$

In Figure 17.34, nodes v_1 and v_2 and their subtrees have been highlighted. All the leaf node descendents of v_1 are frozen nodes, and all the leaf node descendents of v_2 are unfrozen nodes. Let $\mathcal{A} \subset \{0,1,\ldots,N-1\}$ be the information set (the unfrozen bits) and let $\mathcal{F} = \mathcal{A}^c$ be the frozen bits. We say that a node v in the tree is a *rate one node* with respect to $\mathcal{A}$ if the leaf node descendants of v are all information bits, that is, $\mathcal{I}_v \subseteq \mathcal{A}$. Such nodes are designated as $\mathcal{N}^1$ nodes. Similarly, we say that a node v in the tree is a *rate zero node* with respect to $\mathcal{A}$ if the leaf node descendants of v are all frozen bits, that is, $\mathcal{I}_v \subseteq \mathcal{F}$. These nodes are the $\mathcal{N}^0$ nodes. In Figure 17.34, node v_1, and in fact all the white nodes, are rate zero nodes; node v_2 and all the black nodes are rate one nodes. The nodes that are not in $\mathcal{N}^0$ or $\mathcal{N}^1$ (colored in gray on the tree) having rate $0 < R < 1$ are called the $\mathcal{N}^R$ nodes.

Intuitively, since the rate zero nodes are frozen, there no need to do any decoding on them. The entire subtree rooted at v_1 requires no computation, since all its nodes are zero rate nodes. This modification to the decoding algorithm results in some reduction of computational complexity.

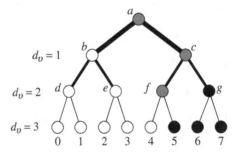

Figure 17.33: A tree labeled to illustrate the notation for simplified successive cancellation decoding.

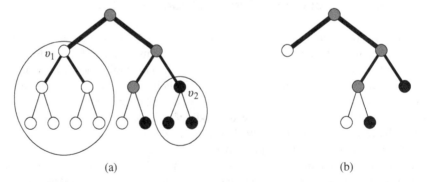

(a)   (b)

Figure 17.34: Identifying rate one nodes (black) and a rate zero nodes (white) in the tree, and the reduced tree. (a) Rate one nodes and rate zero nodes; (b) the reduced tree.

Further simplifications are possible. With the tree structure in mind, we associate to each node v a "constituent code" with a generator as follows. Let G_n denote the generator matrix for a polar code of block length 2^n where, for example (neglecting the bit-reverse permutation matrix),

$$G_1 = F = \begin{bmatrix} 1 & 0 \\ 1 & 1 \end{bmatrix} \quad G_2 = F^{\otimes 2} = \begin{bmatrix} 1 & 0 & 0 & 0 \\ 1 & 1 & 0 & 0 \\ 1 & 0 & 1 & 0 \\ 1 & 1 & 1 & 1 \end{bmatrix}.$$

Assign to each node v a constituent generator G^v obtained from taking the rows i and columns i of G_{n-d_v} for $i \in \mathcal{I}_v \cap \mathcal{A}$.

Example 17.36 For the labeling in Figure 17.33, with $\mathcal{A} = \{5, 6, 7\}$

$$G^b = [\quad] \quad G^d = [\quad] \quad G^e = [\quad] \quad \text{(empty matrix for zero-rate node)}$$
$$G^c = G_2 \quad G^f = [1] \quad G^g = G_1.$$

$\square$

At a rate one node, the constituent generator is simply the square matrix G_{n-d_v}, which is invertible with $G_{n-d_v}^{-1} = G_{n-d_v}$.

A modified decoding algorithm is obtained as follows. Let α_v be the message vector to a rate one node v such as node v_2 in Figure 17.34(a). When v is activated, it immediately calculates β_v by simply quantizing the result as

$$\beta_v = h(\alpha_v),$$

where $h(\cdot)$ is applied to each element of α_v. Then the bit indices in $\mathcal{I}_v$ are decoded as

$$\hat{u}[\min \mathcal{I}_v], \ldots, \hat{u}[\max \mathcal{I}_v]) = \beta_v G^v.$$

The decoder for a rate-one constituent code simply hard-quantizes its soft input values and computes the inverse of the encoding operation (which is the same as the encoding operation).

Example 17.37 In Figure 17.33, the message $\alpha_g = \alpha_{c_r}$ to node g has two components (see (17.56)). These are thresholded to bit values using $\beta_g = h(\alpha_{c_r})$, then un-encoded as

$$(\hat{u}[6], \hat{u}[7]) = \beta_v \begin{bmatrix} 1 & 0 \\ 1 & 1 \end{bmatrix}.$$

$\square$

None of the lower decoders at nodes $u \in V_v \setminus \{v\}$ need to be activated — the information at the highest rate one node in a subtree is immediately transformed to the decoded bit values. The modified algorithm replaces laboriously computed soft information propagated through the intervening layers with easily computed hard information at the leaf nodes of V_v. The result of this observation is that the decoding on the full tree can be reduced to decoding on a reduced tree, as shown in Figure 17.34(b).

This modified decoder produces the same decoding result as if the fully decoding algorithm were employed. Why does this work? It can be verified on a case-by-case basis that if both x and y are nonzero real numbers,

$$h(x \boxplus y) = h(x) \oplus h(y), \tag{17.95}$$

where h is an instance of the quantization function defined in (17.47). That is, computing the log-likelihood computation $x \boxplus y$ then quantizing it is equivalent to quantizing both x and y then adding modulo 2. The proof that the modified decoder produces the same decoding result proceeds by induction, starting at level $d_v = n - 1$, the level above the leaf nodes. For such a node v,

$$\beta_{v_l} = h(\alpha_{v_l}) \quad \text{and} \quad \beta_{v_r} = h(\alpha_{v_r}). \tag{17.96}$$

Using (17.54) and (17.95),

$$h(\alpha_{v_l}[i]) = h(\alpha_v[2i]) \oplus h(\alpha_v[2i+1]).$$

Using (17.55) and (17.96),

$$\begin{aligned}
h(\alpha_{v_r}[i]) &= h(\alpha_v[2i](1 - 2h(\alpha_{v_l}[2i])) + \alpha_v[2i+1]) \\
&= h(\alpha_v[2i](1 - 2(h(\alpha_v[2i]) \oplus h(\alpha_v[2i+1]))) + \alpha_v[2i+1]) \\
&= h(\alpha_v[2i+1]),
\end{aligned}$$

where the last equality is verified by considering each of the four cases

$$(\alpha_v[2i] > 0, \alpha_v[2i+1] > 0), \quad (\alpha_v[2i] > 0, \alpha_v[2i+1] < 0),$$
$$(\alpha_v[2i] < 0, \alpha_v[2i+1] > 0), \quad (\alpha_v[2i] < 0, \alpha_v[2i+1] < 0).$$

The β messages are computed as follows:

$$\begin{aligned}
\beta_v[2i] &= \beta_{v_l}[i] \oplus \beta_{v_r}[i] = h(\alpha_{v_l}[i]) \oplus h(\alpha_{v_r}[i]) \\
&= h(\alpha_v[2i+1]) \oplus h(\alpha_v[2i+1]) \oplus h(\alpha_v[2i]) = h(\alpha_v[2i]) \\
\beta_v[2i+1] &= \beta_{v_r}[i] = \beta_{v_r}[i] = h(\alpha_{v_r}[i]) = h(\alpha_v[0]).
\end{aligned}$$

Thus, at a rate one node at depth $d_v = n - 1$,

$$\beta_v[i] = h(\alpha_v[i]) \quad \text{for all } i.$$

For rate one nodes at $d_v < n - 1$, we can proceed inductively. Assume that (17.96) holds at depth d (the inductive hypothesis). For a rate one node at depth $d - 1$, its children are also rate one nodes at a depth d which, based upon the inductive hypothesis, satisfy (17.96), so the steps in the proof above apply.

17.11.1 Modified SC Decoding

The discussion above results in decoding simplifications for rate zero and rate one subtrees. Are there simplifications that can be applied to the $\mathcal{N}^R$ nodes with $0 < R < 1$, such as node f in Figure 17.33? One approach is to do ML decoding. In general, a decoder for a binary block code C of dimension k estimates the transmitted codeword based on the received information $\mathbf{y}$ as $\hat{\mathbf{x}}$, where

$$\hat{\mathbf{x}} = \arg \max_{\mathbf{x} \in C} P(\mathbf{y}|\mathbf{x}),$$

where the maximization requires (in principle) a search over 2^k different codewords. When BSPK modulation is used (transmitted values are $\pm a$ for some amplitude a) and the received information is represented using LLR values, this becomes

$$\hat{\mathbf{x}} = \arg \max_{\mathbf{x} \in C} \sum_{i=0}^{n_v - 1} (1 - 2\mathbf{x}[i])\alpha_v[i],$$

where n_v is the number of bits associated with the code at node v, $n_v = 2^{d(v)}$. The complexity of this grows exponentially with the code dimension and linearly with the code length n_v. For some nodes this turns out to be a valid tradeoff, especially since the ML search can be carried out in parallel.

17.12 Relations with Reed–Muller Codes

Arıkan [16] observed connections between polar codes and Reed–Muller (RM) codes. One construction of RM codes is follows. Form the matrix $F^{\otimes n}$, then delete the rows of that matrix which have least weight, until an $K \times N$ matrix of obtained. This is similar to the polar code construction, which similarly selects rows of $F^{\otimes n}$. The difference is that the RM generator selects the information set (rows of $F^{\otimes n}$ retained) in a channel-independent manner, while the polar codes retain rows in a channel-dependent manner. Polar coding is thus more finely tuned to the channel than RM coding is. In fact, Arıkan proves that the RM rule for designing the generator leads to asymptotically unreliable codes under SC decoding.

17.13 Hardware and Throughput Performance Results

Because of the great potential of polar codes there has been considerable research devoted to producing high-speed polar code decoders. The performance of these decoders will only go up, so this list cannot be exhaustive. But a few results are mentioned that are interesting at the time of publication.

- In 2013, [332] reported a throughput of approximately 100 Mbps for a rate 0.9 code of length 16,384 with a 230 MHz clock on an FPGA.

- In 2014, [391] reported a throughput of approximately 1 Gbps for a rate 0.9 code of length 32,768 with a clock of 108 MHz on an FPGA, using fast SSC (that is, SSC with specialized decoders for $\mathcal{N}^R$ nodes).

- By unrolling the SSC into a pipeline (which results in large hardware requirements), a decoder with approximately 100 Gbps throughput was reported in 2015 for a $(1024, 512)$ code [157].

- A survey reporting throughput of 415.7 Gbps is reported in [155].

Other articles of interest reporting on hardware implementations are [264, 389, 390, 393].

Besides hardware implementations, software polar decoders can also operate at high speed, making them very competitive with software implementation of decoders for other codes such as turbo codes or LDPC codes. Decoders operating in excess of 250 Mbps throughput for $(32768, 29492)$ codes have been reported [146,156].

17.14 Generalizations, Extensions, and Variations

Beyond the basic concepts related to polar coding presented here, there are many generalizations and variations. We touch on a few here.

- Arıkan [16] indicated how to extend the polarization idea from binary input channels to channels operating with a q-input set $\mathcal{X} = \{0, 1, \ldots, q - 1\}$. The basic idea is very similar to the polarization we have already seen, with an invertible function (generalizing the two-input/two-output $\oplus$ stage used for binary codes) is used to process blocks of the input data, which then passes through a permuter, then through the individual channels. The encoding and SC decoding complexity for this generalization is still $O(N \log N)$.

- Arıkan also describes how to obtain channels whose length N is not a power of 2, using a decomposition $N = \prod_{i=1}^{n} m_i$. Performance comparisons for non-power-of-2 channels is not provided in Arıkan.

- Arıkan also describes using a factor graph for iterative decoding and doing belief propagation decoding. This idea was explored in [207], which showed that belief propagation decoding can significantly outperform SC decoding, if an appropriate message passing schedule can be established. See also [65].

- An alternative proof of channel polarization is provided in [9], which extends polarization to nonstationary memoryless channels.

- Şaşoğlu *et al.* [395] generalized Arıkan's results to channels where the input alphabet size is prime (not just 2).

- Generalization of polarization to multiple access channels is discussed in [323] and references therein.

Appendix 17.A B_N is a Bit-Reverse Permutation

We begin with an observation. Let A be $m \times n$ and B be $p \times q$ so $C = A \otimes B$ is $mp \times nq$. Using 0-based indexing, the (i,j)th element of C is

$$C_{ij} = A_{\lfloor i/p \rfloor, \lfloor j/q \rfloor} B_{i \pmod p, j \pmod q}. \tag{17.97}$$

For an integer i, $0 \le i < N$, let its binary expansion be written as $i = b_1 b_2 \ldots b_n$, where b_1 is the most significant bit or, more precisely,

$$i = \sum_{j=1}^{n} b_j 2^{n-j}.$$

The ith element of a vector u_0^{N-1} can be denoted as $u_i = u_{b_1 \ldots b_n}$. Similarly, the element A_{ij} of an $N \times N$ matrix can be written as $A_{b_1 \ldots b_n, b'_1 \ldots b'_n}$.

Let A be a $2^m \times 2^m$ matrix and let B be a $2^n \times 2^n$ matrix and let $C = A \otimes B$. Then, referring to (17.97) and expressing the indices in binary,

$$C_{b_1 \ldots b_{n+m}, b'_1 \ldots b'_{n+m}} = A_{b_1 \ldots b_n, b'_1 \ldots b'_n} B_{b_{n+1} \ldots b_{n+m}, b'_{n+1} \ldots b'_{n+m}}. \tag{17.98}$$

The elements of the matrix $F = \begin{bmatrix} 1 & 0 \\ 1 & 1 \end{bmatrix}$ can be expressed as $F_{b,b'} = 1 \oplus b' \oplus bb'$ for $b, b' \in \{0, 1\}$, as can be verified exhaustively. Recursively applying (17.98),

$$F^{\otimes n}_{b_1 \ldots b_n, b'_1 \ldots b'_n} = \prod_{i=1}^{n} F_{b_i, b'_i} = \prod_{i=1}^{n} (1 \oplus b'_i \oplus b_i b'_i). \tag{17.99}$$

Let $v_0^{N-1} = s_0^{N-1} R_N$. As observed in Section 17.4.1,

$$(v_0, v_1, \ldots, v_{N-1}) = (s_0, s_2, \ldots, s_{N-2}, s_1, s_3, \ldots, s_{N-1}).$$

For example, when $N = 8$ and expressing the indices in binary,

$$(v_{000}, v_{001}, v_{010}, v_{011}, v_{100}, v_{101}, v_{110}, v_{111}) = (s_{000}, s_{010}, s_{100}, s_{110}, s_{001}, s_{011}, s_{101}, s_{111}).$$

This shows that the permutation operator R_N acts on s_0^{N-1} to replace the element at index $b_1 \ldots b_n$ with the element in position $b_2 \ldots b_n b_1$, that is, a cyclic shift to the right, so

$$v_{b_1 \ldots b_n} = s_{b_2 \ldots b_n b_1}.$$

Now consider the operator B_N in (17.35). B_N can be shown inductively to be a bit-reverse permutation. The induction is best demonstrated by example. It is known (see, for example, Figure 17.9) that B_4 is a bit-reverse permutation. We will use this to show that B_8 is also a bit-reverse permutation.

$$(u_{000}, u_{001}, u_{010}, u_{011}, u_{100}, u_{101}, u_{110}, u_{111})R_8(I_2 \otimes B_4)$$

$$= (u_{000}, u_{010}, u_{100}, u_{110},\ u_{001}, u_{011}, u_{101}, u_{111})(I_2 \otimes B_4)$$

$$= ((u_{000}, u_{010}, u_{100}, u_{110})B_4, (u_{001}, u_{011}, u_{101}, u_{111})B_4).$$

Using the fact that B_4 is a bit-reverse permutation, we now obtain

$$(u_{000}, u_{100}, u_{010}, u_{110},\ u_{001}, u_{101}, u_{011}, u_{111}),$$

which is a bit-reverse permutation.

A matrix A is invariant under bit-reversal if $A_{b_1 \ldots b_n, b'_1 \ldots b'_n} = A_{b_n \ldots b_1, b'_n, b'_1}$ for every index pair $b_1 \ldots b_n, b'_1 \ldots b'_n$. If A is invariant under bit reversal, $A = B_N^T A B_N$ or, using the fact that $B_N^T = B_N$, $B_N A = A B_T$. Thus, bit-reversal-invariant matrices commute with the bit-reverse permutation.

From (17.99), it follows that $F^{\otimes n}$ is invariant under bit-reversal (just read the product in the reverse order), so that $B_N F^{\otimes n} = F^{\otimes n} B_N$.

Appendix 17.B The Relationship of the Battacharyya Parameter to Channel Capacity

Appendix 17.B.1 Error Probability for Two Codewords

In this section, we develop a bound for the probability of error when ML decoding is used to distinguish between two vectors of length N. This will involve the Battacharyya parameter.

Most of this work will be done with nonbinary alphabets. This will be simplified to binary alphabets at some points. Let $\mathcal{X}$ be the alphabet of input symbols, with $|\mathcal{X}| = q$. Let x_0 and x_1 be symbols from $\mathcal{X}$ transmitted through a channel with transmission probability $W(y|x_i)$. Suppose that x_0 is sent. Under ML decoding, x_0 is decoded if $W(y|x_0) > W(y|x_1)$. Let $\mathcal{Y}_0$ be set of received values y such that the decoder selects x_0:

$$Y_0 = \{y \in \mathbb{R} : W(y|x_0) > W(y|x_1)\}.$$

Then the probability of error when message x_0 is sent is

$$P_{e,0} = \sum_{y \in Y_0^c} W(y|x_0). \tag{17.100}$$

Since for $y \in Y^c$, $W(y|x_1) \geq W(y|x_0)$, it follows that for s in the range $0 < s < 1$, $W(y|x_1)^s \geq W(y|x_0)^s$, so

$$W(y|x_0) \leq W(y|x_0)^{1-s} W(y|x_1)^s \quad 0 < s < 1.$$

Substituting this into (17.100), we obtain

$$P_{e,0} \leq \sum_{y \in Y_1^c} W(y|x_0)^{1-s} W(y|x_1)^s \leq \sum_y W(y|x_0)^{1-s} W(y|x_1)^s. \tag{17.101}$$

Similarly,

$$P_{e,1} \leq \sum_y W(y|x_1)^{1-r} W(y|x_0)^r \quad 0 < r < 1. \tag{17.102}$$

Substituting $r \to 1-s$ in (17.102) gives (17.101), resulting in the same bounds for $P_{e,0}$ and $P_{e,1}$, since s is arbitrary in $[0, 1]$. Thus,

$$P_{e,m} \leq \sum_y W(y|x_0)^{1-s} W(y|x_1)^s \quad m = 0, 1, \quad 0 < s < 1.$$

Let the sum be denoted as

$$Z(W, s) = \sum_y W(y|x_0)^{1-s} W(y|x_1)^1,$$

so that

$$P_{e,m} \leq Z(W, s) \quad m = 0, 1 \quad 0 < s < 1.$$

The tightest bound is obtained when s is selected to minimize the $Z(W, s)$. It can be shown that $Z(W, s)$ is convex in s and, for symmetric channels, the minimum values occurs when $s = \frac{1}{2}$. For such symmetric channels, then, let

$$Z(W) = Z(W, s)\big|_{s=\frac{1}{2}} = \sum_y \sqrt{W(y|x_0) W(y|x_1)}.$$

This is the *Battacharyya parameter*. Then

$$P_{e,m} \leq Z(W). \tag{17.103}$$

The smaller the Battacharyya parameter is, the lower the probability of error.

Appendix 17.B.2   Proof of Inequality (17.59)

We prove here not only the inequality

$$I(W) \geq \log \frac{2}{1 + Z(W)},$$

which applies to binary channels, but the more general form

$$I(W) \geq \log \frac{q}{1 + (q-1)Z(W)},$$

which is pertinent to channels with q-ary inputs. This section builds on the results of the preceding section. Consider an information transmission system having M messages to be transmitted, each of which is represented by a codeword $\mathbf{x}$ of length N of symbols $x_i \in \mathcal{X}$.[4] For a message m, the codeword $\mathbf{x}_m$ representing it is drawn at random according to the distribution $Q_N(\mathbf{x})$. A codeword $\mathbf{x}_m$ is transmitted and a vector $\mathbf{y}$ is received, which consists of N symbols each from the alphabet $\mathcal{Y}$ (which may not be a binary alphabet).

Let $P[\text{error}|m, \mathbf{x}_m, \mathbf{y}]$ denote the probability of error conditioned on a message number m entering the system, and the selection of $\mathbf{x}_m$ as the mth codeword and on the reception of $\mathbf{y}$, where $\mathbf{y}$ is selected according to the transition probability $W_N(\mathbf{y}|\mathbf{x}_m)$. Let $\bar{p}_{e,m}$ denote the average probability of error for the mth message, averaged over the random selections of $\mathbf{x}_m$ and the received $\mathbf{y}$. Then

$$\bar{p}_{e,m} = \sum_{\mathbf{x}_m \in \mathcal{X}^N} \sum_{\mathbf{y} \in \mathcal{Y}^N} Q_N(\mathbf{x}_m) W_N(\mathbf{y}|\mathbf{x}_m) P[\text{error}|m, \mathbf{x}_m, \mathbf{y}]. \tag{17.104}$$

---

[4] For our purposes here, it is possible to take $N = 1$. The argument with arbitrary $N > 1$ is the random coding argument and leads, if continued beyond our argument here, to the channel coding theorem, and hence makes a more plausible system. See [147, Section 5.6].

A ML decoder selects the $\mathbf{x}$ such that $W_N(\mathbf{y}|\mathbf{x})$ is the largest. A decoding error occurs if message m is input and $\mathbf{x}_m$ is transmitted but $W_N(\mathbf{y}|\mathbf{x}_{m'}) > W_N(\mathbf{y}|\mathbf{x}_m)$ for some $m' \neq m$. Thus, let $A_{m'}$ denote the event that $W_N(\mathbf{y}|\mathbf{x}_{m'}) \geq W_N(\mathbf{y}|\mathbf{x}_m)$. From this definition,

$$P(A_{m'}) = \sum_{\mathbf{x}'_m : W_N(\mathbf{y}|\mathbf{x}_{m'}) \geq W_N(\mathbf{y}|\mathbf{x}_m)} Q_N(\mathbf{x}_{m'}) \leq \sum_{\mathbf{x}'_m \in \mathcal{X}^N} Q_N(\mathbf{x}_{m'}) \frac{W_N(\mathbf{y}|\mathbf{x}_{m'})^s}{W_N(\mathbf{y}|\mathbf{x}_m)^s} \quad \text{for any } s > 0. \quad (17.105)$$

The probability of the error event can be expressed using the events $A_{m'}$ as

$$P[\text{error}|m, \mathbf{x}_m, \mathbf{y}] \leq P\left(\bigcup_{m' \neq m} A_{m'}\right). \quad (17.106)$$

Here the inequality follows since a ML decodes does not necessarily make an error if $W_N(\mathbf{y}|\mathbf{x}_{m'}) = W_N(\mathbf{y}|\mathbf{x}_m)$ for some m'. We will now invoke a generalization of the union bound:

$$P\left(\bigcup_m A_m\right) \leq \left[\sum_m P(A_m)\right]^\rho, \quad \text{any } \rho, 0 < \rho \leq 1. \quad (17.107)$$

This bound is straightforward to show. By the union bound and the properties of probabilities,

$$P\left(\bigcup_m A_m\right) \leq \begin{cases} \sum_{m=1}^M P(A_m) \\ 1. \end{cases}$$

If $\sum_m P(A_m)$ is less than 1, then it is smaller than $\left(\sum_m P(A_m)\right)^\rho$ for $0 < \rho \leq 1$. On the other hand, if $\sum_m P(A_m) \geq 1$, then $\left[\sum_m P(A_m)\right]^\rho \geq 1$ for these ρ. In either case, the inequality (17.107) results.

Applying the inequalities (17.107) and (17.105)–(17.106) we obtain

$$P[\text{error}|m, \mathbf{x}_m, \mathbf{y}] \leq \left[(M-1) \sum_{\mathbf{x} \in \mathcal{X}^N} Q_N(\mathbf{x}) \frac{W_N(\mathbf{y}|\mathbf{x})^s}{W_N(\mathbf{y}|\mathbf{x}_m)^s}\right]^\rho.$$

Substituting this into (17.104) gives

$$\overline{P}_{e,m} \leq (M-1)^\rho \sum_{\mathbf{y} \in \mathcal{Y}^N} \left[\sum_{\mathbf{x}_m \in \mathcal{X}^N} Q_N(\mathbf{x}_m) W_N(\mathbf{y}|\mathbf{x}_m)^{1-s\rho}\right] \left[\sum_{\mathbf{x} \in \mathcal{X}^N} Q_N(\mathbf{x}) W_N(\mathbf{y}|\mathbf{x})^s\right]^\rho.$$

Setting $s = 1/(1+\rho)$ (which can be shown to minimize the bound) and using $\mathbf{x}$ as the dummy variable of summation we end up with the bound

$$\overline{P}_{e,m} \leq (M-1)^\rho \sum_{\mathbf{y} \in \mathcal{Y}^N} \left[\sum_{\mathbf{x} \in \mathcal{X}^N} Q_N(\mathbf{x}) W_N(\mathbf{y}|\mathbf{x})^{1/(1+\rho)}\right]^{1+\rho}.$$

For our purposes it will suffice to assume that each symbol is selected independently and that the channel is memoryless so that

$$Q_N(\mathbf{x}) = \prod_{n=1}^N Q(x_n) \quad W_N(\mathbf{y}|\mathbf{x}) = \prod_{n=1}^N W(y_n|x_n).$$

This leads to

$$\overline{P}_{e,m} \leq (M-1)^\rho \left[\sum_{y \in \mathcal{Y}} \left[\sum_{x \in \mathcal{X}} Q(x) W(y|x)^{1/(1+\rho)}\right]^{1+\rho}\right]^N.$$

Define now the quantity

$$E_0(\rho, Q) = -\log \sum_{y \in \mathcal{Y}} \left[\sum_{x \in \mathcal{X}} Q(x)W(y|x)^{1/1+\rho} \right]^{1+\rho} \tag{17.108}$$

so that

$$\overline{p}_{e,m} \leq (M-1)^\rho \exp[-NE_0(\rho, Q)].$$

To prove the bounds related to the Battacharyya parameter and the capacity, our attention now turns to the function $E_0(\rho, Q)$. Let

$$I(Q, W) = \sum_{y \in \mathcal{Y}} \sum_{x \in \mathcal{X}} Q(x)W(y|x) \log \frac{W(y|x)}{\sum_{x'} Q(x')W(y|x')}.$$

$I(Q, W)$ is the mutual information for the channel W with input data selected according to the distribution Q. When $|\mathcal{X}| = 2$ (binary source) and $Q(x) = \frac{1}{2}$ for $x = 0, 1$, we get the quantity $I(W)$ defined in (17.1) and (17.57). The following theorem describes some relationships between $E_0(\rho, Q)$ and $I(Q, W)$.

Theorem 17.38 *[147, Theorem 5.6.3]*

$$E_0(\rho, Q) \geq 0 \quad for \ \rho \geq 0, \tag{17.109}$$

$$I(Q, W) = \left. \frac{\partial E_0(\rho, Q)}{\partial r} \right|_{\rho=0} \quad and \quad I(Q, W) \geq \frac{\partial E_0(\rho, Q)}{\partial \rho} > 0 \quad for \ \rho \geq 0, \tag{17.110}$$

$$\frac{\partial E_0(\rho, Q)}{\partial \rho} \leq 0 \quad for \ \rho \geq 0. \tag{17.111}$$

The proof of this theorem is given below. Here, we explore some implications of it. The typical shape of the function is shown in Figure 17.35. From (17.110), the initial slope of $E_0(\rho, Q)$ is $I(Q, W)$. Due to the concavity of the function, $E_0(\rho, Q)$ curves downward away from this initial slope. The result is that then $E_0(\rho, Q)$ is evaluated at $\rho = 1$, for any Q

$$E_0(1, Q) \leq I(Q, W). \tag{17.112}$$

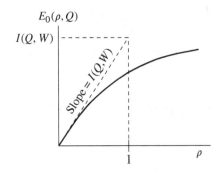

Figure 17.35: Plot of $E_0(\rho, Q)$.

With $q = 2$, expanding the definition of $E_0(\rho, Q)$ in (17.108) at $\rho = 1$ and with $Q(x) = \frac{1}{2}$ for $x = 0, 1$, which we denote as $E_0(1, \frac{1}{2})$,

$$E_0\left(1, \frac{1}{2}\right) = -\log \sum_{y \in \mathcal{Y}} \left[\frac{1}{2}\sqrt{W(y|0)} + \frac{1}{2}\sqrt{W(y|1)}\right]^2$$

$$= -\log \sum_{y \in \mathcal{Y}} \frac{1}{4}W(y|0) + \frac{1}{4}\sqrt{W(y|0)W(y|1)} + \frac{1}{4}W(y|1)$$

$$= -\log \frac{1}{2} + \frac{1}{2}\sum_{y \in \mathcal{Y}} \sqrt{W(y|0)W(y|1)} = \log \frac{2}{1 + \sum_y \sqrt{W(y|0)W(y|1)}}$$

$$= \log \frac{2}{1 + Z(W)}.$$

Hence,

$$I(W) \geq \log \frac{2}{1 + Z(W)},$$

which establishes (17.59).

Similarly, for other values of q, set each probability $Q(x) = \frac{1}{q}$. Denoting this as $E_0(1, \frac{1}{q})$, and taking $\mathcal{X} = \{0, 1, \ldots, q-1\}$:

$$E_0\left(1, \frac{1}{q}\right) = -\log \sum_{y \in \mathcal{Y}} \left[\frac{1}{q}\sum_{x \in \mathcal{X}}\sqrt{W(y|x)}\right]^2$$

$$= -\log \sum_{y \in \mathcal{Y}} \left[\frac{1}{q^2}\left(\sum_{y \in \mathcal{Y}} W(y|x) + \sum_{x,x' \in \mathcal{X}: x \neq x'} \underbrace{\sum_{y \in \mathcal{Y}}\sqrt{W(y|x)W(y|x')}}_{Z(W_{\{x,x'\}})}\right)\right]^2$$

$$= -\log \frac{1}{q} + \frac{q-1}{q}\underbrace{\frac{1}{q(q-1)}\sum_{x,x' \in \mathcal{X}: x \neq x'} Z(W_{\{x,x'\}})}_{Z(W)}$$

$$= \log \frac{q}{1 + (q-1)Z(W)}.$$

Proof *of Theorem* **17.38**. (See [147, Appendix 5B].) It is straightforward to verify from (17.108) that $E_0(0, Q) = 0$. By differentiation, it is straightforward to show that

$$\left.\frac{\partial E_0(\rho, Q)}{\partial r}\right|_{\rho=0} = I(Q, W).$$

For the rest of the proof, we will rely on the following fact ([147, p. 193]): Let

$$\big[Q(0), \ldots, Q(K-1)\big]$$

be a probability vector and let $a_0, \ldots, a_{K-1}$ be non-negative numbers. Then the function

$$f(s) = \log \left[\sum_{k=0}^{K-1} Q(k) a_k^{1/s} \right]^s$$

is nonincreasing and convex in s for $s > 0$. The convexity of $f(s)$ means that for $r > 0$, $s > 0$ and $t = \lambda s + (1 - \lambda)r$ for $0 < \lambda < 1$,

$$f(t) \leq \lambda f(s) + (1 - \lambda)f(r).$$

Exponentiating both sides of this, we obtain

$$\left[\sum_k Q(k) a_k^{1/t} \right]^t \leq \left[\sum_k Q(k) a_k^{1/s} \right]^{s\lambda} \left[\sum_k Q(k) a_k^{1/r} \right]^{r(1-\lambda)}. \tag{17.113}$$

Applying this in (17.108), we see that

$$\left[\sum_k Q(k) W(j|k)^{1/(1+\rho)} \right]^{1+\rho}$$

is nonincreasing with ρ and hence (since log is monotonic increasing), $E_0(\rho, Q)$ is nondecreasing, establishing (17.109).

To establish (17.111), it is sufficient to show that $E_0(\rho, Q)$ is concave in ρ, which is done as follows. Let $\rho_1 > 0$ and $\rho_2 > 0$, and let λ satisfy $0 < \lambda < 1$. Let $\rho = \rho_1 \lambda + \rho_2 (1 - \lambda)$. From (17.113),

$$\sum_j \left[\sum_k Q(k) W(j|k)^{1/(1+\rho)} \right]^{1+\rho} \leq \sum_j \left[\sum_k Q(k) W(j|k)^{1/(1+\rho_1)} \right]^{(1+\rho_1)\lambda}$$

$$\times \sum_j \left[\sum_k Q(k) W(j|k)^{1/(1+\rho_2)} \right]^{(1+\rho_2)(1-\lambda)}. \tag{17.114}$$

Hölder's inequality says that

$$\sum_j a_j b_j \leq [\sum_j a_j^{1/\lambda}]^\lambda [\sum_j a_j^{1/(1-\lambda)}]^{1-\lambda}.$$

Applying this to the right-hand side of (17.114) gives

$$\sum_j \left[\sum_k Q(k) W(j|k)^{1/(1+\rho)} \right]^{1+\rho} \leq \left[\sum_j \left[\sum_k Q(k) W(j|k)^{1/(1+\rho_1)} \right]^{1+\rho_1} \right]^\lambda$$

$$\times \left[\sum_j \left[\sum_k Q(k) W(j|k)^{1/(1+\rho_2)} \right]^{1+\rho_2} \right]^{1-\lambda}.$$

Taking the negative logarithm of both sides yields

$$E_0(\rho, Q) \geq \lambda E_0(\rho_1, Q), +(1 - \lambda)E_0(\rho_2, Q),$$

so $E_0(\rho, Q)$ is concave in ρ. □

Appendix 17.B.3   Proof of Inequality (17.60) [16]

For any B-DMC $W : \mathcal{X} \rightarrow \mathcal{Y}$, define the variational distance between the distributions as

$$d(W) = \frac{1}{2} \sum_{y \in \mathcal{Y}} |W(y|0) - W(y|1)|. \tag{17.115}$$

Let the output alphabet be $\mathcal{Y} = \{1, 2, \ldots, m\}$, and express the capacity (17.57) as

$$I(W) = \sum_{i=1}^{m} \frac{1}{2} \left[P_i \log_2 \frac{P_i}{\frac{1}{2}P_i + \frac{1}{2}Q_i} + Q_i \log_2 \frac{Q_i}{\frac{1}{2}P_i + \frac{1}{2}Q_i} \right],$$

where $P_i = W(i|0)$ and $Q_i = W(i|1)$. Each bracketed term can be written as

$$f(x) = x \log_2 \frac{x}{x+\delta} + (x + 2\delta) \log_2 \frac{x+2\delta}{x+\delta},$$

where $x = \min(P_i, Q_i)$ and $\delta = \frac{1}{2}|P_i - Q_i|$. To maximize $f(x)$ with respect to x take the derivative and find that

$$\frac{df(x)}{dx} = \frac{1}{2} \log \frac{\sqrt{x(x+2\delta)}}{x+\delta}.$$

The numerator is the geometric mean of the numbers x and $(x + 2\delta)$ and the denominator is the arithmetic mean of the numbers x and $(x + 2\delta)$. The arithmetic/geometric mean inequality [318, p. 874] says that the geometric mean is less than or equal to the arithmetic mean, so that $df(x)/dx \leq 0$. The maximum occurs when $x = 0$, in which case $f(0) = 2\delta$, so $f(x) \leq 2\delta$. This means that

$$I(W) \leq \sum_{i=1}^{m} \frac{1}{2}|P_i - Q_i| = \sum_{i=1}^{m} \delta_i = d(W). \tag{17.116}$$

Let $\delta = \sum_{i=1}^{m} \delta_i$.

The Battacharyya parameter $Z(W)$ can be expressed in terms of the P_i and Q_i and δ_i as follows. Let $R_i = (P_i + Q_i)/2$. Then

$$Z(W) = \sum_{i=1}^{m} \sqrt{(R_i - \delta_i)(R_i + \delta_i)} = \sum_{i=1}^{m} \sqrt{R_i^2 - \delta_i^2}.$$

$Z(W)$ is upper-bounded by the maximizing $\sum_{i=1}^{m} \sqrt{R_i^2 - \delta_i^2}$, subject to the constraints that $0 \leq \delta_i \leq R_i$ and $\sum_{i=1}^{m} \delta_i = \delta$. To do the maximization, compute the derivatives

$$\frac{\partial Z}{\partial \delta_i} = -\frac{\delta_i}{\sqrt{R_i^2 - \delta_i^2}} \qquad \frac{\partial^2 Z}{\partial \delta_i^2} = -\frac{R_i^2}{\sqrt[3/2]{R_i^2 - \delta_i^2}}.$$

Thus, $Z(W)$ is a decreasing concave function of δ_i for each δ_i in the range $0 \leq \delta_i \leq R_i$. The constrained optimization problem can be expressed as

$$\text{minimize } f_0(\delta_1, \ldots, \delta_m) = -\sum_{i=1}^{m} \sqrt{R_i - \delta_i^2}$$

$$\text{subject to } f_i(\delta_i) = \delta_r - R_i \leq 0, \quad i = 1, 2, \ldots, m$$

$$h = \sum_{i=1}^{m} \delta_i - \delta = 0.$$

The Lagrangian for this problem is

$$L(\delta_1, \ldots, \delta_m, \lambda_1, \ldots, \lambda_m, \nu) = -\sum_{i=1}^{m} \sqrt{R_i^2 - \delta_i^2} + \sum_{i=1}^{m} \lambda_i f_i(\delta_i) + \nu \left(\sum_{i=1}^{m} \delta_i - \delta \right).$$

Taking the gradient with respect to the vector of δ_i results in

$$\frac{\partial L}{\partial \delta} = \begin{bmatrix} -\dfrac{\partial Z}{\partial \delta_1} \\ \vdots \\ -\partial Z \delta_m \end{bmatrix} + \begin{bmatrix} \lambda_1 \\ \vdots \\ \lambda_m \end{bmatrix} + \nu \begin{bmatrix} 1 \\ \vdots \\ 1 \end{bmatrix} = \mathbf{0}. \tag{17.117}$$

The slackness condition of the Karush–Kuhn Tucker (KKT) [49, Section 5.5.3] also require that

$$\lambda_i f_i(\delta_i) = 0,$$

with $\lambda_i = 0$ if $f_i(\delta_i) < 0$ (the ith constraint is inactive). Taking this as the case, the elements of (17.117) result in

$$\frac{\partial Z}{\partial \delta_i} = \nu \quad \text{for } i = 1, 2, \ldots, m.$$

That is, each partial has the same value. Using the derivatives computed above,

$$-\frac{\delta_i}{\sqrt{R_i^2 + \delta_i^2}} = \nu,$$

which results in $\delta_i = R_i \sqrt{\nu^2/(1 + \nu^2)}$. Enforcing the constraint $\sum_{i=1}^{m} \delta_i = \delta$ using the fact that $\sum_{i=1}^{m} R_i = 1$, it follows that $\sqrt{\nu^2/(1 + \nu^2)} = \delta$. This means that the maximum of $Z(W)$ occurs when $\delta_i = \delta R_i$, and this maximum value is $\sum_{i=1}^{m} \sqrt{R_i^2 - \delta^2 R_i^2} = \sqrt{1 - \delta^2} = \sqrt{1 - d(W)^2}$.

In summary,

$$Z(W) \leq \sqrt{1 - d(W)^2}.$$

Turning this around,

$$d(W) \leq \sqrt{1 - Z(W)^2}. \tag{17.118}$$

Combining this with (17.116), we have $I(W) \leq \sqrt{1 - Z(W)^2}$.

Appendix 17.C   Proof of Theorem 17.12

Let $W'(F(y_0, y_1)|u_1)$ denote the transition probability for the W' channel.

For the proof of (17.66), Arıkan makes use of a very clever inequality. It can be verified algebraically that

$$[\sqrt{(\alpha\beta + \delta\gamma)(\alpha\gamma + \delta\beta)}]^2 + \underbrace{2\sqrt{\alpha\beta\delta\gamma}(\sqrt{\alpha} - \sqrt{\delta})^2(\sqrt{\beta} - \sqrt{\gamma})^2}_{(*)}$$

$$= [(\sqrt{\alpha\beta} + \sqrt{\delta\gamma})(\sqrt{\alpha\gamma} + \sqrt{\delta\beta}) - 2\sqrt{\alpha\beta\delta\gamma}]^2.$$

Since the term (*) is ≥ 0, this leads to the inequality

$$[\sqrt{(\alpha\beta + \delta\gamma)(\alpha\gamma + \delta\beta)}]^2 \leq [(\sqrt{\alpha\beta} + \sqrt{\delta\gamma})(\sqrt{\alpha\gamma} + \sqrt{\delta\beta}) - 2\sqrt{\alpha\beta\delta\gamma}]^2. \tag{17.119}$$

Write $Z(W')$ as

$$Z(W') = \sum_{y_0,y_1} \sqrt{W'(F(y_0,y_1)|0)W'(F(y_0,y_1|1))}$$

$$= \frac{1}{2}\sum_{y_0,y_1} \sqrt{W(y_0|0)W(y_1|0) + W(y_0|1)W(y_1|1)}$$

$$\times \sqrt{W(y_0|0)W(y_1|1) + W(y_0|1)W(y_1|0)}$$

(using (17.61)).

Now let $\alpha(y_0) = W(y_0|0)$, $\beta(y_1) = W(y_1|0)$, $\delta(y_0) = W(y_0|1)$ and $\gamma(y_1) = W(y_1|1)$ and write

$$Z(W') = \frac{1}{2}\sum_{y_0,y_1} \sqrt{\alpha(y_0)\beta(y_2) + \delta(y_0)\gamma(y_1)}\sqrt{\alpha(y_0)\gamma(y_1) + \delta(y_0)\beta(y_1)}.$$

Using the inequality in (17.119),

$$Z(W') \le \underbrace{\sum_{y_0,y_1} \frac{1}{2}(\sqrt{\alpha(y_0)\beta(y_1)} + \sqrt{\delta(y_0)\gamma(y_1)})(\sqrt{\alpha(y_0)\gamma(y_1)} + \sqrt{\delta(y_0)\beta(y_1)})}_{(**)}$$

$$\underbrace{- \sum_{y_0,y_1} \sqrt{\alpha(y_0)\beta(y_1)\delta(y_1)\gamma(y_1)}}_{(***)}. \tag{17.120}$$

It is straightforward to show that

$$\sum_{y_0,y_1} \alpha(y_0)\sqrt{\beta(y_1)\gamma(y_1)} = \frac{1}{2}Z(W), \tag{17.121}$$

and, similarly, each of the four terms in the expansion of (**) is equal to $Z(W)$, so that (**) is equal to $2Z(W)$. Similarly, it can be shown that (***) is equal to $Z(W)^2$.

Let $W''(F(y_0,y_1),u_0|u_1)$ denote the transition probability for the W'' channel. To prove (17.67):

$$Z(W'') = \sum_{y_0,y_1,u_0} \sqrt{W''(F(y_0,y_1),u_0|u_1=0)W''(F(y_0,y_1),u_0|u_1=1)}$$

$$= \sum_{y_0,y_1,u_0} \frac{1}{2}\sqrt{W(y_0|u_0)W(y_1|u_1=0)W(y_0|u_0 \oplus 1)W(y_1|u_1=1)}$$

(using (17.62))

$$= \sum_{y_1} \sqrt{W(y_1|u_1=0)W(y_1|u_1=1)} \sum_{u_0}\frac{1}{2}\sum_{y_0}\sqrt{W(y_0|u_0)W(y_0|u_0 \oplus 1)}.$$

For any value of u_0, the inner sum is equal to $Z(W)$. So the sum over u_0 gives $Z(W)$, absorbing the factor $\frac{1}{2}$ since there are two terms in that sum. The outer sum over y_1 is also equal to $Z(W)$, giving $Z(W') = Z(W)^2$.

To prove (17.68), we first establish a kind of convexity result for $Z(W)$, then apply a version of Minkowski's inequality.

First, let $\mathcal{J}$ be a set of indices, and let $\{W_j : \mathcal{X} \to \mathcal{Y}, j \in \mathcal{J}\}$ denote a collection of B-DMCs with channel transition probabilities $W_j(y|x)$. Let Q be a probability distribution on $\mathcal{J}$, $\sum_j Q_j = 1$. Define (here) $W : \mathcal{X} \to \mathcal{Y}$ as the channel with transition probabilities

$$W(y|x) = \sum_{j \in \mathcal{J}} Q_j W_j(y|x). \tag{17.122}$$

The channel W thus works like this: Pick a channel W_j according to Q, then transmit on that channel.
Claim:

$$\sum_{j \in \mathcal{J}} Q_j Z(W_j) \le Z(W).$$

Proof of claim:

$$Z(W) = \sum_y \sqrt{W(y|0)W(y|1)} = -1 + \frac{1}{2} \sum_y \left[\sum_x \sqrt{W(y|x)} \right]^2 \tag{17.123}$$

$$= -1 + \frac{1}{2} \sum_y \left[\sum_x \left(\sum_{j \in \mathcal{J}} Q_j W_j(y|x) \right)^{1/2} \right]^2, \tag{17.124}$$

which can be readily verified by expanding the sum on the right of (17.123). A version of *Minkowski's inequality* [147, p. 524] says that for positive numbers a_{jk} and a distribution Q,

$$\left[\sum_j Q_j \left(\sum_k a_{jk} \right)^{1/r} \right]^r \le \sum_k \left(\sum_j Q_j a_{jk}^{1/r} \right)^r$$

for $r < 1$.

Now applying this claim to (17.124) with $r = 1/2$, we get

$$Z(W) \ge -1 + \frac{1}{2} \sum_y \sum_{j \in \mathcal{J}} Q_j \left[\sum_x \sqrt{W_j(y|x)} \right]^2 = \sum_{j \in \mathcal{J}} Q(j) Z(W_j). \tag{17.125}$$

Using (17.61),

$$W(F(y_0, y_1)|u_0) = \frac{1}{2} [\underbrace{W(y_0|u_0)W(y_1|0)}_{W_0(y_0, y_1|u_0)} + \underbrace{W(y_0|u_0 \oplus 1)W(y_1|1)}_{W_1(y_0, y_1|u_0)}].$$

The channel W' is thus seen to be a combination of channels of the sort in (17.122), with B-DMCs W_0 and W_1 as identified. Since $Z(W_0) = Z(W_1) = Z(W)$, applying (17.125) gives

$$Z(W') \ge \frac{1}{2}(Z(W_0) + Z(W_1)) = Z(W).$$

It can furthermore be argued that $Z(W') = Z(W'')$ if and only if $I(W) = 0$.

17.15 Exercises

1. For a $BEC(p)$ channel show that $I(W) = 1 - p$.
2. For a $BSC(p)$ channel show that $I(W) = 1 - H_2(p)$.
3. For a $BEC(p)$ channel show that $Z(W) = p$.
4. For a $BSC(p)$ channel show that $Z(W) = \sqrt{4p(1-p)}$.

5. For $\alpha(y_0)$, $\beta(y_1)$, and $\gamma(y_1)$ as defined in Appendix 17.C, show that (17.121) is true.

6. In Equation (17.120), show that each of the term labeled (**) is equal to $Z(\mathsf{W})$. Also show that the term labeled (***) is equal to $Z(\mathsf{W})^2$.

17.16 References

The theory of polar codes as described here was presented in [16] and this chapter draws much from that. The presentation here has benefitted from the insights of Emre Telatar [437]. Discussion of successive cancellation decoding benefitted from [461].

Systematic encoding was described first in [17]. Three different algorithms for systematic encoding were described in [460]. The presentation in Section 17.8 is their **EncoderA**. Another variation on this, which reports only $O(N)$ complexity is [68]. The fast systematic decoding discussion is from [390].

List decoding was described in [431] and the coverage here closely follows their description. The C++ implementation is a close transcription of their pseudocode, filling in some omissions.

A description of a log-likelihood ratio-based formulation is provided in [499]. Our formulation more closely follows [22], which also provides a description of hardware considerations and comparisons. Insights related to AEP come from [324]. Simplified SC decoding is described in [7]. Our discussion benefitted from [169] and [392].

Part VI

Applications

Chapter 18

Some Applications of Error Correction in Modern Communication Systems

18.1 Introduction

Error-correction coding is ubiquitously used in modern communication systems. This chapter highlights how a few technological systems use error-correction coding to give a sense of the practical scale of "real" codes and how different methods of error-correction coding are combined together to make real systems.

The variety of systems that could be explored here is enormous. For example, quick response (QR) codes employ Reed–Solomon codes. Depending on the manufacturer, flash memories employ different codes, such as LDPC, Reed–Solomon, or BCH. But the systems that are described here in some detail are related to broad-based communications technologies.

18.2 Digital Video Broadcast T2 (DVB-T2)

The DVB-T2 standard describes channel coding and modulation for digital terrestrial TV. As a full-fledged communication system, it makes use of topics introduced in this book in several ways, including scrambling, CRC codes, and error correction [105]. Of the many system components involved in this standard, we discuss here only the forward error-correction components. This consists of concatenated coding, with a BCH as the outer code and an LDPC code as the inner code. (This is one of the changes between the DVB-T2 standard compared to the earlier DVB standard, which uses Reed–Solomon codes as the outer code and a convolutional code as the inner code, with convolutional interleaving [104].) Actually, the LDPC code is an irregular repeat-accumulate (IRA) code.

The general FEC coding structure is shown in Figure 18.1. K_{BCH} bits are BCH-encoded to produce N_{BCH} bits. These are further LDPC-encoded to produce N_{LDPC} bits. There are two codeword lengths for forward error correction (FEC) frame: a "normal" FECFRAME of $N_{LDPC} = 64{,}800$ bits, and a "short" FECFRAME of $N_{LDPC} = 16{,}200$ bits.

The system is parameterized to deal with various block sizes and rates. The coding parameters for a normal FECFRAME are shown in Table 18.1 and the coding parameters for a short FECFRAME are shown in Table 18.2.

18.2.1 BCH Outer Encoding

The BCH generator polynomial for the outer codes, capable of correcting t errors, is obtained by multiplying together the first t minimal polynomials to obtain the specified amount of error correction. For the normal codes, these minimal polynomials are shown in Table 18.3. For the short codes, these minimal polynomials are shown in Table 18.4.

Error Correction Coding: Mathematical Methods and Algorithms, Second Edition. Todd K. Moon
© 2021 John Wiley & Sons, Inc. Published 2021 by John Wiley & Sons, Inc.
Companion website: www.wiley.com/go/Moon/ErrorCorrectionCoding

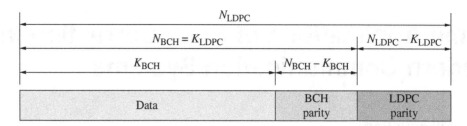

Figure 18.1: FEC encoding structure (see [105, Figure 12]).

Table 18.1: Coding Parameters for a Normal Frame $N_{\text{LDPC}} = 64{,}800$ (See [105, Table 6(a)]

LDPC Code Rate	K_{BCH}	$N_{\text{BCH}} = K_{\text{LDPC}}$	BCH t-Error Correction	$N_{\text{BCH}} - K_{\text{BCH}}$	N_{LDPC}
1/2	32,208	32,400	12	192	64,800
3/5	38,688	38,880	12	192	64,800
2/3	43,040	43,200	10	160	64,800
3/4	48,408	48,600	12	192	64,800
4/5	51,648	51,840	12	192	64,800
5/6	53,840	54,000	10	160	64,800

Table 18.2: Coding Parameters for a Short Frame $N_{\text{LDPC}} = 16{,}200$ (See [105, Table 6(b)]

LDPC Code Rate	K_{BCH}	$N_{\text{BCH}} = K_{\text{LDPC}}$	BCH t-Error Correction	$N_{\text{BCH}} - K_{\text{BCH}}$	N_{LDPC}
1/4	3072	3240	12	168	16,200
1/2	7032	7200	12	168	16,200
3/5	9552	9720	12	168	16,200
2/3	10,632	10,800	12	168	16,200
3/4	11,712	11,880	12	168	16,200
4/5	12,432	12,600	12	168	16,200
5/6	13,152	13,320	12	168	16,200

18.2.2   LDPC Inner Encoding

Let $\mathbf{i} = (i_0, i_1, \ldots, i_{K_{\text{LDPC}}-1})$ be the result of the outer BCH encoding. This is *systematically* encoded into a codeword

$$\mathbf{c} = (i_0, i_1, \ldots, i_{K_{\text{LDPC}}-1}, p_0, p_1, \ldots, p_{N_{\text{LDPC}}-K_{\text{LDPC}}-1}).$$

The "LDPC" code in the standard is actually an IRA code. The standard provides tables describing the interleaving of the different parities. One such table is shown in Table 18.5 for the rate 2/3

Table 18.3: BCH Minimal Polynomials for Normal Codes ($N_{\text{LDPC}} = 64{,}800$)
(See [105, Table 7(a)])

$g_1(x)$	$1 + x^2 + x^3 + x^5 + x^{16}$
$g_2(x)$	$1 + x + x^4 + x^5 + x^6 + x^8 + x^{16}$
$g_3(x)$	$1 + x^2 + x^3 + x^4 + x^5 + x^7 + x^8 + x^9 + x^{10} + x^{11} + x^{16}$
$g_4(x)$	$1 + x^2 + x^4 + x^6 + x^9 + x^{11} + x^{12} + x^{14} + x^{16}$
$g_5(x)$	$1 + x + x^2 + x^3 + x^5 + x^8 + x^9 + x^{10} + x^{11} + x^{12} + x^{16}$
$g_6(x)$	$1 + x^2 + x^4 + x^5 + x^7 + x^8 + x^9 + x^{10} + x^{12} + x^{13} + x^{14} + x^{15} + x^{16}$
$g_7(x)$	$1 + x^2 + x^5 + x^6 + x^8 + x^9 + x^{10} + x^{11} + x^{13} + x^{15} + x^{16}$
$g_8(x)$	$1 + x + x^2 + x^5 + x^6 + x^8 + x^9 + x^{12} + x^{13} + x^{14} + x^{16}$
$g_9(x)$	$1 + x^5 + x^7 + x^9 + x^{10} + x^{11} + x^{16}$
$g_{10}(x)$	$1 + x + x^2 + x^5 + x^7 + x^8 + x^{10} + x^{12} + x^{13} + x^{14} + x^{16}$
$g_{11}(x)$	$1 + x^2 + x^5 + x^9 + x^{11} + x^{12} + x^{13} + x^{16}$
$g_{12}(x)$	$1 + x + x^5 + x^6 + x^7 + x^9 + x^{11} + x^{12} + x^{16}$

Table 18.4: BCH Minimal Polynomials for Normal Codes
($N_{\text{LDPC}} = 6200$) (See [105, Table 7(b)])

$g_1(x)$	$1 + x + x^3 + x^5 + x^{14}$
$g_2(x)$	$1 + x^6 + x^8 + x^{11} + x^{14}$
$g_3(x)$	$1 + x + x^2 + x^6 + x^9 + x^{10} + x^{14}$
$g_4(x)$	$1 + x^4 + x^7 + x^8 + x^{10} + x^{12} + x^{14}$
$g_5(x)$	$1 + x^2 + x^4 + x^6 + x^8 + x^9 + x^{11} + x^{13} + x^{14}$
$g_6(x)$	$1 + x^3 + x^7 + x^8 + x^9 + x^{13} + x^{14}$
$g_7(x)$	$1 + x^2 + x^5 + x^6 + x^7 + x^{10} + x^{11} + x^{14}$
$g_8(x)$	$1 + x^5 + x^8 + x^9 + x^{10} + x^{14}$
$g_9(x)$	$1 + x + x^2 + x^3 + x^9 + x^{10} + x^{14}$
$g_{10}(x)$	$1 + x^3 + x^6 + x^9 + x^{11} + x^{12} + x^{14}$
$g_{11}(x)$	$1 + x^4 + x^{11} + x^{12} + x^{14}$
$g_{12}(x)$	$1 + x + x^2 + x^3 + x^5 + x^6 + x^7 + x^8 + x^{10} + x^{13} + x^{14}$

code with $N_{\text{LDPC}} = 64{,}800$. Quoting [105, Section 6.1.2.1], the data in this table are to be used as follows.

- Set the parities to 0: $p_0 = p_1 = \cdots = p_{N_{\text{LDPC}} - K_{\text{LDPC}} - 1} = 0$.

Table 18.5: IRA Indices for DVB-T2 Rate 2/3 Code, $N_{\text{LDPC}} = 64,800$ (See [105, Table A.3])

[317 2255 2324 2723 3538 3576 6194 6700 9101 10057 12739 17407 21039]
[1958 2007 3294 4394 12762 14505 14593 14692 16522 17737 19245 21272 21379]
[127 860 5001 5633 8644 9282 12690 14644 17553 19511 19681 20954 21002]
[2514 2822 5781 6297 8063 9469 9551 11407 11837 12985 15710 20236 20393]
[1565 3106 4659 4926 6495 6872 7343 8720 15785 16434 16727 19884 21325]
[706 3220 8568 10896 12486 13663 16398 16599 19475 19781 20625 20961 21335]
[4257 10449 12406 14561 16049 16522 17214 18029 18033 18802 19062 19526 20748]
[412 433 558 2614 2978 4157 6584 9320 11683 11819 13024 14486 16860]
[777 5906 7403 8550 8717 8770 11436 12846 13629 14755 15688 16392 16419]
[4093 5045 6037 7248 8633 9771 10260 10809 11326 12072 17516 19344 19938]
[2120 2648 3155 3852 6888 12258 14821 15359 16378 16437 17791 20614 21025]
[1085 2434 5816 7151 8050 9422 10884 12728 15353 17733 18140 18729 20920]
[856 1690 12787]
[6532 7357 9151]
[4210 16615 18152]
[11494 14036 17470]
[2474 10291 10323]
[1778 6973 10739]
[4347 9570 18748]
[2189 11942 20666]
[3868 7526 17706]
[8780 14796 18268]
[160 16232 17399]
[1285 2003 18922]
[4658 17331 20361]
[2765 4862 5875]
[4565 5521 8759]
[3484 7305 15829]
[5024 17730 17879]
[7031 12346 15024]
[179 6365 11352]
[2490 3143 5098]
[2643 3101 21259]
[4315 4724 13130]
[594 17365 18322]
[5983 8597 9627]
[10837 15102 20876]
[10448 20418 21478]
[3848 12029 15228]
[708 5652 13146]
[5998 7534 16117]
[2098 13201 18317]
[9186 14548 17776]
[5246 10398 18597]
[3083 4944 21021]
[13726 18495 19921]
[6736 10811 17545]
[10084 12411 14432]
[1064 13555 17033]
[679 9878 13547]
[3422 9910 20194]
[3640 3701 10046]
[5862 10134 11498]
[5923 9580 15060]
[1073 3012 16427]
[5527 20113 20883]
[7058 12924 15151]
[9764 12230 17375]
[772 7711 12723]
[555 13816 15376]

[10574 11268 17932]
[15442 17266 20482]
[390 3371 8781]
[10512 12216 17180]
[4309 14068 15783]
[3971 11673 20009]
[9259 14270 17199]
[2947 5852 20101]
[3965 9722 15363]
[1429 5689 16771]
[6101 6849 12781]
[3676 9347 18761]
[350 11659 18342]
[5961 14803 16123]
[2113 9163 13443]
[2155 9808 12885]
[2861 7988 11031]
[7309 9220 20745]
[6834 8742 11977]
[2133 12908 14704]
[10170 13809 18153]
[13464 14787 14975]
[799 1107 3789]
[3571 8176 10165]
[5433 13446 15481]
[3351 6767 12840]
[8950 8974 11650]
[1430 4250 21332]
[6283 10628 15050]
[8632 14404 16916]
[6509 10702 16278]
[15900 16395 17995]
[8031 18420 19733]
[3747 4634 17087]
[4453 6297 16262]
[2792 3513 17031]
[14846 20893 21563]
[17220 20436 21337]
[275 4107 10497]
[3536 7520 10027]
[14089 14943 19455]
[1965 3931 21104]
[2439 11565 17932]
[154 15279 21414]
[10017 11269 16546]
[7169 10161 16928]
[10284 16791 20655]
[36 3175 8475]
[2605 16269 19290]
[8947 9178 15420]
[5687 9156 12408]
[8096 9738 14711]
[4935 8093 19266]
[2667 10062 15972]
[6389 11318 14417]
[8800 18137 18434]
[5824 5927 15314]
[6056 13168 15179]
[3284 13138 18919]
[13115 17259 17332]

- Accumulate the first information bit i_0 at parity bit addresses specified in Table 18.5. Using the first row of the table as indices,

$$p_{317} = p_{317} \oplus i_0 \qquad p_{6700} = p_{6700} \oplus i_0$$

$$p_{2255} = p_{2255} \oplus i_0 \qquad p_{9101} = p_{9101} \oplus i_0$$

$$p_{2324} = p_{2324} \oplus i_0 \qquad p_{10057} = p_{10057} \oplus i_0$$

$$p_{2723} = p_{2723} \oplus i_0 \qquad p_{12739} = p_{12739} \oplus i_0$$

$$p_{3538} = p_{3528} \oplus i_0 \qquad p_{17407} = p_{17407} \oplus i_0$$

$$p_{3576} = p_{3576} \oplus i_0 \qquad p_{21039} = p_{21039} \oplus i_0$$

$$p_{6194} = p_{6194} \oplus i_0$$

- Similarly, for each of the next 359 information bits $i_m, m = 1, 2, \ldots, 359$, accumulate i_m at parity bit addresses $(x + (m \pmod{360})) Q_{\text{LDPC}} \pmod{(N_{\text{LDPC}} - K_{\text{LDPC}})}$, where x denotes the address of the parity bit accumulated corresponding to the first bit i_0, and Q_{LDPC} is a code rate-dependent constant specified in Table 18.6. For rate 2/3, $Q_{\text{LDPC}} = 2/3$. For example, for the information bit i_0, the following parity operations are performed:

$$p_{377} = p_{377} \oplus i_0 \qquad p_{6760} = p_{6760} \oplus i_0$$

$$p_{2315} = p_{2315} \oplus i_0 \qquad p_{9161} = p_{9161} \oplus i_0$$

$$p_{2384} = p_{2384} \oplus i_0 \qquad p_{10117} = p_{10117} \oplus i_0$$

$$p_{2783} = p_{2783} \oplus i_0 \qquad p_{12799} = p_{12799} \oplus i_0$$

$$p_{3598} = p_{3598} \oplus i_0 \qquad p_{17467} = p_{17467} \oplus i_0$$

$$p_{3636} = p_{3636} \oplus i_0 \qquad p_{21099} = p_{21099} \oplus i_0$$

$$p_{6254} = p_{6254} \oplus i_0$$

- For the 361st information bit i_{360}, the addresses of the parity bit accumulators are given in the second row of the table (1958, 2007, ...). In a similar manner, the addresses of the parity bit accumulators for the following 359 information bits are obtained using $(x + (m \pmod{360})) Q_{\text{LDPC}} \pmod{(N_{\text{LDPC}} - K_{\text{LDPC}})}$, where x denotes the address of the parity bit accumulator corresponding to information bit i_{360}, that is, the entries in the second row of the table.

- In a similar manner, for every group of 360 new information bits, a new row from the table is used to find the address of the parity bit accumulators.

Table 18.6: Q_{LDPC} Values for Frames of Normal and Short Length

$N_{\text{LDPC}} = 64;800$	
Code Rate	Q_{LDPC}
1/2	90
3/5	72
2/3	60
3/4	45
4/5	36
5/6	30

$N_{\text{LDPC}} = 16;200$	
Code Rate	Q_{LDPC}
1/4	36
1/2	25
3/5	18
2/3	15
3/4	12
4/5	10
5/6	8

After all of the information bits are exhausted, the final parity bits are obtained as follows:

- Sequentially perform the following operations, starting with $i = 1$:

$$p_i = p_i \oplus p_{i-1} \quad i = 1, 2, \ldots, N_{\text{LDPC}} - K_{\text{LDPC}} - 1.$$

The final content of p_i is the parity bit. (End quote.)

The function `ldpcencode.m` performs this encoding function.

For decoding using message-passing decoding, it is helpful to represent the linear operations as a parity check matrix. Summarizing some of the computations above, a parity check matrix (using 0-based indexing) is produced by the following computations (a small subset is shown). For the columns of H associated with the information bits:

$$H(317, 0) = 1 \qquad H(2255, 0) = 1 \qquad H(2255, 0) = 1, \quad \ldots$$

$$H(377, 1) = 1 \qquad H(2315, 1) = 1 \qquad H(2384, 1) = 1, \quad \ldots$$

$$H(437, 2) = 1 \qquad H(2375, 2) = 1 \qquad H(2444, 2) = 1, \quad \ldots$$

ldpcencode.m

For the columns of H associated with the parity bits:

$$H(0, 43200) = 1 \quad H(1, 43201) = 1 \quad H(2, 43202) = 1 \quad H(3, 43203) = 1, \quad \ldots$$

Using this H matrix, any of the LDPC decoding algorithm can be used on this LDPC code.

This concatenated code is similar to that used in the DVB-S2 (digital video broadcast satellite), which also uses BCH and LDPC (really IRA) codes. (The IRA interleaving details are different between the two standards.)

ldpccodesetup1.m

18.3 Digital Cable Television

Digital cable television is a way of delivering digital video content distinct from wireless transmission. Since cable carries many television channels, it is important to transmit in a way that is bandwidth efficient. And, of course, it is important for the transmission to be virtually error-free. In digital TV, the video data is first compressed (using, for example, MPEG-2 compression), then the resulting digital data are protected using error-correction coding.

One way of achieving this may be similar to the framework shown in Figure 18.2, drawn from the U.S. Patent 5,511,096 (figure 1). It employs concatenated coding, with Reed–Solomon codes as the outer code and convolutional coding as the inner code.

In the patent, the following details are described:

- The Reed–Solomon code is either (127,121) or (128,122), using data in 7-bit bytes.

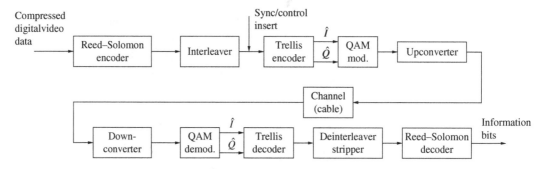

Figure 18.2: Concatenated Reed–Solomon and Trellis coding for television transmission (see [204]).

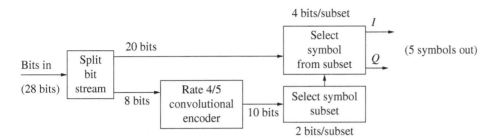

Figure 18.3: Trellis encoder ([204, Figure 2]).

- The interleaver is used to minimize the effects of burst errors.

- A 7-bit synchronization/control symbol is inserted into the stream. When the (127,121) code is used, the symbol is inserted every 10 codewords; when the (128,122) code is used, the symbol is inserted every 20 codewords. With the inclusion of this symbol, the effective rate is (in both cases)

$$R = \frac{\text{symbols out}}{\text{symbols in}} = \frac{20 \cdot 121}{20 \cdot 127 + 1} = \frac{20}{21} \quad R = \frac{10 \cdot 122}{10 \cdot 128 + 1} = \frac{20}{21}.$$

- These blocks are encoded using a "trellis encoder" having rate of either 4/5 or 3/4. The rate 4/5 encoder is used with a 64-QAM constellation and the rate 3/5 encoder is used with a 16-QAM constellation.

- The bits produced by the trellis encoder along the I and Q branches are used to select points in the QAM constellation. This complex baseband symbol produces a baseband waveform which is upconverted for transmission.

The structure of the "trellis encoder" is shown in Figure 18.3, which is the structure used for the 64-QAM system. The input to this system is four 7-bit symbols.[1] These 28 bits are split into 20 uncoded bits and 8 other bits which pass through a rate 4/5 convolutional encoder which produces 10 coded bits, producing a total of 30 bits. Each 64-QAM symbol is selected with a 6-bit index, so these 30 bits determine five symbols.

The 10 coded bits, 2 bits per symbol, are used to select one of four signal subsets for each of five symbols, as illustrated in Figure 18.4. The output of the convolutional encoder may be viewed as a sequence of subsets. For each subset (containing 16 bits), 4 bits out of the 20 uncoded bits are used to select a symbol from its selected subset. Each symbol is represented by its Π (x) component and Q (y) component.

Returning to Figure 18.2, after passing through a channel (which such as the cable, for cable TV) which introduces, among other things, noise (which is assumed to be AWGN), the received signal is down-converted and the complex baseband signal is passed through a QAM demodulator (comprising a matched filter), which produces coordinates in the signal space $\hat{I}$ and $\hat{Q}$. These are passed to a "trellis decoder." The "trellis decoder" is shown in Figure 18.5. The first step in the trellis decoder is what [204] calls a "pruner." The pruner produces two kinds of outputs, an output called "metrics" and an output called "uncoded bits." The metrics are distances from the received point $(\hat{I}, \hat{Q})$ to each subset, i.e., the nearest point in each subset, as suggested by Figure 18.6. These metrics are provided as inputs to a Viterbi decoder, which provides a maximum likelihood estimate of the sequence of subsets. The output of this Viterbi algorithm is a sequence of 2 bit pair which indicate which subset is associated with the received symbol.

---

[1] The patent [204] is scaled differently by a factor of two.

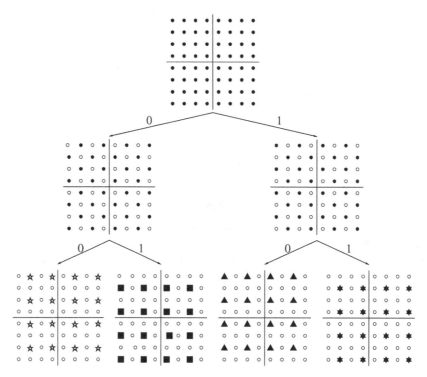

Figure 18.4: Set partition of 64-QAM. At the last stage, different shapes are used to indicate the different subsets. (This decomposition is for example here, and is not indicated in [204].)

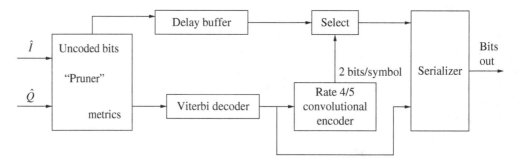

Figure 18.5: Trellis decoder ([204, Figure 3]).

Figure 18.6: Distances from $(\hat{I}, \hat{Q})$ to subsets in the 64-QAM constellation.

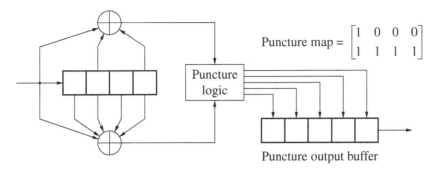

Figure 18.7: Rate 4/5 convolutional encoder.

The other output of the pruner is a sequence of bits corresponding to the uncoded bits that selects a point within a subset, 4 bits per symbol, with one set of 4 bits for each subset. As Figure 18.6 suggests, any of these set of 4 bits could occur with roughly equal likelihood. To select which of these is likely to be the best, the output of the Viterbi decoder is re-encoded using the same encoder used in the trellis encoder. This re-encoded data is used to select a set of the uncoded bits from the pruner, which have been passed through a delay buffer that accounts for the delay in the Viterbi decoder and the re-encoding operation. These bits are placed in order with the output of the Viterbi decoder in the serializer, then output.

The bits of the trellis decoder block are passed through a deinterleaver/stripper. The stripper part removes the synchronization byte (where it occurs) and the deinverleaver puts the bytes back into correct order for the Reed–Solomon decoder. The Reed–Solomon decoder removes any residual errors left after the trellis decoder. Since errors remaining after Viterbi decoding tend to be bursty, the Reed–Solomon decoder is well-suited as an outer code, since it deals well with bursty errors.

Figure 18.7 shows an example of a rate 4/5 convolutional encoder. Four bits are provided into the convolutional structure, which is a rate 1/2 code with memory length, with generators 10101 (25 octal) and 11111 (37 octal). The output of the encoder is then punctured by the puncture map

$$\begin{bmatrix} 1 & 0 & 0 & 0 \\ 1 & 1 & 1 & 1 \end{bmatrix}$$

and the five resulting bits are buffered for output.

18.4 E-UTRA and Long-Term Evolution

The Evolved Universal Telecommunications System (UMTS) Terrestrial Radio Access (E-UTRA) is the air interface of the Third Generation Partnership (3GPP) Long-Term Evolution (LTE) upgrade path for mobile networks. In short, it is a fourth-generation wireless communication standard. Naturally, it employs error-correction coding.

Modern wireless communication systems depend on a variety of technologies up and down a networking protocol stack, including MIMO and space-time coding. The error-correction coding aspects function primarily at layer 1, the physical layer. However, without a reliable physical layer upon which to build the rest of the system, wireless technology as presently widely enjoyed could not exist.

The modulation employed in LTE is orthogonal frequency division multiplexing (OFDM), which employs multiple carriers to carry information from the signal constellation. This can be efficiently implemented using fast Fourier transforms.

Often, real channels are frequency selective, so that some frequency subbands experience different amounts of attenuation (fade). In an OFDM setting, this can present a problem, because entire sets of

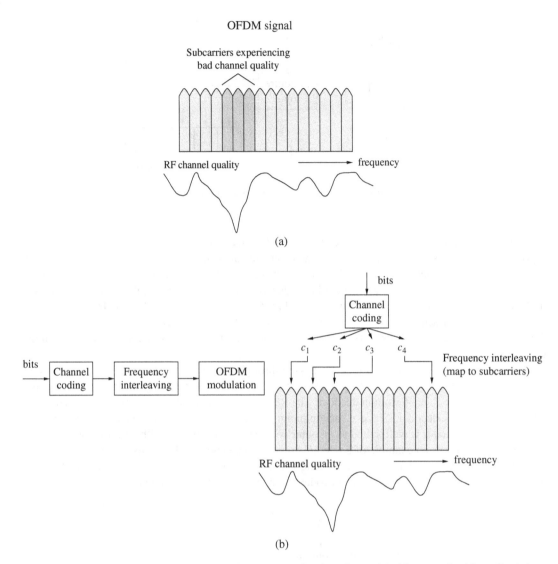

Figure 18.8: OFDM transmission over a frequency-selective channel (without and with coding) (see [87, Section 4.7]). (a) OFDM transmission over a frequency-selective channel; (b) channel coding and interleaving to provide frequency diversity.

subcarriers can be wiped out by a fade. Channel coding can provide an important frequency diversity in such frequency-selective channels. In Figure 18.8(a), there is a representation of several subcarriers (the vertical bars) and the quality of the channel as a function of frequency. A few of the subcarriers experience severe attenuation (low-quality channels). Symbols transmitted on those subcarriers would experience severe degradation. The situation is mitigated by the use of channel coding, as suggested by Figure 18.8(b). Coded spreads information across several symbols. These symbols are then distributed across different frequency bands by an interleaver. A fade experienced by a coded symbol in some subchannel is compensated by information in other coded symbol which do not experience the same fade. This is sometimes referred to as *frequency interleaving*.

LTE uses several channels to perform various communication and control functions. These are summarized in Table 18.7, along with the coding methods they employ.

Table 18.7: Channel Coding Schemes for Transmission and Control Channels [2, Section 5.1.3]

Transmission Channels			
Acronym	Description	Coding Scheme	Rate
UL-SCH	Uplink shared channel	Turbo coding	1/3
DL-SCSH	Downlink shared channel	Turbo coding	1/3
PCH	Paging channel	Turbo coding	1/3
MCH	Multicast channel	Turbo coding	1/3
SL-SCH	Sidelink shared channel	Turbo coding	1/3
SL-DCH	Sidelink discovery channel	Turbo coding	1/3
BCH	Broadcast channel	TB convolutional coding	1/3
SL-BCH	Sidelink broadcast channel	TB convolutional coding	1/3
Control Channels			
Acronym	Description	Coding Scheme	Rate
DCI	Downlink control information	TB convolutional coding	1/3
CFI	Control format indicator	TB convolutional coding	1/3
HI	HARQ indicator	repetition	1/3
UCI	Uplink control indicator	Uci (variable) or TB CC	1/3
SCI	Sidelink control information	TB convolutional coding	1/3

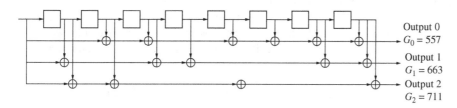

Output 0
$G_0 = 557$
Output 1
$G_1 = 663$
Output 2
$G_2 = 711$

Figure 18.9: Rate 1/3 convolutional encoder for LTE [1, Figure 2].

18.4.1 LTE Rate 1/3 Convolutional Encoder

The rate 1/3 convolutional code uses generators 557, 663, and 711, as shown in Figure 18.9. To drive the final state of a codeword to 0, 8 bits of 0 are added to the end of the code block before encoding, which results in a slight reduction in rate. The state of the encoder is set to 0 before encoding.

18.4.2 LTE Turbo Code

The LTE rate 1/3 turbo code encoder is shown in Figure 18.10. The transfer function for the constituent parallel concatenated convolutional coders is

$$G(X) = \left[1 \quad \frac{1+x^2+x^3}{1+x+x^3} \right].$$

At the beginning of encoding, the shift registers of both encoders are set to 0. The input sequence is $x_1, x_2, x_3, \ldots$. The output from the encoder is taken in the order

$$x_1, z_1, z_1', x_2, z_2, z_2', \ldots, x_K, z_K, z_K',$$

where z_i and z_i' are the outputs from the first and second constituent encoders, and K is the number of input bits.

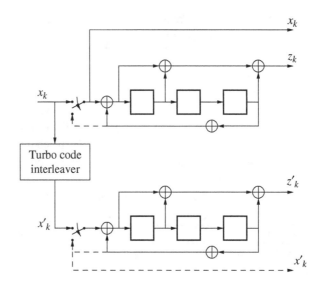

Figure 18.10: LTE rate 1/3 turbo code encoder [1, Figure 3].

Trellis termination is accomplished by moving the upper switch in the figure to lower position (disconnecting the encoder from the input and connecting it to the feedback path). The encoder is then clocked three more times, with the lower constituent encoder disabled. Then the last three tail bits (passed through the interleaver) are used to terminate the second constituent encoder, with the lower switch in lower position. The transmitted bits for trellis termination are [1, Section 4.2.3.2.2]

$$x_{K+1}, z_{K+1}, x_{K+2}, z_{K+2}, x_{K+3}, z_{K+3}, x'_{K+1}, z'_{K+1}, x'_{K+2}, z'_{K+2}, x'_{K+3}, z'_{K+3}.$$

The interleaver (permuter) is specifically described in the standard, and works (essentially) by writing into the rows of a matrix then reading out from the columns of a matrix.

18.5 References

A convenient summary of LTE is provided in (for example) [87]. More complete details, of course, can be found in the standards available online.

Part VII

Space-Time Coding

Chapter 19

Fading Channels and Space-Time Codes

19.1 Introduction

For most of this book the codes have been designed for transmission through either an AWGN channel or a BSC. One exception is the convolutive channel, for which turbo equalization was introduced in Section 14.7. In this chapter, we introduce a coding technique appropriate for Rayleigh flat fading channels. Fading is a multiplicative change in the amplitude of the received signal. As will be shown in Section 19.2, fading is mitigated by means of *diversity*, that is, multiple, independent transmissions of the signal. Space-time coding provides a way of achieving diversity for multiple transmit antenna systems with low-complexity detection algorithms.

A very important "meta-lesson" from this chapter is that the coding employed in communicating over a channel should match the particular requirements of the channel. In this case, space-time codes are a response to the question: Since diversity is important to communicating over a fading channel, how can coding be used to obtain diversity for portable receivers?

A discussion of the fading channel and its statistical model are presented in Section 19.2. In Section 19.3, the importance of diversity in combating fading is presented. Section 19.4 presents space-time codes, which are able to provide diversity with only a single receive antenna and moderate decode complexity. Trellis codes used as space-time codes are presented in Section 19.5.

19.2 Fading Channels

In the channels most frequently used in this book, communication has been from the transmitter directly to the receiver, with only additive noise and attenuation distorting the received signal. In many communication problems, however, the transmitted signal may be subject to multiple reflections. Furthermore, the reflectors and transmitter may be moving with respect to each other, as suggested by Figure 19.1. For example, in an urban environment, a signal transmitted from a cell phone base station may reflect off of buildings, cars, or even trees, so that the signal received at a cell phone may consist only of the superposition of reflected signals. In fact, such impediments are very typical of most wireless channels. The received signal may thus be represented in the (complex baseband) form

$$
\begin{aligned}
r(t) &= \sum_n \alpha_n(t) e^{-j2\pi f_c \tau_n(t)} s(t - \tau_n(t)) + n(t) \\
&= \sum_n \alpha_n(t) e^{-j\theta_n(t)} s(t - \tau_n(t)) + n(t),
\end{aligned}
\tag{19.1}
$$

where $s(t)$ is the transmitted signal, $\alpha_n(t)$ is the attenuation on the nth path (which may be time-varying), $\tau_n(t)$ is the delay on the nth path, and $e^{-j2\pi f_c \tau_n(t)}$ represents the phase change in the carrier with frequency f_c due to the delay, with phase $\theta_n(t) = 2\pi \tau_n(t) f_c$. $\alpha_n(t)$, $\theta_n(t)$, and $\tau_n(t)$ can be considered as random processes. The noise $n(t)$ is a complex, stationary, zero-mean Gaussian random process

Error Correction Coding: Mathematical Methods and Algorithms, Second Edition. Todd K. Moon
© 2021 John Wiley & Sons, Inc. Published 2021 by John Wiley & Sons, Inc.
Companion website: www.wiley.com/go/Moon/ErrorCorrectionCoding

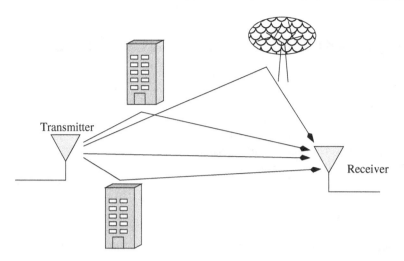

Figure 19.1: Multiple reflections from transmitter to receiver.

with independent real and imaginary parts and $E[n(t)n^*(s)] = N_0\delta(t - s)$. In the limit, if the number of reflectors can be regarded as existing over a continuum (e.g., for signals reflecting off the ionosphere), the received signal can be modeled as

$$r(t) = \int \alpha_s(t)e^{-j\theta_s(t)}s(t - \tau_s(t))\,ds + n(t).$$

Frequently, the delays are similar enough relative to the symbol period that for all practical purposes the delayed signals $s(t - \tau_n(t))$ are the same, so $s_n(t - \tau_n(t)) = s(t - \tau(t))$ for all n. However, even in this case the changes in phase due to delay can be significant. Since f_c is usually rather large (in the megahertz or gigahertz range), small changes in delay can result in large changes in phase.

Example 19.1 A signal transmitted at $f_c = 900$ MHz is reflected from two surfaces in such a way that at some particular instant of time, one signal to receiver travels 0.16 m farther than the other signal. The time difference is therefore

$$\tau = \frac{0.16}{c} = 5.33 \times 10^{-10}\text{ s}$$

and the phase difference is

$$\theta = 2\pi\tau f_c = 3.0159\text{ radians} = 172.8°.$$

The change in phase in the carrier results in a factor of $e^{j2\pi 3.0159} \approx -1$ between the two signals — the two received signals will almost cancel out!   □

Fading in this case is thus due primarily to changes in the phase $\theta_n(t)$. The randomly varying phase $\theta_n(t)$ associated with the factor $\alpha_n e^{-j\theta_n}$ results in signals that at times add constructively and at times add destructively. When the signals add destructively, then *fading* occurs.

If all of the delays are approximately equal, say, to a delay τ, then

$$r(t) = \sum_n \alpha_n(t)e^{-j\theta_n(t)}s(t - \tau) + n(t) = g(t)s(t - \tau) + n(t),\qquad(19.2)$$

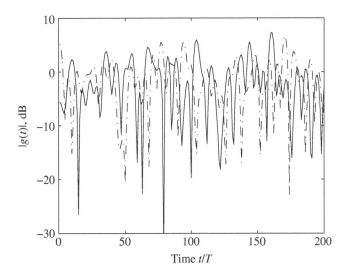

Figure 19.2: Simulation of a fading channel.

where

$$g(t) = \sum_n \alpha_n(t)e^{-j\theta_n(t)} \triangleq g_I(t) + jg_Q(t) \triangleq \alpha(t)e^{-j\phi(t)}$$

is a time-varying complex amplitude factor. The channel transfer function is then $T(t,f) = \alpha(t)e^{-\phi(t)}$, with magnitude response $|T(t,f)| = |g(t)| = \alpha(t)$. Since all frequency components are subjected to the same gain $\alpha(t)$, the channel is said to induce **flat fading**. The channel model for which the space-time codes of this chapter are applicable is flat fading.

The effect of fading on the received signal can be severe. For example, suppose that 90% of the time the signals add constructively, resulting in an SNR at the receiver so that the probability of error is essentially 0, but that 10% of the time the channel introduces a deep fade, so that the probability of error is essentially 0.5. The probability of error averaged over time is then 0.05, much too high for most practical purposes, even though the receiver works perfectly most of the time!

fadeplot.m
jakes.m

As we shall see, the way to combat fading is through diversity, sending multiple copies of the signal in the expectation that not all of the signals will fade simultaneously. Consider, for example, the plot in Figure 19.2, which shows a simulation of $|g(t)|$ (in dB) for a particular channel for two different realizations of the channel. From the plot, it is clear that both of the signals are not necessarily highly attenuated at the same time. If these represented two different paths from transmitter to receiver, there is hope that at least one of the paths would present a reliable channel. Looked at from another point of view, if at one instant of time one channel is bad, at another instant of time, that channel might be good. These observations lead to various forms of diversity.

In *time diversity*, the transmitter sends the same signal at different times, with sufficient delay between symbols that the transmissions experience independent fading. Time diversity may be accomplished using error-control coding in conjunction with interleaving.

A second means of diversity is *frequency diversity*, in which the signal is transmitted using carriers sufficiently separated that the channel over which the signals travel experience independent fading. This can be accomplished using spread spectrum techniques or multiple carriers.

A third means of diversity is *spatial diversity*, in which the signal is transmitted from or received by multiple antennas, whose spatial separation is such that the paths from transmitter antennas to receiver antennas experience independent fading. Spatial diversity has the advantage of good throughput (not requiring multiple transmission for time diversity) and good bandwidth (not requiring broad bandwidth for frequency diversity), at the expense of some additional hardware. Space-time codes are essentially a means of achieving spatial diversity.

19.2.1 Rayleigh Fading

Since the amplitude factor $g(t)$ is the summed effect of many reflectors, it may be regarded (by the central limit theorem) as a complex Gaussian random variable. That is, $g(t) = g_I(t) + jg_Q(t)$ has $g_I(t)$ and $g_Q(t)$ as independent, identically distributed random variables. If there is no strong direct path signal from transmitter to receiver, then these random variables are modeled as zero-mean random variables, so $g_I(t) \sim \mathcal{N}(0, \sigma_f^2)$ and $g_Q(t) \sim \mathcal{N}(0, \sigma_f^2)$, where σ_f^2 is the fading variance. It can be shown that the magnitude $\alpha = |g(t)|$ is *Rayleigh distributed* (see Exercise 19.2), so

$$f_\alpha(\alpha) = \frac{\alpha}{\sigma_f^2} e^{-\alpha^2/2\sigma_f^2} \quad \alpha \geq 0. \tag{19.3}$$

A flat fading channel with magnitude distributed as (19.3) is said to be a **Rayleigh fading channel**.

In the channel model (19.2), it is frequently assumed that τ is known (or can be estimated), so that it can be removed from consideration. On this basis, we write (19.2) as

$$r(t) = g(t)s(t) + n(t).$$

Let this $r(t)$ represent a BPSK-modulated signal transmitted with energy per bit E_b. Suppose furthermore that $g(t) = \alpha(t)e^{-j\phi(t)}$ is such that the magnitude $\alpha(t)$ is essentially constant over at least a few symbols, and that random phase $\phi(t)$ varies slowly enough that it can be estimated with negligible error. This is the *quasistatic* model. Then conventional BPSK detection can be used. This results in a probability of error (see (1.23)) for a particular value of α as

$$P_2(\alpha) = P(\text{bit error}|\alpha) = Q\left(\sqrt{\frac{2\alpha^2 E_b}{N_0}}\right). \tag{19.4}$$

The probability of bit error is then obtained by averaging out the dependence on α:

$$P_2 = \int_0^\infty P_2(\alpha)f_\alpha(\alpha)\,d\alpha.$$

Substituting (19.3) and (19.4) into this integral and integrating by parts (twice) yields

$$P_2 = \frac{1}{2}\left(1 - \sqrt{\frac{\overline{\gamma}_b}{1+\overline{\gamma}_b}}\right), \tag{19.5}$$

where

$$\overline{\gamma}_b = \frac{E_b}{N_0}E[\alpha^2].$$

fadepbplot.m

In Figure 19.3, the line corresponding to $m = 1$ illustrates the performance of the narrowband fading channel, plotted as a function of $\overline{\gamma}_b$ (in dB). Clearly, there is significant degradation compared to BPSK over a channel impaired only by AWGN.

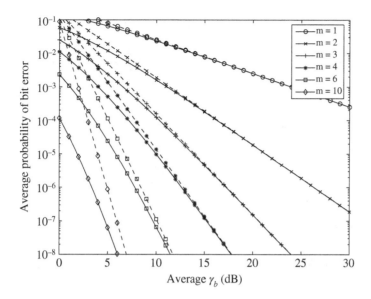

Figure 19.3: Diversity performance of quasi-static, flat-fading channel with BPSK modulation. Solid is exact; dashed is approximation.

19.3 Diversity Transmission and Reception: The MIMO Channel

To provide some background for diversity receivers, let us now consider the somewhat more general problem of transmission through a general linear multiple-input/multiple-output (MIMO) channel. For insight, we first present the continuous-time channel model, then a discrete-time equivalent appropriate for detection (e.g., after filtering and sampling).

Suppose that the signal

$$s_i(t) = \sum_{k=-\infty}^{\infty} a_{ik}\varphi(t - kT)$$

is transmitted from the ith antenna in a system of n antennas, where a_{ik} is the (complex) signal amplitude drawn from a signal constellation for the kth symbol period, and $\varphi(t)$ is the transmitted pulse shape, normalized to unit energy. (See Figure 19.4.) This signal passes through a channel with impulse response $\tilde{h}_{ji}(t)$ and is received by the jth receiver antenna out of m antennas, producing

$$r_j(t) = s_i(t) * \tilde{h}_{ji}(t) + n_j(t) = \sum_{k=-\infty}^{\infty} a_{ik}[\varphi(t - kT) * \tilde{h}_{ji}(t)] + n_j(t).$$

Each $\tilde{h}_{ji}(t)$ may be the response due to scattering and multipath reflections, just as for a single fading channel. The total signal received at the jth receiver due to all transmitted signals is

$$r_j(t) = \sum_{k=-\infty}^{\infty} \sum_{i=1}^{n} a_{ik}[\varphi(t - kT) * \tilde{h}_{ji}(t)] + n_j(t)$$

(assuming that the noise $n_j(t)$ is acquired *at* the receiver, not through the separate channels). Stacking up the vectors as

$$\mathbf{a}(k) = \begin{bmatrix} a_{1,k} \\ a_{2,k} \\ \vdots \\ a_{n,k} \end{bmatrix} \quad \mathbf{r}(t) = \begin{bmatrix} r_1(t) \\ r_2(t) \\ \vdots \\ r_m(t) \end{bmatrix} \quad \mathbf{n}(t) = \begin{bmatrix} n_1(t) \\ n_2(t) \\ \vdots \\ n_m(t) \end{bmatrix},$$

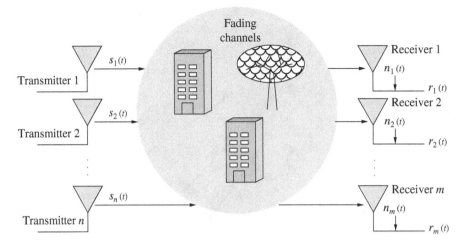

Figure 19.4: Multiple transmit and receive antennas across a fading channel.

we can write

$$\mathbf{r}(t) = \sum_{k=-\infty}^{\infty} \mathbf{H}(t - kT)\mathbf{a}_k + \mathbf{n}(t), \tag{19.6}$$

where $\mathbf{H}(t)$ is the $m \times n$ matrix of impulse responses with

$$h_{ji}(t) = \varphi(t) * \tilde{h}_{ji}(t) = \int_{-\infty}^{\infty} \varphi(\tau)\tilde{h}_{ji}(t - \tau) \, d\tau.$$

If the vector noise process $\mathbf{n}(t)$ is white and Gaussian, with independent components, then the log-likelihood function can be maximized by finding the sequence of vector signals $\mathbf{a} \in S^n$ minimizing

$$J = \int_{-\infty}^{\infty} \|\mathbf{r}(t) - \sum_{k=-\infty}^{\infty} \mathbf{H}(t - kT)\mathbf{a}_k\|^2 \, dt$$

$$= \int_{-\infty}^{\infty} \|\mathbf{r}(t)\|^2 - 2 \sum_{k=-\infty}^{\infty} \mathrm{Re} \left[\mathbf{a}_k^* \int_{-\infty}^{\infty} \mathbf{H}^H(t - kT)\mathbf{r}(t) \, dt \right]$$

$$+ \int_{-\infty}^{\infty} \| \sum_{k} \mathbf{H}(t - kT)\mathbf{a}_k\|^2 \, dt,$$

where $\|\mathbf{x}\|^2 = \mathbf{x}^H\mathbf{x}$ and where ^{H} denotes the transpose-conjugate and * denotes complex conjugation. In this general case, the minimization can be accomplished by a maximum-likelihood vector sequence estimator, that is, a Viterbi algorithm. Let us denote

$$\mathbf{r}_k = \int_{-\infty}^{\infty} \mathbf{H}^H(t - kT)\mathbf{r}(t) \, dt \tag{19.7}$$

as the outputs of a *matrix matched filter*, matched to the transmitted signal and channel. Substituting (19.6) into (19.7), we can write

$$\mathbf{r}_k = \sum_{l=-\infty}^{\infty} \mathbf{S}_{k-l}\mathbf{a}_l + \mathbf{n}_k,$$

where

$$\mathbf{S}_k = \int_{-\infty}^{\infty} \mathbf{H}^H(t - kT)\mathbf{H}(t) \, dt$$

and

$$\mathbf{n}_k = \int_{-\infty}^{\infty} \mathbf{H}^H(t - kT)\mathbf{n}(t) \, dt.$$

19.3.1 The Narrowband MIMO Channel

The formulation of the previous section is rather more general than is necessary for our future development. Consider now the narrowband MIMO channel, in which the frequency response is essentially constant for the signals that are transmitted over the channel. In this case, the transmitted waveform $\varphi(t)$ (transmitted by all antennas) is received as

$$\mathbf{H}(t) = \varphi(t)\mathbf{H}.$$

The matched filter $\mathbf{H}^H(-t)$ can be decomposed into multiplication by $\mathbf{H}^H$ followed by conventional matched filtering with $\varphi(-t)$.

Note that the narrowband case can occur in the case of a flat fading channel, where the channel coefficients h_{ji} are randomly time-varying, due, for example, to multiple interfering signals obtained by scattering.

As a specific and pertinent example, suppose that $s(t) = \sum_k a_k \varphi(t - kT)$ is transmitted (i.e., there is only a single transmit antenna) over a channel, and two receive antennas are used, with

$$r_1(t) = h_1 s(t) + n_1(t) \quad r_2(t) = h_2 s(t) + n_2(t),$$

where h_1 and h_2 are complex and constant over at least one symbol interval. Thus, $\mathbf{H} = \begin{bmatrix} h_1 \\ h_2 \end{bmatrix}$. The receiver first computes

$$\mathbf{H}^H \mathbf{r}(t) = h_1^* h_1 s(t) + h_2^* h_2 s(t) + (h_1^* n_1(t) + h_2^* n_2(t))$$
$$= (|h_1|^2 + |h_2|^2)s(t) + (h_1^* n_1(t) + h_2^* n_2(t)),$$

then passes this signal through the matched filter $\varphi(-t)$, as shown in Figure 19.5, to produce the signal

$$r_k = (|h_1|^2 + |h_2|^2)a_k + n_k,$$

where n_k is a complex Gaussian random variable with $E[n_k] = 0$ and $E[n_k n_k^*] = (|h_1|^2 + |h_2|^2)N_0$. Thus, the maximum likelihood receiver employs the decision rule

$$\hat{a}_k = \arg\min_a |r_k - (|h_1|^2 + |h_2|^2)a|^2.$$

This detector is called a *maximal ratio combiner*, since it can be shown that it maximizes the signal-to-noise ratio.

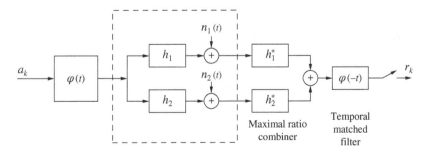

Figure 19.5: Two receive antennas and a maximal ratio combiner receiver.

19.3.2 Diversity Performance with Maximal-Ratio Combining

Let us now consider the performance of the single-transmitter, m-receiver system using maximal ratio combining. Suppose that the signal $a \in S$ is sent. The matched filter output is

$$r_k = \|\mathbf{h}\|^2 a_k + n_k,$$

where $n_k = \mathbf{h}^H \mathbf{n}$ is a complex Gaussian random variable with $E[|n_k|^2] = N_0 \|\mathbf{h}\|^2 = N_0 \sum_{j=1}^{m} |h_j|^2$. Let us define an effective signal-to-noise ratio as

$$\gamma_{\text{eff}} = \|\mathbf{h}\|^2 \frac{E_b}{N_0} = \sum_{j=1}^{m} |h_j|^2 \frac{E_b}{N_0} \triangleq \sum_{j=1}^{m} \gamma_j,$$

where $\gamma_j = |h_j|^2 E_b / N_0$ is the effective SNR for the jth channel. We assume a calibration so that the average SNR is $E[\gamma_j] = E_b / N_0$ for $j = 1, 2, \ldots, m$.

Transmitting from a single antenna then recombining the multiple received signals through a maximal ratio combiner results in a single-input, single-output channel. For BPSK transmission (assuming that the channel varies sufficiently slowly that $\mathbf{h}$ can be adequately estimated) the probability of error as a function of the effective signal-to-noise ratio is

$$P_2(\gamma_{\text{eff}}) = Q(\sqrt{2\gamma_{\text{eff}}}).$$

As for the case of a single fading channel, the overall probability of error is obtained by averaging over channel coefficients. Assume, as for the single fading case, that each coefficient h_i is a complex Gaussian random variable, so γ_i is a χ^2 distribution with 2 degrees of freedom. If each h_i varies independently (which can be assumed if the receive antennas are at least a half wavelength apart), then γ_{eff} is a χ^2 distribution with $2m$ degrees of freedom. The pdf of such a distribution can be shown to be (see, e.g., [333])

$$f_{\gamma_{\text{eff}}}(t) = \frac{1}{(m-1)!(E_b/N_0)^m} t^{m-1} e^{-tN_0/E_b} \quad t \geq 0.$$

The overall probability of error is

$$P_2 = \int_0^\infty f_{\gamma_{\text{eff}}}(t) P_2(t) \, dt.$$

The result of this integral (integrating by parts twice) is

$$P_2 = p^m \sum_{k=0}^{m-1} \binom{m-1+k}{k} (1-p)^k,$$

where

$$p = \frac{1}{2} \left(1 - \sqrt{\frac{\gamma_{\text{eff}}}{1 + \gamma_{\text{eff}}}} \right)$$

is the probability of error we found in (19.5) for single-channel diversity. Figure 19.3 shows the result for various values of m. It is clear that diversity provides significant performance improvement.

At high SNR, the quantity p can be approximated by

$$p \approx \frac{1}{4\gamma_{\text{eff}}}.$$

For $m > 1$, the probability of error can be approximated by observing that $(1-p)^k \approx 1$, so

$$P_2 \approx p^m \sum_{k=0}^{m-1} \binom{m-1+k}{m} = p^m \binom{2m-1}{k} \triangleq K_m p^m. \tag{19.8}$$

Using the $m = 1$ approximation, we find

$$P_2 \approx \left(\frac{1}{4\gamma_{\text{eff}}} \right)^m \binom{2m-1}{m}. \tag{19.9}$$

While the probability of error in an AWGN channel decreases *exponentially* with the signal-to-noise ratio, in a fading channel the probability of error only decreases *reciprocally* with the signal-to-noise ratio, with an exponent equal to the diversity m. We say that this scheme has diversity order m.

19.4 Space-Time Block Codes

We have seen that performance in a fading channel can be improved by receiver diversity. However, in many systems the receiver is required to be small and portable — such as a cell phone or personal digital assistant — and it may not be practical to deploy multiple receive antennas. The transmitter at a base station, however, may easily accommodate multiple antennas. It is of interest, therefore, to develop means of diversity which employ multiple transmit antennas instead of multiple receive antennas. This is what space-time codes provide.

19.4.1 The Alamouti Code

To introduce space-time codes, we present the Alamouti code, an early space-time code and still one of the most commonly used. Consider the transmit diversity scheme of Figure 19.6. Each antenna sends *sequences* of data from a signal constellation S. In the Alamouti code, a frame of data lasts for two symbol periods. In the first symbol time, antenna 1 sends the symbol $a_0 \in S$ while antenna 2 sends the symbol $a_1 \in S$. In the second symbol time, antenna 1 sends the symbol $-a_1^*$ while antenna 2 sends the symbol a_0^*. It is assumed that the fading introduced by the channel varies sufficiently slowly that

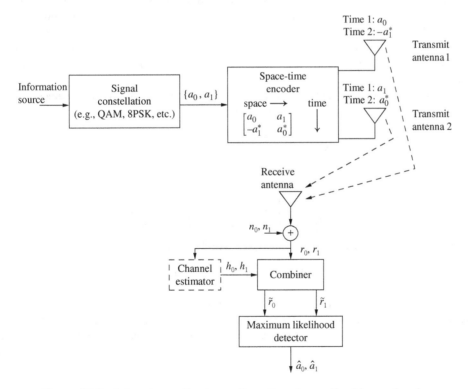

Figure 19.6: A two-transmit antenna diversity scheme: the Alamouti code.

it is *constant* over two symbol times (e.g., the quasistatic assumption applies for the entire duration of the codeword). The channel from antenna 1 to the receiver is modeled as $h_0 = \alpha_0 e^{-j\phi_0}$ and the channel from antenna 2 to the receiver is modeled as $h_1 = \alpha_1 e^{-j\phi_1}$. The received signal for the first signal (i.e., the sampled matched filter output) is

$$r_0 = h_0 a_0 + h_1 a_1 + n_0 \tag{19.10}$$

and for the second signal is

$$r_1 = -h_0 a_1^* + h_1 a_0^* + n_1. \tag{19.11}$$

The receiver now employs a *combining scheme*, computing

$$\begin{aligned} \tilde{r}_0 &= h_0^* r_0 + h_1 r_1^* \\ \tilde{r}_1 &= h_1^* r_0 - h_0 r_1^*. \end{aligned} \tag{19.12}$$

Substituting (19.10) and (19.11) into (19.12), we have

$$\tilde{r}_0 = (|h_0|^2 + |h_1|^2)a_0 + h_0^* n_0 + h_1 n_1^*$$

$$\tilde{r}_1 = (|h_0|^2 + |h_1|^2)a_1 - h_0^* n_1 + h_1^* n_0.$$

The key observation is that $\tilde{r}_0$ *depends only on* a_0, so that detection can take place with respect to this single quantity. Similarly, $\tilde{r}_1$ *depends only on* a_1, again implying a single detection problem.

The receiver now employs the maximum likelihood decision rule on each signal separately

$$\hat{a}_0 = \arg \min_{a \in S} |\tilde{r}_0 - (|h_0|^2 + |h_1|^2)a|^2$$

$$\hat{a}_1 = \arg \min_{a \in S} |\tilde{r}_1 - (|h_0|^2 + |h_1|^2)a|^2.$$

Overall the scheme is capable of sending two symbols over two symbol periods, so this represents a rate 1 code. However, it also provides a diversity of 2. Assuming that the total transmitter power with two antennas in this coded scheme is equal to the total transmitted power of a conventional receiver diversity method, the transmit power must be split into two for each antenna. This power split results in a 3 dB performance reduction compared to $m = 2$ using two receive antennas, but otherwise equivalent performance.

Suppose that, unlike this Alamouti scheme, the combining scheme produced values which are a mixture of the transmitted signals. For example, suppose

$$\tilde{r}_0 = aa_0 + ba_1 + \tilde{n}_0$$

$$\tilde{r}_1 = ca_0 + da_1 + \tilde{n}_1$$

for some coefficients a, b, c, d. We could write this as

$$\tilde{\mathbf{r}} = \begin{bmatrix} a & b \\ c & d \end{bmatrix} \begin{bmatrix} a_0 \\ a_1 \end{bmatrix} + \begin{bmatrix} \tilde{n}_0 \\ \tilde{n}_1 \end{bmatrix} \triangleq A \begin{bmatrix} a_0 \\ a_1 \end{bmatrix} + \begin{bmatrix} \tilde{n}_0 \\ \tilde{n}_1 \end{bmatrix}.$$

Then the maximum likelihood decision rule must maximize *jointly*:

$$[\hat{a}_0, \hat{a}_1] = \arg \min_{\mathbf{a} \in S^2} \|\tilde{\mathbf{r}} - A\mathbf{a}\|^2.$$

The search is over the vector of length 2, so that if the constellation has M points in it, then the search complexity is $O(M^2)$. In the case of m-fold diversity, the complexity rises as $O(M^m)$. This increase of complexity is avoided in the Alamouti code case because of the orthogonality of the encoding matrix.

It is important for computational simplicity that a symbol appears in only one combined received waveform. The remainder of the development of space-time block codes in this chapter is restricted to considerations of how to achieve this kind of separation, using orthogonal designs.

The Alamouti code has been adopted by the IEEE 802.11a and IEEE 802.16a wireless standards.

19.4.2 A More General Formulation

Let us now establish a more general framework for space-time codes, in which the Alamouti scheme is a special case. In the interest of generality, we allow for both transmit and receive diversity, with n transmit antennas and m receive antennas. The code frames exist for l symbol periods. (Thus, for the Alamouti scheme, $n = 2$, $m = 1$, and $l = 2$.) At time t, the symbols $c_i(t)$, $i = 1, 2, \ldots, n$ are transmitted simultaneously from the n transmit antennas. The signal $r_j(t)$ at antenna j is

$$r_j(t) = \sum_{i=1}^{n} h_{j,i} c_i(t) + n_j(t), \quad j = 1, 2, \ldots, m,$$

where the $c_i(t)$ is the coded symbol transmitted by antenna i at time t. The codeword for this frame is thus the sequence

$$\mathbf{c} = c_1(1), c_2(1), \ldots, c_n(1), c_1(2), c_2(2), \ldots, c_n(2), \ldots, c_1(l), c_2(l), \ldots, c_n(l) \tag{19.13}$$

of length nl.

19.4.3 Performance Calculation

Before considering how to design the codewords, let us first establish the diversity order for the coding scheme. Consider the probability that a maximum-likelihood decoder decides in favor of a signal

$$\mathbf{e} = e_1(1), e_2(1), \ldots, e_n(1), e_1(2), e_2(2), \ldots, e_n(2), \ldots, e_1(l), e_2(l), \ldots, e_n(l)$$

over the signal $\mathbf{c}$ of (19.13) which was transmitted, for a given channel state. We denote this probability as

$$P(\mathbf{c} \to \mathbf{e} | h_{j,i}, j = 1, 2, \ldots, m, i = 1, 2, \ldots, n).$$

Over the AWGN channel, this probability can be bounded (using a bound on the Q function) by

$$P(\mathbf{c} \to \mathbf{e} | h_{j,i}, j = 1, 2, \ldots, m, i = 1, 2, \ldots, n) \leq \exp(-d^2(\mathbf{c}, \mathbf{e}) E_s / 4N_0),$$

where

$$d^2(\mathbf{c}, \mathbf{e}) = \sum_{j=1}^{m} \sum_{t=1}^{l} \left| \sum_{i=1}^{n} h_{j,i} (c_i(t) - e_i(t)) \right|^2.$$

Let $\mathbf{h}_j^T = [h_{j,1}, h_{j,2}, \ldots, h_{j,n}]^T$ and $\mathbf{c}_t^T = [c_1(t), c_2(t), \ldots, c_n(t)]^T$ and similarly $\mathbf{e}_t$. Then

$$d^2(\mathbf{c}, \mathbf{e}) = \sum_{j=1}^{m} \mathbf{h}_j^T \left[\sum_{t=1}^{l} (\mathbf{c}_t - \mathbf{e}_t)(\mathbf{c}_t - \mathbf{e}_t)^H \right] \mathbf{h}_j^*.$$

Let

$$A(\mathbf{c}, \mathbf{e}) = \sum_{t=1}^{l} (\mathbf{c}_t - \mathbf{e}_t)(\mathbf{c}_t - \mathbf{e}_t)^H.$$

Then

$$d^2(\mathbf{c}, \mathbf{e}) = \sum_{j=1}^{m} \mathbf{h}_j^T A(\mathbf{c}, \mathbf{e}) \mathbf{h}_j^*,$$

so that

$$P(\mathbf{c} \to \mathbf{e} | h_{j,i}, j = 1, 2, \ldots, m, i = 1, 2, \ldots, n) \leq \prod_{j=1}^{m} \exp(-\mathbf{h}_j^T A(\mathbf{c}, \mathbf{e}) \mathbf{h}_j^* \, E_s / 4N_0).$$

The matrix $A(\mathbf{c}, \mathbf{e})$ can be written as

$$A(\mathbf{c}, \mathbf{e}) = B(\mathbf{c}, \mathbf{e})B^H(\mathbf{c}, \mathbf{e}),$$

where

$$B(\mathbf{c}, \mathbf{e}) = \begin{bmatrix} e_1(1) - c_1(1) & e_1(2) - c_1(2) & \cdots & e_1(l) - c_1(l) \\ e_2(1) - c_2(1) & e_2(2) - c_2(2) & \cdots & e_2(l) - c_2(l) \\ \vdots & & & \\ e_n(1) - c_n(1) & e_n(2) - c_n(2) & \cdots & e_n(l) - c_n(l) \end{bmatrix}. \tag{19.14}$$

In other words, $A(\mathbf{c}, \mathbf{e})$ has $B(\mathbf{c}, \mathbf{e})$ as a square root. It is known (see [202]) that any matrix having a square root is non-negative definite; among other implications of this, all of its eigenvalues are non-negative.

The symmetric matrix $A(\mathbf{c}, \mathbf{e})$ can be written as (see, e.g., [319])

$$VA(\mathbf{c}, \mathbf{e})V^H = D,$$

where V is a unitary matrix formed from the eigenvectors of $A(\mathbf{c}, \mathbf{e})$ and D is diagonal with real non-negative diagonal elements λ_i. Let $\boldsymbol{\beta}_j = V\mathbf{h}_j^*$. Then

$$P(\mathbf{c} \rightarrow \mathbf{e}|h_{j,i}, j = 1, 2, \ldots, m, i = 1, 2, \ldots, n) \leq \prod_{j=1}^{m} \exp(-\boldsymbol{\beta}_j^H D \boldsymbol{\beta}_j E_s / 4N_0)$$

$$= \prod_{j=1}^{m} \exp\left(-\sum_{i=1}^{n} \lambda_i |\beta_{i,j}|^2 E_s / 4N_0\right).$$

Assuming the elements of $\mathbf{h}_i$ are zero mean Gaussian and normalized to have variance 0.5 per dimension, then the $|\beta_{i,j}|$ are Rayleigh distributed with density

$$p(|\beta_{i,j}|) = 2|\beta_{i,j}| \exp(-|\beta_{i,j}|^2).$$

The average performance is obtained by integrating

$$P(\mathbf{c} \rightarrow \mathbf{e}) \leq \int \prod_{j=1}^{m} \exp\left(-\sum_{i=1}^{n} \lambda_i |\beta_{i,j}|^2 E_s / 4N_0\right) \prod_{i,j} 2|\beta_{i,j}| \exp(-|\beta_{i,j}|^2) d|\beta_{1,1}| \cdots d|\beta_{n,m}|.$$

After some effort, this can be shown to be

$$P(\mathbf{c} \rightarrow \mathbf{e}) \leq \left(\frac{1}{\prod_{i=1}^{n}(1 + \lambda_i E_s / 4N_0)}\right)^m. \tag{19.15}$$

Let r be the rank of $A(\mathbf{c}, \mathbf{e})$, so there are $n - r$ eigenvalues of $A(\mathbf{c}, \mathbf{e})$ equal to 0. Then (19.15) can be further approximated as

$$P(\mathbf{c} \rightarrow \mathbf{e}) \leq \left(\prod_{i=1}^{r} \lambda_i\right)^{-m} (E_s / 4N_0)^{-rm}.$$

Comparing with (19.9), we see that the probability of error decreases reciprocally with the signal-to-noise ratio to the rmth power. We have thus proved the following theorem:

Theorem 19.2 *The order of the diversity for this coding is rm.*

From this theorem, we obtain the **rank criterion**: To obtain the maximum diversity mn, the matrix $B(\mathbf{c}, \mathbf{e})$ must of full rank for any pair of codewords $\mathbf{c}$ and $\mathbf{e}$.

The factor $\left(\prod_{i=1}^{r} \lambda_i\right)^{-m}$ in (19.15) is interpreted as the coding advantage. In combination with the diversity from the other factor, we obtain the following two design criteria for Rayleigh space-time codes [435].

- In order to achieve maximum diversity, $B(\mathbf{c}, \mathbf{e})$ of (19.14) must be full rank for any pair of codewords $\mathbf{c}$ and $\mathbf{e}$. The smallest r over any pair of codewords leads to a diversity of rm.

- The coding benefit is maximized by maximizing the sum of the determinants of all $r \times r$ principle cofactors of $A(\mathbf{c}, \mathbf{e}) = B(\mathbf{c}, \mathbf{e})B(\mathbf{c}, \mathbf{e})^H$, since this sum is equal to the product of the determinants of the cofactors.

19.4.3.1 Real Orthogonal Designs

Let us now turn attention to the problem of designing the transmitted codewords. Recall that to minimize decoder complexity, it is desirable to be able to decompose the decision problem so that optimal decisions can be made on the basis of a single symbol at a time, as was possible for the Alamouti code. This can be achieved using *orthogonal designs*. For the moment, we consider only real orthogonal designs which are associated with real signal constellations.

Definition 19.3 A **real orthogonal design** of size n is an $n \times n$ matrix $\mathcal{O} = \mathcal{O}(x_1, x_2, \ldots, x_n)$ with elements drawn from $\pm x_1, \pm x_2, \ldots, \pm x_n$ such that

$$\mathcal{O}^T \mathcal{O} = I \sum_{i=1}^{n} x_i^2 \triangleq IK.$$

That is, $\mathcal{O}$ is proportional to an orthogonal matrix. □

By means of column permutations and sign changes, it is possible to arrange $\mathcal{O}$ so that the first row has all positive signs. Examples of orthogonal designs are

$$
\mathcal{O}_2 = \begin{bmatrix} x_1 & x_2 \\ -x_2 & x_1 \end{bmatrix} \quad
\mathcal{O}_4 = \begin{bmatrix}
x_1 & x_2 & x_3 & x_4 \\
-x_2 & x_1 & -x_4 & x_3 \\
-x_3 & x_4 & x_1 & -x_2 \\
-x_4 & -x_3 & x_2 & x_1
\end{bmatrix}
$$

$$
\mathcal{O}_8 = \begin{bmatrix}
x_1 & x_2 & x_3 & x_4 & x_5 & x_6 & x_7 & x_8 \\
-x_2 & x_1 & x_4 & -x_3 & x_6 & -x_5 & -x_8 & x_7 \\
-x_3 & -x_4 & x_1 & x_2 & x_7 & x_8 & -x_5 & -x_6 \\
-x_4 & x_3 & -x_2 & x_1 & x_8 & -x_7 & x_6 & -x_5 \\
-x_5 & -x_6 & -x_7 & -x_8 & x_1 & x_2 & x_3 & x_4 \\
-x_6 & x_5 & -x_8 & x_7 & -x_2 & x_1 & -x_4 & x_3 \\
-x_7 & x_8 & x_5 & -x_6 & -x_3 & x_4 & x_1 & -x_2 \\
-x_8 & -x_7 & x_6 & x_5 & -x_4 & -x_3 & x_2 & x_1
\end{bmatrix}.
$$

In fact, it is known that these are the *only* orthogonal designs [154]. Each row of an orthogonal design $\mathcal{O}$ is a permutation with sign changes of the $\{x_1, x_2, \ldots, x_n\}$. Let us denote the (i, j)th element of $\mathcal{O}$ as $o_{ij} = x_{\epsilon_i(j)} \delta_i(j)$, where $\epsilon_i(j)$ is a permutation function for the ith row and $\delta_i(j)$ is the sign of the (i, j) entry. Observe that permutations in the orthogonal matrices above are symmetric so that $\epsilon_i(j) = \epsilon_i^{-1}(j)$. By the orthogonality of $\mathcal{O}$,

$$
[\mathcal{O}^T \, \mathcal{O}]_{i,k} = \sum_{l=1}^{n} o_{li} o_{lk} = \begin{cases} \sum_{i=1}^{n} x_i^2 & i = k \\ 0 & \text{otherwise} \end{cases} \triangleq K \delta_{i-k}
$$

or

$$
\sum_{l=1}^{n} x_{\epsilon_l(i)} x_{\epsilon_l(k)} \delta_l(i) \delta_l(j) = K \delta_{i-k}. \tag{19.16}
$$

19.4.3.2   Encoding and Decoding Based on Orthogonal Designs

At the encoder, the symbols $a_1, a_2, \ldots, a_n$ are selected from the (for the moment real) signal constellation $\mathcal{S}$ and used to fill out the $n \times n$ orthogonal design $\mathcal{O}(a_1, a_2, \ldots, a_n)$. At time slot $t = 1, 2, \ldots, n$, the elements of the tth row of the orthogonal matrix are simultaneously transmitted using n transmit antennas. The frame length of the code is $l = n$. At time t, the jth antenna receives

$$r_j(t) = \sum_{i=1}^{n} h_{j,i} c_i(t) + n_j(t)$$

$$= \sum_{i=1}^{n} h_{j,i} \delta_t(i) a_{\epsilon_t(i)} + n_j(t).$$

Now let $l = \epsilon_t(i)$, or $i = \epsilon_t^{-1}(l)$. The received signal can be written as

$$r_j(t) = \sum_{l=1}^{n} h_{j,\epsilon_t^{-1}(l)} \delta_t(\epsilon_t^{-1}(l)) a_l + n_j(t).$$

Let $\mathbf{h}_{j,t}^T = [h_{j,\epsilon_t^{-1}(1)} \delta_t(\epsilon_t^{-1}(1)), \ldots, h_{j,\epsilon_t^{-1}(n)} \delta_t(\epsilon_t^{-1}(n))]$ and $\mathbf{a}^T = [a_1, \ldots, a_n]$. Then

$$r_j(t) = \mathbf{h}_{j,t}^T \mathbf{a} + n_j(t).$$

Stacking the received signals in time, the jth receive antenna receives

$$\mathbf{r}_j = \begin{bmatrix} r_j(1) \\ \vdots \\ r_j(n) \end{bmatrix} = \begin{bmatrix} \mathbf{h}_{j,1}^T \\ \vdots \\ \mathbf{h}_{j,n}^T \end{bmatrix} \mathbf{a} + \begin{bmatrix} n_j(1) \\ \vdots \\ n_j(n) \end{bmatrix} \triangleq H_{j,\text{eff}} \mathbf{a} + \mathbf{n}_j. \tag{19.17}$$

The maximum likelihood receiver computes

$$J(\mathbf{a}) = \sum_{j=1}^{m} \|\mathbf{r}_j - H_{j,\text{eff}} \mathbf{a}\|^2$$

over all vectors $\mathbf{a}$ and selects the codeword with the minimizing value. However, rather than having to search jointly over all $|\mathcal{S}|^n$ vectors $\mathbf{a}$, each component can be selected independently, as we now show. We can write

$$J(\mathbf{a}) = \sum_{j=1}^{m} \|\mathbf{r}_j\|^2 - 2Re \left[\mathbf{a}^H \sum_{j=1}^{m} H_{j,\text{eff}}^H \mathbf{r} \right] + \mathbf{a}^H \left(\sum_{j=1}^{m} H_{j,\text{eff}}^H H_{j,\text{eff}} \right) \mathbf{a}.$$

Using (19.16), we see that each $H_{j,\text{eff}}$ is an orthogonal matrix $\mathcal{O}(h_{j,1}, h_{j,2}, \ldots, h_{j,n})$, so that

$$\sum_{j=1}^{m} H_{r,\text{eff}}^H H_{r,\text{eff}} \triangleq I \sum_{j=1}^{m} K_j \triangleq IK$$

for some scalar K. Let

$$\mathbf{v} = \sum_{j=1}^{m} H_{j,\text{eff}}^H \mathbf{r}.$$

Then minimizing $J(\mathbf{a})$ is equivalent to minimizing

$$J'(\mathbf{a}) = -2Re[\mathbf{a}^H \mathbf{v}] + \|\mathbf{a}\|^2 K.$$

Now let $S_i = -2Rea_i^* v_i + K|a_i|^2$. Minimizing $J'(\mathbf{a})$ is equivalent to minimizing $\sum_{i=1}^{n} S_i$, which amounts to minimizing each S_i separately. Since each S_i depends only on a_i, we have

$$\hat{a}_i = \arg\min_a K|a|^2 - 2Rea^* v_i.$$

Thus, using orthogonal designs allows for using only scalar detectors instead of vector detectors.

Let us now examine the diversity order of these space-time block codes.

Theorem 19.4 *[434] The diversity order for coding with real orthogonal designs is nm.*

Proof The matrix $B(\mathbf{c}, \mathbf{e})$ of Theorem 19.2 is formed by

$$B(\mathbf{c}, \mathbf{e}) = \mathcal{O}(\mathbf{c}) - \mathcal{O}(\mathbf{e}) = \mathcal{O}(\mathbf{c} - \mathbf{e}).$$

Since $\det(\mathcal{O}^T(\mathbf{c} - \mathbf{e})\mathcal{O}(\mathbf{c} - \mathbf{e})) = \left[\sum_i |c_i - e_i|^2\right]^n$ is not equal to 0 for any $\mathbf{c}$ and $\mathbf{e} \neq \mathbf{c}$, $\mathcal{O}(\mathbf{c} - \mathbf{e})$ must be full rank. By the rank criterion, then, the maximum diversity of nm obtains. $\square$

This encoding and decoding scheme provides a way of sending n message symbols over n symbol times, for a rate $R = 1$ coding scheme. However, as mentioned above, it applies only to $n = 2, 4$, or 8.

19.4.3.3 Generalized Real Orthogonal Designs

In the interest of obtaining more possible designs, we now turn to a generalized real orthogonal design $\mathcal{G}$.

Definition 19.5 [434] A **generalized orthogonal design** of size n is a $p \times n$ matrix $\mathcal{G}$ with entries $0, \pm x_1, \pm x_2, \ldots, \pm x_k$ such that $\mathcal{G}^T \mathcal{G} = KI$, where K is some constant. The **rate** of $\mathcal{G}$ is $R = k/p$. $\square$

Example 19.6 The following are examples of generalized orthogonal designs.

$$\mathcal{G}_3 = \begin{bmatrix} x_1 & x_2 & x_3 \\ -x_2 & x_1 & -x_4 \\ -x_3 & x_4 & x_1 \\ -x_4 & -x_3 & x_2 \end{bmatrix} \quad \mathcal{G}_5 = \begin{bmatrix} x_1 & x_2 & x_3 & x_4 & x_5 \\ -x_2 & x_1 & x_4 & -x_3 & x_6 \\ -x_3 & -x_4 & x_1 & x_2 & x_7 \\ -x_4 & x_3 & -x_2 & x_1 & x_8 \\ -x_5 & -x_6 & -x_7 & -x_8 & x_1 \\ -x_6 & x_5 & -x_8 & x_7 & -x_2 \\ -x_7 & x_8 & x_5 & -x_6 & -x_3 \\ -x_8 & -x_7 & x_6 & x_5 & -x_4 \end{bmatrix}$$

$$\mathcal{G}_6 = \begin{bmatrix} x_1 & x_2 & x_3 & x_4 & x_5 & x_6 \\ -x_2 & x_1 & x_4 & -x_3 & x_6 & -x_5 \\ -x_3 & -x_4 & x_1 & x_2 & x_7 & x_8 \\ -x_4 & x_3 & -x_2 & x_1 & x_8 & -x_7 \\ -x_5 & -x_6 & -x_7 & -x_8 & x_1 & x_2 \\ -x_6 & x_5 & -x_8 & x_7 & -x_2 & x_1 \\ -x_7 & x_8 & x_5 & -x_6 & -x_3 & x_4 \\ -x_8 & -x_7 & x_6 & x_5 & -x_4 & -x_3 \end{bmatrix}$$

$$\mathcal{G}_7 = \begin{bmatrix} x_1 & x_2 & x_3 & x_4 & x_5 & x_6 & x_7 \\ -x_2 & x_1 & x_4 & -x_3 & x_6 & -x_5 & -x_8 \\ -x_3 & -x_4 & x_1 & x_2 & x_7 & x_8 & -x_5 \\ -x_4 & x_3 & -x_2 & x_1 & x_8 & -x_7 & x_6 \\ -x_5 & -x_6 & -x_7 & -x_8 & x_1 & x_2 & x_3 \\ -x_6 & x_5 & -x_8 & x_7 & -x_2 & x_1 & -x_4 \\ -x_7 & x_8 & x_5 & -x_6 & -x_3 & x_4 & x_1 \\ -x_8 & -x_7 & x_6 & x_5 & -x_4 & -x_3 & x_2 \end{bmatrix}.$$

$\square$

The encoding for a generalized orthogonal design is as follows. A set of k symbols $a_1, a_2, \ldots, a_k$ arrives at the encoder. The encoder builds the design matrix $\mathcal{G}$ by setting $x_i = a_i$. Then for $t = 1, 2, \ldots, p$, the n antennas simultaneously transmit the n symbols from the tth row of $\mathcal{G}$. In p symbol times, then, k message symbols are sent, resulting in a rate $R = k/p$ code.

In the interest of maximizing rate, minimizing encoder and decoder latency, and minimizing complexity, it is of interest to determine designs having the smallest p possible. A design having rate at least R with the smallest possible value of p is said to be delay-optimal. (The designs of Example 19.6 yield delay-optimal, rate 1 codes.)

A technique for constructing generalized orthogonal designs is provided in [434].

19.4.4 Complex Orthogonal Designs

We now extend the concepts of real orthogonal designs to complex orthogonal designs.

Definition 19.7 A **complex orthogonal design** of size n is a matrix $\mathcal{U}$ formed from the elements $\pm x_1, \pm x_2, \ldots, \pm x_n$, their conjugates $\pm x_1^*, \pm x_2^*, \ldots, \pm x_n^*$, or multiplies of these by $j = \sqrt{-1}$, such that $\mathcal{U}^H \mathcal{U} = (|x_1|^2 + \cdots + |x_n|^2)I$. That is, $\mathcal{U}$ is proportional to a unitary matrix.   □

Without loss of generality, the first row can be formed of the elements $x_1, x_2, \ldots, x_n$.

The same method of encoding is used for complex orthogonal designs as for real orthogonal designs: n antennas send the rows for each of n time intervals.

Example 19.8   The matrix

$$\mathcal{U}_2 = \left. \begin{array}{c} \text{time} \quad \text{space} \rightarrow \\ \Big\downarrow \quad \begin{bmatrix} x_1 & x_2 \\ -x_2^* & x_1^* \end{bmatrix} \end{array} \right.$$

is a complex orthogonal design. As suggested by the arrows, if the columns are distributed in space (across two antennas) and the rows are distributed in time (over different symbol times), this can be used as a space-time code. In fact, this is the Alamouti code.   □

Unfortunately, as discussed in Exercise 19.6, complex orthogonal designs of size n exist only for $n = 2$ or $n = 4$. The Alamouti code is thus, in some sense, almost unique.

We turn therefore to generalized complex orthogonal designs.

Definition 19.9 [434] A **generalized complex orthogonal design** is a $p \times n$ matrix $\mathcal{U}$ whose entries are formed from $0, \pm x_1, \pm x_1^*, \ldots, \pm x_k, \pm x_k^*$ or their product with $j = \sqrt{-1}$ such that $\mathcal{U}^H \mathcal{U} = (|x_1|^2 + \cdots + |x_k|^2)I$.   □

A generalized orthogonal design can be used to create a rate $R = k/p$ space-time code using n antennas, just as for orthogonal designs above.

Example 19.10   The following are examples of generalized complex orthogonal designs.

$$\mathcal{U}_3 = \begin{bmatrix} x_1 & x_2 & x_3 \\ -x_2 & x_1 & -x_4 \\ -x_3 & x_4 & x_1 \\ -x_4 & -x_3 & x_2 \\ x_1^* & x_2^* & x_3^* \\ -x_2^* & x_1^* & -x_4^* \\ -x_3^* & x_4^* & x_1^* \\ -x_4^* & -x_3^* & x_2^* \end{bmatrix} \qquad \mathcal{U}_4 = \begin{bmatrix} x_1 & x_2 & x_3 & x_4 \\ -x_2 & x_1 & -x_4 & x_3 \\ -x_3 & x_4 & x_1 & -x_2 \\ -x_4 & -x_3 & x_2 & x_1 \\ x_1^* & x_2^* & x_3^* & x_4^* \\ -x_2^* & x_1^* & -x_4^* & x_3^* \\ -x_3^* & x_4^* & x_1^* & -x_2^* \\ -x_4^* & -x_3^* & x_2^* & x_1^* \end{bmatrix}.$$

These provide $R = 1/2$ coding using 3 and 4 antennas, respectively.

A rate $R = 3/4$ code using an orthogonal design is provided by [445] is

$$
\mathcal{U}_4 = \begin{bmatrix}
x_1 & -x_2^* & -x_3^* & 0 \\
x_2 & x_1^* & 0 & x_3^* \\
x_3 & 0 & x_1^* & -x_2^* \\
0 & -x_3 & x_2 & x_1
\end{bmatrix}.
$$

□

Higher rate codes are also known using *linear processing orthogonal designs*, which form matrices not by individual elements, but by linear combinations of elements. These produce what are known as *generalized complex linear processing orthogonal designs*.

Example 19.11 Examples of linear processing designs producing $R = 3/4$ codes are

$$
\mathcal{U} = \begin{bmatrix}
x_1 & x_2 & x_3/\sqrt{2} \\
-x_2^* & x_1^* & x_3/\sqrt{2} \\
x_3^*/\sqrt{2} & x_3^*/\sqrt{2} & (-x_1 - x_1^* + x_2 - x_2^*)/2 \\
x_3^*/\sqrt{2} & -x_3^*/\sqrt{2} & (x_2 + x_2^* + x_1 - x_1^*)/2
\end{bmatrix}
$$

$$
\mathcal{U} = \begin{bmatrix}
x_1 & x_2 & x_3/\sqrt{2} & x_3/\sqrt{2} \\
-x_2^* & x_1^* & x_3/\sqrt{2} & -x_3/\sqrt{2} \\
x_3^*/\sqrt{2} & x_3^*/\sqrt{2} & (-x_1 - x_1^* + x_2 - x_2^*)/2 & (-x_2 - x_2^* + x_1 - x_1^*)/2 \\
x_3^*/\sqrt{2} & -x_3^*/\sqrt{2} & (x_2 + x_2^* + x_1 - x_1^*)/2 & -(x_1 + x_1^* + x_2 - x_2^*)/2
\end{bmatrix}
$$

for $n = 3$ and $n = 4$ antennas, respectively. □

19.4.4.1 Future Work

Several specific examples of designs leading to low-complexity decoders have been presented in the examples above. However, additional work in high-rate code designs is still a topic of ongoing research.

19.5 Space-Time Trellis Codes

Trellis codes can also be used to provide diversity. We present here several examples from the literature.

Example 19.12 Consider the coding scheme presented in Figure 19.7. This is an example of *delay diversity*, which is a hybrid of spatial diversity and time diversity. The signal transmitted from two antennas at time t consists of the current symbol a_t and the previous symbol a_{t-1}. The received signal is $r_t = h_0 a_t + h_1 a_{t-1} + n_t$. If the channel parameters $\{h_0, h_1\}$ is known, then an equalizer can be used to detect the transmitted sequence.

Because the encoder has a memory element in it, this can also be regarded as a simple trellis code, so that decoding can be accomplished using the Viterbi algorithm. If this encoder is used in conjunction with an 8-PSK

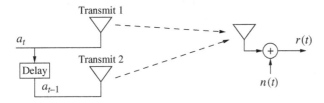

Figure 19.7: A delay diversity scheme.

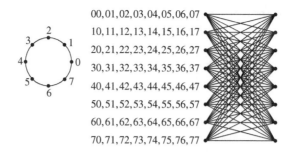

$$00, 01, 02, 03, 04, 05, 06, 07$$
$$10, 11, 12, 13, 14, 15, 16, 17$$
$$20, 21, 22, 23, 24, 25, 26, 27$$
$$30, 31, 32, 33, 34, 35, 36, 37$$
$$40, 41, 42, 43, 44, 45, 46, 47$$
$$50, 51, 52, 53, 54, 55, 56, 57$$
$$60, 61, 62, 63, 64, 65, 66, 67$$
$$70, 71, 72, 73, 74, 75, 76, 77$$

Figure 19.8: 8-PSK constellation and the trellis for a delay-diversity encoder.

signal constellation, then there are 8 states. The trellis and the output sequence are shown in Figure 19.8. The outputs listed beside the states are the pair (a_{k-1}, a_k) for each input. (A similar four-state trellis is obtained for a 4-PSK using delay diversity.)

For a sequence of symbols $a_1, a_2, \ldots, a_n$, a delay diversity coder may also be written as a space-time *block code*, with codeword

$$A(a_1, a_2, \ldots, a_n) = \begin{bmatrix} a_1 & a_2 & a_3 & \cdots & a_{n-1} & a_n & 0 \\ 0 & a_1 & a_2 & a_3 & \cdots & a_{n-1} & a_n \end{bmatrix}.$$

The two zeros in the first and last columns ensure that the trellis begins and ends in the 0 state. By viewing this as a space-time block code, the rank-criterion may be employed. The matrix $B(\mathbf{a}, \mathbf{e}) = A(\mathbf{a}) - A(\mathbf{e})$ is, by the linearity of the coding mechanism, equal to $A(\mathbf{a}')$, where $\mathbf{a}' = \mathbf{a} - \mathbf{e}$. The columns containing the first and last elements of $\mathbf{a}'$ are linearly independent, so B has full rank: This code provides a diversity of $m = 2$ at 2 bits/second/Hz.   □

Example 19.13   In the trellis of Figure 19.8, replace the output mappings with the sequences

$$\begin{array}{ll} \text{State 0:} & 00, 01, 02, 03, 04, 05, 06, 07 \\ \text{State 1:} & 50, 51, 52, 53, 54, 55, 56, 57 \\ \text{State 2:} & 20, 21, 22, 23, 24, 25, 26, 27 \\ \text{State 3:} & 70, 71, 72, 73, 74, 75, 76, 77 \\ \text{State 4:} & 40, 41, 42, 43, 44, 45, 46, 47 \\ \text{State 5:} & 10, 11, 12, 13, 14, 15, 16, 17 \\ \text{State 6:} & 60, 61, 62, 63, 64, 65, 66, 67 \\ \text{State 7:} & 30, 31, 32, 33, 34, 35, 36, 37 \end{array}$$

This corresponds to a delay diversity code, with the additional modification that the delayed symbol is multiplied by -1 if it is odd $\{1, 3, 5, 7\}$. It has been observed [322] that this simple modification provides 2.5 dB of gain compared to simple delay diversity.   □

Example 19.14   Figure 19.9 shows space-time codes for 4-PSK (transmitting 2 bits/second/Hz) using 8, 16, and 32 states. Each of these codes provides a diversity of 2. Figure 19.11(a) shows the probability of error performance (obtained via simulation) for these codes when used with two transmit antennas and two receive antennas. Figure 19.11(b) shows the performance with two transmit antennas and one receive antenna.   □

Example 19.15   Figure 19.10 shows space-time codes for 8-PSK (transmitting 3 bits/second/Hz) using 16 and 32 states (with the code in Example 19.13 being an 8-state code). Each of these codes provides a diversity of 2. Figure 19.12(a) shows the probability of error performance (obtained via simulation) for these codes when used with two transmit antennas and two receive antennas. Figure 19.12(b) shows the performance with two transmit antennas and one receive antenna.   □

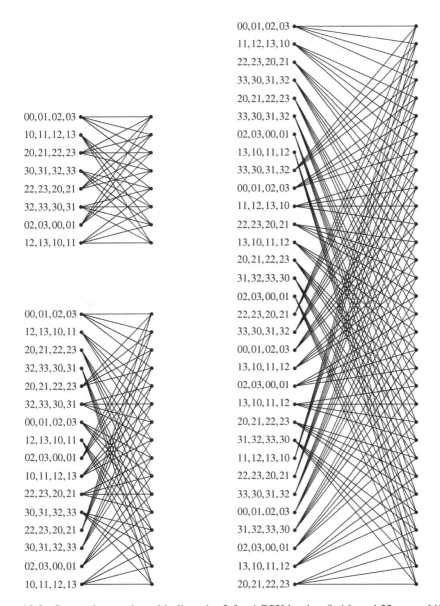

Figure 19.9: Space-time codes with diversity 2 for 4-PSK having 8, 16, and 32 states [435].

19.5.1 Concatenation

Concatenation is also frequently employed in space-time coded systems. In this case, the outer code is frequently a TCM system whose symbols are transmitted via an inner space-time coded system.

19.6 How Many Antennas?

We cannot continue to add antennas without reaching a point of diminishing returns. One argument for the number of antennas is based on channel capacity. It has been proved [139, 436] that the capacity of a multiantenna system with a single receive antenna is a random variable of the form $\log_2(1 + (\chi^2_{2n}/2n)\mathrm{SNR})$, where χ^2_{2n} is a χ^2 random variable with $2n$ degrees of freedom (e.g., formed by summing the squares of $2n$ independent zero-mean, unit-variance Gaussian random variables). By

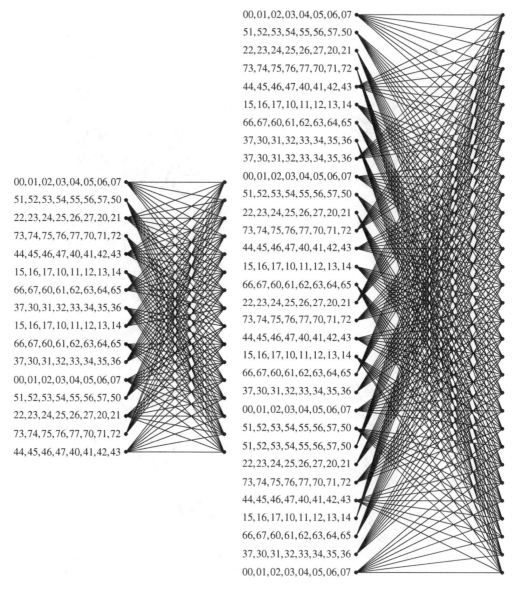

Figure 19.10: Performance of codes with 4-PSK that achieve diversity 2 [435]. (a) Two receive and two transmit antennas; (b) one receive and two transmit antennas.

the law of large numbers, as $n \to \infty$,

$$\frac{1}{2n} \chi_{2n}^2 \to \frac{1}{2}(E[X^2] + E[X^2]) = 1 \text{ where } X \sim \mathcal{N}(0, 1).$$

In practice, the limit begins to be apparent for $n \geq 4$, suggesting that more than four transmit antennas will provide little additional improvement over four antennas. It can also be argued that with two receive antennas, $n = 6$ transmit antennas provides almost all the benefit possible.

However, there are systems for which it is of interest to employ both interference suppression and diversity. In these cases, having additional antennas is of benefit. A "conservation theorem" [26, p. 546] says that

diversity order + number of interferers = number of receive antennas.

As the number of interferers to be suppressed increases, having additional antennas is of value.

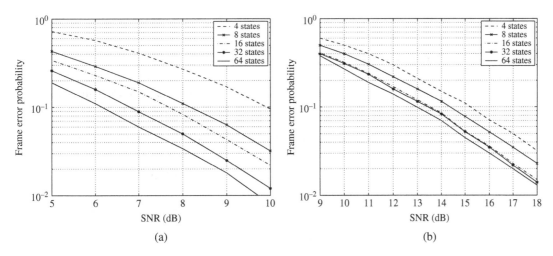

Figure 19.11: Space-time codes with diversity 2 for 8-PSK having 16 and 32 states [435].

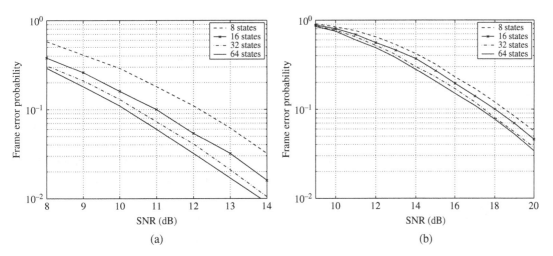

Figure 19.12: Performance of codes with 8-PSK that achieve diversity 2 [435]. (a) Two receive and two transmit antennas; (b) one receive and two transmit antennas.

19.7 Estimating Channel Information

All of the decoders described in this chapter assume that the channel parameters in the form of the $h_{j,i}$ is known at the receiver. Estimating these is viewed for our purposes as signal processing beyond the scope of this book, so we say only a few words regarding the problem.

It is possible to send a "pilot" signal which is known by the receiver, and from this pilot to estimate the channel parameters if the channel is sufficiently static. However, a pilot signal consumes bandwidth and transmitter power and reduces the overall throughput. Another approach is to use differential space-time codes [200, 205], where information is coded in the change of symbols, but at the expense of a 3 dB penalty.

Another approach is to blindly estimate the channel parameters, without using the transmitted symbols. This is developed in [426].

19.8 Exercises

19.1 Consider a transmission scheme in which n transmit antennas are used. The vector $\mathbf{a} = [a_1, a_2, \ldots, a_n]^T$ is transmitted to a single receiver through a channel with coefficients h_i^* so that $r = \mathbf{h}^H \mathbf{a} + n$, where $\mathbf{h} = [h_1, h_2, \ldots, h_n]^T$ and where n is zero-mean AWGN with variance σ^2. Diversity can be obtained by sending the same symbol a from each antenna, so that $\mathbf{a} = a\mathbf{w}$, for some "steering vector" $\mathbf{w}$. The received signal is thus $r = \mathbf{h}^H \mathbf{w} a + n$. Show that the weight vector $\mathbf{w}$ of length $\|\mathbf{w}\| = 1$ which maximizes the SNR at the receiver is $\mathbf{w} = \mathbf{h}/\|\mathbf{h}\|$ and determine the maximum SNR.

19.2 Show that if $G = X + jY$, where $X \sim \mathcal{N}(0, \sigma_f^2)$ and $Y \sim \mathcal{N}(0, \sigma_f^2)$, then $Z = |G| = \sqrt{X^2 + Y^2}$ has density

$$f_Z(z) = \begin{cases} \dfrac{z}{\sigma_f^2} e^{-z^2/2\sigma_f^2} & z \geq 0 \\[2mm] 0 & \text{otherwise.} \end{cases}$$

19.3 Show that if $G = X + jY$, where $X \sim \mathcal{N}(0, \sigma_f^2)$ and $Y \sim \mathcal{N}(0, \sigma_f^2)$, then $A = |G|^2 = X^2 + Y^2$ has density

$$f_A(a) = \begin{cases} \dfrac{1}{2\sigma_f^2} e^{-a/2\sigma_f^2} & a \geq 0 \\[2mm] 0 & \text{otherwise.} \end{cases}$$

A is said to be a *chi-squared* (χ^2) random variable with two degrees of freedom.

19.4 Show that (19.5) is correct.

19.5 Using the 4×4 orthogonal design $\mathcal{O}_4$, show that the matrix $H_{j,\text{eff}}$ of (19.17) is proportional to an orthogonal matrix.

19.6 Let $\mathcal{U}$ be a complex orthogonal design of size n. Show that by replacing each complex variable $x_i = x_i^1 + jx_i^2$ in the matrix with the 2×2 matrix $\begin{bmatrix} x_i^1 & x_i^2 \\ x_i^2 & x_i^1 \end{bmatrix}$, that a $2n \times 2n$ real matrix $\mathcal{O}$ is formed that is a real orthogonal design of size $2n$.

Conclude that complex orthogonal designs of size n exist only if $n = 2$ or $n = 4$.

19.7 Show that a modified delay diversity scheme which uses codewords formed by

$$A = \begin{bmatrix} a_1 & a_2 & \cdots & a_{n-1} & a_n \\ a_n & a_1 & a_2 & \cdots & a_{n-1} \end{bmatrix},$$

which is a tail-biting code, does not satisfy the rank criterion and hence does not achieve full diversity.

19.8 [26] For the set of space-time codes

$$A_1 = \begin{bmatrix} x_1 & x_2^* \\ x_2 & x_1^* \end{bmatrix} \quad A_2 = \begin{bmatrix} x_1 & -x_2 \\ x_2 & x_1 \end{bmatrix} \quad A_3 = \begin{bmatrix} x_1^* & -x_2 \\ x_2^* & x_1 \end{bmatrix} \quad A_4 = \begin{bmatrix} x_1 & x_2 \\ x_2 & x_1 \end{bmatrix}$$

(a) Find the diversity order of each code, assuming that the transmitted symbols are selected independently and uniformly from a 4-QAM alphabet and that the receiver has a single antenna.

(b) Determine which of these codes allows for scalar detection at the receiver.

(c) For those codes having full diversity, determine the coding gain.

19.9   References

Propagation modeling, leading to the Rayleigh channel model, is described in [216]; see also [422], [26], and [352]. The Jakes model which produced Figure 19.2 is described in [216]. Our discussion of MIMO channels, and the discussion of diversity following from it, was drawn from [26]. Additional coding-related discussions relating to multiple-receiver diversity appear in [99,402,425,479,487].

The Alamouti scheme is described in [8]. The generalization to orthogonal designs is described in [434]. The rank criterion is presented following [435]. This paper also presents a thorough discussion of space-time trellis codes and hybrid codes capable of dealing with either slow or fast fading channels.

The paper [435] presents many designs of space-time trellis codes, as does [322]. Combined interference suppression and space-time coding is also discussed in the latter.

References

[1] "3GPP TS 25.222 v15.0.0 3rd Generation Partnership Project; Technical Specification Group Radio Access Network; Multiplexing and channel coding (TDD)," Jun. 2018.

[2] "3GPP TS 36.212 v 15.6.0 3rd Generation Partnership Project; Technical Specification Group Radio Access Network; Evolved Univeral Terrestrial Radio Access (e-utra); Multiplexing and Channel Coding," https://portal.3gpp.org/desktopmodules/Specifications/SpecificationDetails.aspx?specificationId=2426, Jun. 2019.

[3] A. Abbasfar, D. Divsalar, and K. Yao, "*Accumulate Repeat Accumulate Codes*," in *Proceedings of the 2004 IEEE GlobeCom Conference*, Dallas, TX, Nov. 2004.

[4] ——, "Accumulate Repeat Accumulate Codes," *IEEE Trans. Commun.*, vol. **55**, no. 4, pp. 692–702, Apr. 2007.

[5] D. Agarwal and A. Vardy, "The Turbo Decoding Algorithm and its Phase Trajectories," *IEEE Trans. Inf. Theory*, vol. **47**, no. 2, pp. 699–722, Feb. 2001.

[6] S. M. Aji and R. J. McEliece, "The Generalized Distributive Law," *IEEE Trans. Inf. Theory*, vol. **46**, no. 2, pp. 325–343, Mar. 2000.

[7] A. Alamdar-Yazdi and F. R. Kschischang, "A Simplified Successive-Cancellation Decoder for Polar Codes," *IEEE Commun. Lett.*, vol. **15**, no. 12, pp. 1378–1380, Dec. 2011.

[8] S. Alamouti, "A Simple Transmit Diversity Technique for Wireless Communications," *IEEE J. Selected Areas Commun.*, vol. **16**, no. 8, pp. 1451–1458, Oct. 1998.

[9] M. Alsan and E. Telatar, "A Simple Proof of Polarization and Polariztion for Non-Stationary Memoryless Channels," *IEEE Trans. Inf. Theory*, vol. **62**, no. 9, pp. 4873–4878, Sep. 2016.

[10] B. Ammar, B. Honary, Y. Kou, J. Xu, and S. Lin, "Construction of Low-Density Parity-Check Codes Based on Incomplete Designs," *IEEE Trans. Inf. Theory*, vol. **50**, no. 6, pp. 1257–1268, Jun. 2004.

[11] J. B. Anderson and A. Svensson, *Coded Modulation Systems*. New York: Kluwer Academic/Plenum, 2003.

[12] K. Andrews, C. Heegard, and D. Kozen, "A Theory of Interleavers," Cornell University Department of Computer Science, TR97-1634, Jun. 1997.

[13] ——, "Interleaver Design Methods for Turbo Codes," in *Proceedings of the 1998 International Symposium on Information Theory*, Cambridge, MA, 1998, p. 420.

[14] S. Ar, R. Lipton, R. Rubinfeld, and M. Sudan, "Reconstructing Algebraic Functions from Mixed Data," in *Proceedings of the 33rd Annual IEEE Symposium on Foundations of Computer Science*, Pittsburgh, PA, 1992, pp. 503–512.

[15] M. Ardakani, "Efficient Analysis, Design, and Decoding of Low-Density Parity-Check Codes," Ph.D. dissertation, University of Toronto, Electrical and Computer Engineering Department, 2004.

[16] E. Arıkan, "Channel Polarization: A Method for Constructing Capacity-Achieving Codes for Symmetric Binary-Input Memoryless Channels," *IEEE Trans. Inf. Theory*, vol. **55**, no. 7, pp. 3051–3073, Jul. 2009.

[17] ——, "Systematic Polar Encoding," *IEEE Commun. Lett.*, vol. **15**, no. 8, pp. 860–862, Aug. 2011.

[18] E. Arıkan and E. Telatar, "On the Rate of Channel Polarization," in *2009 IEEE International Symposium on Information Theory*, Seoul, Jun 2009, pp. 1493–1495.

[19] D. Augot and L. Pecquet, "A Hensel Lifting to Replace Factorization in List-Decoding of Algebraic-Geometric and Reed–Solomon Codes," *IEEE Trans. Inf. Theory*, vol. **46**, pp. 2605–2614, Nov. 2000.

[20] L. Bahl, J. Cocke, F. Jelinek, and J. Raviv, "Optimal Decoding of Linear Codes for Minimizing Symbol Error Rate," *IEEE Trans. Inf. Theory*, vol. **20**, pp. 284–287, Mar. 1974.

[21] L. R. Bahl, C. D. Cullum, W. D. Frazer, and F. Jelinek, "An Efficient Algorithm for Computing Free Distance," *IEEE Trans. Inf. Theory*, vol. **12**, no. 3, pp. 437–439, May 1972.

[22] A. Balatsoukas-Stimming, M. B. Parizi, and A. Burg, "LLR-Based Successive Cancellation List Decoding of Polar Codes," *IEEE Trans. Signal Process.*, vol. **63**, no. 19, pp. 5165–5179, Oct. 2015.

[23] A. Barbulescu and S. Pietrobon, "Interleaver Design for Turbo Codes," *Electron. Lett.*, vol. **30**, no. 25, p. 2107, 1994.

[24] ——, "Terminating the Trellis of Turbo-Codes in the Same State," *Electron. Lett.*, vol. **31**, no. 1, pp. 22–23, 1995.

[25] J. R. Barry, "The BCJR Algorithm for Optimal Equalization," http://users.ece.gatech.edu/~barry/6603/handouts/Notes[SS1] on the BCJR Algorithm.

[26] J. R. Barry, E. A. Lee, and D. G. Messerschmitt, *Digital Communication*, 3rd ed. Boston: Kluwer Academic, 2004.

[27] G. Battail and J. Fang, "D'ecodage pondéré optimal des codes linéaires en blocs," *Annales des Télécommunications*, vol. **41**, pp. 580–604, Nov. 1986.

[28] R. E. Bellman and S. E. Dreyfus, *Applied Dynamic Programming*. Princeton, NJ: Princeton University Press, 1962.

[29] S. Benedetto, R. Garello, M. Mondin, and M. Trott, "Rotational Invariance of Trellis Codes Part II: Group Codes and Decoders," *IEEE Trans. Inf. Theory*, vol. **42**, pp. 766–778, May 1996.

[30] S. Benedetto and G. Montorsi, "Average Performance of Parallel Concatenated Block Codes," *Electron. Lett.*, vol. **31**, no. 3, pp. 156–158, 1995.

[31] ——, "Design of Parallel Concatenated Convolutional Codes," *IEEE Trans. Commun.*, vol. **44**, no. 5, pp. 591–600, 1996.

[32] ——, "Unveiling Turbo Codes: Some Results on Parallel Concatenated Coding Schemes," *IEEE Trans. Inf. Theory*, vol. **42**, no. 2, pp. 409–428, Mar. 1996.

[33] E. Berlekamp, *Algebraic Coding Theory*. New York: McGraw-Hill, 1968.

[34] E. Berlekamp, "Bounded Distance +1 Soft-Decision Reed-Solomon Decoding," *IEEE Trans. Inf. Theory*, vol. **42**, no. 3, pp. 704–720, May 1996.

[35] E. R. Berlekamp, R. J. McEliece, and H. C. van Tilborg, "On the Inherent Intractability of Certain Coding Problems," *IEEE Trans. Inf. Theory*, vol. **24**, no. 3, pp. 384–386, May 1978.

[36] E. Berlekamp, H. Rumsey, and G. Solomon, "On the Solution of Algebraic Equations over Finite Fields," *Inf. Control*, vol. **10**, pp. 553–564, 1967.

[37] C. Berrou, *Codes, Graphs, and Systems*. Boston: Kluwer Academic, 2002, ch. The Mutations of Convolutional Coding (Around the Trellis), p. 4.

[38] C. Berrou and A. Gaviuex, "Near Optimum Error Correcting Coding and Decoding: Turbo Codes," *IEEE Trans. Commun.*, vol. **44**, no. 10, pp. 1261–1271, Oct. 1996.

[39] C. Berrou, A. Glavieux, and P. Thitimajshima, "Near Shannon Limit Error-Correcting Coding and Decoding: Turbo Codes," in *Proceedings of the 1993 IEEE International Conference on Communications*, Geneva, Switzerland, 1993, pp. 1064–1070.

[40] E. Biglieri, D. Divsalar, P. J. McLane, and M. K. Simon, *Introduction to Trellis-Coded Modulation, with Applications*. New York: Macmillan, 1991.

[41] P. Billingsley, *Probability and Measure*. New York: Wiley, 1986.

[42] G. Birkhoff and S. MacLane, *A Survey of Modern Algebra*, 3rd ed. New York: Macmillan, 1965.

[43] U. Black, *The V Series Recommendations, Protocols for Data Communications*. New York: McGraw-Hill, 1991.

[44] R. E. Blahut, *Fast Algorithms for Digital Signal Processing*. Reading, MA: Addison-Wesley, 1985.

[45] ——, *Theory and Practice of Error Control Codes*. Reading, MA: Addison-Wesley, 1983.

[46] ——, *Algebraic Codes on Lines, Planes, and Curves*. London: Cambridge University Press, 2008.

[47] I. Blake and K. Kith, "On the Complete Weight Enumerator of Reed-Solomon Codes," *SIAM J. Disc. Math*, vol. **4**, no. 2, pp. 164–171, May 1991.

[48] R. Bose and D. Ray-Chaudhuri, "On a Class of Error-Correcting Binary Codes," *Inf. Control*, vol. **3**, pp. 68–79, 1960.

[49] S. Boyd and L. VandenBerghe, *Convex Optimization*. London: Cambridge University Press, 2004.

[50] A. E. Brouwer, "Bounds on the Minimum Distance of q-ary Linear Codes," http://www.win.tue.nl/~aeb/voorlincod.html, 2004.

[51] J. Bucklew and R. Radecke, "On the Monte Carlo Simulation of Digital Communication Systems in Gaussian Noise," *IEEE Trans. Commun.*, vol. **51**, no. 2, pp. 267–274, Feb. 2003.

[52] H. O. Burton, "Inversionless Decoding of Binary BCH Codes," *IEEE Trans. Inf. Theory*, vol. **17**, no. 4, pp. 464–466, Jul. 1971.

[53] H. Burton and E. Weldon, "Cylic Product Codes," *IEEE Trans. Inf. Theory*, vol. **11**, pp. 433–440, Jul. 1965.

[54] J. B. Cain, G. C. Clark, and J. M. Geist, "Punctured Convolutional Codes of Rate $(n - 1)/n$ and Simplified Maximum Likelihood Decoding," *IEEE Trans. Inf. Theory*, vol. **25**, no. 1, pp. 97–100, Jan. 1979.

[55] A. R. Calderbank and N. J. A. Sloane, "An Eight-Dimensional Trellis Code," *IEEE Trans. Info. Theory*, vol. **74**, no. 5, pp. 757–759, May 1986.

[56] ——, "New Trellis Codes Based on Lattices and Cosets," *IEEE Trans. Inf. Theory*, vol. **33**, no. 2, pp. 177–195, Mar. 1987.

[57] M. Cedervall and R. Johannesson, "A Fast Algorithm for Computing Distance Spectrum of Convolutional Codes," *IEEE Trans. Inf. Theory*, vol. **35**, pp. 1146–1159, 1989.

[58] W. Chambers, "Solution of Welch–Berlekamp Key Equation by Euclidean Algorithm," *Electron. Lett.*, vol. **29**, no. 11, p. 1031, 1993.

[59] W. Chambers, R. Peile, K. Tsie, and N. Zein, "Algorithm for Solving the Welch-Berlekamp Key-Equation with a Simplified Proof," *Electron. Lett.*, vol. **29**, no. 18, pp. 1620–1621, 1993.

[60] D. Chase, "A Class of Algorithms for Decoding Block Codes With Channel Measurement Information," *IEEE Trans. Inf. Theory*, vol. **18**, no. 1, pp. 168–182, Jan. 1972.

[61] O. Chauhan, T. Moon, and J. Gunther, "Accelerating the Convergence of Message Passing on Loopy Graphs Using Eigenmessages," in *Proceedings of the 37th Annual Asilomar Conference on Signals, Systems, and Computers*, Monterey, CA, 2003, pp. 79–83.

[62] J. Chen, A. Dholakia, E. Eleftherious, M. Fossorier, and X.-Y. Hu, "Reduced Complexity Decoding of LDPC codes," *IEEE Trans. Commun.*, vol. **53**, no. 8, pp. 1288–1299, Aug. 2005.

[63] L. Chen, L. Lan, I. Djurdjevic, S. Lin, and K. Abdel-Ghaffar, "An algebraic method for constructing quasi-cyclic ldpc codes," in *Proceedings of the International Symposium on Information Theory and its Applications (ISITA)*, Parma, Oct. 2004, pp. 535–539.

[64] ——, "Near-Shannon Limit Quasi-Cyclic Low Density Parity Check Codes," *IEEE Trans. Commun.*, vol. **52**, no. 7, pp. 1038–1042, Jul. 2004.

[65] K. Chen, K. Niu, and J. Lin, "Improved Successive Cancellation Decoding of Polar Codes," *IEEE Trans. Commun.*, vol. **61**, no. 8, pp. 3100–3107, Aug. 2013.

[66] L. Chen, J. Xu, I. Djurdjevic, and S. Lin, "Near-Shannon Limit Quasi-Cyclic Low-Density Parity-Check Codes," *IEEE Trans. Commun.*, vol. **52**, no. 7, pp. 1038–1042, Jul. 2004.

[67] N. Chen and Z. Yan, "Reduced-Complexity Reed–Solomon Decoders Based on Cyclotomic FFTs," *IEEE Signal Process. Lett.*, vol. **16**, no. 4, p. 279, 2009.

[68] G. T. Chen, Z. Zhang, C. Zhong, and L. Zhang, "A Low Complexity Encoding Algorithm for Systematic Polar Codes," *IEEE Commun. Lett.*, vol. **20**, no. 7, pp. 1277–1280, Jul. 2016.

[69] P. Chevillat and J. D.J. Costello, "A Multiple Stack Algorithm for Erasurefree Decoding of Convolutional Codes," *IEEE Trans. Commun.*, vol. **25**, pp. 1460–1470, Dec. 1977.

[70] R. Chien, "Cyclic Decoding Procedures for BoseChaudhuri–Hocquenghem Codes," *IEEE Trans. Inf. Theory*, vol. **10**, pp. 357–363, 1964.

[71] K. L. Chung, *A Course in Probability Theory*. New York, NY: Academic Press, 1974.

[72] S.-Y. Chung, G. D. Forney, Jr., T. J. Richardson, and R. Urbanke, "On the Design of Low-Density Parity-Check Codes within 0.0045 dB of the Shannon Limit," *IEEE Commun. Lett.*, vol. **5**, no. 2, pp. 58–60, Feb. 2001.

[73] S.-Y. Chung, T. J. Richardson, and R. L.Urbanke, "Analysis of Sum-Product Decoding of Low-Density Parity-Check Codes Using Gaussian Approximation," *IEEE Trans. Inf. Theory*, vol. **47**, no. 2, pp. 657–670, Feb. 2001.

[74] T. K. Citron, "Algorithms and Architectures for Error Correcting Codes," Ph.D. dissertation, Stanford, Aug. 1986.

[75] C. A. Cole, S. G. Wilson, E. K. Hall, and T. R. Giallorenzi, "A General Method for Finding Low Error Rates of LDPC Codes," arXiv:cs/0605051v1 [cs.IT] 11 May 2006, Mar. 2018.

[76] J. H. Conway and N. J. A. Sloane, "Fast Quantizing and Decoding Algorithms for Lattice Quantizers and Codes," *IEEE Trans. Inf. Theory*, vol. **28**, no. 2, pp. 227–232, Mar. 1982.

[77] ——, "Voronoi Regions of Lattices, Second Moments of Polytopes, and Quantization," *IEEE Trans. Inf. Theory*, vol. **28**, no. 2, pp. 211–226, Mar. 1982.

[78] ——, "On the Voronoi Regions of Certain Lattices," *SIAM J. Alg. Discrete Methods*, vol. **5**, no. 3, pp. 294–305, Sep. 1984.

[79] ——, *Sphere Packings, Lattices, and Groups*, 2nd ed. New York: Springer-Verlag, 1993.

[80] ——, "A Fast Encoding Method for Lattice Codes and Quantizers," *IEEE Trans. Inf. Theory*, vol. **29**, no. 6, pp. 820–824, Nov. 1983.

[81] ——, "Soft Decoding Techniques for Codes and Lattices, Including the Golay Code and the Leech Lattice," *IEEE Trans. Inf. Theory*, vol. **32**, no. 1, pp. 41–50, Jan. 1986.

[82] T. M. Cover and J. A. Thomas, *Elements of Information Theory*, 2nd ed. New York: Wiley, 2006.

[83] D. Cox, J. Little, and D. O'Shea, *Ideals, Varieties, and Algorithms*. New York: Springer-Verlag, 1992.

[84] ——, *Using Algebraic Geometry*. New York: Springer-Verlag, 1998.

[85] J. Crockett, T. Moon, J. Gunther, and O. Chauhan, "Accelerating LDPC Decoding Using Multiple-Cycle Eigenmessages," in *Asilomar Conference on Signals, Systems, and Computers*, Monterey, CA, Nov. 2004, pp. 1141–1145.

[86] D. Dabiri and I. F. Blake, "Fast Parallel Algorithms for Decoding Reed-Solomon Codes Based on Remainder Polynomials," *IEEE Trans. Inf. Theory*, vol. **41**, no. 4, pp. 873–885, Jul. 1995.

[87] E. Dahlman, S. Parkvall, J. Sköld, and P. Beming, *3G Evolution: HSPA and LTE for Mobile Broadband*. New York, NY: Academic Press, 2008.

[88] F. Daneshgaran, M. Laddomada, and M. Mondin, "Interleaver Design for Serially Concatenated Convolutional Codes: Theory and Applications," *IEEE Trans. Inf. Theory*, vol. **50**, no. 6, pp. 1177–1188, Jun. 2004.

[89] D. G. Daut, J. W. Modestino, and L. D. Wismer, "New Short Constraint Length Convolutional Code Constructions for Selected Rational Rates," *IEEE Trans. Inf. Theory*, vol. **28**, no. 5, pp. 794–800, Sep. 1982.

[90] M. C. Davey and D. J. MacKay, "Low Density Parity Check Codes Over $GF(q)$," *IEEE Comput. Lett.*, vol. **2**, no. 6, pp. 165–167, 1998.

[91] J. R. Deller, J. G. Proakis, and J. H. L. Hansen, *Discrete–Time Processing of Speech Signals*. New York: Macmillan, 1993.

[92] P. Delsarte, "An Algebraic Approach to Coding Theory," Phillips, Research Reports Supplements, no. 10, 1973.

[93] C. Di, D. Proietti, E. Telatar, R. Richardson, and Urbanke, "Finite Length Analysis of Low-Density Parity-Check Codes on the Binary Erasure Channel," *IEEE Trans. Inf. Theory*, vol. **48**, pp. 1570–1579, Jun. 2002.

[94] D. Divsalar, H. Jin, and R. McEliece, "Coding Theorems for Turbo-like Codes," in *Proceedingsof the 36th Annual Allerton Conference*, Monticello, IL, 1998, pp. 201–210.

[95] D. Divsalar, and S. D. C. Jones, "Construction of Protograph LDPC Codes with Linear Minimum Distance," in *International Symposium on Information Theory*, Seattle, WA, 2006.

[96] D. Divsalar, C. Jones, S. Dolinar, and J. Thorpe, "Protograph Based LDPC Codes with Minimum Distance Growing Linearly with Block Size," in *2005 IEEE Global Telecommunications Conference*, St. Louis, MO, 2005.

[97] D. Divsalar and R. McEliece, "Effective Free Distance of Turbo Codes," *Electron. Lett.*, vol. **32**, no. 5, pp. 445–446, Feb. 1996.

[98] D. Divsalar and F. Pollara, "Turbo Codes for Deep-Space Communications," Jet Propulsion Laboratory, JPL TDA Progress Report 42-122, pp. 42–120, Feb. 1995.

[99] D. Divsalar and M. Simon, "The Design of Coded MPSK for Fading Channel: Performance Criteria," *IEEE Trans. Commun.*, vol. **36**, pp. 1013–1021, Sep. 1988.

[100] I. Djurdjevic, J. Xu, K. Abdel-Ghaffar, and S. Lin, "A Class of Low-Density Parity-Check Codes Constructed Based on Reed-Solomon Codes with Two Information Symbols," *IEEE Commun. Lett.*, vol. **7**, no. 7, pp. 317–319, Jul. 2003.

[101] L. Dolecek, P. Lee, Z. Zhang, V. Anantharam, B. Nikolic, and M. Wainright, "Predicting Error Floors of Stuctured LDPC Codes: Deterministic Bounds and Estimates," *IEEE J. Sel Areas Commun.*, vol. **27**, no. 6, pp. 908–917, Aug. 2009.

[102] S. Dolinar and D. Divsalar, "Weight Distributions for Turbo Codes Using Random and Nonrandom Permutations," Jet Propulsion Laboratory, JPL TDA Progress Report 42-121, pp. 42–120, Aug. 1995.

[103] B. Dorsch, "A Decoding Algorithm for Binary Block Codes and *j*-ary Output Channels," *IEEE Trans. Inf. Theory*, vol. **20**, pp. 391–394, May 1974.

[104] "ETSI EN 300 744 v1.6.1 Digital Video Broadcasting (DVB); Framing Structure, Channel Coding and Modulation for Digital Terretrial Television," https://www.etsi.org/deliver/etsi_en/300700_300799/300744/01.06.01_60/en_300744v010601p.pdf, 2009.

[105] "DVB: ETSI EN 302 755 v1.2.1 Digital Video Broadcasting (DVB); Frame Structure Channel Coding and Modulation for a Second Generation Digital Terrestrial Television Broadcasting System (DVB-T2)," https://www.etsi.org/deliver/etsi_en/302700_302799/302755/01.02.01_40/en_302755v010201o.pdf, 2010.

[106] H. El Gamal and J. A. Roger Hammons, "Analyzing the Turbo Decoder Using the Gaussian Approximation," *IEEE Trans. Inf. Theory*, vol. **47**, no. 2, pp. 671–686, Feb. 2001.

[107] E. Eldon, "Euclidean Geometry Cyclic Codes," in *Proceedings of the Symposium on Combinatorial Mathematics*. Chapel Hill, NC: University of North Carolina, Apr. 1967.

[108] M. Elia, "Algebraic Decoding of the (23,12,7) Golay Code," *IEEE Trans. Inf. Theory*, vol. **33**, no. 1, pp. 150–151, Jan. 1987.

[109] P. Elias, "Coding for Noisy Channels," *IRE Conv. Rept. Pt. 4*, New York, NY, pp. 37–47, 1955.

[110] ——, "*List Decoding For Noisy Channels*," Research Laboratory of Electronics, MIT,, Cambridge, MA, Technical Report 335, 1957.

[111] M. Eyuboglu and G. D. Forney, Jr., "Trellis Precoding: Combined Coding, Precoding and Shaping for Intersymbol Interference Channels," *IEEE Trans. Inf. Theory*, vol. **36**, pp. 301–314, Mar. 1992.

[112] D. Falconer, "*A Hybrid Sequential and Algebraic Decoding Scheme*," Ph.D. dissertation. MIT, Cambridge, MA, 1967.

[113] R. M. Fano, "A Heuristic Discussion of Probabilistic Decoding," *IEEE Trans. Inf. Theory*, vol. **9**, pp. 64–73, Apr 1963.

[114] S. Federenko, "A Simple Algorithm for Decoding Reed-Solomon Codes and its Relation to the Welch Berlekamp Algorithm," *IEEE Trans. Inf. Theory*, vol. **51**, no. 3, pp. 1196–1198, Mar. 2005.

[115] ——, "Correction to A Simple Algorithm for Decoding Reed-Solomon Codes and its Relation to the Welch Berlekamp Algorithm," *IEEE Trans. Inf. Theory*, vol. **52**, no. 3, p. 1278, Mar. 2006.

[116] S. Fedorenko, "A Simple Algorithm for Decoding Both Errors and Erasures in Reed–Solomon Codes," in *Proceedings of the Workshop: Coding Theory Days in St. Petersburg*. , Sep. 2008, pp. 18–21.

[117] J. Feldman, M. J. Wainwright, and D. R. Karger, "Using Linear Programming to Decode Binary Linear Codes," *IEEE Trans. Inf. Theory*, vol. **51**, no. 3, pp. 954–972, Mar. 2005.

[118] A. J. Felstrom and K. S. Zigangirov, "Time-Varying Periodic Convolutional Codes with Low-Density Parity-Check Matrix," *IEEE Trans. Inf. Theory*, vol. **45**, no. 6, pp. 2181–2191, Sep. 1999.

[119] G.-L. Feng, "A Fast Special Factorization Algorithm in the Sudan Decoding Procedure for Reed-Solomon Codes," in *Proceedings of the 31st Allerton Conference on Communications, Control, and Computing*, Monticello, IL, 2000, pp. 593–602.

[120] G.-L. Feng and K. K. Tzeng, "A Generalized Euclidean Algorithm for Multisequence Shift-Register Synthesis," *IEEE Trans. Inf. Theory*, vol. **35**, no. 3, pp. 584–594, May 1989.

[121] ——, "A Generalization of the Berlekamp-Massey Algorithm for Multisequence Shift-Register Synthesis with Applications to Decoding Cyclic Codes," *IEEE Trans. Inf. Theory*, vol. **37**, no. 5, pp. 1274–1287, Sep. 1991.

[122] W. Feng and Z. Yu, "Error Evaluator for Inversionless Berlekamp-Massey Algorithm in Reed-Solomon Decoders," United States Patent 7,249,310, Jul. 2007.

[123] M. Ferrari and S. Bellini, "Importance Sampling Simulation of Concatenated Block Codes," *Proc. IEE*, vol. **147**, pp. 245–251, Oct. 2000.

[124] P. Fire, *A Class of Multiple-Error-Correcting Binary Codes For Non-Independent Errors*, Sylvania Report No. RSL-E-2, Sylvania Electronic Defense Laboratory, Reconnaissance Systems Division, Mountain View, CA, Mar. 1959.

[125] G. D. Forney, Jr., "On Decoding BCH Codes," *IEEE Trans. Inf. Theory*, vol. **11**, no. 4, pp. 549–557, Oct. 1965.

[126] ——, *Concatenated Codes*. Cambridge, MA: MIT Press, 1966.

[127] ——, "Generalized Minimum Distance Decoding," *IEEE Trans. Inf. Theory*, vol. **12**, no. 2, pp. 125–131, Apr. 1966.

[128] ——, "The Viterbi Algorithm," *Proc. IEEE*, vol. **61**, no. 3, pp. 268–278, Mar. 1973.

[129] ——, "Convolutional Codes III: Sequential Decoding," *Inf. Control*, vol. **25**, pp. 267–297, Jul. 1974.

[130] ——, "Coset Codes — Part I: Introduction and Geometrical Classification," *IEEE Trans. Inf. Theory*, vol. **34**, no. 5, pp. 1123–1151, Sep. 1988.

[131] ——, "Coset Codes — Part II: Binary Lattices and Related Codes," *IEEE Trans. Inf. Theory*, vol. **34**, no. 5, pp. 1152–1187, Sep. 1988.

[132] ——, "Geometrically Uniform Codes," *IEEE Trans. Inf. Theory*, vol. **37**, pp. 1241–1260, 1991.

[133] ——, "Trellis Shaping," *IEEE Trans. Inf. Theory*, vol. **38**, no. 2, pp. 281–300, Mar. 1992.

[134] ——, "Maximum-Likelihood Sequence Estimation of Digital Sequences in the Presence of Intersymbol Interference," *IEEE Trans. Inf. Theory*, vol. **IT-18**, no. 3, pp. 363–378, May 1972.

[135] ——, "Convolutional Codes I: Algebraic Structure," *IEEE Trans. Inf. Theory*, vol. **16**, no. 6, pp. 720–738, Nov. 1970.

[136] G. D. Forney, Jr., L. Brown, M. V. Eyuboglu, and I. J. LMoran, "The V.34 High-Speed Modem Standard," *IEEE Commun Mag*, vol. **34**, pp. 28–33, Dec. 1996.

[137] G. D. Forney, Jr. and M. Eyuboglu, "Combined Equalization and Coding Using Precoding," *IEEE Commun. Mag.*, vol. **29**, no. 12, pp. 25–34, Dec. 1991.

[138] G. D. Forney, Jr., R. G. Gallager, G. R. Lang, F. M. Longstaff, and S. U. Qureshi, "Efficient Modulation for Band–Limited Channels," *IEEE J. Sel Areas Commun.*, vol. **2**, no. 5, pp. 632–647, Sep. 1984.

[139] G. Foschini and M. Gans, "On Limits of Wireless Communications in a Fading Environment," *Wirel. Pers. Commun.*, vol. **6**, no. 3, pp. 311–355, Mar. 1998.

[140] M. P. Fossorier, F. Burkert, S. Lin, and J. Hagenauer, "On the Equivalence Between SOVA and Max-Log-MAP Decodings," *IEEE Commun. Lett.*, vol. **2**, no. 5, pp. 137–139, May 1998.

[141] M. P. Fossorier and S. Lin, "Chase-Type and GMD-Type Coset Decoding," *IEEE Trans. Commun.*, vol. **48**, pp. 345–350, Mar. 2000.

[142] M. Fossorier and S. Lin, "Soft-Decision Decoding of Linear Block Codes Based on Ordered Statistics," *IEEE Trans. Inf. Theory*, vol. **41**, pp. 1379–1396, Sep. 1995.

[143] ——, "Differential Trellis Decoding of Convolutional Codes," *IEEE Trans. Inf. Theory*, vol. **46**, pp. 1046–1053, May 2000.

[144] J. B. Fraleigh, *A First Course in Abstract Algebra*. Reading, MA: Addison-Wesley, 1982.

[145] B. Friedland, *Control System Design: An Introduction to State-Space Design*. New York: McGraw-Hill, 1986.

[146] B. L. Gal, C. Leroux, and C. Jego, "Multi-gb/s Software Decoding of Polar Codes," *IEEE Trans. Signal Process.*, vol. **63**, no. 2, pp. 349–359, Jan. 2015.

[147] R. G. Gallager, *Information Theory and Reliable Communication*. New York: Wiley, 1968.

[148] ——, "Low-Density Parity-Check Codes," *IRE Trans. Inf. Theory*, vol. **IT-8**, pp. 21–28, Jan. 1962.

[149] ——, *Low-Density Parity-Check Codes*. Cambridge, MA: M.I.T. Press, 1963.

[150] S. Gao, "A new algorithm for decoding Reed-Solomon codes," in *Communications, Information, and Network Security*, V. Bhargava, H. Poor, V. Tarokh, and S. Yoon, Eds. Kluwer, 2003, vol. **712**, pp. 55–68.

[151] S. Gao and M. A. Shokrollahi, "Computing Roots of Polynomials over Function Fields of Curves," in *Coding Theory and Cryptography*, D. Joyner, Ed. Springer-Verlag, 1999, pp. 214–228.

[152] J. Geist, "An Empirical Comparison of Two Sequential Decoding Algorithms," *IEEE Trans. Commun. Tech.*, vol. **19**, pp. 415–419, Aug. 1971.

[153] ——, "Search Properties for Some Sequential Decoding Algorithms," *IEEE Trans. Inf. Theory*, vol. **19**, pp. 519–526, Jul. 1973.

[154] A. Geramita and J. Seberry, *Orthogonal Designs, Quadratic Forms and Hadamard Matrices*, ser. Lecture Notes in Pure and Applied Mathematics, vol. 43. New York and Basel: Marcel Dekker, 1979.

[155] P. Giard, G. Sarkis, A. Balatsoukas-Stimming, Y. Fan, C. Tsui, A. Burg, C. Thibeault, and W. J. Gross, "Hardware Decoders for Polar Codes: An Overview," in *2016 IEEE International Symposium on Circuits and Systems (ISCAS)*, Montreal, QC, May 2016, pp. 149–152.

[156] P. Giard, G. Sarkis, C. Leroux, C. Thibeault, and W. J. Gross, "Low-Latency Software Polar Decoders," *CoRR*, vol. abs/1504.00353, 2015. [Online]. http://arxiv.org/abs/1504.00353

[157] P. Giard, G. Sarkis, C. Thibeault, and W. J. Gross, "237 Gbit/s Unrolled Hardware Polar Decoder," *Electron. Lett.*, vol. **51**, pp. 762–763. 2015.

[158] R. Gold, "Maximal Recursive Sequences with 3-Valued Recursive Cross-Correlation Functions," *IEEE Trans. Info. Theory*, vol. **14**, no. 1, pp. 154–156, 1968.

[159] ——, "Optimal Binary Sequences for Spread Spectrum Multiplexing," *IEEE Trans. Inf. Theory*, vol. **13**, no. 4, pp. 619–621, Oct. 1967.

[160] S. W. Golomb, *Shift Register Sequences*. San Francisco: Holden–Day, 1967.

[161] G. H. Golub and C. F. Van Loan, *Matrix Computations*, 3rd ed. Baltimore, MD: Johns Hopkins University Press, 1996.

[162] M. Gonzàlez-Lopez, L. Castedo, and J. García-Frías, "BICM for MIMO Systems Using Low-Density Generator Matrix (LDGM) Codes," in *Proceedings of the International Conference on Acoustics, Speech, and Signal Processing*. Montreal, QC: IEEE Press, May 2004.

[163] V. Goppa, "Codes on Algebraic Curves," *Soviet Math. Dokl.*, vol. **24**, pp. 170–172, 1981.

[164] ——, *Geometry and Codes*. Dordrecht: Kluwer Academic, 1988.

[165] D. Gorenstein and N. Zierler, "A Class of Error Correcting Codes in p^m Symbols," *J. Soc. Ind. Appl. Math.*, vol. **9**, pp. 207–214, Jun. 1961.

[166] R. Graham, D. Knuth, and O. Patashnik, *Concrete Mathematics*. Reading, MA: Addison-Wesley, 1989.

[167] S. Gravel, "Using Symmetries to Solve Asymmetric Problems," Ph.D. dissertation, Cornell Univerity, 2009.

[168] S. Gravel and V. Elser, "Divide and Concur: A General Approach to Constraint Satisfaction," *Phys. Rev.*, vol. **78**, p. 36706, 2008.

[169] W. Gross, "Are Polar Codes Practical?" https://youtu.be/S3bZOSlNFGo, Feb. 10, 2015.

[170] J. Gunther, M. Ankapura, and T. Moon, "Blind Turbo Equalization Using a Generalized LDPC Decoder," in *Digital Signal Processing Workshop*. Taos Ski Valley, NM: IEEE Press , 2004, pp. 206–210.

[171] F. Guo and H. Henzo, "Reliability Ratio Based Weighted Bit-Flipping Decoding for Low-Density Parity-Check Codes," *IEEE Electron Lett.*, vol. **40**, no. 21, pp. 1356–1358, 2004.

[172] V. Guruswami and M. Sudan, "Improved Decoding of Reed-Solomon Codes and Algebraic Geometry Codes," *IEEE Trans. Inf. Theory*, vol. **45**, no. 6, pp. 1757–1767, Sep. 1999.

[173] D. Haccoun and M. Ferguson, "Generalized Stack Algorithms for Decoding Convolutional Codes," *IEEE Trans. Inf. Theory*, vol. **21**, pp. 638–651, Apr. 1975.

[174] J. Hagenauer, "Rate Compatible Punctured Convolutional Codes and their Applications," *IEEE Trans. Commun.*, vol. **36**, pp. 389–400, Apr. 1988.

[175] ——, "Source-Controlled Channel Decoding," *IEEE Trans. Commun.*, vol. **43**, no. 9, pp. 2449–2457, Sep. 1995.

[176] J. Hagenauer and P. Hoeher, "A Viterbi Algorithm with Soft-Decision Outputs and its Applications," in *Proceedings of. Globecom*, Dallas, TX, Nov. 1989, pp. 1680–1686.

[177] J. Hagenauer, E. Offer, and L. Papke, *Reed Solomon Codes and their Applications*. New York: IEEE Press, 1994, ch. Matching Viterbi Decoders and Reed-Solomon Decoders in a Concatenated System.

[178] ——, "Iterative Decoding of Binary Block and Convolutional Codes," *IEEE Trans. Inf. Theory*, vol. **42**, no. 2, pp. 429–445, Mar. 1996.

[179] D. Haley, A. Grant, and J. Buetefuer, "Iterative encoding of Low-Density Parity-Check Codes," in *Global Communication Conference (GLOBECOM)*. Taipei: IEEE Press, Nov. 2002, pp. 1289–1293.

[180] R. W. Hamming, *Coding and Information Theory*, 2nd ed. Englewood Cliffs, NJ: Prentice-Hall, 1986.

[181] R. Hamming, "Error Detecting and Error Correcting Codes," *Bell Syst. Tech. Jl*, vol. **29**, pp. 41–56, 1950.

[182] A. R. Hammonds, Jr., P. V. Kummar, A. Calderbank, N. Sloane, and P. Solè, "The $\mathbb{Z}_4$-Linearity of Kerdock, Preparata, Goethals, and Related Codes," *IEEE Trans. Inf. Theory*, vol. **40**, no. 2, pp. 301–319, Mar. 1994.

[183] Y. Han, "LDPC Coding for Magnetic Storage: Low-floor Decoding Algorithms, System Design, and Performance Analysis," Ph.D. dissertation, ECE Department, University of Arizona, Aug. 2008.

[184] Y. Han, C. Hartmann, and C. Chen, "Efficient Priority-First Search Maximum-Likelihood Soft-Decision Decoding of Linear Block Codes," *IEEE Trans. Inf. Theory*, vol. **39**, pp. 1514–1523, Sep. 1993.

[185] Y. Han, C. Hartmann, and K. Mehrota, "Decoding Linear Block Codes Using a Priority-First Search: Performance Analysis and Suboptimal Version," *IEEE Trans. Inf. Theory*, vol. **44**, pp. 1233–1246, May 1998.

[186] Y. Han and W. Ryan, "Low-Floor Decoders for LDPC Codes," *IEEE Trans. Commun.*, vol. **57**, no. 5, May 2009.

[187] L. Hanzo, T. Liew, and B. Yeap, *Turbo Coding, Turbo Equalization and Space-Time Coding for Transmission Over Fading Channels*. West Sussex, England: Wiley, 2002.

[188] H. Harashima and H. Miyakawa, "Matched-Transmission Technique for Channels with Intersymbol Interference," *IEEE Trans. Commun.*, vol. **20**, pp. 774–780, Aug. 1972.

[189] C. R. P. Hartmann and L. D. Rudolph, "An Optimum Symbol-by-Symbol Decoding Rule for Linear Codes," *IEEE Trans. Inf. Theory*, vol. **22**, no. 5, pp. 514–517, Sep. 1976.

[190] C. Hartmann and K. Tzeng, "Generalizations of the BCH Bound," *Inf. Contr.*, vol. **20**, no. 5, pp. 489–498, Jun. 1972.

[191] C. Hartmann, K. Tzeng, and R. Chen, "Some Results on the Minimum Distance of Cyclic Codes," *IEEE Trans. Inf. Theory*, vol. **18**, no. 3, pp. 402–409, May 1972.

[192] H. Hasse, "Theorie der höen Differentiale in einem algebraishen Funcktionenköper mit volkommenem Kostantenköerp bei Charakteristic," *J. Reine. Ang. Math.*, pp. 50–54, 175.

[193] C. Heegard, "Randomizer for Byte-Wise Scrambling of Data," United States Patent 5,745,522, Apr. 1998.

[194] C. Heegard and S. B. Wicker, *Turbo Coding*. Boston: Kluwer Academic, 1999.

[195] J. Heller, "Short Constraint Length Convolutional Codes," *Jet Propulsion Labs, Space Programs Summary* 37–54, vol. **III**, pp. 171–177, 1968.

[196] J. Heller and I. M. Jacobs, "Viterbi Decoding for Satellite and Space Communications," *IEEE Trans. Commun. Tech.*, vol. **19**, no. 5, pp. 835–848, Oct. 1971.

[197] F. Hemmati and D. Costello, "Truncation Error Probability in Viterbi Decoding," *IEEE Trans. Commun.*, vol. **25**, no. 5, pp. 530–532, May 1977.

[198] R. W. Hinton, "Finite-Length Scaling of Multi-Edge Type LDPC Ensembles," Ph.D. dissertation, University of Virginia, 2011.

[199] M. Hirotomo, Y. Konishi, and M. Morii, "Approximate Examination of Trapping Sets of LDPC Codes using the Probabilistic Algorithm," in *Proceedingsof the International Symposium on Information Theory and its applications (ISITA)*, Auckland, Dec. 2008, pp. 754–759.

[200] B. Hochwald and W. Sweldons, "Differential Unitary Space-Time Modulation," Bell Labs, Lucent Technology Technical Report, 1999.

[201] A. Hocquenghem, "Codes Correcteurs D'erreurs," *Chiffres*, vol. **2**, pp. 147–156, 1959.

[202] R. A. Horn and C. A. Johnson, *Matrix Analysis*. Cambridge: Cambridge University Press, 1985.

[203] X.-Y. Hu, E. Eleftheriou, and D. Arnold, "Regular and Irregular Progressive Edge-Growth Tanner Graphs," *IEEE Trans. Inf. Theory*, vol. **51**, no. 1, pp. 386–398, Jan. 2005.

[204] Z. Huang and C. Heegard, "Quadrature Amplitude Modulated Data for Standard Bandwidth Television Channel," United States Patent 5,511,096, Apr. 1996.

[205] B. Hughes, "Differential Space-Time Modulation," in *Proceedings of the IEEE Wireless Communications and Networking Conference*, New Orleans, LA, Sep. 1999.

[206] T. W. Hungerford, *Algebra*. New York: Springer-Verlag, 1974.

[207] N. Hussami, S. Korada, and R. Urbanke, "Performance of Polar Codes for Channel and Source Coding," in *Proceediongsof the 2009 IEEE International Symposium on Information Theory*. Seoul: IEEE Press, 2009.

[208] S. Ikeda, T. Tanaka, and S. Amari, "Information Geometry of Turbo and Low-Density Parity-Check Codes," *IEEE Trans. Inf. Theory*, vol. **50**, no. 6, pp. 1097–1114, Jun. 2004.

[209] K. A. S. Immink, "Runlength-Limited Sequences," *Proc. IEEE*, vol. **78**, pp. 1745–1759, 1990.

[210] ——, *Coding Techniques for Digital Recorders*. Englewood Cliffs, NJ: Prentice-Hall, 1991.

[211] K. Immink, *Reed Solomon Codes and their Applications*. New York: IEEE Press, 1994, ch. RS Code and the Compact Disc.

[212] International Telegraph and Telephone Consultive Committee (CCITT), "Recommendation v.29: 9600 Bits per Second Modem Standardized for Use on Point-to-Point 4-Wire Leased Telephone-Type Circuits," in *Data Communication over the Telephone Network "Blue Book"*. Geneva: International Telecommunications Union, 1988, vol. **VIII**, pp. 215–227.

[213] *"IEEE J. Sel. Areas Commun. (Special Issue on Importance Sampling),"* vol. **11**, no. 3, pp. 289–476, Apr. 1993.

[214] I. Jacobs and E. Berlekamp, "A Lower Bound to the Distribution of Computation for Sequential Decoding," *IEEE Trans. Inf. Theory*, vol. **13**, pp. 167–174, Apr. 1967.

[215] N. Jacobson, *Basic Algebra I*. New York: Freeman, 1985.

[216] W. Jakes, *Microwave Mobile Communication*. New York, NY: IEEE Press, 1993.

[217] S. Jayasooriya, M. Shirvanimoghaddam, L. Ong, G. Lechner, and S. Johnson, "A New Density Evolution Approximation for LDPC and Mult-Edge Type LDPC Codes," *IEEE Trans. Commun.*, vol. **64**, no. 10, pp. 4044–4056, Oct. 2016.

[218] F. Jelinek, "An Upper Bound on Moments of Sequential Decoding Effort," *IEEE Trans. Inf. Theory*, vol. **15**, pp. 140–149, Jan. 1969.

[219] ——, "Fast Sequential Decoding Algorithm Using a Stack," *IBM J. Res. Dev.*, pp. 675–685, Nov. 1969.

[220] F. Jelinek and J. Cocke, "Bootstrap Hybrid Decoding for Symmetric Binary Input Channels," *Inf. Control.*, vol. **18**, pp. 261–281, Apr. 1971.

[221] M. Jiang, Z. Shi, and Y. Chen, "An Improvement on the Moodified Weighted Bit Flipping Decoding Algorithm for LDPC Codes," *IEEE Commun. Lett.*, vol. **9**, no. 9, pp. 814–816, 2005.

[222] M. Jiang, C. Zhao, Z. Shi, and Y. Chen, "An Improvement on the Modified Weighted Bit Flipping Decoding Algorithm for LDPC Codes," *IEEE Commun. Lett.*, vol. **9**, no. 9, pp. 814–816, 2005.

[223] H. Jin, A. Khandekar, and R. McEliece, "Irregular Repeat-Accumulate Codes," in *Proceedings 2nd International Symposium on Turbo Codes and Related Topics*, Brest, France, Sep. 2000, pp. 1–8.

[224] O. Joerssen and H. Meyr, "Terminating the Trellis of Turbo-Codes," *Electron. Lett.*, vol. 30, no. 16, pp. 1285–1286, 1994.

[225] R. Johannesson, "Robustly Optimal Rate One-Half Binary Convolutional Codes," *IEEE Trans. Inf. Theory*, vol. 21, pp. 464–468, Jul. 1975.

[226] ——, "Some Long Rate One-Half Binary Convolutional Codes with an Optimum Distance Profile," *IEEE Trans. Inf. Theory*, vol. 22, pp. 629–631, Sep. 1976.

[227] ——, "Some Rate 1/3 and 1/4 Binary Convolutional Codes with an Optimum Distance Profile," *IEEE Trans. Inf. Theory*, vol. 23, pp. 281–283, Mar. 1977.

[228] R. Johannesson and E. Paaske, "Further Results on Binary Convolutional Codes with an Optimum Distance Profile," *IEEE Trans. Inf. Theory*, vol. 24, pp. 264–268, Mar. 1978.

[229] R. Johannesson and P. Stahl, "New Rate 1/2, 1/3, and 1/4 Binary Convolutional Encoders with Optimum Distance Profile," *IEEE Trans. Inf. Theory*, vol. 45, pp. 1653–1658, Jul. 1999.

[230] R. Johannesson and Z.-X. Wan, "A Linear Algebra Approach to Minimal Convolutional Encoders," *IEEE Trans. Inf. Theory*, vol. 39, no. 4, pp. 1219–1233, Jul. 1993.

[231] R. Johannesson and K. Zigangirov, *Fundamentals of Convolutional Coding*. Piscataway, NJ: IEEE Press, 1999.

[232] S. Johnson and S. Weller, "Regular Low-Density Parity-Check Codes from Combinatorial Designs," in *Proceedings of the 2001 Information Theory Workshop*, Cairns, Australia, Sep. 2001, pp. 90–92.

[233] ——, "Construction of Low-Density Parity-Check Codes from Kirkman Triple Systems," in *Global Communications Conference (GLOBECOM)*, Nov. 25–29, 2001, pp. 970–974.

[234] ——, "Regular Low-Density Parity-Check Codes from Combinatorial Designs," in *Information Theory Workshop*, Cairns, 2001, pp. 90–92.

[235] ——, "High-Rate LDPC Codes from Unital Designs," in *Global Telecommunications Conference (GLOBECOM)*. San Francisco, CA: IEEE, 2003, pp. 2036–2040.

[236] ——, "Resolvable 2-Designs for Regular Low-Density Parity Check Codes," *IEEE Trans. Commun.*, vol. 51, no. 9, pp. 1413–1419, Sep. 2003.

[237] C. Jones, S. Dolinar, K. Andrews, D. Divsalar, Y. Zhang, and W. Wyan, "Functions and Architectures for LDPC Decoding," in *IEEE Information Theory Workshop*, Tahoe City, CA, Sep. 2–6 2007, pp. 577–583.

[238] P. Jung and M. Nasshan, "Dependence of the Error Performance of Turbo-Codes on the Interleaver Structure in Short Frame Transmission Systems," *Electron. Lett.*, vol. 30, no. 4, pp. 287–288, Feb. 1994.

[239] T. Kailath, *Linear Systems*. Englewood Cliffs, NJ: Prentice-Hall, 1980.

[240] N. Kamiya, "On Algebraic Soft-Decision Decoding Algorithms for BCH codes," *IEEE Trans. Inf. Theory*, vol. 47, no. 1, pp. 45–58, Jan. 2001.

[241] T. Kaneko, T. Nishijima, and S. Hirasawa, "An Improvement of Soft-Decision Maximum-Likelihood Decoding Algorithm Using Hard-Decision Bounded-Distance Decoding," *IEEE Trans. Inf. Theory*, vol. 43, pp. 1314–1319, Jul. 1997.

[242] T. Kaneko, T. Nishijima, H. Inazumi, and S. Hirasawa, "An Efficient Maximum Likelihood Decoding of Linear Block Codes with Algebraic Decoder," *IEEE Trans. Inf. Theory*, vol. 40, pp. 320–327, Mar. 1994.

[243] T. Kasami, "A Decoding Method for Multiple-Error-Correcting Cyclic Codes by Using Threshold Logics," in *Conference Record of the Information Processing Society of Japan (in Japanese)*, Tokyo, Nov. 1961.

[244] ——, "A Decoding Procedure for Multiple-Error-Correction Cyclic Codes," *IEEE Trans. Inf. Theory*, vol. 10, pp. 134–139, Apr. 1964.

[245] T. Kasami, S. Lin, and W. Peterson, "Some Results on the Weight Distributions of BCH Codes," *IEEE Trans. Inf. Theory*, vol. 12, no. 2, p. 274, Apr. 1966.

[246] T. Kasami, S. Lin, and W. W. Peterson, "Polynomial Codes," *IEEE Trans. Inf. Theory*, vol. 14, no. 6, pp. 807–814, Nov. 1968.

[247] D. E. Knuth, *The Art of Computer Programming*. Reading, MA: Addison-Wesley, 1997, vol. 1.

[248] R. Koetter, "On Algebraic Decoding of Algebraic-Geometric and Cyclic Codes," Ph.D. dissertation, University of Linkoping, 1996.

[249] R. Koetter, A. C. Singer, and M. Tüchler, "Turbo Equalization," *IEEE Signal Process. Mag.*, no. 1, pp. 67–80, Jan. 2004.

[250] R. Koetter and A. Vardy, "The Structure of Tail-Biting Trellises: Minimality and Basic Principles," *IEEE Trans. Inf. Theory*, vol. 49, no. 9, pp. 2081–2105, Sep. 2003.

[251] R. Koetter and A. Vardy, "Algebraic Soft-Decision Decoding of Reed–Solomon Codes," *IEEE Trans. Inf. Theory*, vol. 49, no. 11, pp. 2809–2825, Nov. 2003.

[252] V. Kolesnik, "Probability Decoding of Majority Codes," *Prob. Pered. Inf.*, vol. 7, pp. 3–12, Jul. 1971.

[253] R. Kötter, "Fast Generalized Minimum Distance Decoding of Algebraic-Geometry and Reed–Solomon Codes," *IEEE Trans. Inf. Theory*, vol. 42, no. 3, pp. 721–737, May 1996.

[254] Y. Kou, S. Lin, and M. Fossorier, "Low-Density Parity-Check Codes Based on Finite Geometries: A Rediscovery and New Results," *IEEE Trans. Inf. Theory*, vol. 47, no. 13, pp. 2711–2736, Nov. 2001.

[255] F. R. Kschischang, B. J. Frey, and H.-A. Loeliger, "Factor Graphs and the Sum-Product Algorithm," *IEEE Trans. Inf. Theory*, vol. 47, no. 2, pp. 498–519, Feb. 2001.

[256] L. Lan, Y. Tai, S. Lin, and K. Abdel-Ghaffar, "A Trellis-Based Method for Removal of Cycles from Bipartite Graphs and Construction of Low Density Parity Check Codes," *IEEE Commun. Lett.*, vol. 8, no. 7, pp. 443–445, Jul. 2004.

[257] L. Lan, Y. Tai, S. Lin, B. Memari, and B. Honary, "New Construction of Quasi-Cyclic LDPC Codes Based on Special Classes of BIBDs for the AWGN and Binary Erasure Channels," *IEEE Trans. Commun.*, vol. 56, no. 1, pp. 39–48, Jan. 2008.

[258] L. Lan, L.-Q. Zen, Y. Tai, L. Chen, S. Lin, and K. Abdel-Ghaffar, "Construction of Quasi-Cyclic LDPC Codes for AWGN and Binary Erasure Channels: A Finite Field Approach," *IEEE Trans. Inf. Theory*, vol. 53, no. 7, pp. 2429–2458, Jul. 2007.

[259] L. Lan, L.-Q. Zeng, Y. Tai, S. Lin, and K. Abdel-Ghaffar, "Construction of Quasi-Cyclic LDPC Codes for AWGN and Binary Erasure Channels Based on Finite Fields and Affine Permutations," in *Proceedings of the IEEE Symposium on Information Theory*, Adelaide, Sep. 2005, pp. 2285–2289.

[260] R. Laroia, N. Farvardin, and S. A. Tretter, "On Optimal Shaping of Multidimensional Constellations," *IEEE Trans. Inf. Theory*, vol. **40**, no. 4, pp. 1044–1056, Jul. 1994.

[261] K. Larsen, "Short Convolutional Codes with Maximal Free Distance for Rates 1/2, 1/3 and 1/4," *IEEE Trans. Inf. Theory*, vol. **19**, pp. 371–372, May 1973.

[262] L. Lee, *Convolutional Coding: Fundamentals and Applications*. Boston, MA: Artech House, 1997.

[263] C. Lee and W. Wolf, "Implementation-Efficient Reliability Ratio Based Weighted Bit-Flipping Decoding for LDPC Codes," *IEEE Electron. Lett.*, vol. **41**, no. 13, pp. 755–757, 2005.

[264] C. Leroux, A. J. Raymond, G. Sarkis, and W. J. Gross, "A Semi-Parallel Successive-Cancellation Decoder for Polar Codes," *IEEE Trans. Signal Process*, vol. **61**, no. 2, pp. 289–299, Jan. 2013.

[265] C. Leroux, I. Tal, A. Vardy, and W. Gross, "Hardware Architectures for Successive Cancellation Decoding of Polar Codes," in *Proceedings of the IEEE International Conference oN Acoustics, Speech, and Signal Processing (ICASSP)*, Prague, 2011, pp. 1665–1668.

[266] N. Levanon, *Radar Principles*. New York: Wiley Interscience, 1988.

[267] Z. Li, L. Chen, L. Zeng, S. Lin, and W. Fong, "Efficient Encoding of Quasi-Cyclic Low-Density Parity-Check Codes," *IEEE Trans. Commun.*, vol. **54**, no. 1, pp. 71–81, Jan. 2006.

[268] R. Lidl and H. Niederreiter, *Finite Fields*. Reading, MA: Addison-Wesley, 1983.

[269] ——, *Introduction to Finite Fields and their Applications*. Cambridge: Cambridge University Press, 1986.

[270] T.-C. Lin, P.-D. Chen, and T. Trieu-Kien, "Simplified Procedure for Decoding Nonsystematic Reed-Solomon Codes over $GF(2^m)$ Using Euclid's Algorithm and the Fast Fourier Transform," *IEEE Trans. Commun.*, vol. **57**, no. 6, pp. 1588–1592, 2009.

[271] S. Lin and D. J. Costello, *Error Control Coding: Fundamentals and Applications*. Englewood Cliffs, NJ: Prentice-Hall, 1983.

[272] S. Lin and D. J. Costello, Jr., *Error Control Coding: Fundamentals and Applications*, 2nd ed. Englewood Cliffs, NJ: Prentice-Hall, 2004.

[273] S. Lin, T. Kasami, T. Fujiwara, and M. Fossorier, *Trellises and Trellis-based Decoding Algorithms for Linear Block Codes*. Boston: Kluwer Academic Publishers, 1998.

[274] S. Lin and E. Weldon, "Further Results on Cyclic Product Codes," *IEEE Trans. Inf. Theory*, vol. **6**, no. 4, pp. 452–459, Jul. 1970.

[275] D. Lind and B. Marcus, *Symbolic Dynamics and Coding*. Cambridge: Cambridge University Press, 1995.

[276] J. Lodge, P. Hoeher, and J. Hagenauer, "The Decoding of Multidimensional Codes Using Separable MAP 'Filters'," in *Proceedings of the 16th Biennial Symposium on Communication*. Kingston, ON: Queen's University, May 1992, pp. 343–346.

[277] J. Lodge, R. Young, P. Hoeher, and J. Hagenauer, "Separable MAP 'Filters' for the Decoding of Product and Concatenated Codes," in *Proceedings of the IEEE International Conference on Communication*, Geneva, Switzerland, May 1993, pp. 1740–1745.

[278] T. D. Lookabaugh and R. M. Gray, "High-Resolution Quantization Theory and the Vector Quantizer Advantage," *IEEE Trans. Inf. Theory*, vol. **35**, no. 5, pp. 1020–1033, Sep. 1989.

[279] D. Lu and K. Yao, "Improved Importance Sampling Technique for Efficient Simulation of Digital Communication Systems," *IEEE J. Sel. Areas Commun.*, vol. **6**, no. 1, pp. 67–75, Jan. 1988.

[280] ——, "Improved Importance Sampling Technique for Efficient Simulation of Digital Communication Systems," *IEEE J. Spec. Areas Commun.*, vol. **6**, no. 1, pp. 67–75, Jan. 1988.

[281] M. Luby, "LT codes," in *The 43rd Annual IEEE Symposium on Foundations of Computer Science, 2002. Proceedings*, Nov. 2002, pp. 271–280.

[282] M. G. Luby, M. Miteznmacher, M. A. Shokrollahi, and D. A. Spielman, "Improved Low-Density Parity-Check Codes Using Irregular Graphs," *IEEE Trans. Inf. Theory*, vol. **47**, no. 2, pp. 585–598, Feb. 2001.

[283] M. Luby, M. Mitzenmacher, M. Shokrollahi, D. Spielman, and V. Stemann, "Practical Loss-Resilient Codes," in *Proceedings of the ACM Symposium on Theory of Computing*, 1997, pp. 150–159.

[284] X. Ma and X.-M. Wang, "On the Minimal Interpolation Problem and Decoding RS Codes," *IEEE Trans. Inf. Theory*, vol. **46**, no. 4, pp. 1573–1580, Jul. 2000.

[285] H. Ma and J. Wolf, "On Tailbiting Convolutional Codes," *IEEE Trans. Commun.*, vol. **34**, pp. 104–111, Feb. 1986.

[286] D. J. MacKay, http://www.inference.phy.cam.ac.uk/mackay/CodesFiles.html.

[287] ——, "Near Shannon Limit Performance of Low Density Parity Check Codes," *Electron. Lett.*, vol. **33**, no. 6, pp. 457–458, Mar. 1997.

[288] ——, "Good Error-Correcting Codes Based on Very Sparse Matrices," *IEEE Trans. Inf. Theory*, vol. **45**, no. 2, pp. 399–431, Mar. 1999.

[289] D. MacKay and M. Postol, "Weaknesses of Margulis and Ramanujan-Margulis Low-Density Parity-Check Codes," in *Proceedings of the conference on Mathematical Foundations of Computer Science and Information Technology (MFCSIT)*, Galway, 2002.

[290] D. J. MacKay and R. M. Neal, "Good Codes Based on Very Sparse Matrices," in *Cryptography and Coding 5th IMA Conference*, ser. Lecture Notes in Computer Science, C. Boyd, Ed. Springer, 1995, vol. **1025**, pp. 100–111.

[291] F. MacWilliams, "A Theorem on the Distribution of Weights in a Systematic Code," *Bell Syst. Tech. J.*, vol. **42**, pp. 79–94, 1963.

[292] F. MacWilliams and N. Sloane, *The Theory of Error-Correcting Codes*. Amsterdam: North-Holland, 1977.

[293] G. Margulis, "Explicit Construction of Graphs Without Short Cycles and Low Density Codes," *Combinatorica*, vol. **2**, no. 1, pp. 71–78, 1982.

[294] S. J. Mason, "Feedback Theory — Some Properties of Signal Flow Graphs," *Proceedings IRE*, pp. 1144–1156, Sep. 1953.

[295] J. L. Massey, "Shift-Register Synthesis and BCH Decoding," *IEEE Trans. Inf. Theory*, vol. **IT-15**, no. 1, pp. 122–127, 1969.

[296] ——, "Variable-Length Codes and the Fano Metric," *IEEE Trans. Inf. Theory*, vol. **IT-18**, no. 1, pp. 196–198, Jan. 1972.

[297] J. Massey, *Threshold Decoding*. Cambridge, MA: MIT Press, 1963.

[298] ——, "Coding and Modulation in Digital Communications," in *Proceedings of the International Zurich Seminar on Digital Communications*, Zurich, Switzerland, 1974, pp. E2(1)–E2(4).

[299] J. Massey and M. Sain, "Inverses of Linear Sequential Circuits," *IEEE Trans. Comput.*, vol. **17**, pp. 330–337, Apr. 1968.

[300] R. McEliece, *The Theory of Information and Coding*, ser. Encyclopedia of Mathematics and its Applications. Reading, MA: Addison-Wesley, 1977.

[301] ——, "A Public-Key Cryptosystem Based on Algebraic Coding Theory," JPL, DSN Progress Report 42–44, January and February 1978.

[302] ——, "The Guruswami-Sudan Algorithm for Decoding Reed–Solomon Codes," JPL, IPN Progress Report 42-153, May 15, 2003, http://iprn.jpl.nasa.gov/progress_report/42-153/.

[303] R. J. McEliece, E. R. Rodemich, H. Rumsey, Jr., and L. R. Welch, "New Upper Bounds on the Rate of a Code via the Delsarte-MacWilliams Inequalities," *IEEE Trans. Inf. Theory*, vol. **23**, no. 2, pp. 157–166, Mar. 1977.

[304] R. J. McEliece and J. B. Shearer, "A Property of Euclid's Algorithm and an Application to Padè Approximation," *SIAM J. Appl. Math*, vol. **34**, no. 4, pp. 611–615, Jun 1978.

[305] R. McEliece and L. Swanson, *Reed–Solomon Codes and their Applications*. New York: IEEE Press, 1994, ch. Reed-Solomon Codes and the Exploration of the Solar System, pp. 25–40.

[306] J. Meggitt, "Error Correcting Codes and their Implementations," *IRE Trans. Inf. Theory*, vol. **7**, pp. 232–244, Oct. 1961.

[307] A. Michelson and A. Levesque, *Error Control Techniques for Digital Communication*. New York: Wiley, 1985.

[308] O. Milenkovic, E. Soljanin, and P. Whiting, "Asymptotic Spectra of Trapping Sets in Regular and Irregular LDPC Code Ensembles," *IEEE Trans. Inf. Theory*, vol. **53**, no. 1, pp. 39–55, Jan. 2007.

[309] W. Mills, "Continued Fractions and Linear Recurrences," *Math.Comput.*, vol. **29**, no. 129, pp. 173–180, Jan. 1975.

[310] M. Mitchell, "Coding and Decoding Operation Research," G.E. Advanced Electronics Final Report on Contract AF 19 (604)-6183, Air Force Cambridge Research Labs, Cambridge, MA, Technical Report, 1961.

[311] ——, "Error-Trap Decoding of Cyclic Codes," G.E. Report No. 62MCD3, General Electric Military Communications Department, Oklahoma City, OK, Technical Report, Dec. 1962.

[312] M. Mitzenmacher, "Digital Fountains: A Survey and Look Forward," in *Information Theory Workshop*, San Antonio, TX, 2004, pp. 271–276.

[313] T. Moon, "Wavelets and Lattice Spaces," in *International Symposium on Information Theory*, Whistler, BC, Sep. 17–22 1995, p. 250.

[314] ——, "On General Linear Block Code Decoding Using the Sum-Product Iterative Decoder," *IEEE Commun. Lett.*, vol. **8**, no. 6, pp. 383–385, 2004.

[315] T. K. Moon and S. Budge, "Bit-Level Erasure Decoding of Reed-Solomon Codes Over $GF(2^n)$," in *Proceedings of the Asilomar Conference on Signals and Systems*, Pacific Grove, CA, 2004, pp. 1783–1787.

[316] T. K. Moon, J. S. Crockett, J. H. Gunther, and O. S. Chauhan, "Iterative Decoding using Eigenmessages," *IEEE Trans. Commun.*, vol. **57**, pp. 3618–3628, 2009.

[317] T. Moon and J. Gunther, "On the Equivalence of Two Welch-Berlekamp Key Equations and their Error Evaluators," *IEEE Trans. Inf. Theory*, vol. **51**, no. 1, pp. 399–401, 2004.

[318] T. Moon and W. Stirling, *Mathematical Methods and Algorithms for Signal Processing*. Englewood Cliffs, NJ: Prentice-Hall, 2000.

[319] T. K. Moon and W. C. Stirling, *Mathematical Methods and Algorithms for Signal Processing*. Upper Saddle River, NJ: Prentice-Hall, 2000.

[320] M. Morii and M. Kasahara, "Generalized Key-Equation of Remainder Decoding Algorithm for Reed-Solomon Codes," *IEEE Trans. Inf. Theory*, vol. **38**, no. 6, pp. 1801–1807, Nov. 1992.

[321] D. Muller, "Application of Boolean Switching Algebra to Switching Circuit Design," *IEEE Trans. Comput.*, vol. **3**, pp. 6–12, Sep. 1954.

[322] A. Naguib, N. Seshadri, and A. Calderbank, "Increasing Data Rate over Wireless Channels," *IEEE Signal Process. Mag.*, pp. 76–92, May 2000.

[323] R. Nasser and E. Telatar, "Fourier Analysis of MAC Polarization," *IEEE Trans. Inf. Theory*, vol. **63**, no. 6, pp. 3600–3620, Jun. 2017.

[324] K. Niu, K. Chen, J. Lin, and Q. Zhang, "Polar Codes: Primary Concepts and Practical Decoding Algorithms," *IEEE Commun. Mag.*, vol. **52**, no. 7, pp. 192–203, Jul. 2014.

[325] I. Niven, H. S. Zuckerman, and H. L. Montgomery, *An Introduction to the Theory of Numbers*, 5th ed. New York: Wiley, 1991.

[326] J. Odenwalder, "Optimal Decoding of Convolutional Codes," Ph.D. dissertation, Department of Systems Sciences, School of Engineering and Applied Sciences, University of California, Los Angeles, 1970.

[327] V. Olshevsky and A. Shokrollahi, "A Displacement Structure Approach to Efficient Decoding of Reed–Solomon and Algebraic-Geometric Codes," in *Proceedings of the 31st ACM Symposium on Theory of Computing*, Atlanta, GA, May 1999.

[328] A. V. Oppenheim and R. W. Schafer, *Discrete-Time Signal Processing*. Englewood Cliffs, NJ: Prentice-Hall, 1989.

[329] A. Orlitsky, R. Urbanke, K. Viswanathan, and J. Zhang, "Stopping Sets and the Girth of Tanner Graphs," in *Proceedings of the IEEE International Symposium on Information Theory*, Lausanne, Jun. 2002.

[330] A. Orlitsky and K. Viswanathan, "Stopping Set Distribution of LDPC Code Ensembles," *IEEE Trans. Inf. Theory*, vol. **51**, no. 3, pp. 929–953, 2005.

[331] E. Paaske, "Short Binary Convolutional Codes with Maximal Free Distance For Rate 2/3 and 3/4," *IEEE Trans. Inf. Theory*, vol. **20**, pp. 683–689, Sep. 1974.

[332] A. Pamuk and E. Arıkan, "A Two Phase Successive Cancellation Decoder Architecture for Polar Codes," in *IEEE International Symposium on Information Theory (ISIT)*, Istanbul, 2013, pp. 957–961.

[333] A. Papoulis, *Probability, Random Variables, and Stochastic Processes*, 2nd ed.. New York: McGraw Hill, 1984.

[334] N. Patterson, "The Algebraic Decoding of Goppa Codes," *IEEE Trans. Inf. Theory*, vol. **21**, no. 2, pp. 203–207, Mar. 1975.

[335] L. Perez, J. Seghers, and D. Costello, "A Distance Spectrum Interpretation of Turbo Codes," *IEEE Trans. Inf. Theory*, vol. **42**, pp. 1698–1709, Nov. 1996.

[336] W. Peterson, "Encoding and Error-Correction Procedures for the Bose-Chaudhuri Codes," *IEEE Trans. Inf. Theory*, vol. **6**, pp. 459–470, 1960.

[337] W. W. Peterson, *Error-Correcting Codes*. Cambridge, MA and New York: MIT Press and Wiley, 1961.

[338] W. Peterson and E. Weldon, *Error Correction Codes*. Cambridge, MA: MIT Press, 1972.

[339] S. S. Pietrobon and D. J. Costello, "Trellis Coding with Multidimensional QAM Signal Sets," *IEEE Trans. Inf. Theory*, vol. **29**, no. 2, pp. 325–336, Mar. 1993.

[340] S. S. Pietrobon, R. H. Deng, A. Lafanechère, G. Ungerboeck, and D. J. Costello, "Trellis-Coded Multidimensional Phase Modulation," *IEEE Trans. Inf. Theory*, vol. **36**, no. 1, pp. 63–89, Jan. 1990.

[341] S. Pietrobon, G. Ungerböck, L. Perez, and D. Costello, "Rotationally Invariant Nonlinear Trellis Codes for Two-Dimensional Modulation," *IEEE Trans. Inf. Theory*, vol. **40**, no. 6, pp. 1773–1791, 1994.

[342] M. Plotkin, "Binary Codes with Specified Minimum Distances," *IEEE Trans. Inf. Theory*, vol. **6**, pp. 445–450, 1960.

[343] Y. Polyanskey, "Channel Coding: Non-Asymptotic Fundamental Limits," Ph.D. dissertation, Princeton University, Nov. 2010.

[344] H. V. Poor, *An Introduction to Signal Detection and Estimation*. New York: Springer-Verlag, 1988.

[345] J. Porath and T. Aulin, "Algorithm Construction of Trellis Codes," *IEEE Trans. Commun.*, vol. **41**, no. 5, pp. 649–654, 1993.

[346] A. B. Poritz, "Hidden Markov Models: A Guided Tour," in *Proceedings of ICASSP*, New York, NY 1988.

[347] G. Pottie and D. Taylor, "A Comparison of Reduced Complexity Decoding Algorithms for Trellis Codes," *IEEE J. Sel Areas Commun.*, vol. **7**, no. 9, pp. 1369–1380, 1989.

[348] E. Prange, "Cyclic Error-Correcting Codes in Two Symbols," Air Force Cambridge Research Center, Cambridge, MA, Technical Report TN-57-103, Sep. 1957.

[349] ——, "Some Cyclic Error-Correcting Codes with Simple Decoding Algorithms," Air Force Cambridge Research Center, Cambridge, MA, Technical Report TN-58-156, Apr. 1958.

[350] ——, "The Use of Coset Equivalence in the Analysis and Decoding of Group Codes," Air Force Cambridge Research Center, Cambridge, MA, Technical Report TN-59-164, 1959.

[351] O. Pretzel, *Codes and Algebraic Curves*. Oxford: Clarendon Press, 1998.

[352] J. G. Proakis, *Digital Communications*. New York:McGraw Hill, 1995.

[353] J. G. Proakis and M. Salehi, *Communication Systems Engineering*. Upper Saddle River, NJ: Prentice-Hall, 1994.

[354] ——, *Communication Systems Engineering*. Englewood Cliffs, NJ: Prentice-Hall, 1994.

[355] A. Pusane, A. Jimenez-Feltstrom, A. Sridharam, A. Lentmaier, and M. Ziganarov, "Implementation Aspects of LDPC Convolutional Codes," *IEEE Trans. Commun.*, vol. **56**, no. 7, pp. 1060–1069, Jul. 2008.

[356] M. Püschel and J. Moura, "The Algebraic Approach to the Discrete Cosine and Sine Transforms and their Fast Algorithms," *SIAM J. Comput.*, vol. **32**, no. 5, pp. 1280–1316, 2003.

[357] R. M. Pyndiah, "Near-Optimum Decoding of Product Codes: Block Turbo Codes," *IEEE Trans. Commun.*, vol. **46**, no. 8, pp. 1003–1010, Aug. 1998.

[358] R. Pyndiah, A. Glavieux, A. Picart, and S. Jacq, "Near Optimum Decoding of Product Codes," in *IEEE Global Telecommunications Conference*. San Francisco: IEEE, Nov. 1994, pp. 339–343.

[359] L. R. Rabiner, "A Tutorial on Hidden Markov Models and Selected Applications in Speech Recognition," *Proc. IEEE*, vol. **77**, no. 2, pp. 257–286, Feb. 1989.

[360] T. V. Ramabadran and S. S. Gaitonde, "A Tutorial On CRC Computations," *IEEE Micro*, vol. **8**, no. 4, pp. 62–75, Aug. 1988.

[361] J. Ramsey, "Realization of Optimum Interleavers," *IEEE Trans. Inf. Theory*, vol. **16**, pp. 338–345, May 1970.

[362] I. Reed, "A Class of Multiple-Error-Correcting Codes and a Decoding Scheme," *IEEE Trans. Inf. Theory*, vol. **4**, pp. 38–49, Sep. 1954.

[363] I. Reed, R. Scholtz, T. Truong, and L. Welch, "The Fast Decoding of Reed-Solomon Codes Using Fermat Theoretic Transforms and Continued Fractions," *IEEE Trans. Inf. Theory*, vol. **24**, no. 1, pp. 100–106, Jan. 1978.

[364] I. Reed and G. Solomon, "Polynomial Codes over Certain Finite Fields," *J. Soc. Ind. Appl. Math*, vol. **8**, pp. 300–304, 1960.

[365] I. Reed, T.-K. Truong, X. Chen, and X. Yin, "Algebraic Decoding of the (41,21,9) Quadratic Residue Code," *IEEE Trans. Inf. Theory*, vol. **38**, no. 3, pp. 974–986, May 1992.

[366] I. Reed, X. Yin, and T.-K. Truong, "Algebraic Decoding of (32,16,8) Quadratic Residue Code," *IEEE Trans. Inf. Theory*, vol. **36**, no. 4, pp. 876–880, Jul. 1990.

[367] M. Rice, *Digital Communications: A Discrete-Time Approach*, 2nd ed. (published by author). ISBN 9781790588545, 2017.

[368] T. Richardson, "Multi-Edge type LDPC Codes," Workshop Honoring Professor R. McEliece on his 60th Birthday. Pasadena, CA: California Institute of Technology, May 24–25, 2002.

[369] ——, "Error floors of LDPC codes," in *Proceedings of the 41st Allerton Conference on Communications, Control, and Computing*, , Monticello, IL: Allterton House, Oct. 2003.

[370] T. Richardson and V. Novichkov, "Methods and Apparatus for Decoding LDPC Codes," U.S. Patent 6,633,856, Oct. 14 2003.

[371] T. Richardson and V. Novichkov, "Node Processors For Use in Parity Check Decoders," U.S. Patent 6938196, Aug. 30, 2005, Flarion Technologies.

[372] ——, "Method and Apparatus for Decoding LDPC Codes," U.S. Patent 7,133,853, Nov. 7, 2006.

[373] T. J. Richardson, M. A. Shokrollahi, and R. L. Urbanke, "Design of Capacity-Approaching Irregular Low-Density Parity-Check Codes," *IEEE Trans. Inf. Theory*, vol. **47**, no. 2, pp. 619–637, Feb. 2001.

[374] T. J. Richardson and R. L. Urbanke, "Efficient Encoding of Low-Density Parity-Check Codes," *IEEE Trans. Inf. Theory*, vol. **47**, no. 2, pp. 638–656, Feb. 2001.

[375] T. J. Richardson and R. Urbanke, "The Capacity of Low-Density Parity-Check Codes Under Message-Passing Decoding," *IEEE Trans. Inf. Theory*, vol. **47**, no. 2, pp. 599–618, Feb. 2001.

[376] T. J. Richardson and R. Urbanke, *Iterative Coding Systems*. (available online), Mar. 30, 2003.

[377] T. Richardson and R. Urbanke, *Modern Coding Theory*. Cambridge: Cambridge University Press, 2008.

[378] R. Rivest, A. Shamir, and L. Adleman, "A Method for Obtaining Digital Signatures and Public-Key Cryptosystems," *Commun. ACM*, vol. **21**, no. 2, pp. 120–126, 1978.

[379] P. Robertson, "Illuminating the Structure of Parallel Concatenated Recursive (TURBO) Codes," in *Proceedings of the GLOBECOM*, vol. **3**, San Francisco, CA, Nov. 1994, pp. 1298–1303.

[380] P. Robertson, E. Villebrun, and P. Hoher, "A Comparison of Optimal and Sub-Optimal MAP Decoding Algorithms Operating in the Log Domain," in *Proceedings of the International Conference on Communication (ICC)*, Seattle, WA, Jun. 1995, pp. 1009–1013.

[381] C. Roos, "A New Lower Bound for the Minimum Distance of a Cyclic Code," *IEEE Trans. Inf. Theory*, vol. **29**, no. 3, pp. 330–332, May 1983.

[382] R. M. Roth and G. Ruckenstein, "Efficient Decoding of Reed-Solomon Codes Beyond Half the Minimum Distance," *IEEE Trans. Inf. Theory*, vol. **46**, no. 1, pp. 246–256, Jan. 2000.

[383] L. Rudolph, "Easily Implemented Error-Correction Encoding-Decoding," G.E. Report 62MCD2, General Electric Corporation, Oklahoma City, OK, Technical Report, Dec. 1962.

[384] ——, "Geometric Configuration and Majority Logic Decodable Codes," Master's thesis, Univeristy of Oklahoma, Norman, OK, 1964.

[385] ——, "A Class of Majority Logic Decodable Codes," *IEEE Trans. Inf. Theory*, vol. **13**, pp. 305–307, Apr. 1967.

[386] W. E. Ryan and S. Lin, *Channel Codes Classical and Modern*. Cambridge:Cambridge University Press, 2009.

[387] J. Sadowsky and J. Bucklew, "On Large Deviation Theory and Asymptotically Efficient Monte Carlo Estimation," *IEEE Trans. Inf. Theory*, vol. **36**, no. 3, pp. 579–588, May 1990.

[388] S. Sankaranarayanan, A. Cvetkovic̀, and B. Vasic̀, "Unequal Error Protection for Joint Source-Channel Coding Schemes," in *Proceedings of the International Telemetering Conference (ITC)*, Las Vegas, NV, 2003, p. 1272.

[389] G. Sarkis, P. Giard, A. Vardy, C. Thibeault, and W. J. Gross, "Fast List Decoders for Polar Codes," *IEEE J. Sel. Areas Commun.*, vol. **34**, no. 2, pp. 318–328, Feb. 2016.

[390] G. Sarkis, P. Giard, A. Vardy, C. Thibeault, and W. J. Gross, "Flexible and Low-Complexity Encoding and Decoding of Systematic Polar Codes," *IEEE Trans. Commun.*, vol. **64**, no. 7, pp. 2732–2745, Jul. 2016.

[391] ——, "Fast Polar Decoders: Algorithm and Implementation," *IEEE J. Sel. Areas Commun.*, vol. **32**, no. 5, pp. 946–957, May 2014.

[392] G. Sarkis and W. J. Gross, "Inreasing the Throughput of Polar Decoders," *IEEE Commun. Lett.*, vol. **32**, no. 5, pp. 725–728, Apr. 2013.

[393] G. Sarkis, I. Tal, P. Giard, A. Vardy, C. Thibeault, and W. J. Gross, "Flexible and Low-Complexity Encoding and Decoding of Systematic Polar Codes," *IEEE Trans. Commun.*, vol. **64**, no. 7, pp. 2732–2745, Jul. 2016.

[394] D. V. Sarwate and M. B. Pursley, "Crosscorrelation Properties of Pseudorandom and Related Sequences," *Proc. IEEE*, vol. **68**, no. 5, pp. 593–619, May 1980.

[395] E. Şaşoğlu, E. Telatar, and E. Arıkan, "Polarization for Arbitrary Discrete Memoryless Channels," in *Proceedings of the IEEE Information Theory Workshop*, 2009, pp. 144–148.

[396] J. Savage, "Sequential Decoding — The Computational Problem," *Bell Syst. Tech. J.*, vol. **45**, pp. 149–175, Jan. 1966.

[397] C. Schlegel, *Trellis Coding*. New York: IEEE Press, 1997.

[398] A. Schrijver, *Theory of Linear and Integer Programming*. New York: Wiley, 1987.

[399] M. Schroeder, *Number Theory in Science and Communication: with Applications in Cryptography, Physics, Digital Information*. Berlin:Springer-Verlag, 1986.

[400] R. Sedgewick, *Algorithms*. Reading, MA: Addison-Wesley, 1983.

[401] J. Seghers, "On the Free Distance of TURBO Codes and Related Product Codes," Swiss Federal Institute of Technology, Zurich, Switzerland, Final Report, Diploma Project SS 1995 6613, Aug. 1995.

[402] N. Seshadri and C.-E. W. Sundberg, "Multi-level Trellis Coded Modulation for the Rayleigh Fading Channel," *IEEE Trans. Commun.*, vol. **41**, pp. 1300–1310, Sep. 1993.

[403] K. Shanmugan and P. Balaban, "A Modified Monte Carlo Simulation Technique for Evaluation of Error Rate in Digital Communication Systems," *IEEE Trans. Commun.*, vol. **28**, no. 11, pp. 1916–1924, Nov. 1980.

[404] C. E. Shannon, "A Mathematical Theory of Communication," *Bell Syst. Tech. J.*, vol. **27**, pp. 379–423, 1948.

[405] R. Shao, M. Fossorier, and S. Lin, "Two Simple Stopping Criteria for Iterative Decoding," in *Proceedings of the IEEE Symposium on Information Theory*, Cambridge, MA, Aug. 1998, p. 279.

[406] R. Y. Shao, S. Lin, and M. P. Fossorier, "Two Simple Stopping Criteria for Turbo Decoding," *IEEE Trans. Commun.*, vol. **47**, no. 8, pp. 1117–1120, Aug. 1999.

[407] M. Shao and C. L. Nikias, "An ML/MMSE Estimation Approach to Blind Equalization," in *Proceedings of ICASSP*, vol. **4**. Adelaide: IEEE, 1994, pp. 569–572.

[408] A. Shibutani, H. Suda, and F. Adachi, "Reducing Average Number of Turbo Decoding Iterations," *Electron. Lett.*, vol. **35**, no. 9, pp. 70–71, Apr. 1999.

[409] A. Shiozaki, "Decoding of Redundant Residue Polynomial Codes Using Euclid's Algorithm," *IEEE Trans. Inf. Theory*, vol. **34**, no. 3, pp. 1351–1354, Sep. 1988.

[410] A. Shokrollahi, "Raptor Codes," *IEEE Trans. Inf. Theory*, vol. **52**, no. 6, pp. 2551–2567, Jun. 2006.

[411] J. J. Shynk, *Probability, Random Variables, and Random Processes*. Hoboken, NJ: Wiley, 2003.

[412] R. Singleton, "Maximum Distance q-ary Codes," *IEEE Trans. Inf. Theory*, vol. **10**, pp. 116–118, 1964.

[413] B. Sklar, "A Primer on Turbo Code Concepts," *IEEE Commun. Mag.*, vol. **35**, no. 12, pp. 94–101, Dec. 1997.

[414] P. J. Smith, M. Shafi, and H. Gao, "Quick Simulation: A Review of Importance Sampling Techniques in Communications Systems," *IEEE J. Sel. Areas Commun.*, vol. **15**, no. 4, pp. 597–613, May 1997.

[415] J. Snyders, "Reduced Lists of Error Patterns for Maximum Likelihood Soft Decoding," *IEEE Trans. Inf. Theory*, vol. **37**, pp. 1194–1200, Jul. 1991.

[416] J. Snyders and Y. Be'ery, "Maximum Likelihood Soft Decoding of Binary Block Codes and Decoders for the Golay Codes," *IEEE Trans. Inf. Theory*, vol. **35**, pp. 963–975, Sep. 1989.

[417] H. Song and B. V. Kumar, "Low-Density Parity-Check Codes For Partial Response Channels," *IEEE Signal Process. Mag.*, vol. **21**, no. 1, pp. 56–66, Jan. 2004.

[418] S. Song, B. Zhou, S. Lin, and K. Abdel-Ghaffar, "A Unified Approach to the Construction of Binary and Nonbinary Quasi-Cylic LDPC Codes Based on Finite Fields," *IEEE Trans. Commun.*, vol. **54**, no. 10, pp. 1765–1774, Jan. 2009.

[419] R. Srinivasan, *Importance Sampling: Applications in Communications and Detection*. Berlin: Springer-Verlag, 2002.

[420] P. Staahl, J. B. Anderson, and R. Johannesson, "Optimal and Near-Optimal Encoders for Short and Moderate-Length Tail-Biting Trellises," *IEEE Trans. Inf. Theory*, vol. **45**, no. 7, pp. 2562–2571, Nov. 1999.

[421] H. Stichtenoth, *Algebraic Function Fields and Codes*. Berlin: Springer-Verlag, 1993.

[422] G. Stüber, *Principles of Mobile Communication*, 2nd ed. Boston: Kluwer Academic Press, 2001.

[423] M. Sudan, "Decoding of Reed-Solomon Codes Beyond the Error-Correction Bound," *J. Complex.*, vol. **13**, pp. 180–193, 1997.

[424] Y. Sugiyama, M. Kasahara, S. Hirasawa, and T. Namekawa, "A Method for Solving Key Equation for Goppa Codes," *Inf. Control*, vol. **27**, pp. 87–99, 1975.

[425] C.-E. W. Sundberg and N. Seshadri, "Coded Modulation for Fading Channels: An Overview," *Eur. Trans. Telecommun. Relat.Technol.*, vol. **4**, no. 3, pp. 309–324, May 1993, special issue on Application of Coded Modulation Techniques.

[426] A. Swindlehurst and G. Leus, "Blind and Semi-Blind Equalization for Generalized Space-Time Block Codes," *IEEE Trans. Signal Process.*, vol. **50**, no. 10, pp. 2489–2498, Oct. 2002.

[427] G. Szegö, *Orthogonal Polynomials*, 3rd ed. Providence, RI: American Mathematical Society, 1967.

[428] D. Taipale and M. Pursley, "An Improvement to Generalized-Minimum-Distance Decoding," *IEEE Trans. Inf. Theory*, vol. **37**, pp. 167–172, Jan. 1991.

[429] O. Takeshita and J. D.J. Costello, "New Classes of Algebraic Interleavers for Turbo-Codes," in *International Conference on Information Theory (Abstracts)*, Cambridge, MA, Aug. 1998.

[430] ——, "New Deterministic Interleaver Designs for Turbo Codes," *IEEE Trans. Inf. Theory*, vol. **46**, pp. 1988–2006, Sep. 2000.

[431] I. Tal and A. Vardy, "List Decoding of Polar Codes," *IEEE Trans. Inf. Theory*, vol. **61**, no. 5, pp. 2213–2226, May 2015.

[432] R. Tanner, "A Recursive Approach To Low Complexity Codes," *IEEE Trans. Inf. Theory*, vol. **27**, no. 5, pp. 533–547, Sep. 1981.

[433] R. M. Tanner, "On Quasi-Cyclic Repeat-Accumulate Codes," in *Proceedingsof the 37th Allerton Conference on Communication, Control, and Computing*, Monticello, IL, 1999.

[434] V. Tarokh, H. Jararkhami, and A. Calderbank, "Space-Time Block Codes from Orthogonal Designs," *IEEE Trans. Inf. Theory*, vol. **45**, no. 5, pp. 1456–1467, Jul. 1999.

[435] V. Tarokh, N. Seshadri, and A. Calderbank, "Space-Time Codes for High Data Rate Wireless Communication: Performance Criterion and Code Construction," *IEEE Trans. Inf. Theory*, vol. **44**, no. 2, pp. 744–765, Mar. 1998.

[436] E. Telatar, "Capacity of Multi-Antenna Gaussian Channels," AT&T Bell Labs Internal Technical Memorandum, Jun. 1995.

[437] ——, "The Flesh of Polar Codes," ISIT Plenary Talk, https://youtu.be/VhyoZSB9g0w, Jun. 29, 2017.

[438] S. ten Brink, "Iterative Decoding Trajectories of Parallel Concatenated Codes," in *Third IEEE ITG Conference on Source and Channel Coding*, Munich, Germany, Jan. 2000.

[439] ——, "Rate One-Half Code for Approaching the Shannon Limit by 0.1 dB," *Electron. Lett.*, vol. **36**, pp. 1293–1294, Jul. 2000.

[440] ——, "Convergence Behavior of Iteratively Decoded Parallel Concatenated Codes," *IEEE Trans. Commun.*, vol. **49**, no. 10, pp. 1727–1737, Oct. 2001.

[441] J. Thorpe, "Low Density Parity Check (LDPC) Codes Constructed from Protographs," JPL INP Progress Report 42-154, Aug. 15, 2003.

[442] T. Tian, C. R. Jones, J. D. Villasenor, and R. D. Wesel, "Selective Avoidance of Cycles in Irregular LDPC Code Construction," *IEEE Trans. Commun.*, vol. **52**, no. 8, pp. 1242–1247, Aug. 2004.

[443] T. Tian, J. Villasenor, and R. Wesel, "Construction of Irregular LDPC codes with Low Error Floors," in *Proceedingsof the IEEE International Conference on Communication*, Anchorage, AK, May 2003, pp. 3125–3129.

[444] A. Tietäväinen, "On the Nonexistence of Perfect Codes Over Finite Fields," *SIAM J. Appl. Math.*, vol. **24**, pp. 88–96, 1973.

[445] O. Tirkkonen and A. Hottinen, "Square-Matrix Embeddable Space-Time Block Codes for Communication: Performance Criterion and Code Construction," *IEEE Trans. Inf. Theory*, vol. **44**, no. 2, pp. 744–765, Mar. 2002.

[446] M. Tomlinson, "New Automatic Equalizer Employing Modulo Arithmetic," *Electron. Lett.*, vol. **7**, pp. 138–139, Mar. 1971.

[447] M. Trott, S. Benedetto, R. Garello, and M. Mondin, "Rotational Invariance of Trellis Codes Part I: Encoders and Precoders," *IEEE Trans. Inf. Theory*, vol. **42**, pp. 751–765, May 1996.

[448] T.-K. Truong, J. H. Jeng, and K.-C. Hung, "Inversionless Decoding of Both Errors and Erasures of Reed-Solomon Code," *IEEE Trans. Commun.*, vol. **46**, no. 8, pp. 973–976, Aug. 1998.

[449] M. Tsfasman and S. Vlăduţ, *Algebraic-Geometric Codes*. Dordrecht, The Netherlands: Kluwer Academic Publishers, 1991.

[450] M. Tsfasman, S. Vlăduţ, and T. Zink, "On Goppa Codes Which Are Better than the Varshamov-Gilbert Bound," *Math. Nachr.*, vol. **109**, pp. 21–28, 1982.

[451] M. Tüchler, R. Koetter, and A. C. Singer, "Turbo Equalization: Principles and New Results," *IEEE Trans. Commun.*, vol. **50**, no. 5, pp. 754–766, May 2002.

[452] G. Ungerboeck, "Channel Coding with Multilevel/Phase Signals," *IEEE Trans. Inf. Theory*, vol. **28**, no. 1, pp. 55–67, Jan. 1982.

[453] ——, "Trellis-Coded Modulation with Redundant Signal Sets. Part I: Introduction," *IEEE Commun. Mag.*, vol. **25**, no. 2, pp. 5–11, Feb. 1987.

[454] ——, "Trellis-Coded Modulation with Redundant Signal Sets. Part II: State of the Art," *IEEE Commun. Mag.*, vol. **25**, no. 2, pp. 12–21, Feb. 1987.

[455] G. Ungerböck and I. Csajka, "On Improving Data-Link Performance by Increasing Channel Alphabet and Introducing Sequence Coding," in *IEEE International Symposium on Information Theory*, Ronneby, Sweden, Jun. 1976, p. 53.

[456] A. Valembois and M. Fossorier, "An Improved Method to Compute Lists of Binary Vectors that Optimize a Given Weight Function with Application to Soft Decision Decoding," *IEEE Commun. Lett.*, vol. **5**, pp. 456–458, Nov. 2001.

[457] G. van der Geer and H. van Lint, *Introduction to Coding Theory and Algebraic Geometry*. Basel: Birkhäuser, 1988.

[458] J. van Lint, *Introduction to Coding Theory*, 2nd ed. Berlin: Springer-Verlag, 1992.

[459] H. Vangala, "Polar codes in Matlab," http://www.harishvangala.com or http://www.ecse.monash.edu.au/staff/eviterbo/polarcodes.html.

[460] H. Vangala, Y. Hong, and E. Viterbo, "Efficient Algorithms for Systematic Polar Encoding," *IEEE Commun. Lett.*, vol. **20**, no. 1, pp. 17–19, 2016.

[461] ——, "Practical Introduction to Polar Codes: Part 4 The Decoding," https://youtu.be/s4lzKbDxJpo, Feb. 23, 2016.

[462] H. Vangala, E. Viterbo, and Y. Hong, "A Comparative Study of Polar Code Constructions for the AWGN Channel," *CoRR*, vol. abs/1501.02473, 2015. [Online]. http://arxiv.org/abs/1501.02473

[463] B. Vasic, "Structured Iteratively Decodable Codes Based on Steiner Systems and their Application in Magnetic Recording," in *Global Telecommunications Conference (GLOBECOM)*. San Antonio, TX: IEEE, Nov. 2001, pp. 2954–2960.

[464] B. Vasic, E. Kurtas, and A. Kuznetsov, "LDPC Codes Based on Mutually Orthogonal Latin Rectangles and their Application in Perpendicular Magnetic Recording," *IEEE Trans. Mag.*, vol. **38**, no. 5, pp. 2346–2348, Sep. 2002.

[465] B. Vasic and O. Milenkovic, "Combinatorial Constructions of Low-Density Parity-Check Codes for Iterative Decoding," *IEEE Trans. Inf. Theory*, vol. **50**, no. 6, pp. 1156–1176, Jun. 2004.

[466] S. Verdu, "Optimum Multi-User Signal Detection," Ph.D. dissertation, University of Illinois, 1984.

[467] A. J. Viterbi, "Error Bounds for Convolutional Codes and an Asymptotically Optimum Decoding Algorithm," *IEEE Trans. Info. Theory*, vol. **13**, pp. 260–269, Apr. 1967.

[468] ——, "Convolutional Codes and Their Performance in Communication Systems," *IEEE Trans. Commun. Technol.*, vol. **19**, no. 5, pp. 75–772, Oct. 1971.

[469] A. J. Viterbi, "Approaching the Shannon Limit: Theorist's Dream and Practitioner's Challenge," in *Proceedings of the International Conference on Millimeter Wave and Far Infrared Science and Technology*, Beijing, 1996, pp. 1–11.

[470] ——, "An Intuitive Justification and Simplified Implementation of the MAP Decoder for Convolutional Codes," *IEEE J. Spec Areas Commun.*, vol. **2**, no. 16, pp. 260–264, Feb. 1997.

[471] A. J. Viterbi and J. Omura, *Principles of Digital Communication and Coding*. New York: McGraw-Hill, 1979.

[472] J. von zur Gathen and J. Gerhard, *Modern Computer Algebra*. Cambridge: Cambridge University Press, 1999.

[473] T. Wadayama, K. Nakamura, M. Yagita, Y. Funahashi, S. Usami, and I. Takumi, "Gradient Descent Bit Flipping Algorithms for Decoding LDPC Codes," *IEEE Trans. Commun.*, vol. **58**, no. 6, pp. 1610–1614, Jun. 2010.

[474] N. Wang and R. Srinivasan, "On Importance Sampling for Iteratively Decoded Linear Block Codes," in *Proceedings of the IEEE International Conference on Communications, Circuits, and Systems*, Hong Kong, 2005, pp. 18–23.

[475] L. Wei, "Rotationally Invariant Convolutional Channel Coding with Expanded Signal Space I: 180 Degrees," *IEEE J. Sel. Areas Commun.*, vol. **2**, pp. 659–672, 1984.

[476] ——, "Rotationally Invariant Convolutional Channel Coding with Expanded Signal Space II: Nonlinear Codes," *IEEE J. Sel. Areas Commun.*, vol. **2**, pp. 672–686, 1984.

[477] ——, "Trellis–Coded Modulation with Multidimensional Constellations," *IEEE Trans. Inf. Theory*, vol. **33**, no. 4, pp. 483–501, Jul. 1987.

[478] ——, "Rotationally Invariant Trellis-Coded Modulation with Multidimensional M-PSK," *IEEE J. Sel. Areas Commun.*, vol. **7**, no. 9, pp. 1281–1295, 1989.

[479] L.-F. Wei, "Coded M-DPSK with Built-in Time Diversity for Fading Channels," *IEEE Trans. Inf. Theory*, vol. **39**, pp. 1820–1839, Nov. 1993.

[480] L. R. Welch and E. R. Berlekamp, "Error Correction for Algebraic Block Codes," U.S. Patent Number 4,633,470, Dec. 30, 1986.

[481] N. Wiberg, "Codes and Decoding on General Graphs," Ph.D. dissertation, Linköping University, 1996.

[482] N. Wiberg, H.-A. Loeliger, and R. Kötter, "Codes and Iterative Decoding on General Graphs," *Eur. Trans. Telecommun.*, vol. **6**, pp. 513–525, 1995.

[483] S. B. Wicker, *Error Control Systems for Digital Communications and Storage*. Englewood Cliffs, NJ: Prentice-Hall, 1995.

[484] S. Wicker and V. Bhargava, *Reed Solomon Codes and their Applications*. New York: IEEE Press, 1994.

[485] S. B. Wicker and V. K. Bhargava, *Reed-Solomon Codes and their Applications*. IEEE Press, 1994.

[486] R. J. Wilson, *Introduction to Graph Theory*. Essex, England: Longman Scientific, 1985.

[487] S. Wilson and Y. Leung, "Trellis Coded Phase Modulation on Rayleigh Fading Channels," in *Proceedings of the IEEE ICC*, Montreal, QC, Jun. 1997.

[488] J. K. Wolf, "Efficient Maximum Likelihood Decoding of Linear Block Codes Using a Trellis," *IEEE Trans. Inf. Theory*, vol. **24**, no. 1, pp. 76–80, Jan. 1978.

[489] J. Wozencraft and B. Reiffen, *Sequential Decoding*. Cambridge, MA: MIT Press, 1961.

[490] X.-W. Wu and P. Siegel, "Efficient Root-Finding Algorithm with Application to List Decoding of Algebraic-Geometric Codes," *IEEE Trans. Inf. Theory*, vol. **47**, pp. 2579–2587, Sep. 2001.

[491] Y. Wu, B. D. Woerner, and W. J. Ebel, "A Simple Stopping Criterion for Turbo Decoding," *IEEE Commun. Lett.*, vol. **4**, no. 8, pp. 258–260, Aug. 2000.

[492] B. Xia and W. Ryan, "On Importance Sampling for Linear Block Codes," in *Proceedings of the IEEE International Conference on Communications*, vol. **4**, Anchorage, AK, May 2003, pp. 2904–2908.

[493] B. Xia and W. E. Ryan, "Importance Sampling for Tanner Trees," *IEEE Trans. Inf. Theory*, vol. **51**, no. 6, pp. 2183–2189, Jun. 2005.

[494] H. Xiao and A. Banihashemi, "Improved Progressive-Edge-Growth (PEG) Construction of Irregular LDPC Codes," *IEEE Commun. Lett.*, vol. **8**, no. 12, pp. 715–717, Dec. 2004.

[495] J. Xu, L. Chen, L.-Q. Zeng, L. Han, and S. Lin, "Construction of Low-Density Parity-Check Codes by Superposition," *IEEE Trans. Commun.*, vol. **53**, no. 2, pp. 243–251, Feb. 2005.

[496] J. Xu and S. Lin, "A Combinatoric Superposition Method for Constructive Low-Density Parity-Check Codes," in *Proceedingsof the International Symposium on Information Theory*, vol. **30**, Yokohama, June–July 2003.

[497] J. S. Yedidia, Y. Wang, and S. C. Draper, "Divide and Concur and Difference-Map BP Decoders for LDPC Codes," *IEEE Trans. Inf. Theory*, vol. **57**, no. 2, pp. 786–802, Feb. 2011.

[498] R. W. Yeung, *A First Course in Information Theory*. New York: Kluwer Academic, 2002.

[499] B. Yuan and K. K. Parhi, "Successive Cancellation List Polar Decoding Using Log-Likelihood Ratios," arXiv 14117282, 2014.

[500] E. Zehavi and J. Wolf, "On the Performance Evaluation of Trellis Codes," *IEEE Trans. Inf. Theory*, vol. **32**, pp. 196–202, Mar. 1987.

[501] F. Zhai and I. J. Fair, "New Error Detection Techniques and Stopping Criteria for Turbo Decoding," in *IEEE Canadian Conference on Electronics and Computer Engineering (CCECE)*, Halifax, NS, 2000, pp. 58–60.

[502] W. Zhang, "Finite-State Machines in Communications," Ph.D. dissertation, University of South Australia, 1995.

[503] Y. Zhang, "Design of Low-Floor Quasi-Cyclic IRA Codes and the FPGA Decoders," Ph.D. dissertation, University of Arizona, May 2007.

[504] Z. Zhang, L. Dolecek, B. Nikolic, V. Anantharam, and M. Wainwright, "Investigation of Error Floors of Structured Low-Density Parity Check Codes by Hardware Emulation," in *Proceedings of the IEEE Globecom*, San Francisco, CA, 2006.

[505] J. Zhang and M. Fossorier, "A Modified Weighted Bit-Flipping Decoding of Low-Density Parity-Check Codes," *IEEE Commun. Lett.*, vol. **8**, pp. 165–167, Mar. 2004.

[506] Y. Zhang and W. Ryan, "Structured IRA Codes: Performance, Analysis, and Construction," *IEEE Trans. Commun.*, vol. **55**, no. 5, pp. 837–844, May 2007.

[507] ——, "Toward Low LDPC Floors: A Case Study," *IEEE Trans. Commun.*, vol. **57**, no. 5, pp. 1566–1573, May 2009.

[508] Y. Zhang, W. Ryan, and Y. Li, "Structured eIRA codes," in *Proceedings of the 38th Asilomar Conference on Signals, Systems, and Computing*, Pacific Grove, CA, Nov. 2004, pp. 7–10.

[509] R. E. Ziemer and R. L. Peterson, *Digital Communications and Spread Spectrum Systems*. New York: Macmillan, 1985.

[510] N. Zierler, "Linear Recurring Sequences," *J. Soc. Ind. Appl. Math.*, vol. **7**, pp. 31–48, 1959.

[511] K. S. Zigangirov, "Some Sequential Decoding Procedures," *Prob. Pederachi Inf.*, vol. **2**, pp. 13–25, 1966.

[512] V. Zyablov and M. Pinsker, "Estimation of the Error-Correction Complexity of Gallager Low-Density Codes," *Prob. Pered. Inf.*, vol. **11**, pp. 23–26, Jan. 1975.

Index

Error Correction Coding: Mathematical Methods and Algorithms, Second Edition. Todd K. Moon
© 2021 John Wiley & Sons, Inc. Published 2021 by John Wiley & Sons, Inc.
Companion website: www.wiley.com/go/Moon/ErrorCorrectionCoding